ABOUT OUR COVER

The two double rifles pictured on the front cover of this year's edition were commissioned by New England Arms of Kittery Point, Maine, and built by Arrieta of Spain. Each gun has been made by hand and was designed for use against dangerous game. The model shown on the left is a .375 Holland & Holland magnum caliber with a 25" barrel. The game scenes feature a charging elephant (right) and rhino (left) with a cape buffalo (not shown) on the bottom. The latter is a .470 caliber rifle built in the same painstaking manner and with the same features as the .375 H&H. Both guns were engraved in Italy by master engraver Mauro Dassa. New England Arms introduced this line of engraved "Renaissance" shotguns and rifles, all created by Italy's best engravers, in 1998. Each model is made to a customer's specifications and is engraved by a prominent Italian engraver.

Shooter's Bible

NO. 91
2000 EDITION

ARTICLES EDITOR
William S. Jarrett

SPECIFICATIONS EDITOR
Wayne van Zwoll

PROJECT MANAGER
Dominick S. Sorrentino

PRODUCTION & DESIGN
Lesley A. Notorangelo/D.S.S.

ELECTRONIC IMAGING
Lesley A. Notorangelo/D.S.S.

FIREARMS CONSULTANTS
Bill Meade
Frank Zito

COVER PHOTOGRAPHER
Ray and Matt Wells

PUBLISHER
David C. Perkins

PRESIDENT
Brian T. Herrick

STOEGER PUBLISHING COMPANY

Every effort has been made to record specifications and descriptions of guns, ammunition and accessories accurately, but the Publisher can take no responsibility for errors or omissions. The prices shown for guns, ammunition and accessories are manufacturers' suggested retail prices (unless otherwise noted) and are furnished for information only. These were in effect at press time and are subject to change without notice. Purchasers of this book have complete freedom of choice in pricing for resale.

Published by Stoeger Publishing Company
5 Mansard Court
Wayne, New Jersey 07470

Library of Congress Catalog Card No.: 63-6200
International Standard Book No.: 0-88317-211-9

Manufactured in the United States of America

In the United States:
Distributed to the book trade and to the sporting
goods trade by
Stoeger Industries
5 Mansard Court
Wayne, New Jersey 07470
Tel: 973-872-9500 *Fax:* 973-872-2230

In Canada:
Distributed to the book trade and to the sporting
goods trade by
Stoeger Canada Ltd.
1801 Wentworth Street, Unit 16
Whitby, Ontario, L1N 8R6, Canada

Contents

ARTICLES

A Century Of Shooting--And Then Some   8

Sporting Books Of The 20th Century   17

A Century Of Progress For Shotgunners   26

Handloading: A Century Of Progress   33

Sights And Scopes: A Look Back--And Forward   41

Cartridges--Then And Now   49

The Hunting Knife In The 20th Century   57

Handguns: In The Old Millennium   65

Who's Who In 20th Century Muzzleloaders   77

MANUFACTURER'S SHOWCASE   88

SPECIFICATIONS

Handguns   97

Rifles   189

Shotguns   311

Blackpowder   377

Sights & Scopes   429

Ammunition   477

Ballistics   495

Reloading   519

REFERENCE

Directory of Manufacturers & Suppliers   564

Gunfinder   570

Foreword

In honor of the new millennium, we've asked several of our regular contributors to take a look at the "old" 20th century and retrace the various inventions and improvements that have made the firearms industry what it is today . We open with a piece by a frequent contributor, Wayne van Zwoll, who writes on the subject of *hunting rifles*. [Wayne has taken over the Specifications and Reference sections of this edition, which explains why we're both signing this Foreword]. Another regular contributor, Stephen Irwin, chimes in with a retrospective on the great sporting books of the 20th century. And Tom Tabor, a newcomer to this book, takes a look at how the *shotgun* has evolved since the turn of the century.

Enter Don Lewis, who writes on his favorite topic: *handloading*. Modern technology, he admits, has made the job a lot easier for those who are serious about reloading. On the subject of sights and scopes, we've turned to our Canadian friend, Wilf Pyle, who covers the field--from the iron sight to the sophisticated laser sights. Ralph Quinn, who has always come through on whatever topic we've assigned, zeroes in on the subject of *cartridges*. [Sadly, this is Ralph's final appearance in Shooter's Bible. He passed away in November of 1998 and is sorely missed].

Steve Dick covers the *hunting knife* admirably, comparing the likes of the old "Bowie Hunter" with the high-strength ceramic blades that are slowly emerging. Next Gene Gangarosa Jr. holds forth on the subject of *handguns*, old and new. Those who are interested in the booming muzzleloader industry are urged to take a look at Toby Bridges' article on that subject. And finally, we invite readers to check out the "Manufacturer's Showcase," which immediately follows the article section.

SPECIFICATIONS

For the new millennium H-S Precision Pro-Series 2000 introduces a new 20-inch barrel in .17 Remington and there's a new Weatherby Mark V rifle in 338/378. Both firms now manufacture super-accurate long-range pistols as well. Savage, a long-gun company since the Model 99 rifle appeared a century ago, now offers its "Striker" line of hunting handguns (alas, the 99 is now dead). New revolvers based on the Colt Single Action Army design have also found a ready market in the Cowboy Action fraternity. Kimber and several other manufacturers are capitalizing on the Colt 1911 autoloading pistol, and Smith & Wesson remains the dominant name in double-action revolvers.

Among current bolt-action rifles, detachable box magazines are replacing floorplates, and fluted barrels are trimming rifle weight without sacrificing barrel stiffness. "Woods" chamberings

with big bullets in little cases are out, as hunters buy long-range rifles chambered for the 7STW and the new .300 Remington Ultra Mag. There's renewed interest in older rifles too, thanks in part to the popular "Cowboy Action" events. Marlin and Winchester offer special versions of their 336 and 94 carbines and have also added elegant .22 lever-actions to their lines. Marlin's .45-70 Guide Gun and Winchester's similar 94 are big hits too, along with Sako's widely acclaimed Model 75 series.

In the optics field, Leupold has developed its new "Long Range" scopes, featuring a turret-mounted objective dial that can focus and eliminate parallax without moving your eye from the sight. Leica, Swarovski and Zeiss continue to enter the U.S. market with new scopes sporting American features like rear-focal-plane reticles. For pistol shooters, Burris now markets a high-power variable with long eye relief. Nikon, Pentax and others list heavy reticles for close shooting in thickets. Red dot sights offered by Burris, Leupold and Tasco help hunters and combat shooters take quick, accurate aim. So does Bushnell's Holosight. Ashley Outdoors gives shooters a much-needed selection of trim iron sights designed for minimal target subtention.

On the ammunition front, Remington, Winchester, PMC and Federal are busy tailoring loads for serious hunters and target shooters. Barnes, Nosler, Swift, Trophy Bonded and Woodleigh big game bullets are available in factory loads to augment traditional softpoints and Winchester's Fail Safe. Nosler and Winchester have announced "Supreme" loads with their proven Power Point bullets. Swift's new game bullet, Scirocco, has a ply-tip profile and bonded core that promises flat flight, quick expansion and deep penetration. Nosler's new 30-caliber match bullet is a dead ringer for the tack-driving Sierra 168-grain Match. Hornady's V-Max bullets now come moly-coated. And Speer's dual-core Grand Slam continues to grow. Sabots in rifled shotgun barrels have brought new slugs from Barnes and Remington.

The availability of superb ammunition won't discourage handloaders—not with fine tools made by Dillon, Hornady, Lyman, Redding and RCBS. You'll also appreciate the ballistics tables, not only from industry giants like Remington, Winchester and Federal, but from Weatherby, A-Square, Dakota and Lazzeroni, whose high-performance hunting cartridges define the cutting edge of sporting ammunition design.

We hope you enjoy this edition of SHOOTER'S BIBLE as much as we've enjoyed putting it together!

William S. Jarrett, Articles Editor
Wayne van Zwoll, Specifications Editor

A Century Of Shooting--And Then Some   8
BY WAYNE VAN ZWOLL

Sporting Books Of The 20th Century   17
BY R. STEPHEN IRWIN, M.D.

A Century Of Progress For Shotgunners   26
BY THOMAS C. TABOR

Handloading: A Century Of Progress   33
BY DON LEWIS

Sights And Scopes: A Look Back--And Forward   41
BY WILF E. PYLE

Cartridges--Then And Now   49
BY RALPH F. QUINN

The Hunting Knife In The 20th Century   57
BY STEVEN DICK

Handguns: In The Old Millennium   65
BY GENE GANGAROSA, JR.

Who's Who In 20th Century Muzzleloaders   77
BY TOBY BRIDGES

Articles

A Century Of Shooting --And Then Some

By Wayne Van Zwoll

To understand how far and fast the shooting industry has traveled since the beginning of recorded history, consider that shooting as we know it is less than a thousand years old. The last glacial period ended 10,000 years ago, and Christianity was born 8,000 years later. During all that time, primitive hunters used crude traps to capture their game. Slings, spears and atlatls followed. Then came the bow and arrow, enabling civilized man to make war at a distance. Roman candle fuel, called "Chinese snow," emerged a couple of centuries before an English friar named Roger Bacon first described gunpowder in 1249.

The first guns, as we know them, were crude weapons indeed. Typical was the Swiss culverin, a pipe that required a two-man team: one to direct it and the other to light the charge through a touch-hole. The first trigger mechanisms of any value appeared around 1500. Meanwhile, matchlocks, wheellocks and flintlocks all competed for attention. The flintlock was leagues ahead of the matchlock with respect to reliability, lock time, rate of fire and ease of operation, but it also had an exposed touch-hole. Even with the frizzen covering the pan charge, bad weather could render a gun inoperable. Not until the late 18th century did chemists come up with a better option: shock-sensitive salts called *fulminate*. They could be set off by percussion and, unlike powder, released their energy almost instantly. In 1806 Scotch clergyman Alexander John Forsythe used fulminates to generate a spark in the chamber of a gun. Two years later Swiss gunmaker Johannes Pauly developed a cartridge with a priming mix of fulminate in a paper

cap on its base. Pulling the trigger released a needle that pierced the cap and detonated the fulminate.

Meanwhile, gun designers faced their challenges head-on. Chief among them was fashioning a rifle that could be loaded from the breech. Rifling had appeared in firearms quite early. Target matches in

The Author cycles the action of a new Model 94 Winchester, still popular after a century of service.

Leipzig, Germany in 1498 and in Zurich in 1504 were shot with rifles. By that time lead had become the standard material for balls and bullets. The first breechloaders arrived surprisingly early via a crude, hinged-breech gun built in 1537. Italy's Fresco de Borgia developed a flintlock in 1694, more than 80 years before British Army Major Patrick Ferguson came up with a rifle featuring a cylindrical breech plug that could be lowered on steep threads by turning the trigger guard. It also was a flintlock, as was the first breechloader accepted for military service in the U.S. The blessings of breech loading weren't all realized until self-contained cartridges appeared in the mid-19th century. In 1854 Horace Smith and Daniel Wesson developed a metallic case for the Hunt Volcanic repeating rifle that was to sire Winchester's line of lever-actions. Subsequently Smith and Wesson introduced the .22 Short rimfire, one of the greatest cartridges of all time.

The first centerfire cartridge in the U.S. evolved at Springfield Armory in 1866. The discovery of nitroglycerin in 1846 accelerated firearms development by opening new possibilities in propellants. Nitroglycerin promised more energy and higher velocities from bullets—but its muscle needed harnessing. In the early 1800s the manufacture of primers and propellants kept average life expectancies low. The famous British munitions engineer Charles Eley was blown up in his plant in 1828 while handling priming mixture. About the time of our Civil War a nitroglycerin explosion demolished the German factory of Emanuel Nobel and his son Alfred, who both escaped.. The young Swedish chemist soon came up with a more stable compound called *Kieselguhr*, from which evolved Dynamite.

Guncotton also popped up in the middle of the 19th century. Like nitroglycerin, it posed safety problems as a propellant. During the last half of the 19th century, though, a series of developments harnessed the high energy of nitrated cellulose and nitroglycerin. By the early 1900s Alfred Nobel and Hiram Maxim, working independently, had come up with new propellants. The British War Office, in search of better rifle powder, thus adopted "Cordite." Drawn from the Nobel and Maxim formulas, it was a paste-like substance that could be squeezed through a die to form long, cord-like strands. Smokeless powder followed. Its high operating

This Winchester Model 92 with its folding tang sight was popular at the turn of the century.

pressure increased bullet speed and flattened trajectories. Its almost invisible discharge was hard to spot from a distance and allowed for quick follow-up shots in battle. As smokeless fuel made black powder obsolete, a bright young German inventor named Paul Mauser was improving the rifles he'd designed with breaching mechanisms resembling door locks. His single-shot Model 1871 evolved into the Model 1898, a rifle that quickly dominated military establishments in Europe and South America (and armed Germany through two apocalyptic wars). By the turn of the century, all major military powers were issuing small-bore (264- to 323-caliber) bolt-action rifles chambered for smokeless, bottleneck cartridges. Big game hunters, still wedded to the lever action, witnessed the birthing of rifles whose offspring would wear glass sights and claim animals at distances they wouldn't have even thought of shooting.

THE NEW CENTURY ARRIVES

Since 1900, however, not much has happened in firearms development. Before taking exception to that statement, consider its measure. This century began after the biggest boom in firearms development in history. Between the California Gold Rush of 1849 and the Klondike bonanza of 1898, black powder was supplanted by smokeless, and muzzle-loaders gave way to breech-loading magazine rifles. Rifle scopes saw military service for the first time; jacketed bullets appeared; and bullet velocities doubled. Barrels, once considered adequate if they held at 25,000 psi, soon required proofing at twice that pressure.

Return to the *beginning* of the 19ᵗʰ century and you're deep into the flintlock era. That was before svelte rifles from the Pennsylvania woods were replaced by the stout Plains rifle; before young Eliphalet Remington fired up his father's forge to fashion a flintlock; and before Simeon North was awarded the first government contract for guns with interchangeable parts. Oliver Winchester hadn't yet been born, Jake and Samuel Hawken hadn't reached St. Louis, and Lewis and Clark had yet to start up the Missouri River armed with rifles they soon found were woefully underpowered for grizzly bears. Indeed, the 19ᵗʰ century brought more change to firearms than the six centuries that had, collectively, produced the Kentucky rifle. Flint ignition, black powder and patched balls had given way to magazine rifles, smokeless fuel and jacketed bullets that flew at twice the speed of sound. Now *that* was progress!

By 1900 Arthur Savage had designed his famous lever-action rifle, and John Browning was trying to market his autoloading shotgun to Winchester. Within a decade the new Krag-Jorgensen rifle had stepped aside for the 1903 Springfield and

a cartridge destined to become a standard for big game hunters *for the rest of the century*: the .30-06. It was followed in 1913 by the .375 H&H Magnum. About that time, Charles Newton turned his attention from the .22 High Power and .250-3000 Savage to bigger rounds that performed even then like the magnums of the 1990s.

By the time Winchester unveiled its Model 70 bolt rifle in 1937, four decades after Paul Mauser defined the type, there were no more giants to slay. Sure, rifles, ammunition and optics have continued to improve. More popular autoloaders exist now than the Browning A-5 shotgun and Colt Government .45. But for the most part advances have been incremental compared to the blossoming of the industry during the 19ᵗʰ century —especially its second half. The Gyro-Jet rocket guns that appeared when I was a lad failed to unseat rimfire and centerfire cartridges dating back several decades. Synthetic stocks, cryogenically-treated barrels and Teflon finishes amount to different icings on the same cake. Mauser-style bolt mechanisms still predominate in hunting camps. The .30-06, where its supremacy is challenged at all, gets nipped by short magnums derived from the .300 H&H (c. 1925).

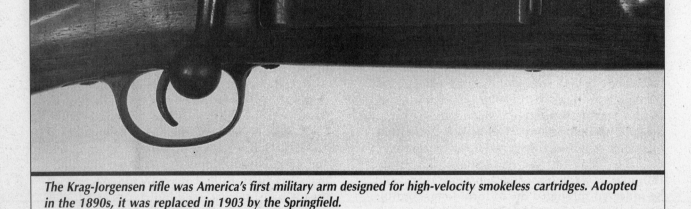

The Krag-Jorgensen rifle was America's first military arm designed for high-velocity smokeless cartridges. Adopted in the 1890s, it was replaced in 1903 by the Springfield.

Since the 1980s new bullets made by Nosler and other recognized companies in the business have increased the effectiveness and versatility of modern rifle cartridges.

This trend of refinement will likely continue. Bold new developments are unlikely in an industry in which truly new developments come at great cost in tooling. Computers may program the mills, drills, routers and indexing spindles that create rifles and ammunition, but real machinery is what moves wood and metal. It's the stuff that defined what Americans used to call *heavy industry*. In fact, many of the same machines that turned out parts and fodder for guns in the wake of Pearl Harbor are still making parts and fodder. Like matrons with new spring hats, these iron behemoths slave away beside control panels ablaze with the latest digital technology.

Even if capitalization wasn't so dear, nostalgic hunters would resist converting to rifles that were radically different from those they grew up with. With rifles that are considered part of the hunting experience, tradition can matter as much as performance. Rifles with "classic" claw extractors and "classic" stocks sell well, as do rifles chambered for "classic" cartridges. The most expensive rifles are still those turned out by craftsmen with traditional materials on actions that are 50 to 100 years old. Some 35 years ago, when Winchester decided sportsmen paid scant attention to esthetics in preference to more "cost-effective" rifles, the company was blown from the saddle of its pinto. The "pre-64" Winchester Models 70 and 94 still command a premium over later versions, though the designers

in New Haven have since brought back the look and even some components of the earlier guns.

Even the belted magnum, once thought to be the case design of the future, has fallen on hard times. New high-octane rounds like Remington's .300 Ultra Mag are now rimless. The current crop of bolt-rifle missiles, while mightier by far than the woods rounds of yesteryear, are not much different in form. Higher ballistic levels matter to modern riflemen; as do the fine points of rifle and cartridge design. Preoccupation with things that promise only marginal improvements in performance signals a flattening of industry growth. Successful manufacturers during the 1990s have walked the chalk-line between traditional and progressive, retaining those features that hold pleasant memories for hunters while pursuing higher performance levels. Accountants may have their say, but gunmakers have learned not to let them dictate deviations from that chalk-line.

Dakota's Don Allen rightly predicted the appeal of the rimless case when he based his proprietary rounds on the .404 Jeffery hull. More recently, John Lazzeroni and Ken Howell have developed stables of rimless cartridges—the former to push performance limits and the latter to offer a selection of .30-06- and mid-length magnum cartridges that can launch heavy bullets at sensible velocities.

Many of the machines found in firearms and ammunition plants date back to the 1940s. Computerized controls make them more efficient. Replacing them would be cost-prohibitive.

Similar to the Hawk line developed by Wyoming riflemen Fred Zeglin and Bob Fulton on the '06 case, the Howell and Howell Express ammo shoots and feeds without special accommodation in ordinary actions. What's common to these and other post-Weatherby proprietary offerings are overlapping performance bands.

When the .270 and .300 Holland & Holland hit the shelves in 1925, it must have seemed a lot like the .30-06. Hunters now suddenly had three similar, flat-shooting big game cartridges to choose from. But today the .270 doesn't seem like the .30-06 at all. The ballistic charts are cluttered with cartridges that are more alike in application and performance; for example, the .243 Winchester and 6mm Remington, the .260 and 7mm-08 Remingtons, and now the .300 Ultra-Mag and .300 Weatherby. This crowded field is the result of manufacturers scurrying to supply new products

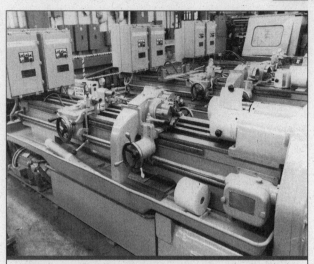

Rifle manufacture is heavy industry, requiring huge capitalization. There's little need now for new firearms factories.

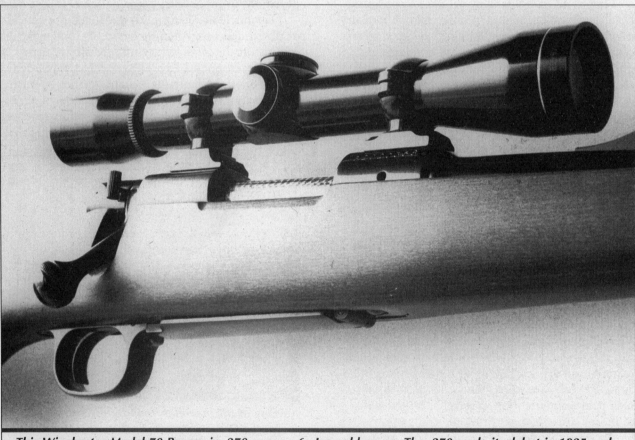

This Winchester Model 70 Ranger in .270 wears a 6x Leupold scope. The .270 made its debut in 1925 and has yet to be surpassed as a deer cartridge.

to boost sales when truly new ideas are wanting. More renditions of fewer rifles can be expected in the near future. Winchester's prewar Model 70s came in a handful of variations and chamberings. Now "The Rifleman's Rifle," along with similar products cataloged by Remington, Savage, Ruger and others, appear in dozens of guises to satisfy every shooter's whim. Stocks, barrels and metal finishes may differ; but the rifles all carry the same mechanism. In fairness, if these rifles were not splendid values to begin with, *someone* would long since have come up with an alternative action. Alas, the costs of producing new actions have grown so high that any start-up company intent on building a low- or mid-priced commercial rifle from scratch would soon founder. The few small firms that design and sell their own actions depend on a coterie of sophisticated customers willing to pay double (or more) the cost of an ordinary one.

Among commercial riflemakers, Sako and Browning have been pioneers in stepping away from successful bolt rifles to fashion new models with different actions. The Browning A-Bolt is a very accurate, serviceable rifle, if not as estheticaly pleasing to the old guard as the lovely (but costly) High-Power built on FN metal. Sako's new Model 75 has a very smooth action, one big enough to handle long magnums. It isn't offered in three sizes like the old

Synthetic stock blanks await the spindles at Thompson/Center's plant.

Sakos, but most hunters are looking toward bigger rounds, not smaller. Like the Browning A-Bolt, Sako's 75 will shoot tiny groups. A close cousin, the Sako TRG, also accepts the outsize .30-378 Weatherby and .338 Lapua cartridges. I'm quite taken with Lapua. Dakota is the only other American firm routinely chambering this elk-crusher.

IMPROVED STOCKS AND SIGHTS ENTER THE NEW WORLD

Synthetic stocks have proved the salvation for corporate giants and custom shops alike. They've eliminated the need for expensive hand-fitting, checkering and finishing of walnut, itself in dwindling supply. Hunters and target shooters have come to accept the utilitarian looks of the synthetics which have, in time, improved in form and feel. Their stability and durability play well to the current crop of shooters in search of higher performance. Tradition, though hardly dead, is becoming redefined.

While the amount of iron in hunting rifles has evolved slowly during this century, the sights on those rifles have undergone a metamorphosis. Iron sights were the rule before World War II and for many years after. Weaver's affordable 330 scope made its appearance along with the New Deal,

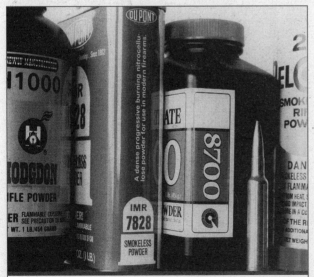

Interest in large-capacity cartridges has prompted development of slow-burning powders that boost velocity within safe pressure limits.

Huge, high-power scopes like this Light Force with illuminated reticle and parallax adjustment are gaining popularity as hunters lean more heavily on their equipment to get game.

but only a few hunters tried it. Noske, Lyman and others grabbed pieces of this infant market with scopes that shared the 330's low magnification and compact tube. Leupold's Pioneer and the early Stith and Kollmorgen scopes converted more shooters to glass sights. All of them were, by today's standards, dim. The reticles moved out of optical center when adjusted for windage and elevation, and under stiff recoil the reticles sometimes broke. Moisture caused fogging. Few rifles were initially tapped for scopes, and surplus rifles from the war years required lower bolt knobs to clear ocular bells.

After World War II, it was discovered that a thin wash of magnesium fluoride on an air-to-glass lens surface could boost brightness dramatically. Now reticles affixed to erector assemblies stayed in the middle of the field. Nitrogen gas in sealed scopes prevented fogging. Steel tubes were replaced by aluminum, and variable magnification became popular. By the late 1950s, when Winchester introduced its long-range .264 and .338 Magnums, scoped hunting rifles were the norm. At the time, the best of them sold for well under $100.

Except for murky barrel-length scopes dating back to the Civil War, the whole history of shooting optics has occurred during the 20th century. From the 3x Weaver, scopes have traveled the way of the rifle cartridge; i.e., always to higher power. Now the 3-9x variable is being supplanted by the 3.5-10x and 4.5-14x (some deer hunters I know even hunt

with 6.5-20x and 6-24x scopes). Such magnification was, a few short years ago, deemed suitable only for competitive shooting at black bullseyes.

During the last couple of decades, range-finding devices, parallax corrections and erector tube locks have become common. Scope tubes, which increased from 7/8 to one inch diameter during the 1950s, have now plumped out to 30mm. Such big pipes sell mostly on appearance, but they also enable shooters to dial in more elevation (assuming erectors of standard size). More elevation range enables shooters to aim center at longer distances, taking advantage of modern cartridges with their greater reach. Mil-dot and other reticles designed for long shooting appear more and more in hunting scopes.

WHY WE HUNT THE WAY WE DO

Driving the trend to far-reaching rifles and more powerful optics is a fundamental change in the way hunters perceive their sport. Having recently completed a study of hunting stories in major outdoors publications dating back to 1932, I looked for indications of a shift in hunting motive to explain or equate changes in the equipment and techniques of big game hunters. What I found validated my premise. In hunting articles of the 1930s, 40s and 50s, writers mainly recounted adventures, detailing camps and travel, companions and weather and the hardships of the hunt. Readers went along vicariously.

According to the author's own surveys, Leupold's 3-9x and 3.5-10x scopes are now the most popular among elk hunters.

Parallax adjustments, once reserved for target scopes, have become common on hunting sights as shooters attempt to reach farther.

Then, beginning in the 1960s, outdoors magazines served their readers a different diet replete with where-to, how-to articles that *taught* hunters how to be more successful. Stories of far-off places that few people could ever visit disappeared and were replaced by articles describing how best to mine the whitewall coverts in one's own backyard. This trend strengthened in the 1970s and '80s, with political issues also gaining in terms of editorial space. Having fun with fellow hunters at a deer camp, making the family part of a hunt, or testing yourself on a solo wilderness trip seemed somehow inadequate now. Records book trophies seemed ever more important. Early articles hardly ever mentioned Boone & Crockett scores, and often the size of a buck was given as live weight, with only incidental mention of antler points or inches. By the 1980s antler score had become important indeed. The traditional contest between the hunter and his game gradually diminished as a key element in stories that focused instead on the exceptional score of an animal pursued or the tactics and techniques used to bring an exceptional beast to bag.

Interviews with dozens of hunters, guides and game managers in the western U.S., Canada and Africa leave no doubt that a hot market for big animals has benefited the game because it has generated an industry in wildlife husbandry. Raising big animals for the harvest is now big business! Ranches in the West that once considered deer and elk as vermin are now charging stiff access fees to hunters keen on having a crack at something besides a yearling. Some cattlemen make more money from hunting leases than they do from raising cattle. Wildlife habitat that was earlier put to other uses is now being conserved, while animals that were once poached are now given protection.

Predictably, the cost of pursuing exceptional animals is rising sharply. The going price for a well-orchestrated pack trip into elk country runs $3500 to $4500. For a better than even chance at a mature bull, the ante goes up to $8000 or more for a hunt on private ground. Hunters who dogged elk mainly for meat at the turn of the century could hardly have imagined such fees. And they'd laugh at the reverent way in which modern hunters talk of antlers. John Plute, who tendered the antlers of an elk he'd killed in 1899 to settle a bar bill, didn't know they'd stand for a century as the largest on record. He would surely have been astonished to learn of the fortunes paid for antlers of such rank these days.

The biological price of raising mature animals in the public or private domain is a lower permissible harvest. As prices for exceptional hunting climb, limited-entry tags on public land become ever harder to draw. When hunters *do* get a crack at a big animal—either by spending lots of money or getting lucky in the draw—they understandably want to make the most of it. Hence the emphasis on more powerful rifles, stronger optics and gadgets like laser rangefinders that further reduce the

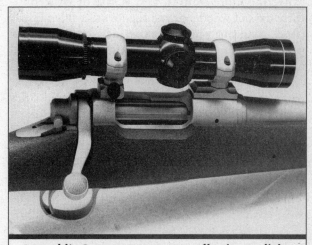

Leupold's Compact scopes are effective on light-weight rifles like this stainless-steel Remington.

The handsome Sako 75 Hunter weighs only 6¹/₈ lbs. with 22" barrel.

chance for a miss. Linking hunter prowess to the size or number of animals shot makes no sense because the best antlers come increasingly from land off limits to most hunters. And among the legions prowling public coverts for trophy-class bone, only a small handful are blessed. Nonetheless, magazines continue to coach readers in the fine points of bugling and cow calling, mock scrapes and antler rattling.

The poor fellow who thinks an outfitter or a technique or a piece of gear will get him a Boone and Crockett antler is fooling himself—even more so if he fails to accept responsibility for the outcome of a hunt. More commonly now, guides, gear and circumstances get blame for hunts that don't turn up the trophy. As the product of the hunt has become more important than the process, hunters spend less time afield while expecting more from it. Less is said or written these days of woodcraft and the joys of wilderness travel. Marksmanship, once considered a vital and practiced skill among hunters, has become a bench exercise. Physical prowess seems less a concern among hunters who rely on guides to find game and who are armed with high-powered rifles and optics that reach across canyons for the kill.

As a part-time guide for hunters in search of large elk and deer in their natural habitat, I've learned that the best hunters are most often those armed with ordinary rifles and costly optics. I recognize them too by their physiques. Even on the dark side of 50, some men have the discipline

to harden their bodies for the hunt. These include men driven by their egos to get the biggest bull in camp or a buck that exceeds the Boone and Crockett minimum. Many in this group also hunt because they like being outside and enjoy the camaraderie peculiar to a big game camp under yellow aspens. Neither type need technology as a crutch, for they realize that no equipment can substitute for marksmanship.

Rifles in the 21st century will surely be more accurate and less esthetically pleasing than those that have gone before. But the Featherweight Winchester 70's and Sako's 75's and the new Weatherby lightweight rifles are handsome indeed! Optics will continue to improve, but not at the rate we've seen during the last 50 years. Big game hunting will become more expensive and more competitive. It will also become more difficult to recruit youths, both boys and girls, in the sport. Still, good times are to be had with fine people and old rifles.

Editor's Note: *We are pleased to have Wayne Van Zwoll on board Shooter's Bible as our new Specifications Editor (see also our staff page and Foreword). It should be noted as well that, in addition to writing this article (his 10th in all for this publication), Wayne has produced a remarkably good book, entitled **Modern Sporting Rifle Cartridges,** published by Stoeger Publishing Company in the spring of 1999. Readers who are interested in this popular subject are urged to take a look.*

Sporting Books Of The 20th Century

By R. Stephen Irwin, M.D.

There are men who love out-of-doors," Theodore Roosevelt wrote in his autobiography in 1913, "who yet never open a book; and other men who love books but to whom the great book of nature is a sealed volume, and the line written therein blurred and illegible. Nevertheless among those men whom I have known the love of books and the love of outdoors, in their highest expression, have usually gone hand in hand."

These men Roosevelt describes as lovers of books and the out-of-doors are fortunate indeed, for sporting literature encompasses a vast and intriguing body of knowledge. Brought to life in these many volumes are stories of great safaris and far-away places; and of experiences that can never again be duplicated on this earth. They include tales of glorious days afield and also of toil, hardship, danger and agonizing loss. In their pages are magnificent trophy animals on unexplored continents and waves of waterfowl passing over virgin marshes. Between their covers lie beauty, reflection and humor—a celebration of the natural world, as it were, and a tribute to the human spirit.

In the earlier days of sport, hunting expeditions were, by necessity, lengthy affairs that lasted typically six months and some as long as two years. To finance such excursions, big game hunters required wealth and good educations, the latter enabling some to become fine writers. Nineteenth century sportsmen seemed to possess a greater sense of appreciation of the terrain and their quarry than did their 20th century counterparts. As such, they were more involved in the entire scope of their expeditions than our contemporary writers. Such lengthy treks permitted a leisurely pace, providing ample time in the evenings for writing and recording the day's events. The heyday of such expeditions occurred between 1830 and 1900 with books stemming from these trips becoming not only hunting accounts, but actual records of each exploration.

G.O. Young's Alaska/Yukon hunting book (Trophies Won and Lost: 1947) is armchair adventure at its best.

The Great Arc of the Wild Sheep

BY JAMES L. CLARK

With a Foreword by S. Dillon Ripley

James L. Clark's The Great Arc of the Wild Sheep (1964) is still ranked among the most authoritative volumes on the subject.

The toll extracted by two world wars and a staggering depression dampened the possibility in the second half of the 20th century for even wealthy sportsmen to undertake traditional safaris. Beginning in the 1930s, as a consequence, fewer sporting books were written. Competition from a proliferation of monthly hunting and fishing magazines also helped suppress the publication of major chronicles.

For the most part, sporting books are of two types: the practical how-to books devoted to discussions of equipment, method and technique; and the polished, literary sporting book more reflective and reminiscent in its content. The latter type chronicled an adventure or told a story. It offered, as the British are fond of saying, "a good read," and was generally more sought after by sporting bibliophiles.

One of the earliest American collectors of sporting books was a naturalist and sheep-hunting fanatic named Charles Sheldon. Born in 1867, he retired from a successful business career at 36 and spent much of the rest of his life traipsing across the mountains and river valleys of British Columbia, the Yukon and Alaska. Five North American animal species have been named in his honor, and with the assistance of his good friend, Teddy Roosevelt, he helped establish Mt. McKinley as a National Park in 1917. On one of his northern treks Sheldon was accompanied by the famous big game painter, Carl Rungius, and the equally well-known African hunter and author Frederick Courtney Selous. What a campfire that must have been to sit around!

Sheldon's unrivaled collection of books was the inspiration in 1930 for a listing of all sporting titles published up to 1925. Entitled *A Bibliography of American Sporting Books*, it was compiled by John C. Phillips and published by Edward Morrill and Son of Boston. Still considered

This 1916 book has a lovely frontispiece (not shown) by big game artist Carl Rungius.

Theodore Roosevelt's African Game Trails (1909) is his best known and most easily obtained volume.

Ernest Thompson Seton's works are sound material for a sporting library. The author was a friend of Teddy Roosevelt and helped establish the Boy Scouts of America.

the standard reference on the subject, it was endorsed by the Boone and Crockett Club. The first of its three parts lists sporting books, followed by conservation titles and a compilation of outdoor periodicals. John C. Phillips, a well known sportsman in the 1930s, also authored *A Natural History of the Ducks.*

Charles Sheldon left his sporting library to his alma mater, Yale University, where it remains an important research source. This collection was not Sheldon's only contribution to sporting literature, however; he authored an outstanding trilogy of books that forms the cornerstone of any collection of books about hunting the north country. *The Wilderness of the Upper Yukon* (1911) dramatizes Sheldon's exploits

around the Pelly River; *The Wilderness of the North Pacific Coast Islands* (1912) describes his hunts in that area; and *The Wilderness of Denali* (1930) details his solitary pursuit of Dall sheep.

These and other men who have created our heritage of sporting literature represent a diverse group in terms of their writing styles, topics and philosophies. They include U.S. Presidents, literary giants, doctors and scientists. There were also the humble and the well-heeled; not to mention eccentric backwoodsmen, business tycoons, athletes and alcoholics. The common thread that brought this diverse group together has been the love of sport and wild places and an affinity for the written word.

THE ROOSEVELT ERA

Theodore Roosevelt (1858-1919) may be better remembered as our 26th president than an outdoorsman, but few men embraced the outdoor life as he did. Certainly he enjoyed an advantaged childhood. His uncle and neighbor as a boy was Robert Barnes Roosevelt, an avid sportsman and conservationist who wrote *Game Fishes of the Northern States and Superior Fishing* (1865). Teddy's father was a founder of the American Museum of Natural History and hosted a parade of writers, adventurers and scientists as dinner guests. Young Teddy grew up reading the books of James Fenimore Cooper, which further whetted his taste for adventure. His socialite parents respected their son's penchant for collecting all sorts of natural history and taxidermy specimens in his room. As a teen Roosevelt hunted waterfowl and shorebirds in the marshes of Long Island and moose in Maine. In 1883 he jumped at the opportunity of going West on a buffalo hunt. The great herds had been pretty well decimated by that date and the hunt was not very successful.

Nonetheless, a seed had been planted and Roosevelt was forever hooked on the rugged sporting life of the American West. He wrote about that first trip west in *The Wilderness Hunter* (1893). The next year, reeling from the death of his young bride and his mother on the same day and in the same house, Teddy headed west again. His destination was the North Dakota Badlands, where he bought a cattle business and founded Elkhorn Ranch near Medora, North Dakota.

The years that followed were so formative as to convince Roosevelt later on that they had made him presidential material. He also flowered from a literary standpoint with the publication of *Hunting Trips of a Ranchman* (1885) and *Ranch Life and the Hunting Trail* (1888). Little in the way of outdoor writing was accomplished during his presidential years (1901-1909), but immediately upon completion of his second term Roosevelt embarked upon his famous zoological safari to Africa for the Smithsonian Institution. That expedition was later chronicled in 1909 in his popular book, *African Game Trails.* Another expedition for the Smithsonian—exploring the River of Doubt (a tributary of the Amazon)— resulted in *Through the Brazilian Wilderness* (1914). That trip, however, probably took years from Roosevelt's life because of malaria and dysentery.

American Big Game In its Haunts

The Book of the Boone and Crockett Club

American Big Game in its Haunts is part of a series called "Books of the Boone and Crockett Club." Authors of note include Theodore and Kermit Roosevelt, George Bird Grinnell, Prentiss N. Gray, Charles Sheldon and others.

George Bird Grinnell (1849-1938) was a close friend of Theodore Roosevelt and his main advisor on conservation matters. Together they founded in 1887 the Boone and Crockett Club, whose purpose was to spearhead an assault on such problems as the dwindling numbers of big game animals, loss of habitat on public lands, and diminishing forest resources. Under the auspices of this new organization, Roosevelt and Grinnell co-authored a series of influential books, including *American Big Game Hunting* (1893), *Trail and Campfire* (1897), and *Hunting in Many Lands* (1895). Today the Boone and Crockett Club remains a major force in conservation causes and is the recognized scoring organization and record keeper for North American big game animals. In 1876 Grinnell joined the staff of *Forest and Stream*, a leading outdoor journal founded in 1868. He eventually became the principal owner of the publication and used it as a mouthpiece to espouse the new conservation ethic. In 1930 it merged with *Field and Stream*, which remains a popular monthly magazine.

Armed with a doctorate in paleontology, Grinnell was a trained scientist and an astute observer. He was on the famous Edward H. Harriman expedition to Alaska, and later he accompanied General George Armstrong Custer as a naturalist on his expedition to the Black Hills in 1874. He became a keen student and expert on various Indian tribes, include the Blackfoot, Cheyenne and Pawnee. In 1886 Grinnell started the Audubon Society, which was designed to prevent the commercial hunting of plumage birds. As a child in Brooklyn, he'd been tutored in natural history by the famous bird painter's wife, so it was really in her honor that he named his fledgling organization. Grinnell's two hunting books, *American Duck Shooting* (1901 and *American Game-Bird Shooting* (1910), are classics in the literature of outdoor sport. Just as Charles Sheldon before him was instrumental in establishing Mt. McKinley National Park in Alaska, so Grinnell became the driving force in creating Glacier National Park in Montana. Many of its peaks, lakes and glaciers were either named by Grinnell or in his honor. He is considered the father of American conservation—and rightly so.

INTO DARKEST AFRICA

Africa, with its tremendous variety and abundance of game animals, has always been a source of intrigue for sportsmen. Not surprisingly, legions of hunters have written books about their adventures on the Dark Continent. Few, if any, have exceeded the story-telling abilities of Frederick Courtney Selous (1851-1917). He had a lively, captivating style and was blessed with an uncanny knack of describing the dangers and drama which were almost daily occurrences in his adventurous life on the African veldt. Selous (pronounced *sell-oo*) was a tenacious hunter and stalker and much admired by Theodore Roosevelt, who referred to him as "the greatest of the world's big game hunters." He was a frequent guest at the White House during Roosevelt's presidency, enthralling his host and his dinner guests with tales of a wild and dangerous life.

George Bird Grinnell wrote American Duck Shooting as well as its companion volume, American Game Bird Shooting. Both represent classics of sporting literature.

Having attended England's famed Rugby College, Selous was capable of fine writing, but he never really took it seriously until after nearly a decade of hunting and adventuring in Africa. In 1881 he wrote *A Hunter's Wanderings in Africa*, which was reprinted many times and became one of the most important books ever written on the subject of African hunting. Several notable titles followed, including *Travel and Adventure in South-East Africa* (1893), in which he described his exploits from 1881-1890; and *Sunshine and Storm in Rhodesia* (1896), an account of his battle experiences in the Second Matabele War. Always the adventurer, Selous secured a commission at age 63 as an intelligence officer during World War I. While serving in East Africa in that capacity, he was shot and killed by a sniper. Fittingly, his grave now lies within the boundaries of the Selous Game Preserve.

One of the greatest writers who ever lived was indisputably Ernest Hemingway (1899-1961). His works are still standard fare on every high school

The works of Robert Ruark, who is often compared to his friend Ernest Hemingway, are extremely collectible.

giant marlin. The book defined an underlying theme in all of Hemingway's works: that man can be destroyed, but he cannot be defeated.

Robert Ruark (1915-1956) certainly ranks among the great outdoor writers. His best known works are *The Old Man and the Boy* (1957) and its sequel, *The Old Man's Boy Grows Older* (1961). *Poor No More* (1959) was somewhat autobiographical and *Something of Value* (1955) was a successful, if controversial novel. Some of Ruark's best works were his African pieces, chiefly *Horn of the Hunter* (1953), *Uhuru: A Novel of Africa* (1962) and *Use Enough Gun* (1966).

Few authors were more knowledgeable than Jack O'Connor (1902-1978), who was gun editor for *Outdoor Life* from 1934 to 1972. A professor of journalism at the University of Arizona, he knew how to write and had the practical experience to back it up. Many of O'Connor's books—chiefly *The Big Game Rifle* (1952), *The Shotgun Book* (1965), *The Art of Hunting Big Game in North*

and college "must read" list. With such literary works to his credit as *A Farewell to Arms* (1929) and *For Whom the Bell Tolls* (1940), Hemingway is sometimes not recognized chiefly as an author of sporting literature. And yet, through all of his novels there runs, to a greater or lesser degree, a strong thread of hunting and fishing. To him, trout in Michigan, ducks in Italy, woodcock in France and pheasants in Idaho were truly the nectar of life.

Hemingway made his first trip to Africa in 1934 and was immediately intoxicated with the beauty of the continent and the daily pursuit of big game animals. From that memorable safari came *The Green Hills of Africa* (1935), containing some of the most exquisite hunting passages ever conceived, followed by *The Snows of Kilimanjaro* (1936). Hemingway's magnum opus, however, was *The Old Man and the Sea* (1952), which told the story of how an aged Cuban fisherman caught a

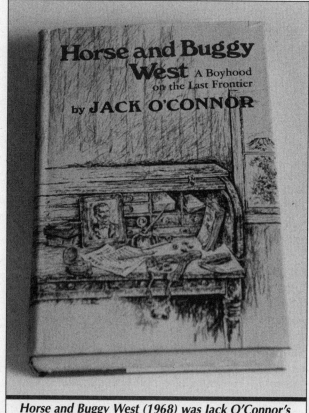

Horse and Buggy West (1968) was Jack O'Connor's last novel.

Few knew Alaska better or wrote about it more superbly than Russell Annabel, a Derrydale Press author.

O'Connor, Roderick Haig-Brown, Preston Jennings and other outdoorsmen and writers of considerable esteem.

Connett, heir to a hat-making business and a Princeton graduate, was a man of impeccable taste. He lavished over details of the books he published and spent time in England acquainting himself with the high quality of sporting books published there. His creed was: "First make a book that is easy to read; second make a book that is dignified and somewhat conversational in style; third make a book in tune with the finest tradition in that class of a book; fourth—and this almost sums up the others—make an honest book; fifth— and most important of all—make a book for the great grandchildren of your present customers." Among the more notable Derrydale titles were *High Country* (1938) by Rutherford G. Montgomery,

America (1967) and others—were extremely popular and are still easily obtained. But his first two novels— *Conquest* (1930) and *Boomtown* (1938)—are scarce and quite pricey. Even his last novel, *Horse and Buggy West* (1968), has become difficult to find. But the rarest of all O'Connor titles is the exquisite limited edition of *Game in the Desert* published in 1939 by Derrydale Press and bound in genuine lizard skin.

COLLECTORS, PRINTERS AND LOVERS OF FINE BOOKS

Everyone knows you can't judge a book by it's cover. A fine story crafted by a skilled author, however, can be enhanced by a publisher's good taste in paper, binding, type and illustration. No publisher better personified these attributes than Eugene V. Connett, who in 1927 established the Derrydale Press (the name, it is said, came from a bottle of whiskey and a map of Ireland). Derrydale exploded like a meteor on the American sporting scene and set a standard that has never been equalled. Among Connett's stable of authors —a group that collectively will probably never be excelled in any period—included Nash Buckingham, Burton Spiller, Roland Clark, Edmund Ware Smith, Russell Annabel, Jack

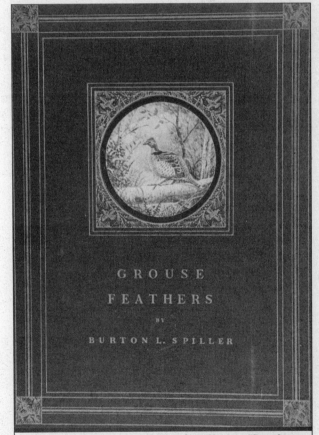

Grouse Feathers by Burton L. Spiller typifies the mastery of fine book publishing for which Derrydale Press was famous.

FRANK C. HIBBEN

18 true stories about exotic and dangerous animals

HUNTING IN AFRICA

Frank C. Hibben, a talented hunter as well as a writer, produced important books in other fields as well, chiefly on archaeology and anthropology.

Tales of a Big Game Guide (1938) by Russell Annabel, *An Artist's Game Bag* (1936) by Lynn Bogue Hunt, *Grouse Feathers* (1935) by Burton L. Spiller, and a bevy of Nash Buckingham titles including *De Shootinest Gent'man* (1934), *Mark Right* (1936), *Ole Miss* (1937) and *Blood Lines* (1938).

Derrydale ceased to exist in 1942 after publishing 221 titles and numerous prints. This small company, despite its struggles to exist during the Depression, not only showcased the finest outdoor writers ever, it produced books that remain masterpieces of publishing art. A fine library of sporting books should have a unifying theme, a certain topic or goal. The most obvious way to do this is to collect all the titles of a particular author along with his or her biography and other works to which the author has contributed chapters or introductions.

Another good way to collect sporting books is by region. Africa is almost too broad, but a sizable library could be put together by specializing in a certain area of the continent, such as the Serengeti. Other collections might concentrate on a favorite outdoor sport, such as bird hunting, or a single specie, such as brown bear or sheep. An artist can also be the basis of a collection. Frederick Remington, for example, illustrated his own book, *Done in the Open* (1898). And for a delightful reading library don't overlook outdoor humor, led by Corey Ford, whose titles include *Minutes of the Lower Forty* (1956) and *Uncle Perk's Jug* (1962).

Just as original paintings are worth more than prints, so are first editions more valuable than

RAY P. HOLLAND

SCATTERGUNNING

Decorations by WILLIAM J. SCHALDACH

ALFRED A. KNOPF, *Publisher, New York*

Ray P. Holland (Scattergunning) was editor of Field and Stream and wrote several classics on hunting with a shotgun.

subsequent ones. Sometimes, though, this is difficult to establish. Books printed in the last 50 years state on the copyright page whether they are first edition, first printing or first issue. Unfortunately, a few publishers further mystify the process with code letters or series of numbers. If the full list of numbers is set forth—say, 1 through 10—it can usually be assumed that the book in question is a first edition.

Pristine dust jackets are worth their weight in gold. When an auction or dealer's catalog denotes "original D.J.," it can be assumed that a given volume will fetch a premium. Dust jackets are placed on books to protect the covers, but ironically their presence and condition seems at least equally important.

In addition to being in excellent condition, private press prints, limited editions and signed copies are desirable qualities of a rare and valuable book. If provenance of note can be attributed to a volume by a handwritten inscription, so much the better. I own a copy of *Hunting the Alaska Brown Bear* (1930) by John W. Eddy, which is signed by the author and inscribed to Colonel Wilson Potter. Posted on the end paper of the upper cover is a book plate decorated with a pronghorn antelope, stating: *Ex libris-Wilson Potter.* Boone and Crockett's *Records of North American Big Game* lists Wilson Potter as the man who took the #3 record antelope, thus importing a nice touch of history to the volume.

PRESERVING OUR LITERARY LEGACY

The sportsmen who became literary legends in the 20th century—Roosevelt, Grinnell, Hemingway, Selous and so many others—were consummate storytellers. They wrote as if they were in their readers' dens telling stories. Their passion for the outdoors and their knowledge of the outdoors created a literary legacy that set the tone for the sporting code and a conservation ethic that has lasted 100 years. What Roosevelt and Charles Sheldon began in the 1890s and 1900s was picked up in mid-century by Jack O'Connor and his contemporaries. Sportsmen and wildlife admirers, not to mention wildlife itself, still benefit from their teachings and writings.

Adventure now comes in smaller packages, such as kayaking a rapids or climbing a rock pinnacle. The fodder of writers like Ruark and Buckingham has been dubbed "hook and bullet press." More often today's outdoor stories are about backpacking,

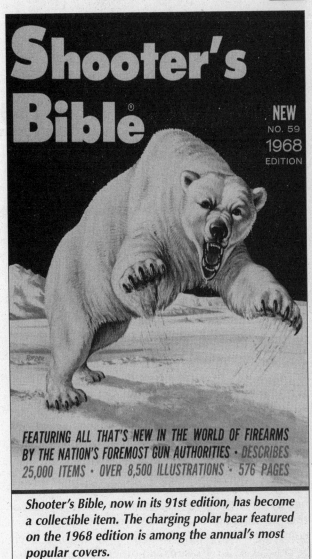

Shooter's Bible, now in its 91st edition, has become a collectible item. The charging polar bear featured on the 1968 edition is among the annual's most popular covers.

mountain biking, skiing and birding, all of which are wonderful sports and deserve wide coverage and encouragement. It must be recognized, however, that a shift in the paradigm of outdoor sport and recreation is at hand.

What direction will sporting literature take as we approach 2000 A.D.? Will new young writers espouse hunting and fishing as wholesome sports? Will the preservation of wild places, the creation of more wetlands and the reclaiming of polluted rivers continue to be popular themes for the new generation to espouse? The books that our children and grandchildren add to their sporting libraries throughout the 21st century will surely tell the tale.

A Century Of Progress For Shotgunners

By Thomas C. Tabor

During the past century and beyond, the shooting sports have changed markedly, but clearly the greatest innovations have occurred in the area of shotgunning. Whether the scattergunners' sport of choice is interrupting the flight of brightly colored clay disks or putting a succulent form of game bird on the dinner table, the past 100 years in shotgunning have witnessed tremendous improvements in the products shooters rely on. Virtually all components of the shotshell have been revamped, altered and improved upon. And yet, while these changes have made shotshells much more dependable and effective, they have in some ways actually worked to the detriment of some shooters.

For example, 40 years ago full-choked shotgun barrels were the norm. The ammunition produced thus far made it imperative to shoot these heavily constricted chokes, particularly while hunting. Even as close as 35 or 40 yards, no other choke could be counted on to produce consistent kills. Today, the same innovative changes that made ammunition better have managed to squeeze shot patterns smaller and smaller. Unfortunately, some shooters still cling to barrels choked full, but for the average shooter a more open choke would greatly improve performance. Surely there are situations that call for full chokes, but usually a modified or improved cylinder remains a better choice.

We have observed with interest as the scattergun of choice for many shooters has gone from doubles—with their barrels finely laid out horizontal to the ground—to stacked tubes with a single, unobstructed sighting plane. Ventilated ribs have now replaced yesterday's solid rib. The idea of a trigger for each barrel has taken a back seat to single triggers that offer shooters the option of which barrel to fire first. The dogleg drop of the butt stock has been made straighter to provide a softer felt recoil. In many cases the hand-checkered, highly figured walnut that took a millennium to grow has been replaced with stocks that were formed in a mold and made of space age plastic.

THE DAYS OF DAMASCUS STEEL

Within the shotshell itself, a major area of change lies in the powder. Even though experiments with smokeless powder were underway as early as the 1600s, it was not until 1886 that a

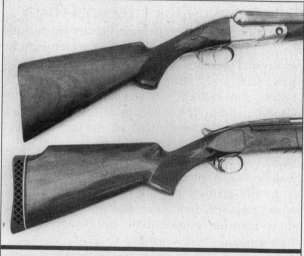

One major change in gun stock design has been the butt stock. Note the difference between the Parker Brothers model (top), built near the turn of the century, and the Browning BT-99 trap stock (bottom).

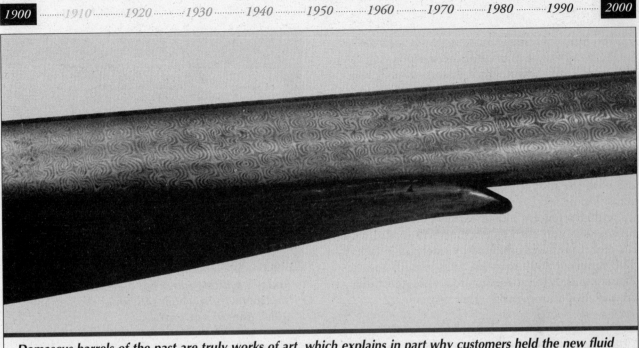

Damascus barrels of the past are truly works of art, which explains in part why customers held the new fluid steel models in such contempt. Unfortunately, Damascus barrels can't stand up to the pressures generated by smokeless powders and should never be used with modern powders.

French chemist named Vielle actually produced the first useable smokeless powder. As the 20th century was ushered in, common use of black powders began to disappear.

With the development of new smokeless powders, not to mention the increase in pressures they generated, gun and barrel manufacturers had no choice but to abandon production of Damascus barrels. The transition from Damascus (sometimes called twist, stub, laminated or a combination of these terms) to a stronger fluid steel (or "weldless barrels" as they were known) was not an easy one for the shooting public to accept. Shooters of that era held the strong belief that Damascus was superior to other forms of steel. They had already been subjected to a less expensive barrel made by welding a strip of flat metal longitudinally around a mandrel. The resulting product did not live up to expectations and was quickly rejected. On the other hand, the time-consuming process of making a Damascus barrel involved twisting and welding many small pieces of wire into larger ones, then forming the barrel by wrapping these wires around a mandrel and forge welding the finished barrel with its swirls of light- and dark-colored metal. The end result was nothing less than a fine piece of artwork.

Even as the days of Damascus were quickly coming to an end, shooters were faced with an over-abundance of the new, undecorated metal barrels—and they weren't ready to accept the change. Many shooters balked at the manufacturer's claims that these new barrels were superior to Damascus in virtually every way, causing growing unrest within the gun manufacturing community. Quick action was definitely called for.

What took place then was a positive step toward public acceptance of the new barrels. The plan was simply to place a superficial, almost lithographic coating to the outside of the barrel, simulating the wire swirls of the old Damascus. Not all manufacturers bought into the plan, but those who did were enough to ensure gradual acceptance of the new steel. Even today these finishes sometimes deceive gun owners into thinking they have a Damascus barrel shotgun, when in fact it is essentially a counterfeit. The best way to determine the truth is to etch the surface with mild acid. If the metal is truly Damascus the acid will not remove the intricate swirls formed by the wire construction. But it the shotgun finish is fake, the acid will quickly eat through the superficial finish, exposing a smooth metal surface.

The problem with Damascus steel barrels lies in the integrity of many hundreds—possibly thousands—of individually welded surfaces. Even when produced by the hands of a real craftsman, slag, scale and other contamination, not to mention poor welds, could weaken the metal's integrity. A good quality Damascus barrel of heavy construction often stood up well to the pressures generated by black powder, but it was never considered safe for use with the modern smokeless powders. In the transition period between Damascus and fluid steel, more than a few Damascus barrels were blown up because shooters tried to fire shotshells loaded with the higher pressures produced by smokeless powders. The barrels of 2000 may not be as beautiful as the Damascus, but the manufacturers were right: they are truly superior in every other way.

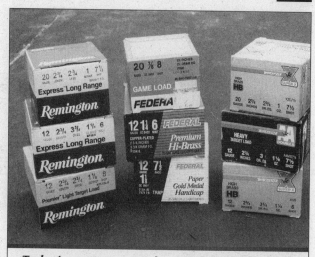

Today's scattergunner has a greater variety of shotshells from which to choose than at any other time in our history.

SHOTSHELL AND CHOKES

Improvements made in the shotshell were not restricted to the powder only. Prior to World War II, most shotshells were loaded with an over-powder wad made of cardboard seated directly on top of the powder. These wads (about 1/8-inch thick) were augmented by a couple of filler wads made of felt or some composition material. The number and thickness of these filler wads were determined simply by how much space had to be filled. Once the shot charge was loaded, a thin cardboard over-shot wad was added, followed by the top of the paper hull.

Roll crimps are a reminder of how shotshells were produced during the first half of the 20th century.

Several problems were associated with the shotshell design of the early to mid-1900s. First, the cardboard over-powder wadding did not provide an efficient or consistent seal during the ignition process. As a result, variations in pressure and velocity were commonplace. In addition, the card that was placed over the shot charge sometimes came into contact with the shot string while in flight, disrupting the shot path and thereby effecting the density of the pattern. This effect was minor, though, compared to the manner in which the shot pattern was opened up as a result of shot deformation. With nothing standing between the vulnerable soft lead of that era and the shotgun bore, deformation was a certainty as the shot made its way down the barrel and through the choke. While a perfectly round piece of shot travels essentially in a straight line, flattened shot often wanders in flight. The result is less uniform and more open shot patterns.

Significant refinements to the shotshell were on the horizon midway through the 1900s. The roll crimp was replaced by the pie or star crimp, thus eliminating the need for the over-shot wad and, in addition, solving the problem of interference during flight. The over-powder wadding was later replaced by a cup-shaped type that provided better sealing capabilities for the gases. For a time these wads were still made from cardboard, but the plastic generation was underway and soon it became apparent that this innovative new product represented the

The cross-section example on the left is a Remington shotshell dating from about the 1950s. It has the old-style felt wadding, unprotected shot column and over-shot card wad. The example on the right is its modern counterpart, including a plastic shot-cup wad.

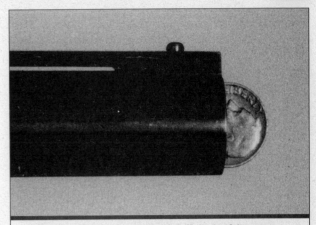

Most shotguns are choked full as is this 1962-vintage Browning. An old method of checking choke construction is to place a dime in the muzzle. If it rides half in and half out, as is the case here, it's a full choke.

wave of the future. Manufacturers used the plastic over-powder wadding with a column of felt filler wads, ensuring better gas seals but doing nothing to protect the shot from deformation within the barrel.

Ironically, even today some shotshell manufacturers resist using the superior one-piece wad, particularly in their field shells. Instead, a cup-shaped over-powder wad is seated, followed by the same filler wads of the past. While these shells do frequently contain a strip of thin plastic surrounding the shot charge, the amount of protection this method provides is minimal compared to the thick-walled modern shot-cup-style wad. Perhaps these recalcitrant manufacturers feel the average shooter benefits from the more open pattern these shells provide.

The advent of the one-piece plastic wad column was possibly the single most important shotshell component improvement to date, coupling as it did a proper gas seal with effective shot protection and ease of loading. Target shooters and hunters alike

These star (or pie) crimps are now the norm for both factory-loaded ammunition and handloads. With the exception of the second star from the top left, these all have the common 8-point crimps (the 6-star crimp is seldom used today).

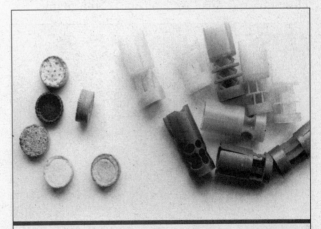

A variety of old felt and cardboard wadding materials commonly used during the first half of the 1900s is shown at left. On the right is a small sampling of the many plastic shot-cup wads in common use today.

now take advantage of what these wads have to offer. In many cases, their pedals flare almost instantly as the wad leaves the barrel, thereby minimizing interference with the shot string.

Improvements in primers and hull design have helped shotgun performance as well. The newer plastic shotshell designs certainly are a big improvement over the old-style paper shells with wads that seemingly disintegrated at the first hint of moisture. The advantages are especially appreciated by shooters who reload their own ammunition. Most plastic hulls today can be reloaded 10 or more times before being discarded.

Even before the new era of shotshells arrived, the ability to change the density and size of a shot pattern without having to change shotguns or barrels became an important consideration. Around 1890, some early attempts to provide versatility were made by incorporating screw-in removable chokes. The real pioneers of these changeable chokes, though, were the products that surfaced in the 1900s, such as the Poly Choke (invented by the late E. Field White) and the Cutts Compensator (after the late U.S. Army Colonel Richard M. Cutts). Various other changeable choke systems surfaced over time, but most were simply variations on either the Cutts or Poly Choke.

The ability to change from a full choke for hunting late season corn field pheasants and then replacing it with an improved cylinder choke for close-quarters quail were obvious. Still, many

A few of the classic hunting shotguns (left to right): Browning's A5 semiauto (12 gauge); Parker's side-by-side D grade (12 gauge); L.C. Smith's side-by-side No. 2 grade (12 gauge); Ithaca's Model 37 pump (12 gauge); Ithaca's Model 37 Pump (20 gauge); and Winchester's Model 12 pump (20 gauge).

This Ithaca Model 37, one of the writer's favorite hunting guns, is frequently used on upland game birds.

shooters disliked the physical appearance of these first attempts at versatility; but trimmer, sleeker designs were on the way. One of the pioneers in this area was Stan Baker, who flared the end of the shotgun barrel slightly, then threaded the inside to accept a screw-in choke tube. While this produced a more pleasing appearance than did the much larger Poly Choke and Cutts systems, the alterations remained clearly visible. A few short years after Baker's innovative work, choke tubes became available with no flaring and no changes to the outside contour of the barrel, the muzzle having been delicately machined and threaded to accept a thin-walled choke tube. Today, most observers cannot tell there's an interchangeable choke tube without looking directly into the muzzle. Soon shooters had the option of purchasing new shotguns with inter-changeable choke systems direct from the factory.

SHOTGUN CLASSICS

The American scattergunner has obviously observed significant changes over the past century, yet today many of the shotguns that were produced early in the 1900s remain true classics. For example, Browning's A5 gas-operated ("square-back" as it is sometimes called) began its career in 1900 and still ranks among the most dependable workhorses of the semiautomatics. The same basic design produced by Remington (as the Model 11) from 1905 to 1949 is still a favorite of waterfowlers especially. Winchester capitalized on the simplicity of this design in 1912 with the now famous Model 12 pump (one of the few pump guns *not* designed by John Browning), now recognized by many shotgunners as the best pump ever made.

The year 1937 proved a good year for Ithaca when it adapted John Browning's unique bottom-ejecting pump design. This lightweight pump, called the Model 37, captured the heart of many upland bird hunters. It was so well accepted that prior to Ithaca's Model 37, Remington had manufactured it under its name (as the Model 17) throughout the

Quality and craftsmanship are what Parker Brothers stood for. This D grade side-by-side came with an optional skeleton butt plate (the center is actually checkered end grain from the stock butt).

1920s and '30s. The Browning version—called the BPS (Browning Pump Shotgun)—was first produced in 1977. It's still marketed by Browning but it is actually made by Miroku of Japan. Ithaca's feather-light version tops the scales at only 5 3/4 pounds, making it light to handle and quick to point. The bottom ejection design is favored especially by hand-loaders simply because the empties are easy to locate.

When talking about classic shotgun designs, it's important to identify some of the important players, even though these classics began their tenure before 1900. While most modern shooters have abandoned the idea of looking down a set of side-by-side barrels, there's still something romantic about actually shooting one. Two of America's best were made by Parker Brothers and L.C. Smith. It takes only a brief look to appreciate the quality of craftsmanship in these firearms. All one has to do is open the action and

Most double triggers are now a part of history. Because of its Damascus steel barrels, this No. 2 grade L.C. Smith shotgun must be restricted to black powder; nevertheless, it still performs effectively in the field after nearly 100 years of service.

close it again. The solid sound of hand-fitted locking lugs snapping firmly into place tells the story of a true craftsman's devotion to his art. The argument can be made that today's shotguns are more practical. The shotguns coming off the assembly lines in the year 2000 are made with much more favorable stock lines and often with attractive and practical ventilated ribs. Certainly they are more effective in the field. Nevertheless, there will always be the desire among sportsmen to fire a quality firearm classic like those produced by L.C. Smith or Parker Brothers. They depict the level of excellence by which other shotguns are judged.

Another area of change has to do with stock drop, which is designed to align the shooter's eye with the barrel. In order to compare the difference between the old and the new, simply invert one of each upside down on a tabletop. With the rib (or top) of the barrel held firmly against the table surface, the differences in drop at the comb and butt are clearly visible. With most older shotguns the drop is much greater than that found on its modern counterpart. By lowering the stock drop and maintaining alignment of the shooter's eye to the bore, the effects of recoil are reduced.

There has also been a significant movement away from wood stocks to plastic or composite type stocks.

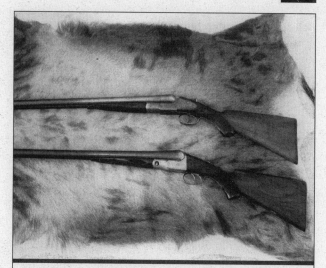

While not too commonly found afield today, but still considered among the best American doubles ever made, are: the sidelock L.C. Smith (top) and boxlock Parker (bottom) shotguns. While not too commonly found afield now, they are still considered among the best American-made doubles ever produced.

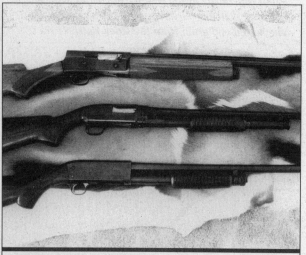

These classic shotguns are still in use (top to bottom): Browning's A5 semiautomatic in 12 gauge; a Winchester Model 12 pump in 20 gauge; and an Ithaca Model 37 bottom ejection pump in 12 gauge.

While no one will claim these stocks are as attractive as a high quality walnut stock, they do provide considerable durability. Foul weather shooters and waterfowlers in particular often prefer these new stocks simply because they offer more resistance to the effects of weather. Many gunmakers are now offering models equipped with this style of stock, and the after-market manufacturers have flooded the marketplace with replacement stocks of the composite design. Half a century or more ago, Stevens produced a single shot model with a plastic stock as a means of cutting production cost. But the timing wasn't right and soon the plastic stock was dropped from Stevens' line.

Today's shooters enjoy distinct advantages over the hunters and target shooters of yesteryear. Shotshells are more dependable, better constructed and capable of unmatched effectiveness. Our contemporary shotguns have barrels made of solid steel that help ensure our safety, along with such terrific features as interchangeable chokes and ventilated ribs. Isn't it ironic, though, that some of the best shotgun designs making their way into the new millennium are the same ones that were designed during the first half of the 20th century?

Handloading:
A Century Of Progress

By Don Lewis

When I was a boy, I remember moving out of our big farm house in the spring of 1931, so it must have been the previous fall when my older brother Dan and I, after finishing our chores, left the house bent on Dan's "mission." I remember walking down a dirt road for over a mile to the home of one of Dan's hunting friends. Most of the details have slipped my mind, but I do recall that my brother had taken some empty shells with him, probably to get them reloaded. The Great Depression had already placed its devastating grip on the nation, and especially on rural folks who worked on farms or in coal mines, brickyards and logging operations. Nothing was moving, and no one had any discretionary income to fritter away on nonessential things like store-bought shells.

Dan's friend, Pete, helped out in his father's business, operating several small hand-dug coal mines. Charges of black powder were used to "shoot down" the coal, and with all of that black powder on hand Pete and Dan were able to reload their black powder shells. On that day, after placing the reloading tools, powder and wad jars (along with Dan's empties) on Pete's dining room table, the operation suddenly came to a halt. Apparently, Pete was short a component (probably some primers), so Dan and I had to leave without any shells. I was only nine at the time, but that episode still sticks in my mind. Little did I realize back then that nearly 70 years later I'd be writing about that experience in a handloading article.

It's worth noting at the outset that the vast majority of hunters in the 1920s and '30s used factory shotshells, even though handloading had been in existence for more than 50 years. The first successful, self-contained metallic cartridge produced in the U.S. was Smith &

Wesson's 22 rimfire Short, which was introduced back in 1857. A rimfire cartridge can't be reloaded because the primer compound is located in the rim of the head. It was sometime around 1868 before a satisfactory centerfire system was developed; then, in 1895, Winchester developed the 30-30 WCF with smokeless powder. Strange as it may seem, black powder cartridges remained popular during the early 1900s; in fact, Winchester was still offering black powder shells until the mid-1930s.

By the late 1800s, repeating shotguns and rifles were on the market. Once multi-shots were available with repeating firearms, hunters and shooters began burning ammo in quantities never dreamed of. It didn't take a degree in ballistics to reach the conclusion that all those empty cases could be refilled instead of being

Loading Machines.

This foot-operated loading machine from Ideal dates back to the "gas light" era. It was probably the forerunner of today's high-speed progressive press.

Ron Bailey, Jr., proudly displays his 500-yard target. All five shots landed in a 1 5/8" group (right photo). The rifle is a Custom 700 Remington (made by Jim Peightal) chambered for 7mm Remington. The scope is a 36X Leupold.

tossed away. Thus were the first hand reloading tools manufactured. From a purely technical standpoint, handloading began when the first firearm was invented. Guns had been around for years, but the matchlock was probably the first true shoulder weapon, making its debut sometime in the 1400s. Firearms history is clouded, but it's reasonable to assume that shoulder weapons were in full swing by the mid-1500s. The first examples were smoothbore muskets loaded by pouring a charge of black powder into the muzzle, then shoving a projectile down on top of the powder. A live coal or red-hot iron was then applied to a touch hole that led into the powder charge, igniting the powder. Through the years, after many design changes and innovations, the smoothbore musket evolved into a rifled flintlock, which came on the scene sometime in the early 1600s. The flintlock was a dependable black powder gun that held the spotlight until the late 1800s, when smokeless powder and the self-contained cartridge put the black powder gun on the back burner for military and hunting purposes.

Obviously, handloading is not a new kid on the block; still, handloading as we know it didn't come into existence until the self-contained centerfire cartridge was invented. At first, reloading tools were somewhat crude, requiring each step to be done by hand, which wasn't so bad considering that large amounts of shells were not needed by early hunters. Today, though, a prairie dog hunter can consume a thousand rounds or more under ideal conditions. Big game hunters can consume a half dozen boxes of ammo in practice sessions prior to opening day. And in the shotgun world, a claybird shooter can go through 15,000 rounds a year without much trouble. Similarly, dedicated dove and waterfowl hunters will fire hundreds of rounds each year. Indeed, modern hunters and shooters have developed an insatiable appetite for shells—and the only sure way to have all the shells you need when you need them is to reload your own.

Handloading became popular as recently as the early 1950s, with the emphasis on saving money. In those days, three shells could be reloaded for the price of one factory round; and purchasing components in large quantities cut the cost even more. That economic fact of life disappeared, though, when handloaders began using scoped rifles to test the accuracy of their reloads. Until the end of World War II, most big game hunters fired less than a dozen or so shots prior to opening day. For hunters east of the Mississippi River, hunting varmints at long range was not top priority shooting. Home reloading introduced thousands of hunters to the benchrest; and group shooting, which was practically unknown to most shooters, became a way of life. Now handloaders quickly took up the challenge, turning out home-reloaded shells that routinely placed five shots in a tight group at 100 yards. Suddenly, the quest for accuracy was in high gear.

Accuracy was understandably the major goal with early handloaders, but it was not often achieved. The reason was pretty simple. First, factory-built rifles and bullets posed problems that made it almost impossible to achieve high degrees of accuracy. With factory rifles being chambered mostly for varmint cartridges, accuracy was not the primary goal. Few, if any, had triggers that were adjustable for preventing free-play and over-travel. A gunsmith could install custom-made adjustable triggers on some types of bolt action rifles, and it was possible to modify a factory trigger to some extent; but modifying a factory-made trigger could not outdo an adjustable trigger. The factory trigger of the "Gas Light Era" was sloppy and hard to pull, drawbacks which made it impossible to achieve the consistent pull weight that made a crisp, lightweight trigger such a vital factor in good accuracy.

Handloaders soon learned that a bullet played a major role in securing tight groups, and that an accurate bullet had to be concentric and free from defects. The reason? When a bullet leaves the case and begins its journey through the barrel, it follows the confines of the bore. Then, after exiting, it spins on its own axis. Should there be even the slightest imperfection in the bullet—some trapped air, foreign particles in the lead or variations in jacket thickness—it cannot fly a true course. As bullet makers began offering match-type bullets, groups started to shrink.

Another factor in achieving accuracy was none other than the shooter himself. When the group-shooting craze first infiltrated the handloading crowd, few shooters and varmint hunters knew anything about how to test reloaded ammunition. Many handloaders thought it was a waste of ammunition because they didn't understand the benefits of testing. The feeling prevailed that "a shell was a shell," and the only things that could be changed were the powder charge and bullet weight. It was generally felt that shooting from a benchrest with the rifle resting solidly on double sandbags was about as challenging as

shooting ducks in a pond. Putting five shots in a tight group at 100 yards didn't seem like much of a feat, but soon most converts to benchrest shooting learned what humility was all about. For every 5-shot, one-inch group fired at 100 yards, there would be ten others that sent anyone's ego in a downward spiral.

By the late 1950s, home reloading was solidly entrenched within the shooting clan, with small shops cranking out reloaded shells by the tens of thousands. Hunters were now fascinated with handloaded shells, but unfortunately a false belief arose to the effect that handloaded ammo was vastly superior to factory shells. That wasn't true then, and it's not true today. It has, however, become a myth that refuses to die. In all fairness, the factory shell is hard to beat. The average handloader who uses the best equipment, components and techniques is hard-pressed to match a factory-made hunting shell; in fact, it's almost impossible to duplicate a factory round.

To begin with, modern high-grade premium cartridges for big game are the result of the latest technology and components. The primers used in high-performance shells, for example, are carefully tested to ensure consistent lots. Moreover, the bullets used by manufacturers may not even be available to reloading buffs. The powders used are bought in huge quantities and tested extensively to find out which lots produce the best results in performance and accuracy. There is no way the average handloader can compete with a factory where thousands of rounds are fired when testing a new varmint round.

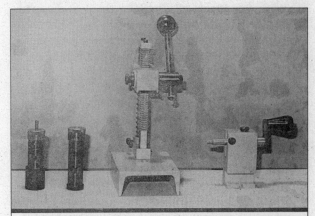

Benchrest shooters use hand-made dies and arbor presses in turning out sophisticated and highly accurate ammo. The setup shown is on a 3/4-inch plywood shelf (nothing is bolted to the bench).

An OAL gauge determines the gap between the ogive of the bullet and the beginning of the rifling section.

The main advantage in reloading your own ammunition lies in the potential for matching a primer/powder/bullet combination with a particular rifle. Factory shells are designed for use in all types of rifles in good condition, whereas a reloaded round can be tailor-made to "fit" a particular rifle. This is not a simple task. Making a case, for instance, is beyond the skills of the average handloader. In its purest sense, handloading entails the refilling of a factory-made case. Normal reloading procedures consist of a few simple operations: the case is resized, the spent primer is removed and replaced, a powder charge is dumped into the case, and a bullet is seated.

With all the improvements made by the ammunition makers, credit must also go to the benchrest shooting clan for bringing rifle accuracy to a level that was unthinkable in the late 1940s. A world-record 200-yard group in 1948 measured just over one-half inch. That's phenomenal shooting, but it represents only one of many half-inch groups produced by today's 200-yard benchrest competitors. Benchresters, who are in large part handloaders, leave no stone unturned when developing an accurate load. They may disagree among themselves over calibers, barrels, triggers and components, but they have worked hard to bring accuracy to a critical level. Today's top benchrest competitors can fire 5-shot groups of less than a hundred-thousandths of an inch at 100 yards (250-thousandth equals one-quarter inch).

The handloading tools used by benchrest competitors are normally custom-made. For example, the resizing die for a given rifle chamber is machined to a mirror finish. Other reloading equipment—including powder measures, primer seaters and outside neck turning tools—are made by specialists. Neil Jones's benchrest Micro Measure is guaranteed to throw charges to one-tenth (plus or minus) of a grain. K&M's primer seating tools have dial indicators measuring to the thousandths of an inch. An Over-All-Length (OAL) gauge offered by Stoney Point establishes the maximum overall cartridge length. Even the top shooting rests are designed for accuracy (as the saying goes, "A good group starts with a good rest"). Home reloaders may not need these custom-made reloading tools and methods for producing top quality hunting ammunition; but long range varmint hunters will certainly benefit from them.

Reloading tools now on the market are a far cry from those used during the black powder era. The old hand-scoop powder and shot measure, plier-type reloading press and hand-cranked closer (a crimping device) have been replaced with metallic and shotshell presses that come close to being fully automated. One good example is the Dillon SL 900 shotshell press, which incorporates a motor-driven case feeder. Once the shell head is full, the handloader simply pulls the handle and drops a wad into the wad guide. With the SL 900 case feeding, resizing brass heads, decapping and seating primers, dropping powder charges, insert-

Tom Peterson of Stoney Point Products demonstrates how to use the OAL gauge.

The "C" frame press is quite strong. In full-length resizing, note that the press ram must touch the bottom of the resizing die to ensure the case is completely in the die.

specifications while, at the same time, removing (decapping) the spent primer. In most presses, a priming arm had to be pushed into a slot in the press ram. When the press handle was lifted, the decapped case came down on the priming arm and a new primer was seated. When all cases were resized and fitted with new primers, a predetermined amount of powder was dropped from the powder measure into each case. The sizing/decapping die was removed and replaced with the bullet seating die. After the seating die was adjusted and each bullet was seated to the correct depth, a bullet was shoved in each case and the shell was finished. It was a time-consuming process, true, but thousands of rounds were cranked out on those early presses.

One of the many innovators was a company offering a double ram press that held both the resizing/decapping die and the bullet-seating die. While it represented an improvement over the single-die press, it was also confusing. A Herter's turret-head press, for example, had six die stations. After the resizing/decapping die, powder measure and bullet seating die were installed, the case was resized, decapped and primed (the first die). The turret was then turned to the powder measure and a powder charge was dropped. At the last station (the seating die), the bullet was

ing wads in the case, dropping the shot and crimping, among other functions, are all done automatically now—and much faster. The SL 900 can crank out 13 shells per minute, which is more than 750 reloads per hour. True, minor mishaps, such as a stuck case in the feed tube, a jammed wad or simple fatigue can reduce that pace considerably, but the dependability and accuracy of this press remain unchallenged.

The famous Lyman 310 Tool held the spotlight until the late 1940s, when new converts to the reloading game switched to C-type presses, which were faster and easier to use. Basically, the C-press (whose frame is shaped like a C) was made from heavy steel or cast iron, rendering it almost indestructible. The reloading process, which required that each step be handled manually, allowed operators to examine a case at each step in the reloading procedure. This consisted of shoving a lubricated empty case into a full-length sizing die, squeezing the empty case back to near-factory

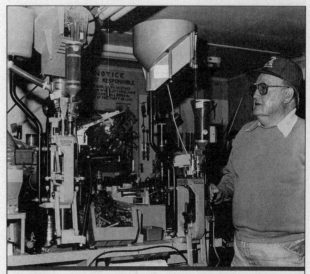

Author Don Lewis poses with a Dillon SL 900 shotshell progressive press (left) and Dillon XL 650 metallic progressive press (right). The SL 900 includes case-activated powder and shot dies. Note the large container of reloaded shotshells to the right of the SL 900 press.

seated and the turret turned back to the resizing/ decapping die. For the reloader, this whole process provided more work and less fun. The only advantage was having three sets of dies for the turret's six stations. If all cases used the same shell holder and primer size—the 30-06, 270 Winchester and 243 Winchester, for example—it was only a matter of turning the turret to the die set for another cartridge.

Die sets for handguns or straight-wall cases required an extra die. Neck expansion did not occur in the resizing die (as in a rifle die) but in a separate die that also bells (flares) the case mouth. All brands of handgun dies now include an expanding die with which to enlarge the case neck to approximately one-thousandth of an inch smaller than bullet size. At the same time, the die flares the case mouth during the crimping process just enough to allow easy entry of the bullet. This is especially important when working with lead bullets, because a non-flared case mouth will shave off the lead.

Since the early 1950s, a flood of reloading tools has hit the market. Belding and Mull introduced their famous "Straightline" model and the Potter Automatic Duplex Machine became popular soon after World War II as well. Lyman's Tru-Line Junior had a huge following and the Hollywood "Senior" was effective in loading shotshell, pistol and rifle shells. Universal's Model III was a turret-type press that cost about $90 back in 1953. C&H offered both C-type and H-type tools, calling them the Big "C" or the Pacific Super Tool.

RCBS (now Blount) probably leads the pack with a host of innovative reloading equipment and reloading dies (including swaging dies for converting conventional rifle cases into wildcat creations). Bear in mind that it takes eight dies for the case-forming process: two tapered expander dies (40 to 45 and 45 to 50) to iron out some of the original shoulder; five case-forming dies; and an inside neck reamer die. After a case has been resized and loaded, it must be

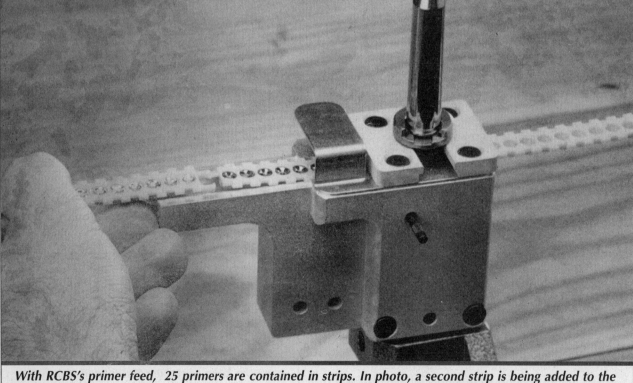

With RCBS's primer feed, 25 primers are contained in strips. In photo, a second strip is being added to the one already in the machine. The primer feed is available in two models: the bench (shown) and press type.

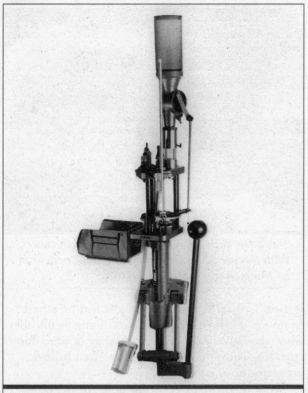

The RCBS Piggyback turns several RCBS single-stage presses into progressive presses, making an inexpensive method for obtaining a top-rated progressive metallic reloading press.

Forty years ago, measuring a bullet's speed was deemed almost impossible for the average handloader, but now reliable and relatively inexpensive chronographs can print out a host of ballistic information, including instrumental velocity, extreme velocity spread and standard deviation. Oehler's Model 43 Personal Ballistic Laboratory (PBL) can fill a computer screen with ballistics readings covering chamber pressure, instrumental velocity and average muzzle velocity for groups fired, plus high and low velocity readings and standard deviation. When a downrange Acoustic Target is used, the Model 43 PBL reports time-of-flight, downrange velocity and the ballistic coefficient of each bullet. The Acoustic Target consists of three microphones attached to each leg of a triangular plastic pipe. As the bullet passes through the triangle, the microphones pick up the bullet's "mach cone" (sonic boom) and relays this information through a cable to the M-43 PBL and on into the computer.

fire-formed to reach a sharp 40-degree shoulder angle. The completed case then can be reloaded using 30-416 Rigby wildcat dies. After fire-forming, and with a total of ten dies and a reaming process in hand, the shell is ready for the woods. With a 180-grain .308 diameter bullet, its muzzle velocity is around 3850 feet per second—almost 900 fps faster than a 180-grain bullet as it leaves the muzzle of a .300 Winchester Magnum.

Today, super-progressive shotshell and metallic cartridge presses are available at prices that don't require mortgaging the farm. RCBS's Ammo-Master, Hornady's Lock-N-Load, Lee's Loadmaster, Dillon's XL650 are all top quality rifle and handgun presses. In addition to Dillon's SL900 progressive shotshell press, other top-of-the-line scattergun presses include MEC's Hustler (900H, Hornady's Apex 3.1 and Ponsness/Warren's Size-O-Matic 900 Elite.

Handloading has also been responsible for introducing the handloader to the ballistic side of shooting.

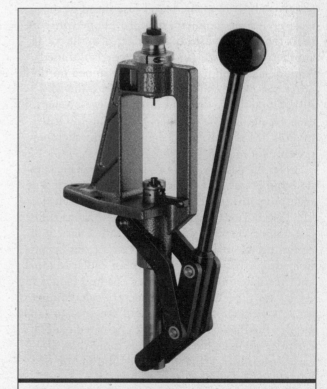

The RCBS single stage Partner Press is light (5 pounds) but strong enough to resize full-length magnum rifle cases. It's equipped with a priming arm with interchangeable prime plugs and sleeves for seating large and small primers alike.

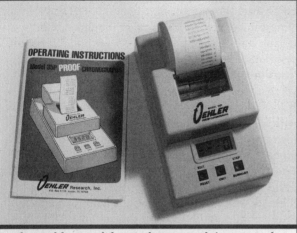

The Oehler Model 35P chronograph is extremely accurate, easy to use, and prints out results on the same type used in adding machines.

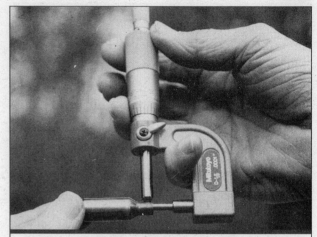

This K&M Ball Mic measures case neck thickness. With this precision measuring tool, case necks can be trimmed to exacting standards.

To obtain chamber pressure readings, a strain gauge is glued to a rifle barrel just ahead of the receiver. A four-conductor modular phone wire connects the cable (two wires are soldered to the gauge, another is grounded, and the 4th wire is not used). A modular telephone connector is crimped on the other end of the cable and plugged into the M-43 PBL. Using this instrument is truly an eye-opener for even experienced handloaders (according to Oehler, 60,000 PSI is considered the maximum chamber pressure for most rifle shells).

Over the past few years a variety of ballistic computer programs have come on the market, including such programs as Oehler Explorer, Barnes Ballistic, On Target, Tioga Engineering and RCBS.Load. The last-named works in conjunction with a variety of reloading manuals including all data from Speer Reloading Manual #12, RCBS Cast Bullet Manual and Accurate Smokeless Powder Loading Guide #1. RCBS.Load performs real trajectory calculations on actual equation of motion and provides an axial view at the impact point with a graduated scale. Its cartridge drawing database covers more than 280 cartridges, plus a great deal more information of benefit to the handloader.

The appeal of handloading today lies not in saving money alone. Modern technology has brought accuracy levels to new heights. Custom-built rifles may be the choice of benchrest competitors, but varmint and big game hunters are enjoying incredible accuracy from factory rifles where high-quality, reloaded ammunition

is used. Critical accuracy is not just for the experts anymore; it can be a realistic goal of any handloader who takes advantage of the vast array of precision reloading equipment and computerized ballistic programs on the market.

What does the 21st century hold for the home reloader? Handloading is no longer simply a pleasant pastime. It's a reliable source of high-quality ammunition. Its imprint, having been clearly defined on the accuracy trail, proves emphatically that the reloaded shell has few peers. After a century of handloading, that's a pretty good sign for the future.

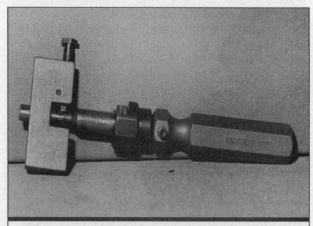

When using the K&M Neck Turning tool, the necks are trimmed on the outside to remove high spots while maintaining the same thickness around the neck of the case wall.

Sights And Scopes:
A Look Back--And Forward

By Wilf E. Pyle

It may have taken more than a few years, but now there remains nothing left to debate: The iron sight has given way to the modern scope. Without the restrictions of iron sights, today's shooters are free to take on shots that were previously considered impossible. No longer sensitive to the whims of weather and without the problems inherent in mounting iron sights on a rifle, the scope is a wonderful—and affordable—instrument indeed. In fact, many younger shooters have never used an iron sight for hunting. Many will argue that, during the last 70 years, the development of the modern scope has made it a must for accurate shooting at all kinds of game by all types of shooters.

The scope was not always the preferred sighting tool. At the turn of the century, iron sights dominated hunting rifles for all but the most specialized shooting. Although scopes have been around since the time of the American Civil War, it was not until midway through the 20th century that they were improved, optically as well as mechanically. Even then, the early scopes remained delicate instruments, difficult to mount and prone to mishaps and lapses in performance. Iron sights were still viewed as reliable, functional and eminently practical for the hunter.

Following World War II, the rifle scope reached levels of development that remained unsurpassed until modern computer assistance was applied to their design and lens manufacturing. Prior to the war, the first scopes to gain popularity in America were the small, delicate $2^1/_2$-power type. In the 1920s, keen-eyed riflemen were importing Zeiss Zielklein and Hensoldt scopes from Germany, but they were difficult to mount properly and the rings lacked universal bases. The reticle was also poorly

designed. It often covered or subtended as much as five inches at 100 yards. California scope builder Rudolph Noske improved these designs and is credited with producing the first American-made scope for big game hunting rifles. Bill Weaver next came along to offer the first inexpensive American-made scope. In its September 1933 issue, *American Rifleman* included the Weaver 3-30 $2^3/_4$-power scope at a retail price of $19 (with mount included). Compare that with the Noske, which sold for $65 at a time when most hunters earned $1 a day, barely enough to buy a pound of butter and a loaf of bread.

This high quality rear sight from an 1886 Winchester carbine was considered the best sighting one could hope for at the turn of the century.

The Weaver scope was one of the first inexpensive scopes produced and marketed in the U.S.

LYMAN LEADS THE WAY

Scopes have evolved greatly since 1840 when New England gunsmith Morgan S. James placed crude, optical sights on his heavy-barreled rifle for long-distance shooting. Snipers on both sides of the American Civil War used small-diameter, barrel-length scopes for picking off distant enemies. As early as 1901, the J. Stevens Arms and Tool Company, which later evolved into Leupold Scopes, began producing scopes. H. M. Pope, the legendary barrel maker, allegedly made a five-power scope measuring 34 inches in length and ³/₄-inch in diameter. Soon scopes were available from a variety of makers.

A good pre-World War II American-made scope was the 2¹/₂-powered Lyman Alaskan. Its 7/8-inch tube, like the Zeiss and Hensoldt models, made possible low mounting on the rifle, provided a wide field of vision, and featured fully enclosed adjustments. It also boasted the first internal windage and elevation adjustment (covered with screw caps to keep the weather out). Its design was promoted by an early gun writer named Philip B. Sharpe. As a result of these developments, Lyman became a serious contender in the scope market, beginning with the purchase of Winchester's manufacturing rights and production equipment with which to produce the early Winchester A5 target sight and mount. Lyman was one of a handful of U.S. companies to make the transition from manufacturing iron sights to producing scope sights with any level of success. For a family-run company that had started out making loading tools and bullet molds, this was

a remarkable accomplishment in modern firearms manufacture and diversification (the Lyman name has remained but the company has disappeared as a manufacturing entity; its products now being produced under license).

COATING AND A CURE FOR FOGGING

About the same time, scope makers in Europe had developed a process for surface-coating optical lenses. It was originally conceived in the 1930s by a German optical designer working for Zeiss. Not all lenses benefited from this technique, however. My personal collection contains two pair of German binoculars my father took from German army personnel during World War II. Although many German field glasses possessed coated lenses, mine didn't; as a result, light transmission was poor.

After single-coat layering became commonplace, multiple layers soon followed. In theory, several coatings on each surface were matched with alternating high and low refractive indexes of light to reduce reflections and allow light to pass. As early as 1943 Germany was producing lens surfaces with three layers of coating. Today many lenses are multicoated to improve light transmission. Coating is now protected by several proprietary processes that essentially cook, stick or oxidize a layer of magnesium fluoride (or combinations of magnesium fluoride) to the lens surfaces. First, a layer of this chemical in the form of

During the early part of the 20th century, the Fecker scope company produced some of the best target scopes, but it never made the transition to hunting scopes.

Large objective lens scopes, which work best in low light situations, are now common.

vapor (not a gas) is baked onto the surface of the lens in an oven or is induced electrically or oxidized onto the lens. This process is often repeated in several layers to achieve better uniformity and light transmission. The result is a lens surface colored slight purple to yellow. This microscopic layer of chemical, some five microns thick, allows more light to pass through the lens, producing a sharper image for superior resolution. For lenses coated on both sides throughout the system, light transmission improves 40 percent.

Another important development in scope making has been the cure for fogging. In the early days, when scopes were used under humid or cold conditions, a vapor collected on the inside of the scope producing a fog that remained until the scope was warmed and the vapor eliminated. Scope manufacturing now prevents fogging by removing moist air during the assembly process. The air is replaced by dry nitrogen and the scope hermetically sealed so the gas can't leak out. This process finally did away with the problem of internal lens fogging.

WEAVER SETS THE STYLE

During the 1950s, scopes underwent remarkable improvements. Bill Weaver is credited with many of these; indeed, it has been noted that Weaver did for scopes what Henry Ford did for cars. Often thought of as a design and marketing genius, he put more scopes with more features in the hands of more shooters than any other manufacturer. His K4 Weaver, for example, following its introduction in 1946, became

the best selling scope of all time. In 1950 the Weaver KV became the first successful variable scope, and in 1954 Weaver pioneered the first nitrogen-filled scope. Many of his improvements were evident in the manufacturing techniques and methods he employed, but they were largely transparent to the average consumer. All combined to provide high quality scopes that were stronger, more reliable, easier to mount, and better performers in the field.

Although Weaver remained with steel tubes well into the 1970s, other scope makers began turning to aluminum tubing—called *duraluminum* or *dural*—to make their scopes lighter. Improved machining of the aluminum created a better shoulder where the lens elements fitted into the tube, thus improving waterproofing and preventing leakage. Another innovation was a rubber gasket material developed by the aviation industry. This substance helped scopes to sustain shocks and ensure stability of the reticle. Internally, adjusted scopes became available as the cost of manufacture improved and demand from shooters grew.

Tube diameter changed, too. The early Weaver 330 and 440 scopes had 3/4-inch tubes, but the scopes made by Zeiss and Hensoldt Zeilklein scopes, plus the Lyman Alaskan, all featured 7/8-inch tubes. When Weaver brought out his "K series" of scopes, including the K-2.5 and K-4, one-inch tubes were standard. This set the style for American-made

Weaver produced some of the first quality long range target scopes for the serious varmint hunter. This ancient Weaver Model K12-1 was a top performer in the 1960s.

scopes, and soon all manufacturers followed Weaver's lead. One-inch tubes were stronger, easier to work with around the cutting machines, and not so easily damaged by strong-arm tactics with scope mounts.

Another problem that plagued scope users in the 20th century was the need for reliable scope mounting equipment. Many German and English mounts were elegant in design, but they were too fragile and unstable. Most fogged completely in damp weather and needed to be removed before any hunting could continue; hence, easy detachment was a necessity. This need led to scope mounts placed high on the rifle, forcing shooters to look under the scope and use the iron sights. But in so doing, the hunter's cheek lost contact with the comb, resulting in poorly placed shots—and extreme displeasure with the scope! This situation really didn't improve until Weaver developed the detachable mount, plus a wide selection of bases. Available in low, medium and high styles, as well as extensions, these mounts were soon in production for over 200 different rifles. Thus did Weaver set the style for top mounting scopes with their wide-spaced mount rings, rigidity, ease of installation, low scope position, easy removal and accurate realignment. To this day his mounts remain detachable, even though scope detachability is no longer a serious issue with hunters.

ENTER THE VARIABLES AND ELECTRONIC SIGHTS

Perhaps the greatest potential in the marketing of scope sights was the variable. For most shooters the

Weaver is credited with providing good quality scopes at a reasonable price, but his invention of bases and mounts are what made modern scope mounting possible.

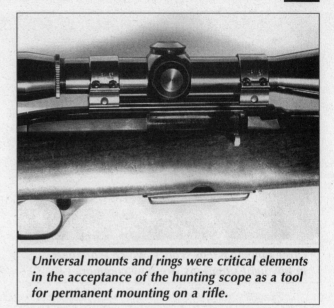

Universal mounts and rings were critical elements in the acceptance of the hunting scope as a tool for permanent mounting on a rifle.

notion that, at the twist of a ring, magnification could be changed from high (for distant shots) to low (for close-in shots) was an appealing idea that made sense. Beginning in the 1950s, the Bausch and Lomb "BALVar" 2$^1/_2$- to 4-power scope became all the rage as hunters demanded a power choice to match field conditions. Most other manufacturers offered variables, but they suffered from reticles that increased in thickness and obscured the target as the power was cranked up. Then Redfield, which had been in business since 1909 (but had only begun making scopes in the 1920s), began offering variable scopes with many different features. By the late 1950s Redfield had developed the constantly centered non-magnifying reticle. Until then, reticles were positioned ahead of the erector lens system, which changes the image to right side up and right reading. As power was increased, the reticle became magnified. Redfield placed the reticle *behind* the erector system; that way, it would stay on center and remain at one size as the power varied. This innovation made the variable scope a more practical instrument for the hunting rifle and provided perhaps the single greatest boon for scope sights. It also allowed scope designers to provide more high-end power choices. Whereas the original variable scopes featured power selections ranging from 2x to 4x, the new scopes reached beyond 10x without blocking out the target.

The next long-term problem was range estimation. To remedy this need, Redfield developed in 1965 a stadia wire housed in the scope body as a means to determine range. This was followed by a Trajectory Compensating System (TCS) which automatically accounted for the ballistic drop of a bullet along its course. Later, in 1970, Redfield offered an extra wide field of view on most of its scopes. While this innovation made the scope look like a TV set, it was well received by gadget-crazy hunters in search of that extra kick from their equipment. Back in 1912, T.K. "Tackhold" Lee had designed the first floating dot reticle for use in a target scope; and by 1939 he was marketing the Lee Dot to interested woodchuck hunters. Today, reticles are available in fine or medium crosshairs, which are quite popular (but difficult to see in bush conditions or low light). The post and crosshair combination, which is easy to see in dimly lit situations, has also come into demand. In long range hunting or in bright light, however, the post may hide part of the target, making the four-plex reticle the most popular reticle. It's wide enough at the edges to be seen in most light conditions, while its center is thin enough so that it doesn't obscure the image during precision shooting.

An interesting offshoot of the modern scope is Aimport's electronic sight, which consistently draws glowing reviews from handgunners and shotgun

Leupold and Stevens, which began work on scopes n the 1940s, was an early producer of hunting scopes designed to meet rugged outdoor conditions.

shooters. In 1981 and 1982 the top shooters at Camp Perry used Aimport's electronic sights on their guns, while several top-place shooters at the Bianch Cup V also adopted them. Unlike conventional scopes, these Swedish-made sights are non-magnifying. The reticle is a luminous red dot that appears to glow as the shooter looks through the lens. He needs only to place the dot on target and the rest is pure physics. With no magnification involved, there are no problems of parallax or resolution to worry about. The battery-operated sight can be used instinctively with both eyes open, making it easy to get the sight on target quickly and reliably with no positioning of the eye. Handgunners especially like the Aimpoint's luminous dot as eye relief and because it eliminates the need to align sights.

Throughout the history and development of the modern rifle scope, there remains a curious relationship between Europe's old-world optic manufacturers and America's modern counterparts. And now Japan and the Pacific rim have also become major sources of precision optics, making a third leg in the import triangle. One in particular—Herters Incorporated—was remarkable for its tenacity and bravado throughout most of the 20th century. Beginning in 1893, Herters imported scopes from Germany and renamed them as part of the U.S. company's own proprietary house brands. Later, the company bought American-made scopes from brand name manufacturers but continued to use proprietary names. Herters was well-known for outlandish claims about its various products and

This Model '70 Winchester is outfitted with a six-power Leupold held in place with Weaver low mount bases, which allow the shooter to get down on the stock quickly.

a propensity for exaggerating the qualities of its products in the company's catalog. Herters' influence in the scope business forced its competitors to handle similar products at slightly lower prices. One of Herters' reticles, incidentally, was its 500-yard Range Reference finder. This reticle was outfitted with several crosshairs and reference screens to show points of aim at yardages from 200 to 500 yards. Herters disappeared as a corporate entity in the late 1970s, but its influence in the scope business can still be felt.

Another option that has proven popular with practical field shooters is the compact scope. First introduced by Leupold in the late 1970s, these scopes are lighter, smaller and less bulky than their larger cousins. They are at home on the current crop of lightweight rifles, which might otherwise look odd when outfitted with the large variable scopes. About the only knock on compact scopes is that, power for power, they offer a reduced field of view compared to full-length types. Redfield offers compacts with an extended field of view, and so the evolution continues.

Gun writers and outdoor fanciers traditionally long for the good old days. As a group, they harbor the notion that today's products are not as good as what they used to be a decade or more ago. This is especially clear where rifles are concerned. Who among us has not longed for a pre-64 Winchester Model 70, even though we all know the 1976 model is probably superior. The same does not hold true for scopes, however. Few of us yearn for an old Noski or a Ziess Zeilklein of the 1950s, nor even a Weaver from the 1960s. In 1936 the great gun scribe Charles Askins wrote: "Generally speaking, a telescope is out of place on a hunting rifle. It is at best a frail instrument which cannot withstand slamming about in a boat or being jolted by a galloping horse. It renders a repeating rifle or an automatic practically nothing but a single shot, and any time the quarry takes a notion to move, no matter if it jumps within twenty-five yards of the gun, the telescope man has a useless tool in hand. All of which, as can readily be conjectured, quite unfits the telescope for use in the woods."

BACK TO THE BASICS

In all fairness to Charles Askins, at the time he wrote those words the iron sight was considered the best way to align rifle and target with accuracy. Today, the most inexpensive way to go is with a middle (or open) sight that is screwed or dovetailed into the rear area of the barrel. These sights offer the same features available

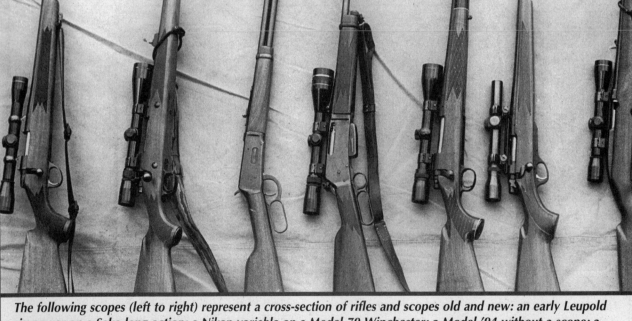

The following scopes (left to right) represent a cross-section of rifles and scopes old and new: an early Leupold six power on a Sako long action; a Nikon variable on a Model 70 Winchester; a Model '94 without a scope; a Browning BLR outfitted with a variable Leupold; a Remington 700 carrying an old Bushnell scope; a Remington Model 600 with a Weaver K4; and a Model 100 Winchester carbine sporting a new Leupold compact.

Compact scopes appeared in the early 1980s, offering less weight and a profile matching the lightweight, carbine-style rifles then coming to market.

at the turn of the century; namely, fast sighting for close-in shots taken in brush or woods, ruggedness, ease of use and weather resistance. Standard issue military rifles in most countries then incorporated some form of iron sight. Even in this modern information age many (including the writer) still prefer a Model '94 Winchester with its original iron sight. A modern scope looks plain silly on these rifles.

Next to the open sight the peep (or aperture) sight has evolved in different ways since the 1900s. Among those rarely seen today (and no longer manufactured) is the tang sight designed to mount on the rear tang of most lever actions rifles. Another is the receiver sight, so-called because of where it is mounted. These sights, which sacrifice ruggedness for greater accuracy and shot placement, allow for adjustments ranging from elementary to precise micrometer and are capable of responding to changes in range, wind direction, ammunition types and light conditions. While often larger or bulkier than a standard sight, aperture sights consume less space in gun cases than the telescope types. They also weigh less.

The peep sight is little more than a hole in a piece of steel through which one sights. Larger holes allow a sight to get on target quickly. In practice, hunters have traditionally favored a large peep hole, while target shooters prefer a small one. By the same token, a large hole is preferred in poor light. But on the target range, where light is often provided, the small aperture is preferred. Generally, the larger the aperture the more coarse the front sight, and vice versa.

RECEIVER SIGHTS

Iron sights have become confined mostly to the back pages of shooting supply catalogs. Target shooters still require them for various competitions, but one has difficulty recalling any hunter going afield with a receiver-mounted sight on a bolt action hunting rifle. For the first half of the 20th century the Lyman 48 was considered the hallmark of receiver sights for hunting. It featured all-steel construction, a low profile design, and precision adjustments (it also had a screw-in disk which many hunters simply unscrewed and looked through the mounting hole). Various aperture sizes up to .125 inch are available for sophisticated shooters. Target shooters select aperture sizes around .05 to .06 inches. My Model 71 bears a flat-sided version of this sight, called the Model 66, featuring a quick release slide. This allows a shooter to return to the original factory sights, an indication that receiver sights were treated somewhat the same as early scopes.

The tang receiver sight was designed for lever action rifles—chiefly Winchester, Marlin, various Remingtons, many single shot models, and the ubiquitous Stevens Model Favorites. Cocking piece sights were also made for Mausers, Krags, Mannlichers and Springfield rifles. These sights were actually products of the previous century, when buffalo hunters using Winchesters and Sharps Borchart long range rifles were outfitted with adjustable peep sights. Winchester, Marlin, Marble's and Lyman all made these sights, which were very accurate and provided an extended sighting plain. They worked best when positioned no

Most lever action rifles are best served without a scope of any kind, forcing the shooter to rely on the oldest form of sight available. This Marlin Model '92 is a fine example of a scope-less rifle.

more than two inches from the eye. The well-known Lyman Model No 1, which appeared in 1870, was awkward to use when folded down and would sometimes tear flesh when the rifle was grabbed for instant action. There was no lateral adjustment, and some claimed the tang mounting destroyed the shooter's hold at the small of the grip. Also, novice shooters taking up-hill shots would allow the rifle stock to slip down slightly when bringing the eye dangerously close to the sight. This caused the shooting press to condemn the tang sight, and it wasn't until late in the 20th century that modern black powder shooters revived the tang.

The receiver sight has a special place in the hearts of hunters. Accuracy with a receiver sight means that one has achieved a level of expertise with the rifle and understands what shooting is all about. The aperture sight remains popular among target shooting circles where rules and regulations govern the choice of sighting equipment. Many hunting peeps are no longer available, but the Williams FP ("finest precision") still holds a prominent place in the market for shooters who seek accuracy without a scope.

THE LASER—PORTENT OF THINGS TO COME

Scopes may have displaced receiver sights, but the future now belongs to the laser sight. A laser produces

Receiver sights hold a fascination for the serious shooter. Hunters who use these sights today are accorded superior knowledge of rifles and game.

a pin-point beam of light and, as a sighting device, it provides illumination of a chosen spot on the target. Quarton, one of the largest manufacturers of visible diode lasers, produces the Beamshot laser sights, often seen on specially outfitted handguns. Among the practical challenges to the laser as a sighting device on a hunting rifle is the need for an electrical power source (current models rely on batteries of limited shelf life). All batteries have a history of underperforming in cold weather. The shooter must also remember to switch the sight on prior to shooting, thus adding another step to an already complicated cycle of sighting, shooting and recovery. Quarton's Beamshot 1000 uses a CR123A Lithium battery with a life of 20 hours in continuous on position. The sighting laser produces a visible beam that is projected on the target. One current concern is the diameter of the beam and its influence on accuracy. A four-inch dot compounds the holding and shooting error on a rifle, producing at best $1\frac{1}{4}$-inch groups at 100 yards (the new Beamshot 1001 produces a $1\frac{1}{2}$-inch dot at 100 yards). Combining a high-powered scope with a laser reticle that can be viewed through the scope is the next step in the evolution of this sighting system.

There is no question that lasers are growing in application and suitability to the hunting rifle. But no matter how well lasers may develop as we move into the new millennium, there will always be a need and demand for rifle scopes.

The modern high power scope is adjustable for parallax, usually by twisting a ring located at the objective end of the scope.

IF YOU THINK "POINTABILITY" DOESN'T MAKE A DIFFERENCE, ASK THE BIRD.

Beretta designed its field O/U's for quick target acquisition. *Their low-profile design and trim stock dimensions* ensure proper *eye-hand alignment,* combining to make them the quickest, most responsive O/U's in the world.

Beretta also designed them

Low-profile action locates barrel lower in the receiver for closer alignment with the shooter's eyes and hands, while reducing felt recoil and barrel rise.

to last, with rugged Monobloc barrel construction and *fully heat-treated receivers.* Replaceable dual conical self-adjusting locking lugs and *hinge pins for the ultimate in durability.* *Nickel-chrome-moly barrels* with hard-chromed bores and chambers dramatically increase corrosion resistance. Mobilchoke® screw-in choke system adds versatility.

The Onyx features a classic blued finish, available in a 3-1/2" magnum model.

The Silver Pigeon is available in 12, 20 and 28 gauge, *chambered for 2-3/4" and 3" shells. Or choose the 686 Onyx* with a classic black receiver or *special matte finish Onyx model* in 12 gauge chambered for 3-1/2" shells. Be sure to explore the full line of *Beretta Sport clothing and accessories* at your Beretta dealer today.

BERETTA
A tradition of excellence since 1526

Beretta U.S.A. Corp., 17601 Beretta Dr., Accokeek, MD 20607, www.beretta.com. For a Beretta Worldwide Catalog of firearms & Beretta Sport clothing and accessories, call 1-800-528-7453 ($3.00 shipping). Visit The Beretta Gallery in New York and Dallas.

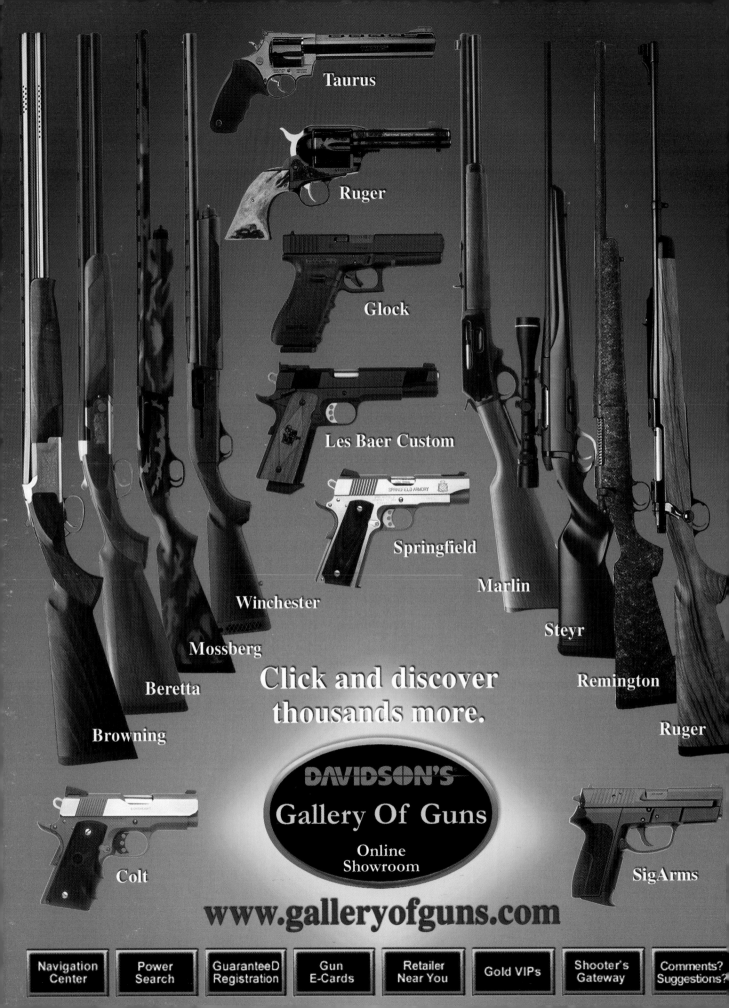

Cartridges--Then And Now

By Ralph F. Quinn

The first really successful self-contained metallic cartridge—consisting of a bullet, case and primer—occurred some 155 years ago when French inventor Flobert developed the .22 rimfire BB cap. Later, in 1858, Smith and Wesson successfully pioneered and marketed the round in the U.S. as the .22 short. A few years later, the first "big bore" rimfire—the .44 Henry—was developed by the New Haven Arms Company for its Henry rifle. The .56-56 Spencer arrived in 1862, followed by Winchester's Model 1866 rifles in .44 Henry and, 26 years later, the first "rimmed" centerfire cartridge: the .30-40 Krag. This round was chambered for Winchester's bolt action rifle and, as the saying goes, the rest is history.

Going from a rimfire to a rimmed centerfire cartridge, however, took lots of time, ingenuity and perseverance, not to mention a new primer design, plus luck and hard cash. Much that transpired in the cartridge business, then as now, could be directly linked to the almighty dollar. Throughout history, the adage, "Produce a better cartridge and they will come," has been a pretty fair assessment of the cartridge business. Likewise, no company can exist for very long without operating at a profit. When sales of a particular cartridge fall below the profit level, the round must eventually be discontinued. And if that cartridge was designed for a particular rifle action, the firearm may suffer a similar fate. Historically, the landscape has been littered with the remains of unsuccessful cartridges. Rifle companies that rose to fame and fortune on the merits of a particular cartridge or rifle, only to fade with the morning sun, include C. Sharps, A.O. Neider; J. Stevens Co., and the Charles Newton Rifle Company. These firms were all headed by firearm experts whose contributions of caliber, cartridge and innovative rifle design endured well into this century.

To gain insight into the subject of "cartridges," both historically and economically, we need to look inside the designs, both rimfire and centerfire, to see what makes each one function. Even though rimfire and centerfire ammo manufactured in the year 2000 outwardly resemble the 1858 S&W Short or the .30-06 Springfield, modern cartridges include chemical, metallurgical technology and production methods that were unavailable in 1900. Comparing an obsolete round with its current edition is like pitting a modern Ford Mustang against the "Tin Lizzy."

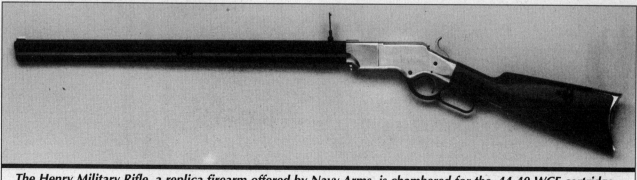

The Henry Military Rifle, a replica firearm offered by Navy Arms, is chambered for the .44-40 WCF cartridge. First offered in 1863, the round made rimfire ammo obsolete.

The 1873 Winchester Style Rifle is another Replica firearm from Navy Arms. Known as the "Gun That Won the West," it's chambered in .44-40, .45 Colt and .357 Mag.

THE RIMFIRE

As the name indicates, rimfires include all cartridges in which the primer compound is sealed in the rim, not in the center of the base (centerfire). Ignition occurs when the rim is indented by the firing pin. Rimfire cases, by design, were not made very strong, since firing depended on crushing the cartridge rim. Black powder loads in .44 Long, for instance, developed modest pressures with 220 grain bullets. Introduced in 1860 as a short range cartridge, it was successful on small to medium game; but when the .44-40 Winchester Centerfire (WCF) cartridge appeared in 1873 the .44 quickly lost ground. The fact that it could be reloaded, and that it was chambered in a number of repeating arms, found favor in the American West. But by the 1920s, the round had become obsolete.

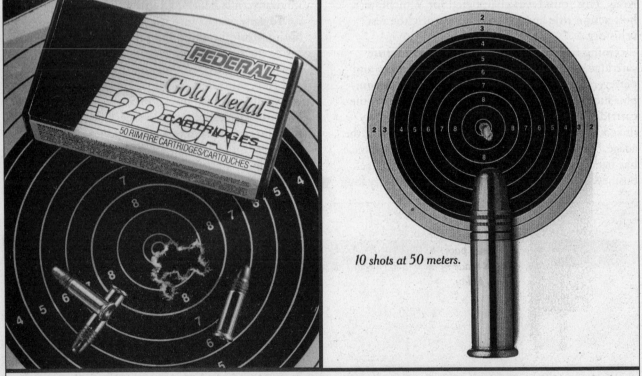

10 shots at 50 meters.

Match .22 rimfire ammo can produce incredible accuracy because of its uniform ignition and shorter lock time. Ultramatch Gold Medal by Federal produced this 50 meter group.

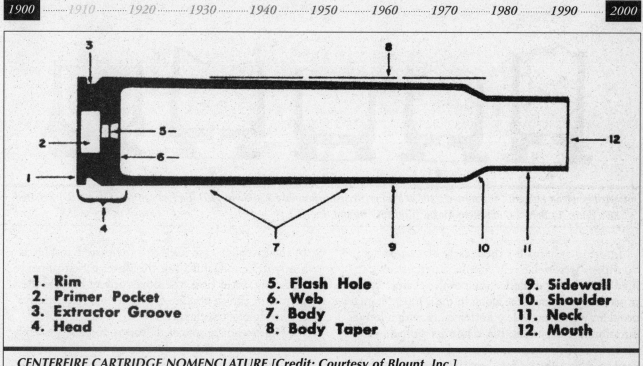

1. Rim
2. Primer Pocket
3. Extractor Groove
4. Head

5. Flash Hole
6. Web
7. Body
8. Body Taper

9. Sidewall
10. Shoulder
11. Neck
12. Mouth

CENTERFIRE CARTRIDGE NOMENCLATURE [Credit: Courtesy of Blount, Inc.]

At one time, several rimfire revolvers and rifles were chambered in .25 Stevens, .32 Long and .38 Long and Extra Long—yet all were discontinued before World War II. Among the most enduring was the .41 Swiss rimfire chambered in the turnbolt Vetterli rifle imported into this country in the early 1900s. This cartridge employed a 334-grain bullet and was, at best, a short range load. Supplies of both rifles and ammo were plentiful at one time, but by the early 1940s most American ammo companies had discontinued the load.

Even though rimfires have suffered historically, their basic design is alive and well due in part to technological advances in both their design and manufacture. In 1959 Winchester introduced the "hot" .22 Magnum Rimfire, which developed in pistols enough energy to equal that of the .38 Special. Within 125 yards it easily surpasses most of the ancient .22 centerfires.

More recently, the .22 Long Rifle has become the most accurate and highly developed rimfire sporting cartridge. The match ammo supplied by Federal in its .22 Gold Medal Ultramatch and British-made Eley Tenex are simply overwhelming in their perfomance. Their secret lies in the uniformity of primer ignition, resulting in shorter lock time. By using the new "Bentz" match reamer by Clymer Sportsman

Team Challenge (STC), shooters today are achieving Olympic performance from semiauto rifles—a feat usually reserved for expensive bolt action rimfires.

THE CENTERFIRE CARTRIDGE AND THE PRIMER

The evolution of the centerfire cartridge, generally considered requisite in the development of modern ammunition, came during the 1860s and 1870s. During this period most, if not all cartridges and rifles evolved in direct response to the demands of the Western frontier. Since rimfires weren't practical to reload and couldn't handle the pressures generated by high velocity loads, buffalo hunters and pioneers looked in another direction. Manufacturers were quick to fill the need by adopting the solid head centerfire case. Breech loaders of various manufacture— i.e., Greene, Hopkins and Allen, Maynard, Spencer and Wesson—were all chambered in .38-40 Ballard, .38-50 Maynard, .38-55 Ballard/Winchester, .44-70 Maynard, 45-70 Sharps, and .50-90 Sharps (the second number indicates grains of powder; the first is caliber diameter). Most of these obsolete loads used black powder as a propellant and were considered "minimal" cartridges for big game by modern standards, yet in their day they were "hot" stuff.

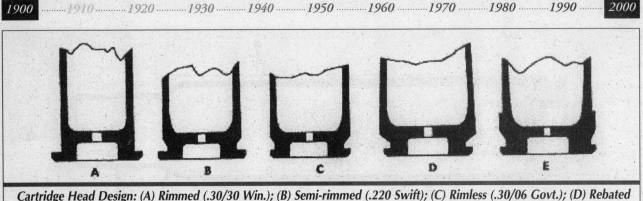

Cartridge Head Design: (A) Rimmed (.30/30 Win.); (B) Semi-rimmed (.220 Swift); (C) Rimless (.30/06 Govt.); (D) Rebated (.284 Win); (E) Belted (7mm Rem Mag.). [Courtesy Blount, Inc.]

Ignition systems for these early black powder cartridges were relatively simple: a percussion cap fired a spark that exploded the powder charge. When smokeless powders came along in the 1900s, the main problem was to provide a hotter spark with a longer duration. No easy task. Black powder primers were made of copper to accommodate the weak firing pins used in early rifles. When breech pressures operated in the 10-20,000 psi range, a harder metal like brass became a necessity. Otherwise, the primer could blow up and cause serious injury or even death.

The modern centerfire primer is an amazingly simple device consisting of a cup, or container, some priming compound and an anvil. Still, its development was one of trial and error. The Boxer design commonly found in the U.S. is completely self-contained, with the anvil as part of the primer. The Berdan Primer, which is preferred in Europe, has no anvil but is part of the cartridge case itself. It's the easiest and least costly to manufacture, but the Boxer is best suited to reloading. Over time, the Boxer primer became the primer of choice because U.S. hunters, trappers and match shooters demanded it.

Those who are so-called "baby boomers" probably have never been exposed to the corrosive priming mix used in early centerfire cartridges. Most of the compounds used contained fulminates of mercury and potassium chlorate. The former is extremely explosive. Once detonated, free mercury combines with the case brass to make it brittle. Eventually, the case cracks or the head separates, making reloading impossible. With black powder loads these chemical effects were not quickly noted; but as smokeless powders became the standard propellant in high-pressure centerfire loads the effect was sudden and catastrophic.

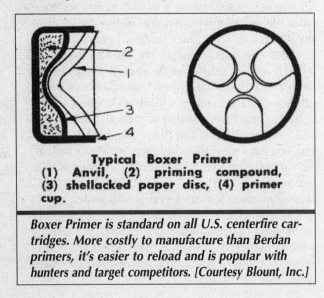

Typical Boxer Primer
(1) Anvil, (2) priming compound, (3) shellacked paper disc, (4) primer cup.

Boxer Primer is standard on all U.S. centerfire cartridges. More costly to manufacture than Berdan primers, it's easier to reload and is popular with hunters and target competitors. [Courtesy Blount, Inc.]

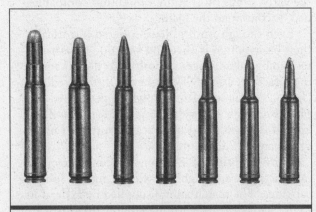

Magnum Primers and slow-burning smokeless powder led Weatherby cartridges into the 21st century. From left: .460, .378, .340, .300, 7mm, .270, .257 Weatherby Magnums.

Initially, the problem was blamed on the smoke-less powder, but the U.S. Ordnance Department, following a series of tests in 1897, found that mercury was the culprit. The following year a new and non-mercuric priming compound was introduced by the U.S. military with commercial ammo companies quick to follow. The new primers, now free of mercury, were based on a potash chlorate which shooters soon discovered caused their rifle bores to rust and become pitted beyond repair. Upon firing, it was found, the potash compound turned into a chlorate salt similar to sodium chloride or common table salt.

By the late 1920s a new priming mix based on lead-styphnate was developed in the U.S., offering shooters a rust-free, non-mercuric primer. Even though RWS, the German ammo firm, had manufactured non-chlorate primers for 20 years and had introduced rust-free rimfire ammo as far back as World War I, U.S. shooters largely ignored the product. After a false start in 1927, however, Remington began changing its earlier Klean-Bore priming to the RWS formula. At last American shooters had a chlorate-free primer to spark their cartridges. By 1931 most U.S. ammo had become salt and mercury free.

In 1944, shortly after the American primer system got rolling, a California rifle maker and ballistics genius named Roy Weatherby achieved high velocities by burning large quantities of powder in blown-out and necked-down cartridges based on the .300 H&H case. Even though Weatherby's idea was revolutionary, the Boxer primer was not suited to the task. The spark issued simply wasn't "hot" enough to ignite the slow-burning powder needed to control peak breech pressures.

To the uninitiated the solution seemed simple: build a bigger fire and the problem would be solved. The trick, however, was to ignite the powder in a way that regulated burn and kept breech pressures within acceptable psi limits. A new, more potent primer was needed. It arrived in the form of the Magnum Primer, which the Speer Cartridge Works had developed for the U.S. military in the 1950s to improve cartridge ignition during cold weather. The Speer team ultimately came up with a priming compound consisting of lead styphnate, aluminum and boron, which retained heat longer and penetrated the coated grains of smoke-less powder. Called the Magnum Primer, it was an instant success and provided a launching pad for the Weatherby cartridge. More important, it introduced the world to magnum cartridges.

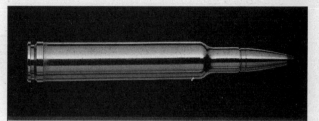

Based on the .300 H&H cartridge, the .300 Weatherby Magnum continues to top magnum chamberings. A dozen or more manufacturers offer the round in their top-end rifles.

With the development of clean and reliable centerfire primers, ammo companies were now free to design case heads capable of withstanding extreme pressures generated in high intensity loads.

But there were problems. As cartridge brass is drawn into successive stages it becomes brittle. Annealing (softening by heat) allows case-forming to proceed smoothly enough, but there's no set formula. If the case is too soft, the brass flows and sticks to the chamber wall upon firing. But if the case is too hard, it becomes brittle and cracks. Ideally, a properly annealed cartridge will expand with pressure to fill the chamber; but when the pressure abates, it should spring back.

To control headspace, centerfire cartridges were rimmed to stop the case from progressing into the chamber. Back in the 1860s, the German Mauser featured a staggered box magazine that led to a rimless case design in which the cartridge shoulder determined headspace. Mauser's belted magnum consisted of a belt in front of the extractor groove, preventing the cartridge from moving into the barrel chamber. It also controlled headspace.

With booming cartridges like the .458 Winchester Magnum, no shoulder is required to control forward movement. Belted straight cases thus have the virtues of a rimmed case that works easily through a Mauser bolt magazine. The .220 Swift has a rebated or semi-rimmed case in which the rim projects above the extractor groove. Older centerfire cartridges (.30/30, .32 Special, .30/40 Krag, .45-70, etc.) are all rimmed with tapered or straight walls, but most cartridges introduced since World War II are rimless or belted with a bottle-neck case design. As breech pressures have risen to 50-60,000 psi, case heads have become thicker and stronger. A cross-sectional view of high intensity loads, such as the .270, 7mm Mag. and .300 Mag., are more strongly constructed at the web base

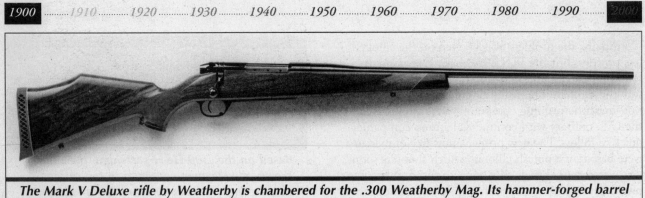

The Mark V Deluxe rifle by Weatherby is chambered for the .300 Weatherby Mag. Its hammer-forged barrel and hand-bedding combine for top accuracy and performance.

and walls than cartridges operating at 38-40,000 psi. Driving bullets faster, farther and more accurately, though, required gun powders with controlled burning, not a constant rate.

ENTER THE SMOKELESS POWDER ERA

A century ago the vast majority of centerfire cartridges in the U.S. were loaded with black powder. Today, though, cartridge listings are universally loaded with smokeless powders—and for good reasons. They come in a variety of forms, compositions, coatings and grain sizes, enough to fulfill virtually any reloading need. All are variants of nitroglycerin and guncotton, either double or single base. Straight nitrocellulose powder contains no nitroglycerin and is produced by dissolving guncotton in ether and alcohol. DuPont, Hodgdon and Hercules all manufacture single base powders.

What type powder should be used for a particular cartridge or bullet combination? I strongly recommend that you borrow or buy the current edition of one of the reloading manuals published by Speer, Hodgdon or Winchester and follow their recommendations. Ballisticians spend countless hours testing a variety of powders best suited to a particular cartridge, with velocities and energies calculated at muzzle and downrange. I once wrote a piece for *Shooter's Bible (1989)* entitled "Brave New World of Computer Ballistics" in which the subject of cartridge and bullet performance-based velocities was explored. A number of programs are now available that can provide armchair ballisticians with an overall view of cartridge performance without firing a shot.

For every cartridge there exists a certain combination of powder and bullet that will develop maximum velocity within safe pressure limits. There is also a combination that produces maximum efficiency in relation to downrange energy. Ideally, shooters seek maximum acceleration while the bullet is in the barrel

without exceeding working pressures. The highest velocity seldom yields the best accuracy, and a slightly heavier bullet at reduced fps will actually retain more energy and velocity at long range.

BULLET SELECTION

Before the advent of smokeless powder and high velocity, bullet selection was mighty important to black powder shooters. With velocities fixed at low fps regardless of caliber, the bullet was responsible for getting the job done. Cast bullets were the norm then, with the old timers lavishing great amounts of time creating the "perfect" projectile. Handloaders liked the idea because lead bullets cost less than jacketed bullets and were just as effective with reduced loads. The standard for black powder loads was an alloy of one part tin to 15 parts lead (one part to 20 was preferred for single-shot rifles). Ultimately, lead bullets evolved into five base types: hollow, plain, zinc washer, half-jacketed and gas-check. The gas-check bullet, which was developed in England around 1900, came to the U.S. in 1905 via the Ideal

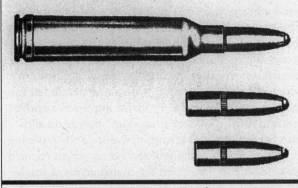

The 7mm Remington Magnum is a long range performer popular with big game hunters. Shown are 175 and 150 grain PSP Spitzers. Belted case is from Winchester's short-magnum group (.264 and .338).

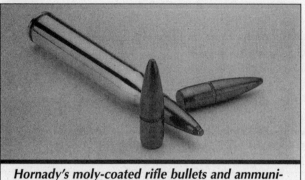

Hornady's moly-coated rifle bullets and ammunition provide exceptional down range performance and optimal expansion.

Manufacturing Company. The gas check itself is a tiny copper cup attached to the bullet base to protect it from the heat and pressures of powder ignition.

When muzzle velocities hit the 2000 fps mark, the jacketed bullet became necessary to protect the bullet base. These bullets are formed by inserting a lead core into a "jacket" made of copper and nickel alloy (cupro-nickel) and swaged together using a hardened steel die. Jacketed bullets are classified as flat-based or boat-tail. The latter has a tapered base to reduce drag and increase long-range performance. These categories are further divided into sub-types based on shape and performance; i.e., round, spitzer and semi-spitzer. Hunting bullets, which are made to allow controlled expansion and energy, include soft and hollow point, silver-tipped and partitioned. The popular Nosler partition bullet is an example of the German H-mantel design in which the front portion expands while the base portion retains its shape.

Today, shooters have a wide choice of excellent bullet designs to choose from. In cartridges with velocities ranging from 2,500 to 4,000 fps, it's a simple matter of matching the caliber to the game. Ammo manufacturers discovered years ago it was impossible to make one bullet do the job on all game in all calibers. The cartridge and bullet lists in the back of this book include multiple listings for nearly every caliber. As a general rule, light bullets in any caliber are made for varmints and small game. Big game bullets are usually heavier, 100 grains or more. The best recommendation is to match gun and bullet to the conditions and game being hunted, then learn how to put the shot where it counts. Don't be too impressed with velocities—heavier bullets retain energy much better than light ones at game ranges. It's the carefully balanced load that brings home the bacon.

CARTRIDGES INTO THE MILLENNIUM

Like all industries in a free market system, the cartridge business is a dynamic, ever-changing one that suffers ups and downs based on the whims and fancies of the shooting public. Trying to predict the future, obviously, is not an exact science, more like reading tea leaves. In the decade following World War II many smokeless centerfire cartridges found their way to the scrap heap, including the little .250/3000 Savage cartridge despite its accuracy and overall excellence. Savage and Ruger made brief production runs, but currently no production rifles are chambered for the round. The .22 Savage Hi Power .25 Remington Rimless, .35 and .405 Winchester, the .24/35, .303 Savage .33 Winchester and .25 and .35 Remington rimless—all have suffered similar fates.

A few old-timers—the .22 Hornet (1920) and .218 Bee (1938)—have enjoyed a revival, thanks to renewed interest by Ruger, AMT, Browning and Uberti. Obviously, a nostalgia factor is working in their favor; as long as their loyal followers continue to climb on board both chamberings will survive well into the 21st century. The great .375 H&H Magnum, king of the African calibers, has been kicking around since 1912; and the light-recoiling 7x57 Mauser is also on the comeback list. In 1920 Remington and Western Cartridge each issued a cartridge loaded with 139-grain bullets @ 2,850 fps and they were instant hits. When sales declined, Remington and Winchester stopped chambering it for their Models 30 and M70, respectively.

Another seemingly ageless cartridge is the .30/30 Winchester. Even though the round was issued in 1895, it continues to sell. U.S. Repeating Arms offers the best

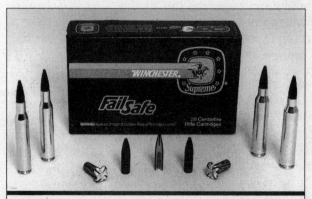

Fail Safe Cartridges and bullets by Winchester offer excellent expansion and performance for future hunters. This cartridge-bullet system was awarded six U.S. patents.

Winchester's Model 70, introduced in 1926, is chambered with the .270 Winchester centerfire cartridge. Long range performance and top accuracy account for its continued success.

selling Model 94 lever action in both standard and classic versions. The .270 and .30/06 continue to dominate cartridge lists as effective big game rounds, even though both calibers were introduced way back in 1926. The M70 bolt chambered in .270 Winchester was a favorite of the legendary gun writer Jack O'Connor, who is largely credited for its popularity. The 30/06 rose to similar stardom, thanks in large part to Griffin and Howe, "Rifle Smiths to Presidents." Many of that company's superbly crafted Customs chambered in .30/06 trod the game fields of the world during the 1930s and 40s, piling up an enviable list of trophies. If I read the cards correctly, both cartridges should enjoy success into the foreseeable future.

Since the magnum craze brought on by the potent .300 Weatherby Magnum in the late 1940s and early 50s, the belted magnums have enjoyed enormous success with hunters worldwide. The .270 Weatherby Magnum (1944) and 7mm Remington Magnum (1962) continue to press on as perennial favorites, as do the .338 Winchester Magnum, Remington's 6.5 (1966) and 8mm Magnums (1978). The .264 Winchester Magnum, however, failed to catch on due to such problems as velocity vs barrel length, barrel erosion and recoil.

The real eye-opener in this lineup is the .458 Winchester, a belted cartridge with straight walls based on the old but excellent .375 H&H Magnum. Introduced in 1958, it was designed for use on the world's toughest and most dangerous game, including cape buffalo, rhino and elephant. Ballistically, it mirrors the famed British 470 Nitro-Express (1907), which is the chambering used in many expensive double rifles. The 500-grain solid plods along at 2,090 fps with 4,850 foot-pounds of energy at the muzzle. Its free recoil in a 10-pound rifle is a whopping 63 foot pounds, definitely not for the faint of heart. Despite its reputation as the undisputed king of the booming Berthas, the cartridge continues to sell so well that some of the world's finest gun manufacturers—Remington, Ruger, Francotte, Winchester and Sauer among them—chamber their top end rifles for it. That fact alone should sustain the load well into the 21st century.

Editor's Note: On the day we received this article by veteran outdoor writer Ralph Quinn, we were informed by his family that Ralph had suffered a fatal heart attack at his home in Parma, Michigan. Ralph began writing regularly for Shooter's Bible some 20 years ago. His work was always well researched and written with great care and expertise. We shall miss him both as a good friend and a true man of the outdoors.

Ruger's No. 1 Tropical rifle is chambered for a number of heavy-hitting magnums: 375 H&H Mag., 458 Win. Mag., 416 Rigby, and 416 Rem. Mag.

The Hunting Knife In The 20ᵗʰ Century

BY STEVEN DICK

When the 20ᵗʰ century began, the American frontier was considered officially tamed. But the last skirmish with the Sioux had taken place less than a decade before, and the buffalo had disappeared only a few years longer. Plenty of rough, lawless land remained along the southwest border, and the wilderness backcountry of the west and Alaska still seemed wild enough for most hunters. For most of the 19ᵗʰ century an oversize hunting knife had been considered an essential back-up weapon for a less than reliable single-shot firearm. Colt's cap and ball revolvers had evened the odds somewhat, but it was the self-contained metallic cartridge firearms of the 1870s that really convinced

the average outdoorsman that a foot-long Bowie knife was no longer needed.

During those final years of the 19ᵗʰ century, three styles of hunting knife dominated the market: the "Bowie Hunter," the butcher-style hunter's sheath knife, and the large single blade folder referred to by modern collectors as the "coke bottle." The Bowie hunter was a scaled-down version of the large fighters that had been popular a few years before the turn of the century. Most featured a 6-inch clip point blade, wide double handguard, and a handle made of stag or wood. Outdoor writers of both past and present may have expressed nothing but scorn for this

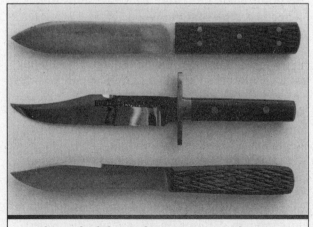

At the end of the 19th century, most hunters carried some form of butcher-style sheath knife (top and bottom), or what we now call the "Bowie Hunter" (center). The last is a smaller version of the fighting blade once popular on the frontier.

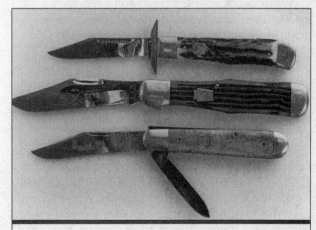

Hunters of the turn of the century who preferred folders to sheath knives usually carried one of three general patterns: (top) a folding guard lock-back; (center) a "Coke Bottle" folding hunter; and (bottom) the basic large two-blade jackknife sometimes referred to as an "English Jack."

Around 1900 Marble's Knives revolutionized the hunting knife market with a series of new designs. From top to bottom: a 1930's Ka-Bar copy of the Marble's Expert; a Ka-Bar copy of the Marble's Woodcraft; a Marble's Ideal; and a Marble's Woodcraft. Nearly every sheath knifemaker copied the Marble's designs at one time or another.

style of knife, but the fact remains that vast numbers of these knives went to the field. A careful look at any of the period photos of Texas Ranger troops will prove that not everyone who carried the Bowie was a greenhorn.

The butcher-style hunting knife, a much more utilitarian cutting tool, can be traced back to the English trade knives carried by the mountainmen in the early part of the 19th century. Most were between 5- and 7-inches long, with either a short clip or spear point. Though bone and stag were used occasionally, the vast majority of handles were plain wood with no handguard. As the name implies, these knives looked like common butcher knives. Cheap and readily available, they appealed to the hunter who didn't care what his tools looked like so long as they got the job done.

The most popular knife among experienced backwoodsmen and wilderness pros was the single blade folding hunter. Many of its owners felt that a 4-inch blade was plenty for most game; moreover, the folder was easy to slip into a coat pocket. While some of these large folders had locking blades similar to modern knives, plain, nonlocking models seem to have been more common, possibly because they were less expensive. Then, around 1900, a Michigan axe-maker by the name of Webster Marble turned the hunting knife market upside down with the introduction of his now legendary "Ideal." It featured a straight, clip point blade with a wide fuller (blood groove), small handguard, and often a stacked leather washer handle. Marble may not have invented this feature, but he was certainly the first to popularize its style. For the next 70 or 80 years the vast majority of fixed blade hunters sold copied Marble's leather handle. One of the most famous knives of the 20th century—the USMC Fighting/Utility (more commonly known as the "kabar")—is basically a militarized version of the Ideal. The same holds true for the Airforce Pilot Survival knife that has been issue in the U.S. military for more than 40 years.

Marble's hunting knife designs dominated the outdoor cutlery market for the next several decades. Its successors were the Expert—a thinner, flat ground clip point blade in 5- and 6-inch versions first offered in 1906—and the Woodcraft in 1915. The latter was a wide, $4\frac{1}{2}$-inch flat ground blade with a continuously curving edge that swept up to a high clip point. Outdoor writers of the day argued end-lessly whether the Expert or the Woodcraft was the perfect hunter's knife (few, if any, liked the thicker bladed Ideal). Again, practically every major cutlery company in the world copied the Expert and the Woodcraft at one time or another.

By 1920 the butcher style hunter was pretty much gone from the scene and the Bowie hunter was fading fast. The coke bottle folding hunter was still around but was soon replaced in popularity by more modern patterns. In 1914 it was discovered by an English firm that adding large amounts of chromium to steel made it "stain-less." Heretofore, all cutlery steels consisted of a simple carbon formula, with rust a common problem on outdoor knives especially. In the early 20s several cutlery companies began experimenting with stainless pocketknives, but it was several more decades before suitable alloys were developed for the manufacture of high quality outdoor knives.

Though few outdoorsmen probably will admit it, sheath knives often serve as a form of ornamental male jewelry. That explains why the ultra-plain wood handle butcher or hunter knives fell from favor, to be replaced by models with shiny brass and steel guards, exotic wood and stag horn handles, and tooled leather sheaths. A plain knife may field dress an animal or perform camp chores successfully, but what looks best on your belt? Still, there has always been a minority of wilderness pros and seasoned hunters who were more interested in getting the job done than in visual flash. For many of these people, the folding knife tucked away in a pocket has always been the answer to their needs.

During the 1920s and 30s, three new folder patterns caught on with this savvy group. The first two both came from Remington Firearms' recent addition of knives to their line of firearms: the two blade Remington R1123 and the single blade lockback R1306. Both models are known by modern collectors as "Bullets," because of the .30 Remington shield set into the handle. The third pattern was apparently introduced originally by W.R. Case Cutlery as simply the "Folding Hunter," a large 5¼-inch closed non-locking two-blade knife. The main

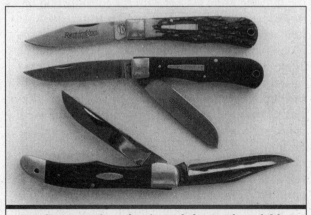

Remington Knives dominated the outdoor folder market in the 1920s and 1930s with their R1306 lockback (top) and R1123 large frame two-bade trapper (middle). Both are modern reproductions. When W.R. Case introduced its Model 6265 two-blade folding hunter (bottom), it was soon copied by most cutlery companies.

The Buck 110 lockback folding hunter (second knife down) was big news when it was introduced in the 1960s. The top knife is a German Puma, the third down is a Canadian Grohmann, and the bottom model is a Japanese-made Kershaw.

blade was normally a saber ground clip point and the second a narrower, straight-backed blade usually referred to as a "skinner." The two handy Remington knives caught on like wildfire during the period between World Wars I and II but dropped from sight after the company discontinued its cutlery business at the start of WWII. Given their near cult status with outdoorsmen, both patterns have become popular reproductions with custom and factory knifemakers over the last couple of decades. The Case style two-blade folding hunter has enjoyed a much longer life span. Like most popular patterns, most cutlery companies copied the Case knife. When I first started working as a forester in the early 1970s, Case 6265s and similar knives from other companies were the most common choice among professional outdoorsmen.

While World War II set the high-water mark for both Marble's and Remington, a number of individual knifemakers got their start during this same period. Handmade knives weren't really new in American history. From the earliest days, in fact, there have always been a few people making handcrafted knives. Hoyt Buck, Bo Randall, Rudy Ruana and William Scagle, among others, were all producing handmade fixed blade hunters in small numbers before the onset of World War II. Few outdoorsmen, however, saw a need at the time for an expensive custom-made knife when there were so many excellent factory models available at much lower prices. Combat knives were something else again. Whereas a soldier could clearly foresee the time when his life might depend on a good blade, few factories turned out much in the way of knives meant for close combat.

The end of the war had several effects on the sporting cutlery scene. First, vast quantities of surplus military sheath knives were dumped on the civilian market at incredibly cheap prices. Though these knives may not have been attractive or ideally shaped for game use, many outdoorsmen were willing to overlook these shortcomings in return for a good bargain. Marble's and other companies specializing in outdoor sheath knives had a difficult time competing, while others like Case, Schrade and Ka-Bar were able to fall back on their lines of folding knives enough to make it through the rough periods.

The many one-man shops that had sprung up during the war suddenly found their market for combat blades disappearing. Most simply shut their doors, but a few, such as Ruana and Randall, were able to survive by turning their production over to sporting blades. Luckily for them, many of the war veterans who had used handmade combat knives during the war years now demanded the same quality in their outdoor blades. Slowly but surely, the custom hunting knife market in the U.S. started to build up.

Despite the hard times for makers of traditional pattern factory sheath knives, a few new names appeared in the postwar era, notably Gerber Legendary Blades and Buck Knives. Rather than copy the classic leather-handled copies of Marble's patterns, Gerber created die-cast aluminum handles and high-speed tool steel blades chrome-plated for

Eventually the pocket carry clip and one-hand opening features were utilized on folding hunters like the Buck Cross-Lock (top) and the Spyderco/Wegner (bottom).

rust protection. Thus was the modern high-tech outdoor knife born.

Buck had existed for many years as a small custom shop, but in 1961 it expanded into a full-fledged commercial knife factory. Like Gerber, Buck's new hunting knife took a fresh path away from Marble's traditional designs and built stainless blades and high-strength plastic handles. The company also cultivated the concept of a premium-grade, factory-made outdoor knife for knowledgeable hunters. Then, in late 1964, Buck completely revolutionized the hunting knife market with the introduction of its lockback 110 Folding Hunter. It featured a totally new pattern of outdoor folder with a heavy brass frame, attractive wood handle and a locking 4-inch blade. The locking folder had been around for centuries, but for some reason it had never caught on to the same degree that non-locking models had. The Buck 110's style and state-of-the-art quality proved just right for the moment. Soon Buck was selling millions of this new folder, with practically every major cutlery factory in the world making their own versions. The lockback folding knife began to replace both the traditional non-locking folding hunter and the fixed blade sheath knife on the belts of American hunters. Once the public had accepted the single blade lockback concept, a flood of new patterns and blade styles were introduced. Even to this day, the factory sheath knife market has not recovered from the snowballing effect of Buck's 110.

The war in Vietnam also provided an opportunity for new names in the custom knife field to get

Two of the best-known custom knifemakers, Randall (top) and Ruana (bottom), made their reputations in the 1940s and early 50s.

a foot in the door. Unlike the 1940s, most of these new companies found a way to keep making knives at the end of the war. While the factory fixed blade may have been considered old-fashioned, many sportsmen were looking to these custom makers for more efficient sheath knife designs, better steels and state-of-the-art heat treatments. Around 1970, Bob Loveless, a custom knifemaker who had been in business since the mid-50s, caught the public's attention with what is now called the "Loveless style drop point hunter" ("drop point" being a fairly modern term for a knife pattern that had doubtless been in use for centuries). In the Loveless version, the spine curved down to meet the edge above the center line of the blade. This made it both handy for skinning and highly efficient for opening game in the field. Loveless knives also featured state-of-the-art steels for superior edge holding as well as tapered blade tangs over flat handle scales for better balance. As with the Buck 110, soon nearly every custom knifemaker had

In the early 1970s, this drop point hunter designed by Bob Loveless took the custom sheath knife market by storm (Photo credit: Weyer of Toledo)

Starting in the 1950s, Gerber pioneered the "high tech" style hunter with an all-metal handle and chrome-plated blade of special M-2 tool steel (center: Gerber Shorty). This began a movement away from the traditional natural materials for knife handles such as leather, stag horn, and wood. Around the same period, the Grohmann Canadian Russell (top) was a popular non-traditional hunter. Gerber continues to offer modern designs of all man-made materials similar to the hunter shown at the bottom.

his own interpretation of the classic Loveless hunter. While the fixed blade sheath knife has never regained the popularity it once had, the Loveless design and its many spin-offs have become the accepted standard for the hunter's blade.

The next major trend in hunting knives was the lightweight but strong thermoplastic-framed folding knife. Gerber was probably the first to introduce this type of knife, with its various Zytel-framed lockbacks, in the early 1980s. The concept quickly caught on with most commercial cutlery companies as a way to produce relatively inexpensive folding knives without reducing blade quality. Zyel also had the effect of weaning outdoor knife users off natural handle materials like wood, stag and bone. Black synthetics made to copy these materials were by far the most popular, but green, camo, day-glow orange, red, blue and many other options became acceptable. This, in turn, set the stage for the fiberglass-based G-10 plastics, carbon fiber and titanium handles that gained popularity in the late 1990s.

Shortly after the thermoplastic-handled lockbacks began to dominate the outdoor market, Spyderco knives created a second major trend with their one-hand opening, serrated edge, spring clip-carry folders. Serrated edges on true hunting knives remain controversial, with most serious outdoorsmen still preferring a conventional straight edge for work on game. The one-hand opening thumb hole feature and the various side mounted pegs and top-mounted disks that followed from other cutlery companies have, on

In the early 1980s Gerber pioneered the Zytel thermoplastic-handled "Bolt-Action" folding hunter (bottom). Most cutlery companies now offer lightweight Zytel folders; including: Cold Steel Voyager (top) and the Outdoor Edge Field-Lite (center).

the other hand, been widely accepted as major improvements in folding knives.

Along with the capability to handcraft a knife to one's personal design (some custom knifemakers are willing to do this, some not), one of the major advantages held by custom knifemakers was their ability to use steel alloys that were unsuitable for mass production techniques. For many years this was true of 154CM, an alloy considered the best of the stainless cutlery steels. Eventually, 154CM was replaced by ATS-34, a Japanese version of the same alloy. Even if a custom hunter resembled a widely available factory knife, the handmade version could offer a blade of ATS-34—or some similar exotic alloy—to gain a distinct advantage in field performance.

In the early 1990s, advances in metal working equipment, such as laser blanking, slowly enabled commercial knifemakers to turn out reasonably priced factory knives from alloys that had once been the sole property of handmakers. Benchmade, Gerber, Spyderco, Kershaw, Columbia River Knife and Tool, among others, now commonly use high performance alloys like ATS-34, ATS-55, BG-42, 440V and 420V in their products. Not only are these the best cutlery steels available, competition between custom knifemakers has driven the price of handmade hunting knives to new lows. A casual search at any large custom knife show will usually produce many functional outdoor blades priced in the same range as the better commercial knives.

Each of these modern fixed blade hunters demonstrate the Loveless influence (top to bottom): Swedish F-1 pilot survival knife; Schrade Pro-Hunter; and Busse Mean Streets.

Possibly because of this competition, hand forging has grown by leaps and bounds among knifecrafters. For those not familiar with the difference, the average commercial or custom knife is cut or ground from a flat bar of steel. Blade forgers, on the other hand, use the age-old method of heating a billet of steel until it is cherry-red hot, then pounding it into rough shape with a hammer on an anvil. Modern bladesmiths tend to prefer power trip hammers over hand hammering, but the result is the same. The old timers, it is said, forged steel primarily to save on precious raw material. The current theory of forging among custom knifemakers states that heating and hammering steel creates a stronger blade, one that has a more compact grain structure, thus increasing edge holding ability over a blade ground from flat bar stock. In most cases only plain carbon steels can be forged, but bladesmiths consider this a plus rather than a disadvantage. Supposedly, simple carbon steels take a keener cutting edge, hold it better and sharpen easier than the best stainless alloys.

Closely related to hand-forging is pattern-welding steel into what is now commonly called "Damascus steel" (the real Damascus steel of ancient times was something altogether different). As in hand forging, steel is heated in a fire and hammered into shape. With "Damascus" steel, two or more dissimilar alloys are twisted together as they are forged. In the hands of a skilled smith, the result is a host of attractive patterns on the steel surface. A good Damascus blade is very strong and flexible with a micro-sawtooth

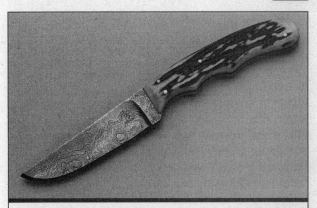

Some custom knifemakers are returning to traditional hand-forging and pattern-welding methods of blade production. This "Damascus" pattern-welded blade is from the forge of Larry Harley. (Photo credit, Weyer of Toledo)

cutting edge that bites into flesh and hide effectively. In addition to its susceptibility to rusting (like all plain carbon steel blades), a Damascus blade requires a lot of handwork to produce, thus driving the price up to astronomical levels.

What is the future of the hunting blade in the new century? The obvious answer is to create steel alloys that are stronger, hold an edge better, sharpen easier, and resist rust forever. Judging by the progress made in the last several decades, my guess is that new steel alloys will probably offer only marginal increases in performance. One possible solution is to create blades from materials other than steel. Titanium has been used on some specialized blades, but it lacks edge-holding compared to normal steel. Cobalt based metals are another possibility under consideration.

The leading post-steel possibility may be some form of ceramic. Several types of ceramic blades have been in use in recent years with mixed results. On the plus side, ceramic is much harder than steel and can hold an edge when cutting through normal flesh and hide for an extremely long time. It is also totally non-corrosive and will not add metal flavors to delicate dishes (this is important to the Japanese). On the downside, most ceramics are only a little less brittle than glass. Drop or flex one a bit too far and it will shatter. Its diamond-like hardness also makes a ceramic difficult to resharpen. Even conventional diamond-surfaced sharpeners seem to chip out the edge rather than honing it. But there

To compete with the many excellent factory knives available, custom makers of the 1990s were quick to utilize new high performance steel alloys: (top) Bob Dozier Elk Hunter in D-2; (center) W.C. Davis hunter in BG-2 stainless; and (bottom) a Melvin Dunn in 440V stainless.

may be some hope for this material in the future. Mad Dog Knives (Prescott, AZ) is now producing a family of knives from what they call "Mirage X" ceramic. While still not as flexible as steel, it will take a mild bend without breaking. It can also be used for light chopping, will hold an edge for an extremely long time and still be resharpened on a diamond hone. For hunters who use their knives for cutting flesh and hides, this could become the ultimate blade material. In any case, it shows how advances can still be made in ceramic technology, bringing closer the day when steel is considered obsolete for knives.

Other questions about the future of knifemaking arise. Will something like a hand-held laser relegate conventional knives to obsolescence in the next century? Will it be possible to place a knife in something equivalent to a microwave oven, set the timer for 30 seconds, and pull out a razor-sharp blade when the bell rings? Only time will tell what marvels lay in store for the simple hunter's knife.

This trio of small custom knives works well on deer-size game: (top) Bob Dozier folder; (center) Dozier "Deer Hunter;" and (bottom) an Ed Chavar. These and other custom knives still offer something extra for the hunter who appreciates fine tools.

Mad Dog Knives' high-strength ceramic bladed hunter represents the future of the hunting knife. (Photo credit, Shannon Lew)

Handguns: In The Old Millennium

By Gene Gangarosa, Jr.

This much can be written with assurance: handgun designers have made more progress during the 20th century than in the 400 or so years of handgun development prior to 1900. By the turn of the century, efforts by the designers centered around two basic but differing markets. On the one hand, there were the large, powerful revolvers that fired heavy lead bullets; and on the other hand, there were the newly developed automatic pistols with their high-velocity jacketed bullets favored by the military. The smaller revolvers and automatic pistols—which were easily concealable under one's clothing but fired smaller, less powerful cartridges—appealed mostly to civilians who sought a reliable means of self-defense. Thus did the handgun evolve throughout the 20th century, centering as it did on these two main types.

The recoil springs on the sleek FN Model 1910 (bottom) and its related Model 1922 (top) are placed around the barrel, an arrangement copied in many later designs.

The revolver clearly held the lead, especially with Smith & Wesson's introduction in 1899 of the Military & Police Model. The early 20th century then witnessed an incredible outpouring of creative effort lavished on the automatic pistol. By the time World War I erupted in 1914, the automatic pistol had matured enough to challenge the revolver—and even replace it in some U.S. armed forces. Its advantages over the revolver included a higher rate of fire, greater accuracy (particularly at extended ranges), and better resistance to dirt, mud and other environmental hazards.

The early success of the automatic pistol was due in part to the efforts of some extremely talented designers, including Fritz Walther (Germany), Tullio Marengoni (Italy), Karel Krynka (Hungary) and, most of all, America's John Browning. These men all helped to make the automatic pistol a rugged, reliable and efficient mechanism. By contrast, modern revolvers, though improved by better metallurgy and greater attention to detail (particularly their safety features), were pretty much unchanged as the 20th century began.

John Browning's Model 1900 automatic pistol—built and marketed by FN in Belgium—was one of the most influential handguns of the early 20th century. More than 700,000 Model 1900 pistols were manufactured by Fabrique Nationale before production ended in 1912. Browning's seminal handgun was one of the earliest automatic pistols to feature a detachable box magazine located in the grip, while other manufactures were still placing theirs in front of the trigger guard. Some even opted for non-detachable magazines loaded rifle-style, with stripper-clipped ammunition pushed down into the open action. Few handgun makers tried to copy the basic design features of the Model 1900, even indirectly, but they all envied FN's success and they all tried to create

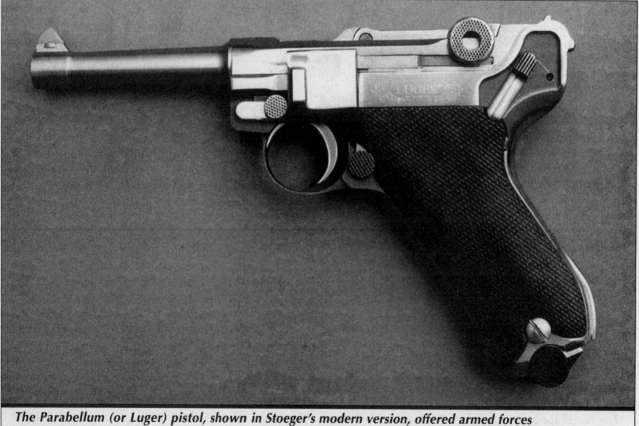

The Parabellum (or Luger) pistol, shown in Stoeger's modern version, offered armed forces a powerful pistol of modern design in the early part of the 20th century.

The first pistol designed by John Browning to become commercially successful was the FN Model 1900. It popularized the small automatic pistol and the .32 ACP cartridge.

competitive handguns of their own. And if that weren't enough, the 7.65mm Browning (.32 ACP) cartridge, originally developed for the Model 1900, became a world standard for small and medium-sized handguns.

Browning followed the Model 1900 with an even better automatic pistol: the FN Model 1903. Slightly larger than the Model 1900, it fired the more powerful 9mm Browning Long cartridge. It also introduced a configuration common to handguns even today: a slide that enveloped the barrel, a recoil spring located on a guide rod underneath the barrel, and a return to the detachable box magazine in the grip. The slightly smaller Colt Model 1903, or Pocket Model M, introduced the .32 ACP round to the U.S. market, followed by John Browning's similar but smaller Model 1905. This new pistol also introduced the 6.35mm Browning (.25 ACP) round, which became still another world standard.

While all these guns sold extremely well (production of each model totaled in the hundreds of thousands), success with the military market mostly eluded the manufacturers. The world's armed forces wanted large, powerful handguns capable of deep penetration. The Parabellum or Luger pistol developed by the Germans was a typical example. Adopted in

1900 in Switzerland in 7.65mm chambering, the Parabellum was brilliantly designed. It featured a reduced-scale Maxim machine gun toggle lock, making it one of the strongest mechanisms ever used in an automatic pistol. On the other hand, the gun was complicated and expensive to produce, but still good enough for the Germans to use as their service standard until 1945. Over two million pistols of this type were ultimately produced in Switzerland and Germany, with a slightly modernized version in stainless steel remaining in production. Even more influential than the Parabellum was its pairing in 1902 with an enlarged cartridge featuring a 9mm bullet. This "9mm Parabellum" cartridge has since become the world's most used automatic pistol and submachine gun cartridge.

Spurred on by the success of the Parabellum (or Luger), Browning turned his creative genius to the perfection of a larger, more powerful military automatic pistol than his earlier efforts for FN and Colt. After a series of false starts, his .45 ACP caliber automatic pistol was adopted by the U.S. armed forces in 1911. Tested in battle during World War I, the Model 1911 underwent minor changes in 1926 and became the Model 1911A1. Sold commercially as the "Colt Government Model," it was produced in the millions. Indeed, the M1911-type pistol is still highly regarded.

FN's High Power model, a Browning design perfected by FN's design team after the inventor's death, has remained in production ever since it was introduced in 1935.

Some lessons learned during World War I soon asserted themselves, with postwar designs appearing in large numbers. Influential among these was the 9mm Parabellum caliber FN High Power pistol, which was introduced in 1935 and eventually became a standard service sidearm in dozens of countries. Another influential design—Walther's Model PP—appeared in 1929. While smaller than the High Power and firing the weaker .32 ACP cartridge, the Model PP introduced an efficient double-action trigger mechanism to the world of automatic pistols. Though double-action revolvers had been in production since the 1850s, the double-action automatic system was applied to automatic pistols only in small numbers before Walther popularized it. The Model PPK, which was even smaller, created a sensation with its double-action trigger.

Walther's crowning effort was the Model P38, a full-sized, double-action pistol suitable for military use. Adopted as Nazi Germany's standard handgun in 1940, this gun went out of production in 1945, returned a decade later, and continued to arm police and military units in over 60 nations before its discontinuance in the late 1990s. Before World War II, several other pistol designs, some of them based on Browning's, had been produced, including the Soviet Tokarev (TT-33), Polish VIS-35 and Finnish Lahti L-35. The latter two pistols helped popularize the 9mm Parabellum cartridge, spreading its use throughout Germany, as did the many submachine guns built from 1918 on.

Revolver designs between the two world wars included the Banker's Special and Detective Special from Colt. Developed from the Police Positive Special revolver of 1908, the Banker's Special (1928-1943) enjoyed only modest success, but the Detective Special proved extremely durable. It was produced from 1927 on and,

The remarkable Makarov pistol, developed by the Soviet Union shortly after World War II, combined advanced design elements from various foreign pistols to produce a simple but durable model.

Beretta's Model 951 Brigadier pistol, shown disassembled, features an open-topped slide, a Beretta feature since the 1920s.

despite being discontinued and reintroduced several times, remains one of the all-time classic handguns of the 20th century. World War II continued the meteoric rise of the automatic pistol. The top models were the Luger, the P38 and the Model 1911A1. As it had in World War I, Spain also contributed several automatic pistols of modified foreign design. Revolvers were by no means dead during World War II, either. The British kept their .38 caliber Webley-type revolvers in production throughout the war, as did Smith & Wesson with its world-famous Military & Police Model.

After World War II the pace of military handgun development slowed, but with a few notable exceptions. One was the Soviet Union's Makarov pistol, which was introduced in 1951 as the *Pistolet Makarova*, or PM, and featured a double-action trigger system. Compared to the Walther, the PM was simpler, stronger and fired a more powerful cartridge: the 9mm Parabellum. The other important military handgun of the early postwar period was the Beretta Model 951. Developed in Italy, it combined the P38's 9mm Parabellum cartridge and efficient breech-locking mechanism with the open-topped slide developed by Beretta. While not well known in the United States, the Model 951 became extremely popular

elsewhere and is still widely distributed in various parts of the world, especially the Middle East. Beretta quit making the Model 951 in 1983, but an Egyptian-made copy, identical except for its markings (called the "Helwan" or "Cadet"), remains in production.

The civilian market, meanwhile, became more influential in the development of new handgun designs. While war-surplus Lugers, P38s, Astras, M1911s and Webleys continued to sell, consumers clamored for new guns. In 1954, Smith & Wesson introduced its own 9mm double-action automatic pistol, later named the Model 39, which combined the design principles made famous by Browning and Walther. It got off to a slow start, but by the 1960s it had become popular among private citizens and police forces, with some armed forces using it as well. Discontinued in 1980, this model set the precedent for all of Smith & Wesson's subsequent large-caliber pistol designs. In 1949, a newcomer—Sturm, Ruger & Company—introduced a .22 Long Rifle caliber automatic pistol that grew rapidly in importance. Intended primarily as a plinker and target pistol, this accurate gun was eventually adopted by the military as well. Modified variants remain in production to this day, and Ruger has gone on to become a major player in the firearms business.

Sturm, Ruger & Company's innovative .22 caliber target pistol remains in production in several modern variants (including this Mark II Target model). Ruger used the success of this gun as a springboard into the lucrative firearms business.

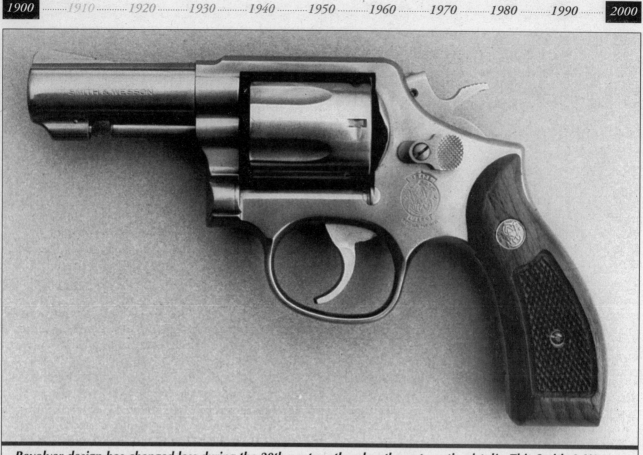

Revolver design has changed less during the 20th century than has the automatic pistol's. This Smith & Wesson Model 65, with its powerful .357 Magnum cartridge and corrosion-resistant stainless steel frame has changed little from S&W's Military & Police Model introduced at the turn of the century.

Among the important revolver designs introduced after World War II was the 5-shot Chief's Special introduced in 1950 by Smith & Wesson. Along with the Centennial and Bodyguard variants, this little gun became extremely popular as a concealed-carry weapon. Some consider the Colt Python, which made its debut in 1955, the finest double-action revolver ever made. That same year Smith & Wesson unveiled its Combat Magnum, or Model 19, offering .357 Magnum firepower on a frame similar to S&W's Military & Police revolver.

Sturm, Ruger & Company also competed aggressively in the revolver field. In 1953, having taken advantage of Colt's decision not to reintroduce its Single Action Army (SAA) revolver, coupled with the increasing popularity of television westerns featuring the SAA in action, Ruger introduced its Single Six revolver, followed by the Super Six, the Bearcat and the Blackhawk. More recent SAA-type revolvers introduced by Ruger include the Vaquero and Bisley models. Ruger's double-action Security Six, which went on the market in 1968, is still considered an excellent service revolver (even though it was replaced in 1987 with the even sturdier Model GP-100).

Development of the automatic pistol fell stagnant in the 1960s, until the terrorist incident at the 1972 Olympics in Munich created a demand for a wholly new handgun design. The requirements demanded by the West German police, which seemed impossibly stringent at the time, nevertheless greatly advanced the state of the art and led to the Walther P5, SIG-Sauer P225 (P6) and Heckler & Koch P7. This trio of automatic pistols, introduced in 1978-1979, offered reliability, accuracy and durability far in advance of earlier 9mm Parabellum pistols.

All three had double-action triggers or, in the case of the P7, an equivalent mechanism. Although it took several decades following its introduction in Walther's P38 prior to World War II, the double-action trigger finally became a fixture on virtually every military automatic pistol made since the late 1970s.

A further round of military handgun testing in Spain in the early 1980s produced a high-capacity magazine based on the High Power pistol (1935). Later, the M9 and M10 pistol trials conducted in the U.S. during the late 1970s and early 1980s confirmed the design trends established earlier in Germany and Spain; namely, the 9mm Parabellum caliber double-action trigger mechanism, a high-capacity magazine, durable construction and extremely high standards of reliability. The pistol chosen by the U.S. military tests—the new M9 (January 1985)—was actually Beretta's Model 92.

Smith & Wesson's small .38 Special J-frame revolver, such as the Model 38 Bodyguard shown here, first appeared in 1950 and still offers excellent performance a half-century later.

While the accuracy of Beretta's Model 92 (adopted in 1985 as the U.S. M9 service pistol) has never been in doubt, its design has remained controversial.

Seven years later, the military seemingly reversed itself by passing over a compact Beretta in favor of the SIG P228 as its M11 pistol.

While automatic pistols have largely supplanted revolvers in most military (and even many police) applications, the revolver is far from dead. In the field of large, high-powered handguns used in hunting, for example, revolvers far outnumber automatic pistols. On the other end of the size scale, few if any automatic pistols can match Smith & Wesson's superb line of J-frame revolvers for reliability, concealability and power. Moreover, with the 10-shot magazine limitation imposed on handguns sold in the U.S. under the so-called "Crime Bill," 6-shot or 7-shot revolvers have become more competitive with the 15-shot automatic pistol (which still outnumber revolvers in

total units produced and number of new models offered). The revolver may not be dead, but it is certainly less vigorous than the automatic pistol. The revolver may have dominated the 19th century, but the automatic pistol has indeed taken over the 20th century.

The most interesting, technologically advanced and controversial handgun development in this century concerns the small, concealable handguns used for self-defense. More changes have occurred in the past ten years in this one area than in any other involving handgun development. People concerned about self-defense now have a choice of small, lightweight but surprisingly effective handguns capable of good accuracy and reliability while firing service cartridges such as the .380 ACP, .38 Special, 9mm Parabellum, .40 S&W,

Continuing its prewar success with aluminum-alloy frames, Walther reintroduced the Model P38 (top) in 1957 with an alloy frame. Beretta, which took almost 20 years longer to perfect its aluminum alloy lightweight frames, finally succeeded with the Model 92 (bottom).

The full-sized polymer-framed Glock 17 (top) has expanded since its introduction in 1983 into a complete line of pistols, including the Model 19 compact service pistol (center) and the Model 26 subcompact concealment pistol (bottom).

10mm—and even the .45 ACP. With concealed-carry handgun licensing spreading throughout the U.S., more consumers than ever demand higher levels of firepower, accuracy and reliability in small, pocket-sized packages. Advanced technology and strong profit potential have enabled handgun manufacturers to create a whole new range of handguns. Like the German guns of the 1970s, these state-of-the-art designs are on the cutting edge of new firearms technology.

The origins of this engineering breakthrough—shrinking big-caliber guns into pocket-sized packages—actually date back to the 1930s. Shortly before World War II, the Walther company in Germany began to experiment with aluminum-alloy frames for its pistols. The .25 caliber Model 8 and .32 caliber PP and PPK pistols, when so lightened, all became fairly popular despite their relatively high cost. Prewar attempts to adapt an aluminum-alloy frame to the more powerful 9mm Parabellum Model HP proved unsuccessful; but in the postwar era Walther, using improved aluminum alloys developed during World War II, found a way to standardize a lightweight alloy frame for

the postwar P38, thus saving six ounces compared to the all-steel version. Other companies soon adapted the aluminum-alloy pistol frame, notably Colt's 9mm Parabellum Commander Model (1949) and Smith & Wesson's contemporary 9mm Model 39 automatic. S&W also tried to develop an all-aluminum revolver, but the stress incurred when firing .38 Special ammunition proved too great. In 1997 Smith & Wesson did finally succeed in creating an all-aluminum revolver, the Model 317 AirLite, which is limited to .22 Long Rifle ammunition.

Despite a track record that now extends more than half a century, aluminum alloy still has its doubters who question the long-term strength and durability of this material compared to an all-steel gun. Even more controversial are the high-tech plastic materials called polymers. Germany's Heckler & Koch had worked with this material in handgun frames during the early 1970s, but it remained for Glock of Austria to make a breakthrough in 1983 with its first pistol with a polymer frame, the Glock Model 17. Light in weight yet impressively strong, Glock has successfully adapted this improved design to a whole range of pistols, both larger and smaller than the original Model 17. A polymer frame flexes more easily than one made of steel or aluminum, thereby

SIG's P239 combines service pistol accuracy, reliability and durability while maintaining its suitability for concealed carry.

compensating in part for the loss of weight in damping recoil. A polymer frame also allows an unusually thin grip, which is always an aid to concealed carry because the grip can now be made in one piece without wooden or plastic stocks.

Titanium, the ultimate handgun material, has not yet been utilized to nearly the extent it could be. Titanium has been limited thus far to small parts requiring high performance, notably firing pins. Compared to steel, titanium is stronger, far more resistant to corrosion and considerably lighter. These attributes, though expensive, make titanium an ideal handgun material.

In their attempts to come up with the ultimate large-caliber small handgun, manufacturers have learned how to reduce slide velocities in their automatic pistols. To do this, slides are made heavier to increase their inertia. Improved spring designs can also ease recoil by pushing forward

Advances in handgun ammunition have elevated palm-sized pistols like the .32 ACP caliber Autauga into serious contenders for close-range firing.

Spanish gunmakers copied many foreign designs, adapting them slightly to suit their production methods and intended use. This Browning-designed "Ruby"-type pistol, copied from the FN Model 1903, was used by French armed forces in World War I.

Kahr's Model MK9 9mm Parabellum pistol (top) and Colt's .380 caliber Pony Pocketlite (bottom) are two state-of-the-art small handguns available in service calibers.

against the slide. Improved slide and spring design explains why SIG's Model P239 outperforms the company's older Model P225, even though it's smaller than the P225. Not only does the Model P239 perform more consistently with 9mm Parabellum ammunition loaded to +P levels, but it's made in the more powerful .357 SIG and .40 S&W calibers (which the P225 cannot shoot). The 239 also offers possibilities for concealed carry, manufacturers having learned how to shrink the large caliber handgun into an even smaller package. New doubled recoil springs, found on compact pistols such as the .380 Colt Pony, Glock" Model 26 and the Kahr MK9, reduce slide velocity while still making possible a light loading stroke when the slide is drawn back.

For decades, gun designers used a breech-locking mechanism on small automatic pistols—particularly .380s—in an effort to reduce recoil. This has allowed still further size reductions over the already small blowback guns offered in the .380 cartridge. Spain was the first to explore this possibility decades ago with its Llama pistol. After another Spanish firm, Star, did the same with its "Starfire" model in the 1950s, Colt took notice. Its 1983-vintage Government Model .380, its even smaller 1987 Mustang and the current Pony all offer the locked-breech .380 caliber pistol, which is no larger than many of the .25 caliber pistols from bygone years.

Reducing pistol size has also caused manufacturers to study the problem of ensuring reliable feed in smaller magazines. Part of the solution relates to how the magazine spring is designed, while others concern the shape of the magazine follower that holds the cartridges in position. The lessons learned in creating reliable, reduced-size magazines will undoubtedly improve the consistency of full-sized magazines in the future.

Improved ammunition has permeated every firearms advance since the 1800s. The development of smokeless powder in the late 1880s made the first workable automatic pistols a real possibility. Subsequent improvements in handgun ammunition have increased the reliability and lethality even of small rounds (notably the .32 ACP, formerly regarded as feeble). Modern technology, which has yielded improved powder formulations and expanding hollowpoint bullet designs, has made the .380 ACP, 9mm Parabellum, .38 Special, .40 S&W and .45 ACP formidable close-range shooters. Whether other promising ammunition breakthroughs—caseless ammunition, for example— will ever percolate down to the handgun level is probably unlikely in the foreseeable future, mostly because of high costs involved. The federal government might underwrite such work and benefit from the design efficiencies of a caseless-ammunition handgun, but the armed forces in general seem satisfied with current levels of handgun performance.

Another area worth commentary are the modern sighting arrangements that promise improved levels of accuracy. Kahr's Model MK9, for exam-

ple, includes an excellent set of iron sights equal to any found on most contemporary service pistols, yet reasonably small and unobtrusive for purposes of concealed carry. Even the sights used on Colt's Pony, which are minimal by current standards, offer a much improved sight picture compared with older .380 caliber pistols like the FN Model 1910. Laser sights, which can project an aiming dot several hundred yards, are growing in popularity among handgunners as they become smaller and handier. One of the best examples is the LaserMax type, which fits into a tunnel bored into the slide in some models for maximum compactness.

These and other developments in the handgun industry truly reflect the results of hard work accomplished during the 20th century. With the ever-increasing pace of technology, it seems safe to say that improvements and innovations in the design of pistols and revolvers worldwide are inevitable. But handgun owners everywhere owe a huge debt of gratitude to the Brownings, Walthers, Berettas and Colts for the pioneering work and creativity they provided over the past 100 years.

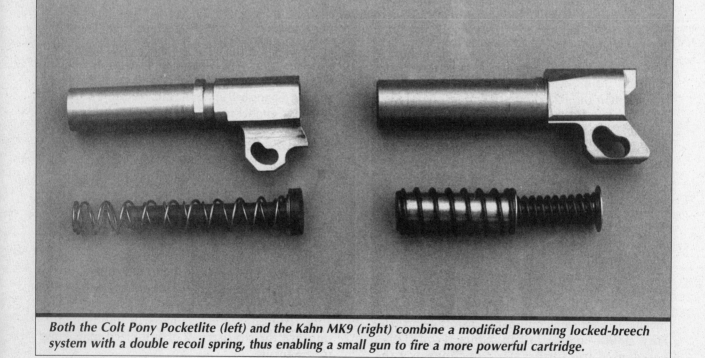

Both the Colt Pony Pocketlite (left) and the Kahn MK9 (right) combine a modified Browning locked-breech system with a double recoil spring, thus enabling a small gun to fire a more powerful cartridge.

Who's Who In 20th Century Muzzleloaders

By Toby Bridges

Today's black powder shooter has more models to choose from than at any other period in history. The variety of high quality, traditionally-styled reproductions and modern in-line percussion frontloading guns available is nothing short of mind-boggling. Depending on one's taste, a muzzleloading shooter or hunter can purchase anything from a 15th century matchlock to a "Brown Bess" flintlock musket from the Revolutionary War era, an 1850's percussion sporting rifle, or an ultra-modern "bolt-action" in-line percussion hunting rifle.

On top of this huge (and growing) selection of muzzleloaders, old and new, is a tremendous line-up of new and old projectiles, accessories, propellants and various black powder gun care products. For those who thrive on the availability of options, these are indeed the "good ol' days." But it was not always so. Only 40 or 50 years ago, shooters had no idea that this centuries-old sport would have the kind of popularity it enjoys as we head into the 21st century.

The fact is, muzzleloading in this country had nearly died by 1900. In a few backwoods regions

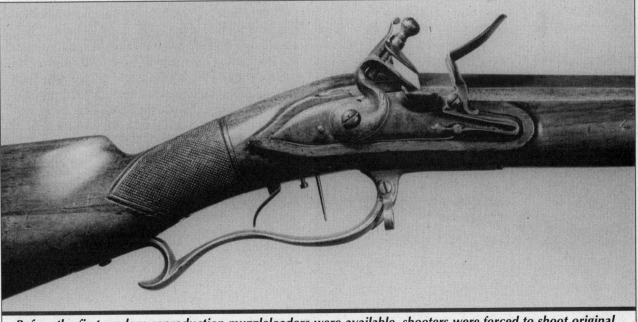

Before the first modern reproduction muzzleloaders were available, shooters were forced to shoot original guns similar to this late German flintlock dating from the early 1800s.

Turner Kirkland poses with some of his favorite muzzleloaders. His Dixie "Squirrel Rifle" first appeared in Dixie Guns Works' 1956 catalog and was listed at $79.50.

One of the first organized muzzleloader shooting matches took place in 1933 when 38 shooters from Indiana, Ohio, Kentucky, Tennessee and West Virginia gathered in southern Indiana. From that meeting evolved the National Muzzle Loading Rifle Association, now headquartered in Friendship, Indiana. It soon grew from a few hundred members to several thousand. The only thing that kept it from growing faster was the lack of modern, safe and affordable muzzleloading guns.

One of the charter members of the N.M.L.R.. was a young traveling salesman from western Tennessee, Turner Edward Kirkland, whose travels took him down the back roads of his native Tennessee and neighboring Arkansas. When the sun set, it often found him far from home, wheeling and dealing with local muzzleloading gun buffs. Kirkland had always been fascinated with these rifles and slowly got others with the same interest involved with the N.M.L.R.A. During the late 1940s, Kirkland, noting that the antique muzzleloaders used by members were invariably in need of springs, screws, and other vital components, began dealing in gun parts. Most were salvaged from junk until he discovered better sources, interestingly enough, in Belgium.

By 1954 Kirkland's business had grown so successful that he quit his sales job and established the now well-known Dixie Gun Works. The company's first 12-page catalog offered muzzleloaders a source for scarce, hard-to-find parts for their old guns. Kirkland soon realized that his catalog subscribers wanted to shoot these guns, not just restore them. And so in late 1955 he

of the Great Smoky Mountains and other remote areas of the country, a small handful of skilled gunsmiths continued to craft long-barreled front loaders, just as they'd been doing for centuries. Barrels were hand forged and slowly rifled on hand-operated rifling benches, and more often than not the lock, trigger and other parts were turned out by hand as well. The small number of "new" muzzleloaders that trickled from these remote areas provided guns for a few shooters during the period roughly covering 1900 to 1950. Most black powder burners of that era were using muzzleloaders made during the 1700s and 1800s.

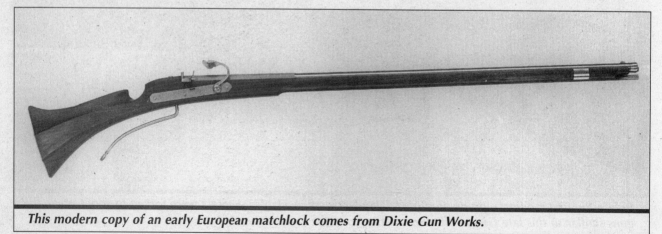

This modern copy of an early European matchlock comes from Dixie Gun Works.

Navy Arms' Italian-made copy of the Colt Model 1851 Navy percussion revolver was the first true reproduction black powder gun.

traveled to Belgium, returning three weeks later with the first prototype of a brand new muzzle-loading rifle. The 1956 edition of Dixie Gun Works' catalog listed this .40 caliber "Squirrel Rifle" in flint or percussion ignition for $79.50. It was the first "production" muzzleloader available to American shooters in nearly a century.

At about the same time, another enterprising young black powder shooter—Val Forgett—developed a love affair with the firearms of the Civil War. In 1957, having garnered a reputation for dealing in .58 caliber muskets, carbines and percussion revolvers dating from the 1850s and '60s, Forgett established the Service Armament Company. As much as he and others enjoyed shooting these old guns, though, Forgett realized that day-to-day service was taking its toll on the 100-year-old antique frontloaders. Therefore, in the fall of 1957 he too began visiting the old armsmaking centers of Europe. His goal: to find a manufacturer ready and willing to produce an entirely new version of the famous Colt Model 1851 percussion revolver. He settled on a region of Italy known as Val Trompia—"the *Valley of the Arms.*"

Forgett's first true "reproduction" black powder guns hit the U.S. market in 1958. These early revolvers were such close copies of the Colt originals that arms collectors shunned the replicas and a few gun magazines even refused to accept

advertising for the Colt knock-offs. Shooters, meanwhile, welcomed the high quality and affordable contemporary revolvers being imported from Italy by a new firm in the firearms business, Navy Arms. The company also introduced in 1960 a modern version of the colorful brass-mounted .58 caliber Remington Zouave rifled musket, the first of many replica muzzleloading long guns to be imported from Italy.

Truly, Turner Kirkland and Val Forgett have earned the title, "Fathers of the Muzzleloading Market." Kirkland's "Dixie Squirrel Rifle" (which lasted until 1979) represented the first modern manufactured muzzleloader offered to the slowly growing ranks of black powder shooters. Val Forgett, on the other hand, was the first to offer a true reproduction of a gun from the past, establishing the replica muzzleloading industry in Italy. Together, these two men laid the cornerstone for an industry that has since manufactured more muzzleloading guns than all the makers of the past combined ever produced. Today's black powder gunmakers have built more Colt percussion revolvers than were ever produced by Colt itself, not to mention more Kentucky rifles than were made by all of the early makers of long rifles combined, more Remington Zouaves than Remington ever dreamed of, and more percussion sporting muzzleloading hunting rifles than were produced by every riflemaker during the 1800s.

Dixie Gun Works' first 12-page catalog offered replacement parts for well-used original muzzle-loaders, such as this early 1800s Kentucky rifle.

About two dozen different muzzleloading gun manufacturers and importers now serve the estimated three million black powder shooters in the U.S. Since the 1960s names like Hopkins & Allen, Replica Arms, Centennial Arms, Richland Arms and others have come and gone. Each one, though, contributed in one way or another to the great selection of muzzleloading guns now available. The following pages describe some of the people, their guns and products that have helped to shape today's muzzleloading industry.

HOPKINS & ALLEN UNDERHAMMER RIFLES (1962)

In 1962 Numrich Arms (West Hurley, NY) introduced the very affordable Hopkins & Allen underhammer percussion rifle. Initially they were available in .45 caliber only, then a few years later in .36 caliber. These rifles were built with a simple, yet very reliable underhammer action with a mainspring doubling as the trigger guard. The design relied on only two moving parts—the hammer and trigger—which enabled the company to build them very economically. To encourage beginning black powder shooters, Numrich Arms packaged the rifles with a ball mold, a flask with a quarter-pound of black powder, 100 percussion caps and a powder measure. The complete package sold for only $44.50 for a rifle with a round barrel and $53.50 for the octagon-barreled model.

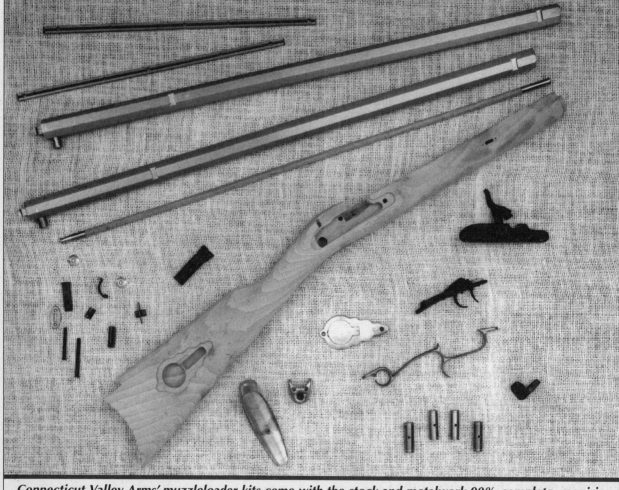

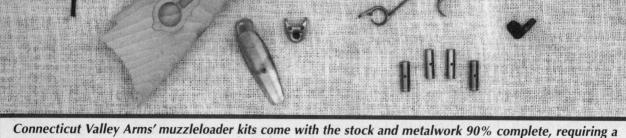

Connecticut Valley Arms' muzzleloader kits come with the stock and metalwork 90% complete, requiring a minimum amount of time and riflemaking skill to complete and finish.

Pyrodex, shown here in its early packaging, was the first successful black powder substitute. It's cleaner burning, less fouling and more readily available than black powder.

THOMPSON/CENTER ARMS "HAWKEN" RIFLE (1970)

In late 1979, gun designer Warren Center sat down at his drawing board and introduced black powder shooters to a truly American-built muzzle-loading rifle—the Thompson/Center "Hawken." Many consider this rifle to be the first serious modern muzzleloading hunting rifle, one that featured a short but accurate 28-inch barrel and a speedy one-turn-in-38 inches rifling twist. The elongated conical bullet was, incidentally, the new Thompson/Center "Maxi-Ball" designed

by Warren Center along with the "Hawken" rifle. Since first hitting the market, this rifle and bullet combination has been a favorite with big game hunters. The Thompson/Center "Hawken" (now available in .45, .50 and .54 calibers) ranks among the best-selling sporting muzzleloaders of all times.

CONNECTICUT VALLEY ARMS RIFLES AND KITS (1971)

In 1971 a new company—Connecticut Valley Arms (CVS)—introduced a line of affordable muzzleloading rifles and pistols along with easily assembled kits of the same guns. Most of the kits came with stocks that were 90% shaped and inletted, requiring only minor additional fitting, sanding and finishing. These CVA kits gave economy-minded shooters an opportunity to participate in the construction of their frontloading guns.

PYRODEX (1975)

In 1975, Dan Pawlak, a chemist from Washington, made the first truly successful black powder substitute, called Pyrodex. This muzzleloading propellant consists primarily of the same properties as black powder, but with some additional ingredients that help make muzzleloaders burn cleaner with less fouling. Pyrodex propellant is a Class B flammable solid, while black powder is a Class A explosive. Thus, gun shops can stock Pyrodex right on their shelves instead of in a fire-proof magazine as required by law. In 1979, Hodgdon Powder Company

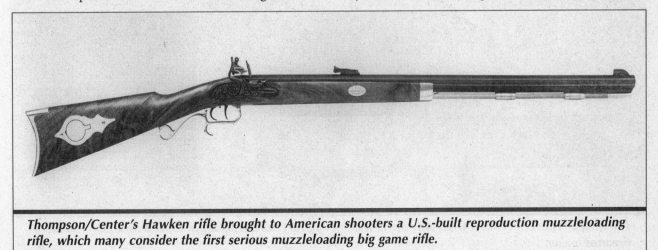

Thompson/Center's Hawken rifle brought to American shooters a U.S.-built reproduction muzzleloading rifle, which many consider the first serious muzzleloading big game rifle.

dedicated a state-of-the-art Pyrodex production facility in Kansas and became its sole producer. Pyrodex has since become the most widely used powder in frontloading guns.

ITHACA HAWKEN (1978)

Ithaca Gun Company entered the muzzleloading market in 1978 with its authentic copy of the famous Hawken rifle, the favorite of American mountain men. The rifle brought to the muzzleloading market a new level of authenticity for shooters who wanted a production muzzleloader with lines and features that more closely copied those of the original. Unfortunately, the muzzleloader was introduced at a bad time for a company

that was financially strapped. When Ithaca closed its doors soon after the rifle hit the market, the Navy Arms Company took over production. It still offers the gun as the "Ithaca-Navy Hawken," the first muzzleloader made by a major modern firearms company.

BUFFALO BULLET COMPANY (1983)

An age-old problem with large, heavy lead conical muzzleloading projectiles had always been poor expansion. These big bullets had a bad habit of punching out the other side of big game without properly expanding and transferring energy. In 1983, Ron Dahlitz produced and marketed the first of his hollow-pointed, muzzleloading

The Ithaca "Hawken" (Navy Arms) was the first contemporary muzzleloader produced by a major modern firearms maker.

big game bullets. Made by Dahlitz's Buffalo
Bullet Company, these new projectiles ensured
better expansion and game-taking performance.
They have also influenced the design of other
muzzleloading bullets, notably Hornady's Great
Plains Bullet.

MUZZLELOAD MAGNUM
PRODUCTS PLASTIC SABOTS (1985)

Black powder shooter Del Ramsey of Harrison,
Arkansas, ended his search for the ultimate muzzleloader hunting projectile by designing a cup-like
plastic sabot. It allowed shooters to load a frontloading big game rifle with modern jacketed
hollowpoint handgun bullets. Ramsey's company—
Muzzleload Magnum Products—began marketing
the sabots in 1985, at the same time taking
on Arkansas' muzzleloader hunting regulations
prohibiting their use. When sabots were first
introduced, the system was illegal in more than a
dozen states. Now, only a few disallow the system

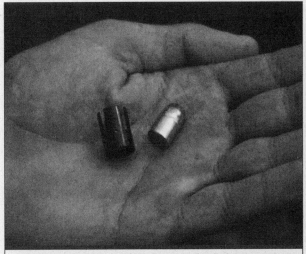

*The plastic sabots from Muzzleload Magnum
Products allow the muzzleloading hunter to load
and shoot modern jacketed handgun bullets. This
system has become the number one choice of
hunters coast to coast.*

*Muzzleload Magnum Products plastic sabots let the muzzleloading hunter load with effective modern jacketed hand-
gun bullets, such as the Speer .45 caliber 260 grain jacketed hollow point, shown with Traditions' Lightning rifle.*

for use during the special muzzleloader hunts. Saboted projectiles are now the number one choice of frontloading hunters coast to coast. Muzzleload Magnum Products packages sabots for .36, .45, .50, .54 and .58 caliber rifles, with Hornady, Modern Muzzleloading, Thompson/Center Arms, Buffalo Bullet Company and others are now selling bullets and sabots as well.

Modern Muzzleloading "Knight" In-Line Rifles (1985)

William "Tony" Knight, a rural gunsmith in northern Missouri, built the first of his now famous MK-85 in-line percussion hunting rifles in 1985. It became the first to incorporate those features sought by today's muzzleloading hunter, including sure-fire ignition, a modern safety system, removable breech plug and a fast rate of rifling twist, all with modern centerfire rifle lines and handling characteristics. Total production of Tony Knight's rifles in 1985 was 25 guns; today, practically every company in the business of building muzzleloading guns has a percussion in-line ignition rifle of similar design in its lineup.

Muzzleloading hunter and outdoor writer Tom Fegely relied on a modern scoped in-line percussion rifle to pull off a 150-yard shot on a record book pronghorn.

The Knight MK-85 provides muzzleloading hunters with all the features needed in a true muzzleloading big game rifle, especially one with the surefire in-line percussion ignition.

BARNES EXPANDER-MZ BULLETS (1995)

Barnes Bullets began offering serious muzzle-loading hunters a saboted big game bullet designed to ensure exceptional expansion and transfer of energy. The all-copper Expander-MZ features an exceptionally deep hollow point for full expansion out to 150 yards, where muzzleloader projectiles usually begin to slow down. Barnes' all-copper construction prevents the bullet from fragmenting when driven into big game with maximum velocity at close range. It's available in several different weights for both .50 and .54 caliber rifles.

REMINGTON MODEL 700ML "BOLT ACTION" MUZZLELOADER (1996)

Having recognized the fast-growing muzzle-loader hunting market, Remington introduced in 1996 its muzzleloading version of the company's well-received Model 700 bolt action centerfire rifle. Called the Model 700ML, it retains the overall lines and handling characteristics of the cartridge models, including the trigger, safety and, to some degree, the bolt. Remington's "bolt-action" in-line percussion rifle is easier to cap than

Randy Brooks, owner of Barnes Bullets, looks over a shipment of his company's revolutionary all-copper muzzleloader big game bullets.

This bull elk was taken by the writer with a single shot from his modern "bolt action" in-line rifle, stuffed with easy-loading Pyrodex Pellets and an all-copper Barnes Expander-MZ bullet.

The Remington Model 700ML combines the popular features of the company's Model 700 centerfire bolt action rifle with a new bolt action in-line percussion ignition system.

standard in-line rifles, has a much faster hammer fall, and features a fast one-turn-in-28 inches rate of rifling twist for exceptional accuracy with a wide range of saboted bullets. The gun proved an overnight success with the new breed of muzzle-loading hunters who are now flocking to the deer woods. Other companies have already followed Remington with similar designs, including Ruger.

PYRODEX PELLETS (1996)

Hodgdon Powder Company introduced its compressed 50 grain Pyrodex Pellets in 1996 primarily to speed up the loading process by eliminating the need to measure each and every powder charge. The pellets—a very precise measurement of Pyrodex propellant—are coated on one end with a sensitive igniter for more positive ignition. Even so, Hodgdon recommends that its pellets be used only in rifles with a surefire in-line percussion ignition system. A small-diameter hole running lengthwise through the center of each pellet allows fire from the ignition system to burn the compressed charge through the center as well as along the sides. Because of their small diameter, these pellets can be used in either .50 or .54 caliber rifles. One pellet (50 grains) makes a

reasonable plinking or target load, while two pellets (100 grains) offers all the punch needed for everything from whitetails to elk. When Hodgdon introduced its 30 grain pellets in 1998, it became possible to use different combinations of 30 and 50 grain pellets, allowing shooters to load with charges ranging from 50 to 150 grains (but not a 70 grain charge).

AUSTIN & HALLECK (1997)

This newly formed company brought a new level of class to muzzleloading with the introduction in 1997 of its Model 420 LR "bolt action" in-line percussion hunting rifle. These new .50 caliber muzzleloaders are built with a streamlined receiver and bolt, plus all the features found on other popular in-line rifles. What sets the Austin & Halleck Model 420 LR apart from the competition is its high quality metal finish and the deluxe curly maple stock with 20 lines-per-inch cut checkering. For slightly more than the asking price of other top in-line frontloaders, Austin & Halleck offers a rifle with all the class of a custom centerfire costing $2,500.

The Austin & Halleck Model 420LR is built with all the class and features of a custom bolt action centerfire.

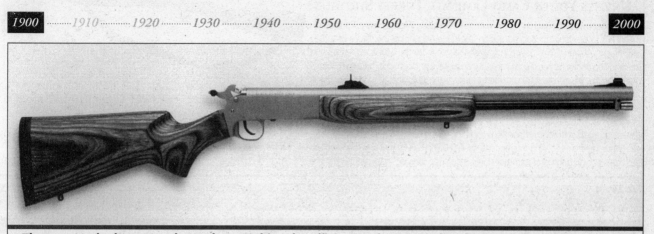

The new Markesbery Muzzle Loaders combine the efficiency of "near" in-line ignition and traditional exposed hammer styling.

NEW TECHNOLOGY IN THE 21ST CENTURY

In 1997, Thompson/Center Arms and Modern Muzzleloading (Knight Rifles) introduced ultra-modern muzzleloading designs said to have a tremendous impact on the muzzleloading market-place. The break-open "Encore" from Thompson/Center and Knight's bolt action "D.I.S.C." rifles were designed to utilize No. 209 shotshell primers for ignition. The primers, which are much hotter than either No. 11 or winged musket caps, ensure more positive ignition. The hotter flame also consumes heavier hunting charges more efficiently.

Both T/C and Knight promote shooting heavy 150 grain powder charges consisting of three 50 grain Pyrodex Pellets. With some sabot and bullet combinations, the two rifles can exceed 2,000 f.p.s., generating more muzzle energy than a .30/06. While such ballistics may quickly catch the eye of muzzleloading hunters in search of the same knockdown power a frontloader can muster, these assets can create a dangerous backlash for an industry that has been relatively free of federal restrictions. In late 1997 the Bureau of Alcohol, Tobacco and Firearms ruled that buyers of the rifles—or any other rifle with a similar primer ignition—must fill out a form No. 4473 (the same as when buying a modern cartridge gun). In early 1998, the Colorado Game Commission banned the use of *all* in-line rifles during the popular muzzleloader big game season held in that state.

A relatively new muzzleloading firm—Markesbery Muzzle Loaders—introduced in 1997 a modified "Outer-Line" system, whose exposed hammer design caused the nipple to be placed at a slight upward angle. This rifle has been declared legal in Colorado, while other states may have since banned true in-line percussion ignition hunting rifles. With Markesbery's design, the standard No. 11 nipple is easily replaced by the company's optional "400 SRP" primer ignition system. This two-piece arrangement allows the use of standard small rifle primers for hotter and weather-proof ignition. Moreover, since the rifle is sold with the nipple installed, the buyer is not required to fill out a form 4473.

A few years ago, Henry Ball (Advanced Firearms & Hunting Supplies) built a true smokeless powder muzzleloader using modern Howa, Sako and Mark-X Mauser centerfire bolt action receivers. His .50 caliber rifles pushed saboted bullets from the muzzle at 2,300 f.p.s. or more, whereas a "sabotless" .45 version developed more than 2,400 f.p.s. with a 300 grain Hornady .452" XTP jacketed hollow point. Ball has since developed a .35 caliber smokeless frontloader that shoots a 250 grain jacketed spire point at over 2,600 f.p.s., generating close to 3,800 ft. lbs. of energy, or about the same amount of punch as a .338 Winchester Magnum!

Since the time when Turner Kirkland and Val Forgett introduced the first "modern made" front-loaders more than 40 years ago, the muzzleloading market has experienced some future shock. The sport has indeed become performance driven. Whether modern technology has gone too far and too fast remains to be seen.

HARRINGTON & RICHARDSON®
UNVEILS YOUTH CAMO LAMINATE TURKEY SHOTGUN

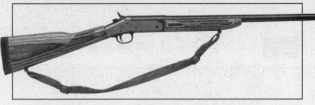

HARRINGTON & RICHARDSON® joins with the NATIONAL WILD TURKEY FEDERATION (NWTF) to produce sponsored edition shotguns enhancing the future of turkey hunting in America. This new shotgun is available in 20 ga. with a 22" barrel and a modified choke for maximum versatility on turkeys and other game. Its 3" chamber handles the heaviest 20 ga. Turkey loads with ease. The polished receiver is laser engraved with the NWTF logo. The hand-checkered stock and forend are made from hardwood laminate with a green, brown and black pattern. Standard features include a ventilated recoil pad, sling swivels and a camo sling. The stock has a special set of youth dimensions for fitting young turkey hunters properly, and it offers greater shooting comfort as well. H&R 1871®'s transfer bar system assures a high degree of hammer down safety for carrying in the field. With the sale of each of these models H&R 1871®, Inc. will make a substantial donation directly to the NWTF to assist the Federation with its vital programs.

For additional information, contact:

H&R 1871, INC. • 600 Industrial Rowe, Gardner, MA 01440
Tel: 978-632-9393 *Fax:* 978-632-2300 *E-Mail:* hr1871@hr1871.com

MANUFACTURERS' SHOWCASE

BEAMSHOT
PROFESSIONAL LASER SIGHTING SYSTEMS™

SIGHTS DESIGNED FOR REVOLVERS

Designed specifically for the special demands of revolver use, BEAMSHOT PROFESSIONAL LASER SIGHTING SYSTEMS will maintain their accuracy in extreme conditions. Constructed of high-grade, lightweight aluminum, they are available in black or silver. BEAMSHOT'S 1000 series and 3000 series have various ranges from 650nm/500 yards to 635nm/800 yards. A special BEAMSHOT 780nm is visible only when viewed through night vision equipment and is for the poice and military only. All BEAMSHOTS are quality constructed and powered by unmatched, continuous "on" operation (20+ hours for the 1000 series). Easily mounted to virtually all revolvers and pistols. One year warranty.

QUARTON USA

7042 Alamo Downs Pkwy, Suite 370, San Antonio, TX 78238
Tel: 800-520-8435 *Fax:* 210-520-8433

NEW ENGLAND FIREARMS®
OFFERS NEW ADULT 22 LB. RIFLE

NEW ENGLAND FIREARMS®'s new NEF Sportster™ 22 LA Rimfire has the great look and feel of the Superlight Handi-Rifle™ but with a rimfire format. The action, made of heat-treated steel, features a properly offset firing pin for reliable rimfire ignition. NEF's transfer bar system assures an extremely high level of hammer down safety when the gun is carried afield. The barrel is 20" long with a thick wall to assure a high degree of accuracy. The barrel does not include sights, but a Weaver-style scope base is standard. An offset hammer extension is supplied for easy cocking when the scope is mounted. The overall finish on metal components is low visibility blue. The stock and forend are high density polymer with a textured non-slip finish. The stock is in a Monte Carlo configuration with a recoil pad standard. The forend is semi-beavertail and has recessed finger panels for an easy grip. Both stock and forend include Uncle Mikes® sling swivel studs.

For additional information, contact:

H&R 1871®, INC.

60 Industrial Rowe, Gardner, MA 01440
Tel: 978-632-9393 *Fax:* 978-632-2300
E-mail: hr1871@hr1871.com

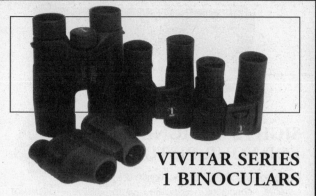

VIVITAR SERIES 1 BINOCULARS

Legendary Quality

The **Series 1** family of premium binoculars is designed for hunters, birdwatchers and serious outdoors enthusiasts. All **Series 1** binoculars feature the same high quality optics found in Vivitar's legendary **Series 1 SLR** camera lenses. **Series 1** models are available in standard and compact designs. With magnifications of 8x and 10x power, and with objective lens sizes from 25mm to 42mm, this line is made for the user who demands the best. Some models are water-proof and all feature an elegant traditional black finish.

VIVITAR CORPORATION
P.O. Box 2559
Newbury Park, CA 91319-8559
www.vivitar.com

GARY REEDER Custom Guns

Gary Reeder Custom Guns, originator of the Ultimate Series of full custom handguns and rifles, including the Tombstone Classic, Doc Holliday Classic, Ultimate Long Colt, Ultimate 41, Ultimate 50, Ultimate Vaquaro, Texas Ranger Classic, and many more. See all our custom guns on our web site at www.reedercustomguns.com. Or contact:

GARY REEDER CUSTOM GUNS
2710 N. Steves Blvd., Suite 22
Flagstaff, Arizona 86004
Tel: 520-526-3313 • *Fax:* 520-527-0840

MANUFACTURERS' SHOWCASE

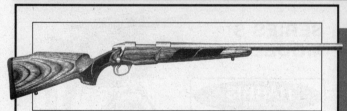

SAKO 75 VARMINT STAINLESS LAMINATED RIFLE

The new Sako 75 Varmint Stainless Laminated Rifle features a mechanical ejector, integral tapered scope mount rails and one-piece forged bolt. Sako's single-stage trigger is adjustable from 2 to 4 pounds of pull. Its safety mechanism allows the rifle to be loaded and unloaded while the safety is engaged. The laminated stock resists temperature change and is extremely durable. The stainless steel barrel is floated for unerring accuracy. Rifles in the #I short action weigh approx. 8 1/8 pounds, while the #III medium action rifles weigh approx. 8 5/8 pounds with a (5+1) round shell capacity.

For further information, contact:

STOEGER INDUSTRIES
5 Mansard Court
Wayne, New Jersey 07470
Tel: 973-872-9500
Fax: 973-872-2230

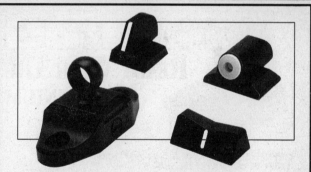

Ashley Outdoors offers the Ashley Express™ Sights for handguns and shotguns, which have four different sight systems including the Ashley Big Dot Tritium Sight. Designed for the fastest possible front sight acquisition. Ashley Aperture™ Ghost-Ring Hunting Sights for centerfire and blackpowder rifles. The rear sight is ultra compact and fully adjustable for windage and elevation. We offer the highly visible Ashley white stripe front sight post or the tritium dot post with the Ashley Aperture™ rear sight for the AR15/M16. Improve your old Mauser with the Ashley Utility Scout Rifle Kit for the Mauser 98 and others.

Ashley Outdoors, Inc.
2401 Ludelle St. • Fort Worth, TX 76105
Tel: 1-888-744-4880 • *Fax:* 1-800-734-7939
www.ashleyoutdoors.com
E-mail: sales@ashleyoutdoors.com

GLASER SAFETY SLUG, INC.

Manufacturers of state-of-the-art personal defense ammunition now available in two bullet styles. The **GLASER BLUE** is available in a full range of handgun calibers from the 25ACP to 45 Colt (including 9mm Makarov and 357 SIG) and four rifle calibers including the .223, .308, .30-06 and 7.62x39. The **GLASER SILVER** is available in a full range of handgun calibers from the .380 ACP to the 45 Colt. Glaser accessories include the Delta cheekpiece and the new night vision Delta Star cheekpiece for the Colt AR-15 rifle, the CAR-15 cheekpiece, and a MG-42 Stock Kit for the Ruger 10/22™.

For a free brochure contact:

GLASER SAFETY SLUG, INC.
P.O. Box 8223
Foster City, CA 94404
Tel: 800-221-3489 *Fax:* 510-785-6685
http://www.safetyslug.com

SIGHTS DESIGNED FOR YOUR PISTOL

Designed specifically for the harsh use and extreme conditions associated with pistols, **BEAMSHOT PROFESSIONAL LASER SIGHTING SYSTEMS** are built to take a beating while maintaining superior accuracy. Available in black or silver, **BEAMSHOT'S** 1000 and 3000 series have various ranges, from 650nm/500 yards to 635nm/800 yards. There's even a special **BEAMSHOT** 780nm visible only when viewed through night vision equipment (for police and military only). All **BEAMSHOTS** are constructed of lightweight, high-grade aluminum, powered by batteries for continuous "on" operation (20+ hours for the 1000 series). Easily mounted to virtually all pistols. One year warranty.

PROFESSIONAL LASER SIGHTING SYSTEMS™

QUARTON USA
7042 Alamo Downs Pkwy, Suite 370, San Antonio, TX 78238
Tel: 800-520-8435 *Fax:* 210-520-8433

MANUFACTURERS' SHOWCASE

TAURUS®

READY WITH THE MILLENNIUM

The affordable compact polymer frame you can trust with your life. A mere 18.7 ounces to carry. Ten rounds in the magazine, one in the chamber, and the lightweight frame makes this lifesaver a must for law enforcement and anyone concerned about personal safety. The double action only Taurus Millennium™ is available with either a blue or stainless steel slide.

www.taurususa.com

SERIES S MODEL L

HARRIS ENGINEERING, INC.

ULTRALIGHT BIPODS
- *Versatile*
- *Sturdy*
- *Light*
- *Fast*

SERIES S BIPODS
Pivoting Bipod with tension adjustment

Harris Bipods clamp quickly and securely to most stud equipped bolt-action rifles. Folding legs have completely adjustable spring-return telescoping extensions. Time proven design and quality manufacture. Thirteen models available plus adapters for various guns.

HARRIS ENGINEERING INC.
999 Broadway • Barlow, Kentucky 42024
Tel: 502-334-3633 • *Fax:* 502-334-3000

MANUFACTURERS' SHOWCASE

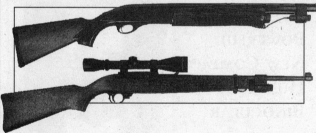
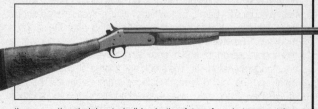

THE CENTURY 2000 DEFENDER "C2K"
FROM BOND ARMS, INC.

The Century 200 Defender ("C2K") is the ultimate in self-defense. With its 3.5" double barrel, the C2K chambers the 3" .410 00 Buck Shot with five pellets. It also features a rebounding hammer, retracting firing pins, crossbolt safety, cammed locking lever, spring-loaded extractor and interchangeable barrels. Choice of caliber includes .410 with 3" chambers and .410/45LC with 2.5" chambers.

For further information, contact:

BOND ARMS, INC.
P.O. Box 1296 • Granbury, TX 76048
Tel: (817) 573-4445 • *Fax:* (817) 573-5636

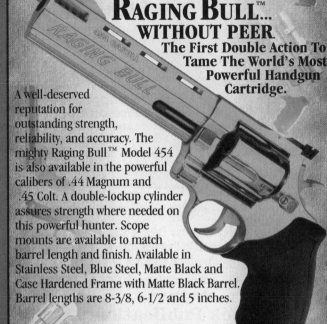

RAGING BULL...
WITHOUT PEER.
The First Double Action To Tame The World's Most Powerful Handgun Cartridge.

A well-deserved reputation for outstanding strength, reliability, and accuracy. The mighty Raging Bull™ Model 454 is also available in the powerful calibers of .44 Magnum and .45 Colt. A double-lockup cylinder assures strength where needed on this powerful hunter. Scope mounts are available to match barrel length and finish. Available in Stainless Steel, Blue Steel, Matte Black and Case Hardened Frame with Matte Black Barrel. Barrel lengths are 8-3/8, 6-1/2 and 5 inches.

www.taurususa.com

MANUFACTURERS' SHOWCASE

NEW ENGLAND FIREARMS®
INTRODUCES NEW SURVIVOR® RIFLE IN .308 WIN

NEW ENGLAND FIREARMS® has added a new heavy barrel .308 Win Survivor® rifle in a matte blue finish to its product line. This cartridge, one of the most popular military rounds in the free world, is now available in even the most remote areas. The .308 Win has an excellent reputation for taking down most North American big game. Its new heavy barrel model includes all the features that have made the Survivor® rifle line so popular. It comes with a heavyweight 22" barrel, factory-fitted with a Weaver-style scope base, and has a hammer extension for cocking when the scope is mounted. The stock and forend are high-density polymer with a thumbhole design for a sure grip. Sling swivels and a nylon sling are standard equipment. The stock has a large storage compartment and the forend is removable for ammo storage. The new .308 Survivor® accepts a wide range of additional rifle and shotgun barrels through the NEF accessory barrel program.

For additional information, contact:

H&R 1871®, INC. • 60 Industrial Rowe, Gardner, MA 01440
Tel: 978-632-9393 *Fax:* 978-632-2300
E-mail: hr1871@hr1871.com

SWIFT'S POWERFUL NEW COMPACT HUNTING BINOCULAR

Swift 818R Trilyte
Rubber Armored - Green Camo
9x, 24HCF - (377 ft.) - 12 oz. R.L.E. 11.48

This 12-ounce roof prism, comouflaged binocular is light enough to effectively use its 9X magnification. Prisms use both BaK-4 and BaK-7 optica glass and are magenta- and aluminum-coated. Green multi-coating is used on the exterior of objective and ocular lenses. Rubber covering provides protection and a comfortabe grip. It is supplied with both objective and eyepiece lens cap and a padded pouch-type case with belt strap.

For more information contact:

SWIFT INSTRUMENTS, INC.
925 Dorchester Avenue
Boston, MA 02125
Tel: (617) 436-2960
Web: www.swift-optics.com
email: swift1@tiac.net

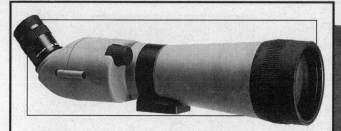

With over 30 years experience in the manufacture of sporting scopes and other precision optical instruments, KOWA has acquired in-depth knowledge about the requirements for field use. The TSN-820 series is waterproof and offers state-of-the-art optics with unmatched quality and ease of use under all conditions. Fully multi-coated optics and an 82mm objective lens produce the ulitmate in bright, clear, high-definition imagery. The superb sharpness is especially noticeable at extended distances and under low-light conditions. We offer 82mm, 60mm and 50mm spotting scopes, and binoculars. Call or write to receive a free brochure.

KOWA OPTIMED INC.
20001 South Vermont Ave.
Torrance, CA 90502
Tel: 310-327-1913
Fax: 310-327-4177
http://www.kowa-scope.com

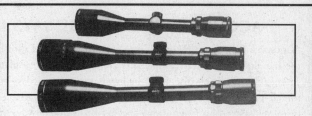

SWIFT INSTRUMENTS NEW PREMIER LINE OF RIFLE SCOPES

The new *Swift Premier* Line constitutes a major and exciting addition to the Swift rifle and pistol scope line. All are brighter than comparabe scopes and offer generous eye relief. They are all hard anodized, waterproof and have Swift's centering Quadraplex reticle. Other features include objective adjustments for parallax and full saddle construction for enhanced strength, elevation and windage adjustments. *Speed Focus* multi-coated optics make it simpler and faster for users to focus on the target. The new *Premier* line consists of six new riflescope models, plus a new pistolscope Model 679M (1.25-4x, 28mm). The riflescope models consist of five 50mm scopes with variable zoom power ranges from 2.5x to 18x, and a 40mm scope with a 3-9x zoom.

For more information contact:
SWIFT INSTRUMENTS, INC.
925 Dorchester Avenue
Boston, MA 02125
Tel: (617) 436-2960
Web: www.swift-optics.com
email: swift1@tiac.net

MANUFACTURERS' SHOWCASE

NOW!!
You can have the ultimate 10/22® accessories by Power Custom, Inc.

Matched Hammer & Sear Pack-
Mfg. by E.D.M. process, carbon steel 56-58RC, precision ground w/hone engagement surfaces. E.P. hammer & disc./sear spg., 2 trigger shims, 2 hammer shims. Repl trigger ret. spg. Allows for 2 1/2 lb. pull. **DROP-IN PARTS**, possible minor fitting **10/22® HS PAC. $55.95**

Detailed Instructions - Dealers Inquire
Manufacturer of Tools, Fixtures and Accessories of Advanced Design for the Professional Gunsmith & Serious Competitor. Send $2 for the Latest Catalog. **MC-VISA-COD**

POWER CUSTOM, INC.
29739 Hwy. J. Dept. SB
Gravois Mills, MO 65037
Ph: 573-372-5864 Fax: 573-372-5799
E-mail: rwpowers@laurie.net

10/22® is a registered trademark of Sturm Ruger, Inc.

TAURUS
VARMINTS BEWARE

The Taurus Raging Hornet™ is here. Varmint-rifle performance and accuracy in a double-action revolver. That's what you get with this unique 8-shot .22 Hornet handgun. The Raging Hornet™ is built with the same massively strong design as our Raging Bull™ revolver, with a signature bright Hornet Yellow grip insert. Scope mount base factory installed.

(Scope and rings not included.)

www.taurususa.com

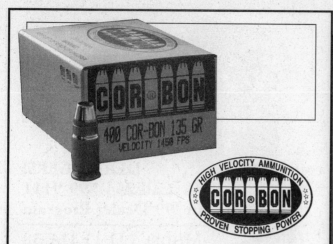

COR-BON is a manufacturer of premium self-defense ammunition for law enforcement, special operations and personal self-defense. In addition, COR-BON *Handgun Hunting* ammunition is offered in various loads, from 10mm to 454 Casull. Plus, a special *Single Shot Hunter* line is specifically designed to give optimum ballistics in the reduced barrel length of high-performance pistols.

COR-BON BULLET CO.
1311 Industry Road
Sturgis, SD 57785
Tel: 800-626-7266 • *Fax:* 800-923-2666
E-mail: COR-BON@STurgis.com

- Fits most firearms
- 5-second access
- Padded interior
- Stainless steel construction
  U.S. and Foreign Patents Pending

For consumer or
dealer information
visit us at:
www.firearmour.com
or call
1-888-GUNLOCK
486-5625

MANUFACTURERS' SHOWCASE

TRIUS
"Setting the Standard for 44 Years"

The TRIUS 1-STEP is almost effortless to use: (1) Set arm and place target on arm without tension; (2) Step on pedal to put tension on arm and release target in one motion. Adjustable without tools, easy cocking, lay-on loading, singles, doubles, plus piggy-back doubles offer unparalleled variety.

Birdshooter: quality at a budget price—now with high-angle retainer. *Model 92:* a bestseller with high-angle clip and can thrower. *TrapMaster:* sit-down comfort plus pivoting action.

TRIUS PRODUCTS INC.
P.O. Box 25, Cleves, OH 45002
Tel: 513-941-5682
Fax: 513-941-7970

CASE GARD SHOTSHELL/ CHOKE TUBE CASE

Carry your shotshells and choke tubes in one convenient compact case. 12 gauge shell boxes can be left open for quick access to your ammo while in the field or at the range. Ideal for shotgun shooting sports. Detachable choke tube case holds up to nine tubes, most factory wrenches and choke lubes. Holds 100 rounds of 12 ga. shotshells. Made of rugged polypropylene. Write to us and send one dollar for our full color catalog. Or visit our Web Sight at www.mtmcase-gard.com.

MTM MOLDED PRODUCTS
P.O. Box 14117
Dayton, OH 45413
Tel: 937-890-7461
Fax: 937-890-1747

95

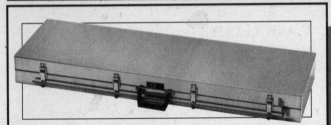

FORREST INC. OFFERS RIFLE/PISTOL MAGAZINES

Whether you're looking for a few spare magazines for that obsolete 22 rifle or pistol, or wish to replace a 10-shot with the higher-capacity pre-ban original, all are available from FORREST INC. With one of the largest selections of magazines, they offer competitive pricing especially for dealers who buy in quantity.

FORREST INC. also stocks parts and accessories for the Colt 1911 45 Auto Pistol, the SKS and MAK-90 rifles, and many U.S. military rifles. One of their specialty parts is firing pins for obsolete weapons.

Call or write for more information and a **FREE** brochure, **DEALERS WELCOME!**

FORREST INC.
P.O. Box 326, Lakeside, CA 92040
Tel: 619-561-5800 *Fax:* 1-888-GUNCLIP
E-mail: SFORR10675@AOL.COM

DERRINGERS!
Call 254-799-9111
for our '99 Dealer Program

NEW! ▶

MODEL LD 11 DA 38
ULTRA LIGHT WEIGHT

Model 1 Series. Stainless Steel; from 22 LR to 45-70
Affordable. Lightweight. Made in USA!
Texas Women 2000 Series & Cowboy 2000 Series

AMERICAN DERRINGER CORP.
127 North Lacy Drive, Waco, Texas 76705
Fax: 254-799-7935
ladyderringer.com
amderringer.com

MANUFACTURERS' SHOWCASE

ALUMINUM TRANSPORT/SHIPPING CASES

ICC, Impact Case Company and KK AIR International offer a complete line of two and three-piece "Flat Style" and "Trunk Style" Protective Aluminum Firearms and Archery Cases. In addition to standard sizes, KK AIR offers special cases in any quantity. NEW PRODUCTS include Cordura Nylon Concealment Duffels and Jackets. All Cases carry a "Lifetime Material and Workmanship Warranty." Before buying any case products or firearm duffels, be sure to check out ICC/KK AIR offerings. For detailed specification sheets describing this rugged equipment, contact:

ICC/KK AIR International

P.O. BOX 9912
Tel: 1-800-262-3322
Fax: 1-509-326-5436

U.S. SHOOTING TEAM

USA BIATHLON TEAM

SPORTSMAN CART BY VERSATILE RACK CO.

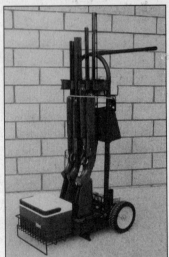

- Holds four long guns
- Heavy duty rubber supports guns
- Room for nine boxes of 12 gauge shells
- Extended handled keeps weapons pointing up and not at the person pulling
- Folds to a compact 33-1/2" x 18" x 14" for easy storage & transport

Call or fax for a free brochure on our gun racks and other accessories. California residents add 8% sales tax. Dealer & distributors welcome. *Visit our Web Site to see this rack and others.* Http://www.versatilegunrack.com

VERSATILE RACK CO.
5761 Anderson Street • Vernon, CA 90058
Tel: 323-588-0137 • *Fax:* 323-588-5067

SERIOUS TRADITION

At the age of twenty-three, John M. Browning was working on the repairs of a single-shot rifle in his

family's gun shop. Disgusted with the design of this fragile single-shot, he turned to his father and said,

"I could make a better gun than this." His father simply replied, "I wish you'd get at it."

One year later John M. Browning had completed his first design — the Model 1885 single-shot rifle.

1885 High Wall

1885 Low Wall

SERIOUS SIMPLICITY

MODEL 1885 HIGH WALL AND LOW WALL

The challenge of a traditional hunt is what it's all about to some shooters. It's the perfection and simplicity that draws them.

But the Model 1885 is more than just a romantic firearm from the past. Its strong falling-block design and detailed engineering make it one of the most dependable and accurate rifles in the field today.

The Model 1885 is available in calibers perfect for big-game. Varmint hunters will also appreciate calibers like 22-250, 22 Hornet and 223. One shot is all you get, but that's all you'll need.

Calibers	Barrel Length	Sight Radius	Overall Length	Approximate Weight	Rate of Twist (R. Hand)
HIGH WALL					
22-250 Rem.	28"	—	43 1/2"	8 lbs. 13 oz.	1 in 14"
270 Win.	28"	—	43 1/2"	8 lbs. 12 oz.	1 in 10"
30-06 Sprg.	28"	—	43 1/2"	8 lbs. 12 oz.	1 in 10"
7mm Rem. Mag.	28"	—	43 1/2"	8 lbs. 11 oz.	1 in 9 1/2"
45-70 Govt.	28"	21 1/2"	43 1/2"	8 lbs. 14 oz.	1 in 20"
LOW WALL					
22 Hornet	24"	—	39 1/2"	6 lbs. 4 oz.	1 in 16"
223 Rem.	24"	—	39 1/2"	6 lbs. 4 oz.	1 in 12"
243 Win.	24"	—	39 1/2"	6 lbs. 4 oz.	1 in 10"

SERIOUS AUTHENTICITY

1885 High Wall Traditional Hunter

1885 Low Wall Traditional Hunter

TRADITIONAL HUNTERS

The history of the American frontier is steeped in romantic tales of lawmen and desperados, of cattle drives and wagon trains and the Model 1885 single shot was there for it.

Because of their rich history, the Model 1885 Low Wall and High Wall Traditional Hunters are a favorite of cowboy action shooters. These were the choice of hunters and shooters when the frontier was young and they are still the choice today.

The crescent butt-plate, tang mounted windage-adjustable peep sight and octagon barrel make the 1885 Traditional Hunter perfect for cowboy action plainsman and precision long-range events.

BROWNING®

Visit your Browning dealer for a
1999 Master Catalog or call 1-800-333-3504.
www.browning.com

Calibers	Barrel Length	Sight Radius	Overall Length	Approximate Weight	Rate of Twist (R. Hand)
HIGH WALL TRADITIONAL HUNTER					
30-30 Win.	28"	31"	44 1/4"	9 lbs.	1 in 12"
38-55	28"	31"	44 1/4"	9 lbs.	1 in 15"
45-70 Govt.	28"	31"	44 1/4"	9 lbs.	1 in 20"
LOW WALL TRADITIONAL HUNTER					
357 Mag.	24"	27"	40 1/4"	6lbs 8oz.	1 in 18 3/4"
44 Mag.	24"	27"	40 1/4"	6lbs 8oz.	1 in 20"
45 Colt	24"	27"	40 1/4"	6lbs 8oz.	1 in 16"

1885 BPCR

1885 BPCR Creedmore

SERIOUS COMPETITION

Creedmore front sight

Vernier rear sight

MODEL 1885 BLACK POWDER CARTRIDGE RIFLE (BPCR)

The Browning BPCR and BPCR Creedmore are designed to give the long-range silhouette shooter a competitive edge. They're ready to go right out of the box with rear soule-type Vernier and front spirit-level Globe sights.

The beginner and experienced shooter will appreciate all the features designed into this complete competition system. Features like a Badger barrel, three aperture sizes for the rear sight and eight interchangeable inserts for the front sight. The Creedmore also has a windage-adjustable front sight. There are no other parts to order — the BPCR is ready for competition.

BROWNING®

Visit your Browning dealer for a 1999 Master Catalog or call 1-800-333-3504.
www.browning.com

Calibers	Barrel Length	Sight Radius	Overall Length	Approximate Weight	Rate of Twist (R. Hand)
BPCR					
40-65	30"	34"	46 1/8"	11 lbs. 7 oz.	1 in 16"
45-70 Govt.	30"	34"	46 1/8"	11 lbs.	1 in 18"
BPCR CREEDMORE TYPE LONG RANGE					
45-90	34"	38"	50 1/8"	11 lbs. 13 oz.	1 in 18"

American Arms	98	H-S Precision	134
American Derringer	99	Israel Arms	134
AMT	100	Kahr Arms	135
Anschutz	102	Kimber	136
Auto-Ordnance	103	Llama	138
Beretta	104	Luger, American Eagle	140
Bernardelli	108	Magnum Research	141
Bersa	108	MOA Maximum	144
Browning	109	Navy Arms	144
Colt	111	New England Firearms	146
Coonan Arms	114	North American Arms	147
Davis	115	Para-Ordnance	148
Downsizer	116	Rossi	150
EMF/Dakota	116	Ruger	151
Entréprise	119	Safari	160
European American Armory	121	Savage	161
FEG	123	Sig Arms	162
Freedom Arms	123	Smith & Wesson	164
Glock	125	Springfield	178
Hämmerli	127	Taurus	180
Harrington & Richardson	128	Thompson/Center	184
Heckler & Koch	129	Uberti	185
Heritage	131	Walther	186
High Standard	131	Wichita Arms	188
Hi-Point	133	Wildey	188

Handguns

*For addresses and phone/fax numbers of manufacturers and distributors included in this section, please turn to **DIRECTORY OF MANUFACTURERS AND SUPPLIERS** on page 564.*

AMERICAN ARMS

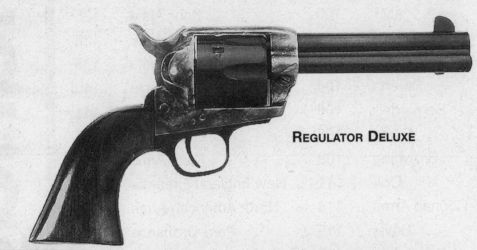

REGULATOR DELUXE

REGULATOR SINGLE ACTION REVOLVER

REGULATOR DELUXE

SPECIFICATIONS
Caliber: 44 Special, 44-40, 45LC
Barrel Length: 4.25" or 5.5"
Features: Blued steel backstrap and trigger guard; hammer block safety;
Prices:
BIRD'S-HEAD GRIP nickel $419.00
Also available:
STOREKEEPER nickel 375.00

REGULATOR SINGLE ACTION

SPECIFICATIONS
Calibers: 45 Long Colt, 44-40, 357 Mag.
Barrel Length: 4.75", 5.5" and 7.5"
Overall Length: 8 1/16"
Weight: 2 lb. 3 oz. (4.75" barrel)
Sights: Fixed
Safety: Hammer block
Features: Brass trigger guard and backstrap; two-cylinder combos avail. (45 L.C./45 ACP and 44-40/44 Special
Prices:
REGULATOR SINGLE ACTION REVOLVER nickel $375.00
    blue 320.00

MATEBA AUTO REVOLVER (not shown)
This firearm incorporates the quickness and handling of a semi-auto pistol with the reliability and accuracy of a revolver. May be fired as a single-action or double-action handgun. When fired, the cylinder and slide assembly move back and the recoil causes the cylinder to rotate. The speed of firing is comparable to a semi-auto pistol. The "auto pistol" aspect of this gun aligns the barrel with the bottom chamber of the cylinder. This reduces recoil allowing the shooter to stay "on target" with the least amount of movement.

SPECIFICATIONS
Caliber: 357
Capacity: 6 rounds
Overall Length: 8.77"
Barrel Length: 4"
Weight: 2.75 lbs.
Features: The mateba has an all blue finish, solid steel alloy frame and walnut grips
Price: $1,295.00
6" barrel 1,349.00

AMERICAN DERRINGER PISTOLS

MODEL 1

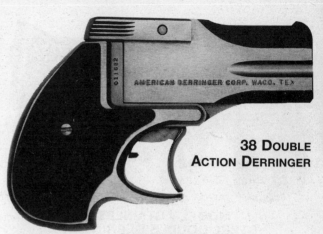

38 DOUBLE ACTION DERRINGER

SPECIFICATIONS

Calibers: See below
Action: Single action w/automatic barrel selection
Capacity: 2 shots **Barrel Length:** 3"
Overall Length: 4.82" **Weight:** 15 oz. (in 45 Auto)
Calibers:

22 Long Rifle w/rosewood grips	$260.00
22 Magnum.	265.00
10mm Auto	280.00
223	420.00
32 Magnum/S&W Long	265.00
32-20	260.00
357 Magnum w/rosewood grips	275.00
357 Maximum w/rosewood grips	285.00
9mm Luger, 38 Special w/rosewood grips	260.00
38 Super w/rosewood grips	275.00
38 Special +P+ (Police)	268.00
38 Special Shot Shells	275.00
38 Special	260.00
380 Auto	255.00
40 S&W, 45 Auto, 30 M-1 Carbine	275.00
45 Colt	325.00
45/.410	338.00
45-70 (single shot)	327.00
44-40 Win., 44 Special	338.00
45 Win. Mag., 44 Magnum, 41 Magnum	400.00
30-30 Win., Comm. Ammo dual calibers	400.00
Engraved Series	1,317.00

MODEL 7 ULTRA LIGHTWEIGHT SINGLE ACTION (7.5 oz.) (not shown)

22 LR, 22 Mag. Rimfire, 32 Mag./32 S&W Long, 38 Special, 380 Auto	$265.00
44 Special	505.00

MODEL 8 TARGET (not shown)

45/410	$425.00
Engraved	1,917.00

SPECIFICATIONS

Calibers: See below **Capacity:** 2 shots **Barrel Length:** 3"
Overall Length: 4.85" **Weight:** 14.5 oz. **Height:** 3.3" **Width:** 1.1"
Finish: Stainless steel **Safety:** Hammerblock thumb
Calibers:

22 LR, 38 Special . . . . , . .	$325.00
9mm Luger	335.00
357 Magnum, 40 S&W	365.00

MODEL 6 STAINLESS STEEL DOUBLE DERRINGER

SPECIFICATIONS

Calibers: See below **Capacity:** 2 shots **Barrel Length:** 6"
Overall Length: 8.2" **Weight:** 21 oz.
Calibers:

22 Win. Mag.	$365.00
357 Mag.	365.00
45 Auto	365.00
45/.410, 45 Colt	375.00

MODEL 10 STAINLESS STEEL BARREL (10 oz.) (not shown)

38 Special	$245.00
45 Auto	270.00
45 Colt	325.00

MODEL 11 LIGHTWEIGHT DOUBLE DERRINGER (11 oz.) (not shown)

22 LR, 22 Mag. Rim., 32 Mag./SW, 38 Special, 380 Auto	$250.00

AMERICAN DERRINGER PISTOLS

MODEL 4

MODEL 4 STAINLESS STEEL DOUBLE DERRINGER

SPECIFICATIONS
Calibers: 45 Colt and 3" .410 **Capacity:** 2 shots
Barrel Length: 4.1" **Overall Length:** 6" **Weight:** 16.5 oz.
Finish: Satin or high-polish stainless steel
Price: $357.00
Also available:
In 357 Mag. $350.00
   357 Maximum 355.00
In 45-70, both barrels 500.00
In 44 Mag. w/oversized grips 445.00
   45/410. .... 365.00
   45 Automatic 355.00
MODEL M-4 ALASKAN SURVIVAL
   in 45-70/45-.410, 45-70/45 Colt 400.00
LADY DERRINGER (Stainless Steel Double)
38 Special 290.00
32 Mag. 305.00
357 Mag. 335.00
45 Colt, 45/410. .... 365.00

AMT PISTOLS

BY GALENA INDUSTRIES, INC.

BACKUP DAO

SPECIFICATIONS
Calibers: 357 SIG, 380 ACP (9mm Short), 38 Super, 400 Corbon, 40 S&W, 45 ACP **Capacity:** 5-shot (40 S&W, 45 ACP); 6-shot (other calibers) **Barrel length:** 3" **Overall length:** 5.75" **Weight:** 23 oz. **Width:** 1" **Features:** Locking-barrel action, checkered fiberglass grips, grooved slide sight
Prices:
In 380 ACP, 40 S&W, 45 ACP, 9mm $319.00
In 38 Super, 357 Sig. 400 Corbon 369.00

BACKUP
(380 OR 9mm SHORT)

1911 GOVERNMENT MODEL

SPECIFICATIONS
Caliber: 45 ACP **Capacity:** 7 shots **Barrel length:** 5"
Overall length: 8.5" **Weight:** 38 oz. **Width:** 1.25"
Sights: Fixed **Features:** Long grip safety; rubber wrap-around Neoprene grips; beveled magazine well; wide adjustable trigger
Price: $399.00
Also available:
1911 HARDBALLER. Same specifications as Standard Model, but with adjustable sights and matte rib. $425.00
400 ACCELERATOR (7" 400 Corbon barrel) 549.00
COMMANDO (40 S&W 4" barrel) 425.00
LONGSLIDE 45 ACP (7" barrel) 499.00

1911 GOVERNMENT

AMT Pistols

By Galena Industries, Inc.

22 Automag II

22 AUTOMAG II RIMFIRE MAGNUM

The only production semiautomatic handgun in this caliber, the Automag II is ideal for the small-game hunter or shooting enthusiast who wants more power and accuracy in a light, trim handgun. The pistol features a bold open-slide design and employs a unique gas-channeling system for smooth, trouble-free action.

SPECIFICATIONS
Caliber: 22 Rimfire Magnum
Barrel lengths: 3 ³/₈", 4.5" or 6"
Magazine capacity: 9 shots (4.5" & 6"), 7 shots (3 ³/₈")
Weight: 32 oz. (6"), 30 oz. (4.5"), 24 oz. (3 ³/₈")
Sights: Adjustable 3-dot *Finish:* Stainless steel
Features: Squared trigger guard; grooved carbon fiber grips; gas channeling system
Price: $399.00

AUTOMAG III

SPECIFICATIONS
Caliber: 30 M1 Carbine
Capacity: 8 shots
Barrel length: 6 ³/₈"
Overall length: 10.5"
Weight: 43 oz.
Sights: Adjustable
Grips: Carbon fiber
Finish: Stainless steel
Price: $499.00

Automag III

AUTOMAG IV

SPECIFICATIONS
Caliber: 45 Win. Mag.
Capacity: 7 shots
Barrel length: 6.5"
Overall length: 10.5"
Weight: 46 oz.
Sights: Adjustable
Grips: Carbon fiber
Finish: Stainless steel
Price: $599.00

Automag IV

ANSCHUTZ PISTOLS

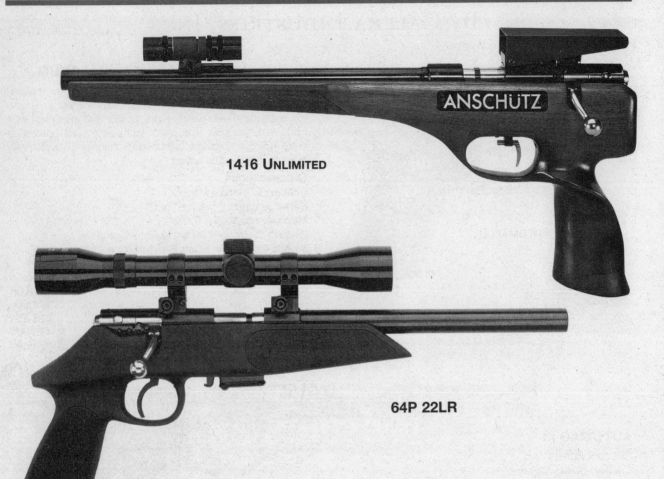

1416 UNLIMITED

64P 22LR

J.G. Anschutz began as a company in 1856, making pistols, rifles and shotguns. Since its rebirth following World War II, the firm has been best known for its fine rimfire target rifles. But there is also a line of bolt-action target pistols with the same features that have put Anschutz rifles in the winner's circle more often than any other rimfires in recent times.

Anschutz silhouette pistols feature a precisely machined single-shot action with left-side bolt handle and fully adjustable trigger (the blade can be moved longitudinally too). The Model 1416 MSP E "Unlimited" has a 14.1-inch barrel and full stock with wide thumb rest and stippling for a better hold in the Creedmoor position. The available Anschutz rear sight (#6836) has click adjustments of .035mm and a folding sight cover. The available front sight (#6523) has an anti-glare tube and three interchangeable inserts. Pistol weight: 14.1 pounds.

A shorter version of the "Unlimited" is the 1416 MSP E "Production" with 9.8-inch barrel that accelerates match-grade .22 bullets to just under the speed of sound. Avoiding the sound barrier helps ensure the greatest bullet stability and best accuracy.

Pistol weight: 3.7 pounds.

The centerfire Anschutz Model 1730 MSP E Field is like the 1416 models in that its trigger is directly below the loading platform, for fine balance. The receiver is grooved, drilled and tapped for scope mounts. The adjustable trigger and grip of this pistol are like those of the 1416s. With its 9.4-inch barrel, the Model 1730 weighs 3.9 pounds.

Price: 1416 MSP E Unlimited **$1,290.00**
1416 MSP E Production **1,290.00**
1730 MSP E Field (not shown). **1,719.00**
Micrometer rear sight **153.80**
Front sight. **49.70**

Anschutz also offers bolt-action repeating pistols on a 64-type action with a right-hand bolt and 9.8-inch barrels. Both the .22 Long Rifle and .22 Magnum versions are grooved, drilled and tapped for scopes. *Pistol weights:* 3.5 pounds.

Price: 64 P .22 LR. **$490.00**
64 P .22 WMR **528.00**
Micrometer rear sight **66.00**
Front sight **22.00**

Auto-Ordnance

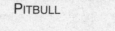

MODEL 1911A1
PITBULL

MODEL 1911A1 THOMPSON

SPECIFICATIONS
Caliber: 45 ACP
Capacity: 7 rounds (45 ACP)
Barrel Length: 5"
Overall Length: 8 1/2"
Weight: 39 oz. (with fixed sights)
Sights: Blade front; rear adjustable for windage
Stock: Checkered plastic with medallion
Prices:
45 ACP, blued $425.00
PIT BULL MODEL (45 ACP w/3 1/2" barrel) 474.50
WW II PARKERIZED PISTOL (45 cal. only) 399.95
DELUXE MODEL (45 cal. only) 438.00
   CUSTOM HIGH POLISH. 585.00

MODEL 1911A1
PARKERIZED

MODEL 1911A1
CUSTOM HIGH POLISH
(5" barrel)

BERETTA PISTOLS

COMPACT FRAME COUGAR PISTOLS

MODEL 8000 (9mm) MODEL 8040 (40 CAL.) MODEL 8045 (45 ACP)

Beretta's 8000/8040/8045 Cougar Series semiautomatics use a proven locked-breech system with a rotating barrel. This design makes the pistol compact and easy to conceal and operate with today's high-powered 9mm, 40 cal. and 45 ACP cal. ammunition. When the pistol is fired, the initial thrust of recoil energy is partially absorbed as it pushes slide and barrel back, with the barrel rotating by cam action against a tooth on the rigid central block. When the barrel has turned about 30 degrees, the locking lugs on the barrel clear the locking recesses, freeing the slide to continue rearward. The recoil spring absorbs the remaining recoil energy as the slide extracts and ejects the spent shell casing, rotates the hammer, and then reverses direction to chamber the next round. By channeling part of the recoil energy into barrel rotation and by partially absorbing the barrel and slide recoil shock through the central block before it is transferred to the frame, the Cougar reduces felt recoil.

SPECIFICATIONS
Calibers: 9mm, 40 S&W, 45 ACP
Capacity: 10 rounds (8 rounds in 45 ACP)
Action: Double/Single or Double Action only
Barrel length: 3.6"
Overall length: 7"
Weight: 32.6 oz.
Overall height: 5.5"
Sight radius: 5.2"
Sights: Front and rear sights dovetailed to slide
Finish: Bruniton/Plastic
Features: Firing-pin block; chrome-lined barrel; short recoil, rotating barrel; anodized aluminum alloy frame
Prices:
Double action only (9mm and 40 cal.) $646.00
Double or Single action (9mm and 40 cal.) 668.00
Double action only (45 ACP) 696.00
Double or Single action (45 ACP) 719.00

**MODEL 8000/8040
COUGAR**

**MODEL 8040
MINI-COUGAR**

MODEL 8000/8040/8045 MINI-COUGAR

SPECIFICATIONS
Caliber: 9mm and 40 S&W
Capacity: 8 rounds
Action: Double/Single or Double Action only
Barrel length: 3.6"
Weight: 27.6 oz. (9mm); 27.4 oz. (40 S&W)
Features: One inch shorter in the grip than the standard Cougar
Prices:
Double action only (9mm & 40 cal.) $646.00
Double or Single actions (9mm & 40 cal.) 668.00

BERETTA PISTOLS

SMALL FRAME PISTOLS

MODEL 3032 TOMCAT

SPECIFICATIONS
Caliber: 32 Auto
Capacity: 7-shot magazine
Barrel length: 2.45"
Overall length: 4.9"
Weight: 14 1/2 oz.
Sights: Blade front, drift-adjustable rear
Features: Double or single action, thumb safety, tip-up barrel for direct loading/unloading, blued or matte finish
Prices:
Matte/Plastic $326.00
Blued/Plastic 355.00

MODEL 3032 TOMCAT

MODEL 21 BOBCAT DA SEMIAUTOMATIC

A safe, dependable, accurate small-bore pistol in 22 LR or 25 Auto. Easy to load with its unique barrel tip-up system.

SPECIFICATIONS
Caliber: 22 LR or 25 ACP
Magazine capacity: 7 rounds (22 LR); 8 rounds (25 ACP)
Overall length: 4.9"
Barrel length: 2.4"
Weight: 11.5 oz. (25 ACP); 11.8 oz. (22 LR)
Sights: Blade front: V-notch rear
Safety: Thumb operated
Grips: Plastic or Walnut
Frame: Forged aluminum
Prices:
Matte/Plastic $242.00
Blued/Plastic 273.00
Nickel/Plastic 316.00
Blued/Engraved/Wood 349.00

MODEL 21 BOBCAT

MODEL 950 JETFIRE
SINGLE-ACTION SEMIAUTOMATIC

SPECIFICATIONS
Calibers: 25 ACP
Barrel length: 2.4"
Overall length: 4.7"
Overall height: 3.4"
Safety: External, thumb-operated
Magazine capacity: 8 rounds
Sights: Blade front; V-notch rear
Weight: 9.9 oz.
Frame: Forged aluminum.
Prices:
Matte/Plastic $220.00
Blued/Plastic 242.00
Nickel/Plastic 300.00
Blued/Engraved/Wood 337.00

MODEL 950 JETFIRE

BERETTA PISTOLS

MEDIUM-FRAME CHEETAH PISTOLS

MODEL 84 CHEETAH

This pistol is pocket size with a large magazine capacity. The first shot (with hammer down, chamber loaded) can be fired by a double-action pull on the trigger without cocking the hammer manually.

The pistol also features a positive thumb safety (designed for both right- and left-handed operation), quick takedown (by means of special takedown button) and a conveniently located magazine release. Black plastic grips. Wood grips extra.

SPECIFICATIONS
Caliber: 380 Auto (9mm Short).
Magazine capacity: 10 rounds. *Barrel length:* 3.8". (approx.) *Overall length:* 6.8". (approx.) *Weight:* 23.3 oz. (approx.). *Sights:* Fixed front; rear dovetailed to slide. *Height overall:* 4.85" (approx.).
Prices: Bruniton/Plastic $543.00
Bruniton/Wood 572.00
Nickel/Wood 615.00

MODEL 84 CHEETAH

MODEL 85 CHEETAH (not shown)

Some basic specifications as the model 84 Cheetah, except has a single line 8-round magazine, ambidextrous safety.
Prices: Bruniton/Plastic $513.00
Bruniton/Wood 545.00
Nickel/Wood 573.00
Also available:
MODEL 87 in 22 LR. *Capacity:* 7 rounds. Straight blow-back open slide design. *Width:* 1.3". *Barrel length:* 3.8". *Overall length:* 6.8". *Overall height:* 4.7". *Weight:* 20.1 oz. *Finish:* Blued with wood $543.00

MODEL 86 CHEETAH

MODEL 86 CHEETAH
SPECIFICATIONS
Caliber: 380 Auto (9mm Short). *Barrel length:* 4.4". *Overall length:* 7.3". *Capacity:* 8 rounds. *Weight:* 23.3 oz. *Sight radius:* 4.9". *Overall height:* 4.8". *Overall width:* 1.4". *Grip:* Walnut. *Features:* Same as other Medium Frame, straight blow-back models, plus safety and convenience of a tip-up barrel (rounds can be loaded directly into chamber without operating the slide).
Price: Bruniton/Wood Grips $545.00

MODEL 89 GOLD STANDARD SA

This sophisticated single-action target pistol features an 8-round magazine, adjustable target sights, and target-style contoured walnut grips with thumbrest.

SPECIFICATIONS
Caliber: 22 LR. *Capacity:* 8 rounds. *Barrel length:* 6". *Overall length:* 9.5". *Height:* 5.3" *Weight:* 41 oz. *Features:* Adjustable target sights, and target style contoured walnut grips with thumbrest
Price: $771.00

MODEL 89 GOLD STANDARD

BERETTA PISTOLS

LARGE FRAME 92/96 SERIES PISTOLS

**MODELS 92FS (9mm)
& 96 (40 Cal.)**

MODEL 92FS COMPACT

MODELS 92FS (9MM) & 96 (40 CAL.)
SPECIFICATIONS
Calibers: 9mm and 40 cal.
Capacity: 10 rounds *Action:* Double/Single
Barrel length: 4.9" *Overall length:* 8.5"
Weight: 34.4 oz. *Overall height:* 5.4"
Overall width: 1.5"
Sights: Integral front; windage adjustable rear; 3-dot or tritium night sights
Grips: Wood or plastic
Finish: Bruniton (also available in blued, stainless, silver or gold)
Features: Chrome-lined bore; visible firing-pin block; open slide design; safety drop catch (half-cock); combat trigger guard; external hammer; reversible magazine release
MODEL BRIGADIER (9mm and 40 cal.). Same as above but with a heavier slide.
Barrel length: 4.3". *Overall length:* 7,8". *Weight:* 35.3 oz.
MODEL 92 COMPACT L TYPE M (9mm)
Barrel length: 4.3" *Overall length:* 7.8" *Weight:* 30.9 oz.

MODEL 96 COMBAT/MODEL 96 STOCK
SPECIFICATIONS
Calibers: 40 *Capacity:* 10 rounds
Action: Single action only (Combat); single/double (Stock)
Barrel length: 4.9" (Stock); 5.9" (Combat)
Overall length: 8.5" (Stock); 9.5" (Combat)
Weight: 35 oz. (Stock); 40 oz. (Combat) *Sights:* 3 interchageable front sights (Stock)
Features: Rubber magazine bumpers; replaceable accurizing barrel bushings; checkered grips; machine-checkered front and backstraps; fitted ABS cases; Brigadier slide; extended frame-mounted safety; competition-tuned trigger and adjustable rear target set and tool set (Combat only)
Prices:
MODEL 96 STOCK (double or single action) $1,407.00
MODEL 96 COMBAT (single action only) 1,634.00
  w/4.9" barrel 1,341.00
COMBAT COMBO (4.9" or 5.9" barrels) 1,599.00

MODEL 92FS COMPACT AND COMPACT TYPE M
SPECIFICATIONS
Same features as the proven 92FS but in a more compact overall size and weight. *Overall length:* 7.8" *Barrel length:* 4.3" *Overall width:* 1.4" *Overall height:* 5.3" *Sight radius:* 5.8" *Weight:* 32.0 oz. Compact, 30.9 oz. Type M (unloaded). Special contoured magazine bottom for improved hand support and control. Compact features a double column magazine, while the Compact Type M features a single column magazine for thinner grip (1.28" instead of 1.39") and reduced weight.
Prices: MODEL 92 FS COMPACT
DA OR **SA** $629.00
MODEL 92FS PLASTIC w/3-Dot sights 629.00
  For wood grips, **add** 37.50
MODEL 92FS Stainless w/3-dot sights 691.00
MODEL 96 w/3-dot sights 629.00
MODEL 92FS BRIGADIER 675.00
MODEL 92FS LIMITED EDITION 2,002.00
  (1 of 470, polished stainless, walnut grips, chrome-plated magazine)

MODEL 96 COMBAT

BERNARDELLI PISTOLS

MODEL P.010 TARGET PISTOL

SPECIFICATIONS

Caliber: 22 LR *Capacity:* 5 or 10 rounds
Barrel length: 5.9" *Weight:* 40 oz.
Sights: Interchangeable front sight; rear sight adjustable for windage and elevation
Sight radius: 7.5"
Features: All steel construction; external hammer with safety notch; external slide catch for hold-open device; inertia safe firing pin; oil-finished walnut grips for right- and left-hand shooters; matte black or chrome finish; pivoted trigger with adjustable weight and take-ups
Price: $899.00

MODEL P.010
TARGET

BERSA AUTOMATIC PISTOLS

THUNDER 380

SPECIFICATIONS

Caliber: 380 ACP *Capacity:* 7 rounds
Barrel length: 3.5" *Overall length:* 6 ⁵⁄₈"
Weight: 23 oz.
Sights: Notched-bar dovetailed rear; blade integral with slide front
Safety: Manual firing pin
Grips: Black polymer
Finish: Blue, satin nickel.
Prices:
Matte $264.95
Satin Nickel 281.95
9-Shot Deluxe 274.95
Also Available:
THUNDER 380 DELUXE (29 oz.; 9 shots)
Price: $274.95

THUNDER 380

SERIES 95

SPECIFICATIONS

Caliber: 32 ACP *Capacity:* 10 rounds
Action: Double *Barrel length:* 3.5"
Overall length: 6 ⁵⁄₈"
Weight: 23 oz.
Sights: Notched-bar dovetailed rear; blade integral with slide front
Safety: Manual firing pin
Grips: Black polymer
Finish: Matte blue, satin nickel, Duo-Tone
Prices:
Matte $248.95
Nickel 264.95
Duo-Tone 259.95

SERIES 95

BROWNING AUTOMATIC PISTOLS

9MM HI-POWER
SINGLE ACTION

HI-POWER SINGLE ACTION

Both the 9mm and 40 S&W models come with either a fixed-blade front sight and a windage-adjustable rear sight or a nonglare rear sight, screw adjustable for both windage and elevation. The front sight is an 1/8-inch-wide blade mounted on a ramp. The rear surface of the blade is serrated to prevent glare. All models have an ambidextrous safety. See table below for specifications and prices.

HI-POWER SPECIFICATIONS 9mm & 40 S&W

MODEL	SIGHTS	GRIPS	BARREL LENGTH	OVERALL LENGTH	OVERALL WIDTH	OVERALL HEIGHT	WEIGHT*	MAG. CAP.	PRICE
Mark III	Fixed	Molded	4.75"	7.75"	1 3/8"	5"	32 oz.	10	$579.00
Standard	Fixed	Walnut	4.75"	7.75"	1 3/8"	5"	32 oz.	10	615.00
Standard	Adj.	Walnut	4.75"	7.75"	1 3/8"	5"	32 oz.	10	668.00
HP-Practical	Fixed	Molded Rubber	4.75"	7.75"	1 3/8"	5"	36 oz.	10	662.00
HP-Practical	Adj.	Molded Rubber	4.75"	7.75"	1 3/8"	5"	36 oz.	10	717.00
Silver Chrome	Adj.	Molded Rubber	4.75"	7.75"	1 3/8"	5"	36 oz.	10	684.00
Capitan (9mm only)	Adj.	Walnut	4.75"	7.75"	1 3/8"	5"	32 oz.	10	728.00

* 9mm weight listed. Overall weight of the 40 S&W Hi-Power is 3 oz. heavier than the 9mm.

BUCK MARK 22 LR SERIES

BUCK MARK STANDARD
(5.5" BARREL)

BUCK MARK PLUS NICKEL

BUCK MARK SPECIFICATIONS

BUCK MARK MODELS	MAG. CAP.	BARREL LENGTH	OVERALL LENGTH	WEIGHT	OVERALL HEIGHT	SIGHT RADIUS	GRIPS	PRICE
Standard	10	5.5"	9.5"	36 oz.	5 3/8"	8"	Molded Composite, Ambidextrous	$265.00
Micro Standard	10	4"	8"	32 oz.	5 3/8"	9 9/16"	Molded Composite, Ambidextrous	265.00
Nickel	10	5.5"	9.5"	36 oz.	5 3/8"	8"	Molded Composite, Ambidextrous	312.00
Micro Nickel	10	4"	8"	32 oz.	5 3/8"	9 9/16"	Molded Composite, Ambidextrous	312.00
Plus Nickel	10	5.5"	9.5"	36 oz.	5 3/8"	8"	Laminated Hardwood	354.00
Micro Plus Nickel	10	4"	8"	32 oz.	5 3/8"	9 9/16"	Laminated Hardwood	354.00
Plus	10	5.5"	9.5"	36 oz.	5 3/8"	8"	Laminated Hardwood	324.00
Micro Plus	10	4"	8"	32 oz.	5 3/8"	9 9/16"	Laminated Hardwood	324.00
Camper	10	5.5"	9.5"	34 oz.	5 3/8"	8"	Composite	234.00
Challenge	10	5.5"	9.5"	25 oz.	5 3/8"	8"	Walnut	296.00
Micro Challenge	10	4"	8"	23 oz.	5 3/8"	6 1/2"	Walnut	296.00

Finishes are matte blue w/polished barrel flats or nickel plated slide and barrel. Pro Target rear sight and 1/8" wide front sight standard.

BROWNING AUTOMATIC PISTOLS

BUCK MARK BULLSEYE

BUCK MARK 5.5 TARGET

BUCK MARK SILHOUETTE

BUCK MARK SPECIFICATIONS (cont.)

BUCK MARK MODELS	MAG. CAP.	BARREL LENGTH	OVERALL LENGTH	WEIGHT	OVERALL HEIGHT	SIGHT RADIUS	GRIPS	PRICE
Bullseye, Standard	10	7.25"	11 ⁵/₁₆"	36 oz.	5 ³/₈"	9 ⁷/₈"	Molded Composite, Ambidextrous	$389.00
Bullseye, Target	10	7.25"	11 ⁵/₁₆"	36 oz.	5 ³/₈"	9 ⁷/₈"	Contoured Rosewood or Wraparound fingergroove	500.00
5.5 Field	10	5.5"	9 ⁵/₈"	35.5 oz.	5 ⁵/₁₆"	8.25"	Contoured Walnut or Wraparound fingergroove	425.00
5.5 Target	10	5.5"	9 ⁵/₈"	35.5 oz.	5 ⁵/₁₆"	8.25"	Contoured Walnut or Wraparound fingergroove	425.00
5.5 Nickel Target	10	5.5"	9 ⁵/₈"	35.5 oz.	5 ⁵/₁₆"	8.25"	Contoured Walnut or Wraparound fingergroove	477.00
5.5 Gold Target	10	5.5"	9 ⁵/₈"	35.5 oz.	5 ⁵/₁₆"	8.25"	Contoured Walnut or Wraparound fingergroove	477.00
Silhouette	10	9 ⁷/₈"	14"	53 oz.	5 ⁵/₁₆"	13"	Contoured Walnut or Wraparound fingergroove	448.00
Varmint	10	9 ⁷/₈"	14"	48 oz.	5 ⁵/₁₆"	no sights	Contoured Walnut Wraparound fingergroove	403.00
Extra Magazine								24.95

COLT AUTOMATIC PISTOLS

COLT .22 SEMIAUTOMATIC DA

SPECIFICATIONS
Caliber: 22 LR
Capacity: 10 rounds
Barrel Length: 6"
Overall Length: 10 1/8"
Weight: 40.5 oz.
Sights: Adjustable
Sight Radius: 7.25"
Grips: Composite Monogrip
Finish: Stainless steel
Price: 377.00

.22 SEMIAUTOMATIC DA

**M1991A1 MKIV
SERIES 80 PISTOLS**

M1991A1 MKIV SERIES 80 PISTOLS

SPECIFICATIONS
Caliber: 45 ACP *Capacity:* 7 rounds
Barrel Length: 5" *Overall Length:* 8.5"
Weight: 38 oz. *Sights:* Fixed
Sight Radius: 6.5" *Grips:* Checkered rubber
Finish: Matte blue
Features: Smooth trigger; 4-way safety
Price: $556.00
Also Available:
COMPACT M1991A1 w/3.5" barrel; *Weight:* 34 oz.. . . . . 556.00
COMMANDER M1991A1 w/4.25" barrel and
  7-round capacity 556.00
Stainless versions 610.00

COLT DEFENDER LIGHTWEIGHT CARRY SERIES 80 SEMIAUTO

SPECIFICATIONS
Caliber: 45 ACP, 40 S&W
Capacity: 7 rounds
Action: Single
Material: Carbon steel and aluminum
Barrel Length: 3"
Overall Length: 6.75"
Weight: 22.5 oz.
Sights: Fixed, white dot front and rear
Sight Radius: 4.75"
Finish: Stainless steel
Features: Pebble finish rubber wraparound w/finger
grooves; firing pin safety; disconnect safety; combat style
hammer, smooth trigger; two magazines
Price: $750.00

**DEFENDER
LIGHTWEIGHT CARRY
SERIES 80 SEMIAUTO**

COLT AUTOMATIC PISTOLS

MKIV SERIES 80 AND 90

MUSTANG .380

MUSTANG .380 POCKETLITE

This backup automatic has four times the knockdown power of 25 ACP automatics. It is a smaller version of the 380 Government Model.

SPECIFICATIONS
Caliber: 380 ACP *Capacity:* 6 rounds
Barrel length: 2.75" *Overall length:* 5.5"
Height: 3.9" *Weight:* 18.5 oz. *Sights:* Fixed
Price: Stainless Steel $529.00
Also available:
MUSTANG POCKETLITE LW380 with aluminum alloy receiver; 12" shorter than standard Govt. 380; weights only 12.5 oz.
Price: $508.00

CUSTOM TACTICAL

CUSTOM TACTICAL MODELS (GOVERNMENT/COMMANDER/OFFICERS)

SPECIFICATIONS
Caliber: 45 ACP *Capacity:* 7 rounds
Action: Single *Barrel Length:* 5"
Overall Length: 8.5" *Weight:* 38 oz.
Sights: Colt, Heine fixed combat or fixed front; Novak carry, Heine fixed combat or Bo Mar adjustable rear
Finish: Matte blue
Prices:
TACTICAL LEVEL I (matte blue). $730.00
TACTICAL LEVEL II (blue). 935.00
TACTICAL LEVEL III (blue). 1,350.00
SPECIAL COMBAT GOVT.. . . . . 1,532.00

COLT REVOLVERS

PYTHON ELITE

The Colt Python custom revolver, suitable for hunting, target shooting and police use, is chambered for the powerful 357 Magnum cartridge. Python features include ventilated rib, wide-spur hammer, trigger and walnut grips, white outline adjustable rear and ramp-type red front sights, grooved.

SPECIFICATIONS
Calibers: 357 Mag./38 Special *Barrel Length:* 6"
Overall Length: 11.5" *Weight:* 43.5 oz. *Features:*
Serrated service trigger; high-polish blue finish; target hammer
Price: $929.00
Stainess Steel. 1,018.00

PYTHON ELITE

SINGLE ACTION ARMY
(Nickel Finish)

THE PEACEMAKER
SINGLE ACTION ARMY REVOLVER

Colt's Custom Gun Shop maintains the tradition of quality and innovation that Samuel Colt began more than a century and a half ago. Single Action Army revolvers continue to be highly prized collectible arms and are offered in full nickel finish or in Royal Blue with color casehardened frame, without engraving, unless otherwise specified by the purchaser. Grips are American walnut.
Price:. $1,213.00
COWBOY SINGLE ACTION REVOLVER, 5.5" 599.00

DS II REVOLVER

SPECIFICATIONS
Caliber: .357 Magnum *Capacity:* 6 rounds
Action: Single/double *Barrel length:* 2"
Overall length: 7" *Grips:* Rubber combat style
Weight: 21 oz. *Sights:* Ramp front; fixed rear
Sight Radius: 4" *Frame:* Stainless steel
Features: Smooth combat trigger; service hammer; satin finish
Price: $435.00

DS II REVOLVER

ANACONDA DOUBLE ACTION

SPECIFICATIONS
Calibers: 44 Magnum/44 Special and 45 Colt
(6" and 8" barrel only)
Capacity: 6 rounds *Barrel Length:* 4", 6" or 8"
Overall Length: 9 ⁵/₈", 11 ⁵/₈", 13 ⁵/₈"
Weight: 47 oz. (4"), 53 oz. (6"), 59 oz. (8")
Sights: Red ramp front; adjustable white outline rear; drilled and tapped for scope mount
Sight Radius: 5.75" (4"), 7.75" (6"), 9.75" (8")
Grips: Rubber combat-style with finger grooves
Finish: Brushed stainless steel
Price: $629.00

ANACONDA
6" BARREL

COONAN ARMS

357 MAGNUM PISTOL
5" BARREL (TOP)
6" BARREL (MIDDLE)
COMPENSATED BARREL (BOTTOM)

357 MAGNUM PISTOL

SPECIFICATIONS
Caliber: 357 Magnum
Magazine Capacity: 7 rounds + 1
Barrel Length: 5" (6" or Compensated barrel optional)
Overall Length: 8.3"
Weight: 48 oz. (loaded)
Height: 5.6"
Width: 1.3"
Sights: Ramp front; fixed rear, adjustable for windage only
Grips: Smooth black walnut (checkered grips optional)

Finish: Stainless steel and alloy steel
Features: Linkless barrel; recoil-operated; extended slide catch and thumb lock
Prices:
With 5" barrel. $735.00
With 6" barrel 768.00
With Compensated barrel. 1015.00
Also available in .41 Magnum 825.00
With checkered walnut grips, Millett W/O
   adj. rear, two-tone Teflon finish 1400.00

"CADET" COMPACT MODEL

SPECIFICATIONS
Caliber: 357 Magnum
Magazine Capacity: 6 rounds + 1
Barrel Length: 3.9"
Overall Length: 7.8"
Weight: 39 oz.
Height: 5.3"
Width: 1.3"
Sights: Ramp front; fixed rear, adjustable for windage only
Grips: Smooth black walnut
Finish: Stainless steel and alloy steel
Features: Linkless bull barrel; full-length guide rod; recoil-operated (Browning falling-block design); extended slide catch and thumb lock for one-hand position
Price: $855.00

"CADET" COMPACT

DAVIS PISTOLS

MODEL D-25 DERRINGER

D-SERIES DERRINGERS

SPECIFICATIONS
Calibers: 22 LR, 22 Mag., 25 Auto, 32 Auto
Capacity: 2 shot *Barrel Length:* 2.4"
Overall Length: 4" *Height:* 2.8" *Weight:* 9.5 oz.
Grips: Laminated wood *Finish:* Black teflon or chrome
Price: $75.00

LONG BORE D-SERIES

SPECIFICATIONS
Calibers: 22 Mag., 9mm, 32 H&R Mag., 38 Special
Capacity: 2 rounds *Barrel Length:* 3.5"
Overall Length: 5.4" *Height:* 3.31" *Weight:* 16 oz.
Price: $104.00
   9mm only. 110.00
Also available:
BIG BORE D-SERIES.
Calibers: 22 WMR, 9mm, 32 H&R Mag., 38 Special.
Barrel Length: 2.75" *Overall Length:* 4.65"
Weight: 14 oz.
Price: $98.00
   9mm only. 104.00

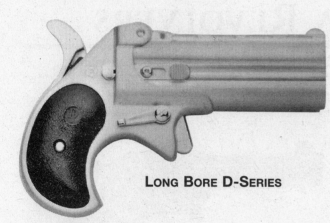

LONG BORE D-SERIES

MODEL P-32

SPECIFICATIONS
Caliber: 32 Auto *Magazine Capacity:* 6 rounds
Barrel Length: 2.8" *Overall Length:* 5.4"
Weight: 22 oz. *Height:* 4"
Grips: Laminated wood *Finish:* Black teflon or chrome
Price: $87.50

MODEL P-380

SPECIFICATIONS
Caliber: 380 Auto *Magazine Capacity:* 5 rounds
Barrel Length: 2.8" *Overall Length:* 5.4"
Height: 4" *Weight:* 22 oz.
Price: $98.00

MODEL P-32

MODEL P-380

DOWNSIZER PISTOLS

MODEL WSP
"WORLD'S SMALLEST PISTOL"

SPECIFICATIONS
Action: Single-shot double-action only
Caliber: 9mm, 40 S&W, 45 ACP, 357 Mag., 357 Sig.
Barrel length: 2.1", tip-up barrel w/o extractor
Overall length: 3.25"
Weight: 11 oz. Height: 2.25"
Width: 0.9"
Materials: Stainless steel; CNC machined from solid bar stock
Price: $359.00

**"WORLD'S
SMALLEST PISTOL"**

EMF/DAKOTA REVOLVERS

E.M.F. HARTFORD SINGLE-ACTION REVOLVERS

Hartford Single Action revolvers are the most authentic of all the Colt reproduction single-actions. All parts are interchangeable with the original Colt 1st and 2nd generation revolvers.

HARTFORD SCROLL-ENGRAVED SINGLE-ACTION REVOLVER

SPECIFICATIONS
Calibers: 45 Long Colt, 357 Magnum, 44-40.
Barrel lengths: 4 5/8", 5.5" and 7.5".
Features: Classic original-type scroll engraving.
Price: $800.00
Nickel 900.00

HARTFORD PINKERTON

SPECIFICATIONS
Caliber: 45 LC *Barrel length:* 4".
Bird's-head grip with ejector tube.
Price: $570.00

HARTFORD MODELS
"CAVALRY COLT" AND "ARTILLERY"

The Model 1873 Government Model Cavalry revolver is an exact reproduction of the original Colt made for the U.S. Cavalry in caliber 45 Long Colt with barrel length of 7.5". The Artillery Model has 5.5" barrel.

Price: $700.00
Also available:
SHERIFF'S MODEL (3.5" barrel) $585.00

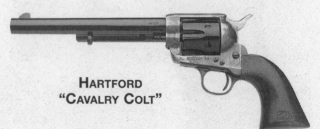

**HARTFORD
"CAVALRY COLT"**

EMF/DAKOTA REVOLVERS

E.M.F. HARTFORD SINGLE-ACTION REVOLVERS

1st and 2nd generations models available. Parts are interchangeable with the original Colts. Forged steel frames, case hardened, steel backstrap & trigger guard. Original blue finish, walnut grips. Barrel lengths: 4.75", 5.5", 7.5", 12" buntline.

1873 HARTFORD "BUNTLINE"
SPECIFICATIONS
Caliber: 45 LC *Barrel Length:* 12"
Features: Steel backstrap & trigger
Price: $670.00

1873 HARTFORD "SIXSHOOTER"
SPECIFICATIONS
Calibers: 45, 357 Magnum, 44-40 *Barrel Lengths:* 4.75",
5.5", 7.5" *Features:* Brass backstrap & trigger guard
Price: $550.00

1873 HARTFORD COMBO "SIXSHOOTER"
Price: $680.00

1895 HARTFORD "BISLEY"
SPECIFICATIONS
Caliber: 45 LC *Barrel Lengths:* 5.5" & 7.5"
Features: Steel backstrap & trigger guard
Price: $600.00

1893 HARTFORD "EXPRESS"
SPECIFICATIONS
Calibers: 45 LC *Barrel Lengths:* 4.75" & 5.5"
Features: Steel backstrap & trigger guard
Price: $570.00

EMF/DAKOTA REVOLVERS

1873 DAKOTA SINGLE ACTION

SPECIFICATIONS
Calibers: 357 Mag., 44-40, 45 Long Colt. *Barrel lengths:* 4.75", 5.5" and 7.5". *Finish:* Blued, case hardened frame. *Grips:* One-piece walnut. *Features:* Classic Colt design, set screw for cylinder pin release; black nickel backstrap and trigger design
Price: $400.00

1873 DAKOTA SINGLE ACTION
WITH 5.5" BARREL

MODEL 1875 "OUTLAW" SINGLE ACTION
(not shown)

SPECIFICATIONS
Calibers: 44-40, 45 Long Colt, 357. *Barrel length:* 5.5" and 7.5". *Finish:* Blued or nickel. *Special features:* Case hardened frame, walnut grips; brass trigger guard; an exact replica of the Remington No. 3 revolver produced from 1875 to 1889.
Price: $575.00

1873 DAKOTA SINGLE ACTION
WITH 7.5" BARREL

1875 REMINGTON SA REVOLVER

MODEL 1875 REMINGTON SINGLE ACTION REVOLVER

SPECIFICATIONS
Features: Factory engraved; case hardened frame
Price:
Blued $575.00
Nickel 740.00

MODEL 1890 REMINGTON POLICE

MODEL 1890 REMINGTON POLICE

SPECIFICATIONS
Calibers: 44-40, 45 Long Colt and 357 Magnum. *Barrel length:* 5.75". *Finish:* Blued or nickel. *Features:* Original design (1891-1894) with lanyard ring in buttstock; case hardened frame; walnut grips
Price: $610.00

ENTRÉPRISE ARMS

TACTICAL P325 PLUS

SPECIFICATIONS

Caliber: .45 ACP, 10 round magazine.
Barrel: 3.25". *Weight:* 37 oz. *Length:* 7.25" overall.
Stocks: Black Ergo Ultra Slim, double diamond checkered grip panels.
Sights: Tactical2 Ghost Ring sight or Novak Lo-mount sight.
Features: Same as the Elite series plus extended ambidextrous thumb safety, front & rear cocking serrations, full length guide rod, barrel throated & frame ramp polished, tuned match extractor, fitted barrel & bushing, stainless steel firing pin, serrated & ramped front sight, slide lapped to frame, dehorned and trigger set at a crisp 4.5 pounds.
Price: $1,049.00

TACTICAL P325 PLUS

ELITE P425 (and P500)

SPECIFICATIONS

Caliber: .45 ACP, 10 round magazine.
Barrel: 4.25" (5" P500) *Weight:* 38 oz. (40 oz. P500)
Length: 7.75" overall.
Stocks: Black Ergo Ultra Slim, double diamond checkered grip panels.
Sights: 3 Dot fixed sights (dovetail cut front sight).
Features: Reinforced dustcover, lowered & flared ejection port, squared trigger guard, adjustable match trigger, bolstered front strap, high grip cut, hardened steel magazine release, high ride beavertail grip safety, steel flat mainspring housing (checkered 20 LPI), checkered slide release, extended thumb lock, EDM skeletonized match hammer & sear, match grade disconnector with polished contact points and Wolff springs throughout.
Price: $739.90

ELITE P425

BOXER P500

SPECIFICATIONS

Caliber: .45 ACP, .40 Cal. *Barrel:* 5". *Weight:* 40 oz.
Length: 8.5" overall. *Stocks:* Black Ergo Ultra Slim, double diamond checkered grip panels.
Sights: Adjustable Competizione "melded" rear sight with dovetail patridge front sight. *Features:* Same as the Elite model plus machined slide parallel rails with polished breech face & barrel channel, front & rear cocking serrations, lowered & flared ejection port, full length stainless steel one piece guide rod with plug, National match barrel 5" Government length, match bushing, stainless steel firing pin, match extractor, oversized firing pin stop, fitted barrel & bushing, slide lapped to frame, barrel throated & frame ramp polished, extractor tuned and trigger set at a crisp 4.5 pounds.
Price: $1,099.00
Also available: MEDALIST P500 (45 ACP and 40 cal.) and TACTICAL P500 (45 cal.)

BOXER P500

ENTRÉPRISE ARMS

MODEL I

MODEL II

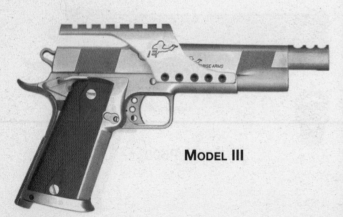

MODEL III

TOURNAMENT SHOOTERS MODEL I
SPECIFICATIONS
Caliber: .45 ACP, 40 cal., 38 Super
Barrel: 5" *Weight:* 40 oz. *Length:* 8.5" overall
Stocks: Black ultra-slim double diamond checkered grip panels
Sights: Adjustable Competizione "melded" rear sight with dovetail Patridge front sight
Features: Same as the Elite model plus oversized magazine release button, ambidextrous thumb lock, flared extended magazine well, fully machined parallel slide rails, polished barrel channel, polished breech face, front & rear cocking serrations, serrated top of slide, stainless steel ramped bull barrel with fully supported chamber, full length stainless steel one piece guide rod with plug, stainless steel firing pin, match extractor, oversized firing pin stop, fitted Bull Barrel, slide lapped to frame, polished ramp, extractor tuned, hard chrome finish and trigger set at a 2 pounds.
Price: $2,300.00

TOURNAMENT SHOOTERS MODEL II
SPECIFICATIONS
Caliber: .45 ACP, 10 round magazine
Barrel: 6" *Weight:* 44 oz. *Length:* 9.5" overall
Stocks: Black ultra slim double diamond checkered grip panels
Sights: Adjustable Competizione "melded" rear sight with dovetail Patridge front sight
Features: Same as the Elite model plus oversized magazine release button, ambidextrous thumb lock, front strap checkered (20 LPI), long slide fully machined, parallel slide rails, polished barrel channel, polished breech face, front & Rear Cocking Serrations, lowered & flared ejection port, serrated top of slide, 6" stainless steel national match barrel, national match bushing, full length stainless steel two piece guide rod with plug, stainless steel firing pin, match extractor, oversized firing pin stop, fitted barrel & bushing, slide lapped to frame, barrel throated & frame pamp polished, extractor tuned, black oxide finish and trigger set at 4.5 pounds.
Price: $2,000.00

TOURNAMENT SHOOTERS MODEL III
SPECIFICATIONS
Caliber: .45 ACP, 40 cal., 38 Super
Barrel: 6" *Weight:* 44 oz. *Length:* 9.5" overall
Stocks: Black ultra slim double diamond checkered grip panels
Features: Same as the Elite model plus fitted barrel and compensator, oversized magazine release button, ambidextrous extended thumb lock, extended slide stop, front strap checkered (20 LPI), trigger guard checkered (20 LPI), frame mounted scope base, flared extended magazine well, slide fully machined, seven port cone-style compensator, full length stainless steel one piece guide rod with plug, stainless steel firing pin, match extractor, oversized firing pin stop, slide lapped to frame, extractor tuned, polished ramp, hard chrome finish and trigger Set at 2 pounds.
Price: $2,700.00

EUROPEAN AMERICAN ARMORY

WITNESS DOUBLE-ACTION PISTOLS

SPECIFICATIONS
Calibers: 9mm, 38 Super, 40 S&W and 45 ACP
Capacity: 10 rounds, (45 ACP)
Barrel length: 4.5"
Overall length: 8.1"
Weight: 33 oz.
Sights: 3-dot; windage adj. rear
Grips: Black rubber
Finish: Blued or Wonder Finish
Prices:
Blue $351.00-359.00
Wonder Finish 366.60

WITNESS GOLD TEAM

SPECIFICATIONS
Calibers: 9mm, 40 S&W, 38 Super, 9X21mm, 45 ACP
Capacity: 10 rounds; (45 ACP)
Barrel length: 5.25" *Overall length:* 10.5"
Weight: 38 oz.
Finish: Hard chrome
Features: Triple chamber comp, S/A trigger, extended safety competition hammer, checkered front strap and backstrap, low-profile competition grips, square trigger guard
Price: $2,150.00
Also available:
WITNESS SILVER TEAM. Same calibers as above. Features double chamber compensator, competition hammer, extended safety & magazine release, blued finish. *O.A. length:* 9.75" *Weight:* 34 oz.
Price: 967.45

WITNESS SUBCOMPACT (not shown)

SPECIFICATIONS
Calibers: 9mm, 40 S&W, 45 ACP. *Capacity:* 10 rounds (9mm); 9 rounds (40 S&W); 8 rounds (45 ACP)
Barrel length: 3.66"
Overall length: 7.24"
Weight: 30 oz.

Finish: Blued or Wonder Finish
Prices:
Blue $351.00
Wonder Finish 366.60
Polymer. 343.20
Ported or Carry Comp 405.60

EUROPEAN AMERICAN ARMORY

EUROPEAN SINGLE ACTION COMPACT

SPECIFICATIONS
Caliber: 380 ACP *Capacity:* 7 rounds
Barrel length: 3.2" *Overall length:* 6.5"
Weight: 26 oz. *Finish:* Blued or Wonder Finish
Features: All-steel construction; automatic ejection; single-
action trigger; European wood grips; rear sight adj. for
windage; positive sighting system
Prices:
Blued Finish. $140.40
Wonder Finish 171.60

EUROPEAN SA COMPACT.

WINDICATOR REVOLVER

SPECIFICATIONS
Calibers: 38 Special, 357 Mag. *Capacity:* 6 rounds
Action: Single/Double action *Barrel length:* 2" or 4"
Sights: Fixed (No-Snag) or windage adj. *Finish:* Blued only
Features: Swing-out cylinder; black rubber grips; hammer
block safety
Prices:
38 SPECIAL w/2" barrel **$173.00**
38 SPECIAL w/4" barrel 187.00
357 MAGNUM w/2" barrel 196.56
357 MAGNUM w/4" barrel 210.00

WINDICATOR REVOLVER

BIG BORE BOUNTY HUNTER
SINGLE ACTION

BIG BORE BOUNTY HUNTER
SINGLE ACTION

SPECIFICATIONS
Calibers: 357 Mag., 45 Long Colt and 44 Mag.
Capacity: 6 rounds *Barrel length:* 4.5" or 7.5"
Sights: Fixed *Weight:* 2.45 lbs. (4.5" bbl.); 2.7 lbs. (7.5" bbl.)
Finish: Blued, color casehardened or nickel
Features: Transfer-bar safety, 3 position hammer; hammer-
forged barrel; walnut grips (polymer grips optional)
Prices: Blued or color casehardened receiver . . . **$286.60**
Nickel 305.76
Also available: In 22 LR/WMR
   (4.75" or 6.75" barrel) w/blue finish 196.56
Nickel 218.40

SMALL BORE BOUNTY HUNTER
(not shown)

SPECIFICATIONS
Caliber: 22 LR/22 WMR
Capacity: 6 or 8 shots
Action: Single action
Barrel length: 4.75" or 6.75" (8 lands and grooves)
Overall length: 9.5" or 11.5"
Height: 5.25"
Weight: 38 oz. (average)
Grips: European walnut
Sights: Fixed
Finish: Blue or nickel
Features: Transfer bar safety
Prices: $187.20
Nickel 205.00

FEG/INTERARMS

MARK II APK $269.00

SPECIFICATIONS
Caliber: 380 ACP
Capacity: 7 rounds
Action: Single or double action
Barrel Length: 3.4"
Overall Length: 6.4"
Height: 4.7"
Width: 1.2"
Weight: 25 oz.
Sights: Windage-adjustable sights
Features: Grooved non-reflective integral sighting rib; safety acts as decocker; thumbrest target grip and field cleaning rod w/padded carrying case included

MARK II APK

MARK II AP $269.00

SPECIFICATIONS
Caliber: 380 ACP
Capacity: 7 rounds
Action: Single or double action
Barrel Length: 3.9"
Overall Length: 6.9"
Height: 4.7"
Width: 1.2"
Weight: 27 oz.
Sights: Windage-adjustable sights
Features: Same as Model APK

MARK II AP22 (not shown) $269.00

SPECIFICATIONS
Caliber: 22 LR
Capacity: 8 rounds
Action: Single or double action
Barrel Length: 3.4"
Overall Length: 6.3"
Height: 4.2"
Width: 1.28"
Weight: 23 oz.
Finish: Blue
Sights: Windage-adjustable sights
Features: Same as Model APK

MARK II AP

FREEDOM ARMS

MODEL 1997 PREMIER GRADE
FIXED SIGHT $1391.00
ADJUSTABLE SIGHT 1492.00

SPECIFICATIONS
Caliber: 357 Magnum
Capacity: 6 shots
Action: Single Action
Barrel Lengths: 5.5" and 7.5"
Sights: Removable front blade; adjustable or fixed rear
Grips: Impregnated hardwood or optional black micanta

MODEL 1997
PREMIER GRADE

FREEDOM ARMS

MODEL 252 REVOLVER
SILHOUETTE CLASS 10" BARREL

SPECIFICATIONS
Caliber: 22 LR (optional 22 Magnum cylinder) *Barrel Lengths:* 5.13", 7.5" (Varmint Class) and 10" (Silhouette Class) *Sights:* Silhouette competition sights (Silhouette Class); adjustable rear express sight; removable front express blade; front sight hood *Grips:* Black micarta (Silhouette Class); black and green laminated hardwood (Varmint Class) *Finish:* Stainless steel *Features:* Dual firing pin; lightened hammer; pre-set trigger stop; accepts all sights and/or scope mounts
Prices:
SILHOUETTE CLASS (10" barrel). $1,600.75
VARMINT CLASS (5.13" & 7.5" barrels) 1,527.00

MODEL 353 REVOLVER
FIELD GRADE 7 1/2" BARREL

SPECIFICATIONS
Caliber: 357 Magnum, 41 Magnum, 44 Magnum *Action:* Single action *Capacity:* 5 shots *Barrel Lengths:* 4.75", 6", 7.5", 9" *Sights:* Removable front blade; adjustable rear *Grips:* Pachmayr Presentation grips (Premier Grade has impregnated hardwood grips *Finish:* Nonglare Field Grade (standard model); Premier Grade brushed finish (all stainless steel)
Prices: FIELD GRADE. $1340.00
PREMIER GRADE, fixed sights 1391.00
   adj. sights 1492.00
   extra cylinder 264.00

SILHOUETTE/COMPETITION MODELS
(not shown)
SPECIFICATIONS
Calibers: 357 Magnum, 41 Rem. Mag. and 44 Rem. Mag.
Barrel Lengths: 9" (357 Mag.) and 10" (41 Rem. Mag., 44 Rem. Mag.)
Sights: Silhouette competition *Grips:* Pachmayr
Trigger: Pre-set stop; trigger over travel screw
Finish: Field Grade
Price: $1417.85

454 CASULL FIELD GRADE

MODEL 555
PREMIER GRADE (50 AE)

454 CASULL & MODEL 555
PREMIER & FIELD GRADES
SPECIFICATIONS
Calibers: 454 Casull, 41 Rem. Mag., 44 Rem. Mag., .475 Linebaugh, 50 AE
Action: Single action *Capacity:* 5 rounds
Barrel Lengths: 4.75", 6", 7.5", 10"
Overall Length: 14" (w/7.5" barrel)
Weight: 3 lbs. 2 oz. (w/7.5" barrel)
Safety: Patented sliding bar
Sights: Notched rear; blade front (optional adjustable rear and replaceable front blade)
Grips: Impregnated hardwood (Premier Grade) or rubber Pachmayr (Field Grade)
Finish: Brushed stainless (Premier Grade); Matte Finish (Field)
Features: ISGW silhouette, Millett competition and express sights are optional; SSK T'SOB 3-ring or 2-ring Leupold scope mount optional; optional cylinder in 454 Casull, 45 ACP, 45 Win. Mag. ($264.00)
Prices:
MODEL FA-454C 475L AND 50AE PREMIER GRADE
W/adjustable sights $1820.00
W/fixed sights 1723.00
357 41 and 44 Magnums w/adjustable sights . . . 1760.00
W/fixed sights 1663.00
MODEL 83 FIELD GRADE
   .454C, 475L, 50 AE, adj. sights. 1400.00

GLOCK

**MODEL 17L
COMPETITION**

**MODEL 19 COMPACT
(Fixed Sight)**

MODEL 19 COMPACT
SPECIFICATIONS
Caliber: 9mm Parabellum *Magazine capacity:* 10 rounds
(15 and 17 rounds optional)* *Barrel length:* 4"
Overall length: 6.85" *Weight:* 21 oz.
Price: Fixed Sight $616.00
Also available: MODEL 21. *Caliber:* 45 ACP. *Capacity:* 10
rounds (13 rounds optional)*
Price: Fixed Sight $688.00

MODEL 20
SPECIFICATIONS
Caliber: 10mm *Magazine capacity:* 10 rounds (15
rounds optional)* *Action:* Double action *Barrel length:*
4.6" *Overall length:* 7.59" *Height:* 5.47" (w/sights)
Weight: 27.68 oz. (empty) *Sights:* Fixed (adjustable
$29.00 add'l) *Features:* 3 safeties, "safe-action" system,
polymer frame
Price: Fixed Sight $668.00

MODEL 24 COMPETITION
SPECIFICATIONS
Caliber: 40 S&W *Capacity:* 10 rounds (15 rounds optional)*
Barrel length: 6.02" *Overall length:* 8.85" *Weight:* 26.7
oz. (empty) *Safety:* Manual trigger safety; passive firing
block and drop safety *Finish:* Matte (Tenifer process); nonglare
Price: . . . . .by special order
w/Compensated Barrel, Fixed Sights . . .by special order
For law enforcement and military use only

MODEL 17L COMPETITION
SPECIFICATIONS
Caliber: 9mm Parabellum
Magazine capacity: 10 rounds (17 and 19 rounds
optional)*
Barrel length: 6.02"
Overall length: 8.85"
Weight: 23.35 oz. (without magazine)
Sights: Fixed (adjustable rear sights **$28.00** add'l)
Price: by special order

MODEL 17 (Not Shown)
SPECIFICATIONS
Caliber: 9mm Parabellum
Magazine capacity: 10 rounds (17 and 19 rounds
optional)*
Barrel length: 4.5" (hexagonal profile with right-hand twist)
Overall length: 7.32"
Weight: 22 oz. (without magazine)
Sights: Fixed (adjustable rear sights **$28.00** add'l)
Price: Fixed Sight $616.00

MODEL 20

MODEL 24 COMPETITION

GLOCK

MODEL 23 COMPACT SPORT/SERVICE MODEL

SPECIFICATIONS
Caliber: 40 S&W *Capacity:* 10 rounds
Barrel length: 4.02"
Overall length: 6.85"
Weight: 21.16 oz.
Price: $616.00
Also available:
MODEL 22 (Sport and Service models)
Caliber: 40 S&W
Capacity: 10 rounds (15 rounds optional)*
Barrel length: 4.5" *Overall length:* 7.32"
Price: Fixed Sight $616.00

MODEL 23

MODEL 29 SUBCOMPACT

SPECIFICATIONS
Caliber: 10 mm auto *Capacity:* 10 rounds
Barrel length: 3.78" *Overall length:* 6.77"
Weight: 24.7 oz. (approx.) *Height:* 4.5"
Finish: Matte (Tenifer process); nonglare
Features: Safe Action trigger system; two magazines provided
Price: $668.00

MODEL 29

MODEL 26

SPECIFICATIONS
Caliber: 9mm *Action:* DA
Capacity: 10 rounds
Barrel length: 3.47" *Overall length:* 6.3"
Weight: 19.77 oz.
Finish: Matte (Tenifer process); nonglare
Features: 3 safeties; Safe Action trigger system; polymer frame
Price: $616.00
Also available:
MODEL 27. Same specifications as Model 26 but in .40 S&W
Capacity: 9 rounds
Price: Fixed Sight $616.00

MODEL 26

MODEL 30 SUBCOMPACT

SPECIFICATIONS
Caliber: 45 ACP
Capacity: 10 rounds (9 round optional)
Barrel length: 3.78"
Overall length: 6.8"
Weight: 24 oz. (approx.)
Height: 4.5"
Finish: Matte (Tenifer process); nonglare
Features: Safe Action trigger system; two magazines provided; magazine has an extended floorplate that serves as a finger rest; 6.7-inch slide
Price: $668.00

MODEL 30

HÄMMERLI U.S.A. PISTOLS

MODEL 160 FREE PISTOL
$2,189.00

SPECIFICATIONS
Caliber: 22 LR *Barrel Length:* 11.3"
Overall Length: 17.5" *Height:* 5.7" *Weight:* 45 oz.
Trigger Action: Infinitely variable set trigger weight;
cocking lever located on left of receiver; trigger length
variable along weapon axis
Locking Action: Martini-type locking action w/side-
mounted locking lever
Barrel: Free floating, cold swaged precision barrel w/low
axis relative to the hand
Ignition: Horizontal firing pin (hammerless) in line w/barrel
axis; firing pin travel 0.15"
Grips: Selected walnut w/adj. hand rest for direct arm to
barrel extension

MODEL 160
FREE PISTOL

MODEL 162 ELECTRONIC PISTOL
$2,410.00

SPECIFICATIONS
Same as **Model 160** except trigger action is electronic.
Features: Short lock time (1.7 milliseconds between
trigger actuation and firing pin impact), light trigger pull,
and extended battery life.

MODEL 162
ELECTRONIC PISTOL

MODEL 208S STANDARD PISTOL
$2,021.00

SPECIFICATIONS
Caliber: 22 LR *Capacity:* 8 rounds *Action:* Single
Barrel Length: 5.9" *Overall Length:* 10" *Height:* 5.9"
Weight: 36.7 oz. *Sight Radius:* 8.2"
Sights: Micrometer rear sight w/notch width; adj. for
windage & elevation; standard front blade
Trigger: Adj. for pull weight, travel, slackweight & creep
Safety: Rotating knob on rear of frame

MODEL 208S
STANDARD PISTOL

MODEL 280 TARGET PISTOL
$1,643.00 ($1,853.00 in 32 S&W)

SPECIFICATIONS
Calibers: 22 LR and 32 S&W
Capacity: 6 rounds (22 LR); 5 rounds (32 S&W)
Action: Single *Barrel Length:* 4.58"
Overall Length: 11.8" *Height:* 5.9"
Weight: (excluding counterweights) 34.6 oz. (22 LR);
 41.8 oz. (32 S&W)
Sight Radius: 8.7" *Sights:* Micrometer adjustable
Grips: Orthopedic type; stippled walnut w/adj. palm shelf
Features: 3 steel & 3 carbon fiber barrel weight; combina-
tion tool; 4 Allen wrenches; dry fire plug; magazine loading
tool; extra magazine
Also available:
MODEL 280 TARGET PISTOL COMBO
Conversion Unit (22 LR) $803.00
In 32 S&W 1,013.00

MODEL 280
TARGET PISTOL

HARRINGTON & RICHARDSON

MODEL 929 SIDEKICK REVOLVER

SPECIFICATIONS
Calibers: 22 Short, Long, Long Rifle
Action: Single and double action
Capacity: 9 rounds
Barrel Length: 6" (w/sighting rib)
Weight: 36 oz.
Sights: Fixed front; fully adjustable rear
Grips: Walnut finished hardwood; nickel medallion
Finish: High-polish blue
Price: $172.95

**MODEL 929
SIDEKICK**

MODEL 939 PREMIER TARGET REVOLVER

SPECIFICATIONS
Calibers: 22 Short, Long, Long Rifle
Capacity: 9 rounds
Barrel Length: 6"
Weight: 36 oz.
Grips: Walnut hardwood; nickel medallion
Sights: Fully adjustable rear; fixed front
Features: Two-piece walnut-stained hardwood western-styled grip frame profile, transfer bar system; made of high-quality ferrous metals
Price: . . . . , . . $189.95

**MODEL 939 PREMIER
TARGET REVOLVER**

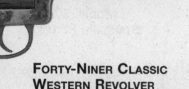

**FORTY-NINER CLASSIC
WESTERN REVOLVER**

FORTY-NINER CLASSIC WESTERN REVOLVER

SPECIFICATIONS
Calibers: 22 Short, Long and Long Rifle
Capacity: 9 rounds
Barrel Length: 5.5" or 7.5" (case colored)
Weight: 36 oz. (5.5" barrel); 38 oz. (7.5" barrel)
Sights: Fixed front; drift-adjustable rear
Grips: Two-piece walnut-stained hardwood; nickel medallion
Price: $189.95

SPORTSMAN 999 REVOLVER

SPECIFICATIONS
Calibers: 22 Short, Long, Long Rifle
Action: Single and double
Capacity: 9 rounds
Barrel Lengths: 4" and 6" (both fluted)
Weight: 30 oz. (4" barrel); 34 oz. (6" barrel)
Sights: Windage adjustable rear; elevation adjustable front
Grips: Walnut-finished hardwood
Finish: Blued
Price: $284.95

**SPORTSMAN 999
REVOLVER**

HECKLER & KOCH

MODEL HK USP 9 &40 UNIVERSAL SELF-LOADING PISTOL

SPECIFICATIONS
Calibers: 9mm and 40 S&W *Capacity:* 10 + 1
Operating System: Short recoil, modified Browning action
Barrel Length: 4.25" *Overall Length:* 7.64"
Weight: 1.74 lbs. (40 S&W); 1.66 lbs. (9mm)
Height: 5.35" *Sights:* Adjustable 3-dot
Grips: Polymer receiver and integral grips
Prices:
9mm & 40 S&W $655.00
  W/control lever on right 676.00
Stainless steel 701.00
  W/control lever on right 722.00
Also available:
HK USP45 TACTICAL PISTOL
  w/cleaning kit & case 965.00

**MODEL HK USP45
TACTICAL PISTOL**

MODEL USP45 UNIVERSAL SELF-LOADING PISTOL

SPECIFICATIONS
Caliber: 45 ACP *Capacity:* 10 rounds
Action: DA/SA or DAO *Barrel Length:* 4.41"
Overall Length: 7.87" *Height:* 5.55" *Weight:* 1.90 lbs.
Grips: Polymer frame & integral grips
Prices: $717.00
Stainless steel 763.00
Also available:
in 9mm and 40 S&W. *Barrel Length:* 4.25". *Overall
Length:* 7.64". *Weight:* 1.75 lbs 655.00
Stainless steel 701.00

**MODEL HK USP45
UNIVERSAL SELF-
LOADING PISTOL**

HK USP COMPACT UNIVERSAL SELF-LOADING PISTOL

SPECIFICATIONS
Calibers: 9mm, 40 S&W, and 45 ACP *Capacity:* 10 rounds
Operating System: Short recoil, modified Browning action
Barrel Length: 3.58" *Overall Length:* 6.81"
Weight: 1.70 lbs. (40 S&W); 1.60 lbs. (9mm)
Height: 5" *Sights:* Adjustable 3-dot
Grips: Polymer frame and integral grips
Prices:
9mm and 40 S&W $685.00
Also available:
Same specifications as above but with stainless
  steel slide: 731.00

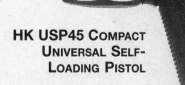

**HK USP45 COMPACT
UNIVERSAL SELF-
LOADING PISTOL**

HECKLER & KOCH

HK USP45 EXPERT

SPECIFICATIONS
Caliber: 45 ACP
Capacity: 10 rounds
Operating System: Short recoil, modified Browning action
Barrel Length: 6.02"
Overall Length: 9.45"
Weight: 2.38 lbs.
Height: 5.90"
Sights: Adjustable 3-dot
Grips & Stock: Polymer frame and integral grips
Prices:
Blued $1,369.00
Stainless Steel 1,441.00

HK USP Expert

MARK 23 SPECIAL OPERATIONS PISTOL (SOCOM)

SPECIFICATIONS
Caliber: 45 ACP
Capacity: 10 rounds
Operating System: Short recoil, modified Browning action
Barrel Length: 5.87"
Overall Length: 9.65"
Height: 5.9"
Weight: 2.66 lbs.
Sights: 3-dot
Grips: Polymer frame & integral grips
Price: $2,055.00

MARK 23 SPECIAL OPERATIONS PISTOL (SOCOM)

MODEL P7M8

MODEL P7M8

SPECIFICATIONS
Caliber: 9mmX19 (Luger)
Capacity: 8 rounds
Barrel Length: 4.13"
Overall Length: 6.73"
Weight: 1.75 lbs. (empty)
Sight Radius: 5.83"
Sights: Adjustable rear
Grips: Plastic *Finish:* Blue or nickel
Operating System: Recoil-operated; retarded inertia slide
Price: $1,222.00

HERITAGE MANUFACTURING

STEALTH COMPACT PISTOL

SPECIFICATIONS
Caliber: 9mm and 40 S&W
Capacity: 10 rounds
Barrel Length: 3.9"
Overall Length: 6.3"
Weight: 20 oz. *Height:* 4.2"
Triggerpull: 4 lbs. *Frame:* Black polymer
Styles: Model C-1000 17-4 Stainess steel slide; Model
C-2000 17-4 Black chrome slide; Model C-1010 17-4
Two-tone stainless steel/black chrome slide
Features: Striker-fire trigger; gas-delayed blow back
action; frame-mounted ambidextrous trigger safety; drop
safety; closed breech safety; magazine disconnect safety
Prices:
9mm $289.95
40 S&W 329.95

ROUGH RIDER SA

SPECIFICATIONS
Caliber: 22 LR or 22 LR/22 WMR
Capacity: 6 rounds *Weight:* 31 to 38 oz.
Barrel Lengths: 4.75", 6.5", 9" (regular grip); 2.75", 3.75",
4.75" (Bird's-Head grip) *Sights:* Blade front, fixed rear
Grips: Exotic hardwood *Finish:* Blue or nickel *Features:*
Rotating hammer block safety; brass accent screws
Prices:
22 LR (4.75", 6.5" bbl.) blued, regular grip. $119.95
22 LR/22 WMR
W/blued finish, regular grip:
4.75" & 6.5" barrels 139.95
9" barrel. 149.95
W/nickel finish, regular grip:
4.75" & 6.5" barrels 159.95
9" barrel. 169.95
W/blued finish, bird's-head grip:
2.75", 3.75" & 4.75" barrels 139.95
W/nickel finish: bird's-head grip:
2.75", 3.75" & 4.75" barrels 159.95

HIGH STANDARD

OLYMPIC RAPID FIRE

SPECIFICATIONS
Caliber: 22 Short *Capacity:* 5 rounds
Barrel length: 4" *Overall length:* 11.5" *Weight:* 46 oz.
Sights: Click-adjustable for windage and elevations (rear);
mounted on vent aluminum rib
Grips: Special International *Finish:* Matte blue
Features: Push-button barrel takedown system; trigger
adj. for weight of pull and travel; gold-plated trigger, slide
stop, safety and magazine release
Price: $1,995.00
Also available:
OLYMPIC MILITARY w/5.5" barrel $590.00

**OLYMPIC
RAPID FIRE**

HIGH STANDARD

SUPERMATIC CITATION

SPECIFICATIONS
Caliber: 22 LR *Capacity:* 10 rounds
Barrel length: 5.5" *Overall length:* 9.5"
Weight: 44 oz. *Finish:* Blued or Parkerized
Features: Optional Universal Mount to replace open-sight rib (deduct $30.00)
Price: $491.00
Also available:
SUPERMATIC CITATION MS. Similar to Citation above, except 10" barrel (14" overall), 54 oz. weight, RPM sights click-adjustable for windage and elevation, checkered right-hand thumbrest and matte blue finish $657.00
TROPHY/CITATION 22 SHORT CONVERSION KIT (incl. barrel w/sight, slide, 2 magazines) $299.00

SUPERMATIC CITATION

OLYMPIC MILITARY

SPECIFICATIONS
Caliber: 22 LR *Capacity:* 10 rounds
Barrel length: 5.5" *Overall length:* 9.5"
Weight: 44 oz. *Finish:* Matte frame
Features: Fully adjustable rear sight; non-adjustable trigger
Price: $590.00

OLYMPIC

SUPERMATIC TROPHY

SPECIFICATIONS
Caliber: 22 LR *Capacity:* 10 rounds
Actions: Recoil-operated semiautomatic
Barrel length: 5.5" bull or 7.25" fluted
Overall length: 9.5 (w/5.5" bbl.) and 11.25" (w/7.25" bbl.)
Weight: 44 oz. (w/5.5" bbl.) and 46 oz. (w/7.25" bbl.)
Sights: Click-adjustable rear for windage/elevation; undercut ramp front *Grips:* Checkered American walnut with right-hand thumbrest (left-hand optional)
Features: Gold-plated trigger; slide lock lever; push-button takedown system; magazine release
Prices: **5.5" BARREL** $569.00
7.25" BARREL 650.00

TROPHY

VICTOR 22 LR

SPECIFICATIONS
Caliber: 22 LR *Capacity:* 10 rounds
Barrel lengths: 4.5" and 5.5"
Overall length: 8.5" and 9.5"
Weight: 45 oz. (w/4.5" bbl.); 46 oz. (w/5.5" bbl.)
Finish: Blued or Parkerized frame
Features: Optional steel rib; click-adjustable sights for windage and elevation; optional barrel weights and Universal Mount (to replace open-sight rib)
Prices: $532.00
  w/5.5" barrel 591.00
Also available:
22 SHORT CONVERSION KIT 5.5" barrel w/vent rib, slide, two magazines $299.00

VICTOR 22 LR

HI-POINT FIREARMS

SEMI-AUTOMATIC HANDGUNS

Hi-Point Firearms offer reliability and accuracy at an affordable price. Hi-Point handguns are sized to feel good in your hand and provide exceptional recoil control. All models feature sleek lines and a scratch-resistant, non-glare military black finish with high-impact grips. New 3-dot sights.

MODEL .380

SPECIFICATIONS
Caliber: .380 ACP
Capacity: 8 shot mag
Action: Single action
Barrel Length: 3.5" alloy steel barrel
Sights: 3 dot sites
Safety: Quick on & off thumb safety
Overall Length: 6.75"
Weight): 29 oz.
Frame: Polymer
Price: $99.00

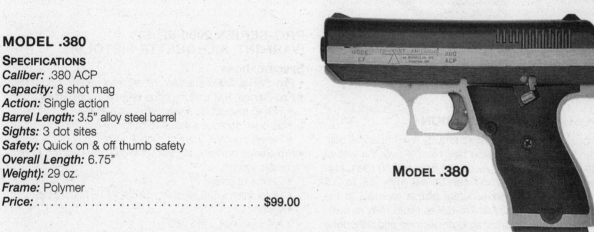

MODEL .380

MODEL 9mm

380 POLYMER

MODEL 9MM

SPECIFICATIONS
Caliber: 9mm Parabellum
Capacity: 9 shots
Barrel length: 4.5"
Overall length: 7.72"
Weight: 39 oz.
Sights: 3-dot type
Features: Quick on-off thumb safety; nonglare military black finish
Price: $139.95

MODEL 380 POLYMER

SPECIFICATIONS
Caliber: 380 ACP *Capacity:* 8 shots *Barrel length:* 3.5"
Price: $79.95
Also available in 45 ACP. Same specifications as the 9mm except w/7-shot capacity and military black finish.
Price: $148.95
MODEL 40 in 40 S&W. Same specifications as the
45 ACP w/8-shot capacity 148.95
MODEL 9mm COMPACT w/3.5" barrel 124.95
Also available w/polymer frame (same price)

H-S PRECISION

H-S SILHOUETTE PISTOL

H-S PRECISION

H-S Precision single-shot pistols employ a right-handle bolt, with handle engineered so the bolt head is over the well of the grip for good balance. As on the Series 2000 rifles, triggers are fully adjustable and can be set from 2.5 to 3.5 pounds pull. These super-accurate pistols are held to the same accuracy standards as Pro-Series rifles. They're available in many chamberings, in both varmint and silhouette versions. The silhouette pistol has a titanium safety shroud and a lighter barrel that is drilled and tapped for sights. It meets IHMSA competition weight requirements.
Price: (either version) **$1,250.00**

PRO-SERIES 2000 VP, SP (VARMINT, SILHOUETTE PISTOLS)

SPECIFICATIONS
- *Pro-Series 2000* stainless steel pistol action, single shot
- *Pro-Series 10X* match grade stainless steel barrel
  - Fluted (except 35 Rem, Silhouette style)
  - Sporter contour, silhouette model
  - Heavy contour, varmint model
- *Pro-Series* synthetic stock, center grip with bedding block chassis system
  - Choice of color
  - Metal finish – Teflon® or Pro-Series PFTE Matte Black
  - Weight*
    - 4.5 pounds, silhouette
    - 5.25 - 5.50 pounds, varmint
- Calibers – 17 Rem, 6mm PPC, 223 Rem, 22-250 Rem, 243 Win, 257 Roberts, 260 Rem, 35 Rem, 308 Winc, 7mm-08 Rem, 7mm BR

ISRAEL ARMS & FIREARMS INT'L

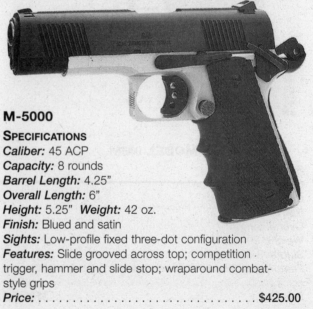

M-2500

SPECIFICATIONS
Calibers: 9mm, 40 S&W
Capacity: 10 rounds
Barrel Length: 3.9"
Overall Length: 7"
Height: 5.4" *Weight:* 34 oz.
Features: Double action; forged steel slide; ambidextrous controls; drop proof safety; chromed barrel; internal automatic safety
Price: **$525.00**

M-5000

SPECIFICATIONS
Caliber: 45 ACP
Capacity: 8 rounds
Barrel Length: 4.25"
Overall Length: 6"
Height: 5.25" *Weight:* 42 oz.
Finish: Blued and satin
Sights: Low-profile fixed three-dot configuration
Features: Slide grooved across top; competition trigger, hammer and slide stop; wraparound combat-style grips
Price: **$425.00**

KAHR ARMS

MODEL K9 PISTOL

All key components of the Kahr K9-frame, slide, barrel, etc. are made from 4140 steel, allowing the pistol to chamber reliably and fire virtually any commercial 9mm ammo, including +P rounds. The frame and sighting surfaces are matt blued, and the sides of the slide carry a polished blue finish.

SPECIFICATIONS
Caliber: 9mm (9x19), 40 S&W **Capacity:** 7 rounds (6 rounds 40 S&W) **Barrel length:** 3.5" **Overall length:** 6" (6.1" 40 S&W) **Height:** 4.5" (4.55" 40 S&W) **Weight (empty):** 25 oz.; 26 oz. (40 S&W) **Grips:** Wraparound soft polymer **Sights:** Drift-adjustable, low-profile white bar-dot combat sights **Finish:** Nonglare matte black finish on slide, frame sighting surfaces, electroless nickel, black titanium, satin hard chrome (matte black, electroless nickel only in 40 S&W) **Features:** Trigger cocking safety; passive firing-pin block; no magazine disconnect; locked breech **Also available:** MODEL MK9 MICRO-COMPACT 9mm. **Overall length:** 5.5" **Barrel length:** 3" **Weight:** 22 oz.

Price:	$605.00
w/night sights	692.00
In duo-tone	749.00
w/night sights	836.00

Prices: K9 PISTOL

Matte black	$538.00
Matte black w/night sights	624.00
Matte electroless nickel	612.00
Electroless nickel w/night sights	699.00
Black titanium	664.00
Black titanium w/night sights	750.00
Matte stainless	588.00
w/night sights	675.00

Prices: LADY K9

Lightened recoil spring, matte black	545.00
W/night sights	631.00
Satin electroless nickel	619.00
Electroless nickel w/night sights	706.00

KBI HANDGUNS

FEG SMC AUTO PISTOL

SPECIFICATIONS
Calibers: 380 ACP
Capacity: 6 rounds
Barrel Length: 3.5"
Overall Length: 6 1/8"
Weight: 18.5 oz.
Stock: Checkered composition w/thumbrest
Sights: Blade front; rear adjustable for windage
Features: Alloy frame; steel slide; double action; blue finish; two magazines and cleaning rod standard
Price: $209.00

FEG SMC

FEG MODEL PJK-9HP (HI-POWER)

SPECIFICATIONS
Caliber: 9mm Luger Parabellum
Magazine capacity: 10 rounds
Action: Single **Barrel Length:** 4.75"
Overall Length: 8" **Weight:** 21 oz.
Grips: Hand-checkered walnut
Safety: Thumb safety
Sights: 3-dot system **Finish:** Blue
Features: One 10-round magazine, cleaning rod
Price: $249.00

FEG MODEL PJK-9HP

KIMBER PISTOLS

CUSTOM
$657.00

CUSTOM STAINLESS
$774.00

SPECIFICATIONS .45 CUSTOM SERIES

	BARREL LENGTH	FINISH	SIGHTS	SIGHT RADIUS	APPROX. WEIGHT	OVERALL LENGTH	MAGAZINE CAPACITY	GRIPS
CUSTOM	5"	Matte Black Oxide	McCormick Low Profile Combat	6.7"	38 oz.	8.7"	7	Black Synthetic
CUSTOM STAINLESS	5"	Satin Stainless Steel	McCormick Low Profile Combat	6.7"	38 oz.	8.7"	7	Black Synthetic
CUSTOM ROYAL	5"	Highly Polished Blue	McCormick Low Profile Combat	6.7"	38 oz.	8.7"	7	Hand Checkered Rosewood
CUSTOM WALNUT	5"	Matte Black Oxide	McCormick Low Profile Combat	6.7"	38 oz.	8.7"	7	Hand Checkered Walnut

CUSTOM WALNUT (NOT SHOWN) – **$670.00**

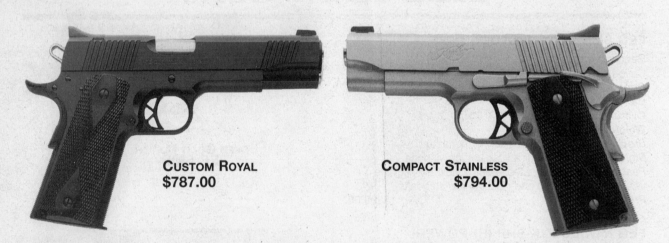

CUSTOM ROYAL
$787.00

COMPACT STAINLESS
$794.00

SPECIFICATIONS .45 COMPACT

	BARREL LENGTH	FINISH	SIGHTS	SIGHT RADIUS	APPROX. WEIGHT	OVERALL LENGTH	MAGAZINE CAPACITY	GRIPS
COMPACT	4"	Matte Black Oxide	McCormick Low Profile Combat	5.7"	34 oz.	7.7"	7	Black Synthetic
COMPACT STAINLESS	4"	Satin Stainless Steel	McCormick Low Profile Combat	5.7"	34 oz.	7.7"	7	Black Synthetic
CUSTOM ALUMINUM	4"	Matte Black	McCormick Low Profile Combat	5.7"	28 oz.	7.7"	7	Black Synthetic

COMPACT (NOT SHOWN) – **$677.00** COMPACT ALUMINUM (NOT SHOWN) – **$677.00**

KIMBER PISTOLS

GOLD MATCH
$1,019.00

CUSTOM TARGET
$745.00

SPECIFICATIONS

	BARREL LENGTH	FINISH	SIGHTS	SIGHT RADIUS	APPROX. WEIGHT	OVERALL LENGTH	MAGAZINE CAPACITY	GRIPS
CUSTOM TARGET	5"	Matte Black Oxide	Kimber Adjustable	6.7"	38 oz.	8.7"	7	Black Synthetic
STAINLESS TARGET	5"	Satin Stainless Steel	Kimber Adjustable	6.7"	38 oz.	8.7"	7	Black Synthetic
GOLD MATCH	5"	Highly Polished Blue	Kimber Adjustable	6.7"	38 oz.	8.7"	8	Hand Checkered Rosewood
STAINLESS GOLD MATCH	5"	Highly Polished Stainless Steel	Kimber Adjustable	6.7"	38 oz.	8.7"	8	Hand Checkered Rosewood

STAINLESS TARGET (NOT SHOWN) – **$863.00** **STAINLESS GOLD MATCH** (NOT SHOWN) – **$1,168.00**

POLYMER
$869.00

POLYMER GOLD MATCH
$957.00

SPECIFICATIONS .45 POLYMERS

	BARREL LENGTH	FINISH	SIGHTS	SIGHT RADIUS	APPROX. WEIGHT	OVERALL LENGTH	MAGAZINE CAPACITY	GRIPS
POLYMER	5"	Matte Black Oxide	McCormick Low Profile Combat	6.7"	34 oz.	8.75"	14	N/A
POLYMER STAINLESS	5"	Satin Stainless Steel Slide	McCormick Low Profile Combat	6.7"	34 oz.	8.75"	14	N/A
POLYMER GOLD MATCH	5"	Matte Black Oxide Slide	Kimber adjustable	6.7"	34 oz.	8.75"	14	N/A
POLYMER STAINLESS GOLD MATCH	5"	Satin Stainless Steel Slide	Kimber adjustable	6.7"	34 oz.	8.75"	14	N/A

POLYMER STAINLESS (NOT SHOWN) – **$948.00** **POLYMER STAINLESS TARGET** (NOT SHOWN) – **$1,036.00**

LLAMA AUTOMATIC PISTOLS

MINI-MAX 45

LLAMA CLASSIC AUTOMATIC PISTOL SPECIFICATIONS

SPECIFICATIONS:	MICRO-MAX	MINI-MAX	GOVERNMENT MODEL
CALIBERS:	.32/.380 ACP	45 Auto	45 Auto
FRAME:	Precision machined from high-strength steel	Precision machined from high-strength steel	Precision machined from high-strength steel
TRIGGER:	Serrated	Serrated	Serrated
HAMMER:	External; wide spur, serrated	External; military style	External; military style
OPERATION:	Straight blow-back	Locked breech	Locked breech
LOADED CHAMBER INDICATOR:	Yes	Yes	Yes
SAFETIES:	Extended manual & grip safeties	Extended manual & beavertail grip safeties	Extended manual & beavertail grip safeties
GRIPS:	Matte black polymer	Anatomically designed rubber grips	Anatomically designed rubber grips
SIGHTS:	Patridge-type front; square-notch rear	3-dot combat sight	3-dot combat sights
SIGHT RADIUS:	4 $\frac{1}{4}$"	6 $\frac{1}{4}$"	6 $\frac{1}{4}$"
MAGAZINE CAPACITY:	8 shots/7 shots	10 shots	10 shots
WEIGHT:	23 oz.	39 oz.	41 oz.
BARREL LENGTH:	3 $\frac{11}{16}$"	4 $\frac{1}{4}$"	5 $\frac{1}{8}$"
OVERALL LENGTH:	6 $\frac{1}{2}$"	7 $\frac{7}{8}$"	8 $\frac{1}{2}$"
HEIGHT:	4 $\frac{3}{8}$"	5 $\frac{7}{16}$"	5 $\frac{5}{16}$"
FINISH:	Standard; Non-glare combat matte. Deluxe: Satin chrome, Duo-tone	Deluxe Blue	Non-glare combat matte Satin chrome, Duo-tone
PRICES:	$264.95	$291.95	$298.95

LLAMA PISTOLS

MiniMax-II 45

Subcompact

Max-I 7-Shot 45 Auto

	COMPACT FRAME	GOVERNMENT MODEL
CALIBERS:	45 Auto	45 Auto
MAG. CAPACITY:	7	7
ACTION:	Single	Single
OPERATION:	Locked breech	Locked breech
BARREL LENGTH:	4 1/4"	5 1/8"
OVERALL LENGTH:	7 7/8"	8 1/2"
WEIGHT:	34 oz.	36 oz.
HEIGHT:	5 7/16"	5 5/16"
FRAME:	Precision machined from high-strength steel	
TRIGGER:	Serrated	Serrated
HAMMER:	Skeletonized combat-style	
LOADED CHAMBER INDICATOR:	Yes	Yes
SAFETIES:	Extended manual & beavertail grip safeties	
SIGHTS:	3-dot combat sights	
SIGHT RADIUS:	6 1/4"	6 1/4"
GRIPS:	Anatomically designed rubber grips	
FINISH:	Non-glare combat matte, Satin chrome, Duo-Tone	

MICRO-MAX/MINI-MAX/MAX-I AUTO PISTOLS

MATTE FINISH
380 Auto 7-Shot $264.95
32 Auto 8-Shot Ultra Lite 264.95
9mm Auto 8-Shot Mini Compact 281.95
40 S&W Auto 7-Shot Mini Compact 281.95
45 Auto 6-Shot Mini Compact 281.95
45 Auto 7-Shot Gov't Model. 291.95

SATIN CHROME FINISH
380 Auto 7-Shot $281.95
9mm Auto 8-Shot Mini Compact 304.95
40 S&W Auto 7-Shot Mini Compact 304.95
45 Auto 6-Shot Mini Compact 304.95
45 Auto 7-Shot Gov't Model. 314.95

DUO-TONE FINISH
45 Auto 7-Shot Gov't Model. 296.95
45 Auto 6-Shot Mini Compact Model 298.95

AMERICAN EAGLE LUGER

AMERICAN EAGLE LUGER®

9mm AMERICAN EAGLE LUGER®
STAINLESS STEEL

It is doubtful that there ever was a pistol created that evokes the nostalgia or mystique of the Luger pistol. Since its beginnings at the turn of the 20th century, the name Luger® conjures memories of the past. Stoeger Industries is indeed proud to have owned the name Luger® since the late 1920s and is equally proud of the stainless-steel version that graces this page.

The "American Eagle" name was introduced around 1900 to capture the American marketplace. It served its purpose well, the name having become legendary along with the Luger® name. The "American Eagle" inscribed on a Luger® also distinguishes a firearm of exceptional quality over some inexpensive models that have been manufactured in the past. Constructed entirely of stainless steel, the gun is available in 9mm Parabellum only, with either a 4" or 6" barrel, each with deeply checkered American walnut grips.

The name Luger®, combined with Stoeger's reputation of selling only quality merchandise since 1918, assures the owner of complete satisfaction.

SPECIFICATIONS
Caliber: 9mm Parabellum
Capacity: 7 + 1
Barrel Length: 4" (P-08 Model); 6" (Navy Model)
Overall Length: 8.25" (w/4" bbl.), 10.25" (w/6" bbl.)
Weight: 30 oz. w/4" barrel, 32 oz. w/6" barrel
Grips: Deeply checkered American walnut
Features: All stainless-steell construction
Price:. $720.00
In matte black 799.00

MAGNUM RESEARCH

MARK XIX COMPONENT SYSTEM

The Mark XIX Component system allows for three caliber changes in two different barrel lengths.

The Desert Eagle Pistol Mark XIX Component System is based on a single platform that transforms into six different pistols–three Magnum calibers, each with a 6-inch or 10-inch barrel. Changing calibers is a simple matter of switching barrels and magazines. (Converting to or from .357 Magnum also involves changing the bolt.)

The barrel design alone sports several improvements. Each barrel is now made of a single piece of steel instead of three. All six barrels, including the optional 10-inch barrels, have a $\frac{7}{8}$" dovetailed design with cross slots to accommodate scope rings; no other scope mounts are required. The .50 A.E.'s new 10-inch barrel will fit existing .50s, as well as the new Mark XIX platform.

Hogue soft rubber grips are standard equipment on the new gun. The pistol's gas operation, polygonal rifling, low recoil and safety features remain the same, as do the Mark VII adjustable trigger, slide release and safety levers.

SPECIFICATIONS
Calibers: 357 Magnum, 44 Magnum and 50 A.E.
Capacity: 9 rounds (357 Mag.); 8 rounds (44 Mag.); 7 rounds (50 A.E.)
Barrel Lengths: 6" and 10"
Overall Length: 10.74" (w/6" bbl.); 14.75" (w/10" bbl.)
Weight: 4 lbs. 6.5 oz. (w/6" bbl.); 4 lbs. 15 oz. (w/10" bbl.) (empty)
Height: 6.25" *Width:* 1.25"
Finish: Standard black
Prices:
357 MAG. w/6" barrel $1099.00
357 MAG. w/10" barrel 1199.00
44 MAG. w/6" barrel 1099.00
44 MAG. w/10" barrel 1199.00
50 A.E. MAG. w/6" barrel 1099.00
50 A.E. w/10" barrel 1199.00

LONE EAGLE SINGLE SHOT

This specialty pistol is designed for hunters, silhouette enthusiasts and long-range target shooters. Available w/interchangeable 14-inch barreled actions. Calibers: 22 Hornet, 22-250, 223 Rem., 243 Win., 30-06, 30-30, 308 Win., 35 Rem., 358 Win., 44 Mag., 444 Marlin, 7mm-08, 7mm Bench Rest., 7.62x39, 260 Rem., 440 Cor-Bon. Features ambidextrous grip, new cocking indicator and lever.

LONE EAGLE

Also available:
Barreled action w/muzzle brake **$418.00**
Barreled action w/chrome finish **$359.00**
Barreled action w/chrome finish, muzzle brake **$469.00**
Ambidextrous grip assembly **$119.00**

MAGNUM RESEARCH

BFR REVOLVER

BFR REVOLVER

"SINGLE-ACTION HUNTING REVOLVER"

For the first time, Magnum Research, Inc., creator of the legendary Desert Eagle Pistol, is offering a revolver. Magnum's BFR (Biggest Finest Revolver) is a single-action hunting revolver manufactured in the United States.

Magnum's BFR is available in two models, Maxine and Little Max, both built to close tolerances entirely of stainless steel. The long-cylindered Maxine fires big-bore calibers - .45/70, .444 Marlin, and .45 Long Colt/.410. Little Max is available in .454 Casull, .45 Long Colt + P, .50A.E., and the unique .22 Hornet. Grouse to grizzly,

squirrel to Kodiak bear, there's a BFR for every job.

Barrels lengths vary. The .45 Long Colt + P is available with a 6.5 or 7.5-inch barrel, the .454 Casull is available with a 6.5, 7.5 or 10-inch barrel, the .45/70 is available with a 7.5 or 10-inch barrel and the .22 Hornet is available with a 7.5 or 10-inch barrel. The .50 A.E. and .45 Long Colt/.410 are available only with a 7.5-inch barrel. The .444 Marlin is available only with a 10-inch barrel.

Price: **$899.00**

ACCESSORIES

BFR821	Hogue Rubber Finger Groove Grips	$34.95
BFR815	Hogue Wood Grips Pau Ferro	74.95
BFR816	Hogue Wood Grips Goncalo Alves	74.95
BFR-AAO	Full Choke Tube (0 marks)	17.00
BFR-AA00	Modified Choke Tube (2 marks)	17.00
BFR-AA1	Scatter Choke Tube (1 mark)	17.00
BFR-AA2	Choke Tube Wrench	5.00
BFR302/W	Millett sights, rear adjustable, white outline	39.95

Standard equipment sights have fixed orange front ramp and rear sight adjustable for windage and elevation.

MAGNUM RESEARCH/ASAI

ONE PRO 45 PISTOL

ONE PRO 45 PISTOL
$649.00

ASIA (Advanced Small Arms Industries) is a Swiss company founded in 1994 and based in Solothurn, an old Swiss City with long tradition in weapon and watch history. All key components of the new **One PRO .45** Series are made from chromium-nickel-molybdenium steel, allowing the pistol to fire any commercially manufactured ammunition, including +P rounds. The **One PRO .45** and **One PRO 400 Cor-Bon** are available with a patented safety system. A decocking lever allows the hammer to be lowered into the safety intercept notch without risk, and a new patented automatic firing pin lock allows the loaded, decocked gun to be carried safely.

SPECIFICATIONS
Caliber: .45 or 400 COR-BON
Capacity: 1
Barrel Length: 3.75" (4.52" in IPSC model)
Overall Length: 7.04"
Height: 5.31"
Weight (empty): 31.1 oz. (23.5 oz. in light alloy frame)
Width: 1.25"

Operation: Short recoil
Trigger Pull DA: 8.6 lbs.
Locking System: Dropping barrel
Features: Conversion kits available (includes recoil spring guide and hard plastic case).
Price: $249.00
    in 400 Cor-Bon Non-Compensated $209.00

BABY EAGLE

The new Baby Eagle FS in 9mm offers a frame-mounted safety and a shorter barrel than the standard Baby Eagle Pistol. The FS is available in standard black, matte hard chrome or brushed hard chrome (as shown). A polymer-frame version is also available. These autoloading pistols are manufactured to the highest quality standards by IMI.
Price: $389.00

MOA MAXIMUM PISTOLS

MAXIMUM SINGLE SHOT

MAXIMUM

This single-shot pistol with its unique falling-block action performs like a finely tuned rifle. The single-piece receiver of stainless steel is mated to a Douglas barrel for optimum accuracy and strength.

SPECIFICATIONS
Calibers: 22 Hornet to 375 H&H
Barrel Lengths: 8.5", 10.5" and 14"
Weight: 3 lbs. 8 oz. (8.5" bbl.); 3 lbs. 13 oz. (10.5" bbl.); 4 lbs. 3 oz. (14" bbl.)
Prices:
Stainless receiver, blued barrel $740.00
Stainless receiver and barrel 818.00
Extra barrels (blue) 235.00
   Stainless 293.00
Muzzle brake 125.00

NAVY ARMS REPLICAS

1873 SINGLE ACTION

1873 "PINCHED FRAME" SA REVOLVER

1873 COLT-STYLE SA REVOLVER

This classic Single Action is the best known of all the "six shooters." From its adoption by the U.S. Army in 1873 to the present, it retains its place as America's most famous revolver.

Calibers: 44-40 or 45 Long Colt
Barrel Lengths: 3", 4.75", 5.5" or 7.5"
Overall Length: 10.75" (5.5" barrel) **Weight:** 2.25 lbs.
Sights: Blade front; notch rear **Grips:** Walnut
Price: $385.00

1873 U.S. CAVALRY MODEL (not shown)

An exact replica of the original U.S. Government issue Colt Single-Action Army, complete with Arsenal stampings and inspector's cartouche.

Caliber: 45 Long Colt **Barrel Length:** 7.5"
Overall Length: 13.25" **Weight:** 2 lbs. 7 oz.
Sights: Blade front; notch rear **Grips:** Walnut
Price: $455.00

1873 "PINCHED FRAME" SA REVOLVER

A replica of the early "pinched frame" Colt Peacemaker, the first run commercial Single Action manufactured in 1873.

Caliber: 45 Long Colt **Barrel Length:** 7.5"
Overall Length: 13.75" **Weight:** 2 lbs. 13 oz. **Sights:** German siver blade front, U-shaped "pinched-frame" rear notch
Price: $415.00

"FLAT TOP" TARGET MODEL SA REVOLVER (not shown)

A fine replica of Colt's rare "Flat top" Single Action Army revolver that was used for target shooting.

Caliber: 45 Long Colt **Barrel Length:** 7.5"
Overall Length: 12.75" **Weight:** 2 lbs. 7 oz.
Sights: Spring-loaded German silver Patridge front, adjustable notch ear.
Grips: Walnut. **Finish:** Blue
Price: $430.00

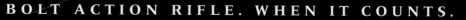

MORE FUN THAN AN EMPTY CAN SHOULD BE.

SERIOUS FUN

 Just because you're in it for fun, doesn't mean you're not serious. Browning introduces three new ways to take your shooting seriously. The Buck Mark Challenge and Challenge Micro feature throwback styling and a smaller grip circumference for shooters who prefer a slimmer grip. The Buck Mark Camper features a rugged matte finish and rubber grips. It is an economic alternative for shooters who insist on Browning quality.

 Of course these new models have all the same high-end features as the rest of the Buck Mark line, like a frame machined from a solid billet of 7075-T6 aluminum and an adjustable Pro-Target sight that has 16 clicks per revolution instead of 12.

 These features are in all 28 Buck Mark Pistol models because we are as serious as you are — serious about quality and serious about fun.

BROWNING®

Visit your Browning dealer for a 1999 Master Catalog or call 1-800-333-3504. www.browning.com

TIKKA

take it to

extremely
Finnish

EXTREMES

NAVY ARMS REPLICAS

1875 SCHOFIELD CAVALRY MODEL REVOLVER

1875 SCHOFIELD REVOLVER

A favorite side arm of Jesse James, the hinged-breech 1875 Schofield revolver was one of the legendary handguns of the Old West.

Caliber: 44-40, 45 LC *Barrel Lengths:* 3" (Hide Out Model), 5" (Wells Fargo Model) or 7" (U.S. Cavalry Model) *Overall Length:* 8.75", 10.75" or 12.75" *Weight:* 2 lbs. 7 oz. *Sights:* Blade front; notch rear *Features:* Top-break, automatic ejector single action
Price: $695.00

NEW MODEL RUSSIAN REVOLVER

NAVY ARMS NEW MODEL RUSSIAN REVOLVER

A replica of the Smith and Wesson Model 3 Russian Third Model top break revolver that was carried by Western Lawman Pat Garrett.

Caliber: .44 Russian *Barrel Lengths:* 6.5"
Overall Length: 12" *Weight:* 2 lbs. 8 oz.
Sights: Blade front; notch rear
Grips: Walnut
Price: $745.00

BISLEY MODEL SINGLE ACTION REVOLVER
(not shown)

Introduced in 1894, Colt's "Bisley Model" was named after the Bisley shooting range in England. Most of these revolvers were sold in the United States and were popular sidearms in the American West at the turn of the century.

This replica features the unique Bisley grip style, low-profile spur hammer, blued barrel and color casehardened frame.

Calibers: 44-40 or 45 Long Colt *Barrel Lengths:* 4.75", 5.5" and 7.5" *Sights:* Blade front, notch rear *Grips:* Walnut
Price: $445.00

NEW ENGLAND FIREARMS

STANDARD REVOLVER
with Swing Out Cylinders

SPECIFICATIONS
Calibers: 22 S, L or LR
Capacity: 9 shots
Barrel Lengths: 3" and 4"
Overall Length: 7" (3" barrel) and 8.5" (4" barrel)
Weight: 25 oz. (3" bbl.) and 28 (4" bbl.)
Sights: Blade front; fixed rear
Grips: American hardwood, walnut finish, NEF medallion
Finish: Blue or nickel
Also available:
In 5-shot, calibers 32 H&R Mag., 32 S&W, 32 S&W Long.
Weight: 23 oz. (3" barrel); 26 oz. (4" barrel). Other specifications same as above.
Prices:
  Blued finish **$143.95**
  Nickel finish (3" bbl. only) **153.95**
STARTER REVOLVER (pull pin cylinder & lanyard ring) in 22 cal.
Capacity: 5 and 9 shot. *Finish:* Blued
Price: **$115.95**

STANDARD MODEL
(22 LR, 3" BARREL)

ULTRA MAG.

ULTRA MODEL
(6" BARREL)

ULTRA AND ULTRA MAG. REVOLVERS

SPECIFICATIONS
Calibers: 22 Short, Long, Long Rifle (Ultra); 22 Win. Mag. (Ultra Mag.)
Capacity: 9 shots (22 LR); 6 shots (22 Win. Mag.)
Barrel Length: 6"
Overall Length: 11" *Weight:* 36 oz.
Sights: Blade on rib front; fully adjustable rear
Grips: American hardwood, walnut finish, NEF medallion
Finish: Blue
Price: **$179.95**
Also available:
LADY ULTRA in 5-shot 32 H&R Magnum. *Barrel Length:* 3"
Overall Length: 7" *Weight:* 31 oz.
Price: **$179.95**

LADY ULTRA

NORTH AMERICAN ARMS

22 LR MINI-REVOLVER
w/NAA HOLSTER GRIP

MINI-REVOLVERS

SPECIFICATIONS (See also table below)
Calibers: 22 Short (1 1/8" bbl. only), 22 LR and 22 Magnum
Capacity: 5-shot cylinder
Grips: Laminated rosewood
Safety: Half-cock safety
Sights: Blade front (integral w/barrel); fixed, notched rear
Material: Stainless steel
Finish: Matte with brushed sides

MINI-MASTER NAA-MMT-M
(22 MAG. 4" BARREL)

MINI-MASTER NAA
BLACK WIDOW

MINI-MASTER SERIES

SPECIFICATIONS (Standard on all models)
Calibers: 22 LR (NAA-MMT-L, NAA-BW-L) and 22 Magnum (NAA-MMT-M, NAA-BW-M)
Barrel: Heavy vent
Rifling: 8 land and grooves, 1:12 R.H. button broach twist
Grips: Oversized black rubber **Cylinder:** Bull
Sights: Front integral with barrel; rear Millett adjustable

white outlined (elelvation only) or low-profile fixed
Prices:
MINI-MASTER NAA-MMT-M $299.00
  w/Fixed sight 281.00
MINI-MASTER NAA BLACK WIDOW
  Adjustable sight $269.00
  Fixed sight 251.00

SPECIFICATIONS: MINI-REVOLVERS & MINI-MASTER SERIES

MODEL	WEIGHT	BARREL LENGTH	OVERALL LENGTH	OVERALL HEIGHT	OVERALL WIDTH	PRICE
NAA-MMT-M	10.7 oz.	4"	7 3/4"	3 7/8"	7/8"	$299.00
NAA-MMT-L	10.7 oz.	4"	7 3/4"	3 7/8"	7/8"	299.00
*NAA-BW-M	8.8 oz.	2"	5 7/8"	3 7/8"	7/8"	251.00
*NAA-BW-L	8.8 oz.	2"	5 7/8"	3 7/8"	7/8"	251.00
NAA-22LR**	4.5 oz.	1 1/8"	4 1/4"	2 3/8"	13/16"	176.00
NAA-22LLR**	4.6 oz.	1 5/8"	4 3/4"	2 3/8"	13/16"	176.00
*NAA-22MS	5.9 oz.	1 1/8"	5"	2 7/8"	7/8"	194.00
*NAA-22M	6.2 oz.	1 5/8"	5 3/8"	2 7/8"	7/8"	194.00

*Available with Conversion Cylinder chambered for 22 Long Rifle **($288.00)** **Available with holster grip **($209.00)**

PARA-ORDNANCE

MODEL P10•45ER
(BLACK)

MODEL P10•45TR
(DUOTONE)

MODEL P10•45SR
(STAINLESS)

P-SERIES PISTOL SPECIFICATIONS *(continued on following page)*

MODEL	CALIBER	BARREL LENGTH	WEIGHT (OZ.)	OVERALL LENGTH)	HEIGHT (W/MAG.)	RECEIVER TYPE	MATTE FINISH	PRICES
P10•40ER	40 S&W	3"	31	6 5/8"	4.5"	Steel	Black	$750.00
P10•40RR	40 S&W	3"	23	6 5/8"	4.5"	Alloy	Black	740.00
P10•40TR	40 S&W	3"	31	6 5/8"	4.5"	Stainless	Duotone	785.00
P10•40SR	40 S&W	3"	31	6 5/8"	4.5"	Stainless	Stainless	799.00
P10•45ER	45 ACP	3"	31	6 5/8"	4.5"	Steel	Black	750.00
P10•45RR	45 ACP	3"	23	6 5/8"	4.5"	Alloy	Black	740.00
P10•45TR	45 ACP	3"	31	6 5/8"	4.5"	Stainless	Duotone	785.00
P10•45SR	45 ACP	3"	31	6 5/8"	4.5"	Stainless	Stainless	799.00
P12•45ER	45 ACP	3.5"	34	7 5/8"	5"	Steel	Black	750.00
P12•45RR	45 ACP	3.5"	26	7 5/8"	5"	Alloy	Black	740.00
P12•45TR	45 ACP	3.5"	34	7 5/8"	5"	Stainless	Duotone	785.00
P12•45SR	45 ACP	3.5"	34	7 5/8"	5"	Stainless	Stainless	799.00
P13•45ER	45 ACP	4.25"	36	7.75"	5.25"	Steel	Black	750.00
P13•45RR	45 ACP	4.25"	28	7.75"	5.25"	Alloy	Black	740.00
P13•45TR	45 ACP	4.25"	36	7.75"	5.25"	Stainless	Duotone	785.00
P13•45SR	45 ACP	4.25"	36	7.75"	5.25"	Stainless	Stainless	799.00

For recreational purposes, magazine capacities are restricted to 10 rounds.

PARA-ORDNANCE

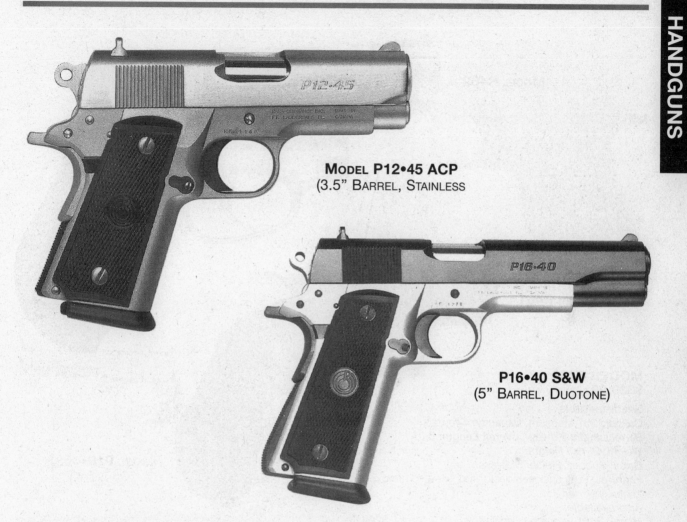

MODEL P12•45 ACP
(3.5" BARREL, STAINLESS

P16•40 S&W
(5" BARREL, DUOTONE)

P-SERIES PISTOL SPECIFICATIONS *(Cont.)*

MODEL	CALIBER	BARREL LENGTH	WEIGHT (OZ.)	OVERALL LENGTH)	HEIGHT (W/MAG.)	RECEIVER TYPE	MATTE FINISH	PRICES
P14•45ER	45 ACP	5"	40	8.5"	5.75"	Steel	Black	$750.00
P14•45RR	45 ACP	5"	31	8.5"	5.75"	Alloy	Black	740.00
P14•45TR	45 ACP	5"	40	8.5"	5.75"	Stainless	Duotone	785.00
P14•45SR	45 ACP	5"	40	8.5"	5.75"	Stainless	Stainless	799.00
P15•40ER	40 S&W	4.25"	36	7.75"	5.25"	Steel	Black	750.00
P15•40RR	40 S&W	4.25"	28	7.75"	5.25"	Alloy	Black	740.00
P15•40TR	40 S&W	4.25"	36	7.75"	5.25"	Stainless	Duotone	785.00
P15•40SR	40 S&W	4.25	36	7.75"	5.25"	Stainless	Stainless	799.50
P16•40ER	40 S&W	5"	40	8.5"	5.75"	Steel	Black	750.00
P16•40TR	40 S&W	5"	40	8.5"	5.75	Stainless	Duotone	785.00
P16•40SR	40 S&W	5"	40	8.5"	5.75"	Stainless	Stainless	799.00

For recreational purposes, magazine capacities are restricted to 10 rounds.

Also available: P109RR 3" or 5" barrel in 9mm: **$740.00**

ROSSI REVOLVERS

MODEL R462

MODEL R461

MODEL R462
$339.00

SPECIFICATIONS
Caliber: 357 Magnum *Capacity:* 6 rounds
Barrel Length: 2" heavy *Overall Length:* 6.87"
Weight: 26 oz. *Height:* 5"
Grips: Rubber *Finish:* Stainless
Features: Fully enclosed ejector rod; serrated ramp
front sight
Also available:
MODEL **R461** w/matte blued finish $299.00

MODEL R352

SPECIFICATIONS
Caliber: 38 Special
Capacity: 5 rounds, swing-out cylinder
Barrel Lengths: 2"
Overall Length: 6.87" (2" barrel)
Weight: 22 oz. (2")
Sights: Ramp front, square-notched rear adjustable
for windage
Grips: rubber (2" barrel only)
Finish: Stainless steel
Price: $299.00
Also available:
MODEL **R351** (not shown) w/matte blue finish **259.00**

MODEL R352

RUGER REVOLVERS

REDHAWK REVOLVER

STAINLESS REDHAWK
MODEL KRH-44

STAINLESS REDHAWK
W/SCOPE (KRH-44R)

SUPER REDHAWK STAINLESS
MODEL KSRH-9

BLUED STEEL REDHAWK REVOLVER

The popular Ruger Redhawk® double-action revolver is available in an alloy steel model with blued finish or high-gloss standard steel in 44 Magnum caliber. Constructed of hardened chrome-moly and other alloy steels, this Redhawk is satin polished to a high luster and finished in a rich blue.

SPECIFICATIONS
Capacity: 6 rounds

CATALOG NUMBER	CALIBER	BARREL LENGTH	OVERALL LENGTH	APPROX. WEIGHT (OUNCES)	PRICE
RUGER BLUED REDHAWK REVOLVER					
RH-445	44 Mag.	5.5"	11"	49	$515.00
RH-44	44 Mag.	7.5"	13"	54	515.00
RH-44R*	44 Mag.	7.5"	13"	54	553.00

Scope model, with Integral Scope Mounts, 1" Ruger Scope rings.

STAINLESS REDHAWK DOUBLE-ACTION REVOLVER

CATALOG NUMBER	CALIBER	BARREL LENGTH	OVERALL LENGTH	APPROX. WEIGHT (OUNCES)	PRICE
RUGER STAINLESS REDHAWK REVOLVER					
KRH-445	44 Mag.	5.5"	11"	49	$574.00
KRH-44	44 Mag.	7.5"	13"	54	574.00
KRH-44R*	44 Mag.	7.5"	13"	54	618.00
KRH-455	45 LC	5.5"	11"	49	574.00
KRH-45	45 LC	7.5"	13"	54	574.00
KRH-45R*	45 LC	7.5"	13"	54	618.00

Scope model, with Integral Scope Mounts, 1" Stainless Steel Ruger Scope rings.

SUPER REDHAWK STAINLESS DOUBLE-ACTION REVOLVER

The Super Redhawk double-action revolver in stainless steel features a heavy extended frame with 7.5" and 9.5" barrels. Cushioned grip panels w/wood inserts provide comfortable, nonslip hold. Comes with case and lock, integral scope mounts and 1" stainless steel Ruger scope rings.

SPECIFICATIONS
Caliber: 44 Magnum, 454 Casull
Barrel Lengths: 7.5" and 9.5"
Overall Length: 13" w/7.5" bbl.; 15" w/9.5" bbl.
Weight (empty): 53 oz. (7.5" bbl.); 11.25" (9.5" bbl.)
Sight radius: 9.5" (7.5" bbl.); 11.25" (9.5" bbl.)
Finish: Stainless steell; satin polished

KSRH-7 (7.5" barrel) $618.00
KSRH-9 (9.5" barrel)) 618.00
KSRH-7454 (7.5" barrel) .454 Casull. 745.00

RUGER SINGLE-ACTION REVOLVERS

VAQUERO SINGLE ACTION
$455.00 (ALL MODELS)

BISLEY-VAQUERO

The original Bisley single-action design developed in the 1890s was created for England's famous target shooting matches held at Bisley Common. Modification and repositioning of the grip to a nearly vertical position greatly reduced a tendency of some standard-frame single-action grips to "ride-up" in the shooter's hand during recoil. Maintaining the same hand positioning on a revolver's grip from shot to shot is an important part of target shooting. The Bisley hammer is lower and has a wide spur. This enables a shooter to cock the hammer with a minimum amount of disturbance to the hand

and revolver position. The Ruger Vaquero has been extremely popular since its introduction a few years ago. Its "color case finish" and fixed sights combined the latest Ruger new model single-action revolver mechanism with the classic appearance of the revolver of a century ago. The design of the Bisley-Vaquero has captured renewed interest among serious single-action target shooters and Cowboy Action Shooters alike. As with the Vaquero, the new Ruger Bisley-Vaquero is based on the Ruger New Model Blackhawk, single-action revolver, in production since 1973.

BISLEY-VAQUERO SINGLE-ACTION REVOLVER

SPECIFICATIONS

Calibers: .44 Magnum and .45 Long Colt
Capacity: 6 rounds
Barrel Length: 5.5" **Overall Length:** 11.375"
Safety: Transfer bar and loading gate interlock
Sights: Blade front; notch rear; fixed
Sights Radius: 6.5"
Weight (Approx.): 40 oz.
Grips: Smooth rosewood with inletted Ruger medallion

Finish: Blued: "color case finish" on frame; polished and blued barrel and cylinder
Features: Instruction manual, lockable plastic case with lock; heat treated Chrome-moly steel frame, barrel and grip (blued version); 400 stainless steel
Prices:
MODELS RBNV-475 AND RBNV-455 . . . . $472.00
MODELS KRBNV-475 AND KRBNV-455 . . . . 512.00
   (Simulated ivory grips **$36.00** additional)

SPECIFICATIONS: VAQUERO SA

CATALOG NUMBER	CALIBER	FINISH*	BARREL LENGTH	OVERALL LENGTH	APPROX. WT (OZ.)	CATALOG NUMBER	CALIBER	FINISH*	BARREL LENGTH	OVERALL LENGTH	APPROX. WT (OZ.)
BNV34	357 Mag.+	CB	4 5/8"	10.25"	39	BNV475	44 Mag.	CB	5.5"	11.5"	40
KBNV34	357 Mag.+	SSG	4 5/8"	10.25"	39	KBNV475	44 Mag.	SSG	5.5"	11.5"	40
BNV35	357 Mag.+	CB	5.5"	11.5"	40	BNV477	44 Mag.	CB	7.5"	13 1/8"	41
KBNV35	357 Mag.+	SSG	5.5"	11.5"	40	KBNV477	44 Mag.	SSG	7.5"	13 1/8"	41
BNV40	44-40	CB	4 5/8"	10.25"	39	BNV44	45 Long Colt	CB	4 5/8"	10.25"	39
KBNV40	44-40	SSG	4 5/8"	10.25"	39	KBNV44	45 Long Colt	SSG	4 5/8"	10.25"	39
BNV405	44-40	CB	5.5"	11.5"	40	BNV455	45 Long Colt	CB	5.5"	11.5"	40
KBNV405	44-40	SSG	5.5"	11.5"	40	KBNV455	45 Long Colt	SSG	5.5"	11.5"	40
BNV407	44-40	CB	7.5"	13 1/8"	41	BNV45	45 Long Colt	CB	7.5"	13 1/8"	41
KBNV407	44-40	SSG	7.5"	13 1/8"	41	KBNV45	45 Long Colt	SSG	7.5"	13 1/8"	41

*Finish: high-gloss stainless steel (SSG); "color-cased finish" on steel cylinder frame w/blued steel grip, barrel and cylinder (CB).
With similated ivory grips: **$548.00 (add **$56.00** for engraved cylinder).

RUGER SINGLE-ACTION REVOLVERS

NEW MODEL BLACKHAWK REVOLVER

NEW MODEL
BLACKHAWK REVOLVER
MODEL KBN-36
STAINLESS STEEL
6 ¹/₂" barrel

SPECIFICATIONS: NEW MODEL BLACKHAWK AND BLACKHAWK CONVERTIBLE

Cat. Number	Caliber	Finish**	Bbl. Length	O.A. Length	Weight (Oz.)	Price
BN34	357 Mag.++	B	4 ⁵/₈"	10 ³/₈"	40	$380.00
KBN34	357 Mag.++	SS	4 ⁵/₈"	10 ³/₈"	40	467.00
BN36	357 Mag.++	B	6.5"	12.25"	42	380.00
KBN36	357 Mag.++	SS	6.5"	12.5"	42	467.00
BN34X*	357 Mag.++	B	4 ⁵/₈"	10 ³/₈"	40	405.00
BN36X*	357 Mag.++	B	6.5"	12.25"	42	405.00
BN44	45 Long Colt	B	4 ⁵/₈"	10.25"	39	380.00
KBN44	45 Long Colt	SS	4 ⁵/₈"	10.25"	39	467.00
BN455	45 Long Colt	B	5.5"	11 ¹/₈"	39	380.00
BN45	45 Long Colt	B	7.5"	13 ¹/₈"	41	380.00
KBN45	45 Long Colt	SS	7.5"	13 ¹/₈"	41	467.00

*Convertible: Designated by an X in the Catalog Number, this model comes with an extra interchangeable .38 Special cylinder; price includes extra cylinder. **Finish: blued (B); stainless steel (SS); high-gloss stainless steel (HGSS); color-cased finish on the steel cylinder frame with blued steel grip, barrel, and cylinder (CB). Also available: Models BN44X and BN455X in .45 Convertible (6-shot). Price: $405.00

RUGER REVOLVERS

NEW SUPER MODEL BLACKHAWK
SINGLE-ACTION REVOLVER

NEW MODEL SUPER BLACKHAWK SINGLE-ACTION REVOLVER

SPECIFICATIONS
Caliber: 44 Magnum; interchangeable with 44 Special
Barrel Lengths: 4 ⁵/₈", 5.5", 7.5", 10.5"
Overall Length: 13 ³/₈" (7.5" barrel)
Weight: 45 oz. (4 ⁵/₈ bbl.), 46 oz. (5.5" bbl.), 48 oz. (7.5" bbl.) and 51 oz. (10.5" bbl.)
Frame: Chrome molybdenum steel or stainless steel
Springs: Music wire springs throughout
Sights: Patridge style, ramp front matted blade 18" wide; rear sight click-adjustable for windage and elevation
Grip Frame: Chrome molybdenum or stainless steel, enlarged and contoured to minimize recoil effect
Trigger: Wide spur, low contour, sharply serrated for convenient cocking with minimum disturbance of grip

Finish: Polished and blued or brushed satin stainless steel
Features: Case and lock included
Prices:
KS45N
   5.5" bbl., brushed or high-gloss stainless **$475.00**
KS458N
   4 ⁵/₈" bbl., brushed or high-gloss stainless **475.00**
KS47N
   7.5" bbl., brushed or high-gloss stainless **475.00**
KS411N 10.5" bull bbl., stainless steel **480.00**
S45N 5.5" bbl., blued **435.00**
S458N 4 ⁵/₈" bbl., blued **435.00**
S47N 7.5" bbl., blued **435.00**
S411N 10.5" bull bbl., blued. **440.00**

FIXED SIGHT NEW MODEL SINGLE-SIX
(W/EXTRA CYLINDER)

FIXED SIGHT NEW MODEL SINGLE-SIX

SPECIFICATIONS
Caliber: 22 LR (fitted with 22 WMR cylinder)
Barrel Lengths: 4 ⁵/₈", 5.5", 6.5", 9.5"; stainless steel model in 5.5" and 6.5" lengths only
Weight (approx.): 33 oz. (with 5.5" barrel); 38 oz. (with 9.5" barrel)
Sights: Patridge-type ramp front sight; rear sight click adjustable for elevation and windage; protected by integral

frame ribs. Fixed sight model available with 5.5" or 6.5" barrel (same prices as adj. sight models).
Finish: Blue or stainless steel *Features:* Case and lock incl.
Prices:
Blue $335.00
   9 ¹/₂" barrel. 335.00
Stainless steel
   (convertible 5.5" and 6.5" barrels only) 415.00

RUGER REVOLVERS

MODEL SP101 SPURLESS DA
$443.00

GP-100 357 MAGNUM
6" HEAVY BARREL

GP-100 DA 357 MAGNUM

The GP-100 is designed for the unlimited use of 357 Magnum ammunition in all factory loadings; it combines strength and reliability with accuracy and shooting comfort. (Revolvers chambered for the 357 Magnum cartridge also accept the 38 Special cartridge.)

SPECIFICATIONS SP101 REVOLVERS

Catalog Number	Caliber	Cap.*	Sights	Barrel Length	Approx Wt. (Oz.)
KSP-221	22 LR	6	A	2.25"	32
KSP-240	22 LR	6	A	4"	33
KSP-241	22 LR	6	A	4"	34
KSP-3231	32 Mag.	6	A	3 1/16"	30
KSP-3241	32 Mag.	6	A	4"	33
KSP-921	9mmx19	5	F	2.25"	25
KSP-931	9mmx19	5	F	3 1/16"	27
KSP-821	38+P	5	F	2.25"	25
KSP-831	38+P	5	F	3 1/16"	27
KSP-321X**	357 Mag.	5	F	2.25"	25
KSP-321XL**	357 Mag.	5	F	2.25"	25
KSP-331X**	357 Mag.	5	F	3 1/16"	27

*Indicates cylinder capacity
**Revolvers chambered for 357 Magnum also accept 38 Special cartridges.
Model KSP-240 has short shroud; all others have full.
L = spurless hammer

SPECIFICATIONS

Catalog Number	Finish	Sights+	Shroud++	Barrel Length	Wt. (Oz.)	Price
GP-141	B	A	F	4"	41	**$440.00**
GP-160	B	A	S	6"	43	**440.00**
GP-161	B	A	F	6"	46	**474.00**
GPF-331	B	F	F	3"	36	**423.00**
GPF-340	B	F	S	4"	37	**423.00**
GPF-341	B	F	F	4"	38	**457.00**
KGP-141	SS	A	F	4"	41	**474.00**
KGP-160	SS	A	S	6"	43	**474.00**
KGP-161	SS	A	F	6"	46	**474.00**
KGPF-330	SS	F	S	3"	35	**457.00**
KGPF-331	SS	F	F	3"	36	**457.00**
KGPF-340	SS	F	S	4"	37	**457.00**
KGPF-341	SS	F	F	4"	38	**457.00**
KGPF-840*	SS	F	S	4"	37	**457.00**
GPF-841*	SS	F	F	4"	38	**457.00**

*38 Special only. B = blued; SS = stainless; A = adjustable; F = fixed. ++ F = full; S = short.

RUGER REVOLVERS

BISLEY SINGLE-ACTION TARGET GUN

BISLEY SINGLE-ACTION TARGET GUN

The Bisley single-action was originally used at the British National Rifle Association matches held in Bisley, England, in the 1890s. Today's Ruger Bisleys are offered in two frame sizes, chambered from 22 LR to 45 Long Colt. These revolvers are the target-model versions of the Ruger single-action line.

Special Features: Unfluted cylinder roll-marked with classic foliate engraving pattern; hammer is low with smoothly curved, deeply checkered wide spur positioned for easy cocking.

Prices:
22 LR $402.00
357 Mag., 44 Mag., 45 Long Colt. 472.00

BISLEY SPECIFICATIONS

Catalog Number	Caliber	Barrel Length	Overall Length	Sights	Approx. Wt. (Oz.)
RB22AW	22 LR	6.5"	11.5"	Adj.	41
RB35W	357 Mag.	7.5"	13"	Adj.	48
RB44W	44 Mag.	7.5"	13"	Adj.	48
RB45W	45 LC	7.5"	13"	Adj.	48

Dovetail rear sight adjustable for windage only.

THE NEW BEARCAT

THE SBC-4 NEW BEARCAT

Originally manufactured between 1958 and 1973, the 22-rimfire single-action Bearcat features an all-steel precision investment-cast frame and patented transfer-bar mechanism. The New Bearcat also has walnut grips with the Ruger medallion.

SPECIFICATIONS
Caliber: 22 LR
Capacity: 6 shots
Barrel Length: 4"
Grips: Walnut
Finish: Blued chrome-moly steel
Price:
    Blued. $330.00

RUGER P-SERIES PISTOLS

MODEL P93 (not shown)

SPECIFICATIONS (See also table below)
Barrel Length: 3.9" **Overall Length:** 7.3"
Height: 5.75" **Width:** 1.5"
Weight: 31 oz.
Sights: 3-dot system; square-notch rear, drift adjustable for windage; square post front (both sights have white dots)
Mechanism: Recoil-operated, double action, autoloading
Features: Oversized trigger guard with curved trigger guard bow; slide stop activated automatically on last shot (w/magazine in pistol); all stainless steel models made with "Terhune Anticorro" steel for maximum corrosion resistance

MODEL KP95D

MODEL P94

SPECIFICATIONS (See also table below)
Barrel Length: 4.5"
Capacity: 10 rounds
Overall Length: 7.5"
Weight: 33 oz. (empty magazine)
Height: 5.5"
Width: 1.5"
Sight Radius: 5"
Sights: 3-dot system
Features: See Model P93

MODEL KP94 9mm
(4.5" Barrel)

SPECIFICATIONS P SERIES PISTOLS

CAT. NUMBER	MODEL	FINISH	CALIBER	MAG. CAP.	PRICE
P89	Manual Safety	Blued	9mm	10	$430.00
KP89	Manual Safety	Stainless	9mm	10	475.00
P89D	Decock Only	Blued	9mm	10	430.00
KP89D	Decock Only	Stainless	9mm	10	475.00
KP89DAO	Double-Action Only	Stainless	9mm	10	475.00
KP90*	Manual Safety	Stainless	45 ACP	7	513.00
KP90D	Decock Only	Stainless	45 ACP	7	513.00
KP93D**	Decock Only	Stainless	9mm	10	520.00
KP93DAO	Double-Action Only	Stainless	9mm	10	520.00
KP94***	Manual Safety	Stainless	9mm	10	520.00
KP94D	Decock Only	Stainless	9mm	10	520.00
KP94DAO	Double-Action Only	Stainless	9mm	10	520.00
KP944	Manual Safety	Stainless	40 Auto	10	520.00
KP944D	Decock Only	Stainless	40 Auto	10	520.00
KP944DAO	Double-Action Only	Stainless	40 Auto	10	520.00
KP95D	Decock Only	Stainless	9mm	10	387.00
KP95DAO	Double-Action Only	Stainless	9mm	10	387.00
P95D	Decock Only	Blued, Stainless Frame	9mm	10	351.00
P95DAO	Double-Action Only	Blued, Stainless Frame	9mm	10	351.00

*Available w/ambidextrous safety, blued (**$454.00**) Model P90.   **Available w/ambidextrous decocker, blued (**$421.50**) Model P93D.
***Available w/ambidextrous safety, blued (**$421.50**) Model P94.

RUGER 22 AUTOMATIC PISTOLS

MARK II STANDARD MODEL

MARK II STANDARD MODEL

The Ruger Mark II models represent continuing refinements of the original Ruger Standard and Mark I Target Model pistols. More than two million of this series of autoloading rimfire pistol have been produced since 1949.

The bolts on all Ruger Mark II pistols lock open automatically when the last cartridge is fired, if the magazine is in the pistol. The bolt can be operated manually with the safety in the "on" position for added security while loading and unloading. A boltstop can be activated manually to lock the bolt open.

The Ruger Mark II pistol uses 22 Long Rifle ammunition in a detachable, 10-shot magazine (standard on all Mark II models except Model 22/45, whose 10-shot magazine is not interchangeable with other Mark II magazines). Designed for easy insertion and removal, the Mark II magazine is equipped with a magazine follower button for convenience in reloading.

For additional specifications, please see chart on the next page.

MARK II GOVERNMENT TARGET MODEL

MARK II TARGET MODEL

RUGER PISTOLS

Model P-4 22/45

Mark II 22/45
w/Zytel Frame

22/45 Target Model P-512

SPECIFICATIONS: RUGER 22 MARK II PISTOLS

Catalog Number	Model*	Finish**	Barrel Length	Overall Length	Approx. Wt. (Oz.)	Price
MK-4	Std.	B	4 3/4"	8 5/16"	35	$252.00
MK-4B	Bull	B	4"	8.25"	38	336.50
KMK-4	Std.	SS	4 3/4"	8 5/16"	35	330.25
KP-4***22/45	Std.	SS	4 3/4"	8 13/16"	28	280.00
P-4	Bull	B	4"	8"	31	237.50
MK-6	Std.	B	6"	10 5/16"	37	252.00
KMK-6	Std.	SS	6"	10 5/16"	37	330.25
MK-678	Target	B	6 7/8"	11 1/8"	42	310.50
KMK-678	Target	SS	6 7/8"	11 1/8"	42	389.00
P-512***22/45	Bull	B	5.5"	9 3/4"	35	237.50
MK-512	Bull	B	5.5"	9 3/4"	42	310.50
KMK-512	Bull	SS	5.5"	9 3/4"	42	389.00
KP-512***22/45	Bull	SS	5.5"	9 3/4"	35	330.00
MK-10	Bull	B	10"	14 5/16"	51	314.50
KMK-10	Bull	SS	10"	14 5/16"	51	393.00
MK-678G	Bull	B	6 7/8"	11 1/8"	46	374.00
KMK-678G	Bull	SS	6 7/8"	11 1/8"	46	448.00
KMK-678GC	Bull	SS	6 7/8"	11 1/8"	45	463.00

*Model: Std.=standard **Finish: B=blued; SS=stainless steel ***22 cartridge, 45 grip angle and magazine latch

SAFARI ARMS PISTOLS

MATCHMASTER

SPECIFICATIONS
Caliber: 45 ACP
Capacity: 7 rounds
Barrel length: 5" or 6"
Overall length: 8.25"
Weight: 40.3 oz.
Finish: Stainless steel or black Parkerized carbon steel
Features: Extended safety & slide stop; wide beavertail grip safety; LPA fully adjustable rear sight; full-length recoil spring guide; squared trigger guide & finger-groove front strap frame; laser-etched walnut grips
Prices:
5" Barrel $595.00
6" Barrel 654.00

ENFORCER

SPECIFICATIONS
Caliber: .45 ACP
Capacity: 6 rounds
Barrel length: 4" conical
Overall length: 7.3"
Height: 4 $^7/_8$"
Weight: 36 oz.
Sight radius: 5.75"
Finish: Stainless steel or matte black Parkerized carbon steel
Features: Beavertail grip safety; extended thumb safety and slide release; smooth walnut stock w/laser-etched Black Widow logo
Price: $630.00

COHORT

SPECIFICATIONS
Caliber: 45 ACP
Capacity: 7 rounds
Barrel length: 4" conical
Overall length: 7.3"
Height: 5.5"
Weight: 37 oz.
Sights: Ramped blade front, LPA adjustable rear
Finish: Stainless steel or black Parkerized carbon steel
Features: Beavertail grip safety; extended thumb safety and slide release; commander-style hammer; smooth walnut stock
Price: $659.00

SAVAGE ARMS

BOLT-ACTION HUNTING HANDGUN

SPECIFICATIONS
Calibers: .223, 22-250, 243, 7mm-08, 260, 308
Capacity: 3 + 1 *Barrel Length:* 14"
Overall Length: 22.5" *Weight:* Approx. 5 lbs.
Sights: None. Drilled and tapped for scope mounts
Stock: Mid-grip, ambidextrous composite, with grooved
forend and dual pillar bedding
Finish: Blued alloy steel
Features: Bolt-action hunting handgun with left hand bolt
and right hand ejection.
Price: **$400.00**

**MODEL 510F
"STRIKER"**

SPECIFICATIONS
Calibers: 223, 22-250
Barrel Length: 14" *Overall Length:* 22.5"
Magazine: Top loading internal
Sights: None. Drilled and tapped for scope mounts
Stock: Mid-grip, ambidextrous composite, with grooved
forend and dual pillar bedding
Finish: Stainless steel
Features: Bolt-action hunting handgun with left hand bolt
and right hand ejection. Adjustable muzzle brake.
Price: **$500.00**

**MODEL 516FSAK
"STRIKER"**

**SAVAGE ARMS INTRODUCES
"SUPER STRIKER" HUNTING HANDGUNS**

The standard Striker action is the basis for an
exciting new handgun with laminated thumbhole
stock, muzzle brake and stainless construction.
• Custom "dual pillar bedded" laminate thumb-
  hole stock
• Left-hand bollt with right-hand ejection
• Fluted 14" stainless steel barrel with Adjustable
  Muzzle Brake (AMB)
• ESP "Engineered Step Performance" Fully
  Adjustable Two-step Trigger System
• Drilled & Tapped for scope mount
Price: **$600.00**

**MODEL
516BSAK
"SUPER
STRIKER"**

SIG ARMS PISTOLS

MODEL P239

SPECIFICATIONS

Calibers: 357 SIG, 9mm, 40 S&W
Capacity: 7 rounds (8 in 9mm)
Barrel Length: 3.6"
Overall Length: 6.6"
Height: 5.2"
Width: 1.2"
Weight (empty): 27.4 oz.
Finish: Nitron Stainless Steel, Two Tone
Prices:
Nitron $595.00
  w/"Siglite" night sights 690.00
Two Tone. 640.00
  "Siglite" night sights 735.00

MODEL P239

MODEL P229S

SPECIFICATIONS

Caliber: 357 SIG *Capacity:* 10 rounds
Action: DA/SA *Barrel Length:* 4.8"
Overall Length: 8.6" *Weight (empty):* 40.6 oz.
Height: 5.7" *Width:* 1.5" *Finish:* Stainless Steel
Price:. $1,320.00

MODEL P229S

MODEL P226

SPECIFICATIONS

Calibers: 357 SIG, 9mm and 40 S&W
Capacity: 10 rounds *Action:* DA/SA or DA only
Barrel Length: 4.4"
Overall Length: 7.7"
Weight (empty): 26.5 oz.; 30.1 oz. in 357 SIG
Height: 5.5" *Finish:* Blue, K-Kote or Two-tone
Prices:
Blackened stainless steel slide $795.00
  w/"Siglite" night sight 885.00
Nickel finish stainless steel slide, DA only
  w/"Siglite" night sights 930.00

MODEL P226

SIG ARMS PISTOLS

MODEL P232

MODEL P232

SPECIFICATIONS
Calibers: 9mm Short (380 ACP) and 32 ACP
Action: DA/SA or DAO
Capacity: 7 rounds (380 ACP); 8 rounds (32 ACP)
Barrel Length: 3.6" **Overall Length:** 6.6"
Weight (empty): 16.2 oz.; (16.4 oz. in 32 ACP)
Height: 4.7" **Width:** 1.2"
Safety: Automatic firing-pin lock **Finish:** Blued or stainless steel
Prices:
Blued finish $485.00
Stainless steel 525.00
w/Stainless slide, alloy frame 505.00
w/"Siglite" night sight, Hogue grips, DA only 560.00

MODEL P229

SPECIFICATIONS
Calibers: 9mm, 357 and 40 S&W
Capacity: 10 rounds
Action: DA/SA or DA only
Barrel Length: 3.8"
Overall Length: 7.1"
Weight (empty): 27.5 oz.
Height: 5.4"
Width: 1.5"
Finish: Blackened stainless steel
Features: Stainless steel slide; automatic firing-pin lock; wood grips (optional); aluminum alloy frame
Prices:
Model P229. . . . . $795.00
w/"Siglite" night sight 885.00
w/Nickel slide 830.00
w/Nickel slide/"Siglite" night sight 925.00

MODEL P229

MODEL P210

SPECIFICATIONS
Calibers: 9mm/.22LR **Rifling lead:** 16"
No. of Grooves: 6 **Barrel Length:** 4.8"
Overall Length: 8.5"
Weight, excl. magazine: 32.0 oz.
Height: 5.4" **Width:** 1.3" **Sight Base:** 6.45"
Magazine, empty: 3.1 oz.
Trigger Pull DA/DAO: 10 lbs. **Trigger:** Single Action
Magazine Capacity: 8 rounds
Trigger Pull SA: 4.5 lbs.
Features: Mechanically-locked, recoil-operated, semiautomatic pistol. Hand-tuned action.
Prices:
P210, Blue $2,100.00
P210, Blue with .22 LR conversion kit 2,400.00

MODEL P210

SMITH & WESSON PISTOLS

COMPACT SERIES

MODEL 3900 COMPACT SERIES

SPECIFICATIONS
Caliber: 9mm Parabellum DA Autoloading Luger
Capacity: 8 rounds
Barrel Length: 3.5"
Overall Length: 6 7/8"
Weight (empty): 25 oz.
Sights: Post w/white dot front; fixed rear adj. for windage only w/2 white dots. Adjustable sight models include micrometer click, adj. for windage and elevation w/2 white dots. Deduct $25 for fixed sights.
Finish: Satin stainless
Prices:
MODEL 3913 . . . . $633.00
MODEL 3913 LADYSMITH (single side) 651.00
MODEL 3953 (double action only) 633.00

MODEL 3913 DA
STAINLESS

MODEL 3913
LADYSMITH

MODEL 6906

MODEL 6900 COMPACT SERIES

SPECIFICATIONS
Caliber: 9mm Parabellum; traditional DA autoloading Luger
Capacity: 12 rounds
Barrel Length: 3.5"
Overall Length: 6 7/8"
Weight (empty): 26.5 oz.
Sights: Post w/white dot front; fixed rear adj. for windage only w/2 white dots
Grips: Curved backstrap
Finish: Blue (Model 6904); satin stainless (Model 6906)
Prices:
MODEL 6904 . . . . $625.00
MODEL 6906 . . . . 688.00
MODEL 6906 Fixed Novak night sight. 801.00
MODEL 6946 DA only, fixed sights 688.00

MODEL 6946 DA
STAINLESS

SMITH & WESSON PISTOLS

FULL-SIZE CENTERFIRE DOUBLE-ACTION PISTOLS

Smith & Wesson's double-action semiautomatic Third Generation line includes the following features: fixed barrel bushing for greater accuracy • smoother trigger pull plus a slimmer, contoured grip and lateral relief cut where trigger guard meets frame • beveled magazine well • ambidextrous safety lever • low-glare bead-blasted finish.

MODEL 4006
WITH FIXED SIGHT

MODEL 4506
ADJUSTABLE SIGHT

MODEL 4046

MODEL 4586
FIXED SIGHT

MODEL 4000 SERIES

SPECIFICATIONS
Caliber: 40 S&W
Capacity: 11 rounds
Barrel Length: 4"
Overall Length: 7.5"
Weight: 38.5 oz. (with fixed sights)
Sights: Post w/white dot front; fixed w/white 2-dot rear
Grips: Straight backstrap
Finish: Stainless steel
Prices:
MODEL 4006 w/fixed sights. $798.00
   Same as above w/adj. sights. 788.00
   w/fixed night sight 880.00
MODEL 4043 DA only (28 oz.) 750.00
MODEL 4046 Fixed sights, DA only (39.5 oz.) 768.00
   Double action only, fixed Tritium night sight 880.00

MODEL 4500 SERIES

SPECIFICATIONS
Caliber: 45 ACP Autoloading DA
Capacity: 8 rounds
Barrel Lengths: 5" (Model 4506); 4.25" (Models 4566 & 4586)
Overall Length: 8.5" (Model 4506)
Weight (empty): 40.5 oz. (Model 4506); 38.5 oz. (Model 4566)
Sights: Post w/white-dot front; fixed rear, adj. for windage only. Adj. sight incl. micrometer click, adj. for windage and elevation w/2 white dots. Add **$29.00** for adj. sights.
Grips: Delrin one-piece wraparound, arched backstrap, textured surface
Finish: Satin stainless
Prices:
MODEL 4506 w/adj. sights, 5" bbl. $830.00
   With fixed sights 798.00
MODEL 4566 w/4.25" bbl., fixed sights 798.00
MODEL 4586 DA only, 4.25" bbl., 39.5 oz.,
   fixed 2-dot rear sight, white dot front 798.00

SMITH & WESSON PISTOLS

FULL-SIZE DOUBLE-ACTION PISTOLS

MODEL 5900 SERIES

SPECIFICATIONS
Caliber: 9mm Parabellum DA Autoloading Luger
Capacity: 15 rounds
Barrel Length: 4"
Overall Length: 7.5"
Weight (empty): 28 oz. (Models 5903, 5904); 37.5 oz. (Model 5906); 38 oz. (Model 5906 w/adj. sight)
Sights: Front, post w/white dot; fixed rear, adj. for windage only w/2 white dots. Adjustable sight models include micrometer click, adj. for windage and elevation w/2 white dots.
Finish: Blue (Model 5904); satin stainless (Models 5903 and 5906)
Prices:
MODEL **5904** Blue. $663.00
MODEL **5906** Satin stainless 765.00
 With fixed sights. 729.00
 With Tritium night sight 841.00
MODEL **5946** Double action only 729.00

MODEL 5906 DA
STAINLESS

MODEL 410

SPECIFICATIONS
Caliber: 40 S&W
Capacity: 10 rounds
Barrel Length: 4"
Overall Length: 7.5"
Weight: 28.5 oz.
Sights: 3-dot sights
Grips: Straight backstrap
Features: Right-hand slide-mounted manual safety; decocking lever; aluminum alloy frame; blue carbon steel slide; nonreflective matte blued finish; beveled edge slide
Price: $500.00

MODEL 410

MODEL 900 SERIES (MODEL 908)

SPECIFICATIONS
Caliber: 9mm
Capacity: 8 rounds
Barrel Lengths: 3.5"
Overall Length: 6 $^{13}/_{16}$"
Weight: 28.8 oz.
Sights: White dot front; fixed 2-dot rear
Grips: Straight backstrap
Safety: External, single side
Finish: Matte blue
Features: Carbon steel slide; alloy frame
Price: $453.00

MODEL 910

SMITH & WESSON PISTOLS

SIGMA SERIES

Smith & Wesson's Sigma Series pistols are a combination of traditional craftmanship and the latest technological advances that allow the guns to be assembled without the usual "fitting" process required for other handguns. The polymer frame provides unprecedented comfort and pointability. The low barrel centerline combined with the ergonomic design reduces muzzle flip and speeds the next shot.

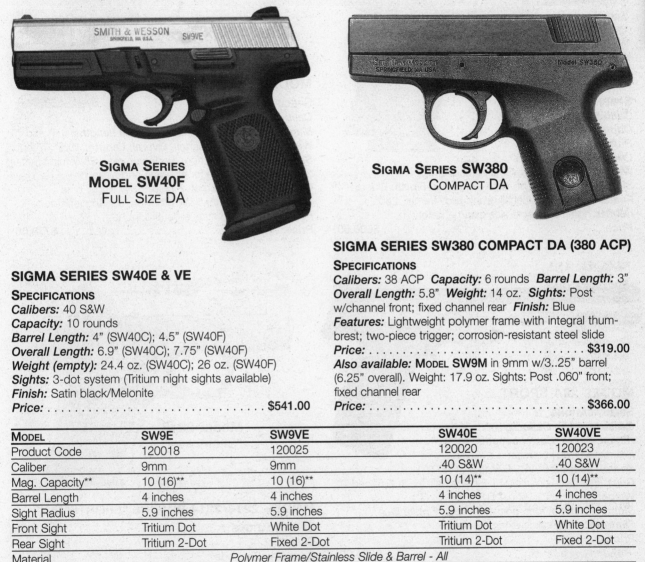

**SIGMA SERIES
MODEL SW40F
FULL SIZE DA**

**SIGMA SERIES SW380
COMPACT DA**

SIGMA SERIES SW40E & VE

SPECIFICATIONS
Calibers: 40 S&W
Capacity: 10 rounds
Barrel Length: 4" (SW40C); 4.5" (SW40F)
Overall Length: 6.9" (SW40C); 7.75" (SW40F)
Weight (empty): 24.4 oz. (SW40C); 26 oz. (SW40F)
Sights: 3-dot system (Tritium night sights available)
Finish: Satin black/Melonite
Price: **$541.00**

SIGMA SERIES SW380 COMPACT DA (380 ACP)

SPECIFICATIONS
Calibers: 38 ACP *Capacity:* 6 rounds *Barrel Length:* 3"
Overall Length: 5.8" *Weight:* 14 oz. *Sights:* Post w/channel front; fixed channel rear *Finish:* Blue
Features: Lightweight polymer frame with integral thumbrest; two-piece trigger; corrosion-resistant steel slide
Price: **$319.00**
Also available: MODEL SW9M in 9mm w/3..25" barrel (6.25" overall). Weight: 17.9 oz. Sights: Post .060" front; fixed channel rear
Price: **$366.00**

MODEL	SW9E	SW9VE	SW40E	SW40VE
Product Code	120018	120025	120020	120023
Caliber	9mm	9mm	.40 S&W	.40 S&W
Mag. Capacity**	10 (16)**	10 (16)**	10 (14)**	10 (14)**
Barrel Length	4 inches	4 inches	4 inches	4 inches
Sight Radius	5.9 inches	5.9 inches	5.9 inches	5.9 inches
Front Sight	Tritium Dot	White Dot	Tritium Dot	White Dot
Rear Sight	Tritium 2-Dot	Fixed 2-Dot	Tritium 2-Dot	Fixed 2-Dot
Material	Polymer Frame/Stainless Slide & Barrel - All			
Finish	Melonite Slide & Barrel	Stainless Slide & Barrel	Melonite Slide & Barrel	Stainless Steel & Barrel
Weight Empty	24.7 oz.	24.7 oz.	24.4 oz.	24.4 oz.
Length	7.25"	7.25"	7.25"	7.25"
Height	5.6"	5.6"	5.6"	5.6"
Width	1.3"	1.3"	1.3"	1.3"
Rifling	1:18.75 RH	1:18.75 RH	1:16 LH	1:16 LH

** High Capacity magazines available for law enforcement or export orders only

SMITH & WESSON PISTOLS

MODEL 457

MODEL 457

SPECIFICATIONS
Caliber: 45 ACP
Capacity: 7 rounds
Barrel Length: 3.75"
Overall Length: 7.25"
Weight: 29 oz. **Grips:** Straight backstrap
Sights: White dot front; fixed 2-dot rear **Finish:** Blued
Features: Carbon steel slide and alloy frame; .260" bobbed hammer; single side external safety
Price: $500.00

MODEL No. 41

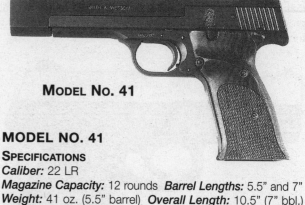

MODEL NO. 41

SPECIFICATIONS
Caliber: 22 LR
Magazine Capacity: 12 rounds **Barrel Lengths:** 5.5" and 7"
Weight: 41 oz. (5.5" barrel) **Overall Length:** 10.5" (7" bbl.)
Sights: Front, 1/8" Patridge undercut; rear, S&W micrometer click sight adjustable for windage and elevation
Grips: Hardwood target **Finish:** S&W Bright blue
Trigger: .365" width; S&W grooving, adj. trigger stop
Features: Carbon steel slide and frame
Price: $778.00

MODEL 22A SPORT

SPECIFICATIONS
Caliber: 22 LR **Capacity:** 10 rounds
Action: Single **Barrel Lengths:** 4", 5.5" (standard or bull barrel and 7")
Overall Length: 8" (4"), 9.5" (5.5"), 11" (7")
Grips: Two-piece polymer (4"); 2-piece Soft Touch (5.5" and 7")
Weight: 28 oz. (4"), 32 oz. (5.5"), 33 oz. (7")
Sights: Patridge front, adjustable rear **Finish:** Blue
Features: Single slide external safety
Prices:
4" $224.00
5.5" 247.00
5.5" Bull Barrel 311.00
5.5" Stainless 287.00
7" 281.00
Also available: in stainless steel (5.5" and 7" only)
Prices:
5.5" Standard $303.00
5.5" Bull Barrel 368.00
7" Standard 334.00

MODEL 2213
"SPORTSMAN"

MODEL 2213/2214 RIMFIRE "SPORTSMAN"

SPECIFICATIONS
Caliber: 22 LR
Capacity: 8 rounds
Barrel Length: 3"
Overall Length: 6 1/8""
Weight: 18 oz.
Sights: Patridge front, adjustable rear
Finish: Stainless steel slide w/alloy frame (Model 2214 has blued carbon steel slide w/alloy frame and blued finish)
Prices:
Blue $284.00
Stainless 330.00

SMITH & WESSON PISTOLS

TSW TACTICAL SERIES

DOUBLE ACTION MODEL 3953TSW

SPECIFICATIONS
Action: Double Action Only
Caliber: 9mm
Capacity: 7 Rounds
Barrel Length: 3.5"
Front Sight: White Dot
Rear Sight: Novak Lo Mount Carry 2-Dot
Grips: Straight Backstrap
Weight: 24.7 oz.
Overall Length: 6 5/8"
Height: 4 7/8" *Width:* 1.00"
Material: Aluminum Alloy/Stainless Steel
Finish: Satin Stainless
Price: $674.00
Also available: **MODEL 3913TSW**
    Same as above but width is 1.30".

MODEL 3953TSW
DOUBLE ACTION

TRADITIONAL DA MODEL 4013TSW

SPECIFICATIONS
Action: Traditional Double Action
Caliber: .40 S&W
Frame: Compact
Capacity: 9 rounds
Barrel Length: 3.5"
Front Sight: White Dot
Rear Sight: Novak Lo Mount Carry 2-Dot
External Safety: Ambidextrous
Grips: Curbed Backstrap
Weight: 26.4 oz. *Overall Length:* 6 7/8"
Height: 5" *Width:* 1.30"
Material: Aluminum Alloy/Stainless Steel
Finish: Satin Stainless
Price: $799.00
Also available: **MODEL 4053STW**
    Same as above but width is 1.24" and weight is 27.2 oz.

MODEL 4013TSW
TRADITIONAL DA

TRADTIONAL DA MODEL 4513TSW

SPECIFICATIONS
Action: Traditional Double Action
Caliber: .45 ACP *Frame:* Compact
Capacity: 6 Rounds *Barrel Length:* 3.75"
Front Sight: White Dot
Rear Sight: Novak Lo Mount Carry 2-Dot
Grips: Straight Backstrap *Weight:* 28 oz.
Overall Length: 6 7/8"
Height: 5" *Width:* 1.30"
Material: Aluminum Alloy/Stainless Steel
Finish: Satin Stainless
Price: $758.00
Also available: **MODEL 4553TSW**
    Same as above but weight is 29 oz. and height is 4 7/8"

MODEL 4513TSW
TRADITIONAL DA

SMALL FRAME

MODEL 60LS LADYSMITH
38 S&W Special

MODEL 37
CHIEFS SPECIAL AIRWEIGHT
38 S&W Special

MODEL 60
38 CHIEFS SPECIAL
Stainless

LADYSMITH HANDGUNS
MODEL 36-LS AND MODEL 60-LS

SPECIFICATIONS
Calibers: 38 S&W Special and 357 Magnum
Capacity: 5 shots *Barrel Lengths:* 2" (2 ¹/₈" 357 Magnum)
Overall Length: 6 ⁵/₁₆" *Weight:* 20 oz. (23 oz. 357 Magnum)
Sights: Serrated ramp front (black pinned ramp in 357 Mag.); fixed notch rear
Grips: Contoured laminated rosewood, round butt
Finish: Glossy deep blue or stainless
Features: Both models come with soft-side LadySmith carry case
Prices:
MODEL 36-LS Blue $425.00
MODEL 60-LS Stainless 479.00

MODEL 36
38 CHIEFS SPECIAL

SPECIFICATIONS
Caliber: 38 S&W Special *Capacity:* 5 shots
Barrel Length: 2" *Overall Length:* 6 ⁵/₁₆"
Weight: 20 oz.
Sights: Serrated ramp front; fixed, square-notch rear
Grips: Uncle Mike's Boot
Finish: S&W blued carbon steel; satin stainless Model 637
Features: .312" smooth combat-style trigger; .240" service hammer
Prices:
MODEL 36 38 CHIEFS SPECIAL $394.00
MODEL 37 CHIEFS SPECIAL AIRWEIGHT:
    Same as Model 36, except finish is blue or
    nickel aluminum alloy. 429.00
MODEL 637 CHIEFS SPECIAL AIRWEIGHT:
    With 2" barrel, synthetic round butt, stainless finish.
    Weight: 13.5 oz. 446.00

MODEL 60
38 CHIEFS SPECIAL, STAINLESS

SPECIFICATIONS
Calibers: 38 S&W Special *Capacity:* 5 shots
Barrel Lengths: 2 1/8" (357 Mag.); 3" full lug (38 S&W Spec.)
Overall Length: 6 ⁵/₁₆" (2 ¹/₈" bbl.)); 7.5" (3" bbl.)
Weight: 23 oz. (2 1/8" barrel); 24.5 oz. (3" full lug barrel)
Sights: Micrometer click rear, adj. for windage and elevation; pinned black front (3" full lug model only); standard sights as on Model 36
Grips: Uncle Mike's Combat *Finish:* Satin stainless
Features: .312" smooth combat-style trigger
Prices:
2 ¹/₈" Barrel $449.00
3" Barrel 476.00

Smith & Wesson Revolvers

Small Frame

MODEL 442
38 SPECIAL

38 CENTENNIAL "AIRWEIGHT" MODEL 442

SPECIFICATIONS
Caliber: 38 S&W Special
Capacity: 5 rounds
Barrel Length: 2" *Overall Length:* 6 $^5/_{16}$"
Weight: 15.8 oz.
Sights: Serrated ramp front; fixed, square-notch rear
Finish: Matte blue
Price: $445.00
Also available:
MODEL 642 CENTENNIAL AIRWEIGHT
  Stainless steel w/2" barrel, synthetic round butt grip,
  double-action only. $460.00
LADYSMITH MODEL (satin stainless). 490.00

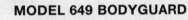

MODEL 649
BODYGUARD

MODEL 649 BODYGUARD

SPECIFICATIONS
Caliber: 38 S&W Special/357 S&W Mag.
Capacity: 5 rounds
Barrel Length: 2 $^1/_8$"
Overall Length: 6 $^5/_{16}$"
Weight: 20 oz.
Sights: Black pinned ramp front; fixed, square-notch rear
Grips: Uncle Mike's Combat
Finish: Satin stainless
Price: $488.00

MODEL 696

MODEL 696

SPECIFICATIONS
Caliber: 44 S&W Special
Capacity: 5 rounds
Action: Single or double action
Barrel Length: 3" *Overall Length:* 8 $^3/_{16}$"
Weight: 48 oz.
Sights: Red ramp front; adjustable white outline rear
Grips: Hogue rubber *Finish:* Satin stainless
Features: .500" target hammer; .400" smooth combat trigger
Price: $509.00

SMALL FRAME

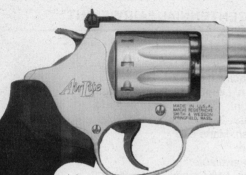

MODEL 317 AIRLITE

MODEL 317 AIRLITE

SPECIFICATIONS
Caliber: 22 LR *Action:* Single or double action
Capacity: 8 rounds *Barrel Length:* 1 ⅞" and 3"
Overall Length: 6 ³/₁₆"
Weight: 9.9 oz. (10.5 oz. w/rubber grip) *Finish:* Clear Cote
Sights: Serrated ramp front; fixed notch rear
Prices:
1 ⅞" barrel w/synthetic grips $451.00
1 ⅞" barrel w/Dymondwood. 484.00
3" barrel w/Dymondwood grip 518.00
3" barrel w/rubber grips 477.00

MODEL 317 LADYSMITH

MODEL 317 LADYSMITH

SPECIFICATIONS
Same as **MODEL 317 AIRLITE** with round butt grip, fixed
sights and Dymondwood grip.
Price: $505.00

MODEL 640

MODEL 640 CENTENNIAL

SPECIFICATIONS
Calibers: 357 Magnum and 38 S&W Special
Action: Double action only
Capacity: 5 rounds
Barrel Length: 1 ⅞" and 2 ⅛"
Overall Length: 6 ¾"
Weight: 23 oz. (1 ⅞" barrel)
Sights: Pinned black ramp front; fixed, square-notch rear
Features: Fully concealed hammer; smooth hardwood
service stock; satin stainless steel finish; round-butt
synthetic grips
Price: $488.00

SMITH & WESSON REVOLVERS

MEDIUM FRAME

MODEL 10
38 MILITARY & POLICE

SPECIFICATIONS
Caliber: 38 S&W Special *Capacity:* 6 shots
Barrel Length: 4" heavy barrel *Overall Length:* 9.25"
Weight: 33.5 oz.
Sights: Front, fixed $^1/_8$" serrated ramp; square-notch rear
Grips: Uncle Mike's Combat *Finish:* S&W blue
Price: $408.00

MODEL 10
HEAVY BARREL

MODEL 64
38 MILITARY &
POLICE STAINLESS

SPECIFICATIONS
Caliber: 38 S&W Special *Capacity:* 6 shots
Barrel Length: 4" heavy barrel, square butt; 3" heavy
barrel, round butt; 2" regular barrel, round butt
Overall Length: 9.25" w/4" bbl.; 7 $^7/_8$" w/3" bbl.;
6 $^7/_8$" w/2" barrel *Weight:* 28 oz. w/2" barrel; 30.5 oz. w/3"
bbl.; 33.5 oz. w/4" barrel *Sights:* Fixed, $^1/_8$" serrated ramp
front; square-notch rear *Grips:* Uncle Mike's Combat
Finish: Satin stainless
Prices:
  2" Bbl. $433.00
  3" & 4" Bbl. 441.00

MODEL 64

MODEL 65 (HEAVY BARREL)
357 MILITARY & POLICE

SPECIFICATIONS
K-frame .357 Magnum with stainless steel frame and 4"
barrel; 6 shots; fixed sights.
Price: $445.00
Also available:
MODEL 65 LADYSMITH
Same specifications as **MODEL 65** but with 3" barrel only
(weights 32 oz.) and rosewood laminate stock; satin stain-
less finish, smooth combat wood grips.
Price: $479.00

MODEL 65

Smith & Wesson Revolvers

Medium Frame

Model 14
K-38 Masterpiece

SPECIFICATIONS
Caliber: 38 S&W Special
Barrel Length: 6" full lug barrel
Overall Length: 11 1/8"
Weight: 41.5 oz.
Sights: Micrometer click rear, adjustable for windage and elevation; pinned blackk Patridge-style front
Grips: Synthetic square butt (on round-butt frame)
Finish: Blue carbon steel
Features: .500 target hammer; .312" smooth combat trigger
Price: **$484.00**

Model 15
38 Combat Masterpiece

SPECIFICATIONS
Caliber: 38 S&W Special
Capacity: 6 shots
Barrel Length: 4"
Overall Length: 9 5/16"
Weight (loaded): 36 oz.
Sights: Serrated ramp front; S&W micrometer click sight adjustable for windage and elevation
Grips: Uncle Mike's Combat
Finish: S&W blue
Features: .375" semi-target hammer; .312" smooth combat-style trigger
Price: **$437.00**
Also available:
Model 67. Same specifications as **Model 15** but with satin stainless finish, red ramp front sight and .375" semi-target hammer.
Price: **$485.00**

Model 617

SPECIFICATIONS
Caliber: 22 Long Rifle *Capacity:* 6 shots
Barrel Length: 4", 6" or 8 3/8"
Overall Length: 9 1/8" (4" barrel); 11 1/8" (6" barrel); 13.5" (8 3/8" barrel)
Weight (loaded): 42 oz. with 4" barrel; 48 oz. with 6" barrel; 54 oz. with 8 3/8" barrel
Sights: Front pinned Patridge; rear, S&W micrometer click sight adjustable for windage and elevation
Grips: Hogue rubber, square butt *Finish:* Satin stainless
Features: Target hammer and trigger; drilled and tapped for scope
Prices:

4" Barrel.	**$478.00**
6" Barrel	**508.00**
8.75" Barrel	**520.00**
6" Bbl. 10-Shot	**524.00**

SMITH & WESSON REVOLVERS

MEDIUM FRAME

MODEL 19

MODEL 19
357 COMBAT MAGNUM

SPECIFICATIONS
Caliber: 357 S&W Magnum
Capacity: 6 shots
Barrel Lengths: 2.5" & 4"
Overall Length: 9.5" w/4" bbl.
Weight: 36 oz. (4" bbl.)
Sights: Serrated ramp front; adjustable black rear
Grips: Uncle Mike's Combat
Finish: S&W bright blue
Prices:
   4" Bbl. 443.00

MODEL 66

MODEL 66
357 COMBAT MAGNUM

SPECIFICATIONS
Caliber: 357 Magnum
Capacity: 6 shots
Barrel Lengths: 4" or 6" with square butt; 2.5" with round butt
Overall Length: 7.5" w/2.5" bbl.; 9.5" w/4" bbl.; 11 ³/₈" w/6" bbl.
Weight: 30.5 oz. w/2.5" bbl.; 36 oz. w/4" bbl.; 39 oz. w/6" bbl.
Sights: Front, ¹/₈"; rear, S&W Red Ramp on ramp base, S&W Micrometer Click, adjustable for windage and elevation
Grips: Uncle Mike's Combat
Trigger: .312" Smooth Combat
Finish: Satin stainless
Prices:
   2.5" Bbl. $484.00
   4" Bbl. 490.00

MODEL 586

MODEL 586
DISTINGUISHED COMBAT MAGNUM

SPECIFICATIONS
Calibers: 357 Magnum and 38 S&W Special
Capacity: 6 shots
Barrel Lengths: 4" or 6"
Overall Length: 9 ⁹/₁₆" w/4" bbl.; 11 ¹⁵/₁₆" w/6" bbl.
Weight: 41 oz. w/4" bbl.; 46 oz. w/6" bbl.
Sights: Front, S&W Red Ramp; rear, S&W Micrometer Click, adjustable for windage and elevation; white outline notch
Grips: Hogue rubber square butt
Finish: S&W Blue
Prices:
   4" Bbl. $480.00
   6" Bbl. 484.00

SMITH & WESSON REVOLVERS

MEDIUM FRAME

MODEL 686

MODEL 686
POWERPORT

SPECIFICATIONS
Same specifications as **MODEL 586** (see preceding page), except also available with 2.5" barrel (35.5 oz.) and 8 ³/₈" barrel (53 oz.). All models have stainless steel finish, combat or target stock and/or trigger; adjustable sights optional.
Prices:

2.5" Barrel	$499.00
8 ³/₈" Barrel	550.00

SPECIFICATIONS
Same general specifications as the **MODEL 686** except this revolver features 6" full lug barrel with intergral compensator, Hogue rubber grips and black-pinned Patridge front sight.
Price: $548.00
Also available:
MODEL 686 PLUS DISTINGUISHED COMBAT MAGNUM
Capacity: 7 rounds **Barrel Lengths:** 2.5", 4" or 6" full lug.
Overall Length: 7.5" – 11 ¹⁵/₁₆" **Weight:** 34.5 oz. – 45 oz.
Prices:

2.5" bbl.	$518.00
4" Barrel	526.00
6" Barrel	534.00

LARGE FRAME

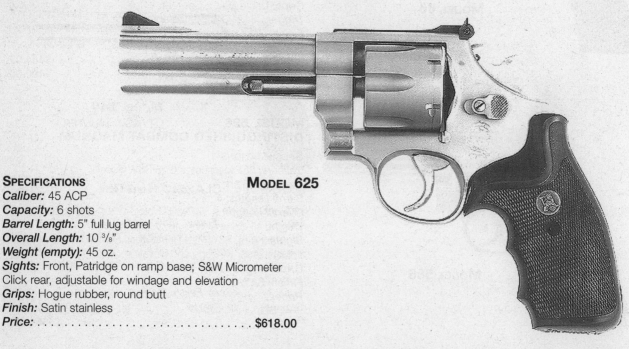

SPECIFICATIONS
MODEL 625

Caliber: 45 ACP
Capacity: 6 shots
Barrel Length: 5" full lug barrel
Overall Length: 10 ³/₈"
Weight (empty): 45 oz.
Sights: Front, Patridge on ramp base; S&W Micrometer Click rear, adjustable for windage and elevation
Grips: Hogue rubber, round butt
Finish: Satin stainless
Price: $618.00

SMITH & WESSON PISTOLS

LARGE FRAME

MODEL 629

MODEL 629
CLASSIC DX

MODEL 629

SPECIFICATIONS
Calibers: 44 Magnum, 44 S&W Special *Capacity:* 6 shots
Barrel Lengths: 4", 6", 8 ³/₈" *Overall Length:* 9 ⁵/₈", 11 ³/₈", 13 ⁷/₈"
Weight (empty): 44 oz. (4" bbl.); 47 oz. (6" bbl.); 54 oz. (8 ³/₈" bbl.)
Sights: S&W Red Ramp front; white outline rear w/S&W Micrometer Click, adjustable for windage and elevation; drilled and tapped
Grips: Hogue rubber *Finish:* Satin stainless steel
Features: Combat trigger, target hammer
Prices: 4" Bbl. $607.00
  6" Bbl. 613.00
  8 ³/₈" Bbl. 627.00

MODEL 629 CLASSIC

SPECIFICATIONS
Calibers: 44 Magnum, 44 S&W Special *Capacity:* 6 rounds
Barrel Lengths: 5", 6.5", 8 ³/₈" *Overall Length:* 10.5", 12", 13 ⁷/₈"
Weight: 51 oz. (5" bbl.); 52 oz. (6.5" bbl.); 54 oz. (8 ³/₈" bbl.)
Grips: Hogue rubber
Prices: 5" & 6.5" Bbl. $650.00
  8 ³/₈" Bbl. 671.00
Also available:
MODEL 629 CLASSIC DX. Same features as the **MODEL 629 CLASSIC** above, plus interchangeable front sights.
  With 6.5" barrel. $835.00
  With 8 ³/₈" barrel. 862.00
MODEL 629 POWERPORT w/6.5" barrel (12" overall length), weighs 52 oz. Patridge front sight, adjustable black blade rear sight.
Price: $650.00

MODEL 657

MODEL 610
CLASSIC HUNTER

MODEL 657 STAINLESS

SPECIFICATIONS
Calibers: 41 Magnum *Capacity:* 6 shots
Barrel Length: 6" *Overall Length:* 11 ³/₈"
Weight (empty): 48 oz.
Sights: Front, pinned ramp on ramp base; black blade rear, adjustable for windage and elevation; drilled and tapped
Grips: Hogue rubber *Finish:* Satin stainless steel
Price: $548.00

MODEL 610 CLASSIC HUNTER

SPECIFICATIONS
Calibers: 10mm *Frame:* N-Large *Capacity:* 6 rounds
Barrel Length: 6.5" *Overall Length:* 12"
Weight: 52 oz.
Sights: Interchangeable front; micrometer click adj. black blade
Grips: Hogue rubber *Finish:* Stainless steel
Feature: Unfluted cylinder
Price: $664.00

SPRINGFIELD PISTOLS

MODEL 1911-A1 PISTOLS

MODEL 1911-A1 CHAMPION 4-INCH

MODEL 1911-A1 STANDARD & LIGHTWEIGHT

SPECIFICATIONS
Calibers: 45 ACP and 38 Super
Capacity: 7 rounds (45 ACP); 9 rounds (38 Super)
Barrel Length: 4" *Overall Length:* 7 $^5/_8$"
Trigger Pull: 5-6.5 lbs. *Sight Radius:* 5.25"
Weight: 34 oz. *Finish:* Parkerized, Blued, Stainless
Prices:
Parkerized **$586.00**
Blued **611.00**
Stainless **645.00**

SPECIFICATIONS
Calibers: 45 ACP, 9mm and 38 Super
Capacity: 8 rounds (45 ACP), 9 rounds (9mm & 38 Super)
Barrel Length: 5"
Overall Length: 8 $^5/_8$"
Weight: 38.5 oz. (31.5 oz. Lightweight)
Features: Walnut grips; Bo-Mar-type sights optional
Prices:
45 ACP Blued **$565.00**
45 ACP Stainless **644.00**
45 ACP Stainless Steel V-12 (ported) **704.00**
45 ACP Lightweight Matte **611.00**
9mm Stainless **660.00**

MODEL 1911-A1 TROPHY MATCH

SPECIFICATIONS
Calibers: 45 ACP and 9mm *Capacity:* 7 rounds
Barrel Length: 5" *Overall Length:* 8 $^5/_8$" *Weight:* 40 oz.
Trigger Pull: 4-5.5 lbs. *Sights:* Fully adjustable target sights
Sight Radius: 6.75" *Finish:* Blued, Bi-tone or stainless
Features: Match grade barrel; Videcki speed trigger; serrated front strap & top of slide
Prices:
Blued **$931.00**
Stainless **975.00**

MODEL 1911-A1 HIGH-CAPACITY STANDARD (not shown)

SPECIFICATIONS
Caliber: 45 ACP
Capacity: 10 rounds (13-round & 17-round capacity available for law enforcement and military use only)
Barrel Length: 5"a
Trigger Pull: 5-6.5 lbs.
Sight Radius: 6.14"
Finish: Blued, stainless or Parkerized
Prices:
45 ACP Parkerized **$660.00**
45 ACP & 9mm Blued **719.00**
45 ACP & 9mm Stainless **764.00**

In addition to the models listed above and in the following pages, Springfield Armory also produces a broad line of customized pistols including the Super Tuned series.
Price: from **$959.00**

SPRINGFIELD PISTOLS

SUPER TUNED SERIES

**CHAMPION 1911-A1
3.5" STAINLESS**

CHAMPION 1911-A1

SPECIFICATIONS
Caliber: 45 ACP **Capacity:** 7 + 1 **Barrel Length:** 4"
Overall Length: 7.75" **Weight:** 36.3 oz. **Sight Radius:** 5.25"
Trigger Pull: 4.4-5.5 lbs. crisp **Grips:** Lightweight combat
Finish: Blue or Parkerized **Sights:** Novak fixed low-mount;
dovetailed serrated ramp front **Features:** Tuned and
polished extractor and ejector; beavertail grip safety;
polished feed ramp and throat barrel
Prices:
Parkerized $959.00
Blued 989.00
Also available: SUPER TUNED V10 1911-A1.
  In stainless $1,119.00
  Bi-tone w/3.5" barrel. 1,049.00
SUPER TUNED STANDARD 1911-A1.
  In stainless w/5" barrel $995.00

ULTRA COMPACT SERIES

HIGH-CAPACITY ULTRA COMPACT MODELS
(not shown)

SPECIFICATIONS
Caliber: 45 ACP and 9mm **Capacity:** 10 rounds (11-
round capacity available for law enforcement and military
use only) **Barrel Length:** 3.5" **Weight:** 33.6 oz.

Sight Radius: 5.25" **Trigger Pull:** 5-6.5 lbs.
Finish: Blue or stainless **Features:** 3-dot fixed combat
sights; flared ejection port; beveled magazine well
Prices:
Stainless $764.00
Mil-Spec Parkerized. 686.00
V-10 (PORTED) ULTRA COMPACT

**1911-A1 V-10
ULTRA COMPACT
BI-TONE**

**MODEL 1911-A1
LIGHTWEIGHT COMPACT**

SPECIFICATIONS
Caliber: 45 ACP **Capacity:** 7 rounds **Barrel Length:** 3.5"
Overall Length: 7.75" **Weight:** 34.8 oz. **Sights:** 3-dot
fixed combat sights **Sight Radius:** 5.25"
Trigger Pull: 5-6.5 lbs. **Finish:** Bi-Tone or Parkerized
Prices:
Parkerized. $569.00

SPECIFICATIONS
Caliber: 45 ACP **Capacity:** 7 rounds
Barrel Length: 4" **Overall Length:** 7.75"
Weight: 32 oz. (27 oz. alloy) **Trigger Pull:** 5-6.5" **Sights:**
3-dot fixed combat sights **Sight Radius:** 5.25"
Finish: Matte
Price: $569.00

TAURUS PISTOLS

SMALL & MEDIUM FRAME

MODEL PT 22

SPECIFICATIONS
Caliber: 22 LR *Action:* Semiautomatic (DA only)
Capacity: 8 shots *Barrel Length:* 2.75"
Overall Length: 5.25" *Weight:* 12.3 oz. *Sights:* Fixed
Safety: Manual *Grips:* Rosewood grip panels
Finish: Blue, nickel, duotone or gold trimmed
Prices:
Blue, Nickel or DuoTone $203.00
Gold Trim 219.00

MODEL PT-25

SPECIFICATIONS
Caliber: 25 ACP *Capacity:* 9 rounds
Action: Double action semiauto
Barrel Length: 2.75" *Overall Length:* 5.25"
Weight: 12.3 oz.
Finish: Blue, stainless steel, duotone or gold trimmed
Sights: Fixed *Features:* Rosewood grip panels; tip-up
barrel; push button magazine release
Prices:
Blue, Nickel or DuoTone $203.00
Blue w/Gold Trim 219.00

MODEL PT 22

MODEL PT-25

MODEL PT-938 COMPACT (not shown)

SPECIFICATIONS
Caliber: 380 ACP *Capacity:* 10 rounds
Action: Double action semiauto
Barrel Length: 3" *Overall Length:* 6.75"
Weight: 27 oz. *Finish:* Blue or stainless steel
Sights: Fixed *Grips:* Checkered rubber grips
Prices:
Blue $453.00
Stainless 469.00

PT 911 COMPACT (not shown)

SPECIFICATIONS
Caliber: 9mm *Capacity:* 10 rounds
Action: Double action semiauto *Barrel Length:* 4"
Overall Length: 7" *Weight:* 28.2 oz.
Safeties: Manual, ambidextrous hammer drop; intercept
notch; firing pin block; chamber load indicator
Grips: Santoprene II *Sights:* Fixed 3-dot combat
Finish: Blue or stainless *Features:* Floating firing pin
Prices:
Blue $453.00
Stainless 469.00
Also available:
PT-111 9MM MILLENNIUM. *Barrel Length:* 3 1/8" *Sights:* Fixed
3-dot *Capacity:* 10 rounds, polymer frame $367.00
Stainless 383.00

**MODEL PT 111
MILLENNIUM**

TAURUS PISTOLS

LARGE FRAME

MODEL PT-92

SPECIFICATIONS

Caliber: 9mm Parabellum *Action:* Semiautomatic double action *Capacity:* 15 + 1 *Hammer:* Exposed
Barrel Length: 5" *Overall Length:* 8.5"
Height: 5.39" *Width:* 1.45" *Weight:* 34 oz. (empty)
Rifling: R.H., 6 grooves *Sights:* Front, fixed; rear, drift adjustable, 3-dot combat *Safeties:* (a) Ambidextrous manual safety locking trigger mechanism and slide in locked position; (b) half-cock position; (c) inertia-operated firing pin; (d) chamber-loaded indicator
Slide: Hold open upon firing last cartridge *Finish:* Blue or stainless steel
Prices:
Blue $508.00
Stainless 523.00
Also available:
MODEL PT-99 Same specifications as Model PT 92, but has micrometer click-adjustable rear sight.
Blue $531.00
Stainless 547.00

MODEL PT-92

MODEL PT-945

SPECIFICATIONS

Caliber: 45 ACP *Capacity:* 8 shots
Action: Semiautomatic double *Barrel Length:* 4.25"
Overall Length: 7.48" *Weight:* 29.5 oz.
Sights: Drift-adjustable front and rear; 3-dot combat
Grips: Checkered rubber
Safety Features: Manual safety; ambidextrous; chamber load indicator; intercept notch; firing-pin block; floating firing pin
Finish: Blue or stainless
Prices:
Blue $484.00
Stainless 500.00
Also available:
MODEL 945C w/factory porting (blue) $523.00
  w/factory porting (stainless) 539.00

MODEL PT-945

MODEL PT-940 (not shown)

SPECIFICATIONS

Caliber: 40 S&W *Action:* Semiautomatic double
Capacity: 10 rounds *Barrel Length:* 4"
Overall Length: 7" *Weight:* 28.2 oz.
Grips: Santoprene II *Sights:* Low-profile 3-dot combat
Finish: Blue or stainless
Features: Factory porting standard
Prices:
Blue $469.00
Stainless 484.00

MODEL PT 99 STAINLESS

TAURUS REVOLVERS

MODEL 44

SPECIFICATIONS
Caliber: 44 Mag. *Capacity:* 6 rounds
Barrel Lengths: 4" (solid rib ported); 6.5" and 8 ³/₈" (vent. rib)
Weight: 44 oz. (4"); 52.5 oz. (6.5"); 57.25 oz. (8 ³/₈")
Sights: Serrated ramp front; rear micrometer click, adjustable for windage and elevation
Grips: Santoprene I
Finish: Blue or stainless steel
Features: Transfer bar safety
Prices:
4" barrel blue, ported solid rib **$447.00**
   stainless steel, ported solid rib **508.00**
6.5" and 8 ³/₈" blue, ported vent. rib **466.00**
   stainless steel, ported vent. rib **530.00**

MODEL 82

SPECIFICATIONS
Caliber: 38 Special *Capacity:* 6 shot
Action: Double *Barrel Length:* 4" heavy barrel
Weight: 34 oz. (4" barrel) *Sights:* Notched rear; serrated ramp front *Grips:* Brazilian hardwood
Finish: Blue or stainless
Prices:
Blue **$297.00**
Stainless **344.00**

MODEL 454
CASULL

MODEL 454 CASULL "RAGING BULL" DA

SPECIFICATIONS
Caliber: 454 Casull *Capacity:* 5 rounds
Barrel Length: 6.5" or 8.375" w/integral vent rib
Overall Length: 12" (6.5" barrel); 14" (8.375" barrel)
Weight: 53 oz. (6.5" barrel); 62.75 oz. (8.375" barrel)
Safety: Transfer bar ignition system
Sights: Black Patridge front blade; micrometer click adj. black rear
Finish: Polished stainless steel or bright blue steel
Grips: Soft black rubber w/recoil-absorbing insert
Features: Ported barrel w/internal gas expansion chamber; front and rear cylinder lock
Prices:
Blue ported **$750.00**
Stainless **820.00**

MODEL 85

SPECIFICATIONS
Caliber: 38 Special *Capacity:* 5 shot
Action: Double *Barrel Length:* 2" and 3"
Weight: 21 oz. (2" barrel) *Sights:* Fixed sights
Grips: Brazilian hardwood *Finish:* Blue or stainless steel
Prices:
Blue **$286.00**
Stainless Steel **327.00**
Also available:
MODEL 85CH. Same specifications and prices as Model 85, except has concealed hammer and 2" barrel only.
MODEL 85UL w/2" barrel only and optional porting; weights 17 oz. Features Ultra-Lite Integral Key Lock
Blue **$311.00**
Stainless **342.00**
MODELS 85CHB2C/85B2C w/2" barrel, blue finish, ported barrels **$305.00**
Stainless **345.00**

TAURUS REVOLVERS

MODEL 941

MODEL 94

SPECIFICATIONS
Caliber: 22 LR *Number Of Shots:* 9
Action: Double *Barrel Lengths:* 2", 3", 4",
and 5" heavy, solid rib *Weight:* 25 oz. (w/4"
barrel) *Sights:* Serrated ramp front; rear
micrometer click adjustable for windage and elevation
Grips: Brazilian hardwood (3", 4", 5")
Finish: Blue or stainless steel
Prices:
Blue $308.00
Stainless Steel 356.00
Also available:
MODEL 941 in 22 Magnum, 8-shot capacity; 2", 3", 4",
5" barrel lengths available; ejector shroud.
In blue $331.00
In stainless steel 384.00

TAURUS

MODEL 445 DOUBLE ACTION

SPECIFICATIONS
Caliber: 44 Special *Capacity:* 5 shots
Barrel Length: 2" *Weight:* 28.25 oz.
Grips: Santoprene I
Sights: Serrated ramp front; notched rear
Finish: Blue or stainless
Features: Optional porting; heavy solid rib barrel
Prices:
Blue $323.00
Stainless 370.00
Also available:
MODEL 445CH. Same specifications as Model 445 but features
concealed hammer

MODEL 608
DOUBLE ACTION

SPECIFICATIONS
Caliber: 357 Magnum *Capacity:* 8
shots *Barrel Lengths:* 4" (heavy solid rib);
6.5" and 8 3/8" (ejector shroud) *Weight:*
51.5 oz. (6.5" barrel) *Grips:* Santoprene I
Sights: Serrated ramp front w/red insert; micrometer
click adjustable *Finish:* Blue or stainless *Features:*
Compensated barrel; transfer bar safety; concealed hammer
Prices:
4" Blue $447.00
4" Stainless 508.00
6.5", 8 3/8" Blue 466.00
6.5", 8 3/8" Stainless 530.00

MODEL 605

SPECIFICATIONS
Caliber: 357 Magnum
Capacity: 5 shot
Barrel Length: 2.25"
Weight: 24.5 oz.
Sights: Notched rear; serrated ramp front
Grips: Santoprene I
Safety: Transfer bar
Finish: Blue or stainless
Features: Optional porting (**$19.00** add'l.)
Prices:
Blue $303.00
Stainless 344.00
Also available:
MODEL 605CH w/concealed hammer and ported barrel
MODELS 605021KL/605029KL w/Integral Key Lock
(**$20.00** add'l.)

THOMPSON/CENTER

ENCORE HUNTER PACKAGE

ENCORE PISTOL
(NOW OFFERED IN STAINLESS STEEL)
SPECIFICATIONS
Calibers: 22-250 Rem., 223 Rem., 243 Win., 260 Rem., 45-70 Gov't., 45 Colt/.410 ga., 270 Win., 7mm BR Rem., 7mm-08 Rem., 7.62X39mm, 308 Win., 30-06 Spfd. 44 Rem. Mag., 444 Marlin **Action:** Single break-open **Barrel lengths:** 12" and 15" **Overall length:** 16.5" (12" bbl.); 19.5" (15" bbl.) **Weight:** 4.25, 12"; 4.5 lbs. (15" bbl.) **Trigger:** Adjustable **Safety:** Automatic hammerblock w/bolt interlock **Grips:** Ambidextrous walnut pistol grip w/finger grooves and butt cap; composite grips as accessory. **Sights:** Adjustable rear; ramp front sight blade **Features:** Interchangeable barrels (12"- **$235.96-258.08**; 15"- **$243.27-274.89** Blued, **$272.85** SST); drilled and tapped for T/C scope mounts; barrel lug welded by electronic beam process
Price: 12" Blued **$527.68-549.80**
   15" barrel Blued 534.99-549.80
   SST 591.42
Also available: ENCORE HUNTER PACKAGE in 22-250 Win., 270 Win., 308 Win. **Barrel length:** 15" **Features:** Weaver-style base and rings, 2.5-7X Recoil Proof pistol scope; blued frame and barrel; black composite grip and forend; soft carry case; no iron sights.
Price: $774.33

THOMPSON/CENTER
CONTENDER SHOOTER'S PACKAGE

SPECIFICATIONS
Calibers: 7-30 Waters, 223 Rem., 30-30 Win., 22 LR Match **Barrel length:** 14" (10" 22 LR Match) **Overall length:** 16" (10" 22 LR Match) **Weight:** 4 lbs. **Features:** Mounted T/C Recoil Proof 2.5 X 7 scope plus carrying case
Price: Blued steel $735.99

CONTENDER SUPER "16" (Not Shown)

SPECIFICATIONS
Calibers: 223 Rem., 45-70 (bull barrel); 45 Colt/.410 ga.
Prices:
Blued (223 Rem.). $500.90
   45-70 Gov't. w/Muzzle Tamer 506.21
   45 Colt/.410 ga. 533.05

CONTENDER SUPER "14"
BULL BARREL MODELS

SPECIFICATIONS
Calibers: 22 LR Match Grade Chamber, 22 Hornet, 223 Rem., 7-30 Waters, 30-30 Win., and 44 Mag. (Blued version also available in 22 Hornet, 222 Rem., 357 Rem. Max.). *See pg. 13 Catalog* **Barrel length:** 14" bull barrel. **Features:** Fully adjustable target rear sight and Patridge-style ramped front sight with 13.5-inch sight radius. **Overall length:** 18.25" **Weight:** 3.5 lbs.
Prices:
Blued **$495.47**
   Match Grade Chamber 506.19
Stainless 550.86
Vent Rib Model (14") in 45 Colt/.410, blue. 530.23
Stainless 584.70
22 LR Match SST 562.66

CONTENDER BULL
BARREL MODELS
These pistols with 10-inch barrel feature fully adjustable Patridge-style iron sights. All stainless steel models (including the Super "14" and Super "16") are equipped with Rynite finger-groove grip with rubber recoil cushion and matching Rynite forend, plus Cougar etching on the steel frame.
Standard calibers available: 22 WMR, 22 Hornet, 22 LR Match, 223 Rem., 30-30 Win., 357 Mag., 44 Mag. and 45 Colt/.410. Custom calibers also available.

Prices:
Bull Barrel Blue **$484.79-495.47**
Bull Barrel Stainless 539.61-550.86
   In 45/.410 - 10 inch SST. 562.32
Vent Rib Model Stainless - 14 inch 584.70
Match Grade Barrel (22 LR only, stainless)
   10-inch 550.86
   14-inch 562.32

UBERTI REPLICAS

1871 ROLLING BLOCK TARGET PISTOL

SPECIFICATIONS
Calibers: 22 LR, 22 Magnum, 22 Hornet and 357 Mag.
Capacity: Single shot
Barrel Length: 9.5" (half-octagon/half-round or full round Navy Style)
Overall Length: 14" *Weight:* 2.75 lbs.
Sights: Fully adjustable rear; ramp front or open sight on Navy Style barrel
Grip and forend: Walnut *Trigger guard:* Brass
Frame: Color case hardened steel
Price: $410.00

1871 ROLLING BLOCK TARGET PISTOL

1873 CATTLEMAN S.A.

SPECIFICATIONS
Calibers: 357 Magnum, 38/40, 44 Sp., 44-40, 45 L.C.
Capacity: 6 shots
Barrel Lengths: 4.75", 5.5", 7.5" round, tapered; 18" (Buntline)
Overall Length: 10.75" w/5.5" barrel
Weight: 2.42 lbs. *Grip:* One-piece walnut
Frame: Color case hardened steel; also available in charcoal blue or nickel
Price: $410.00-475.00
Also available:
45 L.C./45 ACP Convertible $485.00

1873 CATTLEMAN

1875 "OUTLAW"/1890 POLICE

SPECIFICATIONS
Calibers: 357 Magnum, 44-40, 45 ACP, 45 Long Colt
Capacity: 6 shots *Barrel Lengths:* 5.5", 7.5" round, tapered
Overall Length: 13.75" *Weight:* 2.75 lbs.
Grips: Two-piece walnut *Finish:* Color case hardened steel
Price: $435.00
Also available:
In nickel plate $435.00
45 L.C./45 ACP "Outlaw" Convertible. 485.00
45 L.C./45 ACP Police Convertible 475.00

1875 "OUTLAW"/ 1890 POLICE

WALTHER PISTOLS

The Walther double-action system combines the principles of the DA revolver with the advantages of the modern autoloading pistol without the disadvantages inherent in either design.

Models PPK and PPK/S differ only in the overalll length of the barrel and slide. Both models offer the same features, including compact form, light weight, easy handling, and absolute safety. Both models can be carried with a loaded chamber and closed hammer, but ready to fire either single-or double-action. Both models are provided with a live round indicator pin to signal a loaded chamber. An automatic internal safety blocks the hammer to prevent accidental striking of the firing pin, except with a deliberate pull of the trigger. Sights are provided with white markings for high visibility in poor light. Rich Walther blue/black finish is standard, and each pistol is complete with an extra magazine with finger-rest extension.

MODEL PPK & PPK/S

SPECIFICATIONS
Caliber: 380 ACP and 32 ACP
Capacity: 6 rounds (PPK), 7 rounds (PPK/S), 8 rounds (PPK/S in 32 ACP only)
Barrel Length: 3.35"
Overall Length: 6.25"
Weight: 21 oz. (PPK); 23 oz. (PPK/S)
Grips: Plastic
Finish: Walther blue or stainless steel
Price: $540.00

MODEL PP DOUBLE ACTION

SPECIFICATIONS
Calibers: 380 ACP
Capacity: 7 rounds
Barrel Length: 3.85"
Overall Length: 6.75"
Weight: 25 oz.
Grips: Plastic
Finish: Walther blue
Price: $999.00

MODEL PP

MODEL TPH

MODEL TPH DOUBLE ACTION

Walther's Model TPH is considered by government agents and professional lawmen to be one of the top undercover/backup guns available. It is essentially a scaled-down Walther PP-PPK.

SPECIFICATIONS
Calibers: 22 LR and 25 ACP
Capacity: 6 rounds
Barrel Length: 2.85"
Overall Length: 5.37"
Weight: 14 oz.
Width: .89"
Grips: Plastic
Finish: Walther blue or stainless steel
Price: $460.00

WALTHER PISTOLS

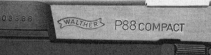

MODEL P 88 COMPACT

The Walther P 88 Compact is a double-action, locked-breech, semiautomatic pistol with an external hammer. Its compact form, light weight and easy handling are combined with the superb performance of the 9mm Luger Parabellum cartridge. The P 88 Compact boasts target-grade accuracy, dual-function controls and comes with two 10-shot double-column magazines.

SPECIFICATIONS
Caliber: 9mm Parabellum
Capacity: 10 rounds
Barrel Length: 3.93" *Overall Length:* 7.25"
Weight: 28 oz. *Width:* 1.32"
Finish: Blue
Price: $900.00

Also available:
MODEL P 5 (not shown)
SPECIFICATIONS
Caliber: 9mm Parabellum
Capacity: 8 rounds *Barrel Length:* 3.62"
Overall Length: 7.1" *Weight:* 28 oz.
Width: 1.26"
Price: $900.00

**MODEL P 88
COMPACT**

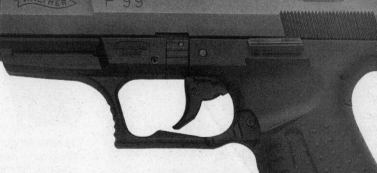

MODEL P 99

MODEL P 99 COMPACT

SPECIFICATIONS
Caliber: 9mm Parabellum, 40 S&W, 9x21
Capacity: 10 rounds
Barrel Length: 4"
Overall Length: 7"
Weight: 25 oz.
Height: 5.37"
Width: 1.2"
Sights: Windage-adjustable micrometer rear; three interchangeable front blades included; optional modular laser sight and halogen flashlight for installation on front rails
Features: Polymer frame; blued slide; customized backstrap; three automatic safeties; cocking and loaded chamber indicator; ambidetrous magazine release levers
Price: $799.00

WICHITA ARMS PISTOLS

SILHOUETTE PISTOL (Right-Hand Rear Grip)

SPECIFICATIONS
Calibers: 308 Win. F.L., 7mm IHMSA and 7mmX308
Barrel length: 14 ¹⁵/₁₆" **Weight:** 4.5 lbs. **Action:** Single-shot bolt action **Sights:** Wichita Multi-Range Sight System **Grips:** Right-hand center walnut grip or right-hand rear walnut grip **Features:** Glass bedded; bolt ground to precision fit; adjustable Wichita trigger
Price: $1,800.00
Also available:
WICHITA CLASSIC SILHOUETTE PISTOL. **Barrel:** 11.25".
Weight: 3 lbs. 15 oz. **Grips:** AAA grade walnut,
 glass bedded $3450.50
ENGRAVED MODEL 4850.00

INTERNATIONAL PISTOL

SPECIFICATIONS
Calibers: 7-30 Waters, 7mm Super Mag., 7R (30-30 Win. necked to 7mm), 30-30 Win., 357 Mag., 357 Super Mag., 32 H&H Mag., 22-RFM, 22 LR **Barrel lengths:** 10" and 14" (10.5" for centerfire calibers) **Weight:** 3 lbs. 2 oz. (10" barrel); 4 lbs. 7 oz. (14" barrel) **Action:** Top-break, single-shot, single action only **Sights:** Partridge front sight; rear sight adjustable for windage and elevation **Grips and Forend:** Walnut **Safety:** Crossbolt
Price: 10" Barrel $775.00
14" Barrel $875.00

WILDEY PISTOLS

WILDEY PISTOLS

These gas-operated pistols are designed to meet the needs of hunters who want to use handguns for big game. The Wildey pistol includes such features as: •Ventilated rib •Reduced recoil •Double-action trigger mechanism •Patented hammer and trigger blocks and rebounding fire pin •Sights adjustable for windage and elevation •Stainless construction •Fixed barrel for increased accuracy •Increased action strength (with 3-lug and exposed face rotary bolt) •Selective single or autoloading capability •Ability to handle high-pressure loads

SPECIFICATIONS
Calibers: 357, 41, 44, 45 & 475 Wildey Magnums and 45 Win. Mag. **Capacity:** 7 shots **Barrel lengths:** 5", 6", 7", 8", 10", 12", 14" **Overall length:** 11" with 7" barrel **Weight:** 64 oz. with 5" barrel **Height:** 6"

SURVIVOR AND GUARDSMAN in 45 Win. Mag.	**Prices**
5", 6" or 7" barrels	$1295.00
8" or 10" barrels	1316.00
12" barrel	1395.00
14" barrel	1895.00
SURVIVOR MODEL in Wildey Mags.	
8" or 10" barrels	$1316.00
12" barrel	1395.00
14" barrel	1895.00

HUNTER MODEL in 45 Win. Mag.	
5", 6" or 7" barrels	$1413.00
8" or 10" barrels	1435.00
12" barrel	1515.00
14" barrel	2015.00
HUNTER MODEL in 475 Wildey Mag.	
8" or 10" barrels	1435.00
12" barrel	1515.00
14" barrel	2015.00
Also available: Interchangeable barrel extension assemblies	
12" barrel	1,515.00
14" barrel	2,015.00

American Hunting	190		L.A.R. Grizzly	227
Anschutz	191		Lazzeroni	228
Arnold	195		Lone Star	229
A-Square	198		Magnum Research	230
Auto-Ordnance	199		Marlin	231
Beretta	200		Mauser	239
Blaser	201		Navy Arms	240
Browning	202		New England Firearms	245
Brown Precision	207		Pedersoli	246
Christensen Arms	209		Prairie Gun Works	246
Colt	211		Remington	247
Cooper Arms	212		Rifles	256
Dakota Arms	213		Rossi	257
EMF	215		Ruger	258
European American Armory	215		Sako	266
Francotte	216		Sauer	272
Harrington & Richardson	216		Savage	273
Harris Gunworks	217		Springfield	284
Heckler & Koch	219		Steyr-Mannlicher	285
Henry Repeating Arms	219		Taylor	286
H-S Precision	220		Thompson/Center	287
Howa	222		Tikka	288
Jarrett	222		Uberti	290
Johannsen	223		Ultra Light Arms	291
KBI/Charles Daly	224		Weatherby	292
Kimber	225		Winchester	298
Krieghoff	227		**NEW!** *Custom Cache*	*304-310*

For addresses and phone/fax numbers of manufacturers and distributors included in this section, please turn to **DIRECTORY OF MANUFACTURERS AND SUPPLIERS** *on page 564.*

AMERICAN HUNTING RIFLES

IN 1999 A MONTANA-BASED COMPANY INTRODUCES A NEW RIFLE AND AN INNOVATIVE LINE OF CARTRIDGES TO MATCH

A BIG GAME RIFLE FOR SERIOUS HUNTERS

The foundation of every AHR rifle is the recently reintroduced pre-1964 Winchester Model 70 Action (other high-quality actions available). Justly famous for its smooth and dependable controlled-round feeding the M70 has a convenient three-position safety and a rugged adjustable trigger. This classic action wears your choice of a claro walnut or all-weather synthetic stock. The classic design in both the walnut and the all-weather stocks, is the creation of master stockmaker Jerry Fisher.

The 24-inch American Hunting Rifles barrel - chrome moly or stainless steel - is rifled with the rate of twist best suited to the premium hunting bullets loaded in each specific cartridge. The outstanding accuracy of these barrels often surpasses that of other production rifles that cost much more.

AHR rifles are available in the standard .270 Winchester and .30-06 Springfield, as well as a wide variety of our own proprietary cartridges from a .220 to a .411. All of our cartridges are based on original designs by Ken Howell, noted writer and author of the popular book, Designing and Forming Custom Cartridges.

Hunters will quickly find that the twelve new Howell cartridges, although designed specifically for hunting varmints and big game, are definitely powerful enough for comparable game on other continents. Designed as a family of cartridges, they offer hunters a wide range of choices for effective knock-down power for each hunter's preferred game species.

Howell cartridges are designed for balanced ballistics and long barrel life - without excessive muzzle blast or recoil - these new cartridges confirm experienced hunters' opinion that belted magnum cases aren't necessary for game-killing power.

A Family of New Cartridges With Roots in Classic Oldies

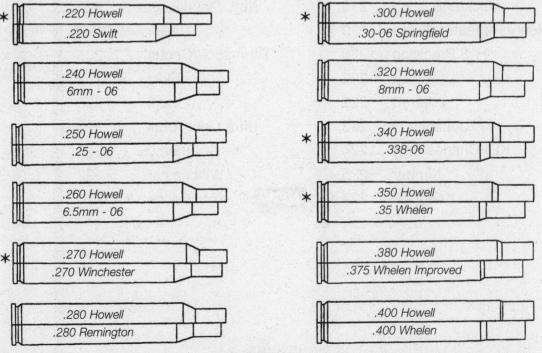

*Available Now

Based on the .30-06 case lengthened to 2.600 inches. Shoulder angles 25°.

ANSCHUTZ

MODEL 2013
SUPER MATCH

Julius Gottfried Anschutz, son of a German gunsmith, founded J.G. Anschutz in 1856 to build pocket pistols, shotguns and rifles. In 1896 the firm moved out of its small workshop into a factory. Five years later Julius Anschutz died, and his sons, Fritz and Otto, assumed control of the business. By 1911 there were 200 people working at the Anschutz plant. When Otto died shortly after the first world war, Fritz and his sons, Rudolf and Max, continued to build the enterprise.

Growth came to an abrupt halt in 1945, when the factory was shut down pursuant to Germany's surrender in World War II. But five years later J.G. Anschutz GmbH was founded to make air pistols and repair firearms. Soon it turned to target rifles and even resumed manufacture of the Flobert-type guns that had been among the firm's original products. Anschutz target rifles began to build a reputation among the world's elite shooters, and the company grew to 250 employees.

In 1968 Dieter Anschutz, a fourth-generation member of the family, became chief executive, as the Anschutz name became more and more prominent in Olympic competition. In 1992 his son, Jochen, became company president. Jochen and Dieter now manage J.G. Anschutz together. An ultra-modern plant in Ulm, Germany produces what have become recognized world-wide as the standard against which all rimfire target rifles and pistols are judged. Anschutz rifles captured all of the gold medals, and all but two of the silver medals in the Barcelona Olympic Games. The company's competition air rifles and pistols have done almost as well as the firearms.

MODEL 2013 "SUPER MATCH"

Since the 1960s, the Model 54 rimfire action has set the standard in competitive three-position and smallbore prone shooting. The current version, with a heavy, rectangular receiver, attaches to the stock with four action screws. This action is the heart of the Model 2013 Super Match Special — and of the 2013 Benchrest, the 2007, 2012, 1907, 1912, and 1913 rifles. It is also featured in the 1808 D-RT Running Target, 54.18 MS Metallic Silhouette and 1808 MS-R Silhouette rifles. Its fine trigger mechanism, close tolerances and extremely fast lock time make it a logical choice for competitive marksmen. Anschutz .22 rimfire barrels, noted for one-hole accuracy, complement the 54 action.

The 2013 Super Match is the latest and most sophisticated in a long line of Super Match rifles for freestyle shooting events. Available in both right- and left-hand versions, it comes with adjustable two-stage match trigger (with safety). The trigger-piece can be moved longitudinally and tilted up to 15 degrees. There's a forearm accessory rail with hand stop and palm rest fitted to the thumbhole stock. A fully adjustable cheekpiece complements a hook butt assembly adjustable for cant, pitch, length and drop. A host of accessories, including match sights and counter-weights is available.

Barrel length: 27.1 inches.
Rifle weight: 14.3 pounds.
Price:. **$3,145.00**
   left-hand 3,299.00

ANSCHUTZ

MODEL 1907

Match 54 action in an economical rifle, with adjustable cheekpiece and butt assembly.
Barrel Length: 25.9 inches
Rifle Weight: 10.5 pounds
Price:. $1,639.00
left-hand 1,726.00

MODEL 1912 "SPORT RIFLE"

Match 54 action in a lightweight international-style rifle engineered to stay under the 6.5kg weight limit. The walnut stock has a forend raiser block, fully adjustable hook buttplate and cheekpiece, and forward hand stop and swivel.
Barrel Length: 25.9 inches.
Rifle Weight: 11.4 pounds.
Price:. $2,250.00
left-hand 2,356.00

MODEL 1808 D-RT "RUNNING TARGET"

A fully adjustable trigger, as per the Model 2013 "Super Match" and lightning-quick lock time help competitors excel on the moving-target range. A removable barrel extension improves smoothness of swing. The stock is specially configured for off-hand shooting, with adjustable cheekpiece and butt assembly.
Barrel Length: 32.6 inches.
Rifle Weight: 9.0 pounds.
Price:. $1,699.00

STOEGER

IGA

DELUXE SERIES
SHOTGUNS

STOEGER

ANSCHUTZ

MODEL 54.18 MS R "SILHOUETTE"

Designed expressly for metallic silhouette shooting, this rifle weighs only 8.1 pounds. The adjustable two-stage trigger is set at 4.4 ounces. The Match 54 action has been modified to accept a 5-shot magazine. A rubber buttpad is standard.
Barrel Length: 22.4 inches
Price:. $1,499.00

MODEL 1827 "FORTNER"

This rifle is built for biathlon competition, an Olympic event that combines skiing and marksmanship. Competitors must shoot twice at the 10-km point, four times at 20 km into the race and twice at a relay point of 7.5 km. Each station requires five shots prone and five standing. The Anschutz 1827 has a straight-pull repeating action to increase speed of fire. It weighs 8.8 pounds and is equipped with magazine holders. The walnut stock features adjustable cheekpiece and butt assembly. A special front sight hood protects the sight and bore from snow.
Barrel Length: 21.6 inches.
Price:. $2,495.00
   left-hand 2,745.00

MODEL 1903

A competitive rifle for riflemen on a budget, the 1903 has a M64-type action with two-stage adjustable trigger. The hardwood stock features a forward accessory rail and an adjustable cheekpiece. The buttplate is vertically adjustable; length of pull can be changed by adding or deleting spacers.
Price: $942.00

ANSCHUTZ

MODEL 1451 (not shown)

An affordable rifle with target-rifle potential, this 5-pound repeater has a trim action, checkered hardwood stock and iron sights on a 21-inch sporter-weight barrel. The receiver is grooved for a scope.

Price: $370.00
  (threaded barrel or tangent rear sight $10 extra each)

MODEL 1710 REPEATING RIFLE (not shown)

A premium-quality .22 sporter, the 1710 is built on the famous Match 54 action. Adjustable sights and trigger, and a high-grade checkered walnut stock, put this rifle in its own class. There's a choice of "classic," "German," and "Monte Carlo" stocks and single-stage or double-set triggers. The

MODEL 1743 HUNTING RIFLE (not shown)

This centerfire rifle in .222 Remington has an Anschutz 54-type action with wing safety and claw extractor. The full-length checkered walnut stock has a Monte Carlo comb. Barrel length: 18 inches. This rifle is also available in a half-

MODEL 1451 R SPORT TARGET

This modestly-priced target rifle has the same action as the 1451 sporter but with a heavier 20-inch barrel adapted to target sights, and a target-style stock with aluminum slide rail and vertically adjustable butt. The two-stage trigger and fast lock time help boost scores. *Weight:* 6.5 pounds.

Price: $486.00
  (target sights $282 extra)

sporter barrel is 22 inches, rifle weight 6.6 pounds. A synthetic-stocked version is available.

Price: **$1,160.00**
  Classic **1,073.00**
  Synthetic. **1,499.00**

stock version with 22-inch barrel (Model 1740) and in .22 Hornet (both stock styles, Models 1730 and 1733). *Weight:* 6.3 and 6.6 pounds, depending on style.

Price: 1743 and 1733. **$1,431.00**
  1740 and 1730. . . . . **1,297.00**

MODEL 2013 "BENCHREST"

Barreled action: Compact connection between barreled action and stock, heavy rectangular receiver attached with 4 action screws. The accuracy of the barreled action and the

extremely short locktime within a range of milliseconds offer best conditions for success. *Barrel:* Cylindrical match barrel *Stock:* Non-stained stock with wide, flat, forend, especially developed for benchrest shooting *Caliber:* .22 l.r. *Barrel length:* 50 cm/19.6" *Rifling:* 50 cm/16.6" *Total length:* 97 cm/38.1" *Weight appr.:* 4,7 kg/10.3 lbs *Version:* Single loader

Price: . . . . **Available upon request**

ARNOLD ARMS RIFLES

AFRICAN SERIES

Arnold Arms designed and builds its own Apollo action with a clever extractor that helps ensure positive function. In its center position, the 3-position safety allows the action to be cycled for loading and unloading without fear of discharge. Squaring and truing operations usually reserved for custom rifles are standard on every Appollo. Lugs are lapped and the action glass bedded for accuracy. The Apollo action is optional on some Arnold rifles.

Most Arnold rifles are built on other actions, in a variety of configurations to satisfy every hunter and target shooter. Match-grade barrels and McMillan synthetic stocks are used throughout, though walnut stocks are available by special order. Rifles are available in chamberings from 223 to 458, including Arnold's own line of high-performance cartridges.

AFRICAN TROPHY

AFRICAN TROPHY

Each rifle features a fully trued and accurized action in chrome-moly matte blued steel with sporting contour match grade barrel and synthetic McMillan stock in either black or camo finish. Each rifle is given the Arnold "Accu*Pro" treatment and is availabe in .223 to .338 magnum calibers as well as most wildcats and the Arnold lines of cartridges.
Prices:
Remington 700 action rifle **$2,595.00**

Winchester M70 action rifle **2,595.00**
Ruger M77 MKII action rifle **2,329.00**
Same rifles as above, but with McMillan
   fibergrain stock . . . . **Add 299.00**
Same as above but with Arnold Sporter
   wanut stock . . . . **Add 79.00**
Same as above but with black teflon coated
   stainless steel barrel . . . . **Add 229.00**

GRAND AFRICAN

GRAND AFRICAN

This line of superbly crafted custom rifles comes with Express sights and barrel band for front sling swivel, and is available in "A" through "AAA" American dark, English walnut, Bastogne, as well as "Exhibition grade. Available in .338 magnum to .458 magnum. Remington 700 action rifles come equipped with a three-position safety and SAKO extractor as a standard upgrade.
Prices:
With McMillan fibergrain synthetic stock **$3,995.00**
With Arnod Walnut Hunter Classic stock. **3,895.00**
With "A" English walnut and ebony forend

and steel grip cap. Start at **6,495.00**
Winchester Model 70 action rifles:
With McMillan fibergrain synthetic stock **3,695.00**
With Arnold Walnut Hunter Classic stock **3,595.00**
With "A" Engllish walnut with ebony forend and
   steel grip cap. Start at **6,195.00**
Ruger M77 MKII action rifles:
With McMillan fibergrain synthetic stock **3,495.00**
With Arnold Walnut Hunter Classic stock **3,395.00**
With "A" Engllish walnut stock with ebony forend
   and steel grip cap. Start at **5,995.00**

ARNOLD ARMS RIFLES

ALASKAN SERIES

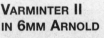

ALASKAN TROPHY

ALASKAN TROPHY
Each rifle features a fully accurized and trued action in stainless steel with a stainless steel match grade sporting contour barrel and choice of McMillan black or camo stock. Barrel lengths available are 22"-24" for non-magnums and 24"-26" for magnums. Chambering are available in all popular cartridges plus most wildcats and the Arnold line of cartridges.
Prices: Remington 700 action rifle **$2,695.00**
Winchester M70 action rifle **2,695.00**
Ruger M77 MKII action rifle **2,329.00**

ALASKAN GUIDE
These rifes come with the same components as the "Alaskan Trophy", but have Express sights and a barrel band for the front sling swivel installed as standard equipment. Available in .338 magnum to .458 magnum.
Prices:
Remington 700 SS action built rifle, upgraded with three-. position safety and SAKO style extractor. . . . **$3,749.00**
Winchester M70 SS action rifle. **3,249.00**
Ruger M77 MKII SS action rifle. **2,879.00**

VARMINTER II IN 6MM ARNOLD

VARMINTER II
With sporter stock and barrel: Fully accurized action with match grade heavy sporter 27" barrel, cryogenically treated, bedded and free-floated in McMillan varminter synthetic stock. Choice of black, woodland, desert or arctic camo. All rifes guaranteed capable of shooting 1/2" groups. Available in all popular varmint cartridges plus many wildcats and the Arnold 6mm and .257 magnums.
Prices:
Remington 70 CM matte blue barreled action . . **$2,595.00**
Remington CM blue with detachable
    box magazine **2,649.00**

Remington SS barreled action **2,695.00**
Remington SS with detachable box magazine. . . **2,695.00**
Winchester M70 CM matte blue
    barreled action **2,595.00**
Winchester M70 SS matte barreled action **2,695.00**
Ruger M77 CM matte blue barreled action **2,329.00**
Ruger M77 SS matte finished barreled action . . . **2,329.00**
Additional selections include:
Arnold laminated varmint stock . . . . **Add 199.00**
McMillan fibergrain synthetic stock . . . . **Add 299.00**
Teflon coated barreled action . . . . **Add 229.00**

ARNOLD ARMS RIFLES

ARNOLD AMS COMPANY manufactures a full line of benchrest, 500-yard, Palma and 1,000-yard match rifles, including prone and x-course models. Only the finest components are used in these rifles, which are custom built to customer specifications and requirements. We offer National Match course rifles in the following calibers .223, .243, 6mm Rem., .308 (7.62 NATO) & 7mm-08. All popuar benchrest cartridge chamberings are available, as well as the magnums and wildcats for 1,000-yard match.

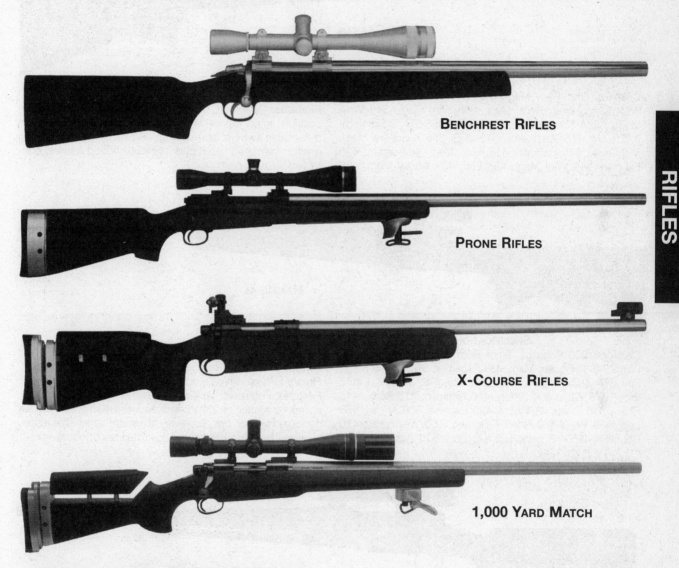

BENCHREST RIFLES

PRONE RIFLES

X-COURSE RIFLES

1,000 YARD MATCH

ARNOLD NEUTRALIZER SERIES RIFLES
(not shown)

Features include Remington 700 action (choice of chrome-moly blued or stainless steel) with detachable box magazine, match grade barrel (chrome-moly or stainless steel) in Palma to heavy varmint contours. McMillan A2 or A3 tactical stocks available in black, woodland, arctic, desert or urban camo. Adjustable cheekpiece standard. SAKO extractor, 3-position safety and thicker recoil lug standard on the Neutraizer rifles, and triggers are set at choice of 2.5 or 3 pounds. Available in .223, .308 and .300 Winchester magnum.

Prices:

Apollo action rifle, includes Jewell trigger **$4,599.00**
Remington 700 action with features
    outlined above. **3,449.00**
Remington 700 action with DBM and 2-position
    safety and Remington extractor **2,959.00**
Winchester Model 70 action **2,949.00**
    Options include Timney, Shilen or Jewell triggers, adjustable buttplate.

A-SQUARE RIFLES

CAESAR

SPECIFICATIONS

Calibers: 7mm Rem. Mag., 7mm STW, 300 Win. Mag., 300 Wby. Mag., 8mm Rem. Mag., 338 Win. Mag., 340 Wby. Mag., 338 A-Square Mag., 358 Norma, 358 STA, 9.3x64mm, 375 H&H, 375 Weatherby, 375 JRS, 375 A-Square Mag., 416 Taylor, 416 Hoffman, 416 Rem. Mag., 404 Jeffery, 425 Express, 458 Win. Mag., 458 Lott, 450 Ackley Mag., 460 Short A-Square, 470 Capstick and 495 A-Square Mag.
Features: Selected Claro walnut stock with oil finish; three-position safety; three-way adjustable target trigger; flush detachable swivels; leather sling; dual recoil lugs; coil spring ejector; ventilated recoil pad; premium honed barrels; contoured ejection port

HANNIBAL

SPECIFICATIONS

Calibers: 300 Pegasus, 8mm Rem. Mag., 338 Win., 340 Wby., 338 A-Square Mag., 338 Excalibur, 358 Norma Mag., 358 STA, 9.3x64, 375 A-Square, 375 JRS, 375 H&H, 375 Wby., 378 Wby., 404 Jeffery, 416 Hoffman, 416 Rem., 416 Rigby, 416 Taylor, 416 Wby., 425 Express, 450 Ackley, 458 Lott, 458 Win., 460 Short A-Square, 460 Weatherby, 470 Capstick, 495 A-Square, 500 A-Square, 577 Tyrannosaur

Barrel Length: 20" to 26".
Length of Pull: 12" to 15.25" **Weight:** 9.5 lbs.-13.25 lbs.
Finish: Deluxe walnut stock; oil finish; matte blue
Features: Flush detachable swivels, leather sling, dual recoil lugs, coil spring ejector, ventilated recoil pad, premium honed barrels, contoured ejection port, three-way adjustable target-style trigger, Mauser-style claw extractor and controlled feed, positive safety

HAMILCAR

SPECIFICATIONS

Calibers: 25-06, 257 Wby., 6.5x55 Swedish, 264 Win., 270 Win., 270 Wby., 7x57 Mauser, 280 Rem., 7mm Rem., 7mm Wby., 7mm STW, 30-06, 300 Win., 300 Wby., 338-06, 9.3x62 **Barrel Length:** 20" to 26" **Length of Pull:** 12" to 15.25" **Weight:** 8.5 lbs. **Finish:** Deluxe walnut stock; oil finish; matte blue **Features:** Flush detachable swivels, leather sling, coil spring ejector, vent. recoil pad; honed barrels; contoured ejection port; target-style adjustable trigger, Mauser-style claw extractor; controlled feed; positive safety
Price: **$3,295.00**
Also available: GENGHIS KHAN MODEL in 22-250, 243 Win., 6mm Rem., 25-06, 257 Wby., 264 Win. Features benchrest-quality heavy taper barrel and coilchek stock. **Weight:** 11 lbs. (w/scope & iron sights)
All Prices: A-square suggests you phone (502-719-3006) for current pricing. Base prices for these semi-custom rifles start at **$3,295.00.**

AUTO-ORDNANCE

SEMIAUTOMATIC RIFLES

THOMPSON MODEL M1 CARBINE

SPECIFICATIONS
Caliber: 45 ACP *Barrel Length:* 16.5"
Overall Length: 38" *Weight:* 11.5 lbs.
Sights: Blade front; fixed rear

Stock: Walnut stock and horizontal foregrip
Features: Side cocking lever; frame and receiver milled from solid steel
Price: $850.00

THOMPSON DELUXE MODEL 1927 A1

SPECIFICATIONS
Caliber: 45 ACP
Barrel Length: 16.5"
Overall Length: 41" *Weight:* 13 lbs.
Sights: Blade front; open rear adjustable

Stock: Walnut stock; vertical foregrip
Also available:
THOMPSON 1927A1C LIGHTWEIGHT (45 Cal.). Same as the 1927 A1 model, but weighs only 9.5 lbs.
Price: $860.00

MODEL 1927 A1 COMMANDO

SPECIFICATIONS
Caliber: 45 ACP
Barrel Length: 16.5"
Overall Length: 41"

Weight: 13 lbs.
Sights: Blade front; open rear (adjustable)
Finish: Black (stock and forend)
Price: $850.00

BERETTA RIFLES

455 EXPRESS

EXPRESS RIFLES

Express Rifles must accomodate large, high pressure cartridges. This requires action and locking systems designed and manufactured with extra strength, all joined with absolute precision for optimum convergence. The SS06 and SS06EELL Over-and Under Express Rifles offer rifled barrels of special steel cold-hammered in three calibers: 9.3x74R, .375 H&H Mag. and .458 Win. Mag. For those wishing to hunt with a traditional shotgun, an extra set of matching 12 gauge barrels is available. Hand-finished, hand-checkered stocks and forends are made from select walnut or walnut briar with a cheekpiece. A special trap door compartment for extra cartridges is fitted inside the stock, and an area under the pistol-grip cap holds a set of spare front sights. The SS-06 is finished with light engraving on the color case-hardened receiver. The SS06 EELL sports a receiver hand-engraved with game scenes, or a color case-hardened version with gold inlaid animals. For additional specifications see the table below.

The 455 Side-by-Side Express Rifle action is made of special high-strength steel and forged with an elongated 60mm plate. This increases the distance between the hinge pin and the three-lug locking system to compensate for stress when shooting. To withstand the pressure of high-powered cartridges, the sealed receiver has reinforced sides, and the top tang extends fully up to the stock comb to strengthen attachment of the stock. An articulated front trigger and automatic blocking device eliminate the possibility of simultaneous discharge. The safety (automatic on request) provides for quick, reliable and positive on/off operation. The Boehler steel barrels are joined with Demibloc chamber system.

SS06 OVER-UNDER EXPRESS RIFLE
SPECIFICATIONS
Calibers: 375 H&H, 458 Win. Mag., 9.3x94R
Barrel length: 24" (12 ga. matching interchangeable barrels available)
Weight: 11 lbs.
Sights: Blade front sight; V-notch rear sight w/folding leaf (claw mounts for Zeiss scope factory fitted and sighted-in at 100 meters)
Price:. $50,000.00
Note: MODEL SS06 EELL is also available in same calibers and features hand-engraved game scenes on the receiver or color case-hardened w/gold inlaid animals. $50,000.00

455 SIDE-BY-SIDE EXPRESS RIFLE
SPECIFICATIONS
Calibers: 375 H&H, 416 Rigby, 458 Win. Mag., 470 N.E., 500 N.E.
Barrel length: 23" - 25"
Weight: 11 lbs.
Sights: Fixed front sight w/folding blade; V-notch rear sight
Price:. $50,000.00
Note: MODEL 455 EELL is also available (same price and calibers) featuring Bulino-style game scene engraving or intricate scroll work and walnut briar stock and forend.

PREMIUM GRADE EXPRESS RIFLE SPECIFICATIONS

MODEL	9.3x 74R	.375 H&H MAG.	CALIBER* .416 RIGBY	.458 H&H MAG.	.470 N.E.	.500 N.E.	BARREL LENGTH (CM/IN)	AVERAGE WEIGHT (KG/LBS)**
SS06	√	√		√			62/24	5.00/11.0
SS06 EELL	√	√		√			62/24	5.00/11.0
455		√	√	√	√	√	60/23 to 65/25	5.00/11.0
455 EELL		√	√	√	√	√	60/23 to 65/25	5.00/11.0

*SS06 EELL Models are available with interchangeable 12 gauge shotgun barrels upon request.
**Weights are approximate, dependent on wood density and barrel length.

BERETTA RIFLES

MATO RIFLES

Beretta's Mato (the Dakota Indian word for "bear") is designed for hunters. Based on the Mauser 98 action, it has a drop-out box magazine that releases quickly. The barrels are machined from high-grade chrome-moly steel. Other features include ergonomic bolt handle, adjustable trigger, wraparound hand checkering and three-position safety.

SPECIFICATIONS

Calibers: 270 Win., 280 Rem., 30-06 Springfield, 7mm Rem. Mag., 300 Win. Mag., 338 Win. Mag., 375 H&H Mag.
Barrel length: 23.6" **Overall length:** 44.5"
Weight: 7.97 lbs. (Deluxe); 8 lbs. (Standard)
Stock: Matte grey composite synthetic (Standard); Triple-X Grade Claro walnut w/hand-rubbed satin oil finish and black forend tip (Deluxe) **Length of pull:** 13.5" **Drop at comb:** .56" **Drop at heel:** .81" **Twist:** 1:10" (1:12" 375 H&H Mag.)
Prices: Standard Synthetic **$1,660.00**
in H&H mag. 2,015.00
Deluxe Synthetic 2,478.00
in H&H Mag. 2,795.00

BLASER RIFLES

MODEL R93 CLASSIC

MODEL R 93 BOLT ACTION SERIES

SPECIFICATIONS (CLASSIC)
Calibers: (interchangeable)
Standard: (22-250, 243 Win., 270 Win., 30-06, 308 Win.
Magnum: 257 Weatherby Mag., 7mm Rem. Mag., 300 Win. Mag., 300 Wby. Mag., 338 Win. Mag., 375 H&H, 416 Rem. Mag..
Barrel lengths: 22" (Standard) and 26" (Magnum)
Overall length: 40" (Standard) and 42" (Magnum)
Weight: (w/scope mounts) 7 lbs. (Standard) and 7.25 lbs. (Magnum) **Safety:** Cocking slide
Stock: Two-piece Custom and Deluxe Walnut recoil pad, hand-cut checkering (18 lines/inch, borderless)
Length of pull: 13.75"

Prices:
CLASSIC $3,495.00
LX 1,795.00
SYNTHETIC 1,495.00
ATTACHÉ 5,125.00
SAFARI SYNTHETIC 2,120.00
SAFARI LX 2,545.00
SAFARI CLASSIC 4,245.00
SAFARI ATTACHÉ 5,875.00
Also available:
SAFARI MODEL. 416 Rem. Mag. only. 24" heavy barrel (42" overall); open sights. **Weight:** 9.5 lbs
Prices: Standard. $3,300.00
Deluxe 3,600.00
Super Deluxe 4,000.00

BROWNING RIMFIRE RIFLES

MODEL BL-22 LEVER-ACTION RIFLE

RIMFIRE RIFLE SPECIFICATIONS

MODEL	CALIBER	BARREL LENGTH	SIGHT RADIUS	OVERALL LENGTH	AVERAGE WEIGHT	PRICE
Semi-Auto 22 Grade I	22 LR	19.25"	16.25"	37"	4 lbs. 12 oz.	**$415.00**
Semi-Auto 22 Grade VI*	22 LR	19.25"	16.25"	37"	4 lbs. 12 oz.	**860.00**
BL-22 Grade I	22 LR, Long, Short	20"	15.875"	36.75"	5 lbs.	**360.00**
BL-Grade II	22 LR, Long, Short	20"	15.875"	36.75"	5 lbs.	**412.00**

Blued or Grayed

22 SEMIAUTOMATIC RIMFIRE RIFLES
GRADES I AND VI (See table above for prices)

SPECIFICATIONS (See also table above)
Capacity: 11 cartridges in magazine, 1 chamber
Safety: Cross-bolt type *Trigger:* Grade I is blued; Grade VI is gold colored *Sights:* Gold bead front, adjustable folding leaf ear; drilled and tapped for Browning scope mounts
Stock & Forearm: Grade I, select walnut with checkering (18 lines/inch); Grade VI, high-grade walnut with checkering (22 lines/inch).

STOCK DIMENSIONS

	SEMI-AUTO	BL-22
Length of Pull	13.75"	13.5"
Drop at Comb	1 ³/₈"	.625"
Drop at Heel	2.375"	2.25"

SEMI-AUTO RIMFIRE GRADE 1

BROWNING RIFLES

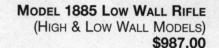

MODEL 1885 LOW WALL RIFLE
(HIGH & LOW WALL MODELS)
$987.00

SPECIFICATIONS MODEL 1885 LOW WALL OR HIGH WALL

CALIBERS*	BARREL LENGTH	SIGHT RADIUS	OVERALL LENGTH	APPROXIMATE WEIGHT	RATE OF TWIST (R. HAND)
HIGH WALL					
22-250 Rem.	28"	—	43.5"	8 lbs. 13 oz.	1 in 14"
270 Win.	28"	—	43.5"	8 lbs. 12 oz.	1 in 10"
30-06 Sprg.	28"	—	43.5"	8 lbs. 12 oz.	1 in 10"
7mm Rem. Mag.	28"	—	43.5"	8 lbs. 11 oz.	1 in 9.5"
45-70 Govt.	28"	21.5"	43.5"	8 lbs. 14 oz.	1 in 20"
454 Casull	28"	—	43.5"	8 lbs. 14 oz.	1 in 20"
LOW WALL					
22 Hornet	24"	—	39.5"	6 lbs. 4 oz.	1 in 16"
223 Rem.	24"	—	39.5"	6 lbs. 4 oz.	1 in 12"
243 Win.	24"	—	39.5"	6 lbs. 4 oz.	1 in 10"
260 Rem.	24"	—	39.5"	6 lbs. 4 oz.	1 in 10"

*Also available in 454 Casull

LOW WALL TRADITIONAL HUNTER

SPECIFICATIONS
Calibers: 357 Mag., 44 Mag., 45 Colt *Barrel Length:* 24"
Overall Length: 40.25" *Sight Radius:* 31" *Weight:* 6 lbs. 8 oz. *Length of Pull:* 13.5"
Price: $1,276.00

MODEL 1885 HIGH WALL TRADITIONAL HUNTER

SPECIFICATIONS
Calibers: 30-30 Win., 38-55 Win., 45-70 Govt.
Barrel Length: 28" *Overall Length:* 44.25" *Weight:* 9 lbs.
Rate of Twist: 1 in 12" (30-30 Win.); 1 in 15" (38-55 Win.);
1 in 20" (45-70 Gov't.)
Price: $1,208.00

MODEL 1885 BPCR
(BLACK POWDER CARTRIDGE RIFLE)

SPECIFICATIONS
Calibers: 40-65, 45-70 Govt. *Barrel Length:* 30" *Overall Length:* 46.125" *Weight:* 11 lbs. (45-70 Govt.); 11 lbs. 7 oz. (40-65) *Sight Radius:* 34" *Rate of Twist:* 1 in 16" (R.H.)
Price: $1,749.00
Also available:
BPCR "CREEDMORE TYPE" LONG RANGE with *Barrel Length:* 34"

BROWNING A-BOLT RIFLES

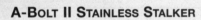

A-BOLT II HUNTER BOLT-ACTION CENTERFIRE RIFLES

BOSS (Ballistic Optimizing Shooting System) is now optional on all A-Bolt II models (except standard and Varmint). BOSS adjusts barrel vibrations to allow a bullet to leave the rifle muzzle at the most advantageous point in the barrel oscillation, thereby fine-tuning accuracy with any brand of ammunition regardless of caliber.

This hard-working rifle features a practical grade of walnut and low-luster bluing. Includes the standard A-Bolt II fast-cycling bolt, crisp trigger, calibrated rear sights and ramp-style front sights. Optional

BOSS on a clean, tapered barrel. Receiver is drilled and tapped for a scope mount; HUNTER model has open sights.

Prices:

w/BOSS, No Sights	$617.00
No Sights	557.00
MICRO HUNTER	
(low-luster blue, shorter barrel and length of pull) without sights	557.00

A-BOLT II STAINLESS STALKER

The barrel, receiver and bolt are machined from solid stainless steel for a high level of corrosion and rust resistance and also

to prolong the life of the rifle bore. The advanced graphite-fiberglass composite stock shrugs off wet weather and rough handling and isn't affected by humidity. A palm swell on both right- and left-hand models offers a better grip. A lower comb directs recoil away from the face. Barrel, receiver and stock have a durable matte finish. The BOSS is optional in all calibers.

A-BOLT II SPECIFICATIONS (See following page for additional A-Bolt II prices)

CALIBER	TWIST (R.H.)	MAGAZINE CAPACITY	HUNTER	GOLD MEDAL.	MEDAL.	MICRO MEDAL.	STAINLESS STALKER	COMP STALKER	VARMINT	ECLIPSE
LONG ACTION MAGNUM CALIBERS										
375 H&H	1:12"	3	—	—	•	—	•	—	—	—
338 Win. Mag.	1:10"	3	•	•	•	•	•	•	—	—
300 Win. Mag.	1:10"	3	•	•	•	•	•	•	—	•
7mm Rem. Mag.	1:9.5"	3	•	•	•	•	•	•	—	•
LONG ACTION STANDARD CALIBERS										
25-06 Rem.	1:10"	4	•	•	•	•	•	•	—	—
270 Win.	1:10"	4	•	•	•	•	•	•	—	—
280 Rem.	1:10"	4	•	•	•	•	•	•	—	—
30-06 Sprg.	1:10"	4	•	•	•	•	•	•	—	—
SHORT ACTION CALIBERS										
243 Win.	1:10"	4	•	•	•	•	•	•	—	•
308 Win.	1:12"	4	•	•	•	•	•	•	•	•+
260 Rem.	1:10"	4	•	•	•	•	•	•	•	•+
7mm-08 Rem.	1:9.5"	4	•	•	•	•	•	•	—	—
22-250 Rem.	1:14"	4	•	•	•	•	•	•	•	•+
223 Rem.	1:12"	6*	•	—	•	•	•	•	•	+

• *Magazine capacity of 223 Rem. models is up to 5 rounds on Micro-Medallion (up to 6 on other models).*
+ = *also available in Varmint version of Eclipse*

A-BOLT II STOCK DIMENSIONS

	MICRO-MED.	GOLD MEDAL.	HUNTER	VARMINT	STALKER	ECLIPSE	ECLIPSE VARMINT M-1000
Length Of Pull	13 5/16"	13 5/8"	13 5/8"	13 3/4"	13 5/8"	14"	14"
Drop At Comb	3/4"	3/4"-1"	3/4"	9/16"	5/8"	7/16"	1/2"
Drop At Heel	1 1/8"	1 3/4"	1 1/8"	7/16"	1/2"	1 1/16"	1"

A-BOLT II AVERAGE WEIGHTS

MODEL	LONG ACTION MAGNUM CALIBERS	LONG ACTION STANDARD CALIBERS	SHORT ACTION CALIBERS
Composite/Stainless Steel	7 lbs. 3 oz.	6 lbs. 11 oz.	6 lbs. 4 oz.
Micro-Medal.			6 lbs. 1 oz.
Gold Medal.	7 lbs. 11 oz.	7 lbs. 3 oz.	
Medallion & Hunter	7 lbs. 3 oz.	6 lbs. 11 oz.	6 lbs. 7 oz.
Varmint			9 lbs.
Eclipse	8 lbs.	7 lbs. 8 oz.	7 lbs. 10 oz.
Eclipse Varmint			9 lbs. 1 oz.
M-1000	9 lbs. 13 oz.		

A-BOLT II GENERAL DIMENSIONS

LENGTH	OVERALL LENGTH	BARREL LENGTH	SIGHT RADIUS*
Long Action Mag. Cal.	46.75"	26"	18"
Long Action Std. Cal.	42.75"	22"	18"
Short Action Cal.	41.75"	22"	16"
Micro-Medallion	39 9/16"	20"**	—
Varmint Models	44.5"	24"	26"

*Open sights available on A-Bolt Hunter and all models in 375 H&H.
**22 Hornet Micro-Medallion has a 22" barrel. BOSS equipped rifles have the same dimensions.

BROWNING RIFLES

A-BOLT II M-1000 ECLIPSE
300 WIN. MAG.

A-BOLT II ECLIPSE MODELS WITH THUMBHOLE STOCK

The proven action and barrel of the A-Bolt II are included in the A-Bolt II Eclipse Series. Each rifle is fitted with a newly designed thumbhole stock configuration. To hold accuracy under changing humidity and precipitation conditions the stock itself is crafted from rugged gray/black, multi-laminated hardwood. This gives the Eclipse a camouflaged look. The custom thumbhole-style stock provides a solid grip and secure feel that adds up to accuracy. The Eclipse is available in two versions: long and short action hunting model with standard A-Bolt II barrel, and a short action varmint version with a heavy barrel. All are BOSS equipped.

A-BOLT II SERIES

	Prices
MEDALLION no sights, BOSS	722.00
MEDALLION no sights	662.00
MEDALLION L.H., no sights, BOSS	748.00
MEDALLION L.H., no sights	688.00
MEDALLION 375 H&H no sights, BOSS.	827.00
VARMINT, hvy. bbl., BOSS, gloss or satin/matte.	853.00

A-BOLT II SERIES

	Prices
STAINLESS STALKER no sights, BOSS	$797.00
STAINLESS STALKER no sights	737.00
STAINLESS STALKER L.H., no sights, BOSS	820.00
STAINLESS STALKER L.H., no sights	760.00
STAINLESS STALKER 375 H&H, BOSS	899.00
STAINLESS STALKER 375 H&H, L.H., BOSS	925.00
COMPOSITE STALKER, no sights, BOSS	640.00
COMPOSITE STALKER, no sights.	580.00
ECLIPSE, no sights, BOSS	941.00
ECLIPSE VARMINT no sights, BOSS	969.00
ECLIPSE M-1000, w/BOSS	969.00

LEFT-HAND A-BOLT II MEDALLION

Only a few popular bolt-action rifles have traditionally been built in left-hand versions. Browning joins a growing movement to accommodate lefties with its A-Bolt II, Boss is available.

SAFETY

The top-mounted safety is perfectly positioned for easy operation. This location also allows the shooter to see the status at any angle.

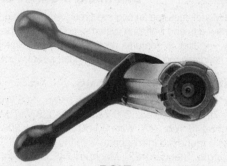

BOLT

The short 60° bolt throw gives you faster follow-up shots and also permits greater clearance between the bolt handle and scope. The flattened bolt knob itself is canted at a 30° angle to fit your hand more naturally.

BROWNING RIFLES

LIGHTNING BLR

SPECIFICATIONS

Calibers: *Long Action*–223 Rem., 270 Win., 30-06 Springfield (7mm Rem. Mag.) 300 Win. Mag. *Short Action*–22-250 Rem., 243 Win., 7mm-08 Rem., 308 Win. **Capacity:** 4 rounds; 3 in magnum calibers **Barrel Length:** *Long Action*–22" (24" magnum calibers) *Short Action*–20" **Overall Length:** *Long* *Action*–42 ⁷/₈" (44 ⁷/₈" magnum calibers) *Short Action*–39.5" **Approximate Weight:** *Long Action*–7 lbs. 4 oz. (7 lbs. 12 oz. magnum calibers) *Short Action*–6 lbs. 8 oz. **Sight Radius:** 17.75" (19.75" magnum calibers)

Prices: Short Action. $600.00
    Long Action 634.00

MODEL BPR PUMP RIFLE

SPECIFICATIONS

Calibers: 243 Win., 308 Win., 270 Win., 30-06 Springfield; 7mm Rem. Mag., 300 Win. Mag. **Capacity:** 4 rounds; 3 in magnum calibers **Action:** Pump action **Barrel Length:** 22" (24" magnum calibers) **Overall Length:** 43"; 45" magnum calibers **Weight:** 7 lbs. 3 oz. (7 lbs. 9 oz. magnum calibers) **Safety:** Crossbolt w/enlarged head **Sight Radius:** 17.5" (19.5" magnum calibers) **Sights:** Adjustable rear sight; hooded front sight w/gold bead **Stock Dimensions:** Length of pull; 13.75"; Drop at comb: 1 ⁵/₈" (1.75" magnum calibers) Drop at heel: 2" **Features:** Drilled and tapped for scope mounts; multiple lug rotating bolt locks directly into barrel; detachable box magazine w/hinged floorplate; single-stage trigger; recoil pad standard; full pistol grip

Price:. $718.00
    Magnum. 772.00

BAR MARK II SAFARI

BAR MARK II SAFARI & LIGHTWEIGHT SEMIAUTOMATIC RIFLES

The BAR Mark II features an engraved receiver, a redesigned bolt release, new gas and buffeting systems, and a removable trigger assembly. Additional features include: crossbolt safety with enlarged head; hinged floorplate, gold trigger; select walnut stock and forearm with cut-checkering and swivel studs; 13.75" length of pull; 2" drop at heel; 1 ⁵/₈" drop at comb; and a recoil pad (magnum calibers only). The New Lightweight model features alloy receiver and shortened barrel. Open sights are standard.

BAR MARK II SPECIFICATONS

Calibers: Standard–243 Win., 25-06, 270 Win., 308 Win.; Magnum–7mm Rem. Mag., 300 Win. Mag., 338 Win. Mag.; Lightweight–243 Win., 270 Win., 30-06 Springfield; 308 Win.
Capacity: 4 rounds; 3 in magnum
Barrel Length: Standard–22"; Magnum–24"; Lightweight–20"
Overall Length: Standard–43"; Magnum–45"; Lightweight–41"
Average Weight: Standard–7 lbs. 6 oz.; Magnum–8 lbs. 6 oz.; Lightweight–7 lbs. 2 oz.
Sight Radius: Standard–17.5"; Magnum–19.5"; Lightweight–15.5"

Prices:
STANDARD CALIBERS: No sights, BOSS $803.00
    Open sights, no BOSS 760.00
    No sights, no BOSS 743.00
MAGNUM CALIBERS: No sights, BOSS. $857.00
    Open sights 814.00
    No sights, no BOSS 797.00
BAR MARK II LIGHTWEIGHT
    No sights, BOSS, Magnum $857.00
    Open sights, no BOSS 760.00
    Open sights, no BOSS Magnum 814.00

BROWN PRECISION RIFLES

PRO-HUNTER RIFLE

Designed for the serious game hunter or guide, this custom version of Brown Precision's Pro-Hunter rifle begins as a Winchester Model 700 Super Grade action with controlled feed claw extractor. The trigger is tuned to crisp let-off at each customer's specified weight. A Shilen Match Grade stainless-steel barrel is custom crowned and hand fitted to the action.

The Pro-Hunter Elite features choice of express rear sight or custom Dave Talley removable peep sight and banded front ramp sight with European dovetail and replaceable brass bead. An optional flip-up white night sight is also available, as is a set of Dave Talley detachable T.N.T. scope mount rings and bases installed with Brown's Magnum Duty 8X40 screws. QD sling swivels are standard.

All metal parts are finished in either matte electroless nickel or black Teflon. The barreled action is glass bedded to a custom Brown Precision Alaskan-configuration fiberglass stock, painted according to customer choice and fitted w/premium 1" buttpad and Dave Talley trapdoor grip cap. Weight ranges from 7 to 15 lbs., depending on barrel length, contour and options.

Optional equipment includes custom steel drop box magazine, KDF or Answer System muzzle brake, Mag-Na-Port, Zeiss, Swarovski or Leupold scope and Americase aluminum hard case.

Prices: **$2,855.00**

PRO-VARMINTER RIFLE

The standard Pro-Varminter is buillt on the Remington 700 or Rremington 40X action (right or left hand) and features a hand-fitted Shilen Match Grade Heavy Benchrest stainless-steel barrel in bright or bead-blasted finish. The barreled action is custom-bedded in Brown Precision's Varmint Special Hunter Bench or 40X Benchrest-style custom fiberglass, Kevlar or graphite stock.

Other standard features include custom barrel length and contour, trigger tuned for crisp pull to customer's specified weight, custom length of pull, and choice of recoil pad. Additional options include metal finishes, muzzle brakes, Leupold (or other) target or varmint scopes.

Prices:
Right-hand Model 700 Action **$2,095.00**
For Left-hand Model, **add** 150.00

BROWN PRECISION RIFLES

HIGH COUNTRY YOUTH RIFLE

This custom rifle has all the same features as the standard High Country rifle, but scaled-down to fit the younger or smaller shooter. Based on the Remington Model 7 barreled action, it is available in calibers 223, 243, 7mm-08, 6mm and 308. The rifle features a shortened fiberglass, Kevlar or graphite stock, which can be lengthened as the shooter grows, a new recoil pad installed and the stock refinished. Custom features/options include choice of actions, custom barrels, chamberings, muzzle brakes, metal finishes, scopes and accessories.

All Youth Rifles include a deluxe package of shooting, reloading and hunting accessories and information to increase a young shooter's interest.

Price: starts at $1395.00

TACTICAL ELITE RIFLE

Brown Precision's Tactical Elite is built on a Remington 700 action and features a bead-blasted Shilen Select Match Grade Heavy Benchrest Stainless Steel barrel custom-chambered for 223 Rem., 308 Win., 300 Win. Mag. (or any standard or wildcat caliber). A nonreflective custom black Teflon metall finish on all metal surfaces ensures smooth bolt operation and 100 percent weatherproofing. The barreled action is bedded in a target-style stock with high rollover comb/cheekpiece, vertical pistol grip and palmswell. The stock is an advanced, custom fiberglass/Kevlar/graphite composite for maximum durability and rigidity, painted in flat black (camouflage patterns are also available). QD sling swivel studs and swivels are standard.

Other standard features include: three-way adjustable buttplate/recoil pad assembly with length of pull, vertical and cant angle adjustments, custom barrel length and contour, and trigger tuned for a crisp pull to customer's specifications. Options include muzzle brakes, Leupold or Kahles police scopes, and others, and are priced accordingly.

Price: $2595.00

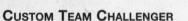

CUSTOM TEAM CHALLENGER

This custom rifle was designed for use in the Chevy Trucks Sportsman's Team Challenge shooting event. It's also used in metallic silhouette competition as well as in the field for small game and varmints. Custom built on the Ruger 10/22 semi-automatic rimfire action, which features an extended magazine release, a simplified bolt release and finely tuned trigger, this rifle is fitted with either a Brown Precision fiberglass or Kevlar stock with custom length of pull up to 15". The stock can be shortened at the butt and later relengthened and repainted to accommodate growing youth shooters. Stock color is also optional. To facilitate shooting with scopes, the lightweight stock has high-comb classic styling. The absence of a cheekpiece accommodates either right- or left-handed shooters, while the stock's flat-bottom, 1 3/4" forearm ensures maximum comfort in both offhand and rest shooting. Barrels are custom-length Shilen Match Grade .920" diameter straight or lightweight tapered.

Prices:
With blued action/barrel. $1,095.00
With blued action/stainless barrel 1175.00
With stainless action/stainless barrel 1225.00

CHRISTENSEN ARMS

CarbonCannon Series

Custom lightweight graphite barreled precision magnum big-game class rifle. All popular Magnum calibers available. Up to 28" long match-grade stainless steel barrel liner, head spaced minimum, accurized action, custom trigger, synthetic or wood stock and fitted for scope mounts. Bedded with graphite barrel free floating. *Weight:* 6.5 to 7.5 lbs. *Accuracy:* 3 shots .5" or less at 100 yards.
Price: $2,950.00

CarbonTactical Series

Custom lightweight graphite, barreled precision tactical-class rifle. All popular calibers available. Up to 28" long match-grade stainless steel barrel liner, head spaced minimum, muzzle break optional, accurized action, custom trigger, synthetic or wood stock and fitted for scope mounts. Bedded with free-floating graphite barrel. *Weight:* 5 to 8 pounds *Accuracy:* 3 shots .5" or less at 100 yards.
Price: $2,950.00

CarbonOne Series

Custom lightweight graphite barreled precision varmint-class rifle. .17 thru .243 calibers available. Up to 28" long match-grade stainless steel barrel liner, head spaced minimum, accurized action, custom trigger, synthetic or wood stock; fitted for scope mounts. Bedded with free-floating graphite barrel. *Weight:* 5.5 to 6.5 lbls. *Accuracy:* 3 shots .5" or less at 100 yards.
Price: $2,950.00

CarbonRanger Series

Custom lightweight long range precision sniper rifle. Available in 50 caliber. Up to 36" long stainless steel barrel liner, chambered to minimum tolerances. E.D.M. precision machined Omni Wind Runner accurized action (or an action of choice), custom trigger, retractable stock. 5 shots 8" at 1000 yards. Like all graphite-barreled Christensen rifles, the CarbonRanger shoots tight groups even after repeated firing.
Prices: $10,625.00

CHRISTENSEN ARMS

CARBONLITE SERIES

Custom ultra-lightweight graphite, barreled precision mountain-class rifle. .17 and .243 calibers available. Up to 28" long match-grade stainless steel barrel liner, head spaced minimum, accurized action, custom trigger, synthetic or wood stock and fitted for scope mounts. Bedded with free-floating graphite barrel that retains accuracy through better heat dissipation.
Weight: 4.5 to 5.5 lbs. **Accuracy:** 3 shots .5" or less at 100 yards (shoots straight when barrel is hot).
Price:. $2,950.00

CARBONKING SERIES

Custom lightweight graphite, barreled precision hunting-class rifle. .25 thru .308 calibers available. Up to 28" long match-grade stainless steel barrel liner, head spaced minimum, accurized action, custom trigger, synthetic or wood stock and fitted for scope mounts. Bedded with free-floating graphite barrel.
Weight: 6 to 7 pounds
Accuracy: 3 shots .5" or less at 100 yards (shoots straight when barrel is hot).
Price:. $2,950.00

CARBONCHALLENGER THUMBHOLE

Custom ultra-lightweight graphite barreled precision target and small-game rimfire-class rifle. Up to 20" long match-grade stainless steel barrel liner, semi-auto action, custom trigger, synthetic or wood stock and fitted for scope mounts. Bedded with action free floating.
Weight: 3 to 5 pounds
Accuracy: 3 shots .5" or less at 50 yards.
Price:. $2,950.00

COLT RIFLES

LIGHTWEIGHTS

The Colt Match Target Lightweight semiautomatic rifle fires from a closed bolt, is easy to load and unload, and has a buttstock and pistol grip made of tough nylon. A round, ribbed handguard is fiberglass-reinforced to ensure better grip control.
Calibers: 223 Rem.

Barrel Length: 16"
Overall Length: 34.5" (35.5" in 7.62 X 39mm)
Weight: 6.7 lbs
Capacity: 5 rounds (7.62 X 39mm); 8 rounds (223 Rem. and 9mm)
Price: $1,010.00

COMPETITION H-BAR

MATCH TARGET RIFLES
The Colt Target and H-Bar rifles are range-selected for top accuracy. They have a 3-9x rubber armored variable-power scope mount, carry handle with iron sight, Cordura nylon case and other accessories.
Caliber: 223 Rem.
Barrel Length: 20: (16" H-BAR II)
Overall Length: 39" (34.5" H-BAR II)

Weight: 8.5 lbs (Competition/Match H-Bar); 8 lbs. (Target H-BAR); 7.5 lbs. (Target); 7.1 lbs. (H-Bar II)
Capacity: 8 rounds
Prices:
MATCH TARGET.......................... $1,040.00
MATCH TARGET H-BAR.................... 1,085.00
COMPETITION H-BAR 1,090.00
COMPETITION H-BAR II.................. 1,065.00

COLT ACCURIZED RIFLE (not shown)
SPECIFICATIONS
Caliber: 223 Rem.
Capacity: 8 rounds
Action: Semiauto; gas operated; locking bolt
Barrel Length: 24" heavy
Overall Length: 43"

Weight: 9.25 oz.
Rifling Twist: 1 turn in 9", 6 grooves
Trigger: Smooth
Finish: Matte black w/matte stainless steel barrel
Features: Flattop upper receiver for low scope mount (1" rings)
Price: $1,295.00

COOPER ARMS RIFLES

VARMINT EXTREME SERIES

MODEL 21 VARMINT EXTREME

MODEL 21 VARMINT EXTREME

SPECIFICATIONS
Calibers: 17 Rem., 17 Mach IV, 221 Fireball, 222 Rem., 222 Rem. Mag., 22 PPC, 223 **Barrel Length:** 24"
Stock: AAA Claro walnut; flared oval forearm
Other specifications same as Model 36 RF.

Price:	$1,750.00
Also available:	
MODEL 21 CUSTOM CLASSIC	$1,950.00
MODEL 21 WESTERN CLASSIC	2,195.00

MODEL 22 VARMINT EXTREME

MODEL 22 REPEATER CUSTOM CLASSIC

MODEL 22 SINGLE SHOT VARMINT EXTREME

SPECIFICATIONS
Calibers: 22-250, 220 Swift, 243, 25-06, 308, 6mm PPC
Capacity: Single shot **Barrel Length:** 24"
Action: 3 front locking lugs; glass-bedded
Trigger: Single-stage Match, fully adjustable; Jewell 2-stage (optional)
Stock: McMillan black-textured synthetic, beaded, w/Monte Carlo cheekpiece; 4-panel checkering

Pachmayr recoil pad
Price:

MODEL 22 VARMINT EXTREME	$1,795.00
Also available:	
MODEL 22 BR-50 BENCH REST	
(w/Jewell Trigger)	$2,195.00
MODEL 22 REPEATER CUSTOM CLASSIC	2,675.00

DAKOTA ARMS

DAKOTA 10 SINGLE SHOT

SPECIFICATIONS

Calibers: Most rimmed/rimless commercially loaded types
Barrel Length: 23" **Overall Length:** 39.5" **Weight:** 6 lbs.
Features: Receiver and rear of breech block are solid steel without cuts or holes for maximum lug area (approx. 8 times more bearing area than most bolt rifles); crisp, clean trigger pull; removable trigger plate allows action to adapt to single-set triggers; straight-line coil-spring action and short hammer fall combine for fast lock time; smooth, quiet top tang safety blocks the striker forward of the main spring; strong, positive extractor and manual ejector adapted to rimmed/rimless cases. XX grade oil-finished English, Bastogne or Claro walnut stock.

Price:.	$3,195.00
BARRELED ACTIONS.	2,050.00
ACTIONS ONLY	1,675.00

Also Available:

DAKOTA 10 MAGNUM SINGLE SHOT	$3,495.00
Barreled actions	2,050.00
Actions only	1,775.00

DAKOTA 76 RIFLES
SPECIFICATIONS

Calibers:
SAFARI GRADE: 338 Win. Mag., 300 Mag., 375 H&H Mag., 458 Win. Mag.
CLASSIC GRADE: 22-250, 257 Roberts, 270 Win., 280 Rem., 30-06, 7mm Rem. Mag., 338 Win. Mag., 300 Win. Mag., 375 H&H Mag., 458 Win. Mag.
AFRICAN GRADE: 404 Jeffery, 416 Dakota, 416 Rigby, 450 Dakota
Barrel Lengths: 21" or 23" (Classic); 23" only (Safari); 24" (African) **Weight:** 7.5 lbs. (Classic); 9.5 lbs. (African); 8.5 lbs. (Safari) **Safety:** Three-position striker-blocking safety allows

DAKOTA 76 AFRICAN GRADE

bolt operation with safety on **Sights:** Ramp front sight; standing-leaf rear **Stock:** Choice of X grade oil-finished English, Bastogne or Claro walnut (Classic); choice of XXX grade oil-finished English or Bastogne walnut w/ebony forent tip (Safari)

Prices: CLASSIC GRADE	$3,195.00
SAFARI GRADE	4,195.00
AFRICAN GRADE	4,695.00
Barreled Actions: Classic Grade.	2,000.00
Safari Grade	2,350.00
African Grade	2,950.00
Actions: Classic Grade	1,750.00
Safari Grade	1,900.00
African Grade	2,500.00

DAKOTA ARMS TRAVELER

The Dakota Traveler rifle can be easily broken down and carried in a small case or conventional suitcase, with the largest portion of the disassembled rifle being the barrel. With additional barrels available in a wide range of calibers, it offers great convenience for the traveling hunter.

The Traveler is based on the long-proven Dakota 76 design, and is stocked in checkered walnut. It features threadless disassembly–there are no threads to wear or stretch, no interrupted cuts and no possibility of headspace increasing even after repeated assembly and disassemblly. Because of the Traveler's rigid design, it can be quickly taken down without disturbing the scope and mounts, assuring consistent, repeatable accuracy.

Additional barrels/calibers can be fitted on the same action, providing true worldwide hunting capability. Three families of actions are available: standard length, including the .257 Roberts, .25-06, 7x57, .270, .280, .30-06, .338-06 and .35 Whelen; short magnums, including the 7mm Rem. Mag., .300 Win. Mag., .338 Win. Mag., 416 Taylor and .458 Win. Mag.; and Dakota short magnums that include-their proprietary 7mm, .300, .330 and .375 Dakota cartridges.

Prices: CLASSIC	$3,995.00
SAFARI	4,995.00

DAKOTA ARMS

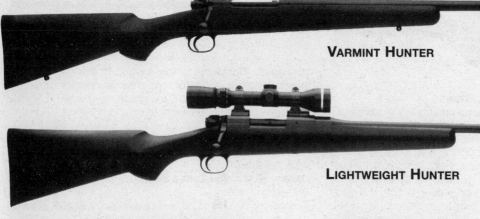

VARMINT HUNTER

LIGHTWEIGHT HUNTER

DAKOTA 97 VARMINT, LONG RANGE & LIGHTWEIGHT HUNTER RIFLES

DAKOTA HUNTER SERIES BOLT ACTION RIFLES (not shown)

97 LONG RANGE HUNTER

Fibergass stock, 2 sling swivel studs, 1" black recoil pad, 13 5/8 length of pull, overall weight 7.7 lbs., overall length 45" to 47", calibers 25-06 through 375 Dakota. RH only.

Price: **$1,795.00**

97 LIGHTWEIGHT HUNTER

Fibergass stock, 2 sling swivel studs, 1" black recoil pad, 12 5/8 length of pull, overall weight approximately 6-6 1/2 lbs., overall length 43", calibers 22-250 through 330, RH only.

97 VARMINT HUNTER

Walnut-stocked round short-action solid-bottom single shot, 24" chrome-moly barrel #4, adjustable trigger, 13 5/8 length of pull, 1/2" black pad, approximate weight 8 lbs, calibers 17 Rem through 22-250, RH only.

Price: w/semi-fancy wood stock **$2,195.00**
w/semi-fancy wood stock, checkering, floor plate **2,495.00**
Barreled action **1,300.00**

LONG BOW TACTICAL E.R. (ENGAGEMENT RIFLE)

SPECIFICATIONS

Caliber: 338 Lapua Mag., 300 Dakota Mag., 330 Dakota Mag.

Action: Blind magazine

Barrel Length: 28" stainless steel

Overall Length: 50"-51"

Length Of Pull: 12 $7/8$"-14 $3/8$"

Weight: 13.7 lbs. (w/o scope)

Stock: McMillan fiberglass (black or olive drab green); matte finish

Features: Adjustable cheekpiece; 3 sling swivel studs; bipod spike in forend; controlled round feeding; claw extraction system; one-piece optical rail; 3-position firing pin block safety; deployment kit; muzzlebrake

Price: **$4,250.00**
Action only **2,500.00**

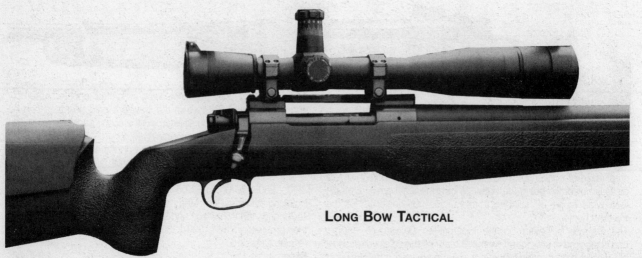

LONG BOW TACTICAL

EMF REPLICA RIFLES

1860 HENRY RIFLE

SPECIFICATIONS
Calibers: 44-40 and 45 LC *Barrel length:* 24.25";
upper half-octagonal w/magazine tube in one-piece steel
Overall length: 43.75" *Weight::* 9.25 lbs.

Stock: Varnished American walnut
Features: Polished brass frame; brass buttplate
Price: $1,230.00

MODEL 1866 YELLOW BOY RIFLE & CARBINE

These exact reproductions of guns used over 100 years
ago are available in 45 Long Colt, 38 Special and 44-40.
Both carbine and rifle are offered with blued finish, walnut
stock and brass frame.
Prices:
Rifle $920.00
Carbine 900.00

MODEL 1873 SPORTING RIFLE

SPECIFICATIONS
Calibers: 357, 44-40, 45 Long Colt *Barrel length:* 24.25"
octagonal *Overall length:* 43.25" *Weight::* 8.16 lbs.
Features: Magazine tube in blued steel; frame is casehard-
ened steel; stock and forend are walnut
Price $1,150.00

Also available:
MODEL 1873 CARBINE. Same features as
the 1873 Sporting Rifle, except in 45 Long Colt only
with 19" barrel, overall length 38.25" and weight 7.38 lbs.
Price: $1,150.00

EUROPEAN AMERICAN ARMORY

HW 660 WEIHRAUCH RIMFIRE TARGET RIFLE (SINGLE SHOT)

SPECIFICATIONS
Caliber: 22 LR *Barrel length:* 26" *Overall length:* 45.33"
Weight: 10.8 lbs. *Finish:* Blue *Stock:* European walnut

w/adjustable black rubber buttplate and comb
Features: Adjustable match trigger; left-handed stock
available; aluminum adjustable sling swivel; adj. vertical
and lateral cheekpiece; rear sight click-adjustable for
windage and elevation; aluminum forend rail; polished
feed ramp; external thumb safety
Price: $998.40
Laminated 1,045.20

FRANCOTTE RIFLES

August Francotte rifles are available in all calibers for which barrels and chambers are made. All guns are custom made to the customer's specifications; there are no standard models. Most bolt-action rifles use commercial Mauser actions; however, the magnum action is produced by Francotte exclusively for its own production. Side-by-side and mountain rifles use either boxlock or sidelock action. Francotte system sidelocks are back-action type. Options include gold and silver inlay, special engraving and exhibition and museum grade wood. Francotte rifles are distributed in the U.S. by Armes de Chasse (see Directory of Manufacturers and Distributors for details).

BOLT-ACTION RIFLE

SPECIFICATIONS
Calibers: 9.3x62, 375 H&H, 416 Rigby, others
Barrel length: To customer's specifications
Weight: 8 to 12 lbs., or to customer's specifications
Stock: A wide selection of wood in all possible styles according to customer preferences; prices listed below do not include engraving or select wood.
Engraving: Per customer specifications
Sights: All types of sights and scope

BOLT-ACTION RIFLES	Prices
Standard Bolt Action 9.3x62	$7,000.00
Magnum Action 375 H&H, 416 Rigby	8,900.00

BOXLOCK SIDE-BY-SIDE DOUBLE RIFLES	Prices
Std. boxlock double rifle (9.3X74R, 8X57JRS, 7X65R, etc.)	$12,700.00
Std. boxlock double (Magnum calibers)	27,500.00

SIDELOCK S/S DOUBLE RIFLES	
Std. sidelock double rifle (9.3X74R, 8X57JRS, 7X65R, etc.)	$17,500.00
Std. sidelock double (Magnum calibers)	27,250.00

MOUNTAIN RIFLES	
Standard boxlock	$12,000.00
Std. boxlock (Mag. & rimless calibers)	Price on request
Standard sidelock (7RM and .243 WM)	36,334.00

HARRINGTON & RICHARDSON

ULTRA VARMINT

ULTRA SINGLE-SHOT RIFLES
SPECIFICATIONS
Calibers: 223 Rem. & 243 (Varmint), 25-06, 308 Win. and 357 Rem. Max. **Action:** Break-open; side lever release; positive ejection **Barrel Length:** 22" (308 Win., 357 Rem. Max.); 24" bull barrel (223 Rem. Varmint; 26" (25-06) **Weight:** 7 to 8 lbs. **Sights:** None (scope mount included) **Length Of Pull:** 14.25" **Drop At Comb:** 1.25" **Drop At Heel:** 1 1/8" **Forend:** Semibeavertail **Stock:** Monte Carlo; hand-checkered curly maple; Varmint model has light laminate stock **Features:** Sling swivels on stock and forend; patented transfer bar safety; automatic ejection; hammer extension; rebated muzzle
Price:

Ultra Varmint	$254.95

Also available:
ULTRA COMP in 30-06 and 270 Win. **Barrel Length:** 24".

Weight: 7-8 lbs. Camo laminate stock.	289.95

HARRIS GUNWORKS RIFLES

SIGNATURE SERIES

CLASSIC SPORTER

SPECIFICATIONS
Calibers:
Model SA: 22-250, 243, 257 Roberts, 6mm Rem., 6mm BR, 7mm BR, 7mm-08, 284, 308, 350 Rem. Mag.
Model LA: 25-06, 270, 280 Rem., 30-06, 35 Whelen
Model MA: 7mm STW, 7mm Rem. Mag., 300 Win. Mag., 300 Weatherby, 300 H&H, 338 Win., 340 Weatherby, 375 H&H, 416 Rem., 416 Hoffman, 416 Taylor, 458 Win., 458 Lott, 257 Wby. Mag., 358 Norma, 358 STA
Capacity: 4 rounds; 3 rounds in magnum calibers
Weight: 7 lbs.; 7 lbs. 9 oz. in long action
Barrel lengths: 22", 24", 26"
Options: Wood stock, optics, 30mm rings, muzzle brake, steel floor plate, iron sights
Price: $2,700.00

STAINLESS SPORTER

Same basic specifications as the Classic Sporter, but with stainless steel action and barrel. It is designed to withstand the most adverse weather conditions. Accuracy is guaranteed (3 shot in 1/2" at 100 yards). Choice of wood, laminate or Gunworks fiberglass stock.
Price: $2,900.00

ALASKAN

SPECIFICATIONS
Calibers: **Model LA:** 270, 280, 30-06, 35 Whelen
Model MA: 7mm Rem. Mag., 300 Win. Mag., 300 H&H, 300 Weatherby, 338 Win., 340 Weatherby, 375 H&H, 416 Rem., 416 Taylor, 458 Win., 458 Lott

Other specifications same as the Classic Sporter, except Harris action is fitted to a match-grade barrel, complete with single-leaf rear sight, barrel band front sight, 1" detachable rings and mounts, steel floorplate, electroless nickel finish. Monte Carlo stock features cheekpiece, palm swell and special recoil pad.
Price: $3,800.00
Also available:
Stainless Steel Receiver, **add** $150.00

.300 PHOENIX

SPECIFICATIONS
Caliber: 300 Phoenix. *Barrel length:* 27 1/2". *Weight:* 12 1/2 lbs. *Stock:* Fiberglass with adjustable cheekpiece.
Feature: Available in left-hand action.
Price: $3,380.00

HARRIS GUNWORKS RIFLES

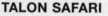

TALON SAFARI

SPECIFICATIONS
Calibers:
Magnum: 300 Win., 300 Weatherby, 300 H&H, 338 Win., 340 Weatherby, 375 H&H, 404 Jeffrey, 416 Rem., 416 Hoffman, 416 Taylor, 458 Win., 458 Lott

Super Magnum: 300 Phoenix, 338 Lapua, 378 Wby., 416 Rigby, 416 Wby., 460 Wby.
Other specifications same as the Classic Sporter, except for match-grade barrel, positive extraction Harris Safari action, quick detachable 1" scope mounts, positive locking steel floorplate, multi-leaf express sight, barrel band ramp front sight, barrel band swivels, and Harris Safari stock.
Prices:
MAGNUM $3,900.00
SUPER MAGNUM 4,200.00

NATIONAL MATCH RIFLE

SPECIFICATIONS
Calibers: 308, 7mm-08
Mag. Capacity: 5 rounds
Weight: Approx. 11 lbs. (12 1/2 lbs. w/heavy contour

barrel). Available for right-hand shooters only. Features Harris fiberglass stock with adjustable buttplate, stainless steel match barrel with barrel band and Tompkins front sight; Harris repeating bolt action with clip slot and Canjar trigger. Barrel twist is 1:12".
Price: $3,500.00

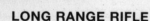

LONG RANGE RIFLE

SPECIFICATIONS
Calibers: 300 Win. Mag., 300 Phoenix, 7mm Rem. Mag., 338 Lapua
Barrel length: 26"

Weight: 14 lbs.
Available in right-hand only. Features a fiberglass stock with adjustable butt plate and cheekpiece. Stainless steel match barrel comes with barrel band and Tompkins front sight. Harris solid bottom single-shot action and Canjar trigger. Barrel twist is 1:12".
Price: $3,620.00

HARRIS BENCHREST RIFLE (not shown)

SPECIFICATIONS
Caliber: 6mm PPC, 243, 6mm BR, 6mm Rem., 308. Built to individual specifications to be competitive in hunter, light varmint and heavy varmint classes. Features solid bottom

or repeating bolt action, Canjar trigger, fiberglass stock with recoil pad, stainless steel match-grade barrel and reloading dies. Right- or left-hand models.
Price: $3,050.00

HECKLER & KOCH RIFLES

MODEL HK PSG-1 HIGH PRECISION MARKSMAN'S RIFLE

SPECIFICATIONS
Caliber: 308 (7.62mm) *Capacity:* 5 rounds
Barrel Length: 25.6" *Overall Length:* 47.5"

Rifling: 4 groove, polygonal *Twist:* 12", right hand
Weight: 17.8 lbs. *Height:* 8.26 lbs. *Sights:* Hensoldt
6X42 telescopic *Stock:* Matte black, high-impact plastic
Finish: Matte black, phosphated *Features:* Aluminum
case; tripod; sling; adj. buttstock and contoured grip
Price: $10,811.00

HENRY REPEATING ARMS

HENRY RIFLE

SPECIFICATIONS
Calibers: 22 S, L, LR *Capacity:* 15 rounds (22 LR); 17 rds. (22
L); 21 rds. (22 S) *Barrel Length:* 18.25" *Overall Length:* 36.5"
Weight: 5.5 lbs. *Stock:* American Walnut *Sights:* Adjustable rear;
hooded front *Features:* Grooved receiver for scope mount
Price: (also carbine and youth model) $229.95

HENRY PUMP ACTION .22

Henry Repeating Arms expands its family of .22 rifles with the
introduction of the Henry Pump Action .22. Made in America, this
rifle features an American walnut stock, grooved receiver for a
scope mount and adjustable rear sight.
Capacity: 15-rounds .22 long rifle
Barrel Length: 18.25" *Weight:* 5.5 lbs.
Price: $249.95

U.S. SURVIVAL RIFLE .22

SPECIFICATIONS
Calibers: 22 long rifle *Capacity:* 9-shot *Barrel Length:* 16.25"
Overall Length: 35.25" *Sights:* Adjustable rear sight *Features:*
Barrel and action fit in floating waterproof stock; comes with two
8-round magazines
Price: $165.00

H-S PRECISION

In 1978 Tom Houghton bought Atkinson Gun Company and combined it with H-S Engineering to form H-S Precision, Inc., in Prescott, Arizona. Two years later the firm began manufacturing test barrels for Winchester, and two years after that H-S began producing Fiberthane rifle stocks. In 1984 the company came up with an aluminum bedding block, now used on all its Pro-Series stocks, which appeared in 1985. They feature a blend of fiberglass, Kevlar and unidirectional carbon fiber. In 1988 H-S Precision developed a take-down rifle, receiving the patent two years later when the firm moved to Rapid City, South Dakota. There Tom Houghton and his crew updated both engineering and manufacturing with CAD and CNC technology. In 1994 the 15,000-square-foot facility grew with the addition of 10,000 square feet designated for stock production only.

By this time H-S was manufacturing synthetic stocks for both Remington and Winchester. It was also building custom rifles with its own super-accurate cut-rifled barrels. Law enforcement agencies were steady patrons. In 1996 the plant expanded by another 25 percent; the next year the series 2000 single-shot pistol appeared, followed by series 2000 rifles on the company's own actions.

The H-S Precision Pro-Series 2000 action combines many of the best features of the Winchester Model 70 and Remington 700 rifles. Available in two lengths, it is the heart of several H-S Precision semi-custom rifles, including a take-down model. Rifles of 30 caliber and smaller are guaranteed to shoot 1/2-inch groups at 100 yards. Big-bore rifles are guaranteed to shoot into one minute of angle.

3-Position Safety with safety indicator and cocking indicator

Action body machined from heat-treated 17-4PH Stainless steel, 42-43 Rc

Tang Mounted Bolt Release lever

One piece bolt body machined from heat-treated 4142, 42-45 Rc

Stainless Steel Floorplate and SS Detachabe Magazine box with center feed design for positive cartridge feeding

Trigger fully adjustable between 2.5-3.5 pounds; Designed and manufactured by **H-S Precision**.

Bolt handle machined with 360° ring, silver soldered to the bolt body

Semi-Cone Bolt Head with a claw extractor totally enclosed in the bolt head

Hardened steel-tipped aluminum firing pin with speed lock spring

H-S PRECISION

PRO-SERIES 2000

PHR (PROFESSIONAL HUNTER RIFLE)

The Pro-Series 2000 PHR is a slightly heavier version of the Pro-Series 2000 SPR rifle. Because of the larger magnum calibers, available for the Pro-Series 2000 PHR the increased weight is a necessity. The Pro-Series 2000 PHR is designed to handle the new "super magnums" such as the 300 RemUltra Mag or the 338 Lapua.

FEATURES
• *Pro-Series 2000* stainless steel action, magnum only

• *Pro-Series 2000* stainless steel floorplate with detachable magazine • 3 rounds in the magazine box
• *Pro-Series 10X* match grade stainless steel barrel • Fluted (except 416 Rigby) • 24" or 26" magnum contour • Optional muzzle brake • Built in recoil reducer • Choice of color • Metal finish – Teflon® or *Pro-Series* PFTE Matte Black • Weight* – 7.75 - 8.25 pounds • Calibers – 7mm STW, 300 Win Mag, 300 Rem Ulltra Mag, 338 Win Mag, 416 Rem Mag, 375 H&H Mag, 338/300 Ultra Mag, 375/300 Ultra Mag, 338 Lapua, 416 Rigby
• *Pro-Series* synthetic stock with ful length bedding block chassis system, sporter style

VTD (VARMINT TAKE-DOWN SYSTEM)

Pro Series 2000 Take-Down rifles are covered by the same 1/2 minute of angle accuracy and repeatability guarantee as all other Pro-Series 2000 rifles (3 shots at 100 yards). Pro-Series 2000 Take-down rifle systems are tested for accuracy and repeatability with factory match ammunition.

FEATURES
• *Pro-Series 2000* stainless steel action, long or short
• *Pro-Series* stainless steel floorplate with detachable

magazine • 4 rounds in the magazine box, standard calibers • 3 rounds in the magazine box, magnum calibers
• *Pro-Series 10X* match grade stainless steel barrel • Fluted • 23.5" varmint contour • Optional muzzle brake • PSV29B - long action • Choice of color • Metal finish – Teflon® or *Pro-Series* PFTE Matte Black • Weight* – 8.50 - 9.00 pounds • Calibers – 308 Win, 300 Win Mag • Options • Additional caliber capabillity by adding a second barrel
• *Pro-Series* synthetic stock with ful length bedding block chassis system, varmint style

HTR (HEAVY TACTICAL RIFLE)

FEATURES
• *Pro-Series 2000* stainless steel action, long or short
• *Pro-Series* stainless steel floorplate with detachable magazine • 4 rounds in the magazine box, standard calibers • 3 rounds in the magazine box, magnum calibers • 3 rounds in the magazine box, 338 Lapua
• *Pro-Series 10X* match grade stainless steel barrel, heavy

barrel • Fluted • 24" heavy contour • Optional muzzle brake
• *Pro-Series* synthetic stock with ful length bedding block chassis system, tactical style • PST25 - short action, fully adjustable length of pull and cheek piece • PST26 - long action, fully adjustable length of pull and cheek piece • Choice of color • Metal finish – Teflon® or *Pro-Series* PFTE Matte Black • Weight* – 10.75 - 11.25 pounds • Calibers – 308 Win, 300 Win Mag, 338 Lapua

Prices: Sporter, with 2000 action $1,645.00
Sporter, with customer's M70 or M700 action 1,100.00
Pro-Hunter, with 2000 action 1,795.00
Varmint, with 2000 action 1,695.00
Varmint, with customer's M70 or M700 action 1,200.00
Pro-Hunter Take-Down, with 2000 action and one barrel. 1,895.00
Varmint Take-Down, with 2000 action and one barrel . . . 1,795.00

Varmint Take-Down, with 2000 action and two barrels
  (same head size) 2,795.00
Varmint Take-Down, with 2000 action and two barrels
  (different head sizes) 2,995.00
Additional barrels, same head size 1,000.00
Additional barrels, different head sizes 1,200.00
Tactical rifles priced on request only.

RIFLES

HOWA LIGHTNING RIFLES

LIGHTNING BOLT-ACTION RIFLE

The rugged mono-bloc receivers on all Howa rifles are machined from a single billet of high carbon steel. The machined steel bolt boasts dual-opposed locking lugs and triple relief gas ports. Actions are fitted with a button-release hinged floorplate for fast reloading. Premium steel sporter-weight barrels are hammer-forged. A silent sliding thumb safety locks the trigger for safe loading or clearing the chamber. The stock is ultra-tough polymer.

SPECIFICATIONS
Calibers: 22-250, 223, 243, 270, 308, 30-06, 300 Win. Mag., 338 Win. Mag., 7mm Rem. Mag. *Capacity:* 5 rounds (3 in Magnum) *Barrel length:* 22" (24" in Magnum) *Overall length:* 42.5" *Weight:* 7.5 lbs. (7.7 lbs. in Magnum) *Finish:* Blue
Price: **STANDARD MODEL** $435.00
  In Magnum calibers 455.00
STAINLESS 485.00
  In Magnum calibers 505.00
  HUNTER *(hardwood stock, checkered) add $20.00*
VARMINT (222, 223, 22-250) 465.00
  Stainless 525.00
  hardwood stock add $20.00
  Barreled actions 325.00-395.00

JARRETT CUSTOM RIFLES

MODEL NO. 1

Jarrett's Standard Hunting Rifle incorporates a McMillan's fiberglass stock match-grade barre and Reminton 70 or Winchester 70 action.
Price: $3,050.00

WALKABOUT (not shown)

This lightweight rifle is based on Remington's Model 7 (or Short 700) receiver. It is available in any short-action caliber and is pillar-bedded into a McMillan Model 7-style or Mountain stock.
Price: $3,050.00

MODEL NO. 3 COUP DE GRACE

Same specifications as the Standard model, but includes a muzzlebreak kit and weatherproofing metal finish. Model 70-style bolt release installed on a Rem. 700.
Price: $3,695.00

MODEL NO. 3

MODEL NO. 4 (not shown)

This model—the "Professional Hunter"—is based on a Winchester controlled round-feed Model 70. It features a quarter rib and iron sights and comes with two Leupold scopes with quick-detachable scope rings. A handload is developed for solids and soft points (40 rounds each). It is then pillar-bedded into a McMillan fiberglass stock. Available in any Magnum caliber. Comes with takedown rifle case.
Price: $6,200.00

JOHANNSEN EXPRESS RIFLES

Three models are available - the "Classic Safari", the "Safari" and the "Tradition". The first of the three, the "Classic Safari", is the choice of preference for those interested in stalking the Big Five. Equipped with a scope, the "Safari" offers exceptionally reliable accuracy during the day or under poor light conditions. The "Tradition" is ideal for the globe-trotting big-game hunter. All models are available in various calibers with standard and custom features, and each rifle is produced individually. When you buy a Johannsen Express Rifle, you get true custom work.

TRADITION

"SAFARI"
Double square bridge action without thumbcut. 4-lb. double-pull trigger. Three-position safety with horizontal lever. Bolt handle close to side of action. Especially suitable for EXPERT scope mount. 2-mm silver bead combined with fold-away 4-mm Holland & Holland-type ivory bead. Express sight with two leaves. Safari-style stock with 1-3/4"/2-1/2" drop. Oil finish. 26" barrel. Length overall 47". Weight from approx. 8 lbs. 6 oz. depending upon caliber. **Standard calibers:** .375 H & H Magnum, 4-shot, or .416 Rigby, 3-shot.
Price: $10,250.00

Magazine capacities, maximum:

CALIBER	NORMAL FLOORPLATE	RIGBY FLOORPLATE
.300 Weatherby Magnum	4	5
.338-378 Weatherby Magnum	3	4
.375 H & H Magnum	4	5
.416 Rigby	3	4
.450 Dakota	3	4
.500 Jeffery	3	4

Other calibers upon request.

HOLLAND & HOLLAND-TYPE NIGHT SIGHT
The "Classic Safari" and "Safari" models come with a 4-mm ivory bead that can be flipped up to cover the 2-mm silver bead under poor light conditions.

EXPRESS SIGHT
The rear sight with its two leaves fits into a special ring base. The rear sight base extends around the barrel and has the second recoil shoulder on the underside, which is important for large-bore rifles.

"CLASSIC SAFARI"
Single square bridge action with thumbcut. 4-lb. double-pull trigger. Three-position wing safety. Traditional bolt handle. 2-mm silver bead combined with a fold-away 4-mm Holland & Holland-type ivory bead. Express sight with two leaves. Safari-style stock with 1-3/4"/2-1/2" drop. Oil finish. 24" barrel. Length overall 45". Weight from approx. 8 lbs. 3 oz. depending upon caliber. **Standard calibers:** .375 H & H Magnum, 4-shot, or .416 Rigby. 3-shot.
Price: $9,500.00

"TRADITION"
Double square bridge action without thumbcut. Adjustable-pull single-set trigger. Three-position safety with horizontal lever. Low bolt handle. Especially suitable for EXPERT scope mount. "Masterpiece" front sight base with 2.5-mm fluorescent bead. Express sight with two leaves. Stock with straight comb and 1-3/4"/2" drop. Oil finish. 26" barrel. Length overall 47". Weight from approx. 8 lbs. depending upon caliber. **Standard calibers:** .300 Weatherby Magnum, 4-shot, .375 H & H Magnum, 4-shot.
Price: $10,550.00

WING SAFETY – The "Classic Safari" features a wing safety with "safe" and "fire" clearly indicated in gold.
PEEP SIGHT – For precision sighting with open sights - or to compensate for less than perfect vision - the peep sight mounted on the cocking piece can be raised into position.

KBI/Charles Daly Rifles

Model CDGA 6345 Empire Grade Semiautomatic

Model CDGA 4103 Field Grade Bolt Action

Standard M-20P Semiautomatic

Model M-12Y Youth Bolt Action

KBI/CHARLES DALY RIFLE SPECIFICATIONS

Item No.	Capacity	Caliber	Barrel Length	Length	Overall Price
FIELD GRADE					
CDGA 4103	6	22LR	22 5/8"	41"	$124.00
CDGA 4164	10	22LR	20 1/4"	40 1/2"	124.00
CDGA 4238	Single Shot	22LR	16 1/4"	32"	143.00
CDGA 4279	6	22LR	17 1/2"	34 3/8"	136.00
SUPERIOR GRADE					
CDGA 5047	6	22LR	22 5/8"	41 1/4"	179.00
CDGA 5159	5	22 MRF	22 5/8"	41 1/4"	199.00
CDGA 5261	5	22 Hornet	22 5/8"	41 1/4"	349.00
CDGA 5302	10	22LR	20 1/4"	40 1/2"	199.00
EMPIRE GRADE					
CDGA 6116	6	22LR	22 5/8"	41 1/4"	329.00
CDGA 6208	5	22 MRF	22 5/8"	41 1/4"	349.00
CDGA 6270	5	22 Hornet	22 5/8"	41 1/4"	449.00
CDGA 6345	10	22LR	20 1/4"	40 1/4"	309.00

KIMBER RIFLES

MODEL 82C 22 LR CLASSIC

MODEL 82C 22 LR

Prices:

CLASSIC	$920.00
STAINLESS CLASSIC	970.00
SVT (SHORT/VARMINT/TARGET)	730.00
HS (HUNTER SILHOUETTE).	$730.00
VARMINT STAINLESS (LTD. ED.)	1,030.00
SUPERAMERICA	1,490.00
CUSTOM MATCH	2,168.00

MODEL 82C 22 LR SPECIFICATIONS

MODEL:	MODEL 82C CLASSIC	MODEL 82C SVT	MODEL 82C SUPERAMERICA	MODEL 82C HS
WEIGHT:	6.5 lbs.	7.5 lbs.	6.5 lbs.	7 lbs.
OVERALL LENGTH:	40.5"	36.5"	40.5"	42.5"
ACTION TYPE:	Rear Locking Repeater	Rear Locking Single Shot	Rear Locking Repeater	Rear Locking Repeater
CAPACITY:	4-Shot Clip 5 & 10 Shot (opt.)		4-Shot Clip 5 & 10 Shot (opt.)	4-Shot Clip 5 & 10 Shot (opt.)
TRIGGER: **PRESSURE**	Fully Adjustable Set at 2.5 lbs.	Fully Adjustable Set at 2.5 lbs.	Fully Adjustable Set at 2.5 lbs.	Fully Adjustable Set at 2.5 lbs.
BARREL LENGTH: **GROOVES** **TWIST**	22" 6 16"	18" Fluted 6 16"	22" 6 16"	24" 6 16"
STOCK: **GRADE WALNUT** **CHECKERING (LPI)** **COVERAGE**	A Claro 18 Side Panel	A Claro None NA	AAA Claro 22 Full Coverage Wrap Around	AA French 22 Full Coverage Wrap Around
LENGTH OF PULL	13 ⅝"	13 ⅝"	13 ⅝"	13 ⅝"
METAL FINISH:	Polished & Blued	Stainless steel bbl. Matte blued action	Polished & Blued	Matte "rust" type blue

MODEL SVT

MODEL HS

RIFLES

KIMBER RIFLES

MODEL 84 C SINGLE SHOT VARMINT

MODEL 84C

The Kimber Model 84C is a scaled-down mini-Mauser with controlled round feeding. Like other Kimber rifles, the 84C action is machined from solid steel. Designed for the .223 Rem. family of cartridges, it is available in both single shot and repeater versions. Every Model 84C is test-fired for accuracy at the factory. Each rifle must shoot a 5-shot group measuring .400" or less center-to-center at 50 yards.

Prices:

SINGLE SHOT VARMINT .223 CALIBER	$1,032.00
in .17 Caliber	1,117.00
CLASSIC	1,275.00
SUPERAMERICA	1,770.00
VARMINT STAINLESS	1,390.00

MODEL 84C SPECIFICATIONS

MODEL:	MODEL 84C SINGLE SHOT VARMINT	MODEL 84C CLASSIC	MODEL 84C SUPERAMERICA	MODEL 84C VARMINT STAINLESS
CALIBERS:	17 Rem., 223 Rem.	222 Rem., 223 Rem.	17 Rem., 222 Rem. 223 Rem.	223 Rem.
WEIGHT:	7.5 lbs.	6.75 lbs.	6.75 lbs.	7.5 lbs.
OVERALL LENGTH:	43.5"	40.5"	40.5"	42.5"
ACTION TYPE:	Front Locking Single Shot	Front Locking Controlled Feed Repeater Hinged floorplate 5-shot box magazine	Front Locking Controlled Feed Repeater Hinged floorplate 5-shot box magazine	Front Locking Controlled Feed Repeater Hinged floorplate 5-shot box magazine
TRIGGER: PRESSURE	Fully Adjustable Set at 2.5 lbs.	Fully Adjustable Set at 2.5 lbs.	Fully Adjustable Set at 2.5 lbs.	Fully Adjustable Set at 2.5 lbs.
BARREL LENGTH: GROOVES TWIST	25" (Fluted) 6 17 Rem.-10"/223 Rem.-12"	22" 6 222 Rem.-12"/223 Rem.-12"	22" 6 17 Rem.-10"/222 Rem.-12" 223 Rem.-12"	24" (Fluted) 6 12"
STOCK: GRADE WALNUT CHECKERING (LPI) COVERAGE	A Claro 18 Side Panel	A Claro 18 Side Panel	AAA Claro 22 Full Coverage Wrap Around	A Claro 18 Side Panel
LENGTH OF PULL	13 5/8"	13 5/8"	13 5/8"	13 5/8"
METAL FINISH:	Stainless steel barrel, Matte blue action	Polished & Blued	Polished & Blued	Stainless steel barrel, Matte blue action

MODEL 84C SUPERAMERICA REPEATER

KRIEGHOFF DOUBLE RIFLES

CLASSIC SIDE-BY-SIDE DOUBLE RIFLE

Krieghoff's Classic Side-by-Side offers many standard features, including: Schnable forearm...classic English-style stock with rounded cheekpiece...UAS anti-doubling device...extractors...1" quick-detachable sling swivels...Decelerator recoil pad...short opening angle for fast loading ...compact action with reinforced sidewalls...sliding, self-adjusting wedge for secure bolt...large underlugs...automatic hammer safety...horizontal firing-pin placement...Purdey-style extension between barrels.

SPECIFICATIONS
Calibers: Standard—7x65R, 308 Win., 30-06, 8x57 JRS, 8X75 JRS, 9.3X74R; *Magnum*—375 Flanged Mag. N.E., 470 N.E., 500 N.E., 500/.416 N.E.
Action: Cocking device for optimum safety
Barrel length: 23.5"
Trigger: Double triggers with steel trigger guard
Weight: 7.5 to 11 lbs. (depending on caliber and wood density) *Options:* 21.5" barrel; engraved sideplates

Prices:
STANDARD $7,850.00
Interchangeable barrels
   (installed, w/extra forearm) 4,500.00
MAGNUM 9,450.00
Interchangeable barrels 5,500.00

L.A.R. GRIZZLY RIFLE

BIG BOAR COMPETITOR

BIG BOAR COMPETITOR

SPECIFICATIONS
Caliber: 50 BMG
Capacity: Single shot
Action: Bolt action, bull pup, breechloading
Barrel length: 36"
Overall length: 45 1/2" *Weight:* 30.4 lbs.
Safety: Thumb safety

Features: All-steel construction; receiver made of 4140 alloy steel, heat-treated to 42 R/C; bolt made of 4340 alloy steel; low recoil (like 12 ga. shotgun)
Prices: $2,570.00
PARKERIZED 2,670.00
NICKEL FRAME 2,820.00
FULL NICKEL 2,920.00

LAZZERONI RIFLES

These state-of-the-art rifles feature 17-4 stainess steel receivers with two massive locking lugs, a match-grade 416R stainless steel barrel, fully adjustable benchrest-style trigger and a Lazzeroni-designed synthetic stock that is hand-bedded using aluminum pillar blocks. Included is a precision-machined floorplate/triggerguard assembly.

MODEL L2000ST

SPECIFICATIONS
Calibers: 6.17 (243) Flash™; 6.53 (257) Scramjet™; 6.71 (264) Blackbird™; 7.21 (284) Firehawk; 7.82 (308) Warbird; 8.59 (338) Titan; 9.53 (375) Saturn™; 10.57 (416) Meteor™
Capacity: 4 rounds (1 in chamber)

MODEL L2000ST-28 (not shown)
A 28-inch-barrled rifle chambered in 7.82 (308) Warbird and scoped with a Schmidt & Bender 4-16x50 Precision Hunter scope with Mil Dot reticle in Lazzeroni rings.

Barrel Length: 27" (24" in Saturn & Meteor)
Overall Length: 47.5" (44.5" Saturn & Meteor)
Weight: 8.1 lbs. (10 lbs. in Saturn & Meteor)
Stock: Lazzeroni fiberglass sporter; right or left hand available; "fibergrain" finish on Saturn & Meteor stock
Prices:
MODEL L2000ST $4,195.00
SATURN & METEOR 4,195.00

MODEL L2000SA
LIGHTWEIGHT MOUNTAIN RIFLE

SPECIFICATIONS
Calibers: 6.17 (243) Spitfire™; 6.71 (264) Phantom™; 7.21 (284) Tomahawk™; 7.82 (308) Patriot™; 8.59 (338) Galaxy™
Capacity: 4 rounds (1 in chamber Tomahawk, Patriot, Galaxy); 5 rounds (1 in chamber Spitfire, Phantom)
Barrel Length: 24" Fluted (except Galaxy)
Overall Length: 42.5"
Weight: 6.8 lbs.
Stock: Lazzeroni Slimline Stock
Price:
MODEL L2000SA $4,195.00

MODEL L2000SP

SPECIFICATIONS
Calibers: 6.17 (243) Flash™; 6.53 (257) Scramjet™; 6.71 (264) Blackbird™; 7.21 (284) Firehawk; 7.82 (308) Warbird™; 8.59 (338) Titan™

Capacity: 4 rounds (1 in chamber)
Barrel Length: 25" (21" Ladies and Youth)
Overall Length: 45.5" (40.5" Ladies and Youth)
Weight: 7.8 lbs.
Stock: Lazzeroni fiberglass thumbhole (right hand only)
Price:
MODEL L2000SP $4,195.00

LONE STAR RIFLE CO., INC.

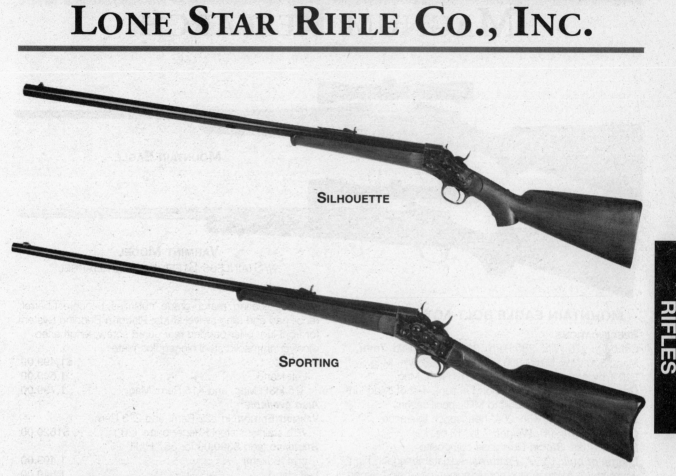

SILHOUETTE

SPORTING

Lone Star specializes in rolling block rifles, a design popularized by Remington after the Civil War. Some buffalo hunters used rolling blocks because, like the fabled Sharps, they could handle large, powerful cartridges. Now Lone Star is building commercial and custom rifles on these actions. Styles available include:
• Black Powder Silhouette • Creedmoor • Sporting
• Deluxe Sporting • Buffalo Rifle • Custer Commemorative
• Gove Underlever • Cowboy Action

Standard rifles are available in three configurations and come with round barrels, single trigger, case-colored actions and straight-grained American walnut stocks. The match-grade barrels are the same as those used on custom models. Chamberings for the standard rifles include:
• 40-60 and 45-70 in the Silhouette model
• 30-40 Krag in the Sporting model 32-40, 38-55, 40-65, 45-70 and 45 Long Colt in the Cowboy Action model
Price: standard rifles **$1,495.00**

Custom rifles can be ordered with a host of options in various hunting and target configurations.
Chamberings include (but are not limited too):
• 32-40 • 38-55 • 40-65 • 40-70 • 45-70 • 45-90
• 45-110 • 50-70 • 50-90
Price: custom rifles . . . . **$1,600.00 and up**
All Lone Star rifles are built entirely in the United States.

COWBOY ACTION

MAGNUM RESEARCH

MOUNTAIN EAGLE

VARMINT MODEL
W/STAINLESS STEEL KRIEGER BARREL

MOUNTAIN EAGLE BOLT-ACTION RIFLE

SPECIFICATIONS

Calibers: 270 Win., 280 Rem., 30-06 Springfield, 7mm Mag., 300 Wby. Mag., 300 Win. Mag., 338 Win. Mag., 340 Wby. Mag., 375 H&H Mag., 416 Rem. Mag. *Capacity:* 5-shot magazine (long action); 4-shot (Magnum action) *Action:* SAKO-built to MRI specifications *Barrel length:* 24" with .004" headspace tolerance *Overall length:* 44" *Weight:* 7 lb. 13 oz. *Sights:* None *Stock:* Fiberglass composite *Length of pull:* 13 ⁵/₈" *Features:* Adjustable trigger; high comb stock (for mounting and scoping); one-piece forged bolt; free-floating, match-grade, cut-rifles, benchrest barrel; recoil pad and sling swivel studs; Platform Bedding System for front lug; pillar-bedded rear guard screw; lengthened receiver ring; solid steel hinged floorplate

Price:. **$1,499.00**
  Left Hand **1,549.00**
  375 H&H Mag. and 416 Rem. Mag. **1,799.00**
Also available:
VARMINT EDITION. In 222 Rem. and 223 Rem.
  with stainless steel Krieger barrel (26") **$1629.00**
STANDARD (add **$300.00** for 357 H&H
  or 416 Rem) **1,499.00**
Left Hand. **1,549.00**

MODEL 7022 SEMI-AUTO

Magtech Model 7022 is a new 22-caliber rimfire semi-auto clip-fed blow-back repeater also produced with the same quality and crafts-manship of all Magtech products. Reliable function is guaranteed by exact fitting tolerances between bolt and receiver, and double extrac-tors. Accuracy is enhanced with an 8-groove 18" free floating ordnance grade heat-treated steel barrel. Safety features include: a convenient cross bolt safety that blocks the hammer; a hammer that can only hit the firing pin when the bolt it totally closed, and a bolt that remains in the open position after the last shot. The bolt may be kept in the open position even if the magazine is withdrawn. Receiver and trigger guard are manufactured in light die casting aluminum alloy and finished with a black electroforetic painting. Magazine lock can be easily operated by either hand and gun is supplied with one 10-shot magazine. Rear sight is adjustable for both elevation and windage and may be tilted forward to allow the installation of scopes with diameter up to 32 mm. Two 6-48 screws are used for assembling the rear sight and the space between them are exacting to other USA made rear sights. Front sight is fixed with removable steel hood. Receiver is milled to accept standard 3/8" scope mounts. The full-length stock is made from selected Brazilian hardwood and hand finished.

Model	Action	Caliber	Capacity	Barrel	Weight	Overall Length
7022	Semi-Auto	.22LR	10-Shot Clip Mag.	18" Long with 8-Groove Rifling	4.8 lbs	37"

Started Importing Late '98

MARLIN 22 RIFLES

MODEL 60

SPECIFICATIONS
Caliber: 22 Long Rifle **Capacity:** 14-shot tubular magazine **Barrel Length:** 22" **Overall Length:** 40.5" **Weight:** 5.5 lbs. **Sights:** Ramp front sight with brass bead and Wide-Scan hood; adjustable open rear, receiver grooved for scope mount

Action: Self-loading; side ejection; manual and automatic "last-shot" hold-open devices; receiver top has serrated, nonglare finish; crossbolt safety **Stock:** One-piece Maine birch Monte Carlo stock, press-checkered, with full pistol grip; Mar-Shield® finish

Price:	$168.00
Stainess	212.00
Stainess, synthetic stock	229.00
Stainess, laminated stock	265.00

MODEL 70PSS "PAPOOSE"

Action: Self-loading; side ejection; manual bolt hold-open; crossbolt safety; stainless-steel breech bolt and barrel **Sights:** Screw adjustable open rear; ramp front; receiver grooved for scope mount **Stock:** Black fiberglass-filled synthetic with abbrev. forend, nickel-plated swivel studs **Price:** $272.00

SPECIFICATIONS
Caliber: 22 Long Rifle **Capacity:** 7-shot clip **Barrel Length:** 16.25" **Overall Length:** 35.25" **Weight:** 3.25 lbs.

MODEL 7000

SPECIFICATIONS
Caliber: 22 LR **Capacity:** 10 shots **Action:** Self-loading; side ejection **Barrel Length:** 18" heavy target; recessed muzzle (16 grooves) **Overall Length:** 37" **Weight:** 5.25 lbs.

Stock: Monte Carlo black fiberglass-filled synthetic **Sights:** No sights; receiver grooved for scope mount (1" scope ring mounts standard) **Features:** Manual bolt hold-open; crossbolt safety; steel charging handle **Price:** $225.00
Also available: MODEL 795. Same as Model 7000 but w/screw-adjustable open rear sight w/brass bead; no scope mount **Weight:** 4.5 lbs. $159.00

MODEL 995SS

SPECIFICATIONS
Caliber: 22 LR only **Capacity:** 7-shot nickel-plated clip magazine **Action:** Same as Model 70PSS **Barrel Length:** 18" stainless steel w/Micro-Groove Rifling (16 grooves) **Overall Length:** 37" **Weight:** 4.5 lbs. **Sights:** Same as Model 70PSS **Stock:** Monte Carlo black fiberglass synthetic w/nickel-plated swivel studs and molded-in checkering **Price:** $255.00

MARLIN BOLT-ACTION RIFLES

MARLIN 15YN "LITTLE BUCKAROO™"
SINGLE SHOT 22 BEGINNER'S RIFLE

SPECIFICATIONS

Caliber: 22 Short, Long or Long Rifle *Capacity:* Single shot *Action:* Bolt action; easy-load feed throat; thumb safety; red cocking indicator *Barrel Length:* 16.25" (16 grooves) *Overall Length:* 33.25" *Weight:* 4.25 lbs.

Sights: Adjustable open rear; ramp front sight *Stock:* One-piece walnut-finished press-checkered Maine birch Monte Carlo w/full pistol grip; tough Mar-Shield® finish
Price: **$188.00**
    Model 15N w/standard-length stock **188.00**

MODEL 25MN

SPECIFICATIONS

Caliber: 22 WMR (not interchangeable w/other 22 cartridges) *Capacity:* 7-shot clip magazine *Barrel Length:* 22" with Micro-Groove® rifling *Overall Length:* 41"

Weight: 6 lbs. *Sights:* Adjustable open rear; ramp front sight; receiver grooved for scope mount
Stock: One-piece walnut finished press-checkered Maine birch Monte Carlo w/full pistol grip; Mar-Shield® finish; swivel studs
Price: **$216.00**
    Model 25N in .22 Long Rifle **189.00**

MODEL 81TS

SPECIFICATIONS

Caliber: 22 Short, Long or Long Rifle *Capacity:* Tubular magazine holds 25 Short, 19 Long, 17 Long Rifle cartridges

Barrel Length: 22" w/Micro-Groove® rifling (16 grooves) *Overall Length:* 41" *Weight:* 6 lbs. *Sights:* Screw-adjustable open rear; ramp front *Stock:* Monte Carlo black fiberglass-filled synthetic w/swivel studs and molded-in checkering
Price: **$187.00**
    w/scope **193.00**

MODEL 883

SPECIFICATIONS

Caliber: 22 WMR (not interchangeable with other 22 cartridges) *Capacity:* 12-shot tubular magazine with patented closure system *Action:* Bolt action; positive thumb safety;

red cocking indicator *Barrel Length:* 22" with Micro-Groove® rifling (20 grooves) *Overall Length:* 41" *Weight:* 6 lbs. *Sights:* Adjustable folding semibuckhorn rear; ramp front with Wide-Scan hood™; receiver grooved for scope mount *Stock:* Checkered Monte Carlo American black walnut with full pistol grip; rubber buttpad; swivel studs; tough Mar-Shield® finish
Price: **$298.00**

MARLIN BOLT-ACTION RIFLES

MODEL 883SS
(STAINLESS STEEL)

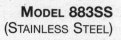

SPECIFICATIONS
Same as Model 883, except with stainless barrel and receiver, laminated two-tone brown Maine birch stock with nickel-plated swivel studs and rubber rifle buttpad
Price: $317.00

MODEL 882L

Laminated hardwood Monte Carlo w/Mar-Shield® finish
Features: Swivel studs; rubber rifle butt pad; receiver grooved for scope mount; positive thumb safety; red cocking indicator
Price: $304.00
　　Model 882SSV stainless, walnut 286.00
　　Model 882SS stainless, synthetic w/"fire" sights . . . 305.00

SPECIFICATIONS
Caliber: 22 WMR (not interchangeable with other 22 cartridges) **Capacity:** 7-shot clip magazine **Barrel Length:** 22" Micro-Groove® **Overall Length:** 41" **Weight:** 6.25 lbs. **Sights:** Ramp front w/brass bead and removable Wide-Scan™ hood; adj. folding semibuckhorn rear **Stock:**

MODEL MR-7B

rifling and recessed muzzle **Overall Length:** 43" **Weight:** 7.25 lbs. **Sights:** Without sights **Stock:** Maine birch pistol grip stock w/cut checkering; swivel studs; rubber rifle butt pad; Mar-Shield® finish
Price: $483.00

SPECIFICATIONS
Caliber: 270 Win. and 30-06 Springfield **Capacity:** 4-shot blind magazine **Barrel Length:** 22" w/6-groove precision

MODEL MR-7

blade **Stock:** American black walnut w/cut checkering; Mar-Shield™ finish **Features:** 3-position safety; shrouded striker; red cocking indicator; drilled and tapped receiver, rubber recoil pad
Price: $643.00

SPECIFICATIONS
Calibers: 25-06 Rem., 270 Win., 30-06 Sprfd, 280 Rem. **Action:** Bolt action **Capacity:** 4-shot detachable box magazine **Barrel Length:** 22" (6-groove rifling), recessed muzzle **Overall Length:** 43" **Weight:** 7.5 lbs. **Sights:** Rear, optional Williams streamlined ramp w/brass bead; front, Williams

MARLIN SELF-LOADING RIFLES

MODEL 922M SELF-LOADER

SPECIFICATIONS

Caliber: 22 WMRF **Capacity:** 5-shot nickel-plated magazine **Barrel Length:** 20.5" Micro-Groove **Overall Length:** 39.75" **Weight:** 6.5 lbs. **Sights:** Adjustable folding semi-buckhorn rear sight; ramp front sight w/brass bead and removable Wide-Scan™ hood **Stock:** Monte Carlo American black walnut checkered stock w/rubber rifle butt pad and swivel studs **Features:** Garand type safety; magazine safety; receiver sandblasted to prevent glare; manual bolt hold-open; automatic last-shot bolt hold-open

Price: **$429.00**

MODEL 9 CAMP CARBINE

SPECIFICATIONS

Caliber: 9mm **Capacity:** 10-shot clip **Action:** Self-loading. Manual bolt hold-open. Garand-type safety, magazine safety, loaded chamber indicator. Solid-top, machined steel receiver is sandblasted to prevent glare, and is drilled/tapped for scope mounting. **Barrel Length:** 16.5" with Micro-Groove® rifling **Overall Length:** 35.5" **Weight:** 6.75 lbs. **Sights:** Adjustable folding rear, ramp front sight with high-visibility, orange front sight post; Wide-Scan™ hood. **Stock:** Press-checkered walnut-finished hardwood w/pistol grip; tough Mar-Shield™ finish; rubber rifle buttpad; swivel studs

Price: **$443.00**
Model 45 in .45 ACP, 7-shot magazine **443.00**

MARLIN LEVER-ACTION .22 RIFLE

MARLIN GOLDEN 39AS

Introduced in 1891, the Marlin lever-action 22 is the oldest shoulder gun still being manufactured.

SOLID RECEIVER TOP. You can easily mount a scope on your Marlin 39 by screwing on the machined scope adapter base provided. The screw-on base is a neater, more versatile method of mounting a scope on a 22 sporting rifle. The solid top receiver and scope adapter base provide a maximum in eye relief adjustment. If you prefer iron sights, you'll find the 39 receiver clean, flat and sandblasted to prevent glare. Exclusive brass magazine tube

MICRO-GROOVE® BARREL. Marlin's famous rifling system of multi-grooving has consistently produced fine accuracy because the system grips the bullet more securely, minimizes distortion, and provides a better gas seal.

And the Model 39 maximizes accuracy with the heaviest barrels available on any lever-action 22.

SPECIFICATIONS

Caliber: 22 Short, Long and Long Rifle **Capacity:** Tubular magazine holds 26 Short, 21 Long and 19 LR cartridges
Action: Lever; solid top receiver; side ejection; one-step takedown; deeply blued metal surfaces; receiver top sandblasted to prevent glare; hammer block safety; rebounding hammer **Barrel:** 24" with Micro-Groove® rifling (16 grooves) **Overall Length:** 40" **Weight:** 6.5 lbs. **Sights:** Adjustable folding semibuckhorn rear, ramp front sight with Wide-Scan™ hood; solid top receiver tapped for scope mount or receiver sight; scope adapter base; offset hammer spur for scope use—works right or left **Stock:** Two-piece cut-checkered American black walnut w/fluted comb; full pistol grip and forend; blued-steel forend cap; swivel studs; grip cap; Mar-Shield® finish; rubber buttpad

Price: **$481.00**

MARLIN SPECIALTY GUNS

COWBOY GUN

MARLIN 336 COWBOY GUN

Available in 30/30 and 38/55, this rifle has a 24-inch octagon barrel and 6-shot full-length magazine. The checkered, straight-grip walnut stock has a hard-rubber butt. Ballard-type rifling gives fine accuracy with cast bullets. Marble open sights add a traditional touch. *Length:* 42-1/2 inches, *Weight:* 7-1/2 pounds
Price: $658.00

GARDEN GUN

MARLIN GARDEN GUN

The Garden Gun is a mini-shotgun chambered for the .22 Winchester Magnum shotshell. A 22-inch smooth bore barrel, 7-shot box magazine and hardwood stock make this ideal pest gun for orchard and yard as well as gardens. *Length:* 41", *Weight:* 6 pounds.
Price: $223.00

MARLIN 7000T WITH SCOPE

MARLIN 7000T

This accurate, autoloading .22 has a Micro-Groove target barrel 18" long. The nickel-plated box magazine holds 10 rounds. The red, white and blue laminated birch stock accepts forend accessories on an aluminum tail. A rubber buttplate is adjustable for drop, length of pull and cant. *Length:* 37", *Weight:* 7-1/2 pounds.
Price: $442.00

MARLIN LEVER-ACTION RIFLES

444P OUTFITTER

MARLIN 444P AND 1895G

The 444P "Outfitter" and 1895G "Guide Gun" are chambered in .444 Marlin and .45-70 respectively. They feature 2/3-length magazines (5-shot and 4-shot capacity), straight-grip walnut stocks with cut checkering, recoil pads and porting at the muzzle to reduce kick. The Guide Gun received Petersen Publishing's 1998 prestigious "Rifle of the Year" award. **Length:** 37" (barrel 18.5") **Weight:** 6.75 pounds **Price:** (with sights) $572.00

1897CB COWBOY

MARLIN 1897 COWBOY

This .22 rimfire with 24" octagon barrel is built on a Model 39 action. The full-length magazine holds 26 short, 21 long and 19 long rifle rounds. A two-level scope adapter lets you add 3/4- or 7/8-inch scopes as well as standard 1" models. Marble open sights and a quick-takedown receiver are standard, as is a checkered, straight-grip walnut stock. **Overall length:** 40", **Weight:** 6-1/2 pounds. **Price:** $648.00

MARLIN LEVER-ACTION CARBINES

MODEL 1894 COWBOY II

SPECIFICATIONS
Calibers: 357 Mag./38 Special, 44-40, 44 Mag./44 Special, 45 LC
Action: Lever action w/squared finger lever

Capacity: 10-shot tubular magazine
Barrel Length: 24" tapered octagon (6 grooves)
Overall Length: 41.5" **Weight:** 7.5 lbs.
Sights: Adjustable semi-buckhorn rear; carbine front
Stock: Straight-grip American black walnut w/cut-checkering and hard rubber buttplate
Features: Mar-Shield™ finish; blued steel forend cap; side ejection; blued metal surfaces; hammer block safety
Price: $723.00

MARLIN 1894S

SPECIFICATIONS
Calibers: 44 Rem. Mag./44 Special
Capacity: 10-shot tubular magazine
Action: Lever action w/square finger lever; hammer block safety

Barrel Length: 20" w/deep-cut Ballard-type rifling
Sights: Ramp front sight w/brass bead; adjustable semi-buckhorn folding rear and Wide-Scan™ hood; solid-top receiver tapped for scope mount or receiver sight
Overall Length: 37.5" **Weight:** 6 lbs.
Stock: Checkered American black walnut stock w/Mar-Shield® finish; blued steel forend cap; swivel studs
Price: $486.00

MARLIN 1894CS 357 MAGNUM

SPECIFICATIONS
Calibers: 357 Magnum, 38 Special
Capacity: 9-shot tubular magazine
Action: Lever action w/square finger lever; hammer block safety; side ejection; solid top receiver; deeply blued metal

surfaces; receiver top sandblasted to prevent glare
Barrel Length: 18.5" w/deep-cut Ballard-type rifling (6 grooves)
Sights: Adjustable semibuckhorn folding rear, ramp front w/brass bead and Wide-Scan™ hood; solid top receiver tapped for scope mount or receiver sight; offset hammer spur for scope use-adjustable for right or left hand
Overall Length: 36" **Weight:** 6 lbs.
Stock: Cut-checkered straight-grip two-piece American black walnut Mar-Shield® finish; swivel studs; rubber rifle buttpad
Price: $486.00

RIFLES

MARLIN LEVER-ACTION CARBINES

MARLIN 1895SS

SPECIFICATIONS
Caliber: 45-70 Government
Capacity: 4-shot tubular magazine
Action: Lever action; hammer block safety; receiver top sandblasted to prevent glare
Barrel: 22" w/deep-cut Ballard-type rifling
Sights: Ramp front sight w/brass bead; adjustable semibuckhorn folding rear and Wide-Scan™ hood; receiver tapped for scope mount or receiver sight
Overall Length: 40.5" **Weight:** 7.5 lbs.
Stock: Checkered American black walnut pistol-grip stock w/rubber rifle buttpad and Mar-Shield® finish; swivel studs
Price: $566.00
Also available:
MODEL 1895G "GUIDE GUN" WITH PORTED BARREL. Same caliber, capacity, action, sights. Stock has straight grip, ventilated recoil pad. **Barrel Length:** 18.5" **Overall Length:** 37" **Weight:** 6.75 lbs.
Price: $572.00

MARLIN 336CS

SPECIFICATIONS
Calibers: 30-30 Win., and 35 Rem.
Capacity: 6-shot tubular magazine
Action: Lever action w/hammer block safety; deeply blued metal surfaces; receiver top sandblasted to prevent glare
Barrel: 20" Micro-Groove® barrel
Sights: Adjustable folding semibuckhorn rear; ramp front sight w/brass bead and Wide-Scan™ hood; tapped for receiver sight and scope mount; offset hammer spur for scope use (works right or left)
Overall Length: 38.5" **Weight:** 7 lbs.
Stock: Checkered American black walnut pistol-grip stock w/fluted comb and Mar-Shield® finish; rubber rifle buttpad; swivel studs
Price: $474.00
Model 30 AS 30-30 onlly, birch stock. 405.00

MODEL 444SS

SPECIFICATIONS
Caliber: 444 Marlin
Capacity: 5-shot tubular magazine
Barrel: 22" w/deep-cut Ballard-type rifling
Overall Length: 40.5" **Weight:** 7.5 lbs.
Stock: Checkered American black walnut pistol grip stock with rubber rifle buttpad; swivel studs
Sights: Ramp front sight with brass bead and Wide-Scan™ hood; adjustable semibuckhorn folding rear; receiver tapped for scope mount or receiver sight
Price: $566.00

MARLIN 22 TARGET RIFLE

MODEL 2000L

SPECIFICATIONS

Caliber: 22 LR only
Capacity: Single shot
Action: Bolt action; thumb safety; patented two-stage target trigger; red cocking indicator
Barrel Length: 22" heavy, selected Micro-Groove w/match chamber and recessed muzzle

Overall Length: 41" *Weight:* 8 lbs.
Sights: Fully adjustable target rear peep sight; hooded front sight w/10 aperture inserts
Stock: Laminated black/grey w/ambidextrous pistol grip; butt plate adjustable for length of pull, height, angle; aluminum forearm
Price: $656.00

MAUSER RIFLES

MODEL 96 BOLT ACTION

MODEL 96

SPECIFICATIONS
Calibers: 243 Win., 25-06, 270 Win., 30-06 S'fld, 308 Win., 7mm Rem. Mag., 300 Win. Mag.
Capacity: 5 rounds
Action: Sliding bolt action
Barrel length: 22" (24" magnum)
Overall length: 42" (44" magnum)
Weight: 6.25 lbs.
Safety: Rear tang, 3-position
Trigger: Single *Stock:* Checkered walnut
Sights: None; drilled and tapped for Rem. 700 scope mounts and bases

Features: Quick-detachable 1" sling swivels; 16 locking lugs
Price: $699.00
Also available:
MODEL SR 86 W/28.75" barrel in 308 Win. w/muzzle brake; adjustable black laminated thumbhold stock w/bipod rail. *Weight:* 13.6 lbs. $11,795.00
MODEL M94 w/22" barrel (24" magnum) in 25-06 Rem., 243 Win., 308 Win., 270 Win., 30-06 S'fld, 7mm Rem. Mag., 300 Win. Mag. Features aluminum bedding block, interchangeable barrels ($799.00), combo or single-set trigger, detachable mag., walnut stock. *Weight:* 7.25 lbs. $2,295.00

NAVY ARMS REPLICA RIFLES

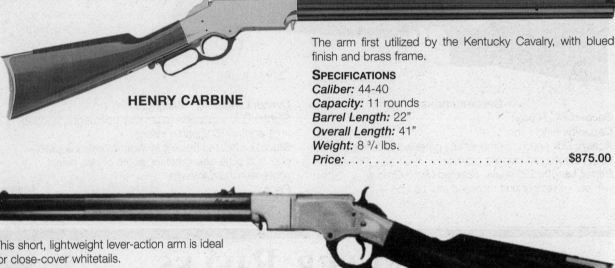

HENRY CARBINE

The arm first utilized by the Kentucky Cavalry, with blued finish and brass frame.

SPECIFICATIONS
Caliber: 44-40
Capacity: 11 rounds
Barrel Length: 22"
Overall Length: 41"
Weight: 8 ³/₄ lbs.
Price: $875.00

This short, lightweight lever-action arm is ideal for close-cover whitetails.

SPECIFICATIONS
Caliber: 44-40
Capacity: 8 rounds
Barrel Length: 16 ¹/₂"
Overall Length: 34 ¹/₂"
Weight: 7 lbs. 7 oz.
Price: $875.00

HENRY TRAPPER MODEL

1866 "YELLOWBOY" RIFLE

The 1866 model was Oliver Winchester's improved version of the Henry rifle. Called the "Yellowboy" because of its polished brass receiver, it was popular with Indians, settlers and cattlemen alike.

SPECIFICATIONS
Caliber: 38 Special, 44-40, 45 Colt
Barrel Length: 24" full octagon *Overall Length:* 42.5"
Weight: 8.25 lbs. *Sights:* Blade front; open ladder rear
Stock: Walnut
Price: $685.00

HENRY MILITARY RIFLE

This Civil War replica features a highly polished brass frame and blued barrel; sling swivels to the original specifications are located on the left side.

SPECIFICATIONS
Caliber: 44-40 or 45 Colt *Capacity:* 13 rounds
Barrel Length: 24"
Overall Length: 43"
Weight: 9.25 lbs. *Stock:* Walnut
Price: $895.00

IRON FRAME HENRY

SPECIFICATIONS
Caliber: 44-40
Capacity: 13 rounds
Barrel Length: 24"
Overall Length: 43"
Weight: 9 lbs.
Stock: Walnut
Finish: Blued or casehardened *Feature:* Iron frame
Price: $945.00

NAVY ARMS REPLICA RIFLES

1866 "YELLOWBOY" CARBINE

This is the "saddle gun" varient of the Yellowboy rifle.

SPECIFICATIONS
Caliber: 38 Special, 44-40 or 45 Colt
Barrel Length: 19" round *Overall Length:* 38.25"
Weight: 7.25 lbs. *Sights:* Blade front; open ladder rear
Stock: Walnut
Price: $675.00

REPLICA 1873 WINCHESTER RIFLE
(not shown)

Known as "The Gun That Won the West," the 1873 was the most popular lever-action rifle of its time. This fine replica features a casehardened receiver.

SPECIFICATIONS
Caliber: 357 Mag., 44-40 or 45 Colt
Barrel Length: 24" *Overall Length:* 43"

Weight: 8.25 lbs.
Sights: Blade front; open ladder rear
Stock: Walnut
Price: $820.00
Also available: 1873 CARBINE
(19" barrel) $800.00
1873 "BORDER MODEL" RIFLE
(20" Oct. barrel) 820.00

REPLICA 1873 WINCHESTER SPORTING RIFLE

This replica of the elegant Winchester 1873 Sporting Rifle features a checkered pistol grip, buttstock, casehardened receiver and blued octagonal barrel.

SPECIFICATIONS
Caliber: 357 Mag. (24" bbl. only), 44-40 or 45 Colt
Barrel Length: 24" or 30"
Overall Length: 48 ³/₄" (w/30" barrel)
Weight: 8 lbs. 14 oz.
Sights: Blade front; buckhorn rear
Prices:
30" Barrel. $960.00
24" Barrel. 930.00

1873 SPRINGFIELD CAVALRY CARBINE

A reproduction of the classic U.S. "Trapdoor" Springfield carbine used by the 7th Cavalry at The Battle of Little Big Horn.

SPECIFICATIONS
Caliber: 45-70 Government *Barrel Length:* 22"
Overall Length: 40.5" *Weight:* 7 lbs.
Sights: Blade front, military ladder rear
Stock: Walnut *Features:* Saddle bar with ring
Price: $870.00
Also available:
1873 SPRINGFIELD INFANTRY RIFLE (32.5" bbl.) $995.00

RIFLES

NAVY ARMS REPLICA RIFLES

1874 SHARPS CAVALRY CARBINE

This cavalry carbine version of the Sharps rifle features a side bar and saddle ring.

SPECIFICATIONS
Caliber: 45-70 percussion
Barrel Length: 22"
Overall Length: 39"
Weight: 7 ³/₄ lbs.
Sights: Blade front; military ladder rear
Stock: Walnut
Price: $935.00

1874 SHARPS SNIPER RIFLE

This replica of the 1874 three-band sharpshooter's rifle was a popular target rifle at the Creedmoor military matches and was the issue longarm of the New York State Militia.

SPECIFICATIONS
Caliber: 45-70 *Barrel Length:* 30"
Overall Length: 46 ³/₄" *Weight:* 8 lbs. 8 oz.
Stock: Walnut
Features: Double-set triggers; casehardened receiver; patchbox and furniture
Price: $1,115.00
Also available:
SINGLE TRIGGER INFANTRY MODEL. $1,060.00

SHARPS PLAINS RIFLE (not shown)

SPECIFICATIONS
Caliber: 45-70 *Barrel Length:* 32" octagonal
Overall Length: 49" *Weight:* 9 lbs. 8 oz.

Sights: Blade front, ladder rear (optional tang sight avail.)
Stock: Walnut *Features:* Color casehardened receiver and furniture; double-set triggers
Price: $1,050.00

SHARPS BUFFALO RIFLE

This deluxe version of the rifle that came to be known simply as "buffalo gun" was favored by market hunters on the Great Plains after the Civil War.

SPECIFICATIONS
Caliber: 45-70 or 45-90 *Barrel Length:* 28" octagonal
Overall Length: 46" *Weight:* 10 lbs. 10 oz.
Sights: Blade front, ladder rear (tang sight optional w/set triggers only–**$65.00**
Stock: Walnut
Features: Color casehardened receiver and furniture; double-set trigger
Price: $1,090.00

NAVY ARMS REPLICA RIFLES

KODIAK MK IV DOUBLE RIFLE

SPECIFICATIONS
Caliber: 45-70 **Barrel Length:** 24" **Overall Length:** 39 ³/₄"
Weight: 10 lbs. 3 oz. **Sights:** Bead front, folding-leaf express rear **Stock:** Checkered European walnut
Features: Color case hardened locks, breech and hammers; semi-regulated barrels
Price: $3,125.00
Also available: DELUXE KODIAK MK IV DOUBLE RIFLE (shown) with browned barrels and hand-engraving on satin frame and fittings.
Price: $4,000.00

1892 BRASS FRAME RIFLE

SPECIFICATIONS
Calibers: 44-40 or 45 Colt
Barrel Length: 24.25" octagonal
Weight: 7.25 lbs.
Sights: Blade front; semi-buckhorn rear
Stock: American walnut
Price: $495.00

1892 SHORT RIFLE

Replica of the "Texas Special" 92 Winchester that featured a 20" full octagonal barrel. Available with color case hardened or blue receiver and furniture.

SPECIFICATIONS
Calibers: 357 Mag., 44-40 or 45 Colt
Barrel Length: 20" octagon **Weight:** 6.25 lbs.
Sights: Blade front; semibuckhorn rear
Stock: American walnut
Price: $495.00

1892 RIFLE (not shown)
SPECIFICATIONS
Caliber: 357 Mag., 44-40 or 45 Colt
Barrel Length: 24.25" octagon
Weight: 7 lbs.

Sights: Blade front; semi-buckhorn rear
Stock: American walnut
Price: $495.00

RIFLES

NAVY ARMS REPLICA RIFLES

NO. 2 CREEDMOOR TARGET RIFLE

This reproduction of the Remington No. 2 Creedmoor Rifle features a color case hardened receiver and steel trigger guard, tapered octagon barrel, and walnut forend and butt-stock with checkered pistol grip.

SPECIFICATIONS
Caliber: 45-70
Barrel Length: 30", tapered
Overall Length: 46"
Weight: 9 lbs.
Sights: Globe front, adjustable Creedmoor rear
Stock: Checkered walnut stock and forend
Price: $900.00

REMINGTON-STYLE ROLLING BLOCK BUFFALO RIFLE

This replica of the rifle used by buffalo hunters and plainsmen of the 1800s features a case hardened receiver, solid brass trigger guard and walnut stock and forend. The tang is drilled and tapped to accept the optional Creedmoor sight.

SPECIFICATIONS
Caliber: 45-70
Barrel Length: 26" or 30"; full octagon or half-round
Sights: Blade front, open notch rear
Stock: Walnut stock and forend
Feature: Shown with optional 32.5" Model 1860 brass telescopic sight **$210.00**; Compact Model (18"): **$200.00**
Price: 650.00
Also available:
With casehardened steel (no brass furniture) 745.00

GREENER LIGHT MODEL HARPOON GUN

Designed for large game fish, the Greener Harpoon gun utilizes the time-proven Martini action. The complete outfit consists of gun, harpoons, harpoon lines, line release frames, blank cartridges and cleaning kit, all housed in a carrying case.

SPECIFICATIONS
Caliber: 38 Special (blank)
Barrel Length: 20" *Overall Length:* 36"
Weight: 6 lbs. 5 oz.
Stock: Walnut
Price: $995.00

NEW ENGLAND FIREARMS RIFLES

SYNTHETIC HANDI-RIFLE

New England Firearms® Handi-Rifle now features a black Monte Carlo synthetic stock and forend. This version includes a factory-mounted scope base and an offset hammer extension to ease cocking when a scope is mounted. The rifles all include the patented NEF Transfer Bar System, which virtually eliminates the possibility of accidental discharge. A wide range of additional rifle barrels are available for factory retrofitting through NEF's Accessory Barrel Program.

SPECIFICATIONS

Calibers: 22 Hornet, 223 Rem., 243 Win., 270 Win., 280 Rem., 30-30 Win., 30-06 Springfield; 44 Rem. Mag., 45-70 Gov't **Action:** Break-open; side lever release; automatic ejection **Barrel Length:** 22" (26" in 270 Win.) **Overall Length:** 38" (40" in 270 Win.) **Length Of Pull:** 14.25" **Drop At Heel:** 2.25" **Drop At Comb:** 1.5" **Weight:** 7 lbs. **Sights:** Ramp front; fully adjustable rear; tapped for scope mount **Stock:** High density polymer; black matte finish; sling swivels; recoil pad
Price: $219.95
  In 270 Win. 224.95

SUPER LIGHT YOUTH HANDI-RIFLE™

In 1998 New England Firearms introduced a youth version of its Superlight Handi-Rifle in 22 Hornet. Proper gun fit is provided by a special youth-sized, lightweight synthetic stock and forend. Weight is further reduced with a new Super Light taper on the quick handling barrel. The matte black synthetic stock and forend feature a non-slip finish plus a sling, swivels and recoil pad. Other features include the patented New England Firearms Transfer Bar System, which virtually eliminates the possibility of accidental discharge. As a young shooter grows, New England Firearms offers a variety of adult-sized rifle and shotgun barrels for factory retrofitting.

SPECIFICATIONS

Caliber: 22 Hornet **Action:** Single shot; break-open; side lever release; automatic ejection **Barrel Length:** 20" **Overall Length:** 33" **Drop At Heel:** 1 1/8" **Drop At Comb:** 1 1/8" **Length Of Pull:** 11.75" **Weight:** 5 1/3 lbs. **Sights:** Ramp front; fully adjustable rear; tapped for scope mount **Stock:** High density polymer; black matte finish; sling swivels; recoil pad
Price: $219.95

PEDERSOLI REPLICA RIFLES

ROLLING BLOCK TARGET RIFLE

SPECIFICATIONS
Calibers: 45-70 and 357 **Barrel length:** 30" octagonal (blued)
Weight: 9 1/2 lbs. (45-70); 10 lbs. (357) **Sights:** Adjustable rear sight; tunnel modified front (all models designed for fitting of Creedmoor sight)
Prices: $740.00
w/Creedmoor sight 810.00
Also available: CAVALRY, INFANTRY, LONG RANGE CREEDMOOR
Prices: . . . . $675.00–$900.00

SPECIFICATIONS
Caliber: 54 **Barrel length:** 22" round (6 grooves)
Overall length: 39" **Weight:** 7.5 lbs.
Sights: Fully adjustable rear; fixed front
Price: w/Patchbox. $940.00
Also available:
SHARPS 1859 MILITARY RIFLE (set trigger, 30" barrel, 8.4 lbs.).
Price:. $1,150.00

SHARPS CARBINE MODEL 766

SPECIFICATIONS
Calibers: 45-70, 9.3x74R, 8x57JSR **Barrel length:** 22" (24" 45-70) **Overall length:** 39" (40.5" 45-70)
Weight: 8.24 lbs. (9.7 lbs. 45/70)
Price: $3,125.00
Also available:
KODIAK MARK IV w/interchangeable 20-gauge barrel
Price:. $4,125.00

KODIAK MARK IV DOUBLE RIFLE

PRAIRIE GUN WORKS

MODEL M-15 ULTRA LITE (not shown)

SPECIFICATIONS
Caliber: Most Short Action calibers
Action: Remington 700 Short Action
Barrel length: 22" Douglas Match Grade
Length of pull: 13.5" **Weight:** 4.5-5.25 lbs.
Stock: Fiberglass-Kevlar composite w/integral recoil lug; recoil pad installed **Finish:** Black or grey textured finish
Sights: Custom aircraft-grade aluminum scope mounts

Features: Trigger set and polished for 3 lb. pull; bolt fluted, hollowed and tapped w/Ultra Lite custom firing pin and bolt shroud
Price:. $1,750.00
Also available:
MODEL M-18. Same specifications and price as Model M-15, except chambered for long-action calibers (up to 340 Weatherby)

REMINGTON BOLT-ACTION RIFLES

MODEL 700 BDL DM

MODEL 700 BDL DM

The **MODEL 700 DM** (Detachable Magazine) models feature detachable 4-shot magazines (except the 3-shot magnum-caliber models), stainless-steel latches, latch springs and magazine boxes. **MODEL 700 BDL DM** rifles feature the standard Remington BDL barrel contour with 22" barrels on standard-caliber models and 24" barrels on magnum-caliber rifles. All barrels have a hooded front sight and adjustable rear sight. Additional features include polished blued-metal finish, high-gloss, Monte Carlo-style stock, white line spacers, 20 lines-per-inch checkering, recoil pad and swivel studs. All models feature fine-line engraving on receiver front rings, rear bridges, non-ejection receiver sides and floorplates. For calibers, see Model 700 table.

Prices: MODEL 700 BDL DM $639.00
  Magnum 665.00
  Stainless DM Magnum 729.00

MODEL 700 BDL SS

MODEL 700 BDL

This Model 700 features the Monte Carlo American walnut stock finished to a high gloss with fine-cut checkering. Also includes a hinged floorplate, sling swivel studs, hooded ramp front sight and adjustable rear sight. Also available in stainless synthetic version (Model 700 BDL SS) with stainless-steel barrel, receiver and bolt plus synthetic stock for maximum weather resistance. For additional specifications, see Model 700 table.

MODEL 700 BDL
Prices:
In 17 Rem., 7mm Rem. Mag., 300 Win. Mag.,
  .300 Rem Ultra Mag $612.00
In 222 Rem., 22-250 Rem., 223 Rem., 243 Win.,
  25-06 Rem., 270 Win., 30-06. . . . . 585.00
In 338 Win. Mag.. . . . . 612.00
Left Hand in 270 Win., 30-06. . . . . 612.00
Left Hand in 7mm Rem. Mag.. . . . . 639.00
MODEL BDL SS (Stainless Synthetic)
In 270 Win. 30-06.. . . . . 641.00
In 7mm Rem. Mag., 300 Win. Mag.. . . . . 668.00
In 338 Win. Mag. and 375 H&H Mag. 668.00

MODEL 700 BDL SS DM-B

Available in *calibers:* 7mm Rem. Mag., 7mm STW, 300 Win. Mag., *Barrel length:* 25.5" (magnum contour barrel). Stainless synthetic detachable magazine with muzzle brake.
Price: $789.00

REMINGTON BOLT-ACTION RIFLES

MODEL 700 VLS
(VARMINT LAMINATED STOCK)

The **MODEL 700 BDL VLS** features a stainless barrel, laminated synthetic stock, hinged magazine floorplate and sling swivel studs. *Barrel length: 26" Overall Length:* 46.5" *Weight:* 9 lbs. *Length of pull:* 13 ³/₈" *Drop at comb:* .5" *Drop at heel:* ³/₈"

Price:	$715.00
Left Hand.	715.00
Magnum	741.00

MODEL 700 "SENDERO SPECIAL"

Remington's Sendero rifle combines the accuracy features of the Model 700 Varmint Special with long action and magnum calibers for long-range hunting. The 26-inch barrel has a heavy varmint profile and features a spherical concave crown. For additional specifications, see table on the following page.

Price:	$705.00
Magnum	732.00

MODEL 700 SENDERO SF
(Stainless Fluted)

This version of the Model 700 Sendero features satin-finished stainless steel receiver and bolt and a 26-inch heavy stainless barrel with six longitudinal flutes designed to improve heat dissipation and reduce gun weight (8.5 lbs.). A spherical, concave crown protects the muzzle. Other features include a composite synthetic fiberglass stock, graphite reinforced by du Pont Kevlar, and a full-length aluminum bedding block.

Price:	$852.00
Magnum	879.00

MODEL 700 ADL
(not shown)

Synthetic model has a fiberglass-reinforced synthetic stock, positive checkering, straight comb, raised cheekpiece and black rubber recoil pad. Stock and blued metalwork have a non-reflective black matte finish.

Price:	$492.00
Magnum	519.00

(See also table on the following page for prices, calibers and additional specifications)

REMINGTON BOLT-ACTION RIFLES

MODEL 700 BDL SS DM
(Stainless/Synthetic)

MODEL 700/CALIBERS
Prices: MOUNTAIN DM 25-06, 260 Rem., 270 Win.,
280 Rem., 7mm-08, 30-06 . . . . $639.00
SENDERO 25-06, 270 Win. 705.00
7mm Rem. Mag., 300 Win. Mag. 732.00
SENDERO SF 25-06. 852.00

7mm Rem. Mag., 7mm STW,
300 Win. Mag., 300 Wby. Mag. 879.00
BDL SS DM 25-06 Rem., 260 Rem., 270 Win.,
280 Rem., 7mm-08, 30-06, 308 Win. 702.00
7mm Rem. Mag., 300 Win. Mag. and
300 Wby. Mag. 729.00

MODEL 700™ CENTERFIRE RIFLE SPECIFICATIONS

CALIBERS	MAGAZINE CAPACITY	BARREL LENGTH	TWIST (R-H) 1 TURN IN	MOUNTAIN RIFLE (DM)	SENDERO	SENDERO SF	BDL STAINLESS SYNTHETIC DM	BDL SS	DM-B	BDL LSS
17 Rem.	5	24"	9"							
220 Swift	4	26"	14"							
222 Rem.	5	24"	14"							
22-250 Rem.	4	24"	14"							
223 Rem.	5	24"	12"							
243 Win.	4	22"	9 1/8"							
	4	24"	9 1/8"							
25-06 Rem.	4	24"	10"		●	●	●			
	4	22"	10"	●						
260 Rem.	4	24"	9"	●			●			
270 Win.	4	22"	10"	●						
	4	22"	10"							
	4	24"	10"		●		●	●		●LH
280 Rem.	4	22"	9 1/4"	●						
	4	24"	9 1/4"				●			
7mm-08 Rem.	4	22"	9 1/4"	●						
	4	24"	9 1/4"							
7mm Rem. Mag.	3	24"	9 1/4"		●	●		●	●	●RH/LH
	3	24"	9 1/4"							●
7mm STW	3	24"	9 1/2"			●			●	
30-06	4	22"	10"	●						
	4	24"	10"				●	●		●LH
308 Win.	4	22"	10"							
	4	24"	12"				●			
300 Win. Mag.	3	24"	10"		●	●	●	●		●RH/LH
	3	24"	12"						●	
300 Wby. Mag.	3	24"	12"			●	●			
300 Rem. Ultra Mag.	3	24"	12"			●		●		●RH/LH
338 Win. Mag.	3	24"	10"					●		
375 H&H Mag.	3	24"	12"					●		

All Model 700™ rifles come with sling swivel studs. The BDL, ADL, and Seven™ are furnished with sights. The BDL Stainless Synthetic, LSS, Mountain Rifle, Classic, Sendero and Varmint guns have clean barrels. All Remington CF rifles drilled and tapped for scope mounts.

RIFLES

MODEL 700/CALIBERS *(cont.)*
Prices:

BDL SS DM-B 7mm Rem., 7mm STW,
300 Win. Mag. **$789.00**
BDL Stainless Synthetic 270 Win., 30-06 ..... **641.00**
7mm Rem. Mag., 300 Win. Mag., 300 Ultra Mag.,
338 Win. Mag., 375 H&H Mag. **668.00**
LLS 7mm Rem. Mag., 300 Win. Mag. **715.00**
BDL 270 Win. LH, 30-06 LH, 300 Win. Mag.,
338 Win. Mag. **612.00**
222 Rem., 22-250, 223 Rem., 243 Win.,
25-06, 270 Win., 30-06. .... **585.00**
7mm Rem. Mag. LH. **639.00**
BDL .17 Rem., 7mm Rem. Mag., 300 Win. Mag.,
300 Rem Ultra Mag., 338 Win. Mag... .... **612.00**
BDL DM 243 Win., 25-06 Rem., 270 Win., 280 Rem., . .

7mm-08 Rem., 30-06. .... **$639.00**
7mm Rem. Mag. 300 Win. Mag... .... **665.00**
270 Win. LH. **665.00**
7mm Rem. Mag. LH, 300 Win. Mag. LH. **692.00**
ADL 270 Win., 30-06, 308 Win. **492.00**
7mm Rem. Mag.. .... **519.00**
ADL Synthetic 223 Rem. 22-250, 243 Win., 270 Win.,
30-06, 308 Win. **425.00**
7mm Rem. Mag., 300 Win. Mag. **452.00**
VLS 22-25 Rem., 223 Rem., 243 Win., 6mm Rem.,
260 Rem., 7mm-08 Rem., 308 Win. **625.00**
VS w/26" Heavy Barrel in 22-250 Rem.,
223 Rem., 243 Win., 308 Win... .... **732.00**
w/26" Fluted Barrel in 22-250 Rem., 223 Rem.,
308 Win. **852.00**
Ported barrels 22-250, 220 Swift, 308 Win... .... **872.00**

MODEL 700™ CENTERFIRE RIFLE SPECIFICATIONS (cont.)

Calibers	Magazine Capacity	Barrel Length	Twist (R-H) 1 Turn In	BDL	BDL (DM)	ADL	ADL Synthetic	VLS* 26" Heavy BBL	VS (Varmint Synthetic) 26" Heavy BBL	VS 26" Stainless Fluted BBL
17 Rem.	5	24"	9"	●					LH only	
220 Swift	4	26"	14"							
222 Rem.	5	24"	14"	●						
22-250 Rem.	4	24"	14"	●			●	●	●	●
223 Rem.	5	24"	12"	●			NEW	●	●	●
243 Win.	4	20"	9 1/8"	●	●		NEW			
	4	22"	9 1/8"				●	●		
6mm Rem	4	22"	9 1/8"					●		
25-06 Rem.	4	24"	10"	●						
	4	22"	10"							
260 Rem.	4	24"	9"					NEW		
270 Win.	4	22"	10"	●LH/RH	●	●	●			
	4	22"	10"							
	4	24"	10"							
280 Rem.	4	22"	9 1/4"		●					
	4	24"	9 1/4"							
7mm-08 Rem.	4	22"	9 1/4"		●					
	4	24"	9 1/4"					●		
7mm Rem. Mag.	3	24"	9 1/4"	●LH/RH	●	●	●			
	3	24"	9 1/4"							
7mm STW	3	24"	9 1/2"							
30-06	4	22"	10"	●LH/RH	●	●	●			
	4	22"	10"							
308 Win.	4	20"	10"			●	●			
	4	22"	12"				●	●	●**	NEW**
300 Win. Mag.	3	24"	10"	●	●		NEW			
	3	24"	12"							
300 Wby. Mag.	3	24"	12"							
300 Rem. Ultra Mag.	3	24"	12"	●						
338 Win. Mag.	3	24"	10"	●						
375 H&H Mag.	3	24"	12"							

*Varmint Laminated Stock (also available in 6mm Rem.) **Available w/24" barrel

REMINGTON BOLT-ACTION RIFLES

MODEL 700 CLASSIC (.17 Rem.)

Since Remington's series of Model 700 Classics began in 1981, the company has offered this model in a special chambering each year.

The Model 700 Classic features an American walnut, straight-combed stock without a cheekpiece for rapid mounting, better sight alignment and reduced felt recoil. A hinged magazine flloorplate, sling swivel studs and satin wood finish with cut-checkering are standard, along with 24" barrel (44.5" overall) and 1:10" twist (no sight). Receiver drilled/tapped for scope mounts.
Price: **$612.00**

MODEL 700 MOUNTAIN DM (DETACHABLE MAGAZINE) RIFLE

The Remington Model 700 MTN DM rifle features the traditional mountain rifle-styled stock with a pistol grip pitched lower to position the wrist for a better grip. The cheekpiece is

designed to align the eye for quick, accurate sighting. The American walnut stock has a handrubbed oil finish and comes with a brown recoil pad and deep-cut checkering. The Model 700 MTN DM also features a lean contoured 22" barrel that helps reduce total weight to 6.75 pounds (no sights). All metalwork features a glass bead-blasted, blued-metal finish. ***Calibers:*** 25-06 Rem., 260 Rem., 270 Win., 280 Rem., 7mm-08 Rem., and 30-06 Springfield.
Price: **$639.00**

MODEL 700 ALASKAN WILDERNESS RIFLE (AWR)

This custom-built rifle has the same rate of twist and custom magnum barrel contour as the African Plains Rifle below, but

features a Kevlar-reinforced composite stock. ***Calibers:*** 7mm Rem. Mag., 7mm STW, .300 Rem. Ultra Mag., 300 Win. Mag., 300 Wby. Mag., 338 Win. Mag., 375 H&H Mag. ***Capacity:*** 3 shots ***Barrel length:*** 24" ***Overall Length:*** 44.5" ***Weight:*** 6 lbs. 12 oz.
Price: **$1,445.00**

MODEL 700 AFRICAN PLAINS RIFLE (APR)

The custom-built Model 700 APR rifle has a laminated classic wood stock and the following specifications.

Calibers: 7mm Rem. Mag., 300 Win. Mag., 300 Wby. Mag., 300 Rem. Ultra Mag., 338 Win. Mag., 375 H&H Mag. ***Capacity:*** 3 shots ***Barrel length:*** 26" ***Overall Length:*** 46.5" ***Weight:*** 7.75 lbs. ***Rate Of Twist:*** R.H. 1 turn in 9.25" (7mm Rem. Mag.); 10" (300 Win. Mag. and 338 Win. Mag.); 12" (30 Wby. Mag. and 375 H&H Mag.)
Price: **$1,554.00**

REMINGTON BOLT-ACTION RIFLES

MODEL 700 SAFARI KS
$1,140.00

MODEL 700 SAFARI
W/MONTE CARLO STOCK

MODEL 700™ SAFARI GRADE bolt-action rifles provide big-game hunters with a choice of either wood or synthetic stock. Model 700 Safari Monte Carlo (with Monte Carlo comb and cheekpiece) and Model 700 Safari Classic (with straight-line classic comb and no cheekpiece) are the satin-finished wood-stock models. Both are decorated with hand-cut checkering 18 lines to the inch and fitted with two reinforcing crossbolts covered with rosewood plugs. The Monte Carlo model also has rosewood pistol-grip and

forend caps. All models are fitted with sling swivel studs and 22" or 24" barrels. Synthetic stock has simulated wood-grain finish, reinforced with Kevlar® (KS).
Calibers: 8mm Rem. Mag., 375 H&H Magnum, 416 Rem. Mag. and 458 Win. Mag. **Capacity:** 3 rounds. **Avg. Weight:** 9 lbs. **Overall Length:** 44.5" **Rate of Twist:** 10" (8mm Rem. Mag.); 12" (375 H&H Mag.); 14" (416 Rem. Mag., 458 Win. Mag.)
Price: $1,197.00
  CUSTOM KS SAFARI. 1,378.00
  LH CUSTOM KS SAFARI 1,453.00

MODEL 40-XR KS TARGET RIMFIRE POSITION RIFLE W/KEVLAR STOCK
Action: Bolt action, single shot
Caliber: 22 Long Rifle rimfire, single loading
Barrel: 24" medium weight target barrel countersunk at muzzle. Drilled and tapped for target scope blocks. Fitted with front sight base
Bolt: Artillery style with lockup at rear; 6 locking lugs, doublle extractors
Overall Length: 43.5"
Average Weight: 100.5 lbs.
Sights: Optional at extra cost; Williams Receiver No. FPTK and Redfield Globe front match sight
Safety: Positive serrated thumb safety
Receiver: Drilled and tapped for receiver sight

Trigger: Adjustable from 2 to 4 bls.
Stock: Position style with Monte Carlo, cheekpiece and thumb groove; five-way adj. buttplate and full-length guide rail
Price: $1,585.00
Also Available:
MODEL 40-XR BR with 22" stainless-steel barrel (heavy contour), 22 LR match chamber and bore dimensions. Receiver and barrel drilled and tapped for scope mounts (mounted on green, duPont Kevlar reinforced fiberglass benchrest stock. Fully adjustable trigger (2 oz. trigger optional).
Price: $1,688.00
(Additional target rifles are available through Remington's Custom Shop.)

REMINGTON RIFLES

MODEL SEVEN

Every **MODEL SEVEN** is built to the accuracy standards of the famous Model 700 and is individually test fired to prove it. Its tapered 18.5" Remington special steel barrel is free floating out to a single pressure point at the forend tip. A fully enclosed bolt and extractor system, ramp front and fully adjustable rear sights and sling swivel studs are standard. The Youth Model features a hardwood stock that is 1 inch shorter for easy control. Chambered in 243 Win. and 7mm-08 for less recoil. See table at right for additional specifications.

Prices:

18.5" Barrel	$585.00
20" Barrel	641.00
Youth	479.00
Stainless Synthetic	641.00

SPECIFICATIONS MODEL SEVEN™

CALIBERS	CLIP MAG. CAPACITY	BARREL LENGTH	OVERALL LENGTH	TWIST R-H 1 TURN IN	AVG. WT. (LBS.)
223 Rem.*	5	18.5"	37 ³/₄"	12"	6 ¹/₄"
243 Win.	4	18.5"	37 ³/₄"	9 ¹/₈"	6 ¹/₄"
	4	18.5"	36 ³/₄" (Youth)	9 ¹/₈"	6
	4	20"	39 ¹/₄"	9 ¹/₈"	6 ¹/₄"
260 Rem.*	4	18.5"	37 ³/₄"	9"	6 ¹/₄"
7mm-08 Rem.	4	18.5"	37 ³/₄"	9 ¹/₄"	6 ¹/₄"
	4	18.5"	36 ³/₄" (Youth)	9 ¹/₄"	6
	4	20"	39 ¹/₄"	9 ¹/₄"	6 ¹/₄"
308 Win.	4	18.5"	37 ³/₄"	10"	6 ¹/₄"
	4	20"	39 ¹/₄"	10"	6 ¹/₄"

Stock Dimensions: 13 ³/₁₆" length of pull, ⁹/₁₆" drop at comb, ⁵/₁₆" drop at heel. youth gun has 12.5" length of pull. 17. Rem. provided without sights.
Note: New Model Seven Mannlicher and Model Seven KS versions are availlable from the Remington Custom Shop through your local dealer.
*Also available in 20" barrel (stainless only).

RIFLES

MODEL 7400 (HIGH GLOSS STOCK)

Calibers: 243 Win., 270 Win., 280 Rem., 30-06, 30-06 Carbine, 308 Win.
Capacity: 5 centerfire cartridges (4 in the magazine, 1 in the chamber); extra 4-shot magazine available

Action: Gas-operated; receiver drilled and tapped for scope mounts **Barrel Lengths:** 22" (18.5" in 30-06 Carbine) **Weight:** 7.5 lbs. (7.25 lbs. in 30-06 Carbine) **Overall Length:** 42" **Sights:** Standard blade ramp front; sliding ramp rear **Stock:** Satin or high-gloss (270 Win. and 300-06 only walnut stock and forend; curved pistol grip; also available with Special Purpose nonreflective finish (270 Win. and 30-06 only) **Length Of Pull:** 13 ³/₈"
Drop At Heel: 2.25" **Drop At Comb:** 1 ¹³/₁₆"
Price: $573.00

MODEL 7600 (HIGH GLOSS STOCK)

The Model 7600 shares nearly the same specifications as the Model 7400 featured above, except the 7600 is pump action.
Drop At Heel: ¹⁵/₁₆"
Drop At Comb: ⁹/₁₆"
Price: $540.00

REMINGTON RIMFIRE RIFLES

MODEL 541-T BOLT ACTION

This heavy-barreled box-fed .22 has a reputation for accuracy among sillhouette shooters. Its checkered walnut stock and a crisp trigger complement a clean barrel contour.
Price: $465.00
HEAVY BARREL 492.00
MODEL 581-S 239.00

MODEL 552 BDL SPEEDMASTER

The rimfire semiautomatic 552 BDL Deluxe sports Remington custom-impresses checkering on both stock and forend. Tough Du Pont RK-W lifetime finish brings out the lustrous beauty of the walnut while protecting it. Sights are ramp-style in front and rugged big-game type fully adjustable in rear.
Price: $340.00

MODEL 572 BDL FIELDMASTER

Features of this rifle with big-game feel and appearance are: Du Pont's tough RK-W finish; centerfire-rifle-type rear sight fully adjustable for both vertical and horizontal sight alignment; big-game style ramp front sight; Remington impressed checkering on both stock and forend.
Price: $353.00

(See following page for additional specifications.)

REMINGTON RIMFIRE RIFLES

MODEL 597 SERIES

Remington's new autoloading rimfire rifles–the Model 597™ Series–are made for those outdoorsmen who view rimfire shooting as a serious activity. They are available in three versions, offering a choice of carbon or stainless steel barreled actions, synthetic or laminated wood stocks, and chambering for either standard 22 Long Rifle or 22 Magnum ammo. All three M597™ rifles feature beavertail-style forends rounded with finger grooves for hand-filling control. The top of the receiver blends into the pistol grip, creating a rimfire autoloader that points like a shotgun but aims like a rifle. Features include a bolt guidance system of twin steel rails for smooth bolt travel and functional reliability. The 20-inch barrels are free-floated for consistent accuracy with all types of rimfire ammunition. A new trigger design creates crisp let-off for autoloading rifles. Bolts on the two 22 LR versions are nickel-plated. The magnum-version bolt is constructed of a special alloy steel to provide controlled, uniform function with magnum cartridges. All receivers are grooved for standard tip-off mounts and are also drilled and tapped for Weaver-type bases. Adjustable open sights and one-piece scope mount rails are standard, as are spare magazine clips.

RIMFIRE RIFLE SPECIFICATIONS

MODEL	ACTION	BARREL LENGTH	OVERALL LENGTH	AVERAGE WT. (LBS.)	MAGAZINE CAPACITY
597™	Auto	20"	40"	5.5	10-Shot Clip
597™ LSS	Auto	20"	40"	5.5	10-Shot Clip
597™ Mag.	Auto	20"	40"	5.5	8-Shot Clip
522 Viper	Auto	20"	40"	4 $5/8$	10-Shot Clip
541-T	Bolt	24"	42.5"	5 $7/8$*	5-Shot Clip
541-T HB Heavy Barrel	Bolt	24"	42.5"	6.5*	5-Shot Clip
552 BDL Deluxe Speedmaster	Auto	21"	40"	5 $3/4$	15 Long Rifle
572 BDL Deluxe Fieldmaster	Pump	21"	40"	5.5	15 Long Rifle
581-S	Bolt	24"	42.5"	5 $7/8$	5-Shot Clip

RIFLES

MODEL 597 (22 LR CARBON STEEL)

The M597™ is chambered for 22 Long Rifle ammunition and matches Remington's carbon steel barrel with a strong, lightweight, alloy receiver. All metal has a non-reflective, matte black finish. The rifle is housed in a one-piece, dark gray synthetic stock.
Price: $159.00

MODEL 597™ LSS

The M597™ LSS (Laminated Stock Stainless) has a satin-finished stainless steel barrel and matching, gray-tone alloy receiver. Chambered for 22 LR cartridges. Its stock is of laminated wood in light and dark brown tones.
Price: $212.00
W/Laminated Stock 265.00

MODEL 597™ MAGNUM

Chambered for 22 Win. Mag. rimfire cartridges, the M597™ MAGNUM features a carbon steel barrel, alloy receiver and black synthetic stock.
Price: $305.00
W/Laminated Stock 359.00

RIFLES, INC.

CUSTOM RIFLES

CLASSIC MODEL

SPECIFICATIONS

Calibers: Customized for varmint, target or hunter specifications, up to 375 H&H
Action: Remington or Winchester stainless steel controlled-round feed with lapped bolt

Barrel Length: 24"-26" depending on caliber; stainless-steel match grade, lapped
Weight: 6.5 lbs. (approx.)
Stock: Pillar glass bedded; laminated fiberglass, finished with textured epoxy
Features: Fine-tuned adjustable trigger; hinged floor-plate trigger guard
Price:. $1,800.00
    left hand 1,900.00

SAFARI MODEL

SPECIFICATIONS

Action: Winchester Model 70 controlled-round feed; hand lapped and honed bolt; drilled and tapped for 8X40 base screws
Barrel Length: 23"-25" depending on caliber; stainless-steel match grade, lapped

Weight: 9 lbs. (approx.)
Muzzle Break: Stainless Quiet Slimbrake
Metal Finish: Matte stainless or black Teflon
Stock: Pillar glass bedded; double reinforced laminated fiberglass/graphite; finished with textured epoxy
Features: Fine-tuned adjustable trigger; hinged floor-plate
Options: Drop box for additional round; express sights; barrel band; quarter ribs
Price:. $2,400.00
    w/Options $3,470.00

LIGHTWEIGHT STRATA STAINLESS MODEL

SPECIFICATIONS

Calibers: Up to 375 H&H **Action:** Stainless Remington; fluted, tapped and handle-hollowed bolt; aluminum bolt shroud **Barrel Length:** 22"-24" depending on caliber; stainless-steel match grade **Weight:** 4.75 lbs. (approx.)
Stock: Pillar glass bedded; laminated Kevlar/Boron/Graphite,

finished with textured epoxy **Features:** Matte stainless metal finish; aluminum blind or hinged floorplate trigger guard; custom Protektor pad
Price:. $2,400.00
    left hand 2,550.00
Also Available: LIGHTWEIGHT 70 in calibers up to 375 H&H.
Barrel Length: 22" to 24" (depending on caliber)) stainless steel match grade. **Weight:** 5.75 lbs. **Stock:** Pillar glass bedded; laminated Kevlar/Graphite/Boron finished with textured epoxy. Trigger is fine-tuned.
Price:. $2,300.00
    left hand 2,450.00

ROSSI RIFLES

PUMP-ACTION GALLERY GUNS

MODEL M62 SAC CARBINE

SPECIFICATIONS
Caliber: 22 LR *Capacity:* 11 rounds *Barrel Length:* 16.5"
Overall Length: 32.5" *Weight:* 4.6 lbs. *Finish:* Blue or nickel
Prices: Blue $240.00
    Nickel 250.00

MODEL M62 SA

SPECIFICATIONS
Caliber: 22 LR *Capacity:* 13 rounds *Barrel Length:* 23"
Overall Length: 39 1/4" *Weight:* 5 lbs. *Finish:* Blue or nickel
Prices: Blue $240.00
    Nickel 250.00
    w/octagonal bbl.. . . . . 250.00
Also available:
MODEL 59 22 MAGNUM (10 rds., blue only) $280.00

MODEL M92SRC LEVER-ACTION OLD WEST CARBINES

MODEL 92 LARGE LOOP

MODEL M92 SRC

SPECIFICATIONS
Caliber: 38 Special or 357 Magnum, *Capacity:* 10 rounds
Barrel Length: 20" *Overall Length:* 37.5"
Weight: 5.7 lbs. *Finish:* Blue
Price: $360.00
Also available: MODEL M92 SRC in 45 LC w/24" half-
ocatgonal barrel 429.00
MODEL M92 SRS in 38 Spec., 357 Mag. & 44 Mag.
w/16" barrel, 8-shot magazine. *Overall Length:* 33".
Weight: 5.5 lbs. (also w/large loop) 360.00
MODEL M92 CARBINE w/16" barrel, 8-shot magazine.
Weight: 5.5 lbs. 360.00
MODEL M92 STAINLESS 415.00

RUGER CARBINES

MODEL 10/22RBI

RUGER 10/22 MAGNUM

This .22 Magnum autoloader uses a heavy bolt in a blow-back mechanism that feeds from the proven 10/22 rotary magazine. Integral scope bases augment open sights. The carbine-style walnut stock and 18.5" barrel make this a fast-handling rimfire.
Length: 37" *Weight:* 6.5 lbs.

MODEL PC9

After several years of research, Ruger engineers combined 10/22 and P-series technology to create an autoloading rifle that uses popular pistol cartridges and Ruger pistol magazines. This handy carbine meets the needs of personal defense, sporting use, law enforcement and security agencies. Advanced synthetics and precision investment-casting technologies allow for improved performance and substantially reduced costs. The Ruger Carbine has a chrome-moly steel barrel, receiver, slide and recoil springs, and features a checkered Zytell stock with rubber buttplate. Adjustable open sights and patented integral scope mounts are standard. The Ruger Carbine also features a combination firing-pin block and slide lock. Trigger engagement is required for the firing pin to strike the primer. The slide locks to prevent chambering or ejection of a round if the riflle is struck on the buttpad. This safety system is backed up by a manual crossbolt safety located at the rear of the trigger guard. A slide stop locks the slide open for inspection and cleaning.

MODEL PC9 AUTOLOADING CARBINE

SPECIFICATIONS
Caliber: 9 x 19mm/40 auto *Capacity:* 10 rounds
Action: Mass impulse delayed blowback
Barrel Length: 15.25" *Overall Length:* 34.75"
Weight: 6 lbs. 4 oz. *Trigger Pull:* Approx. 6 lb.
Rifling: 6 grooves, 1 turn in 10" RH
Stock: du Pont "Zytel" matte black
Finish: Matte black oxide
Sights: Blade front, open rear plus provision for scope mounts (ghost ring version also available)
Sight Radius: 12.65"
Safety: Manual push-button crossbolt safety (locks trigger mechanism) and internal firing-pin block safety
Features: Bolt lock to prevent accidental unloading or chambering of a cartridge; steel barrel, receiver, slide and recoil spring unit w/black composite stock
Price: $555.00
  w/Ghost Ring Receiver Sight 580.00

RUGER CARBINES

RUGER MINI-14/5

Mechanism: Gas-operated, semiautomatic. **Materials:** Heat-treated chrome molybdenum and other alloy steels as well as music wire coil springs are used throughout the mechanism to ensure reliability under field-operating conditions. **Safety:** The safety blocks both the hammer and sear. The slide can be cycled when the safety is on. The safety is mounted in the front of the trigger guard so that it may be set to Fire position without removing finger from trigger guard. **Firing pin:** The firing pin is retracted mechanically during the first part of the unlocking of the bolt. The rifle can only be fired when the bolt is safely locked. **Stock:** One-piece American hardwood reinforced with steel liner at stressed areas. Sling swivels standard. Handguard and forearm separated by air space from barrel to promote cooling under rapid-fire conditions. **Field stripping:** The Carbine can be field-stripped to its eight (8) basic sub-assemblies in a matter of seconds and without use of special tools.

RUGER MINI-14
SPECIFICATIONS
Caliber: 223 (5.56mm) **Barrel Length:** 18.5"
Overall Length: 37 1/4" **Weight:** 6 lbs. 8 oz.
Magazine: 5-round, detachable box magazine
Sights: Rear adj.for windage/elevation.
Prices: MINI-14/5 Blued $542.00
K-MINI-14/5 Stainless Steel 597.00
(Scopes rings not included)

MINI-14/5R RANCH RIFLE

SPECIFICATIONS
Caliber: 223 (5.56mm) **Barrel Length:** 18.5"
Overall Length: 37 1/4" **Weight:** 6 lbs. 8 oz.
Magazine: 5-round detachable box magazine.

Sights: Fold-down rear sight; 1" scope rings (factory machined scope mount system available on all Ranch models)
Prices: MINI-14/5R Blued $584.00
K-MINI-14/5R Stainless Steel 639.00

MINI-THIRTY

This modified version of the Ruger Ranch rifle is chambered for the 7.62 x 39mm Soviet service cartridge. Designed for use with telescopic sights, it features low, compact scope-mounting for greater accuracy and carrying case, and a buffer in the receiver. Sling swivels are standard.

SPECIFICATIONS
Caliber: 7.62 x 39mm **Barrel Length:** 18.5"
Overall Length: 37 1/8" **Weight:** 6 lbs. 14 oz. (empty)
Magazine Capacity: 5 shots **Rifling:** 6 grooves, R.H. twist, 1:10"
Finish: Blued or stainless
Stock: One-piece American hardwood w/steel liners in stressed areas
Sights: Blade front; peep rear (factory machined scope mount system available on all Ranch models).
Prices: Blued $584.00
Stainless Steel 639.00

RUGER CARBINES

STANDARD 10/22 CARBINE

MODEL K10/22RP "ALL WEATHER"

MODEL K10/22RBI
INTERNATIONAL CARBINE STAINLESS

MODEL 10/22T TARGET

Construction of the 10/22 Carbine is rugged and follows the Ruger design practice of building a firearm from integrated sub-assemblies. For example, the trigger housing assembly contains the entire ignition system, which employs a high-speed, swinging hammer to ensure the shortest possible lock time. The barrel is assembled to the receiver by a unique dual-screw dovetail system that provides unusual rigidity and strength—and accounts, in part, for the exceptional accuracy of the 10/22.

SPECIFICATIONS
Mechanism: Blow-back, semiautomatic. *Caliber:* 22 LR, high-speed or standard-velocity loads. *Magazine:* 10-shot capacity, exclusive Ruger rotary design; fits flush into stock. *Barrel:* 18.5", assembled to the receiver by dual-screw dovetail mounting for added strength and rigidity. *Overall Length:* 37 1/4". *Weight:* 5 lbs. *Sights:* 1/16" brass bead front; single folding-leaf rear, adjustable for elevation; receiver drilled and tapped for scope blocks or tip-off mount adapter (included). *Trigger:* Curved finger surface, 3/8" wide. *Safety:* Sliding cross-button type; safety locks both sear and

hammer and cannot be put in safe position unless gun is cocked. *Stocks:* 10/22 RB is birch; 10/22 SP Deluxe Sporter is American walnut. *Finish:* Polished all over and blued or anodized or brushed satin bright metal.

Prices:
MODEL 10/22 RB STANDARD
(Birch carbine stock) $225.00
MODEL 10/22 DSP DELUXE
(Hand-checkered American walnut) 274.00
MODEL K10/22 RB STAINLESS 268.00
MODEL K10/22 RBI INTERNATIONAL CARBINE w/full-length
hardwood stock, stainless-steel bbl. 282.00
MODEL 10/22 RBI INTERNATIONAL CARBINE
w/blued barrel 262.00
MODEL 10/22T TARGET (no sights) Hammer-
forged barrel, laminated target-style stock 392.50
w/stainless steel 440.00
MODEL K10/22RP stainless "All Weather"
w/synthetic stock 268.00

RUGER SINGLE-SHOT RIFLES

The following illustrations show the variations currently offered in the Ruger No. 1 Single-Shot Rifle Series. Ruger No. 1 rifles have a Farquharson-type falling-block action and select American walnut stocks. Pistol grip and forearm are hand-checkered to a borderless design. Price for any listed model is **$719.00** (except the No. 1 RSI International Model: **$734.00**). Barreled Actions (blued only): **$488.00**

NO. 1A LIGHT SPORTER
Calibers: 243 Win., 270 Win., 30-06, 7x57mm. ***Barrel Length:*** 22". ***Sights:*** Adjustable folding-leaf rear sight mounted on quarter rib with ramp front sight base and dovetail-type gold bead front sight; open. ***Weight:*** 7 1/4 lbs.

NO. 1S MEDIUM SPORTER
Calibers: 218 Bee, 7mm Rem. Mag., 300 Win. Mag., 338 Win. Mag., 45-70. ***Barrel Length:*** 26" (22" in 45-70). ***Sights:*** (same as above). ***Weight:*** 8 lbs. (7 1/4 lbs. in 45-70).

NO. 1B STANDARD RIFLE
Calibers: 218 Bee, 22 Hornet, 22-250, 220 Swift, 223, 243 Win., 6mm Rem., 25-06, 257 Roberts, 270 Win., 270 Wby. Mag., 7mm Rem. Mag., 280, 30-06, 300 Win. Mag., 300 Wby. Mag., 338 Win. Mag. ***Barrel Length:*** 26". ***Sights:*** Ruger 1" steel tip-off scope rings. ***Weight:*** 8 lbs.

NO. 1V SPECIAL VARMINTER
Calibers: 22-250, 220 Swift, 223, 25-06, 6mm. ***Barrel Length:*** 24" (26" in 220 Swift). ***Sights:*** Ruger target scope blocks, heavy barrel and 1" tip-off scope rings. ***Weight:*** 9 lbs.
Also available:
NO. 1H TROPICAL RIFLE (24" heavy barrel w/sights) in 375 H&H Mag., 458 Win. Mag., 416 Rigby and 416 Rem. Mag.
NO 1. RSI INTERNATIONAL (20" lightweight barrel and full-length stock) in 243 Win., 270 Win., 30-06 and 7x57mm

RUGER BOLT-ACTION RIFLES

MODEL 77/44 RS

Chambered in .44 Magnum, the new 77/44 is a short (18.5" barrel), lightweight (6 lbs.) deluxed grade carbine based on the same action used in the 77/22 (see preceeding page). Action features right-hand turning bolt with 90-degree bolt throw.
Capacity: 4 rounds
Price: **$575.00**

MARK II SERIES

MODEL M-77RL MKII

MODEL M-77RL MKII ULTRA LIGHT

This big-game, bolt-action rifle encompasses the traditional features that have made the Ruger M-77 one of the most popular centerfire rifles in the world. It includes a sliding top tang safety, a one-piece bolt with Mauser-type extractor and diagonal front mounting system. American walnut stock is hand-checkered in a sharp diamond pattern. A rubber recoil pad, pistol-grip cap and studs for mounting quick detachable sling swivels are standard. Available in both long- and short-action versions, with Integral Base Receiver and 1" Ruger scope rings. **Calibers:** 223, 243, 257, 270, 30-06, 308. **Barrel length:** 20". **Weight:** Approx. 6 lbs.
Price: **$640.00**

MODEL M-77R MKII

Integral Base Receiver, 1" scope rings. No sights.
Calibers: (Long action) 6mm Rem., 6.5x55mm, 7x57mm, 257 Roberts, 270, 280 Rem., 30-06 (all with 22" barrels); 7mm Rem. Mag., 300 Win. Mag., 338 Win. Mag. (all with 24" barrels); and (Short Stroke action) 223, 243, 308 (22" barrels).
Weight: Approx. 7 lbs.
Price: **$599.00**

Also available: M-77LR MKII (Left Hand).
Calibers: 270, 30-06, 7mm Rem. Mag., 300 Win. Mag
Price:. **599.00**

MODEL M-77RS MKII (not shown)

Integral Base Receiver, Ruger steel 1" rings, open sights.
Calibers: 243, 25-06, 270, 7mm Rem. Mag., 30-06, 300 Win. Mag., 308, 338 Win. Mag., 458 Win. Mag.
Weight: Approx. 7 lbs.
Price: **$667.00**

RUGER BOLT-ACTION RIFLES

MODEL 77/22RH HORNET
$499.00 ($509.00 77/22 RSH w/Sights)

The Model 77/22RH is Ruger's first truly compact centerfire bolt-action rifle. It features a 77/22 action crafted from heat-treated alloy steel. Exterior surfaces are blued to match the hammer-forged barrel. The action features a right-hand turning bolt with a 90-degree bolt throw, cocking on opening. Fast lock time (2.7 milliseconds) adds to accuracy. A three-position swing-back safety locks the bolt; in its center position firing is blocked, but bolt operation and safe loading and unloading are permitted. When fully forward, the rifle is ready to fire. The American walnut stock has recoil pad, grip cap and sling swivels installed. One-inch diameter scope rings fit integral bases.

SPECIFICATIONS
Caliber: 22 Hornet
Capacity: 6 rounds (detachable rotary magazine)
Barrel length: 20" **Overall length:** 40"
Weight: 6 lbs. (unloaded)
Sights: Single folding-leaf rear; gold bead front
Length of pull: 13 3/4"
Drop at heel: 2 3/4" Drop at comb: 2"
Finish: Polished and blued, matte, nonglare receiver top
Also available: MODEL K77/22VHZ Varmint w/stainless-steel heavy barrel, laminated American hardwood stock.
Price: (w/o sights) $545.00

MODEL 77/22RS

MODEL K77/22BVZ VARMINT

MODEL 77/22 RIMFIRE RIFLE

The Ruger 22-caliber rimfire 77/22 bolt-action rifle has been built especially to function with the patented Ruger 10-Shot Rotary Magazine concept. The magazine throat, retaining lips and ramps that guide the cartridge into the chamber are solid alloy steel that resists bending or deforming.

The 77/22 weighs just under six pounds. Its heavy-duty receiver incorporates the integral scope bases of the patented Ruger Scope Mounting System with 1-inch Ruger scope rings. With the 3-position safety in its "lock" position, a dead bolt is cammed forward, locking the bolt handle down. In this position the action is locked closed and the handle cannot be raised.

All metal surfaces are finished in nonglare deep blue or satin stainless. Stock is select straight-grain American walnut, hand checkered and finished with durable polyurethane.

An All-Weather, all-stainless steel **MODEL K77/22RS** features a stock made of glass-fiber reinforced Zytel.
Weight: Approx. 6 lbs.

SPECIFICATIONS
Calibers: 22 LR and 22 Magnum. **Barrel length:** 20".
Overall length: 39 1/4". **Weight:** 6 lbs. (w/o scope, magazine empty). **Feed:** Detachable 10-Shot Ruger Rotary Magazine.
Prices: 77/22R Blue, w/o sights, 1" Ruger rings . **$483.00**
77/22RM Blue, walnut stock, plain barrel,
  no sights, 1" Ruger rings, 22 Mag. **483.00**
77/22RS Blue, sights included, 1" Ruger rings . . . **491.00**
77/22RSM Blue, American walnut, iron sights **491.00**
K77/22-RP Synthetic stock, stainless steel, plain
  barrel with 1" Ruger rings **483.00**
K77/22-RMP Synthetic stock, stainless steel,
  plain barrel, 1" Ruger rings **483.00**
K77/22-RSP Synthetic stock, stainless steel, gold
  bead front sight, folding-leaf rear, Ruger 1"rings . **491.00**
K77/22RSMP Synthetic stock, metal sights,
  stainless **491.00**
K77/22VBZ Varmint Laminated stock, scope
  rings, heavy barrel, stainless **509.00**

RUGER BOLT-ACTION RIFLES

MODEL K77RBZ MKII

MODEL K77RBZ MKII
Stainless steel, laminated stock, scope rings, no sights.
SPECIFICATIONS
Calibers: 223, 22-250, 243, 270 Win., 7mm Rem. Mag., 308, 30-06, 300 Win. Mag., 338 Win. Mag.
Price: $636.00

MODEL K77RSBZ MKII

MODEL K77RSBZ MKII
Stainless steel, laminated stock, scope rings, open sights.
Calibers: 243, 270 Win., 7mm Rem. Mag., 30-06, 308 Win. Mag., 338 Win. Mag.
Price: $700.00
Also available:
MODEL K77RBZ MKII
Stainless steel, laminated stock, scope rings
Calibers: 223, 22-250, 243, 270, 280, 7mm Mag., 308, 30-06, 300 Win. Mag., 338 Win. Mag.
Price: $636.00

MODEL M-77RSI MKII

MODEL M-77RSI MKII INTERNATIONAL
International full-length stock, Integral Base Receiver, open sights, Ruger 1" steel rings. *Calibers:* 243, 270, 30-06, 308
Barrel Length: 18.5" *Weight:* Approx. 6 lbs.
Price: $674.00

RUGER BOLT-ACTION RIFLES

MARK II SERIES (w/THREE POSITION SAFETY/FIXED EJECTORS)

MODEL M-77VT MK II HEAVY BARREL TARGET

MODEL M-77VT MK II HEAVY-BARREL TARGET

Features Mark II stainless-steel bolt action, gray matte finish, two-stage adjustable trigger. No sights.

SPECIFICATIONS
Calibers: 22-250, 220 Swift, 223, 243, 25-06 and 308.
Barrel Length: 26", hammer-forged, free-floating stainless steel. *Weight:* 9 ³/₄ lbs. Stock: Laminated American hardwood with flat forend.
Price: KM-77VT MKII $718.00

M-77 MARK II ALL-WEATHER

M-77 II MARK II ALL-WEATHER

KM-77RP MK II ALL-WEATHER Receiver w/integral dovetails to accommodate Ruger 1" rings, no sights, stainless steel, synthetic stock.
Calibers: 223, 22-50, 243, 25-06, 270, 280, 30-06, 7mm Rem. Mag., 300 Win. Mag., 308, 338 Win. Mag. **$599.00**
MODEL K77RSP MKII Receiver w/integral dovetails to accommodate Ruger 1" rings, metal sights, stainless steel, synthetic stock.
Calibers: 243, 270, 7mm Rem. Mag., 30-06, 300 Win. Mag., 338 Win. Mag. *(scope not included)* **667.00**

RUGER 77 RSM MK II MAGNUM RIFLE

This "Bond Street" quality African safari hunting rifle features a sighting rib machined from a single bar of steel; Circassian walnut stock with black forend tip; steel floorplate and latch; a new Ruger Magnum trigger guard with floorplate latch designed flush with the contours of the trigger gurad (to eliminate accidental dumping of cartridges); a three-position safety Express rear sight; and front sight ramp with gold bead sight. Also available in Express Model (long action, no heavy barrel).

Calibers: 375 H&H, 416 Rigby. *Capacity:* 4 rounds (375 H&H) and 3 rounds (416 Rigby). *Barrel Length:* 22" *Overall Length:* 42 ¹/₈" *Barrel Thread Diameter:* 1¹/₈" *Weight:* 9 ¹/₄ lbs. (375 H&H); 10 ¹/₄ lbs. (416 Rigby).
Price: $1,620.00
Also available: EXPRESS RIFLE. *Calibers:* 270, 7mm, 30-06, 300 Win. Mag., 338 Win. Mag. *Features:* Deluxe wood, solid rib, long action, scope rings.
Price: $1,620.00

SAKO RIFLES

SAKO 75

SAKO 75 HUNTER

The SAKO 75 Hunter is the first rifle to offer an action furnished with both a bolt with three locking lugs and a mechanical ejector. This combination results in unprecedented smoothness and reliability. The sturdy receiver helps to zero the rifle with different bullets and loads. The new bolt provides a solid, well-balanced platform for the cartridge. The traditional safety catch is either on or off. Cartridge removal or loading is done by pressing a separate bolt release button in front of the safety. No need to touch the safety to remove a cartridge and then disengage it by mistake under difficult or stressful conditions. The new cold hammer-forged barrel is manufactured in an advanced custom-built robotic cell. The New SAKO features a totally free-floating barrel. Instead of checkering, this all-stainless, all-weather model has soft rubbery grips molded in the stock to provide a firmer, more comfortable hold than with conventional synthetic stocks. The selected moisture stabilized high-grade walnut ensures quality and craftsmanship. Other features include:

- Five bolt siding guides
- 70° Bolt Lift
- Totally free-floating cold hammer-forged barrel
- Positive safety system with separate bolt release button for safe unloading

- Detachable staggered 5-round magazine
- Five (5) action sizes for perfect cartridge match
- All-Stainless metal parts and All-Weather synthetic stock with special grips
- Selected moisture stabilized walnut stock with hand-crafted checkering
- Integral scope rails

Prices:
SAKO 75 HUNTER
22"barrel (17 Rem., 222 Rem., 223 Rem., 22-250 Rem., 243 Win., 7mm-08, 308 Win., 25-06 Rem., 270 Win., 280 Win., 30-06) **$1,134.00**
24" barrel (7mm Rem. Mag., 300 Win. Mag., 338 Win. Mag., 375 H&H Mag., 416 Rem. Mag. **1,164.00**
26" barrel (270 Wby. Mag., 7mm STW, 7mm Wby. Mag., 300 Wby. Mag., 340 Wby.) **1,164.00**

SAKO 75 STAINLESS SYNTHETIC
22" barrel (22-250 Rem., 243 Win., 308 Win., 7mm-08 25-06 Rem., 270 Win., 30-06) **$1,224.00**
24" barrel (7mm Rem. Mag., 300 Win. Mag., 338 Win. Mag., 375 H&H Mag. **1,257.00**
26" barrel (7mm STW), .300 Wby. Mag.

SAKO 75 STAINLESS SYNTHETIC

SAKO RIFLES

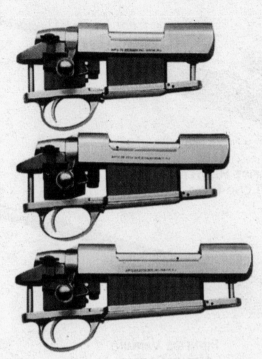

SAKO 75 ACTIONS

Sako 75 actions are designed for maximum performance while maintaining graceful lines, strength and reliability. Each of the action sizes is manufactured for a specific range of calibers. The Sako 75 is the first to offer a bolt with three locking lugs and a mechanical ejector while maintaining a bolt lift of only 70°. Five guiding surfaces prevent the bolt from binding and provide ultra smooth-operation. The two-position safety is located conveniently behind the bolt handle. A separate button in front of the safety allows the bolt to be opened while the safety is on. The detachable magazine can be loaded through the ejection port. When you're building a custom rifle you can't go wrong when you select either our carbon steel or stainless steel actions. The end result will be one of the finest custom rifles in the world.

SAKO 75 VARMINT RIFLE

SAKO 75 VARMINT RIFLE

The new SAKO 75 Varmint Rifle uses only the highest grade steel in the construction of the action, bolt, barrel and all internal parts. SAKO cold hammer-forges heavy-weight bar stock into one of the truest, most accurate barrels available. The 24" barrel is matched to the appropriate action size to eliminate excessive weight. The barreled action assembly is then cradled into a specially designed stock and is free floating for greater accuracy. The matte lacquered walnut stock features a beavertail forearm for additional stability and support when shooting from sandbags or whenever top accuracy is necessary. The SAKO 75 is the first and only rifle with three locking lugs and a mechanical ejector. Other SAKO features include a one-piece forged bolt with five gliding surfaces, a detachable magazine, and a smooth 70 degree bolt lift.

Calibers:
Short Action—17 Rem., 222 Rem., 223 Rem.
Medium Action—22-250 Rem., 22 PPC 6 PPC
Price:. $1,299.00

SAKO RIFLES

**FINNFIRE HUNTER
22 LONG RIFLE**

**FINNFIRE VARMINT
HEAVY BARREL**

FINNFIRE 22 LR BOLT-ACTION RIFLE

SAKO of Finland, acclaimed as the premier manufacturer of bolt-action centerfire rifles, presents its 22 Long Rifle Finnfire. Designed by engineers who use only state-of-the-art technology to achieve both form and function and produced by craftsmen to exacting specifications, this premium grade bolt-action rifle exceeds the requirements of even the most demanding firearm enthusiast.

The basic concept in the design of the Finnfire was to make it as similar to its "big brothers" as possible—just scaled down. For example, the single-stage adjustable trigger is a carbon copy of the trigger found on any other big-bore hunting model. The 22-inch barrel is cold-hammered to ensure superior accuracy.

SPECIFICATIONS
Overall length: 37 1/2" *Weight:* 5 1/4 lbs. (Hunter, Sporter) ; 7 1/2 lbs. (Varmint) *Rate of twist:* 16 1/2"
Other outstanding features include:
- European walnut stock
- Luxurious matte lacquer finish
- 50° bolt lift
- Free-floating barrel
- Integral 11mm dovetail for scope mounting
- Two-position safety that locks the bolt
- Cocking indicator
- Five-shot detachable magazine
- Ten-shot magazine available
- Available with open sights
Price:
  SPORTER $924.00
  HUNTER 789.00
  VARMINT 888.00

COMMITMENT TO EXCELLENCE — A SAKO TRADITION

SAKO RIFLES

DELUXE BOLT-ACTION RIFLE

SAKO 75 DELUXE BOLT-ACTION RIFLE

All the fine-touch features you expect of the deluxe grade SAKO are here: **1**-Reliable safety sysem with a separate bolt release button. **2**-First ever bolt with three locking lugs and a mechanical ejector. Five guiding surfaces prevent bolt binding and provide smooth operation. Four action sizes for perfect cartridge fit. **3**-Totally free-floating cold hammer forged barrel for ultimate accuracy. Test with a slip of paper. **4**-Sako Deluxe 75 Hunting Rifle has stainless steel lined staggered magazine with hinged floorplate and aluminum follower for faultless operation. Positive feeding angle is only 3-5 degrees. **5**-Fancy grade, high-grained walnut. Old-world craftmanship Rosewood pistol grip cap with silver inlay. **6**-Classic detail–Rosewood fore-end tip. And of course the accuracy, reliability and superior field performance for which SAKO is so justly famous are still here too. It's all here—it just weighs less than it used to. Think of it as more for less.

In addition, the scope mounting system on these SAKOS are among the strongest in the world. Instead of using separate bases, a tapered dovetail is milled into the receiver, to which the scope rings are mounted. A beautiful system that's been proven by over 20 years of use. SAKO Original Scope Mounts and SAKO scope rings are available in low, medium and high in one-inch and 30mm.

Prices:

ACTION I
in 17 Rem., 222 Rem. & 223 Rem. **$1,644.00**
ACTION III
In 22-250 Rem., 243 Win., 7mm-08 and
   308 Win. **1,644.00**
ACTION IV
In 25-06 Rem., 270 Win., 280 Rem., 30-06 . . . . **1,644.00**
ACTION V
In 270 Wby. Mag., 7mm Rem. Mag., 300 Win.
   Mag. and 338 Win. Mag. **1,674.00**
In 7mm STW, 300 Wby. Mag., .340 Wby. Mag.,
   375 H&H Mag., 416 Rem. Mag. **1,674.00**

SAKO 75 STAINLESS WALNUT

SAKO 75 ACTION

SAKO 75 STAINLESS WALNUT

Detachable box magazine, checkered walnut stock, standard and magnum chamberings.
Price:
22" 270, 30-06 . . . . **$1,224.00**
24" 7mm Rem. Mag., 300 Win. Mag., 338 Win. Mag. . . . **1,257.00**
26" 7mm STW, 300 Wby. **1,257.00**

SAKO RIFLES

MODEL TRG-21

SAKO, known for manufacturing the finest and most accurate production sporting rifles available today, presents the ultimate in sharpshooting systems: the sleek **TRG-21 TARGET RIFLE.** Designed for use when nothing less than total precision is demanded, this SAKO rifle features a cold-hammer forged receiver, "resistance-free" bolt, stainless-steel barrel and a fully adjustable polyurethane stock. Chambered in .308 Win. A wide selection of optional accessories is also available. Designed, crafted and manufactured in Finland.

- Cold-hammer forged receiver
- "Resistance-free" bolt
- Cold-hammer forged, stainless steel barrel
- Three massive locking lugs
- 60° bolt lift
- Free-floating barrel
- Detachable 10-round magazine

- Fully adjustable cheekpiece
- Infinitely adjustable buttplate
- Adjustable two-stage trigger pull
- Trigger adjustable for both length and pull
- Trigger also adjustable for horizontal or vertical pitch
- Safety lever inside and trigger guard
- Reinforced polyurethane stock

Optional features:
- Muzzle brake
- Quick-detachable one-piece scope mount base
- Available with 1" or 30mm rings
- Collapsible and removable bipod rest
- Quick-detachable sling swivels
- Wide military-type nylon sling

Price:. **$2,699.00**
Also available:
TRG-41 in 338 Lapua Mag. **$3,099.00**

MODEL TRG-S

The TRG-S has been crafted and designed around SAKO's highly sophisticated and extremely accurate TRG-21 Target Rifle (above). The "resistance-free" bolt and precise balance of the TRG-S, plus its three massive locking lugs and short 60-degree bolt lift, are among the features that attract the shooter's attention. Also of critical importance is the cold-hammer forged receiver—unparalleled for strength and durability. The detachable 5-round magazine fits securely into the polyurethane stock. The stock, in turn, is molded around a synthetic skeleton that provides additional support and maximum rigidity. *Calibers: Standard*—270 Win., 30-06; *Magnum*—7mm Rem. Mag., 7mm STW, 300 Win Mag., 300 Wby., 30-378 Wby. Mag., 338 Win. Mag., 338 Lapua.

Price:
STANDARD CALIBERS **$825.00**
MAGNUM CALIBERS 865.00

SAKO RIFLES

SAKO 75 RIFLE MODELS

Model	Action	Total Length Inches	Barrel Length Inches	Weight Lbs.	17 Rem (10")	222 Rem (14")	223 Rem (12")	22 PPC USA (14")	6 PPC USA (11")	22-250 Rem (10")	243 Win (9.5")	7mm-08 Rem (11")	308 Win (10")	25-06 Rem (9")	270 Win (10")	280 Rem (10")	30-06 (11")	270 Wby Mag (10")	7mm Rem Mag (9.5")	7mm Wby Mag (9.5")	7mm STW (9.5")	300 Win Mag (11")	300 Wby Mag (11")	338 Win Mag (10")	340 Wby Mag (10")	375 H&H Mag (12")	416 Rem Mag (14")	Matte Lacquered	Lacquered	Oiled	Injection Moulded	Open Sights	Without Sights	Single Stage Trigger	Detachable	Fixed	Magazine Capacity
75 Hunter	I	41¾	22	6⅜	•	•	•																						•	+		+	•	•	•	+	6
	II	42 5/16	22 7/16	7																									•	+		+	•	•	•	+	5
	III	42⅞	22 7/16	7¼						•	•	•	•																•	+		+	•	•	•	+	5
	IV	43¾	22⅞	7 15/16										•	•	•	•												•	+		+	•	•	•	+	5
	V	45⅝	24⅜	8⅝														•	•	•	•	•							•	+		+	•	•	•	+	4
	V	45⅝	24⅜	9																						•	•	•	•			+	•	•	•	+	4
75 Deluxe	I	41¾	22	6⅜	•	•	•																								•		+	•	•	•	•	6
	II	42 5/16	22 7/16	7																											•		+	•	•	•	•	5
	III	42⅞	22 7/16	7¼						•	•	•	•																		•		+	•	•	•	•	5
	IV	43¾	22⅞	7 15/16										•	•	•	•														•		+	•	•	•	•	5
	V	45⅝	24⅜	8⅝														•	•	•	•	•	•	•	•					•		+	•	•	•	•	4
	V	45⅝	24⅜	9																						•	•	•		•		+	•	•	•	•	4
75 Varmint	I	45⅝	24	8⅜	•	•	•																						•				•	+	•		6
	II	45⅞	24	8⅝																									•				•	+	•		5
	III	46½	24	8 13/16				•	•	•																			•				•	+	•		5
	IV	46⅞	24	9																									•				•	+	•		5
	V	47¼	24	9¼																									•				•	+	•		4
75 Hunter Stainless	III	42⅞	22 7/16	7																									•	+	+	+		•	•	•	5
	IV	43¾	22⅞	7¾											•		•												•	+	+	+		•	•	•	5
	V	45⅝	24⅜	8⅜															•			•		•	•				•	+	+			•	•	•	4
75 Synthetic Stainless	III	42⅞	22 7/16	7							•	•	•	•																	•		•	•	•	+	5
	IV	43¾	22⅞	7¾											•		•														•		•	•	•	+	5
	V	45⅝	24⅜	8⅜															•			•		•	•	•					•		•	•	•	+	4
75 Varmint Laminated Stainless	I	43¼	23⅝	8⅛		•	•																					•					•	+	•		6
	III	44	23⅝	8⅝				•	•	•																		•					•	+	•		5

• = as standard   + = as option
26" Barrel Standard on 7mm STW & Weatherby calibers.

SAUER RIFLES

MODEL 90

SPECIFICATIONS
Calibers: 22-250, 243 Win., 25-06, 270, 30-06, 308 Win.; *Supreme Magnum calibers:* 7mm Rem. Mag., 300 Win. Mag., 300 Wby. Mag., 338 Win. Mag., and 375 H&H
Barrel Length: 23.6"; 26" (Supreme Magnum)
Overall Length: 42.5"; 46.5" (Supreme Magnum)
Weight: 7.5 lbs.; 7.7 lbs. (Supreme Magnum)
Sights: None furnished; drilled and tapped for scope mount
Stock: Monte Carlo cut with sculptured cheekpiece, hand-

MODEL 90 SUPREME

checkered pistol grip and forend, rosewood pistol grip cap and forend tip, black rubber recoil pad, and fully inletted sling swivel studs.
Features: Rear bolt cam-activated locking lug action; jeweled bolt with an operating angle of 65°; fully adjustable gold-plated trigger; chamber loaded signal pin; cocking indicator; tang-mounted slide safety with button release; bolt release button (to operate bolt while slide safety is engaged); detachable 3 or 4-round box magazine; sling slide scope mounts; leather sling (extra)
Prices:
Standard **$1,350.00**
Magnum **1,382.00**

MODEL SHR 970 SYNTHETIC

SPECIFICATIONS
Calibers: 270 Win., 30-06 S'field **Capacity:** 4 rounds
Barrel Length: 22" **Overall Length:** 41.9" **Weight:** 7.2 lbs.
Sights: Drilled and tapped for scope base
Stock: Reinforced synthetic stock, rubber butt pad, QD swivel studs
Price: **$499.00**

SAUER .458 SAFARI

The Sauer .458 Safari features a rear bolt cam-activated locking-lug action with a low operating angle of 65°. It has a gold plated trigger, jeweled bolt, oil finished bubinga stock and deep luster bluing. Safety features include a press

bottom slide safety that engages the trigger sear, toggle joint and bolt. The bolt release feature allows the sportsman to unload the rifle while the safety remains engaged to the trigger sear and toggle joint. The Sauer Safari is equipped with a chamber loaded signal pin for positive identification. Specifications include: **Barrel Length:** 24" (heavy barrel contour). **Overall Length:** 44". **Weight:** 10 lb. 6 oz. **Sights:** Williams open sights (sling swivels included).
Price: **$1,995.00**

MODEL 202 SUPREME BOLT ACTION (not shown)

SPECIFICATIONS
Calibers: 25-06 Rem., 243 Win., 270 Win., 308, 30-06 S'field; *Supreme Magnum calibers:* 7mm Rem. Mag., 300 Win. Mag., 300 Wby. Mag., 375 Win. Mag.
Action: Bolt takedown **Capacity:** 3 rounds
Barrel Length: 23.6"; 26" (Supreme Magnum)
Overall Length: 44.3"; 46" (Supreme Magnum)
Weight: 7.7 lbs.; 8.4 lbs. (Supreme Magnum)
Stock: Select American claro walnut with high-gloss epoxy finish and rosewood forend and grip caps; Monte Carlo comb with cheekpiece; 22 line-per-inch diamond pattern,

hand-cut checking **Sights:** Drilled and tapped for sights and scope bases **Features:** Adjustable two-stage trigger; polished and jeweled bolt; quick-change barrel; tapered bore; QD sling swivel studs; black rubber recoil pad; Wundhammer palm swell; dual release safety; six locking lugs on bolt head; removable box magazine; fully enclosed bolt face; three gas relief holes; firing-pin cocking indicator on bolt rear
Prices: Standard **$985.00**
Magnum **1,056.00**
Also available: In Left Hand model (270 Win., 30-06 S'field, 7mm Rem. Mag. only) **$1,056.00**
Magnum **1,115.00**

SAVAGE ARMS

CENTERFIRE RIFLES

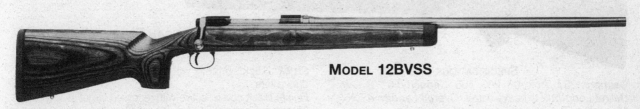

MODEL 12BVSS

MODEL 12BVSS SHORT ACTION VARMINT

SPECIFICATIONS
Calibers: 223 Rem., 22-250 Rem., and 308 Win. Single-shot Model 12FVSS available in 223 Rem. and 22-250 Rem.
Capacity: 5 + 1
Barrel Length: 26" fluted heavy barrel
Overall Length: 46.75"
Magazine: Top loading internal
Weight: 9.5 lbs.

Sights: None. Drilled and tapped for scope mounts
Stock: Laminated hardwood with high comb, ambidextrous grip and ebony tip
Finish: Fluted stainless steel with recessed target style muzzle
Features: Short Action precision long range rifle with dual pillar bedding
Price: $560.00

MODEL 12FVSS

MODEL 12FVSS SHORT ACTION VARMINT

SPECIFICATIONS
Calibers: 223 Rem., 22-250 Rem., and 308 Win. (Single-shot Model 12FVSSs available in 223 Rem. and 22-250 Rem.)
Capacity: 5 *Barrel Length:* 26" heavy barrel
Overall Length: 46.75"
Magazine: Top loading internal *Weight:* 9 lbs.

Sights: None. Drilled and tapped for scope mounts
Stock: Laminated hardwood with high comb, ambidextrous grip and ebony tip
Finish: Fluted stainless steel with recessed target style muzzle
Features: Short Action Long Range rifle with dual pillar bedding and 26" fluted heavy barrel
Price: $534.00

MODEL 12FV

MODEL 12FV SHORT ACTION VARMINT

SPECIFICATIONS
Calibers: 223 Rem., 22-250 Rem., 308 Win.
Capacity: 5
Barrel Length: 26"
Overall Length: 46.75"
Magazine: Top loading internal
Weight: 9 lbs.

Sights: None. Drilled and tapped for scope mounts
Stock: Durable black synthetic with scrolled checkering and dual pillars
Finish: Blued with recesses target style muzzle
Features: Short action varmint rifle with 26" button rifled heavy barrel
Price: $429.00

RIFLES

SAVAGE ARMS

MODEL 10FP SHORT ACTION TACTICAL RIFLE

SPECIFICATIONS

Calibers: 223, 7mm-08, 260, 308 **Capacity:** 5
Barrel Length: 24" heavy barrel **Overall Length:** 43.75"
Magazine: Top loading internal **Weight:** 8 lbs.
Sights: None. Drilled and tapped for scope mounts

Stock: Black synthetic with scrolled checkering and dual pillars
Finish: Black non-reflective with recessed target style muzzle
Features: Short action heavy barrel rifle with twin pillar bedding
Price: $450.00

MODEL 16FSS SHORT ACTION WEATHER WARRIOR

SPECIFICATIONS

Calibers: 223, 243, 7mm-08, 260, 308 **Capacity:** 5
Barrel Length: 22" **Overall Length:** 40.75"
Magazine: Top loading internal **Weight:** 6 lbs.
Sights: None. Drilled and tapped for scope mounts

Stock: Durable black synthetic with scrolled checkering and dual pillars **Finish:** Stainless steel
Features: Short action satin finished 400 series stainless steel barreled action
Price: $515.00

MODEL 10FM SIERRA LIGHTWEIGHT

SPECIFICATIONS

Calibers: 243, 7mm-08, 308
Capacity: 5 + 1 **Barrel Length:** 20"
Overall Length: 41.5" **Magazine:** Top loading internal
Weight: 6.25 lbs. **Sights:** None. Drilled and tapped for

scope mount; bases included
Stock: Lightweight graphite/fiberglass filled composite stock with positive checkering **Finish:** Blued
Features: Blue alloy steel barreled action
Price: $425.00

MODEL 110FP TACTICAL

SPECIFICATIONS

Calibers: 25-06 Rem., 30-06 Spfd., 7mm Rem. Mag., 300 Win. Mag. **Capacity:** 5 rounds (1 in chamber) **Barrel Length:** 24" (w/recessed target-style muzzle) **Overall Length:** 45.5" **Weight:** 8.5 lbs. **Sights:** None; drilled and tapped for scope mount; bases included **Features:** Black matte nonreflective finish on metal parts; bolt coated with titanium nitride; stock made of black graphite/fiberglass-filled composite with positive checkering; left-hand model available

Price: $429.00
Also Available: MODEL 110CY **Calibers:** 223 Rem., 243 Win., 270 Win., 308 Win. **Capacity:** 5 rounds (1 in chamber); top-loading internal magazine. **Barrel Length:** 22" blued. **Overall Length:** 42.5" **Weight:** 6 3/8 lbs. **Sights:** Adjustable; drilled and tapped for scope mounts **Stock:** High comb, walnut-stained hardwood w/cut checkering and short pull.
Price: $450.00

SAVAGE ARMS RIFLES

MODEL 11F SHORT ACTION HUNTER

SPECIFICATIONS
Calibers: 223 Rem., 22-250 Rem., 243 Win., 7mm-08 Rem., 260 Rem., and 308 Win. **Capacity:** 5 **Barrel Length:** 22" standard weight **Overall Length:** 42.75" **Magazine:** Top loading internal **Weight:** 6.75 lbs. **Sights:** Available in right/left hand. Drilled and tapped for scope mounts **Stock:** Durable black synthetic with scrolled checkering and dual pillars **Finish:** Blued
Features: Short Action with dual pillar bedded stock
Price: $395.00

MODEL 11G SHORT ACTION CLASSIC AMERICAN STYLE HUNTER

SPECIFICATIONS
Calibers: 223 Rem., 22-250 Rem., 243 Win., 7mm-08 Rem., 260 Rem., and 308 Win. **Capacity:** 5 **Barrel Length:** 22" **Overall Length:** 42.75" **Magazine:** Top loading internal **Weight:** 6.75 lbs. **Sights:** Available with or without (11GNS) Available in right/left hand. Drilled and tapped for scope mounts **Stock:** American style walnut finished hardwood with fancy scrolled, diamond point checkering and black recoil pad **Finish:** Blued
Price: $374.00

MODEL 10GY SHORT ACTION LADIES/YOUTH RIFLE

SPECIFICATIONS
Calibers: 223 Rem., 243 Win. and 308 Win.
Capacity: 5
Barrel Length: 22" standard weight
Overall Length: 39.25"
Magazine: Top loading internal
Weight: 6.25 lbs.
Sights: None. Drilled and tapped for scope mounts
Stock: American style walnut finished hardwood with cut checkering
Finish: Blued
Price: $374.00

SAVAGE CENTERFIRE RIFLES

LONG RANGE AND SCOUT RIFLES

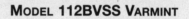

MODEL 112FVSS STAINLESS

SPECIFICATIONS

Calibers: 25-06 Rem., 30-06, 7mm Rem. Mag., 300 Win. Mag. (single-shot model available in 220 Swift, 300 Win. Mag.) **Capacity:** 4 + 1 **Barrel Length:** 26" fluted, stainless steel **Overall Length:** 47.5" **Weight:** 8 7/8 lbs. **Sights:** Graphite/fiberglass-filled composite w/positive checkering
Price: $534.00

MODEL 112BVSS VARMINT

SPECIFICATIONS

Calibers: 25-06, 7mm Rem. Mag., 300 Win Mag., 30-06 Sprgfld., (single-shot model also available in 220 Swift, 300 Win. Mag.) **Capacity:** 4 + 1 **Barrel Length:** 26" fluted heavy barrel, stainless steel **Overall Length:** 47.5" **Weight:** 10 lbs. (approx.) **Sights:** None; drilled and tapped **Stock:** Laminated hardwood w/high comb; ambidextrous grip
Price: $560.00

MODEL 112 BT COMPETITION GRADE

SPECIFICATIONS

Calibers: 223 Rem. and 308 Win. Mag. (single-shot available in 300 Win. Mag.)
Capacity: 5 + 1
Barrel Length: 26"; blackened stainless steel w/recessed target/style muzzle
Overall Length: 47.5"
Weight: 10 7/8 lbs.
Stock: Laminated brown w/straight comb
Price: $1,000.00

NEW SAVAGE "SCOUT" RIFLE-MODEL 10FCM

Ultra-light weight and extremely well balanced, the **NEW 10FCM** SAVAGE "SCOUT" is the ideal rifle for any outdoor situation. Weighing approximately 6 pounds and sporting a 20" barrel, this fast handling carbine is chambered in 7mm-08 and .308. **Features:** DETACHABLE BOX MAGAZINE: Capacity four (4) plus one (1) in the chamber; REMOVABE GHOST RING REAR SIGHT with GOLD BEAD FRONT SIGHT; ONE-PIECE SCOPE MOUNT for long eye relief scope; LARGE BALL BOLT HANDLE; RIFLEMAN'S COMBO SHOOTING SLING/CARRY STRAP WITH Q.D. SWIVEL SET; "Dual Pillar Bedded" synthetic stock
Price: $500.00

Savage Centerfire Rifles

All-Weather 116 Series

Model 116FSS "Weather Warrior"

Savage Arms combines the strength of a black graphite fiberglass polymer stock and the durability of a stainless-steel barrel and receiver in this bolt-action rifle. Major components are made from stainless steel, honed to a low refllective satin finish. Drilled and tapped for scope mounts. Left-hand model available (116FLSS).

SPECIFICATIONS
Calibers: 270 30-06, 7mm Rem. Mag., 300 Win. Mag., 338 Win. Mag. **Capacity:** 4 (7mm Rem. Mag., 300 Win. Mag., 338 Win. Mag.); 5 (270, 30-06) **Barrel Length:** 22" (270, 30-06); 24" (7mm Rem. Mag., 300 Win. Mag., 338 Win. Mag.) **Overall Length:** 43.5"-45.5" **Weight:** 6.5 lbs.
Price: $515.00

Model 116FCS "Weather Warrior"

Calibers: 270, 30-06, 7mm Rem. Mag., 300 Win. Mag. This bolt-action rifle has the same quality features as the Model 116FSS plus a removable box magazine with recessed push-button release for ease in loading and unloading. Left-hand model available.
Price: $560.00

Model 116FCSAK Weather Warrior Rifle

SPECIFICATIONS
Calibers: 270 Win. 30-06 Spfld., 7mm Rem. Mag., 300 Win. Mag. **Capacity:** 5 (standard) 4 (magnum) plus one in chamber **Barrel Length:** 22" **Overall Length:** 43.5" **Magazine:** Detachable staggered box type **Weight:** 7.25 lbs.

Sights: None. Drilled and tapped for scope mount
Stock: Lightweight black synthetic with positive checkering
Finish: Fluted, satin finished stainless steel
Features: Fluted 400 series stainless steel barreled action with Adjustable Muzzle Brake (AMB)
Price: $650.00

Model 116FSK "Kodiak"

Features a compact barrel with "shock suppressor" that reduces average linear recoil by more than 30" without loss of Magnum stopping power. Left-hand model available.

SPECIFICATIONS
Calibers: 270 Win., 30-06 Sprg., 7mm Rem. Mag., 300 Win. Mag., 338 Win. Mag. **Capacity:** 5 rounds (4 in Magnum) **Barrel Length:** 22" **Overall Length:** 43.5" **Weight:** 7 lbs.
Price: $554.00
Also available: MODEL 116FSAK. Same specifications as above except includes adj. muzzle brake.
Price: $585.00

SAVAGE ARMS

MODEL 116SE
SAFARI EXPRESS

SPECIFICATIONS

Calibers: 300 Win. Mag., 338, 458 Win. Mag.
Capacity: 4 rounds (1 in chamber)
Barrel Length: 24" stainless steel w/AMB
Overall Length: 45.5" **Weight:** 8.5 lbs. **Sights:** 3-leaf express **Stock:** Classic-style select-grade walnut w/cut checkering; ebony tip; stainless-steel crossbolts; internally vented recoil pad
Price: $900.00

MODEL 114U

SPECIFICATIONS

Calibers: 270 Win., 30-06 Spfld (22" bbl.); 7mm Rem. Mag., 300 Win. Mag. (24" bbl.) **Overall Length:** 43.5" **Weight:** Approx. 7 lbs. **Rifling Twist:** 1 in 10" (270 Win., 30-6 Spfld., 300 Win. Mag.); 1 in 9.5" (7mm Rem. Mag.) **Features:** High gloss American Walnut Stock with ebony tip; Custom checkering on the grip and forend; High luster blued finish on the barrel, receiver, and bolt handle; Precision laser-etched Savage logo on bolt body; Drilled and tapped for scope mounts
Price: $475.00

MODEL 114CE
"CLASSIC EUROPEAN"

SPECIFICATIONS

Calibers: 270 Win., 30-06 Sprgfld., 7mm Rem. Mag., 300 Win. Mag. **Capacity:** 3 rounds (magnum); 4 rounds (standard); plus 1 in each chamber
Barrel Length: 22" (standard); 24" (magnum)
Overall Length: 43.5" (standard); 45.5" (magnum)

Weight: 7 1/8 lbs. (approx.)
Finish: Oil-finished walnut stock w/schnabel tip, cheekpiece and French skip-line checkering on grip and forend
Features: Rubber recoil pad; pistol-grip cap with gold medallion; high-luster blued finish on receiver barrel and bolt handle; side button release; adjustable metal sights; precision rifled barrel; drilled and tapped
Price: $600.00
Also available:
MODEL 114C "CLASSIC." Same specifications as above except barrel twist is 1 in 10". Plus select grade oil-finished American walnut stock; laser-etched Savage logo on bolt body; custom high lustre blued finish on receiver and bolt handle

SAVAGE RIFLES

HUNTER SERIES 111

MODEL 111GC CLASSIC HUNTER

SPECIFICATIONS

Calibers: 270 Win., 30-06 Springfield, 7mm Rem. Mag., 300 Win. Mag. **Capacity:** 5 rounds (4 rounds in Magnum calibers) **Barrel Length:** 22" (standard) 24" (Magnum) **Overall Length:** 43.5" (45.5" Magnum calibers)

Weight: 6 ³/₈-7 lbs. **Sights:** Adjustable **Stock:** American-style walnut-finished hardwood; cut checkering **Features:** Detachable staggered box-type magazine; left-hand model available
Price: $410.00

MODEL 111FC CLASSIC HUNTER

SPECIFICATIONS

Same specifications as **CLASSIC HUNTER** above, except stock is lightweight graphite/fiberglass-filled composite w/positive checkering. Left-hand model available. **Calibers:** 270 Win., 30-06 Splfd., 7mm Rem. Mag. and 300 Win. Mag.
Price: $420.00

MODEL 111G CLASSIC HUNTER

SPECIFICATIONS

Same specifications as **MODEL 111GC CLASSIC HUNTER**, except available also in **calibers** 25-06, 270 Win., 7mm Rem. Mag., 30-06 Sprgfld., 300 Win. Mag. Stock is American-style walnut-finished hardwood with cut-checkering. Left-hand model available. **YOUTH MODEL** available in 223 Rem., 243 Win., 270 Win., 308 Win.
Price: $374.00

MODEL 111F CLASSIC HUNTER

SPECIFICATIONS

Same specifications as **MODEL 111G CLASSIC HUNTER**, except stock is black nonglare graphite/fiberglass-filled polymer with positive checkering. Left-hand model available.
Price: $395.00

SAVAGE RIFLES

MODEL 93 FSS STAINLESS

SPECIFICATIONS
Caliber: 22 WMR **Capacity:** 5 shots **Barrel Length:** 20.75" (1 in 16 twist) **Overall Length:** 39.5" **Weight:** 5.5 lbs. **Sights:** Front bead sight; sporting rear sight w/step elevator. **Features:** Precision button-rifled, free-floated barrel; black graphite/polymer filled stock w/positive checkering on grip and forend; corrosion and rust-resistant stainless steel barreled action.
Price: $182.00

MODEL 93G MAGNUM

SPECIFICATIONS
Caliber: 22 WMR **Capacity:** 5-shot clip **Barrel Length:** 20.75" **Overall Length:** 39.5" **Weight:** 5.75 lbs. **Stock:** Cut-checkered walnut-stained hardwood. **Sights:** Bead front; sporting rear with step elevator **Feature:** Free-floated precision button rifling.
Price: $150.00

MODEL 93F MAGNUM

SPECIFICATIONS
Calibers: 22 WMR **Capacity:** 5 **Barrel Length:** 20.75" free floated **Overall Length:** 39.5" **Magazine:** 5 shot detachable clip **Weight:** 5 lbs. **Sights:** Bead front sight, adjustable rear. Receiver dovetailed for scope mount **Stock:** Black synthetic with positive checkering **Finish:** Blued, button rifled **Features:** Blue alloy steel barreled action
Price: $145.00

MODEL 93FVSS

SPECIFICATIONS
Caliber: 22 WMR **Capacity:** 5 rounds **Barrel Length:** 21" heavy weight **Overall Length:** 40" **Weight:** 6 lbs. **Sights:** None. Drilled and tapped for scope mount. Weaver style bases included **Stock:** Black synthetic with positive checkering **Finish:** Stainless steel, recessed target style muzzle **Features:** Stainless steel heavy barrel in 22 WMR
Price: $210.00

SAVAGE SPORTING RIFLES

MODEL 64FV
SEMI-AUTOMATIC HEAVY BARREL

SPECIFICATIONS
Caliber: 22 LR *Capacity:* 10 shots
Barrel Length: 21" heavy weight *Overall Length:* 40.75"
Magazine: 10 shot detachable clip *Weight:* 6 lbs.
Sights: None. Weaver style bases included
Stock: Black synthetic with positive checkering
Finish: Blued, button rifled with recessed target style muzzle
Features: Semiauto blue alloy steel barreled action
Price: **$155.00**

MODEL 64F SEMIAUTO

SPECIFICATIONS
Caliber: 22 LR *Capacity:* 10 shots
Action: Semiautomatic side-ejecting
Barrel Length: 20.25" (1 in 16" twist)
Overall Length: 40" *Weight:* 5.5 lbs.
Sights: Front bead; adjustable open rear
Finish: Matte blue *Stock:* Black graphite/polymer synthetic
Features: Detachable clip magazine; free-floated precision
button-rifled barrel
Price: **$115.00**

MODEL 64G SEMIAUTO

SPECIFICATIONS
Caliber: 22 LR *Capacity:* 10-shot clip
Action: Semiautomatic side-ejecting
Barrel Length: 20.25" *Overall Length:* 40"
Weight: 5.5 lbs. *Sights:* Open bead front; adjustable rear
Stock: One-piece, walnut-finish hardwood, Monte Carlo
buttstock w/full pistol grip; checkered pistol grip and forend
Features: Bolt hold-open device; thumb-operated
rotary safety
Price: **$126.00**

SAVAGE SPORTING RIFLES

MARK I-G SINGLE SHOT

SPECIFICATIONS

Caliber: 22 Short, Long or LR **Capacity:** Single shot
Action: Self-cocking bolt action, thumb-operated rotary safety **Barrel Length:** 20.75" **Overall Length:** 39.5"
Weight: 5.5 lbs.
Sights: Open bead front; adjustable rear
Stock: One-piece, walnut-finish hardwood, Monte Carlo buttstock w/full pistol grip; checkered pistol grip and forend
Features: Receiver grooved for scope mounting
Price: $120.00
Also available:
MARK I-G "SMOOTHBORE" (20.75" barrel) 120.00
MARK I-G YOUTH (19" barrel). 120.00

MARK II-FV HEAVY BARREL REPEATER

SPECIFICATIONS

Caliber: 22 LR **Capacity:** 5 shots **Barrel Length:** 21" heavy weight **Overall Length:** 39.75" **Magazine:** 5 shot detachablle clip **Weight:** 6 lbs. **Sights:** None. Weaver style bases included **Stock:** Black synthetic with positive checkering **Finish:** Blued free floated, button rifled with recessed target style muzzle **Features:** Heavy barrel with synthetic stock in 22 LR
Price: $182.00

MARK II-FSS

SPECIFICATIONS

Caliber: 22 LR **Capacity:** 10-shot clip **Barrel Length:** 21" (1 in 16" twist) **Overall Length:** 39.5" **Weight:** 5 lbs.
Stock: Synthetic **Sights:** Bead front sight; adjustable open rear **Features:** Stainless steel barrelled action
Price: $160.00
Also available: MARK II-G w/one-piece walnut-finished Monte Carlo-style hardwood stock, blued steel bolt-action receiver, bead front sight **$132.00**
MARK II-GY LADIES/YOUTH w/19" barrel (37" overall)
Weight: 5 lbs. 132.00
MARK II-GXP w/4x15mm scope (LH model avail.) . 140.00
MARK II-F synthetic stock. 120.00

MARK II-LV

SPECIFICATIONS

Caliber: 22 LR **Capacity:** 10-shot **Barrel Length:** 21" heavy barrel (1 in 16" twist) **Overall Length:** 39.75"
Weight: 6.5 lbs. **Stock:** Grey laminated hardwood stock; cut-checkered **Features:** Precision button rifled with recessed target-style muzzle; machined blued steel barreled action; dovetailed for scope mounting
Price: $210.00

SAVAGE SPORTING RIFLES

MODEL 900TR
TARGET REPEATER

SPECIFICATIONS
Caliber: 22 Long Rifle
Capacity: 5-shot clip magazine
Action: Self-cocking bolt action, thumb-operated rotary safety
Overall Length: 43 ⁵/₈"
Approx. Weight: 8 lbs.
Stock: One-piece, target-type with walnut finish hardwood; comes with shooting rail and hand stop
Sights: Receiver peep sights with 1/4 min. click micrometer adjustments, target front sight with inserts
Price: $415.00

MODEL 24F COMBINATION
RIFLE/SHOTGUN

SPECIFICATIONS MODEL 24F COMBINATION RIFLE/SHOTGUN

MODEL	CALIBER	BARREL LENGTH	OVERALL LENGTH	APPROX. WEIGHT	RIFLING TWIST
24F-20 Gauge - $425.00	22 LR.†	24"	40.5"	8 lbs.	1 in 14"
24F-12 Gauge - $450.00	22 Hornet	24"	40.5"	8 lbs.	1 in 14"
24F-12/410 - $475.00	223 Rem.	24"	40.5"	8 lbs.	1 in 14"
	30-30 Win.	24"	40.5"	8 lbs.	1 in 12"

All 20 gauge models come with modified choke barrel. All 12 gauge models come with Full, Modified & IC choke tubes
†12 Gauge not available in 22 LR.

SPRINGFIELD RIFLES

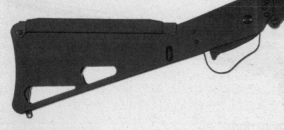

MODEL M-6 SCOUT RIFLE/SHOTGUN COMBO

SPECIFICATIONS
Calibers: 22 LR/.410 and 22 Hornet/.410
Barrel Length: 18.25" (1:15" R.H. twist in 22 LR; 1:13"
R.H. twist in 22 Hornet)
Overall Length: 32"
Weight: 4 lbs.

Sight Radius: 16 ¹/₈" *Finish:* Parkerized or stainless steel
Features: .410 shotgun barrel (2.5" or 3" chamber) choked
Full; drilled and tapped for scope mount with Weaver base;
lockable plastic carry case
Price: $176.00
Stainless Steel. 208.00

M1A STANDARD

SPECIFICATIONS
Calibers: 308 Win./7.62mm NATO (243 or 7mm-08
optional)
Capacity: 5- or 10-round box magazine
Barrel Length: 22"
Rifling: 6 groove, RH twist, 1 turn in 11"
Overall Length: 44 ¹/₃"
Weight: 9.2 lbs.
Sights: Military square post front; military aperture rear,
adjustable for windage and elevation
Sight Radius: 26.75"

Prices:
   Standard w/walnut stock $1,381.00
Also available:
BASIC M1A RIFLE w/painted black fiberglass stock,
   caliber 308/7.62mm only $1,249.00
M1A SCOUT RIFLE w/scope mount and handguard, black
fiberglass stock. $1,459.00
w/walnut stock 1,499.00
National Match (match-grade barrel and trigger) . . . 1,779.00
Super Match (heavy match barrel, special rod
   guide, heavy stock) 2,049.00

M1A-A1 BUSH RIFLE

SPECIFICATIONS
Calibers: 308 Win./7.62mm
Barrel Length: 18" (w/o flash suppressor)
Overall Length: 40.5"
Weight: 8.9 lbs. (9 lbs. w/walnut stock)

Sight Radius: 22.75"
Prices:
w/walnut stock.. .... $1,410.00
w/black fiberglass stock. 1,396.00
w/black laminated stock. 1,466.00

Steyr-Mannlicher Rifles

Steyr SSG-PI

The Steyr SSG features a black synthetic Cycolac stock (walnut optional), heavy Parkerized barrel, five-round standard (and optional 10-round) staggered magazine, heavy-duty milled receiver.

SPECIFICATIONS
Calibers: 243 Win. and 308 Win. *Barrel Length:* 26"
Overall Length: 44.5" *Weight:* 8.5 lbs.

Steyr Scout (not shown)

The Steyr "Jeff Cooper" Scout system is equally effective as a sporter, tactical or survival rifle. Among its features are a spare magazine storage compartment, safe bolt system, roller tang safety and non-skid neutral grey Zytel stock; also an integral bipod, flush sling sockets and forward-mounted Leupold 2.5X Scout Scope.

SPECIFICATIONS
Caliber: 308 Win. (7.62 X 5mm)

Sights: Iron sights; hooded ramp front with blade adjustable for elevation; rear standard V-notch adjustable for windage. *Features:* Sliding safety; 1" swivels.
Prices:
MODEL SSG-PI Cycolac half-stock (26" bbl. with sights in 308 Win.) **$1,695.00**
MODEL SSG-PII (20" or 26" heavy bbl. in 308 Win.) **1,695.00**
MODEL SSG-P-IV URBAN in 308 Win. w/16.75" heavy barrel. **2,660.00**
MODEL SSG-PIIK (20" heavy barrel). **2,295.00**

Capacity: 5 rounds *Barrel Length:* 19" fluted cold-hammer-forged barrel *Overall Length:* 39.57" w/2 buttstock spacers *Weight:* 7 lbs. (w/scope and mounts)
Sights: Factory-installed Leupold 2.5 X 28mm IER
Stock: Synthetic grey Zytel w/13.58" length of pull (adjustable)
Price: **$2,595.00**
   in .276 Steyre. **2,795.00**

SBS (SAFE BOLT SYSTEM) MANNLICHER EUROPEAN MODEL

SPECIFICATIONS
Calibers: 243 Win., 25-06, 308 Win., 270 Win., 7mm-08, 30-06 S'fld, 7mm Rem. Mag., 300 Win. Mag. *Capacity:* 4 rounds (3 rounds in Magnum, Prohunter and Forester); detachable staggered box magazine *Barrel Lengths:* 23.6"; 26" (magnum calibers) *Overall Length:* 44.5"
Weight: 7.5 lbs. *Safety:* 3-position roller safety
Trigger: Single adjustable trigger *Sights:* Ramp front w/balck adjustment for elevations; rear standard V-notch adjustable for windage; drilled and tapped for mounts

Finish: Blued; hand-checkered fancy European oiled walnut stock *Features:* Rotary cold hammer-forged barrel; front locking lug bolt
Prices:
   Standard Calibers (half stock) **$2,795.00**
   Magnum Calibers (half stock) **2,995.00**
   Standard Calibers (half stock carbine) **2,895.00**
   Standard Calibers (full stock) **2,995.00**
Also available:
STEYR SBS PROHUNTER in 243 Win., 25-06, 270 Win., 7mm-08 Rem., 308 Win., 30-06, w/synthetic half stock; no sights **$699.00**
STEYR MAGNUM MODEL in 7mm Rem. Mag. or 300 Win. Mag. w/25.6" barrel **729.00**
STEYR SBS FORESTER in 243 Win, 25-06, 270 Win., 7mm-08 Rem., 308 Win., 30-06 w/23.6" bbl.. . . **719.00**
STEYR SBS FORESTER MAGNUM in 7mm Rem. Mag. or 300 Win. Mag.. . . . . **749.00**

TAYLOR'S RIFLES

Faithful to the original, this "Henry" with its barrel and magazine drawn from one-piece steel, required a good deal of skill to reproduce. Chambered for a cartridge available today, the "Henry" was the first true repeating rifle to be both practical and reliable. Developed from the Volcanic carbines by B. Tyler Henry, inventor of the cartridge, in 1860, this replica would be the pride of its innovator and namesake.

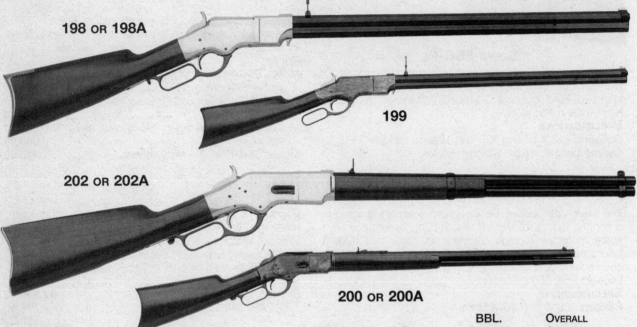

198 OR 198A

199

202 OR 202A

200 OR 200A

198 - HENRY BRASS FRAME 44/40
198A - HENRY BRASS FRAME .45 LC
199-HENRY RIFLE STEEL FRAME 44/40

The first real production of Henry Rifle with the Frame and Butt Plate in Steel. Total production was around 400. The first models had no lever latch. Only a few specimens are available now and they are the most valued by collectors around the world.

Price: wholesale $730.00

MODEL	CAL.	BBL. LENGTH	OVERALL LENGTH	MAGAZINE CAPACITY
198	44/40	24-1/4"	43-3/4"	13-9 shots
198A	45 LC	24-1/4"	43-3/4"	13-9 shots
199	44/40	24-1/4"	43-3/4"	13-9 shots

When Nelson King patented his new loading system he could not have known that he was creating a long, successful line of lever action arms. The "66 Yellowboy" lived the fabulous adventure that was the winning of the west. Its fire power, notable even by today's standards, made this an exceptional weapon.

Price: wholesale $780.00

202 - 1866 YELLOWBOY CARBINE 44/40
202A - 1866 YELLOWBOY CARBINE .45 LC
1866 YELLOW CARBINE

The first gun to carry the Winchester name, strong and light weight was the perfect saddle companion. This is an exceptional collector's piece and a fine shooting gun.

Price: wholesale $565.00

MODEL	CAL.	BBL. LENGTH	OVERALL LENGTH
202	44/40	19"	38 1/4"
202A	45 LC	19"	38 1/4"

200 - 1873 WINCHESTER RIFLE 44/40
200A - 1873 WINCHESTER RIFLE 45 LC
1873 SPORTING RIFLE

This rifle had a long life from 1873-1927. It is probably the only gun to have given its name to a movie. With its steel frame cartridge loading system it was much more powerful than the .44 Henry, and demand quickly pushed its production into the hundreds of thousands.

Price: wholesale $715.00

MODEL	CAL.	BBL. LENGTH	OVERALL LENGTH
200	44/40	24 1/4"	43 1/4"
200A	45 LC	24 1/4"	43 1/4"

5505-FRONT SIGHT GLOBE
Sight has a 3/8" dovetail.

5508-TANG PEEP SIGHT
This tang sight is the famous target and hunting sight of the Old West. This sight has the precision adjustment for windage and elevation. Sight is blue finish and will fit original 1873 Winchester Rifles.

THOMPSON/CENTER RIFLES

CONTENDER CARBINE

SPECIFICATIONS

Available in 5 **calibers:** 22 LR Match, 22 Hornet, 223 Rem., 7x30 Waters, 30-30 Win. **Barrels:** 21 inches, interchangeable. Adjustable iron sights; tapped and drilled for scope mounts. **Weight:** 5 lbs. 3 oz.
Price: $460.00

Also available:
CONTENDER CARBINE w/standard walnut stock in 22 Hornet, 223 Rem. 7x30 Waters 30-30 Win. **$539.04**
CONTENDER CARBINE with Match Grade 22 LR barrel 550.04

ENCORE RIFLE

SPECIFICATIONS

Calibers: 22-250 Rem., .223 Rem., .243 Win., 25-06 Rem., .260 Rem., .270 Win., .280 Rem., .7mm-08 Rem., 7mm Rem. Mag., .308 Win., .30-06 Spfd., .300 Win. Mag., 45-70 Govt. **Action:** Single-shot, break-open **Barrel lengths:** 24" and 26" heavy barrel (.22-250 Rem., 223 Rem., 25-06 Rem., 7mm Rem. Mag., and 300 Win. Mag. only)

Overall length: 38 1/2" (24" barrel); 40 1/2" (26" barrel)
Weight: 6 3/4 lbs. (24"); 7 1/2 lbs. (26")
Trigger: Adjustable for overtravel
Safety: Automatic hammerblock w/bolt interlock
Stock: American walnut with Schnabel forend and Monte Carlo buttstock
Features: Interchangeable barrels, sling swivel studs
Price: $562.00

TIKKA RIFLES

WHITETAIL HUNTER

SPECIFICATIONS

Calibers: 22-250, 223, 243, 308 (Medium); 25-06, 270, 30-06 (Long); 7mm Mag., 300 Win. Mag., 338 Win. Mag.
Capacity: 3 rounds (5 rounds optional); detachable magazine
Barrel Lengths: 22.5" (24.5" Magnum)
Overall Length: 42" (Medium); 42.5" (Long); 44.5" (Magnum)
Weight: 7 lbs. (Medium); 7 ¼ lbs. (Long); 7.5 lbs. (Magnum)

Sights: No sights; integral scope mount rails; drilled and tapped
Safety: Locks trigger and bolt handle
Features: Oversized trigger guard; short bolt throw; customized spacer system; walnut stock with palm swell and matte lacquer finish; cold hammer-forged barrel
Price: $609.00
Magnum 639.00

WHITETAIL HUNTER SYNTHETIC

SPECIFICATIONS

Same specifications as the standard Whitetail Hunter, except with All-Weather synthetic stock.
Price: $598.00
Magnum 624.00

Also available:
WHITETAIL HUNTER STAINLESS SYNTHETIC.
Same specifications as above, except with stainless steel receiver, barrel and bolt. $669.00
In Magnum calibers 699.00

TIKKA RIFLES

CONTINENTAL VARMINT

SPECIFICATIONS
Calibers: 22-250, 223, 308
Capacity: 5 rounds
Barrel Length: 26 *Overall Length:* 46"
Weight: 8 lbs. 10 oz.

Finish: Matte lacquer walnut stock w/palm swell
Features: Recoil pad spacer system; quick-release detachable magazine; beavertail forend; cold hammer-forged barrel; integral scope mount rails; adjustable trigger
Price: $709.00

CONTINENTAL LONG-RANGE HUNTING RIFLE

SPECIFICATIONS
Calibers: 25-06 Rem., 270 Win., 7mm Rem. Mag., 300 Win. Mag.
Capacity: 5 rounds in standard calibers, 4 rounds in magnum calibers
Barrel Length: 26" heavy barrel

Overall Length: 46.5"
Weight: 8 lbs. 12 oz.
Finish: Matte lacquer walnut stock w/palm swell
Features: Same as Continental Varmint model
Price: $709.00
    Magnum Calibers. 739.00

UBERTI REPLICAS

MODEL 1873 SPORTING RIFLE

SPECIFICATIONS
Calibers: 32/20, 357 Magnum, 44-40 and 45 LC. Hand-checkered. Other specifications same as Model 1866 Sporting Rifle. 20" barrel. Also available with 24.25" or 30" octagonal barrel and pistol-grip stock (extra).

Price: $970.00
Also available: With pistol grip. $1,020.00
With pistol grip and 30" barrel. 1,050.00

MODEL 1871 ROLLING BLOCK BABY CARBINE

SPECIFICATIONS
Calibers: 22 LR, 22 Hornet, 22 Magnum, 357 Magnum
Barrel Length: 22" *Overall Length:* 35.5" *Weight:* 4.85 lbs. *Stock and forend:* Walnut *Trigger guard:* Brass
Sights: Fully adjustable rear; ramp front *Frame:* Color-case-hardened steel
Price: $490.00

HENRY RIFLE

SPECIFICATIONS
Calibers: 44-40, 45 LC *Barrel Length:* 24.25" (half-octagon, with tubular magazine) *Overall Length:* 43.75" *Weight:* 9.26 lbs.
Frame: Brass *Stock:* Varnished American walnut
Price: $940.00
44-40 Carbine (22" barrel) 950.00
44-40 Trapper (16.5" or 18.5" barrel). 950.00

MODEL 1866 YELLOWBOY CARBINE

The frist gun to carry the Winchester name, this model was born as the 44-caliber rimfire cartridge Henry and is now chambered for 22 LR and 44-40.

SPECIFICATIONS
Calibers: 22 LR, 22 Magnum, 38 Special, 44-40, 45 L.C.
Barrel Length: 19", round, tapered *Overall Length:* 38.25"
Weight: 7.380 lbs. *Frame:* Brass *Stock and forend:* Walnut
Sights: Vertically adjustable rear; horizontally adjustable front
Price: $760.00
Rifle version. 840.00
Carbine in .22 or .22 Mag. 820.00

ULTRA LIGHT ARMS

**MODEL 20
MOUNTAIN RIFLE**

MODEL 28

MODEL 20 SERIES

SPECIFICATIONS
Calibers (Short Action): 6mm Rem., 17 Rem., 22 Hornet, 222 Rem., 222 Rem. Mag., 22-250 Rem., 223 Rem., 243 Win., 250-3000 Savage, 257 Roberts, 257 Ackley, 7x57 Mauser, 7X57 Ackley, 7mm-08 Rem., 284 Win., 300 Savage, 308 Win., 358 Win.
Barrel Length: 22" **Weight:** 4.75 lbs.
Safety: Two-position safety allows bolt to open or lock with sear blocked
Stock: Kevlar/Graphite composite; choice of 7 or more colors
Price:. **$2,500.00**
Left Hand **2,600.00**

Also Available:
MODEL 24 SERIES (Long Action) in 270 Win., 30-06, 25-06, 7mm Express **Weight:** 5.25 lbs.
Barrel Length: 22". **$2,600.00**
Same as above in Left-Hand Model **2,700.00**
MODEL 28 SERIES (Magnum Action) in 264 Win., 7mm Rem., 300 Win., 338 **Weight:** 5.75 lbs.
Barrel Length: 24". **2,900.00**
Same as above in Left-Hand Model **3,000.00**
MODEL 40 SERIES (Magnum Action) in 300 Wby. and 416 Rigby **Weight:** 7.5 lbs.
Barrel Length: 26". **2,900.00**
Same as above in Left-Hand Model **3,000.00**

MODEL 20 RF

SPECIFICATIONS
Caliber: 22 LR
Barrel Length: 22" (Douglas Premium #1 Contour)
Weight: 5.25 lbs.
Sights: None (drilled and tapped for scope)
Stock: Composite
Features: Recoil pad; sling swivels; fully adjustable Timney trigger; 3-function safety; color options
Price:
Single Shot **$800.00**
Repeater **850.00**

WEATHERBY MARK V RIFLES

MARK V DELUXE

The Mark V Deluxe stock is made of hand-selected American walnut with skipline checkering, traditional diamond-shaped inlay, rosewood pistol-grip cap and forend tip. Monte Carlo design with raised cheekpiece properly positions the shooter while reducing felt recoil. The action and hammer-forged barrel and hand-bedded for accuracy, then deep blued to a high-luster finish. See also specifications tables below and on the following page.

Calibers: **26" Barrel**: In 257 Wby. Mag., 270 Wby. Mag., 7mm Wby. Mag., 300 Wby. Mag. and 340 Wby. Mag. **$1,449.00**
In 378 Wby. Mag. **1,692.00**
28" Barrel: In 416 Wby. Mag. **1,875.00**
In 460 Wby. Mag. **2,193.00**

MARK V® MAGNUM RIFLE SPECIFICATIONS

CALIBER	MODEL	BARRELED ACTION	WEIGHT*	OVERALL LENGTH	MAGAZINE CAPACITY	BARREL LENGTH/ CONTOUR	RIFLING	LENGTH OF PULL	DROP AT COMB	MONTE CARLO	DROP AT HEEL
.257 WBY. MAG.	Mark V Sporter	RH 26"	8 1/2 lbs.	46 5/8"	3+1 in chamber	26" #2	1-10" twist	13 5/8"	1"	1/2"	1 5/8"
	Eurosport	RH 26"	8 1/2 lbs.	46 5/8"	3+1 in chamber	26" #2	1-10" twist	13 5/8"	1"	1/2"	1 5/8"
	Mark V Deluxe	RH 26"	8 1/2 lbs.	46 5/8"	3+1 in chamber	26" #2	1-10" twist	13 5/8"	7/8"	3/8"	1 3/8"
	Euromark	RH 26"	8 1/2 lbs.	46 5/8"	3+1 in chamber	26" #2	1-10" twist	13 5/8"	7/8"	3/8"	1 3/8"
	Lazermark	RH 26"	8 1/2 lbs.	46 5/8"	3+1 in chamber	26" #2	1-10" twist	13 5/8"	7/8"	3/8"	1 3/8"
	Synthetic	RH 26"	8 lbs.	46 5/8"	3+1 in chamber	26" #2	1-10" twist	13 5/8"	7/8"	1/2"	1 1/8"
	Fluted Synthetic	RH 26"	7 1/2 lbs.	46 5/8"	3+1 in chamber	26" #2	1-10" twist	13 5/8"	7/8"	1/2"	1 1/8"
	Stainless	RH 26"	8 lbs.	46 5/8"	3+1 in chamber	26" #2	1-10" twist	13 5/8"	7/8"	1/2"	1 1/8"
	Fluted Stainless	RH 26"	7 1/2 lbs.	46 5/8"	3+1 in chamber	26" #2	1-10" twist	13 5/8"	7/8"	1/2"	1 1/8"
	Accumark	RH 26"	8 1/2 lbs.	46 5/8"	3+1 in chamber	26" #3	1-10" twist	13 5/8"	1"	9/16"	1 1/2"
	SLS	RH 26"	8 1/2 lbs.	46 5/8"	3+1 in chamber	26" #2	1-10" twist	13 5/8"	1"	1/2"	1 5/8"
.270 WBY. MAG.	Mark V Sporter	RH 26"	8 1/2 lbs.	46 5/8"	3+1 in chamber	26" #2	1-10" twist	13 5/8"	1"	1/2"	1 5/8"
	Eurosport	RH 26"	8 1/2 lbs.	46 5/8"	3+1 in chamber	26" #2	1-10" twist	13 5/8"	1"	1/2"	1 5/8"
	Mark V Deluxe	RH 26"	8 1/2 lbs.	46 5/8"	3+1 in chamber	26" #2	1-10" twist	13 5/8"	7/8"	3/8"	1 3/8"
	Euromark	RH 26"	8 1/2 lbs.	46 5/8"	3+1 in chamber	26" #2	1-10" twist	13 5/8"	7/8"	3/8"	1 3/8"
	Lazermark	RH 26"	8 1/2 lbs.	46 5/8"	3+1 in chamber	26" #2	1-10" twist	13 5/8"	7/8"	3/8"	1 3/8"
	Synthetic	RH 26"	8 lbs.	46 5/8"	3+1 in chamber	26" #2	1-10" twist	13 5/8"	7/8"	1/2"	1 1/8"
	Fluted Synthetic	RH 26"	7 1/2 lbs.	46 5/8"	3+1 in chamber	26" #2	1-10" twist	13 5/8"	7/8"	1/2"	1 1/8"
	Stainless	RH 26"	8 lbs.	46 5/8"	3+1 in chamber	26" #2	1-10" twist	13 5/8"	7/8"	1/2"	1 1/8"
	Fluted Stainless	RH 26"	7 1/2 lbs.	46 5/8"	3+1 in chamber	26" #2	1-10" twist	13 5/8"	7/8"	1/2"	1 1/8"
	Accumark	RH 26"	8 1/2 lbs.	46 5/8"	3+1 in chamber	26" #3	1-10" twist	13 5/8"	1"	9/16"	1 1/2"
	SLS	RH 26"	8 1/2 lbs.	46 5/8"	3+1 in chamber	26" #2	1-10" twist	13 5/8"	1"	1/2"	1 5/8"
7MM REM. MAG.	Mark V Sporter	RH 24"	8 lbs.	44 5/8"	3+1 in chamber	24" #2	1-9 1/2" twist	13 5/8"	1"	1/2"	1 5/8"
	Eurosport	RH 24"	8 lbs.	44 5/8"	3+1 in chamber	24" #2	1-9 1/2" twist	13 5/8"	1"	1/2"	1 5/8"
	Synthetic	RH 24"	8 lbs.	44 5/8"	3+1 in chamber	24" #2	1-9 1/2" twist	13 5/8"	7/8"	1/2"	1 1/8"
	Fluted Synthetic	RH 24"	7 1/2 lbs.	44 5/8"	3+1 in chamber	24" #2	1-9 1/2" twist	13 5/8"	7/8"	1/2"	1 1/8"
	Stainless	RH 24"	8 lbs.	44 5/8"	3+1 in chamber	24" #2	1-9 1/2" twist	13 5/8"	7/8"	1/2"	1 1/8"
	Fluted Stainless	RH 24"	7 1/2 lbs.	44 5/8"	3+1 in chamber	24" #2	1-9 1/2" twist	13 5/8"	7/8"	1/2"	1 1/8"
	Accumark	RH 26"	8 1/2 lbs.	46 5/8"	3+1 in chamber	26" #3	1-9 1/2" twist	13 5/8"	1"	9/16"	1 1/2"
	SLS	RH 24"	8 1/2 lbs.	44 5/8"	3+1 in chamber	24" #2	1-9 1/2" twist	13 5/8"	1"	1/2"	1 5/8"
7MM WBY. MAG.	Mark V Sporter	RH 26"	8 1/2 lbs.	46 5/8"	3+1 in chamber	26" #2	1-10" twist	13 5/8"	1"	1/2"	1 5/8"
	Eurosport	RH 26"	8 1/2 lbs.	46 5/8"	3+1 in chamber	26" #2	1-10" twist	13 5/8"	1"	1/2"	1 5/8"
	Mark V Deluxe	RH 26"	8 1/2 lbs.	46 5/8"	3+1 in chamber	26" #2	1-10" twist	13 5/8"	7/8"	3/8"	1 3/8"
	Euromark	RH 26"	8 1/2 lbs.	46 5/8"	3+1 in chamber	26" #2	1-10" twist	13 5/8"	7/8"	3/8"	1 3/8"
	Lazermark	RH 26"	8 1/2 lbs.	46 5/8"	3+1 in chamber	26" #2	1-10" twist	13 5/8"	7/8"	3/8"	1 3/8"
	Synthetic	RH 26"	8 lbs.	46 5/8"	3+1 in chamber	26" #2	1-10" twist	13 5/8"	7/8"	1/2"	1 1/8"
	Fluted Synthetic	RH 26"	7 1/2 lbs.	46 5/8"	3+1 in chamber	26" #2	1-10" twist	13 5/8"	7/8"	1/2"	1 1/8"
	Stainless	RH 26"	8 lbs.	46 5/8"	3+1 in chamber	26" #2	1-10" twist	13 5/8"	7/8"	1/2"	1 1/8"
	Fluted Stainless	RH 26"	7 1/2 lbs.	46 5/8"	3+1 in chamber	26" #2	1-10" twist	13 5/8"	7/8"	1/2"	1 1/8"
	Accumark	RH 26"	8 1/2 lbs.	46 5/8"	3+1 in chamber	26" #3	1-10" twist	13 5/8"	1"	9/16"	1 1/2"
	SLS	RH 26"	8 1/2 lbs.	46 5/8"	3+1 in chamber	26" #2	1-10" twist	13 5/8"	1"	1/2"	1 5/8"
7MM STW	Accumark	RH 26"	8 1/2 lbs.	46 5/8"	3+1 in chamber	26" #3	1-10" twist	13 5/8"	1"	9/16"	1 1/2"
.300 WIN MAG.	Mark V Sporter	RH 24"	8 lbs.	44 5/8"	3+1 in chamber	24" #2	1-10" twist	13 5/8"	1"	1/2"	1 5/8"
	Eurosport	RH 24"	8 lbs.	44 5/8"	3+1 in chamber	24" #2	1-10" twist	13 5/8"	1"	1/2"	1 5/8"
	Synthetic	RH 24"	8 lbs.	44 5/8"	3+1 in chamber	24" #2	1-10" twist	13 5/8"	7/8"	1/2"	1 1/8"
	Fluted Synthetic	RH 24"	7 1/2 lbs.	44 5/8"	3+1 in chamber	24" #2	1-10" twist	13 5/8"	7/8"	1/2"	1 1/8"
	Stainless	RH 24"	8 lbs.	44 5/8"	3+1 in chamber	24" #2	1-10" twist	13 5/8"	7/8"	1/2"	1 1/8"
	Fluted Stainless	RH 24"	7 1/2 lbs.	44 5/8"	3+1 in chamber	24" #2	1-10" twist	13 5/8"	7/8"	1/2"	1 1/8"
	Accumark	RH 26"	8 1/2 lbs.	46 5/8"	3+1 in chamber	26" #3	1-10" twist	13 5/8"	1"	9/16"	1 1/2"
	SLS	RH 24"	8 1/2 lbs.	44 5/8"	3+1 in chamber	24" #2	1-10" twist	13 5/8"	1"	1/2"	1 5/8"

WEATHERBY MARK V RIFLES

MARK V SPORTER

SPECIFICATIONS

Calibers: 26" Barrel: 257 Wby. Mag., 270 Wby. Mag., 7mm Wby. Mag., 300 Wby. Mag. and 340 Wby. Mag. $999.00
24" Barrel: 7mm Rem. Mag., 300 Win. Mag., 338 Win. Mag. and 375 H&H Mag. $999.00
Also available: EUROSPORT. Same specifications and prices but with hand-rubbed satin oil finish.

MARK V® MAGNUM RIFLE SPECIFICATIONS (cont.)

Caliber	Model	Barrelled Action	Weight*	Overall Length	Magazine Capacity	Barrel Length/ Contour	Rifling	Length Of Pull	Drop At Comb	Monte Carlo	Drop At Heel
.300 Wby. Mag.	Mark V Sporter	RH 26"	8 1/2 lbs.	46 5/8"	3+1 in chamber	26" #2	1-10" twist	13 5/8"	1"	1/2"	1 5/8"
	Eurosport	RH 26"	8 1/2 lbs.	46 5/8"	3+1 in chamber	26" #2	1-10" twist	13 5/8"	1"	1/2"	1 5/8"
	Mark V Deluxe	RH 26"	8 1/2 lbs.	46 5/8"	3+1 in chamber	26" #2	1-10" twist	13 5/8"	7/8"	3/8"	1 3/8"
	Euromark	RH 26"	8 1/2 lbs.	46 5/8"	3+1 in chamber	26" #2	1-10" twist	13 5/8"	7/8"	3/8"	1 3/8"
	Lazermark	RH 26"	8 1/2 lbs.	46 5/8"	3+1 in chamber	26" #2	1-10" twist	13 5/8"	7/8"	3/8"	1 3/8"
	Synthetic	RH 26"	8 lbs.	46 5/8"	3+1 in chamber	26" #2	1-10" twist	13 5/8"	7/8"	1/2"	1 1/8"
	Fluted Synthetic	RH 26"	7 1/2 lbs.	46 5/8"	3+1 in chamber	26" #2	1-10" twist	13 5/8"	7/8"	1/2"	1 1/8"
	Stainless	RH 26"	8 lbs.	46 5/8"	3+1 in chamber	26" #2	1-10" twist	13 5/8"	7/8"	1/2"	1 1/8"
	Fluted Stainless	RH 26"	7 1/2 lbs.	46 5/8"	3+1 in chamber	26" #2	1-10" twist	13 5/8"	7/8"	1/2"	1 1/8"
	Accumark	RH 26"	8 1/2 lbs.	46 5/8"	3+1 in chamber	26" #3	1-10" twist	13 5/8"	1"	9/16"	1 1/2"
	SLS	RH 26"	8 1/2 lbs.	46 5/8"	3+1 in chamber	26" #2	1-10" twist	13 5/8"	1"	1/2"	1 5/8"
.338 Win. Mag.	Mark V Sporter	RH 24"	8 lbs.	44 5/8"	3+1 in chamber	24" #2	1-10" twist	13 5/8"	1"	1/2"	1 5/8"
	Eurosport	RH 24"	8 lbs.	44 5/8"	3+1 in chamber	24" #2	1-10" twist	13 5/8"	1"	1/2"	1 5/8"
	Synthetic	RH 24"	8 lbs.	44 5/8"	3+1 in chamber	24" #2	1-10" twist	13 5/8"	7/8"	1/2"	1 1/8"
	Stainless	RH 24"	8 lbs.	44 5/8"	3+1 in chamber	24" #2	1-10" twist	13 5/8"	7/8"	1/2"	1 1/8"
	SLS	RH 24"	8 1/2 lbs.	44 5/8"	3+1 in chamber	24" #2	1-10" twist	13 5/8"	1"	1/2"	1 5/8"
.340 Wby. Mag.	Mark V Sporter	RH 26"	8 1/2 lbs.	46 5/8"	3+1 in chamber	26" #2	1-10" twist	13 5/8"	1"	1/2"	1 5/8"
	Eurosport	RH 26"	8 1/2 lbs.	46 5/8"	3+1 in chamber	26" #2	1-10" twist	13 5/8"	1"	1/2"	1 5/8"
	Mark V Deluxe	RH 26"	8 1/2 lbs.	46 5/8"	3+1 in chamber	26" #2	1-10" twist	13 5/8"	7/8"	3/8"	1 3/8"
	Euromark	RH 26"	8 1/2 lbs.	46 5/8"	3+1 in chamber	26" #2	1-10" twist	13 5/8"	7/8"	3/8"	1 3/8"
	Lazermark	RH 26"	8 1/2 lbs.	46 5/8"	3+1 in chamber	26" #2	1-10" twist	13 5/8"	7/8"	3/8"	1 3/8"
	Synthetic	RH 26"	8 lbs.	46 5/8"	3+1 in chamber	26" #2	1-10" twist	13 5/8"	7/8"	1/2"	1 1/8"
	Stainless	RH 26"	8 lbs.	46 5/8"	3+1 in chamber	26" #2	1-10" twist	13 5/8"	7/8"	1/2"	1 1/8"
	Accumark	RH 26"	8 1/2 lbs.	46 5/8"	3+1 in chamber	26" #3	1-10" twist	13 5/8"	1"	9/16"	1 1/2"
	SLS	RH 26"	8 1/2 lbs.	46 5/8"	3+1 in chamber	26" #2	1-10" twist	13 5/8"	1"	1/2"	1 5/8"
.375 H&H Mag.	Mark V Sporter	RH 24"	8 1/2 lbs.	44 5/8"	3+1 in chamber	24" #3	1-12" twist	13 5/8"	1"	1/2"	1 5/8"
	Eurosport	RH 24"	8 1/2 lbs.	44 5/8"	3+1 in chamber	24" #3	1-12" twist	13 5/8"	1"	1/2"	1 5/8"
	Euromark	RH 24"	8 lbs.	44 5/8"	3+1 in chamber	24" #3	1-12" twist	13 5/8"	1"	1/2"	1 5/8"
	Synthetic	RH 24"	8 lbs.	44 5/8"	3+1 in chamber	24" #3	1-12" twist	13 5/8"	7/8"	1/2"	1 1/8"
	Stainless	RH 24"	8 lbs.	44 5/8"	3+1 in chamber	24" #3	1-12" twist	13 5/8"	7/8"	1/2"	1 1/8"
**.30-378 Wby. Mag.	Accumark	RH 26"	8 1/2 lbs.	46 5/8"	2+1 in chamber	26" #3	1-10" twist	13 5/8"	1"	9/16"	1 1/2"
	Synthetic	RH 26"	8 lbs.	46 5/8"	2+1 in chamber	26" #2	1-10" twist	13 5/8"	7/8"	1/2"	1 1/8"
	Stainless	RH 26"	8 lbs.	46 5/8"	2+1 in chamber	26" #2	1-10" twist	13 5/8"	7/8"	1/2"	1 1/8"
**.338-378 Wby. Mag.	Accumark	RH 26"	8 1/2 lbs.	46 5/8"	2+1 in chamber	26" #3	1-10" twist	13 5/8"	1"	9/16"	1 1/2"
.378 Wby. Mag.	Mark V Deluxe	RH 26"	9 1/2 lbs.	46 5/8"	2+1 in chamber	26" #3	1-12" twist	13 7/8"	7/8"	3/8"	1 3/8"
	Euromark	RH 26"	9 1/2 lbs.	46 5/8"	2+1 in chamber	26" #3	1-12" twist	13 7/8"	7/8"	3/8"	1 3/8"
	Lazermark	RH 26"	9 1/2 lbs.	46 5/8"	2+1 in chamber	26" #3	1-12" twist	13 7/8"	7/8"	3/8"	1 3/8"
**.416 Wby. Mag.	Mark V Deluxe	RH 26"	9 1/2 lbs.	46 3/4"	2+1 in chamber	26" #3	1-14" twist	13 7/8"	7/8"	3/8"	1 3/8"
	Euromark	RH 26"	9 1/2 lbs.	46 3/4"	2+1 in chamber	26" #3	1-14" twist	13 7/8"	7/8"	3/8"	1 3/8"
	Lazermark	RH 26"	9 1/2 lbs.	46 3/4"	2+1 in chamber	26" #3	1-14" twist	13 7/8"	7/8"	3/8"	1 3/8"
**.460 Wby. Mag.	Mark V Deluxe	RH 26"	10 1/2 lbs.	46 3/4"	2+1 in chamber	26" #4	1-16" twist	14"	7/8"	3/8"	1 3/8"
	Lazermark	RH 26"	10 1/2 lbs.	46 3/4"	2+1 in chamber	26" #4	1-16" twist	14"	7/8"	3/8"	1 3/8"

RIFLES

WEATHERBY MARK V RIFLES

MARK V EUROMARK

The Euromark features a hand-rubbed oil finish and Monte Carlo stock of American walnut, plus custom grade, hand-cut checkering with an ebony pistol-grip cap and forend tip.

Prices: 26" Barrel
In Weatherby Magnum calibers 257, 270, 7mm,
   300 and 340 . . . . **$1,599.00**
In 378 Wby. Mag. **1,692.00**
28" Barrel
In 416 Wby. Mag. **1,875.00**
24" Barrel
In 7mm Rem. Mag., 300 Win. Mag., 338 Win. Mag. and
375 H&H Mag. **1,599.00**

MARK V ACCUMARK MAGNUM

Built on the proven performance of the Mark V action, the Accumark is a composite of several field-tested features that help make it the utmost in accuracy, including a hand-laminated raised-comb Monte Carlo synthetic stock by H-S Precison (a combiniation of Kevlar, unidirectional fibers and fiberglass). There's also a molded-in, CNC-machined aluminum bedding plate that stiffens the receiver area of the rifle when the barreled action is secured to the block, providing a solid platform for the action. The Accumark is available in Weatherby Magnum calibers from 257 through 340, 7mm Rem. Mag. and .300 Win. Mag. Please see the specifications on the previous pages for additional information.

Prices: 26" Barrel
In 257, 270, 7mm, 7mm STW, 300, 340
   Magnum calibers **$1,349.00**
28" Barrel
In 30-378 Wby. and 338-378 Magnum
   calibers. **1,549.00**

WEATHERBY MARK V RIFLES

WEATHERBY ULTRALIGHT MAG.

Weatherby's **MARK VR ACCUMARK ULTRA LIGHTWEIGHT** rifle is based on Weatherby's Mark V lightweight action for standard cartridges. It features a chrome moly receiver, bolt and sleeve. To reduce weight, the bolt handle is skeletonized and the flutes on the boot are deeper and wider than those on other Weatherby Mark V rifles. To reduce weight further without sacrificing strength and structural integrity, the follower, floor plate, trigger housing and other non-critical components are made of lighter alloys. A stainless steel 24-inch barrel with weight-reducing flutes increases portability while maintaining velocity. A recessed target crown on the barrel enhances accuracy. The Ultra Lightweight also features a specially designed Monte Carlo stock with a pillar bedding system. Hand-laminated of Kevlar and fiberglass materials to provide a sure grip, the stock is teamed with a Pachmayr decelerator pad to dampen recoil. Stock colors are dark gray with black spiderwebbing. Additional specifications include **Calibers:** .243 Winchester, 7mm-08 Remington, .308 Winchester, .25-06 Remington, .270 Winchester, .280 Remington, .30-06 Springfield, and .240 Weatherby Mag. **Overall length:** 44" and 46". **Weight:** about 6 lbs.

Prices:
24" Barrel: 243, 240 Wby., 25-06, .270, 7mm-08, .280, .308, .30-06 . . . . **$1,199.00**
26" Barrel: 257 Wby., 270 Wby., 7mm Rem., 300 Wby., .300 Win. **1,299.00**

WEATHERBY LEFT HAND ACCUMARK

Weatherby's **MARK VR ACCUMARK LIGHTWEIGHT** is a standard cartridge rifle designed for hunting varmints, deer and other big-game animals with extended-range accuracy. A lightweight version of Weatherby's legendary Mark V Magnum action, its lightweight action is scaled and designed specifically for standard cartridges, with six locking lugs compared to the Magnum action's nine. Both feature a short 54-degree bolt lift. Action metalwork is black oxide coated with a bead blast matte finish to eliminate glare. Six deep flutes help lighten the overall barrel weight without reducing stiffness while increasing the surface area of the barrel by 40 percent. This helps extend barrel life by reducing heat buildup in the barrel. Muzzle diameter is .722. The barrel, which has a low-lustre brushed finish, is free floated and includes a recessed target crown. Trigger presettings are four pounds of pull with .012-.015 of an inch of sear engagement for extremely crisp and consistent let-off. The trigger is fully adjustable for sear engagement and let-off weight. The Accumark Lightweight also features a composite stock made of Kevlar and fiberglass. The bedding block is computer-designed and CNC-machined from aircraft quality aluminum. This system stiffens the receiver area of the rifle when the barreled action is secured into the block. The combination of CNC machining and precision molding of the bedding block into the stock helps ensure perfect fit and alignment of the barreled action. The hand-laminated, raised-comb Monte Carlo stock is black with gray spiderwebbing.

Additional specifications include:
Calibers: .22-250 Remington, .243 Winchester, 240 Wby., 25-06, 270, .280, .308, .30-06, 7mm-08. **Barrel length:** 24". **Overall length:** 44". **Weight:** 7.5 lbs.
Price: **$1,249.00**

WEATHERBY MARK V RIFLES

LAZERMARK

LAZERMARK

A custom-carved walnut stock distinguishes this Weatherby. Traditional high-gloss finish.

Prices: 26" Barrel
In Weatherby Magnum calibers 257, 270, 7mm,
   300 and 340 . . . . **$1,699.00**

378 Wby. Mag. **1,807.00**
28" Barrel
416 Wby. Mag. **1,986.00**
460 Wby. Mag. **2,333.00**

MARK V STAINLESS

MARK V MAGNUM STAINLESS

Features 400 Series stainless steel. The action is hand-bedded to a lightweight, injection-molded synthetic stock.

Prices: MARK V STAINLESS
24" Barrel
.22-250, .243, .240 Wby., 25-06, .270, .280,
   7mm-08, .30-06, .308 . . . . **$899.00**
7mm Rem. Mag., 300 Win. Mag., 338 Win.
   Mag. and 375 H&H Mag. **999.00**

26" Barrel
Weatherby Magnum calibers 257, 270, 7mm
   Rem. Mag., 300 and 340 . . . . **$999.00**
28" Barrel
30-378 Wby. Mag. **1,149.00**
Also available:
MODEL SLS (Stainless Laminated Sporter) **1,249.00**
FLUTED STAINLESS **1,149.00**
FLUTED SYNTHETIC **949.00**

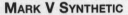

MARK V SYNTHETIC

MARK V SYNTHETIC

Features an injection-molded synthetic stock with dual-tapered checkered forearm. Comes with custom floorplate release/trigger guard assembly and engraved flying "W" monogram.

Prices: MARK V SYNTHETIC
24" Barrel
.22-250, .243, .240 Wby, .25-06, .270, 7mm-08,
   .280, .30-06, .308 . . . . **$699.00**
7mm Rem. Mag., 300 Win. Mag., 338 Win.
   Mag. and 375 H&H Mag. **799.00**
26" Barrel
Weatherby Magnum calibers 257, 270, 7mm,
   300 and 340 . . . . **799.00**
28" Barrel
30-378 Wby. Mag. **949.00**

For complete specifications on the above rifles, please see the tables on the preceding pages.

WEATHERBY MARK V RIFLES

MARK V SPORTER

MARK V RIFLES

Virtually identical in design to the
Mark V magnum action, Weatherby's
lightweight version is shorter, narrower and lighter than the
original. It accommodates up to 30-06 length cartridges,
including the 240 Weatherby Magnum. For complete specifications, see table below.

MARK V CARBINE

Prices: LIGHTWEIGHT SYNTHETIC (24" barrel)
22-250 to 308 Win. Mag. **$699.00**
CARBINE MODEL (20" in 243 Win., 7mm-08
Rem., 308 Win.) **699.00**

MARK V® RIFLE SPECIFICATIONS

Caliber	Model	Barrelled Action	Weight*	Overall Length	Magazine Capacity	Barrel Length/ Contour	Rifling	Length Of Pull	Drop At Comb	Monte Carlo	Drop At Heel
.240 WBY. MAG.	Mark V Sporter	RH 24"	6 3/4 lbs.	44"	5+1 in chamber	24" #1	1-10" twist	13 5/8"	3/4"	3/8"	1 1/8"
	Mark V Stainless	RH 24"	6 1/2 lbs.	44"	5+1 in chamber	24" #1	1-10" twist	13 5/8"	3/4"	3/8"	1 1/8"
	Mark V Synthetic	RH 24"	6 1/2 lbs.	44"	5+1 in chamber	24" #1	1-10" twist	13 5/8"	3/4"	3/8"	1 1/8"
	Accumark	RH 24"	7 lbs.	44"	5+1 in chamber	24" #3	1-10" twist	13 5/8"	3/4"	3/8"	1 1/8"
	Accumark Ultra Lightweight	RH 24"	5 3/4 lbs.	44"	5+1 in chamber	24" #2	1-10" twist	13 5/8"	3/4"	3/8"	1 1/8"
.22-250 REM.	Mark V Sporter	RH 24"	6 3/4 lbs.	44"	5+1 in chamber	24" #1	1-14" twist	13 5/8"	3/4"	3/8"	1 1/8"
	Mark V Stainless	RH 24"	6 1/2 lbs.	44"	5+1 in chamber	24" #1	1-14" twist	13 5/8"	3/4"	3/8"	1 1/8"
	Mark V Synthetic	RH 24"	6 1/2 lbs.	44"	5+1 in chamber	24" #1	1-14" twist	13 5/8"	3/4"	3/8"	1 1/8"
	Accumark	RH 24"	7 lbs.	44"	5+1 in chamber	24" #3	1-14" twist	13 5/8"	3/4"	3/8"	1 1/8"
	Mark V Stainless Carbine	RH 20"	6 lbs.	40"	5+1 in chamber	20" #1	1-14" twist	13 5/8"	3/4"	3/8"	1 1/8"
	Mark V Synthetic Carbine	RH 20"	6 lbs.	40"	5+1 in chamber	20" #1	1-14" twist	13 5/8"	3/4"	3/8"	1 1/8"
.243 WINCHESTER	Mark V Sporter	RH 24"	6 3/4 lbs.	44"	5+1 in chamber	24" #1	1-10" twist	13 5/8"	3/4"	3/8"	1 1/8"
	Mark V Stainless	RH 24"	6 1/2 lbs.	44"	5+1 in chamber	24" #1	1-10" twist	13 5/8"	3/4"	3/8"	1 1/8"
	Mark V Synthetic	RH 24"	6 1/2 lbs.	44"	5+1 in chamber	24" #1	1-10" twist	13 5/8"	3/4"	3/8"	1 1/8"
	Accumark	RH 24"	7 lbs.	44"	5+1 in chamber	24" #3	1-10" twist	13 5/8"	3/4"	3/8"	1 1/8"
	Accumark Ultra Lightweight	RH 24"	5 3/4 lbs.	44"	5+1 in chamber	24" #2	1-10" twist	13 5/8"	3/4"	3/8"	1 1/8"
	Mark V Stainless Carbine	RH 20"	6 lbs.	40"	5+1 in chamber	20" #1	1-10" twist	13 5/8"	3/4"	3/8"	1 1/8"
	Mark V Synthetic Carbine	RH 20"	6 lbs.	40"	5+1 in chamber	20" #1	1-10" twist	13 5/8"	3/4"	3/8"	1 1/8"
7MM-08 REM.	Mark V Sporter	RH 24"	6 3/4 lbs.	44"	5+1 in chamber	24" #1	1-9 1/2" twist	13 5/8"	3/4"	3/8"	1 1/8"
	Mark V Stainless	RH 24"	6 1/2 lbs.	44"	5+1 in chamber	24" #1	1-9 1/2" twist	13 5/8"	3/4"	3/8"	1 1/8"
	Mark V Synthetic	RH 24"	6 1/2 lbs.	44"	5+1 in chamber	24" #1	1-9 1/2" twist	13 5/8"	3/4"	3/8"	1 1/8"
	Accumark	RH 24"	7 lbs.	44"	5+1 in chamber	24" #3	1-9 1/2" twist	13 5/8"	3/4"	3/8"	1 1/8"
	Accumark Ultra Lightweight	RH 24"	5 3/4 lbs.	44"	5+1 in chamber	24" #2	1-9 1/2" twist	13 5/8"	3/4"	3/8"	1 1/8"
	Mark V Stainless Carbine	RH 20"	6 lbs.	40"	5+1 in chamber	20" #1	1-9 1/2" twist	13 5/8"	3/4"	3/8"	1 1/8"
	Mark V Synthetic Carbine	RH 20"	6 lbs.	40"	5+1 in chamber	20" #1	1-9 1/2" twist	13 5/8"	3/4"	3/8"	1 1/8"
.308 WINCHESTER	Mark V Sporter	RH 24"	6 3/4 lbs.	44"	5+1 in chamber	24" #1	1-12" twist	13 5/8"	3/4"	3/8"	1 1/8"
	Mark V Stainless	RH 24"	6 1/2 lbs.	44"	5+1 in chamber	24" #1	1-12" twist	13 5/8"	3/4"	3/8"	1 1/8"
	Mark V Synthetic	RH 24"	6 1/2 lbs.	44"	5+1 in chamber	24" #1	1-12" twist	13 5/8"	3/4"	3/8"	1 1/8"
	Accumark	RH 24"	7 lbs.	44"	5+1 in chamber	24" #3	1-12" twist	13 5/8"	3/4"	3/8"	1 1/8"
	Accumark Ultra Lightweight	RH 24"	5 3/4 lbs.	44"	5+1 in chamber	24" #2	1-12" twist	13 5/8"	3/4"	3/8"	1 1/8"
	Mark V Stainless Carbine	RH 20"	6 lbs.	40"	5+1 in chamber	20" #1	1-12" twist	13 5/8"	3/4"	3/8"	1 1/8"
	Mark V Synthetic Carbine	RH 20"	6 lbs.	40"	5+1 in chamber	20" #1	1-12" twist	13 5/8"	3/4"	3/8"	1 1/8"
.25-06 REM.	Mark V Sporter	RH 24"	6 3/4 lbs.	44"	5+1 in chamber	24" #1	1-10" twist	13 5/8"	3/4"	3/8"	1 1/8"
	Mark V Stainless	RH 24"	6 1/2 lbs.	44"	5+1 in chamber	24" #1	1-10" twist	13 5/8"	3/4"	3/8"	1 1/8"
	Mark V Synthetic	RH 24"	6 1/2 lbs.	44"	5+1 in chamber	24" #1	1-10" twist	13 5/8"	3/4"	3/8"	1 1/8"
	Accumark	RH 24"	7 lbs.	44"	5+1 in chamber	24" #3	1-10" twist	13 5/8"	3/4"	3/8"	1 1/8"
	Accumark Ultra Lightweight	RH 24"	5 3/4 lbs.	44"	5+1 in chamber	24" #2	1-10" twist	13 5/8"	3/4"	3/8"	1 1/8"
.270 WINCHESTER	Mark V Sporter	RH 24"	6 3/4 lbs.	44"	5+1 in chamber	24" #1	1-10" twist	13 5/8"	3/4"	3/8"	1 1/8"
	Mark V Stainless	RH 24"	6 1/2 lbs.	44"	5+1 in chamber	24" #1	1-10" twist	13 5/8"	3/4"	3/8"	1 1/8"
	Mark V Synthetic	RH 24"	6 1/2 lbs.	44"	5+1 in chamber	24" #1	1-10" twist	13 5/8"	3/4"	3/8"	1 1/8"
	Accumark	RH 24"	7 lbs.	44"	5+1 in chamber	24" #3	1-10" twist	13 5/8"	3/4"	3/8"	1 1/8"
	Accumark Ultra Lightweight	RH 24"	5 3/4 lbs.	44"	5+1 in chamber	24" #2	1-10" twist	13 5/8"	3/4"	3/8"	1 1/8"
.280 REM.	Mark V Sporter	RH 24"	6 3/4 lbs.	44"	5+1 in chamber	24" #1	1-10" twist	13 5/8"	3/4"	3/8"	1 1/8"
	Mark V Stainless	RH 24"	6 1/2 lbs.	44"	5+1 in chamber	24" #1	1-10" twist	13 5/8"	3/4"	3/8"	1 1/8"
	Mark V Synthetic	RH 24"	6 1/2 lbs.	44"	5+1 in chamber	24" #1	1-10" twist	13 5/8"	3/4"	3/8"	1 1/8"
	Accumark	RH 24"	7 lbs.	44"	5+1 in chamber	24" #3	1-10" twist	13 5/8"	3/4"	3/8"	1 1/8"
	Accumark Ultra Lightweight	RH 24"	5 3/4 lbs.	44"	5+1 in chamber	24" #2	1-10" twist	13 5/8"	3/4"	3/8"	1 1/8"
.30-06 SPRINGFIELD	Mark V Sporter	RH 24"	6 3/4 lbs.	44"	5+1 in chamber	24" #1	1-10" twist	13 5/8"	3/4"	3/8"	1 1/8"
	Mark V Stainless	RH 24"	6 1/2 lbs.	44"	5+1 in chamber	24" #1	1-10" twist	13 5/8"	3/4"	3/8"	1 1/8"
	Mark V Synthetic	RH 24"	6 1/2 lbs.	44"	5+1 in chamber	24" #1	1-10" twist	13 5/8"	3/4"	3/8"	1 1/8"
	Accumark	RH 24"	7 lbs.	44"	5+1 in chamber	24" #3	1-10" twist	13 5/8"	3/4"	3/8"	1 1/8"
	Accumark Ultra Lightweight	RH 24"	5 3/4 lbs.	44"	5+1 in chamber	24" #2	1-10" twist	13 5/8"	3/4"	3/8"	1 1/8"

WINCHESTER BOLT-ACTION RIFLES

CLASSIC FEATHERWEIGHT

MODEL 70 CLASSIC MODELS WITH PRE-'64 TYPE ACTION

Suggested Retail Right Handed	Left Handed	Caliber	Magazine Capacity*	Barrel Length	Nominal Overall Length	Nominal Length of Pull	Nominal Drop at Comb	Nominal Drop at Heel	Nominal Weight (Lbs.)	Rate of Twist 1 Turn In	Features
CLASSIC FEATHERWEIGHT (BLUED)											
$639	—	22-250 Rem.	5	22"	42"	13-1/2"	9/16"	7/8"	7	14"	Walnut Stock
639	—	243 Win.	5	22	42	13-1/2	9/16	7/8	7	10	Walnut Stock
639	—	6.5 x 55mm Swed.	5	22	42	13-1/2	9/16	7/8	7	8	Walnut Stock
639	—	308 Win.	5	22	42	13-1/2	9/16	7/8	7	12	Walnut Stock
639	—	7mm-08 Rem.	5	22	42	13-1/2	9/16	7/8	7	10	Walnut Stock
639	—	270 Win.	5	22	42-1/2	13-1/2	9/16	7/8	7-1/4	10	Walnut Stock
639	—	280 Rem.	5	22	42-1/2	13-1/2	9/16	7/8	7-1/4	10	Walnut Stock
639	—	30-06 Spfld.	5	22	42-1/2	13-1/2	9/16	7/8	7-1/4	10	Walnut Stock

Stainless Models available in 22-250, 243, 308, 270, 30-06.

For additional capacity, add one round in chamber when ready to fire. Drops are measured from center line of bore. Rate of twist: RH.

MODEL 70 CUSTOM MODELS

Item Number	UPC Code	Caliber	Magazine Capacity	Barrel Length	Nominal Overall Length	Nominal Length of Pull	Nominal Drop at Comb	Nominal Drop at Heel	Nominal Weight (Lbs.)	Rate of Twist 1 Turn In	Features	One Rifle	Three Or More Rifles	Sugg. Retail
CUSTOM AFRICAN EXPRESS														
535-912148 *NEW*	13948	340 Weath. Mag.	4	24"	45"	14"	5/8"	3/8"	9-3/4"	12"	Express Sights	$3,213	$2,835	$3,780
535-912150 *NEW*	13949	358 STA	4	24"	45"	14"	5/8"	3/8	9-3/4"	12"	Express Sights	3,213	2,835	3,780
535-912138 *NEW*	13950	375 H&H	4	24"	45"	14"	5/8"	3/8	9-3/4"	12"	Express Sights	3,213	2,835	3,780
535-912139 *NEW*	13951	416 Rem. Mag.	4	24"	45"	14"	5/8"	3/8	9-3/4"	14"	Express Sights	3,213	2,835	3,780
535-912144 *NEW*	13952	458 Win. Mag.	4	22"	45"	14"	5/8"	3/8	9-3/4"	14"	Express Sights	3,213	2,835	3,780
CUSTOM SAFARI EXPRESS														
535-911148 *NEW*	13943	340 Weath. Mag.	3	24"	45"	13-3/4"	9/16"	1/2"	9-1/2"	10"	Express Sights	$2,206	$1,946	$2,595
535-911150 *NEW*	13944	358 STA	3	24"	45"	13-3/4"	9/16"	1/2"	9-1/2"	12"	Express Sights	2,206	1,946	2,595
535-911138 *NEW*	13945	375 H&H	3	24"	45"	13-3/4"	9/16"	1/2"	9-1/2"	12"	Express Sights	2,206	1,946	2,595
535-911139 *NEW*	13946	416 Rem. Mag.	3	24"	45"	13-3/4"	9/16"	1/2"	9-1/2"	14"	Express Sights	2,206	1,946	2,595
535-911144 *NEW*	13947	458 Win. Mag.	3	22	43"	13-3/4"	9/16"	1/2"	9-1/2"	14"	Express Sights	2,206	1,946	2,595
CUSTOM MANNLICHER														
535-913249 *NEW*	13953	260 Rem.	4	19"	38-3/8"	13-3/4"	5/8"	1"	6-3/4"	9"	Sights Optional	$2,295	$2,025	$2,700
535-913220 *NEW*	13954	308 Win.	4	19"	38-3/8"	13-3/4"	5/8"	1"	6-3/4"	12"	Sights Optional	2,295	2,025	2,700
535-913218 *NEW*	13955	7mm-08	4	19"	38-3/8"	13-3/4"	5/8"	1"	6-3/4"	10"	Sights Optional	2,295	2,025	2,700
ULTIMATE CLASSIC (also in left-hand versions)														
535-900225	13918	25-06 Rem.	5	24"	44-3/4"	13-3/4"	5/8"	9/16"	7-1/2"	10"	B&R	$2,113	$1,865	$2,486
535-900229	13919	264 Win. Mag.	3	26"	46-3/4"	13-3/4"	5/8"	9/16"	7-3/4"	9"	B&R	2,113	1,865	2,486
535-900226	13920	270 Win.	5	24"	44-3/4"	13-3/4"	5/8"	9/16"	7-1/2"	10"	B&R	2,113	1,865	2,486
535-900227 *NEW*	13931	280 Rem.	5	24"	44-3/4"	13-3/4"	5/8"	9/16"	7-1/2"	10"	B&R	2,113	1,865	2,486
535-900228	13922	30-06 Spfld.	5	24"	44-3/4"	13-3/4"	5/8"	9/16"	7-1/2"	10"	B&R	2,113	1,865	2,486
535-900251	13956	338-06	5	24"	44-3/4"	13-3/4"	5/8"	9/16"	7-1/2"	10"	B&R	2,113	1,865	2,486
535-900247	13951	35 Whelen	5	24"	44-3/4"	13-3/4"	5/8"	9/16"	7-1/2"	16"	B&R	2,113	1,865	2,486
535-900230	13923	7mm Rem. Mag.	3	26"	46-3/4"	13-3/4"	5/8"	9/16"	7-3/4"	9-1/2"	B&R	2,113	1,865	2,486
535-900231	13924	7mm STW	3	26"	46-3/4"	13-3/4"	5/8"	9/16"	7-3/4"	10"		2,113	1,865	2,486
535-900233	13925	300 Win. Mag.	3	26"	46-3/4"	13-3/4"	5/8"	9/16"	7-3/4"	10"	B&R	2,113	1,865	2,486
535-900235	13932	300 H&H	3	26"	46-3/4"	13-3/4"	5/8"	9/16"	7-3/4"	10"		2,113	1,865	2,486
535-900234 *NEW*	13926	300 Weath. Mag.	3	26"	46-3/4"	13-3/4"	5/8"	9/16"	7-3/4"	10"		2,113	1,865	2,486
535-900236	13927	338 Win. Mag.	3	26"	46-3/4"	13-3/4"	5/8"	9/16"	7-3/4"	10"	B&R	2,113	1,865	2,486

WINCHESTER BOLT-ACTION RIFLES

MODEL 70 CLASSIC SUPER GRADE

MODEL 70 CLASSIC MODELS WITH PRE-'64 TYPE ACTION *(Continued from previous page)*

SUGGESTED RETAIL RIGHT HANDED	LEFT HANDED	CALIBER	MAGAZINE CAPACITY*	BARREL LENGTH	NOMINAL OVERALL LENGTH	NOMINAL LENGTH OF PULL	NOMINAL DROP AT COMB	NOMINAL DROP AT HEEL	NOMINAL WEIGHT (LBS.)	RATE OF TWIST I TURN IN	FEATURES
CLASSIC LAMINATED (STAINLESS)											
$745	—	270 Win.	5	24"	44-3/4"	13-3/4"	9/16"	13/16"	8	10"	Gray/Black Laminated Stock
745	—	30-06 Spfld.	5	24	44-3/4	13-3/4	9/16	13/16	8	10	Gray/Black Laminated Stock
745	—	7mm Rem. Mag.	3	26	46-3/4	13-3/4	9/16	13/16	8-1/4	9-1/2	Gray/Black Laminated Stock
745	—	300 Win. Mag.	3	26	46-3/4	13-3/4	9/16	13/16	8-1/4	10	Gray/Black Laminated Stock
745	—	338 Win. Mag.	3	26	46-3/4	13-3/4	9/16	13/16	8-1/4	10	Gray/Black Laminated Stock

For additional capacity, add one round in chamber when ready to fire. Drops are measured from center line of bore. Rate of twist: RH.

SPECIFICATIONS & PRICES: MODEL 70 CLASSIC MODELS

SUGGESTED RETAIL RIGHT HANDED	LEFT HANDED	CALIBER	MAGAZINE CAPACITY*	BARREL LENGTH	NOMINAL OVERALL LENGTH	NOMINAL LENGTH OF PULL	NOMINAL DROP AT COMB	NOMINAL DROP AT HEEL	NOMINAL WEIGHT (LBS.)	RATE OF TWIST I TURN IN	FEATURES
CLASSIC SAFARI EXPRESS											
$950	$981	375 H&H Mag.	3	24"	44-3/4"	13-3/4"	9/16"	1 5/16"	8-1/2	12"	Sights, Walnut Stock
950	—	416 Rem. Mag.	3	24	44-3/4	13-3/4	9/16	1 5/16	8-1/2	14	Sights, Walnut Stock
950	—	458 Win. Mag.	3	22	42-3/4	13-3/4	9/16	1 5/16	8-1/4	14	Sights, Walnut Stock
CLASSIC SUPER GRADE											
$880	—	270 Win.	5	24"	44-3/4"	13-3/4"	9/16"	13/16"	7-3/4	10"	B&R, Walnut Stock
880	—	30-06 Spfld.	5	24	44-3/4	13-3/4	9/16	13/16	7-3/4	10	B&R, Walnut Stock
880	—	7mm STW	3	26	46-3/4	13-3/4	9/16	13/16	8	9-1/2	B&R, Walnut Stock
880	—	300 Win. Mag.	3	26	46-3/4	13-3/4	9/16	13/16	8	10	B&R, Walnut Stock
880	—	338 Win. Mag.	3	26	46-3/4	13-3/4	9/16	13/16	8	10	B&R, Walnut Stock
CLASSIC SPORTER LT (BLUED)											
$636	—	25-06 Rem.	5	24"	44-3/4"	13-3/4"	9/16"	13/16"	7-3/4	10"	Walnut Stock
636	—	264 Win. Mag.	3	26	46-3/4	13-3/4	9/16	13/16	8	9	Walnut Stock
636	$668	270 Win.	5	24	44-3/4	13-3/4	9/16	13/16	7-3/4	10	Walnut Stock
636	668	30-06 Spfld.	5	24	44-3/4	13-3/4	9/16	13/16	7-3/4	10	Walnut Stock
636	668	7mm STW	3	26	46-3/4	13-3/4	9/16	13/16	8	9-1/2	Walnut Stock
636	668	7mm Rem. Mag.	3	26	46-3/4	13-3/4	9/16	13/16	8	9-1/2	Walnut Stock
636	668	300 Win. Mag.	3	26	46-3/4	13-3/4	9/16	13/16	8	10	Walnut Stock
636	—	300 Weath. Mag.	3	26	46-3/4	13-3/4	9/16	13/16	8	10	Walnut Stock
636	668	338 Win. Mag.	3	26	46-3/4	13-3/4	9/16	13/16	8	10	Walnut Stock

WINCHESTER BOLT-ACTION RIFLES

MODEL 70 BLACK SHADOW

MODEL 70 STEALTH

SPECIFICATIONS & PRICES: MODEL 70 CLASSIC MODELS *(Cont.)*

Suggested Retail Right Handed	Left Handed	Caliber	Magazine Capacity*	Barrel Length	Nominal Overall Length	Nominal Length of Pull	Nominal Drop at Comb	Nominal Drop at Heel	Nominal Weight (Lbs.)	Rate of Twist I Turn In	Features
CLASSIC STAINLESS (COMPOSITE)											
$693	—	270 Win.	5	24"	44-3/4"	13-3/4"	9/16"	13/16"	7-1/4	10"	Composite Stock
693	—	30-06 Spfld.	5	24	44-3/4	13-3/4	9/16	13/16	7-1/4	10	Composite Stock
693	—	7mm Rem. Mag.	3	26	46-3/4	13-3/4	9/16	13/16	7-1/2	9-1/2	Composite Stock
693	—	300 Win. Mag.	3	26	46-3/4	13-3/4	9/16	13/16	7-1/2	10	Composite Stock
693	—	300 Wby.	3	26	46-3/4	13-3/4	9/16	13/16	7-1/2	10	Composite Stock
693	—	338 Win. Mag.	3	26	46-3/4	13-3/4	9/16	13/16	7-1/2	10	Composite Stock
758	—	375 H&H Mag.	3	24	44-3/4	13-3/4	9/16	13/16	7-1/4	12	Sights, Composite Stock
CLASSIC COMPACT											
$640	—	243 Win.	4	20"	39-1/2"	13"	9/16"	3/4"	6-1/2	10"	Walnut Stock
640	—	308 Win.	4	20	39-1/2	13	9/16	3/4	6-1/2	12	Walnut Stock
640	—	7mm-08 Rem.	4	20	39-1/2	13	9/16	3/4	6-1/2	9-1/2	Walnut Stock
CLASSIC LAREDO											
$787	—	7mm Rem. Mag.	3	26	46-3/4	13-3/4	5/8	1/2	9-1/2	9-1/2	Composite Stock
787	—	300 Win. Mag.	3	26	46-3/4	13-3/4	5/8	1/2	9-1/2	10	Composite Stock

MODEL 70 PUSH FEED MODELS

Suggested Retail Right Handed	Left Handed	Caliber	Magazine Capacity*	Barrel Length	Nominal Overall Length	Nominal Length of Pull	Nominal Drop at Comb	Nominal Drop at Heel	Nominal Weight (Lbs.)	Rate of Twist I Turn In	Features
HEAVY BARREL VARMINT											
$795	—	223 Rem.	6	26	46	13-1/2	3/4	1/2	10-3/4	9	Accu Block
795	—	22-250 Rem.	5	26	46	13-1/2	3/4	1/2	10-3/4	14	Accu Block
795	—	243 Win.	5	26	46	13-1/2	3/4	1/2	10-3/4	10	Accu Block
795	—	308 Win.	5	26	46	13-1/2	3/4	1/2	10-3/4	12	Accu Block
HEAVY BARREL VARMINT (FLUTED BARREL)											
$932	—	223 Rem.	6	26	46	13-1/2	3/4	1/2	10-1/4	9	Accu Block
932	—	22-250 Rem.	5	26	46	13-1/2	3/4	1/2	10-1/4	14	Accu Block
932	—	243 Win.	5	26	46	13-1/2	3/4	1/2	10-1/4	10	Accu Block
932	—	308 Win.	5	26	46	13-1/2	3/4	1/2	10-1/4	12	Accu Block
BLACK SHADOW®											
$467	—	270 Win.	5	22"	42-3/4"	13-3/4"	9/16"	13/16"	7-1/4	10"	Composite Stock
467	—	30-06 Spfld.	5	22	42-3/4	13-3/4	9/16	13/16	7-1/4	10	Composite Stock
467	—	7mm Rem. Mag.	3	24	42-3/4	13-3/4	9/16	13/16	7-1/4	9-1/2	Composite Stock
467	—	300 Win. Mag.	3	22	42-3/4	13-3/4	9/16	13/16	7-1/4	10	Composite Stock
RANGER™											
$503	—	223 Rem.	6	22"	42"	13-1/2"	9/16"	7/8"	6-3/4	12"	Sights, Hardwood Stock
503	—	243 Win.	5	22	42	13-1/2	9/16	7/8	6-3/4	10	Sights, Hardwood Stock
503	—	270 Win.	5	22	42-1/2	13-1/2	9/16	7/8	7	10	Sights, Hardwood Stock
503	—	30-06 Spfld.	5	22	42-1/2	13-1/2	9/16	7/8	7	10	Sights, Hardwood Stock
503	—	7mm Rem. Mag.	3	24	44-1/2	13-1/2	9/16	7/8	7-1/2	9-1/2	Sights, Hardwood Stock
RANGER™ COMPACT											
$496	—	22-250 Rem.	6	22"	41"	12-1/2"	3/4"	1"	6-1/2	12"	Truglo Sights, Hardwood Stock
496	—	243 Win.	5	22	41	12'1/2	3/4	1	6-1/2	10	Truglo Sights, Hardwood Stock
496	—	308 Win.	5	22	41	12'1/2	3/4	1	6-1/2	12	Truglo Sights, Hardwood Stock

WINCHESTER LEVER-ACTION CARBINES/RIFLES

MODEL 94 STANDARD WALNUT RIFLE
The top choice for lever-action styling and craftsmanship. Metal surfaces are highly polished and blued. American walnut stock and forearm have a protective stain finish with precise-cut wraparound checkering. It has a 20-inch barrel with hooded blade front sight and semibuckhorn rear sight.

MODEL 94 WALNUT TRAPPER CARBINE
With 16-inch short-barrel lever action and straight forward styling. Compact and fast handing in dense cover, it has a 5-shot magazine capacity (9 in 45 Colt or 44 Rem. Mag./44 S&W Special). *Calibers:* 30-30 Win., 357 Mag., 45 Colt, and 44 Rem. Mag./44 S&W Special.

MODEL 94

Suggested Retail	Caliber	Magazine Capacity*	Barrel Length	Overall Length	Nominal Length of Pull	Nominal Drop at Comb	Nominal Drop at Heel	Nominal Weight (Lbs.)	Rate of Twist I Turn In	Features
BLACK SHADOW										
$363	30-30 Win.	4	24"	42-1/8	13-3/4	3/4"	3/4"	6-1/2	12"	Comp. Hunting Stock, Rifle Sights, SL
363	30-30 Win.	4	20	38-1/8	13-3/4	3/4	3/4	6-1/4	12	Comp. Hunting Stock, Rifle Sights, SL
374	44 Rem. Mag., & 44 S&W Spec.	5	20	38-1/8	13-3/4	3/4	3/4	6-1/4	38	Comp. Hunting Stock, Rifle Sights, SL
BLACK SHADOW® BIG BORE										
$374	444 Marlin	4	20"	38-1/8"	13-3/4"	3/4"	3/4"	6-1/2	38"	Comp. Hunting Stock, Rifle Sights, SL
RANGER COMPACT										
$354	30-30 Win.	5	16"	33-1/4"	12-1/2"	1-1/8"	1-3/4"	5-7/8	12"	Rifle Sights, SL
354	357 Mag.	9	16	33-1/4	12-1/2	1-1/8	1-3/4	5-7/8	16	Rifle Sights, SL
LEGACY										
423	30-30 Win.	7	24	42-1/8	13-1/2	1-1/8	1-7/8	6-3/4	12	PG, Rifle Sights, SL
423	357 Mag.	12	24	42-1/8	13-1/2	1-1/8	1-7/8	6-3/4	16	PG, Rifle Sights, SL
423	45 Colt	12	24	42-1/8	13-1/2	1-1/8	1-7/8	6-3/4	38	PG, Rifle Sights, SL
423	44 Rem. Mag. & 44 S&W Spec.	12	24	42-1/8	13-1/2	1-1/8	1-7/8	6-3/4	38	PG, Rifle Sights, SL
RANGER										
$334	30-30 Win.	6	20"	38-1/8"	13-1/2"	1-1/8"	1-7/8"	6-1/4	12"	Rifle Sights, SL
WALNUT										
$4099	30-30 Win. checkered	6	20"	38-1/8"	13-1/2"	1-1/8"	1-7/8"	6-1/4	12"	Rifle Sights
379	30-30 Win. not checkered	6	20"	38-1/8"	13-1/2"	1-1/8"	1-7/8"	6-1/4	12"	Rifle Sights
429	44 Mag. checkered	6	20"	38-1/8"	13-1/2	1-1/8	1-7/8	6-1/4	38"	Rifle Sights
TRAILS END										
$415	44-40 Win.	11	20"	38-1/8"	13-1/2"	1-1/8"	1-7/8"	6-1/2	36"	Rifle Sights, SL
415	357 Mag.	11	20	38-1/8	13-1/2	1-1/8	1-7/8	6-1/2	16	Rifle Sights, SL
415	44 Rem. Mag. & 44 S&W Spec.	11	20	38-1/8	13-1/2	1-1/8	1-7/8	6-1/2	38	Rifle Sights, SL
415	45 Colt	11	20	38-1/8	13-1/2	1-1/8	1-7/8	6-1/2	38	Rifle Sights, SL
BIG BORE										
$421	444 Marlin	6	20"	38-1/8"	13-1/2"	1-1/8"	1-7/8"	6-1/2	38	Rifle Sights, LL
TRAPPER										
$379	30-30 Win.	5	16"	34-1/4"	13-1/2"	1-1/8"	1-7/8"	6	12	Rifle Sights, SL
400	44 Rem. Mag. & 44 S&W Spec.	9	16	34-1/4	13-1/2	1-1/8	1-7/8	6	38	Rifle Sights, SL
400	357 Mag.	9	16	34-1/4	13-1/2	1-1/8	1-7/8	6	16	Rifle Sights, SL
400	45 Colt	9	16	34-1/4	13-1/2	1-1/8	1-7/8	6	38	Rifle Sights, SL
WRANGLER										
$400	30-30 Win.	5	16"	34-1/4"	13-1/2"	1-1/8"	1-7/8"	6	12"	Rifle Sights, LL
421	30-30 Win.	9	16"	34-1/4"	13-1/2	1-1/8	1-7/8"	6	12"	Rifle Sights, LL
421	45 Colt	9	16	34-1/4	13-1/2	1-1/8	1-7/8	6	38	Rifle Sights, LL
TIMBER CARBINE										
$520	444 Marlin	5	17-3/4"	36"	13-1/2"	1-1/8"	1-7/8"	6	12	Rifle Sights

Bushnell 4X32 scope and see-thre mounts available.

WINCHESTER RIFLES

LEVER ACTION

MODEL 94 RANGER

MODEL 94 RANGER is an economical version of the Model 94. Lever action is smooth and reliable. In 30-30 Winchester, the rapid-firing six-shot magazine capacity provides two more shots than most other centerfire hunting rifles. *Also available:* **RANGER COMPACT** in 30-30 Win. and 357 Mag. See also Specifications table.
Price: $334.00

MODEL 94 BIG-BORE WALNUT

Lever-action speed and angled ejection provide hunters with improved performance. Available in 444 Marlin in walnut and Black Shadow versions. See also Specification table.
Price: $421.00

MODEL 94 TRAILS END

SPECIFICATIONS
Calibers: 357 Mag., 44 Rem. Mag., 45 Colt. *Capacity:* 11 shot magazine. *Barrel length:* 20". *Overall length:* 38 1/8". *Weight:* 6.5 lbs. Features include rifle sights and standard loop or large loop. Now available in 44-40 Win.
Prices:
Standard Loop Lever $415.00
Large Loop Lever 415.00

MODEL 94 LEGACY
Standard Loop Lever

SPECIFICATIONS
Calibers: 30-30 Win., 357 Mag., 44 Rem. Mag., 45 Colt. *Capacity:* 6 shots (30-30 Win.); 11 shots (other calibers); add 1 shot for 24" barrel. *Barrel length:* 20" or 24". *Overall length:* 42 1/8" w/24" barrel. *Weight:* 6.75 lbs. Features include pistol-grip stock, rifle sights and standard loop lever.
Price: $423.00

WINCHESTER RIFLES

MODEL 9422 LEVER-ACTION RIMFIRE RIFLES

Positive lever action and bolt design ensure feeding and chambering from any shooting position. The bolt face is T-slotted to guide the cartridge with complete control from magazine to chamber. Receivers are grooved for scope mounting. Stock and forearm are checkered American walnut with high-luster finish and straight-grip design. Internal parts are carefully finished for smoothness of action.

MODEL 9422 WALNUT

MODEL 9422 WALNUT MAGNUM gives exceptional accuracy at longer ranges than conventional 22 rifles. It is designed specifically for the 22 WMR and holds 11 cartridges.

Otherwise same basic specifications as the 9422 Walnut. Considered one of the world's finest production sporting arms, this lever-action holds 21 Short, 17 Long or 15 Long Rifle rimfire cartridges. *Barrel length:* 20.5". *Overall length:* 37 1/8". *Weight:* 6.25 lb. Features rifle sights.

MODEL 9422 WINCAM™ MAGNUM features laminated nonglare, green-shaded stock and forearm. American hardwood stock is bonded to withstand all climates. Holds 11 22 WMR cartridges and has same basic specifications as the 9422 Walnut Magnum.

MODEL 9422 WINTUFF™ RIFLE

Includes all features and specifications of standard Model 94 plus tough laminated hardwood styled for the brush-gunning hunter who wants good concealment and a carbine that can stand up to all kinds of weather. In standard and magnum rimfire.

MODEL 9422

Suggested Retail	Caliber	Magazine Capacity*	Barrel Length	Overall Length	Length of Pull	Nominal Drop at Comb	Nominal Drop at Heel	Nominal Weight (Lbs.)	Rate Of Twist 1 Turn In	Features
WINTUFF™										
$423	22 Rimfire	21 Short, 17 Long, 15 Long Rifle	20-1/2"	37-1/8"	13-1/2"	1-1/8"	1-7/8"	6-1/4	16"	R. Sights
474	22 WMR	11	20-1/2	37-1/8	13-1/2	1-1/8	1-7/8	6-1/4	16	R. Sights
LEGACY										
$454	22 Rimfire	21 Short, 17 Long, 15 Long Rifle	22-1/2"	39-1/8"	13-1/2"	1-1/8"	1-7/8"	6	16"	Pistol Grip Stock, R.S.
473	22 WMK	21 Short, 17 Long, 15 Long Rifle	22-1/2"	39-1/8"	13-1/2"	1-1/8"	1-7/8"	6	16"	Pistol Grip Stock, R.S.
WALNUT										
$423	22 Rimfire	21 Short, 17 Long, 15 Long Rifle	20-1/2"	37-1/8"	13-1/2"	1-1/8"	1-7/8"	6	16"	R. Sights
444	22 WMR	11	20-1/2	37-1/8	13-1/2	1-1/8	1-7/8	6	16	R. Sights
448	22 Rimfire	21 Short, 17 Long, 15 Long Rifle	20-1/2	37-1/8	13-1/2	1-1/8	1-7/8	6	16	R. Sights, Large Loop
TRAPPER										
$423	22 Rimfire	15 Short, 12 Long, 11 Long Rifle	16-1/2"	33-1/8"	13-1/2"	1-1/8"	1-7/8"	5-3/4	16"	R. Sights
444	22 WMR	8	16-1/2	33-1/8	13-1/2	1-1/8	1-7/8	5-3/4	16	R. Sights

CUSTOM CACHE

David Miller Marksman rifle on Winchester M70 action, with Miller's scope mounts and 6.5-20x Leupold

This new section of Shooter's Bible will feature custom guns from the most prestigious of the world's small shops. Mass production of interchangeable parts, and the factory manufacture of small arms didn't come about until the 19th century. Until then, all guns were essentially unique unto themselves, though basic mechanisms and styles were shared among many makers. The custom gun survives because connoisseurs of firearms want something better than can be had from factory assembly lines, and they're willing to pay for the hand labor.

In its true sense, "custom" means built to order, with the customer dictating the gun's features and dimensions. There are practical limits to custom orders, of course. Few shops will offer an action to the buyer's specifications. They are constrained by the costs of designing and building actions (as well as by patents and the fact that most of the best actions are already in production) to use what is already available from major arms suppliers. To say that a rifle is not really a custom rifle because it employs a Remington 700 action is being too severe.

A fine example of custom rifle building is David Miller's work, shown on this page. David has been making rifles for most of his adult life. Until recently, he was best known for his fine rendering of hand-fashioned classic-style bolt rifles. Several were highlights at annual conventions of Safari Club International. A few years ago he put together a rifle for his own special type of hunting: Coues deer at long range in the desert hinterlands south of his Tucson shop. The rifle featured a laminated stock, not the exquisite English walnut his customers were used to seeing. It had a Winchester Model 70 action, pillar bedded for accuracy, and a long fluted barrel chambered in .300 Weatherby Magnum. David used his own scope mounts to attach a 6.5-20x Leupold scope with special range-finding reticle. Fellow hunters saw and shot the rifle and wanted a copy. Now David and partner Curt Crum are busy building both the full-custom Classic rifle and the new Marksman. A stickler for rifles that shoot well, David puts the best components and workmanship into both rifles. The Marksman lacks only the options, detailing and fine walnut of the custom Classic. David routinely shoots deer at ranges beyond the capability of most hunters. He insists that with practice and the right rifle (a Marksman!), long-distance shooting can put more venison on the table. His collection of records-class Coues deer show that his Marksman gets lots of use. (Base price for this rifle is **$9,000**. For quotes on options and on the Classic rifle, contact David at 3131 E. Greenlee Rd., Tucson AZ 85716.)

The gunmakers featured in this se tion are not the only competent craftsmen in the field. Indeed, there are gunmakers, stockers, metalsmiths and engravers practicing today whose work is the best of its kind ever seen. Quality standards (and prices) continue to climb. In future editions of Shooter's Bible, you'll find the best of the best in custom guns.

ROGER BIESEN

RIFLEMAKER

Roger Biesen built this classic-style 6.5-06 on a Model 70 Winchester Action and scoped it with a 6x Burris. Biesen rifles are true custom rifles. Prices start at about $3500.

Of all the names in riflemaking, Biesen is among the best known. Al Biesen, a Wisconsin native who moved to Spokane Washington in the 1940s, established his reputation by building rifles for Outdoor Life Shooting Editor, the late Jack O'Connor. Considered the dean of gun writers during the postwar decades that produced a boom in big game hunting, O'Connor was taken not only with Biesen's workmanship, but the lines and feel and function of his rifles. While other able gunmakers have crafted rifles in what has become known as the "classic" style, Al Biesen is among few who can claim to have defined it.

Now Al's son, Roger is carrying on the Biesen tradition. He has been building guns fulltime for more than a decade, in the same Spokane shop used by his father. Roger's guns show the same attention to detail, the same graceful sweep of line that characterizes earlier Biesen rifles. They have the same "gunny" feel, deliver the same fine accuracy. Roger accommodates customer preferences in just about every detail but also offers suggestions. Al is there for a third opinion too, with gunbuilding experience that predates World War II. Like his father, Roger does both the wood and metal work on guns, most of which are bolt-action sporting rifles. Roger points out that he also enjoys the variety of working on shotguns.

Roger Biesen does much of his hand-checkering at home, where his daughter, Paula is establishing a name for herself as a firearms engraver. Paula's floorplates and gripcaps adorn many Biesen rifles, and her work has appeared on guns commissioned for auction by the National Rifle Association, the Rocky Mountain Elk Foundation and Safari Club International. Lately Paula has been asked to engrave rifle barrels and receivers too. Her most challenging project is a rifle Al Biesen is building for himself. "It's a Model 70 Winchester in .30-06," she says. "The wood is a beautiful piece of French walnut that Grandpa squirreled away in 1968. It is really a privilege to work on something like this, but there's also a lot of pressure to come up with a unique design and to execute it very, very well. Grandpa could have gone to the best of engravers."

Paula's modesty belies her talent. Her artistry shows clearly in clean flowing scroll and lifelike animals. She favors animal scenes. "You learn tricks," she says. "Like never setting an animal face-on so you have to make left and right sides exactly the same. But knowing what not to do isn't enough. Achieving fluid forms with a chisel is much tougher than with a paint brush or a pencil. You must breath life into steel by cutting it. You have no colors to help, and three-dimensional effects require lots of astute chisel work. There's no way to brush over or erase a bad mistake."

Paula works at home partly because she's a wife and mom. But partly it's because home has fewer distractions than the shop where Al and Roger work their magic on rifles. "Customers are always stopping in to see Dad or Grandpa, says Paula. "And they talk a lot. Really a lot."

D'Arcy Echols and Co.

"Legend" Dangerous Game Version

D'Arcy Echols, a riflemaker in Utah, is well known in the custom gun fraternity where he has been active for the past 20 years. In 1997 a customer suggested that D'Arcy build a commercial rifle that functioned and shot as well as his custom rifles but that was a bit less expensive. The result is D'Arcy's "Legend" rifle, with the heart of a Winchester Model 70 Classic action and the metalsmithing that has made Echols custom rifles a hallmark of dependability. A McMillan synthetic stock, designed especially for this rifle, adds durability and trims cost. D'Arcy offers three versions of the "Legend."

The standard model comes in 7mm Remington, 300 Winchester, 300 Weatherby, 338 Winchester Magnum chamberings. Cryogenically-treated Krieger chrome-moly barrels complement the M70 action, which D'Arcy modifies to hold four rounds in the magazine instead of the usual three. He also lengthens the loading port for easy access. When fitting the barrel, he remachines then laps the recoil lug seats and lugs, and squares up the receiver face and bolt face. He repins the trigger and bolt stop and grinds sear surfaces for a crisp, consistent 3 1/4-pound trigger pull. The scope base holes are enlarged to accept 8-40 screws, and he installs his own Weaver-style bases.

D'Arcy pillar-beds the actions in the McMillan stocks, which feature a high, straight comb and cheekpiece, functional checkering, an open grip and a cast-off butt to put the shooter's eye right behind the scope. Length of pull is to order. All steel gets a matte blue finish. D'Arcy shoots each rifle a minimum of 40 times to confirm feeding, safety and accuracy.

The Dangerous Game rifle, available in 375 H&H and 416 Remington Magnums, as well as .458 Lott, has a barrel-mounted front swivel and additional action work to ensure flawless feeding with big roundnose bullets. Otherwise it is like the standard model. Iron sights can be ordered.

The Long Range rifle, available in 300 Weatherby Magnum only, has a 26-inch fluted Krieger barrel of slightly heavier dimensions (.750 at the muzzle). Barrel lengths on other Legend rifles depend on chambering and customer special requests.

Prices:

LEGEND $4,500.00
DANGEROUS GAME *(illustrated above)* 4,750.00
LONG RANGE 4,600.00
D'Arcy Echols still builds a limited number of walnut-stocked
   custom rifles *(illustrated, below)* . . . . **Prices on request**

CUSTOM RIFLE

PATRICK HOLEHAN

GUNMAKER

Patrick Holehan Classic Hunter (top) and Safari Hunter (bottom) show the clean, graceful lines of the entire Hunter Series. Both wear Swarovski scopes.

Arizona gunmaker Patrick Holehan is an exuberant young man with a wide smile and a firm handshake. He is also a serious student of classic hunting rifles and a craftsman with an eye for perfection. His tenure in the gunmaking business is not long; but his work reflects the skills of a true professional. Patrick has an artist's sense of proportion. His stocks show grace and elegance in slender contours that stop just short of racy. He is keen to do his best work always, a requisite in what has become a very competitive industry. Patrick Holehan's checkering shows the attention to detail that distinguishes accomplished craftsmen from people who want to become famous building rifles.

While Holehan rifles are custom projects, Patrick offers several basic variations of what he calls the Hunter Series. All are based on Classic Winchester Model 70 actions, and all come with either hand-made walnut or fiberglass stocks that are pillar bedded and reinforced. Patrick trues barrel seating surfaces, laps the locking lugs, hones and polishes the feed ramp and bolt race. He builds up the receiver ring and bridge to a "double square bridge" configuration that accepts quick-release scope rings. Patrick likes cryogenically-treated barrels and uses only those of highest quality. Barrel lengths and contours, like magazine style and capacity, vary with model. Customers can order from a long list of options. The standard Classic Hunter retails for $3350 with a fiberglass stock, $4050 with a wood stock. The Long Range Hunter is in the same price range, as is the Light Weight Hunter with standard magazine. The Light Weight Hunter with blind magazine costs about $300 less. The Safari Hunter retails for $3800 and $4550 with fiberglass and wood stocks. Patrick Holehan also offers both wood and fiberglass stocks as an interchangeable set with all rifle models. Additional cost varies. Holehan rifles are available in any standard chambering and wildcats that will fit the Model 70 action.

STEVEN DODD HUGHES

GUNMAKER

After three years of gunsmithing school, Steven Dodd Hughes started working as a full-time professional custom gunmaker in 1978. For more than a decade, his focus was building muzzleloading firearms from patterns of the 18th and 19th century. Hughes now speciaizes in early cartridge guns creating one-of-a-kind single-shot rifles, double-barrel shotguns and a few high-grade lever action rifes. Current projects include a Winchester Model 1873 .44-40 in a Deluxe 1 of 1000 style, sidelock SXS shotguns based on European metalwork and custom Dakota single-shot rifles

with a 1920's London flair. Other projects include fancy Marlin lever guns, boxlock "game gun" shotguns and Winchester High Wall and Low Wall custom rifles from .22 to .45-70. Delivery time usuallly runs from 1 1/2 to 2 years and Hughes's base price is about $10,000. He does no bolt-action rifle work of any kind. Hughes has also written numerous magazine articles about the custom gun trade and contributes the *"Fine Gunmaking"* column for Shooting Sportsman Magazine. His book *Fine Gunmaking: Double Shotguns* was published by Krause Pub. in 1998.

Hughes designed this custom Winchester High Wall as if it had been created in a London gunshop Circa 1920. It has a 24" octagon barrel with integral quarter-rib and front sight base and weighs 7-1/4 lbs. Stocked in English Walnut, everything is new except the original Winchester action.

A Stevens 44 1/2 mid-range target rifle in 32-40 sports metalwork and stockmaking by Steven Dodd Hughes.

A completely custom M-39A by Hughes follows the theme of the 1897 Deluxe Marlin rimfire rifles. The stock is English Walnut with the distinctive Marlin "S" curve grip profile.

MAURICE OTTMAR

GUNMAKER

Maurice Ottmar grew up on a farm in central Washington. He began working on guns part-time, then turned to building his own custom rifles. They got such good reviews from his customers that he eventually left the farm and set up shop as a full-time rifle-builder in nearby Coulee City, just south of Grand Coulee Dam. Gun fanciers from all over the country have visited Maurice in this small, quiet town. He is one of a handful of gun-builders nationwide who can excel at both wood and metal work. Unlike most stockmakers who turn their blanks on pantographs to save labor, Maurice cuts his stocks from the blank. "That way I'm not limited to established patterns," he says. "I can give the customer just what he or she wants."

Maurice specializes in top-quality custom rifles on bolt and dropping-block single-shot actions, though he has worked on a wide variety of sporting guns. He has an eye for style and can reproduce a German or English "look," or evoke a period in history with his craftsmanship.

He prefers to work on rifles chambered for practical hunting cartridges like the .30-06.

The two rifles featured here illustrate the attention to line and detail that characterizes Maurice Ottmar's work. The Hagn single-shot (top) features Terry Wallace engraving, but Maurice did all the other metal work and fashioned the stock from an exquisite piece of English walnut. The 12x Leupold scope on the quarter-rib complements the chambering: .220 Swift.

The bolt-action rifle (bottom) is based on a much-modified Remington Enfield, with some metal work by Tom Burgess. It's a .404 Jeffery with a low-power scope in quick-detach rings. The stock, of dark Moroccan walnut, is all Maurice's. Like the wood on the Hagn Swift, it features 26-line-per-inch checkering in a difficult point pattern. Maurice located the forward sling swivel on the barrel to protect the shooter's hand under recoil. The straight bolt handle and conservative trigger blade are in keeping with the rifle's understated elegance.

GENE SIMILLION

RIFLEMAKER

Coloradan Gene Simillion has been building custom sporting rifles for nearly 20 years. He grew up near renowned stockmaker Keith Stegall and says he got the inspiration to craft rifle stocks from Keith. Later, Gene honed his wood- and metal-working skills in college, graduating with a teaching degree in industrial arts.

"That wasn't too smart," Gene says with a frown. "I should have figured out beforehand that teachers work during hunting season." Gene started building rifles full-time, then spent a year in Kalispell under the tutelage of crack stockmaker Jerry Fisher. Gene also credits Montanan Tom Burgess with teaching him a lot about custom metal-smithing. "I'm a student of good workmanship," he says. "So I've paid attention to the likes of Monte Mandarino, D'Arcy Echols and Don Klein."

Gene Simillion notes that little has changed in the stye of his work since the early days. "The clean, classic look is as popular as ever–maybe even more so. I like to think I'm better at the job now." On any project, Gene's aim is to produce a rifle with "accuracy, flawless function, and elegant beauty." He says the main difference between custom rifles and the best factory-built guns is in the detailing.

Two grades of rifles come from Gene's Gunnison, Colorado shop. The Premier Rifle is a true custom effort, built to each customer's exact specifications. Gene prefers to use new Model 70 Winchester Classic actions but will substitute pre-64 Model 70s, Mauser 98s, Remington 700s and others on request. Gene installs his own scope bases. A hand-checkered bolt knob and screwless sling swivel studs are standard. Magnum rifles get a second recoil lug and a crossbolt, a custom magazine box and follower. Extended magazines are an option–so too quarter ribs and iron sights. Stocks are of the finest walnut, hand-checkered in point or fleur-de-lis patterns..

SIMILLION PREMIER RIFLE	$7,500.00
MAGNUMS	8,000.00

A less costly custom rifle is Gene's Classic Hunter. Built only on the new Winchester 70 Classic action, it also features new bottom metal and a top-quality, cut-rifled barrel hand-bedded in a high-grade checkered walnut stock with screwless swivel bases. The Classic Hunter shows less detailing than the Premier, and the customer has fewer options. Gene came up with this rifle a couple of years ago to bridge the gap between true custom rifles and the semi-custom factory-built rifles like those produced by Dakota.

STANDARD CLASSIC HUNTER	$5,400.00
MAGNUMS	6,000.00
HEAVY MAGNUMS (.375 H&H and up)	6,500.00

Gene Simillion Premier Rifle, .270 on a Winchester Model 70 action with Leupold 2-7x scope.

Gene Simillion Premier Rifle, 7x57 Mauser on a Mauser 98 action with Zeiss 4x scope.

Gene Simillion Premier Rifle, .338 Magnum on a Mauser 98 action with Leupold 1.5-5x scope.

American Arms	312		Marocchi	341
AYA	315		Merkel	342
Benelli	317		New England Arms (FAIR)	349
Beretta	320		New England Firearms	350
Browning	325		Perazzi	352
Charles Daly	330		Piotti	354
Dakota Arms	332		Remington	355
A.H. Fox	332		Rizzini	363
Francotte	333		Ruger	364
Garbi	333		Savage	365
Harrington & Richardson	334		Sigarms	365
Heckler & Koch/Fabarms	335		SKB	366
Ithaca	337		Stoeger IGA	368
Krieghoff	338		Weatherby	372
Marlin	340		Winchester	374

shotguns

*For addresses and phone/fax numbers of manufacturers and distributors included in this section, please turn to **DIRECTORY OF MANUFACTURERS AND SUPPLIERS** on page 564.*

AMERICAN ARMS SHOTGUNS

SILVER I OVER AND UNDER
(W/Fixed Chokes & Extractors)

Features polished white frame w/outline engraving; blued trigger guard, top lever and forward latch; radiused rubber recoil pad.

SILVER II
(W/Choke Tubes & Automatic Selective Ejectors)

Same features as Silver I, but with more refined engraving. Models in 16, 20 and .410 gauge have fixed chokes.

SILVER SPORTING
(Ported, w/Choke Tubes)

SPECIFICATIONS

Model	Gauge	Bbl. Length	Chamber	Chokes	Avg. Weight	Prices
Silver I	12	26" – 28"	3"	IC/M-M/F	6 lbs. 15 oz.	$649.00
	20	26" – 28"	3"	IC/M-M/F	6 lbs. 12 oz.	649.00
	28	26"	2.75"	IC/M	5 lbs. 14 oz.	679.00
	.410	26"	3"	IC/M	6 lbs. 6 oz.	679.00
Silver II*	12	26" – 28"	3"	CT-3	6 lbs. 15 oz.	769.00
	16	26"	2.75"	IC/M	6 lbs. 13 oz.	769.00
	20	26"	3"	CT-3	6 lbs. 12 oz.	769.00
	28	26"	2.75"	IC/M	5 lbs. 14 oz.	815.00
	.410	26"	3"	IC/M	6 lbs. 6 oz.	815.00
Sporting**	12	29" – 30"	2.75"	CTS	7 lbs. 6 oz.	965.00

CT-3 Choke Tubes IC/M/F Cast Off = 3/8" CTS = SK/SK/IC/M   Silver I and II: Pull = 14 1/8"; Drop at Comb = 1 3/8"; Drop at Heel = 2 3/8"
Silver I and II: Pull = 14 1/4"; Drop at Comb = 1 1/2"; Drop at Heel = 2 1/2"   * 2 Barrel Set: **$115.00** **Silver Upland Lite (12 and 20 ga.) = *$925.00***

AMERICAN ARMS SHOTGUNS

BRITTANY SIDE-BY-SIDE

SPECIFICATIONS
Gauges: 12, 20
Chamber: 3"
Chokes: CT-3

Barrel Length: 26"
Weight: 6 lbs. 7 oz. (20 ga.); 6 lbs. 15 oz. (12 ga.)
Features: Engraved case-colored frame; single selective trigger with top tang selector; automatic selective ejectors; manual safety; hard chrome-lined barrels; walnut English-style straight stock and semi-beavertail forearm w/cut checkering and oil-rubbed finish; ventilated rubber recoil pal; and choke tubes with key
Price: $885.00

GENTRY SIDE-BY-SIDE

Features boxlocks with engraved English-style scrollwork on side plates; one-piece, steel-forged receiver; chrome barrels; manual thumb safety; independent floating firing pin.

SPECIFICATIONS
Gauges: 12, 20, 28, .410
Chamber: 3" (except 28 gauge, 2.75")

Barrel Lengths: 26", choked IC/M (all gauges; 28", choked M/F (12 and 20 gauges)
Weight: 6 lbs. 15 oz. (12 ga.); 6 lbs. 7 oz. (20 and .410 ga.); 6 lbs. 5 oz. (28 ga.)
Drop At Comb: 1 $^3/_8$"
Drop At Heel: 2 $^3/_8$"
Other Features: Fitted recoil pad; flat matted rib; walnut pistol-grip stock and beavertail forend with hand-checkering; gold front sight bead
Prices:
12 or 20 ga. $750.00
28 or .410 ga. 795.00

SHOTGUNS

PHANTOM SYNTHETIC

SPECIFICATIONS
Gauge: 12 **Barrel:** 24"/26"/28", cold hammered forged chrome lined with bright blue finish **Choke:** IC-M-F
Chamber: 3" **Features:** Gas operated semi-automatic shoots 2 3/4" or 3" shells interchangeably. Approved for steel shot, checkered synthetic forend and stock, screw-in choke tubes (3), magazine cut-off for quick unloading and safety, five round magazine.
Price: $439.00

PHANTOM HOME PROTECTION

SPECIFICATIONS
Gauge: 12 **Barrel:** 19" threaded barrel for external choketubes (2), and swivel studs **Choke:** SK, M, F
Chamber: 3" **Features:** Same as Phantom Synthetic
Price: $449.00

PHANTOM WOOD STOCK

SPECIFICATIONS
Gauge: 12 **Barrel:** 24"/26"/28", cold hammered forged chrome lined with bright blue finish **Choke:** IC-M-F
Chamber: 3" **Features:** Same as Phantom Synthetic, except for checkered walnut forend and stock
Price: $439.00

AMERICAN ARMS SHOTGUNS

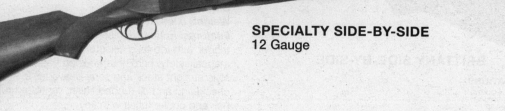

SPECIALTY SIDE-BY-SIDE
12 Gauge

SPECIALTY OVER/UNDER
12 Gauge

SPECIALTY CAMO (SILVER WT/OU)

SPECIFICATIONS

Features nonreflective Mossy Oak "Breakup" Camo pattern. Specifications same as WS/OU 12 ga., including auto selective ejectors and AA1 choke tubes (IC-M-F).

SPECIFICATIONS

MODEL	GAUGE	BBL. LENGTH	CHAMBER	CHOKES	AVG. WGT.	PRICES
WT/OU	10	26"	3.5"	CT-2	9 lbs. 10 oz.	$995.00
WS/OU	12	28"	3.5"	CT-3	7 lbs. 2 oz.	799.00
WT/OU Camo	12	26"	3.5"	CT-3	7 lbs.	885.00
TS/SS	12	26"	3.5"	CT-3	7 lbs. 6 oz.	799.00

CT-3 Choke Tubes IC/M/F. CT-2 = Choke tubes F/F. Drop at Comb = 1 ¹/₈"; Drop at Heel = 2 ³/₈"

AYA SHOTGUNS

SIDELOCK SHOTGUNS

AYA sidelock shotguns are fitted with London Holland & Holland system sidelocks, double triggers with articulated front trigger, automatic safety and ejectors, cocking indicators, bushed firing pins, replaceable hinge pins and chopper lump barrels. Stocks are of figured walnut with hand-cut checkering and oil finish, complete with a metal oval on the buttstock for engraving of initials. Exhibition grade wood is available as are many special options, including a true left-hand version and self-opener. Available from Armes de Chasse (see Directory of Manufacturers and Suppliers). **Barrell lengths:** 26", 27", 28", 29" and 32". **Weight:** 5 to 7 pounds, depending on gauge.

MODEL	Prices
MODEL 1: Sidelock in 12 and 20 ga. w/special engraving and exhibition quality wood	$6,895.00
DELUXE	7,495.00
MODEL 2: Sidelock in 12, 16, 20, 28 ga. and .410 bore	3,295.00
MODEL 53: Sidelock in 12, 16 and 20 ga. with 3 locking lugs and side clips	4,602.00
MODEL 56: Sidelock in 12 ga. only with 3 locking lugs and side clips	7,595.00
MODEL XXV/SL: Sidelock in 12 and 20 ga. only w/Churchill-type rib	3,892.00

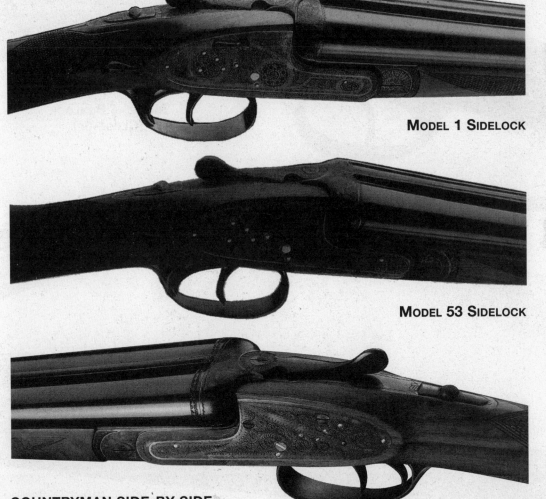

MODEL 1 SIDELOCK

MODEL 53 SIDELOCK

COUNTRYMAN SIDE-BY-SIDE

SPECIFICATIONS
Gauges: 12 and 10 **Barrel lengths:** 26", 27" or 28" **Length of pull:** up to 15" **Features:** Selective ejectors; automatic safety; Cordura covered case; hand-detachable side locks; disc set starters; chopper lump barrels; hand-rubbed select Spanish walnut stock with hand-cut checkering.
Price: $2,295.00

AYA SHOTGUNS

BOXLOCK SHOTGUNS

AYA boxlocks use the Anson & Deeley system with double locking lugs, incorporating detachable cross pin and separate plate to allow easy access to the firing mechanism. Barrels are chopper lump, firing pins are bushed, plus automatic safety and ejectors and metal oval for engraving of initials. Other features include disc set strikers, replaceable hinge pin, split bottom plate.

Barrel lengths: 26", 27" and 28"

Weight: 5 to 7 pounds, depending on gauge.

MODEL	Price
MODEL XXV BOXLOCK: 12 and 20 gauge only	$2,635.00
MODEL 4 BOXLOCK: 12, 16, 20, 28, .410 ga.	1,695.00
MODEL 4 DELUXE BOXLOCK: Same gauges as above	2,995.00

MODEL 4 BOXLOCK
(CLOSE-UP)

MODEL XXV BOXLOCK

MODEL XXV BOXLOCK

BENELLI SHOTGUNS

SLUG GUN

LH SUPER BLACK EAGLE

SUPER BLACK EAGLE (LEFT-HAND VENT RIB AND SLUG GUN SHOWN)

Benelli's Super Black Eagle shotgun offers the advantage of owning one 12-gauge auto that fires every type of 12 gauge currently available. It has the same balance, sighting plane and fast-swinging characteristics whether you're practicing on the sporting clays course with light target loads or touching off a 3 1/2" Magnum steel load at a high-flying goose. The Super Black Eagle also features a specially strengthened steel upper receiver mated to the barrel to endure the toughest shotgunning. The alloy lower receiver keeps the overall weight low. Distinctive high-gloss or satin walnut stocks and a choice of full finish or blued metal add up to a universal gun for all shotgun hunting and sports.

Stock: Satin walnut (28") with drop adjustment kit; high-gloss walnut (26") with drop adjustment kit; or synthetic stock

Finish: Matte black finish on receiver, barrel and bolt (28"); blued finish on receiver and barrel (26") with bolt mirror polished

Features: Montefeltro rotating bolt with dual locking lugs. For additional specifications, see table on folllowing page.

Prices: Wood Satin $1,255.00
Synthetic 1,245.00

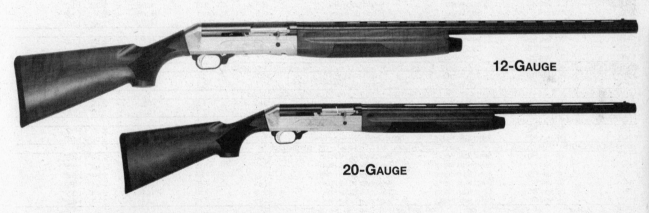

12-GAUGE

20-GAUGE

LEGACY (20- AND 12-GAUGE SHOWN)

Features lower alloy receiver and upper steel receiver cover and interchangeable barrel with mid-point bead and red light-gathering bar front sight. Also Benelli's inertia recoil operating system; cartridge drop lever (to indicate "hammer-cocked condition; set of 5 choke tubes for use with lead or steel shot); chambered round removable without emptying the magazine; handles all 2 3/4" and 3" shells within gauge with over 1 1/2 oz. of shot. **Price:** $1,320.00

SPORT MODEL

Features 28" barrel, interchangeable ribs, Montefeltro style fore-arm, adjustable butt pad, oil finish stock, optional shell catcher.
Price: $1,315.00

SHOTGUNS

BENELLI SHOTGUNS

EXECUTIVE TYPE II

EXECUTIVE SERIES

Engraved I $4,950.00
Engraved II 5,600.00
Engraved III 6,550.00

BENELLI SHOTGUN SPECIFICATIONS

Item #	BBL Length	Stock	Receiver	Length	Weight (Lbs.)	Pull	Drop: Heel/Comb	Mag. Cap.
SUPER BLACK EAGLE - 12 Gauge (fires 3 1/2"-3"-2 3/4" shells) - 5 choke tubes - mid & front bead sights - ventilated buttpad								
10055	26" Vent Rib-Ltd. Ed.	Satin Walnut	Upper Steel/Lower Nickel Finish	47.63	7.4	14.25	2 1/2" / 1 5/8"	3
10000	28" Vent Rib	Satin Walnut	Upper Steel/Lower Alloy	49.63	7.5	14.25	2 1/2" / 1 5/8"	3
10010	26" Vent Rib	Satin Walnut	Upper Steel/Lower Alloy	47.63	7.4	14.25	2 1/2" / 1 5/8"	3
10005	26" Vent Rib	Satin Walnut	Upper Steel/Lower Alloy	47.63	7.4	14.25	2 1/2" / 1 5/8"	3
10015	28" Vent Rib	Synthetic	Upper Steel/Lower Alloy	49.63	7.5	14.25	2 1/2" / 1 5/8"	3
10020	26" Vent Rib	Synthetic	Upper Steel/Lower Alloy	47.63	7.4	14.25	2 1/2" / 1 5/8"	3
10025	24" Vent Rib	Synthetic	Upper Steel/Lower Alloy	45.63	7.3	14.25	2 1/2" / 1 5/8"	3
10040	28" Vent Rib	Camo	Upper Steel/Lower Alloy	49.63	7.5	14.25	2 1/2" / 1 5/8"	3
10045	26" Vent Rib	Camo	Upper Steel/Lower Alloy	47.63	7.4	14.25	2 1/2" / 1 5/8"	3
10050	24" Vent Rib	Camo	Upper Steel/Lower Alloy	45.63	7.3	14.25	2 1/2" / 1 5/8"	3
10075	28" Vent Rib-LH	Synthetic	Upper Steel/Lower Alloy	49.63	7.5	14.25	2 1/2" / 1 5/8"	3
10070	26" Vent Rib-LH	Synthetic	Upper Steel/Lower Alloy	47.63	7.4	14.25	2 1/2" / 1 5/8"	3
10065	24" Vent Rib-LH	Synthetic	Upper Steel/Lower Alloy	45.63	7.3	14.25	2 1/2" / 1 5/8"	3
10090	28" Vent Rib-LH	Camo	Upper Steel/Lower Alloy	49.63	7.5	14.25	2 1/2" / 1 5/8"	3
10085	26" Vent Rib-LH	Camo	Upper Steel/Lower Alloy	47.63	7.4	14.25	2 1/2" / 1 5/8"	3
10080	24" Vent Rib-LH	Camo	Upper Steel/Lower Alloy	45.63	7.3	14.25	2 1/2" / 1 5/8"	3
SUPER BLACK EAGLE SLUG - 12 Gauge (fires 3"-2 3/4" shells) - rifled barre - drilled/tapped receiver, adj. rifle sights - ventilated buttpad								
10030	24" Rifled Bore	Satin Walnut		45.63	7.6	14.25	2 1/2" / 1 5/8"	3
10035	24" Rifled Bore	Upper Steel/Lower Alloy		45.63	7.6	14.25	2 1/2" / 1 5/8"	3
MONTEFELTRO - 12 Gauge (fires 3"-2 3/4" shells) - 5 choke tubes - front sight bead - 4 round magazine capacity - ventilated buttpad								
10800	28" Vent Rib	Satin Walnut	Bued/1 piece alloy	49.5	7.1	14.375	2 3/8" / 1 1/2"	
10810	26" Vent Rib	Satin Walnut	Bued/1 piece alloy	47.5	6.9	14.375	2 3/8" / 1 1/2"	
10820	24" Vent Rib	Satin Walnut	Bued/1 piece alloy	45.5	6.8	14.375	2 3/8" / 1 1/2"	
10805	28" Vent Rib - LH	Satin Walnut	Bued/1 piece alloy	49.5	7.1	14.375	2 3/8" / 1 1/2"	
10815	26" Vent Rib - LH	Satin Walnut	Bued/1 piece alloy	47.5	6.9	14.375	2 3/8" / 1 1/2"	
MONTEFELTRO - 20 Gauge (fires 3"-2 3/4" shells) - 5 choke tubes - front sight bead - 4 round magazine capacity - ventilated buttpad								
10830	26" Vent Rib	Satin Walnut	Bued/1 piece alloy	47.5	5.6	14.25	2 1/4" / 1 1/2"	
10835	24" Vent Rib	Satin Walnut	Bued/1 piece alloy	45.5	5.5	14.25	2 1/4" / 1 1/2"	
10840	26" Vent Rib	Camo Wood	Camo/1 piece alloy	47.5	5.6	14.25	2 1/4" / 1 1/2"	
MONTEFELTRO - 20 Gauge Short Stocked (fires 3"-2 3/4" shells) - 5 choke tubes - front sight bead - 4 rd. mag. Capacity - ventilated buttpad								
10831	26" Vent Rib	Satin Walnut	Bued/1 piece alloy	45.7	5.4	12.5	2 1/8" / 1 1/2"	
10836	24" Vent Rib	Satin Walnut	Bued/1 piece alloy	43.7	5.3	12.5	2 1/8" / 1 1/2"	
LEGACY- 12 Gauge (fires 3"-2 3/4" shells) - 5 choke tubes - mid & front bead sights - 4 round magazine capacity - rubber buttpad								
10400	28" Vent Rib	Select Satin Walnut	Upper Steel/Lower Nickel Finish	49.63	7.5	14.25	2 1/2" / 1 1/2"	
10405	26" Vent Rib	Select Satin Walnut	Upper Steel/Lower Nickel Finish	47.63	7.4	14.25	2 1/2" / 1 1/2"	
LEGACY- 20 Gauge (fires 3"-2 3/4" shells) - 5 choke tubes - mid & front bead sights - 4 round magazine capacity - rubber buttpad								
10420	26" Vent Rib	Select Satin Walnut	Upper Steel/Lower Nickel Finish	47.63	6	14.25	2 1/2" / 1 1/2"	
10425	24" Vent Rib	Select Satin Walnut	Upper Steel/Lower Nickel Finish	45.63	5.8	14.25	2 1/2" / 1 1/2"	
SUPER BLACK EAGLE - 12 Gauge (fires 3 1/2"-3"-2 3/4" shells) - 5 choke tubes - mid & front bead sights - ventilated buttpad								
11420	28" Vent Rib	Select Satin Walnut	Steel/Lower Nickel Finish	49.63	7.85	14.5	2 1/4" / 1 3/8"	
11400	26" Vent Rib	Select Satin Walnut	Steel/Lower Nickel Finish	47.63	7.75	14.5	2 1/4" / 1 3/8"	
11430	28" Vent Rib	Select Satin Walnut	Steel/Lower Nickel Finish	49.63	7.85	14.5	2 1/4" / 1 3/8"	
11405	26" Vent Rib	Select Satin Walnut	Steel/Lower Nickel Finish	47.63	7.75	14.5	2 1/4" / 1 3/8"	
11440	28" Vent Rib	Select Satin Walnut	Steel/Lower Nickel Finish	49.63	7.85	14.5	2 1/4" / 1 3/8"	
11410	26" Vent Rib	Select Satin Walnut	Steel/Lower Nickel Finish	47.63	7.75	14.5	2 1/4" / 1 3/8"	
SPORT - 12 Gauge (fires 3"-2 3/4" shells) - 5 choke tubes - mid & front bead sights - 4 round magazine capacity								
10610	28" Vent Rib (w/2 ribs)	Select Satin Walnut	Matte/1 piece alloy	49.63	7.1	14.375	2 1/4" / 1 7/16"	
10615	26" Vent Rib (w/2 ribs)	Select Satin Walnut	Matte/1 piece alloy	47.63	6.9	14.375	2 1/4" / 1 7/16"	
M1 FIELD - 12 Gauge (fires 3"-2 3/4" shells) - 5 choke tubes - front bead sights - 3 round magazine capacity - ventilated buttpad								
11000	28" Vent Rib	Satin Walnut	Matte/1 Piece Alloy	49.5	7.4	14.375	2 1/4" / 1 3/8"	
11010	26" Vent Rib	Satin Walnut	Matte/1 Piece Alloy	47.5	7.3	14.375	2 1/4" / 1 3/8"	
11035	28" Vent Rib	Camo	Camo/1 piece alloy	49.5	7.4	14.375	2 1/4" / 1 3/8"	
11040	26" Vent Rib	Camo	Camo/1 piece alloy	47.5	7.3	14.375	2 1/4" / 1 3/8"	
11045	24" Vent Rib	Camo	Camo/1 piece alloy	45.5	7.2	14.375	2 1/4" / 1 3/8"	
11050	21" Vent Rib	Camo	Camo/1 piece alloy	42.5	7	14.375	2 1/4" / 1 3/8"	
11005	28" Vent Rib	Synthetic	Matte/1 Piece Alloy	49.5	7.4	14.375	2 1/4" / 1 3/8"	
11015	26" Vent Rib	Synthetic	Matte/1 Piece Alloy	47.5	7.3	14.375	2 1/4" / 1 3/8"	
11020	24" Vent Rib	Synthetic	Matte/1 Piece Alloy	45.5	7.2	14.375	2 1/4" / 1 3/8"	
11025	21" Vent Rib	Synthetic	Matte/1 Piece Alloy	42.5	7	14.375	2 1/4" / 1 3/8"	
M1 FIELD SLUG - 12 Gauge (fires 3"-2 3/4" shells) - rifled barrel - drilled/tapped sights - 3 round magazine capacity - ventilated buttpad								
11060	24" Rifled Bore	Synthetic	Matte/1 Piece Alloy	45.63	7.6	14.375	2 1/4" / 1 3/8"	
NOVA PUMP - 12 Gauge (fires 3 1/2"-3"- 2 3/4" shells) - 3 choke tubes - mid & front bead sights - 4 round mag. capacity								
20015	28" Vent Rib	Camo Synthetic	Camo	49.5	8	14.25		
20018	26" Vent Rib	Camo Synthetic	Camo	47.5	7.9	14.25		
20021	24" Vent Rib	Camo Synthetic	Camo	45.5	7.8	14.25		
20000	28" Vent Rib	Synthetic	Synthetic	49.5	8	14.25		
20003	26" Vent Rib	Synthetic	Synthetic	47.5	7.9	14.25		
20006	24" Vent Rib	Synthetic	Synthetic	45.5	7.8	14.25		
NOVA PUMP SLUG - 12 Gauge (fires 3 1/2"- 3"- 2 3/4" shells) - smooth bore rifle sights								
20050	18.5	Synthetic	Synthetic		7.2	14.25		

BENELLI SHOTGUNS

MODEL M1 SUPER 90 SERIES

M1 SUPER 90 FIELD W/REALTREE

The M1 Field 12-gauge shotgun combines the M1 Super 90 receiver with a choice of polymer or walnut stocks, including

a camouflaged model with an Xtra Brown pattern sealed on the matte finish metal and polymer stock. Available in 21", 24", 26" or 28" barrels with vent rib.

M1 SUPER 90 FIELD W/REALTREE
Camo finish, camo polymer buttstock
and forearm $990.00

MODEL M1 SUPER 90 FIELD

Also available:
MODEL M1 SUPER 90 TACTICAL w/18 1/2" bbl. $875.00
With pistol-grip stock, ghost ring sights 950.00

PRACTICAL SUPER 90, 26" barrel, ghost ring sight,
synthetic stock 1,175.00
MODEL M1 SUPER 90 FIELD (polymer stock)
w/21", 24", 26", 28" bbl. 900.00
MODEL M3 SUPER 90 PUMP/AUTO SERIES
Standard stock, 19 3/4" barrel 1,040.00
w/Ghost Ring Sight and standard stock 1,080.00

MONTEFELTRO SUPER 90 VENT RIB

Prices:
12 Ga.—24", 26", or 28" Barrel
(20 ga.—24" or 26" barrel only) $925.00
Left Hand w/26" or 28" Barrel 945.00
20 ga. w/Camo Wood, 26" VR 1,010.00

See table on the preceding page for all Benelli specifications.

BENELLI SHOTGUN SPECIFICATIONS *(Continued from previous page)*

ITEM #	BBL LENGTH	STOCK	CHOKE	SIGHTS	MAG. CAP.	OVERALL LENGTH	WEIGHT (LBS.)	DROP: HEEL/COMB
M1 SPECIAL USE - 12 Gauge (fires 3"-2 3/4" shells) - matte/1 piece alloy receiver - ventilated buttpad - Pull - 14 3/8"								
11255	Practical 26"	Synthetic	F, M, IC••	Mil. Ghost Ring	9	47.63	7.6	2 1/4" / 1 3/8"
11215	Tactical 18.5"	Pistol Grip	F, M, IC••	Std. Ghost Ring	5	39.75	7	
11216	Tactical 18.5"	Synthetic	F, M, IC••	Std. Ghost Ring	5	39.75	7	2 1/4" / 1 3/8"
11200	Tactical 18.5"	Synthetic	F, M, IC••	Rifle	5	39.75	6.7	
11201	Tactical 18.5"	Pistol Grip	F, M, IC••	Rifle	5	39.75	6.7	
11260	Tactical M 18.5"	Pistol Grip	F, M, IC••	Mil. Ghost Ring	5	39.75	7.1	
11261	Tactical M 18.5"	Synthetic	F, M, IC••	Mil. Ghost Ring	5	39.75	7.1	2 1/4" / 1 3/8"
11600	M3 Conv. 19.75"	Synthetic	Cyl. Bore	Rifle	5	41	7.2	2 1/4" / 1 3/8"
11601	M3 Conv. 19.75"	Pistol Grip	Cyl. Bore	Rifle	5	41	7.2	
11605	M3 Conv. 19.75"	Synthetic	Cyl. Bore	Std. Ghost Ring	5	41	7.4	2 1/4" / 1 3/8"
11606	M3 Conv. 19.75"	Pistol Grip	Cyl. Bore	Std. Ghost Ring	5	41	7.4	
11245	Entry 14"	Synthetic	Cyl. Bore	Rifle	5	35.5	6.6	
11247	Entry 14"	Pistol Grip	Cyl. Bore	Rifle	5	35.5	6.6	
11225	Entry 14"	Pistol Grip	Cyl. Bore	Std. Ghost Ring	5	35.5	6.7	
11227	Entry 14"	Synthetic	Cyl. Bore	Std. Ghost Ring	5	35.5	6.7	2 1/4" / 1 3/8"

ITEM #	BBL LENGTH	BBL RIFLING	CALIBER	GRIP	LENGTH OF SIGHT LINE	HEIGHT/WIDTH	TRIGGER ACTION	WEIGHT (LBS.)	MAG. CAP.
MP95E/MP90S - Semi-automatic fixed barrel operation - inertia blow-back system - sequential loading with magazine feed - sq. sectioned sights									
30000	4.4"	R.H. Pitch 18"	22 LR	Anatomical, Amb., Fixed	8.75"	5.25/2"	single, completely adj.	2.5	6
30100	4.4"	R.H. Pitch 18"	32 WC	Anatomical, Amb., Fixed	8.75"	5.25/2"	single, completely adj.	2.65	5
30200	4.4"/Blue	R.H. Pitch 18"	22 LR	Anatomical, Amb., Fixed	8.75"	5.25/1.75"	single w/release spring	2.5	6,9
30300	4.4"/Chrome	R.H. Pitch 18"	22 LR	Anatomical, Amb., Fixed	8.75"	5.25/1.75"	single w/release spring	2.5	6,9
30400	4.4"/Blue	R.H. Pitch 18"	32 WC	Anatomical, Amb., Fixed	8.75"	5.25/1.75"	single w/release spring	2.65	5
30500	4.4"/Chrome	R.H. Pitch 18"	32 WC	Anatomical, Amb., Fixed	8.75"	5.25/1.75"	single w/release spring	2.65	5

BERETTA SHOTGUNS

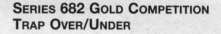

SERIES 682 GOLD COMPETITION TRAP OVER/UNDER

MODEL 682 GOLD TRAP w/ADJUSTABLE STOCK

These 12 gauge Model 682 Trap guns feature adjustable gold-plated, single-selective sliding trigger; low-profile improved boxlock action; manual safety w/barrel selector; 2.75" chambers; auto ejector; competition recoil pad buttplate; hand-checkered walnut stock.
Weight: Approx. 8 lbs. **Barrel Lengths/Chokes:** 30 Imp. Mod./Full (Black); 30" or 32" Mobilchoke® (Black); Top Single 32" or 34" Mobilchoke®; "Live Bird" (Flat rib, Silver);

Combo: 30" or 32" Mobilchoke® (Top), 30" IM/F (Top), 32" Mobilchoke® (Mono), 30" or 32" Mobilchoke® ported
Prices:

MODEL 682 GOLD TRAP	$2,910.00
MODEL 682 GOLD TRAP COMBO	3,845.00
MODEL 682 GOLD "LIVE BIRD"	2,910.00
MODEL 682 GOLD TRAP w/Adjustable Stock	3,725.00
TOP COMBO	4,555.00

MODEL 682 GOLD COMPETITION SKEET O/U

This 12-gauge skeet gun sports a hand-checkerd premium walnut stock w/silver oval for initials, forged and hardened receiver w/Greyston finish, manual safety with trigger selector, auto ejector, silver inlaid on trigger guard.
Action: Low-profile hard chrome-plated boxlock **Trigger:**

Single adjustable sliding trigger **Barrels:** 28" bllued barrels with 2.75" chambers **Stock dimensions:** Length of pull 14.75"; drop at comb 1 3/8"; drop at heel 2.25" **Sights:** fluorescent front and metal middle bead **Weight:** Approx. 7.5 lbs.
Price: (incl. fitted case) $2,850.00

MODEL 682 GOLD SPORTING

These competition-stye sporting clays feature 28" or 30" barels with four flush-mounted screw-in choke tubes (Full, Modified, Improved Cylinder and Skeet), pllus hand-checkered stock and forend of fine walnut, 2.75" or 3" chambers and adjustable trigger. MODEL 682 GOLD features Greystone finish–an ultra-durable finish in gunmetal grey w/gold accents. MODEL 686 ONYX SPORTING has black matte receiver and MODEL 686 SILVER

PIGEON SPORTING has coin silver receiver with scroll engraving.
Prices:

682 GOLD SPORTING	$2,910.00
PORTED	3,035.00
686 ONYX SPORTING	1,500.00
686 SILVER PIGEON SPORTING	1,795.00
COMBO	2,210.00

BERETTA SHOTGUNS

MODEL 687 SILVER PIGEON SPORTING

This sporting over/under features enhanced engraving pattern, schnabel forend and an electroless nickel finished receiver. *Chamber:* 3". Mobilchoke® screw-in tube system. *Gauges:* 12, 20 and 28 (Field Models)
Prices:
MODEL 687 SILVER PIGEON SPORTING $2,575.00
MODEL 687 SILVER PIGEON SPORTING COMBO 3,395.00

MODEL 687 SILVER PIGEON FIELD

The **687** features Mobilchoke® in 12 and 20 gauge; strong boxlock action handsomely tooled with engraved gamescene receiver, fine-quality walnut stock accented with silver monogram plate, selective auto ejectors and fitted case.
Price: $2,115.00

MODEL 687EELL DIAMOND PIGEON (not shown)
MODEL 687EELL COMBO (20 and 28 ga.)

In 12, 20 or 28 ga., this model features the Mobilchoke® engraved choke system, a special premium walnut stock and silver receiver with engraved sideplate.
Prices:
MODEL 687 EELL DIAMOND PIGEON $5,215.00
MODEL 687EELL COMBO (20 and 28 ga.) 5,815.00
Also available:
MODEL 687 EEL DIAMOND PIGEON TRAP O/U $4,815.00
MODEL 687EELL DIAMOND PIGEON SKEET 4,785.00
TRAP TOP MONO (Full) 5,055.00
TRAP TOP MONO FMCT 5,105.00
DIAMOND PIGEON SPORTING (12 ga.). 5,310.00
4-BARREL SET 8,405.00

MODEL 687EL GOLD PIGEON FIELD (not shown)

Features game-scene engraving on receiver with gold highlights. Available in 12, 20 gauge (28 ga. and .410 in small frame).

SPECIFICATIONS
Barrels/Chokes: 26" and 28" with Mobilchoke®
Action: Low-profile improved boxlock
Weight: 6.8 lbs. (12 ga.)
Trigger: Single selective with manual safety
Extractors: Auto ejectors
Prices:
MODEL 687EL (12, 20, 28 ga.; 26" or 28" bbl.) . . . $3,670.00
MODEL 687EL SMALL FRAME (28 ga./.410). 3,835.00
MODEL 687EL SPORTING (12 ga. only) 4,470.00

MODEL ULTRALIGHT OVER/UNDER

SPECIFICATIONS
Stock: Select walnut *Features:* Nickel finish receiver w/game scene engraving; black rubber recoil pad; single selective trigger
Price: $1,740.00
Also available:
ULTRALIGHT DELUXE w/matte electroless nickel finish receiver w/gold game scene engraving; walnut stock and forend; light aluminum alloy receiver reinforced w/titanium breech plate
Price: $1,925.00

BERETTA SHOTGUNS

MODEL 686 ONYX

SPECIFICATIONS
Gauges: 12, 20
Chambers: 3" and 3.5"
Barrel Lengths: 26"" and 28"
Chokes: Mobilchoke® screw-in system

Weight: 6 lbs. 12 oz. (12 ga.); 6.2 lbs. (20 ga.)
Stock: American walnut with recoil pad (English stock available)
Features: Automatic ejectors; matte black finish on barrels and receiver to reduce glare
Price:.................................. $1,470.00

PINTAIL

This 12-gauge semiautomatic shotgun with short-recoil operation is available with 24" or 26" barrels and Mobilchoke®. Finish is nonreflective matte on alll exposed wood and metal surfaces; receiver is aluminum alloy.

SPECIFICATIONS
Barrel Lengths: 24", 26"; 24" Slug
Weight: 7.3 lbs.

Stock: Checkered selected hardwood
Sights: Bead front
Price:................................. $780.00
Also Available:
PINTAIL RIFLED SLUG featuring fully rifed barrel w/1 in 28" twist. Upper receiver and barrel permanently joined as one unit.
Price:.................................. $1,000.00

MODEL 1201 FP RIOT

This all-weather semiautomatic shotgun features an adjustable polymer stock and forend with recoil pad. Lightweight, it sports a unique weather-resistant matte black finish to reduce glare, resist corrosion and aid in heat dispersion; short recoil action for light and heavy loads.

SPECIFICATIONS
Gauge: 12 **Chamber:** 3" **Capacity:** 6 rounds   **Choke:** Cylinder (fixed) **Barrel Length:** 18" **Weight:** 6.3 lbs. **Sights:** Blade Front; adjustable rear
Price:.................................. $760.00
w/Tritium Sights 840.00

BERETTA SHOTGUNS

FIELD GRADE SEMIAUTOMATICS

MODEL AL390 SILVER MALLARD

**MODEL AL390 SILVER MALLARD
SYNTHETIC STOCK**

MODEL AL390 CAMO

SPECIFICATIONS

Gauges: 12; Silver Mallard 12 and 20; Youth 20 ga. only; 3" chamber

Chokes: Mobilchoke® tubes; CL (Cylinder choke on Silver Mallard Slug only); fixed chokes available on request

Barrel Lengths: 24", 26", 28", 30" (22" and 24" Silver Mallard Slug only)

Overall Length: 41.7" (22" Slug model only); 44.1" w/24" Youth bbl.; 47.6" w/28" bbl.

Weight: 6.4 lbs. (Youth); 6.8 lbs. (Slug); 7.2-7.5 lbs. (other 12 ga. models)

Features: All models equipped with vent, field-type rib, except Slug model, which has no rib. Silver Mallard is available w/matte, satin finish & cut checkering on stock & forend. Silver Mallard Slug comes w/special rifle sights and shorter barrels. Camo has Advantage camouflage w/eight different earth tones, natural shapes and open areas to produce four patterns in one (limb, leaf, bark, sky)

Prices:

FIELD GRADE MODELS

AL390 SILVER MALLARD (12 or 20 ga.) $860.00

AL390 SILVER MALLARD–MATTE, BLACK SYNTHETIC
   OR SLUG (12 ga. only) 860.00

AL390 GOLD MALLARD (12 and 20 ga.) 1,025.00

AL390 CAMO (12 ga. only) 994.00

AL390 YOUTH (20 ga. only) 860.00

BERETTA SHOTGUNS

MODEL AL390 SPORTING

MODEL AL390 TRAP

SPECIFICATIONS
Gauges: 12 and 20 (Sporting and Gold Sporting; 12 ga. only (Trap and Skeet); 20 ga. only (Youth/Collection); 3" chamber *Chokes:* Mobilchoke® tubes; MC/Fixed on Trap; Fixed on Skeet *Barrel Lengths:* 26" (Youth only)); 26" and 28" (Skeet); 28" and 30" (Sporting, Gold Sporting & Trap); 32" avail. on Trap only *Overall Length:* 47.8" w/28" bbl. *Weight:* 7.6 lbs. (approx.) *Features:* All models equipped with wide vent rib. **Trap** has white front and mid-rib bead sights, Monte Carlo stock, special trap recoil pad. **Skeet** has Skeet stock, interchangeable rubber skeet pad. **Sporting** has slim competition stock, rounded receiver, interchangeable rubber sporting-type recoil pad. **Gold Sporting** has engraved receiver w/gold-filled game scenes, "PB" logo, satin black or silver side panels. **Sport Sporting** collection has multi-colored stock and forend, plus anti-glare matte black finish w/scroll engraving.
Prices: COMPETITION TRAP MODELS
AL39 TRAP (MCT) $900.00

FULL CHOKE 890.00
PORTED (MCT) 1,005.00

COMPETITION SKEET MODELS
AL390 SKEET $890.00
   PORTED 995.00
AL390 SUPER SKEET Semiauto 1,160.00

COMPETITION SPORTING:
AL390 SPORT SPORTING
   Semiauto 12 & 20 ga. $900.00
   PORTED 995.00
AL390 SPORT DIAMOND SPORTING
   Semiauto (12 ga.) 3,865.00
AL390 SPORT SPORTING COLLECTION
   Semiauto (12 ga.). . . . . Price On Request
AL390 GOLD SPORTING. 1,115.00
AL390 YOUTH. 900.00
AL390 YOUTH COLLECTION. TBA

MODEL 470 SILVER HAWK SIDE-BY-SIDE

SPECIFICATIONS
Gauge: 12 and 2 *Chamber:* 3"
Action: Low profile, improved box lock
Choke: IC/IM, M/F *Barrel Length:* 26" and 28" *Weight:* 6.5 lbs. (12 ga.); 5.9 lbs. (20 ga.)
Sights: Metal front bead *Stock:* Select walnut, checkered

Features: Silver satin chrome finish on receiver, trigger guard, forend iron, top lever, trigger, trigger plate and safety/select lever; hand-chased scroll, engraving on receiver, top lever, forend iron and triggerguard; gold inlaid hawk's head on top lever.
Price:. $3,210.00

BROWNING AUTOMATIC SHOTGUNS

GOLD CLASSIC STALKER

**GOLD SPORTING CLAYS
12 GAUGE**

BROWNING GOLD SHOTGUNS have been called the most versatile autoloaders on the market, with a unique gas metering system that lets you shoot light 2.75" shells or heavy loads from 3.5" hulls. A huge assortment of barrels, stocks and sights adapts this shotgun to all upland game, waterfowl and deer hunting situations. There's even a 10-gauge version. The gun's quick pointing qualities and reliability has already made it a favorite of hunters and clay target shooters–a fitting heir to the now-discontinued **BROWNING AUTO 5.**

**GOLD HUNTER, STALKER AND CAMO SEMIAUTOMATIC SHOTGUNS: $772.00
SPORTING CLAYS: $798.00 DEER HUNTER: $839.00 ($909.00 IN MOSSY OAK BREAK UP CAMO)**

SPECIFICATIONS GOLD 12 AND 20

GAUGE	MODEL	BARREL LENGTH	OVERALL LENGTH	AVERAGE WEIGHT	CHOKES AVAILABLE
12	Hunting	30"	50.5"	7 lbs. 9 oz.	Invéctor-Plus
12	Hunting	28"	48.5"	7 lbs. 6 oz.	Invector-Plus
12	Hunting	26"	46.5"	7 lbs. 3 oz.	Invector-Plus
20	Hunting	28"	48.25"	6 lbs. 14 oz.	Invector
20	Hunting	26"	46.25"	6 lbs. 12 oz.	Invector

DEER GUN

SPECIFICATIONS GOLD 10 HUNTING & STALKER: $1,059.00

CHAMBER	BARREL LENGTH	OVERALL LENGTH	AVERAGE WEIGHT	CHOKES
3.5	30"	52"	10 lbs. 13 oz.	Standard Invector
3.5	28"	50"	10 lbs. 10 oz.	Standard Invector
3.5	26"	48"	10 lbs. 7 oz.	Standard Invector

Extra barrels: 24, 26, 28, 30" – 12 gauge 3.5": $356.00, Mossy Oak Camo: $379.00 • 24,26,28, 30" – 12 and 20 gauge 3": $290.00, Mossy Oak Camo:$314.00

BROWNING CITORI SHOTGUNS

CITORI GRADE I HUNTING
12 GAUGE 3.5" MAGNUM

Grade I = Blued steel w/scroll engraving
Grade III = Grayed steel w/light relief **Grade VI** = Blued or grayed w/engraved ringneck pheasants and mallard ducks;
GL (Gran Lightning) = High-grade wood w/satin finish

CITORI PRICES (all Invector-Plus chokes unless noted otherwise)
HUNTING MODELS (w/pistol-grip stock, beavertail forearm, high-gloss finish) 12 ga., 3.5" Mag.,28" & 30" barrels .. **$1,489.00**
Same as above in 12 & 2 ga. w/3" chamber 26", 28", 30" barrels **1,388.00**
SPORTING HUNTER 12 ga., 3.5" Mag., 28 & 36" barrels . **1,595.00**
Same as above in 12 & 20 ga. 3" chamber, 26", 28", 36" barrels **1,500.00**
SATIN HUNTER in 12 ga., 3.5" chamber, 28" barrel **1,420.00**
Same as above w/3" chamber (26" barrel available) . **1,318.00**
WHITE LIGHTNING 12 & 20 ga., Grade I, 3" chamber. . . **1,478.00**

LIGHTNING MODELS (w/classic rounded pistol grip, Lightning-style forearm) Grade I, 12 & 2 ga., 3" chamber 26" & 28" barrels **1,432.00**
Same as above in Grade GL **1,963.00**
Grade III. **2,127.00**
Grade VI **3,095.00**
MICRO LIGHTNING MODEL (20 Ga.) Grade I, 2.75" chamber, 24" barrel. **1,486.00**
SUPERLIGHT MODELS (w/straight-grip stock, slimmed-down Schnabel forearm; 2.75" chamber, 12 or 20 ga.)
Grade I **1,442.00**
Grade III. **2,127.00**
Grade VI **3,095.00**
LIGHTNING MODELS w/Standard Invector chokes (Lightning models only, 28 and .410 ga., 2.75" chamber, 26" & 28" barrels)
Grade I **1,489.00**
Grade GL **2,068.00**
Grade III. **2,377.00**
Grade VI **3,334.00**
Grade I Superlight Feather 12 ga. **1,592.00**
XS 12,20 (28, .410) . . . . **2,011 (2,077.00)**
UPLAND SPECIAL (12 & 20 ga.)
Grade I only, 24" barrel. **1,442.00**

CITORI FIELD MODEL SPECIFICATIONS

GAUGE	MODEL	CHAMBER	BARREL LENGTH	OVERALL LENGTH	AVERAGE WEIGHT	CHOKES AVAILABLE 1	GRADES AVAILABLE
12	Hunter	3.5" Mag.	30"	47"	8 lbs. 10 oz.	Invector-Plus	I
12	Hunter	3.5" Mag.	28"	45"	8 lbs. 9 oz.	Invector-Plus	I
12	Sporting Hunter	3.5" Mag.	30"	47"	8 lbs. 9 oz.	Invector-Plus	I
12	Sporting Hunter	3"	28"	45"	8 lbs. 5 oz.	Invector-Plus	I
12	Hunter	3"	30"	47"	8 lbs. 4 oz.	Invector-Plus	I
12	Hunter	3"	28"	45"	8 lbs. 1 oz.	Invector-Plus	I
12	Hunter	3"	26"	43"	7 lbs. 15 oz.	Invector-Plus	I
12	Sporting Hunter	3"	30"	47"	8 lbs. 5 oz.	Invector-Plus	I
12	Sporting Hunter	3"	28"	45"	8 lbs. 1 oz.	Invector-Plus	I
12	Sporting Hunter	3"	26"	43"	7 lbs. 13 oz.	Invector-Plus	I
12	Lightning	3"	28"	45"	8 lbs. 1 oz.	Invector-Plus	I, GL, III, VI
12	Lightning	3"	26"	43"	7 lbs. 15 oz.	Invector-Plus	I, GL, III, VI
12	White Lightning	3"	28"	45"	8 lbs. 1 oz.	Invector-Plus	I
12	White Lightning	3"	26"	43"	7 lbs. 13 oz.	Invector-Plus	I
12	Superlight	2.75"	28"	45"	6 lbs. 12 oz.	Invector-Plus	I, III, VI
12	Superlight	2.75"	26"	43"	6 lbs. 11 oz.	Invector-Plus	I, III, VI
12	Upland Special	2.75"	24"	41"	6 lbs. 9 oz.	Invector-Plus	I
12	Superlight Feather	2.75"	26"	41"	6 lbs. 6 oz.	Invector-Plus	I
20	Hunter	3"	28"	45"	6 lbs. 12 oz.	Invector-Plus	I
20	Hunter	3"	26"	43"	6 lbs. 10 oz.	Invector-Plus	I
20	Lightning	3"	28"	45"	6 lbs. 14 oz.	Invector-Plus	I, GL, III, VI
20	Lightning	3"	26"	43"	6 lbs. 9 oz.	Invector-Plus	I, GL, III, VI
20	Lightning	3"	24"	41"	6 lbs. 6 oz.	Invector-Plus	I
20	Micro Lightning	2.75"	24"	41"	6 lbs. 3 oz.	Invector-Plus	I
20	Superlight	2.75"	26"	43"	6 lbs. 3 oz.	Invector-Plus	I, III, VI
20	Upland Special	2.75"	24"	41"	6 lbs.	Invector-Plus	I
28	Lightning	2.75"	28"	45"	6 lbs. 11 oz.	Invector	I
28	Lightning	2.75"	26"	43"	6 lbs. 10 oz.	Invector	I, GL, III, VI
28	Superlight	2.75"	26"	43	6 lbs. 10 oz.	Invector	I, III, VI
.410	Lightning	3"	28"	45"	7 lbs.	Invector	I
.410	Lightning	3"	26"	43"	6 lbs. 14 oz.	Invector	I, GL, III, VI
.410	Superlight	3"	28"	45"	6 lbs. 14 oz.	Invector	I
.410	Superlight	3"	26"	43"	6 lbs. 13 oz.	Invector	I, III, VI

1. Full & Modified Choke installed; Improved Cylinder and wrench included. GL=Gran Lightning grade. New XS Models available in all 4 gauges, 28" and 30" barrels; weights from 6 lbs. 7 oz. to 8 lbs. 2 oz.

BROWNING CITORI SHOTGUNS

LIGHT SPORTING MODEL 802ES

Sporting 12 ga. O/U. *Barrel Length:* 28"
Overall Length: 45.5". Invector-Plus stainlless steel choke tubes. *Weight:* 7 lbs. 5 oz.
Price: $1,965.00

CITORI MODEL 425 SPORTING CLAYS

MODELS 425 AND ULTRA SPORTER (Not shown) (all Invector-Plus)

MODEL 425 (12 & 20 Ga.)
Grade I, 28", 30", 32" bbls. $1,855.00
Grade GC (Golden Clays) 3,507.00
For adjustable comb, **add** 210.00

MODEL WSSF 12 Ga. only, 28" barrel, teal wood
or walnut stock 1,855.00
ULTRA SPORTER (12 Ga. only)
Grade I, Blue or Gray, 28", 30", 32" bbls. $1,800.00
Grade GC 28", 30", 32" barrels 3,396.00
For adjustable comb, **add** 210.00
*WSSF = Women's Shooting Sports Foundation

425 & ULTRA SPORTER SPECIFICATIONS

MODEL	CHAMBER	BARREL LENGTH	OVERALL LENGTH	AVERAGE WEIGHT	CHOKES AVAILABLE	GRADES AVAILABLE
425						
12 ga.	2.75"	32"	49.5"	7 lbs. 15 oz.	Invector-Plus	Gr. I, Golden Clays
12 ga.	2.75"	30"	47.5"	7 lbs. 14 oz.	Invector-Plus	Gr. I, Golden Clays
12 ga.	2.75"	28"	45.5"	7 lbs. 13 oz.	Invector-Plus	Gr. I, Golden Clays
20 ga.	2.75"	30"	47.5"	6 lbs. 13 oz.	Invector-Plus	Gr. I, Golden Clays
20 ga.	2.75"	28"	45.5"	6 lbs. 12 oz.	Invector-Plus	Gr. I, Golden Clays
WSSF 12 ga. Paint	2.75"	28"	45.5"	7 lbs. 4 oz.	Invector-Plus	Custom WSSF Exclusive
WSSF 12 ga. Walnut	2.75"	28"	45.5"	7 lbs. 4 oz.	Invector-Plus	Gr. I
Ultra Sporter						
12 ga. Sporter	2.75"	32"	49"	8 lbs. 4 oz.	Invector-Plus	Gr. I, Golden Clays
12 ga. Sporter	2.75"	30"	47"	8 lbs. 2 oz.	Invector-Plus	Gr. I, Golden Clays
12 ga. Sporter	2.75"	28"	45"	8 lbs.	Invector-Plus	Gr. I, Golden Clays
Light Sporting 802 ES						
12 ga. Sporter	2.75"	28"	45"	7 lbs. 5 oz.	Invector-Plus 802 ES Tubes*	Gr. I

*Sporting Clays models: One modified, one Improved Cylinder and one Skeet tube supplied. Other chokes available as accessories. *Choke tubes included with 802 ES (Six tubes total)*

SPECIFICATIONS SPECIAL SPORTING CLAYS, TRAP & SKEET & LIGHTNING SPORTING (prices on following page)

GAUGE	MODEL	CHAMBER	BARREL LENGTH	OVERALL LENGTH	AVERAGE WEIGHT	CHOKES	GRADES AVAILABLE
Special							
12	Sporting Clays	2.75"	32"	49"	8 lbs. 5 oz.	Inv.-Plus	I, Golden Clays
12	Sporting Clays	2.75"	30"	47"	8 lbs. 3 oz.	Inv.-Plus	I, Golden Clays
12	Sporting Clays	2.75"	28"	45"	8 lbs. 1 oz.	Inv.-Plus	I, Golden Clays
12	Conventional Trap	2.75"	32"	49"	8 lbs. 11 oz.	Inv.-Plus	I, III, Golden Clays
12	Monte Carlo Trap	2.75"	32"	49"	8 lbs. 10 oz.	Inv.-Plus	I, III, Golden Clays
12	Skeet	2.75"	30"	47"	8 lbs. 7 oz.	Inv.-Plus	I, III, Golden Clays
12	Skeet	2.75"	30"	47"	8 lbs. 6 oz.	Inv.-Plus	I, III, Golden Clays
12	Skeet	2.75"	28"	45"	8 lbs.	Inv.-Plus	I, III, Golden Clays
12	Skeet	2.75"	26"	43"	7 lbs. 15 oz.	Inv.-Plus	I
20	Skeet	2.75"	28"	45"	7 lbs. 4 oz.	Inv.-Plus	I, III, Golden Clays
20	Skeet	2.75"	26"	43"	7 lbs. 1 oz.	Inv.-Plus	I
28	Skeet	2.75"	28"	45"	6 lbs. 15 oz.	Invector	I, III, Golden Clays
28	Skeet	2.75"	26"	43"	6 lbs. 10 oz.	Invector	I
.410	Skeet	2.5"	28"	45"	7 lbs. 6 oz.	Invector	I, III, Golden Clays
.410	Skeet	2.5"	26"	43	7 lbs. 3 oz.	Invector	I
Lightning Sporting*							
12	Sporting Clays	3"	30"	47"	8 lbs. 8 oz.	Inv.-Pus	I, Golden Clays
12	Sporting Clays	3"	28"	45"	8 lbs. 6 oz.	Inv.-Plus	I, Golden Clays

BROWNING CITORI SHOTGUNS

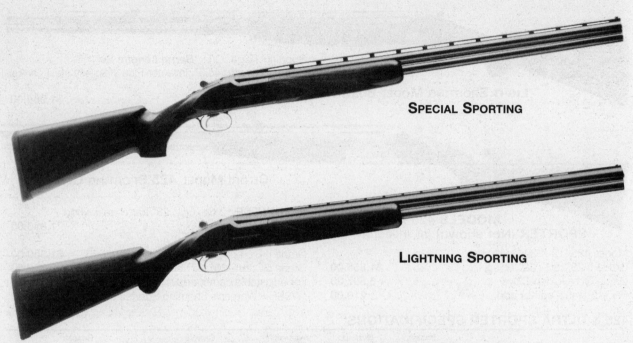

SPECIAL SPORTING

LIGHTNING SPORTING

CITORI SPECIAL SPORTING AND LIGHTNING SPORTING

Many of these lively over/under shotguns are available with ported barrels, adjustable combs, the option of high or low ribs. Prices on request to Browning.

Prices:
SPECIAL SPORTING
Grade I, ported barrels $1,636.00

LIGHTNING SPORTING
Grade I, high rib, ported bbl., 3" **$1,636.00**
Grade I, high rib, adj. comb **1,856.00**
Golden Clays, high rib, adj. comb **3,507.00**
SPORTING HUNTER
Grade I, 3.5" chamber, tapered rib, 12 ga. **$1,595.00**
Grade I, 3" chamber, 12 & 20 ga., tapered rib. . . **1,500.00**

(See previous page for specifications)

CITORI SPECIAL TRAP

SPECIAL TRAP MODELS

Prices:
12 GAUGE, INVECTOR-PLUS, PORTED BARRELS
Grade I, Monte Carlo stock $1,658.00
Grade III, Monte Carlo stock 2,310.00
Golden Clays, Monte Carlo stock. 3,434.00

SPECIAL SKEET MODELS

Prices:
12 & 20 GAUGE, INVECTOR-PLUS, PORTED BARRELS
Grade I, high post rib $1,658.00
Grade III, high post rib 2,310.00
Golden Clays, high post rib 3,434.00
28 GA. AND .410 BORE STD. INVECTOR
Grade I, high post rib $1,627.00
Grade III, high post rib. 2,316.00
Golden Clays, high post rib 3,356.00

BROWNING SHOTGUNS

BT-100 TRAP

BT-100 SINGLE BARREL TRAP

GRADE I, INVECTOR-PLUS

Monte Carlo stock.	$2,095.00
Adjustable comb	2,315.00
Full choke barrel	2,046.00
Full choke barrel, adj. comb	2,266.00
Thumbhole stock	2,384.00
Full choke barrel	2,337.00

LOW LUSTER

Grade I, 12 ga., 32" and 34", adj. trigger pull,
conventional satin stock 1,667.00

STAINLESS, INVECTOR-PLUS

Monte Carlo stock.	2,536.00
Adjustable comb	2,756.00
Full choke barrel	2,487.00
Full choke barrel, adj. comb	2,707.00
Thumbhole stock	2,825.00
Full choke barrel	2,778.00
TRIGGER ASSEMBLY REPLACEMENT	552.00

STOCK DIMENSIONS BT-100

	ADJUSTABLE CONVENTIONAL	THUMBHOLE	MONTE CARLO
Length of Pull	14 3/8"	14 3/8"	14 3/8"
Drop at Comb	Adj.*	1.75"	1 9/16"
Drop at Monte Carlo	—	1.25"	1 7/16"
Drop at Heel	Adj.*	2 1/8"	2"

*Adjustable Drop at Comb and Heel.

BPS 3.5" MAGNUM
(12 Gauge)

BPS SPECIFICATIONS

GAUGE	MODEL	CHAMBER	CAPACITY[2]	BARREL LENGTH	OVERALL LENGTH	AVERAGE WEIGHT	CHOKES AVAILABLE[1]
10 Mag	Hunter & Stalker	3.5"	4	30, 28, 26, 24"	46-52"	9.25-9.5 lbs.	Invector
12, 3.5" Mag	Hunter	3.5"	4	30, 28, 26, 24"	45-51"	7.5-8.5 lbs.	Invector-Plus
12, 3.5" Mag	Stalker	3.5"	4	30, 28, 26, 24"	45-51"	7.5-8.5 lbs.	Invector-Plus
12	Hunter & Stalker	3"	4	30"	50.75"	7 lbs. 12 oz.	Invector-Plus
12	Hunter & Stalker	3"	4	28"	48.75"	7 lbs. 11 oz.	Invector-Plus
12	Hunter & Stalker	3"	4	26"	46.75"	7 lbs. 10 oz.	Invector-Plus
12	Standard Buck Special	3"	4	24"	44.75"	7 lbs. 10 oz.	Slug/Buckshot
12	Upland Special	3"	4	22"	42.5"	7 lbs. 8 oz.	Invector-Plus
12	Hunter & Stalker	3"	4	22"	42.5"	7 lbs. 7 oz.	Invector-Plus
12	Game Gun Turkey Special	3"	4	20.5"	40 7/8"	7 lbs. 7 oz.	Invector
12	Game Gun Deer Special/Rifled	3"	4	20.5"	40 7/8"	7 lbs. 7 oz.	Fully Rifled Barrel
12	Game Gun Deer Special/Smooth	3"	4	20.5"	40 7/8"	7 lbs. 7 oz.	Special Inv./Rifled
12	Game Gun Cantilever Mount	3"	4	20.5"	40 7/8"	7 lbs. 9 oz.	Fully Rifled
20	Hunter	3"	4	28"	48.75"	7 lbs. 1 oz.	Invector-Plus
20	Hunter	3"	4	26"	46.75"	7 lbs.	Invector-Plus
20	Micro	3"	4	22"	41.75"	6 lbs. 11 oz.	Invector-Plus
20	Upland Special	3"	4	22"	42.75"	6 lbs. 12 oz.	Invector-Plus
28	Hunter	2.75"	4	28"	48.75"	7 lbs. 1 oz.	Invector
28	Hunter	2.75"	4	26"	46.75"	7 lbs.	Invector

BPS FIELD MODEL PRICES

SPECIFICATIONS
Prices:

HUNTER 3" chamber 26", 28", 30" barrels	$444.00
STALKER, w/synthetic stock.	444.00
Camo	514.00
GAME GUN Deer Special (20.5" barrel) w/5" rifled slug choke tube	516.00

w/barrel for sabot slugs	548.00
TURKEY SPECIAL w/X-Full Turkey choke tube.	482.00
SMALL GAUGE FIELD (28 gauge, 28" or 26")	444.00
MAGNUM MODELS Hunting & Stalker Grades (10 ga. and 12 ga.) w/3.5" Mag. chamber (26" and 28" barrels).	532.00
w/Mossy Oak camo finish	602.00

CHARLES DALY SHOTGUNS

IMPORTED BY K.B.I., INC.

FIELD OVER/UNDER

FIELD HUNTER OVER/UNDER

SPECIFICATIONS

Gauges: 12, 20, 28 and .410 (3" chambers); 28 ga. (2.75")
Barrel Lengths/Chokes: 28" Mod./Full; 26" IC/Mod.; .410 ga. Full/Full **Weight:** Approx. 7 lb. **Stock:** Checkered walnut pistol-grip and forend **Features:** Blued engraved receiver; chrome-moly steel barrels, gold single-selective trigger, automatic safety, extractors, gold bead front sight

Prices: FIELD HUNTER - 12 or 20 ga. $749.00
28 ga. 809.00
.410 ga. 849.00
FIELD HUNTER AE w/auto-ejectors (not available in 12 or 20 ga.)
28 ga. 889.00
.410 ga. 929.00
FIELD HUNTER AE-MC. Same as Field Hunter but w/5 choke tubes (12 and 20 ga. only) 949.00
SUPERIOR HUNTER AE. Gold single-sellective trigger, gold bead front sight, silver engraved receiver. 28 ga. 1,059.00
.410 ga. 1,099.00
SUPERIOR HUNTER AE-MC. Same as above in 12 and 20 ga. w/5 choke tubes 1,139.00

SUPERIOR SPORTING

SPECIFICATIONS

Gauges: 12 (3" chambers) **Barrel Lengths/Chokes:** 28" & 30" with multi-choke (5 tubes) **Weight:** Approx. 7 lb.

Stock: Checkered walnut pistol-grip buttstock w/semi-beavertail forend **Features:** Silver engraved receiver, ported chrome-moly steel barrels, gold single-selective trigger, automatic safety, auto-ejectors, red bead front sight
Prices: SUPERIOR SPORTING $1,219.00
SUPERIOR TRAP-MC. Same as above
(2.75" chamber) 30" bbl. only 1,259.00

EMPIRE EDL HUNTER

SPECIFICATIONS

Gauges: 12, 20, .410 ga. (3" chambers); 28 ga. (2.75")
Barrel Lengths/Chokes: 26" & 28"–5 multi-choke tubes in 12 & 20 ga.; 26" IC/M in 28 ga.; 26" Full/Full in .410 ga.
Weight: Approx. 7 lb. **Sights:** Red bead front; metal bead center **Stock:** Checkered walnut pistol-grip buttstock

w/semibeavertail forend **Features:** Silver engraved receiver, full sideplate, chrome-moly steel barrels, gold single-selective trigger, automatic safety, auto-ejector, recoil pad
Prices: EMPIRE EDL HUNTER
12 or 20 ga. $1,549.00
28 ga. 1,509.00
.410 ga. 1,509.00
EMPIRE SPORTING. 12 only, w/30" and 28" ported barrels, no metal bead center sight 1,449.00
EMPIRE TRAP-MC. 12 ga. w/30" bbl. (unported) metal bead center sight, recoil pad 1,489.00

DIAMOND COMPETITION

Prices: DIAMOND SPORTING MC-5
12 only, 28" or 30" bbl. $5,629.00
DIAMOND TRAP AE. 6,429.00
DIAMOND TRAP MONO AE-MC. 6,349.00

CHARLES DALY SHOTGUNS

IMPORTED BY K.B.I., INC.

FIELD HUNTER SIDE BY SIDE

SPECIFICATIONS
Gauges: 10, 12, 20 and .410 (3" chambers); 28 ga. (2.75")
Barrel Lengths/Chokes: 32" Mod./Mod.; 30" Mod./Full; 28" Mod./Full; 26" IC/Mod.; .410 ga. Full/Full **Weight:** Approx. 6 lbs.-11.4 lbs. **Stock:** Checkered walnut pistol-grip and forend **Features:** Silver engraved receiver; gold single-selective trigger in 10, 12 and 20 ga.; double trigger in 28 and 410 ga.; automatic safety, extractors, gold bead front sight. Imported from Spain

Prices:

10 ga.	$949.00
12 or 20 ga.	789.00
28 or .410 ga.	829.00

FIELD HUNTER-MC (5 multi-choke tubes)

12 or 20 ga.	899.00

SUPERIOR GRADE (not shown)

SPECIFICATIONS
Gauges: 12 and 20; 3" chambers
Barrel Lengths/Chokes: 28" Mod./Full; 26" IC/Mod.
Weight: Approx. 7 lb. **Stock:** Checkered walnut pistol-grip buttstock and splinter forend
Features: Silver engraved receiver, chrome-lined steel barrels, gold single trigger, automatic safety, extractors, gold bead front sight

Prices:

SUPERIOR HUNTER (12 and 20)	$999.00
28 gauge	1,049.00

EMPIRE HUNTER

Same as above w/hand-checkered stock auto ejectors, game scene engraved receiver	1,299.00

DIAMOND DL HUNTER (not shown)

SPECIFICATIONS
Gauges: 12, 20, .410 ga. (3" chambers; 28 ga. (2.75")
Barrel Lengths/Chokes: 28" Mod./Full; 26" IC/Mod.; 26" Full/Full in .410 ga. **Weight:** Approx. 5-7 lbs.
Stock: Select fancy European walnut, English-styled, beavertail forend, hand-checkered, hand-rubbed oil finish
Features: Fine steel drop-forged action with gas escape valves; fine steel demiblock barrels w/concave rib; selective auto ejectors, hand-detachable double safety sidelocks w/hand-engraved rose and scrollwork; front-hinged trigger, casehardened receiver. Imported from Spain.

Prices:

DIAMOND DL 12 or 20 ga.	$6,749.00
28 or .410 ga.	7,049.00

RIFLE/SHOTGUN COMBINATION GUNS

SPECIFICATIONS
Gauge/Calibers: 12/22 Hornet, 223 Rem., 30-06 Sprgfld.
Barrel Length/Choke: 23.5", shotgun choke IC
Weight: Approx. 7.5 lbs.
Stock: Checkered walnut pistol-grip buttstock and semi-beavertail forend

SUPERIOR COMBINATION

Features: Silver engraved receiver forged and milled from a solid block of high-strength steel; chrome-moly steel barrels, double trigger, extractors, sling swivels, gold bead front sight

Prices:

SUPERIOR COMBINATION	$1,209.00
EMPIRE COMBINATION. Same as above w/deluxe walnut European-style comb/cheekpiece, slim forend	1,729.00

DAKOTA ARMS INC.

DAKOTA ARMS AMERICAN LEGEND
(LIMITED EDITION)

DAKOTA LEGEND SHOTGUNS

PREMIER GRADE
Exhibition Engllish Walnut wood, French Grey Finish, 50% coverage engraving, straight grip, splinter forend, hand rubbed oil finish, double trigger, 27" barrels, game rib with gold bead, selective ejectors, choice of chokes, and Americase.
Price: $12,000.00

LEGEND GRADE
Special Selection English Walnut, 27" barrel, game rib, straight grip, splinter forend, double triggers, round aciton, French Grey finish, selective ejectors, checkered butt, stock oval, full coverage scroll engraving, choice of chokes, gold bead, oak and leather case.
Price: $18,000.00

A.H. FOX SHOTGUNS

DE GRADE ENGRAVED SHOTGUN

CUSTOM BOXLOCKS

SPECIFICATIONS
Gauges: 16, 20, 28 and .410 *Barrel:* Any barrel lengths and chokes; rust blued Chromox or Krupp steel barrels *Weight:* 5 /to 6/lbs. *Stock:* Custom stock dimensions including cast; hand-checkered Turkish Circassian walnut stock and forend with hand-rubbed oil finish; straight grip, full pistol grip (with cap), or semi-pistol grip; splinter, schnabel or beavertail forend; traditional pad, hard rubber plate, checkered, or skeleton butt *Features:* Boxlock action with automatic ejectors; scalloped, rebated and color casehardened receiver; double or Fox single selective trigger; hand-finished and hand-engraved. This is the same gun that was manufactured between 1905 and 1930 by the A.H. Fox Gun Company of Philadelphia, PA, now manufactured in the U.S. by the Connecticut Shotgun Mfg. Co. (New Britain, CT).

Prices:*
CE GRADE	$9,500.00
XE GRADE	11,000.00
DE GRADE	13,500.00
FE GRADE	18,500.00
EXHIBITION GRADE	26,000.00

Grades differ in engraving and inlay, grade of wood and amount of hand finishing needed.

FRANCOTTE SHOTGUNS

CLOSE-UP OF BOXLOCK S6

**"CUSTOM"
BOXLOCKS/SIDELOCKS**

There are no standard Francotte models, since every shotgun is custom made in Belgium to the purchaser's individual specifications. Features and options include Anson & Deeley boxlocks or Auguste Francotte system sidelocks. All guns have custom-fitted stocks. Available are exhibition-grade stocks as well as extensive engraving and gold inlays. U.S. agent for Auguste Francotte of Belgium is Armes de Chasse (see Directory of Manufacturers and Distributors).

SPECIFICATIONS
Gauges: 12, 16, 20, 28, .410; also 24 and 32
Chambers: 2 1/2", 2 3/4" and 3" *Barrel length:* To customer's specifications *Forend:* To customer's specifications *Stock:* Deluxe to exhibition grade; pistol, English or half-pistol grip
Prices: BASIC BOXLOCK $11,090.00
BASIC BOXLOCK (28 & .410 ga.) 15,250.00
BASIC SIDELOCK 27,935.00
BASIC SIDELOCK (28 & .410 ga.) 31,552.00

GARBI SIDELOCK SHOTGUNS

MODEL 100 SIDELOCK

MODEL 101

MODEL M100 SIDELOCK

Like this Model 100 shotgun, all Spanish-made Garbi models are Holland & Holland pattern sidelock ejector guns with chopper lump (demibloc) barrels. They are built to English gun standards with regard to design, weight, balance and proportions, and all have the characteristic "feel" associated with the best London

guns. Garbi's offer fine 24-line hand-checkering, with outstanding quality wood-to-metal and metal-to-metal fit. The Model 100 is available in 12, 16, 20 and 28 gauge and sports Purdey-style fine scroll and rosette engraving, partly done by machine.
Price: MODEL 100 SIDELOCK $4,300.00
Also available: MODEL 101 . . . .$5,550.00
MODEL 103A 6,850.00
MODEL 103B 9,750.00
MODEL 103A ROYAL 10,850.00
MODEL 103B ROYAL 13,750.00

MODEL 200

The Model 200 double is available in 12, 16, 20 or 28 gauge; features Holland-pattern ejector design, heavy-duty locks, heavy proof, Continental-style floral and scroll engraving, walnut stock.
Price: $9,350.00

HARRINGTON & RICHARDSON

SINGLE-BARREL SHOTGUNS

TOPPER MODEL 098

SPECIFICATIONS

Gauges: 12, 20 and .410 (3" chamber); 16 and 28 ga. (2.75" chamber) *Barrel Lengths:* 26" and 28" *Weight:* 5 to 6 lbs. *Action:* Break-open; side lever release; automatic ejection *Stock:* Full pistol grip; American hardwood; black finish with white buttplate spacer *Length Of Pull:* 14.5"
Price: **$117.95**

TOPPER JUNIOR CLASSIC

SPECIFICATIONS

Same specifications as the Standard Topper, but with 22" barrel, hand checkered American black walnut stock and 12.5" pull. *Gauges:* 20, 28, and .410.
Price: **$146.95**

.410 TAMER SHOTGUN

This barreled .410 snake gun features single-shot action, transfer-bar safety and high-impact synthetic stock and forend. Stock has a thumbhole design that sports a full pistol grip and a recessed open side, containing a holder for storing ammo. Forend is modified beavertail configuration. Other features include a matte, electroless nickel finish.
Weight: 5-6 lbs. *Barrel Length:* 20" (3" chamber)
Choke: Full
Price: **$124.95**

ULTRA SLUG HUNTER

Features: 12-gauge 24" barrel, 3" chamber, fully rifled heavy slug barrel (1:35" twist); Monte Carlo stock and forend of American hardwood w/dark walnut stain; matte black receiver; transfer-bar system; scope rail, swivels and sling; ventilated recoil pad.
Price: **$211.95**

Also available:
ULTRA YOUTH SLUG HUNTER. Features 12-gauge barrel blank underbored to 20 gauge and shortened to 22"; factory-mounted Weaver-style scope base; reduced Monte Carlo stock of American hardwood with dark walnut stain; vent recoil pad, sling swivels and black nylon sling.
Price: **$209.95**

HECKLER & KOCH SHOTGUNS

FABARM SERIES

RED LION SEMIAUTOMATIC

CLASSIC LION GRADE I

Prices:

RED LION Semiautomatics 12 ga.	$804.00
GOLD LION Semiautomatic 12 ga.	914.00
FP6 Pump Action 12 ga.	499.00
MAX LION O/U.	1,807.00
BLACK LION COMPETITION 12 & 20 ga.	1,529.00
SILVER LION O/U 12 & 20 ga.	1,146.00
ULTRA MAG LION O/U 12 ga.	1,120.00
SUPER LIGHT LION O/U 12 ga.	1,053.00
CLASSIC LION GRADE II S/S.	2,110.00
GRADE I	1,488.00

SPECIFICATIONS

DESCRIPTION & ARTICLE NUMBER	GAUGE (CHAMBER)	OPERATION	MAGAZINE CAPACITY*	BARREL LENGTH	OVERALL LENGTH	WEIGHT (IN POUNDS)	CHOKE	RECEIVER FINISH	STOCK	SIGHTS
Red Lion #14120	12 (3in)	semi-automatic gas operated	3	24 in.	45.5 in.	7	C,IC,M,IM,F**	matte	gloss walnut	red front bar
Red Lion #16130	12 (3 in.)	semi-automatic gas operated	3	26 in.	47.5 in.	7.1	C,IC,M,IM,F**	matte	gloss walnut	red front bar
Red Lion #18120	12 (3 in.)	semi-automatic gas operated	3	28 in.	49.5 in.	7.2	C,IC,M,IM,F**	matte	gloss walnut	red front bar
Gold Lion #14220	12 (3 in.)	semi-automatic gas operated	3	24 in.	45.5 in.	6.9	C,IC,M,IM,F**	matte	oil finished walnut with olive grip cap	red front bar
Gold Lion #16220	23 (3 in.)	semi-automatic gas operated	3	26 in.	47.5 in.	6	C,IC,M,IM,F**	matte	oil finished walnut with olive grip cap	red front bar
Gold Lion #18220	12 (3 in.)	semi-automatic gas operated	3	28 in.	49.5 in.	7.2	C,IC,M,IM,F**	matte	oil finished walnut with olive grip cap	red front bar
FP6 #40621	12 (3 in.)	pump action	5	20 in.	41.25 in.	6.6	cylinder, barrel threaded for chokes	matte	polymer	blade front
Max Lion #26320	12 (3 in.)	over-and-under	n/a	26 in.	47.5 in.	7.4	C,IC,M,IM,F**	silver	walnut	red front bar
Max Lion #28320	12 (3 in.)	over-and-under	n/a	28 in.	49.5 in.	7.6	C,IC,M,IM,F**	silver	walnut	red front bar
Max Lion #23320	12 (3 in.)	over-and-under	n/a	30 in.	51.5 in.	7.8	C,IC,M,IM,F**	silver	walnut	red front bar
Max Lion 20 Gauge #26300	20 (3 in.)	over-and-under	n/a	26 in.	47.6 in.	6.8	C,IC,M,IM,F**	silver	walnut	red front bar
Max Lion 20 Gauge #28300	20 (3 in.)	over-and-under	n/a	28 in.	49.6 in.	7	C,IC,M,IM,F**	silver	walnut	red front bar
Black Lion Competition #26420	12 (3 in.)	over-and-under	n/a	26 in.	47.5 in.	7	C,IC,M,IM,F**	black	deluxe walnut	red front bar
Black Lion Competition #28420	12 (3 in.)	over-and-under	n/a	28 in.	49.5	7.4	C,IC,M,IM,F**	black	deluxe walnut	red front bar
Black Lion Competition #23420	12 (3 in.)	over-and-under	n/a	30 in.	51.5 in.	7.8	C,IC,M,IM,F**	black	deluxe walnut	red front bar
Black Lion Competition 20 Ga. #26400	20 (3 in.)	over-and-under	n/a	26 in.	47.6 in.	6.8	C,IC,M,IM,F**	black	deluxe walnut	red front bar
Black Lion Competition 20 Ga. #28400	20 (3 in.)	over-and-under	n/a	28 in.	49.6 in.	7	C,IC,M,IM,F**	black	deluxe walnut	red front bar
Silver Lion #26520	12 (3 in.)	over-and-under	n/a	26 in.	47.5 in.	7.2	C,IC,M,IM,F**	silver	walnut	red front bar
Silver Lion #28520	12 (3 in.)	over-and-under	n/a	28 in.	49.5 in.	7.5	C,IC,M,IM,F**	silver	walnut	red front bar
Silver Lion #23520	12 (3 in.)	over-and-under	n/a	30 in.	51.5 in.	7.7	C,IC,M,IM,F**	silver	walnut	red front bar
Silver Lion 20 Gauge #26500	20 (3in.)	over-and-under	n/a	26 in.	47.6 in.	6.8	C,IC,M,IM,F**	silver	walnut	red front bar
Silver Lion 20 Gauge #28500	20 (3 in.)	over-and-under	n/a	28 in.	49.6 in.	7.1	C,IC,M,IM,F**	silver	walnut	red front bar
Ultra Mag Lion #58520	20 (3 in.)	over-and-under	n/a	28 in.	50 in.	7.9	SS-F,SS-M,C,IC,M,IM,F**	silver	black colored walnut	red front bar
Super Light Lion #64520	12 (3 in.)	over-and-under	n/a	24 in.	45.5 in.	6.5	C,IC,M,IM,F**	silver	walnut	red front bar
Classic Lion Grade I #38320	12 (3 in.)	side-by-side	n/a	26 in.	47.6 in.	7	C,IC,M,IM,F**	silver	walnut	red front bar
Classic Lion Grade II #36520	12 (3 in.)	side-by-side	n/a	26 in.	47.6 in.	7.2	C,IC,M,IM,F**	silver	walnut	red front bar

*Magazine capacity given for 2.75 inch shells, size variations among some brands may result in less capacity.
**Cylinder, Improved Cylinder, Modified, Improved Modified, Full, SS-F (Steel Shot-Full) SS-M (Steel Shot-Modified)Specifications & models subject to change without notice.

SHOTGUNS

HECKLER & KOCH SHOTGUNS

FABARM SERIES

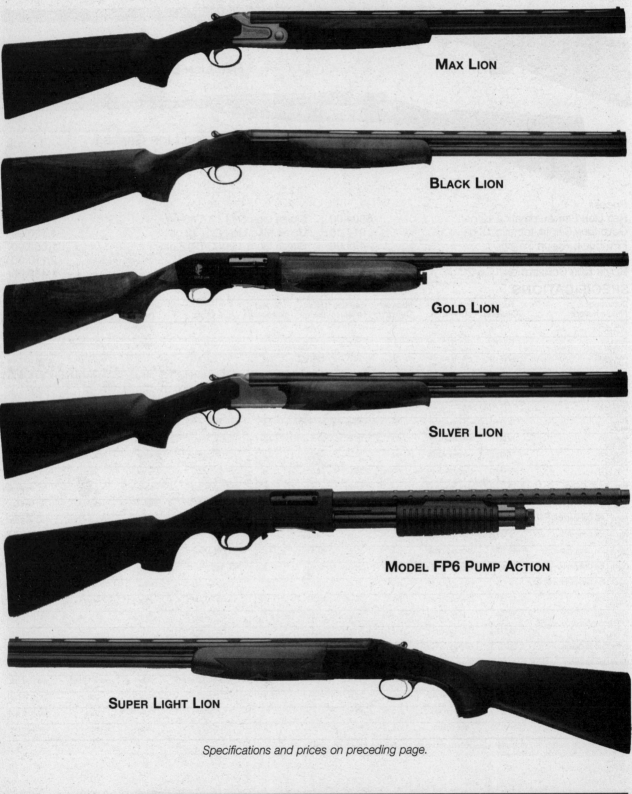

MAX LION

BLACK LION

GOLD LION

SILVER LION

MODEL FP6 PUMP ACTION

SUPER LIGHT LION

Specifications and prices on preceding page.

ITHACA SHOTGUNS

MODEL 37 DEERSLAYER II 12 GA.

SPECIFICATIONS
Gauges: 12 or 20 (3" chamber)
Capacity: 5 rounds
Barrel Lengths: 20" or 25"
Choke: Rifled bore; smooth bore
Weight: 7 lbs.
Stock: Monte Carlo cut-checkered walnut stock and forend
Price: $565.95

CLASSIC 37

SPECIFICATIONS
Features corncob ringtail forearm, sunburst recoil pad, American walnut stock, screw-in choke tubes.
Price: $695.95

MODEL 37 TURKEYSLAYER

SPECIFICATIONS
Gauge: 12
Barrel Lengths: 22" (3" chamber)
Choke/Bore: Turkey Tightshot choke tube
Capacity: 5 rounds
Weight: 7 lbs.
Stock: Monte Carlo
Features: Four camouflage options
Price: $565.95

MODEL 37 ENGLISH VERSION

SPECIFICATIONS
Gauge: 20 (3" chamber)
Barrel Lengths: 24", 26", 28" and 30"
Choke/Bore: 3 choke tubes (Full, Mod., Imp. Cyl.)
Capacity: 5 rounds
Weight: 7 lbs.
Price: $545.95

KRIEGHOFF SHOTGUNS

(See following page for additional Specifications and Prices)

MODEL K-80 SPORTING CLAY

MODEL K-80 TRAP, SKEET, SPORTING CLAY AND LIVE BIRD

Barrels: Made of Boehler steel; free-floating bottom barrel with adjustable point of impact; standard Trap and Live Pigeon ribs are tapered step; standard Skeet, Sporting Clay and International ribs are tapered or parallel flat.

Receivers: Hard satin-nickel finish; casehardened; blue finish available as special order

Triggers: Wide profile, single selective, position adjustable.

Weight: 8 1/2" lbs. (Trap); 8 lbs. (Skeet)

Ejectors: Selective automatic

Sights: White pearl front bead and metal center bead

Stocks: Hand-checkered and epoxy-finished Select European walnut stock and forearm; stocks available in seven different styles and dimensions

Safety: Push button safety located on top tang.

Also available:

SKEET SPECIAL 28" and 30" barrel; tapered flat or 8mm rib; 5 choke tubes.

Price: Standard $7,575.00

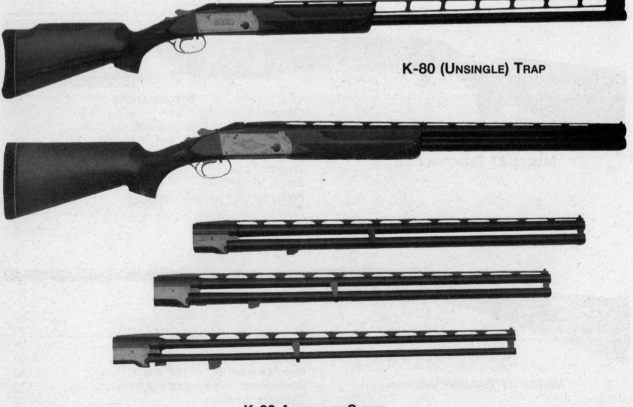

K-80 (UNSINGLE) TRAP

**K-80 AMERICAN SKEET
(4-BARREL SET)**

KRIEGHOFF SHOTGUNS

SPECIFICATIONS AND PRICES MODEL K-80 *(see also preceding page)*

Model	Description	Bbl. Length	Choke	Standard	Bavaria	Danube	Gold Target	Extra Barrels
TRAP	Over & Under	30"/32"	IM/F	$7,375.00	$12,525.00	$23,625.00	$27,170.00	$2,900.00
		30"/32"	CT/CT	8,025.00	13,175.00	24,275.00	27,820.00	3,550.00
	Unsingle	32"/34"	Full	7,950.00	13,100.00	24,200.00	27,745.00	3,575.00
	Combo	30" + 34"	IM/F&F	10,475.00	15,625.00	26,725.00	30,270.00	
	(Top Single)	32" + 34"	CT/CT&CT	11,550.00	16,700.00	27,800.00	31,345.00	
		30" + 32"						
	Combo	30" + 34"	IM/F&F	9,975.00	15,125.00	26,225.00	29,770.00	2,950.00
	(Unsingle)							
		32" + 34"	CT/CT&CT	11,050.00	16,200.00	27,300.00	30,845.00	3,375.00

Optional Features:
Screw-in chokes (Top or Unsingle)   **$425.00**
Single factory release   425.00
Double factory release   **750.00**

Model	Description	Bbl. Length	Choke	Standard	Bavaria	Danube	Gold Target	Extra Barrels
SKEET	4-Barrel Set	28"/12 ga.	Tula					$2,990.00
		28"/20 ga.	Skeet					2,880.00
		28"/28 ga.	Skeet	$16,950.00	$22,100.00	$33,200.00	$36,745.00	2,990.00
		28"/.410 ga.	Skeet					2,880.00
	2-Barrel Set	28"/12 ga.	Tula	11,840.00	16,990.00	28,090.00	31,635.00	4,150.00
	Lightweight	28" + 30"/12 ga.	Skeet	6,900.00	N/A	N/A	N/A	2,650.00
	1-Barrel Set	28"	Skeet	8,825.00	13,975.00	25,075.00	28,620.00	4,150.00
	International	28"/12 ga.	Tula	7,825.00	12,975.00	24,075.00	27,620.00	2,990.00
	Skeet Special			7,575.00	12,725.00	23,825.00	27,370.00	3,300.00
SPORTING CLAYS	Over/Under w/screw-in tubes (5)	28" + 30" + 32"/ 12 ga. 30" Semi-Light	Tubes IC/ICTF	$8,150.00	$13,300.00	$24,400.00	$27,945.00	$2,900.00

*Optional engravings: Super Scroll – **$1,995.00**; Gold Super Scroll – **$4,450.00**; Parcours – **$2,100.00**; Parcours Special – **$3,950.00***

MODEL KS-5

The KS-5 is a single barrel trap gun made by KRIEGHOFF, Ulm/Germany and marketed by Krieghoff International. Standard specifications include: 12 gauge, 2 3/4" chamber, ventilated tapered step rip, and a casehardened receiver (satin gray finished in electroless nickel). The KS-5 features an adjustable point of impact from 50/50 to 70/30 by means of different optional fronthangers. Screw-in chokes and factory adjustable comb stocks are available options. An adjustable rib (AR) and comb stock (ADJ) are standard features.

The KS-5 is available with pull trigger or optional factory release trigger, adjustable externally for poundage. The KS-5 can be converted to release by the installation of the release parts. To assure consistency and proper functioning, release triggers are installed ONLY by Krieghoff International. Release parts are NOT available separately. These shotguns are available in Standard grade only. Engraved models can be special ordered.

Prices:
KS-5 32" or 34" barrel, Full choke, case $3,695.00
KS-5 SPECIAL 32" or 34" barrel, Full choke,
   AR ADJ, cased 4,695.00
Options available:
KS-5 SCREW-IN CHOKES (M, IM, F), add to
   base price $425.00
KS-5 FACTORY ADJ (adjustable comb stock),
   add to base price $395.00
Other Features and Accessories:
KS-5 REGULAR BARREL $2,100.00
KS-5 SPECIAL BARREL (F) 2,750.00
KS-5 SCREW-IN CHOKE BARREL 2,525.00
KS-5 SPECIAL SCREW-IN CHOKE BARREL 3,175.00
KS-5 FACTORY ADJUSTABLE STOCK 1,145.00
KS-5 STOCK 750.00
KS-5 FOREARM 290.00
KS-5 RELEASE TRIGGER (INSTALLED) 295.00
KS-5 FRONTHANGER 70.00
KL-5 ALUMINUM CASE 425.00
KS-5 INDIVIDUAL CHOKE TUBES 75.00

MARLIN SHOTGUNS

MODEL 512 SLUGMASTER

SPECIFICATIONS
Gauge: 12 (up to 3" shells)
Capacity: 2-shot box magazine (+1 in chamber)
Action: Bolt action; thumb safety; red cocking indicator
Barrel Length: 21" rifled (1:28" right-hand twist)
Overall Length: 41.75" *Weight:* 8 lbs. (w/o scope and mount)

Sights: Adjustable folding semi-buckhorn rear; ramp front with brass bead and removable cutaway Wide-Sacn® hood; receiver drilled and tapped for scope mount
Stock: Walnut finished, press-checkered Maine birch w/pistol grip and Mar-Shield® finish, swivel studs, vent, recoil pad
Price: $361.00

MODEL 50DL

SPECIFICATIONS
Gauge: 12 ga. (2.75" or 3" chamber)
Capacity: 2-shot clip *Action:* Bolt action
Barrel Length: 28" (Modified choke)
Overall Length: 48.75" *Weight:* 7.5 lbs.

Sights: Brass bead front; U-groove rear
Stock: Black synthetic w/ventilated rubber recoil pad
Features: Thumb safety; red cocking indicator; swivel studs
Price: **$330.00**
   Goose Gun (36" full-choke barrel, 8 pounds). . . . **385.00**

MODEL 512P
AND PORTED BARREL

MODEL 512P
SPECIFICATIONS
Guage: 12 (up to 3" shells)
Capacity: 2-shot box magazine (+1 in chamber)
Action: Bolt action; thumb safety; red cocking indicator
Barrel Length: 21" rifled (1:28" right-hand twist) and ported
Overall Length: 41.75"
Weight: 8 lbs. (w/o scope and mount)

Sights: Adjustable rear, ramp front fire sights with high-visibility fiber-optic inserts and cutaway Wide-Scan® hood; receiver drilled and tapped for scope mount
Stock: Black fiberglass-filled synthetic w/molded-in checkering and padded black nylon sling
Prices: $366.00

MAROCCHI SHOTGUNS

CONQUISTA
(12 GAUGE, 2.75" CHAMBERS)

CONQUISTA SPORTING CLAYS GRADE III

The Marocchi shotguns listed below all feature 10mm concave ventilated upper rib; Classic middle rib (Classic Doubles has vent middle rib); competition white front sight and automatic extractors/ejectors.

MODELS	PRICES
CONQUISTA SPORTING	$1,995.00-3,599.00
SPORTING LEFT	2,120.00-3,995.00
LADY SPORT	2,120.00-2,300.00
CONQUISTA TRAP	1,995.00-3,599.00
CONQUISTA SKEET	1,995.00-3,599.00
CLASSIC DOUBLES	1,598.00

SPECIFICATIONS CONQUISTA SHOTGUNS (all 12 Gauge)

	CONQUISTA SPORTING	SPORTING LEFT	LADY SPORT	CONQUISTA TRAP	CONQUISTA SKEET	CLASSIC DOUBLES
BARRELS						
Gauge	12	12	12	12	12	12
Chamber	2 3/4"	2 3/4"	2 3/4"	2 3/4"	2 3/4"	2 3/4"
Barrel Length	28",30",32"	28",30",32"	28",30"	29",30"	28	30"
Chokes	Contrechokes	Contrechokes	Contrechokes	Full/Full	Skeet/Skeet	Contre Plus
TRIGGER						
Trigger type	Instajust Selective	Instajust Selective	Instajust Selective	Instajust	Instajust Selective	Instajust Selective
Trigger Pull (Weight)	3.5 - 4.0 lb.s	3.5 - 4.0 lb.s	3.5 - 4.0 lb.s	3.5 - 4.0 lb.s	3.5 - 4.0 lb.s	3.5 - 4.0 lb.s
Trigger Pull (Length)	14 1/2" - 14 7/8"	14 1/2" - 14 7/8"	13 7/8" - 14 1/4"	14 1/2" - 14 7/8"	14 1/2" - 14 7/8"	14 1/4" - 14 5/8"
STOCK						
Drop at comb	1 7/16"	1 7/16"	1 11/32"	1 9/32"	1 1/2"	1 3/8"
Drop at heel	2 3/16"	2 3/16"	2 9/32"	1 11/16"	2 3/16"	2 1/8"
Cast at heel	3/16" Off	3/16" Off	3/16" Off	3/16" Off	3/16" Off	N/A
Cast at toe	3/8" Off	3/8" On	3/8" Off	5/16" Off	3/16" Off	N/A
Stock			Select Walnut			
Checkering	20 lines/inch	20 lines/inch	20 lines/inch	20 lines/inch	20 lines/inch	18 lines/inch
OVERALL						
Length Overall	45" - 45"	45" - 49"	44 3/8"-46 3/8"	47" - 49"	45"	47"
Weight Approx.*	7 7/8 lbs.	7 7/8 lbs.	71/2 lbs.	8 1/4 lbs.	7 3/4 lbs.	8 1/8 lbs.

MERKEL SHOTGUNS

OVER/UNDER SHOTGUNS

Merkel over-and-unders were the first hunting guns with barrels arranged one above the other, and they have since proved to be able competitors of the side-by-side gun. Merkel superiority lies in the following details:

- Available in 12, 16 and 20 gauge (28 ga. in Model 201E with 26 ¾" barrel)
- Lightweight (6.4 to 7.28 lbs.)
- The high, narrow forend protects the shooter's hand from the barrel in hot or cold climates
- The forend is narrow and therefore lies snugly in the hand to permit easy and positive swinging
- The slim barrel line provides an unobstructed field of view and thus permits rapid aiming and shooting
- The over-and-under barrel arrangement gives straight-line recoil, eliminating the torque and lateral deflection of side-by-sides

MODEL 2001EL

MODEL 303EL SIDELOCK

MERKEL OVER/UNDER SHOTGUN

SPECIFICATIONS
Gauges: 12, 16, 20, 28
Barrel Lengths: 26.75" and 28"
Weight: 6.4 to 7.28 lbs.
Stock: English or pistol grip in European walnut
Features: All models include three-piece forearm, automatic ejectors, Kersten double crossbolt lock, Blitz action and single selective or double triggers.
Prices:
MODEL 2001EL
  12, 20, 28 . . . . $6,495.00
  2001EL Sporter 6,495.00

MODEL 2000EL Kersten double cross-bolt lock; scroll engraved silver-grey receiver; modified Anson & Deeley box action; ejectors; single or double triggers, luxury grade wood; pistol grip or English-style stock.
  12 ga., 20 . . . . **5,195.00**
  2000EL Sporter **5,195.00**
MODEL 2002EL Same features as Model 2000EL but with hunting scenes w/arabesque engraving
  12 ga. 28"; 20 ga. and 28 ga., 26.75" **9,995.00**
SIDELOCKS
MODEL 303 Double trigger, auto ejectors, straight or pistol grip. 12, 20, 28 . . . . **19,995.00**

MODEL 2002EL

MERKEL SHOTGUNS

SIDE-BY-SIDE SHOTGUNS

MODEL 47E BOXLOCK

MODEL 147EL BOXLOCK

SPECIFICATIONS
Gauges: 12 and 20 (28 ga. in Models 147E and 147S)
Barrel Lengths: 26" and 28" (25.5" in Models 47S and 147S)
Weight: 6-7 lbs. *Stock:* English or pistol grip in European walnut *Features:* Models 47E and 147E are boxlocks; Models 47S and 147S are sidelocks. All guns have cold hammer-forged barrels, double triggers, double lugs and Greener crossbolt locking systems and automatic ejectors.
Prices:
MODEL 47E (Holland & Holland ejectors) **$2,695.00**
MODEL 122 (H&H ejectors, engraved
   hunting scenes **4,495.00**

MODEL 147E (engraved hunting scenes)
   12, 16 & 20 ga. **3,395.00**
   28 ga. **3,695.00**
MODEL 147EL
   12, 16 & 20 ga. **4,195.00**
   28 ga. **4,495.00**
MODEL 47SL SIDELOCK (H&H ejectors) **5,395.00**
MODEL 147SL SIDELOCK 12, 16, 20 & 28 ga. **6,695.00**
MODEL 147SSL **7,995.00**
MODEL 247S
   (English-style engraving) **6,995.00**
MODEL 447SL **8,995.00**

MODEL 147SL SIDE-BY-SIDE

MODEL 247SL SIDELOCK

MOSSBERG PUMP SHOTGUNS

MODEL 500 SPORTING

All Mossberg Model 500 pump-action shotguns feature 3" chambers, Milspec tough, lightweight alloy receivers with "top thumb safety." Standard models includes 6-shot capacity with 2 3/4" shells, cut-checkered stock, Quiet Carry forend, gold trigger, engraved receiver, blued Woodland Camo or Marinecote metal finish and the largest selection of accessory barrels. Ten-year limited warranty.

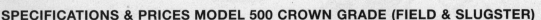

MODEL 500 SPORTING

SPECIFICATIONS & PRICES MODEL 500 CROWN GRADE (FIELD & SLUGSTER)

Ga.	Stock #	Bb;/ Length	Barrel Type	Sights	Chokes	Stock	Length O/A	Wt.	Q.D. Studs	Notes	Prices
12	54220	28"	Vent rib, ported	2 Beads	Accu-Choke	Walnut Finish	48"	7.2		IC, Mod. & Full Tubes	$321.00
20	54132	Bantam 22"	Vent Rib	2 Beads	Accu-Choke	Walnut Finish	42"	6.9		Mod. Tube Only, Bantam Stock	321.00
20	54136	26"	Vent Rib	2 Beads	Accu-Choke	Walnut Finish	46"	7.0		IC, Mod. & Full Tubes	321.00
.410	50112	Bantam 24"	Vent Rib	2 Beads	Full	Synthetic	43"	6.8		Fixed Choke, Bantam Stock	321.00
.410	58104	24"	Vent Rib	2 Beads	Full	Walnut Finish	44"	6.8		Fixed Choke	321.00
12	54232	24"	Trophy Slugster™ Ported	Scop Mount	Rifled Bore	Walnut Finish	44"	7.3	Y	Dual-Comb™ Stock	380.00
12	54244	24"	Slugster, ported	Rifle	Rifled Bore	Walnut Finish	44"	7.0	Y		351.00
12	54844	24"	Slugster, ported	Rifle	Rifled Bore	Walnut Finish	44"	7.0	Y		380.00
20	54233	24"	Trophy Slugster™ Ported	Scope[e Mount	Rifled Bore	Walnut Finish	44"	s6.9	Y	Dual-Comb™ Stock	380.00
20	58252	Bantam 24"	Slugster	Rifle	Rifled Bore	Walnut Finish	44"	s6.9	Y	Bantam Stock	351.00

SPECIFICATIONS MODEL 500 COMBOS

12	54243	28" 24"	Vent rib, ported Trophy Slugster™ ported	2 Beads Scope Mount	Accu-Choke Rifled Bore	Walnut Finish	48"	7.2	Y	IC, Mod. & Full Tubes Dual-Comb™ Stock	438.00
12	54264	24"	Vent rib, ported Slugster, ported	2 Beads Rifle	Accu-Choke Rifled Bore	Walnut Finish	48"	7.2	Y	IC, Mod. & Full Tubes	421.00
20	54282	26" 24"	Vent Rib Slugster, ported	2 Beads Rifle	Accu-Choke Rifled Bore	Walnut Finish	46"	7.0	Y	IC, Mod. & Full Tubes	405.00
12	54169	28" 18.5"	Vent rib, ported Plain	2 Beads Bead	Accu-Choke Cyl. Bore	Walnut Finish	48"	7.2		IC, Mod. & Full Tube Pistol Grip Kit	370.00
20	54188	22" 24"	Vent Rib Slugster, ported	2 Beads Rifle	Accu-Choke Rifled Bore	Walnut Finish	42"	7.0		IC, Mod. & Full Tubes Bantam Stock & Forearm	398.00

Also available: #54158, same as #54264 but w/o Q.D. studs. $385.00

SPECIFICATIONS 500/590 MARINER & 500 SPECIAL PURPOSE

Gauge	Barrel Length	Sight	Stock #	Finish	Stock	Capacity	Overall Length	Weight	Notes	Price
MODEL 500/590 MARINER™ (CYLINDER BORE BARRELS)										
12	18.5"	Bead	50273	Marinecote™	Synthetic	6	38.5"	6.8	Includes Pistol Grip	$424.00
12	20"	Bead	50299	Marinecote™	Synthetic	9	40"	7.0	Includes Pistol Grip	438.00
MODEL 500 SPECIAL PURPOSE (CYLINDER BORE BARRELS) PERSUADER/CRUISER										
12	18.5"	Bead	50411	Blue	Synthetic	6	38.5"	6.8	Includes Pistol Grip	290.00
12	18.5"	Bead	50440	Blue	Pistol Grip	6	28"	5.6	Includes Heat Shield	290.00
20	18.5"	Bead	50452	Blue	Synthetic	6	38.5"	6.8	Includes Pistol Grip	289.00
20	18.5"	Bead	50450	Blue	Pistol Grip	6	28"	5.6		282.00
.410	18.5"	Bead	50455	Blue	Pistol Grip	6	28"	5.3		289.00
12	20"	Bead	50579	Blue	Synthetic	8	40"	7.0	Includes Pistol Grip	290.00
12	20"	Bead	50580	Blue	Pistol Grip	8	40"	7.0		290.00

MOSSBERG PUMP SHOTGUNS

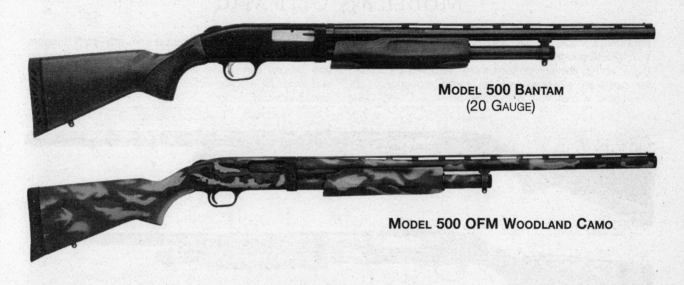

MODEL 500 BANTAM
(20 GAUGE)

MODEL 500 OFM WOODLAND CAMO

SPECIFICATIONS MODEL 500 WOODLAND CAMO (6-SHOT)

12	52193	28"	Vent rib, ported	2 Beads	Accu-Choke	Synthetic	48"	7.2	Y	IC, Mod. & Full Tubes	$346.00
	Turkey			Fiber optic	XX						
12	52195	24"	Vent Rib, Ported	sights	Full Choke	Synthetic					361.00
	Bantam Turkey				X						
20	58235	22"	Vent Rib		Full Choke	Synthetic					361.00

MODEL 500 SPECIAL HUNTER

| 12 | 56420 | 28" | Vent Rib, Ported | | Accu-Choke | Synthetic | | | | | $314.00 |
| 20 | 56436 | 26" | Vent Rib | | Accu-Choke | Synthetic | | | | | 314.00 |

SPECIFICATIONS MODELS 590 SPECIAL PURPOSE, 500/590 GHOST RING™, AND HS 410

GAUGE	BARREL LENGTH	SIGHT	STOCK #	FINISH	STOCK	CAPACITY	OVERALL LENGTH	WEIGHT	NOTES	PRICE
MODEL 590 SPECIAL PURPOSE (CYLINDER BORE BARRELS)										
12	20"	Bead	50645	Blue	Synthetic	9	40"	7.2	w/Acc. Lug & Heat Shield	351.00
12	20"	Bead	50660	Parkerized	Synthetic	9	40"	7.2	w/Acc. Lug & Heat Shield	405.00
12	20"	Bead	50665	Parkerized	Speed Feed	9	40"	7.2	w/Acc. Lug & Heat Shield	439.00
MODEL 500/590 GHOST RING™ (CYLINDER BORE BARRELS)										
12	18.5"	Ghost Ring™	50402	Blue	Synthetic	6	38.5"	6.8		$343.00
12	18.5"	Ghost Ring™	50517	Parkerized	Synthetic	6	38.5"	6.8		398.00
12	20"	Ghost Ring™	50663	Parkerized	Synthetic	9	40"	7.2	w/Acc. Lug	460.00
12	20"	Ghost Ring™	50668	Parkerized	Speed Feed	9	40"	7.2	w/Acc. Lug	495.00
HS 410 HOME SECURITY (SPREADER CHOKE)										
.410	18.5"	Bead	50359	Blue	Synthetic	6	39.5"	6.6	Includes Vertical Foregrip	$303.00

SHOTGUNS

MOSSBERG PUMP SHOTGUNS

MODEL 835 ULTI-MAG

Mossberg's Model 835 Ulti-Mag pump action shotgun has a 3 1/2" 12-gauge chamber but can also handle standard 2 3/4" and 3" shells. Field barrels are overbored and ported for optimum patterns and felt recoil reduction. Cut-checkered walnut and walnut-finished stocks and Quiet Carry™ forearms are standard, as are gold triggers and engraved receivers. Camo models are drilled and tapped for scope and feature detachable swivels and sling. All models include a Cablelock™ and 10-year limited warranty.

MODEL 835 ULTI-MAG

MODEL 835 ULTI-MAG COMBO

SPECIFICATIONS AND PRICES MODEL 835 ULTI-MAG (12 GAUGE, 6 SHOT)

GA	STOCK NO.	BARREL LENGTH	TYPE	SIGHTS	CHOKE	FINISH	STOCK	O.A. LENGTH	W.	STUDS	NOTES	PRICE
ULTI-MAG™ 835 CROWN GRADE												
12	68220	28"	Vent Rib, Ported	2 Beads	Accu-Mag	Blue	Walnut Finish	48.5"	7.7		Mod. Tube Only	$344.00
12	68225	24"	Vent Rib, Ported	2 Beads	Accu-Mag	Matte	Walnut Finish	44.5"	7.3		X-Full Tube	360.00
12	68244	28"	Vent Rib, Ported	2 Beads	Accu-Mag	Blue	Walnut	48.5"	7.7		Mod. Tube only	461.00
		24"	Trophy Slugster™ Ported	Scope Mount	Rifled Bore						Dual-Comb™ Stock	
12	68223	28"	Vent Rib, Ported	2 Beads	Accu-Mag	Blue	Walnut	48.5"	7.7		Mod. Tube only	461.00
		24"	Slugster, Ported	Rifle	Rifled Bore							

GA	STOCK NO.	BARREL LENGTH	TYPE	CHOKE	FINISH	STOCK	PRICE
CAMO							
12	62040-6	24"	Vent Rib, Ported, Fiber Optic Sights	Ulti-Full Only	Rt. X-Tra Brown	Synthetic	492.00
12	62439-8	24"	Vent Rib, Ported, Fiber Optic Sights	Ulti-Full Only	M.O. Shadow Branch	Synthetic	492.00
12	68230-5	24"	Vent Rib, Ported	Ulti-Full Only	Woodlands	Synthetic	380.00
12	68143-8	24"	Combo, Vent Rib, Ported	Ulti-Full Only	Woodlands	Dual Comb®	490.00
		24"	Integral Scope Base, Ported	Fully Rifled Bore	Woodlands		
12	62445-9	28"	Vent Rib, Ported	Hunter Set	M.O. Shadow Grass	Synthetic	547.00
12	68231-2	24"	Vent Rib, Ported, Fiber Optic Sights	Ulti-Full Only	Woodlands	Synthetic	407.00
12	68235-0	28"	Vent Rib, Ported	Mod Only	Woodlands	Synthetic	380.00
12	68243-5	24"	Combo, VR, Ported, Fiber Optic Sights	Ulti-Full Only	Woodlands	Synthetic	537.00
12		24"	Fiber Optic Rifle Sights, Ported	Fully Rifled Bore	Woodlands		
MODEL 835® SPECIAL HUNTER™							
12	67116-3	26"	Vent Rib, Ported	Mod Only	Parkerized	Synthetic (Black)	345.00
12	66720-3	28"	Vent Rib, Ported	Mod Only	Parkerized	Synthetic (Black)	345.00

MOSSBERG SHOTGUNS

MODEL 9200 w/VENT RIB

SPECIFICATIONS AND PRICES MODEL 9200 (12 Gauge, 5 Shot)

Ga	Stock No.	Bbl. Length	Barrel Type	Sights	Choke	Finish	Stock	Length O.A.	Wt.	Q.D. Studs	Notes	Prices
MODEL 9200 CROWN GRADE												
12	49420	28"	Vent Rib, Ported	2 Beads	Accu-Choke	Blue	Walnut	48"	7.7		IC, Mod. & Full Tubes	$550.00
12	49435	22"	Vent Rib	2 Beads	Accu-Choke	Blue	Walnut	42"	7.2		IC/Mod., Full Bantam	550.00
12	49404	26"	Vent Rib		Accu-Choke & Skeet	Blue	Walnut					588.00

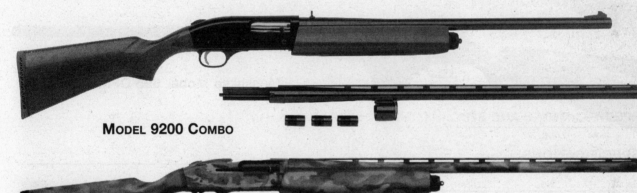

MODEL 9200 COMBO

MODEL 9200 OFM WOODLAND CAMO

MODEL 9200 CAM

Ga	Stock No.	Bbl. Length	Barrel Type	Sights	Choke	Finish	Stock	Length O.A.	Wt.	Q.D. Studs	Notes	Prices
12	49491	28"	Vent Rib	2 Beads	Accu-Choke	OFM Woodland	Synthetic	48"	7.7	Y	IC, Mod. & Full Tubes	$531.00
12		28"	Vent Rib	2 Beads	Accu-Choke	OFM Woodland	Synthetic	48"	7.7	Y	IC, Mod. & Full Tubes	613.00
	49466	24"	Slugster	Rifle	Rifle Bore	OFM Woodland						
12	49443	28"	Vent Rib	2 Beads Scope	Accu-Choke	Blued	Walnut	48"	7.7		IC, Mod. & Full Tubes	644.00
		24"	Trophy Slugster™	Mount	Rifled Bore						Dual-Comb™ Stock	
12	49464	28"	Vent Rib	2 Beads	Accu-Choke	Blued	Walnut	48"	7.7		IC, Mod., & Full Tubes	624.00
		24"	Slugster	Rifle	Rifled Bore							
12	Turkey			Fiber		OFM						515.00
	49431	24"	Vent Rib	Optic	XX-Full	Woodland	Synthetic					
12	Turkey			Fiber		Mossy						628.00
	49439	24"	Vent Rib	Optic	XX-Full	Oak	Synthetic					
MODEL 9200 SPECIAL HUNTER												
12	46420	28"	Vent Rib		Accu-Choke	Matte	Syn. Black					$470.00
MODEL 9200 JUNGLE GUN AUTOLOADER												
12	49047	18.5"	Plain, w/ bead sight		Cyc. bore		Synthetic					$674.00

MOSSBERG SHOTGUNS

MODEL 695 BOLT ACTION

The 3-inch chambered 12-gauge Model 695 bolt-action shotgun features a 22-inch barrel and rugged synthetic stock. This combination delivers the fast handling and fine balance of a classic sporting rifle. Every Model 695 comes with a two-round detachable magazine and Weaver-style scope bases to give hunters the advantage of today's specialized slug and turkey optics. Mossberg's fully rifled slug barrels are specially "ported" to help soften the recoil and reduce muzzle jump. Mossberg's pioneering involvement with turkey hunting has generated the development of the special Extra-full Accu-Choke Tube. The Model 695 Turkey Gun provides the precise pattern placement to make the most of this remarkably tight patterning choke tube. Non-rotating dual claw extractors ensure reliable ejection and feeding. Ten-year limited warranty.

MOSSBERG MODEL 695 BOLT ACTION

MOSSBERG MODEL 695 OFM CAMO

SPECIFICATIONS

Gauge	Model No.	Barrel Length	Barrel Type	Sights	Finish	Stock	Choke	Price
12	59001	22"	Rifled Ported	Rifle	Matte	Black Synthetic	Cyl. Bore	$329.00
12	59802	22"	Rifled Ported	Rifle	Matte	Synthetic	Cyl. Bore	351.00
12	59011	22"	Rifled Ported	Rifle	Matte	Black Synthetic	Cyl. Bore	460.00

*Includes Bushnell 1.5X-4.5X scope and Protecto case

MOSSBERG LINE LAUNCHER

The line Launcher (20" barrel) is the first shotgun devoted to rescue and personal safety. It provides an early self-contained rescue opportunity for boaters, police and fire departments, salvage operations or whenever an extra-long throw of line is the safest alternative. This shotgun used a 12-gauge blank cartridge to propel a convertible projectile with a line attached. With a floating head attached, the projectile will travel 250 to 275 feet. Removing the floating head increases the projectile range to approx. 700 feet.

Prices: $926.00
LAUNCHER KIT 617.00

NEW ENGLAND ARMS FAIR

(FABRICA ARMI DI ISIDORO RIZZINI)

NEW ENGLAND ARMS FAIR *(Fabrica Armi di Isidoro Rizzini)* shotguns: Boxlock, fullly chrome-lined monoblock barrels with vent ribs, choke tubes standard on 12, 16, 20 gauge guns (fixed chokes on 28 and .410), hand-checkered Turkish walnut, single selective triggers, automatic safety and ejectors, straight or semi-pistol grip,

custom options available.
Prices:

M500	$2,250.00
M600	2,995.00
M702	3,995.00
M900	3,995.00

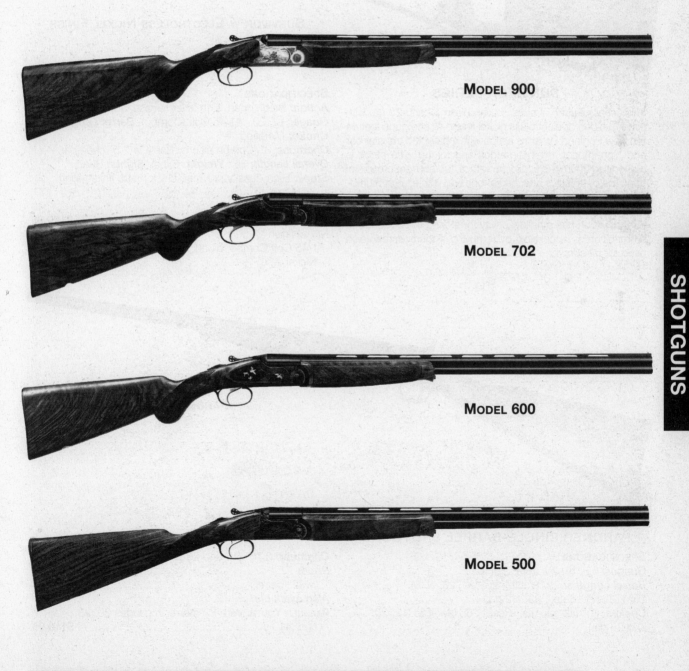

MODEL 900

MODEL 702

MODEL 600

MODEL 500

NEW ENGLAND FIREARMS

SURVIVOR w/ELECTROLESS NICKEL FINISH

SURVIVOR SERIES

This series of survival arms is available in 12 and 20 ga. with either a blued or electroless nickel finish. All shotguns feature the New England Firearms action with a patented transfer bar and high-impact, synthetic stock and forend. The stock is a modified thumbhole design with a full and secure pistol grip. The buttplate is attached at one end with a large thumbscrew for access to a large storage compartment holding a wide variety of survival gear or extra ammunition. The forend, which has a hollow cavity for storing three rounds of ammunition, is accessible by removing a thumbscrew (also used for takedown).

SPECIFICATIONS
Action: Break open, side-lever release, automatic ejection
Guage: 12, 20, .41/45 Colt (Combo) **Barrel Length:** 22"
Choke: Modified
Chamber: 3" (Combo also available w/2.5" chamber)
Overall Length: 36" **Weight:** 6 lbs. **Sights:** Bead
Stock: High-density polymer, black matte finish, sling swivels
Prices:
Blued finish $129.95
Nickel finish 146.95
.41/45 Colt Combo, blued 161.95
  Nickel 175.95

PARDNER YOUTH

PARDNER SINGLE-BARREL SHOTGUNS

SPECIFICATIONS
Guages: 12, 16, 20, 28 and .410
Barrel Lengths: 22" (Youth); 26" (20, 28, .410); 28" (12 and 16 ga.), 32" (12 ga.)
Chokes: Full (alll gauges, except 28); Modified (12, 20 and 28 ga.)

Chamber: 2.75" (16 and 28 ga.); 3" (all others)
Price: $102.95
  w/32" barrel 117.95
Also available:
PARDNER YOUTH. With 22" barrel in gauges 20, 28 and .410 . . . . $110.95

New England Firearms

TURKEY GUN w/24" BARREL, TK2 CHOKE TUBE

TURKEY GUN

SPECIFICATIONS
Guage: 10 (3.5" chamber) *Choke:* Full
Barrel Length: 28" *Overall Length:* 44"
Weight: 9.5 lbs. *Sights:* Bead sights
Stock: American hardwood; walnut or camo finish; full
pistol grip; ventilated recoil pad. *Length Of Pull:* 14.5"

Price: $149.95
w/Camo Paint, Swivels & Sling 159.95
w/32" Barrel, Camo Paint, Swivels & Sling....... 179.95
Also Available:
TURKEY GUN. With 24" screw-in barrel, turkey Full choke,
black matte finish, swivels and sling $184.95

SPECIAL PURPOSE
WATERFOWL SINGLE SHOT (10 ga.)

This sporting shotgun features a 32" barrel, (48" overall),
Modified choke, camo paint finish, swivels and sling.
Weight: 9.5 lbs.
Price: $179.95

TRACKER II RIFLED SLUG GUN

SPECIFICATIONS
Guages: 12 and 20 (3" chamber)
Choke: Rifled bore
Barrel Length: 24" *Overall Length:* 40"
Weight: 6 lbs. *Sights:* Adjustable rifle sights

Length Of Pull: 14.5" *Stock:* American hardwood; walnut
or camo finish; full pistol grip; recoil pad; sling swivel studs
Price: $139.95
Also available:
TRACKER SLUG GUN w/Cylinder Bore:.......... 129.95

PERAZZI SHOTGUNS

The heart of the Perazzi line is the classic over/under, whose barrels are soldered into a monobloc that holds the shell extractors. At the sides are the two locking lugs that link the barrels to the action, which is machined from a solid block of forged steel. Barrels come with flat, step or raised ventilated rib. The finely checkered walnut forend is available with schnabel, beavertail or English styling, and the walnut stock can be of standard, Monte Carlo, Skeet or English design. Double or single nonselective or selective triggers. Sideplates and receiver are masterfully engraved.

OVER/UNDER GAME MODELS

GAME MODEL MX20C

GAME MODELS MX8, MX12, MX16, MX20, MX8/20, MX28 & MX410

SPECIFICATIONS
Gauges: 12, 20, 28 & .410
Chambers: 2.75"; also available in 3"
Barrel Lengths: 26" and 27.5"
Weight: 6 lbs. 6 oz. to 7 lbs. 4 oz.
Trigger Group: Nondetachable with coil springs and selective trigger
Stock: Interchangeable and custom; schnabel forend
Prices:

STANDARD GRADE	$5,500.00 - $17,330.00
SC3 GRADE	14,690.00 - 23,340.00
SCO GRADE	25,020.00 - 33,730.00
SCO GOLD GRADES	28,220.00 - 36,870.00

SCO SIDEPLATE ENGRAVING
(applicable to MX8 and MX12 models of any version)

AMERICAN TRAP SINGLE BARREL MODELS

MODEL MX5

AMERICAN TRAP SINGLE-BARREL MODELS MX15, MX15L & MX5

SPECIFICATIONS
Gauge: 12
Chamber: 2.75"
Barrel Lengths: 32" and 34"
Weight: 8 lbs. 6 oz.
Choke: Full

Trigger Group: Detachable and interchangeable with coil springs
Stock: Interchangeable and custom made
Forend: Beavertail
Prices:

MX5	$5,500.00
MX15	7,380.00
MX15L	8,940.00

PERAZZI SHOTGUNS

COMPETITION OVER/UNDER SHOTGUNS
Olympic, Double Trap, Skeet, Pigeon & Electrocibles

MODEL MX10

MODEL DB81 TRAP

MX8 SPORTING

MX8 SKEET

SHOTGUNS

SPECIFICATIONS STANDARD GRADE
Gauges: 12 and 20
Barrel Lengths: 27.5", 28 ³/₈", 29.5", 30.75", 31.5"
Prices:
MX8 12 ga., removable trigger group 29.5",
  30.75" and 31.5" barrels **$8,670.00**
MX10 12 & 20 ga., w/adj. stock and rib 29.5",
  30.75" and 31.5" bbl.. . . . . **11,050.00**
MX11 12 ga., removable trigger group 29.5",
  30.75" and 31.5" bbl. **8,180.00**
MX8/20 20 ga. removable trigger group
  26.75", 27.5", 28 ³/₈", 29.5", 30.75"
  and 31.5" barrels. **8,670.00**
MX8 12 ga. w/adj. trigger, 28 ³/₈", 29.5",
  31.5" barrels **9,180.00**
MX8 SPORTING 12 ga. w/external selector
  and 5 chokes; 27.5", 28 ³/₈", 29.5",
  and 31.5" barrels. **9,600.00**
MX8 CLASSIC 12 ga. **10,950.00**
MX8 SPECIAL 12 ga. w/adjustable trigger, 29.5",
  and 31.5" barrels. **9,180.00**

DB81 SPECIAL w/adjustable trigger 29.5",
  30.75"and 31.5" barrels **9,450.00**
Note: PIGEON & ELECTROCIBLE MODELS available in MX1B,
MX-8, MX-5, MX10 & MX11 only w/27.5", 28.75", 29.5" &
31.5" barrels. **$5,750.00-11,470.00**
Also Available:
SC3 GRADE (Models MX8, MX10,
  MX10/20, MX8/20, MX8 Special,
  DB81 Spec.) **$14,690.00-17,850.00**
SCO GRADE (same models as
  SC3 Grade). **25,020.00-27,550.00**
SCO GOLD GRADE
  (same models as above) **28,220.00-30,040.00**
SCO GRADE SIDEPLATES
  (same models as above) **38,360.00-38,780.00**
SCO GOLD GRADE SIDEPLATES
  (same models above). **44,540.00-44,960.00**

PIOTTI SHOTGUNS

One of Italy's top gunmakers, Piotti limits its production to a small number of hand-crafted, best-quality double-barreled shotguns whose shaping, checkering, stock, action and barrel work meets or exceeds the standards achieved in London before WWII. All of the sidelock models exhibit the same overall design, materials and standards of workmanship; they differ only in the quality of the wood, shaping and sculpturing of the action, type of engraving and gold inlay work and other details. The Model Piuma differs from the other shotguns only in its Anson & Deeley boxlock design. Piotti's new over/under model appears below.

SPECIFICATIONS
Gauges: 10, 12, 16, 20, 28, .410 *Chokes:* As ordered *Barrels:* 12 ga., 25" to 32"; other gauges, 25" to 30"; chopper lump (demi-bloc) barrels with soft-luster blued finish; level, file-cut rib or optional concave *Action:* Boxlock, Anson & Deeley; Sidelock, Holland & Holland pattern; both have automatic ejectors, double triggers with yielding front trigger (non-selective single trigger optional), coin finish or optional color casehardening *Stock:* Hand-rubbed oil finish on straight grip stock with checkered butt (pistol grip optional) *Forend:* Classic (splinter); optional beavertail *Weight:* 5 lbs. 4 oz. (.410 ga.) to 8 lbs. 4 oz. (12 ga.)

SIDELOCK OVER/UNDER
Available in 12 or 20 ga. w/2.75" or 3" chambers and 26" to 32" barrels. Weight varies from 6 lbs. to 6 lbs. 12 oz. (20 ga.) and 7-8 lbs. (12 ga.). Single or double triggers. Circassion (Turkish) wood
Price: And up depending on engraving $42,500.00

MODEL PIUMA BOXLOCK
Anson & Deeley boxlock ejector double with chopper lump (demi-bloc) barrels, and scalloped frame. Very attractive scroll and rosette engraving is standard.
Price: $13,400.00

MODEL KING NO. 1 SIDELOCK
Best-quality Holland & Holland pattern sidelock ejector double with chopper lump barrels, choice of rib, very fine, full coverage scroll engraving with small floral bouquets, finely figured wood.
Price: $25,600.00

MODEL KING EXTRA
(not shown)
Best-quality Holland & Holland pattern sidelock ejector double with chopper lump barrels, choice of rib and bulino game-scene engraving or game-scene engraving with gold inlays; engraved and signed by a master engraver.
Price: And up depending on engraving $31,800.00

MODEL LUNIK SIDELOCK
Best quality Holland & Holland pattern sidelock ejector double with chopper lump (demi-bloc) barrels, choice of rib, Renaissance-style, large scroll engraving in relief, finely figured wood.
Price: $27,500.00

REMINGTON SHOTGUNS

CUSTOM MODEL 396 SPORTING

CUSTOM MODEL 396 OVER/UNDER SHOTGUN (SKEET AND SPORTING CLAYS)

The Model 396 is produced in 12-gauge Skeet and Sporting Clays versions. Chrome-moly barrels in both versions have lengthened forcing cones, are fitted with side ribs, and have a flat 10-millimeter-wide parallel vent rib. Barrel lengths are 28" or 30". All barrels are fitted for the interchangeable Rem Choke system. Skeet and Improved Skeet choke tubes are supplied for the Model 396 Skeet, and four choke tubes—Skeet, Improved Skeet, Improved Cylinder and Modified configurations—for the Model 396 Sporting. The Sporting Clays version also features factory porting on both barrels.

The barrels and side ribs are finished with high-polished deep bluing. The receiver and sideplates, trigger guard, top lever and forend metal are finished with gray nitride coloring.

Extensive scroll work appears on the receiver, trigger guard, tang, hinge pins and forend metal. The sideplates include detailed renditions of a pointer and setter on the left and right sides, respectively. Identifying individual versions of the Model 396 on both sideplates are the words "Sporting" or "Skeet" in script lettering.

Stocks on both models are selected from fancy American walnut and given a soft satin finish. Several stock design features are specifically adapted to clay target shooting, including a wider, target-style forend, a comb with larger radius and a universal palm swell on the pistol grip.

SPECIFICATIONS
Gauge: 12 *Chamber:* 2.75" *Choke:* Rem Choke
Length of pull: 14 ³/₁₆" *Drop at comb:* 1¹/₂"
Drop at heel: 2.25"
Barrel lengths: 28" and 30"
Overall lengths: 45" and 47"
Weight: 7.5 lbs. and 7³/₈ lbs.
Prices:
MODEL 396 SPORTING $2,126.00
MODEL 396 SKEET 1,993.00

MODEL 870 SPECIAL PURPOSE

MODEL 870 SPECIAL PURPOSE MARINE MAGNUM

Remington's MODEL 870 SPECIAL PURPOSE MARINE MAGNUM is a versatile, multipurpose security gun featuring a rugged synthetic stock and extensive, electroless nickel plating on all metal parts. This new shotgun utilizes a standard 12-gauge Model 870 receiver with a 7-round magazine exten-sion tube and an 18" cylinder barrel (38.5" overall) with bead front sight. The receiver, magazine extension and barrel are protected (inside and out) with heavy-duty, corrosion-resistant nickel plating. The synthetic stock and forend reduce the effects of moisture. The gun is supplied with a black rubber recoil pad, sling swivel studs, and positive checkering on both pistol grip and forend. *Weight:* 7.5 lbs.
Price: $500.00

REMINGTON SHOTGUNS

MODEL 870 EXPRESS "YOUTH" GUN

The **MODEL 870 EXPRESS "YOUTH" GUN** has been specially designed for youths and smaller-sized adults. It's a 20-gauge lightweight with a 1-inch shorter stock and 21-inch barrel. Yet it is still all 870, complete with REM Choke and ventilated rib barrel. Also available with a 20" fully rifled, rifle-sighted deer barrel.

SPECIFICATIONS
Barrel length: 21" ***Stock Dimensions:*** Length of pull 12.5" (including recoil pad); drop at heel; 2.5" drop at comb 1 ⁵/₈"
Overall length: 39" (40.5" w/deer barrel) ***Average weight:*** 6 lbs.
Choke: REM Choke-Mod. (vent-rib version).
Price:
20-Gauge Lightweight **$305.00**
w/Deer Barrel **339.00**
Price:
w/Real Tree Advantage camo stock and forend . . . **372.00**

MODEL 870 EXPRESS SYNTHETIC HOME DEFENSE

This shotgun is designed specifically for home defense use. The 12-gauge pump-action shotgun features an 18" plain barrel with Cylinder choke and front bead sight. Barrel and action have the traditional Express-style metal finish. The synthetic stock and forend have a textured black, nonreflective finish and feature positive checkering.

SPECIFICATIONS
Capacity: 4 rounds.
Price: **$292.00**

MODEL 870 EXPRESS COMBO

The **MODEL 870 EXPRESS** in 12 and 20 gauge offers all the features of the standard Model 870, including twin-action bars, quick changing 28" barrels, REM Choke and vent rib plus low-luster, checkered hardwood stock and no-shine finish on barrel and receiver. The Model 870 Combo is packaged with an extra 20" deer barrel, fitted with rifle sights and fixed, Improved Cylinder choke (additional REM chokes can be added for special applications). The 3-inch chamber handles all 2.75" and 3" shells without adjustment. ***Weight:*** 7.5 lbs.
Price: **$399.00**
Also available: w/26" REM choke barrel w/vent rib and 20" fully rifled deer barrel w/rifle sights (12 and 20 ga.).
Weight: 7.5 lbs.
Price: **439.00**

REMINGTON PUMP SHOTGUNS

MODEL 870 EXPRESS

MODEL 870 EXPRESS features the same action as the Wingmaster and is available with 3" chamber and 26" or 28" vent-rib barrel. It has a hardwood stock with low-luster finish and solid buttpad. Choke is Modified REM Choke tube and wrench. *Overall length:* 48.5" (28" barrel). *Weight:* 7.25" lbs (26" barrel).

Prices: 12 & 20 ga. $305.00
Left Hand 12 ga. 332.00
w/Black Synthetic Stock & Forend
   (Right Hand only) 312.00

MODEL 870 EXPRESS TURKEY GUN

The **MODEL 870 EXPRESS TURKEY GUN** boasts all the same features as the Model 870 Express, except has 21" vent-rib barrel and Turkey Extra-Full REM Choke.

Price: $319.00
Now available:
   w/stock and forend in Advantage Camo 372.00

MODEL 870 EXPRESS DEER GUN

This 12-gauge, pump action deer gun is for hunters who prefer open sights. Features a 20" barrel, quick-reading iron sights, fixed Imp. Cyl. choke and Monte Carlo stock. Also available with fully rifled barrel.

Price: With Rifle Sights $300.00
   Fully Rifled 339.00

MODEL 870 EXPRESS SUPER MAGNUM
(not shown)

For those who seek the power and range of 12 gauge 3.5" magnum shotshells, the new **MODEL 870 EXPRESS SUPER MAGNUM** represents a good value. In addition to having the strength and reliability of the Model 870 Wingmaster, this model has the added versatility of handling 12 ga. 2.75" to 3.5" loads. The existing breech bolt and receiver have been designed to accommodate the big shells (capacity: 3 (3.5") and 4 (2.75" or 3") shells. Also available is a Turkey Camo shotgun with a 23" vent rib and 3.5" chamber with a synthetic stock and forend, plus checkering and vented recoil pad. Fully camouflaged with Real Tree Advantage. Remington also offers Synthetic and Combo models

Prices: **MODEL 870 EXPRESS SUPER MAGNUM** $345.00
   TURKEY CAMO 465.00
   Synthetic Model (26" vent rib) 352.00
Combo (20" fully rifled deer barrel and 26" vent rib
   w/wood stock and forend, vented recoil pad . . . 479.00

SHOTGUNS

REMINGTON SHOTGUNS

MODEL 870 WINGMASTER

MODEL 870 WINGMASTER
12 Gauge, Light Contour Barrel

This restyled **870 "WINGMASTER"** pump has cut-checkering on its satin-finished American walnut stock and forend for confident handling, even in wet weather. Also available in Hi-Gloss finish. An ivory bead "Bradley"-type front sight is included. Rifle is available with 26", 28" and 30" barrel with REM Choke and handles 3" and 2.75" shells interchangeably.

SPECIFICATIONS
Overall length: 46.5" (26" barrel), 48.5" (28" barrel), 50.5" (30" barrel).
Weight: 7.25 lbs. (w/26" barrel).
Price: $532.00
Also available:
MODEL 870 WINGMASTER. 20 Ga. Lightweight (6.5 lbs.), American walnut stock and forend.
Price: $532.00

MODEL 11-87 PREMIER DEER GUN

Price:
With Cantilever Scope Mount and Fully Rifled
21" Barrel (Satin Finish) $759.00

MODEL 11-87 PREMIER SPORTING CLAYS

MODEL 11-87 PREMIER SPORTING CLAYS

Remington's **MODEL 11-87 PREMIER SPORTING CLAYS** features a target-grade, American walnut competition stock with a length of pull that is 3/16" longer and 1/4" higher at the heel. The tops of the receiver, barrel and rib have a nonreflective matte finish. The rib is medium high with a stainless mid-bead and ivory front bead. The barrel (26" or 28") has a lengthened forcing cone to generate greater pattern uniformity; and there are 5 REM choke tubes—Skeet, Improved Skeet, Improved Cylinder, Modified and Full. All sporting clays choke tubes have a knurled end extending .45" beyond the muzzle for fast field changes. Both the toe and heel of the buttpad are rounded.

SPECIFICATIONS
Weight: 7.5 lbs. (26"); 7 5/8 lbs. (28")
Price: $833.00
Nickel Plated 905.00

REMINGTON AUTO SHOTGUNS

MODEL 11-87 PREMIER AUTOLOADER

Remington's redesigned 12-gauge **MODEL 11-87 PREMIER AUTOLOADER** features new, light-contour barrels that reduce both barrel weight and overall weight (more than 8 ounces). The shotgun has a standard 3-inch chamber and handles all 12-gauge shells interchangeably— from 2.75" field loads to 3" Magnums. The gun's interchangeable REM choke system includes Improved Cylinder, Modified and Full chokes.

Select American walnut stocks with fine-line, cut-checkering in satin or high gloss finish are standard. Right-hand models are available in 26", 28" and 30" barrels (left-hand models are 28" only). A two-barrel gun case is supplied.
Prices:
Light Contour Barrel $692.00
Left Hand, 28" Barrel 743.00
Also available:
MODEL 11-87 PREMIER SC (Sporting Clays) 779.00
MODEL 11-87 SC NP (Nickel Plated) 827.00

MODEL 11-87 PREMIER TRAP
(12 Gauge)

A 30" trap barrel (50.5" overall) offers trap shooters a REM Choke system with three interchangeable choke constrictions: trap full, trap extra full, and trap super full.
Weight: 8.75 lbs.
Price: $788.00

MODEL 11-87 PREMIER SKEET
(12 Gauge)

This model features American walnut wood and distinctive cut checkering with satin finish, plus new two-piece buttplate. REM Choke system includes option of two skeet chokes—skeet and improved skeet. Trap and skeet guns are designed for 12-gauge target loads and are set to handle 2.75" shells only. *Barrel length:* 26" *Overall length:* 46" *Weight:* 8 1/8 lbs.
Price: $765.00

REMINGTON AUTO SHOTGUNS

MODEL 11-87 SPS
(Special Purpose Wood or Synthetic)
12 Gauge Autoloader, 3" Chamber/REM/Chokes
26" or 28" Vent-Rib Barrels

Price: Wood $705.00
Synthetic 692.00

MODEL 11-87 SPST TURKEY GUN
12 Gauge Autoloader, 3" Chamber All-Black
Synthetic Stock Extra-Full REM Choke Turkey Tube

Price: $705.00
w/Mossy Oak Break-Up Camo Finish 805.00

MODEL 11-87 SPS SPECIAL PURPOSE SYNTHETIC ALL-BLACK DEER GUN

Features the same finish as other SP models plus a padded, camo-style carrying sling of Cordura nylon with QD sling swivels. Barrel is 21" (41" overall) with rifle sights and rifled and IC choke (handles all 2.75" and 3" rifled slug and buckshot loads as well as high-velocity field and magnum loads; does not function with light 2.75" field loads). *Weight:* 8.5 lbs.
Price: 3" Magnum $725.00
Fully Rifled Cantilever 772.00

REMINGTON AUTO SHOTGUNS

MODEL 1100 AUTOLOADING SHOTGUNS

The Remington **MODEL 1100** is a 5-shot gas-operated autoloader with a gas-metering system designed to reduce recoil. This design enables the shooter to use 2 ³/₄-inch standard velocity "Express" and 2 ³/₄-inch Magnum loads without gun adjustments. Barrels, within gauge and versions, are interchangeable. All 12- and 20-gauge versions include REM™ Choke; interchangeable choke tubes in 26" and 28" (12 gauge only) barrels. American walnut stocks come with design fine-line checkering and a scratch-resistant finish.

MODEL 1100 SPECIAL FIELD (12 & 20 Ga.)
Price: $665.00

MODEL 1100 LT-20
Price: (synthetic only) $505.00
Also Available:
MODEL **1100 LT-20 YOUTH** (synthetic only) 505.00

MODEL 1100 SYNTHETIC (20 Gauge)
Price: $505.00
Also Available:
MODEL **1100 SYNTHETIC FR RS**
  (fully rifled, rifle sights) 475.00
MODEL **1100 SYNTHETIC FR CL**
  (fully rifled, cantilever) 585.00

MODEL 1100 SYNTHETIC 12 Gauge
Price: $505.00

REMINGTON AUTO SHOTGUNS

MODEL 11-96 EURO LIGHTWEIGHT

Based on the Model 11-87™ action, the Model 11-96™ features modifications to the 11-87 action to reduce the overall weight of the 26" barrel version (from 7 ⁵/₈ lbs. to just 6 ⁷/₈ lbs.). These modifications include changing the profile of the receiver and shortening the magazine assembly (capacity of 3 shells).

This shotgun is now available with 26" or 28" barrels and features Remington's pressure-compensated, low-recoil gas system, which handles both 2.75" field and 3" magnum shells interchangeably; three flush-fitting REM™ chokes (for steel or lead shot) are supplied. Each gun has fine-line embellishments on the receivers and cut-checkered, Claro walnut stocks and forends. Barrels are chrome-moly steel with chrome-plated bores and 6mm vent ribs.

Price: $852.00

SP-10 MAGNUM SHOTGUN

Remington's **SP-10 MAGNUM** is the only gas-operated semi-automatic 10-gauge shotgun made today. Engineered to shoot steel shot, the SP-10 delivers up to 34 percent more pellets to the target than standard 12-gauge shotgun and steel shot combinations. This autoloader features a vented, noncorrosive, stainless-steel gas system, in which the cylinder moves—not the piston. This reduces felt recoil energy by spreading the recoil over a longer time. The receiver is machined from a solid billet of ordnance steel for total integral strength. The SP-10 has a 3/8" vent rib with mid and front sights for a better sight plane. The American walnut stock and forend have a protective, low-gloss satin finish for reduced glare, and positive deep-cut checkering. The receiver and barrel have a matte finish, and the stainless-steel breech bolt features a non-reflective finish. The SP-10 also has a brown vented recoil pad and a padded camo sling of Cordura nylon. **Barrel lengths/choke:** 26" or 30"/REM Choke. **Overall length:** 51.5" (30" barrel) and 47.5" (26" barrel). **Weight:** 11 lbs. (30" barrel) and 10.75 lbs. (26" barrel).

Price: $1,116.00

Also available: SP-10 Magnum in Turkey Camo NWTF 25th Anniversary.

Price: 1,229.00

MODEL SP-10 MAGNUM CAMO
10 Gauge Autoloader with 23" Vent-Rib Barrel and Mossy Oak Break-Up Camo Pattern
Price: $1,229.00

RIZZINI SHOTGUNS

PREMIER SPORTING EL
(12 GAUGE)

UPLAND EL
(20 GAUGE)

Rizzini builds a well-finished boxlock ejector over/under that is available in all gauges and in many different configurations. Rizzini guns are manufactured in Marcheno, Italy, in the famous Val Trompia gunmaking region. All Rizzini guns have special steel barrels that are proof-tested at 1200 Bars, as well as pattern-tested at the factory. The guns are built in field, sporting clays and express rifle configurations.

The **ARTEMIS** and **PREMIER** are production guns built to standard specifications. The EL models, which include the Upland EL, the Sporting EL and the High Grades feature higher grade wood, checkering and hand finishing.

FIELD guns are available with case-colored or coin-finish actions with straight grips or round knob semi-pistol grips. Also available are multi-gauge field sets with .410, 28 or 20 gauge barrels in any combination. These sets are available in EL or High Grade level guns. On custom orders, stock dimensions, chokes and barrel length may be specified. Screw-in chokes are available on 12 and 20 gauge guns.

SPORTING guns, in 12 and 20 gauge only, feature heavier weight and a target-style rib, stock and forearm. The Sporting models are available in three versions: Premier Sporting, Sporting EL and S790EL.

High Grade models, built with or without sideplates, are available in four engraving styles, including game scenes and gold inlays.

Prices:
SPORTING EL (12 gauge)	$3,250.00
UPLAND EL (20 gauge)	2,850.00
S790 EMEL HIGH GRADE	8,750.00
ARTEMIS EL HIGH GRADE	12,650.00

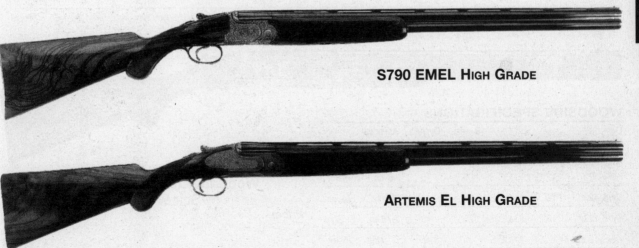

S790 EMEL HIGH GRADE

ARTEMIS EL HIGH GRADE

RUGER OVER/UNDER SHOTGUNS

RED LABEL OVER/UNDER SHOTGUN
(INC. SCREW-IN CHOKES)

Price:................................ $1,276.00

SPORTING CLAYS OVER/UNDER
MODEL KRL-2036 (20 Ga. shown above)
Price: w/Screw-in Chokes & 30" Barrels $1,415.00

SPECIFICATIONS RED LABEL AND SPORTING CLAYS OVER/UNDERS

CATALOG NUMBER	GAUGE	CHAMBER	CHOKE*	BARREL LENGTH	OVERALL LENGTH	LENGTH PULL	DROP COMB	DROP HEEL	SIGHTS**	APPROX. WT. (LBS.)	TYPE STOCK
KRL-1226	12	3"	F,M,IC,S+	26"	43"	14 1/8"	1 1/2"	2 1/2"	GBF	7 3/4	Pistol Grip
KRL-1227	12	3"	F,M.IC,S+	28"	45"	14 1/8"	1 1/2"	2 1/2"	GBF	8	Pistol Grip
KRLS-1226	12	3"	F,M,IC,S+	26"	43"	14 1/8"	1 1/2"	2 1/2"	GBF	7 1/2	Straight
KRLS-1227	12	3"	F,M.IC,S+	28"	45"	14 1/8"	1 1/2"	2 1/2"	GBF	7 3/4	Straight
KRL-1236	12	3"	M,IC,S+	30"	47"	14 1/8"	1 1/2"	2 1/2"	GBF/GBM	7 3/4	Pistol Grip
KRL-2029	20	3"	F,M,IC,S+	26"	43"	14 1/8"	1 1/2"	2 1/2"	GBF	7	Pistol Grip
KRL-2030	20	3"	F,M,IC,S+	28"	45"	14 1/8"	1 1/2"	2 1/2"	GBF	7 1/4	Pistol Grip
KRLS-2029	20	3"	F,M,IC,S+	26"	43"	14 1/8"	1 1/2"	2 1/2"	GBF	6 3/4	Straight
KRLS-2030	20	3"	F,M,IC,S+	28"	45"	14 1/8"	1 1/2"	2 1/2"	GBF	7	Straight
KRL-2036	20	3"	M,IC,S+	30"	47"	14 1/8"	1 1/2"	2 1/2"	GBF/GBM	7	Pistol Grip
KRLS-2826	28	2 3/4"	F,M,IC,S+	26"	43"	14 1/8"	1 1/2"	2 1/2"	GBF	5 7/8	Straight
KRLS-2827	28	2 3/4"	F,M,IC,S+	28"	45"	14 1/8"	1 1/2"	2 1/2"	GBF	6	Straight
KRL-2826	28	2 3/4"	F,M,IC,S+	26"	43"	14 1/8"	1 1/2"	2 1/2"	GBF	6	Pistol Grip
KRL-2827	28	2 3/4"	F,M,IC,S+	28"	45"	14 1/8"	1 1/2"	2 1/2"	GBF	6 1/8	Pistol Grip

*F-Full, M-Modified, IC-Improved Cylinder, S-Skeet. +Two skeet chokes standard with each shotgun. **GBF-Gold-Bead Front Sight, GBM-Gold-Bead Middle

WOODSIDE SPECIFICATIONS

CATALOG NUMBER	GAUGE	CHOKE*	BARREL LENGTH	OVERALL LENGTH	APPROX. WT.	STOCK
KWK-1226	12	F,M,IC,S	26"	43"	7.75 lbs.	Pistol
KWS-1227	12	F,M,IC,S	28"	45"	8 lbs.	Pistol
KWS-1226	12	F,M,IC,S	26"	43"	7.5 lbs.	Straight
KWS-1227	12	F,M,IC,S	28"	45"	7.75 lbs.	Straight
KWS-1236	12	F,M,IC,S	30"	47"	7.75 lbs.	Pistol

WOODSIDE OVER/UNDER SHOTGUN
(W/SCREW-IN CHOKES)

Price:................................ $1,758.00

SAVAGE SHOTGUNS

MODEL 210FT "MASTER SHOT" SHOTGUN

SPECIFICATIONS
Gauge: 12 **Choke:** Full choke tube **Barrel length:** 24"
Overall length: 43.5" **Weight:** 7.5 lbs.

Finish: Advantage™ camo pattern
Features: Barrel threaded for interchangeable Winchester-style choke tubes; drilled and tapped for scope mounting; positive checkering; ventilated rubber recoil pad and swivel studs; bead front sight with U-notch blade rear; short-lift 60° bolt rotation, controlled round feed; triple front locking lugs
Price: $440.00

MODEL 210F SLUG GUN

Also available:
210F "MASTER SHOT" SLUG GUN (12 gauge). Features full-length baffle; 24" barrel chambered for 2.75" or 3" shells; three-position, top tang rifle-style safety; no sights; 1 in 35" twist (8-groove precision button rifling).
Price: $380.00

SIG ARMS SHOTGUNS

MODEL SA5

MODEL SA3 OVER/UNDER

SPECIFICATIONS
Gauge: 12 (3" chamber)
Choke: Full, Modified & Improved Cylinder
Action: Automatic ejectors w/single selective trigger
Barrel lengths: 26" and 28" w/vented rib
Weight: 6.8 lbs. **Length of pull:** 14.5"

Drop at comb: 1.5" **Drop at heel:** 2.5"
Stock: Medium gloss select-grade walnut
Finish: Low-luster nickel
Features: Hand checkering (18 lines per inch); chrome-lined bores; screw-in multi-choke system; hardened monobloc; rolled game scenes on receiver
Prices:
MODEL SA3 FIELD $1,335.00
  SPORTING MODEL 1,675.00
MODEL SA5 FIELD 2,670.00
  SPORTING MODEL 3,185.00

SHOTGUNS

SKB Shotguns

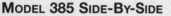

Model 385 Side-By-Side

Model 385 features silver nitride receiver with engraved scroll and game scene design; solid boxlock action w/double locking lugs; single selective trigger; selective automatic ejectors; automatic safety; sculpted American walnut stock; pistol or English straight grip; semi-beavertail forend; stock and forend finished w/18-line fine checkering; standard series choke tube system; solid rib w/flat matte finish and metal front bead. For additional specifications, see table below.

Price:. **$1,799.00**
Field Set. 2,579.00

Also available:

Model 485 Series. Features engraved upland game scene; semi-fancy American walnut stock and beavertail forend; raised vent rib with flat matte finish.

Price:. **$2,439.00**
Field Set. 3,479.00

SPECIFICATIONS MODEL 385 & 485

FIELD MODELS

Gauge	Chamber	Barrel Length	Overall Length	Inter Choke	Sights	Rib Width	Stock	Average Weight* 385	Average Weight* 485
12	3"	28"	44 1/2"	STND-A	MFB	5/16"	PISTOL	7 lb. 3 oz.	7 lb. 1 oz.
12	3"	28"	44 1/2"	STND-A	MFB	5/16"	ENGLISH	7 lb. 1 oz.	7 lb. 5 oz.
12	3"	26"	42 1/2"	STND-A	MFB	5/16"	PISTOL	7 lb. 1 oz.	7 lb. 5 oz.
12	3"	26"	42 1/2"	STND-A	MFB	5/16"	ENGLISH	7 lb. 0 oz.	7 lb. 4 oz.
20	3"	26"	42 1/2"	STND-B	MFB	5/16"	PISTOL	6 lb. 10 oz.	6 lb. 14 oz.
20	3"	26"	42 1/2"	STND-B	MFB	5/16"	ENGLISH	6 lb. 10 oz.	6 lb. 14 oz.
28	2 3/4"	26"	42 1/2"	STND-B	MFB	5/16"	PISTOL	6 lb. 13 oz.	7 lb. 2 oz.
28	2 3/4"	26"	42 1/2"	STND-B	MFB	5/16"	ENGLISH	6 lb. 13 oz.	7 lb. 2 oz.

2 BARREL FIELD SETS

Gauge	Chamber	Barrel Length	Overall Length	Inter Choke	Sights	Rib Width	Stock	Average Weight* 385	Average Weight* 485
20	3"	26"	42 1/2"	STND-B	MFB	5/16"	PISTOL	6 lb. 10 oz.	
28	2 3/4"	26"	42 1/2"	STND-B	MFB	5/16"	PISTOL	6 lb. 13 oz.	
20	3"	26"	42 1/2"	STND-B	MFB	5/16"	ENGLISH	6 lb. 10 oz.	
28	2 3/4"	26"	42 1/2"	STND-B	MFB	5/16"	ENGLISH	6 lb. 13 oz.	

*Weights may vary due to wood density. Specifications may vary. *INTER-CHOKE SYSTEMS: COMP - Competition series includes Mod., Full, Imp. Cyl. STND-A - Standard series includes Mod., Full, Imp. Cyl. STND-B- Standard series includes Imp. Cyl., Mod. Skeet STOCK DIMENSIONS: Length of Pull - 14 1/8" Drop at Comb - 1 1/2" Drop at Heel - 2 3/4" ✓MFB-Metal Front Bead

Model 505
$1,049.00 (Field)
$1,149.00 (Sporting Clays)

505 FIELD OVER AND UNDERS

Gauge	Chamber	Barrel Length	Overall Length	Inter Choke	Sights	Rib Width	Average Weight*
12	3"	28"	45 3/8"	STND-A	MFB	3/8"	7 lb. 12 oz.
12	3"	26"	45 3/8"	STND-B	MFB	3/8"	7 lb. 11 oz.
20	3"	26"	45 3/8"	STND-B	MFB	3/8"	6 lb. 10 oz.

505 SPORTING CLAYS

Gauge	Chamber	Barrel Length	Overall Length	Inter Choke	Sights	Rib Width	Average Weight* 505
12	3"	30"	47 3/8"	STND-B	CP/WFB	15/32" CH/STP	8 lb. 5 oz.
12	3"	28"	45 3/8"	STND-B	CP/WFB	15/32" CH/STP	8 lb. 1 oz.

*Weights may vary due to wood density. Specifications may vary. *INTER-CHOKE SYSTEMS: STND-A-Standard series includes Full, Mod, Imp. Cyl. STND-B- Standard series includes Imp. Cyl., Mod, Skeet STOCK DIMENSIONS: Length of Pull-14 1/8" Drop at Comb-1 1/2" Drop at heel-2 3/16" **MFB-Metal Front Bead**

SKB SHOTGUNS

MODEL 585 AND 785 SERIES

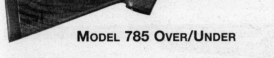

MODEL 785 OVER/UNDER

The SKB 785 Series features chrome-lined chambers and bores, lengthened forcing cones, chrome-plated ejectors and competition choke tube system.

MODEL 785   *Prices*
FIELD(12 & 20 ga.) $1,949.00
   28 or .410 ga. 2,029.00

TWO-BARREL FIELD SET (12 & 20 ga.) 2,829.00
   20/28 ga. or 28/.410 ga 2,929.00
SKEET (12 or 20 ga.) .2,029.00
   28 or .410 ga. 2,069.00
   2-Bbl. Set 2,929.00
SPORTING CLAYS (12 or 20 ga.) 2,099.00
   28 gauge 2,169.00
   2-Barrel Set (12 or 20 ga.) 2,999.00
TRAP (Monte Carlo or Std.) 2,029.00
   2-Barrel Trap Combo 2,829.00

TRAP MODELS

GAUGE	STOCK	BARREL√ LENGTH	OVERALL LENGTH	INTER CHOKE	SIGHTS√	785 RIB WIDTH	585 RIB WIDTH	AVERAGE WEIGHT* 785	585	MANUFACTURERS ID# 785	585
12	STND	30"	47 3/8"	COMP-A	CP/WFB	15/32" CH/STP	3/8" STP	8 lb. 15 oz.	8 lb. 7 oz.	A7820CVTN	A5820CVTN
12	MONTE	30"	47 3/8:	COMP-A	CP/WFB	15/32" CH/STP	3/8" STP	9 lb. 0 oz.	8 lb. 7 oz.	A7820CVTM	A5420CVTM
12	STND	32"	49 3/8"	COMP-A	CP/WFB	15/32" CH/STP	3/8" STP	9 lb. 1 oz.	8 lb. 10 oz.	A7822CVTN	A5822CVTN
12	MONTE	32"	49 3/8:	COMP-A	CP/WFB	15/32" CH/STP	3/8" STP	9 lb. 1 oz.	8 lb. 9 oz.	A7822CVTM	A5822CVTM
TRAP COMBO'S – STANDARD											
12	STND	O/U-30"	47 3/8"	COMP.	CP/WFB	15/32" CH/STP	3/8" STP	8 lb. 15 oz.	8 lb. 6 oz.	A7820TN/7822	A5820TN/5822
12	STND	S/O-32"	49 3/8"	COMP.	CP/WFB	15/32" CH/STP	3/8" STP	9 lb. 0 oz.	8 lb. 6 oz.		
12	STND	O/U-30"	47 3/8"	COMP.	CP/WFB	15/32" CH/STP	3/8"STP	9 lb. 0 oz.	8 lb. 4 oz.	A7820TN/7824	A5820TN/5824
12	STND	S/O-34"	51 3/8"	COMP.	CP/WFB	15/32" CH/STP	3/8"STP	9 lb. 1 oz.	8 lb. 6 oz.		
12	STND	O/U-32"	49 3/8"	COMP.	CP/WFB	15/32" CH/STP	3/8" STP	9 lb. 0 oz.	8 lb. 7 oz.	A7822TN/7824	A5822TN/5824
12	STND	S/O-34"	51 3/8"	COMP.	CP/WFB	15/32" CH/STP	3/8" STP	9 lb. 1 oz.	8 lb. 8 oz.		
TRAP COMBO'S – MONTE CARLO											
12	MONTE	O/U-30"	47 3/8"	COMP.	CP/WFB	15/32" CH/STP	3/8" STP	8 lb. 15 oz.	8 lb. 6 oz.	A7820TM/7822	A5820TM/5822
12	MONTE	S/O-32"	49 3/8"	COMP.	CP/WFB	15/32" CH/STP	3/8" STP	9 lb. 0 oz.	8 lb. 6 oz.		
12	MONTE	O/U-30"	47 3/8"	COMP.	CP/WFB	15/32" CH/STP	3/8"STP	8 lb. 15 oz.	8 lb. 4 oz.	A7820TM/7824	A5820TM/5824
12	MONTE	S/O-34"	51 3/8"	COMP.	CP/WFB	15/32" CH/STP	3/8"STP	9 lb. 1 oz.	8 lb. 6 oz.		
12	MONTE	O/U-32"	49 3/8"	COMP.	CP/WFB	15/32" CH/STP	3/8" STP	9 lb. 0 oz.	8 lb. 7 oz.	A7822TM/7824	A5822TM/5824
12	MONTE	S/O-34"	51 3/8"	COMP.	CP/WFB	51/32" CH/STP	3/8" STP	9 lb. 1 oz.	8 lb. 9 oz.		

*Weights may vary due to wood density. Specifications may vary. *INTER-CHOKE SYSTEMS COMP. - Competition series includes Full, Mod., Imp. Cyl. STND. B - Standard series includes Imp. Cyl. Mod. and Skeet STOCK DIMENSIONS Length of Pull - 13 1/2" Drop at Comb - 1/1/2" Drop at Heel - 2 1/4" √MFB - Metal Front Bead

YOUTH & LADIES

GAUGE	CHAMBER	BARREL LENGTH	OVERALL LENGTH	INTER CHOKE	SIGHTS√	RIB WIDTH	AVERAGE WEIGHT* 785	585	MANUFACTURERS ID# 785	585
12	3"	28"	44 1/2"	COMP.	MFB	3/8"		7 lb. 11 oz.		A5828CFY
12	3"	26"	42 1/2"	COMP.	MFB	3/8"		7 lb. 9 oz.		A5826CFY
20	3"	26"	42 1/2"	STND-B	MFB	3/8"		6 lb. 7 oz.		A5806CFY
SKEET MODELS										
12	3"	30"	47 1/4"	COMP.	CP/WFB	3/8"	8 lb. 9 oz.	8 lb. 1 oz.	A7820CV	A5820CV
12	3"	28"	45 1/4"	COMP.	CP/WFB	3/8"	8 lb. 6 oz.	7 lb. 12 oz.	A7828CV	A5828CV
20	3"	28"	45 1/4"	STND.	CP/WFB	5/16"	7 lb. 2 oz.	6 lb. 15 oz.	A7808CV	A5808CV
28	2.75"	28"	45 1/4"	STND.	CP/WFB	5/16"	7 lb. 5 oz.	6 lb. 15 oz.	A7888CV	A5888CV
410	3"	28"	45 1/4"	SK/SK	CP/WFB	5/16"	7 lb. 5 oz.	7 lb. 0 oz.	A7848CV	A5848V
3 BARREL SKEET SETS										
20	3"	28"	45 1/4"	STND.	CP/WFB	5/16"	7 lb. 2 oz.	6 lb. 15 oz.		
28	2.75"	28"	45 1/4"	STND.	CP/WFB	5/16"	7 lb. 5 oz.	7 lb. 0 oz.	A78088	A58088
410	3"	28"	45 1/4"	SK/SK	CP/WFB	5/16"	7 lb. 5 oz.	7 lb. 0 oz.		

*Weights may vary due to wood density. Specifications may vary. *INTER-CHOKE SYSTEMS: COMP. - Competition series includes 2 -SKI/SCI, 1-Mod/SCIV STND - Standard series includes Skeet, Skeet and Imp. Cyl. NOTE: 785's Are Equipped with Step-Up Style Ribs STOCK DIMENSIONS: Length of Pull - 14 1/8" Drop at Comb - 1 1/2" Drop at Heel - 2 3/16" √CP/WFB - Center Post/White Front Bead

SHOTGUNS

STOEGER IGA SHOTGUNS

COACH GUN

ENGRAVED COACH GUN

The **IGA CLASSIC SIDE-BY-SIDE COACH GUN** sports a 20-inch barrel. Lightning fast, it is the perfect shotgun for hunting upland game in dense brush or close quarters. This endurance-tested workhorse of a gun is designed from the ground up to give you years of trouble-free service. Two massive underlugs provide a super-safe, vise-tight locking system for lasting strength and durability. The mechanical extraction of spent shells and double-trigger mechanism

assures reliability. The automatic safety is actuated whenever the action is opened, whether or not the gun has been fired. The polish and blue is deep and rich, and the solid sighting rib is matte-finished for glare-free sighting. Chrome-moly steel barrels with micro-polished bores give dense, consistent patterns. Nickel finish is now available. The classic stock and forend are of durable hardwood...oil finished, hand-rubbed and hand-checkered.

Improved Cylinder/Modified choking and its short barrel make the IGA coach gun the ideal choice for hunting in close quarters, security and police work. Three-inch chambers.

Prices: In 12 and 20 Gauge or .410 Bore....... $415.00
Nickel, shown 464.00
Also available with Engraved Stagecoach scene
on the stock:............................... 479.00

UPLANDER LADIES SIDE-BY-SIDE

UPLANDER LADIES SIDE-BY-SIDE
Crafted specifically with women in mind, IGA's new model features a lightweight 20 gauge with 24" barrel and is equipped with IC/M choke tubes. The durable 13" Brazilian hardwood stock is fitted with a ventilated pad to reduce recoil. Standard features include extractors, double triggers and automatic safety.
Price: $485.00

UPLANDER YOUTH SIDE-BY-SIDE (not shown)
IGA's new Youth gun is a lightweight .410 gauge with 24" barrels bored modified and full. Both barrels will handle 2 ½'' or 3" shells. The 13" Brazilian hardwood stock includes a recoil pad. Standard features include double triggers, extractors and an automatic safety (activated when the gun is open). This shotgun is easy to load, light to carry and safe to handle with a second shot available when needed.
Price: $446.00

UPLANDER IGA SIDE-BY-SIDE (not shown)
The **IGA SIDE-BY-SIDE** is a rugged shotgun, endurance-tested and designed to give years of trouble-free service. A vise-tight, super-safe locking system is provided by two massive under-lugs for lasting strength and durability. Two design features that make the IGA a standout for reliability are its positive mechanical extraction of spent shells and its traditional double-trigger mechanism. The safety is automatic in that every time the action is opened, whether or not the gun has been fired, the safety is actuated. The polish and bluing are deep and rich. The solid sighting rib carries a machined-in matte finish for glare-free sighting. Barrels are of chrome-moly steel with micro-polished bores to give dense, consistent patterns. Your choice of traditional stock or the legendary English-style stock. Both are of durable Brazilian hardwood, oil-finished, hand-rubbed and hand-checkered.
Prices:
In 12, 20, 28 Gauge or .410 Bore. $434.00
In 12 and 20 Gauge w/Choke Tubes........... 474.00
Also available with English stock w/choke tubes (IC/M) and fixed (M/M).

See table on page 371 for additional specifications

STOEGER IGA SHOTGUNS

CONDOR I OVER/UNDER SINGLE TRIGGER

The **IGA CONDOR I O/U SINGLE TRIGGER** is a workhorse of a shotgun, designed for maximum dependability in heavy field use. The super-safe lock-up system makes use of a sliding underlug, the best system for over/under shotguns. A massive monobloc joins the barrel in a solid one-piece assembly at the breech end. Reliability is assured, thanks to the mechanical extraction system. Upon opening the breech, the spent shells are partially lifted from the chamber, allowing easy removal by hand. IGA barrels are of chrome-moly steel with micro-polished bores to give tight, consistent patterns. They are specifically formulated for use with steel shot where Federal migratory bird regulations require. Atop the barrel is a sighting rib with an anti-glare surface. The buttstock and forend are of durable hardwood, hand-checkered and finished with an oil-based formula that takes dents and scratches in stride.

The **IGA CONDOR I** over/under shotgun is available in 12 and 20 gauge with 26- and 28-inch barrels with choke tubes and 3-inch chambers.
Price: w/Choke Tubes $559.00

CONDOR SUPREME SINGLE SELECTIVE TRIGGER

The **IGA CONDOR SUPREME** truly compliments its name. The stock is selected from upgraded Brazilian walnut, and the hand-finished checkering is sharp and crisp. A matte-laquered finish provides a soft warm glow, while maintaining a high resistance to dents and scratches. A massive monoblock joins the barrel in a solid one-piece assembly at the breech end. Upon opening the breech, the automatic ejectors cause the spent shells to be thrown clear of the gun. The barrels are of moly-chrome steel with micro-polished bores to give tight, consistent patterns; they are specifically formulated for use with steel shot. Choke tubes are provided. Also, a single, selective trigger and barrel rib with both mid- and front bead.
Price: $629.00

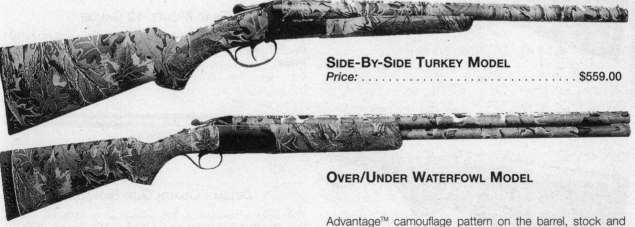

SIDE-BY-SIDE TURKEY MODEL
Price: $559.00

OVER/UNDER WATERFOWL MODEL

The 12-gauge **SIDE-BY-SIDE TURKEY MODEL** features IGA's new Advantage™ camouflage finish, plus double triggers, 3" chamber with 24" barrel and wide beavertail forend. The 30" barrel over/under **WATERFOWL MODEL** also features the new Advantage™ camouflage pattern on the barrel, stock and forend, plus single trigger, automatic ejector and Full/Full flush-mounted choke tubes and ventilated recoil pad. *Also available:* **TURKEY MODEL O/U** w/26" barrel in camouflage.
Price: $729.00

See table on page 371 for additional specifications

SHOTGUNS

STOEGER IGA SHOTGUNS

DELUXE UPLANDER SIDE-BY-SIDE

Offered in 12 and 20 gauge with internal choke tubes along with 28 and .410 gauge with 26" fixed chokes; semi-fancy American walnut stock and forend; wood is finished in matte lacquer and stocks are fitted with a soft black recoil pad; front and mid-rib bead sight, gold double trigger and positive extractor are standard.

Price: 12 & 20 gauge $559.00
28 & .410 gauge 519.00

DELUXE HUNTER CLAY

Features include a matte lacquer finish, select grade semi-fancy American walnut stock and forend with a black target-style recoil pad. Also red bead front and mid-rib beads ensure accuracy. Over/under barrels are 28 inches long with 3" chambers.

Price: $699.00

TRAP MODEL 12 GAUGE

Features single selective trigger, automatic ejectors, raised rib. Full and IM choke tubes

Price: $699.00

DELUXE COACH GUN SIDE/SIDE

The Deluxe version of the Coach Gun featured earlier, this 12-gauge side-by-side features 20" barrels with 3" chambers, IC/M chokes, gold double trigger, vented rubber recoil pad; weighs 6.75 lbs.

Price: $499.00

See table on following page for additional specifications

STOEGER IGA SHOTGUNS

STOEGER IGA SHOTGUNS	GAUGE					BARREL LENGTH					CHOKES		SPECIFICATIONS					SAFETY		BUTT-PLATES		DIMENSIONS			
	12	16	20	28	.410	20"	22"	24"	26"	28"	Fixed	Choke Tubes	Chamber	Weight (lbs.)	Extractors	Ejectors	Triggers	Manual	Automatic	Molded	Rubber-Ventilated	Length of pull	Drop of comb	Drop of heel	Overall length
COACH GUN Side by Side	■		■		■	■					IC/M		3"	6 3/4	■		D.T.		■	■		14 1/2"	1 1/2"	2 1/2"	36 1/2"
COACH GUN Nickel	■		■		■	■					IC/M		3"	6 3/4	■		D.T.		■	■		14 1/2"	1 1/2"	2 1/2"	36 1/2"
COACH GUN Engraved	■		■		■	■					IC/M		3"	6 3/4	■		D.T.		■	■		14 1/2"	1 1/2"	2 1/2"	36 1/2"
COACH GUN Deluxe	■					■					IC/M		3"	6 3/4	■		D.T.		■		■	14 1/2"	1 1/2"	2 1/2"	36 1/2"
UPLANDER Side by Side	■		■						■		IC/M		3"	6 3/4	■		D.T.		■	■		14 1/2"	1 1/2"	2 1/2"	42"
UPLANDER Side by Side	■		■							■	M/F		3"	6 3/4	■		D.T.		■	■		14 1/2"	1 1/2"	2 1/2"	42"
UPLANDER Side by Side		■		■					■		IC/M		2 3/4"	6 3/4	■		D.T.		■	■		14 1/2"	1 1/2"	2 1/2"	42"
UPLANDER Side by Side	■		■							■	M/F		3"	6 3/4	■		D.T.		■	■		14 1/2"	1 1/2"	2 1/2"	45 1/2"
UPLANDER Side by Side	■		■						■		IC/M		3"	6 3/4	■		D.T.		■	■		14 1/2"	1 1/2"	2 1/2"	42"
UPLANDER Side by Side				■					■		F/F		3"	6 3/4	■		D.T.		■	■		14 1/2"	1 1/2"	2 1/2"	42"
UPLANDER English			■					■			IC/M		3"	6 3/4	■		D.T.		■	■		14 1/2"	1 1/2"	2 1/2"	40"
UPLANDER English				■				■			M/M		3"	6 3/4	■		D.T.		■	■		14 1/2"	1 1/2"	2 1/2"	40"
UPLANDER Ladies			■					■			IC/M		3"	6 3/4	■		D.T.		■		■	13"	1 1/2"	2 1/2"	40"
UPLANDER Youth				■				■			M/F		3"	6 3/4	■		D.T.		■		■	13"	1 1/2"	2 1/2"	40"
UPLANDER Deluxe	■									■	M/F		3"	6 3/4	■		D.T.		■		■	14 1/2"	1 1/2"	2 1/2"	44"
UPLANDER Deluxe			■						■		IC/M		3"	6 3/4	■		D.T.		■		■	14 1/2"	1 1/2"	2 1/2"	42"
UPLANDER Deluxe				■					■		IC/M		2 3/4"	6 3/4	■		D.T.		■		■	14 1/2"	1 1/2"	2 1/2"	42"
UPLANDER Deluxe					■				■		M/F		3"	6 3/4	■		D.T.		■		■	14 1/2"	1 1/2"	2 1/2"	42"
CONDOR I Over / Under	■		■						■		IC/M		3"	8	■		S.T.	■			■	14 1/2"	1 1/2"	2 1/2"	43 1/2"
CONDOR I Over / Under	■		■							■	M/F		3"	8	■		S.T.	■			■	14 1/2"	1 1/2"	2 1/2"	45 1/2"
CONDOR II Over / Under	■								■		IC/M		3"	8	■		D.T.	■		■		14 1/2"	1 1/2"	2 1/2"	43 1/2"
CONDOR II Over / Under	■									■	M/F		3"	8	■		D.T.	■		■		14 1/2"	1 1/2"	2 1/2"	45 1/2"
CONDOR Supreme	■		■						■		IC/M		3"	8		■	S.T.	■			■	14 1/2"	1 1/2"	2 1/2"	43 1/2"
CONDOR Supreme	■		■							■	M/F		3"	8		■	S.T.	■			■	14 1/2"	1 1/2"	2 1/2"	45 1/2"
UPLANDER Camo	■							■			F/F		3"	6 3/4	■		D.T.		■	■		14 1/2"	1 1/2"	2 1/2"	40"
CONDOR Supreme Camo	■								■		F/F		3"	8		■	S.T.	■			■	14 1/2"	1 1/2"	2 1/2"	45 1/2"
HUNTERS-CLAYS	■									■	IC M/F		3"	8		■	S.T.	■			■	14 1/2"	1 1/2"	2 1/2"	45 1/2"

SHOTGUNS

WEATHERBY SHOTGUNS

ATHENA GRADE V CLASSIC FIELD

The Athena features a boxlock action and sidelock-type plates with fine floral engraving. The hinge pivots are made of high-strength steel alloy. The locking system employs the Greener crossbolt design. The single selective trigger is mechanically operated for a fully automatic switchover, allowing the second barrel to be fired on a subsequent trigger pull, even during a misfire. The selector lever, located in front of the trigger, enables the shooter to fire the lower barrel or upper barrel first.

The breech block is hand-fitted to the receiver. Every Athena is equipped with a matted, ventilated rib and bead front sight. Ejectors are fully automatic. The safety is a slide type located on the upper tang atop the pistol grip. Each stock is carved from Claro walnut, with fine-line hand-checkering and high-luster finish. Trap model has Monte Carlo stock only. See the Athena and Orion table on the following page for additional information and specifications.

GRADE IV CHOKES
Fixed Choke
Field, .410 Gauge
Skeet, 12 or 20 Gauge
IMC Multi-Choke
Field, 12, 20 or 28 Gauge
Trap, 12 Gauge
Trap, single barrel, 12 Gauge
Trap Combo, 12 Gauge
Prices: ATHENA GRADE III $1,849.00
ATHENA GRADE IV 2,259.00
ATHENA GRADE V 2,599.00

ORION GRADE II CLASSIC FIELD

ORION GRADES I, II & III OVER/UNDERS
For greater versatility, the Orion incorporates the integral multichoke (IMC) system. Available in Extra-full, Full, Modified, Improved Modified, Improved Cylinder and Skeet, the choke tubes fit flush with the muzzle without detracting from the beauty of the gun. Three tubes are furnished with each gun. The precision hand-fitted monobloc and receiver are machined from high-strength steel with a highly polished finish. The boxlock design uses the Greener cross-bolt locking system and special sears maintain hammer engagement. Pistol grip stock and forearm are carved of Claro walnut with hand-checkered diamond inlay pattern and high-gloss finish. Chrome-moly steel barrels, and the receiver, are deeply blued. The Orion also features selective automatic ejectors, single selective trigger, front bead sight and ventilated rib. The trap model boasts a curved trap-style recoil pad and is available with Monte Carlo stock only.

Weight: 12 ga. Field, 7 1/2 lbs.; 20 ga. Field, 7 1/2 lbs.; Trap, 8 lbs.
See following page for prices and additional specifications.

UPLAND IMC MULTI-CHOKE
Grade I
IMC Multi-Choke, Field, 12 or 20 Gauge $1,329.00
Grade II
Fixed Choke, Field, .410 Gauge 1,399.00
Fixed Choke, Skeet, 12 or 20 Gauge 1,399.00
IMC Multi-Choke, Field, 12, 20 or 28 Gauge 1,399.00
IMC Multi-Choke, Trap, 12 Gauge 1,399.00
Sporting Clays (12 ga.)
Sporting and Field Sporting 1,499.00
Super Sporting 1,749.00
Grade III
IMC Multi-Choke, Field, 12 or 20 Gauge 1,699.00

WEATHERBY SHOTGUNS

**ORION GRADE II CLASSIC FIELD
12 GAUGE OVER/UNDER**

ORION SUPER SPORTING CLAYS O/U

ORION III FIELD

Prices:

ORION I	$1,329.00
ORION II CLASSIC FIELD	1,399.00
ORION II SPORTING CLAYS	1,499.00
ORION III FIELD & CLASSIC FIELD	1,699.00

Also available:
ORION SUPER SPORTING CLAYS (SSC) O/U 12 Ga.
Barrel Length: 28", 30", 32". Features include Integral Multi-Choke (IMC) system, including five interchangeable screw-in stainless steel Briley choke tubes; Claro walnut stock w/Sporter style pistol grip. *Weight:* 8 lbs.
Price: $1,749.00

WEATHERBY SHOTGUN SPECIFICATIONS

Model	Gauge	Chamber	Barrel Length	Overall Length	Length Of Pull	Drop At Heel	Drop At Comb	Bead Sight	Approx. Weight (lbs.)
Athena Grade IV Field	12	3"	28" or 26"	45" or 43"	14.25"	2.5"	1.5"	Brilliant front	6.5-8
	20	3"	28" or 26"	45" or 43"	14.25"	2.5"	1.5"	Brilliant front	6.5-8
Athena Grade V Classic Field	12	3"	28" or 26"	45" or 43"	14.25"	2.25"	1.5"	Brilliant front	6.5-8
	20	3"	28" or 26"	45" or 43"	14.25"	2.25"	1.5"	Brilliant front	6.5-8
Orion Upland	12	3"	28" or 26"	45" or 43"	14.25"	2.25"	1.5"	Brilliant front	6.5-8
	20	3"	28" or 26"	45" or 43"	14.25"	2.25"	1.5"	Brilliant front	6.5-8
Orion Grade I Field	12	3"	30", 28" or 26"	47", 45" or 43"	14.25"	2.5"	1.5"	Brilliant front	6.5-8
	20	3"	28" or 26"	45" or 43"	14.25"	2.5"	1.5"	Brilliant front	6.5-8
Orion Grade II Classic Sporting	12	3"	30" or 28"	47" or 45"	14.25" 14.25"	2.25"	1.5" 1.5"	Midpoint w/white front	7.5-8
Orion Grade II Sporting	12	3"	30" or 28"	47" or 45"	14.25"	2.25"	1.5"	Midpoint w/white front	7.5-8
Orion Grade II Classic Field	12	3"	30", 28" or 26"	47", 45" or 43"	14.25"	2.25"	1.5"	Brilliant front	6.5-8
	20	3"	28" or 26"	45" or 43"	14.25"	2.25"	1.5"	Brilliant front	6.5-8
	28	2.75"	26"	43"	14.25"	2.25"	1.5"	Brilliant front	6.5-8
Orion Grade III Classic Field	12	3"	28" or 26"	45" or 43"	14.25"	2.25"	1.5"	Brilliant front	6.5-8
	20	3"	28" or 26"	45" or 43"	14.25"	2.25"	1.5"	Brilliant front	6.5-8
Orion Grade III English Field	12	3"	28"	45"	14.25"	2.5"	1.5"	Brilliant front	7-7.5
	20	3"	28" or 26"	45" or 43"	14.25"	2.5"	1.5"	Brilliant front	6.5-7
Orion Grade III Field	12	3"	28" or 26"	45" or 43"	14.25"	2.25"	1.5"	Brilliant front	6.5-8
	20	3"	28" or 26"	45" or 43"	14.25"	2.25"	1.5"	Brilliant front	6.5-8

WINCHESTER SHOTGUNS

NEW SUPER X2 TURKEY 3.5"

Nothing in turkey hunting is more important than shot placement and pattern density. The new Super X2 Magnum 3 1/2" Turkey version has all the handling advantages of the Super X2 design. Like a 24" barrel combined with the short receiver. Center balance lets you hold with greater steadiness and less fatigue. The stock, receiver, barrel, bolt, bolt handle, carrier—every exposed part—have a no-luster, no-glare finish that won't give you away. The back-bored barrel fitted with an extra-full extended choke tube offers extreme pattern density. And the standard 3-dot TRUGLO® fiber optic sights give you an instant advantage, with more precise shot placement in early morning low-light conditions. And of course, the gas-operated action reduces the kick of recoil noticeably, something no recoil-operated gun can ever offer.

NEW SUPER X2 3.5"

For a long time, a semiauto that handled 3 1/2" shells was only a waterfowler's dream. Now there's the new Winchester Super X2. In addition to 3 1/2" chambers, you get the recoil reduction, faster follow-ups and greater comfort that only comes with gas operation. You need the versatility to shoot light 2 3/4" teal loads to the heaviest 3 1/2" goose loads. You need the balanced handling that comes with an all-alloy receiver. The pointability that comes from a shorter receiver length. The weather-resistant durability of a composite stock. And the consistent pattern density when shooting steel, Bismuth or Tungsten shot that you get with the famous Invector® Plus choke system and a back-bored barrel. The level of complexity is low and the operating range of each component high...so that an extreme level of reliability is achieved. This is the gun for the kind of weather only a waterfowler will put up with.

SUPER X2 SHOTGUNS

Item Number	Gauge	Barrel Length & Type	Chamber	Shotshell Capacity	Choke(s)	Overall Length	Nominal Length Of Pull	Nominal Drop At Comb	Nominal Drop At Heel	Nominal Weight (Lbs.)	Features	Suggested Retail
SUPER X2 SHOTGUNS												
3-1/2" MODELS												
3-1/2" Magnum (Black Synthetic Stock)												
511-001252 *NEW*	12	24"	3-1/2" Mag.	5	Invector(3)	45"	14-1/4"	1-3/4"	2"	7-1/4	Studs, VR	$855
511-001250 *NEW*	12	26	3-1/2 Mag.	5	Invector(3)	47"	14-1/4	1-3/4	2	7-1/2	Studs, VR	855
511-001248 *NEW*	12	28	3-1/2 Mag.	5	Invector(3)	49"	14-1/4	1-3/4	2	7-3/4	Studs, VR	855
3-1/2" Turkey (Black Synthetic Stock)												
511-002253 *NEW*	12	24"	3-1/2" Mag.	5	Invector XF	45"	14-1/4"	1-3/4"	2"	7-1/4	Studs, VR, TRUGLO®	867
3-1/2" Camo Waterfowl (Mossy Oak Shadow Grass)												
511-003246 *NEW*	12	28"	3-1/2" Mag	5	Invector(3)	49"	14-1/4"	1-3/4"	2"	7-1/4	Studs, VR	938
3" MODELS												
3" Magnum Field (Walnut Stock)												
511-004350 *NEW*	12	26"	3" Mag.	5	Invector(3)	47"	14-1/4"	1-3/4"	2"	7-1/4	VR	$725
511-004346 *NEW*	12	28	3 Mag.	5	Invector(3)	49	14-1/4	1-3/4	2	7-3/8	VR	725
3" Magnum (Black Synthetic Stock)												
511-001350 *NEW*	12	26"	3" Mag.	5	Invector(3)	47"	14-1/4"	1-3/4"	2"	7-1/4	Studs, VR	725
511-001346 *NEW*	12	28	3 Mag.	5	Invector(3)	49	14-1/4	1-3/4	2	7-3/8	Studs, VR	725

WINCHESTER SHOTGUNS

MODEL 1300 RANGER LADIES/YOUTH PUMP-ACTION SHOTGUN

MODEL 1300 RANGER 12 GAUGE DEER COMBO
22" Rifled w/Sights & 28" Vent-Rib Barrels

MODEL 1300

Suggested Retail	Gauge	Barrel Length & Type	Chamber	Shotshell Capacity*	Choke	Overall Length	Nominal Length of Pull	Nominal Drop at Comb	Nominal Drop at Heel	Nominal Weight (Lbs.)	Features
FIELD MODELS											
UPLAND											
$361	12	24"VR	3" Mag.	5	W3	45	14	1-1/2	2-1/2	7	Walnut Stock, MBF
WALNUT											
$361	12	28"VR	3" Mag.	5	W3	49"	14"	1-1/2"	2-1/2"	7-3/8	Walnut Stock, MBF
361	12	26VR	3" Mag.	5	W3	47	14	1-1/2	2-1/2	7-1/8	Walnut Stock, MBF
BLACK SHADOW (SYNTHETIC STOCK)											
310	12	28VR	3" Mag.	5	WIM	49	14	1-1/2	2-1/2	7-1/4	MBF
310	12	26VR	3" Mag.	5	WIM	47	14	1-1/2	2-1/2	7	MBF
310	20	26VR	3" Mag.	5	WIM	47	14	1-1/2	2-1/2	6-7/8	MBF
RANGER MODELS											
RANGER											
$325	12	28"VR	3" Mag.	5	W3	49"	14"	1-1/2"	2-1/2"	7-3/8	MBF
325	20	28VR	3" Mag.	5	W3	49	14	1-1/2	2-1/2	7-1/8	MBF
RANGER COMPACT											
$325	12	24VR	3" Mag.	5	W3	44	13"	1-1/2	2-3/8	6-5/8	UP, MBF
325	20	22VR	3" Mag.	5	W3	42	13"	1-1/2	2-3/8	6-5/8	UP, MBF
RANGER DEER COMBO (CYLINDER DEER BARREL AND EXTRA VENT RIB BARREL)											
$399	12	22 Smooth	3" Mag.	5	Cyl	42-3/4	14	1-1/2	2-1/2	6-7/8	SB, D&T, Rifle Sights
399	12	38VR	3" Mag.	5	W3	49	14	1-1/2	2-1/2	7-3/8	MBF
RANGER DEER COMBO (RIFLED DEER BARREL AND EXTRA VENT RIB BARREL)											
$422	12	22 Rifled	3" Mag.	5	Rifled Barrel	42-3/4	14	1-1/2	2-1/2	6-7/8	SB,D&T,Rifle Sights
422	12	28VR	3" Mag.	5	W3	49	14	1-1/2	2-1/2	7-3/8	MBF
TURKEY MODELS											
TURKEY BLACK SHADOW SYNTHETIC STOCK											
$310	12	22VR	3" Mag.	5	WXF	43	14	1-1/2	2-1/2	6-5/8	D&T,MBF
310	12	22 VR	3" Mag.	5	WIF	43	14	1-1/2	2-1/2	6-5/8	D&T,MBF
DEER MODELS											
DEER (WALNUT STOCK)											
$425	12	22"Rifled	3" Mag.	5	Rifled Barrel	42-3/4"	14"	1-1/2	2-1/2"	6-7/8	Studs,B&R,D&T,Rifle Sights
DEER BLACK SHADOW (SYNTHETIC STOCK)											
310	12	22" Smooth	3" Mag.	5	WIC	43	14	1-1/2	2-1/2	6-7/8	Studs,D&T,Rifle Sights
334	12	22 Rifled	3" Mag.	5	Rifled Barrel	42-3/4	14	1-1/2	2-1/2	6-3/4	D&T,Rifle Sights

*Includes one shotshell in chamber. For Model 1300 Feature & Choke and Barrel Abbreviations see following page.

SHOTGUNS

WINCHESTER SECURITY SHOTGUNS

These tough 12-gauge shotguns provide backup strength for security and police work as well as all-around utility. The action is one of the fastest pumps made. It features a front-locking rotating bolt for strength and secure, single-unit lockup into the barrel. Twin-action slide bars prevent binding.

The shotguns are chambered for 3-inch shotshells. They handle 3-inch Magnum, 2.75-inch Magnum and standard 2.75-inch shotshells interchangeably. They have a crossbolt safety, walnut-finished hardwood stock and forearm, black rubber buttpad and plain 18-inch barrel with Cylinder Bore choke. All are ultra-reliable and easy to handle.

Special chrome finish on Police and Marine guns are actually triple-plated: first with copper for adherence, then with nickel for rust protection, and finally with chrome for a hard finish. This triple-plating assures durability and quality. Both guns have a forend cap with swivel to accommodate sling.

MODEL 1300 DEFENDER

SPECIFICATIONS MODEL 1300 DEFENDER

SUGGESTED RETAIL	GAUGE	BARREL LENGTH & TYPE	CHAMBER	SHOTSHELL CAPACITY*	CHOKE	OVERALL LENGTH	NOMINAL LENGTH OF PULL	NOMINAL DROP AT COMB	NOMINAL DROP AT HEEL	NOMINAL WEIGHT (LBS.)	FEATURES
DEFENDER MODELS											
COMBO, HARDWOOD STOCK AND SYNTHETIC PISTOL GRIP, 5 SHOT											
$393	12	18"	3 Mag.	5	Cyl.	29-1/8"	—	—	—	5-5/8	Studs, MBF
	12	28VR	3" Mag.	5	WIM	49	14	1-1/2	2-1/2	7-3/8	Studs, MBF
HARDWOOD STOCK, 8 SHOT											
308	12	18	3" Mag.	8	Cyl.	39-1/2	14	1-1/2	2-1/2	6-3/4	Studs, MBF
SYNTHETIC PISTOL GRIP, 8 SHOT											
308	12	18	3" Mag.	8	Cyl.	29-1/8	—	—	—	5-1/2	Studs, MBF
SYNTHETIC STOCK, 8 SHOT											
308	12	18	3" MAG.	8	Cyl..	39-1/2	14	1-1/2	2-1/2	6-3/8	Studs, Truglo
	20	18	3" MAG.	8	Cyl.	39-1/2	14	1-1/2	2-1/2	6-1/2	Studs, Truglo
STAINLESS MARINE SYNTHETIC STOCK											
485	12	18	3" Mag.	7	Cyl.	39-1/2	14	1-1/2	2-1/2	6-3/8	Studs, MBF
CAMP DEFENDER											
345	12	22	3" Mag.	5	Cyl.	42-3/4	14	1-1/2	2-1/2	6-7/8	Studs, Rifle Sights

Model 1300 Feature Abbreviations: *MBF=Metal bead front, Rifle=Rifle type front and rear sights. Rifle sights=Adjustable rear sight and ramp style front sight. SB=Scope Bases Included. B&R=Scope, Bases and Rings included. D&T=Drilled and tapped to accept scope bases. Studs=Buttstock and magazine cap sling studs provided (sling loop on pistol grip models).*
Model 1300 Choke and Barrel Abbreviations: *VR=Ventilated rib. W3W=WinChoke, Extra Full, Full and Modified Tubes. W3=WinChoke, Full, Modified and Improved Cylinder Tubes. Cyl.=Non-WinChoke, choked Cylinder Bore. WIM=Modified Tube. WIC=Cylinder Choke Tube. WF=Full Choke Tube. WXF=Extra Full Choke Tube. Smooth=Non-Rifled Bore.*

American Frontier Firearms 378
Austin & Halleck 380
Cabela's 381
Colt Blackpowder Arms 382
CVA 385
Dixie 388
EMF Hartford 394
Euroarms of America 396
Gonic Arms 400
Lyman 401
Markesbery 403
Modern Muzzleloading 404
Navy Arms 406
Pedersoli 413
Remington 414
Ruger 415
Thompson/Center 416
Traditions 419
Uberti 427

*For addresses and phone/fax numbers of manufacturers and distributors included in this section, please turn to **DIRECTORY OF MANUFACTURERS AND SUPPLIERS** on page 564.*

AMERICAN FRONTIER FIREARMS

1871-2 OPEN-TOP FRONTIER MODEL

1871-2 OPEN-TOP FRONTIER MODEL

Available in 38 or 44 caliber with non-rebated cylinder, 7.5"
and 8" round barrels; standard-finish high-polish blued steel
parts, color case hardened hammer and walnut varnished
navy-sized grips.
Price: $795.00

1871-2 OPEN-TOP TIFFANY MODEL

1871-2 OPEN-TOP TIFFANY MODEL

Available in 38 and 44 calibers, non-rebated cylinder, 4.75",
5.5", 7.5" and 8" round barrels; Tiffany grips; silver and gold
finish with engraving.
Price: $995.00

REMINGTON NEW ARMY CAVALRY MODEL

REMINGTON NEW ARMY CAVALRY MODEL

Available in 38, 44, and 45 calibers with 5.5", 7.5" and 8"
barrels; high-polish blued finish, color case hardened
hammer. Comes with an ejector assembly, loading gate
and government inspector's cartouche on left grip and
sub-inspector's initials on various other parts.
Price: . . . . : $795.00

POCKET REMINGTON

POCKET REMINGTON

Available in 22, 32, and 38 calibers with 3.5" barrel, with or
without ejector rod or gate, high-polish blued steel parts,
color case hardened hammer, varnished walnut grips.
Price: and up $495.00

AMERICAN FRONTIER FIREARMS

RICHARDS 1851 MODEL NAVY CONVERSION

Available in 38 and 44 calibers with non-rebated cylinder, 4.75", 5.5" & 7.5" octagon barrels, colorcase hardened hammer and trigger, ramrod and plunger, blued steel backstrap and trigger guard; walnut varnished navy-sized grips (Note: No ejector rod assembly on this model)
Price: $695.00

RICHARDS 1851 MODEL NAVY CONVERSION

RICHARDS 1860 ARMY MODEL CONVERSION

Available in 38 or 44 caliber with rebated cylinder with or without ejector assembly; 4.75", 5.5" and 7.5" round barrels, standard finishes are high-polish blued steel parts (including backstrap); trigger guard is silver-plated brass; colorcase hardened hammer and trigger, walnut varnished army-sized grips.
Price: $695.00

RICHARDS AND MASON CONVERSION 1851 NAVY MODEL

RICHARDS AND MASON CONVERSION 1851 NAVY MODEL

Available in 38 and 44 calibers with Mason ejector assembly and non-rebated cylinder, 4.75", 5.5" and 7.5" octagon barrels, high-polish blued steel parts, colorcase hammer and trigger, blued steel backstrap and trigger guard with ejector rod; varnished walnut grips.
Price: $695.00

POCKET RICHARDS AND MASON NAVY CONVERSION

POCKET RICHARDS AND MASON NAVY CONVERSION

Available in 32 caliber, non-rebated cylinder, five shot, high-polish blued steel parts, silver-plated brass backstrap and trigger guard with ejector assembly, colorcase hardened hammer and trigger, varnished walnut grips.
Price: and up $495.00

RICHARDS 1860 ARMY MODEL CONVERSION

RICHARDS 1861 MODEL NAVY CONVERSION

Same as 1860 Model, except with non-rebated cylinder and navy-sized grips. All blue with silver trigger guard and backstrap.
Price: $695.00

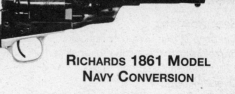

RICHARDS 1861 MODEL NAVY CONVERSION

BLACK POWDER

AUSTIN & HALLECK RIFLES

MODEL 320 LR/SS

MODEL 420 LR CLASSIC

MODEL 420 LR MONTE CARLO

SPECIFICATIONS
Caliber: 50 *Action:* In-line percussion (removable weather shroud) *Barrel Length:* 26" (1:28"); 8 lands & grooves; octagon to .75" tapered round *Overall length:* 47.5" *Weight:* 7 7/8 lbs. *Length of pull:* 13.5" *Stock:* Select grade tiger-striped curly maple (Classic model has filled-grain luster finish w/pistol grip cap; Monte Carlo has filled-grain high-gloss finish) *Features:* Match grade target triggers w/trigger block safety; 1" recoil pad; scope not included

Prices:
MODEL 420 LR MONTE CARLO & CLASSIC STANDARD . . $518.00
   Stainless Steel Standard 613.00
   Fancy Stainless Steel 689.00
   Hand Select 729.00
   Hand Select Stainless Steel 825.00
   Exhibition Grade 1300.00
MODEL 320 LR BLU w/SYNTHETIC STOCK 455.00
MODEL 320 LR S/S 506.00

MOUNTAIN RIFLE

MOUNTAIN RIFLE

SPECIFICATIONS
Caliber: 50 percussion or flintlock
Barrel length: 32" (1:66 roundball or 1:28 bullet twist); 1" octagonal; rust brown finish
Overall length: 49"
Weight: 7.5 lbs.

Stock: Select grade tiger-striped curly maple; filled-grain luster finish
Sights: Fixed buckhorn rear; silver blade brass bead front
Features: Double throw adjustable set triggers
Price: Std. percussion $509.00
   Hand Select percussion 604.00
   Std. flint 534.00
   Hand select flint 629.00

CABELA'S RIFLES

LIGHTNING FIRE SIDE-LOCK MUZZLELOADING RIFLE

This 50-caliber beauty is taking the hunting and target-shooting world by storm. Our Lightning Fire nipple system uses a musket nipple and musket percussion caps to deliver a huge blast of fire (five times the fire of standard #11 caps) to the powder for instantaneous and complete powder ignition. We've also redesigned the flash channel, replacing the fire-slowing right-angle turns with a smooth, natural curving channel that allows the fire to travel unimpeded to the powder so there's less delay between the hammer strike and firing. An exceptional hunting rifle, the Lightning Fire readily shoots two Pyrodex pellets or a wide range of black powder (or black-powder equivalent) charges. The 28 3/4" round barrel features a fast 1-in-32" rifling which provides optimum twist for superior accuracy with bullets and saboted bullets. The windage-and-elevation-adjustable rear sight and ramp front sight both feature bright fiber-optics for rapid, easy target acquisition, even in low-light conditions. Other features: sling swivels, color case-hardened lock, rubber recoil pad and virtually unbreakable ramrod. Wt: 7.85 lbs. .50 Caliber only..
Price: $249.99

LIGHTNING FIRE RIFLE

Developed by Cabela's, this firearm produces muzzle velocities of over 2,100 fps using Hodgdon Pyrodex Pellets and 250 grain saboted bullets. Ignition is enhanced with a musket nipple and percussion caps that deliver five times the spark of standard #11 caps.

SPECIFICATIONS INCLUDE: 24" fluted barrel (blued or stainless), 1 turn in 32" twist rate. Laminated wood stock. *Overall Length:* 43". Fully adjustable rear sight, drilled and tapped for scope mounts. *Weight:* 7.25 lbs. (stainless); 7 lbs. (blue)
Price:
Blue. $269.99
Stainless 399.99

BLUE RIDGE RIFLE

From the era of the American long rifle (1760-1840) comes the design for this faithful reproduction. The so-called "squirrel rifle" by necessity had to be accurate to handle small, often distant targets and Cabela's Blue Ridge rifles live up to that tradition. Precision-rifled 39" browned octagonal barrels with 1-in-48" twist deliver exceptional precision with patched round balls and will handle conical bullets surprisingly well. 8 lands and grooves. Percussion models have drum and bolster system. Flintlocks have large, sure-spark frizzen and ample priming pan. Locks are color case-hardened. Adjustable double-set, double-phase triggers. Buttplate and trigger guard are polished brass.

ORDER NO. PERCUSSION	CAL.	OVERALL LENGTH	BARREL LENGTH	WT. LBS.	GROOVE & LANDS	GUN ONLY PRICE	KIT PRICE
HJ-21-0007-036	.36 Cal	55"	39"	7 3/4	7	$349.99	$389.99
HJ-21-0007-050	.50 Cal	55"	39"	7 1/4	8	$349.99	$389.99
FLINTLOCK							
HJ-21-0008-036	.36 Cal	55"	39"	7 3/4	7	$379.99	$419.99
HJ-21-0008-045	.45 Cal	55"	39"	7 1/4	8	$379.99	$419.99
HJ-21-0008-050	.50 Cal	55"	39"	7 1/4	8	$379.99	$419.99

KODIAK EXPRESS DOUBLE RIFLE

Early explorers of Africa and Asia often had to rely on large-bore express rifles like this handsome sidelock replica featuring oil-finished, hand-checkered European walnut stock with case hardened steel buttplate. Ramp-mounted, adjustable folding double rear sights, ramp front sight, drilled and tapped for folding tang sight. Color-case hardened lock, blued top tang and trigger guard are all polished and engraved. *Calibers:* 50 and 58 *Barrels:* 28" with 1:48" twist (regulated at 75 yards); blued. *Overall Length:* 45.25" *Weight:* 9.3 lbs.
Price: $599.99

COLT BLACKPOWDER ARMS

SIGNATURE SERIES

COLT 1847 WALKER

SPECIFICATIONS
Caliber: 44
Barrel length: 9" *Overall length:* 15.5"
Weight: 73 oz. (empty)
Sights: Fixed blade front sight *Sight radius:* 12.25"
Stock: One-piece walnut
Finish: Colt blue with color case hardened frame; hammer, lever and plunger
Price: **$419.95**

COLT THIRD MODEL DRAGOON

SPECIFICATIONS
Caliber: 44 percussion
Barrel length: 7.5" *Overall length:* 13.75"
Weight: 66 oz. (empty)
Sight: Fixed blade front *Sight radius:* 10.75"
Stock: One-piece walnut *Finish:* Colt blue with color case hardened frame; hammer, lever and plunger
Price: **$419.95**
Also available with steel backstrap and fluted cylinder: **$540.00**

COLT WALKER 150TH ANNIVERSARY MODEL

SPECIFICATIONS
Caliber: 44 *Weight:* 4 lbs. 9 oz.
Barrel length: 9"
Cylinder length: 2 7/16"
Finish: Color case hardened frame and hammer; smooth wooden grips
Features: Colt's Signature Series 150th anniversary re-issue carries the identical markings as the original 1847 Walker. "U.S. 1847" appears above the barrel wedge, exactly as on the Walkers produced for service in the Mexican War. The cylinder has a battle scene depicting 15 Texas Rangers defeating a Comanche war party using the first revolver invented by Sam Colt. This Limited Edition features original A Company No. 1 markings embellished in gold. Serial numbers begin with #221, a continuation of A Company numbers.
Price: **$599.95**

COLT WALKER 150TH ANNIVERSARY

COLT 1849 POCKET REVOLVER

SPECIFICATIONS
Caliber: 31
Barrel length: 4" Overall length: 9.5"
Weight: 24 oz. (empty)
Stock: One-piece walnut
Finish: Colt blue and color case hardened frame
Price: **$389.95**

COLT 1851 NAVY

SPECIFICATIONS
Caliber: 36
Barrel length: 7.5" *Overall length:* 13 1/8"
Weight: 40.5 oz. (empty)
Sights: Fixed blade front *Sight radius:* 10"
Stock: Oiled American walnut
Finish: Colt blue and color case hardened frame
Price: **$399.95**

COLT BLACKPOWDER ARMS

SIGNATURE SERIES

COLT 1860 ARMY

A continuation in production of the famous cap-and-ball revolver used by the U.S. Cavalry with color case hardened frame, hammer and loading lever. Blued backstrap and brass trigger guard, roll-engraved cylinder and one-piece walnut grips

SPECIFICATIONS

Caliber: 44 *Barrel length:* 8" *Overall length:* 13.75"
Weight: 42 oz. (empty) *Sights:* Fixed blade front
Sight radius: 10.5" *Stock:* One-piece walnut
Finish: Colt blue with color case hardened frame; hammer, lever and plunger
Price: $399.95

COLT MODEL 1860 ARMY FLUTED CYLINDER

The first Army revolvers shipped from Hartford were known as the "Cavalry Model"—with fluted cylinder, color case hardened frame, hammer, loading lever and plunger. Features blued barrel, backstrap and cylinder; brass trigger guard, fluted cylinder, one-piece walnut grip and a 4-screw frame (cut for optional shoulder stock)

SPECIFICATIONS

Caliber: 44 percussion *Barrel length:* 8"
Overall length: 13.75" *Weight:* 42 oz. (empty)
Sight: Fixed blade front *Sight radius:* 10.5"
Stock: One piece walnut *Finish:* Colt blue with color casehardened frame; hammer, lever and plunger
Price: $399.95

COLT 1861 NAVY

A personal favorite of George Armstrong Custer, who carried a pair of them during the Civil War. Loading lever and plunger; blued barrel, cylinder backstrap and trigger guard; roll-engraved cylinder; one-piece walnut grip.

SPECIFICATIONS

Caliber: 36 percussion *Barrel length:* 7.5"
Overall length: 13 1/8" *Weight:* 42 oz. (empty)
Sight: Fixed blade front *Sight radius:* 10"
Stock: One-piece walnut *Finish:* Colt blue with color case hardened frame; hammer, lever and plunger
Price: $399.95

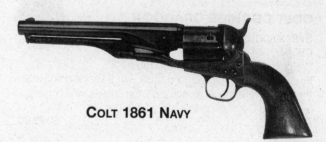

COLT 1861 NAVY

TRAPPER MODEL 1862 POCKET POLICE

TRAPPER MODEL 1862 POCKET POLICE

The first re-issue of the rare and highly desirable Pocket Police "Trapper Model." The Trapper's 3.5" barrel without attached loading lever makes it an ideal backup gun, as well as a welcome addition to any gun collection. Color case-hardened frame and hammer; silver-plated backstrap and trigger guard; blued semi-fluted cylinder and barrel; one-piece walnut grip. Separate 4 5/8" brass ramrod.

SPECIFICATIONS

Caliber: 36 *Barrel length:* 3.5" *Overall length:* 8.5"
Weight: 20 oz. (empty) *Sight:* Fixed blade front
Sight radius: 6" *Stock:* One-piece walnut
Finish: Colt blue with color casehardened frame and hammer
Price: $389.95

BLACK POWDER

COLT BLACKPOWDER ARMS

COLT MODEL 1861 MUSKET

Manufactured to original specifications using modern steels, this re-issue has the authentic Colt markings of its Civil War predecessor. Plus triangular bayonet.

SPECIFICATIONS
Caliber: .58
Barrel length: 40"
Overall length: 56"

Weight: 9 lbs. 3 oz. (empty)
Sights: Folding leaf rear; steel blade front
Sight Radius: 36"
Stock: One piece
Finish: Bright steel lockplate, hammer, buttplate, bands, ramrod and nipple; blued rear sight
Price: $569.95

COLT COCHISE DRAGOON

SPECIFICATIONS
Caliber: .44
Weight: 4 lbs. 4 oz.   **Barrel length:** 7.5"
Features: Colt Black Diamond finish with 24 karat gold Indian-theme embellishments (peace pipe, tomahawk, wild horses, buffalo and Cochise portrait carved into blackhorn grips)
Price: $995.00

COLT 1861 CUSTER

SPECIFICATIONS
Caliber: .36
Weight: 42 oz. (empty)
Barrel length: 7.5"
Features: 70% Nimschke-style engraving, carved rosewood grip and antique silver finish
Price: $995.00

COLT 1860 GOLD U.S. CAVALRY

SPECIFICATIONS
Caliber: .44
Weight: 42 oz. (empty)
Barrel length: 8"
Features: 24 karat gold-plated cylinder with U.S. Cavalry crossed sabres emblem and gold barrel bands
Price: $667.50

CVA Revolvers/Pistols

1851 NAVY REVOLVER BRASS FRAME

SPECIFICATIONS
Caliber: 44
Barrel length: 7.5" octagonal; hinged-style loading lever
Overall length: 13"
Weight: 44 oz.
Cylinder: 6-shot, engraved
Sights: Post front; hammer notch rear
Grip: One-piece walnut
Finish: Solid brass frame, trigger guard and backstrap; blued barrel and cylinder; color case hardened loading lever and hammer
Price: $129.95

1858 ARMY REVOLVER

SPECIFICATIONS
Caliber: 44
Cylinder: 6-shot, engraved
Barrel length: 8" octagonal
Overall length: 13"
Weight: 38 oz.
Sights: Blade front; adjustable target
Grip: Two-piece walnut
Price:
Brass Frame $144.95

KENTUCKY PISTOL

SPECIFICATIONS
Caliber: 50 percussion
Barrel: 9.75", rifled, octagonal
Overall length: 15.5"
Weight: 40 oz.
Finish: Blued barrel, brass hardware
Sights: Brass blade front; fixed open rear
Stock: Select hardwood
Ignition: Engraved, color case hardened percussion lock, screw adjustable sear engagement
Accessories: Brass-tipped, hardwood ramrod; stainless-steel nipple or flash hole liner
Prices:
Finished. $149.95
Percussion Kit 109.95

HAWKEN PISTOL

SPECIFICATIONS
Caliber: 50 percussion
Barrel length: 9.75", octagonal
Overall length: 16.5"
Weight: 50 oz.
Trigger: Early-style brass
Sights: Beaded steel blade front; fully adjustable rear (click adj. screw settings lock into position)
Stock: Select hardwood
Finish: Solid brass wedge plate, nose cap, ramrod thimbles, trigger guard and grip cap
Prices:
Finished. $149.95
Kit. 119.95
Laminated stock 159.95

CVA RIFLES/SHOTGUNS

ST. LOUIS HAWKEN RIFLE

SPECIFICATIONS
Calibers: 50 and 54 percussion or flintlock (50 cal. only)
Barrel: 28" octagonal 15/16" across flats; hooked breech; rifling one turn in 66", 8 lands and deep grooves
Overall length: 44" **Weight:** 8 lbs.
Sights: Dovetail, beaded blade front: adjustable open hunting-style dovetail rear
Stock: Select hardwood with beavertail cheekpiece
Triggers: Double set; fully adjustable trigger pull

Finish: Solid brass wedge plates, nose cap, ramrod thimbles, trigger guard and patchbox
Prices:
50 Caliber Flintlock. $234.95
50 Caliber Flintlock Left Hand (finished) 249.95
Also available:
PLAINSMAN (FLINTLOCK RIFLE) w/26" barrel.
Caliber: 50. **Weight:** 6.5 lbs.
Price: $159.95

TRAPPER SINGLE-BARREL SHOTGUN

SPECIFICATIONS
Gauge: 12 percussion
Barrel length: 28" round, chrome-lines bore; hooked breech
Choke: European Modified
Overall length: 46" Weight: 6 lbs.
Trigger: Early-style steel

Lock: Color Casehardened; engraves with V-type main-spring, bridle and fly
Sights: Brass bead front (no rear sight)
Stock: Select hardwood
Features: Color casehardened engraved lockplate; ventilated recoil pad, fiberglass ramrod and rear swivel
Price: $239.95

CLASSIC TURKEY DOUBLE-BARREL SHOTGUN

SPECIFICATIONS
Gauge: 12 percussion
Barrel length: 28" round, chrome-lined bore; double button-style breech
Choke: European Modified **Overall length:** 45"
Weight: 9 lbs. **Triggers:** Hinged, gold-tone double triggers
Lock: Color casehardened; engraves with V-type main-

spring, bridle and fly
Sights: Brass bead front (no rear sight)
Stock: Select hardwood; wraparound forearm with bottom screw attachment
Features: Ventilated recoil pad; rear sling swivel; fiberglass ramrod
Price: $459.95

CVA RIFLES

IN-LINE MUZZLELOADING RIFLES

ACCUBOLT PRO

SPECIFICATIONS
Caliber: 50 **Barrel Length:** 24"
Rifling: 1:26" **Weight:** 7.5 lbs.
Price: $559.95

Also Available:
Same model as above w/hammer
  forged barrel 339.95

FIREBOLT® w/ADVANTAGE CAMO

FIREBOLT™ SERIES

SPECIFICATIONS
Calibers: 50 (1:32" rifling) and (54 (1:32")
Barrel length: 24" **Weight:** 7 lbs. **Finish:** Matte blue
or stainless **Stock:** Synthetic, Synthetic w/Advantage
Camo, Thumbhole

Prices:
SYNTHETIC STOCK W/STAINLESS BARREL $299.95
SYNTHETIC STOCK W/MATTE BLUE BBL. 249.95
SYNTHETIC STOCK SNIPER CAMO. 279.95
SYNTHETIC STOCK ADVANTAGE CAMO/MATTE BLUE . . . 279.95
THUMBHOLE STOCK W/MATTE BLUE. 279.95

STAG HORN RIFLE
SPECIFICATIONS
Calibers: 50 and 54
Lock: In-line chrome-plated steel percussion bolt
Barrel length: 24" round (1:32") **Overall length:** 42"

Weight: 7 lbs. **Sights:** Blued steel beaded blade front;
Williams "Hunter" sight rear
Stock: Synthetic Dura-Grip stock w/pistol grip
Features: Removable breech plug; oversized black trigger
guard; bottom screw barrel attachment;
black synthetic ramrod w/black tips
Price: $134.95

DIXIE

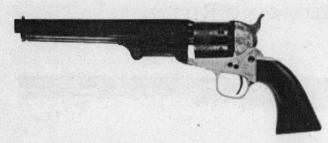

1851 NAVY BRASS-FRAME REVOLVER

This 36-caliber revolver was a favorite of the officers of the Civil War. Although called a Navy type, it is somewhat misnamed since many more of the Army personnel used it. Made in Italy; uses .376 mold or ball to fit and number 11 caps. Blued steel barrel and cylinder with brass frame.
Price:
Plain Model $139.95

SPILLER & BURR 36 CALIBER BRASS-FRAME REVOLVER

The 36-caliber octagonal barrel on this revolver is 7 inches long. The six-shot cylinder chambers mike .378, and the hammer engages a slot between the nipples on the cylinder as an added safety device. It has a solid brass trigger guard and frame with backstrap cast integral with the frame, two-piece walnut grips and Whitney-type casehardened loading lever.
Price: $159.95
Kɪт 149.95

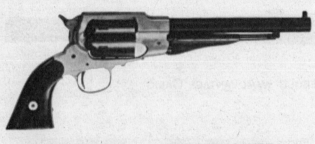

REMINGTON 44 ARMY REVOLVER

All steel external surfaces finished bright blue, including 8" octagonal barrel (hammer is casehardened). Polished brass guard and two-piece walnut grips are standard.
Price: $150.00

1860 ARMY REVOLVER

The Dixie 1860 Army has a half-fluted cylinder and its chamber diameter is .447. Use .451 round ball mold to fit this 8-inch barrel revolver. Cut for shoulder stock.
Price: $196.00

WALKER REVOLVER

This 4 1/2-pound, 44-caliber pistol is the largest cap and ball revolver commercially built during the 19th century. Steel backstrap; guard is brass with Walker-type rounded-to-frame walnut grips; all other parts are blued. Chambers measure .445 and take a .450 ball slightly smaller than the original.
Price: $225.00

"WYATT EARP" REVOLVER

This 44-caliber revolver has a 12-inch octagon rifled barrel and rebated cylinder. Highly polished brass frame, backstrap and trigger guard. The barrel and cylinder have a deep blue luster finish. Hammer, trigger, and loading lever are casehardened. Walnut grips. Recommended ball size is .451.
Price: $150.00

DIXIE

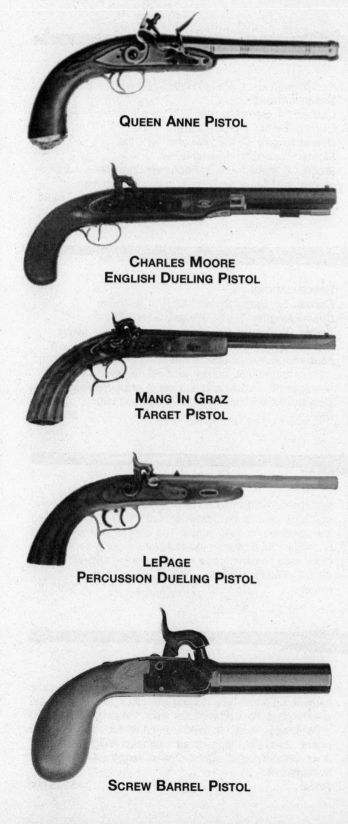

QUEEN ANNE PISTOL

CHARLES MOORE ENGLISH DUELING PISTOL

MANG IN GRAZ TARGET PISTOL

LEPAGE PERCUSSION DUELING PISTOL

SCREW BARREL PISTOL

QUEEN ANNE PISTOL

Named for the Queen of England (1702-1714), this flintlock pistol has a 7 1/2" barrel that tapers from rear to front with a cannon-shaped muzzle. The brass trigger guard is fluted and the brass butt on the walnut stock features a grotesque mask worked into it. *Overall length:* 13". *Weight:* 2.25 lbs.
Price: $225.00
KIT 175.00

CHARLES MOORE ENGLISH DUELING PISTOL

This reproduction of an English percussion dueling pistol, created by Charles Moore of London, features a European walnut halfstock with oil finish and checkered grip. The 45-caliber octagonal barrel is 11" with 12 grooves and a twist of 1 in 15". Nose cap and thimble are silver. Barrel is blued; lock and trigger guard are color casehardened.
Price: FLINT $385.00
PERCUSSION 323.95

MANG TARGET PISTOL

Designed specifically for the precision target shooter, this 38-caliber pistol has a 10 7/16" octagonal barrel with 7 lands and grooves. Twist is 1 in 15". Sights: Blade front dovetailed into barrel; rear mounted on breechplug tang, adjustable for windage. *Overall length:* 17 1/4". *Weight:* 2 .5 lbs.
Price: $786.00

LePAGE PERCUSSION DUELING PISTOL

This 45-caliber percussion pistol features a blued 10" octagonal barrel with 12 lands and grooves; a brass-bladed front sight with open rear sight dovetailed into the barrel; polished silver-plated trigger guard and butt cap. Right side of barrel is stamped "LePage á Paris." Double-set riggers are single screw adjustable. *Overall length:* 16". *Weight:* 2.5 lbs.
Price: $259.95

SCREW BARREL (FOLDING TRIGGER) PISTOL

This little gun, only 6 1/2" overall, has a unique loading system that eliminates the need for a ramrod. The barrel is loosened with a barrel key, then unscrewed from the frame by hand. The recess is then filled with 10 grains of FFFg black powder, the .445 round ball is seated in the dished area, and the barrel is then screwed back into place. The .245X32 nipple uses #11 percussion caps. The pistol also features a sheath trigger that folds into the frame, then drops down for firing when the hammer is cocked. Comes with color case hardened frame, trigger and center-mounted hammer.
Price: $126.95
KIT 95.00

BLACK POWDER

DIXIE

SHARPS MODEL 1859 CARBINE

About 115,000 Sharps New Model 1859 carbines and its variants were made during the Civil War. Characterized by durability and accuracy, they became a favorite of cavalrymen on both sides. Made in Italy by David Pedersoli & Co.

SPECIFICATIONS
Caliber: 54 *Barrel length:* 22" (1 in 48" twist); blued, round barrel has 7-groove rifling
Overall length: 37 1/2" *Weight:* 7 3/4 lbs.
Sights: Blade front; adjustable rear
Stock: Oil-finished walnut *Features:* Barrel band, hammer, receiver, saddle bar and ring all color casehardened
Price: **$775.00**

SHARPS NEW MODEL 1859 MILITARY RIFLE

Initially used by the First Connecticut Volunteers, this rifle is associated mostly with the 1st U.S. (Berdan's) Sharpshooters. There were 6,689 made with most going to the Sharpshooters (2,000) and the U.S. Navy (2,780). Made in Italy by David Pedersoli & Co.

SPECIFICATIONS
Caliber: 54 *Barrel length:* 30" (1 in 48" twist)
Overall length: 45 1/2" *Weight:* 9 lbs.
Sights: Blade front; rear sight adjustable for elevations and windage
Features: Buttstock and forend straight-grained oil finished walnut; three barrel bands, receiver, hammer, nose cap, lever, patchbox cover and butt are all color case hardened; sling swivels attached to middle band and butt
Price: **$895.00**

1874 SHARPS LIGHTWEIGHT HUNTER RIFLE

This Sharps rifle in 45-70 Government caliber has a 30" octagon barrel with blued matte finish (1:18" twist). It also features an adjustable hunting rear sight and blade front, making it ideal for blackpowder hunters. The tang is drilled and threaded for tang sights. The oil-finished military-style buttstock has a blued metal buttplate. Double-set triggers. Color case hardened receiver and hammer. *Overall length:* 49 1/2". *Weight:* 10 lbs.
Price: **$995.00**

1874 SHARPS SILHOUETTE MODEL

This rifle in .40-65 and .45-70 caliber has a shotgun-style buttstock with a pistol grip and a metal buttplate. The 30-inch tapered octagon barrel is blued and has a 1 in 18" twist. The receiver, hammer, lever and buttplate are color case hardened. Ladder-type hunting rear and blade front sights are standard. Four screw holes are in the tang: two with 10 x 28 threads, two with metric threads, for attaching tang sights. Double set triggers are standard. *Weight* is 10 lbs. 3 oz. without target sights. *Overall length:* 47 1/2". Also available in 45-70
Price: **$995.00**

DIXIE

DIXIE TENNESSEE MOUNTAIN RIFLE

This 50-caliber rifle features double-set triggers with adjustable set screw, bore rifled with 6 lands and grooves, barrel of 15/16 inch across the flats, brown finish and cherry stock. *Overall length:* 41 1/2 inches. Right- and left-hand versions in flint or percussion.
Prices:
PERCUSSION OR FLINTLOCK $575.00
KIT 495.00

PENNSYLVANIA RIFLE

A lightweight at just 8 pounds, the 41 1/2" blued rifle barrel is fitted with an open buckhorn rear sight and front blade. The walnut one-piece stock is stained a medium darkness that contrasts with the polished brass buttplate, toe plate, patch-box, sideplate, trigger guard, thimbles and nose cap. Featuring double-set triggers, the rifle can be fired by pulling only the front trigger, which has a normal trigger pull of 4 to 5 pounds; or the rear trigger can first be pulled to set a spring-loaded mechanism that greatly reduces the amount of pull needed for the front trigger to kick off the sear in the lock. The land-to-land measurement of the bore is an exact .450: the recommended ball size is .445.
Overall length: 51 1/2".
Prices: PERCUSSION OR FLINTLOCK $472.00
KIT (Flint or Perc.) 415.00

HAWKEN RIFLE (Not Shown)

Blued barrel is 15/16" across the flats and 30" in length with a twist of 1 in 64". Stock is of walnut with a steel crescent buttplate, halfstock with brass nosecap. Double-set triggers, front-action lock and adjustable rear sight. Ramrod is equipped with jag. *Overall length:* 46 1/2". *Weight:* about 8 lbs., depending on the caliber; shipping weight is 10 lbs. Available in either finished gun or kit. *Calibers:* 45, 50 and 54.
Price: $250.00
KIT 205.00

WAADTLANDER RIFLE (Not Shown)

This authentic re-creation of a Swiss muzzloading target rifle features a heavy octagonal barrel (31") that has 7 lands and grooves. *Caliber:* 45. Rate of twist is 1 turn in 48". Double-set triggers are multi-lever type and are easily removable for adjustment. Sights are fitted post front and tang-mounted Swiss-type diopter rear. Walnut stock, color case hardened hardware, classic buttplate and curved trigger guard complete this reproduction. The original was made between 1839 and 1860 by Marc Bristlen, Morges, Switzerland.
Price: $1,412.00

DOUBLE-BARREL MAGNUM MUZZLELOADING SHOTGUN (Not Shown)

A full 10, 12 or 20 gauge, high-quality, double-barreled percussion shotgun with 30-inch browned barrels. Will take the plastic shot cups for better patterns. Bores are choked Modified and Full. Lock, barrel tang and trigger are case-hardened in a light gray color and are nicely engraved.

Prices:
12 GAUGE $449.00
12 GAUGE KIT 375.00
10 GAUGE MAGNUM (right-hand = Cyl.,
    left-hand = Mod.) 495.00
10 GAUGE MAGNUM KIT 395.00
20 GAUGE 495.00

DIXIE

KODIAK MARK IV .45-70 DOUBLE BARREL RIFLE

Patterned after a classic, limited edition 19th century Colt double rifle, the Kodiak Mark IV has been designed for hunters and collectors. The 24-inch, browned barrels are semi-regulated and topped with a triple leaf. The adjustable rear sight is marked for 100, 200 and 300 yards, providing an option of sighting for various ranges with different loads. Locks, receiver, triggerguard and hammers are color case hardened. The two-piece stock is made from European walnut; forearm and pistol grip are checkered. The buttstock has a cheekpiece and a solid, red rubber pad. Sling swivels are standard. **Weight:** 10 lbs. **Overall length:** 40"
Price: $2,495.00

1873 TRAPDOOR CARBINE

1873 TRAPDOOR SPRINGFIELD

1873 SPRINGFIELD RIFLE AND CARBINE

Developed from the Allin Conversion of Springfield muskets from the Civil War, 1873 Springfield "Trapdoors" became the firearms that finished the winning of the west. Adopted in 1873 and immediately issued to troops on the frontier, the Trapdoor was the final single shot, blackpowder rifle of the U.S. military, later supplanted by the adoption of the .30-.40 Krag-Jorgensen.

RIFLE
Caliber: 45-70. **Barrel length:** 32.5" round. 1-22 twist; 3 groove rifling; all furniture blued; sling swivels; open sights; ladder style elevation rear adjustable to 500 yards. **Overall length:** 52" **Weight:** 8.5 lbs. Walnut stock
Price: $995.00

CARBINE
Caliber: 45-70. **Barrel length:** 22" round. 1-22 twist; 3 groove rifling; all furniture blued; saddle bar and ring; open sights; ladder style elevation rear adjustable to 400 yards. **Overall length:** 41" **Weight:** 8.5 lbs. Walnut stock.
Price: $895.00

OFFICER'S MODEL
Caliber: 45-70. **Barrel length:** 26" round. 1-18 twist; 6 groove rifling; pewter ramrod tip and nosecap; color case hardened hammer and lock; walnut stock; checkered wrist and forearm; single set trigger; fully adjustable tang sight. **Overall length:** 45" **Weight:** 8 lbs.
Price: $1,025.00

DIXIE

U.S. MODEL 1861
SPRINGFIELD PERCUSSION RIFLE-MUSKET

An exact re-creation of an original rifle produced by Springfield National Armory, Dixie's Model 1861 Springfield 58-caliber rifle features a 40" round, tapered barrel with three barrel bands. Sling swivels are attached to the trigger guard bow and middle barrel band. The ramrod has a trumpet-shaped head with swell; sights are standard military rear and bayonet-attachment lug front. The percussion lock is marked "1861" on the rear of the lockplate with an eagle motif and "U.S. Springfield" in front of the hammer. "U.S." is stamped on top of buttplate. All furniture is "National Armory Bright."
Overall length: 55 13/16". **Weight:** 8 lbs.
Prices: **$595.00**
KIT **525.00**

1862 THREE-BAND ENFIELD RIFLED MUSKET

One of the finest reproduction percussion guns available, the 1861 Enfield was widely used during the Civil War in its original version. This rifle follows the lines of the original almost exactly. The 58-caliber musket features a 39-inch barrel and walnut stock. Three steel barrel bands and the barrel itself are blued; the lockplate and hammer are case colored and the remainder of the furniture is highly polished brass. The lock is marked, "London Armory Co." **Weight:** 10.5 lbs. **Overall length:** 55".
Prices: **$495.00**
KIT **425.00**

U.S. MODEL 1816 FLINTLOCK MUSKET

The U.S. Model 1816 Flintlock Musket was made by Harpers Ferry and Springfield Arsenal from 1816 until 1864. It had the highest production of any U.S. flintlock musket and after conversion to percussion saw service in the Civil War. It has a 69-caliber, 42" smoothbore barrel held by three barrel bands with springs. All metal parts are finished in "National Armory Bright." The lockplate has a brass pan and is marked "Harpers Ferry" vertically behind the hammer, with an American eagle placed in front of the hammer. The bayonet lug is on top of the barrel and the steel ramrod has a button-shaped head. Sling swivels are mounted on trigger guard and middle barrel band.
Overall length: 56.5"
Weight: 9.75 lbs.
Price: **$725.00**

1858 TWO-BAND ENFIELD RIFLE

This 33-inch barrel version of the British Enfield is an exact copy of similar rifles used during the Civil War. The 58-caliber rifle sports a European walnut stock, deep blue-black finish on the barrel, bands, breech-plug tang and bayonet mount. The percussion lock is color case hardened and the rest of the furniture is brightly polished brass.
Price: **$475.00**

BLACK POWDER

EMF HARTFORD REVOLVERS

SHERIFF'S MODEL 1851

MODEL 1860 ARMY REVOLVER

SPECIFICATIONS
Caliber: 44 Percussion *Barrel length:* 8"
Overall length: 13 ⅝" *Weight:* 41 oz.
Frame: Case hardened
Finish: High-luster blue with walnut grips
Price: Brass Frame $160.00
Also available:
CASED SET with steel frame, wood case, flask
  and mould $375.00
  Engraved cased set (brass frame only) 315.00
FLUTED CYLINDER MODEL (steel frame only) 380.00

1860 ARMY BRASS FRAME CASED SET
Price: $300.00

HARTFORD 1863 TEXAS DRAGOON

SPECIFICATIONS
Caliber: 44
Barrel length: 7" (round)
Overall length: 14"
Weight: 4 lbs.
Finish: Steel casehardened frame
Price: $330.00

SHERIFF'S MODEL 1851 REVOLVER

SPECIFICATIONS
Caliber: 44 Percussion
Ball diameter: .376 round or conical, pure lead
Barrel length: 5" *Overall length:* 10.5" *Weight:* 39 oz.
Sights: V-notch groove in hammer (rear); truncated
cone in front
Percussion cap size: #11
Prices:
Brass $150.00
Steel 200.00

MODEL 1860 ARMY

HARTFORD MODEL 1862 POLICE REVOLVER

SPECIFICATIONS
Caliber: 36 Percussion
Capacity: 5-shot
Barrel length: 6.5"
Prices:
Steel $250.00
Brass 170.00

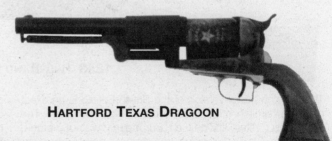

HARTFORD TEXAS DRAGOON

EMF HARTFORD REVOLVERS

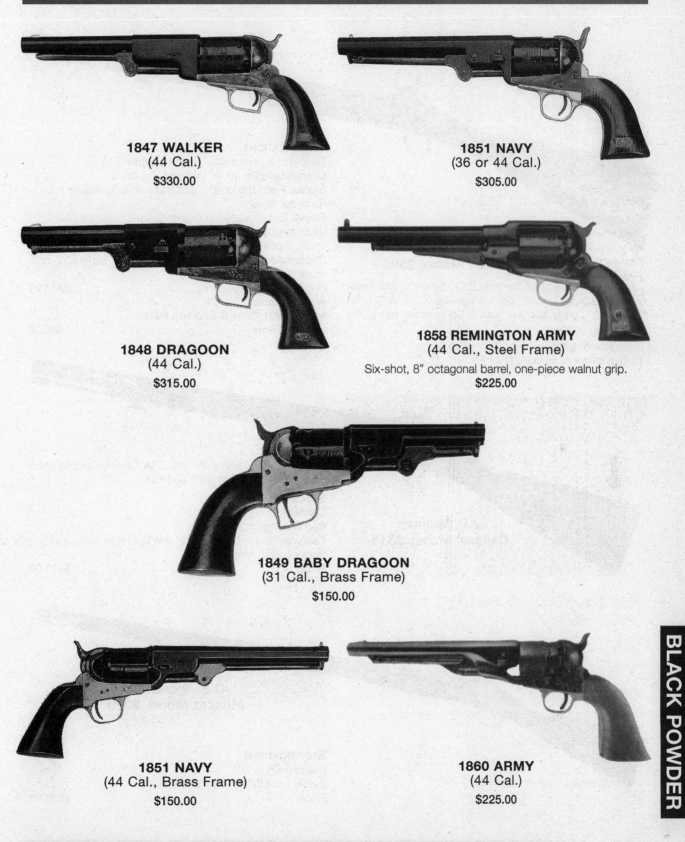

1847 WALKER
(44 Cal.)
$330.00

1851 NAVY
(36 or 44 Cal.)
$305.00

1848 DRAGOON
(44 Cal.)
$315.00

1858 REMINGTON ARMY
(44 Cal., Steel Frame)
Six-shot, 8" octagonal barrel, one-piece walnut grip.
$225.00

1849 BABY DRAGOON
(31 Cal., Brass Frame)
$150.00

1851 NAVY
(44 Cal., Brass Frame)
$150.00

1860 ARMY
(44 Cal.)
$225.00

BLACK POWDER

EUROARMS OF AMERICA

COOK & BROTHER
CONFEDERATE CARBINE MODEL 2300

Classic re-creation of the rare 1861, New Orleans-made Artillery Carbine. The lockplate is marked "Cook & Brother N.O. 1861" and is stamped with a Confederate flag at the rear of the hammer.

SPECIFICATIONS
Caliber: 58 percussion *Barrel Length:* 24"
Overall Length: 40 1/3" *Weight:* 7.5 lbs.
Sights: Fixed blade front and adjustable dovetailed rear
Ramrod: Steel
Finish: Barrel is antique brown; buttplate, trigger guard, barrel bands, sling swivels and nose cap are polished brass; stock is walnut
Recommended ball sizes: .575 r.b., .577 Minie and .580 maxi; uses musket caps
Price: $447.00
Also available:
MODEL 2301 COOK & BROTHER FIELD
with 33" barrel 480.00

J.P. MURRAY
CARBINE MODEL 2315

Replica of an extremely rare CSA Cavalry Carbine based on an 1841 design of parts and lock.

SPECIFICATIONS
Caliber: 58
Barrel Length: 23"
Features: Brass barrel bands and buttplate; oversized trigger guard; sling swivels
Price: $453.00

C.S. RICHMOND
MUSKET MODEL 2370

SPECIFICATIONS
Caliber: 58
Barrel Length: 40" with three bands
Price: $530.00

EUROARMS OF AMERICA

LONDON ARMORY COMPANY ENFIELD P-1858 2-BAND RIFLE MUSKET MODEL 2270

SPECIFICATIONS
Caliber: 58 percussion
Barrel Length: 33", blued and rifled
Overall Length: 49"
Weight: 8.5 to 8.75 lbs., depending on wood density
Stock: One-piece walnut; polished "bright" brass buttplate, trigger guard and nose cap; blued barrel bands
Sights: Inverted 'V' front sight; Enfield folding ladder rear
Ramrod: Steel
Price: $470.00

LONDON ARMORY COMPANY ENFIELD P-1861 MUSKETOON MODEL 2280

SPECIFICATIONS
Caliber: 58; Minie ball
Barrel Length: 24"; round high-luster blued barrel
Overall Length: 40.5"
Weight: 7 to 7.5 lbs., depending on density of wood
Stock: Seasoned walnut stock with sling swivels
Ramrod: Steel
Ignition: Heavy-duty percussion lock
Sights: Graduated military-leaf sight
Furniture: Brass trigger guard, nose cap and buttplate; blued barrel bands, lock plate, and swivels
Price: $415.00

LONDON ARMORY COMPANY 3-BAND ENFIELD P-1853 RIFLED MUSKET MODEL 2260

SPECIFICATIONS
Caliber: 58 percussion
Barrel Length: 38", blued and rifled
Overall Length: 54"
Weight: 9.5 to 9.75 lbs., depending on wood density
Stock: One-piece walnut; polished "bright" brass buttplate, trigger guard and nose cap; blued barrel bands
Ramrod: Steel; threaded end for accessories
Sights: Traditional Enfield folding ladder rear sight; inverted 'V' front sight
Price: $480.00
Also available:
MODEL 2261 w/white barrel, satin finish 520.00

BLACK POWDER

EUROARMS OF AMERICA

U.S. 1803 HARPERS FERRY FLINTLOCK RIFLE MODEL 2305

SPECIFICATIONS
Caliber: 54 Flintlock
Barrel Length: 35", octagonal
Features: Walnut half stock with cheekpiece; browned barrel
Price: $640.00

U.S.1841 MISSISSIPPI RIFLE MODEL 2310

SPECIFICATIONS
Calibers: 54 and 58 percussion
Barrel Length: 33", octagonal
Features: Walnut stock; brass barrel bands and buttplate; sling swivels
Price: $500.00

U.S. MODEL 1863 REMINGTON ZOUAVE RIFLE (2-BARREL BANDS)

SPECIFICATIONS
Caliber: 58 percussion
Barrel Length: 33", octagonal
Overall Length: 48.5"
Weight: 9.5 to 9.75 lbs.
Sights: U.S. Military 3-leaf rear; blade front
Features: Two brass barrel bands; brass buttplate and nose cap; sling swivels
Price: $430.00

U.S. MODEL 1861 SPRINGFIELD RIFLE

SPECIFICATIONS
Caliber: 58 percussion
Barrel Length: 40"
Features: 3 barrel bands
Price: $530.00

EUROARMS OF AMERICA

MODEL 1005

ROGERS & SPENCER ARMY REVOLVER MODEL 1006 (Target)

SPECIFICATIONS

Caliber: 44; takes .451 round or conical balls; #11 percussion cap *Weight:* 47 oz. *Barrel Length:* 7.5"
Overall Length: 13.75" *Finish:* High gloss blue; flared walnut grip; solid frame design; precision-rifled barrel
Sights: Rear fully adjustable for windage and elevation; ramp front sight
Price: $239.00

ROGERS & SPENCER REVOLVER LONDON GRAY MODEL 1007 (Not Shown)

Revolver is the same as Model 1005, except for London Gray finish, which is heat treated and buffed for rust resistance; same recommended ball size and percussion caps.

Price: $245.00
Also available: MODEL 1120 COLT 1851 NAVY Steel or brass frame. 36 cal. *Barrel Length:* 7.5" octagonal.
Overall Length: 13" *Weight:* 42 oz.
Price: 156.00
MODEL 1210 COLT 1860 ARMY Steel frame. 44 percussion
Overall Length: 10 ⁵⁄₈" or 13 ⁵⁄₈" *Weight:* 41 oz.
Price: 177.00

ROGERS & SPENCER REVOLVER MODEL 1005

SPECIFICATIONS

Caliber: 44 Percussion; #11 percussion cap
Barrel Length: 7.5" *Overall Length:* 13.75" *Weight:* 47 oz.
Sights: Integral rear sight notch groove in frame; brass truncated cone front sight
Finish: High gloss blue; flared walnut grip; solid frame design; precision-rifled barrel *Recommended ball diameter:* .451 round or conical, pure lead
Price: $227.00

MODEL 1006

REMINGTON 1858 NEW MODEL ARMY ENGRAVED MODEL 1040 (Not Shown)

Classical 19th-century style scroll engraving on this 1858 Remington New Model revolver.

SPECIFICATIONS

Caliber: 44 Percussion; #11 cap *Barrel Length:* 8"
Overall Length: 14.75" *Weight:* 41 oz. *Sights:* Integral rear sight notch groove in frame; blade front sight
Recommended ball diameter: .451 round or conical, pure lead
Price: $275.00

REMINGTON 1858 NEW MODEL ARMY REVOLVER MODEL 1020

This model is equipped with blued steel frame, brass trigger guard in 44 caliber.

SPECIFICATIONS

Weight: 40 oz. *Barrel Length:* 8" *Overall Length:* 14.75"
Finish: Deep luster blue rifled barrel; polished walnut stock; brass trigger guard.
Price: $200.00
Also available: MODEL 1010 Same as Model 1020, except w/6.5" barrel and in 36 caliber: $200.00

MODEL 1010
(36 Cal. W/6.5" barrel)

GONIC ARMS

MODEL 93 RIFLE SERIES

MOUNTAIN CLASSIC

MOUNTAIN THUMBHOLE

DELUXE

MODEL 93 MOUNTAIN CLASSIC RIFLE

SPECIFICATIONS
Caliber: 50 Magnum
Barrel Length: 26" 4140 chrome-moly blued satin or 416 stainless steel w/matte finish; 1-in-24" twist
Length Of Pull: 14"
Trigger: Single, adjustable w/side safety
Weight: 6.5 to 7 lbs.
Sights: Open or peep sights, fully adjustable for windage and elevation; ramp front w/gold bead and protector hood

Stock: Walnut or laminated (left or right hand)
Features: Unbreakable ram rod; classic cheekpiece; three-point pillar bedding system; 1" decelerator recoil pad; sling swivel studs; E-Z-Load Muzzle System w/muzzle break
Price:. $2,132.00
Also Available:
MODEL 93 MOUNTAIN THUMBHOLE RIFLE w/same specification and features as above, but w/thumbhole Monte Carlo rollover cheekpiece, beavertail forend and palm swell grip.
Price:. 2,132.00

MODEL 93 RIFLE

Gonic Arm's blackpowder rifle has a unique loading system that produces better consistency and utilizes the full powder charge of the specially designed penetrator bullet (2,650 foot-pounds at 1,600 fps w/465-grain .500 bullet).

SPECIFICATIONS
Caliber: 50 Magnum
Barrel Lengths: 26"
Overall Length: 43"
Weight: 6 to 6.5 lbs.
Sights: Open hunting sights (adjustable)
Features: Walnut-stained hardwood stock; adjustable trigger;

nipple wrench; drilled and tapped for scope bases; ballistics and instruction manual

Prices:
Open Sights $500.57
Stainless w/Open Sights. 603.04
Also Available:
MODEL 93 SAFARI CLASSIC RIFLE w/classic walnut
    stock, open sights 1,612.00
MODEL 93 DELUXE w/grey laminated stock;
    Weaver scope base; open sights; E-Z-Load
    Muzzle System. 660.25

LYMAN RIFLES

LYMAN COUGAR-IN-LINE STAINLESS

LYMAN COUGAR-IN-LINE RIFLE

The **LYMAN COUGAR IN-LINE** rifle is designed for the serious blackpowder hunter who wants a rugged and accurate muzzleloader with the feel of a centerfire bolt-action rifle. The Cougar In-Line is traditionally styled with a walnut stock and blued barrel and action. Available in 50 and 54 caliber. Features include a 22" barrel with 1:24" twist and shallow rifling grooves; dual safety system (equipped with a bolt safety notch in receiver and a sliding thumb safety that disables the trigger mechanism); drilled and tapped for Lyman 57

WTR receiver sight; fully adjustable trigger; sling swivel studs installed; unbreakable Delrin ramrod; modern folding-leaf rear and bead front sights; rubber recoil pad.
Price: **$299.95**
Also available in **stainless steel** on all major parts. Features same as standard version. Stock is semi-Schnabel forend with black Hard Kote finish.
Price: **$382.95**

DEERSTALKER STAINLESS

DEERSTALKER RIFLE

LYMAN'S DEERSTALKER rifle incorporates • higher comb for better sighting plane • nonglare hardware • 24" octagonal barrel • case hardened sideplate • Q.D. sling swivels • Lyman sight package (37MA beaded front, fully adjustable fold-down 16A rear) • walnut stock with black recoil pad • single trigger. Left-hand models available (same price). *Calibers:* 50 and 54, flintlock or percussion. *Weight:* 7.5 lbs.

Price: Percussion **$304.95**
    Left-Hand 319.95
    Flintlock 329.95
    Left Hand 344.95
DEERSTALKER STAINLESS. Features all stainless steel parts, plus walnut stock, recoil pad, Delrin ramrod, Lyman front and rear hunting sights.
Price: **$384.95**

LYMAN RIFLES

GREAT PLAINS RIFLE

GREAT PLAINS HUNTER

The **GREAT PLAINS** has a 32-inch deep-grooved barrel and 1 in 66" twist to shoot patched round balls. Blued steel furniture including the thick steel wedge plates and toe plate; correct lock and hammer styling with coil spring dependability; a walnut stock w/o patchbox. A Hawken-style trigger guard protects double-set triggers. Steel front sight and authentic buckhorn styling in an adjustable rear sight. Fixed primitive rear sight also included. **Calibers:** 50 and 54.

Price:
Percussion	$429.95
Kit	349.95
Flintlock	454.95
Kit	374.95
Left-Hand Model Percussion	439.95
Left-Hand Model Flintlock	464.95

Also available:
GREAT PLAINS HUNTER. Same features as standard rifle but with 1 in 32" twist and shallow rifling groove for shooting modern sabots and black powder hunting bullets.

Price:
Percussion	$429.95
Flintlock	$454.95

LYMAN TRADE RIFLE

The **LYMAN TRADE RIFLE** features a 28-inch octagonal barrel, rifled 1 turn at 48 inches, designed to fire both patched round balls and the popular maxi-style conical bullets. Polished brass furniture with blued finish on steel parts; walnut stock; hook breech; single spring-loaded trigger; coil-spring percussion lock; fixed steel sights; adjustable rear sight for elevation also included. Steel barrel rib and ramrod ferrule. **Caliber:** 50 and 54 percussion and flint.

Overall Length: 45"

Price:
Percussion	$299.95
Flintlock	$324.95

MARKESBERY MUZZLE LOADERS

Markesbery's Black Bear, Grizzly Bear and Brown Bear rifles are made of eight cast, polished molded parts, coupled with an all-cast receiver and trigger guard. Pillow mount system with interchangeable barrels in 36, 45, .50 and 54 calibers. All rifles are constructed with Markesbery's **MAGNUM HAMMER IN-LINE IGNITION SYSTEM**, the 400 SRP (small rifle primer) system or optional No. 11 cap and nipple. This system, along with a 1-26" twist button precision 24" rifle barrel, is available in either 4140 or stainless steel models. All models have a double safety system with half cock and cross bolt hammer safeties. Marble adjustable sights with double adjustment features, hammer thumb rest and rubber recoil pad are standard.

The Black Bear is made of a two-piece, handcrafted hardwood walnut, black laminate and green laminate pistol grip. *Weight:* 6.5 lbs. *Overall Length:* 38.5". The Brown and Grizzly Bear models offer custom-checkered Monte Carlo (Grizzly Bear two-piece or Brown Bear one-piece) thumbhole stocks. *Overall Length:* 38.5" *Weight:* 6.5 lbs. (Brown Bear is 6.75 lbs.). Both models are available in black composite, crotch walnut, Mossy Oak Treestand™, Xtra-B™ and Xtra-G™. Finishes are available in glossy black blued, matte and stainless steel. All models support a solid aluminum ram rod with brass jag and bullet starter.

Price: **BLACK BEAR** (two-piece pistol grip stock)
(depending on stock). **$536.63-573.73**

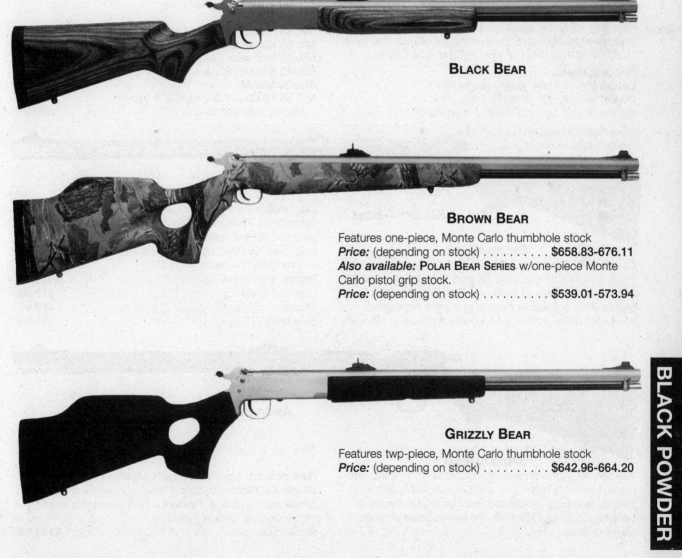

BLACK BEAR

BROWN BEAR

Features one-piece, Monte Carlo thumbhole stock
Price: (depending on stock) **$658.83-676.11**
Also available: **POLAR BEAR SERIES** w/one-piece Monte Carlo pistol grip stock.
Price: (depending on stock) **$539.01-573.94**

GRIZZLY BEAR

Features twp-piece, Monte Carlo thumbhole stock
Price: (depending on stock) **$642.96-664.20**

Modern Muzzleloading

MK-86 12 Gauge Shotgun

MK-85 Stalker

MK-85 AND MK-86 KNIGHT RIFLES

The MK-85 muzzleloading rifles (designed by William A. "Tony" Knight) are handcrafted, lightweight rifles capable of 1 1/2-inch groups at 100 yards. They feature a one-piece, inline bolt assembly, patented double-safety system, Timney featherweight deluxe trigger system, recoil pad, and Green Mountain barrels (1 in 28" twist in 50 and 54 caliber).

SPECIFICATIONS
Calibers: 50 and 54 *Barrel length:* 24"
Overall length: 43" *Weight:* 7 lbs.
Sights: Adjustable high-visibility open sights

Stock: Classic walnut, laminated or composite
Features: Swivel studs installed; hard anodized aluminum ramrod; combo tool; hex keys.
Prices:
MK-85 HUNTER Walnut Stock $549.95
MK-85 KNIGHT HAWK 769.95
MK-85 PREDATOR (Stainless) Laminated Stock 649.95
MK-85 STALKER Black Composite Stock 569.95
Also available:
MK-86 12 GAUGE SHOTGUN (22" barrel),
  black composite stock 599.95

KNIGHT T-BOLT

SPECIFICATIONS
Caliber: 50 *Barrel Length:* 22" (blued or matte stainless) or 26" (matte stainless only) *Overall Length:* 41" *Length of pull:* 14.5" *Rate of twist:* 1 in 28" *Weight:* 6 lbs.
Sights: Fully adjustable mettalic rear sight; front ramp and bead; drilled and tapped for scope mounting *Stock:*

Composite (Black Mossy Oak Break Up or Bill Jordan's Advantage) *Features:* Sling swivel studs installed; patented double safety system; stainless steel breech plug; patented Red Hot nipple; adjustable Knight trigger; In-Line ignition system
Prices: Blue Break-Up $449.95
Stainless Break-Up 519.95
Stainless 469.95
Blue only 399.95

AMERICAN KNIGHT

SPECIFICATIONS
Caliber: 50 *Action:* Patented double safety system; one-piece removable hammer assembly; removable stainless steel breech plug w/patented Red Hot nipple *Barrel Length:* 22" Green Mountain rifle barrel; blued or matte stainless steel

Rate of twist: 1 in 28" *Overall Length:* 41" *Weight:* 6 lbs.
Stock: Full dimension hollow black composite stock; sling swivel studs installed *Features:* Non-adjustable Knight trigger; In-Line ignition system
Price: Blued only $199.95

MODERN MUZZLELOADING

MODEL LK-93 WOLVERINE

SPECIFICATIONS
Calibers: 50 and 54
Barrel length: 22"; blued rifle-grade steel (1:28" twist)
Overall length: 41" *Weight:* 6 lbs.
Sights: Adjustable high-visibility rear sight; drilled and tapped for scope mount

Stock: Lightweight Fiber-Lite molded stock
Features: Patented double-safety system; adjustable Accu-Lite trigger; removable breechplug; stainless-steel hammer
Prices:
Blued $269.95
Stainless 389.95
Blued Advantage or Break-Up 319.95
Stainless Advantage or Break-up 419.95
Value Pack 299.95

LK-93 THUMBHOLE WOLVERINE

SPECIFICATIONS
Calibers: 50 and 54
Barrel length: 22" rifle-grade steel (1:28" twist)
Overall length: 41" *Weight:* 6 lbs. 4 oz.

LK-93 THUMBHOLE WOLVERINE w/MOSSY OAK CAMO

Features: Patented double safety system: adjustable Accu-Lite trigger; removable breech plug; stainless steel hammer
Prices:
Blued w/Black Stock $309.95
Blued w/Camo Stock. 359.95
Stainless Steel w/Black Stock. 379.95
Stainless Steel w/Camo Stock 429.95

DISC RIFLE

SPECIFICATIONS
Caliber: 50
Action: Patented double safety system; turn bolt style
Barrel length: 24" (Green Mountain barrel; blued or matte stainless rifle grade steel)
Overall length: 43" *Rate of twist:* 1 in 28"
Length of pull: 14.5" *Weight:* 14 oz.
Sights: Metallic rear sight; front ramp and bead

Stock: Compositte (Black Mossy Oak Break-Up); Bill Jordan's Advantage w/rubber recoil pad; checkered forearm and palm swell pistol grip;
Features: Fully adjustable Knight trigger; In-Line ignition system; one-piece removable bolt assembly; removable stainless steel breech plug
Prices:
Blue $449.95
Stainless 519.95
Mossy Oak Advantage or Break-Up (Blued). 499.95
Mossy Oak Advantage or Break-Up (Stainless) . . . 569.95

NAVY ARMS REVOLVERS

LE MAT CAVALRY MODEL

LE MAT NAVY MODEL

LE MAT REVOLVERS

Once the official sidearm of many Confederate cavalry officers, this 9-shot .44-caliber revolver with a central single-shot barrel of approx. 65 caliber gave the cavalry man great firepower. *Barrel Length:* 7 ⅝" *Overall Length:* 14" *Weight:* 3 lbs. 7 oz.

CAVALRY MODEL $595.00
NAVY MODEL 595.00
ARMY MODEL 595.00
18TH GEORGIA (engraving on cylinder,
  display case) 795.00
BEAUREGARD (hand-engraved cylinder and frame;
  display case and mold) 1,000.00

LE MAT ARMY MODEL

1862 NEW MODEL POLICE

1862 NEW MODEL POLICE

This is the last gun manufactured by the Colt plant in the percussion era. It encompassed all the modifications of each gun, starting from the early Paterson to the 1861 Navy. It was favored by the New York Police Dept. for many years. Fluted and rebated cylinder, 36 cal., 5 shot. This replica features brass trigger guard and backstrap. Case hardened frame, loading lever and hammer. *Barrel Length:* 5.5"

1862 POLICE $290.00
LAW AND ORDER SET 365.00

ROGERS & SPENCER REVOLVER

This revolver features a six-shot cylinder, octagonal barrel, hinged-type loading lever assembly, two-piece walnut grips, blued finish and case hardened hammer and lever. *Caliber:* 44 *Barrel Length:* 7.5" *Overall Length:* 13.75" *Weight:* 3 lbs.

ROGERS & SPENCER $245.00

COLT 1847 WALKER

COLT 1847 WALKER

The 1847 Walker replica comes in 44 caliber with a 9-inch barrel. Weight: 4 lbs. 8 oz. Features include: rolled cylinder scene; blued and case hardened finish; and brass guard. Proof tested.

COLT 1847 WALKER $275.00
SINGLE CASED SET 405.00
DELUXE CASED SET 540.00

ROGERS & SPENCER REVOLVER

NAVY ARMS REVOLVERS

FIRST MODEL DRAGOON REVOLVER

An improved version of the 1847 Walker, the First Model has a shorter barrel and cylinder as well as a loading lever latch. Used extensively during the Civil War. *Caliber:* 44 *Barrel Length:* 7.5" *Overall Length:* 13.75" *Weight:* 4 lbs. *Sights:* Blade front, notch rear. *Grip:* Walnut

FIRST MODEL DRAGOON $275.00
Also available:
THIRD MODEL DRAGOON w/oval trigger guard
    and cylinder stop 275.00

**FIRST MODEL
DRAGOON REVOLVER**

1851 NAVY "YANK"

A favorite of "Wild Bill" Hickok, the 1851 Navy was originally manufactured by Colt from 1850 through 1876. This model was the most popular of the Union revolvers, mostly because it was lighter and easier to handle than the Dragoon. *Barrel Length:* 7.5" *Overall Length:* 14" *Weight:* 2 lbs. *Rec. Ball Diam.:* .375 R.B. (.451 in 44 cal) *Calibers:* 36 and 44 *Capacity:* 6 shot *Features:* Steel frame, octagonal barrel, cylinder roll-engraved with Naval battle scene, backstrap and trigger guard are polished brass.

1851 NAVY "YANK" $155.00
KIT 125.00
SINGLE CASED SET 280.00
DOUBLE CASED SET 455.00

REB MODEL 1860

A modern replica of the confederate Griswold & Gunnison percussion Army revolver. Rendered with a polished brass frame and a rifled steel barrel finished in a high-luster blue with genuine walnut grips. All Army Model 60s are completely proof-tested by the Italian government to the most exacting standards. *Calibers:* 36 and 44. *Barrel Length:* 7.25" *Overall Length:* 13" *Weight:* 2 lbs. 10 oz.-11 oz. *Features:* Brass frame, backstrap and trigger guard, round barrel.

REB MODEL 1860 . . . . $115.00
SINGLE CASED SET 235.00
DOUBLE CASED SET 365.00
KIT 90.00

1860 ARMY

The 1860 Army satisfied the Union Army's need for a more powerful .44-caliber revolver. The cylinder on this replica is roll engraved with a polished brass trigger guard and steel strap cut for shoulder stock. The frame, loading level and hammer are finished in high-luster color case hardening. Walnut grips. *Weight:* 2 lbs. 9 oz. *Barrel Length:* 8" *Overall Length:* 13 5/8" *Caliber:* 44. *Finish:* Brass trigger guard, steel backstrap, round barrel, creeping lever, rebated cylinder, engraved Navy scene.

1860 ARMY $175.00
SINGLE CASED SET 300.00
DOUBLE CASED SET 490.00
KIT 155.00

BLACK POWDER

NAVY ARMS REVOLVERS

1858 NEW MODEL ARMY REMINGTON-STYLE, STAINLESS STEEL

Exactly like the standard 1858 Remington (below) except that every part except for the grips and trigger guard is manufactured from corrosion-resistant stainless steel. This gun has all the style and feel of its ancestor with all of the conveniences of stainless steel. *Caliber:* 44

1858 REMINGTON STAINLESS	$270.00
SINGLE CASED SET	395.00
DOUBLE CASED SET	680.00

REB 60 SHERIFF'S MODEL

REB 60 SHERIFF'S MODEL

A compact version of the Reb Model 60 Revolver. The Sheriff's model version became popular because the shortened barrel was fast out of the leather. This is actually the original snub nose, the predecessor of the detective specials or belly guns designed for quick-draw use. *Calibers:* 36 and 44

REB 60 SHERIFF'S MODEL	$115.00
KIT	90.00
SINGLE CASED SET	235.00
DOUBLE CASED SET	365.00

DELUXE NEW MODEL 1858 REMINGTON-STYLE 44 CALIBER (not shown)

Built to the exact dimensions and weight of the original Remington 44, this model features an 8" barrel with progressive rifling, adjustable front sight for windage, all-steel construction with walnut stocks and silver-plated trigger guard. Steel is highly polished and finished in rich blue. Barrel Length: 8" Overall Length: 14.25" Weight: 2 lbs. 14 oz.

DELUXE NEW MODEL 1858	$415.00

1858 NEW MODEL ARMY REMINGTON-STYLE REVOLVER

This rugged, dependable, battle-proven veteran with its top strap and rugged frame was considered the Magnum of Civil War revolvers, ideally suited for the heavy 44 charges. Blued finish.

Caliber: 44. *Barrel Length:* 8"
Overall Length: 14.25" *Weight:* 2 lbs. 8 oz.

NEW MODEL ARMY REVOLVER	$170.00
SINGLE CASED SET	290.00
DOUBLE CASED SET	480.00
KIT	150.00

Also available:

BRASS FRAME	$125.00
BRASS FRAME KIT	115.00
SINGLE CASED SET	250.00
DOUBLE CASED SET	395.00

NAVY ARMS

PERCUSSION KENTUCKY PISTOL

FLINTLOCK KENTUCKY PISTOL

The Kentucky Pistol is truly a historical American gun. It was carried during the Revolution by the Minutemen and was the sidearm of "Andy" Jackson in the Battle of New Orleans. Navy Arms Company has conducted extensive research to manufacture a pistol representative of its kind, with the balance and handle of the original for which it became famous. *Caliber:* 45

FLINTLOCK $225.00
SINGLE CASED FLINTLOCK SET. 350.00
DOUBLE CASED FLINTLOCK SET 580.00
PERCUSSION 215.00
SINGLE CASED PERCUSSION SET 335.00
DOUBLE CASED PERCUSSION SET. 550.00

1805 HARPERS FERRY FLINTLOCK PISTOL

Of all the early American martial pistols, Harpers Ferry is one of the best known and was carried by both the Army and the Navy. Navy Arms Company has authentically reproduced the Harper's Ferry to the finest detail, providing a well-balanced and well-made pistol.

Weight: 2 lbs. 9 oz. *Barrel Length:* 10" *Overall Length:* 16"
Caliber: 58 *Finish:* Walnut stock; case-hardened lock; brass-mounted browned barrel.

HARPERS FERRY. $310.00
SINGLE CASED SET 355.00

NAVY ARMS RIFLES

1859 SHARPS CAVALRY CARBINE

This percussion version of the Sharps is a copy of the popular breechloading Cavalry Carbine of the Civil War. It features a patchbox and bar and saddle ring on left side of the stock. **Caliber:** 54 **Barrel Length:** 22" **Overall Length:** 39" **Weight:** 7.75 lbs. **Sights:** Blade front; military ladder rear. **Stock:** Walnut
SHARPS CAVALRY CARBINE $940.00
Also available:
1859 SHARPS INFANTRY RIFLE (54 cal.) 1,030.00

SMITH CARBINE

The Smith Carbine was considered one of the finest breechloading carbines of the Civil War period. The hinged breech action allowed fast reloading for cavalry units. Available in either the Cavalry Model (with saddle ring and bar) or Artillery Model (with sling swivels). **Caliber:** 50 **Barrel Length:** 21.5" **Overall Length:** 39" **Weight:** 7.75 lbs. **Sights:** Blass blade front; folding ladder rear **Stock:** American walnut
SMITH CARBINE. $600.00

1861 SPRINGFIELD RIFLE

One of the most popular Union rifles of the Civil War, the 1861 model featured the 1855-style hammer. The lockplate on this replica is marked "1861, U.S. Springfield." **Caliber:** 58 **Barrel Length:** 40" **Overall Length:** 56" **Weight:** 10 lbs. **Finish:** Walnut stock with polished metal lock and stock fitting.
1861 SPRINGFIELD RIFLE $550.00

1862 C.S. RICHMOND RIFLE

This model was manufactured by the Confederacy at the Richmond Armory utilizing 1855 Rifle Musket parts captured from the Harpers Ferry Arsenal. This replica features the unusual 1855 lockplate, stamped "1862 C.S. Richmond, V.A." **Caliber:** 58 **Barrel Length:** 40" **Overall Length:** 56" **Weight:** 10 lbs. **Finish:** Walnut stock with polished metal lock and stock fittings.
1862 C.S. RICHMOND RIFLE $550.00

NAVY ARMS

PENNSYLVANIA LONG RIFLE

This new version of the Pennsylvania Rifle is an authentic reproduction of the original model. Its classic lines are accented by the long, browned octagon barrel and polished lockplate. **Caliber:** 32 or 45 (flint or percussion.) **Barrel Length:** 40.5"

Overall Length: 56.5" **Weight:** 7.5 lbs. **Sights:** Blade front; adjustable Buckhorn rear **Stock:** Walnut
PENNSYLVANIA LONG RIFLE Flintlock $485.00
  Percussion. 475.00

BROWN BESS MUSKET

Used extensively in the French and Indian War, the Brown Bess Musket proved itself in the American Revolution as well. This fine replica of the "Second Model" is marked "Grice" on the lockplate. **Caliber:** 75 **Barrel Length:** 42" **Overall Length:** 59" **Weight:** 9.5 lbs. **Sights:** Lug front **Stock:** Walnut

BROWN BESS MUSKET $815.00
KIT $690.00
Also available:
BROWN BESS CARBINE **Caliber:** 75 **Barrel Length:** 30"
Overall Length: 47" **Weight:** 7.75 lbs. $815.00

1803 HARPERS FERRY RIFLE

This 1803 Harpers Ferry rifle was carried by Lewis and Clark on their expedition to explore the Northwest territory. This replica of the first rifled U.S. Martial flintlock features a browned

barrel, case hardened lock and a brass patchbox. **Caliber:** 54
Barrel Length: 35" **Overall Length:** 50.5" **Weight:** 8.5 lbs.
1803 HARPERS FERRY RIFLE $630.00

"BERDAN" 1859 SHARPS RIFLE

A replica of the Union sniper rifle used by Col. Hiram Berdan's First and Second U.S. Sharpshooters Regiments during the Civil War. **Caliber:** 54 **Barrel Length:** 30" **Overall Length:** 46.75" **Weight:** 8 lbs. 8 oz. **Sights:** Military-style ladder rear; blade front **Stock:** Walnut **Features:**

Double-set trigger, case hardened receiver; patchbox and furniture.
"BERDAN" 1859 SHARPS RIFLE $1,095.00
Also available:
SINGLE TRIGGER INFANTRY MODEL 1,030.00

BLACK POWDER

NAVY ARMS

1858 ENFIELD RIFLE

In the late 1850s the British Admiralty, after extensive experiments, settled on a pattern rifle with a 5-groove barrel of heavy construction, sighted to 1,100 yards, designated the Naval rifle, Pattern 1858. *Caliber:* 58 *Barrel Length:* 33"

Weight: 9 lbs. 10 oz. *Overall Length:* 48.5" *Sights:* Fixed front; graduated rear. *Stock:* Seasoned walnut w/solid brass furniture.
1858 ENFIELD RIFLE $450.00

1861 MUSKETOON

The 1861 Enfield Musketoon was the favorite long arm of the Confederate Cavalry. *Caliber:* 58 *Barrel Length:* 24" *Weight:* 7 lbs. 8 oz. *Overall Length:* 40.25" *Sights:* Fixed front; grad-

uated rear. *Stock:* Seasoned walnut with solid brass furniture.
1861 MUSKETOON. $405.00
KIT 365.00

STEEL SHOT MAGNUM SHOTGUN

This shotgun, designed for the hunter who must use steel shot, features engraved polished lockplates, English-style

checkered walnut stock (with cheekpiece) and chrome-lined barrels.
Gauge: 10 *Barrel Length:* 28"
Overall Length: 45.5" *Weight:* 7 lbs. 9 oz.
Choke: Cylinder/Cylinder

STEEL-SHOT MAGNUM SHOTGUN. $585.00

T&T SHOTGUN

This Turkey and Trap side-by-side percussion shotgun, choked Full/Full, features a genuine walnut stock with checkered wrist and oil finish, color case hardened locks and blued barrels.

Gauge: 12 *Barrel Length:* 28"
Overall Length: 44" *Weight:* 7.5 lbs.

T&T SHOTGUN $560.00

Also available:
UPLAND SHOTGUN (not shown) same basic specifications as T&T Model, but with cylinder bore choking.
   Upland Shotgun 560.00

PEDERSOLI

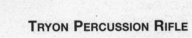

PEDERSOLI "PISTOL LE PAGE" .45 INTERNATIONAL FLINTLOCK TARGET PISTOL

PISTOL LE PAGE

SPECIFICATIONS
Caliber: .45
Barrel Length: 10.5"
Twist: 1-in-18" twist
Trigger: Single set
Weight: 2.5 lbs. (also in .44 smoothbore)
Stock: Walnut
Prices: $675.00
    Percussion model in 36, 38 or 44 caliber **565.00**

PEDERSOLI TRYON PERCUSSION RIFLE

TRYON PERCUSSION RIFLE

SPECIFICATIONS
Caliber: 45, 50 and 54 *Barrel Length:* 32"
Twist: 1-in-48" twist (1-in-66" twist for .54 bore)
Weight: 9.5 lbs.
Also available: Creedmoor version with fast-twist barrel (1-in-21, 451 caliber) and target sights (shown).
Prices: Standard $595.00
    Creedmoor. **780.00**

PEDERSOLI "MANG IN GRÄZ" PERCUSSION PISTOL

MANG IN GRÄZ

SPECIFICATIONS
Caliber: 38 or 44
Barrel Length: 11"
Twist: 1-in-15" (38) or 1-in-18" (44) twist
Weight: 2.5 lbs.
Stock: Walnut
Prices: $995.00

BLACK POWDER

REMINGTON RIFLES

MODEL 700 ML

MODEL 700 MLS STAINLESS

MODEL 700 ML AND MLS IN-LINE MUZZLELOADING RIFLES

Remington began building flintlock muzzleloaders in 1816. These two in-line muzzleloading rifles have the same cocking action and trigger mechanism as the original versions. The difference comes from a modified bolt and ignition system. The Model 700 ML has a traditionally blued carbon-steel barreled action. On the Model 700 MLS the barrel, receiver and bolt are made of 416 stainless steel with a non-reflective, satin finish. Each is set in a fiberglass-reinforced synthetic stock fitted with a Magnum-style recoil pad. One end of the solid aluminum ramrod is recessed into the forend and the outer end is secured by a barrel band. Instead of an open chamber, the breech is closed by a stainless-steel plug and nipple. In the internal structure of the modified bolt, the firing pin is replaced by a cylindrical rod that is cocked by normal bolt lift. It is released by pulling the trigger to strike a

#11 percussion cap seated on the nipple. Lock time is 3.0 milli-seconds. Barrels are rifled with a 1 in 28" twist. The barrels are fitted with standard adjustable iron sights; receivers are drilled and tapped for short-action scope mount.

SPECIFICATIONS:
Barrel length: 24"
Overall Length: 44.5"
Weight: 7.75 lbs.
Length Of Pull: 13 3/8"
Drop At Comb: .5"
Drop At Heel: 3/8"
Prices:
MODEL ML. $372.00
MODEL MLS STAINLESS $469.00
Also available:
w/Mossy Oak Break-up camo stock 405.00
Stainless Steel. 503.00

MODEL 700 ML YOUTH

The MODEL 700 ML YOUTH rifle offers the same design as the 70 ML, but with a shorter (12 3/8") length of pull. Includes a blued, satin-finished carbon steel 21" barrel (38.5" overall), action and bolt, plus fiberglass-reinforced Model 700 stock w/rubber recoil pad; drilled and tapped for short-action scope mounts; ram rod stored in forend.
Price:. $372.00

RUGER

OLD ARMY CAP AND BALL
FIXED SIGHT

OLD ARMY CAP AND BALL

This Old Army cap-and-ball revolver is reminiscent of the Civil War era martial revolvers and those used by the early frontiersmen in the 1800s. This Ruger model comes in both blued and stainless-steel finishes and features modern materials, technology and design throughout, including steel music-wire coil springs. Fixed or adjustable sights.

SPECIFICATIONS
Caliber: 45 (.443" bore; .45" groove)
Barrel Length: 7.5"
Weight: 2 7/8 lbs.
Rifling: 6 grooves, R.H. twist (1:16")
Sights: Fixed, ramp front; topstrap channel rear
Percussion cap nipples: Stainless steel (#11)
Price: $435.00
Stainless Steel 475.00

MODEL 77/50 ALL WEATHER

MODEL 77/50 RS

MODEL 77/50 RSBBZ STAINLESS STEEL ALL-WEATHER BLACK POWDER RIFLE

SPECIFICATIONS

Caliber: .50 *Action:* Bolt action In-line muzzle loader
Finish: Non-glare matte stainless steel finish
Barrel Length: 22" 400 series stainless steel
Overall Length: 41.5"
Rifling: 8 grooves, right hand twist (1-turn-in-28")
Safety: Three-position wing safety
Sights: Single folding leaf rear; gold bead front; rear receiver drilled and tapped for peep sights
Stock: Black/gray laminated American hardwood w/rubber buttpad; studs for sling swivels
Length Of Pull: 13.75" *Drop At Comb:* 1.78"

Drop At heel: 1.94" *Weight (approx.):* 6.5 lbs. (unloaded)
Features: Operator's manual, set of 1" stainless steel scope range; standard breech plug wrench; bolt disassemble tool; cleaning tube; right hand 90° turn bolt
Price: $596.00
Also available:
MODEL 77/50 RS. Same specifications as above, except finish is matte blue and stock is birch w/rubber buttpad 429.00
MODEL 77/50 RSO. Same specifications as above, except for following: *Drop at Comb:* 1 22/32" *Drop At Heel:* 1 6/32"
Stock: Straight gripped, checkered American black walnut stock, w/curved buttplate 550.00
Stainless, synthetic stock 575.00

THOMPSON/CENTER

BLACK MOUNTAIN MAGNUM (not shown)

The new .50 caliber Black Mountain Magnum™ is designed to handle magnum loads of up to 150 grains of FFg black powder or the Pyrodex equivalent volume. It also handles three 50-grain Pyrodex pellets with impressive results. Shooting a Mag Express Sabot with 240-grain XTP bullet, a 150-grain load produces a muzzle velocity of 2203 feed per second. The Black Mountain Magnum™ has a musket cap nipple, the hottest ignition available in a traditional-style muzzleloader. Standard nipples with #11 or #11 Magnum percussion caps can also be used.

The blued, 26-inch barrel is button rifled with a 1-in-28-inch twist to maximize performance with conica projectiles. It is equipped with Thompson/Center's exclusive QLA™ muzzle system for easy loading, even without a short starter. Tru-Glo™ fiber optic sights allow hunters to take advantage of productive dawn and dusk hunting time. Hunters who prefer to use a riflescope will appreciate that the rifle is drilled and tapped for easy scope mounting. The new sidelock rifle is stocked with a tough, durable Rynite® stock.
Price: $347.00

PENNSYLVANIA HUNTER FLINTLOCK RIFLE

The 28" barrel on this model is cut rifled (.010" deep) with 1 turn in 66" twist. Its outer contour is octagonal. Sights are fully adjustable for both windage and elevation. Stocked with select American black walnut; metal hardware is blued steel. Features a hooked breech system and coilspring lock, plus T/C's QLA™ Muzzle System for improved accuracy and easier reloading. *Caliber:* 50. *Overall length:* 45". *Weight:* Approx. 7.50 lbs.
Price: PENNSYLVANIA HUNTER FLINTLOCK $417.15

PENNSYLVANIA HUNTER FLINTLOCK CARBINE

Thompson/Center's Pennsylvania Hunter Flintlock Carbine is 50-caliber with 1:66" twist and cut-rifling. It was designed specifically for the hunter who uses patched round balls only and hunts in thick cover or brush. The 21" barrel is octagonal. Features T/C's QLA™ Muzzle System. *Overall length:* 38". *Weight:* 6.5 lbs. *Sights:* Fully adjustable open hunting-style rear with bead front. *Stock:* Select American walnut. *Trigger:* Single hunting-style trigger. *Lock:* Color cased, coil spring, with floral design.
Price: PENNSYLVANIA HUNTER FLINTLOCK CARBINE . $406.03

THE NEW ENGLANDER RIFLE

This percussion rifle features a 26" round, 50- or 54-caliber rifled barrel (1 in 48" twist). Contains T/C's QLA™ Muzzle System. *Weight:* 7 lbs. 15 oz.
Prices: NEW ENGLANDER RIFLE $335.00
12 GAUGE ACCESSORY SHOTGUN BARREL
(27") w/IC Choke Tube 184.00

THOMPSON/CENTER

ENCORE 209 X 50
MAGNUM MUZZLELOADING RIFLE

SPECIFICATIONS

Caliber: .50 **Action:** Break-open action muzzleloader **Ignition:** 209 shotgun primer **Barrel Length:** 26" with QLA Muzzle System **Twist:** 1 in 28" **Overall Length:** 40.5" **Weight:** 7 lbs. **Sights:** Tru-Glo adjustable rear fiber optic

sight; ramp-style fiber optic front sight **Safety:** Automatic hammerblock w/ bolt interlock **Finish:** Blued **Stock:** American walnut with schnabel forend and Monte Carlo buttstock **Features:** Barrel interchangeable with Encore rifles; equipped with sling swivel studs; accepts magnum charges of up to 150 grains of black powder or Pyrodex equivalent (or three 50-grain Pyrodex Pellets).
Price: Blued/Walnut $581.12
  ($256.58 accessory muzzleloading barrel only-blued)
Complete Gun-SST/Composite 634.20
Accessory barrel only-SST 294.97

BLACK DIAMOND
MUZZLELOADING RIFLE

SPECIFICATIONS

Caliber: .50 **Ignition:** In-line ignition using Flame Thrower musket cap nipple or No. 11 nipple **Barrel:** Free-floated, 22.5" barrel with QLA **Twist:** 1 in 18" **Overall Length:** 41.5" **Weight:** 6 lbs. 9 oz. **Safety:** Patented sliding thumb safety **Sights:** Tru-Glo Fiber Optic adjustable rear sight; Fiber Optic ramp-style front sight **Stock:** Black Rynite stock with molded-in checkering and pistol grip cap **Loading:** Accepts magnum charges of up to 150 grains of black powder or Pyrodex equivalent, or three 50-grain

Pyrodex Pellets **Features:** Removable universal breech plug; Aluminum ram rod; sling swivel studs; rubber recoil pad; musket nipple wrench, 5-pack or T/C Mag Express Sabots, and No. 11 nipple standard
Prices: Blued w/walnut stock $333.32
Blued w/Rynite Stock 304.00
Stainless 362.57
Also Available: BLACK DIAMOND PREMIUM PACK (includes T-Handle Short Starter, 10 Mag Express Sabots, rifle powder measure, In-line U-View Capper, Super Jag, ball and bullet puller, 2 Quick Shots, breech plug wrench, Hunter's Field Pouch, Lube-N-Clean Kit, Gorilla Grease).
Prices:
Blued $339.16
Stainless 397.96

SYSTEM 1
MUZZLELOADING RIFLE

SPECIFICATIONS

Calibers: .50 and .54 (accessory barrels available in .32, .58, and 12-gauge shotgun) **Ignition:** In-line ignition using No. 11 nipple or accessory Flame Thrower Musket Cap nipple **Barrel:** Free-floated, interchangeable 26" barrels with QLA **Twist:** 1 in 38" (1 in 48" in .32 cal. only) **Overall Length:** 44" **Weight:** 7.5 lbs. (.50 cal.) **Safety:** Patented sliding thumb safety **Sights:** Adjustable leaf style rear; ramp style white bead front **Stock:** American Walnut, black composite, or Advantage camo composite **Loading:** Accepts magnum charges of up to 150 grains of black

powder or Pyrodex equivalent, or three 50-grain Pyrodex Pellets **Features:** Removable universal breech plug; synthetic ram rod; sling swivel studs; rubber recoil pad; Weaver-style scope bases, takedown tool, Allen wrench, and 5 all-lead sabots standard
Prices:
Blued/Walnut $396.27
Stainless Steel/Composite 440.84
Stainless Steel/Advantage 479.41
Accessory Barrels Blued 176.90
Stainless Steel 220.42

BLACK POWDER

THOMPSON/CENTER

THE HAWKEN 50 AND 54 CALIBER

Similar to the famous Rocky Mountain rifles made during the early 1800s, the Hawken is intended for serious shooting. Button-rifled for ultimate precision, the Hawken is available in 45-, 50- or 54-caliber percussion or 50- caliber flintlock. It features a hooked breech, double-set triggers, first-grade American walnut stock, adjustable hunting sights, solid brass trim and color casehardened lock. Beautifully decorated; comes equipped with T/C's QLA™ Muzzle System. *Weight:* Approx. 8.5 lbs.
Prices:
HAWKEN CAPLOCK 50 or 54 caliber. $461.65
HAWKEN FLINTLOCK 50 caliber 472.77

THUNDERHAWK SHADOW

Thompson/Center's in-line caplock rifle, the Thunder Hawk Shadow combines the features of an old-time caplock with the look and balance of a modern bolt-action rifle. The in-line ignition system ensures fast, positive ignition, plus an adjustable trigger for a crisp trigger pull. The 24-inch barrels have an adjustable rear sight and bead-style front sight (barrel is drilled and tapped to accept T/C's Thunder Hawk scope rings. Weaver-style base and rings, or Quick-Release Mounting System). The stock is American black walnut with rubber recoil pad and sling swivel studs. Rifling is 1:38" twist, designed to fire patched round balls, conventional conical projectiles and sabot bullets. Includes T/C's QLA™ Muzzle System. *Weight:* Approx. 7 lbs. *Calibers:* 50, 54.
Prices:
Blued steel w/black composite stock $294.53

SST THUNDERHAWK SHADOW

THUNDERHAWK SHADOW VALUE PACK-COMPOSITE/BLUED

Includes .50 caliber ThunderHawk blued with composite stock, T-Handle Short Starter, (10) Sabots, (1) Rifle Powder Measure, (1) Star-7 Capper, (3) Quick Shots, (1) Nipple Wrench, (1) Cleaning Jag, (1) Expediter Field Cleaning Kit and Hunters Field Pouch in Advantage Camo
Price: $373.74

THUNDERHAWK SHADOW VALUE PACK-COMPOSITE/SST

Includes .50 caliber ThunderHawk SST with Composite stock, T-Handle Short Starter, (10) Sabots, (1) Rifle Powder Measure, (1) Star-7 Capper, (3) Quick Shots, (1) Nipple Wrench, (1) Cleaning Jag, (1) Expediter Field Cleaning Kit and Hunters Field Pouch in Advantage Camo
Price: $424.48

TRADITIONS PISTOLS

PIONEER PISTOL

SPECIFICATIONS

Caliber: 45 percussion *Barrel length:* 9 $5/8$" octagonal with tenon; $13/16$" across flats, rifled 1 in 16", fixed tang breech *Overall length:* 15" *Weight:* 1lb. 15 oz. *Sights:* Blade front; fixed rear *Trigger:* Single *Stock:* Beech, rounded *Lock:* V-type mainspring *Features:* German silver furniture; blackened hardware

Price: $140.00
Kit. 116.00

WILLIAM PARKER PISTOL

SPECIFICATIONS

Caliber: 50 percussion (1:20") *Barrel length:* 10 $3/8$" octagonal (15/16" across flats) *Overall length:* 17.5" *Weight:* 2 lbs. 5 oz. *Sights:* Brass blade front; fixed rear *Stock:* Walnut, checkered at wrist *Triggers:* Double set; will fire set and unset *Lock:* Adjustable sear engagement with fly and bridle; V-type mainspring *Features:* Brass percussion cap guard; polished hardware, brass inlays and separate ramrod

Price: $256.00

TRAPPER PISTOL

SPECIFICATIONS

Caliber: 50 percussion or flintlock (1:20") *Barrel length:* 9 $3/4$"; octagonal (7/8" across flats) with tenon *Overall length:* 15.5" Weight: 2 lbs. 14 oz. *Stock:* Beech *Lock:* Adjustable sear engagement with fly and bridle *Triggers:* Double set, will fire set and unset *Sights:* Primitive-style adjustable rear; brass blade front *Furniture:* Solid brass; blued steel on assembled pistol

Price:
Percussion. $183.00
Percussion Kit 139.00
Flintlock. 197.00

TRADITIONS PISTOLS

BUCKHUNTER PRO ALL-WEATHER

BUCKHUNTER PRO BLUED
w/WALNUT STOCK

BUCKHUNTER PRO-IN-LINE PISTOLS

SPECIFICATIONS
Calibers: 50 and 54 Percussion
Barrel length: 9.5" round (removable breech plug);
1:20" twist *Overall length:* 14.25" (also available w/12.5"
barrel in wood) *Weight:* 3.2 oz. (.50); 3.1 oz. (54); 3.4 oz.

(wood) *Trigger:* Single *Sights:* Fold-down adjustable rear;
beaded blade front *Stock:* Walnut or All-Weather
Features: Blued or C-Nickel furniture; PVC ramrod; drilled
and tapped for scop mounting; coil mainspring; thumb safety
Price: **$219.00**
   w/All-Weather Stock **234.00**
   fluted nickel w/muzzle brake **277.00**

KENTUCKY PISTOL

SPECIFICATIONS
Caliber: 50 Percussion (1:20") *Barrel length:* 10"
octagon (7/8" flats); fixed tang breech; 1:20" twist
Overall length: 15" *Weight:* 2 lbs. 8 oz. *Trigger:* Single
Sights: Fixed rear; blade front *Stock:* Beechwood
Features: Brass furniture; wood ramrod; kit available
Price: **$131.00**
   Kit **101.00**

TRADITIONS

SINGLE ACTION REVOLVERS

1875 SCHOFIELD

SPECIFICATIONS
Caliber: 44/40, 45 Schofield, 45 LC
Action: Single
Barrel Length: 5.5" blued
Features: Steel frame and trigger guard; walnut grip
Price: $659.00

SHERIFF'S REVOLVERS

SPECIFICATIONS
Caliber: 45 LC
Action: Single
Barrel Length: 4.75" blued
Features: Steel frame and trigger guard
Price: $369.00
w/checkered walnut grips. 429.00

1858 STARR

In 1858 the U.S. Government commissioned Ebenezor Townsend Starr to produce 20,000 of his new revolvers in .44 caliber. Often called a gun too modern for its time, Starr's New York factory produced several versions, it features a reliable mechanism that can be operated double-action.

SPECIFICATIONS
Caliber: .44 *Action:* Double action *Barrel Length:* 6"
Features: Steel strap
Price: $395.00

1873 COLT SINGLE ACTION REVOLVERS

SPECIFICATIONS
Calibers: 22, 45 LC, 357 Mag., 44/40 *Action:* Single
Barrel Lengths: 4.75", 5.5", 7.5" blued
Features: Walnut grips; steel frame and trigger guard
Price: $339.00
w/brass trigger guard in 4.75" and 5.75"
   (45 LC and 357 Mag.), 44-40 .... 299.00
w/brass trigger guard and nickel frame in 4.75"
   and 5.75" (45 LC). 379.00
w/black quard and strap, simulated ivory grips 45LC 349.00
w/antique silver guard and strap, walnut grips 45LC. . . 395.00

BLACK POWDER

TRADITIONS

DEERHUNTER RIFLES

DEERHUNTER RIFLE

DEERHUNTER COMPOSITE RIFLE

SPECIFICATIONS
Calibers: 32, 50 and 54 percussion
Barrel length: 24" octagonal **Rifling twist:** 1:48"
(percussion only); 1:66" (flint or percussion)
Overall length: 40"
Weight: 6 lbs. (6 lbs. 3 oz. in Small Game rifle)
Trigger: Single **Sights:** Fixed rear; blade front

Features: PVC ramrod; blackened furniture; inletted
wedge plates
Prices:
Percussion w/blued barrel **$160.00**
Percussion w/nickel barrel **152.00**
Flintlock w/nickel barrel **175.00**
Flintlock w/select hardwood stock **182.00**
PANTHER (50 cal.) w/All-Weather composite stock,
   fixed blade sights **116.00**

PANTHER RIFLE
All-Weather Composite Stock

TRADITIONS

HAWKEN WOODSMAN

SPECIFICATIONS
Calibers: 50 and 54 percussion or flint (50 caliber only)
Barrel length: 28" (octagonal); hooked breech; rifled 1 turn in 48" (1 turn in 66" in 50 caliber also available)
Overall length: 44.5"
Weight: 7 lbs. 11 oz.
Triggers: Double set; will fire set or unset

Lock: Adjustable sear engagement with fly and bridle
Stock: Beech
Sights: Beaded blade front; hunting-style rear, fully screw adjustable for windage and elevation
Furniture: Solid brass, blued steel or blackened (50 cal. only); unbreakable ramrod
Prices:
Percussion. $219.00
Flint 248.00

PENNSYLVANIA RIFLE

SPECIFICATIONS
Caliber: 50
Barrel length: 401/4"; octagonal (7/8" across flats) with 3 pins; rifled 1 turn in 66"
Overall length: 57" *Weight:* 8 lbs. 8 oz.
Lock: Adjustable sear engagement with fly and bridle

Stock: Walnut, beavertail style
Triggers: Double set; will fire set and unset
Sights: Primitive-style adjustable rear; brass blade front
Furniture: Solid brass, blued steel
Prices:
Percussion. $462.00
Flintlock 469.00

SHENANDOAH RIFLE

The Shenandoah Rifle captures the frontier styling and steady performance of Tradition's Pennsylvania Rifle in slightly shorter length and more affordable price. Choice of engraved and color case hardened flintlock or percussion V-type mainspring lock with double-set triggers. The full-length stock in walnut finish is accented by a solid brass curved buttplate, inletted patch box, nose cap, thimbles, trigger guard and decorative furniture.

SPECIFICATIONS
Caliber: 50 (1:66") flint or percussion
Barrel length: 33.5" octagon
Overall length: 49.5"
Weight: 7 lbs. 3 oz.
Sights: Buckhorn rear, blade front
Stock: Beech
Prices:
Percussion. $337.00
Flintlock 351.00

TRADITIONS

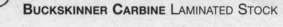

BUCKSKINNER CARBINE LAMINATED STOCK

BUCKSKINNER CARBINE

SPECIFICATIONS
Caliber: 50 percussion or flintlock
Barrel length: 21": octagonal-to-round with tenon; 15/16"
across flats; 1:66" twist (flintlock) and 1:20" (percussion)

Overall length: 36.25" Weight: 5 lbs. 15 oz.
Sights: Hunting-style, click adjustable rear; beaded blade
front with white dot *Trigger:* Single
Features: Blackened furniture: German silver ornamenta-
tion; sling swivels; unbreakable ramrod
Prices:
Flintlock **204.00**
Laminated Stock, Flintlock. **279.00**

KENTUCKY RIFLE

SPECIFICATIONS
Caliber: 50 percussion
Barrel length: 33.5" octagon (7/8" flats); fixed tang;
1:66" twist

Overall length: 49" *Weight:* 7 lbs.
Trigger: Single *Tenons:* 2 pins
Stock: Beechwood
Sights: Fixed rear; blade front
Features: Brass furniture; ramrod; inletted wedge plates;
toe plate; V-mainspring
Price: **$219.00**
Kit. **175.00**

TENNESSEE RIFLE

SPECIFICATIONS
Caliber: 50 flintlock or percussion
Barrel length: 24" octagon (7/8" across flats); hooked
breech; 1:32" twist (percussion)

Overall length: 401/2" *Weight:* 6 lbs.
Sights: Fixed rear; blade front
Stock: Beechwood
Features: Brass furniture; ramrod; inletted wedge plate;
stock inlays; toe plate; V-mainspring
Prices:
Percussion. **$219.00**

TRADITIONS

LIGHTNING BOLT-ACTION RIFLES

Traditions' series of Lightning Bolt rifles includes a variety of models of blued, chemical-nickel, stainless or Ultra-Coat with Teflon barrels. Stock choices are beech, brown laminated, All-Weather Composite, Advantage™Camo, X-Tra brown Camo or Break-up Camo. All models come with rugged synthetic ramrods, adjustable triggers, adjustable hunting sights, drilled and tapped barrels and field-removable stainless breech plugs.

LIGHTNING w/CHECKERED COMPOSITE STOCK
Fluted Stainless Steel Barrel w/Muzzle Break
Price: $336.00

LIGHTNING w/ALL-WEATHER COMPOSITE STOCK
Price: . . . . $204.00-$277.00
    w/Brown Laminated stock 380.00

LIGHTNING w/ADVANTAGE™, (OR BREAK UP™ OR SHADOW BRANCH™ OR HARDWOOD™) CAMO COMPOSITE STOCK
Price: $248.00
    w/select hardwood stock 219.00

LIGHTNING™ BOLT-ACTION RIFLES WITH LIGHTNING FIRE SYSTEM™ AND FIBER OPTIC SIGHTS

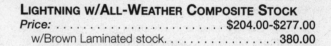

Model Number	Stock	Caliber	Barrel	Rate of Twist	Sights	Ramrod	Overall Length	Weight
R60002	Select Hardwood	.50p	24" Blued	1:32	Fiber Optic	Aluminum	43"	7 lb. 4 oz.
R61002	AW Composite	.50p	24" Blued	1:32	Fiber Optic	Aluminum	43"	7 lb.
R61048	AW Composite	.54p	24" Blued	1:48	Fiber Optic	Aluminum	43"	6 lb. 12 oz.
R61848	AW Composite	.54p	24" Stainless	1:48	Fiber Optic	Aluminum	43"	7 lb. 4 oz.
R62802	Brown Laminate	.50p	24" Stainless	1:32	Fiber Optic	Aluminum	43"	7 lb. 12 oz.
R610022	AW Comp/Advantage	.50p	24" Blued	1:32	Fiber Optic	Aluminum	43"	7 lb.
R610025	AW Comp/Break-Up	.50p	24" Blued	1:32	Fiber Optic	Aluminum	43"	7 lb.
R61702	AW Composite	.50p	24" Fluted Stainless/Muzzle Brake	1:32	Fiber Optic	Aluminum	43"	7 lb.
R610020	AW Composite	.50p	24" Blued/Muzzle Brake	1:32	Fiber Optic	Aluminum	43"	7 lb.
R618075	AW Comp/Break-Up	.50p	24" Stainless	1:32	Fiber Optic	Aluminum	43"	7 lb.

All composite stocks are checkered

TRADITIONS

BUCKHUNTER PRO™ IN-LINE RIFLES

BUCKHUNTER PRO™ IN-LINE RIFLE
w/Walnut-Stained Stock

BUCKHUNTER PRO™ IN-LINE RIFLE
w/Black Composite Stock, Stainless Barrel, Optional Scope

Traditions has upgraded its Buckhunter In-line ignition rifles and shotguns with the Buckhunter Pro series. The guns feature an adjustable trigger, thumb safety and a choice of Ultracoat Teflon, C-Nickel, blued or stainless steel barrels. New slimmed-down matte black composite stocks are available as are two camouflage patterns, laminated, thumbhole or walnut-stained stocks. All Buckhunter Pros have field-removable stainless steel breech plugs and improved adjustable hunting sights. The Buckhunter Pro rifles are available in 50 caliber (1:32") or 54 caliber (1:48") for use with conical and saboted bullets.

Prices: . . . . **$175.00 - $299.00**

BUCKHUNTER IN-LINE COMPOSITE RIFLE

SPECIFICATIONS
Calibers: 50 (1:32") and 54 (2:48") percussion *Barrel*
length: Blued 24" round *Overall length:* 42" *Weight:* 7 lbs. 6 oz. *Stock:* All-Weather Composite (matte black)
Sights: Beaded blade front; fully adjustable rear
Features: Blackened furniture; PVC ramrod; stainless steel removable breech plug; optional Redi-Pak (includes composite powder flask with valve dispenser, powder measure, two universal fast loaders, 5-in-1 loader, cleaning jab and patches, ball puller, 20 conical bullets, in-line nipple wrench
Price: **$149.00**

BUCKHUNTER PRO™ IN-LINE RIFLES WITH FIBER OPTIC SIGHTS

Model Number	Stock	Caliber	Barrel	Rate of Twist	Sights	Overall Length	Weight
R50002	Select Hardwood	.50p	24" Blued	1:32	Fiber Optic	43"	7 lb. 5
R51102	AW Composite	.50p	24" Blued	1:32	Fiber Optic	43"	7 lb. 4 oz.
R51148	AW Composite	.54p	24" Blued	1:48	Fiber Optic	43"	7 lb. 1 oz.

Replacement drop-in black and composite stocks available FCS50101   All composite stocks are checkered

BUCKHUNTER™ IN - LINE RIFLES

Model Number	Stock	Caliber	Barrel	Rate of Twist	Sights	Overall Length	Weight
R42102	AW Composite	.50p	24" Blued	1:32	Adj/BB	43"	7 lb.
R42148	AW Composite	.54p	24" Blued	1:48	Adj/BB	43"	6 lb. 14 oz.

UBERTI REVOLVERS

PATERSON REVOLVER

Manufactured at Paterson, New Jersey, by the Patent Arms Manufacturing Company from 1836 to 1842, these were the first revolving pistols created by Samuel Colt. All early Patersons featured a five-shot cylinder, roll-engraved with one or two scenes, octagon barrel and folding trigger that extends when the hammer is cocked.

SPECIFICATIONS
Caliber: 36
Capacity: 5 shots (engraved cylinder)
Barrel Length: 7.5" octagonal
Overall Length: 11.5"
Weight: 2.552 lbs.
Frame: Color casehardened steel
Grip: One-piece walnut
Price: $399.00
w/Lever. 435.00

PATERSON REVOLVER

1st MODEL DRAGOON REVOLVER

SPECIFICATIONS
Caliber: 44
Capacity: 6 shots
Barrel Length: 7.5" round forward of lug
Overall Length: 13.5"
Weight: 4 lbs.
Frame: Color case hardened steel
Grip: One-piece walnut
Price: $325.00
Also available:
2ND MODEL DRAGOON w/square cylinder bolt shot. . 325.00
3RD MODEL DRAGOON w/loading lever latch, brass
    backstrap, cut for shoulder stock 325.00
WHITNEYVILLE DRAGOON w/7.5" barrel. 360.00

1st MODEL DRAGOON

WALKER REVOLVER

SPECIFICATIONS
Caliber: 44
Barrel Length: 9" (round in front of lug)
Overall Length: 15.75"
Weight: 4.41 lbs.
Frame: Color case hardened steel
Backstrap: Steel
Cylinder: 6 shots (engraved with "Fighting Dragoons" scene)
Grip: One-piece walnut
Price: $370.00

WALKER REVOLVER

UBERTI REVOLVERS

1851 NAVY REVOLVER

SPECIFICATIONS
Caliber: 36
Barrel length: 7 1/2" (octagonal, tapered)
Cylinder: 6 shots (engraved)
Overall length: 13"
Weight: 2 3/4 lbs.
Frame: Color case hardened steel
Backstrap and trigger guard: Steel
Grip: One-piece walnut
Price: $295.00
Also available:
1851 SQUAREBACK OR OVAL. 270.00

1851 NAVY REVOLVER

1858 REMINGTON NEW ARMY 44 REVOLVER

Prices:
8" barrel, open sights $295.00
With stainless steel and open sights 385.00
TARGET MODEL w/black finish 329.00
TARGET MODEL w/stainless steel 420.00
Also available:
1858 NEW NAVY (36 cal.). 270.00
1858 NEW ARMY REVOLVING CARBINE (18" bbl.) 420.00

**1858 REMINGTON
NEW ARMY TARGET MODEL**

1860 ARMY REVOLVER

SPECIFICATIONS
Caliber: 44
Barrel length: 8" (round, tapered)
Overall length: 13 3/4"
Weight: 2.65 lbs.
Frame: One-piece, color case hardened steel
Trigger guard: Brass
Cylinder: 6 shots (engraved)
Grip: One-piece walnut
Price: $270.00
Also available:
1860 ARMY FLUTED. 295.00

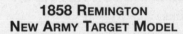

1860 ARMY REVOLVER

1861 NAVY REVOLVER

SPECIFICATIONS
Caliber: 36
Capacity: 6 shots
Barrel length: 7 1/2"
Overall length: 13"
Weight: 2.75 lbs.
Grip: One-piece walnut
Frame: Color case hardened steel
Prices: 1861 NAVY CIVIC. $270.00
1861 NAVY FLUTED 295.00

1861 NAVY REVOLVER

Aimpoint 430
Ashley Outdoors 431
Bausch & Lomb 432
BSA 436
Burris 438
Bushnell 441
Laseraim 442
Leica 443
Leupold 444
Nikon 449
Pentax 451
Quarton 453
Sako 454
Schmidt & Bender 455
Simmons 458
Swarovski & Kahles 463
Tasco 465
Weaver 468
Williams 470
Zeiss 473

Sights & Scopes

For addresses and phone/fax numbers of manufacturers and distributors included in this section, please turn to **DIRECTORY OF MANUFACTURERS AND SUPPLIERS** on page 564.

AIMPOINT SIGHTS

AIMPOINT 5000-XD SIGHT

SPECIFICATIONS
System: Parallax free
Optical: Anti-reflex coated lenses
Adjustment: 1 click = 1/4 inch at 100 yards
Length: 5.5-6"
Weight: 5.8 oz.
Objective diameter: 36mm
Mounting system: 30mm rings
Magnification: 1X
Material: Anodized aluminum; black or camo finish
Diameter of dot: 3" at 100 yds. or Mag Dot reticle, 10" at 100 yards.
Price: $285.00

SERIES 3000 UNIVERSAL

SPECIFICATIONS
System: 100% parallax free
Weight: 6 oz.
Length: 6.25"
Magnification: 1X
Scope attachment: 3X
Eye relief: Unlimited
Battery choices: 2X Mercury SP 675 1X Lithium or DL 1/3N
Material: Anodized aluminum, black finish
Mounting: 1" Rings (Medium or High)
Price: Black $232.00

AIMPOINT 5000 2-POWER XD

SPECIFICATIONS
System: Parallax free
Optical: Anti-reflex coated lens
Adjustment: clock = 1/4" at 100 yards
Length: 7"
Weight: 9 oz.
Objective diameter: 47mm
Diameter of dot: 1.5" at 100 yards
Mounting system: 30mm rings
Magnification: 2X
Material: Anodized aluminum; black finish
Price: $378.00

AIMPOINT COMP XD

SPECIFICATIONS
System: 100% Parallax free
Optics: Anti-reflex coated lenses
Eye relief: Unlimited *Batteries:* 3 x 1.5V silver oxide
Adjustment: 1 click = 1/4-inch at 100 yards
Length: 4 $^{3}/_{8}$" *Weight:* 4.75 oz.
Objective diameter: 36mm
Dot diameter: 7, 10, or 15 MOA
Mounting system: 30mm rings
Magnification: 1X
Material: Black, blue or stainless finish
Also available with 3-minute Dot with Flip Up lens covers and captive metal adjustment covers.
Price: $317.00
Comp MXD 3, 7 or 10 MOA 392.00
Comp ML XD 3, 7 or 10 MOA 359.00

ASHLEY OUTDOORS

SIGHTS AND ACCESSORIES

**ASHLEY EXPRESS
SIGHT SYSTEM**

ASHLEY EXPRESS™
Ashley Express™ Sight System. Available for most guns
- Fastest acquisition of front sight
- Designed for high stress shooting in poor light
- Low profile and snag free

Price: Ashley Big Dot Tritium Sight
  Set for Glocks $90.00

**ASHLEY
BACKUP
POWER ROD
FOR MUZZLELOADERS**
Price: $40.00

ASHLEY APERTURE™ GHOST RING HUNTING SIGHTS
- Fully adjustable for windage and elevation
- Available for most rifles including blackpowder
- Minimum gunsmithing for most installations; matches most existing mounting holes
- Compact design, CNC machined from steel and heat treated
- Perfect for low light conditions and offers minimal target obstruction

Price: Ashley Aperture Ghost Ring Hunting
  Sight Set $90.00
Available for most rifles including blackpowder

**GHOST RING SIGHTS FOR RIFLES
AND CARBINES**
Price: $0.00

**ASHLEY UTILITY SCOUT RIFLE KIT FOR
MAUSER 98 & OTHERS**
Price: $325.00

BAUSCH & LOMB RIFLESCOPES

ELITE 3000 — 5X-15X

ELITE™ 3000 RIFLESCOPES

Model	Special Feature	Actual Magni-fication	Obj. Lens Aperature (mm)	Field of View @ 100yds (ft.)	Weight (oz)	Length	Eye Relief (in.)	Exit Pupil (mm)	Click Value @ 100yds (in.)	Adjust Range @ 100yds (in.)	Selection	Suggested Retail
30-2632G	Handgun (30-2632S Silver Finish)	2x-6x	32	10-4	10	9	20	16-5.3	.25	50	Constant 20" eye relief At all powers w/max. recoil resistance	$417.95
30-2732G	(30-2732M Matte Finish)	2x-7x	32	44.6-12.7	12	11.6	3	12.2-4.6	.25	50	Compact variable for close-in brush ormed. range shooting. Excellent for shotguns	$303.95
30-3940G	(30-3940M Matte Finish, 30-3940S Silver Finish)	3x-9x	40	33.8-11.5	13	12.6	3	13.3-4.4	.25	50	For the full range of hunting. From varmint to big game. Tops in versatility.	$319.95
30-3950G	(30-3950M Matte Finish)	3x-9x	50	31.5-10-5	19	15.7	3	16-5.6	.25	50	All purpose variable with extra brightness.	$382.95
30-3955E	European Reticle Matte Finish	3x-9x	50	31.5-10.5	22	15.6	3	16-5.6	.36	70	Large exit pupil and 30mm tube for max. brightness.	$592.95
30-4124A	Adjustable Objective	4x-12x	40	26.9-9	15	13.2	3	10-3.33	.25	50	Medium to long-range variable makes a superb choice for varmint or big game	$417.95
30-5155M	Adjustable Objective	5x-15x	50	21-7	24	15.9	3	10-3.3	.25	40	Large objective for brightness	$471.95
30-3951M	Command Post Reticle	3x-9x	50	31.5-10.5	19	15.7	3	16-5.6	.25	50	Switch instantly from fine crosshairs to thick 3-pos reticle for low light shooting	$583.95

ELITE 4200 — 2.5-10X40

ELITE 4200

ELITE™ 4200 RIFLESCOPES WITH RAINGUARD™

Model	Special Feature	Actual Magni-fication	Obj. Lens Aperature (mm)	Field of View @ 100yds (ft.)	Weight (oz)	Length	Eye Relief (in.)	Exit Pupil (mm)	Click Value @ 100yds (in.)	Adjust Range @ 100yds (in.)	Selection	Suggested Retail
42-1636M	Matte Finish	1.5x-6x	36	61.8-16.1	15.4	12.8	3	14.6-6	.25	60	Compact wide angle for close-in & brush hunting. Max. brightness. Execel. for shotguns	$560.95
42-2104G	(40-2104M Matte Finish, 40-2104S Silver Finish)	2.5x-10x	40	41.5-10.8	16	13.5	3	15.6-4	.25	50	All purpose hunting scope w/4x zoom range for close-in brush & long range shooting	$592.95
42-3640A	Adjustable Objective	36x	40	3	17.6	15	3.2	1.1	.125	30	Ideal benchrest scope.	$880.95
42-4165M	Matte Finish	4x-16x	50	26-7.2	22	15.6	3	12.5-3.1	.25	50	The ultimate varmint, airgun and precision shooting scope. Parallax focus from 10 meter to infinity.	$768.95
42-6244A	Adjustable Objective, Sunshade (40-6244M Matte Finish)	6x-24x	40	18-4.5	20.2	16.9	3	6.7-1.7	.125	26	Varmint, target & silhouette long range shooting and airgun. Parallax focus adjust. for pinpoint accuracy. Parallax focus from 10 meter to infinity.	$672.95
42-6243A	Adjustable Objective and 1/4" MOA dot reticle	6-24x	40	18-4.5	20.2	16.9	3	6.7-1.7	.125	26	Varmint, target and silhouette long range shooting and airgun. Parallax focus adjust for pinpoint accuracy. Parallax focus from 10 meter to infinity.	$672.95

BAUSCH & LOMB/BUSHNELL

SPORTVIEW® 3X-9X

BUSHNELL SPORTVIEW® RIFLESCOPES

Model	Special Feature	Actual Magni-fication	Obj. Lens Aperature (mm)	Field of View @ 100yds (ft.)	Weight (oz)	Length	Eye Relief (in.)	Exit Pupil (mm)	Click Value @ 100yds (in.)	Adjust Range @ 100yds (in.)	Selection	Suggested Retail
79-0412	Adjustable objective	4x-12x	40	27-9	14.6	13.1	3.2	10-3.3	.25	60	Long range.	$141.95
79-1393	(79-1398 Matte) (79-1393S Matte Silver)	3x-9x	32	38-14	10	11.75	3.5	10.7-3.6	.25	50	All purpose variable	$68.95
79-1403	(79-1403S Silver)	4x	32	29	9.2	11.75	4	8	.25	60	General purpose.	$56.95
79-1545		1.5x-4.5x	21	69-24	8.6	10.7	3	14-4.7	.25	60	Low power variable ideal for close-in brush or medium range shooting	$86.95
79-3940	Wide angle (79-3940M Matte)	3x-9x	40	42-15	12.5	12	3	4.4	.25	50	Excellent for use at any range.	$95.95
79-6184	Adjustable objective	6x-18x	40	19.1-6.8	15.9	14.5	3	6.7-2.2	.25	50	Excellent varmint scope.	$170.95
SPORTVIEW® AIR RIFLE SERIES												
79-0004	Adjustable objective w/rings	4x	32	31	11.2	11.7	4	8	.25	50	General purpose for air rifle and rimfire.With range focus & target adjustments	$97.95
79-0039	Adjustable objective, with rings	3x-9x	32	38-13	11.2	10.75	3.5	10.6-3.5	.25	60	Air rifle, rimfire with range focus adjustments and target adjustments	$116.95
SPORTVIEW® SHOTGUN SCOPES W/CIRCLE-X RETICLE												
79-1548	Circle-X reticle	1.5x-4.5x	32	71-25	11.8	10.4	3.5	21-7	.25		Turkey hunting, shotgun slugs and muzzleloading	$104.95
79-2538	Circle-X reticle	2.5	32	45	10	11	3	12.8	.25		Short range brush scope, turkey hunting	$76.95
SPORTVIEW® RIMFIRE SERIES												
79-1416	3/4" tube	4x	15	17	3.6	10.7	3.5	3.8	Friction	60	General purpose.	$11.95
79-3720	3/4" tube	3x-7x	20	23-11	5.7	11.3	2.6	6.7-2.9	Friction	50	All purpose variable.	$36.95
.22 VARMINT™ WITH RINGS												
79-0428	With rings (79-0428M Matte)	4x	28	25	8.5	7.6	3	7	.5	52	Compact for .22's	$75.95
79-3950M	Wide angle (matte)	3x-9x	50	41-15	12.9	12.5	3	17-5.5	.25	50	Excellent all purpose low light scope	$164.95

BAUSCH & LOMB/BUSHNELL

**3X-9X (40MM) TROPHY®
WIDE ANGLE RIFLESCOPE**

BUSHNELL TROPHY® RIFLESCOPES

Model	Special Feature	Actual Magnification	Obj. Lens Aperature (MM)	Field of View @ 100YDS (FT.)	Weight (OZ)	Length	Eye Relief (IN.)	Exit Pupil (MM)	Click Value @ 100YDS (IN.)	Adjust Range @ 100YDS (IN.)	Selection	Suggested Retail
73-1500	Wide Angle	1.75x-5x	32	68-23	12.3	10.8	3.5	18.3-1.75x	.25	120	Shotgun, black powder or centerfire. Close-in brush hunting.	$243.95
73-3940	Wide angle 73-3940S Silver	3x-9x	40	42/14-14/5	13.2	11.7	3	13.3-4.44	.25	60	All purpose variable, excellent for use from close to long range. Circular view provides a definite advantage over "TV screen" type scopes for running game-uphill or down.	$159.95
73-3941	Illuminated reticle with back-up crosshairs	3x-9x	40	37-12.5	16	13	3	13.3-4.4	.25	70	Variable intensity light control Battery Sony CR 2032 or equivalent	$410.95
73-3942	Long mounting length designed for long-action rifles	3x-9x	42	42-14	13.8	12	3	14-4.7	.25	40	7" mounting length.	$164.95
73-3949	Wide angle with Circle-x™ Reticle	3x-9x	40	42-14	13.2	11.7	3	13.3-4.4	.25	60	Matte finish, Ideal low light reticle.	$170.95
73-4124	Wide angle, adjustable objective (73-4124M Matte)	4x-12x	40	32-11	16.1	12.6	3	10-3.3	.25	60	Medium to long range variable for varmint and big game. Range focus adjustment. Excellent air riflescope.	$285.95
73-4154M	Semi-turret target adjustments	4x-15x	40	26.8-7.7	18.7	13.7	3	10-2.6	.25	40	Medium to long range variable. Focus adjustment from 10mm to infinity.	$337.95
73-6184	Semi-turret target adjustments, adjustable objective	6x-18x	40	17.3-6	17.9	14.8	3	6.6-2.2	.125	40	Long-range varmint centerfire or short range air rifle target precision accuracy.	$360.95
TROPHY® HANDGUN SCOPES												
73-0232	(73-0232S Silver)	2x	32	20	7.7	8.7	9	16	.25	90	Designed for target and short to med. range hunting. Magnum recoil resistant.	$202.95
73-2632	(73-2632S Silver)	2x-6x	32	11-4	10.9	9.1	18	16-5.3	.25	50	18 inches of eye relief at all powers	$268.95
TROPHY® SHOTGUN/HANDGUN SCOPES												
73-1420	Turkey Scope with Circle-x™ Reticle	1.75x-4x	32	73-30	10.9	10.8	3.5	18.8	.25	120	Ideal for turkey hunting, slug guns or blackpowder guns. Matte finish.	$237.95
73-1421	Brush Scope with Circle-x™ Reticle	1.75x-4x	32	73-30	10.9	10.8	3.5	18-8	.25	120	Ideal for turkey hunting, slug guns or blackpowder guns. Matte finish.	$237.95
TROPHY® AIR RIFLESCOPES												
73-4124	Wide angle, adjustable objective (73-4124M Matte)	4x-12x	40	32-11	16.1	12.6	3	10-3.3	.25	60	Medium to long range variable for varmint and big game. Range focus adjustment. Excellent air riflescope.	$285.95
73-6184	Semi-turret target adjustments, adjustable objective	6x-18x	40	17-6	17.9	14.8	3	6.6-2.2	.125	40	Long-range varmint centerfire or short range air rifle target precision accuracy.	$360.95

BAUSCH & LOMB/BUSHNELL

**BUSHNELL®
HOLOsight®**

BUSHNELL® HOLOsight®

The BUSHNELL® HOLOsight® delivers instant target acquisition, improved accuracy, and can be tailored to virtually any shooting discipline. How does it work? A hologram of a reticle pattern is recorded on a heads-up display window. When illuminated by laser (coherent) light, a holographic image becomes visible at the target plane - where it remains in focus with the target. Critical eye alignment is not required and multi-plane focusing error is eliminated. With the BUSHNELL® HOLOsight®, simply look through the window, place the reticle image on the target and shoot. The use of holographic technology allows the creation of virtually any image as a reticle pattern, in either two or three dimensions. Shooters have the flexibly to design reticles in any geometric shape, size and in any dimension to enhance a specific shooting discipline. Since no light is cast on the target, use of the BUSHNELL® HOLOsight® is completely legal in most hunting, target and competition areas.

BUSHNELL HOLOSIGHT® SPECIFICATIONS

OPTICS	MAGNI-FICATION @ 100 YDS	FIELD OF VIEW FT @ 100 YDS	WEIGHT (OZ/G)	LENGTH (IN/MM)	EYE RELIEF (IN/MM)	BATTERIES	WINDAGE CLICK VALUE IN @100 YDS MM@ 100M	ELEVATION CLICK VALUE IN @100 YDS MM@ 100M	BRIGHTNESS ADJUSTMENT SETTINGS
Holographic	1x	Unlimited	8.7/247	6/152	1/2" to 10 ft. 13 to 3048 mm	2 Type N 1.5 Volt	.25 M.O.A./ 7mm @100m	.5 M.O.A./ 14mm@100m	20 levels

MODEL	DESCRIPTION		SUGGESTED RETAIL
50-0021	HOLOsight Model 400	HOLOsight with mounts for Weaver rail and standard reticle.	$567.95
50-0020	HOLOsight Model 400 (without reticle)	HOLOsight with mounts for Weaver rail and no reticle. Reticle must be purchased separately.	$478.95
50-0002	HOLOsight 2X adapter	Increases effective range of HOLOsight	$248.95

MODEL	RETICLE	DESCRIPTION	USES	
HOLOsight® RETICLES				
Included w/50-0021	Standard	2-Dimensional 65 M.O.A. ring with one M.O.A. dot and tick marks.	General all-purpose handguns, rifles, slug guns, and wing shooting	$111.95
50-0122	Dual Rings	2-Dimensional design with two rings (20 M.O.A. & 90 M.O.A.)	Wing shooting, 20" IPSC targets, slug and turkey guns	$111.95
50-0123	Open Crosshairs	2-Dimensional all-purpose design which does not cover up the target area. Inner circle covers 30" at 100 yards.	General all purpose handguns, short range rifles, slug guns and wing shooting	$111.95
50-0125	Dot	1 M.O.A. Dot	Precision rifle, handgun, and slug gun shooting.	$111.95

BSA SCOPES

6-24x50

The BSA name once reserved for superior rifles and motorcycles is now appearing on rifle scopes. The Catseye line, with multi-coated objective and ocular lenses and a European-style reticle for shooting in dim light, includes several models:

• 4x44 • 1.5-4.5x32 • 3-10x44 • 3.5-10x50 • 4-16x50
• 6-24x50 *shown* $219.95
A parallax-compensating lens snaps onto the 4x44 to improve target focus at short yardage.

BSA CATSEYE CE 6-24X50

SPECIFICATIONS
Magnification: 6x-24x **Objective Lens Diameter:** 50mm
Exit Pupil Range: 8.3-2.1 **Field of View at 100 yd:** 16'-3'
Optimum Eye Relief: 3" **Length/Weight:** 16"/23 oz.
Price: $219.95
The Twilight Performance Factor (TPF) is a mathematical expression of a scope's ability to show detailled images in low-light conditions. Normally, the higher the number the better. **BSA's Catseye CE 6-24x50** has a TPF of 17.3 at 6x and a bright 34.7 at 24x.

BSA PLATINUM PT 8-32 X 44 TS

SPECIFICATIONS
Magnification: 8x-32x **Objective Lens Diameter:** 44mm
Exit Pupil Range: 5.5-1.4 **Field of View at 100 yd:** 11'-3.5'
Optimum Eye Relief: 3" **Length/Weight:** 17.25"/19.5 oz.
Price: $239.95

BSA PLATINUM 24 X 44 TS

SPECIFICATIONS
Magnification: 24x **Objective Lens Diameter:** 44mm
Exit Pupil Range: 1.8 **Field of View at 100 yd:** 4.5'
Optimum Eye Relief: 3" **Length/Weight:** 16.25"/17.9 oz.
Price: $189.95

BSA Platinum target scopes are fitted with finger-adjustable windage and elevation dials that move point of impact in 1/8-minute clicks. Two sunshades–3-inch and 5-inch–are standard and can be screwed together for shooting in strong backlight. This scope line includes:

• 24x44 . . . . $189.95
• 36x44 • 6-24x44 • 10-50x60
• 8-32x44 . . . . 239.95

BSA SCOPES

2.5x20

BSA Deer Hunter scopes, from a 2.5x20 (shown) to a 2.5-10x44 offer value for the big game hunter on a budget.
Prices: from **$59.95**
The Contender series of target scopes offers top-of-the line features like 1/8-minute click adjustments at a moderate price.
6-24x40 . . . . **$144.95**

BSA DEERHUNTER PT 8-32X44

SPECIFICATIONS
Magnification: 8x-32x **Objective Lens Diameter:** 44mm
Exit Pupil Range: 5.5-1.4 **Field of View at 100 yd:** 11'-3.5'
Optimum Eye Relief: 3" **Length/Weight:** 17.25"/19.5 oz.
Price: **$69.95**

BSA DEERHUNTER DH 2.5X20

SPECIFICATIONS
Magnification: 2.5x **Objective Lens Diameter:** 20mm
Exit Pupil Range: 8 **Field of View at 100 yd:** 72'
Optimum Eye Relief: 6" **Length/Weight:** 7.5"/7.5 oz.
Price: **$59.95**

BSA CONTENDER CT 6-24X40 TS

SPECIFICATIONS
Magnification: 6x-24x **Objective Lens Diameter:** 40mm
Exit Pupil Range: 6.7-1.7 **Field of View at 100 yd:** 16'-4'
Optimum Eye Relief: 3" **Length/Weight:** 15.5"/20 oz.
Price: **$144.95**
The **BSA Contender CT 6-24x40 TS** features TPFs from 15.5 at 6x to 31 at 24x.

BURRIS SCOPES

BLACK DIAMOND RIFLESCOPES

MODEL 3X-12X-50mm

Burris's new Black Diamond line includes six models of a 30mm main tube 3-12X50mm with various finishes, reticles, and adjustment knobs. These riflescopes have easy-to-grip rubber-armored parallax-adjust rings, an adjustable and resettable adjustment dial, and an internal focusing eyepiece. Other features include fully multi-coated lens surfaces, 110 inches of internal adjustment, four times magnification range, and 3.5" to 4" of eye relief. Alll models come in a non-reflective matte black finish.

SPECIFICATIONS
Models: 3-12X50mm/6-24x50
Field of View (feet @ 100yds.): 34'-12'/18-6
Optimum eye relief: 3.5"-4.0"/3.5-4
Exit Pupil: 13.7mm-4.2mm/7.6-2.1
Click adjust value (@ 100 yds.): .25"/.125
Max. internal adj. (@ 100 yds.): 100"/52

Clear objective diameter: 50mm/50mm
Ocular end diameter: 42mm/42mm
Weight: 25 oz./25 oz.
Length: 13.8"/16.2"
Reticles available: Plex, German 3P#1, German 3P#4, Mil-Dot
Prices: 3-12x
Plex w/matte finish **$854.00**
Plex w/matte finish, Posi-Lock **917.00**
German 3P#1 reticle w/matte finish **881.00**
German 3P#4 reticle w/matte finish **881.00**
Plex w/matte finish, Tactical Knobs **890.00**
Mil-Dot reticle w/matte finish, Tactical Knobs **999.00**
Prices: 6-24x
Fine Plex **$926.00**
Mil Dot **1,069.00**
Ballistic MDot **1,069.00**

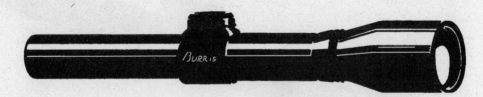

2.7X SCOUT SCOPE
W/Precision Clock Adjustments

SCOUT SCOPES
Made for hunters who need a 7- to 14 inch eye relief to mount just in front of the ejection port opening, allowing hunters to shoot with both eyes open. The 15-foot field of view and 2.75X magnification are ideal for brush guns and handgunners. Also ideal for the handgunner that uses a "two-handed hold." Rugged, reliable and 100% fog proof.

MODELS	Prices
1X XER Plex (matte)	$290.00
1X XER Plex (camo)	316.00
1.5X Heavy Plex (matte)	301.00
2.75X Plex (black)	301.00
2.75X Heavy Plex (matte)	310.00

BURRIS SCOPES

SIGNATURE SERIES

All models in the Signature Series have **HI-LUME** (multi-coated) lenses for maximum light transmission. Many models also feature **POSI-LOCK** to prevent recoil shift and protect against loss of zero from rough hunting use. It allows the shooter to lock the internal optics of the scope in position after the rifle has been sighted in.

8X-32X SIGNATURE

6X-24X

8X-32X

4X-16X

BLACK DIAMOND™ – 30MM SCOPES

ITEM	MODEL	RETICLE	FINISH	FEATURES	LIST	DEALER
200900	3X-12X-50mm	Plex	mat	PA	854	598
200901	3X-12X-50mm	Plex	mat	Posi-Lock/PA	917	641
200902	3X-12X-50mm	3P#1	mat	PA	881	616
200903	3X-12X-50mm	3P#4	mat	PA	881	616
200910	3X-12X-50mm	Plex	mat	Target/PA	890	623
200911	3X-12X-50mm	Mil-Dot	mat	Target/PA	999	699
200930N	6X-24X-50mm	Fine Plex	mat	Target/PA	926	648
200931N	6X-24X-50mm	Mil-Dot	mat	Target/PA	1069	748
200932N	6X-24X-50mm	Ballistic MDot	mat	Target/PA	1069	748

SIGNATURE SERIES® SCOPES

ITEM	MODEL	RETICLE	FINISH	FEATURES	LIST	DEALER
200500	4X	Plex	blk		366	256
200510	6X	Plex	blk		405	283
200511	6X	Plex	mat		423	296
200700	1.5X-6X	Plex	blk		474	332
200701	1.5X-6X	Plex	mat		492	344
200706	1.5X-6X	Plex	mat	Posi-Lock®	538	376
200711N	1.5X-6X	Electro-Dot®	mat		593	414
200712N	1.5X-6X	Electro-Dot®	mat	Posi-Lock®	638	446
200550	2X-8X	Plex	blk		547	383
200551	2X-8X	Plex	mat		565	395
200553	2X-8X	Plex	blk	Posi-Lock®	593	414
200554	2X-8X	Plex	mat	Posi-Lock®	611	427
200600	3X-9X	Plex	blk		560	391
200601	3X-9X	Plex	mat		578	404
200597	3X-9X	Plex	blk	Posi-Lock®	605	423
200598	3X-9X	Plex	mat	Posi-Lock®	623	436
200596	3X-9X	Plex	nic	Posi-Lock®	632	442
200580	3X-9X	Electro-Dot®	blk		660	462
200581	3X-9X	Electro-Dot®	mat		678	474
200590	3X-9X	Electro-Dot®	blk	Posi-Lock®	706	493
200591	3X-9X	Electro-Dot®	mat	Posi-Lock®	724	506
200574	3X-9X-50mm	Plex	blk		620	434
200573	3X-9X-50mm	Mil-Dot	mat	Target Knobs	728	509
200571	3X-9X-50mm	Plex	mat	Posi-Lock®	658	460
200572	3X-9X-50mm	Mil-Dot	mat	Posi-Lock®	747	523

ITEM	MODEL	RETICLE	FINISH	FEATURES	LIST	DEALER
200630	2.5X-10X	Plex	blk	Posi-Lock/PA	682	477
200631	2.5X-10X	Plex	mat	Posi-Lock/PA	700	490
200633	2.5X-10X	Plex	nic	Posi-Lock/PA	709	496
200610	3X-12X	Plex	blk	PA	677	474
200611	3X-12X	Plex	mat	PA	695	486
200614	3X-12X	Plex	blk	Posi-Lock/PA	726	508
200615	3X-12X	Plex	mat	Posi-Lock/PA	744	520
200750	4X-16X	Plex	blk	PA	709	496
200751	4X-16X	Plex	mat	PA	727	509
200761	4X-16X	Fine Plex	mat	PA	727	509
200762	4X-16X	Fine Plex	blk	Target/PA	749	524
200763	4X-16X	Fine Plex	mat	Target/PA	764	534
200764	4X-16X	Mil-Dot	mat	Target/PA	892	624
200756	4X-16X	Plex	mat	Posi-Lock/PA	779	554
200765N	4X-16X	Electro-Dot®	mat	PA	828	579
200766N	4X-16X	Electro-Dot®	mat	Posi-Lock/PA	879	615
200800	6X-24X	Plex	blk	PA	727	509
200804	6X-24X	Plex	mat	PA	746	521
200803	6X-24X	Fine Plex	blk	Target/PA	764	534
200806	6X-24X	Fine Plex	mat	Target/PA	782	547
200811	6X-24X	Fine Plex	nic	Target/PA	791	553
200814	6X-24X	Mil-Dot	mat	Target/PA	910	636
200816N	6X-24X	Ballistic MDot	mat	Target/PA	910	636
200815	6X-24X	1"-.25" Dot	mat	Target/PA	819	572
200812	6X-24X	Plex	blk	Posi-Lock/PA	780	546
200813	6X-24X	Plex	mat	Posi-Lock/PA	799	558
200820	6X-24X	Electro-Dot®	blk	PA	828	579
200821	6X-24X	Electro-Dot®	mat	PA	846	592
200850	8X-32X	Fine Plex	blk	Target/PA	782	547
200860	8X-32X	Fine Plex	mat	Target/PA	800	560
200866	8X-32X	Fine Plex	nic	Target/PA	810	566
200851	8X-32X	Peep Plex™	blk	Target/PA	800	560
200853	8X-32X	1"-.25" Dot	mat	Target/PA	837	585
200854	8X-32X	Mil-Dot	mat	Target/PA	928	649
200855	8X-32X	Fine Plex	blk	Posi-Lock/PA	837	585
200856	8X-32X	Fine Plex	mat	Posi-Lock/PA	855	598

Finish: BLK=Gloss Black, MAT=Matte, CAM=Camo, NIC=Nickel. Features: PA=Parallax Adjustable, Target=Target-type adjustment knobs All scopes come with Storm Queen-style lens covers. Item number with "N" afterward are new for 1999

BURRIS SCOPES

FULLFIELD SCOPES
FIXED POWER WITH HI-LUME LENSES

3X-9X GLOSS ELECTRO-DOT

3X-9X GLOSS

3X-9X MATTE

2.5X SHOTGUN SCOPE

Item	Model	Reticle	Finish	Features	List	Dealer
200310	4X	Plex	blk		263	184
200311	4X	Plex	mat		281	196
200316	4X	Plex	nic		290	203
200350	6X	Plex	blk		279	195
200354	6X	Plex	blk	PA	321	224
200357	6X HBR	Fine Plex	blk	Target/PA	438	306
200360	6X HBR	Fine Xhair	blk	Target/PA	438	306
200362	6X HBR	2.7" Peep	mat	Target/PA	438	306
200358	6X HBR	.375" Dot	blk	Target/PA	474	332
200375	2X-7X	Plex	blk		359	251
200376	2X-7X	Plex	mat		377	264
200378	2X-7X	Plex	nic		386	270
200385	3X-9X	Plex	blk		368	258
200387	3X-9X	Plex	mat		387	270
200388	3X-9X	Plex	nic		396	277
200389	3X-9X	Plex	camo		421	295
200384	3X-9X	Plex	mat	PA	397	278
200383	3X-9X	Plex	nic	PA	407	284
200390	4X-12X	Plex	blk		485	339
200393	4X-12X	Fine Plex	blk	Target/PA	521	365
200394	4X-12X	Fine Plex	mat	Target/PA	540	377

FULLFIELD® SCOPES

Item	Model	Reticle	Finish	Features	List	Dealer
200402	1.5X shotgun	Plex	mat		299	209
200403	1.5X shotgun	Plex	camo		334	233
200413	2.5X shotgun	Plex	mat		308	215
200414	2.5X shotgun	Plex	camo		343	240
200010	4X	Plex	blk		314	219
200014	4X	Plex	mat		332	232
200050	6X	Plex	blk		343	240
200054	6X	Plex	mat		361	252
200094	12X	Fine Plex	blk	Target/PA	463	324
200060	1.75X-5X	Plex	blk		374	261
200061	1.75X-5X	Plex	mat		392	274
200020	2X-7X	Plex	blk		399	279
200024	2X-7X	Plex	mat		418	292
200030	3X-9X-38mm	Plex	blk		356	249
200034	3X-9X-38mm	Plex	mat		356	249
200028	3X-9X-38mm	Plex	nic		383	268
200140	3X-9X-40mm	Plex	blk		379	265
200141	3X-9X-40mm	Plex	mat		397	278
200142	3X-9X-40mm	Plex	nic		406	284
200134	3X-9X-40mm	Electro-Dot®	blk		487	340
200135	3X-9X-40mm	Electro-Dot®	mat		505	353
200150	3X-9X-50mm	Plex	blk		427	299
200151	3X-9X-50mm	Plex	mat		445	311
200152	3X-9X-50mm	Plex	nic		454	318
200045	3.5X-10X-50mm	Plex	blk		496	347
200046	3.5X-10X-50mm	Plex	mat		514	360
200048	3.5X-10X-50mm	Plex	nic		523	366
200070	4X-12X	Plex	blk	PA	503	352
200071	4X-12X	Fine Plex	blk	PA	503	352
200072	4X-12X	Fine Plex	mat	PA	521	365
200103	6X-18X	Fine Plex	blk	PA	527	368
200109	6X-18X	Fine Plex	mat	PA	545	381
200104	6X-18X	Fine Plex	blk	Target/PA	563	394
200108	6X-18X	Peep Plex™	mat	PA	563	394

RIMFIRE/AIRGUN SCOPES

Item	Model	Reticle	Finish	Features	List	Dealer
200313	4X	Plex	blk	PA	306	214
200352	6X	Plex	blk	PA	323	226
200384	3X-9X	Plex	mat	PA	397	278
200383	3X-9X	Plex	nic	PA	407	284
200393	4X-12X	Fine Plex	blk	Target/PA	521	365
200394	4X-12X	Fine Plex	mat	Target/PA	540	377
200858	8X-32X	Plex	blk	Target/PA	802	561
200859	8X-32X	Fine Plex	mat	Target/PA	820	574

COMPACT SCOPES

Item	Model	Reticle	Finish	Features	List	Dealer
200424	1X XER	Plex	mat		290	203
200423	1X XER	Plex	camo		316	221
200432	1X-4X XER	Plex	mat		377	264

HANDGUN SCOPES

Item	Model	Reticle	Finish	Features	List	Dealer
200424	1X XER	Plex	mat		290	203
200423	1X XER	Plex	camo		316	221
200220	2X	Plex	blk		257	180
200229	2X	Plex	nic		275	193
200222	2X	Plex	blk	Posi-Lock®	293	205
200228	2X	Plex	mat	Posi-Lock®	302	211
200227	2X	Plex	nic	Posi-Lock®	311	218
200235	4X	Plex	blk		288	201
200232	4X	Plex	blk	Posi-Lock®	324	226
200237	4X	Plex	nic		306	214
200263	10X Target/PA	Plex	blk	Target	447	313
200210	1.5X-4X	Plex	blk		352	246
200214	1.5X-4X	Plex	nic		370	259
200208	1.5X-4X	Plex	blk	Posi-Lock®	388	271
200213	1.5X-4X	Plex	nic	Posi-Lock®	406	284
200290	2X-7X	Plex	blk		390	273
200291	2X-7X	Plex	mat		399	279
200293	2X-7X	Plex	blk	PA	431	301
200298	2X-7X	Plex	nic		408	285
200294	2X-7X	Plex	blk	Posi-Lock®	425	298
200297	2X-7X	Plex	nic	Posi-Lock®	443	310
200281	3X-9X	Plex	blk	PA	440	308
200300	3X-9X	Plex	nic	PA	458	320
200288	3X-9X	Plex	blk	Posi-Lock/PA	475	333
200289	3X-9X	Plex	nic	Posi-Lock/PA	493	345
200306	3X-12X	Plex	blk	PA	493	345
200307	3X-12X	Plex	mat	PA	502	351
200308	3X-12X	Plex	nic	PA	511	358
200305	3X-12X	Fine Plex	blk	Target/PA	529	370

SCOUT SCOPES

Item	Model	Reticle	Finish	Features	List	Dealer
200424	1X XER	Plex	mat		290	203
200423	1X XER	Plex	camo		316	221
200277	1.5X	Heavy Plex	blk		301	210
200278	1.5X	Heavy Plex	mat		301	210
200270	2.75X	Plex	blk		301	210
200271	2.75X	3P#1	blk		310	217
200269	2.75X	Heavy Plex	mat		310	217

SPEEDOT™ 135 SIGHTS

Item	Model	Reticle	Finish	Features	List	Dealer
300200	1X-35mm	3 MOA Dot	mat		282	198
300201	1X-35mm	11 MOA Dot	mat		282	198

BUSHNELL SCOPECHIEF® RIFLESCOPES

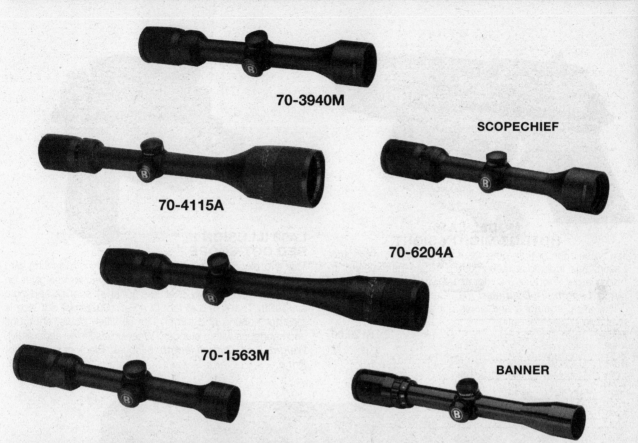

70-3940M

SCOPECHIEF

70-4115A

70-6204A

70-1563M

BANNER

BUSHNELL SCOPECHIEF® RIFLESCOPES

Model	Special Feature	Actual Magnification	Obj. Lens Aperature (mm)	Field of View ft @ 100yds/m	Weight (oz/g)	Length (in/mm)	Eye Relief (in/mm)	Exit Pupil (mm)	Click Value in @ 100yds mm @ 100m	Adjust Range in @ 100yds m @ 100m	Selection	Suggested Retail
70-1563M	Matte Finish	1.5x-6x	32	74/24.6@1.5x 20/6.7@6x	14.4/408	10.7/272	3.5/89	14@1.5x 5.3@6x	.25/7	100/2.8	Ideal shotgun, close range scope.	$337.95
70-3104M	Matte Finish	3.5x-10x	40	43/14.3@3.5x 15/5.0@10x	17/482	13/330	3.5/89	12@3.5x 4.2@10x	.25/7	50/1.4	6 inch mounting length	$293.95
70-3940M	Matte Finish	3x-9x	40	42/14.0@3x 14/4.7@9x	16/454	11.5/292	3.5/89	13.3@3x 4.4@9x	.25/7	90/2.5	Standard, all purpose scope	$255.95
70-4145A	Matte Finish, Adj. Objective, Sunshade	4x-14x	50	31/103@4x 9/3.0@14x	23/652	14.1/358	3.5/89	12.5@4x 3.6@14x	.25/7	50/1.4	Higher magnification with longer objective for enhanced brightness at longer ranges.	$408.95
70-6204A	Matte Finish, Adj. Objective, Sunshade	6x-20x	40	21/7.0@6x 6/2.0@20x	21/595	15.75/400	3.5/89	6.6@6x 2.0@20x	.25/7	40/1.1	High magnification for target shooting and varminting.	$583.95

BUSHNELL BANNER RIFLESCOPES

Model	Special Feature	Actual Magnification	Obj. Lens Aperature (mm)	Field of View ft @ 100yds/m	Weight (oz/g)	Length (in/mm)	Eye Relief (in/mm)	Exit Pupil (mm)	Click Value in @ 100yds mm @ 100m	Adjust Range in @ 100yds m @ 100m	Selection	Suggested Retail
71-1545	Wide Angle	1.5x-4.5x	32	67-23	10.5	10.5	3.5	17-7	.25	60	Ideal Shotgun and median to short range scope.	$116.95
71-3944	Black powder scope w/extended eye relief and Circle-x@ reticle	3x-9x	40	36-13	12.5	11.5	4	13-4.4	.25	60	Specifically designed for black powder and shotguns	$120.95
71-3948	Ideal scope for multi purpose guns	3x-9x	40	40-74	13	12	3	13.3-4.4	.25	60	General purpose.	$113.95
71-3950	Large objective for extra brightness in low light	3x-9x	50	31-10	19	16	3	16-5.6	.25	50	Low light conditions	$186.95
71-4124	Adjustable objective	4x-12x	40	29-11	15	12	3	10-3.3	.25	60	Ideal scope for long-range shooting.	$157.95
71-6185	Adjustable objective	6x-18x	50	17-6	18	16	3	8.3-2.8	.25	40	Long range varmint and target scope.	$209.95

Laseraim Arms Inc.

MODEL LA16
HOTDOT MIGHTY SIGHT
Ten times brighter than other laser sights, Laseraim's Hotdot Lasersights include a rechargeable NICad battery and in-field charger. Produce a 2" dot at 100 yards with a 500-yard range. *Length:* 2". *Diameter:* .75". Can be used with hand-guns, rifles, shotguns and bows. Fit all Laseraim mounts. Available in black or satin.
Price: **$129.00**

LA93 ILLUSION III™
RED DOT SCOPE
This two-piece design offers more flexibility in mounting with less added overall weight. The 30mm objective lens gives an increased field of veiw over traditional 1" scopes and zero eye relief. The 4 m.o.a. (about 4" at 100 yards) dot size is ideal for hunting and target. Fits all rifles, bows, shotguns and handguns with a standard Weaver base (sold separately). *Weight:* 5 oz. *Overall length:* 6 inches. Black or satin finish.
Price: **$129.00**

GI HOT CUSTOM LASERS
The GI HOT (Hotdot® laser) has been custom-designed for Glock models 17 to 30. It allows a two-handed shooting grip by locating the laser close to the bottom of the frame. This patented system internalizes the wires, leaving a clean, easy-to-use laser that conforms to the pistol and makes sighting a breeze. A pressure-sensitive pad turns the laser on and off. Four button-cell batteries power it up to one hour continuously. The Easy-lock™ windage & elevation system makes sighting quick and reliable. GI HOT range = 500 yds. *Length:* 1.5". *Weight:* 2 oz.
Price: **$229.00**

LA70 SHOTLESS LASER BORE SIGHTER™
(Not shown)
The **LA70 SHOTLESS LASER BORE SIGHTER™** facilitates sight-ing to near perfect accuracy without wasting a shot. To check the center of the bore, simply rotate the laser on axis of the gun bore. The LA70 is equipped with a rotational **LASERAIM™** with constant ON switch and six arbors fitting calibers 22 thru 45, 12-gauge shotguns and muzzleloaders (50 and 54 cal.). *Length:* 8" (w/laser and arbor).
Price: **$169.00**

LEICA ULTRAVID RIFLESCOPES

LEICA, the world-renowned maker of high-quality cameras, binoculars and spotting scopes has earned the reputation of producing German-engineered optics with unsurpassed optical performance and mechanical precision. The LEICA ULTRAVID Riflescopes have created a complete hunting product line for the serious outdoor enthusiast. These riflescopes are designed to withstand the most extreme conditions–from frigid Alaskan bays to scorching Kalahari sands. All models provide exceptionally brilliant, high-contrast images, thanks to LEICA's Multi-Coated glass with "ballistic tough" ion-assisted coatings. The lenses are precisely positioned in a durable, one-piece 30mm housing machined from a single block of aircraft-grade aluminum to withstand accidents of all kinds. Waterproofed up to 33 feet and nitrogen-purged to provide a lifetime of fog-proof use, LEICA's ULTRAVID riflescopes are finished in a hard, anodized black matte with titanium accents. In addition, the power selector and diopter adjustment covers feature "soft touch" rubber tactile surfaces for a positive grip even with gloved hands or wet fingers.

1.75-6x 32mm

3.5x-10x 42mm

4.5x-14x 42mm "F"

SPECIFICATIONS

MODEL	WEIGHT	LENGTH	FIELD OF VIEW FT. @ 100 YD.		OPTIMUM EYE RELIEF		ADJUSTMENT RANGE @ 100 YARDS	PRICES
			LOW	HIGH	LOW	HIGH		
1.75x-6x by 32 mm	14 ounces	11.25 inches	47 inches	18	4.8 inches	3.7	55 inches	$699.00
3.5x-10x by 42 mm	16 ounces	12.62 inches	29.5 inches	10.7	4.6 inches	3.6	51 inches	$799.00
4.5x-14x by 42 mm F	18 ounces	12.28 inches	20.8 inches	7.4	5.0 inches	3.7	67 inches	$899.00

LEUPOLD RIFLESCOPES

VARI-X III LINE

The Vari-X III scopes feature a power-changing system that is similar to the sophisticated lens systems in today's finest cameras. Improvements include an extremely accurate internal control system and a sharp sight picture. All lenses are coated with Multicoat 4. Reticles are the same apparent size throughout the power range and stay centered during elevation/windage adjustments. Eyepieces are adjustable and fog-free. Reticles are also available in German #1, German #1 European, German #4, Post and Duplex, and Leupold Dot.

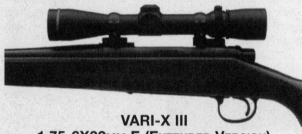

**VARI-X III
1.75-6X32MM E (EXTENDED VERSION)**

VARI-X III 1.5-5X20mm
This selection of hunting powers is for ranges varying from very short to those at which big game is normally taken. The field at 1.5X lets you get on a fast-moving animal quickly. With magnification at 5X, medium and big game can be hunted around the world at all but the longest ranges.
Duplex or Heavy Duplex $610.70
In black matte finish 632.10
Also available:
VARI-X III 1.75-6X32mm. Matte finish 653.60

VARI-X III 2.5-8X36mm
This is an excellent range of powers for almost any kind of game, including varmints. The top magnification provides resolution for practically any situation.
Duplex $651.80
In matte or silver finish 673.20
Mil Dot (Matte) 807.10

VARI-X III 3.5-10X40mm
The extra power range makes these scopes the optimum choice for year-around big game and varmint hunting. The adjustable objective model, with its precise focusing at any range beyond 50 yards, also is an excellent choice for some forms of target shooting.
Duplex $671.40
With matte or silver finish 692.90

VARI-X III 3.5-10X50mm
The hunting scope is designed specifically for low-light situations. The 3.5X10-50mm scope, featuring lenses coated with Multicoat 4, is ideal for twilight hunting because of its efficient light transmission. The new scope delivers maximum available light through its large 50mm objective lens, which translates into an exit pupil that transmits all the light the human eye can handle in typical low-light circumstances, even at the highest magnification
Duplex or Heavy Duplex $769.60
With matte or silver finish 791.10

VARI-X III 4.5-14X40mm (Adj. Objective)
This model has enough range to double as a hunting scope and as a varmint scope.
Duplex or Heavy Duplex $750.00
With matte finish 771.40
Same as above with 50mm adj. obj., Duplex or Heavy
Duplex; matte finish only 869.60

VARI-X III 6.5-20X50mm Varmint

VARI-X III 6.5-20X40mm (Adj. Objective)
This scope has a wide range of power setting, with magnifications useful to hunters of all types of varmints. Can be used for any kind of big-game hunting where higher magnifications are an aid. Side-focus adjustment allows shooters to eliminate parallax while in shooting position without taking their eyes off the target.
Gloss finish $791.10
With matte or silver finish 812.50
Also available:
VARMINT (target knob) $892.90
6.5-20X50MM ADJ. OBJ. w/duplex matte finish. . . 910.70
6.5-20X50MM ADJ. OBJ. w/Mil Dot matte finish . . 1,044.60

VARI-X III 8.5-25X40mm

VARI-X III 8.5-25X40mm (Adj. Objective)
Features one-piece main tube of T-6061 aluminum, 1/4-minute click adjustments, Multicoat 4™ lens coating.
With matte finish $846.40
Target Model 900.00
(Leupold Dot about $54.00 extra)

LEUPOLD

The Vari-X II line offers magnesium fluoride-coated lenses for improved light transmission, continuous tension adjustment dials with increments as fine as 1/2 minute of angle, a locking eyepiece for reliable ocular adjustment, and a sealed, nitrogen-filled interior for fog-free reliability. Many models are available with Dot, CPC, German #1, German #4, and Post & Duplex reticles in addition to Duplex.

VARI-X II 1-4X20mm DUPLEX

This scope, the smallest of Leupold's VARI-X II line, is noted for its large field of view: 70 feet at 100 yards.
Gloss finish only. $380.40
Vari-X II 1-4x 20 Shotgun (heavy Duplex) matte . . 401.80

1-4X20mm Duplex

VARI-X II 2-7X33mm DUPLEX

A compact scope, no larger than the Leupold M8-4X, offering a wide range of power. It can be set at 2X for close ranges in heavy cover or zoomed to maximum power for shooting or identifying game at longer ranges.
Vari-X II 2-7x 33 Shotgun (heavy Duplex) matte . . 412.50

2-7X33mm Duplex

VARI-X II 3-9X50mm

This LOV scope delivers a 5.5mm exit pupil for low-light visibility: $494.60
Matte finish 516.10

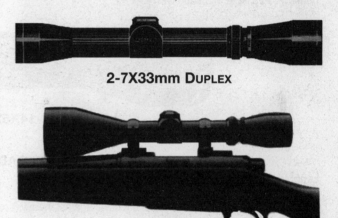

3-9X50mm

VARI-X II 3-9X40mm DUPLEX

A wide selection of powers offers the right combination of field of view and magnification to fit most hunting conditions. Many hunters use the 3X or 4X setting most of the time, cranking up to 9X for positive identification of game or for extremely long shots. The adjustable objective eliminates parallax and permits precise focusing on any object from less than 50 yards to infinity for extra-sharp definition.
Gloss finish $416.10
In matte, silver 437.50
Tactical (Mil Dot, matte) 650.00

3-9X40mm Duplex

VARI-X II 4-12X40mm (Adj. Objective)

The ideal answer for big game and varmint hunters alike. At 12.25 inches, the 4X12 is virtually the same length as Vari-X II 3X9. New fixed objective has same long eye relief and is factory-set to be free of parallax at 150 yds.
Gloss finish $573.20
Matte or silver finish 594.60
3/4 Mil. Dot (gloss) 707.10
3/4 Mil. Dot (matte) 728.60

4-12X40mm

VARI-X II 6-18X40mm Adj. Obj. Target

Features target-style click adjustments, fully coated lenses, adj. objective for parallax-free shooting from 50 yards to infinity.
In matte. $630.40
Target Dot Model 683.90
Target Dot w/Target knobs 737.50

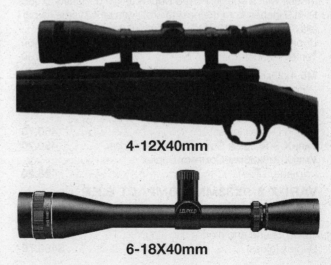

6-18X40mm

LEUPOLD SCOPES

LEUPOLD PREMIER SCOPES (LPS)

The Leupold Premiere Scope (LPS) line features 30mm maintubes, fast-focus eye-pieces, armored power selector dials that can be read from the shooting position, a 4-inch constant eye relief, Diamondcoat lenses for increased light transmission scratch resistance, and finger adjustable, low profile elevation and windage adjustments.

LPS 1.5-6x42mm
A wide field of view and a generous magnification range make this scope an outstanding choice for all big game hunting. Available in a satin finish.

Duplex (satin) $1,476.80
German #1 or German #4 (satin) 1,530.40

LPS 3.5-14x52mm Adj. Obj.
With a magnification range from 3.5x to 14x, this scope works for all types of hunting. The adjustable objective dial, with increments printed on the slope of the objective bell, can be read without leaving the shooting position. Available in a satin finish.
Duplex (satin) $1,569.60
Target Dot, German #1, German #4 (satin) 1,623.20
3/4 Min. Mil. Dot (satin) 1,703.60

LPSTM 3.5-14X52mm Adj. Obj.

SHOTGUN & MUZZLELOADER SCOPES (not shown)

Leupold shotgun scopes are parallax-adjusted to deliver precise focusing at 75 yards. Each scope features a special Heavy Duplex reticle that is more effective against heavy, brushy backgrounds. All scopes have matte finish.

Prices:
VARI-X II 1-4X20mm MODEL HEAVY DUPLEX $396.40
M8-4X33mm HEAVY DUPLEX 383.90
VARI-X III 2-7X33mm HEAVY DUPLEX 428.60

COMPACT SCOPES

M8 2.5-20MM COMPACT
This small scope presents the shooter with an enormous field of view for fast target acquisition. It also features generous elevation and windage adjustment. Standard models are parallax adjusted to 100 yards. The Turkey Ranger model, with a special Post & Duplex reticle designed to subtend 9 inches from the post to crosswire at 40 yards, is parallax adjusted to 40 yards. Offered in a matte finish.
Duplex or Heavy Duplex (matte) $300.00
Turkey Ranger (matte) 353.60

M8 4x28MM COMPACT RIMFIRE SPECIAL
Fine Duplex (gloss) 367.90
VARI-X 2-7x28MM COMPACT Duplex (gloss) 460.70
VARI-X 2-7x28MM COMPACT RIMFIRE SPECIAL
Fine Duplex (gloss) 460.70
VARI-X 3-9x33MM COMPACT Duplex (gloss) 460.70
VARI-X 3-9x33MM COMPACT Duplex
(matte, silver) 498.20

VARI-X 3-9X33MM COMPACT E.F.R.
With an adjustable objective capable of setting parallax as close as 10 meters, this scope is perfectly suited to .22 rimfire silhouette and air rifle shooting.
Duplex (gloss) $460.70

M8-2.5x20MM COMPACT

4X COMPACT & 4 RF SPECIAL

2-7 COMPACT

3-9 COMPACT SILVER

LEUPOLD SCOPES

TACTICAL MODELS

6x42mm AO TACTICAL SCOPE

The Leupold 6x42mm features 1/4-minute click target-style adjustments for precise corrections in the field. Adjustment travel for windage or elevation is 76 inches. The combination of an exact 6X magnification, adjustable objective and target-style adjustments make it an excellent choice for Hunter Benchrest Competitions as well. Leupold's exclusive Multicoat 4 lens coating is applied to all air-to-glass surfaces to provide the 6X42mm maximum light transmission.
Length: 12" **Weight:** 11.5 ounces
Two reticles styles: classic Duplex or a 3/4-minute Military Dot. Black matte finish.
Matte finish $628.60
With 3/4-minute Military Dot 762.50

MARK 4 MI 10x40 (MATTE)/MARK 4 MI 16x40 (MATTE)
MARK 4 MI 10x40 (MATTE)
Duplex 1,735.70
Mil Dot 1,869.60
VARI-X II 3-9x40 (MATTE)
Duplex 516.10
Mil Dot 650.00
VARI-X III 3.5-10x40 (MATTE)
Duplex 771.40
Mil Dot 905.40
VARI-X III 4.5-14x40 AO (MATTE)
Duplex 850.00
Mil Dot 983.80

FIXED POWER SCOPES

M8-4X

The 4X delivers a widely used magnification and a generous field of view $371.40
In black matte finish 392.90
Shotgun (heavy Duplex) matte 371.40

M8-4X33

M8-6X

The 6X extends the range for big-game hunting and doubles in some cases as a varmint scope $394.60

M8-6X36

M8-6X42mm

Large 42mm objective lens features a 7mm exit pupil for increased light-gathering capability. Recommended for varmint shooting at night.
Duplex or Heavy Duplex $491.10
In matte finish 512.50

M8-6X42mm

M8-12X40MM STANDARD (Adj. Obj.)

Outstanding optical qualities, resolution and magnification make the 12X a natural for the varmint shooter. Adjustable objective is standard for parallax-free focusing.
Duplex $550.00
With CPC reticle or Dot 651.80

M8-12X40mm STANDARD

LEUPOLD RIFLESCOPES

LONG-RANGE MODELS

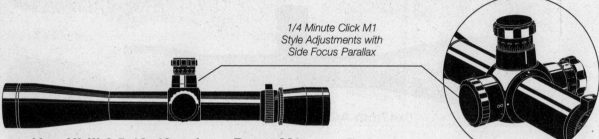

1/4 Minute Click M1 Style Adjustments with Side Focus Parallax

VARI-X® III 3.5-10x40MM LONG RANGE M1

VARI-X III 3.5-10X40MM LONG RANGE TACTICAL M1

This scope combines the bold 1/4 minute of angle target dial design of the Leupold Mark 4 M1 scopes with the 30 mm maintube and side parallax dial of a long range scope to produce a low profile, close mounted tactical scope of remarkable versatility not only as a tactical scope, but as a sporting scope as well. Available in an all matte (including the Leupold Golden Ring) finish.

Duplex (matte)........................ **$1,108.90**
Target Dot (matte)..................... **1,162.50**
3/4 Min. Mil. Dot (matte) **1,242.90**

VARI-X III 4.5-14X50MM LONG RANGE

With the increasing popularity of long range shooting, special scopes have been developed to accommodate the additional adjustment necessary to success in this discipline. The 4.5-14x50mm Long Range models with their 30mm maintubes, target style adjustment knobs, and side mounted parallax dials offer the shooter everything necessary to achieve success at great distances.

VARI-X III 4.5-14x50MM LONG RANGE TARGET Fine Duplex (silver).............................. **$1,012.50**
VARI-X III 4.5-14x50MM LONG RANGE TARGET
Target Dot (silver)..................... **1,066.10**
VARI-X III 4.5-14x50MM LONG RANGE TACTICAL
Fine Duplex (matte) **1,037.50**
VARI-X III 4.5-14x50MM LONG RANGE TACTICAL
Target Dot (matte) **1,091.10**

LEUPOLD GILMORE RED DOT SIGHTS

The Leupold Gilmore Red Dot Sights feature a compact frame that is easily mounted on any type of firearm, from shotguns and muzzleloaders to rifles and pistols. Eleven dot intensity settings and three different dot sizes available, unlimited eye relief, and 1/3 minute of angle elevation and windage.

LG-1

2 Minute Dot (matte and silver two tone) **$278.60**

LG-35

Offered in either solid matte black or a two tone matte and silver finish.

4 Minute Dot (matte, matte and silver two tone) **$421.40**
8 Minute Dot (matte and silver two tone) **421.40**

VARI-X III 4.5-14x50MM LONG RANGE TACTICAL
3/4 Min. Mil. Dot (matte)................. **1,171.40**

VARI-X III 6.5-20X40MM E.F.R. TARGET

For those situations, such as air rifle or rimfire silhouette, where normal adjustable objective ranges are simply too distant, Leupold offers the EFR (Extended Focus Rifle) model of the 6.5-20. With this model, parallax distances as close as 10 meters can be set.

Fine Duplex (matte) **$883.90**
Target Dot (matte) **937.50**

VARI-X III 6.5-20X50MM LONG RANGE TARGET

Designed with a 30mm maintube to provide additional elevation and windage adjustment, and featuring target style adjustment dials and a side mounted parallax dial, this scope offers the long range shooter impressive magnification and convenient adjustment mechanisms.

Fine Duplex (matte, silver) **$1,117.90**
Target Dot (matte,silver).................. **1,171.40**
3/4 Min. Mil. Dot (matte) **1,251.80**

VARI-X III 8.5-25X50MM LONG RANGE TARGET

With a 30mm maintube to provide additional elevation and windage adjustment, target style adjustment dials, and a side mounted parallax dial, this scope offers the long range shooter impressive magnification and convenient adjustment mechanisms.

Fine Duplex (matte) **$1,208.90**
Target Dot (matte)...................... **1,262.50**

LG-35, 35MM RED DOT SIGHT

NIKON MONARCH SCOPES

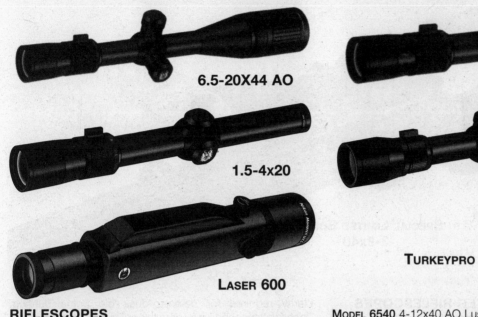

6.5-20X44 AO

2-7X32

1.5-4x20

5.5-16x44AO

LASER 600

TURKEYPRO

RIFLESCOPES

MODEL **6500** 4x40 Lustre $284.00
MODEL **6505** 4x40 Matte 304.00
MODEL **6510** 2-7x32 Lustre 367.00
MODEL **6515** 2-7x32 Matte 387.00
MODEL **6520** 3-9x40 Lustre 371.00
MODEL **6525** 3-9x40 Matte 391.00
MODEL **6530** 3.5-10x50 Lustre 554.00
MODEL **6535** 3.5-10x50 Matte 572.00

MODEL **6540** 4-12x40 AO Lustre 476.00
MODEL **6545** 4-12x40 AO Matte 496.00
MODEL **6550** 6.5-20x44 AO Lustre 591.00
MODEL **6555** 6.5-20x44 AO Matte 612.00
MODEL **6570** 6.5-20x44 HV 591.00
MODEL **6575** 6.5-20x44 HV 612.00

HANDGUN SCOPES

MODEL **6560** 2x20 EER Black Lustre $213.00
MODEL **6565** 2x20 EER Silver 233.00

MONARCH™ UCC RIFLESCOPE SPECIFICATIONS

Model	4x40	2-7x32	3-9x40	3.5-10x50	4-12x40 AO	6.5-20x44 AO	6.5-20x44 AO Hunting	2x20 EER
Lustre	#6500	#6510	#6520	#6530	#6540	#6550	#6570	#6560
Matte	#6505	#6515	#6525	#6535	#6545	#6555	#6575	-
Silver	-							#6565
Actual Magnification	4x	2x-7x	3x-9x	3.5x-10x	4x-12x	6.5x-19.46x	6.5x-19.46x	1.75x
Objective Diameter	40mm	32mm	40mm	50mm	40mm	44mm	44mm	20mm
Exit Pupil	10mm	16-4.6mm	13.3-4.4mm	14.3-5mm	10-3.3mm	6.7-2.2mm	6.7-2.2mm	10mm
Eye Relief	89mm 3.5 in.	101-93mm 3.9-3.6 in.	93-90mm 3.6-3.5 in.	100-98mm 3.9-3.8 in.	92-87mm 3.6-3.4 in.	89-81mm 3.5-3.1 in.	89-81mm 3.5-3.1 in.	670-267mm 26.4-10.5 in.
Field of View at 100 yards	26.9 ft.	44.5-12.7 ft.	33.8-11.3 ft.	25.5-8.9 ft.	25.6-8.5 ft.	16.1-5.4 ft.	16.1-5.4 ft.	22.0 ft.
Tube Diameter	25.4mm 1 in.	25.4mm 1 in.	25.4mm 1 in.	25.4mm 1 in.	25.4mm 1 in.	25.4mm 1 in.	25.4mm 1 in.	25.4mm 1 in.
Objective Tube Diameter	47.3mm 1.86 in.	39.3mm 1.5 in	47.3mm 1.86 in.	57.3mm 2.2 in.	53.1mm 2.09 in.	54mm 2.13 in.	54mm 2.13 in.	25.4mm 1 in.
Eyepiece O.D. Diameter	38mm 1.5 in.	38mm 1.5 in.	38mm 1.5 in.	38mm 1.5 in.	38mm 1.5 in.	38mm 1.5 in.	38mm 1.5 in.	35.5mm 1.4 in.
Length	297mm 11.7 in.	283mm 11.1 in.	312mm 12.3 in.	350mm 13.7 in.	348.5mm 13.7 in.	373mm 14.6 in.	373mm 14.6 in.	207mm 8.1 in.
Weight	315 g. 11.2 oz.	315 g. 11.2 oz.	355 g. 12.6 oz.	435 g. 15.5 oz.	475 g. 16.9 oz.	565 g. 20.1 oz.	565 g. 20.1 oz.	185 g. 6.6 oz.
Adjustment Graduation	¼:1 Click ½:1 Div.	¼:1 Click ¼:1 Div.	¼:1 Click ¼:1 Div.	¼:1 Click ¼:1 Div.	¼:1 Click ¼:1 Div.	⅛:1 Click ⅛:1 Div.	⅛:1 Click ⅛:1 Div.	¼:1 Click ½:1 Div.
Max. Internal Adjustment (moa)	120	70	55	45	45	38	38	120
Parallax Setting (yards)	100	100	100	100	50 to infinity	50 to infinity	50 to infinity	100

NIKON BUCKMASTER RIFLESCOPES

SPECIAL LIMITED EDITION
3-9x40

NIKON BUCKMASTER RIFLESCOPES

Nikon has teamed with Buckmasters to produce a limited edition riflescope line. The first products in this line are a 3-9x40 variable, a large objective 3-9x50 variable and a 4x40 fixed power scope. Built to withstand the toughest hunting conditions, the new scopes integrate shockproof, fogproof and waterproof construction, plus numerous other features seldom found on riflescopes in this price range. Nikon's Brightvue™ anti-reflective system of high-quality, multicoated lenses provides over 93% anti-reflection capability for high levels of light transmission and optical clarity required for dawn-to-dusk big game hunting. These riflescopes are parallax-adjusted at 100 yards and have durable matte finishes that reduce glare while afield. They also feature positive steel-to-brass, quarter-minute-click windage and elevation adjustments for instant, repeatable accuracy and a Nikoplex® reticle for quick target acquisition.

Prices:
MODEL 6405 4x40 BUCKMASTER $237.00
MODEL 6425 3-9x40 BUCKMASTER 299.00
MODEL 6435 3-9x50 BUCKMASTER 439.00

SPECIFICATIONS

	4x40	3-9x40	3-9x50
MODEL	#6405	#6425	#6435
Actual Magnification	4x	3x-9x	3x-9x
Objective Diameter	40mm	40mm	50mm
Exit Pupil	10mm	13.3-4.4mm	16.7-5.5mm
Eye Relief	3.5 in.	3.6-3.5 in.	3.6-3.5 in.
Field of View at 100 yards	26.9 ft.	33.8-11.3 ft.	33.8-11.3 ft.
Tube Diameter	1 in.	1 in.	1 in.
Objective Tube Diameter	1.86 in.	1.86 in.	2.2 in.
Eyepiece O.D. Diameter	1.5 in.	1.5 in.	1.5 in.
Length	11.7 in.	12.3 in.	12 in.
Weight	11.2 oz.	12.6 oz.	12.7 oz.
Adjustment Graduation	1/4: 1 Click 1/2: 1 Div.	1/4: 1 Click 1/4: 1 Div.	1/4: 1 Click 1/4: 1 Div.
Max. Internal Adjustment (moa)	120	55	55
Parallax Setting (yards)	100	100	100

PENTAX SCOPES

LIGHTSEEKER II RIFLESCOPES

4X-16XAO LIGHTSEEKER II
$844.00

3X-9X LIGHTSEEKER II
$636.00 (Glossy) $660.00 (Matte)

6X-24XAO LIGHTSEEKER II
$878.00

Features:

- **Scratch-resistant outer tube.** Under ordinary wear and tear, the outer tube is almost impossible to scratch.
- **High Quality cam zoom tube.** No plastics are used. The tube is made of a bearing-type brass with precision machined cam slots. The zoom control screws are precision-ground to 1/2 of one thousandth tolerance.
- **Leak Prevention.** The power rings are sealed on a separate precision-machined seal tube. The scopes are then filled with nitrogen and double-sealed with heavy-duty "O" rings, making them leak-proof and fog-proof.
- **Excellent eyepieces.** The eyepiece lenses have a greater depth of field than most others. Thus, a more focused target at 100, 200 or 500 yards is attainable. Most Pentax Riflescopes are available in High Gloss, Matte or Satin Chrome finish.

PENTAX CORPORATION expands its extensive line of scopes by adding a Mil-Dot reticle option to three of its current models. The Mil-Dot reticle is an extremely accurate device for estimating range up to 1,000 yards, which increases the degree of accuracy for the shooter. First featured on the **PENTAX** 8.5X-32X Lightseeker, Mil-Dot reticles are now also available on the 3X-9X, 4X-16X, and 6X-24X Lightseeker scopes.

The Mil-Dot reticle looks like a standard crosshair, with the addition of four oval dots radiating in each direction from the center. The distance from each dot to the next is one mil, or one yard at one thousand yards. If the shooter knows the height or width of the target or other nearby object, the range to the target can be estimated accurately by making a simple calculation or referring to a Mil-Dot chart.

PENTAX RIFLESCOPES

LIGHTSEEKER RIFLESCOPES

**2.5 LIGHTSEEKER SG PLUS
MOSSY OAK® BREAK-UP SCOPE**

**ZERO-X/V SG PLUS
TURKEY STILL-TARGET COMPETITION**

LIGHTSEEKER RIFLESCOPE SPECIFICATIONS

MODEL	OBJECTIVE DIAMETER (MM)	EYEPIECE DIAMETER (MM)	EXIT PUPIL (MM)	EYE RELIEF (IN.)	FIELD OF VIEW (FT 100 YD)	ADJUSTMENT GRADUATION (IN 100YD)	MAXIMUM ADJUSTMENT (IN 100 YD)	LENGTH (IN.)	WEIGHT (OZ.)	RETICLE*	RECOMMENDED USE**	PRICES
LIGHTSEEKER 1.75X-6X	35	36	15.3-5	3.5-4.0	71-20	1/2	110	10.75	13.0	HP	BG,DG,SG/P	$546.00
LIGHTSEEKER 2X-8X	39	36	11.0-4.0	3.5-4.0	53-17	1/3	80	11.7	14.0	P	BG,DG,SG/P	594.00
LIGHTSEEKER 3X-9X	43	36	12.0-5.0	3.5-4.0	36-14	1/4	50	12.7	15.0	P or HP	BG	628.00
LIGHTSEEKER 3.5X-10X	50	36	11.0-5.0	3.5-4.0	29.5-11	1/4	50	14.0	19.5	HP, P	BG,V	652.00
LIGHTSEEKER 4X-16X AO	44	36	10.4-2.8	3.5-4.0	33-9	1/4	35	15.4	22.7	FP or MD, HP, P	T,V,BG	816.00
LIGHTSEEKER 6X-24X AO	44	36	6.9-2.3	3.5-4.0	18-5.5	1/8	26	16.0	23.7	FP or MD	T,V	856.00
LIGHTSEEKER 8.5X-32X AO	44	36	5.0-1.4	3.5-4.0	13-3.8	1/8	26	17.2	24.0	FP or MD	T,V	944.00
LIGHTSEEKER 2.5X SG PLUS	25	36	7.0	3.5-4.0	55	1/2	60	10.0	9.0	DW	BG,DG,TK	350.00
LIGHTSEEKER ZERO-X SG PLUS	27	35	19.5	4.5-15	51	1/2	196	8.9	7.9	DW	BG,DG,TK	372.00
LIGHTSEEKER ZERO-X/V SG PLUS	27	35	19.5-5.5	3.5-7	53.8-15	1/2	129	8.9	10.3	CP or HP	BG,DG,TK	454.00
LIGHTSEEKER ZERO-X/V SG PLUS TURKEY STILL-TARGET COMPETITION	27	35	19.5-5.5	3.5-7	53.8-1.5	1/2	129	8.9	10.3	CP or HP	BG,DG,TK	476.00

All scope tubes measure 1 inch in diameter. Scopes are available in high-gloss black, matte black, satin chrome or camouflage, depending on model. *P = Penta-Plex FP = Fine-Plex DW = Deepwoods Plex D = Dot HP = Heavy Plex MD = Mil Dot **BG = Big Game SG/P = Small Game/Pinking V= Varmint DG = Dangerous Game T = Target TK = Turkey Add $20 for matte finish

QUARTON BEAMSHOT SIGHTS

BEAMSHOT 1000 ULTRA/SUPER

SPECIFICATIONS

Size: .75" X 2 ³/₅" (overall length)
Weight: 3.8 oz. (incl. battery & mount)
Construction: Aluminum 6061 T6
Finish: Black anodized *Cable length:* 5"
Range: 500 yards *Power:* <5mW Class IIIA Laser
Wave length: 650nm (Beamshot 1000U-635nm)
Power supply: 3V Lithium battery
Battery life: Approx. 20 hrs. (continuous)
Dot size: 5" at 10 yds.; 4" at 100 yds.
Prices:
STANDARD $50.00
SUPER 60.00
ULTRA 80.00
BORE SIGHT ARBOR 1 (.22-.264 DIAM.) 99.00
BORE SIGHT ARBOR 2 (.264-.308 DIAM.) 99.00
BORE SIGHT ARBOR 3 (.308-.35 DIAM.) 99.00

1000 (PLUS RV2 MOUNT)

1000 (PLUS P1A MOUNT)

BEAMSHOT 3000

SPECIFICATIONS

Size: ³/₅" X 2 (overall length)
Weight: 2 oz. (incl. battery)
Construction: Aluminum 6061 T6
Finish: Black *Cable length:* 5"
Range: 300 yards *Power:* <5mW Class IIIA Laser
Wave length: 670nm
Power supply: 3 SR44 silver oxide watch battery
Battery life: Approx. 4 hrs. (continuous)
Dot size: 0.5" at 10 yds.; 4" at 100 yds.
Prices:
SUPER $60.00
ULTRA 80.00

3000 (PLUS P4 MOUNT)

SAKO SCOPE MOUNTS

"ORIGINAL" SCOPE MOUNTS

"ORIGINAL" SCOPE MOUNTS

SAKO's "Original" scope mounts are designed and engineered to exacting specifications, which is traditional to all SAKO products. The dovetail mounting system provides for a secure and stable system that is virtually immovable. Unique to this Sako mount is a synthetic insert that provides maximum protection against possible scope damage. It also affords additional rigidity by compressing itself around the scope. Manufactured in Finland.

Prices:
1" LOW, MEDIUM & HIGH
   (Short, Medium & Long Action) **$98.00**
30mm LOW, MEDIUM & HIGH
   (Short, Medium & Long Action) **116.00**
1" MEDIUM & HIGH EXTENDED BASE
   SCOPE MOUNTS **154.00**

SCOPE MOUNTS

These SAKO scope mounts are lighter, yet stronger than ever. Tempered steel allows the paring of every last gram of unnecessary weight without sacrificing strength. Like the original mount, these rings clamp directly to the tapered dovetails on Sako rifles, thus eliminating the need for separate bases. Grooves inside the rings preclude scope slippage even under the recoil of the heaviest calibers. Nicely streamlined and finished in a rich blue-black to complement any Sako rifle.

Prices:
Low, medium, or high (1") **$116.00**
Medium or high (30mm) **135.00**

"NEW" SCOPE MOUNTS

SCHMIDT & BENDER RIFLE SCOPES

2.5-10X56 VARIABLE POWER SCOPE
$1390.00

Also available:

1.25-4X20 VARIABLE POWER SCOPE	$995.00
1.5-6X42 VARIABLE POWER SCOPE	1125.00
3-12X42 VARIABLE POWER SCOPE	1290.00
3-12X50 VARIABLE POWER SCOPE	1360.00

Note: All variable power scopes have glass reticles and are available in steel and aluminum

Also available:

4X36 FIXED POWER SCOPE
1" Steel Tube w/o Mounting Rail	$760.00

6X42 FIXED POWER SCOPE
Steel Tube w/o Mounting Rail	835.00

8X56 FIXED POWER SCOPE
Steel Tube w/o Mounting Rail	960.00

10X42 FIXED POWER SCOPE
Steel Tube w/o Mounting Rail	955.00

L.E.R. 1.25-4X20

The Safari is designed for use on magnum rifles and for hunting large game. A newly designed ocular results in a longer eye relief, providing a wide field of view (31.5 yards at 200 yards).

Magnification: 1.25-4X
Objective lens diameter: 12.7-20mm
Field of view at 100m: 32m-10m; at 100 yards: 96'-16'
Objective housing diameter: 30mm
Scope tube diameter: 30mm
Twilight factor: 3,7-8,9
Lenses: hard multi-coating
Click value 1 click @100 meters: 15mm; @100 yards: .540"
Also available: 3-12X42 and 4-16X50
Price: $995.00

VARMINT

Designed for long-range target shooters and varmint hunters, Schmidt & Bender 4-16X50 "Varmint" riflescope features a precise parallax adjustment located in a third turret on the left side of the scope, making setting adjustments quick and convenient. The fine crosshairs of Reticle No. 6 and 8 cover only 1.5mm at 100 meters (.053" at 100 yards) throughout the entire magnification range.

Magnification: 4-16X   *Objective lens diameter:* 50mm
Field of view at 100m: 7.5-2.5m; at 100 yards: 22.5'-7.5'
Objective housing diameter: 57mm
Scope tube diameter: 30mm   *Twilight factor:* 14-28
Lenses: Hard multi-coating
Click value 1 click @100 meters: 10mm; @100 yards: .360"
Price: $1,525.00

POLICE/MARKSMAN RIFLESCOPES

This line of riflescopes was designed specifically to meet the needs of the precision sharpshooter. It includes fixed-power scopes in 6X42 and 10X42 magnifications and variable-power scopes in 1.5-6X42, 3-12X42 and 3-12X50 configurations. The 3-12X50 is available in two models: Standard (for shooting to 500 yards) and a military version (MIL) designed for ranges up to 1000 yards. Each scope is equipped with two elevation adjustment rings: a neutral ring with 1/4" 100-yard clicks, which can be matched to any caliber and bullet weight, and a second ring calibrated for a

POLICE/MARKSMAN
3.12X50mm w/DETACHABLE
RUBBER SUNSHADE AND
BRYANT P-RANGEFINDING RETICLE

308 (7.62 NATO) bullet. The 1.5-6X42 is calibrated for the 150-grain bullet, while rings on other scopes are calibrated for the 168-grain bullet. The military elevation adjustment ring has 1" @100-yard clicks, except for the MIL scope which has 1/2" @100-yard clicks.

6X42	$900.00
10X42	950.00
1.5-6X42	1,200.00
3-12X42	1,360.00
3-12X50	1,400.00
3-12X50 MI	1,425.00

SCHMIDT & BENDER

SCOPES FOR LONG RANGE SHOOTING

PRECISION HUNTER

PRECISION HUNTER

Very accurate rifles, high-speed cartridges and modern bullets make it possible to shoot very accurately at long distances...IF you have the right scope. Your scope must let you see your target clearly. It must help you determine the distance, bullet drop, and wind drift, and it must do it quickly and precisely.

Our new **PRECISION HUNTER** scopes combine the legendary optical quality of S&B hunting scopes, the most appropriate magnification ranges, and a sophisticated mil-dot reticle (developed by the U.S. Marine Corps) with a bullet drop compensator to give you the ability and confidence to place an accurate shot at up to 500 yards. Three different models are available:

4-16 X 50 PRECISION HUNTER SCOPE WITH PARALLAX ADJUSTMENT

Set on 4 power, the mil-dot reticle with fine crosshairs and four posts allows quick target acquisition.

Turned up to 16 power, the mil-dots become visible and can be used for range, trajectory and windage calculations. The top-mounted bullet drop compensator has 5mm (1/5") clicks, permitting quick adjustments up to 500 yards.

The windage adjustment also has 5mm (1/5") clicks, allowing for precise sighting in.

The standard elevation adjustment knob has graduations and numbers that allow you to create a meaningful distance chart for your preferred caliber. A blank elevation knob can be special-ordered with markings you can specify after sighting in your rifle.

A parallax adjustment is conveniently located in a third turret on the left side. This allows you to easily make necessary adjustments with the rifle shouldered, ready to shoot.
Price:. **$1,555.00**

3-12 X 50 PRECISION HUNTER

Identical to the 4-16 x 50 with mil-dot reticle but 1cm (2/5") clicks and no parallax adjustment. It is factory-adjusted to be parallax free at 200 meters.
Price:. **$1,285.00**

2.5-10 X 56 PRECISION HUNTER

Identical to the 3-12 x 50, but with 1 cm (2/5") clicks for windage and elevation adjustment and with our Reticle No. 9, which makes it suitable for dangerous game.
Price:. **$1,325.00**

SCHMIDT & BENDER

POLICE/MARKSMAN II

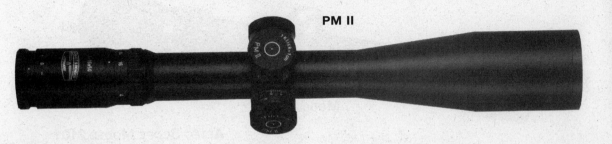

PM II

SPECIFICATIONS

	10 x 42	3-12 x 50	3-12 x 50 W/PARALLAX ADJ.	3-12 x 50 ILLLUMINATED	4-16 x 50 W/PARALLAX ADJ.
Magnification	10x	3-12x	3-12x	3-12x	4-16x
Field of View	4m	11.1-4.2m	11.1-4.2m	11.1-4.2m	7.5-2.5m
(100m/100yd)	12'	33.3-12.6'	33.3-12.6'	33.3-12.6'	22.5-7.5'
Objective					
Diameter	42mm	50mm	50mm	50mm	5mm
Exit Pupil	4.2mm	14.3-4.3mm	14.3-4.3mm	14.3-4.3mm	12.5-3.1mm
(mm/inches)	.165"	.563-.169"	.563-.169"	.563-.169"	.492"-.122"
Twilight Factor	20.5	11.4-24.5	11.4-24.5	11.4-24.5	14-28
Eye Relief	95mm	995mm	95mm	95mm	95mm
(mm/inches)	3.74"	3.74"	3.74"	3.74"	3.74"
Middle Tube					
Diameter	30mm	34mm	34mm	34mm	34mm
Weight	520g	7600g	810g	780g	880g
(gram/lb., oz.)	1 lb. 2 oz.	1 lb. 2.5 oz.	1 lb. 12.5 oz.	1 lb. 11.5 oz.	1 lb. 15 oz.
Adj. Range @	*270 cm/97"	200 cm/72"	200 cm/72"	200 cm/72"	185 cm/67"
(100m/100 yd)	**250 cm/990"	180 cm/64.8"	180 cm/64.8"	180 cm/64.8"	170 cm/61.2"
	***130 cm/46.8"	130 cm/46.8"	130 cm/46.8"	130 cm/46.8"	130 cm/46.8"

*Using the very ends of the elevation adjustment will reduce the windage adjustment range **Sighting-in adjustment range without restriction of windage
***With adjustment knob locked in place

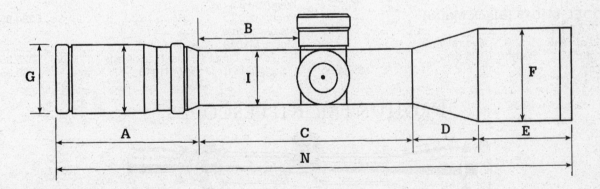

DIMENSIONS

MODEL	A	B	C	D	E	F	G	I	N
10x42	98mm	56mm	139mm	55mm	54mm	50mm	43mm	30mm	346mm
	3.858"	2,204"	5.472"	2.165"	2.126"	1.969"	1.693"		13.622"
3-12x50	101.3mm	68.3mm	145.4mm	43.5mm	64.8mm	57mm	43mm	34mm	355mm
	3.988"	2.689"	6.076"	1.713"	3.354"	2.244"	1.693"		13.976"
4-16x50	101.3mm	68.3mm	145.4mm	85.2mm	75.5mm	57mm	43mm	34mm	405.7mm
	3.988"	2.689"	6.076"	1.713"	3.354"	2.244"	1.693"		15.972"

SIMMONS SCOPES

AETEC

MODEL 2101

MODELS 2100/2101/2102
2.8-10X44 WA
Field of view: 44'-14' *Eye relief:* 5"
Length: 11.9" *Weight:* 15.5 oz. *Reticle:* Truplex
Price: $315.95

AETEC SCOPE MODEL 2101
2.8-10x44 WA ASPHERICAL LENS SYSTEM
w/SUNSHADE, BLACK MATTE (not shown)

Also available: MODEL 2104 – 3.8-12X44 WA/AO
Aspherical Lens System w/sunshade, black matte
Price: $343.95

44 MAG RIFLESCOPES

MODEL M1044 (Black Matte)
3-10X44mm
Field of view: 34'-10.5' *Eye relief:* 3"
Length: 12.75" *Weight:* 15.5 oz.
Price: $224.95

MODEL M1050DM
44 DIAMOND MAG (Black Matte)
RANGE-CALCULATING SMART RETICLE
(Black Matte)
3.8-12X44mm
Field of view: 26'-9' *Eye relief:* 3"
Length: 13.08" *Weight:* 16.75 oz.
Price: $315.95

MODEL M1045 (Black Matte)
4-12X44mm
Field of view: 29.5'-9.5' *Eye relief:* 3"
Length: 13.2" *Weight:* 18.25 oz.
Price: $274.95

MODEL M1050DM

MODEL M1047 (Black Matte)
6.5-20X44mm
Field of view: 14'-5'
Eye relief: 2.6"-3.4"
Length: 12.8"
Weight: 19.5 oz.
Price: $284.95
Also available:
MODEL M1048
6.5-20X44 Target Turrets Black Matte (¹/₈" MOA) . **$325.95**
Sunshade for M1047/M1048 . . . . $9.95

PROHUNTER RIFLESCOPES

MODEL 7710

MODEL 7710
3-9X40mm Wide Angle Riflescope
Field of view: 36'-13'
Eye relief: 3" *Length:* 12.6"
Weight: 13.5 oz. *Features:* Truplex reticle; silver matte finish
Price: $131.95

(Same in black matte or black polish, Models 7711 and 7712)
Also available:
MODEL 7700 2-7X32 Black Matte $121.95
MODEL 7716 4-12X40 Black Matte AO 155.95
MODEL 7721 6-18X40 AO Black Matte 172.95
MODEL 7740 6X40 Black Matte 114.95

SIMMONS SCOPES
(featuring Extra Large 50mm Obj. Lenses)

PRO 50 RIFLESCOPES

MODEL 8800

SIMMONS #8830 PRO 50 SCOPE 2.5-10x50MM
SPECIFICATIONS
Magnification: 2.5-10X *Field Of View:* 30.5'-11'
Eye Relief: 3" *Length:* 12.75" *Weight:* 17 oz.
Reticle: Truplex *Finish:* Black matte
Price: $142.95

MODEL #8800
SPECIFICATIONS
Magnification: 4-12X *Field Of View:* 27'-9'
Eye Relief: 3.5" *Length:* 13.2" *Weight:* 18.25 oz.
Reticle: Truplex *Finish:* Black matte
Price: $210.95

MODEL #8810 (not shown)
SPECIFICATIONS
Magnification: 6-18X
Field Of View: 17'-5.8'
Eye Relief: 3.6"
Length: 13.2"
Weight: 18.25 oz.
Reticle: Truplex
Finish: Black matte
Price: $229.95

PROHUNTER PISTOL SCOPES

MODEL 7738 (4X)

MODEL 7732 (2X)

MODEL #7732/7733 (Silver Matte)
SPECIFICATIONS
Magnification: 2X
Field Of View: 22'
Eye Relief: 9-17"
Length: 8.75"
Weight: 7 oz.
Reticle: Truplex
Finish: Black matte
Price: $131.95

MODEL #7738/7739 (Silver Matte)
SPECIFICATIONS
Magnification: 4X
Field Of View: 15'
Eye Relief: 11.8-17.6"
Length: 9"
Weight: 8 oz.
Reticle: Truplex
Finish: Black matte
Price: $141.95

SIMMONS SCOPES

*Simmons' **Whitetail Classic Series** features fully coated lenses and glare-proof BlackGranite finish.*

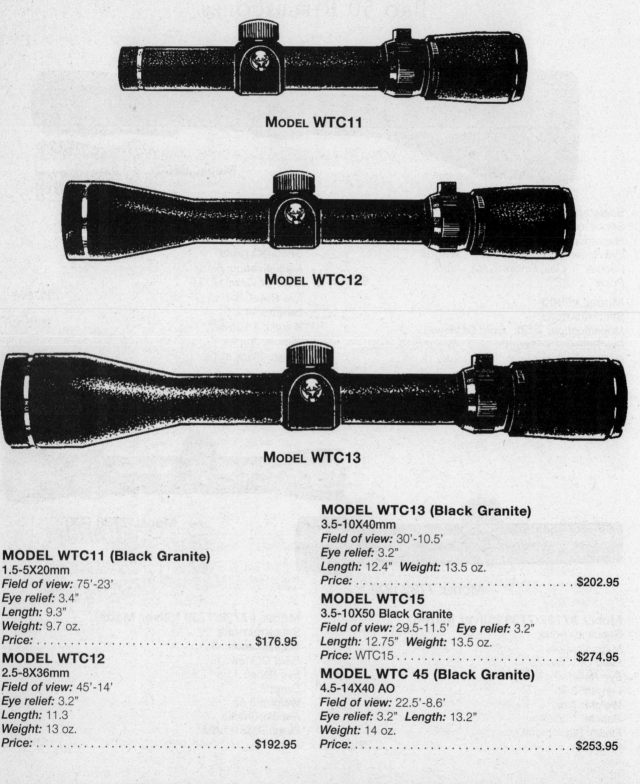

MODEL WTC11

MODEL WTC12

MODEL WTC13

MODEL WTC11 (Black Granite)
1.5-5X20mm
Field of view: 75'-23'
Eye relief: 3.4"
Length: 9.3"
Weight: 9.7 oz.
Price: $176.95

MODEL WTC12
2.5-8X36mm
Field of view: 45'-14'
Eye relief: 3.2"
Length: 11.3'
Weight: 13 oz.
Price: $192.95

MODEL WTC13 (Black Granite)
3.5-10X40mm
Field of view: 30'-10.5'
Eye relief: 3.2"
Length: 12.4" *Weight:* 13.5 oz.
Price: $202.95

MODEL WTC15
3.5-10X50 Black Granite
Field of view: 29.5-11.5' *Eye relief:* 3.2"
Length: 12.75" *Weight:* 13.5 oz.
Price: WTC15 . . . . $274.95

MODEL WTC 45 (Black Granite)
4.5-14X40 AO
Field of view: 22.5'-8.6'
Eye relief: 3.2" *Length:* 13.2"
Weight: 14 oz.
Price: $253.95

SIMMONS SCOPES

GOLD MEDAL SILHOUETTE/VARMINT SERIES

Simmons Gold Medal Silhouette/Varmint Riflescopes are made of state-of-the-art drive train and erector tube design, a new windage and elevation indexing mechanism, camera-quality 100% multicoated lenses, and a super smooth objective focusing device. High silhouette-type windage and elevation turrets house 1/8 minute click adjustments. The scopes have a black matte finish and choice of dot or crosshair reticle and are fogproof, waterproof and shockproof.

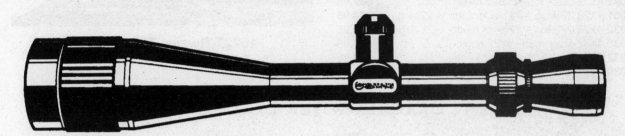

MODEL 23002

MODEL #23002
6-20X44mm AO
Field of view: 18.5'-5' *Eye relief:* 2.6-3.4"
Length: 14.75" *Weight:* 19.75 oz.

Feature: 100% Multi-Coat Lens System, black matte finish, obj. focus
Price: Crosshair $570.95
Also available:
MODEL 23012 (dot reticle) $570.95

GOLD MEDAL HANDGUN SERIES

Simmons Gold Medal handgun scopes offer long eye relief, light weight, high resolution, non-critical head alignment, compact size and durability to withstand the heavy recoil of today's powerful handguns. In black and silver finishes, all have fully multicoated lenses and a Truplex reticle.

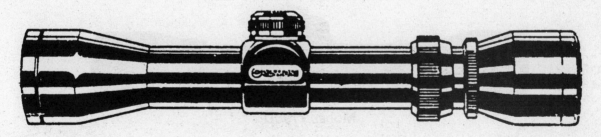

MODEL 22001

MODEL #22001
2.5-7X28mm
Field of view: 11'-4' *Eye relief:* 15.7"-19.7"
Length: 9.3" *Weight:* 9 oz.
Feature: Truplex reticle, 100% Multi-Coat Lens System, black polished finish.

Price: $264.95
Also Available:
MODEL #22004 2X20 . . . . 202.95
MODEL #22008 1.5-4X28 (black matte) 253.95

SIMMONS SCOPES

1022T RIMFIRE TARGET SCOPE

Magnification: 3-9X32mm WA/AO
Finish: Black matte
Features: Adjustable for windage and elevation; adjustable objective lens, target knobs
Price: $161.95
Also available:
1022 4X32 black matte w/22 rings $67.95
1031 4X28 22 Mag Mini black matte w/22 rings . . . 74.95
1032 4X28 22 Mag Mini silver matte w/22 rings . . . 76.95
1033 4X32 silver matte w/22 rings 70.95
1037 3-9X32 silver matte w/22 rings. 80.95
1039 3-9X32 black matte w/22 rings 78.95

1022T RIMFIRE TARGET SCOPE

BLACKPOWDER SCOPES

MODEL BP2732M

MODEL BP2732M

Magnification: 2-7X32 **Finish:** Black matte
Field of view: 57.7'-16.6' 100 yards **Eye relief:** 3"
Reticle: Truplex **Length:** 11.6" **Weight:** 12.4 oz.
Price: $131.95
Also available:
MODELS BP400M/400S
4X20 Black Matte or Silver Matte, Long Body

Field of view: 28' **Eye relief:** 5.0"
Length: 10.25" **Weight:** 8.7 oz. **Reticle:** Truplex
Price: $45.95

MODELS BPO420M/420S

4X20 Octagon Body
Field of view: 19.5' **Eye relief:** 4"
Length: 7.5" **Weight:** 8.3 oz. **Reticle:** Truplex
Price: $110.95

SHOTGUN SCOPES

MODEL 7790D

MODELS 21004/7790D

Magnification: 4X32
Finish: Black matte
Field of view: 16' (Model 21004); 17' (Model 7790D)
Eye relief: 5.5"
Reticle: Truplex (Model 21004); ProDiamond (Model 7790D)
Length: 8.5" (8.8" Model 21004)
Weight: 8.75 oz. (9.1 oz. Model 7790D)

Prices:
MODEL 21004 . . . . $80.95
MODEL 7790D 110.95
Also available:
MODEL 21005 2.5X20 Black matte (Truplex reticle). . . . $59.95
MODEL 7789D 2X32 Black matte
(ProDiamond reticle) 100.95
MODEL 7791D 1.5-5X20 WA Black matte
(ProDiamond reticle) 131.95

SWAROVSKI & KAHLES RIFLESCOPES

SWAROVSKI HUNTER PH SERIES

(Prices on following page)

3-12X50

2.5-10X42

SPECIFICATIONS HUNTER PH SERIES (*see* following page for additional PH Models)

Type	Magnification	Effective Objective Lens Diameter MM	Exit Pupil Diameter MM	Eye Relief IN/MM	Field Of View FT/100YDS M/100M	Field Of View DEGREES	Subjective Field Of View DEGREES	Dioptric Correction DPT	Twilight Performance Acc. to DIN 58388	Impact Point Correction Per Click IN/100YDS MM/100M	Max. Elevation/ Windage Adjustment Range IN/100YDS	Length IN	Weight (approx.) S OZ/G	Weight (approx.) L OZ/G	Weight (approx.) LS OZ/G
PF															
6x42	6x	42	7	3.15 80	21 7	4	23.2	+2-3	15.9	0.36 10	47	12.83	17.3 490	12.0 340	13.4 380
8x50	8x	50	6.25	3.15 80	15.6 5.2	3	23.2	+2-3	20	0.36 10	40	13.94	21.5 610	14.8 420	15.9 450
8x56	8x	56	7	3.15 80	15.6 5.2	3	23.2	+2-3	21.2	0.36 10	47	14.29	24.0 680	16.6 470	17.6 500
PV															
1.25-4x24	1.25-4x	24	12.5-6	3.15 80	98.4-31.2 32.8-10.4	18.6-6	23.2	+2-3	3.5-9.8	0.54 15	119	10.63	16.2 460	12.7 360	13.8 390
1.5-6x42	1.5-6x	42	13.1-7	3.15 80	65.4-21 21.8-7	12.4-4	23.2	+2-3	4.2-15.9	0.36 10	79	12.99	20.8 590	16.2 460	17.5 495
2.5-10x42	2.5-10x	42	13.1-4.2	3.15 80	39.6-12.6 13.2-4.2	7.5-2.4	23.2	+2-3	7.1-20.5	0.36 10	47	13.23	19.8 560	15.2 430	16.4 465
2.5-10x56	2.5-10x	56	13.1-5.6	3.15 80	39.6-12.3 13.2-4.1	7.5-2.4	23.2	+2-3	7.1-23.7	0.36 10	47	14.72	24.5 695	18.7 53	20.1 570
3-12x50	3-12x	50	13.1-4.2	3.15 80	33-10.5 11-3.5	6.3-2	23.2	+2-3	8.5-24.5	0.36 10	40	14.33	22.4 635	16.9 480	18.3 520
PF-N															
8x50	8x	50	6.25	3.15 80	15.6 5.2	3	23.2	+2-3	20	0.36 10	40	13.94	21.5 610	14.8 420	15.9 450
8x56	8x	56	7	3.15 80	15.6 5.2	3	23.2	+2-3	21.2	0.36 10	47	14.29	24.0 680	16.6 470	17.6 500

SWAROVSKI & KAHLES RIFLESCOPES

6-24X50mm PROFESSIONAL HUNTER "PH" RIFLESCOPE

Swarovski's 6-24X500mm "PH" riflescope was developed for long-range target, big-game and varmint shooting. Its waterproof parallax adjustment system should be popular with whitetail "Bean Field Shooters" and long-range varmint hunters looking for a choice of higher powers in a premium rifle scope and still deliver accuracy. The new scope will also appeal to many bench rest shooters who compete in certains classes where power and adjustment are limited. A non-magnifying, fine plex reticle and an all-new fine crosshair reticle with 1/8" MOA dot are available in the 6-24X50mm scope. Reticle adjustment clicks are 1/6" (minute) by external, waterproof target knobs. The internal optical system features a patented coil spring suspension system for dependablle accuracy and positive reticle adjustment. The objective bell, 30mm middle tube, turret housing and ocular bell are machined from one solid bar of aluminum.

Price: **$1,665.50**

PRICES PH SERIES RIFLESCOPES

PF 6x42 (4A, 7A) **$921.11**	
PF 8x50 (4A, 7A) **954.44**	
w/illum reticle (4N, PLEXN) **1,343.33**	
PF 8x56 (4A, 7A) **998.89**	
w/illum reticle (4N, PLEXN) **1,388.88**	
PH 1.25-4x24 (4A) **998.89**	
PH 1.5-6x42 (4A, 7A) **1,132.22**	
aluminum only (#24) **1,165.56**	
PH 2.5-10x42 (4A, 7A) **1,298.89**	
aluminum only (PLEX) **1,298.89**	

PH 2.5-10x56 (4A, 7A) **1,398.89**	
aluminum only (PLEX) **1,398.89**	
w/illum reticle (4N, PLEXN) **1,765.55**	
PH 3-12x50 (4A, 7A) **1,376.67**	
aluminum only (PLEX) **1,376.67**	
w/illum reticle (4N, PLEXN) **1,698.88**	
PH 6-24x50 (aluminum only) (PLEX, DOT, FINE) . **1,665.56**	
Same as above w/4, PLEX **1,532.22**	
Kahles 3-9x42 . . . . **549.00**	
Swarovski 3-9x36 AV **680.00**	

SPECIFICATIONS HUNTER PH SERIES (cont.)

TYPE	MAGNIFICATION	EFFECTIVE OBJECTIVE LENS DIAMETER	EXIT PUPIL DIAMETER	EYE RELIEF	FIELD OF VIEW FT/100YDS M/100M	FIELD OF VIEW DEGREES	SUBJECTIVE FIELD OF VIEW DEGREES	DIOPTRIC CORRECTION DPT	TWILIGHT PERFORMANCE ACC. TO DIN 58388	IMPACT POINT CORRECTION PER CLICK IN/100YDS MM/100M	MAX. ELEVATION/ WINDAGE ADJUSTMENT RANGE IN/100YDS	LENGTH IN	WEIGHT (APPROX.) S oz/G	L oz/G	LS oz/G
		MM	MM	IN/MM											
PV-N															
2.5-10x56	2.5-10x	56	13.1-5.6	3.15 80	39.6-12.3 13.2-4.1	7.5-2.4	23.2	+2-3	7.1-23.7	0.36 10	47	14.72 374	24.5 695	18.7 530	20.1 570
3-12x50	3-12x	50	13.1-4.2	3.15 80	33-10.5 11-3.5	6.3-2	23.2	+2-3	8.5-24.5	0.36 10	40	14.33 392	22.4 635	16.9 480	18.3 520
PVS															
6-24x50 P	6-24x	50	8.3-2.1	3.15 80	18.6-5.4 6.2-1.8	3.5-1	23.2	+2-3	7.1-34.6	0.17 4.8	E: 43 W: 25	15.43 392	- -	24.5 695	- -
Nova-A															
4x32 A	4x	32	8	3.15 80	30 10	5.7	22.8	+2-5	11.3	0.25 7	100	11.42 29	- -	10.8 305	- -
6x36 A	6x	36	6	3.15 80	21 7	4	22.8	+2-5	14.7	0.25 7	90	11.93 303	- -	11.5 325	- -
1.5-4.5x20 A	1.5-4.5x	20	12.7-4.4	3.35 85	75-25.8 25-8.6	14.2-4.9	22.7	+2-5	4.2-9.4	0.25 7	110	9.53 242	- -	10.6 300	- -
3-9x36 A	3-9x	36	12-4	3.35 85	39-13.5 13-4.5	7.4-2.6	22.7	+2-5	8.5-18	0.25 7	60	11.93 303	- -	13.0 370	- -
3-10x42 A	3.3-10x	42	12.6-4.2	3.35 85	33-11.7 11-3.9	6.3-2.2	22.7	+2-5	9.3-2.5	0.25 7	50	12.52 318	- -	13.7 390	- -
AV															
3-9x36	3-9x	36	12-4	3.5 85	43-15.2 14-5.1	- -	-	-	-	-	70	11.62	- -	11.8 33	- -
Kahles															
3-9x42	3-9	42	14-4.7	3.5 89	43-15.2 14-5.1	- -	-	-	-	-	70	12.36	- -	12.7 360	- -

S: Steel • L: Alloy • LS: Alloy with rail

TASCO SCOPES

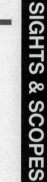

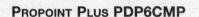

PROPOINT PLUS PDP6CMP

PROPOINT® MULTI-PURPOSE SCOPES

Tasco's ProPoint is a true 1X-30mm scope with electronic red dot reticle that features unlimited eye relief, enabling shooters to shoot with both eyes open. It is available with a 3X booster and also has application for rifle, shotgun, bow and black powder. The compact version (PDP2) houses a lithium battery pack, making it 1.25 inches narrower than previous models and lighter as well (5.5 oz.). A mercury battery converter is provided for those who prefer standard batteries. Tasco's 3X booster with crosshair reticle weights 6.1 oz. and is 5.5 inches long.

SPECIFICATIONS PROPOINT SCOPES

MODEL	POWER	OBJECTIVE DIAMETER	FINISH	RETICLE	FIELD OF VIEW @ 100 YDS.	EYE RELIEF	TUBE DIAM.	SCOPE LENGTH	SCOPE WEIGHT	PRICES
PDP2	1X	25mm	Black Matte	5 M.O.A. Dot	40'	Unlimited	30mm	5"	5.5 oz.	**$254.65**
PDP2ST	1X	25mm	Stainless	5 M.O.A. Dot	40'	Unlimited	30mm	5"	5.5 oz.	254.65
PDP2BD	1x	25mm	Black Matte	10 M.O.A. Dot	40'	Unlimited	30mm	5"	5.5 oz.	254.65
PDP2BDST	1X	25mm	Stainless	10 M.O.A. Dot	40'	Unlimited	30mm	5"	5.5 oz.	254.65
PDP3	1X	25mm	Black Matte	5 M.O.A. Dot	52'	Unlimited	30mm	5"	5.5 oz.	305.60
PDP3ST	1X	25mm	Stainless	10 M.O.A. Dot	52'	Unlimited	30mm	5"	5.5 oz.	305.60
PDP3BD	1X	25mm	Black Matte	10 M.O.A. Dot	52'	Unlimited	30mm	5"	5.5 oz.	305.60
PDPBDST	1X	25mm	Stainless	10 M.O.A. Dot	52'	Unlimited	30mm	5"	5.5 oz.	305.60
PDP3CMP	1X	30mm	Black Matte	10 M.O.A. Dot	68'	Unlimited	33mm	4.75"	5.4 oz.	390.45
PDP5CMP	1X	45mm	Black Matte	4,8,12,16 M.O.A. Dot	82'	Unlimited	47mm	4"	8 oz.	
PDP6CMP	1X	30mm	Black Matte	10 M.O.A. Dot	72'	Unlimited	38mm	3"	5.8 oz.	390.45

TASCO SCOPES

WORLD CLASS PLUS RIFLESCOPES

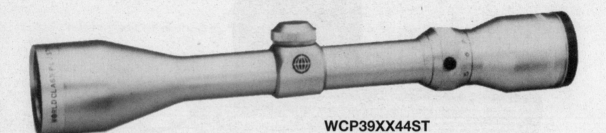

WCP39XX44ST

SPECIFICATIONS WORLD CLASS PLUS RIFLESCOPES

MODEL	POWER	OBJECTIVE DIAMETER	FINISH	RETICLE	F.O.V. @ 100 YD.S	EYE RELIEF	TUBE DIAMETER	LENGTH	WEIGHT	PRICES
WCP4X44	4X	44mm	Black Gloss	30/30	32'	3.25"	1"	12.75"	13.5 oz.	$237.70
DWCP4X44	4X	44mm	Black Matte	30/30	32'	3.25"	1"	12.75"	13.5 oz.	237.70
WCP39X44	3X-9X	44mm	Black Gloss	30/30	39'-14'	3.5"	1"	12.75"	15.8 oz.	407.45
DWCP39X44	3X-9X	44mm	Black Matte	30/30	39'-14'	3.5"	1"	12.75"	15.8 oz.	407.45
WCP39X44ST	3X-9X	44mm	Stainless Steel	30/30	39'-14'	3.5"	1"	12.75"	15.8 oz.	407.45
WCP3.510X50	3.5X-10X	50mm	Black Gloss	30/30	30'-10.5'	3.75"	1"	13"	17.1 oz.	492.35
DWCP3.510X50	3.5X-10X	50mm	Black Matte	30/30	30'-10.5'	3.75"	1"	13"	17.1 oz.	492.35
DWCP832X50	8X-32X	50mm	Black Matte	Crosshair* (1/8 M.O.A.)	13'-4'	3"	1"	14.5"	25.1 oz.	560.00
DWCP1040X50	10X-40X	50mm	Black Matte	Crosshair* (1/8 M.O.A.)	11'-2.5'	3"	1"	14.5"	25.3 oz.	611.00

*With 1/8 M.O.A.

OPTIMA 2000

OPTIMA 2000

What makes this newest ProPoint so revolutionary is that, unlike previous ProPoints, it does not have a tube design. It's smaller (only 1 1/2") and lighter (only 1/2 oz.) than any other sighting device. It's also extremely durable and rugged. After thousands of test rounds it held its point of aim and its one-piece, dovetailed-style slide mount remained immovable. Its red dot was always on, with no time lost turning it on. While used primarily on pistols, the Optima 2000 can be mounted on shotguns for skeet or trap shooting or for duck hunting. It also works well on rifles for close-cover hunting. Optima 2000 is available with a bright, in-focus 3.5 or 7 M.O.A. dot on the same plane as iron sights for fast target acquisition.
Price: . . . . **Available on request**

TASCO RIFLESCOPES

MODEL 1.75X-5X

WORLD CLASS™ WIDE-ANGLE® RIFLESCOPES

Features:
- 25% larger field of view
- Fully coated for maximum light transmission
- 1/4-minute clicks
- Waterproof, shockproof, fogproof
- Free haze filter lens caps
- TASCO's unique World Class Lifetime Warranty

WORLD CLASS, WIDE-ANGLE VARIABLE ZOOM RIFLESCOPES

Model No.	Power	Objective Diameter	Finish	Reticle	F.O.V. @100 Yds.	Eye Relief	Tube Diameter	Length	Weight
RIFLESCOPES									
WA13.5X20	1X-3.5X	20mm	Black Gloss	30/30	103'-13'	3"	1"	9.75"	11.1 oz.
WA1.755X20	1.75X-5X	20mm	Black Gloss	30/30	72'-24'	3"	1"	10.5"	10 oz.
WA27X32	2X-7X	32mm	Black Gloss	30/30	56'-17'	3.25"	1"	11.5"	12 oz.
R-DWC39X40*	3X-9X	40mm	Black Matte	30/30	41'-15'	3"	1"	12.75"	13 oz.
R-WA39X40*	3X-9X	40mm	Black Gloss	30/30	41'-15'	3"	1"	12.75"	13 oz.
R-WA39X40TV*	3X-9X	40mm	Black Gloss	30/30 TV	41'-15'	3"	1"	12.75"	13 oz.
WA39X40ST	3X-9X	40mm	Stainless	30/30	41'-15'	3"	1"	12.75"	13 oz.
RIFLESCOPE & BINOCULAR COMBO: R-DWC39X50									
DWC39X50**	3X-9X	50mm	Black Matte	30/30	41'-13'	3"	1"	12.5"	15.8 oz.*
WC1025RB**	10X	25mm	Black Rubber	N/A	355' @ 100 yds.	12mm	N/A	4.5"	8.8 oz.

MAG-IV 4X-16X50mm

MAG-IV-50™ RIFLESCOPES

Tasco's MAG-IV™ riflescopes now feature large 50mm objective lenses that transmit even more light than the MAG-IV with 40mm objectives and are especially designed for dawn and dusk use. The additions to the MAG-IV line include three high-quality variable scopes: the 4X-16X50mm, the 5X20X50mm and the 5X-20X50mm with bullet drop compensation. All three models have Super-Con® multi-layered lens coating, fully coated optics, and black matte finish.

Tasco's MAG-IV scopes feature windage and elevation adjustments with 1/4-minute clickstops and an Opti-Centered® 30/30 range-finding reticle. This adjustment system allows the reticle to remain centered in the feld of view (an "image moving" system as opposed to a "reticle moving" system). Finished in black gloss.

Prices:

MODEL W416X50 .... $127.80
MODEL W520X50 .... 144.50
MODEL W520X50 BDC 155.60
Also available:
**MAG-IV RIFLESCOPES 3X-12X40mm,
4X-16X40mm, 6X-24X40mm** $254.65

TITAN™ RIFLESCOPES

Tasco's Titan™ riflescopes are equipped with unusually large 42mm and 52mm objective lenses that can transmit more light than standard 40mm lenses for dim early morning and dusk conditions. Three variable scopes—the 1.5X-6X42mm, the 3X-9X42mm and the 3X-12X52mm—are available with 30/30 reticles and feature lenses with five-layer multi-coating for greater image contrast and clarity. Titan scopes also have finger-adjustable windage and elevation controls. Waterproof, shockproof and fogproof, these scopes feature all-weather lubrication of each moving part

for smooth functioning in any climate condition. Finished in matte black.

Now available in 1.25-4.5X26mm for close range hunting; features a German reticle and five-layer multi-coating, long eye relief and wide field of view.

Prices:

1.25-4.5X26mm $594.00
3-9X42mm 645.00
1.5X-6X42mm 679.00
3X-12X52mm 763.95

WEAVER SCOPES

T-SERIES TARGET/VARMINT T-36

T-SERIES TARGET/VARMINT SCOPES - Fixed-power scopes featuring Weaver's patented Micro-Trac adjustment system utilizing a dual-spring, four-bearing contact design that allows independent movement of windage and elevation. Optics are fully multi-coated, delivering premium image clarity in virtually all light conditions. Adjustable objective lens allows for zero parallax from 50' to infinity. Choice of fine cross hair or dot reticles. Scopes come with sunshade, extra pair of oversize benchrest adjustment knobs, and screw-in metal lens caps.

Model: T-36
Magnification/Objective: 36X40mm
Field Of View: 3.0' **Eye Relief:** 3.0"
Length: 15.1" **Weight:** 16.7 oz.
Reticle: 1/8 or 3/8 MOA Dot, Fine Crosshair
Finish: Matte black or silver
Price: $793.95

Model: T16 (not shown)
Magnification/Objective: 16X40mm
Field Of View: 6.5' **Eye Relief:** 3.0"
Length: 15.1" **Weight:** 16.7 oz.
Reticle: 3/4 MOA Dot, Varminter Crosshair
Finish: Matte black
Price: $780.95

Model: T-24 (not shown)
Magnification/Objective: 24X40mm
Field Of View: 4.4' **Eye Relief:** 3.0"
Length: 15.1" **Weight:** 16.7 oz.
Reticle: 1/2 or 1/8 MOA Dot, Fine Crosshair
Finish: Matte black
Price: $787.95

Model: T-10 (not shown)
Magnification/Objective: 10X40mm
Field Of View: 9.3' **Eye Relief:** 3.0"
Length: 15.1" **Weight:** 16.7 oz.
Reticle: 1 1/4 MOA Dot, Varminter Crosshair
Finish: Matte black
Price: $774.95

T-SERIES MODEL T-6 RIFLESCOPE

Weaver's T-6 competition rifle scope is only 12.7 inches long and weighs less than 15 ounces. Magnification is six-power. All optical surfaces are fully multi-coated for maximum clarity and light transmission. The T-6 features Weaver's Micro-Trac precision adjustments in 1/8-minute clicks to ensure parallel tracking. The protected target-style turrets are a low-profile configuration combining ease of adjustment with weight reduction. A 40mm adjustable objective permits parallax correction from 50 feet to infinity without shifting the point of impact. A special AO lock ring eliminates bell vibration or shift. The T-6 comes with screw-in metal lens caps and features a competition matte black finish.
Reticles: dot, Fine Crosshair
Price: $424.95

WEAVER SCOPES

MODEL #49837

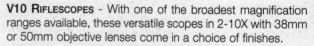

V16 RIFLESCOPES - The V16 is popular for a variety of shooting applications, from close shots that require a wide field of view to long-range varmint or benchrest shooting. Adjustable objective allows a parallax-free view from 30 feet to infinity. Features one-piece tube for strength and moisture resistance and multicoated lenses for clear, crisp images. Two finishes and three reticle options.

MODEL #49837
Magnification/Objective: 4-16X42mm
Field Of View: 26.8'-6.8' *Eye Relief:* 3.1"
Length: 13.9" *Weight:* 16.5 oz.
Reticle: Choice of Dual-X, 1/4 MOA Dot, or Fine Crosshair
Finish: Matte black
Price: Black $424.95

V10 RIFLESCOPES - With one of the broadest magnification ranges available, these versatile scopes in 2-10X with 38mm or 50mm objective lenses come in a choice of finishes.

MODEL #49810 (not shown)
Magnification/Objective: 2-10X38mm
Field Of View: 38.5-9.5" *Eye Relief:* 3.4-3.3" *Length:* 12.2"
Weight: 11.2 oz. *Reticle:* Dual-X *Finish:* Matte black
Price: $258.95
Also Available:
In gloss black, **MODEL #49910** 252.95
Silver, **MODEL #49710** 258.95

MODEL #49938 (not shown)
Magnification/Objective: 2-10X50mm
Field Of View: 40.2-9.2" *Eye Relief:* 2.9-2.8" *Length:* 13.75"
Weight: 15.2 oz. *Reticle:* Dual-X *Finish:* Matte black
Price: $357.95
Also Available:
In gloss black, **MODEL #49937** 346.95
Silver, **MODEL #49939** 357.95

V24 6X24 VARMINT SCOPE

RIMFIRE 4X MATTE SCOPE

V24 6X24 VARMINT SCOPE - Weaver's V24 Varmint scope is the big brother of the V16, one of Weaver's most popular scopes. The V24 zooms from 6 to 24 power, has a 42mm adjustable objective and a special varmint reticle. Reticle adjustments are in precise, 1/8-minute clicks for precision positioning. One-piece tube design and intelligent engineering make the V24 lighter than comparable high-quality scopes. Like the V16, the new scope has generous eye relief, multi-coated optics for maximum light transmission, and comes with a matte black finish. An optional 4-inch sun shade is available for shooting in critical light conditions.
Price: $494.95

RIMFIRE SCOPE 2.5-7X
Lenses are multi-coated for bright, clear low-light performance and the one-piece tube design is shockproof and waterproof.
Prices:
49622 2.5-7x Rimfire Matte $171.95
49623 2.5-7x Rimfire Silver. 172.95

RIMFIRE SCOPE 4X
Fixed 4x scope is ideal for a variety of shooting applications. It's durable, light-weight and waterproof.
Prices:
49620 4x Rimfire Matte $148.95
49621 4x Rimfire Silver. 151.95

WILLIAMS

FP SERIES

Internal micrometer adjustments have positive internal locks. The FP is strong, rugged, dependable. The alloy used to manufacture this sight has a tensile strength of 85,000 pounds. Yet, the FP is light and compact, weighing only 1-1/2 ounces.

For big game hunting, the FP will outsell all other makes and models of receiver sights put together.

Many rifles are now being drilled and tapped at the factory for installation of the FP.

Target knobs are available on all models of the FP receiver sight if desired.

Prices:

For most models $59.95
Target knobs 71.20
Mini 14 w/sub-base 100.91

FP-GR-TK
on Remingto 581

FP-KNIGHT-TK
SILVER on MK-85

FP-AG-TK
on Beeman
Air Rifle

FP-94 SE shown
on Winchester
94 Side Eject

FP MINI-14-TK
WITH SUB-BASE

FP RECEIVER SIGHT OPTIONS

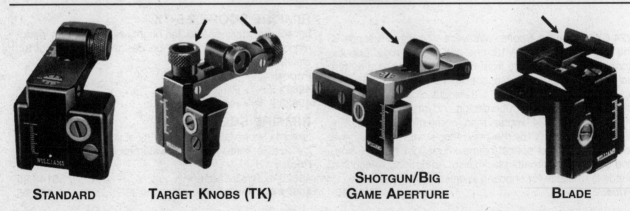

STANDARD   **TARGET KNOBS (TK)**   **SHOTGUN/BIG GAME APERTURE**   **BLADE**

WILLIAMS

Open Sights

WGOS SERIES

- Made from high tensile strength Aluminum. Will not rust.
- All parts milled - no stampings.
- Streamlined and lightweight with tough anodized finish.
- Dovetailed windage and elevation - Easy to adjust, positive locks.
- Interchangeable blades available in four heights and four styles.

Price: . . . . $15.68 to 21.80

Blades are sold separately, except "U" blades are available installed on WGOS octagon T/C and CVA.

Price: $6.37

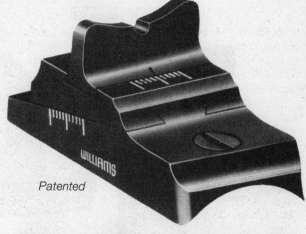

Patented

"SQ"   **"U"**   **"V"**   **"B"**

Receiver Sights

WGRS SERIES

- Compact Low Profile
- Lightweight, Strong, Rustproof
- Positive Windage and Elevation Locks

In most cases these sights utilize dovetail or existing screws on top of receiver for installation. They are made from an aluminum alloy that is stronger than many steels. Light. Rustproof. Williams quality throughout.

Price: most models $30.85

WGRS-KN on MK-85 Knight Rifle

OPEN SIGHT BLADES FOR THE GUIDE RECEIVER SIGHT

The WGRS receiver sight can be converted to an open sight by installing a 1/4" WGOS blade in place of the aperture holder.

WGRS-CVA on CVA Apolllo

"GHOST RING"
Shotgun aperture available For WGRS receiver sights. Sold separately.

WILLIAMS

5D SERIES

5D SERIES
- *For Big Game Rifles, 22's, Shotguns*
- *Positive Windage and Elevation Locks*
- *Lightweight, Strong, Accurate*
- *Williams Quality Throughout - Rustproof*

Available for most of the more popular rifles and shotguns - the inexpensive, quality-made 5D sight. These sights have the same strength, lightweight, and neat appearance, but without the micrometer adjustments. Designed for rugged hunting use, the 5D sights are dependable and accurate. Positive locks. Clear unobstructed vision. No knobs or side plates to blot out shooter's field of vision. Wherever possible, the manufacturers' mounting screw holes in the receivers of the guns have been utilized for easy installation. The upper staff of the Williams 5D sight is readily detachable. It is only necessary to loosen one screw so that the upper staff slides easily in the close-fitting dovetail. The angular bushing locks this upper staff in a positive manner. A set screw is provided as a stop screw so that the sight will return to absolute zero upon detaching and reattaching. The material used in the manufacture of the Williams 5D sight is one of the highest grade alloys obtainable. Laboratory tests show that the material used has a tensile strength approximately 25% greater than mild steels.

Price: Most 5D models. **$31.47**

TARGET FP SERIES

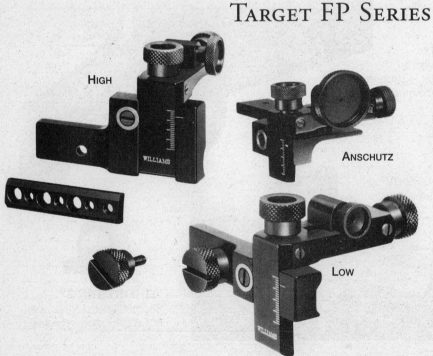

HIGH

ANSCHUTZ

LOW

WILLIAMS

TARGET - FP (HIGH)

Adjustable From 1.250" to 1.750"
Above Centerline of Bore.
Price: **$77.15**

TARGET FP-ANSCHUTZ

Designed to fit many of the Anschutz Lightweight .22 Cal. Target and Sporter Models. No Drilling and Tapping required.
Price: **$73.90**

TARGET - FP (LOW)

Adjustable From .750" to 1.250"
Above Centerline of Bore.
Price: **$77.15**

ZEISS RIFLESCOPES

THE "Z" SERIES

DIAVARI-C 3-9X36
$615.00
NEW LIGHTER VERSION OF THE
GERMAN-MADE SCOPE NOW
BUILT IN THE U.S.A.

DIAVARI-C 3-9X36T (not shown)
$815.00 ($845.00 Silver)

DIATAL-Z 6X42 T
$955.00

DIAVARI-Z 1.5-6X42 T
$1,240.00

DIATAL-Z 3-12X56 T
$1,575.00 ($1,810.00 w/
Illuminated #8 Reticle)

DIAVARI-Z 2.5-10X48 T
(not shown)
$1,465.00

DIATAL-Z 8X56 T
$1,135.00

DIAVARI-Z 1.25-4x24
(not shown)
$1,085.00

ZM/Z SERIES RIFLESCOPE SPECIFICATIONS

MODEL	DIATAL-ZM/Z 6X42T	DIAVARI-ZM/Z 1.5-6x42 T	DIAVARI-ZM/Z 3-12x56 T	DIATAL-ZM/Z 8x56 T	DIAVARI-ZM/Z 2.5-10x48 T	DIAVERA-ZM/Z 1.25-4x24	DIAVARI-C 3-9x36
Magnification	6X	1.5 X 6X	3X 12X	8X	2.5X-10X	1.25-4X	3X 9X
Effective obj. diam.	42mm/1.7"	19.5/0.8" 42/1.7"	38/1.5" 56/2.2"	56mm/2.2"	33/1.30" 48/1.89"	NA	30.0/1.2" 36.0/1.4"
Diameter of exit pupil	7mm	13mm 7mm	12.7mm 4.7mm	7mm	13.2mm 4.8mm	12.6mm 6.3mm	10.0 4.0mm
Twilight factor	15.9	4.2 15.9	8.5 25.9	21.2	7.1 21.9	3.54 9.6	8.5 18.0
Field of view at 100 m/ ft. at 100 yds.	6.7m/20.1'	18/54.0' 6.5/19.5'	9.2/27.6' 3.3/9.9'	5m/15.0'	11.0/33.0 3.9/11.7	32 10	12.0/36.0 4.3/12.9
Approx. eye relief	8cm/3.2"	8cm/3.2"	8cm/3.2"	8cm/3.2"	8cm/3.2"	8cm/3.2"	3.5"
Click-stop adjustment 1 click - (cm at 200 m)/ (inch at 100 yds)	1cm/0.36"	1cm/0.36"	1cm/0.36"	1cm/0.36"	1cm/0.36"	1cm/0.36"	107/0.25"
Max adj. (elv./wind.) at 100m (cm) at 100 yds.	187	190	95	138	110/39.6	300	135/49
Center tube dia.	25.4mm/1"	30mm/1.18"	30mm/1.18"	25.4mm/1"	30mm/1.18"	30mm/1.18"	25.4/1.0"
Objective bell dia.	48mm/1.9"	48mm/1.9"	62mm/2.44"	62mm/2.44"	54mm/2.13"	NA	44.0/1.7
Ocular bell dia.	40mm/1.57"	40mm/1.57"	40mm/1.57"	40mm/1.57"	40mm/1.57"	NA	42.5/1.8
Length	324mm/12.8"	320mm/12.6"	388mm/15.3"	369mm/14.5"	370mm/14.57"	290mm/11.46"	
Approx. weight: ZM	350g/15.3 oz.	586g/20.7 oz.	765g/27.0 oz.	550g/19.4 oz.	715g/25.2 oz.	490g/17.3 oz.	NA
Z	400g/14.1 oz.	562g/19.8	731g/25.8 oz.	520g/18.3 oz.	680g/24 oz.	NA	430g/15.2 oz.

ZEISS RIFLESCOPES

DIAVARI C 3-9x36 MC

Introduced in 1981, the Diavari C 3-9x 36 quickly gained the respect and admiration of the North American hunter. In 1997, Zeiss moved production of this favorite scope to the USA to provide hunters with a more affordable alternative. If you are in the market for performance - on a budget, the Diavari C 3-9 x 36 MC is the logical choice. The new MC coating boasts a minimum of 90% light transmission and superb image brillance. And when compared to other scopes in its price range, the Diavari C 3-9 x 36 MC offers extraordinary value.

POWER	3-9x	EYE RELIEF (inch)	3.5
EFFECTIVE OBJECTIVE DIAMETER (mm)	30-36	CENTER TUBE DIAMETER (inch)	1
EXIT PUPIL DIAMETER (mm)	10-4	OBJECTIVE BELL DIAMETER (inch)	1.7
TWILIGHT FACTOR	8.5-18	LENGTH (inch)	11.2
FIELD OF VIEW AT 100 YARDS (feet)	36-12.9	WEIGHT (ounces)	15.2
MINIMUM SQUARE ADJUSTMENT RANGE		PARALLAX FREE (yards)	100
AT 100 YARDS (inch)	48.6	*Price:*	.$615.00

ZEISS HAS THE RIGHT RETICLE FOR YOU

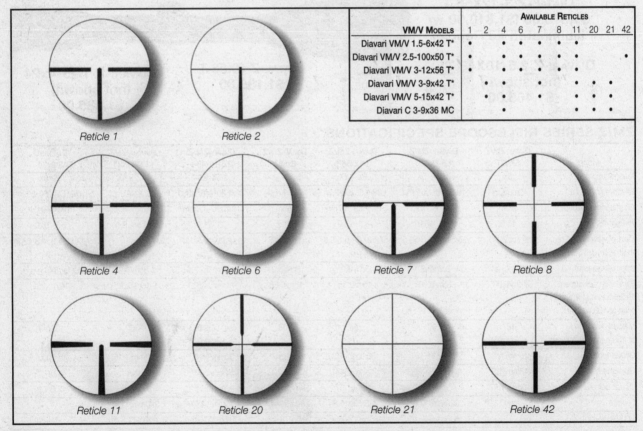

VM/V Models	Available Reticles									
	1	2	4	6	7	8	11	20	21	42
Diavari VM/V 1.5-6x42 T*	•	•	•	•	•	•				
Diavari VM/V 2.5-100x50 T*		•	•	•	•	•	•			•
Diavari VM/V 3-12x56 T*	•	•	•		•	•		•	•	•
Diavari VM/V 3-9x42 T*	•	•	•		•	•		•	•	•
Diavari VM/V 5-15x42 T*	•	•	•		•	•		•	•	•
Diavari C 3-9x36 MC		•						•	•	•

Reticle 1

Reticle 2

Reticle 4

Reticle 6

Reticle 7

Reticle 8

Reticle 11

Reticle 20

Reticle 21

Reticle 42

If you already own a Zeiss riflescope, Zeiss may be abe to change the reticle for you. For more information contact your local Zeiss representative.

ZEISS RIFLESCOPES

DIAVARI VM/V 3-9x42 T*

Over the years, the 3-9x power range has proven its staying power. Still the favorite power range of North American hunters, the new Diavari VM/V 3-9 x 42 T* will be the overwhelming choice of the traditionalist. The 42 mm objective, coupled with the newly developed optical system and famous Zeiss T* coating, will extend your hunting day. Whether your quarry is elk, Dall sheep or Boone and Crockett white-tail, the VM/V Diavari 3-9 x 42T* offers top quality and the right magnification.

POWER	3-9x	**EYE RELIEF** (inch)	3.74
EFFECTIVE OBJECTIVE DIAMETER (mm)	30-42	**CENTER TUBE DIAMETER** (inch)	1
EXIT PUPIL DIAMETER (mm)	10-4.7	**OBJECTIVE BELL DIAMETER** (inch)	1.89
TWILIGHT FACTOR	8.5-18.4	**LENGTH** (inch)	13.3
FIELD OF VIEW AT 100 YARDS (feet)	39.6-13.2	**WEIGHT** (ounces)	14.8-14
MINIMUM SQUARE ADJUSTMENT RANGE		**PARALLAX FREE** (yards)	109.4
AT 100 YARDS (inch)	49.7	*Price:* $1,249.95

DIAVARI VM/V 5-15x42 T*

If you enjoy testing your long range shooting skills, you are going to love this new scope. Precise windage and elevation adjustments make the new Diavari VM/V 5 - 15 x 42 T* the perfect companion for your favorite target or varmint rifle.

Designed for years of trouble free service, its rugged adjustment system gives you fast, accurate and repeatable adjustments. By aligning the optical and mechanical axes, Zeiss ensures you have the full range of adjustment.

POWER	5-15x	**EYE RELIEF** (inch)	3.74
EFFECTIVE OBJECTIVE DIAMETER (mm)	42-42	**CENTER TUBE DIAMETER** (inch)	1
EXIT PUPIL DIAMETER (mm)	8.4-2.8	**OBJECTIVE BELL DIAMETER** (inch)	1.89
TWILIGHT FACTOR	14.1-25.1	**LENGTH** (inch)	13.3
FIELD OF VIEW AT 100 YARDS (feet)	23.7-7.8	**WEIGHT** (ounces)	14.9-14
MINIMUM SQUARE ADJUSTMENT RANGE		**PARALLAX FREE** (yards)	109.4
AT 100 YARDS (inch)	30	*Price:* $1,499.95

ZEISS RIFLESCOPES

DIAVARI VM/V 3-12x56 T*

In the quiet haze of dawn or the fleeting light of sunset, a riflescope is put to the ultimate test. Under these conditions, the Diavari VM/V 3-12x56 T* establishes its reputation for unrivaled performance. The patented Zeiss T* anti-reflection coating is designed to transmit the optimum percentage of light throughout the spectral range to take full advantage of your eye's sensitivity. Weighing in at a mere 13.5 ounces, the VM/V 3-12x56 T* won't slow you down. 30mm tube.

POWER	3-12x	EYE RELIEF (inch)	3.54
EFFECTIVE OBJECTIVE DIAMETER (mm)	44.0-56	CENTER TUBE DIAMETER (inch)	1.18
EXIT PUPIL DIAMETER (mm)	14.7-4.7	OBJECTIVE BELL DIAMETER (inch)	2.44
TWILIGHT FACTOR	8.5-25.9	LENGTH (inch)	13.54
FIELD OF VIEW AT 100 YARDS (feet)	37.5-10.4	WEIGHT (ounces)	17.8/16.8
MINIMUM SQUARE		PARALLAX FREE (yards)	109.4
ADJUSTMENT RANGE		*Price:* $1,599.95	
AT 100 YARDS (inch)	36.7	w/illuminated reticle 2,049.95	

ZEISS–PREMIUM SPORTS OPTICS

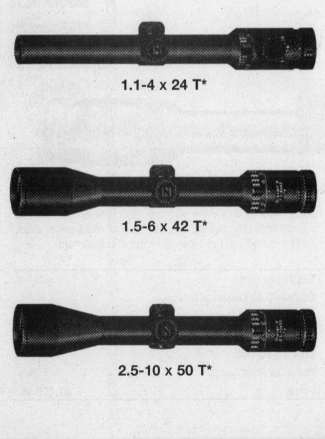

1.1-4 x 24 T*

1.5-6 x 42 T*

2.5-10 x 50 T*

DIAVARI 1.1-4 X 24 T* VM/V
- Compact riflescope with 108 ft. field of view at 1.1 power
- Extremely lightweight - ideal for safari rifles
- With illuminated varipoint reticle for fast target acquisition clearly visible also in critical lighting conditions
- Especially designed for running shots and hunting in heavy brush
- Available with bullet drop compensator
- Eye relief: 3.74 in.

Price:............................... $1,799.95

DIAVARI 1.5-6 X 42 T* VM/V
- Excellent choice for white-tail or moose hunter
- Compact and easy to handle
- Lightest scope of its class
- 72 ft. field of view - largest field of view in premium class
- Easy-grip adjustment knob
- Available with bullet drop compensator
- Eye relief: 3.54 in.

Price:............................... $1,349.95

DIAVARI 2.5-10 X 50 T* VM/V
- High powered riflescope with superior twilight performance
- Light, compact with a wide field of view
- Available with an illuminated reticle
- Easy-grip adjustment knob
- Excellent choice for world-wide all-round hunting
- Available with bullet drop compensator
- Eye relief: 3.54 in.

Price:............................. $1,549.95
w/illuminated reticle 1,999.95

CENTERFIRE PISTOL & REVOLVER AMMUNITION

Federal	478
Hornady	482
PMC	483
Winchester	490

CENTER RIFLE AMMUNITION

Federal	478, 479
Hornady	480, 481
PMC	483, 484
Remington	485, 486
Winchester	490, 492

RIMFIRE AMMUNITION

RWS	489
Winchester	491

SHOTSHELL AMMUNITION

Federal	478
PMC	483, 484
Remington	486
Rottweill	487
Winchester	490

Ammunition

*For addresses and phone/fax numbers of manufacturers and distributors included in this section, please turn to **DIRECTORY OF MANUFACTURERS AND SUPPLIERS** on page 564.*

FEDERAL AMMUNITION

Federal's 1999-2000 line-up includes ammunition and components for big game and wildfowl hunters and personal defense.
Some examples:

PREMIUM BARNES EXPANDER SABOT SLUG

The expansive hollow point of the Barnes Expander delivers expansion 150% greater than conventional sabot slugs and groups 2.5" or better at 100 yards.

PREMIUM SABOT SLUG
In a rifled barrel, Premium Sabot Slugs are capable of 2.5" groups at 100 yards.

PREMIUM RIFLED SLUG
Federal Premium Rifled Slugs feature helix ribbing and the unique Hydra-Shok hollow point.

PREMIUM PERSONAL DEFENSE PISTOL

This jacketed hollow point load comes in clear plastic packaging that offers protection against moisture and rough treatment. Also new is a .357 Magnum handgun load.

PREMIUM SLUGS

Federal's Premium Slug line includes three highly accurate, highly effective slugs: rifled slug for smoothbores, copper-plated sabot slug for rifled barrels or rifled choke tubes and the Barnes Expander Sabot Slug for fully rifled barrels. The rifled slug delivers 2" groups at 50 yards, while both sabot styles consistently group as tight as 2.5" at 100 yards.

PREMIUM WOODLEIGH WELDCORE CENTERFIRE RIFLE (NOT SHOWN)

Federal has expanded this load, which has been popular throughout Europe and Africa for big game and safari hunting since 1988, to include eight new Premium Centerfire and High Energy loads featuring an Australian legend called Woodleigh Weldcore. This load features a bonded-core bullet with a special heavy jacket for extra penetration power. Weight retention of 80-85% provides the energy needed to drop big game in its tracks.

PREMIUM TUNGSTEN-IRON TURKEY SHOTSHELL

This turkey load has the pellet energy of lead, a velocity of 1300 feet per second, and good penetration. Tight patterns and excellent penetration assure success of this load among turkey hunters. Tungsten-Polymer loads offer the same deadly performance to waterfowlers.

FEDERAL CENTERFIRE RIFLE AMMUNITION

PREMIUM LOAD BULLET SELECTION

PREMIUM CENTERFIRE RIFLE

Combining the world's best brand-name bullet designs with our advanced delivery systems, Federal Premium performs better than handloads, right out of the box.

TROPHY BONDED BEAR CLAW®

Excellent for small to heavy game.
Only Federal offers this famous Jack Carter design in a factory load. The jacket and core are 100% fusion bonded. Superb accuracy, 95% weight retention, deep penetration and reliable expansion from 25 yards to extreme ranges.

TROPHY BONDED SLEDGEHAMMER®

Excellent for large and dangerous game.
Also a Jack Carter design, this bonded bronze solid delivers maximum stopping power. The flat nose minimizes deflection for a straight, deep wound cavity.

BARNES XLC COATED-X BULLET™

Superb stopping power for small to large game.
New for 1999-2000, this hard-hitting design features a 100% copper bullet, four petal expansion and hollow cavity 1/3 the bullet length for deep penetration and 100% weight retention. Heat cured dry film lubricant prevents copper fouling, reduces bore friction and won't rub off on hands.

WOODLEIGH® WELDCORE

Smaller calibers are excellent for medium to large game. Larger calibers are favored for very large or dangerous game.
Safari hunters have long respected this bonded Australian bullet for its superb accuracy and excellent stopping power. Its special heavy jacket provides 80-85% weight retention.

NOSLER® PARTITION®

A proven favorite for medium to large game.
The tapered H-shaped brass jacket of the Nosler Partition allows the front half of the bullet to mushroom on impact while the rear core remains intact, providing additional penetration and stopping power.

SIERRA GAMEKING® BOAT-TAIL

Long-range choice for varmints to big game.
The tapered design of the Sierra GameKing Boat-Tail provides extremely flat trajectories while offering higher retained velocity and downrange energy for excellent stopping power. Reduced wind drift makes it a good choice for long-range shots.

NOSLER BALLISTIC TIP®

Especially for long-range shots at varmints, predators and small to medium game.
Proven fast, flat-shooting, wind-defying performance. Color-coded polycarbonate tip provides easy identification, prevents deformation in the magazine and drives back on impact for explosive expansion and immediate energy transfer.

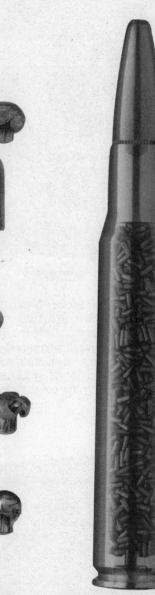

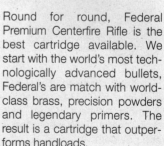

Round for round, Federal Premium Centerfire Rifle is the best cartridge available. We start with the world's most technologically advanced bullets, Federal's are match with world-class brass, precision powders and legendary primers. The result is a cartridge that outperforms handloads.

AMMUNITION

HORNADY AMMUNITION

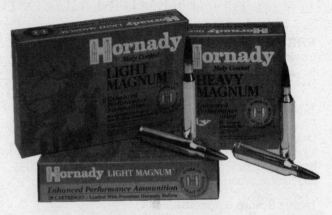

Hornady's moly-coated **LIGHT MAGNUM** ammo achieves more energy, flatter trajectory and velocities up to 200 feet per second faster than standard ammo. That same performance is now available in .280 Remington and 7mm Remington Magnum. With Light Magnum and Heavy Magnum, greater velocity is achieved from standard cartridges with no additional heat and pressure. The addition of molybdenum disulfide to these bullets cuts friction and eliminates copper fouling in the bore—more rounds can be fired without stopping to clean the rifle.

Hornady's **SST (SUPER SHOCK TIPPED)** bullets feature a premium polymer tip which, along with its profile, combine to improve the SST's ballistic coefficient. The result: greater velocity and better accuracy. Upon impact, the tip is pushed backward into the lead core to initiate immediate expansion. The specially designed jacket grips and controls the expanding core, allowing the bullet to reach its optimum mass and momentum.

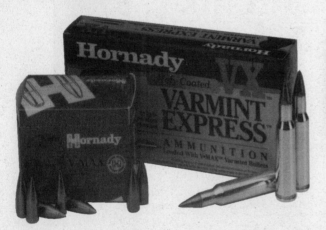

Hornady's **VARMINT EXPRESS** ammunition now features moly-coated V-MAX bullets, which offer faster speeds in most calibers. Other features include high quality brass cases, hand-inspection, individually selected primers and powders.

The effectiveness of Hornady's factory-loaded rifle match ammunition is assured by hand-selection and matching for premium uniformity. Cases, powder and primer are all loaded so as to guarantee superb ignition and pinpoint accuracy. These match cartridges are loaded with either Hornady **A-MAX** or **BTHP** match bullets, all available with high-performance moly-coating that reduces barrel wear and increases speed.

HORNADY

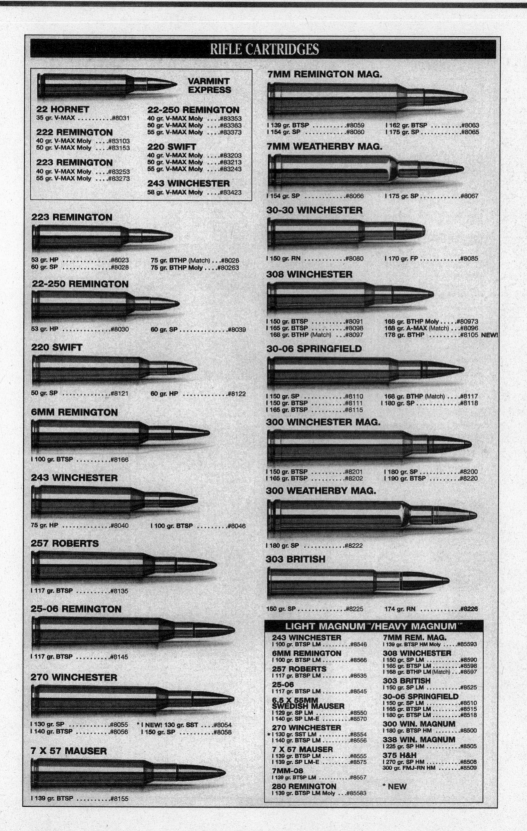

RIFLE CARTRIDGES

VARMINT EXPRESS

22 HORNET
35 gr. V-MAX . . . . #8031

222 REMINGTON
40 gr. V-MAX Moly . . . . #83103
50 gr. V-MAX Moly . . . . #83153

223 REMINGTON
40 gr. V-MAX Moly . . . #83253
55 gr. V-MAX Moly . . . #83273

22-250 REMINGTON
40 gr. V-MAX Moly . . . . #83353
50 gr. V-MAX Moly . . . . #83363
55 gr. V-MAX Moly . . . . #83373

220 SWIFT
40 gr. V-MAX Moly . . . . #83203
50 gr. V-MAX Moly . . . . #83213
55 gr. V-MAX Moly . . . . #83243

243 WINCHESTER
58 gr. V-MAX Moly . . . . #83423

223 REMINGTON
53 gr. HP . . . . #8023
60 gr. SP . . . . #8028
75 gr. BTHP (Match) . . . #8026
75 gr. BTHP Moly . . . . #80263

22-250 REMINGTON
53 gr. HP . . . . #8030
60 gr. SP . . . . #8039

220 SWIFT
50 gr. SP . . . . #8121
60 gr. HP . . . . #8122

6MM REMINGTON
I 100 gr. BTSP . . . . #8166

243 WINCHESTER
75 gr. HP . . . . #8040
I 100 gr. BTSP . . . . #8046

257 ROBERTS
I 117 gr. BTSP . . . . #8135

25-06 REMINGTON
I 117 gr. BTSP . . . . #8145

270 WINCHESTER
I 130 gr. SP . . . . #8055
I 140 gr. BTSP . . . . #8056
* I NEW! 130 gr. SST . . . . #8054
I 150 gr. SP . . . . #8058

7 X 57 MAUSER
I 139 gr. BTSP . . . . #8155

7MM REMINGTON MAG.
I 139 gr. BTSP . . . . #8059
I 154 gr. SP . . . . #8060
I 162 gr. BTSP . . . . #8063
I 175 gr. SP . . . . #8065

7MM WEATHERBY MAG.
I 154 gr. SP . . . . #8066
I 175 gr. SP . . . . #8067

30-30 WINCHESTER
I 150 gr. RN . . . . #8080
I 170 gr. FP . . . . #8085

308 WINCHESTER
I 150 gr. BTSP . . . . #8091
I 165 gr. BTSP . . . . #8098
168 gr. BTHP (Match) . . #8097
168 gr. BTHP Moly . . . . #80973
168 gr. A-MAX (Match) . . #8096
178 gr. BTHP . . . . #8105 NEW!

30-06 SPRINGFIELD
I 150 gr. SP . . . . #8110
I 150 gr. BTSP . . . . #8111
I 165 gr. BTSP . . . . #8115
168 gr. BTHP (Match) . . . #8117
I 180 gr. SP . . . . #8118

300 WINCHESTER MAG.
I 150 gr. BTSP . . . . #8201
I 165 gr. BTSP . . . . #8202
I 180 gr. SP . . . . #8200
I 190 gr. BTSP . . . . #8220

300 WEATHERBY MAG.
I 180 gr. SP . . . . #8222

303 BRITISH
150 gr. SP . . . . #8225
174 gr. RN . . . . #8226

LIGHT MAGNUM™/HEAVY MAGNUM™

243 WINCHESTER
I 100 gr. BTSP LM . . . . #8546

6MM REMINGTON
I 100 gr. BTSP LM . . . . #8566

257 ROBERTS
I 117 gr. BTSP LM . . . . #8535

25-06
I 117 gr. BTSP LM . . . . #8545

6.5 X 55MM SWEDISH MAUSER
I 129 gr. SP LM . . . . #8550
I 140 gr. SP LM-E . . . . . . #8570

270 WINCHESTER
* I 130 gr. SST LM . . . . #8554
I 140 gr. BTSP LM . . . . . . #8556

7 X 57 MAUSER
I 139 gr. BTSP LM . . . . . . #8555
I 139 gr. SP LM-E . . . . . . #8575

7MM-08
I 139 gr. BTSP LM . . . . #8557

280 REMINGTON
I 139 gr. BTSP LM Moly . . . . #85583

7MM REM. MAG.
I 139 gr. BTSP HM Moly . . . . #85593

308 WINCHESTER
I 150 gr. SP LM . . . . #8590
I 165 gr. BTSP LM . . . . . . #8598
I 168 gr. BTHP LM (Match) . . #8597

303 BRITISH
I 150 gr. SP LM . . . . #8525

30-06 SPRINGFIELD
I 150 gr. SP LM . . . . #8510
I 165 gr. BTSP LM . . . . . . #8515
I 180 gr. BTSP LM . . . . . . #8518

300 WIN. MAGNUM
I 180 gr. BTSP HM . . . . . . #8500

338 WIN. MAGNUM
I 225 gr. SP HM . . . . #8505

375 H&H
I 270 gr. SP HM . . . . #8508
300 gr. FMJ-RN HM . . . . #8509

* NEW

AMMUNITION

HORNADY

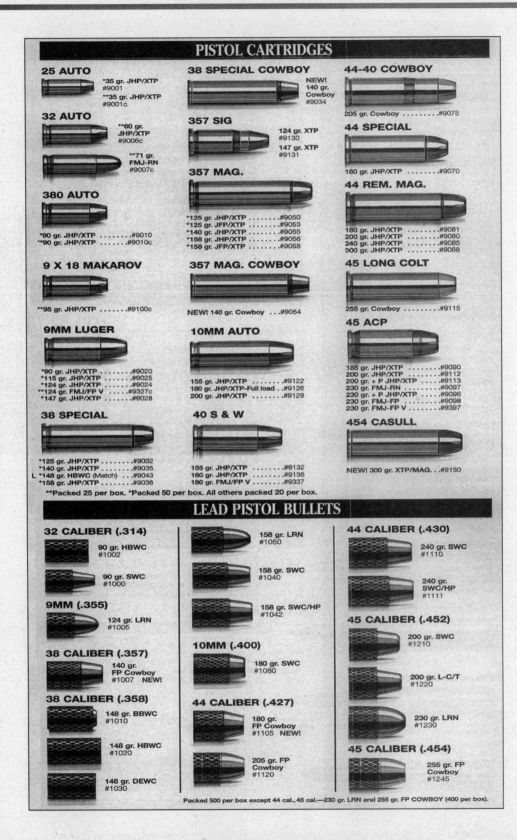

PISTOL CARTRIDGES

25 AUTO
*35 gr. JHP/XTP #9001
**35 gr. JHP/XTP #9001c

32 AUTO
**60 gr. JHP/XTP #9006c
**71 gr. FMJ-RN #9007c

380 AUTO
*90 gr. JHP/XTP . . . .#9010
**90 gr. JHP/XTP . . . .#9010c

9 X 18 MAKAROV
**95 gr. JHP/XTP . . . .#9100c

9MM LUGER
*90 gr. JHP/XTP . . . .#9020
*115 gr. JHP/XTP . . . .#9025
*124 gr. JHP/XTP . . . .#9024
*124 gr. FMJ/FP V . . . .#9327c
*147 gr. JHP/XTP . . . . . .#9028

38 SPECIAL
*125 gr. JHP/XTP . . . .#9032
*140 gr. JHP/XTP . . . .#9035
L *148 gr. HBWC (Match) . . .#9043
*158 gr. JHP/XTP . . . . . .#9036

38 SPECIAL COWBOY
NEW! 140 gr. Cowboy #9034

357 SIG
124 gr. XTP #9130
147 gr. XTP #9131

357 MAG.
*125 gr. JHP/XTP . . . .#9050
*125 gr. JFP/XTP . . . .#9053
*140 gr. JHP/XTP . . . .#9055
*158 gr. JHP/XTP . . . .#9056
*158 gr. JFP/XTP . . . .#9058

357 MAG. COWBOY
NEW! 140 gr. Cowboy . . .#9054

10MM AUTO
155 gr. JHP/XTP . . . .#9122
180 gr. JHP/XTP-Full load . .#9126
200 gr. JHP/XTP . . . .#9129

40 S & W
155 gr. JHP/XTP . . . .#9132
180 gr. JHP/XTP . . . .#9136
180 gr. FMJ/FP V . . . .#9337

44-40 COWBOY
205 gr. Cowboy . . . .#9075

44 SPECIAL
180 gr. JHP/XTP . . . .#9070

44 REM. MAG.
180 gr. JHP/XTP . . . .#9081
200 gr. JHP/XTP . . . .#9080
240 gr. JHP/XTP . . . .#9085
300 gr. JHP/XTP . . . .#9088

45 LONG COLT
255 gr. Cowboy . . . .#9115

45 ACP
185 gr. JHP/XTP . . . .#9090
200 gr. JHP/XTP . . . .#9112
200 gr. + P JHP/XTP . . . . . .#9113
230 gr. FMJ-RN . . . .#9097
230 gr. + P JHP/XTP . . . . . .#9096
230 gr. FMJ-FP . . . .#9098
230 gr. FMJ-FP V . . . .#9397

454 CASULL
NEW! 300 gr. XTP/MAG. . . .#9150

**Packed 25 per box. *Packed 50 per box. All others packed 20 per box.

LEAD PISTOL BULLETS

32 CALIBER (.314)
90 gr. HBWC #1002
90 gr. SWC #1000

9MM (.355)
124 gr. LRN #1005

38 CALIBER (.357)
140 gr. FP Cowboy #1007 NEW!

38 CALIBER (.358)
148 gr. BBWC #1010
148 gr. HBWC #1020
148 gr. DEWC #1030

158 gr. LRN #1050
158 gr. SWC #1040
158 gr. SWC/HP #1042

10MM (.400)
180 gr. SWC #1080

44 CALIBER (.427)
180 gr. FP Cowboy #1105 NEW!
205 gr. FP Cowboy #1120

44 CALIBER (.430)
240 gr. SWC #1110
240 gr. SWC/HP #1111

45 CALIBER (.452)
200 gr. SWC #1210
200 gr. L-C/T #1220
230 gr. LRN #1230

45 CALIBER (.454)
255 gr. FP Cowboy #1245

Packed 500 per box except 44 cal., 45 cal.—230 gr. LRN and 255 gr. FP COWBOY (400 per box).

PMC

PMC (Precision Made Cartridges) is the same firm as Eldorado Cartridge Company — a name that may be phased out. The company may not claim the volume of business that accrues to Winchester, Remington or Federal, but it is a fast-growing enterprise whose product line continues to expand. At this writing the firm offers more than 50 handgun loads, from .25 Auto to .44 Magnum, including five specifically for Cowboy Action shooting. The centerfire rifle stable includes cowboy action loads in .30-30 and .45-70, plus a wide variety of hunting and match ammunition from .222 Remington to .375 H&H Magnum. The selection of .22 rimfire rounds features hunting, plinking and match loads.

PMC offers a broad choice of bullet styles. In pistol ammo, there's the quick-opening Starfire hollowpoint, a traditional jacketed hollowpoint, a jacketed softpoint and a full-metal-jacket (hardball) bullet — plus lead wadcutter, semi-wadcutter and round-nose options. Rifle bullets include the Barnes X-Bullet, .30-30 Starfire hollowpoint, Sierra boat-tail hollowpoint, Sierra boat-tail softpoint, pointed softpoint, softpoint, flat-nose softpoint and full metal jacket.

PMC also manufactures shotshells, from light dove and quail and target loads to heavy steel-shot loads for geese.

One more thing that PMC has: A rural Nevada plant that offers test-firing opportunities right out the back door.

PMC has entered the popular Cowboy Action game with an assortment of low-recoil ammunition that speeds recovery for a second shot. The Lite Clay Target shotshell works at this game as well as at hand-thrown clay targets. The firm offers Cowboy Action pistol and rifle rounds in .38 Special, .357 Magnum, .44 Special, .44-40 Winchester, .45 Colt, .30-30 and .45-70 Government.

PMC rifle cartridges include hunting loads for heavy-hitters like the .338 Winchester and .375 H&H magnums as well as for varmint rounds like the .222 and .223. There are match loads for cartridges commonly used in competition. Bullet choices for big game hunters include a wide variety of softpoint and hollowpoint designs — for example, the Barnes X-Bullet and Sierra boat-tails.

PMC handgun ammunition is loaded for target, hunting and personal defense. The firm's own Starfire bullet dumps energy right away with quick, violent expansion. It is available in nine pistol cartridges, from .380 Auto to .44 magnum. Target rounds include a new 180-grain FMJ .40 S&W. There's also a low-cost practice load for the .357 SIG; it features a 124-grain FMJ bullet.

PMC

After an absence of several years, PMC Ammunition has brought back its Moderator Subsonic .22 Long Rifle Hollow Point cartridge. Because its subsonic velocity of 1000 feet per second eliminates the sharp "crack" made by a bullet as it reaches supersonic speeds, the Moderator offers the advantage of a low report. The reliable expansion resulting from the bullet's deep hollow point makes it a good choice for small game hunting.

High velocity steel shotshells in both 2.75-inch and 3-inch magnum lengths have been added to the PMC shotshell line for 1999. Both shell lengths are constructed with strong, ribbed plastic hulls, and feature a maximum powder charge for the power and reach needed by goose hunters. The 2.75-inch shells are loaded with 1 1/8 ounces of steel shot, and come in BB, #2, #3, and #4 shot sizes, while the 3-inch magnums have a 1.25 ounce steel shot charge in BBB, BB, #2, #3 and #4 shot sizes. Velocities are listed at 1365 feet per second for the 2.75-inch shells, 1425 feet per second for the 3-inch magnum shells.

PMC Ammunition introduces a new 9mm Starfire "Lite" load for those who prefer high velocity loads for home and personal defense or law enforcement use. The new high performance cartridge features a 95 grain hollow point bullet with a muzzle velocity of 1250 feet per second. In spite of its high velocity, the light bullet means low recoil, allowing fast, on-target second shots. Like those in other PMC Starfire cartridges, this bullet owes its broad expansion to the unique rib-and-flute cavity in the deep hollow point, and a notched jacket to encourage mushrooming.

PMC has added two BlitzKing varmint loads to the company's Silver Line rifle cartridges. The new loads feature the Sierra BllitzKingTM varmint bullet with green acetal resin (polycarbonate) tip. The varmint cartridges are available in .223 Remington and .22-250 Remington, each with a 50 grain bullet. Muzzle velocity for the .223 is 3300 feet per second, and the .22-250 exits the muzzle at 3725 feet per second, PMC also offers varmint loads with the Sierra 55 grain hollow point boat tail bullet in .223 and .22-250, and in .243 with an 85 grain Sierra HPBT.

REMINGTON AMMUNITION

REMINGTON® INTRODUCES
NON-BELTED MAGNUM–THE .300 ULTRA MAG

PREMIER® ULTRA MAG CENTERFIRE RIFLE AMMUNITION

Remington has introduced a powerful, flat-shooting big game cartridge named the .300 Remington Ultra Mag. The new round delivers one of the highest levels of velocity and energy ever offered in a commercially-produced, non-belted magnum. It's the first of a new series of high-power, non-belted Magnums planned by Remington to become the ultimate flat-shooting long-range performers of the 21ˢᵗ Century.

The .300 Remington Ultra Mag is based on an original but slightly modified .404 Jeffery case. Necking down the case mouth to .30 caliber produces a 30-degree shoulder angle that permits positive headspacing on the shoulder alone. Use of the .404 Jeffery case also provides two other significant advantages. One is its generous case capacity, allowing a greater volume of slow-burning, magnum-compatible powders that deliver exceptional performance at normal pressures. By comparison, it has 13 percent more case capacity than the .300 Weatherby Magnum and 20 percent more capacity than the .300 Win. Magnum. The other advantage of the .300 Remington Ultra Mag is its relatively straight-line, slightly tapered, beltless body, that creates easier, more reliable feeding and a more uniform chamber fit for improved accuracy.

The new cartridge will be loaded with a 180-grain Nosler® Partition® bullet at a muzzle velocity of 3300 fps from a 26-inch barrel. Use of the tough, deep penetrating, but reliably expanding Nosler® Partition® extends effective performance of this powerful round over an extremely wide spread of ranges. The .300 Remington Ultra Mag's retained energy of 2145 ft-lbs at 500 yards is still adequate for effective performance on elk with proper bullet replacement. Because range estimation errors are magnified at such distances Remington recommends stalking closer. But this new Magnum is a remarkable range-shrinker. Sighting in a .300 Remington Ultra Mag just 2 inches high at 100 yards will deliver the bullet less than 3 inches low at 300 yards.

Simultaneous with its own introduction, the .300 Remington Ultra Mag will be chambered in nine different Model 700™ bolt action rifles, all with 26-inch barrels to derive maximum ballistic performance from the exceptional case capacity of the new Magnum cartridge.

COMPARATIVE ENERGY & TRAJECTORY OF .300 REMINGTON ULTRA MAG VS. STANDARD .300 MAGNUM CARTRIDGES

ENERGY COMPARISON IN FT-LBS.

Cartridge	Muzzle	100 Yds.	200 Yds.	300 Yds.	400 Yds.	500 Yds.
.300 Rem. Ultra Mag, 180-gr. Partition	4352	3802	3313	2878	2490	2144**
.300 Rem. Ultra Mag, 180-gr. Partition	4221	3686	3210	2786	2407	2071*
.300 Win. Mag 180-gr. PSP	3501	3011	2578	2196	1859	1565*
.300 Weatherby Mag., 180-gr. PSP	3890	3284	2758	2301	1905	1565*

*From 26-inch barrel **From 24-inch barrel

TRAJECTORY COMPARISON IN INCHES, ZEROED @ 250 YARDS

Cartridge	Muzzle	100 Yds.	200 Yds.	300 Yds.	400 Yds.	500 Yds.
.300 Rem. Ultra Mag, 180-gr. Partition	-1.5	1.9	1.7	-2.8	-12.1	-26.9**
.300 Rem. Ultra Mag, 180-gr. Partition	-1.5	2.0	1.7	-2.9	-12.5	-27.9*
.300 Win. Mag 180-gr. PSP	-1.5	2.2	1.9	-3.4	-15.0	-34.4*
.300 Weatherby Mag., 180-gr. PSP	-1.5	2.4	2.0	-3.4	-14.9	-33.6*

*From 24-inch barrel **From 26-inch barrel

PREMIER® BALLISTIC TIP® .300 WIN. MAG./180-GR.

REMINGTON® ADDS .300 WIN. MAG. LOADING TO PREMIER® BALLISTIC TIP® AMMUNITION LINE

In 1999, Remington is adding another outstanding big game caliber to its line of Premier® Ballistic Tip® centerfire ammunition. The newest addition to this highly versatile ammunition group is the .300 Win. Mag., loaded with a 180-grain Nosler® Ballistic Tip® bullet.

The pointed polycarbonate tip, in conjuction with a boat tail base, creates an exceptionally low drag factor that retains velocity and flattens trajectory over extended ranges. In addition, the combination of the tip with the bullet's progressively-tapered jacket, lead alloy core and heavy jacket base, provides effective expansion with deep penetration.

This type of performance, backed by a high muzzle velocity of 296 feet per second, creates the most effective and versatile combination of range-shrinking flat trajectory and high retained energy ever formulated for the .300 Win. Mag. cartridge. This addition now expands Remington's Premier® Ballistic Tip® ammunition line to 11 loadings in 10 calibers from .243 Win. to .338 Win. Mag.

REMINGTON AMMUNITION

REMINGTON® INTRODUCES PREMIER® PARTITION® CENTERFIRE AMMUNITION LINE

PREMIER® PARTITION CENTERFIRE RIFLE AMMUNITION

Remington has introduced a new line of Premier® Partition centerfire ammunition built on the use of highly regarded Nosler® Partition® bullets. The original dual-core bullet design, Nosler® Partition® has set the standard for reliabe performance on tough game for over 50 years. In today's world of specialized bullets, there are those that excel in either accuracy, flat trajectory, reliable expansion or high weight retention. There are none that combine all these performance features, under virtually all hunting situations, as well as Nosler® Partition®. In 1999, Remington's new Premier® Partition® line brings the reliable, accurate performance of these famous bullets to seven popular calibers for use on medium to heavy big game species.

REMINGTON® PREMIER® PARTITION® CENTERFIRE AMMUNITION				
	VELOCITY (FPS)**		ENERGY (FT-LBS)	
CARTRIDGE	MUZZLE	300 YDS.	MUZZLE	300 YDS.
.260 Remington, 125-Gr. Partition	2875	2285	2294	1449
.270 Win. 150-Gr. Partition	2850	2282	2705	1734
7mm Rem. Mag., 160-Gr. Partition	2950	2381	3091	2014
.308 Win. 180-Gr. Partition	2620	2089	2743	1744
.30-06 Spngfld. 180-Gr. Partition	2700	2160	2913	1864
.300 Win. Mag., 180-Gr. Partition*	2960	2291	3501	2097
.338 Win. Mag., 210-Gr. Partition	2830	2179	3734	2214

*Protected Point **From 24-inch test barrel

IMPROVED COPPER SOLID™ SABOT SLUGS

REMINGTON® IMPROVES DESIGN AND PERFORMANCE 12-GAUGE COPPER SOLID™ SABOT SLUGS

Already accurate and effective, Remington's 12-gauge Copper Solid™ slug has been designed to provide more reliable and uniform expansion and even higher weight retention. The hollow point cavity is now formed by six, separate petals in an inwardly-curved, spiral design. Upon impact, these petals mushroom open quickly to twice the diameter of the 58-caliber slug body. However, they remain intact, with no separation for deep, reliable penetration. Groups from rifled barrels stay within 3 inches at 100 yards.

These improved 12-gauge Copper Solid™ sabot slugs weigh one ounce. They are loaded in 12-gauge, 2 3/4-inch shells at a muzzle velocity of 1450 feet per second, and in three-inch shells, at 1550 feet per second.

NITRO-STEEL™ HIGH VELOCITY MAGNUM WATERFOWL LOADS

NEW PREMIER® NITRO-STEEL™ HIGH VELOCITY WATERFOWL LOADS INTRODUCED BY REMINGTON®

Remington has announced a new line of Premier® Nitro-Steel™ High Velocity waterfowl loads specifically designed to retain greater long-range energy with larger-size steel pellets. Because steel is lighter and has only about two-thirds the specific density of lead, larger pellets are required for comparable effectiveness. However, the larger steel pellets have greater wind resistance than smaller lead pelllets and slow down faster in flight. Remington Premier Nitro Steel HV loads have the muzzle velocity to counteract this. They deliver more energy for larger birds and reduce the required forward allowance for longer shots.

These new Premier® High Velocity steel loads will be produced in five specifications: a 12-gauge, 3-inch Magnum with 1 1/8 ounces of BB, 2 or 4 shot at 1500 feet per second; a 12-gauge 3 1/2-inch Magnum with 1 3/8 ounces of BB shot at 1450 feet per second; and a 10-gauge, 3 1/2-inch Magnum load with 1 3/8 ounces of BB shot, also at a muzzle velocity of 1450 feet per second.

ROTTWEIL BRENNEKE CARTRIDGES

Original Brenneke® Golden Slug 12 GA 3" Magnum

DISTANCE (YDS)	VELOCITY (FT/SEC)	ENERGY 1-3/8 oz. (FT/LBS)	TIME OF FLIGHT (MILLISEC.)
Muzzle	1476	2913	0
25	1286	2209	54
50	1138	1730	117
75	1036	1436	186
100	965	1244	261

Brenneke MP 12 GA 2-3/4"

DISTANCE (YDS)	VELOCITY (FT/SEC)	ENERGY 1-3/8 oz. (FT/LBS)
Muzzle	1510	2215
25	1300	1640
50	1135	1250
75	1036	1025
100	950	890

Original Brenneke® 12 & 20 GA., 410 Bore 3" Magnum

DISTANCE (YDS)	VELOCITY (FT/SEC) 12 GA	ENERGY (FT/LBS) 1-3/8 oz.	1 oz.	1/4 oz.	TIME OF FLIGHT (MILLISEC.)
Muzzle	1502	3017	2117	780	0
25	1300	2261	1591	502	54
50	1144	1749	1239	342	115
75	1037	1438	1026	259	184
100	936	1240	888	213	259

Origina Brenneke Slug 12, 16, & 20 GA Magnum, 2-3/4"

DISTANCE (YDS)	VELOCITY (FT/SEC) 12 GA	ENERGY (FT/LBS) 12 GA	16 GA	20 GA	TIME OF FLIGHT (MILLISEC.)
Muzzle	1590	2745	2320	2080	0
25	1365	2025	1710	1530	51
50	1190	1540	13000	1165	110
75	1060	1220	1030	925	176
100	975	1035	875	780	250

RWS Centerfire Cartridges

Bullets And Ballistics For Norma

VULKAN

Vulkan bullets are strengthened by the folded jacket at the front. The folds protect the tip from deformation. The bullet penetrates before expansion starts. Subsequently, mushrooming to double the original diameter follows rapidly. *1. Reinforced rear jacket with lead core lock. 2. Crimping groove for secure seating in the case. 3. Thin forward jacket with internal notches. 4. Jacket folded into the lead core. 5. Antimony hardened lead core.*

SOFT POINT

Soft Point bullets have optimum ballistic shape. They offer good penetration and mushroom well even on smaller game. The Soft Point is an excellent all-around bullet particularly suitable for small and medium game. *1. Reinforced rear jacket. 2. Crimping groove for secure seating in the case. 3. Thin forward jacket. 4. Antimony hardened lead core.*

The design of the DK bullet is the result of Dynamit Nobel's extensive ballistics research. Special laboratory tests, in conjunction with extensive practical field trials, support this.

Manufactured at considerable expense, DK bullets barely splinter, mushroom in a controlled manner, have a residue body of over 50 percent, and will always produce an exit hole. A true twin core that separates to perform two separate functions upon impact, penetration and a high degree of impact force, combine to give the DK a clear advantage over more conventional bullets.

The DK is tailored exactly to the hunting conditions that hunters are faced with: medium shot distance, small to large game, and close game-reserve boundaries. The range of top-quality rifle cartridges with the traditional RWS symbol has been expanded, thanks to the new DK Bullet!

The RWS cone point bullet was designed and developed after exhaustive studies dealing with various bullet shapes and their ballistic behavior; in the laboratory as well as in the field.

A carefully engineered matching of casing and core material and an aerodynamically favorable bullet shape have been paired to produce a controlled mushrooming of the bullet and a largely uniform yield of energy in the body of the game. Mushrooming, caused by the formation of vanes, amounts to almost twice caliber size.

The rear groove, which joins the lead core and casing, controls mushrooming and preserves effective residual body to give it killing power.

Due to external shape, the RWS cone point bullet is largely insensitive to small obstacles, such as brush, in the path of its trajectory.

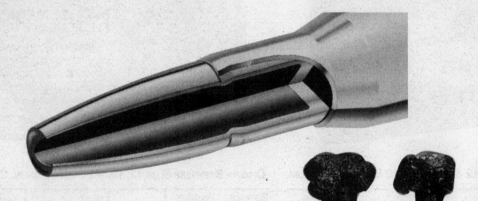

NORMA ORYX

This is a completely new type of bullet, designed to meet the ever increasing need of hunters. The jacket and core are bonded together through a chemical process. This ensures a very high residue weight, even in hard targets. Despite the solid construction, mushrooming starts early. The Oryx bullet delivers excellent deep energy transfer and is suitable for big and medium sized game.

- *Bonded bullet-lead core soldered into copper jacket*
- *Good penetration*
- *Exceptional expansion, combined with bonding, results in deep wound channel and minimal meat damage*
- *Very high weight retention*

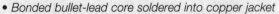

RWS RIMFIRE CARTRIDGES

GECO .22 L.R. RIFLE

Combining quality and cost effectiveness this rimfire ammunition is made in the RWS Nuremberg factory to exacting standards. Perfect for informal target shooting and entry level competition.

GECO .22 L.R. PISTOL

The same quality and affordability as the rifle version but with a reduced velocity. For the pistol shooter looking for muzzle control.

RWS .22 L.R. RIFLE MATCH

Perfect for the club level target competitor. Accurate and affordable.

RWS .22 L.R. TARGET RIFLE

An ideal training and field cartridge, the .22 Long Rifle Target also excels in informal competitions. The target .22 provides the casual shooter with accuracy at an economical price.

RWS .22 L.R. SUBSONIC HOLLOW POINT

Subsonic ammunition is a favorite ammunition of shooters whose shooting range is limited to where the noise of a conventional cartridge would be a problem.

RWS .22 L.R. HV HOLLOW POINT

A higher velocity hollow point offers the shooter greater shocking power in game, suitable for both small game and vermin.

RWS .22 MAGNUM HOLLOW POINT

The soft point allows good expansion on impact while preserving the penetration characteristics necessary for larger vermin and game.

RWS .22 MAGNUM FULL JACKET

Outstanding penetration characteristics of this cartridge allow the shooter to easily tackle game where penetration is necessary.

TECHNICAL DATA

Cartridges	Bullet Style	Bullet Weight (Grains)	Max. Chamber Pressure (PSI)	Velocity (Ft./Sec.)			Energy (Ft./Lbs.)			Open Sight At	Trajectory inches above (+) or below (-) line of sight				Scope Sighted				
				Muzzle	50y	100y	Muzzle	50y	100y		25 yds	50 yds	75 yds	100yds	In At	25 yds	50 yds	75 yds	100 yds
.22 L.R. R 50	Lead	40	25.600	1.070	970	890	100	80	70	--	--	--	--	--	--	--	--	--	--
.22 Short R 25	Lead	28	18.500	560	490	---	20	15	--	--	--	--	--	--	--	--	--	--	--
.22 L.R. Geco Rifle	Lead	40	25.600	1.080	990	900	100	8/5	70	50 yds.	+0.6		-3.1	-8.7	50 yds	+0.1		-2.5	-7.5
.22 L.R. Rifle Match	Lead	40	25.600	1.035	945	860	95	80	65	50 yds.	+0.7		-3.2	-9.0	50 yds	+0.1		-2.6	-7.8
.22 L.R. Target Rifle	Lead	40	25.600	1.080	990	900	100	85	70	50 yds.	+0.6		-3.1	-8.7	50 yds	+0.1		-2.5	-7.5
.22 L.R. Subsonic	Hollow Point	40	25.600	1.000	915	835	90	75	60	50 yds.	+0.8		-3.4	-4.7	50 yds	+0.2		+2.8	-8.5
.22 L.R. HV Hollow point	Lead coppered	40	25.600	1.310	1.120	990	150	110	85		--	--	--	--	--	--	--	--	--
.22 Magnum	Soft Point	40	25.600	2.020	1.710	1.430	360	260	180	100 yds.	+0.6	+1.3	+1.1	0	100 yds	-0.3	+0.7	+0.8	0
.22 Magnum	Full Jacket	40	25.600	2.020	1.710	1.430	360	260	180	100 yds.	+0.6	+1.3	+1.1	0	100 yds	-0.3	+0.7	+0.8	0

WINCHESTER AMMUNITION

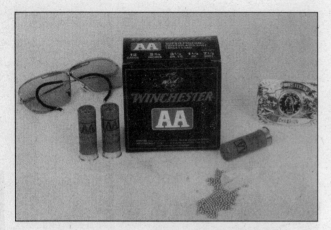

WINCHESTER® HEAVY UPLAND AND AA® SUPER PIGEON LOADS

Winchester Ammunition offers three new AA® Super Pigeon loads to replace previously obsoleted pigeon loads by Winchester. The rounds feature Winchester's time-proven AA components, including a one-piece hull, a plastic one-piece wad, Winchester's famous 209 primer, and clean-burning Ball Powder®. In addition, Winchester has improved the payload with extra-hard copper-plated pellets for hard-hitting performance. The three new loads contain 3 1/4 dram of powder and 1 1/4 oz. of shot in shot sizes 6, 7 1/2, or 8, with a muzzle velocity of 1250 fps. Two 2.75" 12-gauge loads with 1.25 oz. of 7.5 or 8 shot have been added to the popuar Upand line of 12, 16 and 20 gauge shotshells for hunters.

WINCHESTER INTRODUCES WINCLEAN TOTALLY NON-TOXIC CENTERFIRE AMMUNITION

Winchester Ammunition has expanded its offerings of non-lead alternatives for centerfire ammunition with the addition of WinClean to SuperClean™ NT. Both feature soft point bullets using cores made of tin, which is completely safe and totally non-toxic. Tin, in a pistol bullet, performs much like lead and will not ricochet like other non-toxic alternatives. The WinClean first five offerings from Winchester SuperClean NT uses Winchester's lead-free, nickel-plated cup primer, which is very sensitive and ignites well even with light or off-center firing pin hits. Initial WinClean offerings: 115-gr. 9mm, 125-gr. 38 Spl., 165-gr. 40 S&W, 180-gr. 40 S&W, 185-gr. 45 Auto, 230-gr. 45 Auto.

WINCHESTER® INTRODUCES NEW MEDIUM VELOCITY 454 CASULL ROUND

Winchester Ammunition is responding to the introduction of several new guns in the marketplace with the addition of its Super-X® 454 Casull, medium velocity 250-gr., jacketed hollow point round. A recently introduced 454 double-action revolver at a very attractive price is generating a great deal of new interest in this caliber. Other companies may introduce similar guns in 1999.

The new load from Winchester delivers a 250-gr. bullet at 1300 fps with 938 ft.-lb. of energy and will be an excellent practice round with reduced recoil. It will also be a good hunting round choice with plenty of power for medium sized big game like whitetail deer. The energy level of this medium velocity compares to other loads as follows:

Load	Muzzle Energy (Ft-Lbs)
454 Casull 260 Partition	1871
New 454 Casull 250 JHP	938
44 Remington Magnum 240 HSP	741

WINCHESTER AMMUNITION

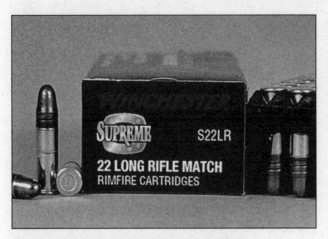

WINCHESTER® INTRODUCES NEW SUPREME® 22LR MATCH AMMUNITION

Winchester Ammunition has a new offering for the high-end match grade 22 rimfire ammunition category with a new Supreme Match 22 long rifle cartridge. The new Winchester Supreme Match 22 long rifle ammunition is produced to the quality and performance standards shooters have come to expect from Winchester Supreme ammunition.

The new load was originally designed by the Australian division of Winchester. Rimfire ammunition developments at this facility include the Winchester 22 Power-Point round that is popular with 22 target shooters and varmint hunters.

The Supreme 22 match was designed for outstanding accuracy. Each case is blade trimmed for greater consistency of bullet pull and overall length. The propellant is a graded ball powder that ensures consistent ignition and pressures. A 40-gr. lubricated bullet is selected from batch lots produced on state-of-the-art presses. The bullet is annealed and aged for greater molecular stability, resulting in optimum accuracy. Velocity is a consistent 1080 fps at the muzzle.

WINCHESTER® IMPROVES PROVEN DESIGN WITH SUPREME® HIGH VELOCITY POWER-POINT® PLUS CENTERFIRE RIFLE AMMUNITION

After several years of unprecedented success with its Supreme Centerfire product line, Winchester Ammunition is breaking the Supreme price barrier in 1999. Winchester is offering the "ultimate" deer load at an affordable price level, but with Supreme features and benefits. The new line, Supreme High Velocity Power-Point Plus, combines the dependability of the known and respected Power-Point bullet with the improved aspects of Supreme.

The workhorse Power-Point line was developed by Winchester almost 40 years ago to deal with then-common problems in centerfire rifle ammunition of inconsistent bullet performance and related bullet failure. The Power-Point bullet design offers an exposed soft lead-alloy nose with a strategically notched metal jacket with controlled expansion for a massive energy release and good weight retention.

The new moly coat on the bullet reduces copper fouling and helps increase velocities about 100 fps over the Super-X loadings. Down-range performance and knockdown power will get a substantial boost.

Initial offerings in the new Supreme line will include:

CARTRIDGE	SYMBOL	BULLET WT. GRS.
223 Remington	SHV223R2	64
243 Winchester	SHV2432	100
270 Winchester	SHV2705	130
7mm Remington Mag.	SHV7MMR1	150
30-30 Winchester	SHV30306	150
30-06 Springfield	SHV30064	180
300 Winchester Mag.	SHV30WM2	180
308 Winchester	SHV3085	150

WINCHESTER® EXPANDS SUPREME® LINE WITH .22 HORNET

In 1998 Winchester Ammunition added several products designed for varmint hunting to the Supreme line. For 1999, Winchester continues the trend with a new 22 Hornet Supreme moly-coated bullet cartridge that will be the fastest Hornet offered commercially and more bad news for varmints everywhere. The new Winchester load develops a muzzle velocity of 3050 fps, with a 34-grain hollowpoint bullet, compared to the standard Hornet velocity of 2690 fps.

WINCHESTER AMMUNITION

WINCHESTER® EXPANDS 7MM LINES FOR 1999

The popularity of 7mm guns and ammo has prompted Winchester to add 7mm STW cartridges under both the Supreme and Super-X banners. In Supreme, Winchester presents a Ballistic Silvertip 140-gr. bullet and a Fail Safe 160-gr. entry. Both come in nickel-plated cases. The Ballistic Silvertip is Lubalox coated, while the Fail Safe version wears a moly coat. The Super-X line now includes a 7mm STW 150-gr. Power-Point bullet in a brass case.

The 7mm STW was developed by Shooting Times Field Editor, Layne Simpson. The round has velocities 200-300 fps higher than the 7mm Remington Mag. The Ballistic Silvertip and Fail Safe bullets are perfectly designed for this high-performance round.

NEW SUPREME® PARTITION GOLD™ BULLET NOW AVAILABLE IN 45-70

Shooters and hunters are seeing a resurgence of some old calibers and one of the most popular is the 45-70. Several gun companies are now offering rifles in this caliber.

The 45-70 has also become popular among guides who carry a backup rifle for dangerous game. Many of these guides have modified lever-action guns with shorter ported barrels, but still use outdated rifle bullets or even cartridges with conventional handgun bullets.

Winchester Ammunition has introduced a new 300-gr. Partition Gold bullet that is perfect for these guide guns and hunting in general. The bullet delivers both expansion and penetration.

The bullet is a flat-nosed design that mushrooms like the Partition handgun bullet. Retained weight, superior penetration, and bullet integrity will make it a popular choice for all big game.

WINCHESTER® AND NOSLER® INC. TEAM UP ON A NEW SUPREME 308 COMPETITION LOAD

Winchester Ammunition and Nosler, Inc. continue to produce outstanding products through their alliance.

The latest product from the Winchester and Nosler team is a new 308 competition round in the Supreme rifle cartridge line. This load utilizes a brand new 168-gr. "J-Y" hollow point boattail bullet developed by Nosler. The extremely concentric and uniform J4 bullet jacket is famous among benchrest shooters.

Seven items now in the Winchester line have been converted to seasonal items in 1999:

CARTRIDGE	SYMBOL	BULLET WT. GRS.	BULLET TYPE
284 Winchester	X2842	150	Power-Point
300 H&H Magnum	S300HX	180	Fail Safe®
*32-20 Winchester	X32201	100	Lead
356 Winchester	X3561	200	Power-Point
375 Winchester	X375W	200	Power-Point
375 H&H Magnum	X375HX	270	Fail Safe
375 H&H Magnum	S375HXA	300	Fail Safe

WINCHESTER AMMUNITION

SUPERCLEAN NT™ (NON-TOXIC)
REDUCED HAZARD AMMUNITION

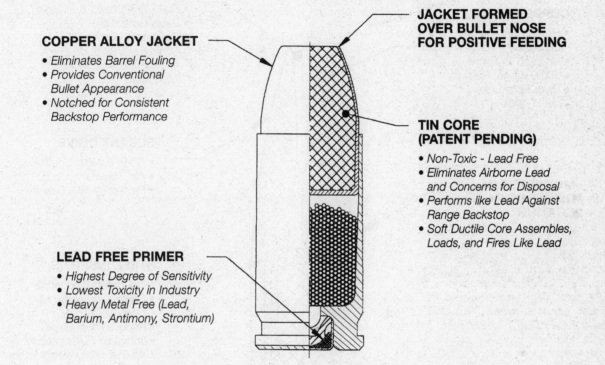

COPPER ALLOY JACKET
- *Eliminates Barrel Fouling*
- *Provides Conventional Bullet Appearance*
- *Notched for Consistent Backstop Performance*

JACKET FORMED OVER BULLET NOSE FOR POSITIVE FEEDING

TIN CORE (PATENT PENDING)
- *Non-Toxic - Lead Free*
- *Eliminates Airborne Lead and Concerns for Disposal*
- *Performs like Lead Against Range Backstop*
- *Soft Ductile Core Assembles, Loads, and Fires Like Lead*

LEAD FREE PRIMER
- *Highest Degree of Sensitivity*
- *Lowest Toxicity in Industry*
- *Heavy Metal Free (Lead, Barium, Antimony, Strontium)*

SUPERCLEAN NT™ CARTRIDGES ASSEMBLED WITH TIN CORE PROJECTILES AND LEAD-FREE PRIMERS COST-EFFECTIVE CHOICE FOR TRAINING APPLICATIONS

CALIBER	BULLET WT. (GRAINS)	MUZZLE VELOCITY (FPS)
9mm Luger	105	1200
38 SPL	110	975
357 MAG	110	1650
40 S&W	140	1200
45 AUTO	140	1050
5.56mm	55	3150
357 SIG	105	1350

9MM LUGER (1005) TIN ACCURACY AND CENTER OF IMPACT TESTING VS. 9MM LUGER (115) FMJ Q4239
3x10 SHOT TARGETS AT 50 YARDS

	E.S. (IN)	MISMATCH (IN)	(MILS)
9mm Luger (105) TIN	0.86"	0.2"	0.11"
9mm Luger (115) FMJ	3.55"	–	–

WINCHESTER AMMUNITION

SUPREME® FAIL SAFE®

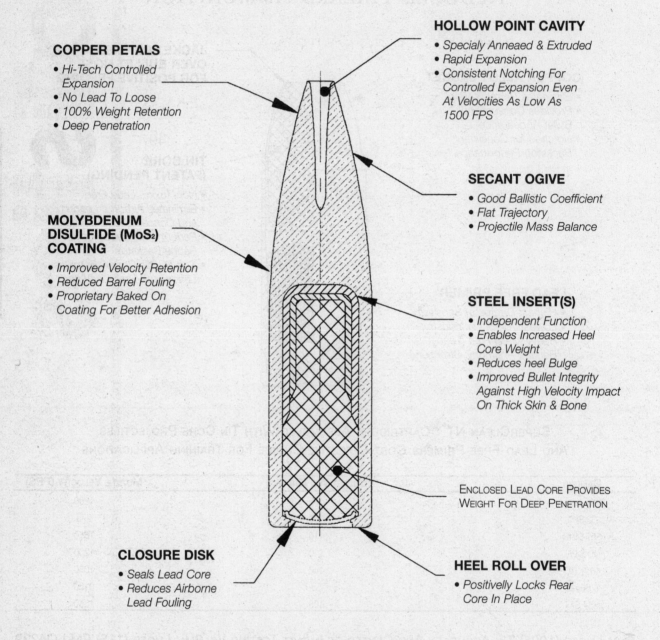

HOLLOW POINT CAVITY
- Specialy Anneaed & Extruded
- Rapid Expansion
- Consistent Notching For Controlled Expansion Even At Velocities As Low As 1500 FPS

COPPER PETALS
- Hi-Tech Controlled Expansion
- No Lead To Loose
- 100% Weight Retention
- Deep Penetration

SECANT OGIVE
- Good Ballistic Coefficient
- Flat Trajectory
- Projectile Mass Balance

MOLYBDENUM DISULFIDE (MoS2) COATING
- Improved Velocity Retention
- Reduced Barrel Fouling
- Proprietary Baked On Coating For Better Adhesion

STEEL INSERT(S)
- Independent Function
- Enables Increased Heel Core Weight
- Reduces heel Bulge
- Improved Bullet Integrity Against High Velocity Impact On Thick Skin & Bone

ENCLOSED LEAD CORE PROVIDES WEIGHT FOR DEEP PENETRATION

CLOSURE DISK
- Seals Lead Core
- Reduces Airborne Lead Fouling

HEEL ROLL OVER
- Positivelly Locks Rear Core In Place

FAIL SAFE DESIGN ENABLES USE OF LIGHTWEIGHT BULLETS
FOR FLATTER TRAJECTORY AND DEEP PENETRATION WITHIN A GIVEN CALIBER

Ballistics

CENTERFIRE PISTOL & REVOLVER BALLISTICS

Federal	499
Remington	514

CENTER RIFLE BALLISTICS

A-Square	496
Dakota Arms	497
Federal	498, 500-502
Lazzeroni	497
Norma	503-505
PMC	506-509
Remington	510
Sako	515
Weatherby	516
Winchester	517, 518

SHOTSHELL BALLISTICS

Federal	487

A-SQUARE BALLISTICS

Cartridge	Weight	Type	Velocity (fps) Mzl.	100	200	300	400	500	Energy (ft. lbs.) Mzl.	100	200	300	400	500	Bullet Path Mzl.	100	200	300	400	500
.22 PPC	52	BERGER	3300	2952	2629	2329	2049		1257	1006	798	626	485		-1.50	+1.26	ZERO	-6.27	-19.06	
6mm PPC	68	BERGER	3100	2751	2428	2128	1850		1451	1143	890	684	516		-1.50	+1.55	ZERO	-7.52	-22.64	
7mm REM	175	MONO	2860	2557	2273	2008	1771		3178	2540	2008	1567	1219		-1.50	+1.92	ZERO	-8.68	-25.89	
7mm STW	140	NOS B-TIP	3450	3254	3067	2888	2715	2550	3700	3291	2924	2592	2292	2021	-1.50	+2.42	+3.04	ZERO	-7.27	-19.23
7mm STW	160	NOS PAR	3250	3071	2900	2735	2576	2422	3752	3351	2987	2657	2357	2084	-1.50	+2.83	+3.50	ZERO	-8.16	-21.45
7mm STW	160	SBT	3250	3087	2930	2778	2631	2490	3752	3385	3049	2741	2460	2202	-1.50	+2.78	+3.42	ZERO	-7.97	-20.92
.30-06	180	M & D-T	2700	2365	2054	1769	1524		2913	2235	1687	1251	928		-1.50	+2.39	ZERO	-10.64	-32.41	
.30-06	220	MONO	2380	2108	1854	1623	1424		2767	2171	1679	1287	990		-1.50	+3.14	ZERO	-13.56	-39.90	
.300 WIN	180	M & D-T	3120	2756	2420	2108	1820		3890	3035	2340	1776	1324		-1.50	+1.55	ZERO	-7.57	-22.90	
.300 WBY	180	M & D-T	3180	2811	2471	2155	1863		4041	3158	2440	1856	1387		-1.50	+1.46	ZERO	-7.21	-21.85	
.300 WBY	220	MONO	2700	2407	2133	1877	1653		3561	2830	2223	1721	1334		-1.50	+2.28	ZERO	-9.82	-29.75	
.300 PEG	180	SBT	3500	3319	3145	2978	2817	2663	4896	4401	3953	3544	3172	2833	-1.50	+2.28	+2.89	ZERO	-6.79	-18.04
.300 PEG	180	NOS PAR	3500	3295	3100	2913	2734	2563	4896	4339	3840	3392	2988	2624	-1.50	+2.34	+2.96	ZERO	-7.10	-18.86
.300 PEG	180	M & D-T	3500	3103	2740	2405	2095		4896	3848	3001	2312	1753		-1.50	+1.06	ZERO	-5.70	-17.51	
8mm REM	220	MONO	2800	2501	2221	1959	1718		3829	3055	2409	1875	1442		-1.50	+2.05	ZERO	-9.10	-27.56	
.338-06	200	NOS B-TIP	2750	2553	2364	2184	2011		3358	2894	2482	2118	1796		-1.50	+1.90	ZERO	-8.22	-23.63	
.338-06	250	SBT	2500	2374	2252	2134	2019		3496	3129	2816	2528	2263		-1.50	+2.36	ZERO	-9.27	-26.01	
.338-06	250	D T	2500	2222	1963	1724	1507		3496	2742	2139	1649	1261		-1.50	+2.78	ZERO	-11.90	-35.51	
.338 WIN	250	SBT	2700	2568	2439	2314	2193	2075	4046	3659	3302	2972	2669	2390	-1.50	+4.44	+5.15	ZERO	-11.73	-30.62
.338 WIN	250	TRIAD	2700	2407	2133	1877	1653		4046	3216	2526	1956	1516		-1.50	+2.28	ZERO	-9.82	-29.75	
.340 WBY	250	SBT	2820	2684	2552	2424	2299	2179	4414	3999	3615	3261	2935	2635	-1.50	+3.98	+4.63	ZERO	-10.57	-27.82
.340 WBY	250	TRIAD	2820	2520	2238	1976	1741		4414	3524	2781	2166	1683		-1.50	+2.00	ZERO	-8.98	-26.79	
.338 A-SQ	200	NOS B-TIP	3500	3266	3045	2835	2634	2442	5440	4737	4117	3568	3081	2648	-1.50	+2.42	+3.08	ZERO	-7.46	
.338 A-SQ	250	SBT	3120	2974	2834	2697	2565	2436	5403	4911	4457	4038	3652	3295	-1.50	+3.07	+3.72	ZERO	-8.47	-22.10
.338 A-SQ	250	TRIAD	3120	2799	2500	2220	1958		5403	4348	3469	2736	2128		-1.50	+1.49	ZERO	-7.05	-20.37	
.338 EXCALBR	200	NOS B-TIP	3600	3361	3134	2920	2715	2520	5755	5015	4363	3785	3274	2820	-1.50	+2.23	2.87	ZERO	-6.99	-18.67
.338 EXCALBR	250	SBT	3250	3101	2958	2819	2684	2553	5863	5339	4855	4410	3998	3618	-1.50	+2.72	3.35	ZERO	-7.78	-20.35
.338 EXCALBR	250	TRIAD	3250	2922	2618	2333	2066	1818	5863	4740	3804	3021	2370	1834	-1.50	+1.30	ZERO	-6.35	-19.20	-40.10
.358 NORMA	275	TRIAD	2700	2394	2108	1842	1653		4451	3498	2713	2072	1668		-1.50	+2.32	ZERO	-10.06	-29.75	
.358 STA	275	TRIAD	2850	2562	2292	2039	1764		4959	4009	3208	2539	1899		-1.50	+1.90	ZERO	-8.58	-26.11	
9.3x62	286	TRIAD	2360	2089	1844	1623	1369		3538	2771	2157	1670	1189		-1.50	+3.04	ZERO	-13.12	-42.16	
9.3x64	286	TRIAD	2700	2391	2103	1835	1602		4629	3630	2808	2139	1631		-1.50	+2.33	ZERO	-10.11	-30.77	
9.3x74R	286	TRIAD	2360	2089	1844	1623			3538	2771	2157	1670			-.90	+3.61	ZERO	-14.02		
.375 H&H	300	SBT	2550	2415	2284	2157	2034	1914	4331	3884	3474	3098	2755	2441	-1.50	+5.24	+5.99	ZERO	-13.33	-34.26
.375 H&H	300	TRIAD	2550	2251	1973	1717	1496		4331	3375	2592	1964	1491		-1.50	+2.70	ZERO	-11.72	-35.13	
.375 WBY	300	SBT	2700	2560	2425	2293	2166	2043	4856	4366	3916	3503	3125	2779	-1.50	+4.49	+5.22	ZERO	-11.91	-31.08
.375 WBY	300	TRIAD	2700	2391	2103	1835	1602		4856	3808	2946	2243	1710		-1.50	+2.33	ZERO	-10.11	-30.77	
.375 JRS	300	SBT	2700	2560	2425	2293	2166	2043	4856	4366	3916	3503	3125	2779	-1.50	+4.49	+5.22	ZERO	-11.91	-31.08
.375 JRS	300	TRIAD	2700	2391	2103	1835	1602		4856	3808	2946	2243	1710		-1.50	+2.33	ZERO	-10.11	-30.77	
.375 A-SQ	300	SBT	2920	2773	2631	2494	2360	2231	5679	5123	4611	4142	3710	3314	-1.50	+3.70	+4.36	ZERO	-9.80	-26.01
.375 A-SQ	300	TRIAD	2920	2596	2294	2012	1762		5679	4488	3505	2698	2068		-1.50	+1.83	ZERO	-8.49	-25.49	
.378 WBY	300	SBT	2900	2754	2612	2475	2342	2214	5602	5051	4546	4081	3655	3264	-1.50	+3.76	+4.41	ZERO	-9.99	-26.47
.378 WBY	300	TRIAD	2900	2577	2276	1997	1747		5602	4424	3452	2656	2034		-1.50	+1.87	ZERO	-8.69	-25.92	
.450/.400 (3")	400	TRIAD	2150	1910	1690	1490			4105	3241	2537	1972			-.90	+4.39	ZERO	-16.52		
.450/.400 (3¼")	400	TRIAD	2150	1910	1690	1490			4105	3241	2537	1972			-.90	+4.39	ZERO	-16.52		
.416 TAYLOR	400	TRIAD	2350	2093	1853	1634	1443		4905	3892	3049	2371	1849		-1.50	+3.19	ZERO	-13.62	-39.83	
.416 REM	400	TRIAD	2380	2122	1879	1658	1464		5031	3998	3136	2440	1903		-1.50	+3.08	ZERO	-13.22	-38.71	
.416 HOFF	400	TRIAD	2380	2122	1879	1658	1464		5031	3998	3136	2440	1903		-1.50	+3.08	ZERO	-13.22	-38.71	
.416 RIMMED	400	TRIAD	2400	2140	1897	1673			5115	4069	3194	2487			-.90	+3.31	ZERO	-13.19		
.416 RIGBY	400	TRIAD	2400	2140	1897	1673	1478		5115	4069	3194	2487	1940		-1.50	+3.02	ZERO	-12.95	-37.99	
.416 WBY	400	TRIAD	2600	2328	2073	1834	1624		6004	4813	3816	2986	2343		-1.50	+2.49	ZERO	-10.49	-31.56	
.404 JEFFERY	400	TRIAD	2150	1901	1674	1468	1299		4105	3211	2489	1915	1499		-1.50	+4.14	ZERO	-16.45	-49.10	
.425 EXPRESS	400	TRIAD	2400	2136	1888	1662	1465		5115	4052	3167	2454	1906		-1.50	+3.09	ZERO	-13.07	-38.34	
.458 WIN	465	TRIAD	2220	1999	1791	1601	1433		5088	4127	3312	2646	2121		-1.50	+3.57	ZERO	-14.69	-42.46	
.450 N.E. (3¼")	465	TRIAD	2190	1970	1765	1577			4952	4009	3216	2567			-.90	+4.33	ZERO	-15.40		
.450 #2	465	TRIAD	2190	1970	1765	1577			4952	4009	3216	2567			-.90	+4.33	ZERO	-15.40		
.458 LOTT	465	TRIAD	2380	2150	1932	1730	1551		5848	4773	3855	3091	2485		-1.50	+2.99	ZERO	-12.46	-36.45	
.450 ACKLEY	465	TRIAD	2400	2169	1950	1747	1567		5947	4857	3927	3150	2534		-1.50	+2.93	ZERO	-12.17	-35.75	
.460 SH. A-SQ.	500	TRIAD	2420	2198	1987	1789	1613		6501	5362	4385	3553	2890		-1.50	+2.87	ZERO	-11.59	-34.25	
.460 WBY	500	TRIAD	2580	2349	2131	1923	1737		7389	6126	5040	4107	3351		-1.50	+2.43	ZERO	-9.96	-29.45	
.500/.465 N.E.	480	TRIAD	2150	1928	1722	1533			4926	3960	3160	2505			-.90	+4.28	ZERO	-16.03		
.470 N.E.	500	TRIAD	2150	1912	1693	1494			5132	4058	3182	2478			-.90	+4.38	ZERO	-16.48		
.470 CAP	500	TRIAD	2400	2172	1958	1761	1553		6394	5236	4255	3445	2678		-1.50	+2.91	ZERO	-11.88	-36.06	
.475 #2 N.E.	480	TRIAD	2200	1964	1744	1544			5158	4109	3240	2539			-.90	+4.09	ZERO	-15.63		
.475 #2 JEFF	500	TRIAD	2200	1966	1748	1550			5373	4291	3392	2666			-.90	+4.07	ZERO	-15.58		
.505 GIBBS	525	TRIAD	2300	2063	1840	1637			6166	4962	3948	3122			-.90	+3.61	ZERO	-14.18		
.500 N.E. (3")	570	TRIAD	2150	1928	1722	1533			5850	4703	3752	2975			-.90	+4.28	ZERO	-16.03		
.495 A-SQ	570	TRIAD	2350	2117	1896	1693	1513		6989	5671	4552	3629	2899		-1.50	+3.10	ZERO	-13.02	-37.83	
.500 A-SQ	600	TRIAD	2470	2235	2013	1804	1620		8127	6654	5397	4336	3495		-1.50	+2.74	ZERO	-11.29	-33.47	
.577 N.E.	750	TRIAD	2050	1811	1595	1401			6998	5463	4234	3267			-.90	+4.94	ZERO	-18.48		
.577 TYRNSR	750	TRIAD	2460	2197	1950	1723	1516		10077	8039	6335	4941	3825		-1.50	+2.85	ZERO	-12.12	-35.95	
.600 N.E.	900	TRIAD	1950	1680	1452	1336			7596	5634	4212	3564			-.90	+5.61	ZERO	-20.74		
.700 N.E.	1000	MONO	1900	1669	1461	1288			8015	6188	4740	3685			-.90	+5.78	ZERO	-22.22		

DAKOTA ARMS BALLISTICS

BALLISTIC COMPARISONS

7mm Dakota	140 Gr.	160 Gr.
7mm Dakota	3400	3200
280 Rem	3000	2840
7 Rem Mag	3150	2950
7MM Wea	3225	3100

300 Dakota	165 Gr.	180 Gr.	200 Gr.
300 Dakota	3250	3200	3050
30-06	2800	2700	2600
300 Win	3100	2960	2825
300 Wea	3200	3120	2950

330 Dakota	225 Gr.	250Gr.
330 Dakota	3000	2900
338 Win	2785	2660
340 Wea	2950	2850

375 Dakota	270 Gr.	300 Gr.
375 Dakota	2850	2650
375 HH	2690	2530

416 Dakota	400 Gr.
416 Dakota	2550
416 Rig	2370
416 Rem	2400

450 Dakota	500 Gr.
450 Dakota	2550
458 Win	2040
458 Lott	2300

LAZZERONI BALLISTICS

CARTRIDGE	BULLET		VELOCITY in Feet per Second						ENERGY In Foot-Pounds						PATH OF BULLET Above or below line-of-sight of riflescopes mounted 1.5" above bore				
Cartridge	Weight Grains	Bullet Type	Muzzle	100 Yards	200 Yards	300 Yards	400 Yards	500 Yards	Muzzle	100 Yards	200 Yards	300 Yards	400 Yards	500 Yards	100 Yards	200 Yards	300 Yards	400 Yards	500 Yards
6.53 (.257) SCRAMJET™	85	B/T	3960	3652	3365	3096	2844	2605	2961	2517	2137	1810	1526	1281	1.7	2.4	0.0	−6.0	−16.4
	100	PART	3740	3465	3208	2965	2735	2516	3106	2667	2285	1953	1661	1406	2.1	2.7	0.0	−6.7	−17.9
7.21 (7mm/.284) FIREHAWK™	140	PART	3580	3349	3130	2923	2724	2534	3985	3488	3048	2656	2308	1997	2.2	2.9	0.0	−7.0	−18.6
	160	A/FR	3385	3167	2961	2763	2574	2393	4072	3565	3115	2713	2354	2034	2.6	3.3	0.0	−7.8	−20.9
7.82 (.308) WARBIRD™	150	PART	3680	3432	3197	2975	2764	2563	4512	3923	3406	2949	2546	2188	2.1	2.7	0.0	−6.6	−17.9
	180	PART	3425	3220	3026	2839	2661	2489	4689	4147	3661	3224	2831	2477	2.5	3.2	0.0	−7.5	−19.8
	200	A/FR	3290	3105	2928	2758	2594	2435	4808	4283	3808	3378	2988	2635	2.7	3.4	0.0	−7.9	−21.1
8.59 (.338) TITAN™	200	B/T	3430	3211	3002	2803	2613	2430	5226	4579	4004	3491	3033	2624	2.5	3.2	0.0	−7.6	−20.3
	225	PART	3235	3031	2836	2650	2471	2299	5229	4591	4021	3510	3052	2642	3.0	3.6	0.0	−8.6	−22.9
	250	A/FR	3100	2908	2725	2549	2379	2216	5336	4697	4123	3607	3143	2726	3.3	4.0	0.0	−9.3	−24.8
10.57 (.416) METEOR™	400	A/FR	2730	2532	2342	2161	1987	1823	6621	5695	4874	4147	3508	2951	1.9	0.0	−8.3	−24.0	−48.7

PART = Partition*   A/FR = Swift A-Frame   B/T = Ballistic Tip*

Note: This table was calculated by computer using a standard modern technique to predict trajectories and recoil energies from the best available cartridge data. Figures shown are expected to be reasonably accurate; however, the shooter is cautioned that performance will vary because of variations in rifles, ammunition, atmospheric conditions and altitude. Velocities were determined using 27-inch barrels; shorter barrels will reduce velocity by 30 to 85 fps per inch of barrel removed. Trajectories were computed with the line-of-sight 1.5 inches above the bore centerline. *B.C.:* Ballistic Coefficient supplied by the bullet manufacturers. Partition and Ballistic Tip are registered trademarks of Nosler, Inc.

BALLISTICS

FEDERAL RIFLE BALLISTICS

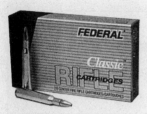

If you're looking for depth of choice in a quality ammunition, you've come to the right place. Twenty-eight calibers, five bullet types, and over 75 years of reliability add up to one thing - the Classic Centerfire line. From flat-and-fast varmint loads, to the .45-70 Government, there is something here for every rifle shooter. And each load has all the right ingredients for success, from high-quality Hi-Shok and Sierra Pro-Hunter bullets, down to our specially selected powders, hot primers and famous brass casings.

CLASSIC® CENTERFIRE RIFLE

Usage	Federal Load No.	Caliber	Bullet Wgt. In Grains	Bullet Wgt. In Grams	Bullet Style**	Factory Primer No.	Velocity In Feet Per Second (To Nearest 10 FPS) Muzzle	100Yds	200Yds	300Yds	400Yds	500Yds	Energy In Foot-Pounds (To Nearest 5 Foot-Pounds) Muzzle	100Yds	200Yds	300Yds	400Yds	500Yds
1	222A	222 Rem. (5.56x43mm)	50	3.24	Hi-Shok Soft Point	205	3140	2600	2120	1700	1350	1110	1095	750	500	320	200	135
5	222B	222 Rem. (5.56x43mm)	55	3.56	FMJ Boat-Tail	205	3020	2740	2480	2230	1990	1780	1115	915	750	610	485	385
1	223A	223 Rem. (5.56x45mm)	55	3.56	Hi-Shok Soft Point	205	3240	2750	2300	1910	1550	1270	1280	920	650	445	295	195
5	223B	223 Rem. (5.56x45mm)	55	3.56	FMJ Boat-Tail	205	3240	2950	2670	2410	2170	1940	1280	1060	875	710	575	460
1	22250A	22-250 Rem.	55	3.56	Hi-Shok Soft Point	210	3680	3140	2660	2220	1830	1490	1655	1200	860	605	410	270
1	243AS	243 Win. (6.18x51mm)	80	5.18	Sierra Pro-Hunter SP	210	3350	2960	2590	2260	1950	1670	1995	1550	1195	905	675	495
2	243B	243 Win. (6.18x51mm)	100	6.48	Hi-Shok Soft Point	210	2960	2700	2450	2220	1990	1790	1945	1615	1330	1090	880	710
1	6AS	6mm Rem.	80	5.18	Sierra Pro-Hunter SP	210	3470	3060	2690	2350	2040	1750	2140	1665	1290	980	735	540
2	6B	6mm Rem.	100	6.48	Hi-Shok Soft Point	210	3100	2830	2570	2330	2100	1890	2135	1775	1470	1205	985	790
2	2506BS	25-06 Rem.	117	7.58	Sierra Pro-Hunter SP	210	2990	2730	2480	2250	2030	1830	2320	1985	1645	1350	1100	885
2	270A	270 Win.	130	8.42	Hi-Shok Soft Point	210	3060	2800	2560	2330	2110	1900	2700	2265	1890	1565	1285	1045
2	270B	270 Win.	150	9.72	Hi-Shok Soft Point RN	210	2850	2500	2180	1890	1620	1390	2705	2085	1585	1185	870	640
2	270GS	270 Win.	130	8.42	Sierra Pro-Hunter SP	210	3060	2830	2600	2390	2190	2000	2705	2305	1960	1655	1390	1155
2	6555B	6.5x55 Swedish	140	9.07	Hi-Shok Soft Point	210	2600	2400	2220	2040	1860	1700	2100	1795	1525	1285	1080	900
2	7A	7mm Mauser (7x57mm Mauser)	175	11.34	Hi-Shok Soft Point RN	210	2440	2140	1860	1600	1380	1200	2315	1775	1340	1000	740	565
2	7B	7mm Mauser (7x57mm Mauser)	140	9.07	Sierra Pro-Hunter SP	210	2660	2450	2260	2070	1890	1730	2200	1865	1585	1330	1110	930
2	708CS	7mm-08 Rem.	150	9.72	Sierra Pro-Hunter SP	210	2650	2440	2230	2040	1860	1690	2340	1980	1660	1390	1150	950
2	280B	280 Rem.	150	9.72	Hi-Shok Soft Point	210	2890	2670	2460	2260	2060	1880	2780	2370	2015	1695	1420	1180
2	280CS	280 Rem.	140	9.07	Sierra Pro-Hunter SP	210	2990	2740	2500	2270	2060	1860	2770	2325	1940	1605	1320	1070
2	7RA	7mm Rem. Magnum	150	9.72	Hi-Shok Soft Point	215	3110	2830	2570	2320	2090	1870	3220	2670	2200	1790	1450	1160
3	7RB	7mm Rem. Magnum	175	11.34	Hi-Shok Soft Point	215	2860	2650	2440	2240	2060	1880	3180	2720	2310	1960	1640	1370
3	7RJS	7mm Rem. Magnum	160	10.37	Sierra Pro-Hunter SP	215	2940	2730	2520	2320	2140	1960	3070	2640	2260	1920	1620	1360
1	30CA	30 Carbine (7.62x33mm)	110	7.13	Hi-Shok Soft Point RN	205	1990	1570	1240	1040	920	840	965	600	375	260	210	175
2	762398	7.62x39mm Soviet	123	7.97	Hi-Shok Soft Point	210	2300	2030	1780	1550	1350	1200	1445	1125	860	655	500	395
2	3030A	30-30 Win.	150	9.72	Hi-Shok Soft Point FN	210	2390	2020	1680	1400	1180	1040	1900	1355	945	650	460	355
2	3030B	30-30 Win.	170	11.01	Hi-Shok Soft Point RN	210	2200	1900	1620	1380	1190	1060	1830	1355	990	720	535	425
1	3030C	30-30 Win.	125	8.10	Hi-Shok Hollow Point	210	2570	2090	1660	1320	1080	960	1830	1210	770	480	320	260
2	3030FS	30-30 Win.	170	11.01	Sierra Pro-Hunter SP	210	2200	1820	1500	1240	1060	960	1830	1255	845	575	425	345
2	300A	300 Savage	150	9.72	Hi-Shok Soft Point	210	2630	2350	2100	1850	1630	1430	2305	1845	1460	1145	885	685
2	300B	300 Savage	180	11.66	Hi-Shok Soft Point	210	2350	2140	1940	1750	1570	1410	2205	1825	1495	1215	985	800
2	308A	308 Win. (7.62x51mm)	150	9.72	Hi-Shok Soft Point	210	2820	2530	2260	2010	1770	1560	2650	2140	1705	1345	1050	810
2	308B	308 Win. (7.62x51mm)	180	11.66	Hi-Shok Soft Point	210	2620	2390	2180	1970	1780	1600	2745	2290	1895	1555	1270	1030
2	308HS	308 Win. (7.62x51mm)	180	11.66	Sierra Pro-Hunter SP	210	2620	2410	2200	2010	1820	1650	2745	2315	1940	1610	1330	1090
2	3006A	30-06 Springfield (7.62x63mm)	150	9.72	Hi-Shok Soft Point	210	2910	2620	2340	2080	1840	1620	2820	2280	1825	1445	1130	875
3	3006B	30-06 Springfield (7.62x63mm)	180	11.66	Hi-Shok Soft Point	210	2700	2470	2250	2040	1850	1660	2915	2435	2025	1665	1360	1105
1	3006CS	30-06 Springfield (7.62x63mm)	125	8.10	Sierra Pro-Hunter SP	210	3140	2780	2450	2140	1850	1600	2735	2145	1660	1270	955	705
3	3006HS	30-06 Springfield (7.62x63mm)	220	14.25	Sierra Pro-Hunter SP RN	210	2410	2130	1870	1630	1420	1250	2835	2215	1705	1300	985	760
3	3006JS	30-06 Springfield (7.62x63mm)	180	11.66	Sierra Pro-Hunter SP RN	210	2700	2350	2020	1730	1470	1250	2915	2200	1630	1190	860	620
2	3006SS	30-06 Springfield (7.62x63mm)	150	9.72	Sierra Pro-Hunter SP	210	2910	2640	2380	2130	1900	1690	2820	2315	1880	1515	1205	950
2	3006TS	30-06 Springfield (7.62x63mm)	165	10.69	Sierra Pro-Hunter SP	210	2800	2560	2340	2130	1920	1730	2875	2410	2005	1655	1360	1100
3	300WBS	300 Win. Magnum	180	11.66	Sierra Pro-Hunter SP	215	2960	2750	2540	2340	2160	1980	3500	3010	2580	2195	1860	1565
2	300WGS	300 Win. Magnum	150	9.72	Sierra Pro-Hunter SP	215	3280	3030	2800	2570	2360	2160	3570	3055	2600	2205	1860	1560
2	303AS	303 British	180	11.66	Sierra Pro-Hunter SP	210	2460	2230	2020	1820	1630	1460	2420	1995	1625	1315	1060	850
2	303B	303 British	150	9.72	Hi-Shok Soft Point	210	2690	2440	2210	1980	1780	1590	2400	1980	1620	1310	1055	840
2	32A	32 Win. Special	170	11.01	Hi-Shok Soft Point	210	2250	1920	1630	1370	1180	1040	1910	1395	1000	710	520	410
2	8A*	8mm Mauser (8x57mm JS Mauser)	170	11.01	Hi-Shok Soft Point	210	2360	1970	1620	1330	1120	1000	2100	1465	995	670	475	375
3	338ES	338 Win. Magnum	225	14.58	Sierra Pro-Hunter SP	215	2780	2570	2360	2170	1980	1800	3860	3290	2780	2340	1960	1630
2	C357G	357 Magnum	180	11.66	Hi-Shok Hollow Point	100	1550	1160	980	860	770	680	960	535	385	295	235	185
2	35A	35 Rem.	200	12.96	Hi-Shok Soft Point	210	2080	1700	1380	1140	1000	910	1920	1280	840	575	445	370
3	375A	375 H&H Magnum	270	17.50	Hi-Shok Soft Point	215	2690	2420	2170	1920	1700	1500	4340	3510	2810	2220	1740	1355
4	375B	375 H&H Magnum	300	19.44	Hi-Shok Soft Point	215	2530	2270	2020	1790	1580	1400	4265	3425	2720	2135	1665	1295
2	C44A	44 Rem. Magnum	240	15.55	Hi-Shok Hollow Point	150	1760	1380	1090	950	860	790	1650	1015	640	485	395	330
2	4570AS	45-70 Government	300	19.44	Sierra Pro-Hunter HP FN	210	1880	1650	1430	1240	1110	1010	2355	1815	1355	1015	810	680

*Only for use in barrels intended for .323 inch diameter bullets. Do not use in 8x57mm J Commission Rifles (M1888) or in sporting or other military arms of .318 inch bore diamter.

**RN = Round Nose SP = Soft Point FN = Flat Nose FMJ = Full Metal Jacket HP = Hollow Point

Usage Key: 1 = Varmints, predators, small game 2 = Medium game 3 = Large, heavy game 4 = Dangerous game 5 = Target shooting, training, practice 6 = Self Defense

FEDERAL BALLISTICS

Federal offers what may be the industry's most comprehensive lineup of handgun ammunition. A wide assortment of bullet profiles and weights, in a broad range of calibers, assures that there is a Classic load for every situation, from self-defense to hunting to target shooting.

CLASSIC BULLET STYLES

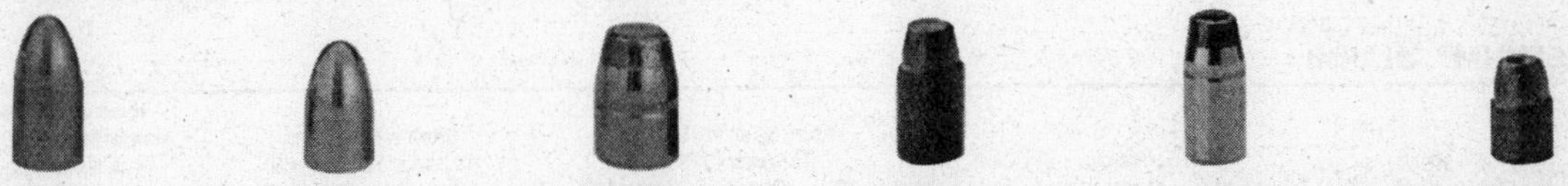

| Lead Round Nose | Full Metal Jacket | Hi-Shok Jacketed Soft Point | Lead Semi-Wadcutter | Hi-Shok Jacketed Hollow Point | Semi-Wadcutter Hollow Point |

CLASSIC® AUTOMATIC PISTOL

Usage	Federal Load No.	Caliber	Bullet Wgt. In Grains	Bullet Wgt. In Grams	Bullet Style*	Factory Primer No.	Velocity Muzzle	25Yds	50Yds	75Yds	100Yds	Energy Muzzle	25Yds	50 Yds	75Yds	100Yds	Mid-Range 25Yds	50Yds	75Yds	100Yds	Test Barrel Length Inches
5,6	C25AP	25 Auto (6.35mm Browning)	50	3.24	Full Metal Jacket	200	760	750	730	720	700	65	60	60	55	55	0.5	1.9	4.5	8.1	2
5,6	C32AP	32 Auto (7.65mm Browning)	71	4.60	Full Metal Jacket	100	910	880	860	830	810	130	120	115	110	105	0.3	1.4	3.2	5.9	4
5,6	C380AP	380 Auto (9x17mm Short)	95	6.15	Full Metal Jacket	100	960	910	870	830	790	190	175	160	145	130	0.3	1.3	3.1	5.8	3¾
6	C380BP	380 Auto (9x17mm Short)	90	5.83	Hi-Shok JHP	100	1000	940	890	840	800	200	175	160	140	130	0.3	1.2	2.9	5.5	3¾
6	C9MKB	9mm Makarov (9x18 Makarov)	90	5.83	Hi-Shok JHP	100	990	950	910	880	850	195	180	165	155	145	0.3	1.2	2.9	5.3	3¾
5,6	C9AP	9mm Luger (9x19mm Parabellum)	124	8.03	Full Metal Jacket	100	1120	1070	1030	990	960	345	315	290	270	255	0.2	0.9	2.2	4.1	4
6	C9BP	9mm Luger (9x19mm Parabellum)	115	7.45	Hi-Shok JHP	100	1160	1100	1060	1020	990	345	310	285	270	250	0.2	0.9	2.1	3.8	4
6	C9MS	9mm Luger (9x19mm Parabellum)	147	9.52	Hi-Shok JHP	100	980	950	930	900	880	310	295	285	265	255	0.3	1.2	2.8	5.1	4
6	C357S2	357 Sig	125	8.10	Full Metal Jacket	100	1350	1270	1190	1130	1080	510	445	395	355	325	0.2	0.7	1.6	3.1	4
6	C40SWA	40 S&W	180	11.66	Hi-Shok JHP	100	990	960	930	910	890	390	365	345	330	315	0.3	1.2	2.8	5.0	4
6	C40SWB	40 S&W	155	10.04	Hi-Shok JHP	100	1140	1080	1030	990	950	445	400	365	335	315	0.2	0.9	2.2	4.1	4
6	C10C	10mm Auto	180	11.66	Hi-Shok JHP	150	1030	1000	970	950	920	425	400	375	355	340	0.3	1.1	2.5	4.7	5
6	C10E	10mm Auto	155	10.04	Hi-Shok JHP	150	1330	1230	1140	1080	1030	605	515	450	400	360	0.2	0.7	1.8	3.3	5
6	C45A	45 Auto	230	14.90	Full Metal Jacket	150	850	830	810	790	770	370	350	335	320	305	0.4	1.6	3.6	6.6	5
6	C45C	45 Auto	185	11.99	Hi-Shok JHP	150	950	920	900	880	860	370	350	335	315	300	0.3	1.3	2.9	5.3	5
6	C45D	45 Auto	230	14.90	Hi-Shok JHP	150	850	830	810	790	770	370	350	335	320	300	0.4	1.6	3.7	6.7	5

*JHP = Jacketed Hollow Point

CLASSIC® REVOLVER

Usage	Federal Load No.	Caliber	Bullet Wgt. In Grains	Bullet Wgt. In Grams	Bullet Style*	Factory Primer No.	Velocity Muzzle	25Yds	50Yds	75Yds	100Yds	Energy Muzzle	25Yds	50 Yds	75Yds	100Yds	Mid-Range 25Yds	50Yds	75Yds	100Yds	Test Barrel Length Inches
5	C32LA	32 S&W Long	98	6.35	Lead Wadcutter	100	780	700	630	560	500	130	105	85	70	55	0.5	2.2	5.6	11.1	4
5	C32LB	32 S&W Long	98	6.35	Lead Round Nose	100	710	690	670	650	640	115	105	100	95	90	0.6	2.3	5.3	9.6	4
6	C32HRA	32 H&R Magnum	95	6.15	Lead Semi-Wadcutter	100	1030	1000	940	930	900	225	210	195	185	170	0.3	1.1	2.5	4.7	4½
6	C32HRB	32 H&R Magnum	85	5.50	Hi-Shok JHP	100	1100	1050	1020	970	930	230	210	195	175	165	0.2	1.0	2.3	4.3	4½
5	C38B	38 Special	158	10.23	Lead Round Nose	100	760	740	720	710	690	200	190	185	175	170	0.5	2.0	4.6	8.3	4-V
5,6	C38C	38 Special	158	10.23	Lead Semi-Wadcutter	100	760	740	720	710	690	200	190	185	175	170	0.5	2.0	4.6	8.3	4-V
1,6	C38E	38 Special (High-Velocity+P)	125	8.10	Hi-Shok JHP	100	950	920	900	880	860	250	235	225	215	205	0.3	1.3	2.9	5.4	4-V
1,6	C38F	38 Special (High-Velocity+P)	110	7.13	Hi-Shok JHP	100	1000	960	930	900	870	240	225	210	195	185	0.3	1.2	2.7	5.0	4-V
1,6	C38G	38 Special (High-Velocity+P)	158	10.23	Semi-Wadcutter HP	100	890	870	860	840	820	280	265	260	245	235	0.3	1.4	3.3	5.9	4-V
5,6	C38H	38 Special (High-Velocity+P)	158	10.23	Lead Semi-Wadcutter	100	890	870	860	840	820	270	265	260	245	235	0.3	1.4	3.3	5.9	4-V
1,6	C38J	38 Special (High-Velocity+P)	125	8.10	Hi-Shok JSP	100	950	920	900	880	860	250	235	225	215	205	0.3	1.3	2.9	5.4	4-V
2,6	C357A	357 Magnum	158	10.23	Hi-Shok JSP	100	1240	1160	1100	1060	1020	535	475	430	395	365	0.2	0.8	1.9	3.5	4-V
1,6	C357B	357 Magnum	125	8.10	Hi-Shok JHP	100	1450	1350	1240	1160	1100	580	495	430	370	335	0.1	0.6	1.5	2.8	4-V
5	C357C	357 Magnum	158	10.23	Lead Semi-Wadcutter	100	1240	1160	1100	1060	1020	535	475	430	395	365	0.2	0.8	1.9	3.5	4-V
1,6	C357D	357 Magnum	110	7.13	Hi-Shok JHP	100	1300	1180	1090	1040	990	410	340	290	260	235	0.2	0.8	1.9	3.5	4-V
2,6	C357E	357 Magnum	158	10.23	Hi-Shok JHP	100	1240	1160	1100	1060	1020	535	475	430	395	365	0.2	0.8	1.9	3.5	4-V
2	C357G	357 Magnum	180	11.66	Hi-Shok JHP	100	1090	1030	980	930	890	475	425	385	350	320	0.2	1.0	2.4	4.5	4-V
2,6	C357H	357 Magnum	140	9.07	Hi-Shok JHP	100	1360	1270	1200	1130	1080	575	500	445	395	360	0.2	0.7	1.6	3.0	4-V
1,6	C41A	41 Rem. Magnum	210	13.60	Hi-Shok JHP	150	1300	1210	1130	1070	1030	790	680	585	540	495	0.2	0.7	1.8	3.3	4-V
1,6	C44SA	44 S&W Special	200	12.96	Semi-Wadcutter HP	150	900	860	830	800	770	360	330	305	285	260	0.3	1.4	3.4	6.3	6½-V
2,6	C44A	44 Rem. Magnum	240	15.55	Hi-Shok JHP	150	1180	1130	1080	1050	1010	740	675	625	580	550	0.2	0.9	2.0	3.7	6½-V
1,2	C44B	44 Rem. Magnum	180	11.66	Hi-Shok JHP	150	1610	1480	1370	1270	1180	1035	875	750	640	555	0.1	0.5	1.2	2.3	6½-V
1,6	C45LCA	45 Colt	225	14.58	Semi-Wadcutter HP	150	900	880	860	840	820	405	385	370	355	340	0.3	1.4	3.2	5.8	5½

+P ammunition is loaded to a higher pressure. Use only in firearms recommended by the gun manufacturer. "V" indicates vented barrel to simulate service conditions.
**JHP = Jacketed Hollow Point HP = Hollow Point JSP = Jacketed Soft Point
Usage Key: 1 = Varmints, predators, small game 2 = Medium game 3 = Large, heavy game 4 = Dangerous game 5 = Target shooting, training, practice 6 = Self Defense

FEDERAL BALLISTICS

The newest addition to Federal's Premium Slug line is the Premium Barnes Expander Sabot Slug, which expands up to 150% more than conventional sabot slugs and groups 2-1/2" or better from a fully rifled barrel at 100 yards.

The Premium Sabot Slug load features a unique copper-coated Hydra-Shok slug stabilized by a two-piece sabot sleeve. In addition to its potent punch, this slug delivers accuracy, producing groups of 2-1/2" or smaller at 100 yards from rifled barrels or choke tubes.

And for smoothbore shooters, Federal offers the Premium Rifled Slug, a helix-ribbed Hydra-Shok slug also available in a low recoil load that's great for smaller folks and those new to the sport.

PREMIUM® SLUGS

Federal Load No.	Gauge	Shell Length Inches	Shell Length MM	Slug Type*	Slug Weight Ounces	Slug Weight Grains	Dram. Equiv.	Velocity In Feet Per Second (To Nearest 10 FPS) Muzzle	25 Yds	50 Yds	75 Yds	100 Yds	125 Yds	Energy In Foot-Pounds (To Nearest 5 Foot-Pounds) Muzzle	25 Yds	50 Yds	75 Yds	100 Yds	125 Yds	Height Of Slug Trajectory In Inches Above Or Below Line Of Sight If Zeroed At + Yards. Sights .5 Inches Above Bore Line 25 Yds	50 Yds	75 Yds	100 Yds	125 Yds	Test Barrel Length Inches
PREMIUM® BARNES EXPANDER SABOT SLUGS																									
NEW P151XS	12	3	76	Barnes Sabot	1	438	Mag.	1525	1450	1390	1330	1270	1210	2260	2055	1870	1710	1560	1325	+1.3	+2.0	+1.6	⊕	-3.0	30
P150XS	12	2¾	70	Barnes Sabot	1	438	Max.	1450	1380	1320	1260	1210	1160	2045	1860	1695	1545	1420	1310	+1.4	+2.2	+1.8	⊕	-3.3	30
NEW P207XS	20	3	76	Barnes Sabot	¾	325	Mag.	1450	1380	1320	1260	1200	1150	1515	1375	1250	1140	1040	960	+1.5	+2.3	+1.8	⊕	-3.3	30
PREMIUM® SABOT SLUGS																									
P151SS	12	3	76	Hydra-Shok Sabot HP	1	438	Mag.	1550	1440	1340	1250	1180	1110	2335	2020	1750	1530	1345	1205	+1.4	+2.2	+1.8	⊕	-3.3	30
P154SS	12	2¾	70	Hydra-Shok Sabot HP	1	438	Max.	1450	1350	1260	1180	1120	1070	2045	1775	1545	1360	1215	1100	+1.6	+2.5	+2.0	⊕	-3.8	30
P207SS	20	3	76	Hydra-Shok Sabot HP	⅝	275	Mag.	1450	1330	1230	1140	1070	1020	1285	1080	920	795	705	630	+1.7	+2.6	+2.2	⊕	-4.0	30
P203SS	20	2¾	70	Hydra-Shok Sabot HP	⅝	275	Max.	1400	1290	1190	1110	1050	1000	1200	1010	860	750	670	610	+1.8	+2.8	+2.3	⊕	-4.3	30
PREMIUM® RIFLED SLUGS																									
P127LRS**	12	2¾	70	Hydra-Shok HP	1	438	Max.	1300	1200	1110	1050	1000	—	1645	1390	1205	1070	965	—	+0.5	⊕	-2.3	-6.5	—	30
P127RS	12	2¾	70	Hydra-Shok HP	1	438	Max.	1610	1460	1330	1220	1140	—	2520	2075	1725	1455	1255	—	+0.3	⊕	-1.5	-4.3	—	30

**HP = Hollow Point **Low Recoil Slug. These trajectory tables were calculated by computer using the best available data for each load. Trajectories are representative of the nominal behavior of each load at standard conditions (59° F temperature; barometric pressure of 29.53 inches; altitude at sea level). Shooters are cautioned that actual trajectories may differ due to variation in altitude, atmospheric conditions, guns, sights, and ammunition.*

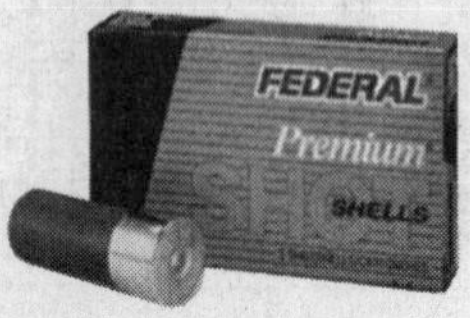

In many parts of the country, buckshot is still the old favorite. But the way Federal makes buckshot is anything but old fashioned. Hard, copper-plated buckshot is nestled in buffer, in a long-range shot cup. Pellets stay rounder and fly truer. Plus, the patented method of spiral stacking pellets provides patterns that stay dense farther out than any other buckshot on the market.

PREMIUM® BUCKSHOT

Federal Load No.	Gauge	Shell Length Inches	Shell Length MM	Dram Equiv.	Muzzle Velocity	Shot Sizes
P108	10	3½	89	Magnum	1100	18 Pellets – 00 Buck
P135	12	3½	89	Magnum	1100	18 Pellets – 00 Buck
P158	12	3	76	Magnum	1225	10 Pellets – 000 Buck
P158	12	3	76	Magnum	1210	15 Pellets – 00 Buck
P158	12	3	76	Magnum	1040	24 Pellets – 1 Buck
P158	12	3	76	Magnum	1210	41 Pellets – 4 Buck
P156	12	2¾	70	Magnum	1290	12 Pellets – 00 Buck
P156	12	2¾	70	Magnum	1250	34 Pellets – 4 Buck
P154	12	2¾	70	Max.	1325	9 Pellets – 00 Buck

Performance and reliability are a must for home defense situations. Premium Personal Defense shotshells deliver fast-opening patterns with reduced recoil, for better firearm control.

PREMIUM® PERSONAL DEFENSE

Federal Load No.	Gauge	Shell Length Inches	Shell Length MM	Dram Equiv.	Muzzle Velocity	Shot Charge Wgt. Ounces	Shot Charge Wgt. Grams	Shot Sizes
PD12	12	2¾	70	3	1140	1¼	35.44	2
PD20	20	2¾	70	2½	1140	1	28.35	2

(10 round boxes)

TAKE COMFORT IN QUALITY

When things get tense in a home defense situation, everyone is a beginner. Premium Personal Defense shotshell ammunition was designed with that fact in mind. It features a specially engineered payload that opens rapidly and offers optimized penetration. The amount of recoil has also been reduced to improve firearm control. It's the best ammunition for the worst cicumstances.

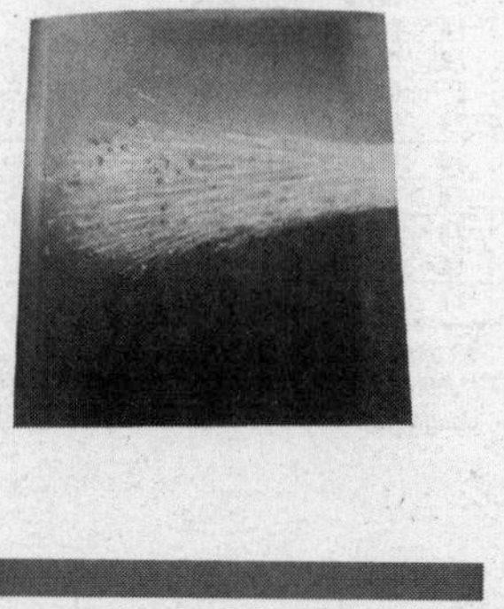

Gelatin test conducted at 15 feet.

Federal Rifle Ballistics

Premium Bullet Styles

Trophy Bonded Bear Claw — Trophy Bonded Sledgehammer — Woodleigh Weldcore — Barnes XLC Coated-X Bullet — Nosler Partition — Sierra GameKing — Nosler Ballistic Tip

Premium® Centerfire Rifle

Usage	Federal Load No.	Caliber	Bullet Wgt. in Grains	Bullet Wgt. in Grams	Bullet Style*	Factory Primer No.	Velocity in Feet per Second (To Nearest 10 FPS) Muzzle	100 Yds.	200 Yds.	300 Yds.	400 Yds.	500 Yds.	Energy in Foot-Pounds (To Nearest 5 Foot-Pounds) Muzzle	100 Yds.	200 Yds.	300 Yds.	400 Yds.	500 Yds.
1	P223E	223 Rem. (5.56x45mm)	55	3.56	Sierra GameKing BTHP	205	3240	2770	2340	1950	1610	1330	1280	935	670	465	315	215
NEW 2	P223T2	223 Rem.	55	3.56	Trophy Bonded Bear Claw**	205	3100	2630	2210	1830	1500	1240	1175	845	595	410	275	185
1	P22250B	22-250 Rem.	55	3.56	Sierra GameKing BTHP	210	3680	3280	2920	2590	2280	1990	1655	1315	1040	815	630	480
2	P22250T1	22-250 Rem.	55	3.56	Trophy Bonded Bear Claw**	210	3600	3080	2610	2190	1810	1490	1585	1155	835	580	400	270
2	P220T1	220 Swift	55	3.56	Trophy Bonded Bear Claw**	210	3700	3170	2690	2270	1880	1540	1670	1225	885	625	430	290
2	P243C	243 Win. (6.16x51mm)	100	6.48	Sierra GameKing BTSP	210	2960	2760	2570	2380	2210	2040	1950	1690	1460	1260	1080	925
1	P243D	243 Win. (6.16x51mm)	85	5.50	Sierra GameKing BTHP	210	3320	3070	2830	2600	2380	2180	2080	1770	1510	1280	1070	890
NEW 2	P243E	243 Win. (6.16x51mm)	100	6.48	Nosler Partition**	210	2960	2730	2510	2300	2100	1910	1945	1650	1395	1170	975	805
1	P243F	243 Win. (6.16x51mm)	70	4.54	Nosler Ballistic Tip	210	3400	3070	2760	2470	2200	1950	1795	1465	1185	950	755	590
2	P6C	6mm Rem.	100	6.48	Nosler Partition	210	3100	2860	2640	2420	2220	2020	2135	1820	1545	1300	1090	910
2	P257B	257 Roberts (High-Velocity + P)	120	7.77	Nosler Partition	210	2780	2560	2360	2160	1970	1790	2060	1750	1480	1240	1030	855
2	P2506C	25-06 Rem.	117	7.58	Sierra GameKing BTSP	210	2990	2770	2570	2370	2190	2000	2320	2000	1715	1485	1240	1045
2	P2506D	25-06 Rem.	100	6.48	Nosler Ballistic Tip	210	3210	2960	2720	2490	2280	2070	2290	1940	1640	1380	1150	955
2	P2506E	25-06 Rem.	115	7.45	Nosler Partition	210	2990	2750	2520	2300	2100	1900	2285	1930	1620	1350	1120	915
2	P2506T1	25-06 Rem.	115	7.45	Trophy Bonded Bear Claw	210	2990	2740	2500	2270	2050	1850	2285	1910	1590	1310	1075	870
2	P257WBA	257 Weatherby Magnum	115	7.45	Nosler Partition	210	3150	2900	2660	2440	2220	2020	2535	2145	1810	1515	1260	1040
2	P257WBT1	257 Weatherby Magnum	115	7.45	Trophy Bonded Bear Claw	210	3150	2880	2640	2400	2180	1970	2535	2125	1775	1470	1210	990
2	P6555T2	6.5X55 Swedish	140	9.07	Trophy Bonded Bear Claw**	210	2550	2350	2160	1980	1810	1650	2020	1720	1450	1220	1015	845
NEW 2	P260A	260 Rem.	140	9.07	Sierra Gameking BTSP	210	2750	2570	2390	2220	2060	1900	2350	2045	1775	1535	1315	1125
NEW 2	P260T1	260 Rem.	140	9.07	Trophy Bonded Bear Claw	210	2750	2540	2340	2150	1970	1800	2350	2010	1705	1440	1210	1010
2	P270C	270 Win.	150	9.72	Sierra GameKing BTSP	210	2850	2660	2480	2300	2130	1970	2705	2355	2040	1760	1510	1290
2	P270D	270 Win.	130	8.42	Sierra GameKing BTSP	210	3060	2830	2620	2410	2220	2030	2700	2320	1980	1680	1420	1190
2	P270E	270 Win.	150	9.72	Nosler Partition	210	2850	2590	2340	2100	1880	1670	2705	2225	1815	1470	1175	930
2	P270F	270 Win.	130	8.42	Nosler Ballistic Tip	210	3060	2840	2630	2430	2230	2050	2700	2325	1990	1700	1440	1210
NEW 2	P270H	270 Win.	130	8.42	Barnes XLC Coated-X Bullet	210	3060	2840	2620	2420	2220	2040	2705	2320	1985	1690	1425	1200
2	P270T1	270 Win.	140	9.07	Trophy Bonded Bear Claw	210	2940	2700	2480	2260	2060	1860	2685	2270	1905	1590	1315	1080
2	P270T2	270 Win.	130	8.42	Trophy Bonded Bear Claw	210	3060	2810	2570	2340	2130	1930	2705	2275	1905	1585	1310	1070
2	P270WBA	270 Weatherby Magnum	130	8.42	Nosler Partition	210	3200	2960	2740	2520	2320	2120	2955	2530	2160	1835	1550	1300
2	P270WBB	270 Weatherby Magnum	130	8.42	Sierra GameKing BTSP	210	3200	2980	2780	2580	2400	2210	2955	2570	2230	1925	1655	1415
2	P270WBT1	270 Weatherby Magnum	140	9.07	Trophy Bonded Bear Claw	210	3100	2840	2600	2370	2150	1950	2990	2510	2100	1745	1440	1175
2	P730A	7-30 Waters	120	7.77	Sierra GameKing BTSP	210	2700	2300	1930	1600	1330	1140	1940	1405	990	685	470	345
2	P7C	7mm Mauser (7x57mm Mauser)	140	9.07	Nosler Partition	210	2660	2450	2260	2070	1890	1730	2200	1865	1585	1330	1110	930
2	P708A	7mm-08 Rem.	140	9.07	Nosler Partition	210	2800	2590	2390	2200	2020	1840	2435	2085	1775	1500	1265	1060
2	P708B	7mm-08 Rem.	140	9.07	Nosler Ballistic Tip	210	2800	2610	2430	2260	2100	1940	2440	2135	1840	1590	1360	1165
2	P764A	7x64 Brenneke	160	10.37	Nosler Partition	210	2650	2480	2310	2150	2000	1850	2495	2180	1895	1640	1415	1215
2	P280A	280 Rem.	150	9.72	Nosler Partition	210	2890	2690	2490	2310	2130	1960	2780	2405	2070	1770	1510	1275
2	P280T1	280 Rem.	140	9.07	Trophy Bonded Bear Claw	210	2990	2630	2310	2040	1730	1480	2770	2155	1655	1250	925	680
2	P7RD	7mm Rem. Magnum	150	9.72	Sierra GameKing BTSP	215	3110	2920	2750	2580	2410	2250	3220	2850	2510	2210	1930	1690
3	P7RE	7mm Rem. Magnum	165	10.69	Sierra GameKing BTSP	215	2950	2800	2650	2510	2370	2230	3190	2865	2570	2300	2050	1825
3	P7RF	7mm Rem. Magnum	160	10.37	Nosler Partition	215	2950	2770	2590	2420	2250	2090	3090	2715	2375	2075	1800	1555
2	P7RG	7mm Rem. Magnum	140	9.07	Nosler Partition	215	3150	2930	2710	2510	2320	2130	3085	2660	2290	1960	1670	1415
2	P7RH	7mm Rem. Magnum	150	9.72	Nosler Ballistic Tip	215	3110	2910	2720	2540	2370	2200	3220	2825	2470	2150	1865	1610
3	P7RT1	7mm Rem. Magnum	175	11.34	Trophy Bonded Bear Claw	215	2860	2600	2350	2120	1900	1700	3180	2625	2150	1745	1400	1120
3	P7RT2	7mm Rem. Magnum	160	10.37	Trophy Bonded Bear Claw	215	2940	2660	2390	2140	1900	1680	3070	2505	2025	1620	1280	1005
3	P7RT3	7mm Rem. Magnum	140	9.07	Trophy Bonded Bear Claw	215	3150	2910	2680	2460	2250	2060	3085	2630	2230	1880	1575	1310
3	P7WBA	7mm Weatherby Magnum	160	10.37	Nosler Partition	215	3050	2850	2650	2470	2290	2120	3305	2880	2505	2185	1885	1600
3	P7WBB	7mm Weatherby Magnum	160	10.37	Sierra GameKing BTSP	215	3050	2880	2710	2560	2400	2250	3305	2945	2615	2320	2050	1805
3	P7WBT1	7mm Weatherby Magnum	160	10.37	Trophy Bonded Bear Claw	215	3050	2730	2420	2140	1880	1640	3305	2640	2085	1630	1255	955
3	P7STWA	7mm STW	160	10.37	Sierra GameKing BTSP	215	3200	3020	2850	2670	2530	2380	3640	3245	2890	2570	2275	2010
3	P7STWT1	7mm STW	150	9.72	Trophy Bonded Bear Claw	215	3250	3010	2770	2560	2350	2150	3520	3010	2565	2175	1830	1535
2	P3030D	30-30 Win.	170	11.01	Nosler Partition	210	2200	1900	1620	1380	1190	1060	1830	1355	990	720	535	425
2	P308C	308 Win. (7.62x51mm)	165	10.69	Sierra GameKing BTSP	210	2700	2520	2330	2160	1990	1830	2670	2310	1990	1700	1450	1230
3	P308E	308 Win. (7.62x51mm)	180	11.66	Nosler Partition	210	2620	2430	2240	2060	1890	1730	2745	2355	2005	1700	1430	1200
2	P308F	308 Win. (7.62x51mm)	150	9.72	Nosler Ballistic Tip	210	2820	2610	2410	2220	2040	1860	2650	2270	1935	1640	1380	1155
3	P308J	308 Win. (7.62x51mm)	180	11.66	Woodleigh Weldcore SP	210	2620	2390	2170	1960	1770	1590	2745	2280	1880	1540	1250	1010
3	P308T1	308 Win. (7.62x51mm)	165	10.69	Trophy Bonded Bear Claw	210	2700	2440	2200	1970	1760	1570	2670	2185	1775	1425	1135	900
2	P3006D	30-06 Spring (7.62x63mm)	165	10.69	Sierra GameKing BTSP	210	2800	2610	2420	2240	2070	1910	2870	2490	2150	1840	1580	1340
3	P3006F	30-06 Spring (7.62x63mm)	180	11.66	Nosler Partition	210	2700	2500	2320	2140	1970	1810	2915	2510	2150	1830	1550	1350
2	P3006G	30-06 Spring (7.62x63mm)	150	9.72	Sierra GameKing BTSP	210	2910	2690	2480	2270	2070	1880	2820	2420	2040	1710	1430	1180
3	P3006L	30-06 Spring (7.62x63mm)	180	11.66	Sierra GameKing BTSP	210	2700	2540	2380	2220	2080	1930	2915	2570	2260	1975	1720	1495
2	P3006P	30-06 Spring (7.62x63mm)	150	9.72	Nosler Ballistic Tip	210	2910	2700	2490	2300	2110	1940	2820	2420	2070	1760	1485	1245
2	P3006Q	30-06 Spring (7.62x63mm)	165	10.69	Nosler Ballistic Tip	210	2800	2610	2430	2250	2080	1920	2870	2495	2155	1855	1585	1350
3	P3006W	30-06 Spring (7.62x63mm)	180	11.66	Woodleigh Weldcore SP	210	2700	2470	2240	2030	1830	1650	2915	2430	2010	1645	1340	1085
NEW 3	P3006Z	30-06 Spring (7.62x63mm)	180	11.66	Barnes XLC Coated-X Bullet	210	2700	2530	2360	2200	2040	1890	2915	2550	2220	1930	1670	1430
3	P3006T1	30-06 Spring (7.62x63mm)	165	10.69	Trophy Bonded Bear Claw	210	2800	2540	2290	2050	1830	1630	2870	2360	1915	1545	1230	975
3	P3006T2	30-06 Spring (7.62x63mm)	180	11.66	Trophy Bonded Bear Claw	210	2700	2460	2220	2000	1800	1610	2915	2410	1975	1605	1290	1035
3	P300WC	300 Win. Magnum	200	12.96	Sierra GameKing BTSP	215	2830	2680	2530	2380	2240	2110	3560	3180	2830	2520	2230	1970
3	P300WT4	300 Win. Magnum	150	9.72	Trophy Bonded Bear Claw	215	3280	2980	2700	2430	2190	1950	3570	2450	2420	1970	1590	1270
3	P300WBC	300 Weatherby Magnum	180	11.66	Sierra GameKing BTSP	215	3190	3010	2830	2660	2490	2330	4065	3610	3195	2820	2480	2175
3	P35WT1	35 Whelen	225	14.58	Trophy Bonded Bear Claw	210	2600	2400	2200	2020	1840	1670	3375	2865	2420	2030	1690	1400

+P ammunition is loaded to a higher pressure. Use only in firearms recommended by the gun manufacturer.

**BTHP = Boat-Tail Hollow Point BTSP = Boat-Tail Soft Point SP = Soft Point **Moly-Coat = New, Molybdenum disulfide dry film lubricant*

Usage Key: 1 = Varmints, predators, small game 2 = Medium game 3 = Large, heavy game 4 = Dangerous game 5 = Target shooting, training, practice 6 = Self Defense

FEDERAL RIFLE BALLISTICS

PREMIUM® HIGH ENERGY RIFLE

Usage	Federal Load No.	Caliber	Bullet Wgt. in Grains	Bullet Wgt. in Grams	Bullet Style*	Factory Primer No.	Velocity in Feet per Second (to nearest 10 FPS) Muzzle	100 Yds.	200 Yds.	300 Yds.	400 Yds.	500 Yds.	Energy in Foot-Pounds (to nearest 5 foot-pounds) Muzzle	100 Yds.	200 Yds.	300 Yds.	400 Yds.	500 Yds.
2	P270T3	270 Win.	140	9.07	Trophy Bonded Bear Claw	210	3100	2860	2620	2400	2200	2000	2990	2535	2140	1785	1500	1240
NEW 2	P270G	270 Win.	150	9.72	Sierra GameKing BTSP	210	3000	2800	2620	2430	2260	2090	2995	2615	2275	1975	1700	1460
NEW 2	P708T1	7mm-08 Rem.	140	9.07	Trophy Bonded Bear Claw	210	2950	2660	2390	2140	1900	1680	2705	2205	1780	1420	1120	875
NEW 2	P280T2	280 Rem.	140	9.07	Trophy Bonded Bear Claw	210	3150	2850	2570	2300	2050	1820	3085	2520	2050	1650	1310	1030
3	P308T2	308 Win. (7.62x51mm)	165	10.69	Trophy Bonded Bear Claw	210	2870	2600	2350	2120	1890	1690	3020	2485	2030	1640	1310	1040
3	P308G	308 Win. (7.62x51mm)	180	11.66	Nosler Partition	210	2740	2550	2370	2200	2030	1870	3000	2600	2245	1925	1645	1395
3	P308L	308 Win. (7.62x51mm)	180	11.66	Woodleigh Weldcore SP	210	2740	2500	2280	2060	1860	1680	3000	2500	2075	1705	1385	1120
3	P3006T3	30-06 Spring (7.62x63mm)	180	11.66	Trophy Bonded Bear Claw	210	2880	2630	2380	2160	1940	1740	3315	2755	2270	1855	1505	1210
NEW 3	P3006T4	30-06 Spring (7.62x63mm)	165	10.69	Trophy Bonded Bear Claw	210	3140	2860	2590	2340	2100	1880	3610	2990	2460	2010	1625	1300
3	P3006R	30-06 Spring (7.62x63mm)	180	11.66	Nosler Partition	210	2880	2690	2500	2320	2150	1980	3315	2880	2495	2150	1845	1570
3	P3006X	30-06 Spring (7.62x63mm)	180	11.66	Woodleigh Weldcore SP	210	2880	2640	2400	2180	1970	1780	3315	2775	2310	1905	1560	1265
NEW 3	P3006Y	30-06 Spring (7.62x63mm)	165	10.69	Sierra GameKing BTSP	210	3140	2900	2670	2450	2240	2050	3610	3075	2610	2200	1845	1535
3	P300WT3	300 Win. Mag.	180	11.66	Trophy Bonded Bear Claw	215	3100	2830	2580	2340	2110	1900	3840	3205	2660	2190	1780	1445
3	P300WE	300 Win. Mag.	200	12.96	Nosler Partition	215	2930	2740	2550	2370	2200	2030	3810	3325	2885	2495	2145	1840
3	P300WG	300 Win. Mag.	180	11.66	Woodleigh Weldcore SP	215	3100	2830	2580	2340	2120	1910	3840	3210	2685	2185	1795	1450
3	P300WBT3	300 Weatherby Magnum	180	11.66	Trophy Bonded Bear Claw**	215	3330	3080	2850	2750	2410	2210	4430	3785	3235	2750	2320	1950
3	P300WBB	300 Weatherby Magnum	180	11.66	Nosler Partition**	215	3330	3110	2910	2710	2520	2340	4430	3875	3375	2835	2540	2180
2	P303T1	303 British	180	11.66	Trophy Bonded Bear Claw**	210	2590	2350	2120	1900	1700	1520	2680	2205	1795	1445	1160	920
3	P338T2	338 Win. Mag.	225	14.58	Trophy Bonded Bear Claw	215	2940	2690	2450	2230	2010	1810	4320	3610	3000	2475	2025	1640
3	P338B	338 Win. Mag.	250	16.20	Nosler Partition	215	2800	2610	2420	2250	2080	1920	4350	3775	3260	2805	2395	2035
3	P338G	338 Win. Mag.	250	16.20	Woodleigh Weldcore SP	215	2800	2610	2420	2240	2070	1910	4350	3770	3255	2795	2385	2025
4	P375T3	375 H & H Magnum	300	19.44	Trophy Bonded Bear Claw	215	2700	2440	2190	1960	1740	1540	4855	3960	3195	2550	2020	1585

*SP = Soft Point **Moly-Coat = New, Molybdenum disulfide dry film lubricant BTSP = Boat-Tail Soft Point

PREMIUM® SAFARI® RIFLE

Usage	Federal Load No.	Caliber	Bullet Wgt. in Grains	Bullet Wgt. in Grams	Bullet Style*	Factory Primer No.	Velocity in Feet per Second (to nearest 10 FPS) Muzzle	100 Yds.	200 Yds.	300 Yds.	400 Yds.	500 Yds.	Energy in Foot-Pounds (to nearest 5 foot-pounds) Muzzle	100 Yds.	200 Yds.	300 Yds.	400 Yds.	500 Yds.
3	P300HA	300 H&H Magnum	180	11.66	Nosler Partition	215	2880	2620	2380	2150	1930	1730	3315	2750	2260	1840	1480	1190
3	P300WB2	300 Win. Magnum	180	11.66	Nosler Partition	215	2960	2700	2450	2210	1990	1780	3500	2905	2395	1955	1585	1270
3	P300WT1	300 Win. Magnum	200	12.96	Trophy Bonded Bear Claw	215	2800	2570	2350	2150	1950	1770	3480	2935	2460	2050	1690	1385
3	P300WT2	300 Win. Magnum	180	11.66	Trophy Bonded Bear Claw	215	2960	2700	2460	2220	2000	1800	3500	2915	2410	1975	1605	1290
3	P300WF	300 Win. Magnum	180	11.66	Woodleigh Weldcore SP	215	2960	2700	2460	2230	2010	1800	3500	2915	2415	1990	1610	1300
3	P300WBA	300 Weatherby Magnum	180	11.66	Nosler Partition	215	3190	2980	2780	2590	2400	2230	4055	3540	3090	2670	2305	1985
3	P300WBT1	300 Weatherby Magnum	180	11.66	Trophy Bonded Bear Claw	215	3190	2950	2720	2500	2290	2100	4065	3475	2955	2500	2105	1760
3	P300WBT2	300 Weatherby Magnum	200	12.96	Trophy Bonded Bear Claw	215	2900	2670	2440	2230	2030	1830	3735	3150	2645	2200	1820	1490
3	P338A2	338 Win. Magnum	210	13.60	Nosler Partition	215	2830	2600	2390	2180	1980	1800	3735	3160	2655	2215	1835	1505
3	P338B2	338 Win. Magnum	250	16.20	Nosler Partition	215	2660	2470	2300	2120	1960	1800	3925	3395	2925	2505	2130	1805
3	P338T1	338 Win. Magnum	225	14.58	Trophy Bonded Bear Claw	215	2800	2560	2330	2110	1900	1710	3915	3265	2700	2220	1800	1455
3	P338F	338 Win. Magnum	250	16.20	Woodleigh Weldcore SP	215	2660	2470	2290	2120	1960	1800	3925	3385	2920	2495	2120	1795
3	P340WBT1	340 Weatherby Magnum	225	14.58	Trophy Bonded Bear Claw	215	3100	2840	2600	2370	2150	1940	4800	4035	3375	2800	2310	1885
4	P375F	375 H&H Magnum	300	19.44	Nosler Partition	215	2530	2320	2120	1930	1750	1590	4265	3585	2995	2475	2040	1675
4	P375T1	375 H&H Magnum	300	19.44	Trophy Bonded Bear Claw	215	2530	2280	2040	1810	1610	1425	4265	3450	2765	2190	1725	1350
4	P375T2	375 H&H Magnum	300	19.44	Trophy Bonded Sledgehammer	215	2530	2160	1820	1520	1280	1100	4265	3105	2210	1550	1090	810
2	P458A	458 Win. Magnum	350	22.68	Soft Point	215	2470	1990	1570	1250	1060	950	4740	3065	1915	1205	870	705
4	P458B	458 Win. Magnum	510	33.04	Soft Point	215	2090	1820	1570	1360	1190	1080	4945	3730	2790	2080	1605	1320
4	P458C	458 Win. Magnum	500	32.40	Solid	215	2090	1870	1670	1480	1320	1190	4850	3880	3085	2440	1945	1585
4	P458T1	458 Win. Magnum	400	25.92	Trophy Bonded Bear Claw	215	2380	2170	1960	1770	1590	1430	5030	4165	3415	2785	2255	1825
4	P458T2	458 Win. Magnum	500	32.40	Trophy Bonded Bear Claw	215	2090	1870	1660	1480	1310	1180	4850	3870	3065	2420	1915	1550
4	P458T3	458 Win. Magnum	500	32.40	Trophy Bonded Sledgehammer	215	2090	1860	1650	1460	1300	1170	4850	3845	3025	2365	1865	1505
4	P416A	416 Rigby	410	26.57	Woodleigh Weldcore SP	216	2370	2110	1870	1640	1440	1280	5115	4050	3165	2455	1895	1485
4	P416B	416 Rigby	410	26.57	Solid	216	2370	2110	1870	1640	1440	1280	5115	4050	3165	2455	1895	1485
4	P416T1	416 Rigby	400	25.92	Trophy Bonded Bear Claw	216	2370	2150	1940	1750	1570	1410	4990	4110	3350	2715	2190	1760
4	P416T2	416 Rigby	400	25.92	Trophy Bonded Sledgehammer	216	2370	2120	1890	1660	1460	1290	4990	3975	3130	2440	1895	1480
NEW 4	P416RT2	416 Rem. Magnum	400	25.92	Trophy Bonded Sledgehammer	216	2400	2150	1920	1700	1500	1330	5115	4110	3260	2565	2005	1575
4	P416RT1	416 Rem. Magnum	400	25.92	Trophy Bonded Bear Claw	216	2400	2180	1970	1770	1590	1420	5115	4215	3440	2785	2245	1800
4	P470A	470 Nitro Express	500	32.40	Woodleigh Weldcore SP	216	2150	1890	1650	1440	1270	1140	5130	3965	3040	2310	1790	1435
4	P470B	470 Nitro Express	500	32.40	Woodleigh Weldcore Solid	216	2150	1890	1650	1440	1270	1140	5130	3965	3040	2310	1790	1435
4	P470T1	470 Nitro Express	500	32.40	Trophy Bonded Bear Claw	216	2150	1940	1740	1560	1400	1260	5130	4170	3360	2695	2160	1750
4	P470T2	470 Nitro Express	500	32.40	Trophy Bonded Sledgehammer	216	2150	1940	1740	1560	1400	1260	5130	4170	3360	2695	2160	1750

**SP = Soft Point Sledgehammer = Sledgehammer Solid

PREMIUM® VARMINT RIFLE

Usage	Federal Load No.	Caliber	Bullet Wgt. in Grains	Bullet Wgt. in Grams	Bullet Style*	Factory Primer No.	Velocity in Feet per Second (to nearest 10 FPS) Muzzle	100 Yds.	200 Yds.	300 Yds.	400 Yds.	500 Yds.	Energy in Foot-Pounds (to nearest 5 foot-pounds) Muzzle	100 Yds.	200 Yds.	300 Yds.	400 Yds.	500 Yds.
1	P223F	223 Rem. (5.56x45mm)	55	3.56	Nosler Ballistic Tip	205	3240	2870	2530	2220	1920	1660	1280	1005	780	600	450	335
NEW 1	P223J	223 Rem.	55	3.56	Sierra BlitzKing	205	3240	2870	2520	2200	1910	1640	1280	1005	775	590	445	330
NEW 1	P223K	223 Rem.	52	3.37	Sierra MatchKing BTHP	205	3300	2860	2460	2090	1760	1470	1255	945	700	505	360	250
NEW 1	P223V1	223 Rem.	50	3.24	Speer TNT HP	205	3300	2860	2450	2080	1750	1460	1210	905	670	480	340	235
NEW 1	P22250C	22-250 Rem.	55	3.56	Sierra BlitzKing	210	3680	3270	2890	2540	2220	1920	1655	1300	1020	790	605	450
1	P22250V	22-250 Rem.	40	2.59	Sierra Varminter HP	210	4000	3320	2720	2200	1740	1360	1420	980	660	430	265	165
NEW 1	P220A	220 Swift	55	3.56	Sierra BlitzKing	210	3800	3370	2990	2630	2310	2000	1765	1390	1090	850	650	490
1	P220V	220 Swift	52	3.37	Sierra MatchKing BTHP	210	3830	3370	2960	2600	2230	1910	1690	1310	1010	770	575	420
NEW 1	P243V1	243 Win. (6.16x51mm)	70	4.54	Speer TNT HP	210	3400	3040	2700	2390	2100	1830	1795	1435	1135	890	685	520
1	P2506V	25-06 Rem.	90	5.83	Sierra Varminter HP	210	3440	3040	2680	2340	2030	1750	2365	1850	1435	1100	825	610

*BTHP = Boat-Tail Hollow Point HP = Hollow Point • Usage Key: 1 = Varmints, predators, small game 2 = Medium game 3 = Large, heavy game 4 = Dangerous game 5 = Target shooting, training, practice 6 = Self Defense • TNT is a trademark of Speer.

NORMA CENTERFIRE BALLISTICS

BALLISTIC DATA

CALIBER	BULLET TYPE / BULLET WEIGHT GRAM/GRAINS / PRODUCT NUMBER	BALL. CO-EFFICIENT	VELOCITY FEET/SEC				ENERGY FOOT POUNDS				ZERO RANGE YARDS	HEIGHT OF TRAJECTORY ABOVE LINE OF SIGHT IF SIGHTED IN A + YARDS. FOR SIGHTS 1,6 INCH ABOVE BORE.					WIND DRIFT IN INCHES FOR A 10 M.P.H. CROSS WIND.		
			MUZZLE	V100 YDS	V200 YDS	V300 YDS	MUZZLE	E100 YDS	E200 YDS	E300 YDS		50 YDS	100 YDS	150 YDS	200 YDS	300 YDS	100 YDS	200 YDS	300 YDS
.220 SWIFT	Soft point 3.2 gram/50 grains Product no. 15701	.185	4019	3380	2826	2335	1794	1268	887	605	100 150 200	-0.5 -0.4 -0.1	+ 0.2 0.7	-0.3 + 0.8	-1.5 -1.1 +	-7.3 -6.8 -5.1	1.2	5.1	12.6
.222 Rem.	Soft point 3.2 gram/50 grains Product no. 15711	.185	3199	2667	2193	1771	1136	790	534	348	100 150 200	-0.3 0.0 0.6	+ 0.6 1.7	-0.9 + 1.6	-3.4 -2.1 +	-14.1 -12.2 -9.1	1.6	6.9	17.2
	Full jacket 3.2 gram/50 grains Product no. 15713	.198	2789	2326	1910	1547	864	601	405	266	100 150 200	-0.1 0.4 1.1	+ 1.0 2.5	-1.5 + 2.2	-4.9 -2.9 +	-19.6 -16.6 -12.2	1.8	7.9	19.8
	Soft point 4.0 gram/62 grains Product no. 15716	.214	2887	2457	2067	1716	1148	831	588	405	100 150 200	-0.2 0.2 0.9	+ 0.8 2.1	-1.3 + 1.9	-4.2 -2.6 +	-16.7 -14.2 -10.4	1.5	6.5	16.5
.22-250	Soft point 3.4 gram/53 grains Product no. 15733	.237	3707	3234	2809	1716	1618	1231	928	690	100 150 200	-0.4 -0.3 0.0	+ 0.3 0.6	-0.4 + 0.9	-1.7 -1.2 +	-7.9 -7.1 -5.3	1.0	4.3	10.3
5,6x52 R	Soft point 4.6 gram/71 grains Product no. 15604	.268	2789	2446	2128	1835	1227	944	714	531	100 150 200	-0.2 0.3 0.9	+ 0.9 2.1	-1.3 + 1.9	-4.3 -2.5 +	-16.2 -13.7 -9.9	1.3	5.5	13.2
.243 Win.	Full jacket 6.5 gram/100 grains Product no. 16002	.357	3018	2747	2493	2252	2023	1677	1380	1126	100 150 200	-0.3 0.0 0.5	+ 0.6 1.5	-0.9 + 1.4	-3.0 -1.9 +	-11.7 -9.9 -7.1	0.8	3.5	8.3
	Soft point 6.5 gram/100 grains Product no. 16003	.357	3018	2748	2493	2252	2023	1677	1380	1126	100 150 200	-0.3 0.0 0.5	+ 0.6 1.5	-0.9 + 1.4	-3.0 -1.9 +	-11.7 -9.9 -7.1	0.8	3.5	8.3
6,5 JAP	Alaska 10.1 gram/156 grains Product no. 16532	.326	2067	1832	1615	1423	1480	1162	904	701	100 150 200	0.4 1.3 2.6	+ 2.0 4.4	-2.9 + 3.7	-8.8 -4.9 +	-31.0 -25.2 -17.8	1.5	6.8	16.0
6,5 Carcano	Alaska 10.1 gram/156 grains Product no. 16535	.326	2428	2169	1926	1702	2043	1630	1286	1004	100 150 200	0.0 0.7 1.5	+ 1.3 1.8	-1.9 + 2.5	-5.8 -2.2 +	-21.1 -11.7 7.8	1.3	5.3	12.8
6,5x55	Vulkan 9.0 gram/139 grains Product no. 16558	.325	2854	2569	2302	2051	2515	2038	1636	1298	100 150 200	-0.2 0.2 0.7	+ 0.7 1.8	-1.1 + 1.7	-3.7 -2.2 +	-14.0 -11.7 -8.4	1.0	4.2	10.0
	Nosler 9.1 gram/140 grains Product no. 16559	.467	2789	2592	2403	2223	2419	2089	1796	1536	100 150 200	-0.2 0.2 0.7	+ 0.7 1.8	-1.1 + 1.6	-3.6 -2.1 +	-13.2 -11.0 -7.8	0.7	2.9	6.9
	TXP Line, Swift 10.1 gram/156 grains Product no. 16541	.345	2526	2276	2040	1818	2196	1782	1432	1138	100 150 200	0.0 0.6 1.3	+ 1.1 2.6	-1.7 + 2.2	-5.3 -3.0 +	-18.8 -15.4 -10.9	1.0	4.8	11.2
	Alaska 10.1 gram/156 grains Product no. 16552	.276	2559	2245	1953	1687	2269	1746	1322	986	100 150 200	0.0 0.5 1.3	+ 1.1 2.7	-1.7 + 2.3	-5.4 -3.1 +	-19.9 -16.5 -11.9	1.4	5.9	14.5
	Vulkan 10.1 gram/156 grains Product no. 16556	.354	2644	2395	2159	1937	2422	1987	1616	1301	100 150 200	-0.1 0.4 1.0	+ 0.9 2.2	-1.4 + 2.0	-4.5 -2.6 +	-16.5 -13.6 -10.6	0.9	4.3	10.0
	Oryx 10.1 gram/156 grains Product no. 16562	.348	2559	2308	2070	1848	2269	1845	1485	1183	100 150 200	-0.1 0.5 1.2	+ 1.1 2.5	-1.6 + 2.2	-5.0 -2.9 +	-18.1 -14.9 -9.7	1.1	4.6	11.0
.270 Win.	Soft point 8.4 gram/130 grains Product no. 16902	.359	3140	2862	2601	2354	2847	2365	1953	1600	100 150 200	-0.3 0.1 0.4	+ 0.5 1.3	-0.7 + 1.3	-2.7 -1.7 +	-10.5 -9.0 -6.5	0.8	3.4	7.9
	Soft point 9.7 gram/150 grains Product no. 16903	.373	2799	2555	2323	2104	2610	2175	1798	1475	100 150 200	-0.2 0.2 0.7	+ 0.8 1.9	-1.1 + 1.7	-3.7 -2.2 +	-13.9 -11.7 -8.3	0.9	3.7	8.9
7x57	Soft point 9.7 gram/150 grains Product no. 17002	.421	2690	2479	2278	2087	2411	2048	1729	1450	100 150 200	-0.2 0.3 0.9	+ 0.8 2.0	-1.3 + 1.8	-4.1 -2.4 +	-14.9 -12.3 -8.8	0.8	3.4	8.0
7x57 R	Full jacket 9.7 gram/150 grains Product no. 17006	.441	2690	2489	2296	2112	2411	2063	1756	1486	100 150 200	-0.2 0.3 0.9	+ 0.8 2.0	-1.3 + 1.8	-4.0 -2.4 +	-14.7 -12.2 -8.6	0.8	3.2	7.6
	Soft point 10.0 gram/154 grains Product no. 17005	.425	2625	2417	2219	2030	2357	1999	1684	1410	100 150 200	-0.1 0.3 1.0	+ 0.9 2.2	-1.4 + 1.9	-4.4 -2.5 +	-15.8 -13.1 -9.3	0.8	3.5	8.3
7 MM Rem. Mag.	Vulkan 11.0 gram/170 grains Product no. 17024	.353	3018	2747	2493	2252	3439	2850	2346	1914	100 150 200	-0.3 0.0 0.5	+ 0.6 1.5	-0.9 + 1.4	-3.0 -1.9 +	-11.7 -9.9 -2.8	0.9	3.6	8.4
	Oryx 11.0 gram/170 grains Product no. 17023	.321	2887	2601	2333	2080	3147	2555	2055	1634	100 150 200	-0.2 0.2 0.7	+ 0.7 1.8	-1.1 + 1.6	-3.7 -2.2 +	-13.7 -11.5 -8.2	1.0	4.0	9.8
	Plastic point 11.0 gram/170 grains Product no. 17027	.378	3018	2762	2519	2290	3439	2880	2394	1980	100 150 200	-0.3 0.0 0.5	+ 0.6 1.5	-0.9 + 1.4	-3.0 -1.8 +	-11.4 -9.7 -7.0	0.8	3.3	7.8
7x64	Soft point 10.0 gram/154 grains Product no. 17103	.422	2821	2605	2399	2203	2722	2321	1969	1660	100 150 200	-0.2 0.2 0.7	+ 0.7 1.8	-1.1 + 1.6	-3.5 -2.1 +	-13.1 -11.0 -7.8	0.8	3.2	7.6
	Vulkan 11.0 gram/170 grains Product no. 17018	.353	2756	2501	2259	2031	2868	2361	1927	1558	100 150 200	-0.2 0.2 0.8	+ 0.8 2.0	-1.2 + 1.8	-4.0 -2.4 +	-14.8 -12.4 -8.8	0.9	4.0	9.4
	Oryx 11.0 gram/170 grains Product no. 17020	.324	2756	2481	2222	1979	2868	2324	1864	1478	100 150 200	-0.1 0.3 0.9	+ 0.9 2.1	-1.3 + 1.8	-4.2 -2.4 +	-15.4 -12.8 -9.2	1.0	4.3	10.0
	Plastic point 11.0 gram/170 grains Product no. 17019	.378	2756	2519	2294	2081	2868	2396	1987	1635	100 150 200	-0.2 0.2 0.8	+ 0.8 2.0	-1.2 + 1.7	-3.9 -2.3 +	-14.4 -12.0 -8.6	0.9	3.7	8.7

Ballistic Data

Caliber	Bullet Type / Bullet Weight gram/grains / Product Number	Ball. Co-Efficient	Velocity Feet/Sec Muzzle	V100 yds	V200 yds	V300 yds	Energy Foot Pounds Muzzle	E100 yds	E200 yds	E300 yds	Zero Range Yards	Trajectory 50 yds	100 yds	150 yds	200 yds	300 yds	Wind Drift 100 yds	200 yds	300 yds
7x65R	Plastic point 11.0 gram/170 grains Product no. 17028	.373	2625	2390	2167	1956	2602	2157	1773	1445	100	-0.1	+	-1.4	-4.5	-16.4			
											150	0.4	0.9	+	-2.6	-13.6	1.0	4.1	9.6
											200	1.0	2.3	2.0	+	-9.7			
	Vulkan 11.0 gram/170 grains Product no. 17029	.335	2657	2392	2143	1909	2666	2161	1734	1377	100	-0.1	+	-1.5	-4.6	-16.8			
											150	0.4	1.0	+	-2.7	-13.9	1.1	4.5	10.8
											200	1.1	2.3	2.0	+	-9.9			
	Oryx 11.0 gram/170 grains Product no. 17022	.312	2657	2378	2115	1871	2666	2135	1690	1321	100	-0.1	+	-1.5	-4.7	-17.2			
											150	0.4	1.0	+	-2.7	-14.2	1.0	4.5	10.0
											200	1.1	2.3	2.0	+	-10.1			
.280 Rem	Vulkan 11.0 gram/170 grains Product no. 17051	.357	2592	2346	2113	1894	2537	2078	1686	1354	100	0.0	+	-1.5	-4.8	-17.5			
											150	0.5	1.0	+	-2.8	-14.4	1.0	4.4	10.3
											200	1.2	2.4	2.1	+	-10.2			
	Oryx 11.0 gram/170 grains Product no. 17049	.321	2690	2416	2159	1918	2732	2204	1760	1389	100	-0.1	+	-1.4	-4.5	-16.5			
											150	0.4	1.0	+	-2.6	-13.6	1.0	4.5	10.5
											200	1.0	2.2	2.0	+	-9.7			
	Plastic point 11.0 gram/170 grains Product no. 17060	.373	2707	2468	2241	2026	2767	2299	1896	1550	100	-0.1	+	-1.3	-4.2	-15.4			
											150	0.3	0.9	+	-2.5	-12.7	0.9	3.9	9.1
											200	1.0	2.1	1.8	+	-9.1			
7,5x55 Swiss	Soft point 11.7 gram/180 grains Product no. 17511	.404	2651	2432	2223	2025	2810	2364	1976	1639	100	-0.1	+	-1.4	-4.4	-15.8			
											150	0.4	0.9	+	-2.5	-13.1	0.8	3.7	8.6
											200	1.0	2.2	1.9	+	-9.3			
7,62 Russian	Soft point 9.7 g/150 gr Product no. 17637	.287	2953	2622	2314	2028	2905	2291	1784	1370	100	-0.2	+	-1.1	-3.6	-13.7			
											150	0.2	0.7	+	-2.2	-11.5	1.1	4.6	11.2
											200	0.7	1.8	1.6	+	-8.3			
	Soft point 11.7 gram/180 grains Product no. 17634	.406	2575	2360	2154	1960	2651	2226	1856	1536	100	0.0	+	-1.5	-4.7	-17.0			
											150	0.5	1.0	+	-2.7	-14.0	0.8	3.9	9.0
											200	1.2	2.4	2.0	+	-9.9			
.300 Win. Mag.	Soft point 11.7 gram/180 grains Product no. 17680	.406	3018	2780	2555	2341	3641	3091	2610	2190	100	-0.2	+	-0.9	-3.0	-11.4			
											150	0.1	0.6	+	-1.8	-9.6	0.8	3.4	8.1
											200	0.5	1.5	1.4	+	-7.0			
	Plastic point 11.7 gram/180 grains Product no. 17687	.366	3018	2755	2506	2271	3641	3034	2512	2062	100	-0.2	+	-0.9	-3.1	-11.7			
											150	0.1	0.6	+	-1.9	-9.9	0.8	3.4	8.0
											200	0.6	1.6	1.4	+	-7.1			
	TXP Line, Swift 11.7 gram/180 grains Product no. 17519	.400	2920	2688	2467	2256	3409	2888	2432	2035	100	-0.2	+	-1.0	-3.3	-12.4			
											150	0.1	0.7	+	-2.0	-10.4	1.0	3.0	7.5
											200	0.6	1.7	1.5	+	-7.4			
	Vulkan 13.0 gram/200 grains Product no. 17644	.336	2887	2609	2347	2100	3702	3023	2447	1960	100	-0.2	+	-1.1	-3.6	-13.6			
											150	0.2	0.7	+	-2.2	-11.4	0.9	3.7	8.9
											200	0.7	1.8	1.6	+	-8.2			
	Oryx 13.0 gram/200 grains Product no. 17676	.323	3018	2755	2506	2271	4046	3371	2791	2292	100	-0.3	+	-0.9	-3.0	-11.5			
											150	0.1	0.6	+	-1.8	-9.8	0.8	3.4	8.0
											200	0.5	1.5	1.4	+	-7.0			
.30-06	Soft point 9.7 gram/150 grains Product no. 17643	.285	2972	2640	2331	2043	2943	2321	1810	1390	100	-0.2	+	-1.1	-3.5	-13.5			
											150	0.2	0.7	+	-2.1	-11.4	1.1	4.6	11.1
											200	0.7	1.8	1.6	+	-8.2			
	Alaska 11.7 gram/180 grains Product no. 17648	.257	2700	2351	2028	1734	2914	2209	1645	1202	100	-0.1	+	-1.5	-4.8	-18.2			
											150	0.4	1.0	+	-2.8	-15.2	1.4	6.0	14.6
											200	1.1	2.4	2.1	+	-11.0			
	Nosler 11.7 gram/180 grains Product no. 17649	.438	2700	2494	2297	2108	2914	2486	2108	1777	100	-0.1	+	-1.3	-4.1	-14.8			
											150	0.3	0.9	+	-2.4	-12.2	0.8	3.3	7.8
											200	0.9	2.1	1.8	+	-8.7			
.30-06	Plastic point 11.7 gram/180 grains Product no. 17653	.366	2700	2455	2222	2003	2914	2409	1974	1603	100	-0.1	+	-1.4	-4.3	-15.6			
											150	0.4	0.9	+	-2.5	-12.9	0.9	4.0	9.4
											200	1.0	2.1	1.9	+	-9.2			
	Vulkan 11.7 gram/180 grains Product no. 17659	.315	2700	2416	2150	1901	2914	2334	1848	1445	100	-0.1	+	-1.4	-4.5	-16.5			
											150	0.4	0.9	+	-2.6	-13.7	1.1	4.8	11.2
											200	1.0	2.2	2.0	+	-9.8			
	Oryx 11.7 gram/180 grains Product no. 17674	.288	2700	2387	2095	1825	2914	2278	1755	1332	100	-0.1	+	-1.4	-4.5	-17.1			
											150	0.3	0.9	+	-2.7	-14.3	1.1	5.3	12.8
											200	1.0	2.3	2.0	+	-10.2			
	TXP Line, Swift 11.7 gram/180 grains Product no. 17518	.400	2700	2479	2268	2067	2914	2456	2056	1708	100	-0.2	+	-1.3	-4.1	-14.9			
											150	0.3	0.8	+	-2.4	-12.4	0.8	3.2	7.6
											200	0.9	2.0	1.8	+	-8.8			
	Vulkan 13.0 gram/200 grains Product no. 17684	.347	2641	2385	2143	1916	3098	2527	2040	1631	100	-0.1	+	-1.5	-4.6	-16.9			
											150	0.4	1.0	+	-2.7	-13.9	1.0	4.4	10.5
											200	1.1	2.3	2.0	+	-9.9			
	Oryx 13.0 gram/200 grains Product no. 17677	.338	2625	2362	2115	1883	3061	2479	1987	1575	100	-0.1	+	-1.5	-4.7	-17.1			
											150	0.4	1.0	+	-2.7	-14.2	1.1	4.6	11.0
											200	1.1	2.3	2.0	+	-10.1			
.308 Win	Soft Point 9.7 gram/150 grains Product no. 17624	.289	2861	2537	2235	1954	2727	2144	1664	1272	100	-0.2	+	-1.2	-3.9	-14.9			
											150	0.3	0.8	+	-2.3	-12.5	1.2	4.9	11.7
											200	0.8	2.0	1.8	+	-9.0			
	TXP Line, Swift 10.8 gram/165 grains Product no. 17612	.367	2700	2459	2231	2015	2672	2216	1824	1488	100	-0.3	+	-1.3	-4.2	-15.3			
											150	0.3	0.9	+	-2.4	-12.8	0.8	3.5	8.4
											200	0.9	2.1	1.8	+	-9.1			
	Plastic point 11.7 gram/180 grains Product no. 17628	.358	2612	2365	2131	1911	2728	2235	1815	1460	100	0.1	+	-1.5	-4.7	-17.2			
											150	0.5	1.0	+	-2.7	-14.2	1.1	4.4	10.3
											200	1.1	2.4	2.1	+	-10.1			
	Nosler 11.7 gram/180 grains Product no. 17635	.442	2612	2414	2225	2044	2728	2330	1979	1670	100	0.1	+	-1.4	-4.5	-16.0			
											150	0.4	1.0	+	-2.6	-13.1	0.8	3.4	8.0
											200	1.1	2.2	1.9	+	-9.3			
	Alaska 11.7 gram/180 grains Product no. 17636	.257	2612	2269	1953	1667	2728	2059	1526	1111	100	0.0	+	-1.7	-5.3	-19.8			
											150	0.5	1.1	+	-3.1	-16.5	1.4	6.4	15.4
											200	1.3	2.7	2.3	+	-11.9			
	Vulkan 11.7 gram/180 grains Product no. 17660	.305	2612	2325	2056	1806	2728	2161	1690	1304	100	0.0	+	-1.6	-5.0	-18.2			
											150	0.5	1.1	+	-2.9	-15.1	1.2	5.2	12.4
											200	1.2	2.5	2.2	+	-10.8			
	Oryx 11.7 gram/180 grains Product no. 17675	.288	2612	2305	2019	1755	2728	2124	1629	1232	100	-0.1	+	-1.6	-5.0	-18.6			
											150	0.4	1.0	+	-2.9	-15.4	1.3	5.6	13.4
											200	1.2	2.5	2.2	+	-11.1			
	Vulkan 13.0 gram/200 grains Product no. 17683	.347	2461	2215	1983	1767	2690	2179	1747	1387	100	0.1	+	-1.8	-5.6	-20.1			
											150	0.7	1.2	+	-3.2	-16.5	1.2	4.9	11.7
											200	1.5	2.8	2.4	+	-11.7			

Note: "Height of trajectory above line of sight if sighted in A + yards. For sights 1,6 inch above bore." — "Wind drift in inches for a 10 M.P.H. cross wind."

BALLISTIC DATA

Caliber	Bullet Type / Bullet weight gram/grains / Product number	Ball. Co-Efficient	Velocity Feet/Sec Muzzle	V100 YDS	V200 YDS	V300 YDS	Energy Foot Pounds Muzzle	E100 YDS	E200 YDS	E300 YDS	Zero Range, Yards	Trajectory 50 YDS	100 YDS	150 YDS	200 YDS	300 YDS	Wind 100 YDS	200 YDS	300 YDS
.30-30 Win.	Soft point 9.7 gram/150 grains Product no. 17630	.257	2329	2008	1716	1459	1807	1344	981	709	100	0.2	+	-2.3	-7.2	-26.3	1.8	7.6	18.3
											150	1.0	1.6	+	-4.1	-21.7			
											200	2.0	3.6	3.1	+	-15.5			
.308 Norma Mag.	Vulkan 13.0 gram/200 grains Product no. 17650	.337	2903	2624	2361	2114	3744	3058	2476	1985	100	-0.2	+	-1.1	-3.6	-13.4	1.0	4.0	9.4
											150	0.2	0.7	+	-2.1	-11.2			
											200	0.7	1.8	1.6	+	-8.0			
7,65 Arg.	Soft point 11.7 gram/180 grains Product no. 17702	.425	2592	2386	2189	2002	2686	2276	1916	1602	100	-0.1	+	-1.5	-4.6	-16.5	0.9	3.6	8.5
											150	0.5	1.0	+	-2.7	-13.6			
											200	1.1	2.3	2.0	+	-9.6			
.303 British	Soft point 9.7 gram/150 grains Product no. 17712	.316	2723	2438	2170	1920	2470	1980	1569	1228	100	-0.1	+	-1.4	-4.4	-16.2	1.1	4.7	11.1
											150	0.4	0.9	+	-2.6	-13.4			
											200	1.0	2.2	1.9	+	-9.6			
7,7 JAP	Soft point 11.7 gram/180 grains Product no. 17722	.427	2493	2291	2099	1916	2485	2099	1761	1468	100	0.0	+	-1.7	-5.1	-18.2	0.9	3.8	9.0
											150	0.6	1.1	+	-2.9	-14.9			
											200	1.3	2.6	2.2	+	-10.5			
8x57 JS	Soft point 12.7 gram/196 grains Product no. 18003	.305	2526	2244	1981	1737	2778	2192	1708	1314	100	0.0	+	-1.7	-5.4	-19.8	1.3	5.4	13.0
											150	0.6	1.2	+	-3.1	-16.1			
											200	1.4	2.7	2.3	+	-11.6			
	Vulkan 12.7 gram/196 grains Product no. 18020	.347	2526	2276	2041	1821	2778	2256	1813	1443	100	0.0	+	-1.7	-5.2	-18.9	1.1	4.7	11.2
											150	0.6	1.1	+	-3.0	-15.5			
											200	1.3	2.6	2.2	+	-11.0			
	Alaska 12.7 gram/196 grains Product no. 18018	.296	2395	2112	1850	1611	2497	1942	1490	1130	100	0.1	+	-2.1	-6.3	-22.9	1.5	6.0	14.8
											150	0.8	1.4	+	-3.6	-18.8			
											200	1.7	3.2	2.7	+	-13.4			
.338 Win. Mag.	Nosler 16.2 gram/250 grains Product no. 18502	.478	2657	2470	2290	2118	3920	3387	2912	2490	100	-0.1	+	-1.3	-4.2	-15.1	0.8	3.1	7.2
											150	0.4	0.9	+	-2.4	-12.4			
											200	1.0	2.1	1.8	+	-8.7			
.358 Norma Mag.	Woodleigh 16.2 gram/250 grains Product no. 19005	.253	2799	2442	2112	1810	4350	3312	2478	1819	100	-0.1	+	-1.3	-4.4	-16.6	1.4	5.7	13.9
											150	0.3	0.9	+	-2.6	-13.9			
											200	1.0	2.2	1.9	+	-10.0			
9,3x57	Vulkan 15.0 gram/232 grains Product no. 19305	.278	2329	2031	1757	1512	2795	2126	1591	1178	100	0.2	+	-2.3	-7.0	-25.3	1.6	6.9	16.7
											150	0.9	1.5	+	-4.0	-20.8			
											200	1.9	3.5	3.0	+	-14.9			
	Alaska 18.5 gram/286 grains Product no. 19303	.365	2067	1857	1662	1484	2714	2190	1754	1399	100	0.4	+	-2.9	-8.6	-29.9	1.4	6.0	14.2
											150	1.4	1.9	+	-4.8	-24.1			
											200	2.5	4.3	3.6	+	-17.0			
9,3x62	Vulkan 15.0 gram/232 grains Product no. 19317	.278	2625	2327	2049	1792	3551	2791	2164	1655	100	0.0	+	-1.6	-5.0	-18.2	1.3	5.3	12.8
											150	0.5	1.0	+	-2.9	-15.1			
											200	1.2	2.5	2.2	+	-10.8			
	Oryx 15.0 gram/232 grains Product no. 19307	.267	2625	2294	1988	1708	3535	2700	2028	1497	100	-0.1	+	-1.6	-5.1	-19.0	1.4	6.0	14.6
											150	0.5	1.1	+	-3.0	-15.8			
											200	1.2	2.5	2.2	+	-11.4			
	Plastic point 18.5 gram/286 grains Product no. 19314	.376	2362	2141	1931	1736	3544	2911	2370	1914	100	0.1	+	-2.0	-6.1	-21.6	1.2	4.7	11.3
											150	0.8	1.3	+	-3.4	-17.6			
											200	1.6	3.1	2.6	+	-12.4			
	Alaska 18.5 gram/286 grains Product no. 19315	.365	2362	2135	1920	1720	3544	2894	2342	1879	100	0.1	+	-2.0	-6.2	-21.8	1.2	4.8	11.7
											150	0.8	1.4	+	-3.5	-17.8			
											200	1.7	3.1	2.6	+	-12.5			
9,3x74R	Vulkan 15.0 gram/232 grains Product no. 19321	.294	2625	2327	2049	1792	3551	2791	2164	1655	100	0.0	+	-1.6	-5.0	-18.2	1.2	5.3	12.7
											150	0.5	1.0	+	-2.9	-15.1			
											200	1.2	2.5	2.2	+	-10.8			
	Oryx 15.0 gram/232 grains Product no. 19328	.251	2526	2191	1883	1605	3274	2463	1819	1322	100	0.0	+	-1.9	-5.8	-21.5	1.6	6.7	16.1
											150	0.7	1.2	+	-3.3	-17.8			
											200	1.5	2.9	2.5	+	-12.8			
	Alaska 18.5 gram/286 grains Product no. 19320	.365	2362	2135	1920	1720	3544	2894	2342	1879	100	0.1	+	-2.0	-6.2	-21.8	1.2	4.9	11.6
											150	0.8	1.4	+	-3.5	-17.7			
											200	1.7	3.1	2.6	+	-12.5			
	Plastic point 18.5 gram/286 grains Product no. 19325	.365	2362	2135	1920	1720	3544	2894	2342	1879	100	0.1	+	-2.0	-6.2	-21.8	1.2	4.8	11.6
											150	0.8	1.4	+	-3.5	-17.7			
											200	1.7	3.1	2.6	+	-12.5			
.375 H&H Mag.	Soft point 19.4 gram/300 grains Product no. 19502	.257	2549	2211	1900	1619	4329	3258	2406	1747	100	0.0	+	-1.8	-5.7	-21.1	1.6	6.6	16.0
											150	0.6	1.2	+	-3.3	-17.5			
											200	1.4	2.8	2.5	+	-12.6			
	TXP Line, Swift 19.4 gram/300 grains Product no. 19503	.325	2559	2296	2049	1818	4363	3513	2798	2203	100	0.0	+	-1.6	-5.1	-18.6	1.2	4.9	11.6
											150	0.5	1.1	+	-2.9	-15.3			
											200	1.3	2.6	2.2	+	-10.9			
.416 Rigby	TXP Line, Swift 25.9 gram/400 grains Product no. 11069	.367	2350	2127	1917	1721	4906	4021	3266	2632	100	0.1	+	-2.0	-6.1	-21.7	1.2	4.8	11.4
											150	0.7	1.3	+	-3.5	-17.7			
											200	1.6	3.1	2.6	+	-12.5			
.458 Win	TXP Line, Swift 32.4 gram/500 grains Product no. 11120	.361	2116	1903	1705	1524	4972	4023	3228	2578	100	0.3	+	-2.7	-8.1	-28.2	1.4	5.7	13.6
											150	1.2	1.8	+	-4.5	-22.8			
											200	2.4	4.1	3.4	+	-16.1			

All Norma velocity and striking energy data for hunting cartridges have been obtained in 24 inch test barrels. If your barrel is longer or shorter than 2.4 inch, as a rule of thumb, your muzzle velocity changes by 2-3 feets/s. for each 4.0 inch difference. The velocity increases in longer barrels and decreases in shorter. Muzzle velocity of a cartridge also varies from gun to gun, due to different barrel material, length, wear, inside dimensions, etc. Therefore, all data and tables should be considered guides only. Our ballistics data are obtained in barrels representing averages of those available on the market. We calibrate our barrels according to international standards (CIP). We recommed that you zero-in your gun after each change of ammunition. Ammendment: The test barrels are 24 inch. If your barrel is longer or shorter than 24 inch, as a rule of thumb, your muzzle velocity changes by 15-25 f/s per inch difference.

BALLISTICS

PMC – Centerfire Rifle Ballistics

CALIBER	ITEM NO.	BULLET TYPE	WEIGHT (Grain)	VELOCITY (feet/second)					
				Muzzle	100 Yds.	200 Yds.	300 Yds.	400 Yds.	500 Yds.
222 Rem	222B	PSP	50	3044	2727	2354	2012	1651	1269
NEW! 223 Rem	223VB	HPBT	55	3240	2717	2250	1832	1473	1196
223 Rem	223A	FMJ-BT	55	3195	2882	2525	2169	1843	1432
223 Rem	223B	PSP	55	3112	2767	2421	2100	1806	1516
223 Rem	223C	PSP	64	2775	2511	2261	2026	1806	1604
NEW! 22-250 Rem	22-250VB	HPBT	55	3680	3104	2596	2141	1737	1395
22-250 Rem	22-250B	PSP	55	3586	3203	2852	2505	2178	1877
NEW! 243 Win	243VA	HPBT	85	3275	2922	2596	2292	2009	1748
NEW! 243 Win	243HB	SPBT	100	2960	2742	2534	2335	2144	1964
243 Win	243A	PSP	80	2940	2684	2444	2215	1999	1796
243 Win	243B	PSP	100	2743	2507	2283	2070	1869	1680
NEW! 6.5 x 55 Swed	6.5SMA	HPBT	140	2560	2398	2243	2093	1949	1811
NEW! 6.5 x 55 Swed	6.5HB	SPBT	140	2560	2386	2218	2057	1903	1757
6.5 x 55 Swedish	6.5MA	FMJ	144	2650	2370	2110	1870	1650	1450
6.5 x 55 Swedish	6.5MB	PSP	139	2850	2560	2290	2030	1790	1570
270 Win	270XA	X	130	2910	2717	2533	2356	2186	2023
270 Win	270XB	X	150	2700	2541	2387	2238	2095	1957
NEW! 270 Win	270HA	SPBT	130	3050	2830	2620	2421	2229	2047
NEW! 270 Win	270HB	SPBT	150	2850	2660	2477	2302	2134	1973
270 Win	270A	PSP	130	2816	2593	2381	2179	1987	1805
270 Win	270B	PSP	150	2547	2368	2197	2032	1875	1727
7mm Mauser	7MA	PSP	140	2660	2450	2260	2070	1890	1730
7mm Mauser	7MB	SP	175	2440	2140	1860	1600	1380	1200
7mm Rem Mag	7XA	X	140	3000	2808	2624	2448	2279	2116
7mm Rem Mag	7XB	X	160	2800	2639	2484	2334	2189	2049
NEW! 7mm Rem Mag	7HA	SPBT	140	3125	2891	2669	2457	2255	2063
NEW! 7mm Rem Mag	7HB	SPBT	160	2900	2696	2501	2314	2135	1965
7mm Rem Mag	7A	PSP	140	3099	2878	2668	2469	2279	2097
7mm Rem Mag	7B	PSP	160	2914	2748	2586	2428	2276	2130
7mm Rem Mag	7C	PSP	175	2860	2645	2442	2244	2057	1879
7.62 x 39	7.62A	FMJ	123	2350	2072	1817	1583	1368	1171
7.62 x 39	7.62B	PSP	125	2320	2046	1794	1563	1350	1156

ABBREVIATIONS: **X–** X-Bullet   **SFHP–** Starfire Hollow Point   **SP–** Soft Point   **PSP–** Pointed Soft Point   **FNSP–** Flat Nose Soft Point   **FMJ–** Full Metal Jacket

This Ballistics Table was calculated by using current data for each load. Velocity figures are from test barrels; user velocities may vary from those listed. The data in the table represents the approximate behavior of each loading under the following conditions: 59°F., barometric pressure of 29.52 inches, sea level altitude.

PMC – Centerfire Rifle Ballistics

ENERGY (foot/pounds)						Bullet Path (inches)					
Muzzle	100 Yds.	200 Yds.	300 Yds.	400 Yds.	500 Yds.	Muzzle	100 Yds.	200 Yds.	300 Yds.	400 Yds.	500 Yds.
1131	908	677	494	333	197	-1.50	+1.62	0.00	-7.93	-24.54	-54.33
1282	901	618	410	265	175	-1.50	+1.65	0.00	-8.61	-27.67	-62.20
1246	1014	779	574	415	250	-1.50	+1.36	0.00	-6.85	-21.13	-46.03
1182	935	715	539	398	281	-1.50	+1.54	0.00	-7.49	-22.91	-49.12
1094	896	726	583	464	366	-1.50	+2.01	0.00	-8.82	-26.11	-54.08
1654	1176	823	560	368	238	-1.50	+1.08	0.00	-6.30	-20.20	-45.76
1570	1253	993	766	579	430	-1.50	+0.95	0.00	-5.24	-16.05	-34.21
2024	1611	1272	991	761	577	-1.50	+1.31	0.00	-6.51	-19.66	-41.41
1945	1669	1425	1210	1021	856	-1.50	+1.61	0.00	-7.03	-20.46	-41.42
1535	1280	1060	871	709	573	-1.50	+1.66	0.00	-7.48	-22.06	-45.34
1670	1395	1157	951	776	626	-1.50	+2.02	0.00	-8.69	-25.50	-52.26
2037	1788	1563	1361	1181	1020	-1.50	+2.29	0.00	-9.19	-26.35	-52.74
2037	1769	1529	1315	1126	960	-1.50	+2.31	0.00	-9.42	-27.09	-54.25
2425	1950	1550	1215	945	730	-1.50	+2.70	0.00	-10.50	-30.90	-64.00
2515	2025	1615	1270	985	760	-1.50	+2.20	0.00	-8.90	-26.30	-54.50
2444	2131	1852	1602	1379	1181	-1.50	+1.64	0.00	-7.08	-20.40	-41.06
2428	2150	1897	1668	1461	1275	-1.50	+1.97	0.00	-8.07	-23.08	-46.04
2685	2312	1982	1691	1435	1209	-1.50	+1.46	0.00	-6.54	-19.02	-38.52
2705	2355	2043	1765	1516	1296	-1.50	+1.74	0.00	-7.40	-21.41	-43.02
2288	1941	1636	1370	1139	941	-1.50	+1.83	0.00	-7.96	-23.24	-47.33
2160	1868	1607	1375	1171	993	-1.50	+2.35	0.00	-9.54	-27.49	-55.32
2200	1865	1585	1330	1110	930	-1.50	+2.40	0.00	-9.60	-27.30	-53.50
2315	1775	1340	1000	740	565	-1.50	+1.50	-3.60	-18.60	-46.80	-92.80
2797	2451	2141	1863	1614	1391	-1.50	+1.49	0.00	-6.56	-18.93	-37.99
2785	2474	2192	1935	1703	1492	-1.50	+1.78	0.00	-7.41	-21.20	-42.33
3035	2597	2213	1877	1580	1322	-1.50	+1.35	0.00	-6.29	-18.35	-37.23
2987	2582	2222	1903	1620	1371	-1.50	+1.68	0.00	-7.22	-20.98	-42.33
2984	2574	2212	1895	1614	1366	-1.50	+1.35	0.00	-6.22	-18.14	-36.75
3016	2682	2375	2095	1840	1611	-1.50	+1.55	0.00	-6.74	-19.35	-38.67
3178	2718	2313	1956	1644	1372	-1.50	+2.00	0.00	-7.90	-22.70	-45.80
1495	1162	894	678	507	371	+0.60	0.00	-5.00	-26.40	-67.80	-135.00
1493	1161	893	678	505	371	+0.70	0.00	-5.20	-27.50	-70.60	-140.00

FMJ-BT– Full Metal Jacket - Boat Tail

BALLISTICS

PMC – Centerfire Rifle Ballistics

CALIBER	ITEM NO.	BULLET TYPE	WEIGHT (Grain)	VELOCITY (feet/second)				
				Muzzle	50 Yds.	100 Yds.	150 Yds.	200 Yds.
30-30 Win	C3030SFA	SFHP	150	2100	1930	1769	1618	1478
30-30 Win	3030A	FNSP	150	2159	1984	1819	1669	1554
30-30 Win	3030B	FNSP	170	1965	1817	1680	1577	1480
30 Carbine	30A	FMJ	110	1927	1730	1548	1386	1248

CALIBER	ITEM NO.	BULLET TYPE	WEIGHT (Grain)	VELOCITY (feet/second)				
				Muzzle	100 Yds.	200 Yds.	300 Yds.	400 Yds.	500 Yds.
308 Win	308XA	X	150	2700	2504	2316	2135	1964	1801
308 Win	308XB	X	165	2600	2425	2256	2095	1940	1793
NEW! 308 Win	308HA	SPBT	150	2820	2581	2354	2139	1935	1744
NEW! 308 Win	308HC	SPBT	180	2620	2446	2278	2117	1962	1815
NEW! 308 Win	308SMB	HPBT	168	2650	2460	2278	2103	1936	1778
308 Win (7.62 NATO)	308B	FMJ-BT	147	2751	2473	2257	2052	1859	1664
308 Win	308A	PSP	150	2643	2417	2203	1999	1807	1632
308 Win	308C	PSP	180	2410	2223	2044	1874	1714	1561
30-06 Sprg	3006XA	X	150	2750	2552	2361	2179	2005	1840
30-06 Sprg	3006XB	X	165	2750	2569	2395	2228	2067	1914
30-06 Sprg	3006XC	X	180	2650	2487	2331	2179	2034	1894
NEW! 30-06 Sprg	3006HA	SPBT	150	2900	2657	2427	2208	2000	1805
NEW! 30-06 Sprg	306HC	SPBT	180	2700	2523	2352	2188	2030	1879
30-06 Sprg	3006A	PSP	150	2773	2542	2322	2113	1916	1730
30-06 Sprg	3006B	PSP	180	2550	2357	2172	1996	1829	1671
30 M2	3006C	FMJ	150	2773	2542	2322	2113	1916	1730
300 Win Mag	300XA	X	150	3135	2918	2712	2515	2327	2146
300 Win Mag	300XC	X	180	2910	2738	2572	2412	2258	2109
NEW! 300 Win Mag	300HA	SPBT	150	3250	2987	2739	2504	2281	2070
NEW! 300 Win Mag	300HC	SPBT	180	2900	2714	2536	2365	2200	2042
300 Win Mag	300A	PSP	150	3150	2902	2665	2438	2222	2017
300 Win Mag	300B	PSP	180	2853	2643	2446	2258	2077	1906
NEW! 303 British	303HB	SPBT	180	2450	2276	2110	1951	1799	1656
8mm Mauser	8MA	PSP	170	2360	1969	1622	1333	1123	997
338 Win Mag	338XA	X	225	2780	2619	2464	2313	2168	2028
375 H&H Mag	375XA	X	270	2690	2528	2372	2221	2076	1936
375 H&H Mag	375XB	X	300	2530	2389	2252	2120	1993	1870

ABBREVIATIONS: **X**– X-Bullet **SFHP**– Starfire Hollow Point **SP**– Soft Point **PSP**– Pointed Soft Point **FNSP**– Flat Nose Soft Point **FMJ**– Full Metal Jacket

This Ballistics Table was calculated by using current data for each load. Velocity figures are from test barrels; user velocities may vary from those listed. The data in the table represents the approximate behavior of each loading under the following conditions: 59°F., barometric pressure of 29.52 inches, sea level altitude.

PMC – Centerfire Rifle Ballistics

ENERGY (foot/pounds)					Bullet Path (inches)				
Muzzle	50 Yds.	100 Yds.	150 Yds.	200 Yds.	Muzzle	50 Yds.	100 Yds.	150 Yds.	200 Yds.
1469	1240	1042	871	728	-0.50	+0.92	0.00	-3.67	-10.75
1552	1311	1102	928	804	-1.50	+0.35	0.00	-2.97	-9.04
1457	1246	1065	939	827	-1.50	+0.56	0.00	-3.60	-10.69
906	731	585	469	380	-0.50	+1.20	0.00	-4.85	-14.24

ENERGY (foot/pounds)						Bullet Path (inches)					
Muzzle	100 Yds.	200 Yds.	300 Yds.	400 Yds.	500 Yds.	Muzzle	100 Yds.	200 Yds.	300 Yds.	400 Yds.	500 Yds.
2428	2087	1786	1518	1284	1080	-1.50	+2.03	0.00	-8.56	-24.73	-49.99
2476	2154	1865	1608	1379	1177	-1.50	+2.23	0.00	-9.04	-26.04	-52.38
2648	2218	1846	1523	1247	1013	-1.50	+1.89	0.00	-8.18	-23.96	-49.00
2743	2391	2074	1790	1538	1316	-1.50	+2.17	0.00	-8.89	-25.54	-51.32
2619	2257	1935	1649	1399	1179	-1.50	+2.14	0.00	-8.85	-25.59	-51.64
2428	2037	1697	1403	1150	922	-1.50	+2.30	0.00	-9.30	-27.30	-57.90
2326	1946	1615	1331	1088	887	-1.50	+2.23	0.00	-9.39	-27.49	-56.22
2320	1975	1670	1404	1174	973	-1.50	+2.77	0.00	-11.08	-32.04	-64.84
2518	2168	1857	1582	1339	1127	-1.50	+1.95	0.00	-8.17	-23.73	-47.95
2770	2418	2101	1818	1565	1342	-1.50	+1.91	0.00	-7.97	-22.98	-46.14
2806	2472	2171	1898	1652	1433	-1.50	+2.07	0.00	-8.48	-24.34	-48.62
2801	2351	1961	1623	1332	1085	-1.50	+1.74	0.00	-7.66	-22.51	-46.04
2913	2543	2210	1913	1646	1411	-1.50	+2.00	0.00	-8.28	-23.89	-47.94
2560	2152	1796	1487	1222	997	-1.50	+1.94	0.00	-8.39	-24.56	-50.21
2598	2220	1886	1592	1336	1115	-1.50	+2.38	0.00	-9.74	28.20	-57.05
2560	2152	1796	1487	1222	997	-1.50	+1.94	0.00	-8.39	-24.56	-50.21
3273	2836	2449	2107	1803	1534	-1.50	+1.30	0.00	-6.13	-17.71	-35.74
3384	2995	2644	2325	2037	1778	-1.50	+1.61	0.00	-6.89	-19.77	-39.43
3517	2970	2498	2088	1733	1426	-1.50	+1.20	0.00	-5.96	-17.41	-35.55
3361	2944	2571	2235	1935	1666	-1.50	+1.65	0.00	-7.08	-20.34	-40.85
3304	2804	2364	1979	1644	1355	-1.50	+1.31	0.00	-6.21	-18.26	-37.36
3252	2792	2391	2037	1724	1451	-1.50	+1.73	0.00	-7.53	-21.89	-44.29
2399	2071	1779	1521	1294	1096	-1.50	+2.61	0.00	-10.44	-30.14	-60.15
2102	1463	993	671	476	375	-1.50	+1.80	-4.50	-24.30	-63.80	-130.70
3860	3426	3032	2673	2348	2054	-1.50	+1.81	0.00	-7.55	-21.61	-43.11
4337	3831	3371	2957	2582	2247	-1.50	+1.99	0.00	-8.15	-23.39	-46.70
4263	3801	3378	2994	2644	2329	-1.50	+2.31	0.00	-9.15	-26.09	-51.79

FMJ-BT– Full Metal Jacket - Boat Tail

BALLISTICS

REMINGTON BALLISTICS

CENTERFIRE RIFLE BALLISTICS TABLE

PREMIER® ULTRA MAG = PR
PREMIER® PARTITION® = PRP
PREMIER® BOAT TAIL = PRB
PREMIER® SAFARI GRADE = RS
PREMIER® BALLISTIC TIP® = PRT
PREMIER® VARMINT = PRV

These tables were calculated by computer. A standard scientific technique was used to predict trajectories from the best available data for each round. Trajectories shown typify the ammunition's performance at sea level, but note that they may vary due to atmospheric conditions and the equipment.

All velocity and energy figures in these charts have been derived by using test barrels of indicated lengths.

Ballistics shown are for 24" barrels, except those for .30 carbine and .44 Remington Magnum, which are for 20" barrels. These barrel lengths were chosen as representative, as it's impractical to show performance figures for all barrel lengths.

The muzzle velocities, muzzle energies and trajectory data in these tables represent the approximate performance expected of each specified loading. Differences in barrel lengths, internal firearms dimensions, temperatures, and test procedure can produce actual velocities that vary from those given here.

CENTERFIRE RIFLE VELOCITY VS. BARREL LENGTH

MUZZLE VELOCITY RANGE (FT./SEC.)	APPROX. CHANGE IN MUZZLE VELOCITY PER 1" CHANGE IN BARREL LENGTH (FT./SEC.)
2000-2500	10
2500-3000	20
3000-3500	30
3500-4000	40

1. Determine how much shorter, or longer, your barrel is than the test barrel.

2. In the left column of the above table, select the muzzle-velocity class of your cartridge.

3. To the right of that class, read the approximate change in velocity per inch of barrel length.

4. Multiply this number by the difference in the length of your barrel from that of the test barrel.

5. If your barrel is shorter than the test barrel, subtract this figure from the muzzle velocity shown for your cartridge.

6. If your barrel is longer, add this figure to the muzzle velocity shown.

The trajectory figures shown in these ballistic tables are the rise or drop, in inches, of the bullet from a direct line of sight at selected yardage. Sighting-in distances have been set at 100 to 250 yards.

The line of sight used is 1 1/2" above the axis of the bore. Since the rise or drop figures shown at the stated yardage are points of impact, you must hold low for positive figures, high for negative figures.

Many shooters who use the same cartridge often, find it helpful to commit the rise and drop figures for that cartridge to memory, or tape them to their rifle stock. That way, they know instantly the right "hold" as soon as they estimate the target's range.

FOOTNOTES:
Specifications are nominal. Balistics figures established in test barrels.
Individual rifles may vary from test-barrel specifications.
* Inches above or below line of sight. Hold low for positive numbers, high for negative numbers.
† .280 Rem. and 7mm Express® Remington are interchangeable.
‡ Interchangeable in .244 Remington.
¹ Bullet does not rise more than 1" above line of sight from muzzle to sighting-in range.
² Bullet does not rise more than 3" above line of sight from muzzle to sighting-in range.
***Note:** "zero" indicates yardage at which rifle was sighted in.*

Caliber	Index/EDI Number	Wt. (grs.)	Bullet Style
.17 Remington	R17REM	25	Hollow Point Power-Lokt®
.22 Hornet	R22HN1	45	Pointed Soft Point
	R22HN2	45	Hollow Point
.220 Swift	R220S1	50	Pointed Soft Point
	PRV220SA	50	V-Max™, Boat Tail
.222 Remington	R222R1	50	Pointed Soft Point
	R222R3	50	Hollow Point Power-Lokt®
	PRV222RA	50	V-Max™, Boat Tail
.223 Remington	PRV223RA	50	V-Max™, Boat Tail
	R223R1	55	Pointed Soft Point
	R223R2	55	Hollow Point Power-Lokt®
	R223R3	55	Metal Case
	R223R6	62	Hollow Point Match
.22-250 Remington	R22501	55	Pointed Soft Point
	R22502	55	Hollow Point Power-Lokt®
	PRV2250A	50	V-Max™, Boat Tail
.243 Win.	R243W1	80	Pointed Soft Point
	R243W2	80	Hollow Point Power-Lokt®
	R243W3	100	Pointed Soft Point Core-Lokt®
	PRV243WC	75	V-Max™, Boat Tail
	PRB243WA	100	Pointed Soft Point, Boat Tail
	PRT243WC	90	Nosler® Ballistic Tip®
6mm Remington	R6MM4 ‡	100	Pointed Soft Point Core-Lokt®
	PRV6MMRC ‡	75	V-Max™, Boat Tail
	PRB6MMRA ‡	100	Pointed Soft Point, Boat Tail
.25-20 Win.	R25202	86	Soft Point
.250 Savage	R250SV	100	Pointed Soft Point
.257 Roberts	R257	117	Soft Point Core-Lokt®
.25-06 Remington	R25062	100	Pointed Soft Point Core-Lokt®
	R25063	120	Pointed Soft Point Core-Lokt®
6.5x55 Swedish	R65SWE1	140	Pointed Soft Point Core-Lokt®
.260 Remington	PRP260RA ★	125	Nosler® Partition®
	R260R1	140	Pointed Soft Point Core-Lokt®
	PRT260RC	140	Nosler® Ballistic Tip®
.264 Win. Mag.	R264W2	140	Pointed Soft Point Core-Lokt®
.270 Win.	R270W1	100	Pointed Soft Point
	R270W2	130	Pointed Soft Point Core-Lokt®
	R270W3	130	Bronze Point™
	R270W4	150	Soft Point Core-Lokt®
	RS270WA	140	Swift A-Frame™ PSP
	PRB270WA	140	Pointed Soft Point, Boat Tail
	PRT270WB	140	Nosler® Ballistic Tip®
	PRP270WD ★	150	Nosler® Partition®
7mm Mauser (7x57)	R7MSR1	140	Pointed Soft Point Core-Lokt®
7x64	R7X642	175	Pointed Soft Point Core-Lokt®
7mm-08 Remington	R7M081	140	Pointed Soft Point Core-Lokt®
	R7M082	120	Hollow Point
	PRB7M08RA	140	Pointed Soft Point, Boat Tail
	PRT7M08RA	140	Nosler® Ballistic Tip®
.280 Remington	R280R3 †	140	Pointed Soft Point Core-Lokt®
	R280R1 †	150	Pointed Soft Point Core-Lokt®
	R280R2 †	165	Soft Point Core-Lokt®
	PRB280RA	140	Pointed Soft Point, Boat Tail
	PRT280RA	140	Nosler® Ballistic Tip®
7mm Remington Mag.	R7MM2	150	Pointed Soft Point Core-Lokt®
	R7MM3	175	Pointed Soft Point Core-Lokt®
	R7MM4	140	Pointed Soft Point Core-Lokt®
	RS7MMA	160	Swift A-Frame™ PSP
	PRP7MMA ★	160	Nosler® Partition®
	PRB7MMRA	140	Pointed Soft Point, Boat Tail
	PRT7MMC	150	Nosler® Ballistic Tip®
7mm STW	R7MSTW1	140	Pointed Soft Point Core-Lokt®
	RS7MSTWA	140	Swift A-Frame™ PSP

REMINGTON BALLISTICS

Primer Number	Velocity (ft./sec.) Muzzle	100 yds.	200 yds.	300 yds.	400 yds.	500 yds.	Energy (ft.-lbs.) Muzzle	100 yds.	200 yds.	300 yds.	400 yds.	500 yds.	Short-range[1] Trajectory* 50 yds.	100 yds.	150 yds.	200 yds.	250 yds.	300 yds.	Long-range[2] Trajectory* 100 yds.	150 yds.	200 yds.	250 yds.	300 yds.	400 yds.	500 yds.	Barrel Length
7½	4040	3284	2644	2086	1606	1235	906	599	388	242	143	85	-0.3	0.3	zero	-1.3	-3.8	-7.8	1.8	2.3	1.8		-3.3	-16.6	-43.6	24"
6½	2690	2042	1502	1128	948	840	723	417	225	127	90	70	-0.1	zero	-2.1	-7.1	-16.0	-30.0	1.4	zero	-4.3	-12.4	-25.8	-74.2	-162.0	24"
6½	2690	2042	1502	1128	948	840	723	417	225	127	90	70	-0.1	zero	-2.1	-7.1	-16.0	-30.0	1.4	zero	-4.3	-12.4	-25.8	-74.2	-162.0	
9½	3780	3158	2617	2135	1710	1357	1586	1107	760	506	325	204	-0.2	0.3	zero	-1.4	-4.0	-8.2	0.4	1.0	zero	-2.3	-6.2	-20.1	-46.1	24"
9½	3780	3321	2908	2532	2185	1866	1586	1224	939	711	530	387	-0.3	0.3	zero	-1.2	-3.3	-6.7	0.8	0.9	zero	-1.9	-5.0	-15.4	-33.2	24"
7½	3140	2602	2123	1700	1350	1107	1094	752	500	321	202	136	0.1	0.7	zero	-2.3	-6.5	-13.1	1.9	1.7	zero	-3.6	-9.7	-31.7	-72.8	24"
7½	3140	2635	2182	1777	1432	1172	1094	771	529	351	228	152	0.1	0.7	zero	-2.2	-6.2	-12.5	1.8	1.6	zero	-3.5	-9.2	-29.6	-67.1	
7½	3140	2744	2380	2045	1740	1471	1094	836	629	464	336	240	0.1	0.6	zero	-1.9	-5.4	-10.7	1.6	1.5	zero	-3.0	-7.8	-23.9	-51.7	24"
7½	3300	2889	2514	2168	1851	1568	1209	927	701	522	380	273	-0.1	0.5	zero	-1.7	-4.8	-9.4	-0.1	1.3	zero	-2.6	-6.9	-21.2	-45.8	24"
7½	3240	2747	2304	1905	1554	1270	1282	921	648	443	295	197	-0.1	0.6	zero	-2.0	-5.6	-11.2	1.6	1.5	zero	-3.1	-8.2	-26.2	-58.6	
7½	3240	2773	2352	1969	1627	1341	1282	939	675	473	323	220	-0.1	0.6	zero	-1.9	-5.4	-10.7	1.5	1.4	zero	-3.0	-7.9	-24.8	-55.1	24"
7½	3240	2759	2326	1933	1587	1301	1282	929	660	456	307	207	-0.1	0.6	zero	-1.9	-5.5	-11.0	1.6	1.5	zero	-3.1	-8.1	-25.5	-57.0	
7½	3025	2572	2162	1792	1471	1217	1260	911	643	442	298	204	0.2	0.7	zero	-2.3	-6.5	-12.9	1.9	1.7	zero	-3.6	-9.4	-29.9	-66.4	24"
9½	3680	3137	2656	2222	1832	1493	1654	1201	861	603	410	272	-0.2	0.3	zero	-1.4	-4.0	-8.1	1.9	2.4	1.8	zero	-3.3	-15.5	-38.3	
9½	3680	3209	2785	2400	2046	1725	1654	1257	947	703	511	363	-0.2	0.3	zero	-1.3	-3.7	-7.4	1.8	2.2	1.7	zero	-3.0	-13.7	-32.8	24"
9½	3725	3272	2864	2491	2147	1832	1540	1188	910	689	512	372	-0.3	0.3	zero	-1.2	-3.5	-7.0	1.7	2.1	1.6	zero	-2.8	-12.8	-30.4	
9½	3350	2955	2593	2259	1951	1670	1993	1551	1194	906	676	495	-0.1	0.5	zero	-1.6	-4.5	-8.8	2.2	2.7	2.0	zero	-3.5	-15.8	-37.3	
9½	3350	2955	2593	2259	1951	1670	1993	1551	1194	906	676	495	-0.1	0.5	zero	-1.6	-4.5	-8.8	2.2	2.7	2.0	zero	-3.5	-15.8	-37.3	
9½	2960	2697	2449	2215	1993	1786	1945	1615	1332	1089	882	708	0.1	0.7	zero	-2.0	-5.4	-10.4	1.6	1.5	zero	-2.9	-7.5	-22.1	-45.4	24"
9½	3375	3065	2775	2504	2248	2008	1897	1564	1282	1044	842	671	-0.1	0.4	zero	-1.4	-4.0	-7.8	2.0	2.4	1.8	zero	-3.0	-13.3	-30.6	
9½	2960	2720	2492	2275	2069	1875	1945	1642	1378	1149	950	780	0.1	0.7	zero	-1.9	-5.3	-10.1	2.8	3.2	2.3	zero	-3.8	-16.6	-37.6	
9½	3120	2871	2635	2411	2199	1997	1946	1647	1388	1162	966	797	-0.1	0.5	zero	-1.7	-4.5	-8.9	1.4	1.3	zero	-2.5	-6.4	-18.8	-38.3	
9½	3100	2829	2573	2332	2104	1889	2133	1777	1470	1207	983	792	-0.1	0.6	zero	-1.8	-4.8	-9.3	1.4	1.3	zero	-2.6	-6.7	-19.8	-40.8	
9½	3400	3088	2797	2524	2267	2026	1925	1587	1303	1061	856	683	-0.1	0.4	zero	-1.4	-3.9	-7.6	1.9	2.3	1.7	zero	-3.0	-13.1	-30.1	24"
9½	3100	2852	2617	2394	2183	1982	2134	1806	1521	1273	1058	872	-0.1	0.5	zero	-1.7	-4.7	-9.0	1.4	1.3	zero	-2.6	-6.5	-19.1	-38.9	
6½	1460	1194	1030	931	858	797	407	272	203	165	141	121	zero	-3.5	-13.2	-30.0	-54.7	-89.1	zero	-7.9	-22.9	-45.8	-78.5	-173.0	-315.5	24"
9½	2820	2504	2210	1936	1684	1461	1765	1392	1084	832	630	474	-0.1	zero	-1.3	-4.1	-8.7	-15.3	2.0	1.8	zero	-3.6	-9.2	-27.7	-58.6	24"
9½	2650	2291	1961	1663	1404	1199	1824	1363	999	718	512	373	-0.1	zero	-1.6	-5.2	-10.5	-19.5	2.6	2.3	zero	-4.1	-11.7	-36.1	-78.2	24"
9½	3230	2893	2580	2287	2014	1762	2316	1858	1478	1161	901	689	-0.1	0.5	zero	-1.7	-4.6	-9.1	1.3	1.3	zero	-2.6	-6.6	-19.8	-41.7	
9½	2990	2730	2484	2252	2032	1825	2382	1985	1644	1351	1100	887	0.1	0.6	zero	-1.9	-5.2	-10.1	1.6	1.4	zero	-2.8	-7.2	-21.4	-44.1	24"
9½	2550	2353	2164	1984	1814	1654	2021	1720	1456	1224	1023	850	-0.1	zero	-1.5	-4.8	-9.9	-17.0	2.4	2.1	zero	-3.9	-9.8	-27.0	-57.8	24"
9½	2875	2669	2473	2285	2105	1934	2294	1977	1697	1449	1230	1037	0.2	0.7	zero	-2.0	-5.4	-10.4	1.71	1.5	zero	-2.9	-7.4	-21.4	-43.4	
9½	2750	2544	2347	2158	1979	1812	2351	2011	1712	1448	1217	1021	0.3	0.8	zero	-2.3	-6.1	-11.7	1.9	1.7	zero	-3.3	-8.3	-24.0	-47.2	24"
9½	2890	2688	2494	2309	2131	1962	2226	1924	1657	1420	1210	1025	0.2	0.7	zero	-2.0	-5.4	-10.2	1.7	1.5	zero	-2.9	-7.3	-21.1	-42.5	
9½M	3030	2782	2548	2326	2114	1914	2854	2406	2018	1682	1389	1139	0.1	0.6	zero	-1.8	-5.0	-9.6	1.5	1.4	zero	-2.7	-6.9	-20.2	-41.3	24"
9½	3320	2924	2561	2225	1916	1636	2448	1898	1456	1099	815	594	-0.1	0.5	zero	-1.6	-4.6	-9.1	2.3	2.8	2.0	zero	-3.6	-16.2	-38.5	
9½	3060	2776	2510	2259	2022	1801	2702	2225	1818	1472	1180	936	0.1	0.6	zero	-1.8	-5.1	-9.8	1.5	1.4	zero	-2.8	-7.0	-20.9	-43.3	
9½	3060	2802	2559	2329	2110	1904	2702	2267	1890	1565	1285	1046	-0.1	0.6	zero	-1.8	-4.9	-9.5	1.5	1.3	zero	-2.7	-6.8	-20.0	-41.1	
9½	2850	2504	2183	1886	1618	1385	2705	2087	1587	1185	872	639	0.3	0.8	zero	-2.4	-6.7	-13.0	2.0	1.8	zero	-3.6	-9.4	-28.6	-61.2	24"
9½	2925	2652	2394	2152	1923	1711	2659	2186	1782	1439	1150	910	0.2	0.7	zero	-2.1	-5.6	-10.9	1.7	1.5	zero	-3.1	-7.8	-23.2	-48.0	
9½	2960	2749	2548	2355	2171	1995	2723	2349	2018	1724	1465	1237	0.1	0.6	zero	1.9	-5.1	-9.7	1.6	1.4	zero	-2.7	-6.9	-20.1	-40.7	
9½	2960	2754	2557	2366	2187	2014	2724	2358	2032	1743	1487	1262	0.1	0.6	zero	-1.9	-5.0	-9.7	1.6	1.4	zero	-2.7	-6.9	-20.0	-40.3	
9½	2850	2652	2463	2282	2108	1942	2705	2343	2021	1734	1480	1256	0.2	0.7	zero	-2.0	-5.5	-10.5	1.7	1.5	zero	-3.0	-7.5	-21.6	-43.6	
9½	2660	2435	2221	2018	1827	1648	2199	1843	1533	1266	1037	844	-0.1	zero	-1.4	-4.4	-9.1	-15.8	2.2	1.9	zero	-3.6	-9.2	-27.4	-55.3	24"
9½	2650	2445	2248	2061	1883	1716	2728	2322	1964	1650	1378	1144	-0.1	zero	-1.4	-4.3	-9.0	-15.6	2.2	1.9	zero	-3.6	-9.1	-26.4	-53.5	24"
9½	2860	2625	2402	2189	1988	1798	2542	2142	1793	1490	1228	1005	0.2	0.7	zero	-2.1	-5.7	-11.0	1.8	1.6	zero	-3.1	-7.8	-22.9	-46.8	
9½	3000	2725	2467	2223	1992	1778	2398	1979	1621	1316	1058	842	0.1	0.6	zero	-1.9	-5.3	-10.2	1.6	1.4	zero	-2.9	-7.3	-21.7	-44.9	24"
9½	2860	2656	2460	2273	2094	1923	2542	2192	1881	1606	1363	1150	0.2	0.7	zero	-2.0	-5.5	-10.5	1.7	1.5	zero	-3.0	-7.5	-21.7	-43.9	
9½	2860	2670	2488	2313	2145	1984	2543	2217	1925	1663	1431	1224	0.2	0.7	zero	-2.0	-5.4	-10.3	1.7	1.6	zero	-2.9	-7.3	-21.2	-42.6	
9½	3000	2758	2528	2309	2102	1905	2797	2363	1986	1657	1373	1128	0.1	0.6	zero	-1.9	-5.1	-9.8	1.5	1.4	zero	-2.8	-7.0	-20.5	-42.0	
9½	2890	2624	2373	2135	1912	1705	2781	2293	1875	1518	1217	968	0.2	0.7	zero	-2.1	-5.8	-11.2	1.8	1.6	zero	-3.1	-8.0	-23.6	-48.8	
9½	2820	2510	2220	1950	1701	1479	2913	2308	1805	1393	1060	801	-0.1	zero	-1.3	-4.1	-8.6	-15.2	2.0	1.8	zero	-3.6	-9.1	-27.4	-57.8	24"
9½	3000	2789	2588	2395	2211	2035	2797	2418	2081	1783	1519	1287	0.1	0.6	zero	-1.8	-4.9	-9.3	1.5	1.4	zero	-2.7	-6.7	-19.5	-39.4	
9½	3000	2804	2616	2436	2263	2097	2799	2445	2128	1848	1593	1368	0.1	0.6	zero	-1.8	-4.8	-9.2	1.5	1.3	zero	-2.6	-6.8	-19.0	-38.2	
9½M	3110	2830	2568	2320	2085	1866	3221	2667	2196	1792	1448	1160	-0.1	0.5	zero	-1.6	-4.6	-9.0	1.3	1.2	zero	-2.5	-6.6	-20.2	-43.4	
9½M	2860	2645	2440	2244	2057	1879	3178	2718	2313	1956	1644	1372	0.2	0.7	zero	-2.1	-5.6	-10.7	1.7	1.5	zero	-3.0	-7.6	-22.1	-44.8	
9½M	3175	2923	2684	2458	2243	2039	3133	2655	2240	1878	1564	1292	-0.1	0.5	zero	-1.6	-4.4	-8.5	2.2	2.6	1.9	zero	-3.2	-14.2	-32.0	24"
9½M	2900	2659	2430	2212	2006	1812	2987	2511	2097	1739	1430	1166	0.2	0.7	zero	-2.0	-5.5	-10.7	1.7	1.5	zero	-3.0	-7.6	-22.4	-44.7	
9½M	2950	2752	2563	2381	2207	2040	3091	2690	2333	2014	1730	1478	0.6	1.5	1.4	zero	-2.7	-6.9	0.6	zero	-1.9	-5.0	-9.6	-23.6	-44.6	
9½M	3175	2956	2747	2547	2356	2174	3133	2715	2345	2017	1726	1469	-0.1	0.5	zero	-1.6	-4.2	-8.2	2.2	2.6	1.6	zero	-3.1	-13.4	-30.0	
9½M	3110	2912	2723	2542	2367	2200	3222	2825	2470	2152	1867	1612	-0.1	0.5	zero	-1.6	-4.3	-8.3	1.2	1.2	zero	-2.3	-5.9	-17.3	-34.8	
9½M	3325	3064	2818	2585	2364	2153	3436	2918	2468	2077	1737	1441	-0.1	0.4	zero	-1.4	-3.9	-7.6	2.0	2.4	1.7	zero	-2.9	-12.8	-28.8	24"
9½M	3325	3020	2735	2467	2215	1978	3436	2834	2324	1892	1525	1215	-0.1	0.4	zero	-1.5	-4.1	-8.0	2.1	2.5	1.8	zero	-3.1	-13.8	-31.5	

★ New For 1999

BALLISTICS

CENTERFIRE RIFLE BALLISTICS TABLE (cont.)

PREMIER® ULTRA MAG = PR
PREMIER® PARTITION® = PRP
PREMIER® BOAT TAIL = PRB
PREMIER® SAFARI GRADE = RS
PREMIER® BALLISTIC TIP® = PRT
PREMIER® VARMINT = PRV

VENTED TEST-BARREL BALLISTICS

This Remington® patented, industry-accepted method provides data that more precisely reflect actual use of revolver ammunition. It considers cylinder gap, barrel length, powder position, and production tolerances. Although our final values differ from conventional figures, the ammunition is unchanged. Key elements of our patented procedure include: (a) horizontal powder orientation; (b) cylinder gap: .008"; (c) barrel length: 4".

INTERCHANGEABILITY CHART

Cartridges within groups shown are interchangeable. Other substitutions should not be made withour specific recommendation of the firearms manufacturer since improper combinations could resul in firearm damage or personal injury.

RIMFIRE

.22 W.R.F.
.22 Remington Special
.22 Win. Model 1890 in a .22 Win. Mag. Rimfire but not conversely

CENTERFIRE

.25-20 Remington
.25-20 W.C.F.
.25-200 Win.
.25-20 Win. High Speed
.25-20 Marlin
.25 W.C.F.

6mm Rem. (80 & 90 grain)
.244 Remington

.25 Automatic
.25 Auto. Colt Pistol (ACP)
.25 (6.35mm) Automatic Pistol
6.35mm Browning

7mm Express® Remington
.280 Remington

.30-30 Sav.
.30-30 Win.
.30-30 Win. Accelerator® (See Note A)
.30-30 Marlin
.30-30 Win. High Speed
.30-30 W.C.F.

.32 Colt Automatic
.32 Auto. Colt Pistol (ACP)
.32 (7.65mm) Automatic Pistol
7.65mm Automatic Pistol
7.65mm Browning (not interchangeable with 7.65mm Luger)

.32 Short Colt in .32 Long Colt but not conversely (See Note C)

.32 S&W in .32 S&W Long but not conversely

.32 S&W Long
.32 Colt New Police
.32 Colt Police Positive

.32 W.C.F. (See Note A)
.32 Win. (See Note A)
.32-20 Win. High Speed (See Note A)
.32-20 Colt L.M.R.
.32-20 W.C.F. (See Note G)
.32-20 Win. and Marlin

.38 S&W
.38 Colt New Police
.380 Webley

.38 Colt Special
.38 S&W Special
.38 Special Targetmaster®
.38 S&W Special Mid-Range (See Note D)
.38 Special (+P) (See Note B)
.38-44 Special (+P) (See Note B)
.38 Special
.38 Special Flat Point

.38 Short Colt in .38 Long Colt but not conversely. Both can be used in .38 Special

.38 Marlin
.38 Win. (See Note A)
.38 Remington (See Note A)
.38-40 Win.
.38 W.C.F. (See Note A)

.38 Automatic in .38 Super (+P) but not conversely

.380 Automatic
9mm Browning Short (Corto Kurz)

9mm Luger (See Note E)
9mm Parabellum

.44 S&W Special (See Note F)

.44 Marlin
.44 Win.
.44 Remington
.44-40 Win.
.44 W.C.F.

.45-70 Government
.45-70 Marlin, Win.
.45-70-405

Note A: High-speed cartridges must not be used in revolvers. They should be used only in rifles made especially for them.

Note B: Ammunition with (+P) on the case head-stamp is loaded to higher pressure. Use only in firearms designated for this cartridge and so recommended by the gun manufacturer.

Note C: Not for use in revolvers chambered for .32 S&W or .32 S&W Long.

Note D: All .38 Special cartridges can be used in .357 Magnum revolvers but not conversely.

Note E: 9mm sub-machine gun cartridges should not be used in handguns.

Note F: .44 Russian and .44 S&W Special can be used in .44 Remington Magnum revolvers but not conversely.

Note G: Not to be used in Win. M-66 and M-73.

FOOTNOTES:

Specifications are nominal. Balistics figures established in test barrels.

Individual rifles may vary from test-barrel specifications.

* Inches above or below line of sight. Hold low for positive numbers, high for negative numbers.

† .280 Rem. and 7mm Express® Remington are interchangeable.

‡ Interchangeable in .244 Remington.

1 Bullet does not rise more than 1" above line of sight from muzzle to sighting-in range.

2 Bullet does not rise more than 3" above line of sight from muzzle to sighting-in range.

Note: "zero" indicates yardage at which rifle was sighted in.

Caliber	Index/EDI Number	Wt. (grs.)	Bullet
.30 Carbine	R30CAR	110	Soft Point
.30-30 Win. Accelerator®	R3030A	55	Soft Point
.30-30 Win.	R30301	150	Soft Point Core-Lokt®
	R30302	170	Soft Point Core-Lokt®
	R30303	170	Hollow Point Core-Lokt®
.300 Savage	R30SV3	180	Pointed Soft Point Core-Lokt®
	R30SV2	150	Pointed Soft Point Core-Lokt®
.30-40 Krag	R30402	180	Pointed Soft Point Core-Lokt®
.308 Win.	R308W1	150	Pointed Soft Point Core-Lokt®
	R308W2	180	Soft Point Core-Lokt®
	R308W3	180	Pointed Soft Point Core-Lokt®
	PRP308WB ★	180	Nosler® Partition®
	R308W7	168	Boat Tail HP Match
	PRB308WA	165	Pointed Soft Point, Boat Tail
	PRT308WB	165	Nosler® Ballistic Tip®
.30-06 Springfield Accelerator®	R30069	55	Pointed Soft Point
.30-06 Springfield	R30061	125	Pointed Soft Point
	R30062	150	Pointed Soft Point Core-Lokt®
	R30063	150	Bronze Point™
	R3006B	165	Pointed Soft Point Core-Lokt®
	R30064	180	Soft Point Core-Lokt®
	R30065	180	Pointed Soft Point Core-Lokt®
	R30066	180	Bronze Point™
	R30067	220	Soft Point Core-Lokt®
	RS3006A	180	Swift A-Frame™ PSP
	PRP3006A ★	180	Nosler® Partition®
	PRB3006SA	165	Pointed Soft Point, Boat Tail
	PRT3006A	150	Nosler® Ballistic Tip®
	PRT3006B	165	Nosler® Ballistic Tip®
.300 Win. Mag.	R300W1	150	Pointed Soft Point Core-Lokt®
	R300W2	180	Pointed Soft Point Core-Lokt®
	PRP300WA ★	180	Nosler® Partition®
	PRT300WA ★	180	Nosler® Ballistic Tip®
	RS300WA	200	Swift A-Frame™ PSP
	PRB300WA	190	Pointed Soft Point, Boat Tail
.300 Wby. Mag.	R300WB1	180	Pointed Soft Point Core-Lokt®
	RS300WBB	200	Swift A-Frame™ PSP
	PRB300WBA	190	Pointed Soft Point, Boat Tail
.300 Remington Ultra Mag.	PR300UM1 ★	180	Nosler® Partition®
.303 British	R303B1	180	Soft Point Core-Lokt®
7.62x39mm	R762391	125	Pointed Soft Point
.32-20 Win.	R32201	100	Lead
.32 Win. Special	R32WS2	170	Soft Point Core-Lokt®
8mm Remington Mag.	RS8MMRA	200	Swift A-Frame™ PSP
8mm Mauser	R8MSR	170	Soft Point Core-Lokt®
.338 Win. Mag.	R338W1	225	Pointed Soft Point Core-Lokt®
	R338W2	250	Pointed Soft Point Core-Lokt®
	RS338WA	225	Swift A-Frame™ PSP
	PRT338WB	200	Nosler® Ballistic Tip®
	PRP338WC ★	210	Nosler® Partition®
.35 Remington	R35R1	150	Pointed Soft Point Core-Lokt®
	R35R2	200	Soft Point Core-Lokt®
.35 Whelen	R35WH1	200	Pointed Soft Point
	R35WH3	250	Pointed Soft Point
.375 H&H Mag.	R375M1	270	Soft Point
	RS375MA	300	Swift A-Frame™ PSP
.416 Remington Mag.	RS416RA ★	400	Swift A-Frame™ PSP
.44-40 Win.	R4440W	200	Soft Point
.44 Remington Mag.	R44MG2	240	Soft Point
	R44MG3	240	Semi-Jacketed Hollow Point
	R44MG6	210	Semi-Jacketed Hollow Point
	RH44MGA	275	JHP Core-Lokt®
.444 Mar.	R444M	240	Soft Point
.45-70 Government	R4570G	405	Soft Point
	R4570L	300	Jacketed Hollow Point
.458 Win. Mag.	RS458WA	450	Swift A-Frame™ PSP

REMINGTON BALLISTICS

Primer		Velocity (ft./sec.)					Energy (ft.-lbs.)						Short-range[1] Trajectory*						Long-range[2] Trajectory*							Barrel
Number	Muzzle	100 yds.	200 yds.	300 yds.	400 yds.	500 yds.		100 yds.	200 yds.	300 yds.	400 yds.	500 yds.	50 yds.	100 yds.	150 yds.	200 yds.	250 yds.	300 yds.	100 yds.	150 yds.	200 yds.	250 yds.	300 yds.	400 yds.	500 yds.	Length
6½	1990	1567	1236	1035	923	842	967	600	373	262	208	173	0.6	zero	-4.2	-12.9	-27.2	-48.6	zero	-4.2	-12.9	-27.2	-48.6	-116.6	-225.5	20"
9½	3400	2693	2085	1570	1187	986	1412	886	521	301	172	119	-0.1	0.6	zero	-2.2	-6.2	-13.2	1.7	1.6	zero	-3.5	-9.9	-34.3	-83.3	24"
9½	2390	1973	1605	1303	1095	974	1902	1296	858	565	399	316	0.2	zero	-2.4	-7.6	-16.1	-28.8	1.6	zero	-4.3	-12.1	-24.0	-64.2	-133.2	
9½	2200	1895	1619	1381	1191	1061	1827	1355	989	720	535	425	0.3	zero	-2.7	-8.3	-17.1	-29.9	1.8	zero	-4.6	-12.6	-24.5	-62.6	-125.3	24"
9½	2200	1895	1619	1381	1191	1061	1827	1355	989	720	535	425	0.3	zero	-2.7	-8.3	-17.1	-29.9	1.8	zero	-4.6	-12.6	-24.5	-62.6	-125.3	
9½	2350	2025	1728	1467	1252	1098	2207	1639	1193	860	626	482	0.2	zero	-2.3	-7.1	-14.7	-25.9	1.5	zero	-4.0	-10.9	-21.3	-54.8	-110.3	24"
9½	2630	2354	2095	1853	1631	1432	2303	1845	1462	1143	806	685	-0.1	zero	-1.5	-4.8	-10.1	-17.6	2.4	2.1	zero	-4.1	-10.4	-30.9	-64.6	
9½	2430	2213	2007	1813	1632	1468	2360	1957	1610	1314	1064	861	0.1	zero	-1.8	-5.6	-11.6	-18.6	1.2	zero	-3.2	-8.5	-15.0	-39.9	-76.7	24"
9½	2820	2533	2263	2009	1774	1560	2648	2137	1705	1344	1048	810	-0.1	zero	-1.2	-3.9	-8.4	-14.7	2.0	1.7	zero	-3.4	-8.8	-26.2	-54.8	
9½	2620	2274	1955	1666	1414	1212	2743	2066	1527	1109	799	587	-0.1	zero	-1.7	-5.3	-10.7	-19.7	2.6	2.3	zero	-4.1	-11.8	-36.3	-78.2	
9½	2620	2393	2178	1974	1782	1604	2743	2288	1896	1557	1269	1028	-0.1	zero	-1.5	-4.6	-9.5	-16.5	2.3	2.0	zero	-3.8	-9.7	-28.3	-57.8	24"
9½	2620	2436	2259	2089	1927	1774	2743	2371	2039	1774	1485	1257	-0.1	zero	-1.4	-4.4	-9.1	-15.6	2.2	1.9	zero	-3.6	-9.0	-26.0	-52.4	
9½	2680	2493	2314	2143	1979	1823	2678	2318	1998	1713	1460	1239	-0.1	zero	-1.3	-4.1	-8.5	-14.7	2.1	1.8	zero	-3.4	-8.6	-24.7	-49.9	
9½	2700	2497	2303	2117	1941	1773	2670	2284	1942	1642	1379	1152	-0.1	zero	-1.3	-4.1	-8.5	-14.8	2.0	1.8	zero	-3.4	-8.6	-25.0	-50.6	
9½	2700	2613	2333	2161	1996	1838	2672	2314	1995	1711	1460	1239	0.1	zero	-1.3	-4.0	-6.4	-14.4	2.0	1.7	zero	-3.3	-8.4	-24.3	-48.9	
9½	4080	3484	2964	2499	2080	1706	2033	1482	1073	763	528	355	-0.4	0.2	zero	-1.0	-3.0	-6.2	1.4	1.8	1.4	zero	-2.6	-12.2	-30.0	24"
9½	3140	2780	2447	2138	1853	1595	2736	2145	1662	1269	953	706	-0.1	0.6	zero	-1.9	-5.2	-10.1	1.5	1.4	zero	-2.8	-7.4	-22.4	-47.6	
9½	2910	2617	2342	2083	1843	1622	2820	2281	1827	1445	1131	876	0.2	0.7	zero	-2.2	-5.9	-11.4	1.8	1.6	zero	-3.2	-8.2	-24.4	-50.9	
9½	2910	2656	2416	2189	1974	1773	2820	2349	1944	1596	1298	1047	0.2	0.7	zero	-2.0	-5.6	-10.8	1.7	1.5	zero	-3.0	-7.7	-22.7	-46.6	
9½	2800	2534	2283	2047	1825	1621	2872	2352	1909	1534	1220	963	0.3	0.8	zero	-2.3	-6.3	-12.1	2.0	1.7	zero	-3.4	-8.7	-25.9	-53.2	
9½	2700	2348	2023	1727	1466	1251	2913	2203	1635	1192	859	625	-0.1	zero	-1.5	-4.9	-10.3	-18.3	2.4	2.1	zero	-4.3	-11.0	-33.8	-72.8	
9½	2700	2469	2250	2042	1846	1663	2913	2436	2023	1666	1362	1105	-0.1	zero	-1.3	-4.2	-8.8	-15.4	2.1	1.8	zero	-3.5	-9.0	-26.3	-54.0	24"
9½	2700	2485	2280	2084	1899	1725	2913	2468	2077	1736	1441	1189	-0.1	zero	-1.3	-4.2	-8.7	-15.0	2.1	1.8	zero	-3.5	-8.8	-25.5	-52.0	
9½	2410	2130	1870	1632	1422	1246	2837	2216	1708	1301	988	758	0.1	zero	-2.0	-6.2	-12.9	-22.4	1.3	zero	-3.5	-9.5	-18.4	-46.4	-91.6	
9½	2700	2465	2243	2032	1833	1648	2913	2429	2010	1650	1343	1085	-0.1	zero	-1.3	-4.2	-8.9	-15.4	2.1	1.8	zero	-3.6	-9.1	-26.6	-54.4	
9½	2700	2512	2332	2160	1995	1837	2913	2522	2174	1864	1590	1349	-0.1	zero	-1.3	-4.0	-8.4	-14.4	2.0	1.7	zero	-3.3	-8.4	-24.3	-48.9	
9½	2800	2592	2394	2204	2023	1852	2872	2462	2100	1780	1500	1256	0.2	0.8	zero	-2.2	-5.8	-11.2	1.8	1.6	zero	-3.1	-7.9	-23.0	-46.6	
9½	2910	2696	2492	2298	2112	1934	2821	2422	2070	1769	1485	1247	0.1	0.7	zero	-2.0	-5.3	-10.2	1.6	1.5	zero	-2.9	-7.3	-21.1	-42.8	
9½	2800	2609	2426	2249	2080	1919	2873	2494	2155	1854	1588	1350	0.2	0.8	zero	-2.1	-5.7	-10.9	1.8	1.6	zero	-3.1	-7.7	-22.3	-45.0	
9½ M	3290	2951	2636	2342	2068	1813	3605	2900	2314	1827	1859	1565	0.1	0.6	zero	-1.9	-5.1	-9.8	1.6	1.4	zero	-2.8	-7.0	-20.2	-41.0	
9½ M	2960	2745	2540	2344	2157	1979	3501	3011	2578	2196	1424	1095	-0.1	0.5	zero	-1.6	-4.4	-8.7	2.2	2.6	1.9	zero	-3.4	-15.0	-34.4	
9½ M	2960	2725	2503	2291	2089	1898	3501	2968	2503	2087	1744	1440	0.1	0.6	zero	-1.9	-5.2	-10.0	1.6	1.4	zero	-2.8	-7.2	-20.9	-42.7	
9½ M	2960	2774	2595	2424	2259	2100	3501	3075	2692	2348	2039	1762	0.1	0.6	zero	-1.8	-4.9	-9.4	1.5	1.4	zero	-2.6	-6.7	-19.3	-38.7	24"
9½ M	2825	2595	2376	2167	1970	1783	3544	2989	2506	2086	1722	1412	0.2	0.8	zero	-2.2	-5.9	-11.3	1.8	1.6	zero	-3.2	-8.0	-23.5	-47.9	
9½ M	2885	2691	2506	2327	2156	1993	3511	3055	2648	2285	1961	1675	0.1	0.7	zero	-2.0	-5.3	-10.1	1.6	1.5	zero	-2.9	-7.2	-20.8	-41.9	
9½ M	3120	2866	2627	2400	2184	1979	3890	3284	2758	2301	1905	1565	-0.1	0.5	zero	-1.7	-4.6	-8.9	2.4	2.8	2.0	zero	-3.4	-14.9	-33.6	
9½ M	2925	2690	2467	2254	2052	1861	3799	3213	2701	2256	1870	1538	0.1	0.7	zero	-2.0	-5.4	-10.4	2.8	3.2	2.3	zero	-3.9	-17.0	-38.3	24"
9½ M	3030	2830	2638	2455	2279	2110	3873	3378	2936	2542	2190	1878	-0.1	0.6	zero	-1.7	-4.7	-9.0	1.4	1.3	zero	-2.6	-6.4	-18.6	-37.6	
9½ M	3250	3037	2834	2640	2454	2276	4221	3686	3201	2786	2407	2071	0.3	0.6	zero	-1.6	-4.3	-8.2	2.4	2.6	1.8	zero	-3.0	-12.7	-28.5	24"
9½	2460	2124	1817	1542	1311	1137	2418	1803	1319	950	687	517	0.1	zero	-2.0	-5.8	-13.2	-23.3	1.3	zero	-3.1	-9.9	-19.3	-49.9	-100.8	24"
7½	2365	2062	1783	1533	1320	1154	1552	1180	882	652	483	370	0.1	zero	-2.2	-6.7	-14.0	-24.5	1.5	zero	-3.8	-10.4	-20.1	-51.3	-102.5	24"
6½	1210	1021	913	834	769	712	325	231	185	154	131	113	zero	-5.9	-20.0	-43.3	-77.4	-122.4	zero	-11,1	-31.6	-62.6	-104.7	-226.7	-410.6	24"
9½	2250	1921	1626	1372	1175	1044	1911	1393	998	710	521	411	0.3	zero	-2.6	-8.0	-16.7	-29.3	1.7	zero	-4.5	-12.4	-24.1	-62.1	-125.3	24"
9½ M	2900	2623	2361	2115	1885	1672	3734	3054	2476	1987	1577	1241	0.2	0.7	zero	-2.1	-5.8	-11.2	1.8	1.6		-3.1	-8.0	-23.9	-49.6	24"
9½	2360	1969	1622	1333	1123	997	2102	1463	993	671	476	375	0.2	zero	-2.4	-7.6	-16.1	-28.6	1.6	zero	-4.4	-12.0	-23.7	-62.8	-128.9	24"
9½ M	2780	2572	2374	2184	2003	1832	3860	3305	2815	2383	2004	1676	-0.3	0.8	zero	-2.2	-5.9	-11.4	1.9	1.7	zero	-3.2	-8.1	-23.4	-47.5	
9½ M	2660	2456	2261	2075	1898	1731	3927	3348	2837	2389	1999	1663	-0.1	zero	-1.4	-4.3	-8.9	-15.4	2.1	1.9	zero	-3.5	-8.9	-26.0	-52.7	24"
9½ M	2785	2517	2266	2029	1808	1605	3871	3165	2565	2057	1633	1286	-0.1	zero	-1.2	-4.0	-8.5	-14.8	2.0	1.8	zero	-3.5	-8.8	-25.2	-54.1	
9½ M	2950	2724	2509	2303	2108	1922	3866	3295	2795	2357	1973	1641	0.1	0.6	zero	-1.9	-5.2	-10.0	1.6	1.4	zero	-2.8	-7.1	-20.8	-42.4	
9½	2830	2602	2385	2179	1983	1798	3734	3157	2653	2214	1834	1508	-0.2	zero	-1.1	-3.6	-7.7	-13.4	1.8	1.6	zero	-3.1	-7.9	-23.2	-47.4	
9½	2300	1874	1506	1218	1039	934	1762	1169	755	494	359	291	0.3	zero	-2.7	-8.6	-18.2	-32.6	1.8	zero	-4.9	-13.7	-27.1	-72.5	-150.4	24"
9½	2080	1698	1376	1140	1001	911	1921	1280	841	577	445	369	0.5	zero	-3.5	-10.7	-22.6	-40.1	2.3	zero	-6.1	-16.7	-33.0	-86.6	-174.8	
9½ M	2675	2378	2100	1842	1606	1399	3177	2510	1958	1506	1145	869	-0.1	zero	-1.5	-4.7	-9.9	-17.3	2.3	2.0	zero	-4.0	-10.3	-30.8	-64.9	24"
9½ M	2400	2197	2005	1823	1652	1496	3197	2680	2230	1844	1515	1242	0.1	zero	-1.9	-5.7	-11.8	-20.4	1.3	zero	-3.2	-8.6	-16.6	-40.0	-76.3	
9½ M	2690	2420	2166	1928	1707	1507	4337	3510	2812	2228	1747	1361	-0.1	zero	-1.4	-4.5	-9.4	-16.4	2.2	1.9	zero	-3.8	-9.7	-28.7	-59.8	24"
9½ M	2530	2245	1979	1733	1512	1321	4262	3357	2608	2001	1523	1163	-0.1	zero	-1.7	-5.4	-11.4	-19.8	2.7	2.3	zero	-4.6	-11.7	-35.0	-73.6	
9½ M	2400	2175	1962	1763	1579	1414	5115	4201	3419	2760	2214	1775	0.1	zero	-1.9	-5.9	-12.1	-20.8	1.3	zero	-3.3	-8.9	-17.0	-41.9	-80.8	24"
2½	1190	1006	900	822	756	699	629	449	360	300	254	217	zero	-5.8	-20.0	-44.6	-78.6	-126.1	zero	-11.3	-33.1	-64.1	-108.7	-235.2	-422.3	24"
2½	1760	1380	1114	970	878	806	1650	1015	661	501	411	346	zero	-2.1	-8.7	-21.2	-40.6	-67.7	zero	-5.6	-17.0	-35.4	-61.4	-143.0	-269.9	
2½	1760	1380	1114	970	878	806	1650	1015	661	501	411	346	zero	-2.1	-8.7	-21.2	-40.6	-67.7	zero	-5.6	-17.0	-35.4	-61.4	-143.0	-269.9	20"
2½	1920	1477	1155	982	880	802	1719	1017	622	450	361	300	zero	-1.6	-7.1	-17.9	-35.1	-60.2	zero	-4.8	-14.7	-31.2	-55.5	-131.3	-253.7	
2½	1580	1293	1093	976	896	832	1524	1020	730	582	490	422	1.4	zero	-6.6	-19.4	-39.2	-67.5	zero	-6.6	-19.4	-39.2	-67.5	-210.8	-280.8	
9½	2350	1815	1377	1087	941	846	2942	1755	1010	630	472	381	0.2	zero	-3.2	-9.7	-20.8	-37.8	2.2	zero	-5.4	-15.4	-31.4	-86.7	-180.0	24"
9½	1330	1168	1055	977	918	869	1590	1227	1001	858	758	679	zero	-4.0	-14.5	-32.0	-57.5	-90.6	zero	-8.5	-24.0	-47.4	-78.6	-169.4	-301.3	24"
9½	1810	1497	1244	1073	969	895	2182	1492	1031	767	625	533	zero	-1.3	-6.6	-16.5	-32.0	-54.1	zero	-4.6	-13.8	-28.6	-50.1	-115.7	-219.1	
9½ M	2150	1901	1671	1465	1289	1150	4618	3609	2789	2144	1659	1321	0.3	zero	-2.7	-8.2	-16.7	-28.9	1.8	zero	-4.6	-12.2	-23.4	-58.5	-114.7	24"

★ New For 1999

Remington Ballistics

P & R

Golden Saber™ = GS Core-Lokt® Hunting = RH Disintegrator™ Frangible = LF

Caliber	Order No.	Primer No.	Weight (grs.)	Bullet Style	Velocity (ft./sec.) Muzzle	Velocity 50 yds.	Velocity 100 yds.	Energy (ft.-lbs.) Muzzle	Energy 50 yds.	Energy 100 yds.	Mid-range Trajectory 50 yds.	Mid-range Trajectory 100. yds.	B.L.
.25 (6.35mm) Auto. Pistol	R25AP	1½	50	Metal Case	760	707	659	64	56	48	2.0"	8.7"	2"
.32 S&W	R32SW	1½	88	Lead	680	645	610	90	81	73	2.5"	10.5"	3"
.32 S&W Long	R32SWL	1½	98	Lead	705	670	635	115	98	88	2.3"	10.5"	4"
.32 (7.65mm) Auto. Pistol	R32AP	1½	71	Metal Case	905	855	810	129	115	97	1.4"	5.8"	4"
.357 Mag. (Vented Barrel Ballistics)	R357M7	5½	110	Semi-Jacketed Hollow Point	1295	1094	975	410	292	232	0.8"	3.5"	4"
	R357M1	5½	125	Semi-Jacketed Hollow Point	1450	1240	1090	583	427	330	0.6"	2.8"	4"
	GS357MA	5½	125	Brass-Jacketed Hollow Point	1220	1095	1009	413	333	283	0.8"	3.5"	4"
	RH357MA	5½	165	JHP Core-Lokt®	1290	1189	1108	610	518	450	0.7"	3.1"	8 3/8"
	R357M2	5½	158	Semi-Jacketed Hollow Point	1235	1104	1015	535	428	361	0.8"	3.5"	4"
	R357M3	5½	158	Soft Point	1235	1104	1015	535	428	361	0.8"	3.5"	4"
	R357M5	5½	158	Semi-Wadcutter	1235	1104	1015	535	428	361	0.8"	3.5"	4"
	R357M10	5½	180	Semi-Jacketed Hollow Point	1145	1053	985	524	443	388	0.9"	3.9"	8 3/8"
9mm Luger Auto. Pistol	R9MM1	1½	115	Jacketed Hollow Point	1155	1047	971	341	280	241	0.9"	3.9"	4"
	R9MM10	1½	124	Jacketed Hollow Point	1120	1028	960	346	291	254	1.0"	4.1"	4"
	R9MM2	1½	124	Metal Case	1110	1030	971	339	292	259	1.0"	4.1"	4"
	R9MM3	1½	115	Metal Case	1135	1041	973	329	277	242	0.9"	4.0"	4"
	R9MM6	1½	115	Jacketed Hollow Point (+P)‡	1250	1113	1019	399	316	265	0.8"	3.5"	4"
	R9MM8	1½	147	Jacketed Hollow Point (Subsonic)	990	941	900	320	289	264	1.1"	4.9"	4"
	R9MM9	1½	147	Metal Case (Match)	990	941	900	320	289	264	1.1"	4.9"	4"
	LF9MMA	1½	101	Disintegrator™ Plated Frangible	1220	1092	1004	334	267	226	0.9"	3.6"	4"
	GS9MMB	1½	124	Brass-Jacketed Hollow Point	1125	1031	963	349	293	255	1.0"	4.0"	4"
	GS9MMC	1½	147	Brass-Jacketed Hollow Point	990	941	900	320	289	264	1.1"	4.9"	4"
	GS9MMD	1½	124	Brass-Jacketed Hollow Point (+P)‡	1180	1089	1021	384	327	287	0.8"	3.8"	4"
.380 Auto. Pistol	R380AP	1½	95	Metal Case	955	865	785	190	160	130	1.4"	5.9"	4"
	R380A1	1½	88	Jacketed Hollow Point	990	920	868	191	165	146	1.2"	5.1"	4"
	GS380B	1½	102	Brass-Jacketed Hollow Point	940	901	866	200	184	170	1.2"	5.1"	4"
.38 S&W	R38SW	1½	146	Lead	685	650	620	150	135	125	2.4"	10.0"	4"
.38 Special (Vented Barrel Ballistics)	R38S10	1½	110	Semi-Jacketed Hollow Point (+P)‡	995	926	871	242	210	185	1.2"	5.1"	4"
	R38S16	1½	110	Semi-Jacketed Hollow Point	950	890	840	220	194	172	1.4"	5.4"	4"
	R38S2	1½	125	Semi-Jacketed Hollow Point (+P)‡	945	898	858	248	224	204	1.3"	5.4"	4"
	GS38SB	1½	125	Brass-Jacketed Hollow Point (+P)‡	975	929	885	264	238	218	1.0"	5.2"	4"
	R38S3	1½	148	Targetmaster® Lead WC Match	710	634	566	166	132	105	2.4"	10.8"	4"
	R38S5	1½	158	Lead (Round Nose)	755	723	692	200	183	168	2.0"	8.3"	4"
	R38S14	1½	158	Semi-Wadcutter (+P)‡	890	855	823	278	257	238	1.4"	6.0"	4"
	R38S6	1½	158	Semi-Wadcutter	755	723	692	200	183	168	2.0"	8.3"	4"
	R38S12	1½	158	Lead Hollow Point (+P)‡	890	855	823	278	257	238	1.4"	6.0"	4"
.38 Short Colt	R38SC	1½	125	Lead	730	685	645	150	130	115	2.2"	9.4"	6"
.357 Sig.	R357S1	5½	125	Jacketed Hollow Point	1350	1157	1032	506	372	296	0.7"	3.2"	4"
.40 S&W	R40SW1	5½	155	Jacketed Hollow Point	1205	1095	1017	499	413	356	0.8"	3.6"	4"
	R40SW2	5½	180	Jacketed Hollow Point	1015	960	914	412	368	334	1.3"	4.5"	4"
	LF40SWA	5½	141	Disintegrator™ Plated Frangible	1135	1056	996	403	349	311	0.9"	3.9"	4"
	GS40SWA	5½	165	Brass-Jacketed Hollow Point	1150	1040	964	485	396	340	1.0"	4.0"	4"
	GS40SWB	5½	180	Brass-Jacketed Hollow Point	1015	960	914	412	368	334	1.3"	4.5"	4"
.41 Rem. Mag. (Vented BBL Ballistics)	R41MG1	2½	210	Soft Point	1300	1162	1062	788	630	526	0.7"	3.2"	4"
.44 Rem. Mag. (Vented BBL Ballistics)	R44MG5	2½	180	Semi-Jacketed Hollow Point	1610	1365	1175	1036	745	551	0.5"	2.3"	4"
	R44MG2	2½	240	Soft Point	1180	1081	1010	741	623	543	0.9"	3.7"	4"
	R44MG3	2½	240	Semi-Jacketed Hollow Point	1180	1081	1010	741	623	543	0.9"	3.7"	4"
	RH44MGA	2½	275	JHP Core-Lokt®	1235	1142	1070	931	797	699	0.8"	3.3"	6½"
.44 S&W Special	R44SW	2½	246	Lead	755	725	695	310	285	265	2.0"	8.3"	6"
	R44SW1	2½	200	Semi-Wadcutter	1035	938	866	476	391	333	1.1"	4.9"	6"
.45 Colt	R45C	2½	250	Lead	860	820	780	410	375	340	1.6"	6.6"	5"
	R45C1	2½	225	Semi-Wadcutter (Keith)	960	890	832	460	395	346	1.3"	5.5"	5"
.45 Auto.	R45AP1	2½	185	Targetmaster® MC WC Match	770	707	650	244	205	174	2.0"	8.7"	5"
	R45AP2	2½	185	Jacketed Hollow Point	1000	939	889	411	362	324	1.1"	4.9"	5"
	R45AP4	2½	230	Metal Case	835	800	767	356	326	300	1.6"	6.8"	5"
	R45AP7	2½	230	Jacketed Hollow Point (Subsonic)	835	800	767	356	326	300	1.6"	6.8"	5"
	LF45APA	2½	175	Disintegrator™ Plated Frangible	1020	923	851	404	331	281	1.2"	5.1"	5"
	GS45APA	2½	185	Brass-Jacketed Hollow Point	1015	951	899	423	372	332	1.1"	4.5"	5"
	GS45APB	2½	230	Brass-Jacketed Hollow Point	875	833	795	391	355	323	1.5"	6.1"	5"
	GS45APC	2½	185	Brass-Jacketed Hollow Point (+P)‡	1140	1042	971	534	446	388	1.0"	4.0"	5"

‡Ammunition with (+P) on the case headstamp is loaded to higher pressure. Use only in firearms designated for this cartridge and so recommended by the gun manufacturer.

SAKO RIFLE BALLISTICS

Caliber	Grs	Type	Velocity Muzzle	100y	200y	300y	400y	500y	Energy Muzzle	100y	200y	300y	400y	500y	Traj. Muzzle	100y	200y	300y	400y	500y	Box pcs
22 Hornet	45	SPEEDHEAD FMJ	2300	1724	1291	1069	944	861	524	295	165	114	89	74	-1.5	0	-14.3	-47.1	-108.9	-203.5	20
	45	SOFT POINT RN	2300	1724	1291	1069	944	861	524	295	165	114	89	74	-1.5	0	-14.3	-47.1	-108.9	-203.5	20
	42	HOLLOW PIONT	2700	2193	1764	1419	1161	1011	652	428	277	179	120	91	-1.5	0	-6.6	-24.5	-60.1	-120.9	20
22 PPC USA	52	HPBT MATCH	3400	2990	2613	2255	1920	1616	1342	1040	795	592	429	304	-1.5	1.2	0	-6.0	-19.1	-41.8	20
222 Remington	50	SPEEDHEAD FMJ	3200	2663	2182	1776	1447	1192	1135	786	528	350	232	158	-1.5	1.2	0	-10.3	-31.1	-67.3	20
222	50	SOFT POINT P	3200	2663	2182	1776	1447	1192	1135	786	528	350	232	158	-1.5	1.7	0	-10.3	-31.1	-67.3	20
	55	SOFT POINT P	3280	2800	2372	1978	1637	1350	1312	958	686	477	326	222	-1.5	1.4	0	-8.0	-24.8	-54.5	20
	52	HPBT MATCH	3035	2613	2235	1894	1589	1333	1072	795	581	417	294	207	-1.5	1.8	0	-9.0	-27.9	-60.7	20
222 Remington	50	SPEEDHEAD FJM	3230	2690	2207	1798	1466	1207	1159	803	540	359	238	161	-1.5	1.6	0	-10.0	-30.3	-67.0	20
	50	SOFT POINT P	3230	2690	2207	1798	1466	1207	1159	803	540	359	238	161	-1.5	1.6	0	-10.0	-30.3	-67.0	20
	55	SOFT POINT P	3330	2848	2414	2016	1671	1378	1352	989	710	495	340	231	-1.5	1.4	0	-7.7	-23.8	-51.9	20
223 Remington	50	SPEEDHEAD FJM	3230	2690	2207	1798	1466	1207	1159	803	540	359	238	161	-1.5	1.6	0	-10.0	-30.3	-67.0	20
	50	SOFT POINT P	3230	2690	2207	1798	1466	1207	1159	803	540	359	238	161	-1.5	1.6	0	-10.0	-30.3	-67.0	20
	55	SOFT POINT P	3330	2848	2414	2016	1671	1378	1352	989	710	495	340	231	-1.5	1.4	0	-7.7	-23.8	-51.9	20
22-250 Remington	50	SPEEDHEAD FMJ	3770	3168	2639	2168	1751	1396	1579	1113	773	522	340	216	-1.5	1.0	0	-6.0	-19.5	-44.0	20
	50	SOFT POINT P	3770	3168	2639	2168	1751	1396	1579	1113	773	522	340	216	-1.5	1.0	0	-6.0	-19.5	-44.0	20
	55	SOFT POINT P	3660	3146	2681	2255	1871	1533	1631	1206	876	620	426	286	-1.5	1.0	0	-5.9	-18.7	-41.3	20
6PPC USA	70	HPBT MATCH	3200	2740	2407	2090	1793	1527	1481	1156	892	673	495	359	-1.5	1.5	0	-7.2	-22.8	-49.2	20
243 Winchester	90	SPEEDHEAD FJM	2855	2587	2340	2110	1895	1693	1618	1329	1087	884	713	569	-1.5	1.9	0	-8.2	-24.3	-49.9	20
	90	SOFT POINT P	3130	2850	2587	2343	2114	1898	1949	1612	1329	1090	887	715	-1.5	1.5	0	-6.5	-19.5	-40.2	20
6.5X55 Swedish	100	SPEEDHEAD FJM	2625	2270	1946	1651	1397	1196	1533	1147	842	606	434	319	-1.5	2.6	0	-11.9	-36.0	-76.8	20
	139	HPBT MATCH	2790	2648	2512	2381	2252	2129	2396	2161	1945	1746	1563	1396	-1.5	1.7	0	-7.2	-20.5	-40.7	20
	156	SOFT POINT RN	2625	23843	2156	1941	1740	1554	2382	1966	1607	1303	1047	835	-1.5	2.3	0	-9.8	-28.9	-59.7	20
270 WInchester	130	SPEEDHEAD FJM	2820	2506	2212	1938	1687	1463	2290	1805	1407	1080	818	616	-1.5	2.0	0	-9.2	-27.5	-58.3	20
	156	HAMMERHEAD	2755	2470	2208	1967	1743	1538	2625	2111	1685	1338	1051	818	-1.5	2.2	0	-9.3	-27.6	-57.5	20
7x33 Sako	78	SPEEDHEAD FJM	2430	1920	1500	1190	1013	906	1029	643	392	247	179	143	-1.5	0	-8.5	-31.0	-78.8	-158.0	50
	78	SOFT POINT SP	2430	1920	1500	1190	1013	906	1029	643	392	247	179	243	-1.5	0	-8.5	-31.0	-78.8	-158.0	50
7mm Mauser(7x57)	78	SPEEDHEAD FMJ	2950	2324	783	1362	1090	950	1522	943	555	324	208	158	-1.5	2.6	0	-14.9	-50.4	-112.2	20
	170	SOFT POINT SP	2495	2283	2086	1901	1728	1567	2324	1962	1638	1361	1125	925	-1.5	2.6	0	-10.8	-31.1	-63.3	20
7x64	120	SOFT POINT P	3100	2816	2545	2296	2069	1856	2567	2117	1730	1408	1143	920	-1.5	1.4	0	-7.3	-20.9	-42.6	20
	170	HAMMERHEAD	2790	2563	2351	2154	1967	1791	2929	2473	2081	1747	1458	1208	-1.5	1.9	0	-8.2	-23.9	-48.6	20
7x65R	170	HAMMERHEAD	2625	2409	2208	2019	1839	1670	2594	2186	1836	1535	1274	1050	-1.5	2.3	0	-9.4	-27.4	-55.6	20
7mm Remington Mag	170	HAMMERHEAD	2970	2734	2512	2303	2108	1924	3320	2814	2376	1996	1674	1394	-1.5	1.6	0	-7.2	-21.0	-42.5	20
7.62x39 Russian	123	SPEEDHEAD FMJ	2345	2096	1863	1651	1466	1305	1507	1203	951	747	589	466	-1.5	0	-6.5	-23.6	-53.2	-98.5	30
	123	SPEEDHEAD FMJ	2345	2096	1863	1651	1466	1305	1507	1203	951	747	589	466	-1.5	0	-6.5	-23.6	-53.2	-98.5	250
	123	SOFT POINT P	2345	2096	1863	1651	1466	1305	1507	1203	951	747	589	466	-1.5	0	-6.5	-23.6	-53.2	-98.5	30
30-30 Winchester	93	SPEEDHEAD FMJ	2970	2354	1818	1400	1126	976	1811	1138	679	403	260	196	-1.5	0	-4.9	-21.8	-57.7	-117.3	20
	150	SOFT POINT FP	2310	1982	1681	1439	1240	1096	1777	1304	938	688	510	400	-1.5	0	-8.1	-28.3	-65.6	-125.6	20
308 Winchester	93	SPEEDHEAD FMJ	2970	2354	1818	1400	1126	976	1811	1138	679	403	260	196	-1.5	0	-4.9	-21.8	-56.7	-117.3	20
	123	SPEEDHEAD FMJ	2920	2622	2347	2097	1868	1654	2335	1883	1509	1205	955	749	-1.5	1.8	0	-8.4	-24.5	-50.7	20
	123	SOFT POINT P	3035	2734	2455	2194	1958	1738	2523	2047	1650	1318	1050	827	-1.5	1.6	0	-7.6	-22.4	-46.2	20
	156	S-HAMMERHEAD	2790	2563	2353	2158	1973	1800	2689	2271	1914	1610	1346	1120	-1.5	2.0	0	-8.2	-23.9	-48.9	20
	180	HAMEMRHEAD	2610	2382	2169	1971	1786	1612	2725	2273	1885	1556	1277	1041	-1.5	2.4	0	-9.9	-28.6	-58.1	20
	180	S-HAMMERHEAD	2610	2400	2204	2017	1839	1672	2725	2310	1946	1629	1355	1119	-1.5	2.3	0	-9.5	-27.5	-55.8	20
	200	HAMMERHEAD	2445	2210	1990	1782	1588	1415	2660	2172	1762	1414	1122	891	-1.5	2.8	0	-11.3	-33.7	-70.1	20
	123	RANGE	2950	2652	2378	2126	1895	1679	2388	1927	1549	1238	983	772	-1.5	1.8	0	-8.0	-23.7	-49.0	50
	102	SUPER RANGE	3120	2712	2342	2003	1695	1428	2195	1662	1240	907	649	461	-1.5	1.6	0	-8.0	-24.7	-53.7	50
	168	HPBT MATCH	2690	2500	2321	2159	2004	1857	2701	2328	2010	1739	1499	1286	-1.5	2.3	0	-8.5	-24.5	-49.1	20
	190	HPBT MATCH	2525	2372	2224	2080	1940	1806	2688	2369	2082	1822	1585	1373	-1.5	2.4	0	-9.0	-26.3	-52.9	20
7.62x53R	93	SPEEDHEAD FMJ	2970	2354	1818	1400	1126	976	1811	1138	679	403	260	196	-1.5	0	-4.9	-21.8	-56.7	-117.3	20
	123	SPEEDHEAD FMJ	2920	2622	2347	2097	1868	1654	2335	1883	1509	1205	955	749	-1.5	1.8	0	-8.4	-24.5	-50.7	20
	156	S-HAMMERHEAD	2790	2563	2353	2158	1973	1800	2689	2271	1914	1610	1346	1120	-1.5	2.0	0	-8.2	-23.9	-48.9	20
	180	S-HAMMERHEAD	2610	2400	2204	2017	1839	1672	2725	2310	1946	1629	1355	1119	-1.5	2.3	0	-9.5	-27.5	-55.8	20
	200	HAMMERHEAD	2445	2210	1990	1782	1588	1415	2660	2172	1762	1414	1122	891	-1.5	2.8	0	-11.3	-33.7	-70.1	20
	123	RANGE	2950	2652	2378	2126	1895	1679	2388	1927	1549	1238	983	772	-1.5	1.8	0	-8.0	-23.7	-49.0	50
30-06 Springfield	123	SPEEDHEAD FMJ	2920	2622	2347	2097	1868	1654	2335	1883	1509	1205	955	749	-1.5	1.8	0	-8.4	-24.5	-50.7	20
	123	SOFT POINT P	3120	2800	2510	2250	2010	1786	2661	2148	1726	1385	1106	873	-1.5	1.6	0	-7.3	-21.3	-43.9	20
	156	S-HAMMERHEAD	2900	2670	2454	2255	2070	1893	2915	2466	2083	1759	1481	1240	-1.5	1.8	0	-7.8	-22.2	-44.7	20
	180	HAMMERHEAD	2700	2465	2242	2042	1857	1682	2935	2433	2013	1670	1381	1133	-1.5	2.3	0	-9.4	-27.0	-54.5	20
	180	S-HAMMERHEAD	2700	2500	2295	2100	1920	1750	2935	2495	2105	1768	1475	1223	-1.5	2.1	0	-8.7	-25.3	-51.3	20
	220	HAMMERHEAD	2410	2200	2000	1826	1664	1517	2847	2369	1963	1632	1356	1126	-1.5	3.3	0	-12.4	-34.7	-69.6	20
	123	RANGE	2950	2652	2378	2126	1895	1679	2388	1927	1549	1238	983	772	-1.5	1.8	0	-8.0	-23.7	-49.0	50
300 Winchester Mag	156	S-HAMMERHEAD	3150	2905	2673	2453	2243	2044	3430	2918	2470	2080	1740	1445	-1.5	1.3	0	-6.1	-18.1	-37.0	20
	180	S-HAMMERHEAD	2950	2700	2467	2243	2031	1833	3493	2926	2438	2015	1653	1345	-1.5	1.6	0	-7.4	-21.7	-44.4	20
	180	S-HAMMERHEAD	2950	2730	2517	2314	2121	1938	3493	2983	2537	2144	1801	1504	-1.5	1.6	0	-7.1	-20.7	-42.0	20
	168	HPBT MATCH	3020	2816	2622	2438	2260	2090	3400	2959	2566	2217	1905	1630	-1.5	1.5	0	-6.5	-18.8	-38.0	20
8.2x57JRS	200	HAMMERHEAD	2395	2093	1815	1563	1347	1176	2553	1949	1465	1087	807	616	-1.5	3.3	0	-13.9	-42.0	-89.7	20
338 Winchester Mag	250	HAMMERHEAD	2676	2413	2169	1946	1742	1554	3966	3229	2608	21012	1683	1339	-1.5	2.3	0	-10.0	-29.1	-59.7	20
9.3x53R Finnish	256	SOFT POINT RN	2330	2000	1695	1439	1236	1091	3010	2211	1593	1148	847	660	-1.5	3.6	0	-16.9	-50.3	-107.0	20
9.3x62	250	POWERHEAD BARNES	2360	2170	1988	1815	1652	1503	3095	2612	2192	1828	1514	1253	-1.5	3.0	0	-11.8	-34.2	-69.4	10
375 H&H Mag	270	POWERHEAD BARNES	2535	2354	2181	2015	1857		4440	3848	3319	2848	2432.	2066	-1.5	1.9	0	-8.3	-23.8	-48.0	10

SPEEDHEAD=FMJ-Full Metal Jacket
HP = Hollow Point, Varmint, Precision
SP FP = Soft Point Flat Point

HAMMERHEAD=Soft Point Bonded Core
S-HAMMERHEAD=SUPER HAMMERHEAD=Hollow Point Bonded Core
POWERHEAD BARNES = Hollow Piont Solid Copper

HPBT=Hollow Point Boat Tail, Precision
RANGE=Full Metal Jacket
SUPER RANGE = HPBT, Varmint, Precision

SP P=Soft Point Pointed
SP SP = Soft Point Semi Pointed
SP RN = Soft Point Round Nose

BALLISTICS

WEATHERBY BALLISTICS

SUGGESTED USAGE	CARTRIDGE	BULLET Weight Grains	BULLET Type	B/C	VELOCITY in Feet per Second Muzzle	100 Yards	200 Yards	300 Yards	400 Yards	500 Yards	ENERGY in Foot-Pounds Muzzle	100 Yards	200 Yards	300 Yards	400 Yards	500 Yards	PATH OF BULLET 100 Yards	200 Yards	300 Yards	400 Yards	500 Yards
V	.224 Wby.	55	Pt-Ex	.235	3650	3192	2780	2403	2056	1741	1627	1244	944	705	516	370	2.8	3.7	0.0	-9.8	-27.9
V	.240 Wby.	87	Pt-Ex	.327	3523	3199	2898	2617	2352	2103	2397	1977	1622	1323	1069	855	2.7	3.4	0.0	-8.4	-23.3
		90	Barnes-X	.382	3500	3222	2962	2717	2484	2264	2448	2075	1753	1475	1233	1024	2.6	3.3	0.0	-8.0	-21.8
		95	Bst	.379	3420	3146	2888	2645	2414	2195	2467	2087	1759	1475	1229	1017	2.7	3.5	0.0	-8.4	-22.9
M		100	Pt-Ex	.381	3406	3134	2878	2637	2408	2190	2576	2180	1839	1544	1287	1065	2.8	3.5	0.0	-8.4	-23.0
		100	Partition	.384	3406	3136	2882	2642	2415	2199	2576	2183	1844	1550	1294	1073	2.8	3.5	0.0	-8.4	-22.9
V	.257 Wby.	87	Pt-Ex	.322	3825	3472	3147	2845	2563	2297	2826	2328	1913	1563	1269	1019	2.1	2.8	0.0	-7.1	-19.5
M		100	Pt-Ex	.357	3602	3298	3016	2750	2500	2264	2881	2416	2019	1680	1388	1138	2.4	3.1	0.0	-7.7	-21.0
		100	Bst	.393	3602	3325	3066	2822	2590	2370	2881	2455	2087	1768	1490	1247	2.3	3.0	0.0	-7.4	-19.9
		115	Barnes-X	.429	3400	3158	2929	2711	2504	2306	2952	2546	2190	1877	1601	1358	2.7	3.4	0.0	-8.1	-21.7
		117	Rn-Ex	.243	3402	2984	2595	2240	1921	1639	3007	2320	1742	1302	956	690	3.4	4.3	0.0	-11.1	-31.9
		120	Partition	.391	3305	3046	2801	2570	2350	2141	2910	2472	2091	1760	1471	1221	3.0	3.7	0.0	-8.9	-24.3
V	.270 Wby.	100	Pt-Ex	.307	3760	3396	3061	2751	2462	2190	3139	2560	2081	1681	1346	1065	2.3	3.0	0.0	-7.6	-21.0
M		130	Pt-Ex	.409	3375	3123	2885	2659	2444	2240	3288	2815	2402	2041	1724	1448	2.8	3.5	0.0	-8.4	-22.6
		130	Partition	.416	3375	3127	2892	2670	2458	2256	3288	2822	2415	2058	1744	1470	2.8	3.5	0.0	-8.3	-22.4
		140	Bst	.456	3300	3077	2865	2663	2470	2285	3385	2943	2551	2204	1896	1622	2.9	3.6	0.0	-8.4	-22.6
		140	Barnes-X	.462	3250	3032	2825	2628	2438	2257	3283	2858	2481	2146	1848	1583	3.0	3.7	0.0	-8.7	-23.2
		150	Pt-Ex	.462	3245	3028	2821	2623	2434	2253	3507	3053	2650	2292	1973	1690	3.0	3.7	0.0	-8.7	-23.3
		150	Partition	.465	3245	3029	2823	2627	2439	2259	3507	3055	2655	2298	1981	1699	3.0	3.7	0.0	-8.7	-23.2
M	7MM Wby.	139	Pt-Ex	.392	3340	3079	2834	2601	2380	2170	3443	2926	2478	2088	1748	1453	2.9	3.6	0.0	-8.7	-23.7
		140	Partition	.434	3303	3069	2847	2636	2434	2241	3391	2927	2519	2159	1841	1562	2.9	3.6	0.0	-8.5	-23.1
		140	Bst	.485	3302	3092	2892	2700	2517	2341	3389	2972	2599	2267	1969	1703	2.8	3.5	0.0	-8.2	-21.9
		150	Barnes-X	.488	3100	2901	2710	2527	2352	2183	3200	2802	2446	2127	1842	1588	3.3	4.0	0.0	-9.4	-25.3
		154	Pt-Ex	.433	3260	3028	2807	2597	2397	2206	3634	3134	2694	2307	1964	1663	3.0	3.7	0.0	-8.8	-23.8
		160	Partition	.475	3200	2991	2791	2600	2417	2241	3662	3177	2767	2401	2075	1784	3.1	3.8	0.0	-8.9	-23.8
B		175	Pt-Ex	.462	3070	2861	2662	2471	2288	2113	3662	3181	2753	2373	2034	1735	3.5	4.2	0.0	-9.9	-26.5
M	.300 Wby.	150	Pt-Ex	.338	3540	3225	2932	2657	2399	2155	4173	3462	2862	2351	1916	1547	2.6	3.3	0.0	-8.2	-22.6
		150	Partition	.387	3540	3263	3004	2759	2528	2307	4173	3547	3005	2536	2128	1773	2.5	3.2	0.0	-7.7	-20.9
		165	Pt-Ex	.387	3390	3123	2872	2634	2409	2195	4210	3573	3021	2542	2126	1765	2.8	3.5	0.0	-8.5	-23.1
		165	Bst	.475	3350	3133	2927	2730	2542	2361	4111	3596	3138	2730	2367	2042	2.7	3.4	0.0	-8.1	-21.4
B		180	Pt-Ex	.425	3240	3004	2781	2569	2366	2173	4195	3607	3091	2637	2237	1886	3.1	3.8	0.0	-9.0	-24.4
		180	Barnes-X	.511	3190	2995	2809	2631	2459	2294	4067	3586	3154	2766	2417	2103	3.1	3.8	0.0	-8.7	-23.2
		180	Partition	.474	3240	3028	2826	2634	2449	2271	4195	3665	3193	2772	2396	2062	3.0	3.7	0.0	-8.6	-23.1
		200	Partition	.481	3060	2860	2668	2485	2308	2139	4158	3631	3161	2741	2366	2032	3.5	4.2	0.0	-9.8	-26.2
		220	Rn-Ex	.300	2845	2543	2260	1996	1751	1530	3954	3158	2495	1946	1497	1143	4.9	5.9	0.0	-14.6	-40.6
B	.340 Wby.	200	Pt-Ex	.361	3221	2946	2688	2444	2213	1995	4607	3854	3208	2652	2174	1767	3.3	4.0	0.0	-9.9	-27.0
		200	Bst	.502	3221	3022	2831	2649	2473	2305	4607	4054	3559	3115	2716	2358	3.0	3.7	0.0	-8.6	-22.9
		210	Partition	.400	3211	2963	2728	2505	2293	2092	4807	4093	3470	2927	2452	2040	3.2	3.9	0.0	-9.5	-25.7
		225	Pt-Ex	.397	3066	2824	2595	2377	2170	1973	4696	3984	3364	2822	2352	1944	3.6	4.4	0.0	-10.7	-28.6
		225	Barnes-X	.482	3001	2804	2615	2434	2260	2093	4499	3927	3416	2959	2551	2189	3.6	4.3	0.0	-10.3	-27.4
		250	Pt-Ex	.431	2963	2745	2537	2338	2149	1968	4873	4182	3572	3035	2563	2150	3.9	4.6	0.0	-11.1	-29.6
		250	Partition	.473	2941	2743	2553	2371	2197	2029	4801	4176	3618	3120	2678	2286	3.9	4.6	0.0	-10.9	-28.9
MB	.30-378 Wby.	165	Bst	.475	3500	3275	3062	2859	2665	2480	4488	3930	3435	2995	2603	2253	2.4	3.0	0.0	-7.4	-19.5
		180	Barnes-X	.511	3450	3243	3046	2858	2678	2504	4757	4204	3709	3264	2865	2506	2.4	3.1	0.0	-7.4	-19.6
		200	Partition	.481	3160	2955	2759	2572	2392	2220	4434	3877	3381	2938	2541	2188	3.2	3.9	0.0	-9.1	-24.3
MB	.338-378 Wby.	200	Bst	.502	3350	3145	2949	2761	2582	2409	4983	4391	3861	3386	2959	2576	2.7	3.3	0.0	-7.9	-21.0
		225	Barnes-X	.482	3180	2974	2778	2591	2410	2238	5052	4420	3856	3353	2902	2501	3.1	3.8	0.0	-8.9	-24.0
		250	Partition	.473	3060	2856	2662	2475	2297	2125	5197	4528	3933	3401	2927	2507	3.5	4.2	0.0	-9.8	-26.4
B	.378 Wby.	270	Pt-Ex	.380	3180	2921	2677	2445	2225	2017	6062	5115	4295	3583	2968	2438	1.3	0.0	-6.1	-18.1	-37.1
		270	Barnes-X	.503	3150	2954	2767	2587	2415	2249	5948	5232	4589	4013	3495	3031	1.2	0.0	-5.8	-16.7	-33.7
		300	Rn-Ex	.250	2925	2558	2220	1908	1627	1383	5699	4360	3283	2424	1764	1274	1.9	0.0	-9.0	-27.8	-60.0
		300	FMJ	.275	2925	2591	2280	1991	1725	1489	5699	4470	3461	2640	1983	1476	1.8	0.0	-8.6	-26.1	-55.4
A	.416 Wby.	350	Barnes-X	.521	2850	2673	2503	2340	2182	2031	6312	5553	4870	4253	3700	3204	1.7	0.0	-7.2	-20.9	-41.8
		400	Swift A	.391	2650	2426	2213	2011	1820	1644	6237	5227	4350	3592	2941	2399	2.2	0.0	-9.3	-27.1	-56.0
		400	Rn-Ex	.311	2700	2417	2152	1903	1676	1470	6474	5189	4113	3216	2493	1918	2.3	0.0	-9.7	-29.3	-61.2
		400	**Mono	.304	2700	2411	2140	1887	1656	1448	6474	5162	4068	3161	2435	1861	2.3	0.0	-9.8	-29.7	-62.1
A	.460 Wby.	450	Barnes-X	.488	2700	2518	2343	2175	2013	1859	7284	6333	5482	4725	4050	3452	2.0	0.0	-8.4	-24.1	-48.2
		500	Rn-Ex	.287	2600	2301	2022	1764	1533	1333	7504	5877	4539	3456	2608	1972	2.6	0.0	-11.1	-33.5	-71.1
		500	FMJ	.295	2600	2309	2037	1784	1557	1357	7504	5917	4605	3534	2690	2046	2.5	0.0	-10.9	-33.0	-69.6

LEGEND: Pt-Ex = Pointed Expanding   Rn-Ex = Round Nose-Expanding   FMJ = Full Metal Jacket   Swift A = Divided Lead Cavity or "H" Type   Barnes-X = Barnes "X" Flat Base   Bst = Nosler Ballistic Tip®

NOTE: These tables were calculated by computer using a standard modern scientific technique to predict trajectories and recoil energies from the best available data for each cartridge. The figures shown are expected to be reasonably accurate of ammunition behavior under standard conditions. However, the shooter is cautioned that performance will vary because of variations in rifles, ammunition, atmospheric conditions and altitude. • B.C.: Ballistic Coefficients used for these tables were supplied by the bullet's manufacturers. Listed velocities were determined using 26-inch barrels. Velocities from shorter barrels will be reduced by 30 to 65 feet per second per inch of barrel removed. • Trajectories were computed with the line-of-sight 1.5 inches above the bore centerline.

*Partition is a registered trademark of Nosler, Inc. • **Monolithic Solid is a registered trademark of A-Square, Inc. • Barnes X-Bullet® is a registered trademark of Barnes Bullets.

USAGE: V-Varmint   M-Medium Game (Deer, Sheep, Pronghorn, Black Bear)   B-Big Game (Elk, Moose, Grizzly)   A-African Big Game (Elephant, Cape Buffalo, Rhino, Lion)

Winchester Rifle Ballistics

Supreme® Centerfire Rifle Ballistics

	Cartridge	Symbol	Bullet Wt. Grs.	Bullet Type	Game Selector Guide	CXP Guide Number	Barrel Length (In.)	Velocity in Feet Per Second (fps) Muzzle	100	200	300	400	500	Energy in Foot Pounds (ft-lbs.) Muzzle	100	200	300	400	500	Trajectory, Short Range Yards 50	100	150	200	250	300	Trajectory, Long Range Yards 100	150	200	250	300	400	500
NEW	22 Hornet	S22H1	34	Jacketed Hollow Point	V	1	24	3050	2132	1415	1017	852	741	700	343	151	78	55	41	-0.1	0	-1.9	-6.6	-15.5	-29.9	1.2	0	-4.1	-12.4	-26.2	-74.1	-155.6
	220 Swift	SBST220	40	Ballistic Silvertip™	V	1	24	4050	3518	3048	2624	2238	1885	1457	1099	825	611	445	316	-0.4	0	-0.3	-1.3	-3.3	-6.4	0.7	0.7	0	-1.7	-4.4	-13.9	-30.4
	22-250 Remington	SBST22250A	40	Ballistic Silvertip	V	1	24	4150	3591	3099	2658	2257	1893	1530	1146	853	628	453	318	-0.5	0	-0.2	-1.2	-3.1	-6.1	0.6	0.7	0	-1.6	-4.2	-13.4	-29.5
	22-250 Remington	SBST22250	50	Ballistic Silvertip	V	1	24	3810	3341	2919	2536	2182	1859	1611	1239	946	714	529	384	-0.4	0	-0.4	-1.6	-3.9	-7.3	0.8	0.9	0	-1.9	-4.9	-15.2	-32.9
	222 Remington	SBST222	40	Ballistic Silvertip	V	1	24	3370	2915	2503	2127	1786	1487	1009	755	556	402	283	196	-0.3	0	-0.7	-2.6	-5.9	-10.8	1.3	1.2	0	-2.6	-6.9	-21.5	-47.2
	223 Remington	SBST223A	40	Ballistic Silvertip	V	1	24	3700	3166	2693	2265	1879	1540	1216	891	644	456	314	211	-0.4	0	-0.5	-2.0	-4.7	-8.8	1.0	1.0	0	-2.2	-5.8	-18.4	-40.9
	223 Remington	SBST223	50	Ballistic Silvertip	V	1	24	3410	2982	2593	2235	1907	1613	1291	987	746	555	404	289	-0.3	0	-0.7	-2.4	-5.5	-10.0	1.2	1.2	0	-2.5	-6.4	-19.8	-42.8
NEW	223 Remington	SHV223R2*	64	Power-Point Plus™	D	2	24	3090	2684	2312	1971	1664	1398	1357	1024	760	552	393	278	-0.2	0	-1.0	-3.4	-7.4	-13.3	1.7	1.5	0	-3.2	-8.2	-25.4	-55.1
	243 Winchester	SBST243	55	Ballistic Silvertip	V	1	24	4025	3597	3209	2853	2525	2220	1978	1579	1257	994	779	602	-0.5	0	-0.2	-1.2	-3.0	-5.8	0.6	0.7	0	-1.5	-4.0	-12.2	-26.0
	243 Winchester	SBST243A	95	Ballistic Silvertip	D,O/P	2	24	3100	2854	2626	2410	2203	2007	2021	1719	1455	1225	1024	850	-0.3	0	-0.8	-2.8	-6.0	-10.6	1.4	1.3	0	-2.5	-6.4	-18.9	-38.4
NEW	243 Winchester	SHV2432*	100	Power-Point Plus	D,O/P	2	24	3090	2818	2562	2321	2092	1877	2121	1764	1458	1196	972	782	-0.3	0	-0.8	-2.9	-6.3	-11.1	1.4	1.3	0	-2.6	-6.7	-20	-41.1
	25-06 Remington	SBST2506A	85	Ballistic Silvertip	V	1	24	3470	3156	2864	2590	2332	2089	2273	1880	1548	1266	1026	824	-0.4	0	-0.5	-2.0	-4.5	-8.2	1.0	1.0	0	-2	-5.2	-15.7	-32.5
	25-06 Remington	SBST2506	115	Ballistic Silvertip	D	2	24	3060	2825	2603	2390	2188	1996	2391	2038	1729	1459	1223	1017	-0.2	0	-0.8	-2.9	-6.1	-10.8	1.4	1.3	0	-2.6	-6.6	-19.2	-39.1
NEW	270 Winchester	SHV2705*	130	Power-Point Plus	D,O/P	2	24	3150	2881	2628	2388	2161	1946	2865	2396	1993	1646	1348	1094	-0.3	0	-0.8	-2.7	-5.9	-10.4	1.3	1.2	0	-2.5	-6.4	-18.9	-38.8
NEW	270 Winchester	SPG270	150	Partition Gold	D,O/P,M	2	24	2930	2693	2468	2254	2051	1859	2860	2416	2030	1693	1402	1152	-0.2	0	-1.0	-3.3	-7.7	-12.3	1.7	1.5	0	-2.9	-7.4	-21.6	-44.1
	270 Winchester	SBST270	130	Ballistic Silvertip	D	2	24	3050	2828	2618	2416	2224	2040	2685	2309	1978	1685	1428	1202	-0.2	0	-0.8	-2.8	-6.1	-10.7	1.4	1.3	0	-2.6	-6.5	-18.9	-38.4
	270 Winchester	S270X	140	Fail Safe®	D,O/P	3	24	2920	2671	2435	2211	1999	1799	2651	2218	1843	1519	1242	1007	-0.2	0	-1.0	-3.4	-7.2	-12.6	1.7	1.5	0	-3	-7.6	-22.3	-45.7
	280 Remington	SBST280	140	Ballistic Silvertip	D	2	24	3040	2842	2653	2471	2297	2130	2872	2511	2187	1898	1640	1410	-0.2	0	-0.8	-2.8	-6.0	-10.5	1.4	1.3	0	-2.5	-6.3	-18.4	-37.0
	280 Remington	S280XA	140	Fail Safe	D,O/P	2	24	3050	2756	2480	2221	1977	1751	2893	2362	1913	1533	1216	953	-0.2	0	-0.9	-3.1	-6.7	-11.8	1.5	1.4	0	-2.8	-7.2	-21.5	-44.7
	7mm-08 Remington	S708	140	Fail Safe	D,O/P	2	24	2760	2506	2271	2048	1839	1645	2360	1953	1603	1304	1051	841	-0.1	0	-1.3	-4.0	-8.5	-14.9	2.0	1.8	0	-3.5	-8.8	-25.9	-53.2
	7mm-08 Remington	SBST708	140	Ballistic Silvertip	D,O/P	2	24	2770	2572	2382	2200	2026	1860	2386	2056	1764	1504	1276	1076	-0.1	0	-1.2	-3.8	-7.9	-13.7	1.9	1.6	0	-3.2	-8.0	-23.2	-46.9
NEW	7mm STW	SBST7STW*	140	Ballistic Silvertip	D,O/P	2	24	3320	3100	2890	2690	2499	2315	3427	2982	2597	2250	1941	1667	-0.3	0	-0.6	-2.1	-4.7	-8.4	1.1	1.0	0	-2.1	-5.2	-15.2	-30.8
NEW	7mm STW	S7STWX*	160	Fail Safe	D,O/P,M,L	3	24	3150	2894	2652	2422	2204	1998	3526	2976	2499	2085	1727	1481	-0.3	0	-0.8	-2.7	-5.8	-10.3	1.3	1.2	0	-2.5	-6.3	-18.5	-37.8
NEW	7mm Remington Mag.	SHV7MMR1*	150	Power-Point Plus	D,O/P	2	24	3130	2849	2586	2337	2102	1881	3264	2705	2227	1819	1472	1179	-0.3	0	-0.8	-2.8	-6.1	-10..8	1.4	1.3	0	-2.6	-6.6	-19.6	-40.4
NEW	7mm Remington Mag.	SPG7MAG	160	Partition Gold	D,O/P,M,L	3	24	2950	2743	2546	2357	2176	2003	3093	2674	2303	1974	1682	1425	-0.2	0	-0.9	-3.1	-6.6	-11.6	1.6	1.4	0	-2.7	-6.9	-20.1	-40.7
	7mm Remington Mag.	SBST7	150	Ballistic Silvertip	D,O/P	2	24	3100	2903	2714	2533	2359	2192	3200	2806	2453	2136	1853	1600	-0.3	0	-0.8	-2.6	-5.7	-10.0	1.3	1.2	0	-2.4	-6.0	-17.5	-35.1
	7mm Remington Mag.	S7MAGXB	140	Fail Safe	D,O/P	2	24	3150	2861	2589	2333	2092	1866	3085	2544	2085	1693	1361	1083	-0.3	0	-0.8	-2.8	-6.0	-10.7	1.4	1.3	0	-2.6	-6.6	-19.5	-40.5
	7mm Remington Mag.	SBST7A	140	Ballistic Silvertip	D,O/P	2	24	3100	2889	2687	2494	2310	2133	2988	2595	2245	1934	1659	1414	-0.3	0	-0.8	-2.7	-5.8	-10.2	1.3	1.2	0	-2.4	-6.2	-17.9	-38.1
	7mm Remington Mag.	S7MAGX	160	Fail Safe	D,O/P,M,L	3	24	2920	2678	2449	2331	2025	1830	3030	2549	2131	1769	1457	1190	-0.2	0	-1.0	-3.4	-7.1	-12.5	1.7	1.5	0	-2.9	-7.5	-22.0	-44.9
NEW	30-30 Winchester	SHV30306*	150	Power-Point Plus	D	2	24	2480	2095	1747	1446	1209	1053	2049	1462	1017	697	487	369	0.1	0	-2.1	-6.5	-13.8	-24.5	3.3	2.8	0	-5.7	-14.7	-45.7	-98.4
NEW	30-06 Springfield	SHV30061*	150	Power-Point Plus	D,O/P	2	24	3050	2685	2352	2043	1760	1508	3089	2402	1843	1391	1032	757	-0.2	0	-1	-3.3	-7.3	-13	1.7	1.5	0	-3.1	-8	-24.3	-51.9
NEW	30-06 Springfield	SPG3006	150	Partition Gold	D,O/P,M	2	24	2960	2705	2464	2235	2019	1815	2919	2437	2022	1664	1358	1098	-0.2	0	-1.0	-3.3	-7.0	-12.3	1.6	1.5	0	-2.9	-7.4	-21.7	-44.6
	30-06 Springfield	SBST3006	150	Ballistic Silvertip	D,O/P	2	24	2900	2687	2483	2289	2103	1926	2801	2404	2054	1745	1473	1236	-0.2	0	-1.0	-3.3	-7.0	-12.3	1.7	1.5	0	-2.9	-7.3	-21.2	-43.0
	30-06 Springfield	SBST3006A	168	Ballistic Silvertip	D,O/P	2	24	2790	2599	2416	2240	2072	1911	2903	2520	2177	1872	1601	1362	-0.2	0	-1.1	-3.6	-7.6	-13.2	1.8	1.6	0	-3.1	-7.8	-22.5	-45.2
	30-06 Springfield	S3006XB	150	Fail Safe	D,O/P	3	24	2920	2625	2349	2089	1848	1625	2841	2296	1838	1455	1137	880	-0.2	0	-1.1	-3.6	-7.5	-13.4	1.8	1.6	0	-3.2	-8.1	-24.3	-50.5
	30-06 Springfield	S3006XA	165	Fail Safe	D,O/P,M	3	24	2800	2540	2295	2063	1846	1645	2873	2365	1930	1560	1249	992	-0.1	0	-1.2	-3.9	-8.2	-14.4	2.0	1.7	0	-3.4	-8.6	-25.3	-52.3
NEW	30-06 Springfield	SHV30064*	180	Power-Point Plus	D,O/P,M	2	24	2770	2563	2366	2177	1997	1826	3068	2627	2237	1894	1594	1333	-0.1	0	-1.2	-3.8	-8.0	-13.8	1.9	1.7	0	-3.2	-8.1	-23.6	-47.8
	30-06 Springfield	SPG3006A	180	Partition Gold	D,O/P,L	3	24	2790	2581	2382	2192	2010	1838	3112	2664	2269	1920	1615	1350	-0.1	0	-1.2	-3.7	-7.8	-13.6	1.9	1.6	0	-3.2	-8.0	-23.2	-47.1
	30-06 Springfield	S3006X	180	Fail Safe	D,O/P,M,L	3	24	2700	2486	2283	2089	1904	1731	2914	2472	2083	1744	1450	1198	-0.1	0	-1.3	-4.1	-8.6	-14.9	2.1	1.8	0	-3.5	-8.7	-25.5	-51.8
NEW	300 Winchester Mag.	SHV30WM2*	180	Power-Point Plus	D,O/P,M,L	3	24	3070	2846	2633	2430	2236	2051	3768	3239	2772	2361	1999	1681	-0.3	0	-0.8	-2.8	-6.0	-10.6	1.4	1.3	0	-2.5	-6.4	-18.7	-38.0
	300 Winchester Mag.	SBST300	180	Ballistic Silvertip	D,O/P,M,L	3	24	2950	2764	2586	2415	2250	2092	3478	3054	2673	2331	2023	1749	-0.2	0	-0.9	-3.0	-6.5	-11.3	1.5	1.4	0	-2.7	-6.7	-19.4	-38.9
	300 Winchester Mag.	S300WXA	165	Fail Safe	D,O/P,M	3	24	3120	2807	2515	2242	1985	1748	3567	2888	2319	1842	1445	1120	-0.3	0	-0.8	-2.9	-6.4	-11.4	1.5	1.3	0	-2.7	-7.0	-20.9	-43.6
	300 Winchester Mag.	S300WXB	150	Fail Safe	D,O/P	3	24	3260	2943	2647	2370	2110	1867	3539	2884	2334	1871	1483	1161	-0.3	0	-0.7	-2.5	-5.6	-10.0	1.3	1.2	0	-2.4	-6.2	-18.7	-38.9
	300 Winchester Mag.	S300WX	180	Fail Safe	M,L	3	24	2960	2732	2514	2307	2110	1923	3503	2983	2528	2129	1780	1478	-0.2	0	-1.0	-3.2	-6.8	-11.8	1.6	1.4	0	-2.8	-7.1	-20.7	-42.1
	300 Winchester Mag.	SPG300WM	180	Partition Gold	M,O/P,L	3	24	3070	2859	2657	2464	2280	2103	3768	3267	2823	2428	2078	1768	-0.3	0	-0.8	-2.8	-5.9	-10.4	1.4	1.3	0	-2.5	-6.3	-18.3	-37.1
	300 H& H Magnum	S300HX	180	Fail Safe	M,L	3	24	2880	2628	2390	2165	1952	1752	3316	2762	2284	1873	1523	1227	-0.2	0	-1.1	-3.5	-7.5	-13.2	1.8	1.6	0	-3.1	-7.9	-23.2	-47.6
NEW	308 Winchester	SHV3085*	150	Power-Point Plus	D,O/P	2	24	2900	2558	2241	1946	1678	1441	2802	2180	1672	1262	938	692	-0.2	0	-1.2	-3.8	-8.2	-14.6	1.9	1.7	0	-3.4	-8.9	-27.0	-57.4
NEW	308 Winchester	SPG308	150	Partition Gold	D,O/P	2	24	2900	2645	2405	2177	1962	1760	2802	2332	19-27	1579	1282	1032	-0.2	0	-1.1	3.5	-7.4	-13.0	1.7	1.6	0	-3.1	-7.8	22.9	-47.0
	308 Winchester	SBST308	150	Ballistic Silvertip	D,O/P	2	24	2810	2601	2401	2211	2028	1856	2629	2253	1920	1627	1370	1147	-0.2	0	-1.1	-3.6	-7.6	-13.3	1.8	1.6	0	-3.1	-7.8	-22.8	-46.2
	308 Winchester	SBST308A	168	Ballistic Silvertip	D,O/P	2	24	2670	2484	2306	2134	1971	1815	2659	2301	1983	1699	1449	1229	-0.1	0	-1.3	-4.1	-8.6	-14.8	2.1	1.8	0	-3.4	-8.6	-24.8	-50.0
	308 Winchester	S308XA	150	FailSafe	D,O/P,M	3	24	2820	2533	2263	2010	1775	1561	2649	2137	1706	1346	1049	812	-0.1	0	-1.2	-3.9	-8.4	-14.7	2.0	1.7	0	-3.4	-8.8	-26.2	-54.6
	338 Winchester Mag.	SBST338	200	Ballistic Silvertip	D,O/P,M,L	3	24	2950	2724	2509	2303	2108	1922	3864	3294	2794	2355	1972	1640	-0.2	0	-1.0	-3.2	-6.8	-11.9	1.6	1.4	0	-2.8	-7.1	-20.8	-42.3
	338 Winchester Mag.	S338XA	230	Fail Safe	M,L,XL	3	24	2780	2573	2375	2186	2005	1834	3948	3382	2881	2441	2054	1719	-0.1	0	-1.2	-3.8	-7.9	-13.7	1.9	1.7	0	-3.2	-8.1	-23.4	-47.4
NEW	338 Winchester Mag.	SPG338WM	250	Partition Gold	M,L,XL	3	24	2650	2467	2291	2122	1960	1807	3899	3378	2914	25200	2134	1812	-0.1	0	-1.3	-4.2	-8.8	-15.1	2.1	1.8	0	-3.5	-8.7	-25.2	-50.7
	375 H&H Magnum	S375HX	270	Fail Safe	L,XL	4	24	2670	2447	2234	2033	1842	1664	4275	3590	2994	2478	2035	1662	-0.1	0	-1.4	-4.3	-9.0	-15.6	2.2	1.9	0	-3.6	-9.1	-28.7	-54.5
	375 H&H Magnum	S375HXA	300	Fail Safe	L,XL	4	24	2530	2336	2151	1974	1806	1649	4265	3636	3082	2596	2173	1811	0	0	-1.6	-4.8	-10.1	-17.2	2.4	2.1	0	-4.0	-10.0	-26.9	-58.4
NEW	45-70 Government	SPG4570	300	Partition Gold	M,L	3	24	1880	1558	1292	1103	988	910	2355	1616	1112	811	651	551	0	-1.5	-6.5	-15.8	-30.2	-50.4	0	-4.3	-12.9	-26.6	-46.0	-104.9	-193.7

BALLISTICS

WINCHESTER RIFLE BALLISTICS

SUPER-X® CENTERFIRE RIFLE BALLISTICS

Cartridge	Symbol	Bullet Wt. Grs.	Bullet Type	Game Selector Guide	CXP Guide Number	Barrel Length (In.)	Velocity in Feet Per Second (fps) Muzzle	100	200	300	400	500	Energy in Foot Pounds (ft-lbs.) Muzzle	100	200	300	400	500	Trajectory, Short Range Yards 50	100	150	200	250	300	Trajectory, Long Range Yards 100	150	200	250	300	400	500
218 Bee	X218B	46	Hollow Point	V	1	24	2760	2102	1550	1155	961	850	778	451	245	136	94	74	0.3	0	-2.3	-7.2	-15.8	-29.4	1.5	0	-4.2	-12.0	-24.8	-71.4	-155.6
22 Hornet	X22H1	45	Soft Point	V	1	24	2690	2042	1502	1128	948	840	723	417	225	127	90	70	0.3	0	-2.4	-7.7	-16.9	-31.3	1.6	0	-4.5	-12.8	-26.4	-75.6	-163.4
22 Hornet	X22H2	46	Hollow Point	V	1	24	2690	2042	1502	1128	948	841	739	426	230	130	92	72	0.3	0	-2.4	-7.7	-16.9	-31.3	1.6	0	-4.5	-12.8	-26.4	-75.5	-163.3
22-250 Remington	X222501	55	Pointed Soft Point	V	1	24	3680	3137	2656	2222	1832	1493	1654	1201	861	603	410	272	0.2	0.5	0	-1.6	-4.4	-8.7	2.3	2.6	1.9	0	-3.4	-15.9	-38.9
220 Swift	X220S	50	Pointed Soft Point	V	1	24	3870	3310	2816	2373	1972	1616	1663	1226	881	625	432	290	-0.4	0	-0.4	-1.7	-4.1	-7.8	0.8	0.9	0	-2.0	-5.2	-16.7	-37.1
222 Remington	X222R	50	Pointed Soft Point	V	1	24	3140	2602	2123	1700	1350	1107	1094	752	500	321	202	136	0.5	0.9	0	-2.5	-6.9	-13.7	2.2	1.9	0	-3.8	-10.0	-32.3	-73.8
223 Remington	X223RH	53	Hollow Point	V	1	24	3330	2882	2477	2106	1770	1475	1305	978	722	522	369	256	0.3	0.7	0	-1.9	-5.3	-10.3	1.7	1.4	0	-2.9	-7.4	-22.7	-49.1
223 Remington	X223R	55	Pointed Soft Point	V	1	24	3240	2747	2304	1905	1554	1270	1282	921	648	443	295	197	0.4	0.8	0	-2.2	-6.0	-11.8	1.9	1.6	0	-3.3	-8.5	-26.7	-59.6
223 Remington	X223R2	64	Power-Point®	D	2	24	3020	2656	2320	2009	1724	1473	1296	1003	765	574	423	308	0.1	0.7	0	-2.1	-5.8	-11.4	1.7	1.6	0	-3.2	-8.2	-25.1	-53.6
NEW 556 mm	SC556NT	55	Super Clean NT	Training		24	3150	2520	1970	1505	1165	983	1212	776	474	277	166	118	0.5	0	-1.9	-5.6	-11.5	-20.3	2.8	2.3	0	-4.5	-11.9	-38.9	-87.9
225 Winchester	X2251	55	Pointed Soft Point	V	1	24	3570	3066	2616	2208	1838	1514	1556	1148	836	595	412	280	0.2	0.6	0	-1.7	-4.6	-9.0	2.4	2.8	2.0	0	-3.5	-16.3	-39.5
243 Winchester	X2431	80	Pointed Soft Point	V	1	24	3350	2955	2593	2259	1951	1670	1993	1551	1194	906	676	495	0.3	0.7	0	-1.8	-4.9	-9.4	2.6	2.9	2.1	0	-3.6	-16.2	-37.9
243 Winchester	X2432	100	Power-Point	D,O/P	2	24	2960	2697	2449	2215	1993	1786	1945	1615	1332	1089	882	708	0.5	0.9	0	-2.2	-5.8	-11.0	1.9	1.6	0	-3.1	-7.8	-22.6	-46.3
6mm Remington	X6MMR2	100	Power-Point	D,O/P	2	24	3100	2829	2573	2332	2104	1889	2133	1777	1470	1207	983	792	0.4	0.8	0	-1.9	-5.2	-9.9	1.7	1.5	0	-2.8	-7.0	-20.4	-41.7
25-06 Remington	X25061	90	Positive Expanding Point	V	1	24	3440	3043	2680	2344	2034	1749	2364	1850	1435	1098	827	611	0.3	0.6	0	-1.7	-4.5	-8.8	2.4	2.7	2.0	0	-3.4	-15.0	-35.2
25-06 Remington	X25062	120	Positive Expanding Point	D,O/P	2	24	2990	2730	2484	2252	2032	1825	2382	1985	1644	1351	1100	887	0.5	0.8	0	-2.1	-5.6	-10.7	1.9	1.6	0	-3.0	-7.5	-22.0	-44.8
25-20 Winchester #	X25202	86	Soft Point	V	1	24	1460	1194	1030	931	858	798	407	272	203	165	141	122	0	-4.1	-14.4	-31.8	-57.3	-92.0	0	-8.2	-23.5	-47.0	-79.6	-175.9	-319.4
25-35 Winchester	X2535	117	Soft Point	D	2	24	2230	1866	1545	1282	1097	984	1292	904	620	427	313	252	0.6	0	-3.1	-9.2	-19.0	-33.1	2.1	0	-5.1	-13.8	-27.0	-70.1	-142.0
250 Savage	X2503	100	Silvertip®	D,O/P	2	24	2820	2467	2140	1839	1569	1339	1765	1351	1017	751	547	398	0.2	0	-1.6	-4.9	-10.0	-17.4	2.4	2.0	0	-3.9	-10.1	-30.5	-65.2
257 Roberts + P	X257P3	117	Power-Point	D,O/P	2	24	2780	2411	2071	1761	1488	1263	2009	1511	1115	806	576	415	0.8	1.1	0	-2.9	-7.8	-15.1	2.6	2.2	0	-4.2	-10.8	-33.0	-70.0
264 Winchester Mag.	X2642	140	Power-Point	D,O/P	2	24	3030	2782	2548	2326	2114	1914	2854	2406	2018	1682	1389	1139	0.5	0.8	0	-2.0	-5.4	-10.2	1.8	1.5	0	-2.9	-7.2	-20.8	-42.2
6.5 x 55 Swedish	X6555	140	Soft Point	D,O/P	2	24	2550	2359	2176	2002	1836	1680	2022	1731	1473	1246	1048	878	0	0	-1.5	-4.8	-9.8	-16.9	2.4	2	0	-3.9	-9.7	-28.1	-56.8
270 Winchester	X2705	130	Power-Point	D,O/P	2	24	3060	2802	2559	2329	2110	1904	2702	2267	1890	1565	1285	1046	0.4	0.8	0	-2.0	-5.3	-10.1	1.8	1.5	0	-2.8	-7.1	-20.6	-42.0
270 Winchester	X2703	130	Silvertip	D,O/P	2	24	3060	2776	2510	2259	2022	1801	2702	2225	1818	1472	1180	936	0.5	0.8	0	-2.0	-5.5	-10.4	1.8	1.5	0	-2.9	-7.4	-21.6	-44.3
270 Winchester	X2704	150	Power-Point	D,O/P,M	3	24	2850	2585	2336	2100	1879	1673	2705	2226	1817	1468	1175	932	0.6	1.0	0	-2.4	-6.4	-12.2	2.2	1.8	0	-3.4	-8.6	-25.0	-51.4
284 Winchester	X2842	150	Power-Point	D,O/P,M	3	24	2860	2595	2344	2108	1886	1680	2724	2243	1830	1480	1185	940	0.6	1.0	0	-2.4	-6.3	-12.1	2.1	1.8	0	-3.4	-8.5	-24.8	-51.0
7mm-08 Remington	X708	140	Power-Point	D,O/P	2	24	2800	2523	2268	2027	1802	1596	2429	1980	1599	1277	1010	792	-0.1	0	-1.2	-4.0	-8.4	-14.7	2.0	1.8	0	-3.4	-8.8	-26.0	-54.0
7mm Mauser (7x57)	X7MM1	145	Power-Point	D	2	24	2660	2413	2180	1959	1754	1564	2279	1875	1530	1236	990	788	0.2	0	-1.7	-5.1	-10.3	-17.5	1.1	0	-2.8	-7.4	-14.1	-34.4	-66.1
NEW 7mm STW	X7STW1*	150	Power-Point	D,O/P,M	2	24	3250	2957	2683	2424	2181	1951	3519	2913	2398	1958	1584	1269	-0.3	0	-0.7	-2.5	-5.5	-9.8	1.2	1.2	0	-2.4	-6.1	-18.1	-37.4
7mm Remington Mag.	X7MMR1	150	Power-Point	D,O/P,M	2	24	3090	2812	2551	2304	2071	1852	3181	2634	2167	1768	1429	1143	-0.3	0	-0.8	-2.9	-6.3	-11.2	1.5	1.3	0	-2.7	-6.8	-20.2	-41.6
7mm Remington Mag.	X7MMR2	175	Power-Point	D,O/P,M	3	24	2860	2645	2440	2244	2057	1879	3178	2718	2313	1956	1644	1372	0.6	0.9	0	-2.3	-6.0	-11.3	2.0	1.7	0	-3.2	-7.9	-22.7	-45.8
7.62 x 39mm Russian	X76239	123	Soft Point	D,V	2	20	2365	2033	1731	1465	1248	1093	1527	1129	818	586	425	327	0.5	0	-2.6	-7.6	-15.4	-26.7	3.8	3.1	0	-6.0	-15.4	-46.3	-98.4
30 Carbine #	X30M1	110	Hollow Soft Point	V	1	20	1990	1567	1236	1035	923	842	967	600	373	262	208	173	0.9	0	-4.5	-13.5	-28.3	-49.9	0	-4.5	-13.5	-28.3	-49.9	-118.6	-228.2
30-30 Winchester	X30301	150	Hollow Point	D	2	24	2390	2018	1684	1398	1177	1036	1902	1356	944	651	461	357	0.5	0	-2.6	-7.7	-16.0	-27.9	1.7	0	-4.3	-11.6	-22.7	-59.1	-120.5
30-30 Winchester	X30306	150	Power-Point	D	2	24	2390	2018	1684	1398	1177	1036	1902	1356	944	651	461	357	0.5	0	-2.6	-7.7	-16.0	-27.9	1.7	0	-4.3	-11.6	-22.7	-59.1	-120.5
30-30 Winchester	X30302	150	Silvertip	D	2	24	2390	2018	1684	1398	1177	1036	1902	1356	944	651	461	357	0.5	0	-2.6	-7.7	-16.0	-27.9	1.7	0	-4.3	-11.6	-22.7	-59.1	-120.5
30-30 Winchester	X30303	170	Power-Point	D	2	24	2200	1895	1619	1381	1191	1061	1827	1355	989	720	535	425	0.6	0	-3.0	-8.9	-18.0	-31.1	2.0	0	-4.8	-13.0	-25.1	-63.6	-126.7
30-30 Winchester	X30304	170	Silvertip	D	2	24	2200	1895	1619	1381	1191	1061	1827	1355	989	720	535	425	0.6	0	-3.0	-8.9	-18.0	-31.1	2.0	0	-4.8	-13.0	-25.1	-63.6	-126.7
30-06 Springfield	X30062	125	Pointed Soft Point	V	1	24	3140	2780	2447	2138	1853	1595	2736	2145	1662	1269	953	706	0.4	0.8	0	-2.1	-5.6	-10.7	1.8	1.5	0	-3.0	-7.7	-23.0	-48.5
30-06 Springfield	X30061	150	Power-Point	D,O/P	2	24	2920	2580	2265	1972	1704	1466	2839	2217	1708	1295	967	716	0.6	1.0	0	-2.4	-6.6	-12.7	2.2	1.8	0	-3.5	-9.0	-27.0	-57.1
30-06 Springfield	X30063	150	Silvertip	D,O/P	2	24	2910	2617	2342	2083	1843	1622	2820	2281	1827	1445	1131	876	0.6	0.9	0	-2.3	-6.3	-12.0	2.1	1.8	0	-3.3	-8.5	-25.0	-51.8
30-06 Springfield	X30065	165	Pointed Soft Point	D,O/P,M	2	24	2800	2573	2357	2151	1956	1772	2873	2426	2036	1696	1402	1151	0.7	1.0	0	-2.5	-6.5	-12.2	2.2	1.9	0	-3.6	-8.4	-24.4	-49.6
30-06 Springfield	X30064	180	Power-Point	D,O/P,M	2	24	2700	2348	2023	1727	1466	1251	2913	2203	1635	1192	859	625	0.2	0	-1.8	-5.5	-11.2	-19.5	2.7	2.3	0	-4.4	-11.3	-34.4	-73.7
30-06 Springfield	X30066	180	Silvertip	D,O/P,M,L	3	24	2700	2469	2250	2042	1846	1663	2913	2436	2023	1666	1362	1105	0.2	0	-1.6	-4.8	-9.7	-16.5	2.4	2.0	0	-3.7	-9.3	-27.0	-54.9
30-40 Krag	X30401	180	Power-Point	D	2	24	2430	2099	1795	1525	1298	1128	2360	1761	1288	929	673	508	0.4	0	-2.4	-7.1	-14.5	-25.0	1.6	0	-3.9	-10.5	-20.3	-51.7	-103.9
300 Winchester Mag.	X30WM1	150	Power-Point	D,O/P	2	24	3290	2951	2636	2342	2068	1813	3605	2900	2314	1827	1424	1095	0.3	0.7	0	-1.8	-4.8	-9.3	2.6	2.9	2.1	0	-3.5	-15.4	-35.5
300 Winchester Mag.	X30WM2	180	Power-Point	O/P,M,L	3	24	2960	2745	2540	2344	2157	1979	3501	3011	2578	2196	1859	1565	0.5	0.8	0	-2.1	-5.5	-10.4	1.9	1.6	0	-2.9	-7.3	-20.9	-41.9
300 Savage	X3001	150	Power-Point	D,O/P	2	24	2630	2311	2015	1743	1500	1295	2303	1779	1352	1012	749	558	0.3	0	-1.9	-5.7	-11.6	-19.9	2.8	2.3	0	-4.5	-11.5	-34.4	-73.0
303 British	X303B1	180	Power-Point	D	2	24	2460	2233	2018	1816	1629	1459	2418	1993	1627	1318	1060	851	0.3	0	-2.1	-6.1	-12.2	-20.8	1.4	0	-3.3	-8.8	-16.6	-40.4	-77.4
307 Winchester	X3076	180	Power-Point	D,M	2	24	2510	2179	1874	1599	1362	1177	2519	1898	1404	1022	742	554	0.3	0	-2.2	-6.5	-13.3	-22.9	1.5	0	-3.6	-9.6	-18.6	-47.1	-93.7
308 Winchester	X3085	150	Power-Point	D,O/P	2	24	2820	2488	2179	1893	1633	1405	2648	2061	1581	1193	888	657	0.2	0	-1.6	-4.8	-9.8	-16.9	2.4	2.0	0	-3.8	-9.8	-29.3	-62.0
308 Winchester	X3086	180	Power-Point	D,O/P,M	2	24	2620	2274	1955	1666	1414	1212	2743	2066	1527	1109	799	587	0.3	0	-2.0	-5.9	-12.1	-20.9	2.9	2.4	0	-4.7	-12.1	-36.9	-79.1
308 Winchester	X3083	180	Silvertip	M,L	3	24	2620	2393	2178	1974	1782	1604	2743	2288	1896	1557	1269	1028	0.2	0	-1.8	-5.2	-10.4	-17.7	2.6	2.1	0	-4.0	-9.9	-28.9	-58.8
32 Win Special	X32WS2	170	Power-Point	D	2	24	2250	1870	1537	1267	1082	971	1911	1320	892	606	442	356	0.6	0	-3.1	-9.2	-19.0	-33.2	2.0	0	-5.1	-13.8	-27.1	-70.9	-144.3
32-20 Winchester #	X32201	100	Lead	V	1	24	1210	1021	913	834	769	712	325	231	185	154	131	113	0	-6.3	-20.9	-44.9	-79.3	-125.1	0	-11.5	-32.3	-63.6	-106.3	-230.3	-413.3
8mm Mauser (8 x 57)	X8MM	170	Power-Point	D	2	24	2360	1969	1622	1333	1123	997	2102	1463	993	671	476	375	0.5	0	-2.7	-8.2	-17.0	-29.8	1.8	0	-4.5	-12.4	-24.3	-63.8	-130.7
338 Winchester Mag.	X3381	200	Power-Point	D,O/P,M, L	3	24	2960	2658	2375	2110	1862	1635	3890	3137	2505	1977	1539	1187	0.5	0.9	0	-2.3	-6.1	-11.6	2.0	1.7	0	-3.2	-8.2	-24.3	-50.4
348 Winchester	X3483	200	Silvertip	D,M	3	24	2520	2215	1931	1672	1443	1293	2820	2178	1656	1241	925	697	0.3	0	-2.1	-6.2	-12.7	-21.9	1.4	0	-3.4	-9.2	-17.7	-44.4	-87.9
35 Remington	X35R1	200	Power-Point	D	2	24	2020	1646	1335	1114	985	901	1812	1203	791	551	431	360	0.9	0	-4.1	-12.1	-25.1	-43.9	2.7	0	-6.7	-18.3	-35.8	-92.8	-185.5
356 Winchester	X3561	200	Power-Point	D,M	2	24	2460	2114	1797	1517	1284	1113	2688	1985	1434	1022	732	550	0.4	0	-2.3	-7.0	-14.3	-24.7	1.6	0	-3.8	-10.4	-20.1	-51.2	-102.3
357 Magnum #	X3575P	158	Jacketed Soft Point	V,D	2	20	1830	1427	1138	980	883	809	1175	715	454	337	274	229	0	-2.4	-9.1	-21.0	-39.2	-64.3	0	-5.5	-16.2	-33.1	-57.0	-128.3	-235.8
358 Winchester	X3581	200	Silvertip	D,M	3	24	2490	2171	1876	1610	1379	1194	2753	2093	1563	1151	844	633	0.4	0	-2.2	-6.5	-13.3	-23.0	1.5	0	-3.6	-9.7	-18.6	-47.2	-94.1
375 Winchester	X375W	200	Power-Point	D,M	2	24	2200	1841	1526	1268	1089	980	2150	1506	1034	714	527	427	0.6	0	-3.2	-9.5	-19.5	-33.8	2.1	0	-5.2	-14.1	-27.4	-70.1	-138.1
38-40 Winchester #	X3840	180	Soft Point	D	2	24	1160	999	901	827	764	710	538	399	324	273	233	201	0	-6.7	-22.2	-47.3	-83.2	-130.8	0	-12.1	-33.9	-66.4	-110.6	-238.3	-425.6
38-55 Winchester	X3855	255	Soft Point	D	2	24	1320	1190	1091	1018	963	917	987	802	674	587	525	476	0	-4.7	-15.4	-32.7	-57.2	-89.3	0	-8.4	-23.4	-45.6	-75.2	-158.8	-277.4
44 Remington Magnum #	X44MS	210	Silvertip Hollow Point	V,D	2	20	1580	1198	993	879	795	725	1164	670	460	361	295	245	0	-3.7	-13.3	-29.8	-54.2	-87.3	0	-7.7	-22.4	-44.9	-76.1	-168.0	-305.8
44 Remington Magnum #	X44MHSP2	240	Hollow Soft Point	D	2	20	1760	1362	1094	953	861	789	1650	988	638	484	395	332	0	-2.7	-10.2	-23.6	-44.2	-73.3	0	-6.1	-18.1	-37.4	-65.1	-150.3	-282.5
44-40 Winchester #	X4440	200	Soft Point	D	2	24	1190	1006	900	822	756	699	629	449	360	300	254	217	0	-6.5	-21.6	-46.3	-81.8	-129.1	0	-11.8	-33.3	-65.5	-109.5	-237.4	-426.2
45-70 Government	X4570H	300	Jacketed Hollow Point	D,M	2	24	1880	1650	1425	1235	1105	1010	2355	1815	1355	1015	810	680	0	-2.4	-8.2	-17.6	-31.4	-51.5	0	-4.6	-12.8	-25.4	-44.3	-95.5	–
458 Winchester Magnum	X4581	510	Soft Point	L,XL	3	24	2040	1770	1527	1319	1157	1046	4712	3547	2640	1970	1516	1239	0.8	0	-3.5	-10.3	-20.8	-35.6	2.4	0	-5.6	-14.9	-28.5	-71.5	-140.4

Game Selector/CXP Class/Examples: *V-Varmint/1/Prairie dog, coyote, woodchuck • D-Deer/2/Antelope, deer, black bear • O/P-Open or Plains/3/Large,heavy game • L-Large Game/4/Cape Buffalo, elephant • XL-Extra Large Game/M/Match # Acceptable for use in pistols and revolvers also. * Preliminary external ballistic data based upon computer model. Actual field performance may vary.*

Reloading

BULLETS
Barnes 520-522
Federal 523
Hornady 524-526
Nosler 527-530
Sierra 531-533
Speer 534-537
Swift 538
Woodleigh 539, 540

GUNPOWDER
Alliant 541, 542
Hodgdon 543

TOOLS
Dillon 544, 545
Forster 546, 547
Hornady 548, 549
Lyman 550-554
MEC 555, 556
MTM 557
RCBS 558-560
Redding 561, 562

*For addresses and phone/fax numbers of manufacturers and distributors included in this section, please turn to **DIRECTORY OF MANUFACTURERS AND SUPPLIERS** on page 564.*

BARNES BULLETS

In 1989 Barnes introduced the **X-Bullet**. It has since supplanted the company's lead-core softpoints (still made) as a premier big game bullet. Now the **X-Bullet** is also available for handguns, muzzleloaders and shotguns, and for rifles with a special blue dry-film lubricant–the **XLC**.

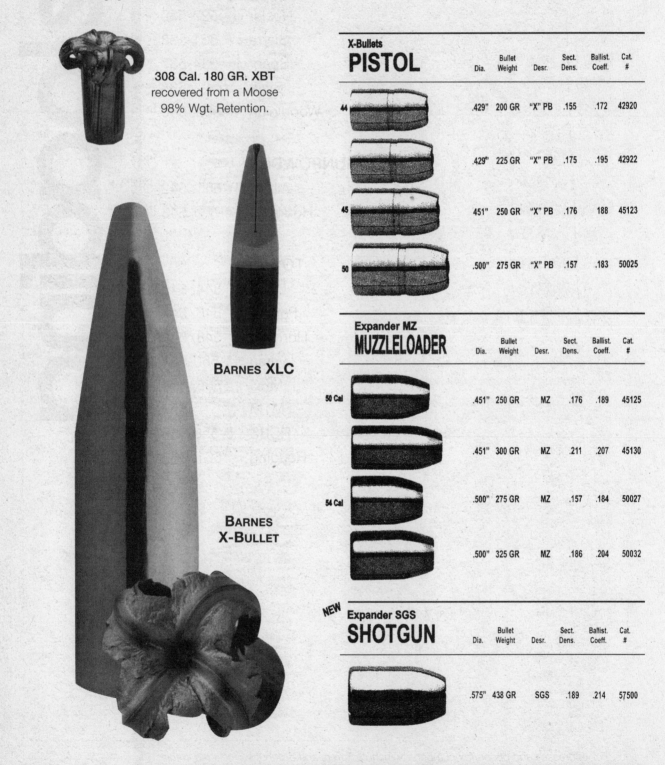

308 Cal. 180 GR. XBT
recovered from a Moose
98% Wgt. Retention.

BARNES XLC

BARNES X-BULLET

X-Bullets
PISTOL

	Dia.	Bullet Weight	Desr.	Sect. Dens.	Ballist. Coeff.	Cat. #
44	.429"	200 GR	"X" PB	.155	.172	42920
	.429"	225 GR	"X" PB	.175	.195	42922
45	451"	250 GR	"X" PB	.176	188	45123
50	.500"	275 GR	"X" PB	.157	.183	50025

Expander MZ
MUZZLELOADER

	Dia.	Bullet Weight	Desr.	Sect. Dens.	Ballist. Coeff.	Cat. #
50 Cal	.451"	250 GR	MZ	.176	.189	45125
	.451"	300 GR	MZ	.211	.207	45130
54 Cal	.500"	275 GR	MZ	.157	.184	50027
	.500"	325 GR	MZ	.186	.204	50032

Expander SGS
SHOTGUN **NEW**

	Dia.	Bullet Weight	Desr.	Sect. Dens.	Ballist. Coeff.	Cat. #
	.575"	438 GR	SGS	.189	.214	57500

BARNES BULLETS

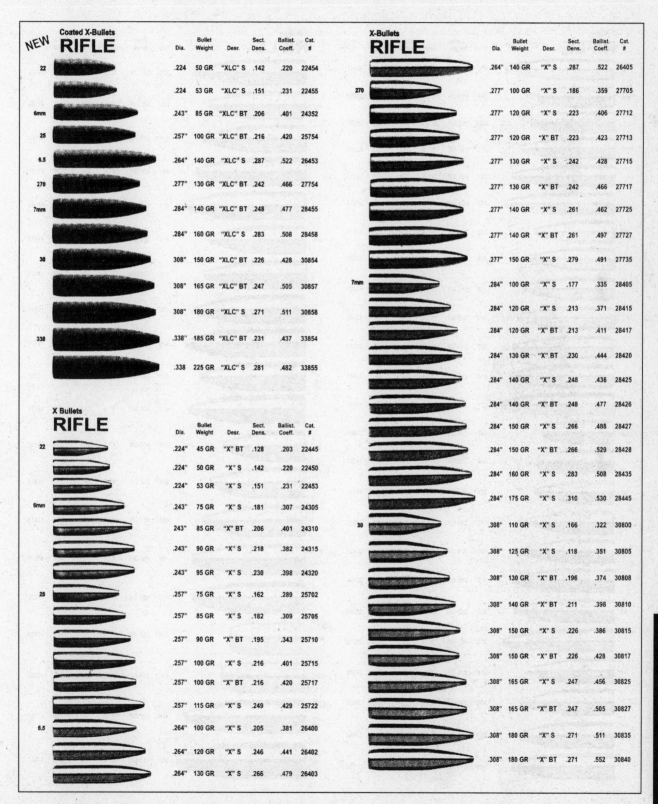

Coated X-Bullets
RIFLE

	Dia.	Bullet Weight	Desr.	Sect. Dens.	Ballist. Coeff.	Cat. #
NEW						
22	.224	50 GR	"XLC" S	.142	.220	22454
	.224	53 GR	"XLC" S	.151	.231	22455
6mm	.243"	85 GR	"XLC" BT	.206	.401	24352
25	.257"	100 GR	"XLC" BT	.216	.420	25754
6.5	.264"	140 GR	"XLC" S	.287	.522	26453
270	.277"	130 GR	"XLC" BT	.242	.466	27754
7mm	.284"	140 GR	"XLC" BT	.248	.477	28455
	.284"	160 GR	"XLC" S	.283	.508	28458
30	308"	150 GR	"XLC" BT	.226	.428	30854
	308"	165 GR	"XLC" BT	.247	.505	30857
	308"	180 GR	"XLC" S	.271	.511	30858
338	.338"	185 GR	"XLC" BT	.231	.437	33854
	.338	225 GR	"XLC" S	.281	.482	33855

X Bullets
RIFLE

	Dia.	Bullet Weight	Desr.	Sect. Dens.	Ballist. Coeff.	Cat. #
22	.224"	45 GR	"X" BT	.128	.203	22445
	.224"	50 GR	"X" S	.142	.220	22450
	.224"	53 GR	"X" S	.151	.231	22453
6mm	.243"	75 GR	"X" S	.181	.307	24305
	243"	85 GR	"X" BT	.206	.401	24310
	.243"	90 GR	"X" S	.218	.382	24315
	.243"	95 GR	"X" S	.230	.398	24320
25	.257"	75 GR	"X" S	.162	.289	25702
	.257"	85 GR	"X" S	.182	.309	25705
	.257"	90 GR	"X" BT	.195	.343	25710
	.257"	100 GR	"X" S	.216	.401	25715
	.257"	100 GR	"X" BT	.216	.420	25717
	.257"	115 GR	"X" S	.249	.429	25722
6.5	.264"	100 GR	"X" S	.205	.381	26400
	.264"	120 GR	"X" S	.246	.441	26402
	.264"	130 GR	"X" S	.266	.479	26403

X-Bullets
RIFLE

	Dia.	Bullet Weight	Desr.	Sect. Dens.	Ballist. Coeff.	Cat. #
	.264"	140 GR	"X" S	.287	.522	26405
270	.277"	100 GR	"X" S	.186	.359	27705
	.277"	120 GR	"X" S	.223	.406	27712
	.277"	120 GR	"X" BT	.223	.423	27713
	.277"	130 GR	"X" S	.242	.428	27715
	.277"	130 GR	"X" BT	.242	.466	27717
	.277"	140 GR	"X" S	.261	.462	27725
	.277"	140 GR	"X" BT	.261	.497	27727
	.277"	150 GR	"X" S	.279	.491	27735
7mm	.284"	100 GR	"X" S	.177	.335	28405
	.284"	120 GR	"X" S	.213	.371	28415
	.284"	120 GR	"X" BT	.213	.411	28417
	.284"	130 GR	"X" BT	.230	.444	28420
	.284"	140 GR	"X" S	.248	.436	28425
	.284"	140 GR	"X" BT	.248	.477	28426
	.284"	150 GR	"X" S	.266	.488	28427
	.284"	150 GR	"X" BT	.266	.529	28428
	.284"	160 GR	"X" S	.283	.508	28435
	.284"	175 GR	"X" S	.310	.530	28445
30	.308"	110 GR	"X" S	.166	.322	30800
	.308"	125 GR	"X" S	.118	.351	30805
	.308"	130 GR	"X" BT	.196	.374	30808
	.308"	140 GR	"X" BT	.211	.398	30810
	.308"	150 GR	"X" S	.226	.386	30815
	.308"	150 GR	"X" BT	.226	.428	30817
	.308"	165 GR	"X" S	.247	.456	30825
	.308"	165 GR	"X" BT	.247	.505	30827
	.308"	180 GR	"X" S	.271	.511	30835
	.308"	180 GR	"X" BT	.271	.552	30840

RELOADING

BARNES BULLETS

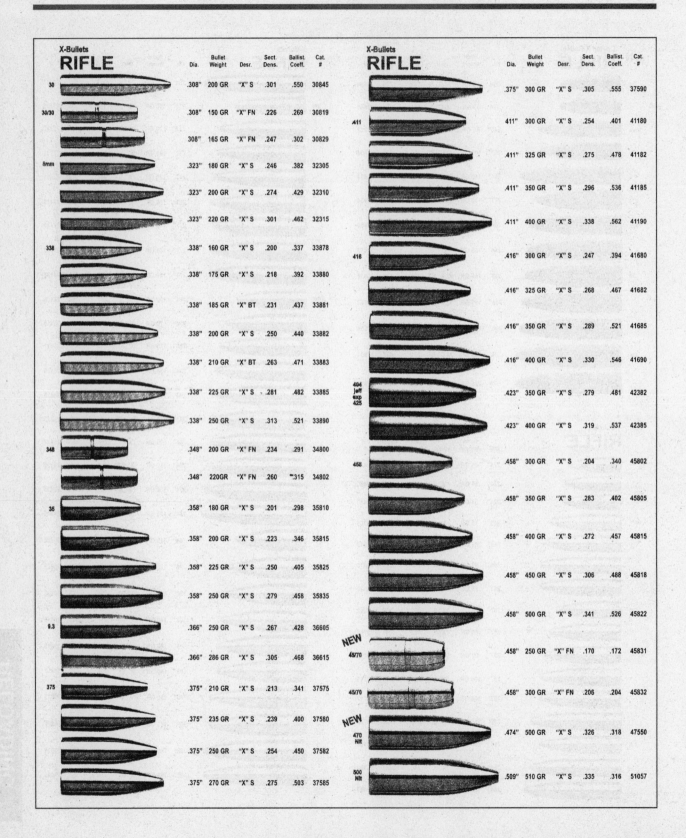

X-Bullets RIFLE

	Dia.	Bullet Weight	Desr.	Sect. Dens.	Ballist. Coeff.	Cat. #
30	.308"	200 GR	"X" S	.301	.550	30845
30/30	.308"	150 GR	"X" FN	.226	.269	30819
	308"	165 GR	"X" FN	.247	.302	30829
8mm	.323"	180 GR	"X" S	.246	.382	32305
	.323"	200 GR	"X" S	.274	.429	32310
	.323"	220 GR	"X" S	.301	.462	32315
338	.338"	160 GR	"X" S	.200	.337	33878
	.338"	175 GR	"X" S	.218	.392	33880
	.338"	185 GR	"X" BT	.231	.437	33881
	.338"	200 GR	"X" S	.250	.440	33882
	.338"	210 GR	"X" BT	.263	.471	33883
	.338"	225 GR	"X" S	.281	.482	33885
	.338"	250 GR	"X" S	.313	.521	33890
348	.348"	200 GR	"X" FN	.234	.291	34800
	.348"	220GR	"X" FN	.260	.315	34802
35	.358"	180 GR	"X" S	.201	.298	35810
	.358"	200 GR	"X" S	.223	.346	35815
	.358"	225 GR	"X" S	.250	.405	35825
	.358"	250 GR	"X" S	.279	.458	35835
9.3	.366"	250 GR	"X" S	.267	.428	36605
	.366"	286 GR	"X" S	.305	.468	36615
375	.375"	210 GR	"X" S	.213	.341	37575
	.375"	235 GR	"X" S	.239	.400	37580
	.375"	250 GR	"X" S	.254	.450	37582
	.375"	270 GR	"X" S	.275	.503	37585

X-Bullets RIFLE

	Dia.	Bullet Weight	Desr.	Sect. Dens.	Ballist. Coeff.	Cat. #
	.375"	300 GR	"X" S	.305	.555	37590
411	411"	300 GR	"X" S	.254	.401	41180
	.411"	325 GR	"X" S	.275	.478	41182
	.411"	350 GR	"X" S	.296	.536	41185
	.411"	400 GR	"X" S	.338	.562	41190
416	.416"	300 GR	"X" S	.247	.394	41680
	.416"	325 GR	"X" S	.268	.467	41682
	.416"	350 GR	"X" S	.289	.521	41685
	.416"	400 GR	"X" S	.330	.546	41690
404 Jeff exp 425	.423"	350 GR	"X" S	.279	.481	42382
	.423"	400 GR	"X" S	.319	.537	42385
458	.458"	300 GR	"X" S	.204	.340	45802
	.458"	350 GR	"X" S	.283	.402	45805
	.458"	400 GR	"X" S	.272	.457	45815
	.458"	450 GR	"X" S	.306	.488	45818
	.458"	500 GR	"X" S	.341	.526	45822
NEW 45/70	.458"	250 GR	"X" FN	.170	.172	45831
45/70	.458"	300 GR	"X" FN	.206	.204	45832
NEW 470 Nit	.474"	500 GR	"X" S	.326	.318	47550
500 Nit	.509"	510 GR	"X" S	.335	.316	51057

FEDERAL RIFLE BULLETS

CLASSIC CENTERFIRE RIFLE

Federal Classic Rifle ammunition is still the choice of many serious hunters who know what it takes to succeed in the field. Whether you choose the Sierra Pro-Hunter®, the most widely reloaded bullet in America, or Federal's renowned Hi-Shok® bullet, you'll get dependable, consistent performance with deadly accuracy and double-caliber expansion.

Soft Point

Soft Point Round Nose

Soft Point Flat Nose

Hollow Point

Full Metal Jacket Boat-Tail

SOFT POINT
Excellent for small game and thin-skinned medium game.
The aerodynamic tip provides flat shooting, and the exposed soft point expands rapidly, even at reduced velocities found at longer ranges.

SOFT POINT ROUND NOSE
A traditional choice for deer and bear in the brush.
A large exposed tip, extra weight, and specially tapered jacket provide controlled expansion, good weight retention, and deep penetration.

SOFT POINT FLAT NOSE
A good choice for light to medium game, even in brush.
Especially designed for rifles with tubular magazines, the flat nose prevents accidental discharge. It also expands reliably and offers deep penetration.

HOLLOW POINT
A great mid-distance load for medium game.
Available in 30-30 Win., 357 Mag., 44 Rem. Mag., and 45-70 Govt., the hollow-point provides hard-hitting accuracy and dramatic expansion.

FULL METAL JACKET BOAT-TAIL
Excellent for fur-bearing animals and target shooting.
The jacket prevents point deformation for smooth, reliable feeding in semi-automatics. The non-expanding bullet leaves a small exit hole for minimal pelt damage.

CLASSIC HANDGUN

Federal offers breadth of selection and quality that are second to none. The lineup includes wadcutters for clean target marking, hollow-point loads favored by law enforcement officials and soft points that are the choice of countless handgun hunters. All are available in a wide variety of calibers to ensure the perfect load for specific needs.

Lead Round Nose
An accurate, economical training round.

Full Metal Jacket
A good choice for recreational shooting.

Hi-Shok Jacketed Soft Point
Good for small to medium-sized game.

Lead Semi-Wadcutter
Good for target shooting and personal defense.

Hi-Shok Jacketed Hollow Point
Excellent for personall defense.

Semi-Wadcutter Hollow Point
For small game and personal defense.

HORNADY RIFLE BULLETS

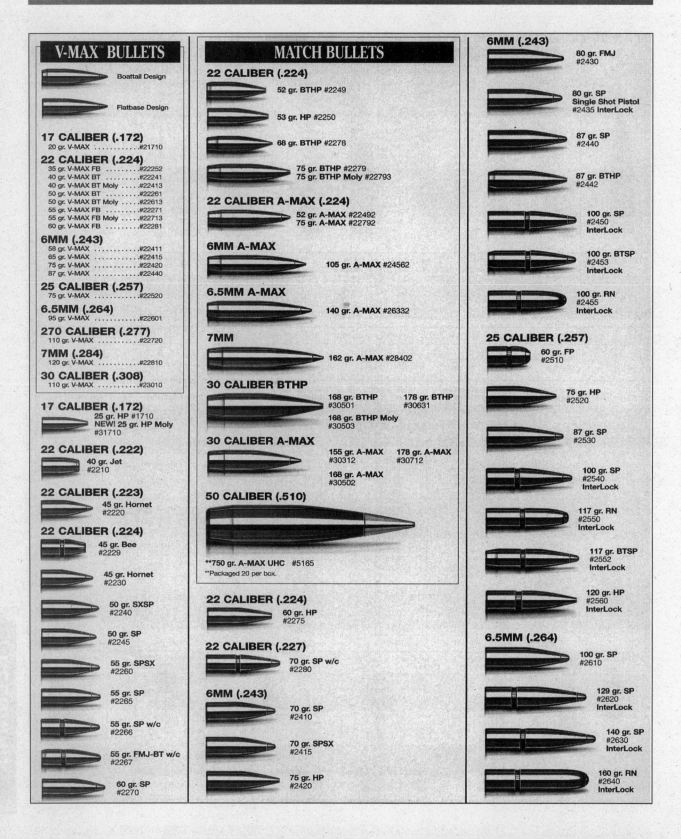

V-MAX™ BULLETS

Boattail Design

Flatbase Design

17 CALIBER (.172)
20 gr. V-MAX ....#21710

22 CALIBER (.224)
35 gr. V-MAX FB ....#22252
40 gr. V-MAX BT ....#22241
40 gr. V-MAX BT Moly ....#22413
50 gr. V-MAX BT ....#22261
50 gr. V-MAX BT Moly ...#22613
55 gr. V-MAX FB ....#22271
55 gr. V-MAX FB Moly ...#22713
60 gr. V-MAX FB ....#22281

6MM (.243)
58 gr. V-MAX ....#22411
65 gr. V-MAX ....#22415
75 gr. V-MAX ....#22420
87 gr. V-MAX ....#22440

25 CALIBER (.257)
75 gr. V-MAX ....#22520

6.5MM (.264)
95 gr. V-MAX ....#22601

270 CALIBER (.277)
110 gr. V-MAX ....#22720

7MM (.284)
120 gr. V-MAX ....#22810

30 CALIBER (.308)
110 gr. V-MAX ....#23010

17 CALIBER (.172)
25 gr. HP #1710
NEW! 25 gr. HP Moly
#31710

22 CALIBER (.222)
40 gr. Jet
#2210

22 CALIBER (.223)
45 gr. Hornet
#2220

22 CALIBER (.224)
45 gr. Bee
#2229

45 gr. Hornet
#2230

50 gr. SXSP
#2240

50 gr. SP
#2245

55 gr. SPSX
#2260

55 gr. SP
#2265

55 gr. SP w/c
#2266

55 gr. FMJ-BT w/c
#2267

60 gr. SP
#2270

MATCH BULLETS

22 CALIBER (.224)
52 gr. BTHP #2249

53 gr. HP #2250

68 gr. BTHP #2278

75 gr. BTHP #2279
75 gr. BTHP Moly #22793

22 CALIBER A-MAX (.224)
52 gr. A-MAX #22492
75 gr. A-MAX #22792

6MM A-MAX
105 gr. A-MAX #24562

6.5MM A-MAX
140 gr. A-MAX #26332

7MM
162 gr. A-MAX #28402

30 CALIBER BTHP
168 gr. BTHP   178 gr. BTHP
#30501   #30631
168 gr. BTHP Moly
#30503

30 CALIBER A-MAX
155 gr. A-MAX   178 gr. A-MAX
#30312   #30712
168 gr. A-MAX
#30502

50 CALIBER (.510)

**750 gr. A-MAX UHC   #5165
**Packaged 20 per box.

22 CALIBER (.224)
60 gr. HP
#2275

22 CALIBER (.227)
70 gr. SP w/c
#2280

6MM (.243)
70 gr. SP
#2410

70 gr. SPSX
#2415

75 gr. HP
#2420

6MM (.243)
80 gr. FMJ
#2430

80 gr. SP
Single Shot Pistol
#2435 InterLock

87 gr. SP
#2440

87 gr. BTHP
#2442

100 gr. SP
#2450
InterLock

100 gr. BTSP
#2453
InterLock

100 gr. RN
#2455
InterLock

25 CALIBER (.257)
60 gr. FP
#2510

75 gr. HP
#2520

87 gr. SP
#2530

100 gr. SP
#2540
InterLock

117 gr. RN
#2550
InterLock

117 gr. BTSP
#2552
InterLock

120 gr. HP
#2560
InterLock

6.5MM (.264)
100 gr. SP
#2610

129 gr. SP
#2620
InterLock

140 gr. SP
#2630
InterLock

160 gr. RN
#2640
InterLock

HORNADY RIFLE BULLETS

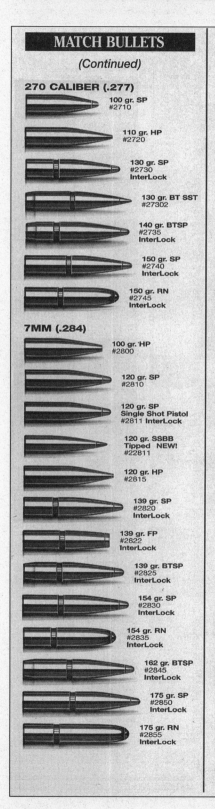

MATCH BULLETS
(Continued)

270 CALIBER (.277)

100 gr. SP
#2710

110 gr. HP
#2720

130 gr. SP
#2730
InterLock

130 gr. BT SST
#27302

140 gr. BTSP
#2735
InterLock

150 gr. SP
#2740
InterLock

150 gr. RN
#2745
InterLock

7MM (.284)

100 gr. HP
#2800

120 gr. SP
#2810

120 gr. SP
Single Shot Pistol
#2811 InterLock

120 gr. SSBB
Tipped NEW!
#22811

120 gr. HP
#2815

139 gr. SP
#2820
InterLock

139 gr. FP
#2822
InterLock

139 gr. BTSP
#2825
InterLock

154 gr. SP
#2830
InterLock

154 gr. RN
#2835
InterLock

162 gr. BTSP
#2845
InterLock

175 gr. SP
#2850
InterLock

175 gr. RN
#2855
InterLock

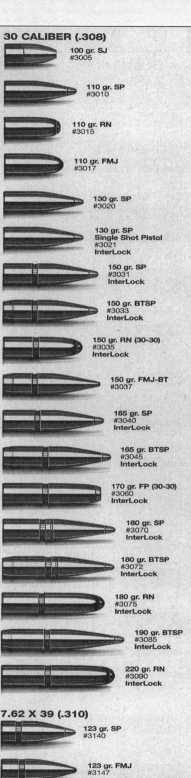

30 CALIBER (.308)

100 gr. SJ
#3005

110 gr. SP
#3010

110 gr. RN
#3015

110 gr. FMJ
#3017

130 gr. SP
#3020

130 gr. SP
Single Shot Pistol
#3021
InterLock

150 gr. SP
#3031
InterLock

150 gr. BTSP
#3033
InterLock

150 gr. RN (30-30)
#3035
InterLock

150 gr. FMJ-BT
#3037

165 gr. SP
#3040
InterLock

165 gr. BTSP
#3045
InterLock

170 gr. FP (30-30)
#3060
InterLock

180 gr. SP
#3070
InterLock

180 gr. BTSP
#3072
InterLock

180 gr. RN
#3075
InterLock

190 gr. BTSP
#3085
InterLock

220 gr. RN
#3090
InterLock

7.62 X 39 (.310)

123 gr. SP
#3140

123 gr. FMJ
#3147

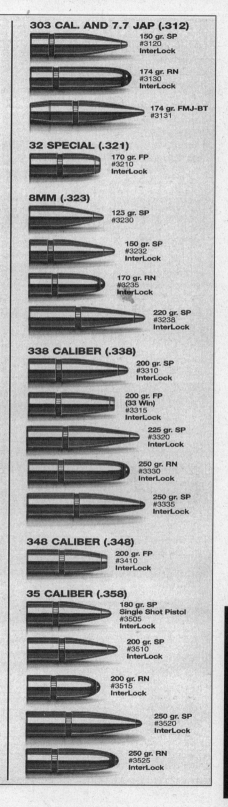

303 CAL. AND 7.7 JAP (.312)

150 gr. SP
#3120
InterLock

174 gr. RN
#3130
InterLock

174 gr. FMJ-BT
#3131

32 SPECIAL (.321)

170 gr. FP
#3210
InterLock

8MM (.323)

125 gr. SP
#3230

150 gr. SP
#3232
InterLock

170 gr. RN
#6235
InterLock

220 gr. SP
#3238
InterLock

338 CALIBER (.338)

200 gr. SP
#3310
InterLock

200 gr. FP
(33 Win)
#3315
InterLock

225 gr. SP
#3320
InterLock

250 gr. RN
#3330
InterLock

250 gr. SP
#3335
InterLock

348 CALIBER (.348)

200 gr. FP
#3410
InterLock

35 CALIBER (.358)

180 gr. SP
Single Shot Pistol
#3505
InterLock

200 gr. SP
#3510
InterLock

200 gr. RN
#3515
InterLock

250 gr. SP
#3520
InterLock

250 gr. RN
#3525
InterLock

RELOADING

HORNADY BULLETS

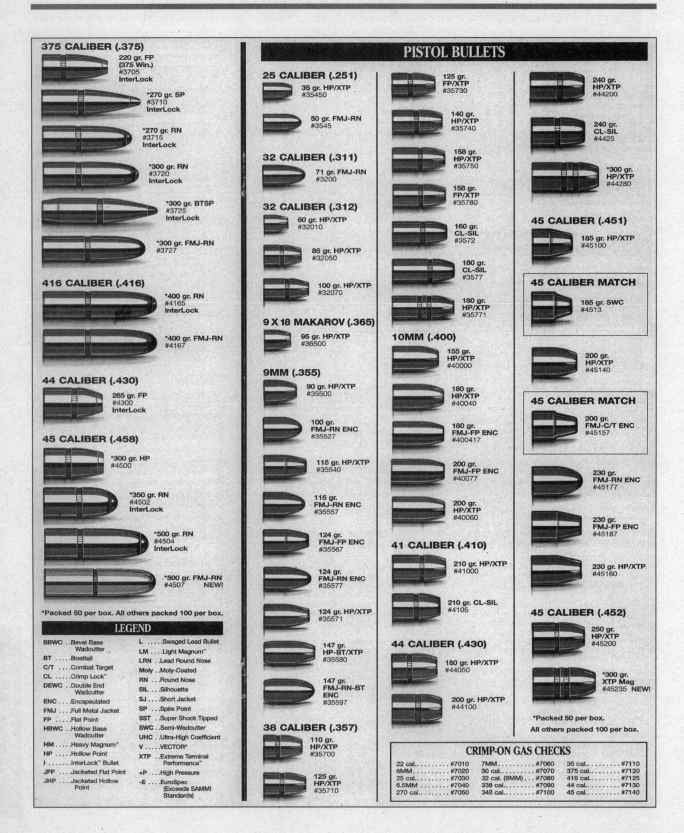

375 CALIBER (.375)

220 gr. FP (375 Win.) #3705 InterLock

*270 gr. SP #3710 InterLock

*270 gr. RN #3715 InterLock

*300 gr. RN #3720 InterLock

*300 gr. BTSP #3725 InterLock

*300 gr. FMJ-RN #3727

416 CALIBER (.416)

*400 gr. RN #4165 InterLock

*400 gr. FMJ-RN #4167

44 CALIBER (.430)

265 gr. FP #4300 InterLock

45 CALIBER (.458)

*300 gr. HP #4500

*350 gr. RN #4502 InterLock

*500 gr. RN #4504 InterLock

*500 gr. FMJ-RN #4507 NEW!

*Packed 50 per box. All others packed 100 per box.

LEGEND

BBWC ..Bevel Base Wadcutter	L .....Swaged Lead Bullet
BT .....Boattail	LM ....Light Magnum™
C/T ....Combat Target	LRN ...Lead Round Nose
CL .....Crimp Lock™	Moly ...Moly-Coated
DEWC ..Double End Wadcutter	RN ...Round Nose
ENC ....Encapsulated	SIL ...Silhouette
FMJ ....Full Metal Jacket	SJ ....Short Jacket
FP .....Flat Point	SP ....Spire Point
HBWC ..Hollow Base Wadcutter	SST ...Super Shock Tipped
HM ....Heavy Magnum™	SWC ...Semi-Wadcutter
HP .....Hollow Point	UHC ...Ultra-High Coefficient
I ....InterLock™ Bullet	V ......VECTOR®
JFP ....Jacketed Flat Point	XTP ...Extreme Terminal Performance™
JHP ....Jacketed Hollow Point	+P ....High Pressure
	-E ....EuroSpec (Exceeds SAMMI Standards)

PISTOL BULLETS

25 CALIBER (.251)

35 gr. HP/XTP #35450

50 gr. FMJ-RN #3545

32 CALIBER (.311)

71 gr. FMJ-RN #3200

32 CALIBER (.312)

60 gr. HP/XTP #32010

85 gr. HP/XTP #32050

100 gr. HP/XTP #32070

9 X 18 MAKAROV (.365)

95 gr. HP/XTP #36500

9MM (.355)

90 gr. HP/XTP #35500

100 gr. FMJ-RN ENC #35527

115 gr. HP/XTP #35540

115 gr. FMJ-RN ENC #35557

124 gr. FMJ-FP ENC #35567

124 gr. FMJ-RN ENC #35577

124 gr. HP/XTP #35571

147 gr. HP-BT/XTP #35580

147 gr. FMJ-RN-BT ENC #35597

38 CALIBER (.357)

110 gr. HP/XTP #35700

125 gr. HP/XTP #35710

125 gr. FP/XTP #35730

140 gr. HP/XTP #35740

158 gr. HP/XTP #35750

158 gr. FP/XTP #35780

160 gr. CL-SIL #3572

180 gr. CL-SIL #3577

180 gr. HP/XTP #35771

10MM (.400)

155 gr. HP/XTP #40000

180 gr. HP/XTP #40040

180 gr. FMJ-FP ENC #400417

200 gr. FMJ-FP ENC #40077

200 gr. HP/XTP #40060

41 CALIBER (.410)

210 gr. HP/XTP #41000

210 gr. CL-SIL #4105

44 CALIBER (.430)

180 gr. HP/XTP #44050

200 gr. HP/XTP #44100

240 gr. HP/XTP #44200

240 gr. CL-SIL #4425

*300 gr. HP/XTP #44280

45 CALIBER (.451)

185 gr. HP/XTP #45100

45 CALIBER MATCH

185 gr. SWC #4513

200 gr. HP/XTP #45140

45 CALIBER MATCH

200 gr. FMJ-C/T ENC #45157

230 gr. FMJ-RN ENC #45177

230 gr. FMJ-FP ENC #45187

230 gr. HP/XTP #45160

45 CALIBER (.452)

250 gr. HP/XTP #45200

*300 gr. XTP Mag #45235 NEW!

*Packed 50 per box.
All others packed 100 per box.

CRIMP-ON GAS CHECKS

22 cal..........#7010	7MM..........#7060	35 cal..........#7110
6MM..........#7020	30 cal..........#7070	375 cal..........#7120
25 cal..........#7030	32 cal. (8MM)...#7080	416 cal..........#7125
6.5MM ....#7040	338 cal..........#7090	44 cal..........#7130
270 cal........#7050	348 cal..........#7100	45 cal..........#7140

NOSLER BULLETS

Bullets for Autos

Cal. Dia.		BULLET WEIGHT AND STYLE	SECT. DENS.	BAL. COEF.	PART#
9mm .355"		90 GR. HOLLOW POINT	.102	.086	42050
		115 GR. FULL METAL JACKET	.130	.103	42059
		115 GR. HOLLOW POINT 250 QUANTITY BULK PACK	.130	.110	43009 44848
38 .357"		115 GR. HOLLOW POINT PRACTICAL PISTOL™ 250 QUANTITY BULK PACK	.129	.110	44835
		135 GR. PRACTICAL PISTOL™ 250 QUANTITY BULK PACK	.151	.149	44836
		150 GR. PRACTICAL PISTOL™ 250 QUANTITY BULK PACK	.168	.157	44839
10mm .400"		135 GR. HOLLOW POINT 250 QUANTITY BULK PACK	.121	.093	44838 44852
		150 GR. HOLLOW POINT	.134	.106	44849
		180 GR. HOLLOW POINT	.161	.147	44837
45 .451"		185 GR. HOLLOW POINT 250 QUANTITY BULK PACK	.130	.142	42062 44847
		230 GR. FULL METAL JACKET	.162	.183	42064

Bullets for Revolvers

		BULLET WEIGHT AND STYLE	SECT. DENS.	BAL. COEF.	PART#
38 .357"		125 GR. HOLLOW POINT 250 QUANTITY BULK PACK	.140	.143	42055 44840
		150 GR. SOFT POINT	.168	.153	42056
		158 GR. HOLLOW POINT 250 QUANTITY BULK PACK	.177	.182	42057 44841
		180 GR. SILHOUETTE 250 QUANTITY BULK PACK	.202	.210	44851
41 .410"		210 GR. HOLLOW POINT	.178	.170	43012
44 .429"		200 GR. HOLLOW POINT 250 QUANTITY BULK PACK	.155	.151	42060 44846
		240 GR. HOLLOW POINT 250 QUANTITY BULK PACK	.186	.173	42061 44842
		240 GR. SOFT POINT	.186	.177	42068
		300 GR. HOLLOW POINT	.233	.206	42069
45 Colt .451"		250 GR. HOLLOW POINT	.176	.177	43013

Partition-HG™

50 cal/250 GR. JHP	.429"	50429	
50 cal/260 GR. JHP	.451"	50260	
54 cal/260 GR. JHP	.451"	54260	
50 cal/300 GR. JPP	.451"	50280	*New*
54 cal/300 GR. JPP	.451"	54280	*New*

S.H.O.T.S.™

50 cal/250 grain JHP	.451"	50250	
50 cal/300 grain JHP	.429"	50300	
54 cal/250 grain JHP	.451"	54250	

High volume shooters can now get Nosler's specially designed plastic muzzleloading sabots in 50-count Bulk Packs:

50 cal. sabots for .429" bullets	50095	*New*
50 cal. sabots for .451" bullets	50096	*New*
54 cal. sabots for .451" bullets	50097	*New*

RELOADING

NOSLER BULLETS

NOSLER PARTITION® BULLETS

The Nosler Partition® bullet earned its reputation among professional guides and serious hunters for one reason: it doesn't fail. The patented Partition® design offers a dual core that is unequallled in mushrooming, weight retention and hydrostatic shock.

Cal. Dia.	BULLET WEIGHT AND STYLE	SECT. DENS.	BAL. COEF.	PART#
6mm .243"	85 GR. SPITZER	.206	.315	16314
	95 GR. SPITZER	.230	.365	16315
	100 GR. SPITZER	.242	.384	35642
25 .257"	100 GR. SPITZER	.216	.377	16317
	115 GR. SPITZER	.249	.389	16318
	120 GR. SPITZER	.260	.391	35643
6.5mm .264"	100 GR. SPITZER	.205	.326	16319
	125 GR. SPITZER	.256	.449	16320
	140 GR. SPITZER	.287	.490	16321
270 .277"	130 GR. SPITZER	.242	.416	16322
	150 GR. SPITZER	.279	.465	16323
	160 GR. SEMI SPITZER	.298	.434	16324
7mm .284"	140 GR. SPITZER	.248	.434	16325
	150 GR. SPITZER	.266	.456	16326
	160 GR. SPITZER	.283	.475	16327
	175 GR. SPITZER	.310	.519	35645
30 .308"	150 GR. SPITZER	.226	.387	16329
	165 GR. SPITZER	.248	.410	16330
	170 GR. ROUND NOSE	.256	.252	16333
	180 GR. PROTECTED POINT	.271	.361	25396

Cal. Dia.	BULLET WEIGHT AND STYLE	SECT. DENS.	BAL. COEF.	PART#
	180 GR. SPITZER	.271	.474	16331
	200 GR. SPITZER	.301	.481	35626
	220 GR. SEMI SPITZER	.331	.351	16332
8mm .323"	200 GR. SPITZER	.274	.426	35277
338 .338"	210 GR. SPITZER	.263	.400	16337
	225 GR. SPITZER	.281	.454	16336
	250 GR. SPITZER	.313	.473	35644
35 .358"	225 GR. SPITZER	.251	.430	44800
	250 GR. SPITZER	.279	.446	44801
9.3mm .366"	286 GR. SPITZER (18.5 GRAM)	.307	.482	44750
375 .375"	260 GR. SPITZER	.264	.314	44850
	300 GR. SPITZER	.305	.398	44845
416 .416"	400 GR. SPITZER	.330	.390	45200 New
45-70 .458"	300 GR. PROTECTED POINT	.204	.199	45325 New
PARTITION-HG™ 38 .357"	180 GR. HOLLOW POINT	.202	.201	35180
44 .429"	250 GR. HOLLOW POINT	.194	.200	44250
45 .451"	260 GR. HOLLOW POINT	.182	.174	45260
	300 GR. PROTECTED POINT	.211	.199	45350 New

NOSLER BULLETS

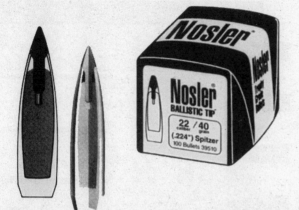

NOSLER BALLISTIC TIP® HUNTING BULLETS

Nosler has replaced the familiar lead point of the Spitzer with a tough polycarbonate tip. The purpose of this new Ballistic Tip® is to resist deforming in the magazine and feed ramp of many rifles. The Solid Base® design produces controlled expansion for excellent mushrooming and exceptional accuracy.

Varmint Bullets

Cal. Dia.	BULLET WEIGHT AND STYLE	SECT. DENS.	BAL. COEF.	PART#
22 .224"	40 GR. SPITZER (ORANGE TIP) 250 CT. VARMINT PAK™	.114	.221	39510 / 39555
	45 GR. HORNET (SOFT LEAD TIP)	.128	.144	35487
	50 GR. SPITZER (ORANGE TIP) New– 250 CT. VARMINT PAK™	.142	.238	39522 / 39557
	55 GR. SPITZER (ORANGE TIP) 250 CT. VARMINT PAK™	.157	.267	39526 / 39560
6mm .243"	55 GR. SPITZER (PURPLE TIP) New– 250 CT. VARMINT PAK™	.133	.276	24055 / 39565
	70 GR. SPITZER (PURPLE TIP) New– 250 CT. VARMINT PAK™	.169	.310	39532 / 39570
25 .257"	85 GR. SPITZER (BLUE TIP)	.183	.331	43004

Hunting Bullets

Cal. Dia.	BULLET WEIGHT AND STYLE	SECT. DENS.	BAL. COEF.	PART#
6mm .243"	95 GR. SPITZER (PURPLE TIP)	.230	.379	24095
25 .257"	100 GR. SPITZER (BLUE TIP)	.216	.393	25100
	115 GR. SPITZER (BLUE TIP)	.249	.453	25115
6.5mm .264"	100 GR. SPITZER (BROWN TIP)	.205	.350	26100
	120 GR. SPITZER (BROWN TIP)	.246	.458	26120

Cal. Dia.	BULLET WEIGHT AND STYLE	SECT. DENS.	BAL. COEF.	PART#
270 .277"	130 GR. SPITZER (YELLOW TIP)	.242	.433	27130
	140 GR. SPITZER (YELLOW TIP)	.261	.456	27140
	150 GR. SPITZER (YELLOW TIP)	.279	.496	27150
7mm .284"	120 GR. FLAT POINT (SOFT LEAD TIP)	.213	.195	28121
	120 GR. SPITZER (RED TIP)	.213	.417	28120
	140 GR. SPITZER (RED TIP)	.248	.485	28140
	150 GR. SPITZER (RED TIP)	.266	.493	28150
30 .308"	125 GR. SPITZER (GREEN TIP)	.188	.366	30125
	150 GR. SPITZER (GREEN TIP)	.226	.435	30150
	165 GR. SPITZER (GREEN TIP)	.248	.475	30165
	180 GR. SPITZER (GREEN TIP)	.271	.507	30180
338 .338"	180 GR. SPITZER (MAROON TIP)	.225	.372	33180
	200 GR. SPITZER (MAROON TIP)	.250	.414	33200
35 .358"	225 GR. WHELEN (BUCKSKIN TIP)	.251	.421	35225

NOSLER BULLETS

BALLISTIC SILVER TIP

CALIBER	DIAMETER	BULLET WEIGHT	SECT. DENS.	BAL. COEF.	PART #
22	.224"	40 grain	.114	.221	51005
22	.224"	50 grain	.142	.238	51010
6mm	.243"	55 grain	.133	.276	51030
6mm	.243"	95 grain	.230	.379	51040
25	.257"	85 grain	.183	.331	51045
25	.257"	115 grain	.249	.453	51050
270	.277"	130 grain	.242	.433	51075
7mm	.284"	140 grain	.248	.485	51105
7mm	.284"	150 grain	.266	.493	51110
30	.308"	150 grain	.226	.435	51150
30	.308"	168 grain	.253	.490	51160
30	.308"	180 grain	.271	.507	51170
338	.338"	200 grain	.250	.414	51200

Ballistic Silvertip, Fail Safe and Partition Gold bullets are made by Nosler for loading in Winchester ammunition in a project known as Combined Technology.

FAIL SAFE

CALIBER	DIAMETER	BULLET WEIGHT	SECT. DENS.	BAL. COEF.	PART #
270	.277"	150 grain	.279	.465	52100
7mm	.284"	160 grain	.283	.475	52150
30	.308"	150 grain	.226	.387	52200
30	.308"	180 grain	.271	.474	52230
338	.338"	250 grain	.313	.473	52280

PARTITION GOLD

CALIBER	DIAMETER	BULLET WEIGHT	SECT. DENS.	BAL. COEF.	PART #
270	.277"	140 grain	.261	.322	53140
7mm	.284"	140 grain	.248	.323	53150
7mm	.284"	160 grain	.283	.382	53160
30	.308"	150 grain	.226	.308	53170
30	.308"	165 grain	.248	.314	53175
30	.308"	180 grain	.271	.391	53180
338	.338"	230 grain	.288	.436	53230
375	.375"	270 grain	.274	.393	53350
375	.375"	300 grain	.305	.441	53360

SIERRA BULLETS

RIFLE BULLETS

.22 Caliber Hornet (.223/5.66MM Diameter)
40 gr. Hornet
Varminter #1100

45 gr. Hornet
Varminter #1110

.22 Caliber Hornet (.224/5.69MM Diameter)
40 gr. Hornet
Varminter #1200

45 gr. Hornet
Varminter #1210

.22 Caliber (.224/5.69MM Diameter)
40 gr. HP
Varminter #1385

40 gr.
BlitzKing #1440

45 gr. SMP
Varminter #1300

45 gr. SPT
Varminter #1310

50 gr. SMP
Varminter #1320

50 gr. SPT
Varminter #1330

50 gr. Blitz
Varminter #1340

50 gr.
BlitzKing #1450

52 gr. HPBT
MatchKing #1410

53 gr. HP
MatchKing #1400

55 gr. Blitz
Varminter #1345

55 gr. SMP
Varminter #1350

55 gr. FMJBT
GameKing #1355

55 gr. SPT
Varminter #1360

55 gr. SBT
GameKing #1365

55 gr. HPBT
GameKing #1390

55 gr.
BlitzKing #1455

60 gr. HP
Varminter #1375

63 gr. SMP
Varminter #1370

69 gr. HPBT
MatchKing #1380
7"-10" TWST BBLS

6MM .243 Caliber (.243/6.17MM Diameter)
55 gr.
BlitzKing #1502

60 gr. HP
Varminter #1500

70 gr. HPBT
MatchKing #1505

70 gr.
BlitzKing #1507

75 gr. HP
Varminter #1510

80 gr. Blitz
Varminter #1515

85 gr. SPT
Varminter #1520

85 gr. HPBT
GameKing #1530

90 gr. FMJBT
GameKing #1535

100 gr. SPT
Pro-Hunter #1540

100 gr. SMP
Pro-Hunter #1550

100 gr. SBT
GameKing #1560

107 gr. HPBT
MatchKing #1570
7"-8" TWST BBLS

.25 Caliber (.257/6.53MM Diameter)
75 gr. HP
Varminter #1600

87 gr. SPT
Varminter #1610

90 gr. HPBT
GameKing #1615

100 gr. SPT
Pro-Hunter #1620

100 gr. SBT
GameKing #1625

100 gr. HPBT
MatchKing #1628

117 gr. SBT
GameKing #1630

117 gr. SPT
Pro-Hunter #1640

120 gr. HPBT
GameKing #1650

6.5MM .264 Caliber (.264/6.71MM Diameter)
85 gr. HP
Varminter #1700

100 gr. HP
Varminter #1710

107 gr. HPBT
MatchKing #1715

6.5MM .264 Caliber (cont.)
(.264/6.71MM Diameter)
120 gr. SPT
Pro-Hunter #1720

120 gr. HPBT
MatchKing #1725

140 gr. SBT
GameKing #1730

140 gr. HPBT
MatchKing #1740

142 gr. HPBT
MatchKing #1742

160 gr. SMP
Pro-Hunter #1750

.270 Caliber (.277/7.04MM Diameter)
90 gr. HP
Varminter #1800

110 gr. SPT
Pro-Hunter #1810

130 gr. SBT
GameKing #1820

130 gr. SPT
Pro-Hunter #1830

135 gr. HPBT
MatchKing #1833

140 gr. HPBT
GameKing #1835

140 gr. SBT
GameKing #1845

150 gr. SBT
GameKing #1840

150 gr. RN
Pro-Hunter #1850

7MM .284 Caliber (.284/7.21MM Diameter)
100 gr. HP
Varminter #1895

120 gr. SPT
Pro-Hunter #1900

130 gr. HPBT
MatchKing #1903

140 gr. SBT
GameKing #1905

140 gr. SPT
Pro-Hunter #1910

150 gr. SBT
GameKing #1913

150 gr. HPBT
MatchKing #1915

160 gr. SBT
GameKing #1920

160 gr. HPBT
GameKing #1925

168 gr. HPBT
MatchKing #1930

SIERRA BULLETS

RIFLE BULLETS

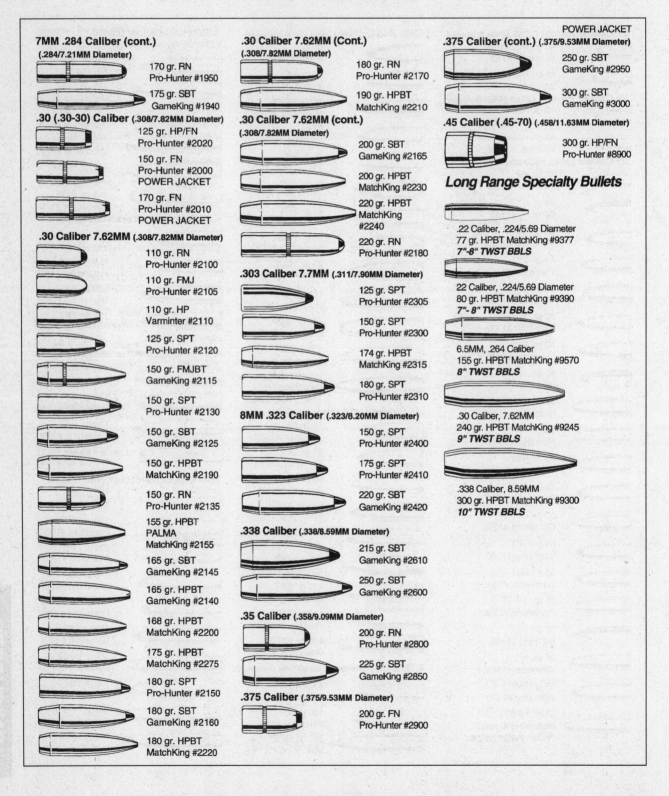

7MM .284 Caliber (cont.)
(.284/7.21MM Diameter)

170 gr. RN
Pro-Hunter #1950

175 gr. SBT
GameKing #1940

.30 (.30-30) Caliber (.308/7.82MM Diameter)

125 gr. HP/FN
Pro-Hunter #2020

150 gr. FN
Pro-Hunter #2000
POWER JACKET

170 gr. FN
Pro-Hunter #2010
POWER JACKET

.30 Caliber 7.62MM (.308/7.82MM Diameter)

110 gr. RN
Pro-Hunter #2100

110 gr. FMJ
Pro-Hunter #2105

110 gr. HP
Varminter #2110

125 gr. SPT
Pro-Hunter #2120

150 gr. FMJBT
GameKing #2115

150 gr. SPT
Pro-Hunter #2130

150 gr. SBT
GameKing #2125

150 gr. HPBT
MatchKing #2190

150 gr. RN
Pro-Hunter #2135

155 gr. HPBT
PALMA
MatchKing #2155

165 gr. SBT
GameKing #2145

165 gr. HPBT
GameKing #2140

168 gr. HPBT
MatchKing #2200

175 gr. HPBT
MatchKing #2275

180 gr. SPT
Pro-Hunter #2150

180 gr. SBT
GameKing #2160

180 gr. HPBT
MatchKing #2220

.30 Caliber 7.62MM (Cont.)
(.308/7.82MM Diameter)

180 gr. RN
Pro-Hunter #2170

190 gr. HPBT
MatchKing #2210

.30 Caliber 7.62MM (cont.)
(.308/7.82MM Diameter)

200 gr. SBT
GameKing #2165

200 gr. HPBT
MatchKing #2230

220 gr. HPBT
MatchKing #2240

220 gr. RN
Pro-Hunter #2180

.303 Caliber 7.7MM (.311/7.90MM Diameter)

125 gr. SPT
Pro-Hunter #2305

150 gr. SPT
Pro-Hunter #2300

174 gr. HPBT
MatchKing #2315

180 gr. SPT
Pro-Hunter #2310

8MM .323 Caliber (.323/8.20MM Diameter)

150 gr. SPT
Pro-Hunter #2400

175 gr. SPT
Pro-Hunter #2410

220 gr. SBT
GameKing #2420

.338 Caliber (.338/8.59MM Diameter)

215 gr. SBT
GameKing #2610

250 gr. SBT
GameKing #2600

.35 Caliber (.358/9.09MM Diameter)

200 gr. RN
Pro-Hunter #2800

225 gr. SBT
GameKing #2850

.375 Caliber (.375/9.53MM Diameter)

200 gr. FN
Pro-Hunter #2900

POWER JACKET

.375 Caliber (cont.) (.375/9.53MM Diameter)

250 gr. SBT
GameKing #2950

300 gr. SBT
GameKing #3000

.45 Caliber (.45-70) (.458/11.63MM Diameter)

300 gr. HP/FN
Pro-Hunter #8900

Long Range Specialty Bullets

.22 Caliber, .224/5.69 Diameter
77 gr. HPBT MatchKing #9377
7"-8" TWST BBLS

22 Caliber, .224/5.69 Diameter
80 gr. HPBT MatchKing #9390
7"- 8" TWST BBLS

6.5MM, .264 Caliber
155 gr. HPBT MatchKing #9570
8" TWST BBLS

.30 Caliber, 7.62MM
240 gr. HPBT MatchKing #9245
9" TWST BBLS

.338 Caliber, 8.59MM
300 gr. HPBT MatchKing #9300
10" TWST BBLS

SIERRA BULLETS

HANDGUN

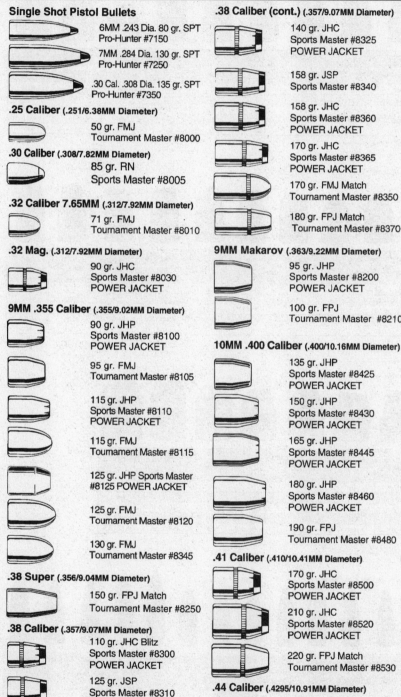

Single Shot Pistol Bullets

6MM .243 Dia. 80 gr. SPT
Pro-Hunter #7150

7MM .284 Dia. 130 gr. SPT
Pro-Hunter #7250

.30 Cal. .308 Dia. 135 gr. SPT
Pro-Hunter #7350

.25 Caliber (.251/6.38MM Diameter)

50 gr. FMJ
Tournament Master #8000

.30 Caliber (.308/7.82MM Diameter)

85 gr. RN
Sports Master #8005

.32 Caliber 7.65MM (.312/7.92MM Diameter)

71 gr. FMJ
Tournament Master #8010

.32 Mag. (.312/7.92MM Diameter)

90 gr. JHC
Sports Master #8030
POWER JACKET

9MM .355 Caliber (.355/9.02MM Diameter)

90 gr. JHP
Sports Master #8100
POWER JACKET

95 gr. FMJ
Tournament Master #8105

115 gr. JHP
Sports Master #8110
POWER JACKET

115 gr. FMJ
Tournament Master #8115

125 gr. JHP Sports Master
#8125 POWER JACKET

125 gr. FMJ
Tournament Master #8120

130 gr. FMJ
Tournament Master #8345

.38 Super (.356/9.04MM Diameter)

150 gr. FPJ Match
Tournament Master #8250

.38 Caliber (.357/9.07MM Diameter)

110 gr. JHC Blitz
Sports Master #8300
POWER JACKET

125 gr. JSP
Sports Master #8310

125 gr. JHC
Sports Master #8320
POWER JACKET

.38 Caliber (cont.) (.357/9.07MM Diameter)

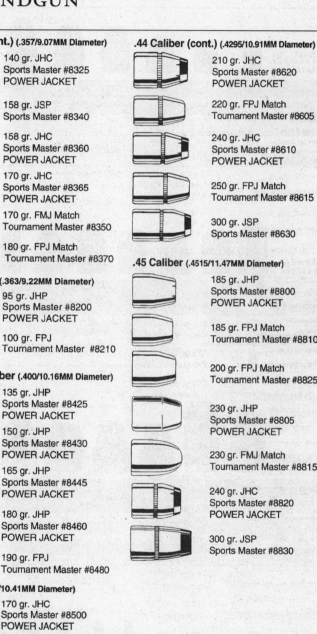

140 gr. JHC
Sports Master #8325
POWER JACKET

158 gr. JSP
Sports Master #8340

158 gr. JHC
Sports Master #8360
POWER JACKET

170 gr. JHC
Sports Master #8365
POWER JACKET

170 gr. FMJ Match
Tournament Master #8350

180 gr. FPJ Match
Tournament Master #8370

9MM Makarov (.363/9.22MM Diameter)

95 gr. JHP
Sports Master #8200
POWER JACKET

100 gr. FPJ
Tournament Master #8210

10MM .400 Caliber (.400/10.16MM Diameter)

135 gr. JHP
Sports Master #8425
POWER JACKET

150 gr. JHP
Sports Master #8430
POWER JACKET

165 gr. JHP
Sports Master #8445
POWER JACKET

180 gr. JHP
Sports Master #8460
POWER JACKET

190 gr. FPJ
Tournament Master #8480

.41 Caliber (.410/10.41MM Diameter)

170 gr. JHC
Sports Master #8500
POWER JACKET

210 gr. JHC
Sports Master #8520
POWER JACKET

220 gr. FPJ Match
Tournament Master #8530

.44 Caliber (.4295/10.91MM Diameter)

180 gr. JHC
Sports Master #8600
POWER JACKET

.44 Caliber (cont.) (.4295/10.91MM Diameter)

210 gr. JHC
Sports Master #8620
POWER JACKET

220 gr. FPJ Match
Tournament Master #8605

240 gr. JHC
Sports Master #8610
POWER JACKET

250 gr. FPJ Match
Tournament Master #8615

300 gr. JSP
Sports Master #8630

.45 Caliber (.4515/11.47MM Diameter)

185 gr. JHP
Sports Master #8800
POWER JACKET

185 gr. FPJ Match
Tournament Master #8810

200 gr. FPJ Match
Tournament Master #8825

230 gr. JHP
Sports Master #8805
POWER JACKET

230 gr. FMJ Match
Tournament Master #8815

240 gr. JHC
Sports Master #8820
POWER JACKET

300 gr. JSP
Sports Master #8830

RELOADING

SPEER HANDGUN/RIFLE BULLETS

Handgun Bullets

Caliber & Type	25 Gold Dot Hollow Pt.	32 Gold Dot Hollow Pt.	9mm Gold Dot Hollow Pt.	9mm Gold Dot Hollow Pt.	9mm Gold Dot Hollow Pt.	9mm Gold Dot Hollow Pt.	357 Sig Gold Dot Hollow Pt.	38 Gold Dot Hollow Pt.	38 Gold Dot Hollow Pt.	9mm Makarov Gold Dot Hollow Pt.	40/10mm Gold Dot Hollow Pt.	40/10mm Gold Dot Hollow Pt.
Diameter	.251"	.311"	.355"	.355"	.355"	.355"	.355"	.357"	.357"	.364"	.400"	.400"
Weight (grs.)	35	60	90	115	124	147	125	125	158	90	155	165
Ballist. Coef.	0.091	0.118	0.101	0.125	0.134	0.164	0.141	0.140	0.168	0.107	0.123	0.138
Part Number	3985	3986	3992	3994	3998	4002	4360	4012	4215	3999	4400	4397
Box Count	100	100	100	100	100	100	100	100	100	100	100	100

Handgun Bullets

Caliber & Type	9mm TMJ	357 Sig TMJ	38 JHP	38 JSP	38 JHP	38 TMJ	38 JHP	38 JHP-SWC	38 TMJ	38 JHP	38 JSP	38 JSP-SWC	38 TMJ-Sil.
Diameter	.355"	.355"	.357"	.357"	.357"	.357"	.357"	.357"	.357"	.357"	.357"	.357"	.357"
Weight	147	125	110	125	125	125	140	146	158	158	158	160	180
Ballist. Coef.	0.208	0.147	0.122	0.140	0.135	0.146	0.152	0.159	0.173	0.158	0.158	0.170	0.230
Part Number	4006	4362	4007	4011	4013	4015	4203	4205	4207	4211	4217	4223	4229
Box Count	100	100	100	100	100	100	100	100	100	100	100	100	100

Handgun Bullets

Caliber & Type	44 TMJ-Sil.	44 Mag. SP	45 TMJ-Match	45 TMJ-Match	45 JHP	45 Mag. JHP	45 TMJ	45 Mag. JHP	45 SP	50 AE HP
Diameter	.429"	.429"	.451"	.451"	.451"	.451"	.451"	.451"	.451"	.500"
Weight (grs.)	240	300	185	200	200	225	230	260	300	325
Ballist. Coef.	0.206	0.213	0.090	0.129	0.138	0.169	0.153	0.183	0.199	0.149
Part Number	4459	4463	4473	4475	4477	4479	4480	4481	4485	4495
Box Count	100	50	100	100	100	100	100	100	50	50

Rifle Bullets

Bullet Caliber & Type	22 Spitzer Soft Point	22 Spire Soft Point	22 Spitzer Soft Point	22 218 Bee Flat Soft Point w/Cann.	22 Spitzer Soft Point	22 "TNT" Hollow Point	22 MHP Hollow Point	22 Hollow Point	22 Hollow Point B.T. Match	22 FMJ B.T. w/Cann.	22 Spitzer Soft Point	22 Spitzer S.P. w/Cann.	22 FMJ B.T. w/Cann.	22 Semi-Spitzer Soft Point	6mm "TNT" Hollow Point	6mm MHP Hollow Point	6mm Hollow Point
Diameter	.223"	.224"	.224"	.224"	.224"	.224"	.224"	.224"	.224"	.224"	.224"	.224"	.224"	.224"	.243"	.243"	.243"
Weight (grs.)	45	40	45	46	50	50	50	52	52	55	55	55	62	70	70	70	75
Ballist. Coef.	0.166	0.144	0.167	0.094	0.231	0.223	0.234	0.225	0.253	0.269	0.255	0.241	0.307	0.214	0.282	0.296	0.234
Part Number	1011	1017	1023	1024	1029	1030	1031	1035	1036	1044	1047	1049	1050	1053	1206	1207	1205
Box Count	100	100	100	100	100	100	100	100	100	100	100	100	100	100	100	100	100

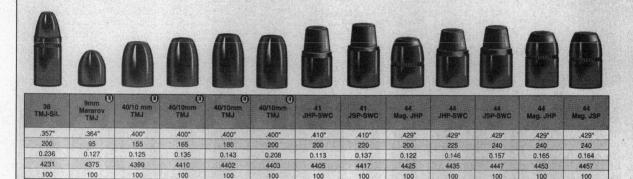

	40/10mm Gold Dot Hollow Pt.	44 Special Gold Dot Hollow Pt.	44 Gold Dot Hollow Pt.	44 Gold Dot Soft Pt.	44 Gold Dot Soft Pt.	45 Gold Dot Hollow Pt.	45 Gold Dot Hollow Pt.	45 Gold Dot Hollow Pt.	25 TMJ	32 JHP	9mm TMJ	9mm TMJ	9mm JHP	9mm Soft Pt.
	.400"	.429"	.429"	.429"	.429"	.451"	.451"	.451"	.251"	.312"	.355"	.355"	.355"	.355"
	180	200	240	240	270	185	200	230	50	100	95	115	115	124
	0.143	0.145	0.175	0.175	0.193	0.109	0.138	0.143	0.110	0.167	0.131	0.177	0.118	0.115
	4406	4427	4455	4456	4461	4470	4478	4483	3982	3981	4001	3995	3996	3997
	100	100	100	100	50	100	100	100	100	100	100	100	100	100

	38 TMJ-Sil.	9mm Mararov TMJ	40/10 mm TMJ	40/10mm TMJ	40/10mm TMJ	40/10mm TMJ	41 JHP-SWC	41 JSP-SWC	44 Mag. JHP	44 JHP-SWC	44 JSP-SWC	44 Mag. JHP	44 Mag. JSP
	.357"	.364"	.400"	.400"	.400"	.400"	.410"	.410"	.429"	.429"	.429"	.429"	.429"
	200	95	155	165	180	200	200	220	200	225	240	240	240
	0.236	0.127	0.125	0.135	0.143	0.208	0.113	0.137	0.122	0.146	0.157	0.165	0.164
	4231	4375	4399	4410	4402	4403	4405	4417	4425	4435	4447	4453	4457
	100	100	100	100	100	100	100	100	100	100	100	100	100

Handgun Bullets-Lead

Caliber & Type	32 HB-WC	9mm RN	38 BB-WC	38 DE-WC	38 HB-WC	38 SWC	38 HP-SWC	38 RN	44 SWC	45 SWC	45 RN	45 SWC
Diameter	.314"	.356"	.358"	.358"	.358"	.358"	.358"	.358"	.430"	.452"	.452"	.452"
Weight (grs.)	98	125	148	148	148	158	158	158	240	200	230	250
Part Number	--	4601	4605	--	4617	4623	4627	4647	4660	4677	4690	4683
Bulk Part No.	4600	4602	4606	4611	4618	4624	4628	4648	4661	4678	4691	4684

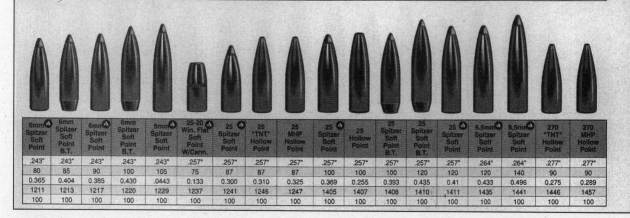

	6mm Spitzer Soft Point	6mm Spitzer Soft Point B.T.	6mm Spitzer Soft Point	6mm Spitzer Soft Point B.T.	6mm Spitzer Soft Point	25-20 Win. Flat Soft Point W/Cann.	25 Spitzer Soft Point	25 "TNT" Hollow Point	25 MHP Hollow Point	25 Spitzer Soft Point	25 Hollow Point	25 Spitzer Soft Point B.T.	25 Spitzer Soft Point B.T.	25 Spitzer Soft Point	6.5mm Spitzer Soft Point	6.5mm Spitzer Soft Point	270 "TNT" Hollow Point	270 MHP Hollow Point
	.243"	.243"	.243"	.243"	.243"	.257"	.257"	.257"	.257"	.257"	.257"	.257"	.257"	.257"	.264"	.264"	.277"	.277"
	80	85	90	100	105	75	87	87	87	100	100	100	120	120	120	140	90	90
	0.365	0.404	0.385	0.430	.0443	0.133	0.300	0.310	0.325	0.369	0.255	0.393	0.435	0.41	0.433	0.496	0.275	0.289
	1211	1213	1217	1220	1229	1237	1241	1246	1247	1405	1407	1408	1410	1411	1435	1441	1446	1457
	100	100	100	100	100	100	100	100	100	100	100	100	100	100	100	100	100	100

RELOADING

SPEER RIFLE BULLETS

Rifle Bullets

Bullet Caliber & Type	270 Hollow Point	270 Spitzer Soft Point B.T.	270 Spitzer Soft Point	270 Spitzer Soft Point B.T.	270 Spitzer Soft Point	7mm MHP Hollow Point	7mm "TNT" Hollow Point	7mm Hollow Point	7mm Spitzer Soft Point	7mm Spitzer Soft Point	7mm Spitzer Soft Point B.T.	7mm Spitzer Soft Point B.T.	7mm Spitzer Soft Point	7mm Match Hollow Point B.T.	7mm Spitzer Soft Point B.T.	7mm Spitzer Soft Point
Diameter	.277"	.277"	.277"	.277"	.277"	.284"	.284"	.284"	.284"	.284"	.284"	.284"	.284"	.284"	.284"	.284"
Weight (grs.)	100	130	130	150	150	110	110	115	120	130	130	145	145	145	160	160
Ballist. Coef.	0.225	0.449	0.408	0.496	0.481	0.355	0.338	0.257	0.386	0.394	0.411	0.502	0.457	0.465	0.556	0.502
Part Number	1447	1458	1459	1604	1605	1615	1616	1617	1620	1623	1624	1628	1629	1631	1634	1635
Box Count	100	100	100	100	100	100	100	100	100	100	100	100	100	100	100	100

Rifle Bullets

Bullet Caliber & Type	30 Spitzer Soft Point B.T.	30 Spitzer Soft Point	30 MHP Hollow Point B.T.	30 Match Hollow Point B.T.	30 Flat Soft Point	30 Round Soft Point	30 Spitzer Soft Point B.T.	30 Spitzer Soft Point	30 Mag-Tip" Soft Point	30 Spitzer Soft Point	303 Spitzer Soft Point w/Cann.	303 Spitzer Soft Point	303 Round Soft Point	32 Flat Soft Point	8mm Spitzer Soft Point
Diameter	.308"	.308"	.308"	.308"	.308"	.308"	.308"	.308"	.308"	.308"	.311"	.311"	.311"	.321"	.323"
Weight (grs.)	165	165	168	168	170	180	180	180	180	200	125	150	180	170	150
Ballist. Coef.	0.477	0.433	0.504	0.480	0.304	0.304	0.540	0.483	0.352	0.556	0.292	0.411	0.328	0.297	0.369
Part Number	2034	2035	2039	2040	2041	2047	2052	2053	2059	2211	2213	2217	2223	2259	2277
Box Count	100	100	100	100	100	100	100	100	100	50	100	100	100	100	100

Grand Slam

Bullet Caliber & Type	6mm GS Soft Point	25 GS Soft Point	6.5mm GS Soft Point	270 GS Soft Point	270 GS Soft Point	7mm GS Soft Point	7mm GS Soft Point	7mm GS Soft Point	30 GS Soft Point	30 GS Soft Point	30 GS Soft Point	30 GS Soft Point	338 GS Soft Point	35 GS Soft Point	375 GS Soft Point
Diameter	.243"	.257"	.264"	.277"	.277"	.284"	.284"	.284"	.308"	.308"	.308"	.308"	.338"	.358"	.375"
Weight (grs.)	100	120	140	130	150	145	160	175	150	165	180	200	250	250	285
Ballist. Coef.	0.351	0.328	0.385	0.345	0.385	0.327	0.387	0.465	0.305	0.393	0.416	0.448	0.431	0.335	0.354
Part Number	1222	1415	1444	1465	1608	1632	1638	1643	2026	2038	2063	2212	2408	2455	2473
Box Count	50	50	50	50	50	50	50	50	50	50	50	50	50	50	50

SPEER RIFLE BULLETS

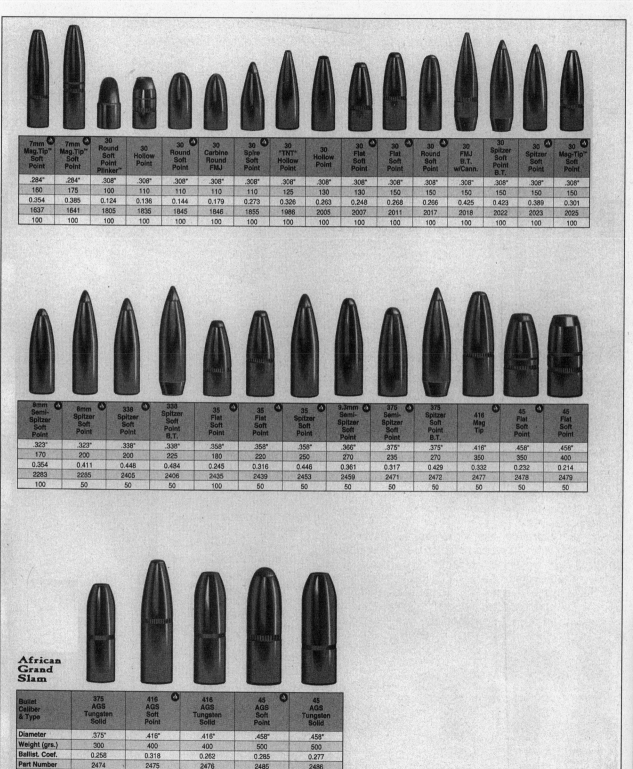

	7mm Mag.Tip™ Soft Point	7mm Mag.Tip™ Soft Point	30 Round Soft Point Plinker™	30 Hollow Point	30 Round Soft Point	30 Carbine Round FMJ	30 Spire Soft Point	30 "TNT" Hollow Point	30 Hollow Point	30 Flat Soft Point	30 Flat Soft Point	30 Round Soft Point	30 FMJ B.T. w/Cann.	30 Spitzer Soft Point B.T.	30 Spitzer Soft Point	30 Mag-Tip™ Soft Point
	.284"	.284"	.308"	.308"	.308"	.308"	.308"	.308"	.308"	.308"	.308"	.308"	.308"	.308"	.308"	.308"
	160	175	100	110	110	110	110	125	130	130	150	150	150	150	150	150
	0.354	0.385	0.124	0.136	0.144	0.179	0.273	0.326	0.263	0.248	0.268	0.266	0.425	0.423	0.389	0.301
	1637	1641	1805	1835	1845	1846	1855	1986	2005	2007	2011	2017	2018	2022	2023	2025
	100	100	100	100	100	100	100	100	100	100	100	100	100	100	100	100

	8mm Semi-Spitzer Soft Point	8mm Spitzer Soft Point	338 Spitzer Soft Point	338 Spitzer Soft Point B.T.	35 Flat Soft Point	35 Flat Soft Point	35 Spitzer Soft Point	9.3mm Semi-Spitzer Soft Point	375 Semi-Spitzer Soft Point	375 Spitzer Soft Point B.T.	416 Mag Tip	45 Flat Soft Point	45 Flat Soft Point
	.323"	.323"	.338"	.338"	.358"	.358"	.358"	.366"	.375"	.375"	.416"	.458"	.458"
	170	200	200	225	180	220	250	270	235	270	350	350	400
	0.354	0.411	0.448	0.484	0.245	0.316	0.446	0.361	0.317	0.429	0.332	0.232	0.214
	2283	2285	2405	2406	2435	2439	2453	2459	2471	2472	2477	2478	2479
	100	50	50	50	100	50	50	50	50	50	50	50	50

African Grand Slam

Bullet Caliber & Type	375 AGS Tungsten Solid	416 AGS Soft Point	416 AGS Tungsten Solid	45 AGS Soft Point	45 AGS Tungsten Solid
Diameter	.375"	.416"	.416"	.458"	.458"
Weight (grs.)	300	400	400	500	500
Ballist. Coef.	0.258	0.318	0.262	0.285	0.277
Part Number	2474	2475	2476	2485	2486
Box Count	25	25	25	25	25

RELOADING

SWIFT

New Swift Scirocco® Polymer-Tipped Bullet Combines Accuracy, Reliable Expansion and Integrity On Virtually All Game At All Velocities

**SWIFT
SCIROCCO™ BONDED**
*30 cal. (.308") 180-gr.
Polymer Tip/Boat Tail Spitzer*

Tapered jacket and proprietary bonding process produce controlled mushrooming with high weight retention. Ideally suited to fast, flat-shooting calibers.

The Swift Bullet Company has designed what it believes is the most versatile and broadly effective hunting bullet ever developed - one that combines the best of all desirable performance features in a single bullet.

The **Scirocco** design starts with its tough, pointed, polymer tip that reduces frontal air resistance, prevents tip deformation, and blends symmetrically into the curved radius of its secant ogive noise section. A moderate 15-degree boat tail base was carefully calculated to reduce drag and enhance seating, while retaining an effective, cross-sectional gas-pressure platform. And the thick base prevents bullet deformation even in high velocity, magnum calibers. The sleekly aerodynamic **Scirocco** shape creates two other significant advantages. One is an extremely high ballistic coefficient of well over 500, depending on caliber. The other, derived from the secant ogive nose, is a comparatively long bearing surface for a sharply pointed bullet, a feature that improves rotational stability.

Inside, the **Scirocco** has a non-frame, bonded-core construction with a pure lead core encased in a tapered, progressively thickening jacket of pure copper. Pure copper was selected because it is more malleable and less brittle than less expensive gilding metal. Both jacket and core are bonded together by Swift's proprietary bonding process so that the bullet expands

**SWIFT
SCIROCCO™ BONDED**
*30 cal. (.308") 180-gr.
Polymer Tip/Boat Tail Spitzer*

without break-up as if the two parts were the same metal. Considerable experimentation and testing was devoted to both the taper and ultimate thickness of the jacket, to create an optimum balance of expansion and weight retention over a wide range of velocities.

In tests, the new bullet mushroomed effectively at velocities as low as 1440 fps, yet stayed together at velocities in excess of 3,000 fps, with over 70 percent weight retention.

Initially, the **Scirocco** is being produced in a 30-caliber 180-grain offering. These bullets are available for order now. Future plans include selection of Swift Scirocco bullets in calibers ranging from .224" to .338" by the end of this year. In conjunction with Swift's highly-regarded A-Frame bullets, the **Scirocco** now gives Swift a complete bullet line for all types of big game hunting.

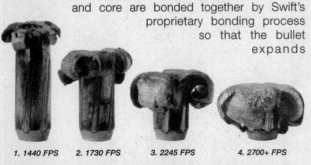

1. 1440 FPS   2. 1730 FPS   3. 2245 FPS   4. 2700+ FPS

Swift Scirocco™ Expands dependably over a wide range of velocities, and maintains high jacket/core integrity.

The SWIFT A-FRAME, noted for deep penetration in tough game, is loaded in Remington Premier ammunition.

WOODLEIGH PREMIUM BULLETS

Calibre Diameter	Bullet	Type	Wt. Gr.	SD	BC	Cat. No.
9.3mm .366"		SN	250	.267	.296	47A
		SN	286	.305	.331	47
		FMJ	286	.305	.324	48
360 No.2 .366"		SN	320	.341	.378	49
		FMJ	320	.341	.362	50
358 Cal. .358"		SN	225	.250	.277	51
		FMJ	225	.250	.298	52
		SN	250	.285	.365	53
		SN	310	.346	.400	54
		FMJ	310	.346	378	55
338 Mag .338"		PP	225	.281	.425	56A
		SN	250	.313	.332	56
		PP	250	.313	.470	56B
		FMJ	250	.313	.326	57
		SN	300	.375	.416	58
		FMJ	300	.375	.398	59
333 Jeffery .333"		SN	250	.322	.400	60
		SN	300	.386	.428	61
		FMJ	300	.386	.419	62
318 Westley Richards .330"		SN	250	.328	.420	63
		FMJ	250	.328	.364	64
8mm .323"		SN	196	.268	.370	64B
		SN	220	.302	.363	64C
		SN	250	.343	.389	64D
303 British .312		SN	215	.316	.359	68
308 Cal. .308"		PP	165	.250	.320	65A
		PP	180	.273	.376	65B
		RN	220	.331	.367	65C
		FMJ	220	.331	.359	65

Calibre Diameter	Bullet	Type	Wt. Gr.	SD	BC	Cat. No.
425 Westley Richards .435"		SN	410	.310	.344	31
		FMJ	410	.310	.336	32
404 Jeffery .423"		SN	400	.319	.354	33
		FMJ	400	.319	.358	34
		SN	350	.279	.357	35
10.75 x68mm .423"		SN	347	.277	.355	36
		FMJ	347	.277	.307	36A
416 Rigby .416"		SN	410	.338	.375	37
		FMJ	410	.338	.341	38
		PP	340	.281	.425	39
450/ 400 Nitro .411" or .408"		SN	400	.338	.384	40
		FMJ	400	.338	.433	41
405 Win .411"		SN	300	.254	.194	71
375 Mag. .375"		PP	235	.239	.331	42A
		RN	270	.275	.305	42
		SP	270	.275	.380	43
		PP	270	.275	.352	43A
		RN	300	.305	.340	44
		SP	300	.305	.425	45
		PP	300	.305	.420	45A
		FMJ	300	.305	.307	46

Woodleigh Premium Bullets

WELDCORE SOFT NOSE

Woodleigh Weldcore Soft Nose bullets are made from 90/100 guilding metal (90% copper: 10% zinc) 1.6 mm thick. All jackets are made by deep drawing through several processes and are specially profiled internally for optimum jacket wall taper. This gives them the feature of reliable controlled expansion. Maximum retained weight is obtained by fusing the pure lead to the guilding metal jacket, hence the name "Weldcore." This minimizes fragmentation of the nose section as it mushrooms.

FULL METAL JACKET

When hunting dangerous game Full Metal Jackets are preferable for maximum penetration. Made from Premium Grade K32, guilding metal clad steel 2mm thick.

The heavy jackets are made by deep drawing, through several processes, producing a jacket which is heavy at the nose section for extra impact resistance. The jacket then tapers towards the base to assist rifling engraving as the bullet enters the bore.

Calibre Diameter	Bullet	Type	Wt. Gr.	SD	BC	Cat. No.
475 No.2 .483"		SN	480	.294	.334	15
		FMJ	480	.294	.326	16
475 Nitro .476"		SN	480	.227	.307	69
		FMJ	480	.227	.257	70
476 Westley Richards .476"		SN	520	.328	.420	18
		FMJ	520	.328	.455	19
470 Nitro .474"		SN	500	.318	.411	20
		FMJ	500	.318	.410	21
465 Nitro .468"		SN	480	.318	.410	22
		FMJ	480	.318	.407	23
450 Nitro .458"		SN	480	.327	.419	24
		FMJ	480	.327	.410	25
458 Mag. .458"		SN	500	.341	.430	26
		SN	550	.375	.480	27
		FMJ	500	.341	.405	28
		FMJ	550	.375	.426	29
		PP	400	.272	.420	30
		RN	350	.238	.305	30A
11.2x72 Schuler .440"		SN	401	.296	.411	67

Calibre Diameter	Bullet	Type	Wt. Gr.	SD	BC	Cat. No.
700 Nitro .700"		SN	1000	.292	.340	A
		FMJ	1000	.292	.340	B
600 Nitro .620"		SN	900	.334	.371	1
		FMJ	900	.334	.334	2
577 Nitro .585"		SN	750	.313	.346	3
		FMJ	750	.313	.351	4
577 BP .585"		SN	650	.271	.320	5
500 Nitro .510"		SN	570	.313	.474	6
		FMJ	570	.313	.434	7
500 BP .510"		SN	440	.242	.336	8
500 Jeffery .510"		SN	535	.304	.460	9
		FMJ	535	.304	.422	10
505 Gibbs .505"		SN	525	.294	.445	11
		FMJ	525	.294	.408	12
475 No.2 Jeffery .488"		SN	500	.300	.420	13
		FMJ	500	.300	.416	14

Alliant Rifle, Shotgun and Pistol Powders

Powder	Relative Quickness	Principal Purpose	Secondary Uses
Bullseye®	10%	Handgun Loads	12 ga. Light Target Loads
Red Dot®	94.1%	Light & Standard 12 & 16 ga. Target Loads	Handgun Loads
American Select®	81.0%	12 ga. Target Loads	Cowboy Action Handgun Loads
Green Dot®	77.9%	Handicap Trap Loads	20 & 28 ga. Target Loads
Unique®	61.6%	All-around Shotshell Powder, 12, 16 & 20 ga.	Handgun Loads
Power Pistol®	58.6%	High Performance 9mm, .40 S&W & 10mm	Moderate Pistol Cartridges
Herco®	56.1%	Heavy Shotshell Loads 10, 12 16, 20 & 28 ga.	Heavy Handgun Loads
Blue Dot®	37.8%	Magnum Shotshell Loads 10, 12, 16, 20 & 28 ga.	Magnum Handgun Loads
Steel™	34.0%	Non-Toxic Hunting Shotshell	2 oz. Turkey Loads
2400®	27.00%	Magnum Handgun Loads	.22 Hornet & 218 Bee
Reloader® 7	19.4%	Light Rifle	45-70 Gov't
Reloader® 15	13.7%	Medium Rifle	Silhouette Rifle
Reloader® 19	11.3%	Standard Rifle	Light Magnum Rifle
Reloader® 22	11.1%	Magnum Rifle	Heavy Bullet Stand Rifle
Reloader® 25	10.5%	Heavy Magnum Rifle	Magnum Rifle

HODGDON SMOKELESS POWDER

PYRODEX PELLETS
Both rifle and pistol pellets eliminate powder measures, speeds shooting for black powder enthusiasts.

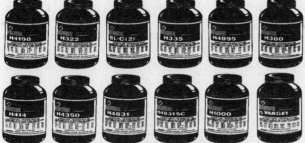

EXTREME H4198
H4198 was developed especially for small and medium capacity cartridges.

EXTREME H322
This powder fills the gap between H4198 and BL-C9(2). Performs best in small to medium capacity cases.

SPHERICAL BL-C2
Best performance is in the 222, and in other cases smaller than 30/06.

SPHERICAL H335®
Similar to BL-C(2), H335 is popular for its performance in medium capacity cases, especially in 222 and 308 Winchester.

EXTREME H4895®
4895 gives desirable performance in almost all cases from 222 Rem. to 458 Win. Reduced loads, to as low as 3/5 maximum, still give target accuracy.

SPHERICAL H380®
This number fills a gap between 4320 and 4350. It is excellent in 22/250, 220 Swift, the 6mm's, 257 and 30/06.

SPHERICAL H414®
In many popular medium to medium-large calibers, pressure velocity relationship is better.

LIL' GUN
This powder was developed specifically for the .410 shotgun but works very well in rifle cartridges like the .22 Hornet and in the .44 magnum.

EXTREME H4350
This powder gives superb accuracy at optimum velocity for many large capacity metallic rifle cartridges.

EXTREME H50 BMG
Designed for the 50 Browning Machine Gun cartridge. Highly insensitive to extreme temperature changes.

EXTREME VARGET
Features small extruded grain powder for uniform metering, plus higher velocities/normal pressures in such calibers as .223, 22-250, 306, 30-06, 375 H&H

TITEGROUP
Excelllent for most straight-walled pistol cartridges, incl. 38 Spec., 44 Spec., 45 ACP. Low charge weights, clean burning; position insenstive and flawless ignition

TITEWAD
This new 12 ga. flattened spherical shotgun powder is ideal for 7/8, 1 and 1 1/8 oz. loads, with minimum recoil and mild muzzle report.

EXTREME H4831®
Outstanding performance with medium and heavy bullets in the 6mm's, 25/06, 270 and Magnum calibers. Also available with shortened grains (H4831SC) for easy metering.

EXTREME H1000 EXTRUDED POWDER
Fills the gap between H4831 and H870. Works especially well in overbore capacity cartridges (1,000-yard shooters take note).

HP38
A fast pistol powder for most pistol loading. Especially recommended for mid-range 38 specials.

CLAYS
Tailored for use in 12 ga., 7/8, 1-oz. and 1 1/8-oz. loads. Also performs well in many handgun applications, including .38 Special, .40 S&W and 45 ACP. Perfect for 1 1/8 and 1 oz. loads.

Universal Clays
Loads nearly all of the straight-wall pistol cartridges as well as 12 ga. 1.25 oz. thru 28 ga. 3/4 oz. target loads.

International Clays
Ideal for 12 and 20 ga. autoloaders who want reduced recoil.

HS-6 AND HS-7
HS-6 and HS-7 for Magnum field loads are unsurpassed, since they do not pack in the measure. They deliver uniform charges and are dense to allow sufficient wad column for best patterns.

H110
A spherical powder made especially for the 30 M1 carbine. H110 also does very well in 357, 44 spec., 44 Mag. or .410 ga. shotshell. Magnum primers are recommended for consistent ignition.

H4227
An extruded powder similar to H110, it is the fastest burning in Hodgdon's line. Recommended for the 22 Hornet and some specialized loading in the 45-70 caliber. Also excellent in magnum pistol and .410 shotgun.

DILLON PRECISION RELOADERS

Dillon Precision is a leader in the shotgun shooting sports market with its SL 900 progressive shotshell reloader. Based on Dillon's proven XL 650 O-frame design, it incorporates the same powerful compound linkage. The automatic case insert system, fed by an electric case collator, ranks high among the new features of this reloader. Adjustable shot and powder bars come as standard equipment. Both the powder and shot bars are case-activated, so no powder or shot can spill when no shell is at that station. Should the operator forget to insert a wad during the reloading process, the SL 900 will not dispense shot into the powder-charged hull. Both powder and shot systems are based on Dillon's adjustable powder bar design, which is accurate to within a few tenths of a grain. These systems also eliminate the need for fixed-volume bushings. Simply adjust the measures to dispense the exact charges required.

The Dillon SL 900 is the first progressive shotshell loader on which it is practical to change gauges. An interchangeable tool-head makes it quick and easy to change from one gauge to another. The SL 900 also has an extra large, remote shot hopper that holds an entire 25-pound bag of shot, making it easy to fill with a funnel. The unique shot reservoir/dispenser helps ensure that a consistent volume of shot is delivered to each shell.

For shotgunners who shoot and load for multiple gauges or different kinds of shooting, the SL 900's interchangeable toolhead feature makes quick work of changing from one gauge to another. It uses a collet-type sizing die that re-forms the base of the shotshell to factory specifications—a feature that ensure reliable feeding in all shotguns. The heat-treated steel crimp die forms and folds the hull before the final taper crimp die radiuses and blends the end of the hull and locks the crimp into place.

MODEL RL550B PROGRESSIVE LOADER

- Accomodates over 120 calibers
- Interchangeable toolhead assembly
- Auto/Powder priming systemsa
- Uses standard 7/8" by 14 dies
- Loading rate: 500-600 rounds per hour

Price: $319.95

MODEL SL900
$799.95

DILLON PRECISION RELOADERS

MODEL SQUARE DEAL B

- Automatic Indexing
- Auto Powder/Priming Systems
- Available in 14 handgun calibers
- Loading rate: 400-500 rounds per hour
- Loading dies standard
- Factory adjusted, ready-to-use

Price: $249.95

MODEL RL 1050

- Automatic indexing
- Auto powder/priming systems
- Automatic casefeeder
- Commercial grade machine
- Swages military primer pockets
- Loading rate: 1000-1200 rounds per hour
- Weighs 54 lbs.
- Eight station

Price: $1,189.95

MODEL XL 650

- New primer system design (uses rotary indexing plate)
- Automatic indexing
- Uses standard 7/8" x 14 dies
- Loading rate: 800-1000 rounds per hour
- Five station interchangeable toolhead

Price: $438.95

MODEL AT-500

- Loads over 40 calibers
- Uses standard 7/8" by 14 dies
- Upgradeable to Model RL 550B
- Interchangeable toolhead
- Switch from one caliber to another in 30 seconds
- Universal shellplate

Price: $191.95

RELOADING

FORSTER RELOADING

CO-AX® BENCH REST® RIFLE DIES

Bench Rest Rifle Dies are glass hard and polished mirror smooth with special attention given to headspace, tapers and diameters. Sizing die has an elevated expander button to ensure better alignment of case and neck.

BENCH REST® DIE SET	$69.98
WEATHERBY BENCH REST DIE SET	69.98
ULTRA BENCH REST DIE SET	92.98
FULL LENGTH SIZER	32.98
BENCH REST SEATING DIE	39.98

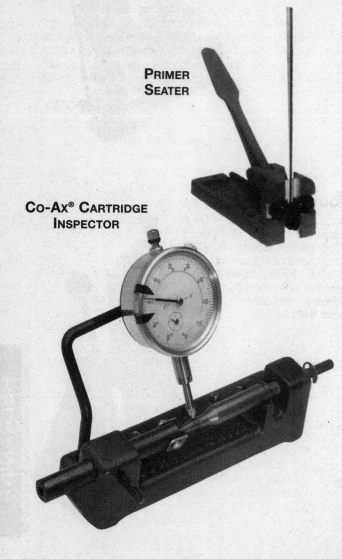

PRIMER SEATER

CO-AX® CARTRIDGE INSPECTOR

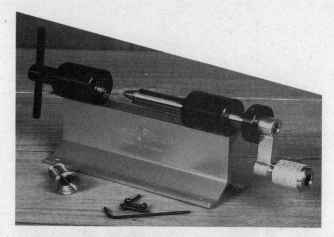

HAND CASE TRIMMER

Shell holder is a Brown & Sharpe-type collet. Case and cartridge conditioning accessories include inside neck reamer, outside neck turner, deburring tool, hollow pointer and primer pocket cleaners. The case trimmer trims all cases, ranging from 17 to 458 Winchester caliber.

Price: $59.00

PRIMER SEATER
With "E-Z-Just" Shellholder

The Bonanza Primer Seater is designed so that primers are seated Co-Axially (primer in line with primer pocket). Mechanical leverage allows primers to be seated fully without crushing. With the addition of one extra set of Disc Shell Holders and one extra Primer Unit, all modern cases, rim or rimless, from 222 up to 458 Magnum, can be primed. Shell holders are easily adjusted to any case by rotating to contact rim or cannelure of the case.

PRIMER SEATER	$69.00
PRIMER POCKET CLEANER	6.98

"CLASSIC 50" CASE TRIMMER (not shown)

Handles more than 100 different big bore calibers–500 Nitro Express, 416 Rigby, 50 Sharps, 475 H&H, etc. *Also available:* .50 BMG Case Trimmer, designed specifically for reloading needs of .50 Cal. BMG Shooters.

Price: "CLASSIC 50" CASE TRIMMER	$84.00
.50 BMG CASE TRIMMER	89.00

CO-AX® CASE AND CARTRIDGE INSPECTOR

One tool to perform three vital measurements. Accurate performance from your ammunition is absolutely dependent on uniformity of both the bullet and the case. Achieving that uniformity is not possible without an accurate, reliable measuring device.

Forster's exclusive Co-Ax® Case & Cartridge Inspector provides you with the ability to ensure uniformity by measuring three critical dimensions: • Neck wall thickness • Case neck concentricity • Bullet runout.

Measurements are in increments of one-thousandth of an inch so accuracy is superb.

The Inspector is unique because it checks both the bullet and case alignment in relation to the centerline (axis) of the entire cartridge or case.

FORSTER RELOADING

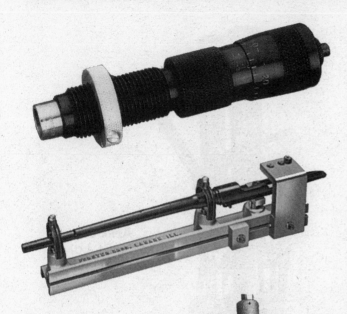

CO-AX LOADING PRESS B-2

BENCH REST POWDER MEASURE

ULTRA BULLET SEATER DIE

Forster's new Ultra Die is available in 56 calibers, more than any other brand of micrometer-style seater. Adjustment is identical to that of a precision micrometer—the head is graduated to .001" increments with .025" bullet movement per revolution. The cartridge case, bullet and seating stem are completely supported and perfectly aligned in a close-fitting chamber before and during the bullet seating operation.
Price: **$62.98**

UNIVERSAL SIGHT MOUNTING FIXTURE

This product fills the exacting requirements needed for drilling and tapping holes for the mounting of scopes, receiver sights, shotgun beads, etc. The fixture handles any single-barrel gun—bolt-action, lever-action or pump-action—as long as the barrel can be laid into the "V" blocks of the fixture. Rifles with tube magazines are drilled in the same manner by removing the magazine tube. The fixture's main body is made of aluminum casting. The two "V" blocks are adjustable for height and are made of hardened steel ground accurately on the "V" as well as the shaft.
Price: **$368.00**

CO-AX® LOADING PRESS MODEL B-2

Designed to make reloading easier and more accurate, this press offers the following features: Snap-in and snap-out die change • Positive spent primer catcher • Automatic self-acting shell holder • Floating guide rods • Working room for right- or left-hand operators • Top priming device seats primers to factory specifications • Uses any standard 7/8"X14 dies • No torque on the head • Perfect alignment of die and case • Three times the mechanical advantage of a "C" press
Price: **$298.00**

BENCH REST POWDER MEASURE

When operated uniformly, this measure will throw uniform charges from 2 1/2 grains Bullseye to 95 grains #4320. No extra drums are needed. Powder is metered from the charge arm, allowing a flow of powder without extremes in variation while minimizing powder shearing. Powder flows through its own built-in baffle so that powder enters the charge arm uniformly.
Price: **$109.98**

HORNADY

APEX 3.1 AUTO SHOTSHELL RELOADER

This versatile shotshell reloader features a new hold-fast shell plate. Other features include: extra-large shot hopper, short linkage arm, automatic dual-action crimp die, swing-out wad guide, and extra-long shot and powder feed tubes. The reloader is now available with Gas-Assist Indexing. With each downstroke of the handle the gas assist cylinder compresses, storing energy. Raise the handle and the gas cylinder transfers its energy to the shellplate, rotating it in one smooth motion, without jerking, and advancing the shells and primers with smooth control regardless of handle speed. The Apex 3.1 Auto Shotshell Loader with Gas Assist is available in four models: 12 ga., 20 ga., 28 ga., and 410 ga.

Prices:

APEX SHOTSHELL LOADER WITH GAS ASSIST
In 12, 20, 28 and .410 gauge **399.95**

APEX 3.1
SHOTSHELL LOADER
w/GAS ASSIST

LOCK-N-LOAD
CLASSIC RELOADING PRESS

LOCK-N-LOAD CLASSIC PRESS

Hornady introduces two new presses that let the operator change dies with a flick of the wrist. This new feature, called Lock-N-Load, is available on Hornady's single stage and progressive reloader models. This bushing system locks the die into the press like a rifle bolt, simply by threading a die into the Lock-N-Load bushing. The die is then inserted into a matching press bushing on the loader and locked in place with a clockwise turn. Instead of threading dies in and out, the operator simply locks and unlocks them with a slight twist. Dies are held firmly in place like a rifle bolt, but release instantly for changing. The die bushing stays with the die and retains the die setting. Single stage reloading has never been simpler with Hornady's new Lock-N-Load Classic press. Instead of screwing dies in, the Lock-N-Load system lets the operator change dies with a simple twist. Die settings remain firm and the die is held perfectly solid in the loader. The Lock-N-Load Classic Press features an easy grip handle, an O-style frame made of high-strength alloy, and a positive priming system that feeds, aligns and seats the primer smoothly and automatically.

Prices:

LOCK-N-LOAD CLASSIC PRESS (includes three die bushings, primer catcher, positive priming system, Automatic Primer Feed and accessories) **$229.95**

HORNADY

LOCK-N-LOAD AUTO PROGRESSIVE PRESS

The Lock-N-Load Automatic Progressive reloading press, featuring the Lock-N-Load bushing system, delivers consistently accurate loaded rounds, changing forever the way handloaders switch from one caliber to another. This task can now be done with a flick of the wrist and allows the operator to stop loading, change dies and start loading another caliber in seconds. Five Lock-N-Load die stations offer the flexibility to add a roll or taper crimp die. Dies and powder measure are inserted into Lock-N-Load die bushings, which lock securely into the press. The bushings remain with the die and powder measure and can be removed in seconds. They also fit on other presses and mount like dies using the Lock-N-Load bushing system. Other features include: Deluxe Powder Measure, Automatic Indexing, Off-Set Handle, Power-Pac Linkage, Case ejector.

LOCK-N-LOAD AUTO PROGRESSIVE PRESS (includes five die
bushings, shellplate, primer catcher, Positive Priming
System, powder drop, Deluxe Powder Measure,
automatic primer feed) $349.95

MODEL 366 AUTO SHOTSHELL RELOADER

The 366 Auto features full-length resizing with each stroke, automatic primer feed, swing-out wad guide, three-state crimping featuring Taper-Loc for factory tapered crimp, automatic advance to the next station and automatic ejection. The turntable holds 8 shells for 8 operations with each stroke. The primer tube filler is fast. The automatic charge bar loads shot and powder. Right- or left-hand operation; interchangeable charge bushings, die sets and Magnum dies and crimp starters for 6 point, 8 point and paper crimps.

MODEL 366 AUTO SHOTSHELL RELOADER:
12, 20, 28 gauge or .410 bore $390.00
PRIMER TUBE FILLER 12.25
POWDER AND SHOT BAFFLES (PER SET) 5.50
RISER LEGS (PER SET) 6.65
SHOT AND POWDER HOPPERS (EACH) 11.30

NEW DIMENSION CUSTOM GRADE RELOADING DIES

Features an Elliptical Expander that minimizes friction and reduces case neck stretch, plus the need for a tapered expander for "necking up" to the next larger caliber. Other recent design changes include a hardened steel decap pin that will not break, bend or crack even when depriming stubborn military cases. A bullet seater alignment sleeve guides the bullet and case neck into the die for in-line benchrest alignment. All New Dimension Reloading Dies include: collar and collar lock to center expander precisely; one-piece expander spindle with tapered bottom for easy cartridge insertion; wrench flats on die body, Sure-Loc™ lock rings and collar lock for easy tightening; and built-in crimper.

NEW DIMENSION CUSTOM GRADE RELOADING DIES:
SERIES I TWO-DIE RIFLE SET $28.40
SERIES I THREE-DIE RIFLE SET 30.00
SERIES II THREE-DIE PISTOL SET (w/Titanium Nitride) .39.70
50 CALIBER BMG DIES (TWO-DIE SET) $260.00
Special die sets also available.

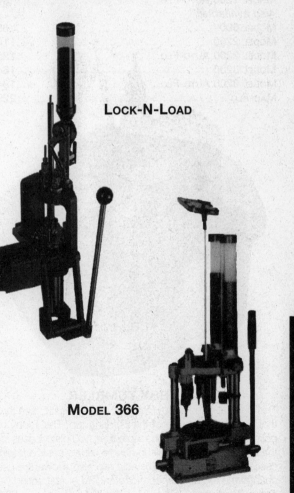

LOCK-N-LOAD

MODEL 366

LYMAN RELOADING TOOLS

MODEL 1200 CLASSIC TURBO TUMBLER

Features a redesigned base and drive system, plus a stronger suspension system and built-in exciters for better tumbling action and faster cleaning

MODEL 1200 CLASSIC	$79.95
MODEL 1200 AUTO-FLO	.99.95
Also available:	
MODEL 600	.69.95
MODEL 2200	.116.50
MODEL 2200 AUTO-FLO	.125.00
MODEL 3200	.164.95
MODEL 3200 AUTO-FLO	.184.95
MAG-FLO	.229.95

"INSIDE/OUTSIDE" DEBURRING TOOL

This unique new tool features an adjustable cutting blade that adapts easily to any rifle or pistol case from 22 caliber to 45 caliber with a simple hex wrench adjustment. Inside deburring is completed by a conical internal section with slotted cutting edges, thus providing uniform inside and outside deburring in one simple operation. The deburring tool is mounted on an anodized aluminum handle that is machine-knurled for a sure grip.

DEBURRING TOOL $13.50

TUBBY TUMBLER

This popular tumbler now features a clear plastic "see thru" lid that fits on the outside of the vibrating tub. The Tubby has a polishing action that cleans more than 100 pistol cases in less than two hours. The built-in handle allows easy dumping of cases and media. An adjustable tab also allows the user to change the tumbling speed for standard or fast action.

TUBBY TUMBLER $54.95

MASTER CASTING KIT

Designed especially to meet the needs of blackpowder shooters, this new kit features Lyman's combination round ball and maxi ball mould blocks. It also contains a combination double cavity mould, mould handle, mini-mag furnace, lead dipper, bullet lube, a user's manual and a cast bullet guide. Kits are available in 45, 50 and 54 caliber.

MASTER CASTING KIT $156.00

LYMAN RELOADING TOOLS

FOR RIFLE OR PISTOL CARTRIDGES

POWER CASE TRIMMER

The new Lyman Power Trimmer is powered by a fan-cooled electric motor designed to withstand the severe demands of case trimming. The unit, which features the Universal™ Chuckhead, allows cases to be positioned for trimming or removed with fingertip ease. The Power Trimmer package includes Nine-Pilot Multi-Pack. In addition to two cutter heads, a pair of wire end brushes for cleaning primer pockets are included. Other features include safety guards, on-off rocker switch, heavy cast base with receptacles for nine pilots, and bolt holes for mounting on a work bench. Available for 110 V or 220 V systems.

Prices: 110 V Model **$187.50**
220 V Model **187.50**

ACCULINE OUTSIDE NECK TURNER
(not shown)

To obtain perfectly concentric case necks, Lyman's Outside Neck Turner assures reloaders of uniform neck wall thickness and outside neck diameter. The unit fits Lyman's Universal Trimmer and AccuTrimmer. In use, each case is run over a mandrel, which centers the case for the turning operation. The cutter is carefully adjusted to remove a minimum amount of brass. Rate of feed is adjustable and a mechanical stop controls length of cut. Mandrels are available for calibers from .17 to .375; cutter blade can be adjusted for any diameter from .195" to .405".

OUTSIDE NECK TURNER w/extra blade, 6 mandrels . . **$28.95**
INDIVIDUAL MANDRELS **4.00**

CRUSHER II PRO KIT

Includes press, loading block, case lube kit, primer tray, Model 500 Pro scale, powder funnel and *Lyman Reloading Handbook.*
STARTER KIT **$154.95**

LYMAN CRUSHER II RELOADING PRESS

The only press for rifle or pistol cartridges that offers the advantage of powerful compound leverage combined with a true Magnum press opening. A unique handle design transfers power easily where you want it to the center of the ram. A 4 1/2-inch press opening accommodates even the largest cartridges.

CRUSH II PRESS
With Priming Arm and Catcher **$112.50**

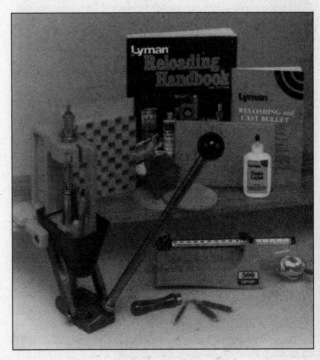

STARTER KIT

LYMAN RELOADING TOOLS

T-MAG II TURRET RELOADING PRESS

With the T-Mag II you can mount up to six different reloading dies on one turret. This means you can have all your dies set up, precisely mounted, locked in and ready to reload at all times. The T-Mag works with all 7/8 x 14 dies. The T-Mag II turret with its quick-disconnect release system is held in rock-solid alignment by a 3/4-inch steel stud.

Also featured is Lyman's Crusher II compound leverage system. It has a longer handle with a ball-type knob that mounts easily for right- or left-handed operation.

T-MAG II PRESS w/Priming Arm & Catcher $154.95
   Extra Turret Head 34.95
Also available:
EXPERT KIT that includes T-MAG II Press, Universal Case Trimmer and pilot Multi-Pak, Model 500 powder scale and Model 50 powder measure, plus accessories and Reloading Manual. Available in calibers 9mm Luger, 38/357, 44 Mag., 45 ACP and 30-06 . . . .$384.95

ELECTRONIC SCALE MODEL LE-1000

Accurate to 1/10 grain, Lyman's new LE: 1000 measures up to 1000 grains of powder and easily converts to the gram mode for metric measurements. The push-button automatic calibration feature eliminates the need for calibrating with a screwdriver. The scale works off a single 9V battery or AC power adapter (included with each scale). Its compact design allows the LE-1000 to be carried to the field easily. A sculpted carrying case is optional. 110 Volt or 220 Volt.

MODEL LE-1000 ELECTRONIC SCALE $259.95
MODEL LE-300 ELECTRONIC SCALE 166.50
MODEL LE-500 ELECTRIC SCALE 183.25

55 CLASSIC BLACK POWDER MEASURE

Lyman's new 55 Classic Powder Measure is ideal for the Cowboy Action Competition or the growing number of black powder cartridge shooters. The large, one pound capacity aluminum reservoir, along with brass powder meter eliminates static. The new internal powder baffel assures highly accurate and consistent charges. The 24" powder compacting drop tube allows the maximum charge in each cartridge. Drop tube works on calibers .38 through .50, and mounts easily to the bottom of the measure. Clamp on back allows easy mounting of the measure at a convenient height, when using long drop tubes.

55 CLASSIC POWDER MEASURE (std model-no tubes) $99.95
55 CLASSIC POWDER MEASURE (with drop tubes) 116.60
POWDER DROP TUBES ONLY .20.95

MODEL LE-500
ELECTRONIC
SCALE

ELECTRONIC
DIGITAL
MICROMETER
$94.95

BLACK POWDER MEASURE

LYMAN RELOADING TOOLS

UNIVERSAL TRIMMER WITH NINE PILOT MULTI-PACK

This trimmer with patented chuckhead accepts all metallic rifle or pistol cases, regardless of rim thickness. To change calibers, simply change the case head pilot. Other features include coarse and fine cutter adjustments, an oil-impregnated bronze bearing, and a rugged cast base to assure precision alignment and years of service. Optional carbide cutter available. Trimmer Stop Ring includes 20 indicators as reference marks.

REPLACEMENT CARBIDE CUTTER $42.00
TRIMMER MULTI-PACK (incl. 9 pilots: 22, 24, 27,
   28/7mm, 30, 9mm, 35, 44 and 4A 64.95
NINE PILOT MULTI-PACK .10.75
POWER PACK TRIMMER .74.95
UNIVERSAL TRIMMER POWER ADAPTER 16.50

DRILL PRESS CASE TRIMMER

Intended for competitive shooters, varmint hunters, and other sportsmen who use large amounts of reloaded ammunition, this new drill press case trimmer consists of the Universal™ Chuckhead, a cutter shaft adapted for use in a drill press, and two quick-change cutter heads. Its two major advantages are speed and accuracy. An experienced operator can trim several hundred cases in an hour, and each will be trimmed to a precise length.

DRILL PRESS CASE TRIMMER $46.50

UNIVERSAL TRIMMER POWER ADAPTER

ACCU-TRIMMER

Lyman's Accu Trimmer can be used for all rifle and pistol cases from 22 to 458 Winchester Magnum. Standard shell-holders are used to position the case, and the trimmer incorporates standard Lyman cutter heads and pilots. Mounting options include bolting to a bench, C-clamp or vise.

ACCU TRIMMER w/9-pilot multi-pak $43.00

ELECTRONIC DIGITAL CALIPER
(not shown)

Lyman's 6" electronic caliper gives a direct digital readout for both inches and millimeters and can perform both inside and outside depth measurements. Its zeroing function allows the user to select zeroing dimensions and sort parts or cases by their plus or minus variation. The caliper works on a single, standard 1.5 volt silver oxide battery and comes with a fitted wooden storage case.

ELECTRONIC CALIPER $94.95

RELOADING

LYMAN RELOADING TOOLS

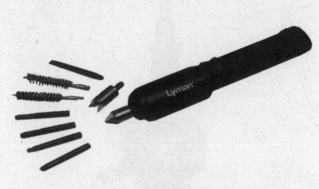

PRO 1000 & 505 RELOADING SCALES

Features include improved platform system; hi-tech base design of high-impact styrene; extra-large, smooth leveling wheel; dual agate bearings; larger damper for fast zeroing; built-in counter weight compartment; easy-to-read beam

PRO 1000 SCALE $57.95
PRO 500 SCALE 41.95

POWER DEBURRING KIT

Features a high torque, rechargeable power driver plus a complete set of accessories, including inside and outside deburr tools, large and small reamers and cleaners and case neck brushes. No threading or chucking required. Set also includes battery recharger and standard flat and phillips driver bits.

POWER DEBURRING KIT $54.95

AUTOSCALE

After setting this new autoscale to the desired powder charge, it dispenses the exact amount of powder with the push of a button, over and over again. Features solid-state electronics and is controlled by a photo transistor to ensure accurate powder charges.

AUTOSCALE $269.95

DELUXE RELOADERS' PRO KIT

Includes Accupress with compound leverage; Pro 505 Scale; Accutrimmer with 9 popular pilots; ram prime die; deburr tool; powder funnel; Quick Spray case lube; shellholders (4); Lyman's 47th *Reloading Handbook.*

DELUXE RELOADERS' PRO KIT $135.00

MEC Shotshell Reloaders

MODEL 600 JR. MARK V

This single-stage reloader features a cam-action crimp die to ensure that each shell returns to its original condition. MEC's 600 Jr. Mark 5 can load 6 to 8 boxes per hour and can be updated with the 285 CA primer feed. Press is adjustable for 3" shells. Die sets are available in 10, 12, 16, 20, 28 and .410 gauges at: **$59.38**
MODEL 600 . . . . **$167.50**

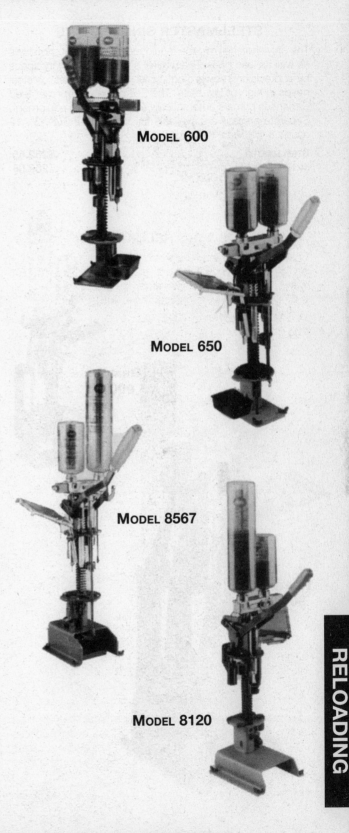

MODEL 600

MODEL 650

MODEL 8567

MODEL 8120

MODEL 650

This reloader works on 6 shells at once. A reloaded shell is completed with every stroke. The MEC 650 does not resize except as a separate operation. Automatic Primer feed is standard. Simply fill it with a full box of primers and it will do the rest. Reloader has 3 crimping stations: the first one starts the crimp, the second closes the crimp, and the third places a taper on the shell. Available in 12, 16, 20 and 28 gauge and .410 bore. No die sets are available.
Price: **$329.39**

MODEL 8567 GRABBER

This reloader features 12 different operations at all 6 stations, producing finished shells with each stroke of the handle. It includes a fully automatic primer feed and Auto-Cycle charging, plus MEC's exclusive 3-stage crimp. The "Power Ring" resizer ensures consistent, accurately sized shells without interrupting the reloading sequence. Simply put in the wads and shell casings, then remove the loaded shells with each pull of the handle. Optional kits to load 3" shells and steel shot make this reloader tops in its field. Resizes high and low base shells. Available in 12, 16, 20, 28 gauge and .410 bore. No die sets are available.
Price: **$472.54**

MODEL 8120 SIZEMASTER

Sizemaster's "Power Ring" collet resizer returns each base to factory specifications. This generation resizing station handles brass or steel heads, both high and low base. An 8-fingered collet squeezes the base back to original dimensions, then opens up to release the shell easily. The E-Z Prime auto primer feed is standard equipment (not offered in .410 bore). Press is adjustable for 3" shells and is available in 10, 12, 16, 20, 28 gauge and .410 bore. Die sets are available at: $88.67 ($104.06 in 10 ga.)
MODEL 8120 . . . . **$252.39**

RELOADING

MEC RELOADING

STEELMASTER SINGLE STATE

The only shotshell reloader equipped to load steel shotshells as well as lead ones. Every base is resized to factory specs by a precision "power ring" collet. Handles brass or steel heads in high or low base. The E-Z prime auto primer feed dispenses primers automatically and is standard equipment. Separate presses are available for 12 gauge 2 3/4", 3", 12 gauge 3 1/2" and 10 gauge.

STEELMASTER $262.65
In 12 ga. 3 1/2" only 289.08

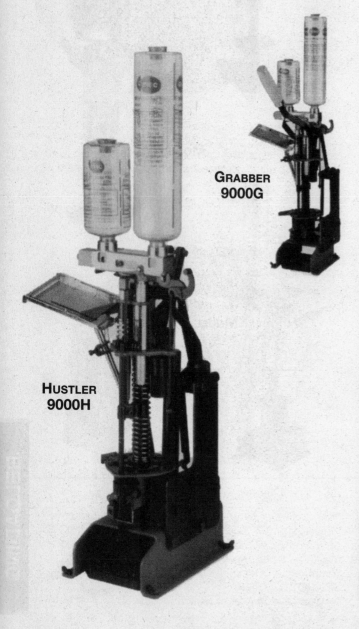

GRABBER 9000G

HUSTLER 9000H

E-Z PRIME "S" AND "V" AUTOMATIC PRIMER FEEDS

From carton to shell with security, these primer feeds provide safe, convenient primer positioning and increase rate of production. Reduce bench clutter, allowing more free area for wads and shells.

- Primers transfer directly from carton to reloader, tubes and tube fillers
- Positive mechanical feed (not dependent upon agitation of press)
- Visible supply
- Automatic. Eliminate hand motion
- Less susceptible to damage
- Adapt to all domestic and most foreign primers with adjustment of the cover
- May be purchased separately to replace tube-type primer feed or to update your present reloader

E-Z PRIME "S" (for Super 600, 650) or
E-Z PRIME "V" (for 600 Jr. Mark V & VersaMEC) . . .$39.71

MEC 9000 SERIES SHOTSHELL RELOADER

MEC's 9000 Series features automatic indexing and finished shell ejection for quicker and easier reloading. The factory set speed provides uniform movement through every reloading stage. Dropping the primer into the reprime station no longer requires operator "feel." The reloader requires only a minimal adjustment from low to high brass domestic shells, any one of which can be removed for inspection from any station. Can be set up for automatic or manual indexing. Available in 12, 16, 20 and 28 gauge and .410 bore. No die sets are available.

MEC 9000H $1,386.09
MEC 9000G SERIES 573.73

MTM Reloading

GUNSMITH'S MAINTENANCE CENTER

MTM's Gunsmiths Maintenance Center (RMC-5) is designed for mounting scopes and swivels, bedding actions or for cleaning rifles and shotguns. Multi-positional forks allow for eight holding combinations, making it possible to service firearm level, upright or upside down. The large middle section keeps tools and cleaning supplies in one area. Individual solvent compartments help to eliminate accidental spills. Cleaning rods stay where they are needed with the two built-in holders provided. Both forks (covered with a soft molded-on rubber pad) grip and protect the firearm. The RMC-5 is made of engineering- grade plastic for years of rugged use.
Dimensions: 29.5" X 9.5"
MODEL RMC-5 . . . .$27.38

PISTOL REST MODEL PR-30

MTM's new PR-30 Pistol Rest will accommodate any size handgun, from a Derringer to a 14" Contender. A locking front support leg adjusts up or down, allowing 20 different positions. Rubber padding molded to the tough polypropylene fork protects firearms from scratches. Fork clips into the base when not in use for compact storage.
Dimensions: 6" x 11" x 2.5
PISTOL REST MODEL PR-30 . . . .$14.58

CARD-GARD WITH WILD CAMO

The CASE-GARD SF-100 holds 100 shotshells in two removable trays. Designed primarily for hunters, this dust and moisture resistant carrier features a heavy-duty latch, fold-down handle, integral hinge and textured finish.
Price:
SF-100 12 or 20 ga.
 WILD CAMO SHOTSHELL BOX $14.62

RCBS RELOADING TOOLS

ROCK CHUCKER PRESS

With its easy operation, outstanding strength and versatility, a Rock Chucker press is ideal for beginner and pro alike. It can also be upgraded to a progressive press with an optional Piggyback II conversion unit.

- Heavy-duty cast iron for easy case-resizing
- 1" ram held in place by 12.5 sq. in. of rambearing surface
- Toggle blocks of ductile iron
- Compound leverage system
- Pins ground from hardened steel
- 1 1/4" - 12 thread for shotshell die kits and Piggyback II
- 7/8" - 14 thread for all standard reloading dies and accessories
- Milled slot and set screws accept optional RCBS automatic primer feed

Price: $130.95

ROCK CHUCKER MASTER RELOADING KIT

For reloaders who want the best equipment, the Rock Chucker Master Reloading Kit includes all the tools and accessories needed. Included are the following: • Rock Chucker Press • RCBS 505 Reloading Scale • Speer TrimPro Manual #12 • Uniflow Powder Measure • RCBS Rotary Case Trimmer-2 • deburring tool • case loading block • Primer Tray-2 • Automatic Primer Feed Combo • powder funnel • case lube pad • case neck brushes • fold-up hex key set • Trim Pro Manual Case Trimmer Kit

Price: $362.95

.50 BMG PACK

Shooters of the .50 BMG need not look for hard-to-find items individually with the new .50 BMG Pack from RCBS®. The Pack includes the press, dies, and accessory items needed, all in one box. The shooter saves money over buying the parts separately. The press is the powerful Ammo Master® Single Stage rigged for 1.5-inch dies. It has a massive 1.5-inch solid steel ram and plenty of height for the big .50. The kit also has a set of RCBS .50 BMG, 1.5-inch reloading dies, including both full-length sizer and seater. Other items are a shell holder, ram priming unit, and a trim die.

Price: $531.95

AMMOMASTER SINGLE STAGE

ROCK CHUCKER

RELOADER SPECIAL-5

RELOADER SPECIAL-5

The Reloader Special press features a comfortable ball handle and a primer arm so that cases can be primed and resized at the same time.

- Compound leverage system
- Solid aluminum black "O" frame offset for unobstructed access
- Corrosion-resistant baked-powder finish
- Can be upgraded to progressive reloading with an optional Piggyback II conversion unit
- 1 1/4" - 12 thread for shotshell die kits and Piggyback II
- 7/8" - 14 thread for all standard reloading dies and accessories

Price: $103.95

AMMOMASTER RELOADING SYSTEM

The AmmoMaster offers the handloader the freedom to configure a press to his particular needs and preferences. It covers the complete spectrum of reloading, from single stage through fully automatic progressive reloading, from .25 Auto to .50 caliber. The AmmoMaster Auto has all the features of a five-station press.

SINGLE STAGE $186.95
AUTO 394.95

RCBS RELOADING TOOLS

APS BENCH-MOUNTED PRIMING TOOL

The APS Bench-Mounted Priming Tool was created for reloaders who prefer a separate, specialized tool dedicated to priming only. The handle of the bench-mounted tool is designed to provide hours of comfortable loading. Handle position can be adjusted for bench height.
Price: **$85.95**

APS PRIMER STRIP LOADER

For those who keep a supply of CCI primers in conventional packaging, the APS primer strip loader allows quick filling of empty strips. Each push of the handle seats 25 primers.
Price: **$21.95**

POW'R PULL BULLET PULLER (not shown)

The RCBS Pow'r Pull bullet puller features a three-jaw chuck that grips the case rim—just rap it on any solid surface like a hammer, and powder and bullet drop into the main chamber for re-use. A soft cushion protects bullets from damage. Works with most centerfire cartridges from .22 to .45 (not for use with rimfire cartridges).
Price: **$25.95**

RELOADING SCALE MODEL 5-0-5

This 511-grain capacity scale has a three-poise system with widely spaced, deep beam notches to keep them in place. Two smaller poises on right side adjust from 0.1 to 10 grains, larger one on left side adjusts in full 10-grain steps. The first scale to use magnetic dampening to eliminate beam oscillation, the 5-0-5 also has a sturdy die-cast base with large leveling legs for stability. Self-aligning agate bearings support the hardened steel beam pivots for a guaranteed sensitivity to 0.1 grains.
Price: **$74.95**

APS BENCH-MOUNTED PRIMING TOOL

APS PRESS-MOUNTED PRIMING TOOL

This APS press-mounted priming tool provides the same features as the bench-mounted tool except it attaches to any single-stage press that accepts standard 7/8" x 14 dies.
Price: **$54.95**

TRIM PRO™ CASE TRIMMER

Cartridge cases are trimmed quickly and easily with a few turns of the RCBS Trim Pro case trimmer. The lever-type handle is more accurate to use than draw collet systems. A flat plate shell holder keeps cases locked in place and aligned. A micrometer fine adjustment bushing offers trimming accuracy to within .001". Made of die-cast metal with hardened cutting blades. The power model is like having a personal lathe, delivering plenty of torque. Positive locking handle and in-line power switch make it simple and safe.
Price: Power **$201.95**
Manual **$66.95**
Also available:
TRIM PRO CASE TRIMMER STAND **$13.95**
CASE HOLDER ACCESSORY **29.95**

RELOADING

RCBS RELOADING TOOLS

POWDER PRO™ DIGITAL SCALE

The RCBS Powder Pro Digital Scale has a 1500-grain capacity. Powder, bullets, even cases with accuracy up to 0.1 grain can be weighed. Includes infra-red data port for transferring information to the Powdermaster Electronic Powder Dispenser and electronic powder trickler. *Price:* $209.95

POWDERMASTER ELECTRONIC POWDER DISPENSER

Works in combination with the RCBS Powder Pro Digital Scale and with all types of smokeless powder. Can be used as a power trickler as well as a powder dispenser. Accurate to one-tenth of a grain.
Price: $220.95

RC-130 MECHANICAL SCALE

The new RC130 features a 130 grain capacity and maintenance-free movement, plus a magnetic dampening system for fast readings. A 3-poise design incorporates easy adjustments with a beam that is graduated in increments of 10 grains and one grain. A micrometer poise measures in 0.1 grain increments with acuracy to ±0.1 grain.
Price: $34.95

POWDER CHECKER (not shown)

Operates on a free-moving rod for simple, mechanical operation with nothing to break. Standard 7/8x14 die body can be used in any progressive loader.
Price: $24.95

ELECTRONIC POWDER TRICKLER (not shown)

Works with Powder Pro scale and Uniflow Powder Measure to ensure charge weights +/- .01 grain.
Price: $195.95

RELOADING SCALE MODEL 10-10
Up to 1010 Grain Capacity

Normal capacity is 510 grains, which can be increased, without loss of sensitivity, by attaching the included extra weight.

Features include micrometer poise for quick, precise weighing, special approach-to-weight indicator, easy-to-read graduation, magnetic dampener, agate bearings, anti-tip pan, and dustproof lid snaps on to cover scale for storage. Sensitivity is guaranteed to 0.1 grains.
Price: $118.95

PARTNER ELECTRONIC POWDER SCALE

Accurate for +/- one-tenth of a grain up to 350 grains and +/- two-tenths from 350 to 750 grains. Large LCD display is angled for easy reading over a wide range of positions. Powered by 9-volt battery.
Price: $150.95

REDDING RELOADING TOOLS

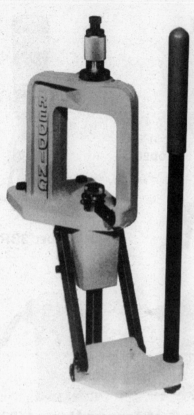

MODEL 721

COMPETITION BUSHING NECK DIE

TYPE S BUSHING NECK DIE

MODEL 721 "THE BOSS" PRESS

This "O" type reloading press features a rigid cast iron frame whose 36° offset provides the best visibility and access of comparable presses. Its "Smart" primer arm moves in and out of position automatically with ram travel. The priming arm is positioned at the bottom of ram travel for lowest leverage and best feel. Model 721 accepts all standard 7/8-14 threaded dies and universal shell holders.

MODEL 721 "THE BOSS" $129.00
   With Shellholder and 10A Dies 165.00
Also available:
BOSS PRO-PAK DELUXE RELOADING KIT. Includes Boss Reloading Press, #2 Powder and Bullet Scale, Powder Trickler, Reloading Dies $336.00
   w/o dies and shellholder 289.50

ULTRAMAG MODEL 7000 (not shown)

Unlike other reloading presses that connect the linkage to the lower half of the press, the Ultramag's compound leverage system is connected at the top of the press frame. This allows the reloader to develop tons of pressure without the usual concern about press frame deflection. Huge frame opening will handle 50 x 3 1/4-inch Sharps with ease.

NO. 700 PRESS, complete $289.50
NO. 700K KIT, includes shell holder and
   one set of dies 334.50

BUSHING-STYLE NECK-SIZING DIES

Redding introduces two new Bushing Style Neck Sizing Dies—a simplified version (dubbed "Type S") and a Competition model—with interchangeable sizing bushings available in .001 increments. The Type S comes in 42 calibers and has an adjustable decapping rod to allow positioning of the bushing to resize only a portion of the neck length, if desired. The Competition Model features a cartridge case that is supported and aligned with the interchangeable sizing bushings before the sizing process begins.

COMPETITION BULLET SEATING DIE $99.00
TYPE S BUSHING NECK DIE 54.00
TYPE S FULL BUSHING DIE 54.00
COMPETITION BUSHING NECK DIE 99.00

METALLIC TURRET RELOADING PRESS MODEL 25000 (not shown)

Extremely rugged, ideal for production reloading. No need to move shell, just rotate turret head to positive alignment. Ram accepts any standard snap-in shell holder. Includes primer arm for seating both small and large primers.

NO. 25 PRESS, complete $298.50
NO. 25K KIT, includes press, shell holder, and one
   set of dies 334.50

REDDING RELOADING TOOLS

MASTER POWDER MEASURE MODEL 3

Universal- or pistol-metering chambers interchange in seconds. Measures charges from 1/2 to 100 grains. Unit is fitted with lock ring for fast dump with large "clear" plastic reservoir. "See-thru" drop tube accepts all calibers from 22 to 600. Precision-fitted rotating drum is critically honed to prevent powder escape. Knife-edged powder chamber shears coarse-grained powders with ease, ensuring accurate charges.

No. 3 Master Powder Measure (specify Universal-
   or Pistol-Metering chamber) $120.00
No. 3K Kit Form, includes both Universal and
   Pistol Chambers 144.00
Bench Stand 27.00

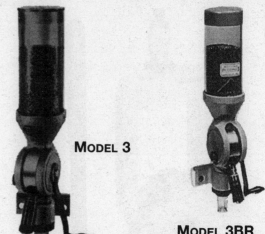

Model 3

Model 3BR

MASTER CASE TRIMMER MODEL 1400

This unit features a universal collet that accepts all rifle and pistol cases. The frame is solid cast iron with storage holes in the base for extra pilots. Both coarse and fine adjustments are provided for case length.

The case-neck cleaning brush and primer pocket cleaners attached to the frame of this tool make it a very handy addition to the reloading bench. Trimmer comes complete with:
- New speed cutter shaft
- Six pilots (22, 6mm, 25, 270, 7mm and 30 cal.)
- Universal collet
- Two neck cleaning brushes (22 thru 30 cal.)
- Two primer pocket cleaners (large and small)

No. 1400 Master Case Trimmer complete $93.00
No. 1500 Pilots 3.90

Master Case Trimmer Model 1400

COMPETITION MODEL BR-30 POWDER MEASURE (not shown)

This powder measure features a new drum and micrometer that limit the overall charging range from a low of 10 grains (depending on powder density) to a maximum of approx. 50 grains. For serious competitive shooters whose loading requirements are between 10 and 50 grains, this is the measure to choose. The diameter of Model 3BR's metering cavity has been reduced, and the metering plunger on the new model has a unique hemispherical or cup shape, creating a powder cavity that resembles the bottom of a test tube. The result: irregular powder setting is alleviated and charge-to-charge uniformity is enhance.

Competition Model BR-30 Powder Measure   . .$180.00

MATCH GRADE POWDER MEASURE MODEL 3BR

Designed for the most demanding reloaders—bench rest, silhouette and varmint shooters. The Model 3BR is unmatched for its precision and repeatability. Its special features include a powder baffle and zero backlash micrometer.

No. 3BR with Universal or
   Pistol Metering Chamber $150.00
No. 3BRK includes both metering chambers 189.00

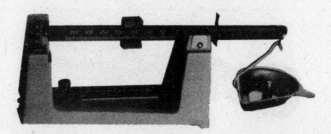

STANDARD POWDER AND BULLET SCALE MODEL RS-1

For the beginner or veteran reloader. Only two counterpoises need to be moved to obtain the full capacity range of 1/10 grain to 380 grains. Clearly graduated with white numerals and lines on a black background. Total capacity of this scale is 380 grains. An over-and-under plate graduate in 10th grains allows checking of variations in powder charges or bullets without further adjustments.

Model No. RS-1 . . . .$49.50
Also available: Master Powder & Bullet Scale. Same as standard model, but includes a magnetic dampened beam swing for extra fast readings. 505-grain capacity . .$75.00

Directory of Manufacturers & Suppliers   564

Gunfinder   570

Reference

DIRECTORY OF MANUFACTURERS AND SUPPLIERS

The following manufacturers, suppliers and distributors of firearms, reloading equipment, sights, scopes, ammo and accessories all appear with their products in the Specifications and/or "Manufacturers' Showcase" sections of this edition of SHOOTER'S BIBLE.

ACCURATE ARMS CO., INC.
5891 Hwy, 230W
McEwen, Tennessee 37101
Tel: 931-729-4207 Fax: 931-729-4211
Web site: www.accuratepowder.com
(see p. 94 in Manufacturers' Showcase)

AIMPOINT (sights, scopes, mounts)
420 West Main St.
Geneseo, Illinois 61254
Tel: 309-944-1702 Fax: 309-944-3676

ALLIANT POWDER (gunpowder)
Route 114, P.O. Box 6
Radford, Virginia 24141
Tel: 800-276-9337 Fax: 540-639-8496

AMERICAN ARMS (handguns; Franchi
shotguns; Uberti handguns, rifles,
blackpowder)
2607 N.E. Industrial Dr.
N. Kansas City, Missouri 64117
Tel: 816-474-3161 Fax: 816-474-1225

AMERICAN DERRINGER CORP. (handguns)
127 North Lacy Drive
Waco, Texas 76705
Tel: 817-799-9111 Fax: 817-799-7935
Web site: www.amderringer.com
(see also p. 96 in Manufacturers' Showcase)

AMERICAN FRONTIER FIREARMS
(black-powder arms)
P.O. Box 744
Aguanga, California 92536
Tel: 909-763-2209 Fax: 909-763-0014

AMERICAN SECURITY PRODUCTS
(AMSEC) (safes)
11925 Pacific Avenue
Fontana, CA 92337
Tel: 800-423-1881 Fax: 909-681-9056
(see p. 94 in Manufacturers' Showcase)

AMT/GALENA INDUSTRIES
(AMT handguns, rifles)
5463 Diaz Street
Irwindale, California 91706
Tel: 626-334-6629 Fax: 626-969-5247

A.G. ANSCHUTZ GmbH
Postfach 1128
D-89001 Ulm, Germany
Tel: 731-40120 Fax: 731-4012700
E-mail: JGA-Info@anschuetz-sport.com

ARMES DE CHASSE (AyA shotguns;
Francotte rifles, shotguns)
P.O. Box 86
Hertford, North Carolina 27944
Tel: 919-426-2245 Fax: 919-426-1557

ARMSCOR (handguns, rifles, shotguns)
Available through K.B.I., Inc.

ARMSPORT, INC. (Bernardelli handguns,
shotguns)
P.O. Box 523066
Miami, Florida 33152-3066
Tel: 305-635-7850 Fax: 305-633-2877

ARNOLD ARMS CO. INC. (rifles)
P.O. Box 1011
Arlington, Washington 98223
Tel: 800-371-1011 Fax: 360-435-7304

A-SQUARE COMPANY INC. (rifles)
One Industrial Park
Bedford, Kentucky 40006
Tel: 502-719-3006 Fax: 502-719-3030

ASHLEY OUTDOORS
2401 Ludelle St.
Fort Worth, TX 76105
Tel: 888-744-4880 Fax: 800-734-7939
Web site: www.ashleyoutdoors.com
(see also p. 89 in Manufacturers' Showcase)

ASTRA (handguns)
Available thru European American Amory

AUSTIN & HALLECK (blackpowder rifles)
1099 Welt
Weston, Missouri 64098
Tel: 816-386-2176 Fax: 816-386-2177

AUTO-ORDNANCE CORP. (handguns, rifles)
Williams Lane
West Hurley, New York 12491
Tel: 914-679-7225 Fax: 914-679-2698

BARNES BULLETS
P.O. Box 215
American Fork UT 84003
Tel: 800-574-9200 Fax: 8001-756-2465
Web site: www.barnesbullets.com

BAUSCH & LOMB/BUSHNELL (scopes)
Sports Optics
9200 Cody
Overland Park, Kansas 66214
Tel: 913-752-3400 Fax: 913-752-3550
Web site: www.bushnell.com

BENELLI
Handguns available through European
American Armory
Shotguns available through Heckler & Koch
Web site: www.benelliusa.com

BERETTA U.S.A. CORP. (handguns, rifles,
shotguns)
17601 Beretta Drive
Accokeek, Maryland 20607
Tel: 301-283-2191 Fax: 301-283-0435
Web site: www.berettausa.com

BERNARDELLI (handguns, shotguns)
Available through Armsport

BERSA (handguns)
Available through Eagle Imports Inc.

ROGER BIESEN
W 5021 Rosewood
Spokane, WA 92008
Tel: 509-328-9340

BLASER USA, INC. (rifles)
Available through Sigarms

BLUE BOOK PUBLICATIONS, INC. (books)
8009 34th Ave. South, Suite 175
Minneapolis, Minnesota 55425
Tel: 612-854-5229 Fax: 612-853-1486
(See p. 91 in Manufacturers' Showcase)

BLOUNT, INC. (RCBS reloading equipment;
Speer bullets; Weaver scopes)
P.O. Box 856
Lewiston, Idaho 83501
Tel: 208-746-2351 Fax: 208-799-3904

BONANZA (reloading tools)
See Forster Products

BOND ARMS INC. (handguns)
P.O. Box 1296
Granbury, Texas 70048
Tel: 817-573-4445 Fax: 817-573-5636
(see p. 92 in Manufacturers' Showcase)

BRENNEKE OF AMERICA LTD.
81 Eades Drive
Irvine, California 40336-9463
Tel: 606-723-1045 Fax: 606-723-3253

BRNO (rifles)
Available through Euro-Imports
Web site: www.zbrojouka.com

BROWN PRECISION, INC. (custom rifles)
7786 Molinos Avenue; P.O. Box 270 W.
Los Molinos, California 96055
Tel: 530-384-2506 Fax: 530-384-1638

BROWNING (handguns, rifles, shotguns,
   blackpowder guns)
One Browning Place
Morgan, Utah 84050
Tel: 801-876-2711 Fax: 801-876-3331
Web site: www.browning.com

BSA
3911 SW 47th Ave., Ste 914
Ft. Lauderdale, FL 33314
Tel: 954-581-2144 Fax: 954-581-3165
E-mail: bsaoptic@bellsouth.net

BURRIS COMPANY, INC. (scopes)
331 East Eighth Street, P.O. Box 1747
Greeley, Colorado 80631
Tel: 970-356-1670 Fax: 970-356-8702
Web site: www.burrisoptics.com

CABELA'S INC. (blackpowder arms)
One Cabela Drive
Sidney, Nebraska 69160
Tel: 308-254-5505 Fax: 308-254-6669

CHRISTENSEN ARMS (rifles)
192 E. 100 N.
Fayette, Utah 84630
Tel: 801-528-7199
Web site: www.christensenarms.com

COLT BLACKPOWDER ARMS CO.
   (blackpowder arms)
110 8th Street
Brooklyn, New York 11215
Tel: 718-499-4678 Fax: 718-768-8052

COLT'S MANUFACTURING CO., INC.
   (handguns, rifles)
P.O. Box 1868
Hartford, Connecticut 06144-1868
Tel: 800-962-COLT Fax: 860-244-1442
Web site: www.colt.com

CONNECTICUT SHOTGUN MFG. CO.
   (A. H. Fox shotguns)
35 Woodland Street, P.O. Box 1692
New Britain, Connecticut 06051-1692
Tel: 860-225-6581 Fax: 860-832-8707

COONAN ARMS (handguns)
1745 Highway 36E
Maplewood, Minnesota 55109
Tel: 612-777-3156 Fax: 612-777-3683

COOPER FIREARMS (rifles)
P.O. Box 114
Stevensville, Montana 59870
Tel: 406-961-8416

COR-BON BULLET COMPANY
1311 Industry Road
Sturgis, South Dakota 57885
Tel: 800-626-7266 Fax: 800-923-2666
(See p. 95 in Manufacturers' Showcase)

CUMBERLAND MOUNTAIN ARMS
   (blackpowder rifles)
1045 Dinah Shore Blvd., P.O. Box 710
Winchester, Tennessee 37398
Tel: 931-967-8414 Fax: 931-967-9199

CVA (blackpowder arms)
5988 Peachtree Corners East
Norcross, Georgia 30071
Tel: 800-320-9412 Fax: 770-242-8546
Web site: www.cva.com

DAEWOO PRECISION (handguns)
Available through Kimber of America

DAKOTA (handguns)
Available through E.M.F. Co., Inc.

DAKOTA ARMS, INC. (rifles, shotguns)
HC 55, Box 326
Sturgis, South Dakota 57785
Tel: 605-347-4686 Fax: 605-347-4459
Web site: www.dakotaarms.com

CHARLES DALY (shotguns)
Available through K.B.I., Inc.

DAVIS INDUSTRIES (handguns)
15150 Sierra Bonita Ln.
Chino, California 91710
Tel: 909-597-4726 Fax: 909-393-9771
Web site: www.davisindguns.com

DESERT EAGLE (handguns)
Available through Magnum Research Inc.

DESERT MOUNTAIN MFG. (rifle rests)
P.O. Box 130184
Coram, Montana 59913
Tel: 800-477-0762 Fax: 406-387-5361
Web site: www.bench-master.com
(see p. 94 in Manufacturers' Showcase)

DILLON PRECISION PRODUCTS
   (reloading equipment)
8009 East Dillon's Way
Scottsdale, Arizona 85260
Tel: 800-223-4570 Fax: 602-998-2786
Web site: www.dillonprecision.com

DIXIE GUN WORKS (blackpowder guns)
P.O. Box 130, Highway 51 S.
Union City, Tennessee 38261
Tel: 901-885-0561 Fax: 901-885-0440

DOWNSIZER CORPORATION (handguns)
P.O. Box 710316
Santee, California 92072-0316
Tel: 619-448-5510 Fax: 619-448-5780

DYNAMIT NOBEL/RWS (Rottweil shotguns)
81 Ruckman Road
Closter, New Jersey 07624
Tel: 201-767-1995 Fax: 201-767-1589

EAGLE IMPORTS, INC. (Bersa handguns)
1750 Brielle Avenue, Unit B1
Wanamassa, New Jersey 07712
Tel: 732-493-0333 Fax: 732-493-0301

D'ARCY ECHOLS
98 West 300 South, P.O. Box 421
Millville, UT 84326
Tel: 435-755-6842

E.M.F. COMPANY, INC. (Dakota handguns;
   Uberti handguns, blackpowder arms)
1900 East Warner Avenue 1-D
Santa Ana, California 92705
Tel: 714-261-6611 Fax: 714-756-0133

ENTRÉPRISE ARMS (handguns)
15861 Business Center Drive
Irwindale, California 91706
Tel: 626-962-8712 Fax: 626-962-4692

ERMA (handguns)
Available through Precision Sales Int'l.

EUROARMS OF AMERICA INC.
   (blackpowder guns)
P.O. Box 3277
Winchester, Virginia 22604
Tel: 540-662-1863

EURO-IMPORTS (Brno handguns)
614 Millar Avenue
El Cajon, California 92020
Tel: 619-442-7005 Fax: 619-442-7005

EUROPEAN AMERICAN ARMORY CORP.
   (Astra handguns; Benelli handguns;
   E.A.A. handguns, rifles)
P.O. Box 1299
Sharpes, Florida 32959
Tel: 800-536-4442 Tel: 407-639-4842
Fax: 407-639-7006
Web site: www.eaacorp.com

FEDERAL CARTRIDGE CO. (ammunition)
900 Ehlen Drive
Anoka, Minnesota 55303-7503
Tel: 612-323-3740 Fax: 612-323-2506
Web site: www.federalcartridge.com

FEG (handguns)
Available through Interarms and K.B.I., Inc.

FIREARMOUR LLC (gunlocks)
2115 Buffalo Heights
Garden City, KS 67846
Tel: 888-486-5625 Fax: 316-276-2456
(see p.95 in Manufacturers' Showcase)

FLINTLOCKS, ETC. (Pedersoli replica rifles)
160 Rossiter Road
Richmond, Massachusetts 01254
Tel: 413-698-3822 Fax: 413-698-3866

FORREST INC.
P.O. Box 326
Lakeside, California 92040
Tel: 619-561-5800 Fax: 1-888-GUNCLIP
E-mail: SFORR10675@AOL.COM
(see also p. 96 in Manufacturers' Showcase)

FORSTER PRODUCTS (reloading)
310 East Lanark Avenue
Lanark, Illinois 61046
Tel: 815-493-6360 Fax: 815-493-2371
Web site: www.forsterproducts.com

A. H. FOX (shotguns)
Available thru Connecticut Shotgun Mfg. Co.

FRANCHI (shotguns)
Available through American Arms

FRANCOTTE (rifles, shotguns)
Available through Armes de Chasse

FREEDOM ARMS (handguns)
One Freedom Lane, P.O. Box 1776
Freedom, Wyoming 83120
Tel: 307-883-2468 Fax: 307-883-2005
Web site: www.freedomarms.com

GARBI (shotguns)
Available through W. L. Moore & Co.

GARY REEDER CUSTOM GUNS
2710 N. Steves Blvd., Suite 22
Flagstaff, Arizona 86004
Tel: 520-526-3313 Fax: 520-527-0840
Web site: www.reedercustomguns.com
(see p. 89 in Manufacturers' Showcase)

GLASER SAFETY SLUG, INC.
(ammunition, gun accessories)
P.O. Box 8223
Foster City, California 94404
Tel: 800-221-3489 Fax: 510-785-6685
(See p. 90 in Manufacturers' Showcase)

GLOCK, INC. (handguns)
6000 Highlands Parkway
Smyrna, Georgia 30082
Tel: 770-432-1202 Fax: 770-437-4710

GONIC ARMS (blackpowder rifles)
134 Flagg Road
Gonic, New Hampshire 03839
603-332-8456 Fax: 603-332-8457

GSI (GUN SOUTH INC.) (Mauser rifles;
Merkel shotguns; Steyr-Mannlicher rifles)
108 Morrow Ave., P.O. Box 129
Trussville, Alabama 35173
Tel: 205-655-8299 Fax: 205-655-7078
Web site: www.gsifirearms.com

H&R 1871 INC. (see Harrington &
Richardson or New England Firearms)

H-S PRECISION
1301 Turbine Drive
Rapid City, SD 57703
Tel: 605-341-3006 Fax: 605-342-8964
Web site: www.hsprecision.com

HÄMMERLI U.S.A. (handguns)
19296 Oak Grove Circle
Groveland, California 95321
Tel: 209-962-5311 Fax: 209-962-5931

HARRINGTON & RICHARDSON
(handguns, rifles, shotguns)
60 Industrial Rowe
Gardner, Massachusetts 01440
Tel: 978-632-9393 Fax: 978-632-2300
(see also p. 88 in Manufacturers' Showcase)

HARRIS ENGINEERING INC. (bipods)
Barlow, Kentucky 42024
Tel: 502-334-3633 Fax: 502-334-3000
(see p. 90 in Manufacturers' Showcase)

HARRIS GUNWORKS (rifles)
3840 N. 28th Ave.
Phoenix, Arizona 85017-4733
Tel: 602-230-1414 Fax: 602-230-1422

HECKLER & KOCH (handguns, rifles; Benelli
and Fabarms shotguns)
21480 Pacific Boulevard
Sterling, Virginia 20166
Tel: 703-450-1900 Fax: 703-450-8160

HENRY REPEATING ARMS CO. (rifles)
110 8th Street
Brooklyn, New York 11215
Tel: 718-499-5600 Fax: 718-768-8056
Web site: www.henryrepeating.com

HERITAGE MANUFACTURING (handguns)
4600 NW 135 St.
Opa Locka, Florida 33054
Tel: 305-685-5966 Fax: 305-687-6721
Web site: www.heritagemfg.com

HI-POINT FIREARMS (handguns)
MKS Supply, Inc.
5990 Philadelphia Drive
Dayton, Ohio 45415
Tel/Fax: 937-275-4991
Web site: www.hi-pointfirearms.com

HIGH STANDARD MFG CO. (handguns)
4601 S. Pinemont, 2148B
Houston, Texas 77041
Tel: 713-462-4200 Fax: 713-462-6437

HODGDON POWDER CO., INC. (gunpowder)
6231 Robinson, P.O. Box 2932
Shawnee Mission, Kansas 66201
Tel: 913- 362-9455 Fax: 913-362-1307
Web site: www.hodgdon.com

PATRICK HOLEHAN
5758 E. 34th St.
Tucson, AZ 85711
Tel: 520-745-0622
E-mail: plholehan@juno.com

HORNADY MANUFACTURING COMPANY
(ammunition, reloading)
P.O. Box 1848
Grand Island, Nebraska 68802-1848
Tel: 308-382-1390 Fax: 308-382-5761
Web site: www.hornady.com

HOWA (rifles)
Available through Interarms

STEVEN DODD HUGHES
P.O. Box 545
Livingston, MT 59047
Tel: 406-222-9377

ICC/KKAIR INTERNATIONAL
P.O. Box 9912
Spokane, Washington 99209
Tel: 800-262-3322 Fax: 509-326-5436
(see p. 96 in Manufacturers' Showcase)

IGA SHOTGUNS
Available through Stoeger Industries

INTERARMS (FEG handguns; Howa rifles;
Rossi handguns, rifles; Star handguns;
Walther handguns)
10 Prince Street, Alexandria, Virginia 22314
Tel: 703-548-1400 Fax: 703-549-7826
Web site: www.interarms.com

ISRAEL ARMS INT'L. INC. (handguns)
5709 Hartsdale
Houston, Texas 77036
Tel: 713-789-0745 Fax: 713-789-7513

ITHACA GUN CO. (shotguns)
891 Route 34-B
Kings Ferry, New York 13081
Tel: 315-364-7171 Fax: 315-364-5134
Web site: www.ithacagun.com

JARRETT RIFLES INC. (custom rifles)
383 Brown Road
Jackson, South Carolina 29831
Tel: 803-471-3616

JOHANNES (Express Rifle)
Reimer Johannsen GmbH
Haart 49, D-24534 Neumuenster
Tel: 49-4321-28747 Fax: 49-4321-29325

KAHR ARMS (handguns)
P.O. Box 220
Blauvelt, New York 10913
Tel: 914-353-5996 Fax: 914-353-7833
Web site: www.kahr.com

K.B.I., INC. (Armscor rifles, handguns,
shotguns; Charles Daly shotguns; FEG
handguns)
P.O. Box 6625
Harrisburg, Pennsylvania 17112
Tel: 717-540-8518 Fax: 717-540-8567
Web site: www.kbi-inc.com

KIMBER MANUFACTURING, INC.
(handguns, rifles)
1 Lawton St.
Yonkers, NY 10705
Tel: 888-243-4522 Fax: 914-964-9340

KOWA OPTIMED, INC. (scopes)
20001 South Vermont Avenue
Torrance, California 90502
Tel: 310-327-1913 Fax: 310-327-4177
(see p. 93 in Manufacturers' Showcase)

KRIEGHOFF INTERNATIONAL INC.
(rifles, shotguns)
337A Route 611, P.O. Box 549
Ottsville, Pennsylvania 18942
Tel: 610-847-5173 Fax: 610-847-8691

L.A.R. MANUFACTURING, INC. (Grizzly
rifles)
4133 West Farm Road
West Jordan, Utah 84088
Tel: 801-280-3505 Fax: 801-280-1972

LASERAIM TECHNOLOGIES INC.
(sights)
721 Main St., P.O. Box 3548
Little Rock, Arkansas 72203-3548
Tel: 501-375-2227 Fax: 501-372-1445

LAZZERONI ARMS CO. (rifles)
P.O. Box 26696
Tucson, Arizona 85726
Tel: 520-577-7500 Fax: 520-624-4250
Web site: www.lazzeroni.com

LEUPOLD & STEVENS, INC.
(scopes, mounts)
14400 N.W. Greenbriar Parkway,
P.O. Box 688
Beaverton, Oregon 97075
Tel: 503-646-9171 Fax: 503-526-1475
Web site: www.leupstv.com

LEICA CAMERA INC. (rifle scopes)
156 Ludlow Avenue
Northvale, New Jersey 07647
Tel: 800-222-0118 Fax: 201-767-8666

LLAMA (handguns)
Available through SGS Importers Int'l

LONE STAR RIFLE CO., INC.
11231 Rose Road
Conroe TX 77303
Tel: 409-856-3363
Web site: www.lonstarrifle.com

LUGER, American Eagle (pistols)
Available through Stoeger Industries

LYMAN PRODUCTS CORP. (rifles,
blackpowder guns, reloading tools)
475 Smith Street
Middletown, Connecticut 06457
Tel: 860-632-2020 Fax: 860-632-1699
Web site: www.lymanproducts.com

MAGNUM RESEARCH INC. (Desert Eagle
handguns; CZ handguns; Brno rifles)
7110 University Avenue N.E.
Minneapolis, Minnesota 55432
Tel: 612-574-1868 Fax: 612-574-0109

MARKESBURY MUZZLELOADERS, INC.
(black-powder guns)
7785 Foundation Drive, Suite 6
Florence, Kentucky 41042
Tel: 606-342-5553- Fax: 606-342-2380

MARLIN FIREARMS COMPANY (rifles,
shotguns, blackpowder)
100 Kenna Drive, P.O. Box 248
North Haven, Connecticut 06473
Tel: 203-239-5621 Fax: 203-234-7991
Web site: www.marlinfirearms.com

MAROCCHI (Conquista shotguns)
Available through Precision Sales Int'l.

MAUSER (rifles)
Available through GSI (Gun South Inc.)

MAVERICK OF MOSSBERG (shotguns)
Available through O. F. Mossberg

MEC INC. (reloading tools)
c/o Mayville Engineering Co.
715 South Street
Mayville, Wisconsin 53050
Tel: 920-387-4500 Fax: 920-387-5802
Web site: www.mayri.com

MERKEL (shotguns)
Available through GSI (Gun South Inc.)
Web site: www.gsifirearms.com

M.O.A. CORP. (handguns)
2451 Old Camden Pike
Eaton, Ohio 45302
Tel: 937-456-3669 Fax: 937-456-9331

MODERN MUZZLELOADING INC.
(Knight rifles)
P.O. Box 130, 234 Airport Rd.,
Centerville, Iowa 52544
Tel: 515-856-2626 Fax: 515-856-2628

WILLIAM L. MOORE & CO. (Garbi and
Piotti shotguns)
31360 Via Colinas, No. 109
Westlake Village, California 91361
Tel: 818-889-4160

O. F. MOSSBERG & SONS, INC. (shotguns)
7 Grasso Avenue; P.O. Box 497
North Haven, Connecticut 06473
Tel: 203-230-5300 Fax: 203-230-5420
Web site: www.mossberg.com

MTM CASE-GUARD (reloading
tools)
P.O. Box 13117, Dayton, Ohio 45413
Tel: 937-890-7461 Fax: 937-890-1747
Web site: www.mtmcase-gard.com
(See p. 95 in Manufacturers' Showcase)

MUZZLELOADING TECHNOLOGIES INC.
(black-powder guns)
25 E. Hwy. 40, Suite 330-12
Roosevelt, Utah 84066
Tel: 435-722-5996 Fax: 435-722-5909

NAVY ARMS COMPANY, INC. (handguns,
rifles, blackpowder guns)
689 Bergen Boulevard
Ridgefield, New Jersey 07657
Tel: 201-945-2500 Fax: 201-945-6859
Web site: www.navyarms.com

NEW ENGLAND ARMS (Rizzini shotguns)
Lawrence Lane, P.O. Box 278
Kittery Point, Maine 03905
Tel: 207-439-0593 Fax: 207-439-6726

NEW ENGLAND CUSTOM GUN SERVICE, LTD.
(Schmidt & Bender Scopes)
438 Willow Brook Road
Plainfield, NH 03781
Tel: 603-469-3450

NEW ENGLAND FIREARMS CO., INC.
(handguns, rifles, shotguns)
60 Industrial Rowe
Gardner, Massachusetts 01440
Tel: 978-632-9393 Fax: 978-632-2300
(See p. 88, 91, 92 in Manufacturers' Showcase)

NIKON INC. (scopes)
1300 Walt Whitman Road
Melville, New York 11747
Tel: 516-547-4200 Fax: 516-547-0309
Web site: www.nikonusa.com

NORTH AMERICAN ARMS (handguns)
2150 South 950 East
Provo, Utah 84606
Tel: 801-374-9990 Fax: 801-374-9998
Web site: www.naaminis.com

NOSLER BULLETS, INC. (bullets)
P.O. Box 671
Bend, Oregon 97709
Tel: 541-382-3921 Fax: 541-388-4667
Web site: www.nosler.com

OLIN/WINCHESTER (ammunition, primers, cases)
427 No. Shamrock
East Alton, Illinois 62024
Tel: 618-258-2936 Fax: 618-258-3609

MAURICE OTTMAR
113 East Fir, P.O. Box 657
Coulee City, WA 99115
Tel: 509-632-5717

PARAGON COMPETITION (Rottweil shotguns)
1330 Glassel
Orange, California 92667
Tel: 714-538-3109

PARA-ORDNANCE (handguns)
980 Tapscott Road
Scarborough, Ontario, Canada M1X 1E7
Tel: 416-297-7855 Fax: 416-297-1289

PARKER REPRODUCTIONS (shotguns)
124 River Road
Middlesex, New Jersey 08846
Tel: 908-469-0100 Fax: 908-469-9692

PEDERSOLI, DAVIDE (replica rifles)
Available through Flintlocks Etc.
Web site: www.davide-pedersoli.com

PENTAX (scopes)
35 Inverness Drive East
Englewood, Colorado 80112
Tel: 303-643-0261 Fax: 303-790-1131
Web site: www.pentax.com

PERAZZI U.S.A. (shotguns)
1207 S. Shamrock Ave.
Monrovia, California 91016
Tel: 626-303-0068 Fax: 626-303-2081

PIOTTI (shotguns)
Available through W. L. Moore & Co.

PMC CARTRIDGES
P.O. Box 62508
12801 U.S. Hwy 95 South 89005
Boulder City, NV 89008-2508
Tel: 702-294-0025 Fax: 702-294-0121

POWER CUSTOM INC. (gun accessories)
29739 Highway, J. Dept. SB
Gravois Mills, MO 65037
Tel: 573-372-5864 Fax: 573-372-5799
(see p. 93 in Manufacturers' Showcase)

PRAIRIE GUN WORKS (rifles)
1-761 Marion St.
Winnipeg, Manitoba, Canada R2J 0K6
Tel: 204-231-2976

PRAIRIE RIVER ARMS LTD.
(blackpowder guns)
1220 North 6th St.
Princeton, Illinois 61356
Tel: 815-875-1616 Fax: 815-875-1402

PRECISION SALES INTERNATIONAL
(Erma handguns; Marocchi shotguns)
P.O. Box 1776
Westfield, Massachusetts 01086
Tel: 413-562-5055 Fax: 413-562-5056
Web site: www.precision-sales.com

PRECISION SMALL ARMS (handguns)
155 Carleton Rd.
Charlottesville, Virginia 22902
Tel: 804-293-6124 Fax: 804-295-0780

QUARTON USA LTD. CO. (laser sights)
7042 Alamo Dawn Parkway, Suite 370
San Antonio, Texas 78238-4518
Tel: 800-520-8435 Fax: 210-520-8433
(see also P. 88, 90, 91 in Manufacturers' Showcase)

RCBS, INC. (reloading tools)
Available through Blount, Inc.

REDDING RELOADING EQUIPMENT
(reloading tools)
1089 Starr Road
Cortland, New York 13045
Tel: 607-753-3331 Fax: 607-756-8445
Web site: www.redding-reloading.com

REMINGTON ARMS COMPANY, INC.
(rifles, shotguns, blackpowder, ammunition)
870 Remington Drive, P.O. Box 700
Madison, North Carolina 27025-0700
Tel: 800-243-9700 Fax: 910-548-7814

RIFLES, INC. (rifles)
873 West 5400 North
Cedar City, Utah 84720
Tel: 435-586-5995 Fax: 435-586-5996

RIZZINI (shotguns)
Available through New England Arms
Web site: www.rizzini.it

ROSSI (handguns, rifles)
Available through Interarms

ROTTWEIL (shotguns)
Available through Paragon Competition

RUGER (handguns, rifles, shotguns, blackpowder guns). See Sturm, Ruger & Company, Inc.

SAFARI ARMS (handguns)
c/o Olympic Arms, Inc.
624 Old Pacific Highway Southeast
Olympia, Washington 98513
Tel: 360-459-7940 Fax: 360-491-3447

SAKO (rifles, actions, scope mounts, ammo)
Available through Stoeger Industries

SAUER (rifles)
c/o Paul Company, Inc.
27385 Pressonville Road
Wellsville, Kansas 66092
Tel: 913-883-4444 Fax: 913-883-2525

SAVAGE ARMS (rifles, shotguns)
100 Springdale Road
Westfield, Massachusetts 01085
Tel: 413-568-7001 Fax: 413-562-7764

SCHMIDT AND BENDER (scopes)
Schmidt & Bender U.S.A.
P.O. Box 134
Meriden, New Hampshire 03770
Tel: 800-468-3450 Fax: 603-469-3471
Web site: www.schmidt-bender.de

SGS IMPORTERS INTERNATIONAL INC.
(Llama handguns)
1750 Brielle Avenue, Unit B1
Wanamassa, New Jersey 07712
Tel: 732-493-0333 Fax: 732-493-0301

SIERRA BULLETS (bullets)
P.O. Box 818
1400 West Henry St.
Sedalia, Missouri 65301
Tel: 660-827-6300 Fax: 660-827-4999
Web site: www.sierrabullets.com

SIGARMS INC. (Sig-Sauer shotguns and handguns, Blaser rifles)
Corporate Park
Exeter, New Hampshire 03833
Tel: 603-772-2302 Fax: 603-772-1481

GENE SIMILLION
220 S. Wisconsin
Gunnison, CO 81230
Tel: 970-641-1126

SIMMONS OUTDOOR CORP. (scopes)
2120 Killarney Way
Tallahassee, Florida 32308-3402
Tel: 904-878-5100 Fax: 904-893-5472

SKB SHOTGUNS (shotguns)
4325 South 120th Street
P.O. Box 37669
Omaha, Nebraska 68137
Tel: 800-752-2767 Fax: 402-330-8029
Web site: www.skbshotguns.com

SMITH & WESSON (handguns)
2100 Roosevelt Avenue, P.O. Box 2208
Springfield, Massachusetts 01102-2208
Tel: 800-331-0852 Tel: 413-747-3299
Fax: 413-747-3677
Web site: www.smith-wesson.com

SPEER (bullets)
Available through Blount, Inc.

SPORTSLINE (stands, rests, totes & seats)
16607 Blanco Rd., Suite 100
San Antonio, TX 78232
Tel: 210-492-8405
(see p. 94 in Manufacturers' Showcase)

SPRINGFIELD INC. (handguns, rifles,
  Aimpoint scopes and sights)
420 West Main Street
Geneseo, Illinois 61254
Tel: 309-944-5631 Fax: 309-944-3676
Web site: www.springfield-armory.com

STAR (handguns)
Available through Interarms

STEYR-MANNLICHER (rifles)
Available through GSI (Gun South Inc.)
Web site: www.gsifirearms.com

STOEGER INDUSTRIES (American Eagle
  Luger; IGA shotguns; Sako ammo, bullets,
  actions, mounts, rifles; Tikka rifles, shotguns)
5 Mansard Court
Wayne, New Jersey 07470
Tel: 800-631-0722 Tel: 973-872-9500
Fax: 973-872-2230

STURM, RUGER AND COMPANY, INC.
  (Ruger handguns, rifles, shotguns,
  blackpowder revolver)
Lacey Place
Southport, Connecticut 06490
Tel: 203-259-4537 Fax: 203-259-2167
Web site: www.ruger-firearms.com

SWAROVSKI OPTIK NORTH AMERICA
(scopes)
2 Slater Rd.
Cranston, Rhode Island 02920
Tel: 401-734-1800 Fax: 401-734-5888

SWIFT BULLET CO. (bullets)
201 Main st., P.O. Box 27
Quinter, Kansas 67752
Tel: 785-754-3959 Fax: 785-754-2359

SWIFT INSTRUMENTS, INC.
  (scopes, mounts)
952 Dorchester Avenue
Boston, Massachusetts 02125
Tel: 800-446-1116 Fax: 617-436-3232
Web site: www.swift-optics.com
(see p. 92, 93 in Manufacturers' Showcase)

TASCO (scopes, mounts)
7600 N.W. 26th Street
Miami, Florida 33122
Tel: 305-591-3670 Fax: 305-592-5895
Web site: www.tascosales.com

TAURUS INT'L, INC. (handguns)
16175 N.W. 49th Avenue
Miami, Florida 33014-6314
Tel: 305-624-1115 Fax: 305-623-7506
Web site: www.taurususa.com
(see p. 90, 91, 92, 93 in Manufacturers' Showcase)

TAYLOR'S & CO. INC. (rifles, carbines)
304 Lenoir Drive
Winchester, Virginia 22603
Tel: 540-722-2017 Fax: 540-722-2018

THOMPSON/CENTER ARMS (handguns,
  rifles, reloading, blackpowder arms)
Farmington Road, P.O. Box 5002
Rochester, New Hampshire 03867
Tel: 603-332-2394 Fax: 603-332-5133
Web site: www.tcarms.com

TIKKA (rifles, shotguns)
Available through Stoeger Industries

TRADITIONS, INC. (blackpowder arms)
P.O. Box 776
Old Saybrook, Connecticut 06475
Tel: 860-388-4656 Fax: 860-388-4657
Web site: www.traditionsmuzzle.com

TRIUS PRODUCTS, INC. (traps, targets)
221 South Miami Avenue, P.O. Box 25
Cleves, Ohio 45002
Tel: 513-941-5682 Fax: 513-941-7970
(see p. 95 in Manufacturers' Showcase)

UBERTI USA, INC. (handguns, rifles,
  blackpowder guns). See also American
  Arms, EMF, Navy Arms
362 Limerock Rd., P.O. Box 509
Lakeville, Connecticut 06039
Tel: 860-435-8068

ULTRA LIGHT ARMS COMPANY (rifles)
214 Price Street, P.O. Box 1270
Granville, West Virginia 26534
Tel: 304-599-5687 Fax: 304-599-5687

U.S. REPEATING ARMS CO. (Winchester
  rifles, shotguns)
275 Winchester Avenue
Morgan, Utah 84050
Tel: 801-876-3440 Fax: 801-876-3737

VERSATILE RACK CO.
5761 Anderson Street
Vernon, CA 90058
Tel: 323-588-0137 Fax: 323-588-5067
(see p. 96 in Manufacturers' Showcase)

VIVITAR CORPORATION (optics)
P.O. Box 2559
Newbury Park, CA 91319-8559
Tel: 805-498-7008 Fax: 805-498-5086
(see p. 89 in Manufacturers' Showcase)

WALTHER (handguns)
Available through Interarms

WEATHERBY, INC. (rifles, shotguns,
  handguns, ammunition)
3100 El Camino Real
Atascadero, California 93422
Tel: 805-466-1767 Fax: 805-466-2527
Web site: www.weatherby.com

WEAVER (scopes, mount rings)
Available through Blount, Inc.

WICHITA ARMS (handguns)
P.O. Box 11371
Wichita, Kansas 67211
Tel: 316-265-0661

WILDEY INC. (handguns)
458 Danbury Road
New Milford, Connecticut 06776
Tel: 860-355-9000 Fax: 860-354-7759

WILLIAMS GUN SIGHT CO.
7389 Lapeer Road
Davison, Michigan 48423
Tel: 810-653-2131

WINCHESTER (ammunition, primers, cases)
Available through Olin/Winchester
Web site: www.winchester.com

WINCHESTER (rifles, shotguns)
Available through U.S. Repeating Arms Co.
Web site: www.winchester-guns.com

WOODLEIGH BULLETS
P.O. Box 15
Murrabit, Victoria
Australia
Handled in U.S. by:
HUNTINGTON DIE SPECIALTIES
P.O. Box 991
Oroville, CA 95965
Tel: 916-534-1210 Fax: 916-534-1212

ZEISS OPTICAL, INC. (scopes)
1015 Commerce Street
Petersburg, Virginia 23803
Tel: 800-338-2984 Fax: 804-733-4024
Web site: www.zeiss.com

GUNFINDER

To help you find the model of your choice, the following index includes every firearm found in this *SHOOTER'S BIBLE* 2000, listed by type of gun.

HANDGUNS
PISTOLS–COMPETITION/TARGET

ANSHUTZ
Models 1416, 64P, 1730 102

BERNARDELLI
Model P.010 Target 108

BROWNING
Buck Mark 5.5 Target 109, 110

COLT
Custom Tactical Models 112

ENTERPRISE ARMS
Models I, II, III 120

GLOCK
Model 17L Competition 125
Model 24 Competition 125

HÄMMERLI
Model 160 Free, Model 162 Electronic 127
Model 208S Standard 127
Model 280 Target, Combo 127

HECKLER & KOCH
USP 45 Expert 130

HIGH STANDARD
Olympic Rapid Fire 131
Citation, Supermatic Citation MS ... 132
Trophy 132

H-S PRECISION
Pro Series 2000 134

KIMBER
Classic 45 Gold Match 137
Custom Target 137
Polymer Gold Match 137

MAGNUM RESEARCH
Lone Eagle Single Shot 141

RUGER
Mark II Target Series 158, 159
P-512 22/45 Target 159

SMITH & WESSON
Model 41 Rimfire 168
Model 22A Sport 168

THOMPSON/CENTER
Contender "Super 14" 184

UBERTI
1871 Rolling Block Target 185

WICHITA ARMS
International, Silhouette 188

PISTOLS–DERRINGERS

AMERICAN DERRINGER
Models 1, 6, 7, 10, 11 99
Model 4, Model M-4 Alaskan Survival 100
Lady Derringer 100

DAVIS
Long-Bore D-Series 115
D-25 Series Derringers 115

DOWNSIZER
Model WSP 116

PISTOLS SEMIAUTOMATIC
See also Pistols Competition/Target

AMT
Automag II, III, IV 101
Backup & 380 Backup II 100
1911 Government 100
1911 Government 45 ACP Longslide 100
1911 Hardballer 100

ARMSCOR *See KBI*

AUTO-ORDNANCE
Model 1911A1 103
WW II Parkerized 103

BENELLI *See European American Armory*

BERETTA
Model 21 Bobcat 105
Model 84 Cheetah 106
Models 85, 86, 87 Cheetah 106
Model 89 Gold Standard 106
Model 92 Series 107
Model 96 107
Model 950 BS Jetfire 105
Model 3032 Tomcat 105
Models 8000/8040
   Cougar & Mini-Cougar 104

BERSA
Series 95 108
Thunder 380, 380 Deluxe 108

BROWNING
Buck Mark 109, 110
Hi-Power 109

COLT
Combat Commander 112
MKIV Series 80 Pistols 112
Colt Defender 111
.22 Semiauto DA 111
Mustang 380, Pocketlite,
   Model LW380 112

COONAN ARMS
"Cadet" Compact 114
357 Magnum Pistol 114

DAVIS
Model P-32 115
Model P-380 115

ENTREPRISE
Elite P425 119
Tactical P500 119
Boxer P500 119

EUROPEAN AMERICAN ARMORY
European SA Compact 122
Witness DA 121
Witness Gold Team, Silver Team ... 121
Witness Subcompact 121

FEG/INTERARMS
Mark II APK, AP, AP22 123

FEG *(See also KBI)*

GLOCK
Model 17 125
Model 19 Compact 125
Model 20 125
Models 22, 23 Compact 126
Models 26, 27 126
Models 29, 30 Subcompacts 126

HECKLER & KOCH
Mark 23 Special 130
Model HK USP 9 & 40 Universal ... 129
Model P7M8 Self-Loading 130
Model USP45 Universal Self-Loading 130
Model USP45 Compact Universal ... 129

HERITAGE MFG.
Stealth Compact 131

HI-POINT FIREARMS
Models 9mm, 9mm Compact & 380
Polymer 133
Models 40, 45 133

HIGH STANDARD
Citation MS 132
Olympic Military 131
Supermatic Citation, MS 132
Trophy 132
Victor 22 LR 132

ISRAEL ARMS
Models M-5000, M-2500 134

KAHR ARMS
Model K9 135

KBI
FEG Model PJK-9HP 135
FEG Model SMC Auto 135
FEG Model SMC-380 135

KIMBER
Model Custom .45 Series ... 136

LLAMA
Government Model (table) ... 138
Maxi-1 7 Shot ... 139
Micro-Max ... 139
Compact ... 138

LUGER
American Eagle ... 140

MAGNUM RESEARCH
Lone Eagle Single Shot ... 141
Mark XIX Component System ... 141
One Pro 45 ... 143
Baby Eagle ... 143

M.O.A.
Maximum ... 144

PARA-ORDNANCE
P Series Pistols (P10, P12, P16) ... 148, 149

RUGER
Mark II Series ... 158, 159
P-Series Pistols (P93, P94,
  P90, P95, P89) ... 157
P-4 22/45 ... 159
Mark II 22/45 ... 159

SAFARI ARMS
Cohort, Enforcer, Matchmaster ... 160

SAVAGE ARMS
"Striker" Models 510F, 516 ... 161

SIG ARMS
Model P210 ... 163
Models P226 ... 162
Models P229, P232, P239 ... 162, 163

SMITH & WESSON
Model 410 ... 166
Model 900 Series ... 166
Models 3900 Compact Series ... 164
Model 457 ... 168
Models 2213, 2214 Sportsman ... 168
Model 4000 Series ... 165
Model 4500 Series ... 165
Model 5900 Series ... 166
Model 6900 Series ... 164
Sigma Series SW40F, SW380 ... 167
TSW Tactical Series (3953TSW,
  4013TSW, 4513TSW) ... 169

SPRINGFIELD
Model 1911 Series ... 178
Ultra Compact Series ... 179
Super Tuned Series ... 179

TAURUS
Models PT 22, PT 25 ... 180
Models PT-92 ... 181
Model PT-911 Compact ... 180
Model PT-945 ... 181
Model PT-938 Compact ... 180
Model PT 940 ... 181

THOMPSON/CENTER
Contender Bull & Octagon Barrels ... 184
Contender Hunter ... 184

Contender "Super 14" & "Super 16" ... 184
Encore ... 184

UBERTI
1871 Rolling Block Target ... 185

WALTHER
Models P 5 DA ... 287
Model P 88 Compact ... 287
Model P 99 Compact ... 287
Models PP, PPK & PPK/S ... 286
Model TPH DA ... 286

WILDEY
Hunter & Survivor ... 188
Guardsman ... 188

REVOLVERS

AMERICAN ARMS
Mateba ... 98
Regulator SA, Deluxe ... 98

ARMSCOR See KBI

COLT
Anaconda DA ... 113
DS II ... 113
The Peacemaker SA Army ... 113
Python Elite ... 113

EMF/DAKOTA
Hartford Pinkerton ... 116
Cavalry Colt/Artillery ... 116
Hartford Single Action Models ... 116
1873 Hartford Buntline ... 117
1873 Hartford Sixshooter ... 117
1895 Hartford Bisley ... 117
1893 Hartford Express ... 117
Model 1873 Dakota SA ... 118
Model 1875 Outlaw ... 118
Model 1890 Remington Police ... 118
Model 1895 SA Remington ... 118

EUROPEAN AMERICAN ARMORY
Big Bore Bounty Hunter ... 122
Windicator DA ... 122
Small Bore Bounty Hunter ... 122

FREEDOM ARMS
Model 1997 Premier Grade ... 123
Model 252 Competition/Silhouette
  /Varmint ... 124
Model 353 Field/Premier ... 124
454 Casull Field/Premier ... 124
Model 555 Field/Premier ... 124

HARRINGTON & RICHARDSON
Model 929 Sidekick 91 ... 128
Model 939 Premier Target ... 128
Model 949 Classic Western ... 128
Sportsman 999 ... 128

HERITAGE MFG.
Rough Rider SA ... 131

MAGNUM RESEARCH
BFR Revolver ... 142

NAVY ARMS
1873 "Pinched Frame" SA ... 144

"Flat Top" Target SA ... 144
1873 U.S. Cavalry ... 144
1873 Colt-Style SA ... 144
1875 Schofield ... 145
Bisley Model SA ... 145
New Model Russian ... 145

NEW England FIREARMS
Standard, Starter Revolver ... 146
Ultra, Ultra Mag & Lady Ultra ... 146

NORTH AMERICAN ARMS
Mini-Master Series ... 147
Mini Revolvers ... 147

ROSSI
Models 352, 461, 462 ... 151

RUGER
Bisley SA Target ... 156
GP-100 357 Mag. ... 155
Model SP101 Spurless ... 155
New Bearcat ... 156
New Model Blackhawk ... 153
New Model Single-Six ... 154
New Model Super Blackhawk ... 154
Fixed Sight New Model Super
  Single-Six ... 154
Redhawk Models (Stainless & Blued) ... 151
Super Redhawk Stainless DA ... 151
Bisley-Vaquero ... 152
Vaquero SA ... 152

SMITH & WESSON
Model 10 Military & Police ... 173
Model 14 K-38 Masterpiece ... 174
Model 15 Combat Masterpiece ... 174
Model 19 Combat Magnum ... 175
Model 36 .38 Chiefs Special ... 170
Models 37 & 637 Chiefs
  Special Airweight ... 170
Model 60 .38 Chiefs Special
  Stainless ... 170
Model 60LS LadySmith ... 170
Model 317 Airlite, LadySmith ... 174
Model 64 M & P Stainless ... 173
Model 65 M & P, LadySmith ... 173
Model 66 Combat Magnum ... 175
Model 67 ... 174
Model 442 .38 Airweight ... 171
Model 586 Distinguished
  Combat Mag. ... 175
Model 617 K-22 Masterpiece ... 174
Model 610 Classic Hunter ... 177
Model 625 ... 176
Model 629, 629 Classic/Classic DX ... 177
Model 629 Powerport ... 177
Model 640 Centennial ... 172
Model 642 Centennial Airweight,
  LadySmith ... 171
Model 649 Bodyguard ... 171
Model 657 Stainless ... 177
Model 686, 686 Plus, 686
  Powerport ... 176
Model 696 ... 171

TAURUS
Model 44 ... 182
Model 82 ... 182
Model 85 Series ... 182
Model 454 Casull "Raging Bull" ... 182
Model 445 DA ... 183

REFERENCE

Model 605	183
Model 608 DA	183
Model 94	183

UBERTI REPLICAS
See also American Arms

1873 Cattleman	185
1875 Outlaw/1890 Police	185

RIFLES

CENTERFIRE BOLT ACTION

AMERICAN HUNTING RIFLE	190
ANSCHUTZ	
Model 1743	191
ARNOLD ARMS	
African Trophy	196
Alaskan Series (Trophy, Alaskan Guide)	195
Grand African	195
Varminter II	196
A-SQUARE	
Bench	197
Prone	197
X-Course	197
1,000 Yard Match	197
Caesar Model	198
Hamilcar & Hannibal	198
BERETTA	
Mato Rifle	201
BIESEN (Roger)	305
BLASER	
Model R 93	201
Safari Models	201
BROWNING	
A-Bolt II Eclipse, Stainless Stalker	205
A-Bolt II Hunter	204
A-Bolt II Medallion	204, 205
BROWN PRECISION	
High Country Youth	208
Pro-Hunter, Pro-Varminter	207
Tactical Elite	208
CHRISTENSEN	
CarbonCannon Series	209
CarbonTactical Series	209
CarbonOne Series	209
CarbonLite Series	210
CarbonKing	210
CarbonRanger	209
COOPER ARMS	
Varmint Extreme Series (Models 21, 22)	212
DAKOTA ARMS	
Dakota 76	213
Dakota 97 Varmint, Lightweight & Long Range Hunter	214
Long Bow Tactical	214
Traveler	213
ECHOLS (D'Arcy)	306

FRANCOTTE	
Bolt-Actions	216
HARRIS GUNWORKS	
Alaskan	217
Benchrest	218
Classic & Stainless Sporters	217
Long Range	218
National Match	218
Talon Safari	218
HOLEHAN (Patrick)	
Custom Models	307
HOWA	
Lightning Bolt Action	222
H-S PRECISION	
Pro-Series 2000 (Professional Hunter, Varmint Takedown, Heavy Tactical)	221
JARRETT	
Models No. 1, 3, 4	222
Walkabout	222
KIMBER	
Model 84 Series	226
JOHANNSEN EXPRESS	
Safari	223
Classic Safari	223
Tradition	223
LAZZERONI	
Models L2000ST/SA/SP	228
MAGNUM RESEARCH	
Mountain Eagle, Varmint Edition	230
MARLIN	
Model MR-7B	233
Model MR-7	233
MAUSER	
Model 96	239
MILLER (David)	
Custom Guns	304
OTTMAR (Maurice)	
Custom Guns	309
REMINGTON	
Model Seven Series	253
Model 700 ADL	248, 249 (table)
Model 700 African Plains	251
Model 700 Alaskan Wilderness	251
Model 700 BDL Series	247, 249
Model 700 Classic	251
Model 700 Mountain DM	249, 251
Model 700 Safari, Safari KS	252
Model 700 Sendero Special, Sendero SF	248, 249, 250
RIFLES, INC.	
Classic	256
Lightweight Strata SS	256
Safari	256
RUGER	
Model 77R Mark II	262
Model RS Mark II	262
Model RL Mark II Ultralight	262

Model RBZ Mark II	264
Model RSBZ Mark II	264
Model RSI Mark II	264
Model VT Mark II	265
Model Mark II All Weather	265
Model Mark II Magnum	265
Model 77/44 RS	264
Model 77/22 RH Hornet	263
Model 77/22 RSH Hornet	263
SAKO	
Model 75 Series (Hunter, Stainless Synthetic)	266, 271
Deluxe, Stainless	269, 271
TRG-21, TRG-41, TRG-S	270 (table)
Varmint	267, 271
SAUER	
Model 90	272
Model SHR 970 Synthetic	272
Model 202 Supreme	272
Model .458 Safari	272
SAVAGE	
Model 12BVSS/12FVSS/12FV Varmint	273
Model 110FP/10FP Tactical	274
Model 10FM Sierra Lightweight	274
Model 10FMC Scout	276
Model 16FSS Weather Warrior	274
Model 11F Hunter	275
Model 10GY Ladies/Youth	275
Model 11G Classic American Style Hunter	275
Model 111 Classic Hunter Series (GC, FC, G, F)	279
Models 112BT Competition, 112BVSS, 112FV, 112FVSS	276
Models 114CE, 114CU Classics	278
Model 116FCS, FSK Kodiak, FSAK, FSS Weather Warriors	277
Model 116SE Safari Express	278
STEYR-MANNLICHER	
Steyr SSG-P1	285
Steyr Scout	285
Model SBS Mannlicher European	285
TIKKA	
Continental Varmint & Long-Range Hunting	289
Whitetail Hunter & Synthetic	288
ULTRA LIGHT ARMS	
Models 20, 24, 28 & 40 Series	291
WEATHERBY	
Mark V Accumark Magnum	294 (table)
Mark V Accumark Standard	295
Mark V Carbine	297
Mark V Deluxe	292 (table)
Mark V Euromark	294
Mark V Lazermark	296
Mark V Magnum Stainless	296
Mark V Sporter	293
Mark V Stainless & Synthetic	296
Mark V Tables	293, 297
Mark V Lightweight	297
Mark V Ultra Lightweight	295
WINCHESTER	
Model 70 Classic Featherweight	298
Model 70 Classic Sporter	299
Model 70 Classic Super Grade	299

Model 70 Custom Classics	298, 299
Model 70 Push Feed	300
Heavy Barrel Varmint	300
Black Shadow	300
Ranger, Ranger Compact	300

CENTERFIRE LEVER ACTION

BROWNING

Model Lightning BLR	206

MARLIN

Model 336 Cowboy	235
Models 336CS	238
Model 444P	236
Model 1894 Cowboy II	237
Models 1894CS & 1894S	237
Model 1895SS	238

ROSSI

Models M92 Large Loop, Stainless	257

WINCHESTER

Model 94 Big-Bore Walnut	302
Model 94 Standard Walnut	301
Model 94 Legacy	302
Model 94 Trail's End	302
Model 94 Ranger Compact	302
Model 94 Walnut Trapper Carbine	301
Model 94 Wrangler	301
Model 94 Timber Carbine	301

CENTERFIRE SEMIAUTOMATIC & SLIDE ACTION

AUTO-ORDNANCE

Thompson Model M1 Carbine	199
Thompson Model 1927 A1 Deluxe, Lightweight and Commando	199

BROWNING

BAR Mark II Safari & Lightweight	206
Model BPR Pump	206

COLT

Accurized	211
Match Target, H-Bar	211

HECKLER & KOCH

Model HK PSG-1 High-Precision	219

MARLIN

Model 9 Camp Carbine	234
Model 922M	234

REMINGTON

Models 7400 & 7600	253

RUGER

Model PC9 Auto	258
Mini-14/5 Carbine, 14/5R Ranch Rifle	259
Model Mini-Thirty	259

SPRINGFIELD

M1A Standard, Nat'l Match, Super Match	284
M1A-A1 Bush	284

CENTERFIRE SINGLE SHOT

BROWNING

Model 1885 Low & High Wall	203
Model BPR Pump	206

DAKOTA ARMS

Dakota 10 Single Shot	213

HARRINGTON & RICHARDSON

Ultra Single Shot Rifles	216

HUGHES (Steven)

Custom	308

L.A.R.

Grizzly Big Boar Competitor	227

LONE STAR

Silhouette	229
Sporting	229
Cowboy Action	229

NAVY ARMS

Greener Harpoon Gun	244

NEW ENGLAND FIREARMS

Synthetic Handi-Rifle	245
Super Light Youth Handi-Rifle	245

OTTMAR (Maurice)

Custom	309

RUGER

No. 1A Light & 1S Medium Sporters	261
No. 1B Standard/1V Special Varminter	261
No. 1H Tropical	261
No. 1RSI International	261

THOMPSON/CENTER

Contender Carbines	287
Encore	287

RIMFIRE BOLT ACTION & SINGLE SHOT

ANSCHUTZ

Model 2013 Supermatch	191
Model 1907	192
Model 1808	192
Model 54.18 MSR Silhouette	193
Model 1827 Fortner	193
Model 1903	193
Model 1451	194
Model 1451R Sport Target	194
Model 2013 Benchrest	194

ARMSCOR See KBI

EUROPEAN AMERICAN ARMORY

HW660 Weihrauch Target	215

KBI/CHARLES DALY

Model CDGA Empire and Field Grades	224
Model M-12Y Youth	224

KIMBER

Model 82C Series	225

MARLIN

Model 81TS	232
Model 15N	232
Model 15YN "Little Buckaroo"	232
Models 25MN & 25N	232
Models 882, 882L	232
Models 883 Magnum, 883SS	234
Model 922 Magnum	234
Model 2000L Target	239
Garden Gun	235

REMINGTON

Models 40-XR KS Target Rimfire	252
Models 541-T	254

RUGER

77/22 Rimfire Series	263

SAKO

Finnfire	268, 271

SAVAGE

Mark I-G Single Shot	282
Model 93G Magnum, 93F Magnum	280
Model 900TR	283

THOMPSON/CENTER

Contender Carbines	287

ULTRA LIGHT

Model 20 RF	291

RIMFIRE LEVER ACTION

BROWNING

Model BL-22	202

HENRY REPEATING ARMS

Henry Rifle	219
Pump Action	219
U.S. Survival	219

HUGHES (Steven) | 308 |

MARLIN

Golden 39AS	234
1897 Cowboy	236

WINCHESTER

Model 9422 Win-Tuff	383
Model 9422 Walnut, Legacy, Trapper	383

RIMFIRE SEMIAUTOMATIC & SLIDE ACTION

BROWNING

22 Semiauto Grades I & VI	202

BROWN PRECISION

Custom Team Challenger	208

KBI/CHARLES DALY

Model CDGA6345	224
Model M-20P	224

MARLIN

Models 60, 60SS	231
Model 7000	231
Model 70PSS "Papoose"	231
Model 922 Magnum	234
Model 995SS	231

REMINGTON

Model 597 Series	255
Model 552 BDL Deluxe Speedmaster	254
Model 572 BDL Fieldmaster	254

ROSSI

Models M62 SA & SAC	257

RUGER

Model 10/22 Series	258

SAVAGE
Model 64 Series (FV, F, G)   281

DOUBLE RIFLES, ACTIONS & DRILLINGS

BERETTA
Express Rifles (5506, 455)   200

FRANCOTTE
Boxlocks/Sidelocks/Mountain   216

KRIEGHOFF
Classic Side-by-Side   227

NAVY ARMS
Kodiak MK IV, Deluxe   243

PEDERSOLI
Kodiak Mark IV   246

SAKO
Actions   267

REPLICA RIFLES

EMF
1860 Henry   215
1866 Yellowboy Carbine/Rifle   215
1873 Sporting Rifle & Carbine   215

NAVY ARMS
1866 "Yellowboy" Rifle & Carbine   240
1873 Springfield Cavalry Carbine   241
1873 Winchester Sporting   241
1874 Winchester-Style Rifle   241
1873 Winchester-Style Carbine & Rifle   241
1874 Sharps Cavalry Carbine
  & Infantry   242
1874 Sharps Sniper   242
1892 Model (brass frame, short rifle)   243
Greener Light Model Harpoon Gun   244
Henry Carbine   240
Henry Iron Frame, Military, Trapper   240
Kodiak MK IV Double, Deluxe   243
No. 2 Creedmoor Target   244
Remington-Style Rolling Block
  Buffalo Rifle   244
Sharps Plains & Buffalo   242

PEDERSOLI
Kodiak Mark IV Double Rifle   246
Rolling Block Target   246
Sharps Carbine Model 766   246

TAYLOR'S
Henry   286
1866 Yellowboy Carbine   286
1873 Winchester Rifle   286
1873 Sporting Rifle   286

UBERTI
Henry Carbine, Rifle   290
Model 1866 Yellowboy Carbine   290
Model 1871 Rolling Block Baby Carbine
290
Model 1873 Sporting Rifle   290

COMPETITION TARGET RIFLES

ANSCHUTZ (See under RIMFIRE
  BOLT ACTION)

ARNOLD
Bench   197
Prone   197
X-Course   197
1000 Yard Match   197

BROWN PRECISION
Custom Team Challenger   208

CHRISTENSEN
Carbon Challenger   210

COLT
Match Target   211
Competition H-Bar   211

EUROPEAN AMERICAN ARMORY
HW660 Weihrauch Target   215

HARRIS GUNWORKS
Benchrest   218
Long Range   218
National Match   218

MARLIN
Model 7000   231
Model 2000L Target   239

REMINGTON
Model 40-XR KS Target Rimfire   252

RUGER
Model 1022T   260

SAVAGE
Model M112BT Competition   276

SPRINGFIELD
MIA National Match, Super Match   284

THOMPSON/CENTER
Contender Carbine   287

RIFLE/SHOTGUN COMBINATIONS
(See SHOTGUNS Shotgun/Rifle Combinations)

SHOTGUNS

AUTOLOADING

AMERICAN ARMS
Phantom   313

BENELLI
Super Black Eagle   317
M1 Super 90 Series   318, 319
Montefeltro Super 90   318, 319
Super Black Eagle/Slug   318

BERETTA
Model A 390 Series   323
Model 1201 FP Riot   322
Pintail, Pintail Rifled Slug   322

BROWNING
Gold Sporting Clays   325
Gold Hunter & Stalker   325
Gold Deer & Camo   325

MOSSBERG
Model 9200 Series   347

REMINGTON
Model 11-87 Premier, Deer Gun   359
Model 11-87 Skeet/Trap   359
Model 11-87 Sporting Clays   359
Model 11-87 SPS   360
Model 11-87 SPS/SPS
  Camo/SPST Turkey   360
Model 1100 Special Field Gun   361
Model 1100 LT-20   361
Model 1100 LT-20 Youth   361
Model SP-10 Magnum, Camo   362

BOLT ACTION

MARLIN
Model 50 DL Goose Gun   340
Model 512 Slugmaster   340
Model 512P (Ported Barrel)   340

MOSSBERG
Model 695 Series   348

SAVAGE
Model 210 FT "Master Shot," 210F Slug
Gun   365

OVER-UNDER

AMERICAN ARMS
Silver I & II, Sporting   312
Specialty Models TS, WS, WT   314

BERETTA
Model 682 Gold Competition
  Skeet & Trap   320
Model 682 Gold Competition Sporting   320
Model 686 Onyx   322
Model 686 Ultralight   321
Model 687 Silver Pigeon Sporting   321
Model 687L Silver Pigeon Field   321
Model 687EL Gold Pigeon Field   321

BROWNING
Citori Field Models   326
Citori Lightning Sporting,
  Special Sporting   327, 328
Citori Special Trap & Skeet   327, 328
Citori Sporting Clays Model 425   327, 328

CHARLES DALY
Field Hunter   330
Superior Sporting   330
Empire EDL Hunter   330

HECKLER & KOCH
Fabarm Series   336
Lion Series   336

KRIEGHOFF
Models K-80 Live Bird, Trap,
  Skeet, Sporting Clays   338, 339
MAROCCHI
Conquista Series   341

MERKEL
Models 2000 Series   342
Models 303 Sidelocks   342
Models 2001, 2002   342

PERAZZI
Competition Series (Electrocibles, Double
  Trap, Pigeon, Mirage, Olympic, Pigeon,
  Skeet, Special/Sporting)   353

Game Models 352
SC3, SCO High Grades 353

PIOTTI Sidelock 354

REMINGTON
Custom Model 396 Skeet & Sporting 355

RIZZINI
Premier Sporting & Upland 363
Model 5700 High Grade 363
Artemis EL High Grade 363

RUGER
Red Label 364
Sporting Clays 364
Woodside O/U 364

SIG ARMS
Models SA3, SA5 365

SKB
Model 505 366
Model 585 Series 367
Model 785 Series 367

STOEGER/IGA
Condor I Single Trigger 369, 371
Deluxe Hunter Clay 370, 371
Trap Model 370, 371
Waterfowl Model 369, 371

WEATHERBY
Athena Grades IV & V 372, 373
Orion Grades I, II, III 372, 373
Orion Super Sporting Clays 272, 373

SIDE-BY-SIDE

AMERICAN ARMS
Brittany 313
Gentry 313
Specialty Model 314

AYA
Boxlock Models 316
Sidelock Models 315
Countryman 315

BERETTA
Model 470 Silver Hawk 324

DAKOTA ARMS
American Legend 332

CHARLES DALY
Field Hunter 331
Superior, Diamond 331

A.H. FOX
Custom Boxlock Models 331

FRANCOTTE
Boxlocks, Sidelocks 333

GARBI
Models 100, 101, 103A/103B, 200 333

IGA (see STOEGER IGA)

HECKLER & KOCH
Fabarm Series
(Classic Lion Grades 1 & 2) 335

MERKEL
Models 47E, 47EL 343
Model 122 343
Models 247S, 447S 343

PIOTTI
Models King Extra & King No. 1 354
Model Lunik Sidelock 354
Model Piuma 354

SKB
Model 385 367
Model 485 366

STOEGER/IGA
Coach Gun 368, 371
Uplander Series 368, 371
Turkey Model 369, 371
Deluxe Uplander 370, 371
Deluxe Coach Gun 370, 371

SINGLE BARREL

BROWNING
BT-100 Series 329

HARRINGTON & RICHARDSON
.410 Tamer Shotgun 334
Model Ultra Slug Hunter 334
Topper Series Models 098 &
Junior Classic 334

KRIEGHOFF
Model KS-5 339

NEW ENGLAND FIREARMS
Pardner/Pardner Youth 350
Special Purpose Waterfowl SS 351
Survivor Series 350
Tracker Slug Gun 351
Tracker II Rifled Slug Gun 351
Turkey & Goose Gun 351

PERAZZI
American Trap Series 352

SLIDE ACTION

ARMSCOR See KBI

BROWNING
BPS Magnum Series 329

HECKLER & KOCH
Fabarm Series (Model FP6) 335

ITHACA
Model 37 Deerslayer II 337
Model 37 Turkeyslayer 337
Classic 37, English Version 337

MOSSBERG
Line Launcher 348
Model HS 410 Home Security 345
Model 500 American Field 344
Model 500 Crown Grade/Combos 344
Model 500 Mariner 344
Model 500 Sporting 344
Model 500 Woodland Camo 345
Model 500/590 Ghost Ring 345
Model 500/590 Special Purpose 345
Model 835 Ulti-Mag 346

REMINGTON
Model 870 Express/Combo
/Deer/Turkey 356, 357
Model 870 Express Syn. Home Defense 356
Model 870 SP Marine Magnum 355
Model 870 Express Youth 356
Model 870 Wingmaster Series 358

WINCHESTER
Model 1300 Deer, Field, Turkey 375
Model 1300 Defender Series 376
Model 1300 Ranger, Ranger Deer,
Ladies'/Youth 375
Model 1300 Marine 376

BLACKPOWDER
MUSKETS, CARBINES & RIFLES

AUSTIN & HALLECK
Mountain Rifle 380
Models 320, 420 380

CABELA'S
Lightning Fire Rifle 381
Blue Ridge Rifle 381
Kodiak Express Double Rifle 390 381

COLT BLACKPOWDER
Colt Model 1861 Musket 384

CVA
Accubolt Pro 387
Firebolt Series 387
Stag Horn Rifle 387
St. Louis Hawken, Plainsman 386

DIXIE
1858 Two-Band Enfield Rifle 393
1859 Sharps New Model
Carbine/Military Rifle 390
1862 Three-Band Enfield Rifled Musket 393
1873 Springfield Rifle/Carbine
& Officer's Model 392
1874 Sharps Lightweight Hunter 390
1874 Sharps Silhouette 390
Hawken 391
Kodiak Mark IV Double Barrel Rifle 392
Pennsylvania Rifle 391
Tennessee Mountain 391
U.S. Model 1816 Flintlock Musket 393
U.S. Model 1861 Springfield Rifle/Musket 393
Waadtlander Model 391

EUROARMS
Cook & Brother Confederate Carbine 396
Cook & Brother Field Model 2301 396
C.S. Richmond Musket Model 2370 396
1803 Harpers Ferry Rifle 398
1841 Mississippi Rifle 398
1861 Springfield 398
1863 Remington Zouave Rifle 398
London Armory Co. Enfield Musketoon 397
London Armory Co. 2-B& Rifle Musket 397
London Armory Co. 3-B&
Enfield Musket 397
London Armory Co. Musket Model 2261 397
Murray, J.P., Carbine Model 2315 396

GONIC
Model 93 Magnum, Mountain Safari 400

LYMAN
Cougar In-Line	401
Deerstalker	401
Great Plains Rifle	402
Trade Rifle	402

MARKESBERY
Black Bear, Brown Bear, Grizzly Bear	403

MODERN MUZZLELOADING
Model LK-93 Wolverine & Thumbhole Wolverine	405
Model MK-85 Grand American, Hunter, Knight Hawk, Predator, Stalker	404
Disc Rifle	405
Knight T-Bolt	404
American Knight	404

NAVY ARMS
1859 Sharps Cavalry Carbine	410
Berdan 1859 Sharps Rifle	411
Brown Bess Musket/Carbine	411
1803 Harpers Ferry	411
1858 Enfield Rifle	412
1861 Musketoon	412
1861 Springfield	410
1862 C.S. Richmond Rifle	410
Pennsylvania Long Rifle	411
Smith Carbine	410

REMINGTON
Model 700 ML & MLS	414
Model 700 ML Youth	414

RUGER
Model 77/50 All-Weather	415

THOMPSON/CENTER
Black Diamond	417
Encore 209x50 Magnum Rifle	417
System 1	417
Hawken	418
New Englander Rifle	416
Pennsylvania Hunter Rifle/Carbine	416
Thunderhawk, Thunderhawk Shadow	418

TRADITIONS
Buckhunter In-Line Rifle Series	426
Buckhunter Pro In-Line Rifles	426
Buckskinner Carbine	424
Deerhunter Rifle Series	422
Lightning Series	425
Hawken Woodsman	423
Kentucky Rifle	424
Panther Rifle	422
Pennsylvania Rifle	423
Shenandoah Rifle	423
Tennessee Rifle	424

PISTOLS

CVA
Hawken, Kentucky	385

DIXIE
LePage Percussion Dueling	389
Mang Target	389
Charles Moore English Dueling	389
Queen Anne	389
Screw Barrel Pistol	389

NAVY ARMS
1805 Harpers Ferry	409
Kentucky Flint/Percussion	409

TRADITIONS
Buckhunter Pro In-Line, All Weather	420
Kentucky	420
William Parker	419
Pioneer, Trapper	419

REVOLVERS

AMERICAN FRONTIER FIREARMS
1871-2 Open-Top Frontier Model	378
1871-2 Open-Top Tiffany Model	378
Remington New Army Cavalry Model	378
Pocket Remington	378
Richards 1851 Model	379
Richards 1860 Army	379
Richards and Mason 1851 Navy	379
Pocket Richards Mason Navy	379
Richards 1861 Model	379

COLT BLACKPOWDER
Colt 1849 Pocket	382
Colt 1851 Navy	382
Colt 1860 Army, Cavalry Model	383
Colt 1861 Navy	383
Colt Third Model Dragoon	382
Colt 1847 Walker	382
Colt Model 1860 Army Fluted Cylinder	383
Colt Cochise Dragoon	384
Colt 1861 Custer	384
Colt 1860 Gold U.S. Cavalry	384
Colt Walker 150th Anniversary Model	382
Trapper Model 1862 Pocket Police	383

CVA
1851 Navy Brass Frame	385
1858 Army Brass Frame	385

DIXIE
1851 Navy	388
1860 Army	388
Remington 44 Army	388
Walker	388
Spiller & Burr	388
"Wyatt Earp"	388

EMF HARTFORD
Model 1851 Sheriff's	394
Model 1860 Army	394
Model 1862 Police	394
1863 Texas Dragoon	394
1847 Walker	395
1849 Baby Dragoon	395
1848 Dragoon	395
1851 Navy	395

EUROARMS
Colt 1851 Navy Model 1120	399
Colt 1860 Army Model 1210	399
Remington 1858 New Model Army Models 1010, 1020, 1040	399
Rogers & Spencer Models 1005, 1006	399
Rogers & Spencer London Gray Model 1007	399

NAVY ARMS
Colt 1847 Walker	406
1851 Navy "Yank"	408

1858 New Model Army Remington Models	408
1860 Army	407
1862 New Model Police	406
Le Mat (Army, Navy, Cavalry, 18th Georgia, Beauregard)	406
Reb Model 1860	407
Reb 60 Sheriff's	408
Rogers & Spencer Models	406
First Model Dragoon	407

RUGER
Old Army Cap & Ball	415

TRADITIONS
1875 Schofield	412
Sheriff's Model	421
1873 Colt SA	421
1858 Starr	421

UBERTI
1851 & 1861 Navy	428
1858 Remington New Army 44	428
1858 Remington New Navy	428
1860 Army	428
1st, 2nd, 3rd Model Dragoons	427
Paterson	427
Walker	427

SHOTGUNS

CVA
Classic Turkey Double	386
Trapper Single Barrel	386

DIXIE
Double Barrel Magnum	391

NAVY ARMS
Model T & T	412
Steel Shot Magnum	412
Upland Shotgun	412

Roland Clark—Top O' The Morning—1931